W9-CSD-311

THRACIA

COELALETAE

RHODOPE

BULGARIA GREECE

TRAUSI

BISTONES

CICONES

Via Egnatia

Porsulis

GALLAISE BRIANTICE

Maronea (Ismarus)

Stryme

Dicaea

Abdera

Crenides (Datum, Philippe)

SATRES

M. PANGAEUS

Thasos

Thasos

MARE THRACICUM

Samothracia

Imbros

Heraclea Sentica

Amphipolis

PIERES

CRESTONIA

MYGDONIA

Thessalonica

ANTHEMUS

CHALCIDICE

Olynthus

Potidaea (Cassandrea)

SITHONIA

PALLENE

Lemnos

Scyros

Scyros

MARE AEGAEUM

Euboea

Oreus (Histiaea)

HELLOPIA

Chalcis

Eretria

Chaeronea
Lebadea
Coronea

Orchomenus

Propontis

Scale 1:2,500,000

© Oxford University Press

Compiled by N. G. L. Hammond in 1967.

Propontis inset:

Plotinopolis

Druzipara

Caenophrurium

Delcus

Bosporus Thracius

Rheba

Phinopolis

Myrileum

Dusae Petra

Hyaroetdes

Pythas

Anthemusia

Discus

Chrysopolis

PAETI

Zirinis

Tzirallum

Selymbria

Cypsela

Drippa

Heraeum (Neon-Didymo-Teichos)

Perinthus (Heraclea)

Rhegium

Byzantium (Constantinopolis)

Calchedon

Dymis (Doriscus)

Aenus

APSINTHII

Zorlani

Cplta

Syracellae

Apri

Zeutera

Ornus

Ganos (Serioteichos)

Myriophytum

Proconnesus

Astacenus Sinus

Pr. Sarpedon

Cypasia

Heraclea Neapolis Aphrodisias

Deris

Lysimachea

Cobrys

Tiristasis (Tyrodiza)

Pytha

Lixus

Proconnesus

Artace

Panormus

Cyzicus

Dascylium Maritimum

Topedium

Prusa

Pythsse Thermae

M. Arganthonius

Cianus Sinus

Cardia

Agora

Pactye

Crithote

Pitya

Priapus

Zelea

Apollonia ad Rhyndacum

Dascylium

Miletopolis

Sestus

Lampsacus

Parium

Coela

Abydus

Dardanus

Madytus

Eion

Araplus

Limnae

DOLONCI

Alopeconnesus

Scyros

Scyros

A HISTORY OF
MACEDONIA

A HISTORY OF
MACEDONIA

VOLUME III
336–167 B.C.

N. G. L. HAMMOND
Hon. Fellow of Clare College, Cambridge

AND

F. W. WALBANK
Hon. Fellow of Peterhouse, Cambridge

CLARENDON PRESS · OXFORD
1988

Oxford University Press, Walton Street, Oxford OX2 6DP

Oxford New York Toronto
Delhi Bombay Calcutta Madras Karachi
Petaling Jaya Singapore Hong Kong Tokyo
Nairobi Dar es Salaam Cape Town
Melbourne Auckland

and associated companies in
Berlin Ibadan

Oxford is a trade mark of Oxford University Press

Published in the United States
by Oxford University Press, New York

British Library Cataloguing in Publication Data
Hammond, N. G. L.
A history of Macedonia.
Vol 3: 336–167 B.C.
1. Macedonia—History—To 168 B.C.
2. Macedonia—History—168 B.C.–1453 A.D.
I. Title   II. Walbank, F. W.
938′.1   DF261.M2
ISBN 0–19–814815–1

Library of Congress Cataloging in Publication Data
(Revised for vol. 3)
Hammond, N. G. L. (Nicholas Geoffrey Lempière), 1907–
A history of Macedonia.
Vol. 3. by N. G. L. Hammond and F. W. Walbank.
Includes bibliographical references.
Contents: v. 1. Historical geography and prehistory—v. 3. 336–167 B.C.
1. Macedonia—History—To 168 B.C.   I. Walbank, F. W.
(Frank William), 1909–   .   II. Title.
DF161.M2H34 1972 938′.1 73–154748
ISBN 0–19–815294–3 (v. 1)
ISBN 0–19–814815–1 (v. 3)

Set by H Charlesworth & Co Ltd, Huddersfield
Printed in Great Britain
at the University Printing House, Oxford
by David Stanford
Printer to the University

In memoriam
GUY THOMPSON GRIFFITH
collegae adiutoris amici
l. m. d.

PREFACE

WHEN THIS VOLUME was in prospect, I realized that a full study of Alexander the Great in terms, not only of Macedonian history, but also of his conquests outside Europe, was essential for an understanding of the development of Macedonia after his death. It was clear that such a study should not be made without an assessment of the sources. In consequence I published *Alexander the Great: King, Commander and Statesman* in 1980 and *Three Historians of Alexander the Great: the so-called vulgate authors, Diodorus, Justin and Curtius* in 1983. At the time when these books were finished, my colleague in Volume II, G. T. Griffith, was in poor health. Although he was not prepared to join in the writing, he was most zealous in reading the early chapters of this volume and he made most valuable comments. He and I were delighted when Professor F. W. Walbank accepted the invitation to be co-author of Volume III. G. T. Griffith maintained his interest in the project until his death in 1985. It is a token of our affection and our respect for his scholarship that we dedicate this book to him.

In September 1983 I was invited to attend the Fourth International Symposium on Ancient Macedonia at Thessaloniki and accepted the invitation with alacrity. I am most grateful to the many colleagues who presented papers and who gave me offprints on that and other occasions. Most of all I have been helped by Dr. M. B. Hatzopoulos, who has an unrivalled knowledge of Macedonian inscriptions and institutions and has travelled widely throughout Macedonia and Thrace. He has been most generous in putting his knowledge at my disposal, reading and criticizing drafts and accompanying me on travels in Western Macedonia and Central Thessaly. He has been an unfailing source of encouragement. Professor M. Andronikos, Professor D. Pantermalis, Mrs. Maria Siganidou, Mrs. Julia Vokotopoulou, Mrs. Koukouli-Chrysanthaki, and many other colleagues in museums and on excavated sites have been most courteous and friendly in showing me their discoveries and their material. Mrs. Fanoula Papazoglou walked with Dr. Hatzopoulos and me in Western Macedonia and discussed problems of topography to our great benefit; and Professor Fano Prendi has been most kind in sending me offprints about discoveries in Albania. I am particularly grateful to the Albanian Government for sending me copies of their archaeological and historical journals.

I am most grateful to the British Academy for a grant which enabled me to study the battles of Cynoscephalae and Pydna on the ground and make other travels. Since 1930 I have been fortunate in becoming familiar, mainly on foot, with northern Greece, southern and central Albania, and some adjacent parts of Yugoslavia and Bulgaria. Visits to the Center for Hellenic Studies in Washington put me in touch with many scholars and especially with Dr. T. Martin, who helped me greatly over Macedonian coinage. In October 1985 I had the honour of being made a Member of the National Hellenic Research Foundation in Athens and of receiving a travel grant in that connection from the British Academy. It was a unique privilege to work with Professor M. B. Sakellariou, Dr. M. B. Hatzopoulos, Dr. L. D. Loukopoulos, and the other distinguished members of the Foundation, and to learn of the progress which is being made towards the publication of the Greek inscriptions of Macedonia and Greek Thrace.

The National Humanities Center awarded me one of its Fellowships for the first term of 1986, and I was able to complete my part of this volume in ideal surroundings in North Carolina and in the congenial company of eminent scholars. I am most grateful to the ladies of the Center who transformed much of my manuscript into faultless typscript—Maggie Blades, Karen Carroll, and Linda Morgan. Since the publication of Volume II in 1979 I have benefited greatly from innumerable discussions with colleagues in many parts of the world, as I have held teaching appointments in America, Australia, and New Zealand and given many lectures on Macedonian topics. But my most valued experience has been co-authorship with F. W. Walbank, whose unrivalled knowledge of Philip V and Perseus has saved me from error on many occasions and enriched my understanding. It has been for me an ideal partnership. Where we have disagreed, we have done so after frank discussion, and we have drawn attention to such disagreements in the text. My last and greatest debt is to my wife, Margaret, who has taken part in all our travels and has treated my absorption in Macedonian matters with indulgence.

It is a pleasure to record my gratitude to Mr. J. K. Cordy, who conveyed to me the invitation of the Clarendon Press to undertake this History of Macedonia and has guided the development of it up to this final stage. He has been most helpful and supportive. Professor Walbank and I are most grateful to Mrs. Sonia Argyle for her careful work with the present volume.

N. G. L. H.

When, following G. T. Griffith's withdrawal, N. G. L. Hammond invited me to join him in Volume III of his *History of Macedonia*, his invitation came at an opportune time and I was happy to accept it.

Hammond was already deeply involved in work connected with Alexander and had published several important studies of military and political matters from 230 B.C. onwards. For my part, I had no wish to return to topics which were my concern nearly fifty years ago, when I was writing *Philip V of Macedon*. On the other hand, I had quite recently become interested in the history of Greece and Macedonia in the earlier decades of the third century, while writing chapters for the new edition of the *Cambridge Ancient History*, Volume 7.1, and I welcomed a chance to look more closely at this period from the Macedonian point of view. So we had no difficulty in arriving at an amicable division of labour and it was quickly decided that I should deal with the years between, roughly, Ipsus and Sellasia.

Throughout, our collaboration has been close. Each of us has read and criticized in detail everything that the other has written. Speaking for myself, this exchange of views continuing at intervals over about five years has been an extremely illuminating and rewarding experience, for which I am immensely grateful. It has also, I hope, helped to improve both our sections of the book. On the few occasions when it has been necessary for each of us to take up a position and yet, after full discussion, we found ourselves in disagreement, we have said so. For the rest, we take separate responsibility for the views expressed in our respective chapters.

The years from 301 to 221 lack good sources and any progress in their elucidation is often bound up with the interpretation of uncertainly dated inscriptions. It has however been my good fortune that it is also a period which has attracted a good deal of attention in recent years and I have been able to draw on the useful monographs of K. Buraselis on Macedonian policy in the Aegean, of H. Heinen on Ptolemy Ceraunus and the Chremonidean War, of O. Picard on Chalcis and the Euboean Confederacy, and of R. Urban on the growth and collapse of the Achaean Confederacy and on Dr. C. Ehrhardt's unpublished thesis on Demetrius II and Antigonus Doson. I should, moreover, have been frequently lost in the morass of third-century chronology but for the basic work of Chr. Habicht on the Athenian archons and G. Nachtergael's study of the Gallic invasion and the Delphic *Soteria*.

I owe a special debt to the organizers of the Fourth International Symposium on Macedonia held in Thessaloniki in September 1983. Their invitation to participate in this congress enabled me to discuss Macedonian problems with many interested scholars, to visit several important museums and to inspect recent work at such sites as Pella and Vergina and, following the Symposium, to drive across Pindus into Epirus as far as Dodona and back through Thessaly to Thessaloniki, thus renewing and extending my acquaintance with areas with which this volume is largely concerned. I was also able to supplement this journey with a visit to Albania in 1985, when my wife and I travelled the length of the Shkumbi valley and visited or revisited some of the main Illyrian sites between Shkodra and Butrint. My work has also been facilitated and advanced by the kindness of many colleagues and friends, too many to name individually, who have sent me copies of their books and articles. My daughter Dorothy Thompson has helped me greatly with advice and bibliography on Ptolemaic (and other) matters and by reading with keener eyes than mine the proofs of my part of the book. In addition, both Professor Hammond and I are grateful to her for help with the coordination of the combined index. Finally, I should like to thank Professors P. Roesch and F. Chamoux for informing me about the important inscription from Xanthus, which mentions Antigonus Doson's attack on Cytinium (see below, pp. 339–40), and Professor J. Bousquet, who generously made the complete text available to me in advance of publication. My main debt, however, remains that to my friend and collaborator, N. G. L. Hammond.

F. W. W.

CONTENTS

PART ONE

(by N. G. L. HAMMOND)

FROM THE DEATH OF PHILIP TO THE BATTLE OF IPSUS

PART THREE

(by N. G. L. HAMMOND)

THE REIGNS OF PHILIP V AND PERSEUS

LIST OF FIGURES

(at end)

Figures 1, 4, 8, 13–15, and 17–19 were made by N. G. L. Hammond on the basis of various British and Greek Staff Maps; Figure 5 was drawn by N G. L. H.; Figures 9 and 11 were made by F. W. Walbank; and Figures 3, 6, 7, and 10 were made by F. W. W. and N. G. L. H. together.

LIST OF PLATES

(at end)

Coins *a*, *b*, *d*, *g*, *h*, *j*, *k*, *l*, *n*, *o*, *p*, and *q* are reproduced by kind permission of the Ashmolean Museum; *c*, *f*, *i*, and *m* of the Fitzwilliam Museum; coin *e* of the Staatliche Museen zu Berlin. Plate II is reproduced by kind permission of Professor M. Andronicos, the photographs for Plate III *a* and *b* by that of Margaret Hammond and Dr M. B. Hatzopoulos respectively. Plate IV is reproduced by kind permission of Professor Ph. Petsas.

ABBREVIATIONS AND
SELECT BIBLIOGRAPHY

Not every title mentioned in notes or text is listed here.
ABBREVIATIONS are those listed in LSJ⁹ except as follows:

A.	Alexander the Great
AAA	Ἀρχαιολογικὰ ἀναλεκτὰ ἐξ Ἀθηνῶν (*Athenian Annals of Archaeology*)
ABAW	*Abhandlungen der Bayerischen Akademie der Wissenschaften*, Phil.-hist. Abteilung
Abh. Berl. Akad.	*Abhandlungen der preussischen Akademie der Wissenschaften, Berlin.* Phil.-hist. Klasse (later '*der deutschen Akademie der Wissenschaften zu Berlin*, Klasse für Sprache, Literatur und Kunst', or 'Klasse für Philosophie, Geschichte, etc.')
Adams and Borza	W. L. Adams and E. N. Borza (edd.), *Philip II, Alexander the Great and the Macedonian heritage* (Washington, 1982)
AM 1, 2, 3	*Ancient Macedonia*, Papers read at the First (Second, Third) International Symposium held in Thessaloniki, 3 vols. (Institute of Balkan Studies. Thessaloniki, 1970, 1977, 1983)
Am. Stud. Pap.	*American Studies in Papyrology*
Anc. Soc.	*Ancient Society*
Andronicos, *V*	M. Andronicos, *Vergina: The Royal Tombs and the Ancient City* (Athens, 1984)
ANSMN	*American Numismatic Society. Museum Notes*
Ant. class.	*L'Antiquité classique*
AR	*Archaeological Reports*
Arch. Eph.	Ἀρχαιολογικὴ Ἐφημερίς
Arr. and Arr., *An.*	Arrian, *Anabasis*
Asheri, *Leggi greche*	D. Asheri, *Leggi greche sul problema dei debiti* (Studi Classici e Orientali 18) (Pisa, 1969)
Atlas	N. G. L. Hammond (ed.), *Atlas of the Greek and Roman World in Antiquity* (Park Ridge, N. J., 1981)
Atti Acc. Torino	*Atti dell'Accademia delle scienze di Torino*
Austin, *HW*	M. M. Austin, *The Hellenistic World from Alexander to the Roman Conquest: a selection of ancient sources in translation* (Cambridge, 1981)
Aymard, Études	A. Aymard, *Études d'histoire ancienne* (Paris, 1967)
Aymard, *Premiers Rapports*	A. Aymard, *Les Premiers Rapports de Rome et de la confédération achaienne (198–189 av. J.-C.)* (Bordeaux, 1938)
Bagnall, *Administration*	R. S. Bagnall, *The Administration of the Ptolemaic Possessions outside Egypt* (Leiden, 1976)

Beloch   K. J. Beloch, *Griechische Geschichte* 4. 1 and 2 (Berlin–Leipzig, 1925–7)

Bengtson, *Gesch.*   H. Bengtson, *Griechische Geschichte von den Anfängen bis in die römische Kaiserzeit* (Handbücher der Altertumswissenschaft, III.4) 4th edn., 1969

Bengtson, *Strat.*   H. Bengtson, *Die Strategie in der hellenistichen Zeit*, 3 vols. (*Münchener Beiträge* 26. 32. 36) (Munich, 1937, 1944, 1952)

Béquignon   Y. Béquignon, *La Vallée du Spercheios des origines au IVᵉ siècle* (Paris, 1937)

Berve   H. Berve, *Das Alexanderreich auf prosopographischer Grundlage*, 2 vols. (Munich, 1926)

Bevan, *Ptol. Dyn.*   E. Bevan, *A History of Egypt under the Ptolemaic Dynasty* (London, 1927)

BMC   *Catalogue of Coins in the British Museum*

Boehringer   Chr. Boehringer, *Zur Chronologie mittelhellenistischer Münzserien, 220–160 v. Chr.* (Antike Münzen und geschnittene Steine 5) (Berlin, 1972)

Borza   E. N. Borza, 'Cleitarchus and Diodorus' account of Alexander', *Proceedings of the African Classical Associations* 11 (1968) 25 ff.

Bosworth   A. N. Bosworth, *A Historical Commentary on Arrian's History of Alexander*, Books 1–3 (Oxford, 1980)

Bouché-Leclercq, *Lagides*   A. Bouché-Leclercq, *Histoire des Lagides*, 4 vols. (Paris, 1903–7)

Briant   P. Briant, *Antigone le Borgne: les débuts de sa carrière et les problèmes de l'assemblée macédonienne* (Paris, 1973)

Briscoe   J. Briscoe, *Commentaries on Livy 31–33 and 34–37* (Oxford, 1973 and 1981)

Brulé   P. Brulé, *La Piraterie crétoise hellénistique* (Paris, 1978)

Bruneau   P. Bruneau, *Recherches sur les cultes de Délos* (Paris, 1970)

Brunt, L   P. A. Brunt (ed.) *Arrian, with an English translation*, 2 vols. (Loeb Library) (Cambridge, Mass.–London, 1976–83)

BS   *Balkan Studies*

Bul. Ark.   *Buletin Arkeologjik*

Bull. épig.   J. and L. Robert, *Bulletin épigraphique* (in *REG*)

Bülow-Jacobsen   A. Bülow-Jacobsen, '*P. Haun* 6. An inspection of the original', *ZPE* 36 (1979) 91–100

Buraselis   K. Buraselis, *Das hellenistische Makedonien und die Ägäis: Forschungen zur Politik des Kassandros und der drei ersten Antigoniden im Ägäischen Meer und in Westkleinasien* (Münchener Beiträge 73) (Munich, 1982)

BUSS   *Buletin per Shkencat Shoqërore* (Tiranë)

BUST   *Buletin i Universitetit Shtetëror të Tiranës, Seria Shkencat Shoqërore* (Tiranë)

C.   Curtius

CA   *Classical Antiquity* (continuation as from 1982 of *CSCA*)

Cabanes   P. Cabanes, *L'Épire de la mort de Pyrrhus à la conquête romaine (272–167 av. J.-C.)* (Besançon–Paris, 1976)

CAH   *Cambridge Ancient History*

Cary   M. Cary, *History of the Greek World from 323 to 146 B.C.* 2nd edn., London–New York, 1951 (with new bibliography by V. Ehrenberg, 1963)

Çeka, *Questions*   H. Çeka, *Questions de numismatique illyrienne* (Tiranë, 1979)

Chron. d'Égypte   *Chronique d'Égypte*

Cloché, *Thèbes*   P. Cloché, *Thèbes de Béotie des origines à la conquête romaine* (Paris, n.d.)

CP   *Classical Philology*

Crampa, *Labraunda*   J. Crampa, *Labraunda. Swedish Excavations and Researches* III. 1–2: *The Greek Inscriptions* (Acta Instituti Atheniensis Regni Sueciae, Series in 4°, V). (Lund, 1969, and Stockholm, 1972)

Cross   G. N. Cross, *Epirus, A Study in Greek Constitutional Development* (Cambridge, 1932)

CSCA   *Californian Studies in Classical Antiquity*

Danov   Christo M. Danov, *Altthrakien* (Berlin–New York, 1976)

Daux   G. Daux, 'Remarques sur la composition du conseil amphictionique', *BCH* 81 (1957) 95–120

Davies, *APF*   J. K. Davies, *Athenian Propertied Families, 600–300 B.C.* (Oxford, 1971)

Délos   *Exploration archéologique de Délos*, vols. by various authors (Paris, 1902–61)

Demetrias I   V. Milojčić and D. Theocharis (edd.), *Demetrias I* (Bonn, 1976)

De Sanctis   G. De Sanctis, *Storia dei romani*, Vols. 1–4. 3 in eight parts (Turin–Florence, 1907–64)

De Sanctis, *Scritti*   G. De Sanctis, *Scritti minori*, 1 (ed. S. Accame) (Rome, 1966)

Dinsmoor   W. B. Dinsmoor, *The Archons of Athens in the Hellenistic Age* (Cambridge, Mass., 1931)

DLZ   *Deutsche Literatur-Zeitung*

Droysen   J. G. Droysen, *Geschichte des Hellenismus*, I. II² (1 and 2), III² (1 and 2) (Gotha, 1877–8)

Durrbach, *Choix*   F. Durrbach, *Choix d'inscriptions de Délos avec traduction et commentaire*, 1. 1–2 (Paris, 1921–3)

Dušanić   S. Dušanić, 'The year of the Athenian archon Archippus II (318/17)'. *BCH* 87 (1965) 128–41

Edson   C. F. Edson, 'Perseus and Demetrius', *Harv. Stud.* 46 (1935) 191–202.

Ehrhardt	C. T. H. R. Ehrhardt, *Studies in the Reigns of Demetrius II and Antigonus Doson* (Diss. SUNY at Buffalo, N.Y., 1975: microfilm)
EHW	E. Van't Dack, P. Van Dessel, and W. Van Gucht (edd.), *Egypt and the Hellenistic World*, Proceedings of the International Colloquium, Leuven, 24–6 May 1982, Studia Hellenistica 27 (Louvain, 1983)
Ellis, *Philip*	J. R. Ellis, *Philip II and Macedonian Imperialism* (London, 1976)
Engels	D. W. Engels, *Alexander the Great and the logistics of the Macedonian army* (Berkeley–Los Angeles–London, 1978)
Ep. Chron.	'Ηπειρωτικὰ Χρονικά (Ioannina)
Epit. Metz	*Epitoma rerum gestarum Alexandri et liber de morte eius*, ed. P. H. Thomas (Leipzig, 1966)
Errington	R. M. Errington, 'From Babylon to Triparadeisos: 323–320 B.C.' *JHS* 90 (1970), 49–77
Errington, *Dawn*	R. M. Errington, *The Dawn of Empire: Rome's Rise to World Power* (London, 1971)
Errington, *Gesch. Mak.*	M. Errington, *Geschichte Makedoniens von den Anfängen bis zum Untergang des Königreiches* (Munich, 1986)
Errington, *Philop.*	R. M. Errington, *Philopoemen* (Oxford, 1969)
Essays Starr	*The Craft of the Ancient Historian: Essays in Honor of Chester G. Starr*, ed. T. W. Earle and J. Ober (New York, 1985)
Étienne and Knoepfler, *Hyettos*	R. Étienne and D. Knoepfler, *Hyettos de Béotie et la chronologie des archontes fédéraux entre 250 et 171 av. J.-C.* (*BCH* Suppl. 2) (Athens, 1976)
Fellmann	W. Fellmann, *Antigonos Gonatas, König der Makedonen, und die griechischen Staaten*, Diss. Würzburg, 1930
Ferguson, *HA*	W. S. Ferguson, *Hellenistic Athens* (London, 1911)
Ferguson Studies	*Athenian Studies Presented to W. S. Ferguson* (Harvard, 1940)
Feyel	M. Feyel, *Polybe et l'histoire de Béotie au IIIe siècle av. notre ère* (Paris, 1941)
Feyel, *Contr.*	M. Feyel, *Contribution à l'épigraphie béotienne* (Le Puy, 1942)
Flacelière	R. Flacelière, *Les Aitoliens à Delphes: contribution à l'histoire de la Grèce centrale au IIIe siècle av. J.-C.* (Paris, 1937)
Fortina	M. Fortina, *Cassandro, re di Macedonia* (Turin, 1965)
Franke	P. R. Franke, 'Zur Finanzpolitik des makedonischen Königs Perseus während des Krieges mit Rom (171–168 v. Chr)', *JNG* 8 (1957) 31–50
Franke, *AE*	P. R. Franke, *Alt-Epirus und das Königtum der Molosser* (Kallmünz Oplf., 1954)
Franke, *Münzen*	P. R. Franke, *Die antiken Münzen von Epirus: Poleis, Stämme und Epeirotischer Bund bis 27 v. Chr.* (Wiesbaden, 1961)
Fraser	P. M. Fraser, *Ptolemaic Alexandria*, 3 vols. (Oxford, 1973)

Fraser, *Samothrace*
P. M. Fraser, *Samothrace* II. 1: *The Inscriptions on Stone* (New York, 1960)

Fraser–Bean
P. M. Fraser and G. E. Bean, *The Rhodian Peraea and Islands* (Oxford, 1954)

Fredricksmeyer
E. A. Fredricksmeyer, 'Alexander, Midas and the oracle at Gordium', *Class. Phil.* 56 (1961) 160–8

Freeman
E. A. Freeman, *History of Federal Government in Greece and Italy*, 2nd edn. by J. B. Bury (London, 1983)

Fuks, *Social Conflict*
A. Fuks, *Social Conflict in Ancient Greece*, ed. M. Stern and M. Amit (Jerusalem–Leiden, 1984)

Fuller
J. F. C. Fuller, *The Generalship of Alexander* (London, 1958)

Gaebler
H. Gaebler, *Die antiken Münzen Nord-Griechenlands* III, *Makedonia und Paionia*, Parts 1–2 (Berlin, 1906–35)

Garnsey and Whittaker
P. Garnsey and C. R. Whittaker (edd.), *Imperialism in the Ancient World* (Cambridge, 1978)

GHI
M. N. Tod, *A Selection of Greek Historical Inscriptions*, Vols. 1² and 2 (Oxford, 1946–8)

Glotz–Roussel–Cohen
G. Glotz, P. Roussel, and R. Cohen, *Histoire grecque* IV. 1: *Alexandre et le démembrement de son empire*, 2nd edn. (Paris, 1945)

Gomme
A. W. Gomme, *The Population of Athens in the Fifth and Fourth Centuries B.C.* (Oxford, 1933)

Goukowsky
P. Goukowsky, *Diodore de Sicile xvii*, Édition Budé (Paris, 1974)

GRBS
Greek, Roman and Byzantine Studies

Griffith
G. T. Griffith (ed.), *Alexander the Great: The Main Problems* (Cambridge, 1966)

Griffith, *Merc.*
G. T. Griffith, *The Mercenaries of the Hellenistic World* (Cambridge, 1935)

Gruen
E. S. Gruen, *The Hellenistic World and the Coming of Rome* (Berkeley, 1984), 2 vols. with consecutive paging.

Gruen, 'Coronation'
E. S. Gruen, 'The coronation of the Diadochoi' in *Essays Starr*, 253–71

Gyioka, *Perseus*
P. G. Gyioka, Περσεύς, ὁ τελευταῖος βασιλεὺς τῶν Μακεδόνων (Thessaloniki, 1975)

H*A*
N. G. L. Hammond, *Alexander the Great, King, Commander and Statesman* (New Jersey, 1980; London, 1981)

Habicht, *Gottmenschentum*
Chr. Habicht, *Gottmenschentum und die griechischen Städte* (Zetemata, 14), 2nd edn. (Munich, 1970)

Habicht, *Studien*
Chr. Habicht, *Studien zur Geschichte Athens in hellenistischer Zeit* (Hypomnemata, 78) (Göttingen, 1982)

Habicht, *Unters.*
Chr. Habicht, *Untersuchungen zur politischen Geschichte Athens im 3. Jahrhundert v. Chr.* (Vestigia, 20) (Munich, 1979)

H*ACI*
N. G. L. Hammond, 'Alexander's campaign in Illyria', *JHS* 94 (1974) 66–87

Hamilton	J. R. Hamilton, *Plutarch, Alexander: A Commentary* (Oxford, 1969)
Hansen	E. V. Hansen, *The Attalids of Pergamon* (Cornell Studies in Classical Philology, 5) 2nd edn. (Ithaca–London, 1973)
Harris	W. V. Harris, *War and Imperialism in Republican Rome 327–70 B.C.* (Oxford, 1979)
Harv. Stud.	*Harvard Studies in Classical Philology*
H*AS*	N. G. L. Hammond, 'The opening campaigns and the battle of the Aoi Stena in the Second Macedonian War', *JRS* 56 (1966) 39–54
H*E*	N. G. L. Hammond, *Epirus* (Oxford, 1967)
Head	B. V. Head, *Historia numorum*, 2nd edn. (Oxford, 1911)
Heiland	P. Heiland, *Untersuchungen zur Geschichte des Königs Perseus von Makedonien (179–168)* (Diss. Jena, 1913)
Heinen, *Unters.*	H. Heinen, *Untersuchungen zur hellenistischen Geschichte des 3. Jahrhunderts v. Chr. Zur Geschichte der Zeit des Ptolemaios Keraunos und zum Chremonideischen Kriege* (*Historia*, Einzelschift 20) (Wiesbaden, 1972)
Heisserer	A. J. Heisserer, *Alexander the Great and the Greeks: The Epigraphic Evidence* (Norman, 1982)
Helly	B. Helly, *Gonnoi II: les inscriptions* (Amsterdam, 1973)
Herman	G. Herman, *Ritualised Friendship and the Greek City* (Cambridge, 1987)
Herzog–Klaffenbach	R. Herzog and G. Klaffenbach, 'Asylieurkunden aus Kos', *Abh. Berl. Akad.* 1952, no. 1
Hesp.	*Hesperia*
Heuss, *VG*	A. Heuss, *Die völkerrechtlichen Grundlagen der römischen Aussenpolitik in republikanischer Zeit* (*Klio*, Beiheft 31) (Leipzig, 1933)
Heuzey, *Olympe*	L. A. Heuzey, *Le Mont Olympe et l'Acarnanie, exploration de ces deux régions* (Paris, 1860)
Heuzey–Daumet	L. A. Heuzey and H. Daumet, *Mission archéologique de Macédoine* (Paris, 1876)
HGE	F. Hiller von Gaertringen (ed.), *Historische griechische Epigramme* (Kleine Texte, 156) (Bonn, 1926)
H*HG*	N. G. L. Hammond, *A History of Greece*, 3rd edn. (Oxford, 1986)
H*HSE*	N. G. L. Hammond, 'The hosts of sacred envoys travelling through Epirus', *Ep. Chron.* 22 (1980) 9–20
HH *Via Egnatia*	N. G. L. Hammond and M. B. Hatzopoulos, 'The Via Egnatia, I', *AJAH* 7 (1982 = 1985) 128–49; 'The Via Egnatia II', ibid. 8 (1983 = 1986) 48–53
H*IRM*	N. G. L. Hammond, 'Illyria, Rome and Macedonia in 229–205 B.C.', *JRS* 58 (1968) 1–21

H*KI*   N. G. L. Hammond, 'The Kingdoms in Illyria *circa* 400–167 B.C.', *BSA* 61 (1966) 239–53

H.–L.   M. B. Hatzopoulos and D. Loukopoulos (edd.), *Philip II of Macedon* (Athens, 1980)

H*MAT*   N. G. L. Hammond, 'The march of Alexander the Great on Thebes in 335 B.C.' in Μέγας Ἀλέξανδρος 2000 χρόνια ἀπὸ τὸν θάνατόν του (Thessaloniki, 1980), 171–81

Holleaux, *Études*   M. Holleaux, *Études d'épigraphie et d'histoire grecques*, ed. L. Robert, 6 vols. (Paris, 1938–68)

Holleaux, *Rome*   M. Holleaux, *Rome et la Grèce et les monarchies hellénistiques au III*^e *siècle av. J.-C. (273–205)* (Paris, 1921)

Hornblower   Jane Hornblower, *Hieronymus of Cardia* (Oxford, 1981)

H*P*   N.G.L. Hammond, 'A note on "pursuit" in Arrian', *CQ* 28 (1978) 136–40

H*PT*   N. G. L. Hammond, '"Philip's tomb" in historical context', *GRBS* 19 (1978) 331–50

H*Pydna*   N. G. L. Hammond, 'The battle of Pydna', *JHS* 104 (1984) 31–47

H*RTV*   N. G. L. Hammond, 'The evidence for the identity of the royal tombs at Vergina' in Adams and Borza, 111–27

H*SD*   N. G. L. Hammond, 'The sources of Diodorus XVI', *CQ* 31 (1937) 79 ff. and 32 (1938) 137 ff.

H*SMO*   N. G. L. Hammond, 'Some Macedonian offices c. 336–309 B.C.', *JHS* 105 (1985) 156–60

H*SPA*   N. G. L. Hammond, 'Some passages in Arrian concerning Alexander', *CQ* 30 (1980) 455–76

H*THA*   N. G. L. Hammond, *Three Historians of Alexander the Great* (Cambridge, 1983)

H*TUS*   N. G. L. Hammond, 'Training in the use of a sarissa and its effect in battle, 359–333 B.C.', *Antichthon* 14 (1980) 53–63

Huss, *Unters.*   W. Huss, *Untersuchungen zur Aussenpolitik Ptolemaios IV.* (Munich, 1976)

H*Venture*   N. G. L. Hammond, *Venture into Greece: with the Guerrillas 1943–44* (London, 1983)

IC   *Inscriptiones Creticae*, ed. M. Guarducci, 4 vols. (Rome, 1935–50)

IGCH   O. Mørkholm, C. M. Kraay, and M. Thompson, *An Inventory of Greek Coin Hoards* (New York, 1973)

Inschr. Ilion   P. Frisch, *Die Inschriften von Ilion* (Bonn, 1975)

Inschr. Priene F. Hiller von Gaertringen, *Die Inschriften von Priene* (Berlin, 1906)

ISE   L. Moretti, *Iscrizioni storiche ellenistiche*, 2 vols. (Florence, 1967–75)

JIAN   *Journal international d'archéologie numismatique*

JNG Jahrbuch für Numismatik und Geldgeschichte

J. Justinus

Kanatsoules D. Kanatsoules, Μακεδονικὴ προσωπογραφία ἀπὸ τοῦ *148 μ.Χ. μέχρι τῶν χρόνων τοῦ M. Κωνσταντίνου* (Thessaloniki, 1955)

Klotzsch C. Klotzsch, *Epirotische Geschichte bis zum Jahre 280 v. Chr.* (Berlin, 1911)

Kromayer, AS J. Kromayer and G. Veith, *Antike Schlachtfelder*, 4 vols. (Berlin, 1902–31)

Launey M. Launey, *Recherches sur les armées hellénistiques*, 2 vols. (Paris, 1949–50)

Leake, NG W. M. Leake, *Travels in Northern Greece*, 4 vols. (London, 1835)

Leschhorn W. Leschhorn, *'Gründer der Stadt': Studien zu einem politisch-religiösen Phänomen der griechischen Geschichte* (Palingenesia, 20) (Stuttgart, 1984)

Lévêque P. Lévêque, *Pyrrhos* (Paris, 1957)

Loeb R E. I. Robson (ed.), *Arrian*, with an English translation, 2 vols. (Loeb Library) (Cambridge, Mass.–London, 1946–9)

Longega G. Longega, *Arsinoe II* (Univ. degli studi di Padova, Pubbl. dell'Ist. di Storia Antica, Vol.6) (Rome, 1968)

Maass M. Maass, *Die Prohedrie des Dionysostheater in Athen* (Munich, 1972)

McCredie J. R. McCredie, *Fortified Camps in Attica* (*Hesperia*, Supplement 11) (Princeton, 1966)

McDonald and Walbank A. H. McDonald and F. W. Walbank, 'The origins of the Second Macedonian War', *JRS* 27 (1937) 180–207

Macedonia *Macedonia, 4000 years of Greek History and Civilization*, ed. M. B. Sakellariou (Athens, 1983)

Magie D. Magie, *Roman Rule in Asia Minor to the End of the Third Century after Christ*, 2 vols. (Princeton, 1950)

Maier, Mauerbauinschriften F.-G. Maier, *Griechische Mauerbauinschriften* 1. *Texte und Kommentare* (Vestigia 1) (Heidelberg, 1959)

Mak. Μακεδονικά

Mamroth, 1928 A. Mamroth, 'Die Silbermünzen des Königs Perseus', *ZfN* 38 (1928) 1–28

Mamroth, 1930 A. Mamroth, 'Die Silbermünzen des Königs Philipps V. von Makedonien', *ZfN* 40 (1930) 277–303

Mamroth, 1935 A. Mamroth, 'Die Bronzemünzen des Königs Philipps V. von Makedonien' *ZfN* 42 (1935) 219–51

Manni E. Manni, *Demetrio Poliorcete* (Rome, 1951)

Martin T. R. Martin, *Sovereignty and Coinage in Classical Greece* (Princeton, 1985)

Meloni, *Perseo*   P. Meloni, *Perseo e la fine della monarchia macedone* (Rome, 1953)

Meritt, *Athenian Year*   B. D. Meritt, *The Athenian Year* (Berkeley–Los Angeles, 1961)

Merker   I. L. Merker, 'The silver coinage of Antigonus Gonatas and Antigonus Doson', *ANSMN* 9 (1960) 39–52

M–G   *Macedonia and Greece in Late Classical and Early Hellenistic Times*, edd. B. Barr-Sharrar and E. N. Borza (Washington, 1982)

Mikalson   J. D. Mikalson, *The Sacred and Civil Calendar of the Athenian Year* (Princeton, N.J., 1975)

Milns   R. D. Milns, 'The army of Alexander the Great', *Alexandre le Grand* (ed. E. Badian): Entretiens Hardt 22, 87–130 (Vandoeuvres–Geneva, 1975)

Moretti   *see ISE*

Müller, *MV*   H. Müller, *Milesische Volksbeschlüsse. Eine Untersuchung zur Verfassungsgeschichte der Stadt Milet in hellenistischer Zeit* (Hypomnemata 47) (Göttingen, 1976)

Mus. Helv.   *Museum Helveticum*

Musti, *Pausania*   D. Musti, *Pausania, guida della Grecia* ([Milan] 1982–)

Nachtergael   G. Nachtergael, *Les Galates en Grèce et les Soteria de Delphes* (Brussels, 1977)

Newell, *Coinages*   E. T. Newell, *The Coinages of Demetrius Poliorcetes* (Oxford, 1927)

Newell, *WSM*   E. T. Newell, *The Coinage of the Western Seleucid Mints from Seleucus I to Antiochus III* (American Numismatic Society: Numismatic Studies 4) 2nd edn. (New York, 1977)

Niese   B. Niese, *Geschichte der griechischen und makedonischen Staaten seit der Schlacht bei Chaeronea*, 3 vols. (Gotha, 1893–1903)

Num. Chron.   *Numismatic Chronicle*

Num. Zeitschr.   *Numismatische Zeitschrift*

OCD^2 *Oxford Classical Dictionary*, 2nd edn., ed. N. G. L. Hammond and H. H. Scullard (Oxford, 1970)

Orth   W. Orth, *Königlicher Machtanspruch und städtische Freiheit* (Munich, 1977)

Otto, *Beiträge*   W. Otto, *Beiträge zur Seleukidischen Geschichte des 3. Jahrhunderts v. Chr.* (*ABAW* 34. 1) (Munich, 1928)

P   Plutarch (followed by title of work normally abbreviated, excepting those listed below)

P*A*   Plutarch, *Life of Alexander*

PAE   Πρακτικὰ τῆ ἐν Ἀθήναις Ἀρχαιολογικῆς Ἑταιρείας

Pagasai und Demetrias   F. Stählin, E. Meyer, and A. Heidner, *Pagasai und Demetrias: Beschreibung der Reste und Stadtgeschichte* (Berlin–Leipzig, 1934)

Papazoglou, *CBT* — Fanoula Papazoglou, *The Central Balkan Tribes in pre-Roman Times* (Amsterdam, 1978)

Parker–Dubberstein — R. A. Parker and N. Dubberstein, *Babylonian Chronology 626 B.C.–A.D. 75* (Brown University Studies 19), 2nd edn. (Providence, R.I., 1956)

P. Bour. — Les Papyrus Bouriant, ed. P. Collart (Paris, 1926)

PCPS — *Proceedings of the Cambridge Philological Society*

P*D* — Plutarch, *Life of Demetrius*

Pearson — L. Pearson, *The Lost Historians of Alexander the Great* (Philological monographs 20) (American Philological Association, 1960)

Pédech, *Méthode* — P. Pédech, *La Méthode historique de Polybe* (Paris, 1964)

Pélékidis — Chr. Pélékidis, *Histoire de l'éphébie attique des origines à 31 av. J.-C.* (Paris, 1962)

Pélékidis, *Μέλετες* — Chr. Pélékidis, *Μέλετες ἀρχαίας ἱστορίας* (Athens, 1979)

Petsas, *Pella* — Ph. Petsas, *Pella* (Thessaloniki, 1978)

P*Eum* — Plutarch, *Life of Eumenes*

P. Haun. — T. Larsen, *Literarische Texte und Ptolemäische Urkunden* (Papyri Graecae Haunienses I) (Copenhagen, 1942)

Picard, *Chalcis* — O. Picard, *Chalcis et la confédération eubéenne: étude de numismatique et d'histoire* (Athens–Paris, 1979)

Pliny, *HN* — Pliny, *Natural History*

P. Lond. 7 — T. C. Skeat (ed.), *Greek Papyri in the British Museum 7, The Zenon Archive* (London, 1974)

Pollitt — J. J. Pollitt, *Art in the Hellenistic Age* (Cambridge, 1986)

Porter — W. H. Porter, *Plutarch's Life of Aratus*, with introduction, notes and appendix (Cork, 1937)

Pouilloux, *Rhamnonte* — J. Pouilloux, *La Forteresse de Rhamnonte: étude de topographie et d'histoire* (Paris, 1954)

P*Ph* — Plutarch, *Life of Phocion*

Préaux — C. Préaux, *Le Monde hellénistique. La Grèce et l'orient de la mort d'Alexandre à la conquête romaine de la Grèce (323–146 av. J.-C.)* (Paris, 1978)

P. Rev. — *Revenue Laws of Ptolemy Philadelphus* ed. B. P. Grenfell. (Oxford, 1896). Re-edited by J. Bingen in *Sammelb.*, Beiheft 1 (Göttingen, 1952)

Price — M. Price, *Coins of the Macedonians* (London, 1974)

Pritchett, *Studies* — W. K. Pritchett, *Studies in Ancient Greek Topography* (Berkeley–Los Angeles), 3 vols. 1 (1965); 2 *Battlefields* (1969); 3 *Roads* (1980)

Proc. 8th Epigr. Conf. — *Πρακτικὰ τοῦ Η΄ Διεθνοῦς Συνεδρίου Ἑλληνικῆς καὶ Λατινικῆς Ἐπιγραφίας* (Athens, 1984)

Pros. Ptol. — W. Peremans, E. Van 't Dack, and others, *Prosopographia Ptolemaica*, 8 vols. (1950–75), 1–5 repr. 1977; 6 (1968); 7–8 (1975) (Studia Hellenistica) (Louvain)

RE	Pauly-Wissowa, *Realencyclopädie der classischen Altertumswissenschaft*
REA	*Revue des études anciennes*
REG	*Revue des études grecques*
Rend. Pont. Acc.	*Atti della Pontificia Accademia Romana di Archeologia: Rendiconti*
RFIC	*Rivista di filologia e d'istruzione classica*
Rhodes	P. J. Rhodes, *The Athenian Boule* (Oxford, 1972)
Rich	J. W. Rich, 'Roman aims in the First Macedonian War', *PCPS* 30 (1984) 126–80
Ritter	H. W. Ritter, *Diadem und Königsherrschaft* (Munich, 1965)
Robert, *Amyzon*	L. Robert, *Les Fouilles d'Amyzon* (Paris, 1983)
Robert, *Hellenica*	L. Robert, *Hellenica. Recueil d'épigraphie, de numismatique et d'antiquités grecques*, 13 vols. (Paris, 1940–65)
Robert, *Num. grecque*	L. Robert, *Études de numismatique grecque* (Paris, 1951)
Robinson Studies	*Studies presented to D. M. Robinson*, 2 vols. (St. Louis, Mo., 1951 and 1953)
Roesch	P. Roesch, *Études béotiennes* (Paris, 1982)
Rostovtzeff, *SEH*	M. Rostovtzeff, *Social and Economic History of the Hellenistic World*, 3 vols. 2nd edn. (Oxford, 1953)
SA	*Studia Albanica*
SBAW	*Sitzungsberichte der bayerischen Akademie der Wissenschaften, Phil.-hist. Abteilung*
Schmitt	*see SVA*
Schubert	R. Schubert, *Die Quellen zur Geschichte der Diadochenzeit* (Leipzig, 1914; repr. Aalen, 1984)
Schwahn	W. Schwahn, *Heeresmatrikel und Landfriede Philipps von Makedonien* (*Klio*, Beiheft 21) (Leipzig, 1930)
SEG	*Supplementum Epigraphicum Graecum*
Seibert, *DV*	J. Seibert, *Hisorische Beiträge zu den dynastischen Verbindungen in hellenistischer Zeit* (*Historia* Einzelschrift 10) (Wiesbaden, 1967)
Seltman, *GC*	C. Seltman, *Greek Coins* (London, 1933)
Shear	T. L. Shear, *Kallias of Sphettos and the Revolt of Athens in 286 B.C.* (*Hesperia*, Supplement 17) (Princeton, N.J., 1978)
Sherk	R. T. Sherk, *Roman Documents from the Greek East: senatus consulta and* epistulae *to the age of Augustus* (Baltimore, 1969).
SIG	W. Dittenberger, *Sylloge Inscriptionum Graecarum*, 3rd edn., 4 vols. (Leipzig, 1915–24)
Simpson	R. H. Simpson, 'Abbreviation of Hieronymus in Diodorus', *AJP* 80 (1959) 370–9
Sitz. Berlin	*Sitzungsberichte der Preussischen Akademie der Wissenschaften*

Sitz. Wien	*Sitzungsberichte der Akademie der Wissenschaften in Wien,* phil.-hist. Klasse
Smith	S. Smith, *Babylonian Historical Texts* (London, 1924)
SNG v	*Sylloge Nummorum Graecorum* v *Ashmolean Museum, Oxford,* Part III *Macedonia* (London, 1976)
Stählin	F. Stählin, *Das hellenistische Thessalien* (Stuttgart, 1924)
StGH	N. G. L. Hammond, *Studies in Greek History* (Oxford, 1973)
Stöckli	W. E. Stöckli, 'Anmerkungen zur Chronologie von Victoriat, Denar, Quinar und Sesterz', *JNG* 25 (1975) 73–90
Studies Edson	*Ancient Macedonian Studies in honor of Charles F. Edson.* *(Thessaloniki, 1981)*
Studies Mihailov	*Studies in honour of G. Mihailov,* ed. A. Fol (forthcoming)
SVA	*Die Staatsverträge des Altertums* III. *Die Verträge der griechisch-römischen Welt von 338 bis 200 v. Chr.* ed. H. H. Schmitt (Munich, 1969)
Symb. Osl.	*Symbolae Osloenses*
TAPA	*Transactions of the American Philological Association*
Tarn	W. W. Tarn, *Alexander the Great,* 2 vols. (Cambridge, 1948)
Tarn, *AG*	W. W. Tarn, *Antigonos Gonatas* (Oxford, 1913)
Tarn, *Bactria*	W. W. Tarn, *The Greeks in Bactria and India,* 2nd edn. (Cambridge, 1951)
Treves, 'Dopo Ipso'	P. Treves, 'Dopo Ipso', *Riv. fil.* 59 (1931) 73–92, 355–76
Trog. *Prol.*	Trogus, *Prologi*
Urban	R. Urban, *Wachstum und Krise des achäischen Bundes: Quellenstudien zur Entwicklung des Bundes von 280 bis 222 v. Chr.* (*Historia* Einzelschrift 35) (Wiesbaden, 1979)
van Effenterre	H. van Effenterre, *La Crète et le monde grec de Platon à Polybe* (Paris, 1948)
Walbank, *A*	F. W. Walbank, *Aratos of Sicyon* (Cambridge, 1933)
Walbank, *C*	F. W. Walbank, *A Historical Commentary on Polybius,* 3 vols. (Oxford, 1957, 1967, 1979)
Walbank, *Ph*	F. W. Walbank, *Philip V of Macedon* (Cambridge, 1940)
Warrior	V. M. Warrior, 'Livy book 42: structure and chronology', *AJAH* 6 (1981) 1–50
Wehrli	C. Wehrli, *Antigonos et Démétrios* (Geneva, 1969)
Welles	C. B. Welles, *Diodorus of Sicily with an English translation* (Loeb Library), Vol. 8 (Book 17) (Cambridge, Mass.–London, 1969)
Welles, *RC*	C. B. Welles, *Royal Correspondence of the Hellenistic Age* (Newhaven, Conn., 1934)
Westlake	H. D. Westlake, *Thessaly in the Fourth Century* (London, 1935)

Wilhelm, *Beiträge*	A. Wilhelm, *Beiträge zur griechischen Inschriftenkunde* (Vienna, 1919)
Will	E. Will, *Histoire politique du monde hellénistique*, 2 vols. (Nancy, 1966–7 (1st edn.), 1979–82 (2nd edn.))
Wirth, *Studien*	G. Wirth, *Studien zur Alexandergeschichte* (Darmstadt, 1985)
Woodhouse	W. J. Woodhouse, *Aetolia, its Geography, Topography and Antiquities* (Oxford, 1897)
Youroukova	Y. Youroukova, *Coins of the Ancient Thracians* (Oxford, 1976)
ZfN	*Zeitschrift für Numismatik*
Zon.	Zonaras
ZPE	*Zeitschrift für Papyrologie und Epigraphik*

PART ONE

FROM THE DEATH OF PHILIP TO THE BATTLE OF IPSUS

I

THE FIRST ACTS OF ALEXANDER AND THE NATURE OF THE EVIDENCE

1. *The election of Alexander as king and the aftermath of Philip's assassination*

MACEDONIAN princes and members of the leading commoner families passed out of childhood at the age of fourteen, and those chosen by the king became Royal Pages. Thus Alexander, born in 356, hunted and fought as a Royal Page beside the king from 342 onwards. Moreover, he was entrusted with high offices of state. At sixteen he acted as the king's deputy in Macedonia, commanded an expeditionary force against the Maedi in the Strymon valley, and founded a city there in his own name, Alexandroupolis. At seventeen he accompanied the king on the Danubian campaign of 339. At eighteen he commanded the left half of the Macedonian line and in particular led the Companion Cavalry at the battle of Chaeronea in 338. He escorted the ashes of the dead to Athens after the battle. At twenty he walked as heir apparent beside the king in the procession of the Macedonian state at Aegeae. Philip advertised his intention in the Greek world too. For when Philip dedicated his Philippeum at Olympia,[1] he placed there only one gold-and-ivory statue of a member of the younger generation in the royal house, that of Alexander, completed probably early in 336. When Philip was assassinated that July, everyone knew he had wished his son Alexander to succeed him. It was normal at this time for a Macedonian prince to marry in his middle twenties. Thus on the death of Perdiccas Philip was unmarried at the age of twenty-three or twenty-four; and a son of that Perdiccas, Amyntas, did not marry until 336, when he was well on in his twenties. The fact that Alexander was unmarried at the age of twenty was of no significance in the matter of succession to the throne.

The decision who was to succeed lay entirely with the Assembly of the Macedonians. Other candidates than Alexander were certain to be considered. There were descendants of senior collateral branches of the royal house, the Temenidae, such as the sons of Aëropus,[2] among

---

[1] Paus. 5.20. 10.

[2] See H*SPA* 457 f., superseding my view in Volume II 15 f.; for the traditional opinion that they were members of the Lyncestian royal house, the Bacchiadae, see Beloch 3. 2. 77. The *hegemon* Aëropus in Polyaen. 4. 2. 3 may have been this Aëropus.

whose forebears were the kings Aëropus II, Archelaus, and Perdiccas II, whereas Alexander's grandfather, Amyntas, had been the first of his branch to become king as Amyntas III. Even among the descendants of Amyntas III the family of Philip was junior to the family of Perdiccas III, and Alexander was junior to the son of Perdiccas, Amyntas, by several years.

This Amyntas was a very strong rival. As a minor in 359 he had been elected king (in the opinion of the present writer[1]) as Amyntas IV, but only to be superseded by Philip. As an adult member, indeed the senior member in his generation, of the royal house he had held high offices of state and was probably leader of the Macedonian embassy to Thebes in 338. It was in recognition of his importance that he was given the hand of Cynane,[2] half-sister of Alexander, by Philip, who hoped thereby to link the two branches of the family and make Amyntas more amenable to the succession of Alexander, Philip's chosen heir.

The Macedonians themselves must have been divided. The supporters of Philip were more likely to support Alexander, because he had already shown brilliant abilities in diplomacy and in war and a restless energy. Yet many were discontented with Philip's policies. They wished to put an end to the transplanting of populations, continuous periods of conscription, promotion of non-Macedonians to high positions, and a deeper and deeper involvement in Greek affairs, quite apart from a war against Persia. On that summer day at Aegeae, when Philip lay dead under the early morning sky, they saw their chance to reverse Philip's policies. As Plutarch expressed it, perhaps without undue exaggeration, 'Macedonia was festering with discontent and was looking to Amyntas and the sons of Aëropus' (*Mor.* 327 c).

The Assembly of the Macedones acted at once. Meeting under arms that very day, they proceeded to elect a king by acclamation. The shout prevailed 'Alexander, son of Philip'. Forthwith he put on the royal robe and received the royal signet-ring. Leading Macedonians, donning their cuirasses, and men of the Royal Guard moved to his side, the Assembly clashed their spears upon their shields, and Alexander marched at the head of the military procession to the palace on the high terrace.[3] Among the first to pledge their loyalty to him by

---

[1] Volume II, 651; *contra* 702 f. (Griffith) and Ellis, *Philip* 23 f.

[2] This is the Attic form of the Macedonian name Cynnana, known from a third-century inscription in Macedonia (*AR* 1982–83. 44).

[3] Andronicos's discovery of the theatre below the terrace of the palace enables us to visualize the scene. The election was probably made where the corpse of Philip lay (as later at the death of A., J. 13. 4. 4), close to the altar dedicated by 'Eurydice, daughter of Sirras' (the form of the name is as I had suggested, and against the view of E. Badian in Adams and Borza 103 n. 14). For the part played by the 'Friends' in the coronation ceremony we may compare *PD* 18. 1. It is possible that Antipater spoke in commendation of A. on this occasion, as stated in Ps.-Callisthenes (rec. Müller) 1. 26.

donning their cuirasses was another Alexander, son of Aëropus, the strongest claimant to the throne in any collateral branch of the royal house. There is no mention of Amyntas having given such a lead.

The immediate duties of Alexander were to investigate the crime and prepare the tomb. Suspicion attached inevitably to those who had killed the assassin and thereby made interrogation of him impossible, namely two Bodyguards related to the royal house, Perdiccas and Leonnatus, and a third Bodyguard, Attalus, the uncle of one of Philip's younger wives, Cleopatra. The fact that horses had been provided for a getaway seemed to suggest the presence of two or three potential killers, and in consequence the intention to kill not only the king, but one or more of his immediate entourage, not on the way to the theatre (for only a last-minute change of plan by Philip had enabled the assassin to strike then), but during the performance in the theatre. All suspects who were available when the trial was held, some weeks perhaps after the event, were brought before the Assembly of the Macedones, sitting as a People's Court, under arms in accordance with traditional procedure. The king acted as prosecutor, the charge being one of high treason. The Assembly was sole judge.

The tattered remains of the text of a Hellenistic history, written on papyrus, which was discovered at Oxyrhynchus in Egypt, refer undoubtedly to some stage of the trial. As tentatively restored by the present writer, the passage translates as follows:

Those with him [viz. Philip] in the theatre and his followers they acquitted and those around the throne. The diviner he [viz. Alexander] delivered to the Macedones to punish, and they crucified him. The body of Philip he delivered to attendants to bury ... [and] by the burial....

The diviner, who had declared the omens favourable that day, fell victim to an occupational hazard. Two other persons were condemned to death as privy to the plot, but they were reserved for later execution, Heromenes and Arrhabaeus, sons of Aëropus. Their brother, the other Alexander, was also accused of complicity, but he was acquitted, as the king did not press the charge. The corpse of the assassin, Pausanias, was produced at the trial, and his three sons were held under arrest, pending execution in accordance with the customary law that male relatives of anyone found guilty of treason were put to death.[1]

By this time the tomb for the dead king was almost completed.[2] It stood just below ground level, close to the tomb—a smaller one—

[1] For references and arguments see HPT 339 f.
[2] For what follows see HPT 331 f. and HRTV 122 with references; also H.-L. 166 f. For different interpretations see W. L. Adams, 'The Royal Macedonian Tomb at Vergina: an historical interpretation', *Ancient World* 3 (1980) 67 f.; P. W. Lehmann in *AJA* 84 (1980) 527 ff.; and P. Green in Adams and Borza 129–51.

in which Amyntas III lay, and the adjacent shrine was destined henceforth to serve for the worship of both Amyntas and Philip as divine beings. The Friends of the dead king had mounted guard in turns. They had laid beside the corpse the emblems of royalty which were to go into the tomb—a diadem of gilded silver, a ceremonial shield of gold, silver, and ivory with a separate bronze cover, and an heirloom, an inscribed tripod won in the games at the Argive Heraeum by an ancestor of Philip *c.* 450 B.C. On the orders of Alexander an exquisite coffer of solid gold had been fashioned, and it was Alexander who chose the rich offerings which were to be laid with the dead: a superb cuirass of iron plates with gold fittings, three sets of gold-engraved greaves, an iron helmet with cheek-pieces, a fine-pommelled sword, twenty silver goblets, many bronze vessels, and a wealth of furniture.

On the appointed day the corpse was cremated on a great pyre. The two sons of Aëropus, wearing their swords as officers, and the horses associated with the assassin were killed and cast upon the flaming pyre, and the three sons of Pausanias were killed at the spot. When the fire had been doused with wine, the charred remains of the king, together with his wreath of gold oak-leaves and acorns, were placed in the gold coffer. It and all the offerings were deposited in the tomb, and the double marble doors were shut and sealed. The charred swords, the charred trappings of the horses, and the spearhead which had killed Philip were laid, together with a few gold acorns from a wreath and a bronze wine-pourer, in a brick tray on the top of the vaulted tomb. The stucco there was still wet. The walls of the chamber had not received the final layer of plaster and the inside of the marble doors was still rough. No one was to enter the tomb of the deified Philip, and no one did until Manolis Andronicos lifted a keystone of the vault and found the contents intact on 8 November 1977.[1]

The building of the antechamber continued. When it was complete, the cremated remains of a young woman aged between twenty-three and twenty-seven were laid in an equally beautiful, but less large, gold coffer; these remains were wrapped in purple cloth, beautifully embroidered with gold thread, and were accompanied by a gold wreath of myrtle leaves and blossoms, in which gold bees and other insects were inset. Conspicuous among the offerings was a gold *gorytos* or quiver-cover and beside it a pile of arrows, testifying that the queen had been a warrior-archer. Four other examples are known, all from Scythia. One from the same mould, and also accompanied by a pile of

---

[1] His recent accounts are in H.-L. 188 ff. and *AAA* 13.1 (1980) 168 ff. At the International Symposium in Thessaloniki in September 1984 he showed the photographs of the injured skull as reconstituted, which are conclusive. See now the report in *JHS* 104 (1984), and see Andronicos, *V.*

arrows, lay in the tumulus burial of a Scythian king at Karagodeo-nachkha; the skeleton of a woman wearing jewelry there was inter-preted as a case of suttee. Two coins of the Scythian king, Atheas, show a mounted archer with this particular type of *gorytos*.[1] We may conjecture that the queen in the antechamber of Philip's tomb was the daughter of the Getic king, Cothelas, or of the Scythian king, Atheas, who had promised to adopt Philip as his heir and to that end would have offered his daughter in marriage. Both were of the right age and both belonged to races in which one of the wives of a king met their death, whether by immolation or self-immolation, and was buried with the dead king.[2]

The antechamber in which she lay received its final coat of plaster, a white dado, and a band of rosettes. The front (Pl. II) had a high doorway of two fine marble leaves and four attached columns, which suggested a sacred building.[3] Between the capitals and the flat top of the façade a fresco portrayed a royal hunt with three men on horseback and seven on foot. Of these only one horseman is of mature years, and he is about to kill the lion; he is evidently the king, Philip. The central place in the picture is taken by a young horseman, riding towards the viewer and wearing a laurel wreath. He is presumably a prince and the commissioner of the painting, i.e. Alexander. On top of the façade there were the remains of a small purificatory fire with bones of small creatures; and it was evidently there that the crucified corpse of the assassin had been displayed to public view.

The richness of the offerings leave us in no doubt that Alexander meant to pay the highest honour to his father. There is nothing here to support the rumours of strong animosity between father and son and of an impoverished treasury. A group of five ivory heads, only an inch high, is of special interest. Of the fourteen found these five have been published, and of them two have been identified by special character-istics; one is a portrait of Philip, showing the scar of the wound which blinded his right eye, and the other of Alexander in his late teens, with the typical poise of the neck and upward gaze of the eyes. If, as is probable, the other three belong to a family group, they represent Amyntas and Eurydice, Philip's parents, and Olympias, wife of Philip and mother of Alexander. To these heads there belonged bodies and

---

[1] See V. Schiltz, 'Deux gorytes identiques en Macédoine et dans le Kouban', *Rev. Arch.* 1979, 305 f.

[2] St. Byz. s.v. *Getia*; J. 9. 2. 1 (Atheas); Hdt. 4. 71. 4 and 5. 5 with How and Wells ad loc. 'like Suttee'. See *HPT* 336 and *HRTV* 123. P. Green disputes the likeness to suttee and doubts whether Atheas would promise the hand of his daughter, in Adams and Borza 148.

[3] Ps.-Callisthenes (ed. G. Kroll) 1. 24. 11 has the best surviving description of the structure: 'Having arranged a rich tomb for him Alexander put the vault (*skenoma*) on it, founding a shrine (*naon*) at the very tomb', where I take the 'shrine' to be the temple-like façade.

FIG. 2. PHILIP'S TOMB: FRESCO OF THE ROYAL HUNT

limbs of gold and ivory. Lifesize statues in gold and ivory of the same five persons were dedicated at Olympia in the Philippeum, a building planned by Philip in the autumn of 338 B.C. The probability is considerable that the figures in the tomb were miniatures of the statues at Olympia. They were placed there in honour of the dead man, just as gold and ivory 'images' (i.e. likenesses) were prepared for the tomb of Hephaestion in 323 B.C. (see D.S. 17. 115. 1). They testify again to the affection of Alexander for his father. Similarly, at Olympia Philip had intended to show the solidarity of the royal family and his own choice of a successor; for he knew that the constitutional decision was to be taken by the Macedonian Assembly.

The verdict of the People's Court and the executions did not put an end to suspicions in Macedonia concerning the assassination of Philip. Had foreign powers promoted the murder? It was learnt soon after the event that Demosthenes, the leader of the anti-Macedonian party at Athens, had had secret information of Philip's death in advance of any official report, had appeared there in festive dress, and had later persuaded the Athenians to vote a crown in honour of Pausanias (P*Demosth* 22. 1). Another pointer to the possible involvement of Demosthenes came in summer 335 B.C. when the Theban leaders were planning a rising and Demosthenes 'was writing to the Macedonian generals in Asia' (ibid. 23. 2), and specifically to Attalus, who,

according to D.S. 17. 5. 1 (drawing on Diyllus), had earlier been in touch with Athens, but now sent Demosthenes' letter to Alexander in the hope of extricating himself. Then, as Macedonia was at war with Persia, it was natural to suspect Persia, itself in touch with Demosthenes. Late in 333 B.C., in the course of diplomatic exchanges, Alexander openly accused Darius of complicity. Nor was it improbable; for by then Darius was believed to have made two attempts to have Alexander killed by members of Alexander's entourage (Arr. 1. 25. 3; 2. 4. 9).

Had other Macedonians than the two sons of Aëropus been involved in planning the assassination? We have already mentioned those three Bodyguards of Philip who had not arrested, but killed, the assassin. Acquitted at the time, they were not made Bodyguards of Alexander, but they were appointed by him to important commands. In particular, Attalus, a dashing soldier and most popular with the army, was sent back to Asia, where he shared the command of the Macedonian forces with Parmenio and an Amyntas—not the son of Perdiccas (J. 9. 5. 9; cf. D.S. 16. 91. 2, omitting Amyntas). But further evidence emerged which seemed to inculpate Attalus. In particular some treasonable correspondence between Demosthenes and 'the generals in Asia' was reported (P*Demosth* 23. 2; D.S. 17. 3. 2, naming Attalus as the recipient). Alexander moved quickly. He sent one of his Friends,

Hecataeus, 'with orders at best to arrest Attalus, and if he could not arrest him, to kill him' (D.S. 17. 2. 5). In the event Hecataeus killed Attalus in autumn 335 (D.S. 17. 5. 2).

As in the case of Pausanias, we may assume that the corpse of Attalus was tried by the Assembly and found guilty of treason, and that the evidence against Attalus was made public. Whether such evidence implicated other members of his family, we do not know; but it is certain that his ward, Cleopatra, the baby she had born to Philip, and those male relatives who had been promoted to high positions by Philip were all put to death (J. 11. 5. 1; cf. 12. 6. 14 'noverca fratresque').[1] It is probable that the decision was taken by the Assembly of the Macedones sitting as a People's Court and condemning the relatives of a convicted traitor in accordance with their customary law (cf. C. 8. 6. 28).

The correspondence between Demosthenes and 'the generals in Asia' involved Amyntas, but not Parmenio, who in Alexander's eyes was above suspicion. This Amyntas, appointed by Philip in 336 and confirmed in a command by Alexander (C. 3. 11. 18), deserted to Persia and entered Persian service. In summer 334 he fled from Ephesus as Alexander advanced, and he was then described by Arrian as the son of Antiochus (1. 17. 9). When this Amyntas deserted, he delivered a letter from Alexander, son of Aëropus, to Darius[2]; and it was in connection with this letter that Darius offered the throne of Macedonia and 1,000 talents of gold to Alexander, son of Aëropus, if he would assassinate Alexander. However, the carrier of the offer fell into the hands of Parmenio, who forwarded him to Alexander in the winter of 334/3 (Arr. 1. 25. 3–4). Alexander convened and consulted the Council of Friends. They advised him to dispose of Alexander, son of Aëropus. Alexander merely imprisoned him. Trial by the Assembly of Macedones came three years later, in 330; he was found guilty of treason and was executed on the spot (C. 7. 1. 5–9; cf. D.S. 17. 32. 1–2 and 80. 2).

The case of Alexander, son of Aëropus, also known from his cantonal citizenship as Alexander Lyncestes,[3] throws much light on the

---

[1] The statement in Paus. 8. 7. 7 that Cleopatra and her child were roasted to death by Olympias is part of Cassander's campaign of vilification and is not historical; so too J. R. Ellis in *M–G* 71.

[2] Bosworth ad loc. doubts this; but A.'s treatment of his namesake is difficult to reconcile with a forged letter, designed to convict him of treason.

[3] The significance of this term has often been misunderstood. For instance, Welles 275 calls him 'a Prince of Lyncus'. The fact is that all Macedones had either a city affiliation or a canton affiliation (see Volume II. 647). The affiliation was sometimes added in order to distinguish a man who had a common name: e.g. Ptolemy Alorites (D.S. 15. 71. 1, regent in 368), Ptolemy of Eordaea (Arr. *Ind.* 18. 5), Leonnatus of Pella, Leonnatus of Orestis, and Leonnatus of Aegeae (Arr. *Ind.* 18. 5–6). Two of these were members of the royal house, and the affiliation simply indicated where they lived and voted in local affairs.

attitude of Alexander. As we have mentioned above, this man had been tried and acquitted, when his two brothers were condemned and executed, shortly after the assassination of Philip. According to Arrian (1. 25. 2) it was Alexander the king who saved him; for it is to be noted that under the customary law he could have been executed as a relative of the two traitors. Indeed, Alexander had complete faith in him; for he gave him a leading position at court, and made him commander first of Thrace and then of the Thessalian cavalry, to which he endeared himself. It was an indication of the high standing of Alexander Lyncestes that he had married a daughter of Antipater, Philip's trusted general and soon to be Alexander's deputy in Macedonia. As I have argued elsewhere,[1] he was treated so well by Alexander because he was a member of the royal house, and it was only the initiative of Atarrhias[2] and the insistence of the Assembly of Macedones that led to his execution.

The desertion of Amyntas, son of Antiochus, may have led to the execution of Amyntas, son of Perdiccas, who had been married shortly before Philip's death to Philip's daughter, Cynane (see above, p. 4). Both Amyntases had been honoured in Boeotia: the son of Perdiccas as 'king of the Macedones' (on my interpretation c. 359–357) at Lebadeia (*IG* VII. 3055), and as *proxenos* shortly before the battle of Chaeronea in 338 at Oropus (*IG* VII. 4251), and the son of Antiochus also as *proxenos* at the same time at Oropus (*IG* VII. 4250).[3] Whatever the evidence against Amyntas, son of Perdiccas, may have been, he was put to death shortly before Alexander set out for Asia (J. 11. 5. 2, evidently referring to this, and 12. 6. 14 'Amyntas consobrinus'), and presumably after being convicted of plotting against Alexander (C. 6. 9. 17 and 10. 24). The wife of Amyntas, Cynane, was not involved in the verdict, nor was her infant daughter by Amyntas, Eurydice, who was subsequently married to Alexander's half-brother, Arrhidaeus.

That the aim of all these measures taken by the king and by the Assembly of Macedones was to secure the throne is not in dispute. Past history was full of precedents. Dynastic plots and killings had been important factors in the weakness of Macedonia in 399–359. Philip had strengthened the kingdom by bringing about the deaths of five

---

[1] H*SPA* 458.
[2] Despite C. 7. 1. 5, who couples Atarrhias' initiative with the words 'undoubtedly by previous arrangement' ('haud dubie ex composito'). C., with the example of the Roman emperors in mind, could hardly have thought otherwise. But since A. acted as prosecutor, he had no need to ask Atarrhias to demand a trial; he could initiate a trial himself, as he did at this time for Amyntas and Simmias (C. 7. 1. 10). The best explanation for Atarrhias acting so is that A. did not wish to bring Alexander Lyncestes to trial.
[3] On these inscriptions see J. R. Ellis, 'Amyntas Perdikka, Philip II and Alexander the Great; a study in conspiracy', *JHS* 91 (1971) 16 ff., and Griffith in Volume II. 702 f.

members of the royal house—Pausanias, Argaeus, Archelaus, Arrhidaeus, and Menelaus—and there is no reason to reject the tradition that these five had been supported by at least three foreign states. The enormous growth of Macedonian power after 359 made the Macedonian throne a greater prize, and rendered Macedonia's enemies more eager than ever to overthrow the expansionist kings, Philip and Alexander. Precedent and probability suggest that Alexander and the Assembly of Macedones acted in accordance with Macedonian standards of justice.

2. *Alexander and the Macedonians*

The sensational nature of these cases has distracted attention from the much more important concerns of Alexander in Macedonia. The Macedonian state, τὸ κοινὸν τῶν Μακεδόνων, consisted of two parts: the elected king exercising the constitutional powers which had evolved over three centuries, known internationally as βασιλεὺς Μακεδόνων; and the assembly of men serving or having served in the king's forces (as opposed to the local militia), known as οἱ Μακεδόνες. Each new king or regent had to impress his personality upon the Macedones. As Philip had done (D.S. 16. 3. 1), Alexander won them over by the eloquence and the appropriateness of his speeches (J. 11. 1. 8).[1] At the outset he promised to adhere to the principles of Philip's reign (17. 2. 2). Later he enuntiated two of his own principles: the king will govern, not by decree, but by persuasion (Arr. 5. 27. 2), and the king will speak nothing but the truth to his people (Arr. 7. 5. 2). Throughout his reign he acted within his constitutional powers, being scrupulous in conducting state sacrifices and observing omens, persuading the Assembly to undertake campaigns (C. 6. 4. 1; 9. 1. 3; *PA* 34. 1) as Philip had done (D.S. 16. 4. 3), bringing suspected traitors before the Assembly as a People's Court[2] and accepting its decision when it acquitted men whom he himself had prosecuted (C. 7. 1. 10–2. 11; Arr. 3. 27. 2). Alexander may be called a democratic king in that he was constantly marching, talking, and fighting in the company of his soldiers, accepted their freedom of speech in the Assembly, as Polybius later remarked (5. 27. 6), and knew and loved them to the end of his days. In return they honoured and venerated him both for his own qualities and as the representative of the only family which in their opinion had

---

[1] One item in his speeches was not, as J. 11. 1. 10 asserts, the remission to the Macedones of all obligations except military service. A. was in no financial position to grant that, and Arr. 1. 16. 5 shows the incorrectness of Justin, the epitomizer of Trogus, who was familiar with Roman donatives.

[2] Except that he kept Alexander Lyncestes under arrest and did not pursue the allegations laid against Philotas in Egypt (Arr. 3. 26. 1, citing Ptolemy and Aristobulus).

a right to rule (C. 10. 7. 15). It was essentially a free society (there
being no trace in Macedonia of the slave-base[1] on which Greek city-
states rested), and the Macedonians (to quote C. 4. 7. 31) 'being
accustomed to the rule of a king, lived with a greater sense of freedom
than any others subject to a monarchy'. The combination of Alexander
the king and his free, but devoted, Macedonians was to create a
dynamic energy which has never been equalled. In 336 he mounted an
intensive training programme for his troops (D.S. 17. 2. 3).

It proved much more difficult for Alexander to choose appropriate
persons to be his Bodyguards, Friends, and Companions, men who
were to feast and drink with him, advise him at his discretion, form his
élite cavalry, and serve him as commanders and administrators. The
difficulty arose partly from the conditions of the past. There was no
hereditary aristocracy in the Macedonian homeland from which a king
might recruit his closest followers; for long before the accession of
Philip the tribal system had been replaced by town-citizenships. There
were no such things as 'barons with local followings'. In Upper
Macedonia there had been separate kingdoms and tribal aristocracies,
but Philip had deliberately dismantled the apparatus of kingship and
dispersed any local groups by transplanting populations, fusing old
and new in his city foundations (J. 8. 5. 7), and creating a unified field
army of men drawn from Lower Macedonia and Upper Macedonia
alike.

When the tribal aristocracies disappeared in the homeland, one of
the Macedonian kings introduced what may be called the School of
Royal Pages, first attested in the reign of Archelaus. In that school the
boys of the royal family and the sons of the Friends, from the age of
fourteen to the age of seventeen inclusive, served the king and were
trained by him in behaviour, hunting, and war. It was a hard school
with exposure to danger and strict discipline, and it proved to be a
remarkable 'seed-bed of commanders and administrators' (C. 8. 6. 6
'seminarium ducum praefectorumque'; cf. 5. 1. 42). It had, however,
its defects. The parents and the boys were where they were only
because a king had chosen them, and the graduation and the future
career of each boy depended upon the favour of the reigning king.
Competition to win his regard was intense, and rivalries were keen
within the school and thereafter (e.g. C. 6. 8. 2). There was no appeal
against the king's decision. If one felt oneself unfairly treated or
thwarted, one had no redress (e.g. D.S. 16. 94. 1; Arr. 4. 13. 3). It is not
surprising that all the attempts or supposed attempts on the lives of
Philip and Alexander came not from the ordinary soldiers among

---

[1] The practices of the Macedonian court alone make this clear; see Volume II. 154.

whom they moved so freely, but from members or graduates of the School of Royal Pages. We may mention from our sources Pausanias, three sons of Aëropus, Amyntas son of Perdiccas, Attalus, Philotas, Dimnus, four sons of Andromenes, Hermolaus, and five other Pages.

Within the School of Royal Pages cliques developed, sometimes with homosexual attachments, and they tended to cluster round potential heirs to the throne. Alexander was himself a product of the school. His closest friends there were Hephaestion, Ptolemy, Nearchus, Erigyius, Laomedon, and Harpalus. When Philip married Cleopatra and a rift developed between Philip and Alexander, the last five of these young men expressed their support of Alexander in some public manner and were banished by Philip in 337. What seemed to have damned their careers turned out to be the key to promotion. For Alexander, as king, was most generous and even proved himself indulgent to those who had supported him through thick and thin.

It was inevitable with this system that certain families distinguished themselves in the service of the king and that something like a hereditary officer class tended to develop. There was also some inbreeding, because such families intermarried with one another and sometimes with members of the royal house. Thus Antipater had daughters married to Alexander Lyncestes, Craterus, Perdiccas, and Ptolemy (all rose to high commands), and Parmenio had daughters married to Coenus and to the Attalus who held command in Asia and was killed by Hecataeus. In a society which assessed as the qualities of manliness the killing of a man in war and the spearing of a wild boar in the hunt the sons of such officer families, who rode from childhood and served in the School of Pages, had every opportunity to reach the top. Together with inbreeding there developed a certain limitation of outlook and lack of elasticity, such as one finds in any officer-producing system, and these became more obvious with the need to expand the armed forces drastically and to induct new racial elements. Alexander was to show later that he was aware of these defects and had recourse to new methods (see p. 93 below). But for the moment, in the weeks following the assassination of Philip, Alexander had to select his own personal Bodyguards and Friends and to keep the officer class on his side.

3. *The election as* hegemon *of the Greek League's forces*

It will be recalled that Alexander sealed off the burial chamber of Philip before its interior was completed. The reason was presumably that he had to pay his last respects to Philip in person, and at the same time he had to take a grip on the situation in Greece immediately and in person.[1] A force of dissident Thessalians was already holding an almost impregnable position in the vale of Tempe on the direct route into Greece (see Fig. 6). Alexander turned the position by a brilliant manœuvre. Crossing the river Peneus lower down, he and his picked men, trained in mountaineering, climbed the sheer face of Mt. Ossa by cutting steps, known as 'Alexander's Ladder', and appeared above the Thessalians who fled and dispersed (Polyaen. 4. 3. 23). Leaving these Thessalians to their own devices, he went to the centre of support, Larissa, where the ruling clan, the Aleuadae, had a record of loyalty, and he emphasized their and his common descent from Heracles and from Achilles and his desire to benefit them. With their aid he sought and obtained election at a meeting of the Thessalian League Council as its president (*archon*) for life (thus succeeding to the position held by his father).[2] He was now able to keep the city-states of Thessaly at peace with one another, control the financial resources of the League, and call up the finest cavalry force by far in Greece. He reaffirmed the close alliance between his country and Thessaly, which had existed since Philip's entry into the Third Sacred War (Isoc. 5. 20).

Next, he convened a meeting of the Amphictyonic Council at Thermopylae; for he was as anxious as Philip had been to establish his influence and to show that he had the support of the Delphic god, Apollo, in his plans for the reconciliation of the Greeks and the invasion of Persia. Since the Macedonians and their supporters in Thessaly and adjacent areas had a majority of the votes, the Council expressed their full support of Alexander. Moreover, the Thessalian League Council and the Amphictyonic Council both passed resolutions (κοινὰ δόγματα) conferring on Alexander the hegemony of the Greeks which his father had held. In other words they put their forces under his command to enforce the conditions of the alliance between the Greeks and the Macedonians. He moved south, not only with the terrifyingly efficient Macedonian army (D.S. 17. 4. 4), but also with some Greek troops and especially the redoubtable Thessalian cavalry, who were ready to attack any state which might break the terms of the peace and the alliance— even Athens, as Aeschines later remarked (3. 161 ἤδη δ' ἐψηφισμένων Θετταλῶν ἐπιστρατεύειν ἐπὶ τὴν ἡμετέραν πόλιν). And it all happened more rapidly than the Athenians and other dissidents had supposed possible; for Alexander marched at speed (J. 11. 2. 5 'citato gradu in Graeciam contendit', and D.S. 17. 4. 4 ὀξείαις ταῖς ὁδοιπορίαις).

[1] The chamber was sealed between the collection of the bones of Philip from the pyre and the collection of other objects from the pyre; for the pieces of gold leaf and the gold acorns missing from the wreath in the gold coffer were found in the brick tray on top of the tomb. The interval of time must have been brief. For another example of the missing part of a wreath being found later in the pyre see Volume I. 190, citing *Mak.* 2 (1941–52) 621.
[2] D.S. 17. 4. 1–3; J. 11. 3. 1–2.

In 336 the relations between the Greeks and the Macedonians were governed by the alliance for all time which had been contracted between the Greeks of the Common Peace and the Macedonians, and by their commitment to a joint war against Persia.[1] The Greeks had appointed Philip *hegemon*—that is, to command the joint forces not only against Persia, but against any violator of the Common Peace of the Greeks, whether within Greece or outside Greece. The death of Philip altered only the last point. Alexander might claim that he 'inherited'[2] the hegemony (D.S. 17. 4. 1 τὴν πατροπαράδοτον ἡγεμονίαν); but in practice he had to ask for it to be conferred upon him (D.S. 17. 4. 9 and Arr. 1. 1. 2). There were already many indications that it would not be his for the asking; for action had been taken, or was about to be taken, by Ambracia, the Aetolian League, Thebes, Argos, Elis, and probably Arcadia. Moreover, a possible leader for this formidable array of dissident states was Athens, where the news of Philip's assassination had been greeted with public jubilation and a crown had been voted to the assassin (not that it would do much for Pausanias); and in addition it was believed that through Demosthenes Athens was in touch with Persia and with Alexander's generals in Asia. It was evident that Athens and Thebes might mount a coalition of resistance which would rival or surpass that of 338, but only if they were given time.

Time was what Alexander refused them. He appeared suddenly in full force outside Thebes, where Philip's garrison was still installed. The Theban move towards resistance collapsed. The Athenians abandoned the countryside and attended to their defences; but at the same time they sent envoys to apologize for not having said earlier that they would support his request for the hegemony. He accepted their apology and swept on to Corinth. Now he needed only the consent of 'those inside the Peloponnese' (Arr. 1. 1. 2). The members of the Council of the Greek League who had acted in Philip's time were assembled at Corinth; in response to an eloquent and persuasive speech by Alexander, a young man of twenty, but backed by the Macedonian army and a force of northern Greeks, the Councillors all voted to appoint him *hegemon* and to proceed with the joint campaign against Persia (D.S. 17. 4. 9 and Plb. 9. 33. 7). Dissidents in the Peloponnese apologized. Only Sparta stayed, as before, out of the Greek League. She declared proudly that it was her way not to be led, but to lead. As no one showed any desire to be led by Sparta, Alexander wisely let her be. The hegemony she had once had was exercised now by Macedonia.

He had gained all he wanted through speed of movement, skilful

---

[1] See Appendix 1 on this subject.
[2] The meaning of πατροπαράδοτον is not legal or literal, but general, as at D.S. 17. 2. 2, when A. asked the Greeks to observe their traditional goodwill, τὴν πατροπαράδοτον εὔνοιαν.

diplomacy, and in the background the mailed fist. By taking piece after piece—the Thessalian League, the Amphictyonic Council, Thebes, and Athens—he had needed only to put the Council of the Greek League in check and threaten the Peloponnese in order to win the game outright without the loss of a pawn. He and his army returned triumphant to Macedonia.

Alexander had fitted two strings to his bow. The Common Peace might not hold, because, as Alexander had seen, the leading states of Greece did not willingly support a system which tied them to the *status quo*. But the Amphictyonic Council offered a more dependable base politically and religiously, as Philip himself had demonstrated. Alexander may have supported now the issue of an Amphictyonic coinage with a head of Demeter and a seated Apollo,[1] and his concern for the prestige of the Amphictyony was to be repaid by the loyalty of its members in the war of Agis III. In matters of justice Alexander, like Philip, took Greek offenders for trial not only to the Council of the Common Peace, but also to the Council of the Amphictyony (Paus. 7. 10. 10). In Greek religion Apollo was particularly Hellenic, and Philip had espoused his cause in two Sacred Wars. Alexander was to pay his tributes to Apollo of Delphi on the bank of the Hyphasis and in his last plans which included the building of a temple at Delphi to cost 1,500 talents.

4. *The evidence: the* King's Journal, *the secondary narratives, and other material*

With the above narrative at our disposal we may consider the sources of information from which it is constructed. Although such a consideration has been omitted or belittled by many recent writers of books on Alexander, it remains an essential element in Alexander-history. The five surviving narratives, written all in the time of the Roman Empire, vary greatly in quality of information and in attitude to Alexander's personality and achievement, and this variation clearly arose to a great extent from the sources which were chosen by these five writers, namely the written accounts composed in the fifty or so years after the death of Alexander. It is of course possible for a modern writer to pick and choose from the five narratives those items that fit a preconceived image of Alexander as, for example, a ruthless dictator, a raging Achilles, or a power-crazy homosexual. But the responsibility of the historian is to take an objective view and to weigh the value of the evidence, piece by piece, in so far as his insight permits. This may result

---

[1] It is uncertain whether A. now or his father, Philip, in 338 inspired the issue of this Amphictyonic coinage. Seltman, *GC* 203, favoured Philip.

in a reconstruction which comes closer to the historical Alexander and his historical achievements.

The *King's Journal, αἱ βασίλειοι Ἐφημερίδες* (Arr. 7. 25. 1), contained a full record of a Macedonian king's actions, sayings, orders, correspondence, etc., set down day by day at the time by a team of secretaries. A Greek called Eumenes (he came from Cardia in the Thracian Chersonese) served Philip as a junior secretary and Alexander as his chief secretary (ἀρχιγραμματεύς). The record had to be accurate, because any official's act might be reviewed in relation to the king's order. Every effort was undertaken to make the record complete; thus when Eumenes lost some documents through a fire, Alexander ordered his satraps and generals to supply copies to Eumenes of what they had written (P*Eum* 2. 3). Any *King's Journal* was both a state archive and personal to the king. It was not open to the public. When a king died, the *Journal* for the years of his reign became a separable unit; thus we hear of the *Alexander-Journal* (*FGrH* 118 Strattis T 1, αἱ Ἀλεξάνδρου Ἐφημερίδες).

It is probable that completed *Journals* of this kind (for instance the *Philip-Journal*) were kept at Aegeae, where the kings were buried. But the *Alexander-Journal*, which was in Babylon when he died, never reached Aegeae; for the corpse, the funerary car, and the adjuncts of the king were intercepted and taken by Ptolemy to Alexandria in Egypt. Access to past *Journals* was granted only, one imagines, by favour of the reigning king in Macedonia and, in the case of the *Alexander-Journal*, of Ptolemy as ruler of Egypt.

The author who comes closest to quoting at some length from the *Alexander-Journal* is Arrian, writing in the second century A.D. Being precise in his use of language, Arrian made a point of using ὧδε to introduce a citation (2. 14. 4 and 16. 8; 5. 1. 4 and 25. 2; 7. 1. 5 and 8. 3) and sometimes ταῦτα to close a citation (2. 15. 1 and 18. 1; 5. 2. 1; 7. 11. 3), whereas he used τοιόσδε and τοιοῦτος to introduce and close a passage which was not an actual citation (e.g. 4. 10. 5 and 11. 1; 5. 27. 1 and 28. 1). In accordance with this practice Arrian introduced a citation concerning Alexander's illness from the *King's Journal* with the words αἱ βασίλειοι ἐφημερίδες ὧδε ἔχουσι (7. 25. 1); and he closed it with the words οὕτως and then ἐπὶ τούτοις (7. 26. 1). The citation is given not in the original words, nor in direct speech, but in Arrian's words and in indirect speech; and it is certainly abbreviated from the original, which would have given *in extenso* the various orders issued by him (7. 25. 2, 4, and 5). At 7. 26. 1 Arrian gives further material from the *King's Journal*, not however in this form of citation, but in a paraphrase intermingled with his own comment. The introductory phrases are now ἀναγέγραπται...ὅτι, λέγουσι [sc. αἱ ἐφημερίδες], λέγουσι δὲ αἱ ἐφημερίδες αἱ βασίλειοι; and Arrian adds two comments, ὡς ἔγωγε δοκῶ and ὡς τοῦτο ἄρα ἤδη ὂν τὸ ἄμεινον.

Thus it is clear from Arrian's practice and his introductory phrases that Arrian is himself making his own version from the text of the *Alexander-Journal.* He goes on to compare his own version with those given by other authors: namely those of Aristobulus and Ptolemy being 'not far from this' (7. 26. 3 οὐ πόρρω δὲ τούτων, 'this' being Arrian's own version),[1] those of some others including a conversation about a successor, and those of yet others adding Alexander's epigrammatic statement that he foresaw a great funerary contest. We see, then, that Arrian went back to the original source in this instance, and that he did not lift the citation from either Aristobulus or Ptolemy.

Whether Arrian had access to a complete copy of the *Alexander-Journal* or read the relevant part in a verbatim excerpt, such as might have been transmitted, for example, by Strattis of Olynthus (*FGrH* 118 T 1), who wrote five books *On the Alexander-Journal*[2], or by one Philinus who preserved two short verbatim citations ἐκ τῶν βασιλικῶν ἐφημερίδων (*FGrH* 117 F 2c), is not material to our present argument. The point is that Arrian, Strattis, and Philinus drew directly or indirectly on the *Alexander-Journal*. To them we may add Plutarch. For he said that it was possible to infer 'from the Journal' that Alexander often hunted foxes and birds for sport (*PA* 23. 3–4); and he gave his own less precise paraphrase of the passage in the *Journal* concerning Alexander's illness (*PA* 76, with the remark at 77. 1 that 'the bulk of this is so written verbatim in the Journal').

Some scholars[3] have supposed that there existed not only the genuine *Alexander-Journal*, but also a fictitious so-called *Alexander-Journal*, and that it was the latter from which the authors we have mentioned were making their citations and paraphrases, they of course being unaware of what these modern scholars have divined. This is an audacious theory; for the ancient writers had before their eyes at least one and (on this theory) even two *Alexander-Journals in extenso* and were

---

[1] The phrase is translated in Loeb R as 'beyond this neither Ptolemaeus nor Aristobulus have recorded', for which not πόρρω, but πορρωτέρω, would be needed; see LSJ[9] s.v. πρόσω. Loeb R's meaning is not found there; and compare for my interpretation πρόσω B II, e.g. πόρρω τῆς ὑποθέσεως, and Arrian's own use at 5. 20. 10 οὐ πόρρω τοῦ ἀληθοῦς 'not far from the truth'. Bosworth 23 supports Loeb R.

[2] The suggestion in Pearson 260 n. 92, that περὶ τῶν Ἀλεξάνδρου Ἐφημερίδων βιβλία πέντε means 'Five books of Diaries on the exploits of Alexander', makes no sense of 'Diaries', unless Strattis wrote daily (for that is the meaning of ἐφημερίδες) and runs counter to all known titles in which 'the exploits of Alexander' are αἱ Ἀλεξάνδρου πράξεις (*FGrH* II B 645) or τὰ περὶ Ἀλέξανδρον (*FGrH* II B 657, 658, 737, 743, 812) and never τὰ Ἀλεξάνδρου. The title περὶ τῶν Ἀλεξάνδρου Ἐφημερίδων, in which Ἀλεξάνδρου precedes the aspect of his activity, is as in περὶ τῆς Ἀλεξάνδρου τελευτῆς and αἱ Ἀλεξάνδρου πράξεις. For what seems to be a fragment of Strattis' work see Hammond's article in *GRBS* 1988.

[3] E.g. L. Pearson in *Historia* 3 (1955) 432 f. and A. E. Samuel in *Historia* 14 (1965) 1 f.

thus in a far better position to judge whether this or that *Journal* was true or fictitious than we who have neither *Journal* before our eyes. And when we realize that the documentation included in either *Alexander-Journal* must have run into many volumes (so many that Strattis wrote five books about it), we may indeed be amazed at the diligence and the inventiveness of the supposed forger of an entire *Alexander-Journal*. Further, it remains wellnigh incredible that the forger could challenge the authenticity and bring about the suppression of the genuine *Alexander-Journal*, composed over thirteen years by the chief secretaries Eumenes and Diodotus (*FGrH* 117 T 1) and their assistants, and kept after Alexander's death as a state archive, which contained many documents written by leading persons who survived for up to forty years and could vouch for or deny the truth of them. The conclusion of the present writer is that there was only one *Alexander-Journal* and that it was genuine.[1]

When Alexander lay dying, the *King's Journal* already contained copies of the written orders which he had given to Craterus and had sent through him to Antipater (Arr. 7. 12. 4; D.S. 18. 4. 1 ἐντολὰς...ἐγγράπτους), and these orders included the building of temples costing 1,500 talents each at six places in Europe and a tomb for Philip 'like the greatest pyramid of Egypt'.[2] As the temples were to mark the triumph of Graeco-Macedonian arms in Asia and the tomb was to honour Philip, there is no doubt that Alexander had discussed these plans with his Friends; for there was nothing secret about them and the plans would be to their liking. A day or two after Alexander's death Perdiccas brought these orders to the Assembly of Macedones (τὸ κοινὸν τῶν Μακεδόνων πλῆθος), and it was these orders among others than the Macedones cancelled (D.S. 18. 4. 6) and the 'Successors'

[1] One of the incidents which set this particular hare upon its long run has been the all-night vigil of some of A.'s Companions in the shrine of Sarapis, cited expressly from αἱ ἐφημερίδες αἱ βασίλειοι (Arr. 7. 26. 2). Here, say some scholars, the forger has betrayed himself; we know better than he; for there was no such shrine at Babylon. To suppose the forger was such an ass as to think there was does not help to explain how his (supposed) forgery imposed on his contemporaries and all antiquity! It is better to note A.'s addiction to Zeus Ammon, A.'s use of Egyptian diviners as 'the most skilled in his opinion at reading the heavens and the stars' (C. 4. 10. 4, just before Gaugamela), and the preparation of A.'s corpse for embalming—by Egyptians (C. 10. 10. 13 'Aegyptii Chaldaeique, iussi corpus suo more curare')—not, as we know from Vergina, a Macedonian royal practice, but certainly one which A. had himself asked to be used in the event of his death. That he believed in Sarapis as a miraculous healer is highly probable, and that his closest Companions should consult Sarapis on his behalf is not surprising. We should note too that Egyptians spread into many parts of Asia and even campaigned as far as India (Arr. *Ind.* 18. 1; 31. 3). There is, then, no difficulty in believing that A. himself had set up a shrine to Sarapis in Babylon, or/and that Egyptians in Babylon, the great metropolis of the Kingdom of Asia, had established the worship of their own god of healing. We should remember too (Suidas s.v. *basilikoi paides*) that Alexander had ordered the training for war of 6,000 'royal boys' in Egypt; these were like the Persian 'Epigonoi' and some may have come to Babylon.

[2] For the genuineness of these plans see *HA* 300 f.

agreed not to implement (18. 4. 1). The idea that Perdiccas brought to the Assembly a forged set of orders and not those issued to Craterus and Antipater and recorded by Eumenes and other secretaries in the current *King's Journal* does not bear inspection. For it would have been an act, not only of dishonesty, but also of folly in Perdiccas, because Eumenes and other Friends could have exposed such a forgery immediately by reference to the *King's Journal* (it existed for precisely that purpose) and later by consulting Craterus and Antipater. Nor was Perdiccas short of enemies, who might have taken such an initiative.

It has been suggested that only the section covering the end of Alexander's life at Babylon survived from a *Journal*, whether genuine or fictitious in itself. This suggestion, highly improbable if the *Journal* was a genuine state archive, is disproved by the fact that Alexander's orders to Craterus, and through him to Antipater, were given not at Babylon, but at Opis (Arr. 7. 12. 4), that Alexander's fox-hunting days (*FGrH* 117 F 1) were not in the Mesopotamian flats, but earlier, and that the reflections of Athenaeus and Philinus on Alexander's sleeping and drinking habits were evidently not based only on his stay at Babylon. Rather it seems that the entire *Journal* survived Alexander's death, and that it was the ultimate source, for instance, of the very great number of details which have come down to us in Arrian's account of the campaign in the Balkans (see p. 50 below).

Let us consider next what use, if any, was made of the *Alexander-Journal* by some historians. The first candidate is Callisthenes of Olynthus, a nephew of Aristotle and an accomplished writer even before he was employed by Alexander to write an account of the Asiatic campaigns. Joining Alexander's entourage in Europe, he was able to describe the crossing into Asia from what he saw for himself and from what he was told by Alexander and others. His aim was to produce not an accurate record, but an account favourable to, and appropriate to, Alexander and his purposes. The *Alexander-Journal*, for instance, will have included the reviewing of the army at the crossing into Asia, no doubt unit by unit, as mentioned by D.S. 17. 17. 3 f. The total given by Callisthenes for Alexander's infantry 'at the crossing into Asia', namely 40,000 men (*FGrH* 124 F 35, 19. 1), was indeed far in excess of the actual number, and therefore was designed to alarm the enemy, who feared Alexander's infantry more than his cavalry. Callisthenes certainly did not take these figures from the *Alexander-Journal*.

For Greeks and Macedonians the crossing of the Hellespont was the historic moment. Alexander was treading in the steps of Agamemnon, Xerxes, and Agesilaus in leading his forces from one continent to the other with a view to conquest. Alexander emphasized the historical associations by a series of acts.[1] In particular, like Xerxes, he reviewed his forces at the Hellespont. Homer had sung of the forces of Agamemnon, and Herodotus had reported the numbering of Xerxes' army and navy at Doriscus, where they first joined one another on European soil.[2] So too the Alexander-historians. Unlike some modern historians, they were not concerned with the number of Macedonian troops already in Asia; for that was no more relevant to their purpose than the strength of Persia's advance forces in Thrace and Macedonia had been to Herodotus. They wrote of the number of men and ships which made the historic crossing with the young king at their head.

The historians themselves made it clear that the numbers they gave referred to the forces at the time of the crossing. 'Callisthenes', as we learn from Plb. 12. 19. 1, 'says that Alexander made the crossing with 40,000 infantry and 4,500 cavalry.' Alexander's military and financial situation and the state of his supplies were given for the start of the campaign by Plutarch (*Mor.* 327 C-D). He cited Callisthenes for the same numbers; Anaximenes of Lampsacus in the Hellespontine area for 43,000 infantry and 5,500 cavalry (*FGrH* 72 F 29); Ptolemy for 30,000 infantry and 5,000 cavalry (*FGrH* 138 F 4); and Aristobulus for 30,000 infantry and 4,000 cavalry.[3] When the secondary sources picked up some of these numbers, they applied them to the proper context, the crossing from Europe to Asia. Thus Livy 9. 19. 5 'ipse traiecisset cum veteranis Macedonibus non plus triginta milibus hominum et quattuor milibus equitum'; J. 11. 6. 2 'in exercitu eius fuere peditum XXXII milia, equitum IV milia quingenti'; Arr. 1. 11. 3 'he sets off for the Hellespont at the head of infantrymen not much more than 30,000 and of cavalrymen exceeding 5,000' (ἐξελαύνει ἐφ' Ἑλλησπόντου...αὐτὸς δὲ ἄγων). The most explicit and detailed is D.S. 17. 17. 3–4. At the Hellespont 'Alexander in person reviewed the accompanying force with exactitude. The findings were 12,000 Macedonians etc.... So many then in number were those who crossed to Asia with Alexander' (αὐτὸς δὲ τὸν ἐξετασμὸν τῆς ἀκολουθούσης δυνάμεως ἀκριβῶς ἐποιήσατο...οἱ μὲν οὖν μετ' Ἀλεξάνδρου διαβάντες εἰς τὴν Ἀσίαν τοσοῦτοι τὸ πλῆθος ἦσαν).

Let us consider now the numbers. The wrong way to approach them is to 'assume that some exclude and others include the troops already in Asia';[4] for not only historical sense, but also the texts themselves show that none of the figures included 'the troops already in Asia'. Nor is it profitable, to use Tarn's phrase, 'to juggle Diodorus' figures about'

---

[1] See HA 67; compare the sacrifice by Agesilaus at Aulis in X. *Hell.* 3. 4. 3.
[2] Hdt. 7. 44–5 and 54–6 for the review, and 59–60 for the numbering.
[3] *FGrH* 139 F 4.
[4] So P. A. Brunt, 'Alexander's Macedonian Cavalry', *JHS* 83 (1963) 34.

in order to diminish the differences.[1] We must face the fact that Alexander did not publish the numbers of the units he reviewed or the totals of his infantry and cavalry when he crossed the Hellespont. Personal experience of war is not necessary for anyone to see that he was wise not to publish the true figures. What he did do was to allow Callisthenes to publish an inflated number of infantry and a reduced number of cavalry in the hope of misleading the enemy. Later, others made their guesses at the totals: Anaximenes, a local man, and Aristobulus, not an officer of the line, but an engineer. It was their guesses which Plutarch took as the extreme examples: '43,000 infantry and 5,000 cavalry' being the guess of Anaximenes (Plutarch reduces Anaximenes' 5,500 to the round thousand), and '30,000 infantry and 4,000 cavalry' being the guess of Aristobulus (P*Mor* 327 D).

The figures which command respect are those in Diodorus, which not only claim to be the findings of the accurate review by Alexander personally, but are consistent with the strengths of various units as they appear later in our sources. The actual total of the infantry of the named units is 32,000 (Diodorus makes a total of 30,000 either because he chose to give a round number in tens of thousands, or because he added up incorrectly); and the actual total of the cavalry units is 5,100 (Diodorus' total of 4,500 is palpably wrong in arithmetic and in fact). What is more remarkable is the record of the strength of individual units. There is only one source for this record, the return of the army's strength, unit by unit, for that day in the *Alexander-Journal*.

Of the contemporary writers whose numbers have survived, only Ptolemy is consistent with the totals of the *Alexander-Journal*, as we have deduced them from Diodorus' figures. This is not surprising, if, as we have argued, Ptolemy had that *Journal* in his possession. When he published the figures, they were taken over by Diyllus, the source of D.S. 17. 17. 3–4 on my analysis, and by Arrian, who tells us that he used Ptolemy and Aristobulus—and here demonstrably[2] Ptolemy; for Arrian's 'not much more than 30,000 infantrymen and cavalrymen exceeding 5,000' is a good fit. It suited Livy's purpose to take the lowest totals of any source, namely those of Aristobulus. Justin, the epitomator of Trogus, is the odd man out, since his two totals are not found together in any of the sources we have cited. I have argued in H*THA* 96 that Trogus' source for the information in J. 11. 6. 2 was Cleitarchus.

Once the official figures for the individual units at the review had

---

[1] This has been widely done, especially of recent years by Brunt, L lxix-lxxi, Goukowsky 179, and Bosworth 98 f. Tarn 2. 156 complicated the figures for the cavalry by introducing a supposed 'Mercenaries' source' which was reliable for some figures, but not for others.

[2] Aristobulus' figures for both infantry and cavalry being entirely different.

been published by Ptolemy from the *Journal*, there was no longer any doubt about the totals of the infantry and the cavalry. It follows that the primary writers who gave different figures had already written when Ptolemy disclosed this information: namely Callisthenes (ob. 328/7), Anaximenes (ob. *c.* 320) and Aristobulus, and in addition, as he is the source of J. 11. 6. 2, Cleitarchus. On the other hand, Diyllus took his numbers (as we find them in Diodorus) from the detailed figures in the work of Ptolemy. He wrote, then, after Ptolemy had published his work.[1]

We may be sure that Alexander numbered the ships also at the Hellespont. Macedonia herself had had a relatively small fleet. Philip, probably in 352, had boldly slipped past twenty Athenian triremes with his own fleet of 'light ships', being penteconters at the most (Polyaen. 4. 2. 22), and he had no doubt increased the number of these and added some triremes, in order to attack Perinthus, for instance, from the sea (see Volume II. 568 n. 4). In 335 Alexander brought up the Danube 'a few warships (ναῦς μακράς) and no great body of marines' (Arr. 1. 3. 3–4). The navy for the expedition to Asia is said by *Itin. Al.* 18 to have mustered at Amphipolis. At the Hellespont the main body of the army was ferried over from Sestus to Abydus by 160 'triremes' (τριήρεσι) and many merchant vessels (Arr. 1. 11. 6). What follows in Arrian is a 'story', and it includes the steering of 'the flagship' (τὴν στρατηγίδα ναῦν) by Alexander himself. This flagship was presumably the leading ship of the Macedonian squadron in the joint navy. In this ship Alexander sailed from Elaeus, not to Abydus, but to the Troad.

According to D.S. 17. 17. 1 (Diyllus), when Alexander reached the Hellespont, he sent the main body across from Europe to Asia, and he himself sailed with sixty 'long ships' (μακραῖς ναυσίν) to the Troad. As we have argued that Diyllus got his figures for the forces from Ptolemy, and as we have seen that Ptolemy was Arrian's source for the crossing (except when a 'story' is introduced), it appears that we can put Arrian and Diodorus together and conclude that the main body crossed in 160 triremes and that Alexander in his flagship led the Macedonian flotilla of sixty 'long ships', which was composed predominantly of penteconters and triaconters.

There is no doubt that the 160 triremes of Arr. 1. 11. 6 is what was later called 'the Greek fleet', τὸ Ἑλληνικὸν ναυτικόν. It appears under that name at Lade and is stated to consist then of 160 ships (Arr. 1. 18. 4). Although Alexander disbanded this navy there, he decided later, in 333, to reconstitute the navy. He ordered 'the allies to provide ships in

---

[1] This is a new approach to an old problem. Pearson is superior to Tarn and others in his treatment of it, but I disagree with some of his conclusions.

accordance with the treaty' (C. 3. 1. 20 'ex foedere naves sociis imperatae'). As Alexander's treaty with the Greeks had not changed in the meanwhile, we should expect the Greeks to provide 160 triremes. This is what we find: in 332 the Aegean islands had been brought under control by 'a fleet of 160 ships' (C. 4. 5. 14 'CLX navium classe'). In the same year Alexander referred to this fleet as 'the fleet of the Greeks' (*GHI* 192, 10–11 τὸ ἄλλο ναοτικὸν τὸ τῶν Ἑλλήνων).

As regards 'the Macedonian fleet',[1] we may make an inference from a statement in J. 11. 6. 2, a passage for which the ultimate source is probably Cleitarchus. Just as he produced idiosyncratic figures for the army, so he gave his own figure for ships in the expeditionary force: 182 ships ('naves centum LXXXII'). Now the actual number of ships must have been observed by many Greeks and others at the time, and there is no reason to suppose that Cleitarchus was mistaken. In that case the number applies only to triremes; and it was general for Greek navies to consist at this time of triremes. We infer, then, that the Macedonian fleet consisted of twenty-two triremes and thirty-eight penteconters and triaconters, and that these accompanied Alexander in his flagship to the Troad. This same fleet of sixty ships appears again in 332, when it was sent to Cos (Arr. 3. 2. 6).[2] It seems that the Macedonian fleet was based on the Hellespont in 334, and it was there again in 333 (C. 3. 1. 19, while the Greek fleet was about to reassemble; and 4. 1. 36, in action in the Hellespont). The triaconters and the one penteconter of which we hear in these early years were evidently units of the Macedonian fleet (Arr. 2. 7. 2, 21. 6, and 20. 2).

That Alexander distinguished the Macedonian fleet and the Greek fleet by name and that he used them separately is not surprising; for he did the same with his army. The former was used mainly to guard the lines of communication, and it is doubtful whether it was ever disbanded. Some of its smaller ships accompanied Alexander in his advance. The Greek fleet was used for the naval offensive, whenever Alexander wished to conduct such an offensive, and its ships were organized in city-state squadrons (D.S. 17. 22. 5, based on Diyllus).[3]

---

[1] I coin the name because Ptolemy referred to the Macedonian part of the army as τὸ Μακεδονικόν (Arr. 3. 26. 4).

[2] Amphoterus commanded this fleet in Arr. 3. 2. 6 and C. 3. 1. 19.

[3] It may be noted that the city-states manned their ships (*GHI* 192, 9–10 πεπληρωμένας τοῖς αὑτῶν τέλεσιν), and no doubt the Macedonians manned their own. The marines were another matter. A. put Macedonian infantrymen on the Greek fleet at Miletus (Arr. 1. 18. 8), and it was their skill and daring which he did not want to risk in a set battle (τήν τε ἐμπειρίαν τῶν Μακεδόνων καὶ τὴν τόλμαν). On the other hand, he regarded the Greek fleet there as inferior in oarsmanship and training to the Persian fleet. C. 4. 4. 2 'delectosque militum imponi' refers to Macedonians boarding ships as marines.

His entire naval force at the crossing over the Hellespont was 220 ships of war and many merchantmen.[1]

Our discussion of the figures for the army and the navy has underlined the importance of source criticism, that is of determining the ultimate source of each item of information which has survived in an extant writer. A short introduction to the various writers is required. Callisthenes we have already described;[2] his *Achievements of Alexander* covered events in Asia to at least the battle of Gaugamela in 331. Cleitarchus, whose father Dinon had written a history of Persia, came from a Greek city in Asia Minor, probably Colophon, and was studying philosophy in mainland Greece while Alexander was in Asia. Lacking any first-hand experience and having no acquaintance with Alexander, Cleitarchus had a journalist's flair for sensational writing and produced a historical novel, partly factual and partly fictional, entitled *The Histories of Alexander* and running into more than twelve books. He was the first writer to offer a full and elaborate study of Alexander, publishing it in parts over more than twenty years with the last part appearing *c.* 290. As we deduced from our consideration of the army numbers in 334, Cleitarchus wrote before Ptolemy did; and this is confirmed by the fact that Cleitarchus credited Ptolemy with saving the life of Alexander at the city of the Malli in 326/5 and that Ptolemy himself denied it in his own work (*FGrH* 137 F 24 and 138 F 26a), and probably also by Cleitarchus' provision of a Roman embassy to wait on Alexander and the lack of any such thing in the work of Ptolemy (137 F 31 and 138 F 29). For Cleitarchus went to live in Alexandria at the invitation of Ptolemy, ruler of Egypt, *c.* 308, and there is no doubt that his last wish was to deny any statement published by Ptolemy. In the judgement of Cicero (137 T 7 and 13), Strabo (F 16), Quintilian (T 6), Curtius (F 24), and Arrian, who narrated some of Cleitarchus' stories (τὰ λεγόμενα), but scorned to mention his name, the work of Cleitarchus showed little or no respect for truth; and where they who knew his work were so unanimous, only the rashest of modern historians will try to whitewash Cleitarchus on the basis of the few fragments we possess.[3] This disregard for truth is not surprising; for we can see from the fragments that his concern was with the extravagant, the emotional, and the fantastic (F 9, 11, 18, 19). His Alexander was an angry, bloodthirsty, ruthless, but romantic, hero in the image of Achilles, his

---

[1] Berve and others have failed to notice the figure for the Macedonian fleet in 334; they seem to put the total of A.'s entire fleet at 160 triremes. For Macedonians using triaconters one may recall the bold reconnaissance at the Pinarus river, the voyage down the Indus, and the voyage of Nearchus.

[2] For the nature of his work see especially M. Plizia, 'Der Titel u.d. Zweck von Kallisthenes' Alexandergeschichte', *Eos* 60 (1972) 263 f.

[3] On these fragments see Borza 25 ff.

battles were epic encounters in Homeric style, his sacked cities were reminiscent of Euripidean plays, and the Macedonians fought best when they had an impassable river or sea behind them. As a Greek, his admiration was for the Greeks rather than for their conquerors, the Macedonians; and the East had the glamour of 'the Orient'.[1]

Marsyas of Pella grew up with Alexander as a Royal Page and presumably as a pupil of Aristotle, so that he was well qualified to write *The Upbringing of Alexander* (this being the main source, no doubt, for Plutarch's account of Alexander's youth in *PA* 4. 8–8. 2). He wrote *The Achievements of Macedonia* from the first king (probably of the Temenid dynasty) onwards in ten books. Although we do not know where it ended, this pioneering work, researched before the overlay of the Hellenistic monarchy, was used probably by Trogus for his 'origines Macedonicae' (*Prol.* 7) and certainly by Curtius for his 'mores Macedonum'. He wrote also[2] *The Affairs of Alexander* in five books down to the summer of 331, the work being unfinished presumably because he was a man of action as a brother of Antigonus Monophthalmus and a commander in 307.

Aristobulus, a Greek (perhaps of Phocis), served throughout as an engineer and as a close friend of Alexander. He wrote his memoirs beginning at the age of eighty-four, as he stated in his introduction (*FGrH* 139 T 3), and he lived to over ninety. His intention was to correct the record (this had been much distorted by Cleitarchus and others). His picture of Alexander's personality, and especially of his 'yearning' ($\pi\delta\theta\sigma s$), was based on an intimate friendship with a man young enough to be his son. He had the scientific interests of the Aristotelian school in botany, zoology, geography, and ethnography. As regards his time of publication, we have already deduced from the figures for the army in 334 that Aristobulus wrote before Ptolemy did. This is confirmed by some points of difference between the two writers. Aristobulus F 5 gave the casualties at the Granicus river as thirty-four, including nine infantrymen; and Arr. 1. 16. 4, following Ptolemy here and not Aristobulus, had twenty-five Companion Cavalry and as rounded numbers sixty cavalry and thirty infantry (the rounding being due probably to Arrian). For the discrepancy the simplest explanation is that Aristobulus wrote from memory first and that Ptolemy published precise numbers from the *Journal* later (if vice versa, surely Aristobulus would have taken Ptolemy's figures). Aristobulus F 15 had

---

[1] Using 'Orient' in the sense of E. W. Said, *Orientalism* (New York, 1978). In fact Cleitarchus was the first of the historical novelists.

[2] This work is mentioned in *FGrH* 135/6 F 2 and F 3; I assume that T 1 is corrupt, there being a lacuna before μέχρι. See W. Heckel, 'Marsyas of Pella, historian of Macedon', *Hermes* 108 (1980) 444 f.

Alexander return from Siwa to Egypt by the same route, but Ptolemy (138 F 9) by the direct route to Memphis; since Ptolemy had not only access to the *Journal*, but also local knowledge and informants, his statement would hardly have been refuted by Aristobulus, who therefore wrote earlier. Aristobulus F 24 differs from Ptolemy F 14 in a matter in which Ptolemy was in command; if he had written after Ptolemy, he would surely have given Ptolemy's version.[1] Other differences are inconclusive (F 25 and 138 F 34, F 33 and 138 F 17, and F 43 and 138 F 20);[2] but in general it would seem that Aristobulus would have deferred to Ptolemy's account in the two of these cases which are purely matters of military detail. As regards the date when Aristobulus completed his work, it was certainly after 301 (F 54 = Arr. 7. 18. 5) and before Ptolemy began; so at any period of some six years between 300 and 285. Whether his earliest work overlapped with the latest volumes of Cleitarchus cannot be determined from the fragments.

Ptolemy, a Macedonian from Eordaea, was a close and loyal friend of Alexander in the School of Pages; and he was exiled by Philip for some demonstration in support of Alexander in 337/6. Restored to favour, he rose rapidly from being a Companion Cavalryman to a command post and then to the top rank as King's Bodyguard (*somatophylax*), and he served continuously and in close friendship with Alexander from beginning to end. Setting himself up as ruler of Egypt, Ptolemy obtained in 321 the corpse of Alexander and, in my opinion, the *Alexander-Journal* which he kept under his own hand. We have already inferred that Ptolemy wrote after Cleitarchus and Aristobulus. It was probably in the last years of his life, between 290 and 283, that he was composing and publishing his work.[3] As a man of outstanding ability, with the greatest possible experience in military and administrative affairs, he had a clearer understanding of Alexander's problems and achievements than any other writer, and he was able to fortify and check his memory by constant reference to the state archive known as the *Alexander-Journal*.

Arrian chose Ptolemy and Aristobulus as indisputably the best authorities, and of the two he preferred to follow Ptolemy for military

---

[1] So too Pearson 167, 'Those differences suggest strongly that Ptolemy wrote after him, not before him; otherwise it is unlikely that the civilian would disagree with the military authority on such matters'. For Aristobulus and Phocis see Pearson in *AJP* 73 (1952) 71 ff.

[2] Pearson 172 argues that in 138 F 20 the sentence οὐδὲ γὰρ εἰκὸς ἀξιόμαχα... was part of Ptolemy's statement. However, the comment οὐδὲ γὰρ εἰκός is a comment by Arrian as is clear also from the finite verb ἦν in section 6. What answers οὐχ ἑξήκοντα μόνα ἅρματα in Ptolemy's argument is ἀλλὰ δισχιλίους γὰρ λέγει ἱππέας... It does not, therefore, show a belief by Arrian that Aristobulus wrote before Ptolemy, as Pearson holds (though I too think he did write before Ptolemy). So too Brunt, L 2. 43 n. 4.

[3] Goukowsky xxxi proposes *c.* 285; *contra* E. Badian in *Gnomon* 33 (1961) 665 f. and R. M. Errington in *CQ* 19 (1969) 233 f.

details and anecdotes (see *FGrH* 138 F 3, F 6, F 18, F 20), the cases of Philotas, Parmenio, and Bessus (F 13, F 14), for the Acesines river (F 22), for Alexander's sacrifice at the Hyphasis (F 23), and for sending cattle to Macedonia (F 18). He used Ptolemy also, in preference to any other, for the description of Alexander's fleet descending the Indus (F 24 ᾧ μάλιστα ἐγὼ ἕπομαι). We have only thirty definite fragments of Ptolemy's work, according to Jacoby, and we know that Arrian's *Anabasis*, greatly abbreviated as compared with Ptolemy's work, rested in part—at times mainly—upon that work; thus we have no secure basis for saying what Ptolemy omitted to mention, and for assuming from the supposed omissions that Ptolemy was lauding himself and blackening his rivals.[1] Arrian had the whole of Ptolemy's work at his disposal and he compared it with other long works which he also had in their entirety. He was far better qualified to form an assessment than we can ever be. His assessment was that Ptolemy was truthful. What Ptolemy does say on two points supports Arrian: that he was not at the city of the Malli, whereas Cleitarchus had said he was (F 26b), and that Perdiccas (later an enemy of Ptolemy) in person started the attack which ended so brilliantly in the capture that same day of Thebes.[2]

All the writers we have listed so far have survived for us only in fragments. What we do possess *in toto*, or nearly *in toto*, is five main accounts, secondary in nature and late in date. Diodorus Siculus, a universal historian writing in the second half of the first century B.C., devoted his seventeenth book to Alexander. Pompeius Trogus, another universal historian, writing in the Augustan age, gave an account of Alexander which is known to us only through an epitome by Justinus, an author probably of the third century A.D. Quintus Curtius wrote a much longer work, *The History of Alexander the Great*, probably in the middle of the first century A.D. Plutarch, the biographer, published his *Alexander* probably between 110 and 115 A.D. And Arrian, who had held the consulship and exercised military command in Cappadocia,

---

[1] Errington, loc. cit., has argued on this assumption. He infers that Ptolemy suppressed any mention of Leonnatus in the matter of the Pages conspiracy from the fact that Arrian does not mention Leonnatus at 4. 13. 7; but Arrian himself is abbreviating, so that one cannot equate Arrian with Ptolemy. On the other hand Errington accepts the account of Curtius as correct at 8. 6. 20–2, a passage deriving probably from more than one source and much elaborated. One might as well blame Ptolemy for omitting to mention Epimenes because Curtius included him.

[2] The account of Perdiccas' bravery and of his being severely wounded in leading an assault on the second stockade is entirely to his credit, and the fact that he did not await A.'s order to attack is not adduced to his discredit by Arrian at 1. 8. 1. A. appreciated courage in action, as all his officers and men knew. Errington, followed by Brunt, L 1. 35 n. 1, suggested that Ptolemy fabricated this incident in order to blame Perdiccas and exonerate A. for the Greek Council's decision to destroy Thebes (*CQ* 19. 237). I gave reasons for rejecting the suggestion in H*A* 309 n. 20; see now J. Roisman in *CQ* 34 (1984) 374 f. A. B. Bosworth, 'Arrian and the Alexander Vulgate' in *Entretiens Hardt* 22 (1975) 14, also held that Ptolemy misrepresented the beginning of the action at Thebes; for my arguments against his view see H*THA* 166 ff.

published his *Alexandri Anabasis* perhaps *c.* 140 A.D.[1] The first four certainly used Cleitarchus extensively and drew also on others. Who those others were is disputed. It must suffice to mention the conclusions of the present writer: namely, for Diodorus a universal historian of the period 357–297 B.C., Diyllus of Athens; for Trogus probably Satyrus, who in the third century B.C. had written lives of famous men; for Curtius several writers including Diyllus, Hegesias, and Trogus; and for Plutarch many writers—especially Callisthenes, Aristobulus, Onesicritus, and Chares—and some letters.[2] The last, Arrian, followed a different procedure.[3] His main sources were Ptolemy and Aristobulus; he regarded their accounts, when in agreement, 'as completely true', and when they differed he chose that which seemed to him 'both worth narrating and not utterly untrustworthy'. In addition he gave some items from other writers. These items were characterized as 'stories', being worthy of mention and not entirely incredible, and some of them certainly came from Cleitarchus, an author whom Arrian never names in the *Anabasis*. It is a measure of Arrian's superiority as a historian that he alone of the five tells us who were his main sources and how we are to recognize the inferior material, 'the stories'.

The narrative sections earlier in this chapter may now be reviewed with the eye of the source critic. The election of Alexander to the throne of Macedon is mentioned by Arrian (1. 25. 2), using Ptolemy and Aristobulus, and the procedure for such an election is known from C. 10. 6–10, a trustworthy passage deriving from eye-witnesses. This is to be preferred to passages which depict Alexander as a stripling and 'Anti-pater' as a 'father substitute' (D.S. 17. 2. 2, 3. 6, 4. 5; P*Demosth* 23. 2; P*A* 11. 6); for they bear the mark of a Greek source, unacquainted with conditions at the Macedonian court. Ptolemy and Aristobulus, as cited by Arr. 3. 26. 1–27. 2, show beyond question the procedure in treason trials in Macedonia;[4] and their evidence is incompatible with the picture of Alexander and Olympias (independently of one another) putting eminent Macedonians to death arbitrarily and autocratically in J. 9. 7. 12; 11. 2. 1–3 and 5. 1–2; 12. 6. 14; Paus. 8. 7. 7; and C. 8. 7. 4–6. The testimony of Macedonian contemporaries, writing for Macedonians, is much more acceptable than these later versions, influenced by Hellenistic and Roman developments. The account which I have given of the death of Philip and the burial at Aegeae is based on D.S. 16. 92. 5–94. 4 and 17. 2. 1 with Arr. 1. 25. 1 and 2. 14. 5, drawn respectively from Diyllus, writing

---

[1] So P. A. Stadter, *Arrian of Nicomedia* (Chapel Hill, 1980) 184 f., refuting Bosworth's proposal to make it a very early work of Arrian.

[2] See the convenient summary in Hamilton liii-lix.

[3] It is clearly stated in the preface to the *Anabasis*.

[4] See also H*SPA* 464 f.

c. 275 as an Athenian familiar with Macedonian procedure, and Ptolemy and Aristobulus, and a letter in the *King's Journal*.[1] In comparison, J. 9. 7, attributable to Trogus' use of a Hellenistic biographer, Satyrus, in my opinion, is worthless, for instance, in the allegation that Olympias, with the connivance of Alexander, impelled Pausanias to assassinate Philip.[2]

For the arrest of Alexander Lyncestes we accord credence to Arr. 1. 25, based on Ptolemy and Aristobulus, and to J. 11. 7. 1 ('indicio captivi') and not to D.S. 17. 32. 1–2, a passage which dated the affair later and introduced a letter from Olympias as the cause, probably due to Cleitarchus. The description of his death in D.S. 17. 80. 2 and C. 7. 1. 5–8 may have come from Diyllus. The rapid move of Alexander in the Tempe pass, described by Polyaenus (4. 3. 23), was of interest only to Ptolemy, the source of several feats of mountaineering in Arrian. Alexander's progress through Greece with much reference to Greek states, and then his election as *hegemon* in D.S. 17. 3–4, have an awareness of Greek affairs which is typical of Diyllus.[3]

If we are correct in our analysis of the ultimate sources behind the late narratives which we possess, then our reconstruction of Alexander's opening months as king rests on a secure foundation. Nor should we forget the contribution of archaeology. The excavation of the royal tombs at Vergina has provided an example of the type of tomb which Plato had already described as appropriate for the leading men of his state in *Laws* 947 D and which was imitated to some degree in Alexander's funerary car (D.S. 18. 26. 5–6).[4] If the burial in the largest tomb is that of Philip II, Alexander did indeed 'expend all possible care on the burial of his father' (D.S. 17. 2. 1); and its proximity to the shrine supports the literary tradition of Philip being worshipped as a god. And the peculiarities of the tombs and the objects found on top of it fit the literary evidence to a remarkable degree.[5] Inscribed stones found in the region of Amphipolis have shown Alexander's interest in land-reclamation there, as literary evidence indicated in the case of Lake Copaïs (Str. 407), and the holding of games in honour of Heracles after the overthrow of Tyre (as reported by Arr. 2. 24. 6).[6] These and other discoveries provide independent confirmation of points in the literary accounts which have been erroneously called in question.

---

[1] For the passages in Book 16 see H*SD* 84 and 89 f.
[2] Although Justin introduced this allegation with the cautionary words 'creditum est etiam' and Plutarch in a similar passage from the same source throws in a λέγεται, this allegation has been accepted by E. Badian in *Phoenix* 17 (1963) 244 f. on what seem to be inadequate grounds.
[3] I summarized the qualities of Diyllus in H*SD* 90.
[4] M. Andronicos in *AAA* 13. 1 (1980) 175, and independently H*RTV* 115.
[5] H*PT* 335 f. and H*SD* 116 f. and 124.
[6] Ch. Koukouli-Chrysanthaki in *Arch. Delt.* 26 (1971) 120 ff.

II

ALEXANDER IN THE BALKAN AREA

1. *The campaign to the Danube*
(See Figure 3)

'THE population of Thrace is greater than that of any country in
the world except India, and if the Thracians were to unite
they would prove themselves invincible and be the strongest
of the nations.' So wrote Herodotus in the fifth century (5. 3). His
words were no less true in 335 B.C., especially if we add for good
measure the Illyrians, Dardanians, and Triballians. For all these
peoples were as reckless of life and as dedicated to warfare as any
Sikhs or Pathans. 'If all these peoples should rise together in revolt,'
wrote Justin of this time (11. 1. 6), 'they could not be held in check.'
It is not surprising, then, that Alexander made a pre-emptive strike
against them in 335. His aim was not just short term; for, as Arrian
alone of our sources remarks, he intended to preclude the possibility
of a rising during his projected absence of uncertain length in Asia, a
campaign for which he had already made his preparations that
winter (1. 1. 3–4).

Arrian's account of the campaign of 335 tells us more about the
Balkan area than accounts of campaigns there in the Hellenistic
period. It is therefore worth reporting it in some detail. I shall put in
inverted commas Alexander's 'orders'. They are to be discussed at the
end of the narrative (p. 49 below), because they may enable us to
identify the source behind Arrian.

The size of the army is not stated. Alexander certainly left considerable forces in Macedonia under the command of Antipater, in case
there was a rising in Greece, and he did not withdraw the forces under
Parmenio's command from Asia. Yet he needed large forces; and in
fact Arrian's mentions of particular units show that Alexander had a
considerable cross-section of the Macedonian field army and only one
non-Macedonian unit, 'the Agrianes' from the upper Strymon valley.
At the most he may have taken 3,000 cavalry, 12,000 heavy infantry,
and 8,000 specialized light infantry.[1] If so, it was a larger Macedonian
force than he was to take to Asia in 334.

---

[1] For this estimate see *HACI* 79 f. We may compare Philip's 30,000 men at Perinthus
according to D.S. 16. 74. 5, drawing on Ephorus.

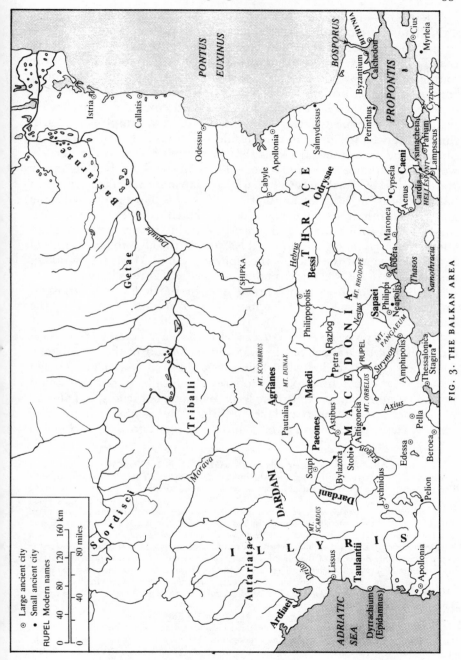

FIG. 3. THE BALKAN AREA

When the intelligence reached him that the Illyrians and the Triballians were planning to rise, he set off from Amphipolis 'with the spring' (in early April) and aimed not at the Morava valley where the Triballi were adjacent to the Illyrian Autariatae, but at the southern slopes of Mt. Haemus, beyond which lay the easternmost conquests of the Triballi.[1] Moreover, he chose an unusual route, in order to crush 'the republican Thracians' and enter the central plain before he was expected there. He marched from Amphipolis north through the Rupel pass and alongside the Strymon to just south of Simitli, and from there it seems that he turned east into the densely wooded mountains of the republican Thracians and reached the upper Nestus river by Razlog (see Fig. 3).[2] Arrian does not mention what happened during his invasion there, but it seems that he reduced some and chased others who fled towards Mt. Haemus. Alexander crossed the Nestus in spring spate, and after the crossing his army covered 240 kilometres (150 miles) within ten days, at first through the highlands of Mt. Rhodope and then across the central plain of Marica.[3] By taking this unusual route Alexander had in effect sliced Thrace in two, so that the tribes of south-eastern Thrace and in particular the strongest group, the Odrysae, had no opportunity of joining forces with the Triballi.

On reaching Mt. Haemus Alexander could have taken a low pass at either end of the range, but he was still in pursuit of the 'republican Thracians' who had fled with their wives, children, and gear.[4] He led his army up to a central pass (probably the Shipka pass), and found that the summit was occupied, not only by those Thracians, but also by well-armed mountaineers of Haemus. They had loaded a number of wagons (with rocks, presumably) and were ready to launch them as

---

[1] The positions of these and other tribes were worked out in H*KI* and they seem to be in agreement with F. Papazoglou in her later and independent work, *CBT* (see the map at the end). The large tribal groups expanded and contracted from time to time, as Strabo remarked (C 315–16).

[2] Reading Φιλιππούπολιν with H rather than Φιλίππους πόλιν with other codices and in Volume I. 198. This is the Philippoupolis in Parorbelia. For this route see H*SPA* 455 f. and Volume I. 193 and 199 (I travelled with Professor G. Toncheva in 1970 from Sandanski via Razlog to Plovdiv). Bosworth 53 misinterprets Arrian in suggesting that these Thracians were the Tetrachoritae (St. Byz. s.v.) of the Haemus range; for in Arrian the invasion of their territory begins before A. crosses the Nestus. They are rather the republican Thracians of Rhodope of Thuc. 2. 96. 2, known for their long knives as μαχαιροφόροι; they appear again in P. *Aem* 18. 5, where the knife was called a ῥομφαία. For 'autonomous' see H*SPA* 456, and add the *abasileutoi Thrakes* of X. *HG* 5. 2. 17.

[3] If we allow one day of rest the rate is 27 km. (17 m.) a day.

[4] Arrian is obscure, because he has abbreviated his source drastically. Either there were two different sets of 'republican Thracians' (as I thought in H*SPA* 457 n. 7), or some of those in the upper Nestus valley had fled to Mt. Haemus. The words ὅσαι ξυνείποντο αὐτοῖς at 1. 1. 13 favour the second alternative.

missiles against any attackers from below.[1] Behind these wagons they had constructed a laager of wagons as a barricade, and they intended to fight from there. This presented Alexander, a young man of twenty years, with his first tactical problem as commander-in-chief. He relied on his own abilities, since he had left Philip's experienced generals in other theatres. Guessing the plans of the Thracians, he 'gave the order' (1. 1. 8) that when the wagons were launched the heavy infantry of the line were either to open ranks and let the wagons pass through the intervals or, where space was cramped, to bend over or lie down and protect themselves by forming a close-set roof of shields, over which the hurtling wagons would pass harmlessly. The men did as they were told, and no life was lost. 'It turned out as Alexander had advised and recommended.' The infantrymen of the line then advanced uphill, shouting their war-cry 'alalai'.

Meanwhile Alexander had 'ordered' (1. 1. 11) the specialist group of Archers to advance ahead of the line on the right, where the going was less difficult, in order to be in a position to enfilade any Thracians who might charge downhill at the main line. This in fact happened, and the Archers' concentrated fire forced the Thracians to withdraw to their barricade of wagons. Alexander himself commanding the Royal Infantry Guard, the Hypaspists, and the Agrianians on the leftward extension of the line, intended to move ahead of the main line and attack the Thracian position on the flank. But in the event the impetuous charge of the main line broke through the Thracians, whose weapons and armour were much inferior, and the force under Alexander did not engage in time (1. 1. 12 fin.). Even so, 1,500 Thracians were killed; and the women, children, and property of the 'republican Thracians' were taken as booty. In this first exercise of supreme command Alexander demonstrated not only his own skill as a tactician, but also the superiority of trained troops against brave, but ill-organized, tribesmen, however numerous, a superiority which Brasidas had shown on a small scale in 424 (Thuc. 4. 125–8). Nor did he make the mistake of Philip, who had kept his booty with the army and then lost it (Volume II. 583). Alexander sent it down to the coastal cities, from which it was no doubt moved to Macedonia.

After crossing the watershed of the Haemus range, Alexander descended into territory now held by the Triballi in the valley of the Lyginus (probably the Rositsa). There he encountered no opposition; for their king Syrmus and his retinue, their women and children, and also the neighbouring Thracians, had fled to an island in the Danube, called Peuce ('Pinetree'), some three days' march from the Lyginus

---

[1] As the text is corrupt, 'mountaineers' is only one of several possibilities. We learn of the loading of the wagons from Polyaen. 4. 3. 11, a passage which derives also from Ptolemy.

valley.[1] Alexander advanced for a day, only to learn that the
Triballian army had doubled back and had cut his communications in
the Lyginus valley. Doubling back himself, at top speed, he caught the
Triballi as they were encamping in a narrow glen. The enemy drew
themselves up in deep formation within the glen, a naturally strong
position for defence. Alexander intended to bring them out into the
open. He 'ordered' (1. 2. 4) the Archers and the Slingers to run ahead
and pepper the front lines of the enemy with their fire. The Triballi
attacked the Archers and pursued them as they withdrew into open
ground. There Alexander was waiting in a prearranged disposition.
For he had 'ordered' (1. 2. 5) Philotas with the cavalry of Upper
Macedonia on the right to charge the advancing Triballi in the flank,
and Heracleides and Sopolis with the cavalry of Bottiaea and Amphipolis to advance on the left. Alexander himself was in the centre in
command of the phalanx, which was drawn up in a deep formation,
and ahead of the phalanx there was a screen of cavalry. The whole
force in the centre now went into the advance. As long as the two
armies engaged with missiles, the Triballi held their own; but when the
phalanx charged with vigour and the cavalry pressed in on the flanks,
using the weight of their horses and wielding their swords, the Triballi
broke and fled back to the river with a loss of 3,000 men. The fall of
darkness and the thickness of the forest prevented the Macedonians
from carrying out the pursuit 'with their usual thoroughness' (1. 2. 7).[2]
They themselves lost eleven cavalrymen and some forty infantrymen
'according to Ptolemy'.

'On the third day' after the battle Alexander reached the Danube.
There, in accordance with earlier planning, a small fleet of Macedonian warships awaited him; they had come via Byzantium, now an
ally, into the Black Sea and along the river (1. 3. 3 κατὰ τὸν ποταμόν).
He manned them at once with archers and infantrymen and attempted
to force a landing on Peuce, but the water-borne force was too small to
overcome the combination of a swift current, steep banks, and tough
opposition. Withdrawing his ships, he decided to cross the Danube,
despite the fact that the opposite bank was held by a large army of
Getae, estimated at 4,000 cavalry and more than 10,000 infantry; for
he felt 'a longing' (*pothos*) to go beyond the Danube, something which
Philip had not done. Secrecy was maintained while local dug-out tree-
trunk boats were brought in and the soldiers' tent-covers of leather
were stuffed with straw to act as floats for rafts (cf. X. *Anab.* 1. 5. 10),

---

[1] There was an island of this name near the mouth of the Danube (Str. 301 and 305), but it is
too far away from the realm of Syrmus; the name was evidently given to more than one island in
the river.

[2] For the specialized nature of the pursuit see H*P*.

and then after dark Alexander began to cross over at a point lower down with 1,500 cavalry and 4,000 infantry. To escape notice was all-important. Towards dawn the Macedonians, still unobserved, mustered in a field of standing grain and advanced upstream, Alexander 'ordering' (1. 4. 1) the infantrymen to part the tall corn with their pikes held at the ready and the cavalry to follow behind. When they came into open ground, he brought the cavalry forward to the right of the infantry, and 'ordered' (1. 4. 2) Nicanor to lead the infantry on in square formation (its left flank was protected by the river). This formation was used when infantry faced a superior force of cavalry, and it was wise in this instance, since the Getae, like the Scythians, were famous for their cavalry tactics and now outnumbered the Macedonian cavalry by more than two to one.

Alexander was relying on the effect of a surprise attack; for the Getae had never supposed that an army could cross the mighty river in a single night! When the squadrons of cavalry, each in wedge formation, galloped forward and the massed pikes of the phalanx in close order bore down upon them, the Getic army broke at the terrifying sight and fled to their poorly fortified base, a Getic town some 5 kilometres away from the river. But Alexander pressed on, his cavalry in front and his phalanx still on open ground near the river in case there was an ambush. The Getae had no time to reorganize themselves. They fled into the steppes, taking as many of their women and children on their horses' cruppers as they could. The booty, including supplies for the Getic army, was sent back under the charge of two brigade-commanders, and sacrifices of thanksgiving were made by Alexander to Zeus the Saviour, Heracles,[1] and the river-god Ister. He then ferried his entire force back by daylight. Not a single man had been lost.

As the news of this fantastic feat of arms spread along the Danube, embassy after embassy came to Alexander, asking for a treaty of friendship with him: first from 'the republican tribes' living near the Danube, then from Syrmus, and finally from the Gauls near the head of the Adriatic Sea.[2] Alexander granted their requests, and oaths of friendship were exchanged. To the Gauls he granted alliance also, and he is said to have called them 'braggarts', because they expressed fear, not of him, but of the heavens falling upon them.[3]

---

[1] Philip had sacrificed to Heracles at the river mouth (Volume II, 582).

[2] Ptolemy in Str. 301 put them on the Adriatic, whereas Arr. 1. 4. 6 placed them on the Ionian Gulf. As Bosworth 64 suggests, Arrian may be 'archaising'. For in the fourth century 'Adrias' and 'Ionian Gulf' were synonymous to Ps.-Scylax 14 and 27.

[3] This was perhaps A.'s misunderstanding of their oath to keep the pact as long as the sky did not fall, the earth open, and the sea rise.

For some weeks after the crossing of the Danube in June[1] we hear nothing about Alexander from Arrian. We can only guess at his activities. He probably made arrangements with the Triballi and the Thracians for the defence of the Danube line against the ever-present danger of invasion by the peoples of the north, especially the Getae and the Scythians, and he may have regulated any frontier disputes between the Triballi and 'the republican tribes of Thracians living near the Danube'. These Thracians lay to the east of the Triballi and extended to the delta of the river; for in Macedonian administrative terms 'Thrace' stopped short of the Triballi (*FGrH* 100 (Dexippus) F 8, 3 and 156 (Arrian) F 1, 7). This was country already known to Alexander; for he had been summoned by Philip to participate in the campaign against the Scythians of Atheas and then against the Triballi (Volume II. 582 ff.). He may now have confirmed or modified pacts made by Philip with the Thracian or Scythian tribes, for instance the Histriani who had been ruled by a king (J. 9. 2. 2),[2] and with the Greek cities on the Black Sea coast. As he intended to use Triballian troops for his impending campaign in Asia, he made arrangements now with Syrmus for the selection and training of these men. Whereas Philip had exacted from the Thracians subjugated in 344 a tribute of one-tenth of their produce payable to the Macedones (D.S. 16. 71. 2), it seems that Alexander did not impose any tribute on the Triballi or on the down-river Thracians; for this would not have been consistent with treaties of 'friendship'. He hoped rather to tie them to Macedonia by the bond of common interest in maintaining a common peace and a common defence.

The economic centre of gravity in Thrace was the great plain of Marica. See Fig. 3. Routes led from it to the region of Sofia and the upper Strymon valley, the habitat of the Agrianes; to the Greek trading cities of the Black Sea coast; and down the valley of the Hebrus to Doriscus and the Greek cities of the Aegean seaboard. Within the plain itself Philip's own town, Philippopolis (Plovdiv), stood at the crossroads of communications, and it is probable that the other 'important towns in advantageous positions' which Philip founded (D.S. 16. 71. 2) were at strategic places on the roads which led out of the plain. The most powerful people among the Thracians were the Odrysae, a group of tribes ruled by the Odrysian royal house, which controlled the route from the plain to Doriscus, its homeland being in the valley of the Artescus (Ardas).

---

[1] Inferred from the crops being tall, but unharvested.

[2] 'Histriani' refers to Thracians or Scythians of the Danubian area and not to Greeks of the Greek city, Istria, as has sometimes been supposed. The 'Istriani' of Arr. *Peripl. M. Eux.* 20. 2 are distinct from, and distant from, Istria in 24. 2. See Volume II. 560 f.

Alexander was certainly on good terms with the Odrysian royal house; for one of his commanders in Asia bore the Odrysian dynastic name Sitalces (Berve no. 712), a squadron of cavalry which was to fight in Asia was recruited from the Odrysian aristocracy, and a force of Odrysian infantrymen was to accompany Alexander in the crossing to Asia (D.S. 17. 17. 4). Alexander must have arranged at this time for the selection and training of these troops. Central Thrace was bound to be an important source of supply for the expeditionary force during its march along the south coast and its early operations in north-west Asia, and later for the garrison forces which were to hold the Hellespontine area as a keypoint in Alexander's lines of communication. He had a chance now to organize local transport and local supplies in advance.

He was interested too in the development of the towns so recently founded by Philip, and he may have strengthened them with new settlers.[1] These towns were typically Macedonian and un-Greek, in that they were not coastal, not exclusive in citizenship, and not independent in political status; and they were of great importance for the spread of Macedonian culture and of Greek commercial ideas and practices.[2] Both the towns and the tribal groups in Thrace administered their own local affairs. For Alexander did not have a bureaucracy of civil servants; the essence of Macedonian government at home and outside it was that the various communities were responsible for their own local administration.

2. *The battle at Pelion in Illyris*

At the end of July Alexander moved his army from the central plain 'towards the Agrianes and the Paeonians' (Arr. 1. 5. 1). The Agrianes belonged in matters of administration not to 'Thrace', but to the north-western area which was controlled from Pella (*FGrH* 100 F 8, 3 and 156 F 1, 7). Their royal house had exceptionally close ties with Alexander; for the king Langarus had shown great affection for Alexander as a boy and had had direct diplomatic relations with him even during Philip's life. Such a bond originated perhaps when Alexander, acting as viceroy in 340, suppressed a rising by the Maedi of the middle Strymon valley and founded there the first of his own new towns, Alexandropolis (Volume II. 558). At the present time Langarus was accompanying Alexander, rather as an associate than as

---

[1] Philip had sent captives to his new towns according to J. 8. 6. 1 (for the numbers see J. 9. 2. 15), and A. may have done this with the women and children of the 'republican Thracians'.
[2] For these cities see D. K. Samsaris, Ὁ ἐξελληνισμὸς τῆς Θράκης κατὰ τὴν Ἑλληνικὴ καὶ Ῥωμαικὴ ἀρχαιότητα (Thessaloniki, 1980) 69 ff.

a subordinate; for Langarus had his own Royal Guard, consisting of the most handsome and most well-armed of his subjects, whom Arrian called 'his Hypaspists' (1. 5. 2).[1] When it came to armed action, he accepted the orders of Alexander as the supreme commander (1. 5. 3). The Paeonians, on the other hand, had been subjugated by Philip and incorporated in the Macedonian kingdom (Volume II. 672). Their royal house enjoyed a favoured status, in that their king, Lyppeus, continued to issue his own royal coinage alongside the coinages of Philip and Alexander, and the squadron of Paeonian cavalry was recruited from the Paeonian aristocracy as an ethnic unit within the kingdom.

The route which Alexander took from the central plain 'towards the Agrianes and the Paeonians' is not given by Arrian, because he has abbreviated his source so drastically. The Autariatae, who hoped to attack Alexander on the march, may have expected him to go via Sofia into the Morava valley, but he went south-west from Sofia, aiming for the territory of the Agrianes in the headwaters of the Strymon (see Figs. 3 and 8). The pass from there to Paeonian territory was by Pautalia (Kjustendil), and from Pautalia he could either head for northern Paeonia and go to Scupi (Skopje) or turn south to Astibus (Štip), the capital of Paeonia. Alexander was probably in Agrianian territory when the news reached him that the Autariatae planned to attack him; that Cleitus, king (as we shall see later) of the Dardanians, whose home territory was Kosovo, had risen in revolt, and that Glaucias, king of the Taulantii, a group of tribes centred on Tirana,[2] had joined the cause of Cleitus. When Alexander asked for detailed information about the Autariatae, the Agrianian king expressed his scorn of them and offered to invade their territory. On receiving Alexander's 'order', he did so successfully (1. 5. 3). Alexander himself marched south-westwards via Astibus to Stobi, near the confluence of the Axius with the Erigon, and then 'beside the Erigon' (its valley being impassable[3]) via Prilep and the Monastir gap into Lyncus

---

[1] Langarus' Hypaspists; not A.'s Hypaspists, as Heisserer 20 n. 27. See Volume II. 414–15 n. 5. The word was not restricted to A.'s army and it may have been used for an infantry soldier with a certain standard of equipment in the forces of the Greek League, e.g. in *GHI* 183, 10 with Tod's comment.

[2] See H*E* 467 f. Bosworth, map facing p. 52, misplaces the Taulantii, inconsistently with his note on p. 66; see H*KI* 247 for their position.

[3] Fuller 224 made A. march up the Erigon valley. This is physically impossible, as travellers' accounts of the Morihovo show (see Heuzey cited in Volume I. 65, and H*ACI* 78 n. 29): I travelled from Stobi to Prilep in 1968 and saw the lower end of the impassable gorge. Bosworth 68 is aware of the impossibility, but falls into confusion over the meaning of παρὰ τὸν Ἐριγόνα which I translated 'near the Erigon' in H*ACI* 78 n. 29. This, Bosworth claims, is 'impossible'; it must mean 'along the river'. But then at 69 and 76 he has A. march παρὰ τὴν Ἐορδαίαν, 'through Eordaea', and avoids translating παρὰ τὰ τῆς Στυμφαίας καὶ Παραναίας ἄκρα as 'through the

where tributaries of the Erigon rise. What led him to take this direction was the news, or the guess, that an enemy army was proceeding south through the corridor of the lakes and was heading for the plain of Koritsa, which was the natural rendezvous for Cleitus and Glaucias, and that thereafter their joint forces would invade Orestis, the adjoining canton of the Macedonian kingdom. Alexander marched on into Orestis, found it intact, and crossed by the Vatochorion pass into Dassaretis, an Illyrian canton. He then advanced northwards towards the enemy army, which was reported to be at Pelion.

No doubt this was country familiar to Alexander. As a Royal Page, he had accompanied Philip on Illyrian campaigns, and then in 337 he had escorted Olympias to Epirus and gone from there to Illyria, where he stayed with one or more kings, perhaps indeed with Glaucias (*PA* 9. 11; J. 9. 7. 5, ed. Seel 'one king'; ed. Ruehl 'kings'). From Illyria Alexander had returned to Macedonia, probably by the most direct and least arduous route, that through the Wolf's pass (see Fig. 4). Pelion lay on the Illyrian side of the Wolf's pass. Lake Little Prespa, since Philip's annexation of land, was on the Macedonian side. In 335 Pelion was 'the strongest city in the region', i.e. in its walled defences (Arr. 1. 5. 5), and it was 'favourably situated for making attacks into Macedonia' (Livy 31. 40. 5). It is to be identified with the fortified hill-site Goricë.[1]

---

peaks' or even 'along the peaks' (1. 7. 5). He does not comment on 1. 4. 4, παρὰ τὸν ποταμόν, where A. led his infantry neither along nor through the river (the Danube), but near to the river on the way towards a city 5 km. distant from the river. If Bosworth wants the Greek for 'along the river' in a literal sense, it is supplied by Arrian at 6. 4. 1, παρὰ τοῦ Ἀκεσίνου ποταμοῦ τὴν ὄχθην πορεύεσθαι.

[1] I argued in Volume 1. 101, on the basis of a journey in 1932 from Florina via Bilisht to Koritsa that 'Pelion should be sought on the eastern side of the plain of Poloskë'; and I went in 1972 with two Albanian archaeologists, Gjerak Karaiskaj and Frano Prendi, to that side of the plain and was able, from Arrian's detailed description, to identify the site of Pelion and the battle. See *HACI* with plates and plans. In 1981 I visited the Greek side of Lake Little Prespa with the Greek archaeologist, Mrs. M. Siganidou, and checked the route from there via Kariai to Florina. The ancient evidence places the campaign, and Pelion in particular, in Illyria (Arr. 1. 7. 3 and 10. 3; D.S. 17. 8. 1; *PA* 11. 6; *PMor* 327A; Livy 31. 40. 4; C. 3. 10. 6; 5. 1. 1; St. Byz. s.v. *Pelion*; and Procop. *Aed.* 4. 4. 75 in Epirus Nova, not in Macedonia). Tarn 1. 6 was alone in placing Pelion on the Macedonian side of the border, apparently because Cleitus 'occupied' Pelion (Tarn thought it had therefore to be Macedonian, but all the word means is that it was not a Dardanian town—in fact the ancient sources call it Dassaretian). Papazoglou, *CBT* placed Pelion by Lake Maliq on the plain of Koritsa in her map; but the physical features of Arrian's account are lacking, and there is no fortified site in the plain. There are three phonetic spellings in Greek of the Illyrian name, if the MSS. are correct: Πέλλιον in Arr. 1. 5. 5, Πήλιον in St. Byz. (so too in Polybius, inferred from Livy loc. cit.), and Πήλεον in Procop. loc. cit. The differences are neither surprising nor 'important', *pace* Bosworth 69; for they are one and the same, being in each case a fortified city, which is rare in this region (Arr. 1. 5. 5 ὀχυρωτάτη; Livy 31. 40. 4 'vi cepit'; Procop. *Aed.* 4. 4. 75 'fortifications repaired'). Bosworth 69 finds the evidence for this western Eordaea in which the river Eordaicus runs (*RE* 5. 2. 2656–7; Volume 1. 95 and *HACI* 76) not 'conclusive'. Topographical evidence is rarely 'conclusive'; but at least there is supporting evidence. There is

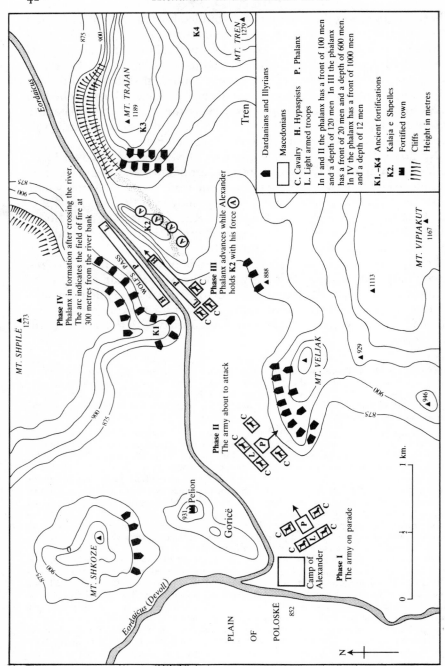

FIG. 4. ALEXANDER'S DISPOSITIONS AT PELION

Alexander found that Cleitus had occupied not only Pelion, but also the surrounding heights which look down on the city and cover the approach to the Wolf's pass. It was evident that he was waiting for Glaucias to arrive. Alexander wanted to strike at Cleitus first. He therefore pitched and fortified a camp on the river Eordaicus in full sight of the enemy, and next morning he moved his army up to the walls of Pelion. He no doubt calculated that this move would bring the Dardanians down from the heights in order to attack him in the flanks and rear. Anyhow it proved so. On one height the Dardanians sacrificed three youths, three girls, and three rams; then they all rushed down the hillsides to converge on the Macedonians. But Alexander promptly about-turned his army, routed the Dardanians, and even captured the height on which the sacrificed victims still lay. He decided next to build a wall round Pelion, so that he could blockade the city and his army could operate inside its own defences (1. 5. 8). Having established his superiority in the plain over the Dardanians of the heights, he would be able to round up supplies and obtain pasture in the plain of Poloskë.

Next day Glaucias, at the head of a large army, came from the plain of Koritsa through the Tsangon pass and joined forces with Cleitus. The situation was reversed: Alexander was heavily outnumbered and faced a serious problem of supply. He acted at once, sending his baggage train of horse-drawn waggons with an escort of cavalry under Philotas to pasture and round up supplies in the plain of Koritsa. They went unopposed through the Tsangon pass, which Glaucias had failed to picket, and proceeded about their business. As Alexander had no doubt anticipated, Glaucias now rectified his mistake and occupied both sides of the pass in the hope of catching Philotas' foraging party

---

none at all for Bosworth's reconstruction. He does not reveal any personal knowledge of the ground. He simply places the river Eordaicus in *Lyncus*, discards the fully attested city and campaign in *Illyria*, and 'conjures up' (to use his own phrase) an unattested city and a campaign in Lyncus inside *Macedonia*. In Bosworth's campaign Cleitus alone invades Macedonia (not waiting for Glaucias); he comes from the north through the Monastir gap to south Lyncus (a march from the Dardanian border of 120 km. through Macedonian territory), unopposed by Antipater's field army or any local forces. Meanwhile Glaucias alone invades Macedonia, is also unopposed, and finds Cleitus some 60 km. inside Macedonia (by a happy chance?). Defeated in south Lyncus, the enemy forces are pursued 'to the mountains of the Taulantii'—some 170 km. away—by A. 'on foot' (p. 73). Such a pursuit is ridiculous; so either one fudges or supposes Arrian to have fudged the evidence. Bosworth prefers to put the blame on Arrian. In fact, he says, A. got no farther than the west side of Lyncus. But what about the Athenian decree congratulating A. on his safe return ἐξ Ἰλλυριῶν (1. 10. 3)? On Bosworth's reconstruction A. has not even set foot in Illyria. Are we to suppose that the Athenian *demos* erred likewise? Bosworth has developed his views in *Studies Edson* 87–97, *M–G* 75–84, and in his *Commentary* 1. 68 f.; I am grateful to him for having shown me a copy of the first article in advance. T. K. P. Sarantes in *Ancient Macedonia* 3. 247 ff. has given a different account of the campaign; it lacks topographical detail, and the fortified town on his Fig. 3 above the Tsangon pass seems to have no actuality on the ground.

on its return.[1] Alexander too divided his forces. Leaving sufficient troops to keep the Dardanian garrison penned up inside Pelion, he marched to the Tsangon pass with the Hypaspists, the Archers, the Agrianians and two squadrons of cavalry—some 5,000 men in all— and cleared the pass. Glaucias' Taulantians did not even put up a fight, and the baggage train returned in safety.

The effect of this success could only be short lived in terms of supply. 'The troops of Cleitus and Glaucias seemed still to have caught Alexander in a difficult position; for they held the commanding heights with large numbers of cavalry, large numbers of javelin-men and slingers, and no small force of heavy-armed infantry as well, while the garrison of Pelion was likely to fall upon the Macedonians as they made off'.[2] Alexander decided to move at once—the very next morning. However, his plan was not to retreat, but to advance through the middle of the enemy forces, thereby keeping them divided and his own men united. In order to do so, he had to deceive the enemy and then seize the narrow passage which he had in mind, namely the Wolf's pass, confined between the river on one side and high cliffs on the other side and admitting only four men abreast at its narrowest point (1. 5. 12).

Next morning the deception was achieved by a superb piece of drill (Figs. 4 and 5). The army paraded on the flat plain[3] without its baggage train, but with its catapults, which led the enemy to expect an assault upon the walls of Pelion. The drill was executed by the phalanx in a solid block of men, 100 men wide and 120 men deep, and by a squadron of 200 cavalrymen on each flank. They moved smartly in complete silence, listening to Alexander's words of command: advancing, retreating, inclining now to the right, now to the left, swinging their serried pike-points now overhead, now to the ready, now to one side, now to the other. The enemy detachments, enjoying a grandstand view from the battlements of Pelion and the surrounding heights, were amazed by the precision of the drill and bewildered by the changing movements. Suddenly Alexander formed the left front of the phalanx into a wedge (*embolon*) and charged the Dardanians on the nearest slopes. They fled at the mere onset. Next he ordered his men to about-turn, utter the battle-cry, and rattle their pikes against their shields,[4]

[1] The Tsangon pass is shown on Pl. XI c in H*ACI*.

[2] This comment was made, not by Arrian who eschews such remarks, but by Ptolemy whom Arrian was following. It is one of the many indications that Ptolemy was a participant in the battle.

[3] See Pl. XI b in H*ACI*.

[4] For this see H*TUS* 59 n. 25; *contra* Markle in *AJA* 82. 492. See now Bosworth 71 f. The wedge is illustrated in H*A* 55 Fig. 4, and discussed by A. M. Devine in *Phoenix* 37 (1983) 210 with Fig. 2.

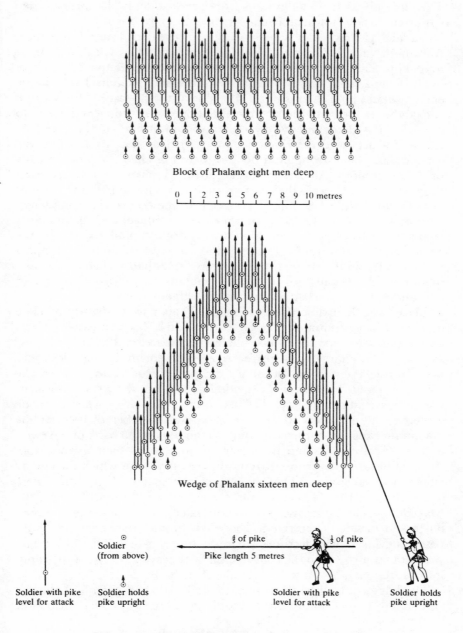

Block of Phalanx eight men deep

0 1 2 3 4 5 6 7 8 9 10 metres

Wedge of Phalanx sixteen men deep

Soldier (from above)

Soldier with pike level for attack

Soldier holds pike upright

⅔ of pike   ⅓ of pike
Pike length 5 metres

Soldier with pike level for attack

Soldier holds pike upright

FIG. 5. THE MACEDONIAN PHALANX IN ACTION

which was the preliminary to a charge by the phalanx of 12,000 men. This time it was the Taulantians who were suddenly the target. They withdrew hastily towards Pelion (1. 6. 4).

Having cleared the flanks of his unrevealed line of advance, Alexander 'ordered' his personal Bodyguards and his own Companions to gallop, carrying their shields, to the enemy-occupied ridge (of Spelle[1]) and fight there half on foot and half on horseback, if the enemy should hold their ground. He rode at their head. At the sight of Alexander in person, the enemy abandoned the ridge and went to reinforce the detachments on either mountainside of the pass. As Alexander occupied the ridge, he was joined by the Archers and the Agrianians, 2,000 strong, and behind them marched the phalanx now in a long column. Alexander 'ordered' the Hypaspists and then each brigade in turn to cross the river on their left, incline left, and form at once in close order (see Fig. 4). When this manœuvre was completed, Alexander's force on the ridge became the rearguard; and the phalanx, facing both ways (in technical terms a 'double phalanx'), held the enemy on the Mt. Shpilë side at bay and was ready to go to the support of Alexander on the ridge. For the enemy forces had rushed down each mountainside, hoping to attack the phalanx as it was crossing and Alexander as he was left behind on the ridge.

Those who had descended from Mt. Trajan were already at close quarters when Alexander charged at the head of his own cavalry force, and at the same time the 12,000 phalangites roared out their battle-cry, as if about to charge through the river. The enemy facing Alexander fled. During their flight Alexander did not pursue them, but led the Agrianians and the Archers at the double towards the river. Conspicuous on his charger, he was the first to cross the river, whereupon he 'ordered' the engineers to fire the maximum number of bolts at the maximum range from their catapults, mounted on the bank of the river, and the Archers to stand in midstream and shoot their arrows from there, in order to cover the rearguard of cavalry upon which the enemy were now converging. The barrage of fire halted them (they were Taulantians led by Glaucias); and while they stayed out of range, the Macedonian cavalry crossed the river to safety. The whole army, united on the north side of the river, proceeded through the widening Wolf's pass into Macedonian territory where pasture was plentiful and supplies were not far away.[2] 'In the course of the withdrawal', i.e. from the camp into Macedonia, 'not a man was killed' (1. 6. 8).

The baggage train with its men and animals had been lost, though Arrian fails to mention it. But not for long. Three days later Alexander

---

[1] See Pl. X in H*ACI*.   [2] See Pl. XI a in H*ACI*.

mounted a night attack. The Dardanians and the Taulantians had not followed him through the Wolf's pass into Macedonian territory. They had assumed that he had fled for good; so now they bivouacked their men over a wide area and did not build field defences or mount guards. Learning of their dispositions (presumably by bold scouting), Alexander came back into the Wolf's pass at night. He crossed the river, leading the Hypaspists, the Agrianians, the Archers, and two phalanx brigades (in all over 7,000 men). He 'had ordered' (1. 6. 10) the rest of his army to follow closely. Moving silently and seeing his chance, Alexander did not wait for the other troops, but sent into action the Archers and the Agrianians, who struck in a deep formation at the very end of the enemy's line, killed many in their beds, and started a panic which became a rout as the infantry line poured through the gap and rolled up the enemy line from east to west. Cleitus and the troops under his immediate command escaped into Pelion, but the rest suffered the full thoroughness of the cavalry pursuit, a Macedonian speciality,[1] with Alexander at the head. It was carried 'up to the mountains of the Taulantii',[2] some 95 kilometres (59 miles) away. Those who escaped did so without their weapons.

On returning from the pursuit, Alexander received the news of a crisis in Greece (see p. 56 below). He led his army southwards, leaving the Macedonian frontier open to invasion. He probably did so in confidence; for such losses had been inflicted upon both the Dardanians and the Taulantians, that they were not prepared to face the part of the field army under Antipater's command and the reserve troops of the western cantons of Macedonia. Cleitus burnt Pelion (perhaps the Dassaretian inhabitants had shown themselves less than friendly to the Dardanian raiders), and he went to join Glaucias in the region of Tirana. They evidently made their submission. Alexander left their royal houses in power; for we hear later that Pyrrhus as a child was sent to Glaucias, and that Pyrrhus as a man married a granddaughter of Cleitus. In 334 a number of Illyrian infantrymen served in Alexander's expeditionary force, and many more Illyrian troops were later to serve in Asia. They went with the acquiescence, we may assume, of Cleitus and Glaucias.

---

[1] See H*P*.

[2] The word order in Arr. 1. 6. 11 makes this translation preferable to 'the pursuit of the Taulantians up to the mountains', as in Brunt, L. 1. 29. For the route via Malik and Gramsh to Elbasan see H*ACI* 85 n. 34 and H*P* 139. I am very grateful to Dr. G. Schlepens for sending me a copy of an article by him and W. Clarysse in *Chron. d'Égypte* 60 no. 119–20 (1985) 30 ff., which connects with this campaign some papyrus fragments from an unidentified Hellenistic historical work. Col. 2, as restored, is incoherent. The name Corragos occurs also in *Arch. Eph.* 1934/5. 118 as the past holder of a royal estate in Eordaea; if Corragos Perdikkou can be restored in col. 2, he will be the man of the *Arch. Eph.* inscription. Col. 3 does not shed any new light on the campaign.

This was the end of an epoch in which the Illyrians had been the greatest threat to Macedonia's very existence. Exceedingly numerous, fearless and well armed, accustomed to live by rapine (C. 3. 10. 9 'rapto vivere assueti'), like their descendants the Albanians in later Turkish times, they had often looted northern Epirus and western Macedonia and had inflicted heavy casualties. If the forces of the Autariatae, the Dardanii, and the Taulantii had made their intended attack earlier in the year when Alexander was campaigning in eastern Thrace, they might well have defeated the army of Antipater and destroyed that margin of military power which alone enabled Alexander to invade Asia. Their mistake had been to move too late and their misfortune was to encounter a master of generalship.

3. *The sources of information and the impact of Alexander on the Balkan peoples*

The narrative of Arrian which describes the Balkan campaign of 335 is of the highest quality. Other accounts are so trivial (e.g. PA 11. 3 'he overran the barbarians' territory to the Danube and defeated Syrmus, king of the Triballi, in a great battle'), that we can conclude that their sources—Cleitarchus, Diyllus, Satyrus, Hegesias, and others—did not describe the campaign, remote as it was from Greek affairs.[1] What we read in Arr. 1. 1. 4 – 6. 11 comes only from Ptolemy and Aristobulus, and almost entirely from Ptolemy, because the interests of Aristobulus were rather in Alexander's personality and in peoples and places than in the details of military action.[2] In some passages Arrian certainly has reproduced Ptolemy's account at comparable length (e.g. on the evasion of the wagons, the tactics at the Lyginus glen, the passage through the cornfield, and the affair at Pelion). In others Arrian has abbreviated so drastically that the meaning is obscure (e.g. Alexander's route to Pelion and the follow-up after the attack by the Archers and the Agrianians at 1. 6. 10). Some events which must have been described in the narrative of Ptolemy are simply omitted (e.g. Alexander's actions on invading the land of the republican Thracians at 1. 1. 5, and between returning from the Danube and setting off for the land of the Agrianes). Then Arrian dates a few events to a particular day or by an interval of so many days (1. 1. 5, 2. 1, 2. 3, 5. 5, and 6. 9). He could do so presumably because the narrative he was following gave the day-by-day sequence of events. On all these grounds we can see that

---

[1] PA 11. 3, Demosthenes was still calling A. 'a mere boy' when he was at the end of his triumphant campaign in the Balkans.

[2] For possible echoes of Aristobulus see HACI 77.

Ptolemy's work was on a much larger scale and much more complete than that of Arrian for this campaign.

Arrian owes to Ptolemy the technical terms for the naming of the various units in the Macedonian army of this time, of the officers commanding them or appointed to particular tasks, and of the territories, places, and rivers which localized the operations. He obtained from him the strength of units at the time, the listing of Macedonian casualties in detail, and the estimated losses of the enemy.[1] Attention is concentratd on Alexander himself and his every action is reported. On the other hand, we are not told what Philotas and Lysanias did with the women and children, where Meleager and Philip took their booty, or what Philotas did on passing through the Tsangon pass. A very remarkable feature of the narrative is the recording of the orders issued by Alexander, which I have put above in inverted commas for ease of reference. There are thirteen instances and, what is more remarkable, in two instances the order was not fulfilled and did not affect the action. One concerned the measures to be taken *if* the enemy on the ridge resisted (in the event they did not, 1. 6. 6), and the other was the order for the rest of the army to follow closely with a view to a joint action, which did not eventuate. These orders were evidently reported for their own sake in Ptolemy's narrative; they are not what a recorder of the actual events would have included in his account.

How was Ptolemy in a position to provide such minutiae of information? Although he enjoyed Alexander's favour, he was at best a junior cavalry officer during the campaign[2] and not aware of the various orders issued by Alexander. His own memories—and we may attribute to him many of the vivid touches, such as some of the women and children of the Getae being carried off on the horses' cruppers, and the sacrificed victims lying there on the hill—were to be overlaid by hundreds of actions in which he took part, not only during Alexander's eventful lifetime, but also in the wars of the Successors, before he came

---

[1] The records of Macedonian casualties, being small, have been regarded sometimes as merely 'propagandist' figures (e.g. Bosworth 217, 254, 312). This is mistaken. A. gave the Macedonian dead a military funeral and informed the relatives (1. 16. 5, Arrian recording the first instance only of a continuous practice); there was no attempt at secrecy, no attempt to mislead his people. He set up bronze statues to those who fell in the first onset at the Granicus river. The small number of casualties in ancient battles on the winning side should not surprise us, if we think of Marathon (some 200) and Pydna (not over 100). Ptolemy (1. 2. 7) cites the losses from the *King's Journal* on my interpretation, not from memory. Arrian is usually (but not at 3. 15. 6) cautious in giving estimates of enemy casualties. He does so for occasions when there was an opportunity for a count. At Pelion there was no such opportunity, as A. had to hasten away, and no estimate is given, whereas an estimate was given at the Haemus pass and at the Lyginus glen. Bosworth 312 criticizes A.'s numbers at 3. 15. 6 without realizing that Arrian was giving the losses in men and horses *only* of A.'s own force (cf. 3. 15. 5 for οἱ ἀμφὶ Ἀλέξανδρον) in the cavalry pursuit.

[2] The Ptolemy who was a *somatophylax* was a different Ptolemy.

to write his account of this campaign some fifty years after the event.
And not only of this campaign, but also of all the campaigns in
Arrian's history and of others which Arrian saw fit to omit. The only
satisfactory explanation is that Ptolemy was drawing upon the *King's
Journal*, in which there was even more detail than he needed. His use of
the *Journal* explains also the concentration on the king's own actions,
the recording of Alexander's orders, and the mentioning of events in
other areas only at the time when they came to Alexander's notice.
Since the *Journal* was an official record and not intended for publica-
tion or for propaganda—that was left to Callisthenes—we have in
Arrian, not only a very detailed, but also an unbiased, record of the
Balkan campaign. There is no attempt to conceal the fact that
Alexander ran short of supplies and came near to disaster at Pelion.

It is easy to underestimate the impact Alexander had on the Balkans
in this campaign and in subsequent years. Philip, of course, had laid
the foundations of conquest and, to some extent, of consolidation. He
had invented the pike and the disciplined formation of the pikemen
(see Fig. 4), which had defeated the hitherto invincible Illyrian armies
of cavalrymen and infantrymen, equipped with metal shield, helmet,
and greaves and with their weapons—javelin, spear, curving cutlass,
and sling—and the dangerous, but less well-organized, Thracians who
prided themselves on their horsemanship and won fame as peltasts
with a lighter shield and longer spear. Philip's victories, especially over
the Illyrians, had been marked by the long pursuits in which the well-
trained Macedonian cavalry inflicted maximum casualties on the
enemy cavalry, that is on the aristocratic leaders of the tribes, and
forced the survivors to recognize Macedon's supremacy in war and
accept Macedonian rule. By these means Philip had created a Balkan
empire, correctly so called because he exercised direct rule and exacted
tribute from his subjects (2. 14. 5 and 7. 9. 3).

There is no indication that Philip placed Illyrians or Thracians on a
level with Macedonians, although he must have employed them as
auxiliary troops, for instance Thracians at Perinthus. On the other
hand, Alexander established an entirely new kind of relationship with
the king of the Agrianians in that, even during Philip's reign, he
became a close friend and had direct communication with him (1. 5.
2). When Alexander succeeded to the throne, a complete trust
developed between the two kings and also between the two peoples; for
Alexander recruited a special group of Agrianian soldiers which was to
win as many battle honours as any unit of the Macedonian army.
When Langarus proved his loyalty by invading and ravaging the
territory of the Autariatae, he was highly honoured by Alexander.
Indeed he was the recipient of 'the greatest gifts that it is customary for

a Macedonian king to bestow on anyone' (1. 5. 4). Nor was this all. Alexander offered him the hand of his own half-sister, Cynane, the widow of Amyntas IV, in marriage, and he agreed to give her to him at a wedding ceremony in Pella. Of course Philip had married Balkan princesses to strengthen new military alliances.[1] This was different because the loyalty of Langarus was assured already. Alexander's spontaneous offer must have made a great impression on the Balkan peoples, even though the wedding did not take place because Langarus fell ill and died. The group of Agrianian soldiers was trusted totally by Alexander; he placed them in the forefront of several actions in the Balkan campaign, and he in person led them out of danger at the Wolf's pass (1. 6. 7).

Alexander's treatment of Langarus and the Agrianians brought an immediate response from 'the most robust and most warlike of the peoples of Europe, Thracians, Paeonians, Illyrians, and Agrianians' (2. 7. 5). Thus Thracian javelin-men under the command of Sitalces, an Odrysian prince, and Odrysian cavalry served as special units comparable in their own expertise to units of the Macedonian kingdom, and the number of Illyrians, Triballians, Agrianians, Tralleis, Odrysae, and Thracians in general who served as soldiers and as settlers in Asia, and especially in the Indus valley, were to be numbered in several tens of thousands.

The wars of Philip and Alexander had a constructive purpose, to enforce peace and develop prosperity. They succeeded to a remarkable extent in the Balkans. Peace certainly brought a booming prosperity. The distribution of Philip's gold and silver coins, which Alexander continued to mint, shows that the trade of the Balkans expanded enormously and ranged far into Central Europe at this period, and that there was for commercial purposes some unification of the peoples who lived between the Danube and the Aegean basin. Like his father, Alexander was interested in promoting land reclamation and flood control,[2] improving farm stock and developing urbanization, whether through his own foundations or through encouraging the formation of native towns. A letter from Alexander early in his reign to the citizens of Philippi made general arrangements for the cultivation of some unused land by Thracian settlers (probably squatters) alongside the citizens of Philippi, and it is clear that his aim was not only to keep the land under production and yielding revenue, but also to provide for

---

[1] The Illyrian Audata, the Getic Meda, and probably the daughter of the Scythian king Atheas (*HPT* 336 n. 19; *contra* P. Green in Adams and Borza 145 n. 44). Philip married 'for military purposes', κατὰ πόλεμον ἐγάμει, or as we should say 'for reasons of policy' (Athen. 13. 557 b-e = Satyrus F 5 in *FHG* 3. 161).

[2] He planned to drain land in the Copaïs basin of Boeotia (Str. 407) and probably near Philippi (see next note).

better relations between the Thracians and the citizens. A detailed survey was to be supervised by two members of a commission (*presbeia*) sent by the king, namely Philotas and Leonnatus.[1]

The construction of roads had been important in Macedonia for military and commercial purposes since the reign of Archelaus (413–399), and the network of roads was extended into Illyria and Thrace by Philip and Alexander. An Albanian archaeologist[2] has identified the earliest phase of what was to become the western part of the Via Egnatia. It was a narrow flagged all-weather road, designed probably in Philip's time, for the movement of cavalry in particular, and from it there were probably side-roads to the forts which Philip built in Illyris. These were 'royal roads', that is, roads of state built by the king. The Thracians too were road-builders (for instance, they worked for Alexander in Pamphylia, 1. 26. 1); and we can be confident that the new towns in Thrace were linked by good roads. There was also an important cultural change in progress. As we have learnt from the excavations at Vergina, the Macedonian court was the cultural leader in the Balkans and rivalled Athens as patron of the arts. Macedonian skills in metalwork, jewelry, weaponry, ivory-carving, portrait-sculpture, painting, and mosaic spread into many parts of Thrace. Athenian tragedians, such as Euripides and Agathon, had written plays at the Macedonian court, and Euphraeus, Aristotle, and Theophrastus lectured and took pupils in Macedonia. The love of Greek literature, and especially of the Attic theatre, which Alexander was able to plant in Asia was carried also into the Balkan area. What has often been called the Hellenization of the Balkans may more accurately be called the Macedonization of the area.

The Greek city-states of the Aegean coast east of the Nestus river and of the Black Sea coast south of the Danube mouth had their own traditions of independence, for which they had fought against the Thracian tribes, the imperial ambitions of Athens, and the expanding power of Macedonia. Philip II was particularly astute in offering to them terms of alliance under which they maintained some form of independence. He had done this even within his kingdom at Amphipolis and at Crenides, renamed Philippi; for both cities operated at first as independent entities, but within the limits of Philip's overall policy. We have a brief description of Philip's campaign in eastern Thrace in 344/3 which is derived probably from a Hellenistic textbook, similar to

---

[1] *Proc. 8th Epigr. Conf.* 259 ff. with the commentary by C. Vatin. The mention of Philotas and Leonnatus dates the letter to 335, since they were to accompany A. to Asia in the spring of 334. A. showed tact in using the term 'embassy', but his recommendations were to be followed.

[2] N. Çeka, cited in my article in *JRS* 64 (1974) 184 f. from his article in *Monumentet* (Tiranë) 1971. 43 f. with Fig. 4.

POxy 1. 12 (D.S. 16. 71. 1–2).[1] Philip, it is stated, defeated the Thracians in several battles and made them tribute-paying subjects of the Macedonians, and he brought the Greek city-states very readily into alliance; for he had freed them from their fear of Thracian raids and he had thereby gained their goodwill. It is clear from this passage that Philip did not make the Greek city-states subject or payers of tribute (as Athens had done), but he left them as free allies in the expectation that a community of interests—particularly commercial interests—would keep them loyal to the alliances. It did not always prove so, since Perinthus and Byzantium opposed him with the help of Persia and Athens in 340. In the settlement of Greek affairs prompted by Philip and confirmed by Alexander at least some of the Greek states on the Thracian coast may have become members of the Common Peace.[2] In 335 Byzantium served as Alexander's naval base, and in 333 when the Persian fleet advanced as far north as Tenedos and Samothrace and even captured Callipolis in the Hellespont (see p. 000 below), the Greek states of Thrace and the Hellespont did not show any support for the Persian cause.

We know little of the Greek city-states on the Adriatic coast, Apollonia and Epidamnus (Dyrrachium), but we can be confident that they entered into alliance with Alexander (see Fig. 8). They benefited from the enforced peace in the hinterland, and they had maintained friendly relations with some of the tribes. The very popular silver coinages of Apollonia and Epidamnus at this time testify to their prosperity and to their trade northwards into central Illyria.[3]

In spring 334 the Illyrian, Triballian, Odrysian, and Agrianian troops who had been selected and trained, reported for duty to Alexander in Amphaxitis, being some 7,500 infantrymen with varied skills and equipment. They were more numerous, slightly, than the Greek infantrymen who were sent to Amphipolis by the Greek League, and they were more often to be entrusted with front-line positions in battle. The Balkan troops and the Macedonians marched together from Amphaxitis via the Kumli valley to Amphipolis. From there, together with the Greek allies and the Greek mercenaries, they marched along the coastal road which was to become famous as the Via Egnatia (see Figs. 1 and 3). It had been built long ago by Xerxes, maintained by the Thracians (Hdt. 7. 115. 3), and probably improved by the Macedonians, and the troops crossed the great rivers 'easily' by

---

[1] See H*SD* 90 f.

[2] *GHI* 177. 30 ... ἀ]πὸ Θραίκης, often added when there was more than one place with the same name (see *SIG* 268 G). In Volume II. 380 Griffith held that Abdera and Aenus were members as allies of A.; but alliance did not always lead to membership.

[3] See H*E* 541.

bridge or by ferry (1. 11. 4). The distance of some 350 miles from
Amphaxitis to Sestus on the Hellespont was covered in twenty days (1.
11. 5), which means a daily march of some 20 miles (32 km.) if we
allow for one day of rest each week. Supplies were no doubt provided
by the Greek cities, and some may have been dumped in advance. The
fleet carried supplies for a month (PA 15. 2 = Duris, *FGrH* 76 F 40), the
siege equipment, and the 'tent' or marquee which Alexander was to
use in Asia as his headquarters. This was to be the most important road
in Europe for the movement of armies and supplies; thus Memnon, for
instance, brought 5,000 cavalrymen from Thrace (C. 9. 3. 21) as
reinforcements for Alexander, then in India, drovers brought splendid
cattle from India to improve the Balkan breed, and large quantities of
bullion for coinage were sent by Alexander to his mint at Amphipolis.
The successes of Philip and Alexander brought undreamt-of prosperity
to this part of Europe.

  The combination of economic prosperity and huge military resources made Thrace a potential source of danger to the central
government. When Alexander planned to invade Asia, he placed
Thrace not under Antipater, but under a separate commander,
Alexander son of Aëropus, who stood very high in his favour and was a
son-in-law of Antipater. His title, 'general of Thrace' (1. 25. 2), shows
that he commanded a standing army which was probably based on
cities founded by Philip and Alexander in the interior, and one of his
functions was to train and equip Thracian forces of infantry and
cavalry for Alexander. Indeed Alexander took more reinforcements
from Thrace than from Macedonia. In 331 the general of Thrace,
called Memnon, 'a man of spirit in command of a powerful army'
(D.S. 17. 62. 5), leagued himself with some Thracians and rose against
the central government. Whatever his aims were, he was outmanœuvred by Antipater who brought the full force of the home army into
Thrace,[1] and he came to terms, which probably included an amnesty
for himself. For in 325 Memnon was the conducting officer for the
5,000 Thracian cavalry who were to join Alexander in Asia. At that
time Macedonia could not have raised so large a force of cavalry. His
successor as general of Thrace, Zopyrion, perhaps for reasons of
personal ambition, crossed the Danube and attacked the Getae and the
Scythians in a major campaign.[2] Undeterred by ominous storms, he

---

[1] D.S. 17. 62. 6 and Polyaen. 4. 4. 1; see D. Kanatsoulis in *Hellenika* 16 (1958-9) 50 ff.

[2] C. 10. 1. 44-5, the better source, gives the date, whereas J. 12. 1. 4 and 2. 16 attached
Zopyrion's disaster to the death of Agis and that of Alexander the Molossian. At J. 2. 3. 4 the
extent of the disaster is stressed. The suggestion of D. M. Pippidi in *AM* 2. 390, that Zopyrion's
expedition was intended to conquer the Greek cities of the north coast of the Black Sea, rests on no
ancient evidence. Indeed it differs from that evidence in Curtius and Justin. So too Danov 365
'der Zug gegen Olbia'.

pressed on with an army of 30,000 men—mainly Thracians—and was totally defeated. The loss of the army prompted the king of the Odrysians, Seuthes III, to bring his people out in revolt, and Thrace was within an ace of breaking away.[1] But the Thracians themselves were not united and a large Macedonian army was soon to return from the East *en route* for home. In 323 Thrace and the neighbouring tribes near the Black Sea were allotted to Lysimachus (*FGrH* 156 (Arrian) F 1, 7).

[1] Although defeated, Seuthes III was left on his throne. He restruck Macedonian coins with his name after 316; it is of interest that Macedonian coins, both silver and bronze, were more in use in the Odrysian area than the coins of Lysimachus. See Youroukova 24. Against Lysimachus Seuthes deployed 8,000 cavalry (D.S. 18. 14. 2), an indication of great wealth; his coins portray his head with a beard and long hair and on the reverse himself on horseback (Youroukova Pl. 11, Figs. 68–72).

III

ALEXANDER AND THE GREEK STATES

As Isocrates saw so clearly, the city-states of the Greek world suffered in his long lifetime from two terrible diseases: revolutionary-faction strife (*stasis*) which, as in modern times, resulted in massacres and in waves of exiles, and inter-state strife exacerbated by rival ideologies and embittered by past rancours to the pitch almost of madness. Plato, too, saw these diseases operating in a seemingly endless succession, a vicious circle, in the Greek states of Sicily.[1] These diseases were already endemic in the states of the Greek mainland, when the rise of Macedonia introduced a complicating factor. The settlement known as the 'Common Peace', which Philip organized and Alexander endorsed (p. 16 above), was intended to make a new start. Its aim was to put an end to faction strife by banning revolutionary methods within the states and to settle disputes between state and state by arbitration and not by war. But achievement was bound to be difficult, even when the Common Peace was fortified by its alliance with Macedonia and its members had the common aim of a war against Persia. No one can have supposed in 336/5 that the two diseases were more than temporarily held in check.

1. *The war with Thebes*

The news which caused Alexander to abandon operations in Illyria at once was indicative of a serious deterioration in the Common Peace. Some men exiled by Philip had returned secretly to Thebes, over-turned the constitution as approved under the terms of the Common Peace, and seized and killed two Macedonian officers of the garrison which had been installed on the Cadmea by Philip. It is to be assumed, though nowhere attested, that the presence of the garrison had been approved by a resolution of the Greek Council. The revolutionary leaders had some grounds for believing that the anti-Macedonian party at Athens, headed by Demosthenes and Lycurgus, and known to be in touch with Persia, might bring Athens into alliance with the dissidents at Thebes, and that both the Aetolian League and some Peloponnesian states might take their side, especially if Persian aid in

---

[1] Isocrates, *Philippus* and *Ep.* 3; Plato, *Ep.* 8, 353 D.

money and ships were to be forthcoming. This situation took priority over any further action in Illyria. Alexander left the plain of Koritsa forthwith.[1]

He marched south (see Fig. 8) alongside Eordaea and the heights of Parauaea, that is, via the Bara pass on the western side of the watershed of the Grammus range and then on the western side of North Pindus; he passed next to the eastern side of the watershed alongside the heights of Tymphaea, down to its frontier with Elimiotis, and then south to Pelinna, a state which was a stalwart supporter of Macedonia (as later in D.S. 18. 11. 1). On this high route in late summer Alexander had at his disposal innumerable flocks of sheep for meat and milk, an abundance of horses and mules, and excellent alpine pastures for his cavalry mounts and transport animals. Fast riders had no doubt ordered Pelinna to have supplies ready for the army. Alexander arrived at Pelinna on the seventh day, having covered some 120 miles as the crow flies. The next stage of the march, again of some 120 miles, took six days (Fig. 6). He proceeded probably on the west side of the plain, away from the main route, then down the Spercheus valley and through the Gates of Thermopylae, so that he encamped at Onchestus, 12 miles from Thebes, at the very time when the Theban leaders first heard that an army had passed through the Gates. It was an amazing example of an army having marched faster than the report of its coming.[2]

At this time the rising was well under way. The central figure was Demosthenes, because he was in communication with Attalus, the disaffected Macedonian general in Asia (D.S. 17. 5. 1; P*Demosth* 23. 2), and with the Persian authorities who sent a large sum to support any rising (300 talents, it was said, in Aeschin. 3. 239, Dinarch. 1. 10 and 18, and D.S. 17. 4. 8). Although the Athenian state did not formally accept a subsidy, Demosthenes certainly made use of the money. It was from Athens that the Theban exiles had set out, and once they had made their coup they were supplied by Athens through Demosthenes with the large quantity of arms and equipment which was needed to put Thebes on a war footing. On the proposal of Demosthenes the Athenian Assembly entered into alliance with Thebes (Aeschin. 3. 238–9)[3] and voted to send an army to help the Thebans. It was at this time probably that the Assembly dispatched one or more envoys to Persia, who fell into Alexander's hands later (C. 3. 13. 15; Arrian mentioned only one at 2. 15. 2). Thus Athens was fully committed,

---

[1] The news had come presumably from Antipater in Lower Macedonia.

[2] Arr. 1. 7. 1–5. For further details see H*MAT* and H*A* 58 with Figs. 5 and 37, which supersede Volume I. 109 f.

[3] The time is given by the expression 'shortly before A.'s crossing to Asia'.

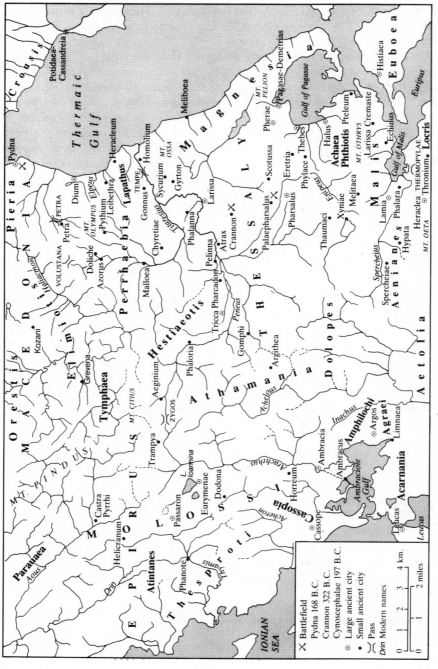

FIG. 6. THESSALY AND ADJACENT REGIONS

except that her army had not yet entered Boeotia. The sudden appearance of a Macedonian army outside Thebes made Athens pause. Her army stayed on Attic soil.

In prompting the Theban exiles and in urging his own people towards war Demosthenes, aided by Lycurgus, made much play with a report that Alexander had been killed and his army had been defeated by the Triballi ([Demades] *On the Twelve Years* 17; J. 11. 2. 8). The significance of Alexander's reported death was not that the Macedonians had lost a gifted commander (for Alexander's military gifts were so little known at Athens that Demosthenes could describe him as 'a boyish Margites' (P*Demosth* 23. 2), but that the *hegemon* of the Common Peace was dead and the Greeks were freed from their oaths to him. Thus the rising could be represented as no breakaway from the Common Peace, but as a rising against Macedonia, admittedly an ally of the Greeks, but not a member of their Common Peace.

At Thebes the new leaders insisted that Alexander was dead, and their forces besieged the symbol of Macedonian domination, the garrison on the Cadmea.[1] When the Macedonian army arrived and Alexander was reported by some to be there, they proclaimed that this Alexander was the son of Aëropus. As he was a man who had nothing to do with the Common Peace, they pressed the citizens to continue the war of liberation (Arr. 1. 7. 2, 6, and 11).

During the first stage of the rising three Peloponnesian states—Arcadia, Argos, and Elis—had also entered into alliance with Thebes, and they had sent some troops, which marched as far as the Isthmus (D.S. 17. 8. 5–6). The diplomatic background in the case of Arcadia is known from Dinarchus 1. 18–20. The alliance was already made when an embassy arrived from Antipater in Macedonia. It had been sent off presumably when Antipater heard of the insurgent movements and relayed the news to Alexander, then in Illyria; and its purpose no doubt was to ask Arcadia to join in suppressing the insurgent movements. The Arcadian League Assembly rejected the embassy. What is more, they dispatched their troops to help Thebes, and it was these troops which met at the Isthmus an embassy of Thebans, who presented themselves as suppliants with olive twigs twined round their herald-wands. They had come 'with difficulty by sea'; for a Macedonian army had arrived unexpectedly at Onchestus, and the envoys had had to avoid Macedonia's allies, Thespiae and Plataea, on the way from Thebes to the Gulf of Corinth. They were as desperate as the Spartan envoy, Pericleidas, had been in 464; for everything depended

---

[1] Consisting of Macedonians and mercenaries; an attempt to bribe the latter is mentioned in Aeschin. 3. 240.

on their allies.[1] Their city, they urged, was not breaking its 'friendship with the Greeks' (of the Common Peace); it was rising against the Macedonians. The Arcadians expressed their sympathy with Thebes and with the cause of Greek freedom; but at the same time, they said, 'we are compelled by the times to give our personal service to Alexander.'[2]

The only hope for the Theban envoys was to bribe the Arcadian general. On learning his price they hastened to Athens to obtain the money from Demosthenes. He refused.[3] By then the Athenian Assembly had decided to abandon Thebes. The Peloponnesian troops soon went home from the Isthmus. In central Greece the Aetolian League Assembly had entered into alliance with Thebes; but its troops did not put in an appearance.

When Alexander arrived at Onchestus, he issued orders to the nearest of the members of the Common Peace whom he could trust—namely the cities of Phocis and in Boeotia Orchomenus, Thespiae, and Plataea—to send their troops to him as *hegemon*. On the next day Alexander moved to the east side of the walled city and encamped. His hopes of a change of heart in Thebes were dashed when some Theban cavalry and light-armed troops sortied and killed a few Macedonians before they withdrew into the city. On the third day, the Phocian and Boeotian contingents having joined him, Alexander led 'the entire force' to the south side and encamped there, so that he lay between the city and any relieving force that might come from Athens and the Peloponnese, and as close as possible to the beleaguered garrison on the Cadmea.

Alexander waited again in the hope of obtaining a peaceful settlement (Arr. 1. 7. 10–11; D.S. 17. 9. 2–4; PA 11. 7). He was prepared to forgive the Theban people and to accept it into the Common Peace, but only on the condition that the insurgent leaders were delivered for trial by the Council of the Common Peace.[4] Inside the city one set of leaders wished to negotiate 'in the public interest', as Arrian put it. But the exiles and those who had invited them to return (and they included some officials of the Boeotian League) urged the people to resist. Their advice was accepted by the people. Even so, Alexander was prepared to wait.

The Theban decision may be judged with hindsight as foolhardy. But the Thebans had considerable grounds for confidence. They

---

[1] I differ here from Griffith in Volume II. 612 n. 3, who stops the Arcadians south of Acrocorinth. For Pericleidas see H*HG* 290.

[2] Dinarch. 1. 20; D.S. 17. 8. 6 mentions the rumour of A.'s army approaching.

[3] So Aeschin. 3. 240 and Dinarch. 1. 20–1.

[4] This can be deduced from A.'s demands of Athens later.

expected Athens to send its army and Demosthenes to supply funds, and they did not know that the troops they were expecting from the Peloponnese and from Aetolia had turned back or never started. Their walled defences were impregnable by the standards of Greek warfare, and the additional field defences which they had constructed were such as had kept the Spartans and their allies at bay in the 370s. Moreover, in terms of manpower the defenders were almost as numerous as the attackers, and they regarded themselves as the finest fighters in Greece. While they held these defences, they would surely capture the beleagu- ered garrison on the Cadmea, and with Macedonian prisoners in their hands they could negotiate with Alexander, if negotiations were needed. But their thoughts were probably of victory, with the enemy trapped between their own forces and the armies of their allies— Athens, Aetolia, Argos, Arcadia, and Elis—and with Persian subsidies to come.

For what followed we rely on the Attic orators for some details and on Arrian for the main account; for the narrative in D.S. 17. 9–13 is a hotch-potch of rhetorical fictions.[1] The action was started on that third day on the initiative of Perdiccas.[2] He had not received an order from Alexander, but he and the Macedonians in general were anxious for the safety of their compatriots in the Cadmea, who were now within hailing distance of the Macedonian lines. So he and his phalangites tore down a section of the outer of the two stockades which had been erected in advance of the city wall, and they then fought their way into the mass of Theban troops who were stationed between the stockades. Amyntas and the men of his brigade followed on their heels. Lest these 3,000 men should be surrounded and cut down, Alexander sent the Archers and the Agrianians, 2,000 in all, to reinforce them. But he himself waited outside the gap in the first stockade, having under his own command 3,000 Guardsmen and Hypaspists in deep formation.

Meanwhile the first wave of Macedonians was failing to break through the second stockade towards the Cadmea, and Perdiccas was carried back severely wounded. The Archers and the men of Perdiccas drove the Theban infantry back along a sunken way between the stockades, but the Thebans delivered a successful counter-attack. As they drove the Macedonians out with considerable casualties through the gap in the stockade, the Thebans pursued eagerly and not in

[1] See H*THA* 13–15.
[2] As stated by Ptolemy (Arr. 1. 8. 1). The suggestion, e.g. in Brunt, L. 1. 35 n. 1, that Ptolemy was censuring Perdiccas, does not seem acceptable, because the brave action of Perdiccas led to a most amazing victory. There is no attempt in Arrian's account to blame Perdiccas for the verdict of the Greeks on Thebes.

formation and fell headlong into the trap Alexander had prepared for
them. The best Macedonian infantry in perfect formation charged and
drove the Thebans back through both stockades and up to the city
wall. Those Thebans who escaped through the gates in the wall failed
to shut the gates in time, and a number of Macedonians got inside the
walls. Of these Macedonians a part joined the garrison on the Cadmea,
and their combined forces advanced into the lower city, while another
part mounted the parapet, so that the main forces could swarm over
the wall and head at speed for the centre of the city. Indiscriminate
and bitter street fighting followed, with some tens of thousands on each
side, Alexander appearing here, there, and everywhere, and the
Macedonian pike outreaching the spear or sword. The panic-stricken
Theban cavalry rode through the gates for the safety of the northern
plain, and the unfortunate infantrymen, 'no longer in any formation',
were cut down 'not so much by the Macedonians as by the Phocians,
the Plataeans, and the other Boeotians'[1]—and some women and
children too, before Alexander managed to halt the action. Greek
sources later estimated the Theban dead at 6,000 and the prisoners at
30,000.[2]

A few hours on one day had brought total disaster to Thebes, the
strongest military state in Greece. The lesson was not lost upon her
allies. Athens dispatched an embassy to congratulate Alexander on his
safe return from Illyria and Triballia and on his suppression of the
Theban revolt. The Aetolians, sending embassies from each tribe and
not from the federal Assembly,[3] asked for pardon; the Arcadians
condemned to death those who had led them into their ill-advised
action; and the Eleans hurriedly recalled those pro-Macedonians
whom they had expelled. We do not know what the Argives did. In
any case the revolt collapsed like a pricked balloon.[4]

What was Alexander to do with the defeated city? He could keep the
decision in his own hands by declaring that the war had been waged
between Macedonia and Thebes with a few of Macedonia's allies
joining in, and he could justify any sentence he might pass on Thebes
by saying that she had broken her treaties of alliance with Macedonia,

---

[1] The implication is that these Greeks were taking no prisoners, whereas the Macedonians
were (Arr. 1. 8. 8).

[2] D.S. 17. 14. 1; *PA* 11. 12; Ael. *VH* 13. 7. Hegesias exaggerates (*FGrH* 142 F 15).

[3] Arr. 1. 10. 1. It was probably the federal Assembly which had voted to join Thebes, and this
was now the way in which the constituent tribes dissociated themselves from the policy. Bosworth
ad loc. holds that the federal system had been disbanded by Philip, but see Volume II. 614 and
615 n. 2.

[4] The sequence of events is not given clearly by Arrian (1. 9. 9 and 1. 10), but it can be
deduced from Arrian's repetition at 1. 10. 1 of πάθος at 1. 9. 1 where it is the slaughter during the
taking of the city, and from the words ἐξ αὐτοῦ τοῦ ἔργου (the fighting in the city) at 1. 10. 2. Thus
these actions preceded the decision by the Council of the Greeks.

not once, but thrice, in 339/8, 336, and 335.[1] Instead, he chose deliberately to set the war and the decision in a general Greek context, and to regard Thebes as both a violator of the Common Peace of the Greeks and a traitor in the joint war of the Greeks and the Macedonians against Persia. Given his choice, it was inevitable that he should refer the decision on Thebes to the Council of the Greeks, and this is what he did (D.S. 17. 14. 1, following Diyllus; J. 11. 3. 8 'in concilio').[2]

The councillors had to decide whether Thebes was justified in her action or whether she was guilty of sacrilege for breaking the oath of the Common Peace and of treason in the war against Persia. They had been elected personally as supporters of the Common Peace,[3] had sworn to uphold its terms, and had voted the war against Persia. While a few might offer excuses for Thebes, the majority would surely find Thebes guilty, and Alexander could rely upon the councillors from the anti-Theban states 'to arrange the affair of Thebes' (Arr. 1. 9. 9).[4] These came not only from Phocis and Boeotia, but also from Thessaly, where the Thessalian League had already declared itself in support of Alexander (Aeschin. 3. 161).[5] To them the intentions of Thebes, if she had succeeded, were all too plain: to reimpose Theban hegemony and to destroy her opponents in Phocis and Boeotia. In fact the majority found Thebes guilty of perjury and of treason.

The Council had next to decide what the penalty for these offences was. Let us consider sacrilege first.[6] Although the oath to respect 'the agreement with Philip' is known to us in *GHI* 177, the penalty for breaking that oath has not been preserved. But we do know of penalties exacted earlier by some Greek states for the breaking of an oath. The execution of all adult males, the enslavement of the rest of the free population, and the razing or repeopling of the site were carried out by Athens on Scione and other 'allies', and without that excuse on Melos and recently Sestus (D.S. 16. 34. 3), and by Thebes on Plataea and recently on Orchomenus; and the less harsh method of total enslave-

---

[1] In 336 A. had not invoked the Council of the Greeks, when there had been insurgent moves (see above, p. 16). Plutarch does not mention the Council now in his account (*PA* 11. 5).

[2] Diodorus' *synhedroi* are those he had just mentioned at 17. 4. 9 and 9. 5, and Justin's *concilium* is that of the Common Peace, 'universae pacis', at 9. 5. 2. There is no point in looking for antecedents in D.S. 11. 55. 5 and 15. 38. 3, and no justification for calling J.'s *concilium* 'a wholly neutral expression', as Bosworth (89 f.) does.

[3] Occasionally, as in the European Parliament, a candidate who was not in favour of the Common Peace may have been elected to the Council. But when Demosthenes offered himself for election as an *eirenophylax* in 338/7, he was not chosen (Aeschin. 3. 159).

[4] J. 11. 3. 8 in describing the meeting calls these states 'Alexandri socii victoriaeque participes'.

[5] Thessalians were not mentioned as taking part in the fighting at Thebes, *pace* Bosworth 77.

[6] The importance of the charge is clear from the fictitious speech of Cleadas in J. 11. 4. 1, where the plea is that because the Thebans thought A. dead they were guilty 'credulitatis, non perfidiae'.

ment or of expulsion was quite frequently applied to Greek and non-Greek peoples, for instance, by Athens. Then in the charter of the Second Athenian Confederacy the stated penalty for breaking one's oath in the case of an individual was 'death or banishment' from confederate territory (*GHI* 123, 59 f.); and sentences of death were indeed passed.[1] We can infer that the penalty for a reneging state is likely to have been similar. For the individual sometimes invoked disaster on his city, if he should break the oath (*GHI* 204, 39 f.). This clause (in the form of 'evil') is found in two Greek treaties and one Macedonian treaty of the fourth century (*GHI* 127, 25 f. and 36 f.; 142, 68 f. and 81; 158, 6).

The penalty for Medism had become proverbial by the fourth century: 'decimation', meaning total destruction, both as proclaimed in the oath of the Greeks in 481 (Hdt. 7. 132. 2; cf. How and Wells ad loc.) and as reaffirmed in the fourth-century copy of the oath before the battle of Plataea (*GHI* 204, 32 f. δεκατεύσω τὴν Θηβαίων πόλιν).[2] Moreover, there was an example of the penalty for Medism in this same year. Gryneum had joined Macedonia in the war against Persia when the Macedonians drove south to free Ephesus from Persian control in 336, and then when Memnon's counter-attack succeeded Gryneum joined Persia. This, it seems, is the background to Parmenio's capture of the town by storm in 335 (D.S. 17. 7. 9). He applied the penalty, *exandrapodismos*, that is the selling of the population as slaves.

With these precedents in mind, the issue before the councillors was probably whether or not the adult males of Thebes should be executed. It was demanded by those who wanted to enforce 'implacable penalties' on Thebes as the destroyer of other cities and the practitioner of Medism in the past and the present (D.S. 17. 14. 2–3; J. 11. 3. 8–11). Among the states whose representatives took this line were those of Phocis and in Boeotia Plataea, Thespiae, and Orchomenus. However, less extreme views prevailed. The Council of the Greeks decided to sell the population as slaves, banish any escapees from Greek territory, raze the city, divide its land among those Greeks who had helped to capture it, garrison the Cadmea, and rebuild and fortify Plataea and Orchomenus.[3]

---

[1] Thus the death sentence was passed on perjurers at Iulis (*GHI* 142, 30). There was no option of exile in *GHI* 138, lines 15, 30, and 49.

[2] J. 11. 3. 10 has the Phocians and the Boeotians cite this oath of the Greeks, when they were discussing the punishment of Thebes in the Council. It was a commonplace; cf. Lycurg. 1. 81.

[3] Hyp. 6. 17; D.S. 17. 14. 3; J. 11. 4. 7; P*A* 11. 5; Arr. 1. 9. 9–10. 'The allies' in 1. 9. 10 are, it seems, the Greeks from the viewpoint of Arrian's Macedonian sources. At 1. 9. 9 Arrian has abbreviated his sources so drastically that he has created the impression that only states which fought in the action at Thebes were represented at the Council. In Diodorus, Justin, and Arr. 1. 9. 10 the full Council seems to be meant, and this surely was what A. wanted.

This decision by the Council of the Greeks of the Common Peace was executed by Alexander (D.S. 17. 14. 4), acting as *hegemon* in command of the forces of the Greeks and of the Macedonians. He made exceptions of those who had voted against the revolt; priests and priestesses, and sacred land; the descendants of Pindar and Pindar's house; *proxenoi* (representatives) of the Macedonian state; guest-friends of Philip and himself; and Timoclea and her children (*PA* 12 tells how she was ravished and killed the ravisher). Later, he permitted Athens to shelter some Theban escapees,[1] and in general he showed clemency to individual Thebans (e.g. Arr. 2. 15. 3). Otherwise the full rigour of the verdict of *andrapodismos* was enforced (2. 15. 3). The sale of the population as slaves raised 440 talents of silver,[2] which was probably devoted to the war against Persia.

Alexander could hardly have expected the sentence on Thebes to be other than it was. While his first desire had been to bring Thebes back into the Common Peace by negotiation, the severe fighting had altered the situation completely. He had now to consider the reactions of his own people to the loss of several hundred Macedonian lives (for D.S. 17. 14. 1 reported the military funeral of more than 500 Macedonians).[3] He had to pay some heed to the complaints and the demands of those members of the Common Peace who had supported him in battle and had suffered casualties in the cause of the Common Peace (D.S. 17. 14. 2; J. 11. 3. 8–9; *PA* 11. 11). He was aware too that would-be insurgents in other states were waiting to judge from the fate of Thebes whether an attempt to fight one's way out of the Common Peace and the Macedonian hegemony was worth the risk. On these considerations Alexander must have judged the sentence to be as satisfactory for his policies as the circumstances permitted.

It is a simplification of the issues to say that Alexander was concerned only to deter the other Greek states (so Diodorus, following Diyllus, Plutarch, and Plb. 4. 23. 8 and 38. 2. 13). But it was this use of the deterrent which did have the very serious effect, that it cheapened the Common Peace. From 335 onwards many Greeks regarded the Common Peace merely as the means by which Alexander involved the Greek states in maintaining his own hegemony and in punishing any insurgents. The hope of a full and willing co-operation between Greeks and Macedonians in preserving peace within Greece and in promoting a national war against Persia was certainly diminished for the time

---

[1] Athens granted them exemption from paying tax as resident aliens (Harpoc. s.v. *isoteles*).

[2] *FGrH* 137 (Cleitarchus) F 1; D.S. 17. 14. 4.

[3] D.S. 17. 61. 3 gave the same number of casualties at the battle of Gaugamela, but non-Macedonians were included in the total then. Street-fighting cost the Macedonians more lives than phalanx battle.

being. It was a hope which may have mattered less to Alexander in 335 than it had done to Philip in 338. For Alexander's eyes were set upon the immediate conquest of Asia.

The failure of Thebes had been due not only to the sheer incompetence of her commanders, but also to her political leaders' misjudgement of the situation in other Greek states. For when it came to the test of war, not one of her allies acted. Fear was no doubt a potent factor, but there were also two interconnected reasons: the division of opinion at home in each state, and the unwillingness of the citizen troops to break their oath and fight against Alexander as *hegemon* of the Greeks. This lack of action was particularly shameful in Athens which had been served so staunchly by Thebes in 339/8 and had herself pushed Thebes into action now. On being congratulated by the Athenians on his suppression of the Theban revolt, Alexander demanded for trial 'before the Council of the Greeks', i.e. of the Common Peace, Demosthenes, Lycurgus, and other politicians whom he named as being no less responsible than the Theban leaders for the rising.[1] During the subsequent debate Phocion proposed that these politicians should surrender themselves in the public interest, but the Assembly decided to ask that Alexander should permit the Athenian lawcourts to judge them. The Athenians chose Demades and Phocion as their spokesmen. Alexander granted the request, except in the case of the mercenary general Charidemus, who then escaped and entered the service of Persia.

2. *The war with Persia*

Alexander had good reason to treat the would-be insurgent states with moderation. He needed them for the invasion of Asia. As *hegemon* he confirmed the size of the contingents which he asked these and other states to prepare that winter for the joint war of the Greeks of the Common Peace and the Macedonians against Persia. It is a proof both of his diplomacy and of the genuine interest of the states in this war that they provided 2,400 cavalry, 7,000 infantry, and 32,000 naval personnel (manning 160 triremes), which made a total more than twice as large as that of the men provided by the Macedonian kingdom. The Greek cavalry and the Greek fleet proved to be of crucial importance. It is a mistake to think of these Greek troops as reluctant or not dependable or as 'hostages' for the behaviour of their

---

[1] Aeschin. 3. 161 κριθῆναι ἐν τῷ τῶν Ἑλλήνων συνεδρίῳ. The names and even the number of the politicians are uncertain; see P*Demosth* 23. 4; P*Ph* 17. 2; and Bosworth 93 f. Evidence of Demosthenes' correspondence with Persia was said to have been found by A. at Sardes (P*Demosth* 20. 4–5).

states at home;[1] for it would have been absurd for Alexander to take a Greek fleet more than three times as large as his own Macedonian fleet, if he had thought it might attack his fleet or sail over to the enemy, as it could have done at any time. The truth is rather that the campaign against Persia under Alexander's leadership did appeal to a very large number of Greeks for both practical and sentimental reasons (cf. D.S. 16. 89. 2). Isocrates had expressed what was probably a widely held view when he proclaimed that such a campaign would bring much profit and some degree of unity to the Greek states, and those who were of his opinion were less alienated by the elimination of Thebes for Medism than modern scholars are apt to be. It is worthy of remark in this context that the author of the speech 'On the articles of Agreement with Alexander' four years later did not even mention the destruction of Thebes[2] in the list of Alexander's wrongdoings in Greece.

In the spring of 334 Alexander, 'entrusted the Greeks to Antipater' (Arr. 1. 11. 3). Antipater was thus authorized to confer with the Council of the Greeks of the Common Peace, act as deputy *hegemon*, and deal with the individual states. He took over a stable situation, in that politicians favouring co-operation with Alexander had come into power in the states since the fall of Thebes. Thus at Athens Antipater dealt mainly with Phocion and Demades, who had headed the last embassy to Alexander; and for some years the people elected Phocion general annually, and they honoured Demades with a bronze statue and free meals at the Prytaneum. Athens' undertaking to put on trial the anti-Macedonian politicians seems to have lapsed, and even an inquiry by the Areopagus Council into the handling of Persian subsidies came to no conclusion; and it is clear from this that the politicians in favour did not feel threatened by those who opposed their policies, namely Demosthenes and Lycurgus and their supporters. It is probable that a similar leadership was exercised in the other member states of the Common Peace in 334–331. The number of politicians and generals who preferred to cross the Aegean Sea and enter the service of Persia were remarkably few.

The forces for the panhellenic expedition were provided by the members of the Common Peace in fulfilment of the alliance with Macedonia in the war against Persia and in accord generally with the assessment which Philip had made in 337 (D.S. 16. 89. 3 διατάξας ἑκάστῃ πόλει τὸ πλῆθος τῶν εἰς συμμαχίαν στρατιωτῶν). The contingents of cavalry and infantry were supplied, it seems, by states of the Greek *mainland* (Sparta and states in Epirus north of Ambracia excepted); for

---

[1] E.g. Heisserer 87, 'compelled to serve in the manner of hostages'.
[2] It became a stock subject for rhetorical display later; see *FGrH* 142 (Hegesias) and J. 11. 4. 1–6.

we hear only of troops from such states (namely, Athens, Thessaly, Phthiotis, Locris, Malis, Phocis, Orchomenus, Thespiae, Argos, Achaea, and Elis) and we may add with probability some light-armed troops from the smaller states of northern Greece (as named or restored in *GHI* 177, Acarnania, Oetaea, Aeniania, Agraeis, Dolopia, and Perrhaebia). The naval contingents came predominantly from the islands (we hear of ships from Euboea and Chios, and islands as far apart as Cephallenia and Thasos are named in *GHI* 177); for Athens supplied only twenty—the same number as Chios was later to supply—and the states of the Peloponnese probably only a few (Arr. 2. 2. 4). The Greek fleet set out with 160 triremes in 334. When it was called up again, it stood at the same strength in the winter of 333/2 (C. 4. 5. 14).

The Greek units, whether military or naval, were equipped at the cost of the member states, and they were of the same standing as the Macedonian units; for the Greeks and the Macedonians were equal partners in an alliance against Persia. Because the supreme command of the joint forces was vested in Alexander,[1] the senior commanders were appointed by him from his own staff, which consisted of Macedonians and some Greeks in his personal service. Thus the Greek fleet was commanded by a Macedonian (Nicanor); and the large army groups—the Thessalian cavalry, the residue of the Greek allied cavalry, and the Greek allied infantry—were each commanded by a native Macedonian such as Alexander Lyncestes and Antigonus or by a Greek who had become a Macedonian (e.g. Erigyius). Commands at the next level, that is of flotillas, cavalry squadrons, and infantry brigades, were held by Greek nationals,[2] and these Greek officers, ranking as *hegemones*, were summoned by Alexander to confer together with the corresponding Macedonian officers, for instance before the battle of Gaugamela (Arr. 3. 9. 3). Thus Alexander was careful to respect the free standing of the Greek allied forces.

Valuable as the Greek and Balkan troops were, they would have achieved nothing by themselves. It was the Macedonian cavalry and the Macedonian phalanx under the generalship of Alexander which made the army invincible in battle. The army which Philip bequeathed to his son has been described in Volume II chapter XII, and we have seen it in action in the Balkan campaign of 335. In the first trial of strength in Asia, at the Granicus river, the Macedonian cavalry used the long lance with a blade at each end to great effect, and an élite group led by Alexander forced its way up a steep river-bank and defeated the finest cavalry Asia could provide. The Macedonian phalanx was able with its long pikes to drive the Persian cavalry off the

---

[1] *GHI* 197 βασιλείο]s Ἀλεξάνδρου στραταγίοντος.   [2] Ibid. Fιλιαρχίοντος.

river-bank, and it then went on to pin down a larger force of Greek hoplites, the best mercenary troops of that period, until the victorious cavalry came up to attack from the flanks and the rear. It was essentially a victory of Macedonian arms, and it was the courage of the Macedonian cavalry which was commemorated by the bronze statues of twenty-five cavalrymen set up at Dium. But the opportunity to do battle was due to the Greek fleet and to the Greek and Balkan supporting troops; and it was the fleet which carried supplies for some 100,000 men afloat and ashore, until the crops ripened in Asia Minor and Miletus was captured. The co-operation of Macedonians and Greeks was commemorated by the inscription on the spoils which were dedicated to Athena on the acropolis of Athens: 'Alexander, son of Philip, and the Greeks, the Lacedaemonians excepted, gave these from the barbarians in Asia.'[1] And the captured Greek mercenaries were sent to do forced labour in Macedonia as traitors to the panhellenic cause of liberation.

At sea there was no established thalassocracy. Since the suicidal Social War of 357–355 and the dissolution of the Second Athenian Confederacy in 338 the nominal control of the Aegean had passed to the organization known as the Common Peace, which aimed *inter alia* to check the increasing practice of piracy (seen e.g. in *GHI* 170, 11). Persia had used money and mercenaries, not ships, to support her interference at Byzantium, and her aim had been to hold the Asian shore with land forces under the command of Mentor and then Memnon. When the news of Alexander's ability and energy reached Darius in the winter of 336/5, he began to prepare for the launching of a large fleet (D.S. 17. 7. 2). In summer 334 that fleet entered the southern Aegean for the first time.[2] By then Alexander's Greek and Macedonian fleets had established control over the Hellespont and the larger islands of the eastern Aegean, and the Persian fleet was unable to prevent Alexander from capturing Miletus (1. 18. 4–5). (See Fig. 7).

However, the Greek fleet of 160 triremes was completely outnumbered by the Persian fleet of 400 warships, and many of its flotillas had had no battle experience since the Social War of 357–355. Alexander took the prudent decision to disband the bulk of the Greek fleet; for it

[1] Arr. 1. 16. 7; *PA* 16. 18. The phrase 'Alexander and the Greeks' occurs again in *GHI* 191, 6–7, where a tyrant at Eresus fought against them; it was probably a standard expression. The Macedonian forces are described also in H*A* 24–34, and the use of the *sarissa* in H*TUS*. The double-ended lance of the cavalryman is well illustrated by P. A. Manti in *Ancient World* 8 (1983) 73 ff.; and for Macedonian types of shield see M. M. Markle in *M–G* 92 ff. For the battle of the Granicus river see my article in *JHS* 100 (1980).

[2] Heisserer 93 and 132 supposed that Persia's fleet was *already* in the Aegean and he talked of Memnon as commander of the Persian fleet in 335. This mistaken belief underlies much of his attempt to re-date constitutional changes in the islands.

was not battle-worthy in itself, it was expensive to maintain, and above all he did not wish to risk losing the Macedonian troops who would have been needed as marines in a set battle.[1] This was not, of course, to abandon the contest at sea. The Macedonian fleet (see p. 71 below) continued to hold the Hellespont, vital not only for Alexander's line of communications with Macedonia, but also for the corn supply of so many Greek states. And the pick of the Greek fleet, being twenty ships from Athens and certain others, stayed with Alexander to transport the siege-train,[2] which was to enable him ultimately 'to defeat the enemy fleet on land'. By the end of 334 it seems that the fleets on both sides returned to their home bases.

'To defeat the enemy fleet on land' was a matter of keeping or gaining control of the land bases without which a fleet of oared ships could not operate. The most important were those of the Hellespont and those of the Greek mainland, the former held by the Macedonian fleet and the latter defended by the members of the Common Peace and overseen by Antipater. On the other hand, Alexander had no means of defending the Aegean islands against the great war fleet of the Persians.

In spring 333 the Persian admiral, Memnon, exploited the weakness of Alexander at sea. His fleet, now of 300 ships, but carrying a formidable force of Greek mercenaries as marines, captured the offshore islands of the eastern Aegean as far north as Lesbos, where Memnon unwisely stopped to besiege Mytilene (Arr. 2. 1. 1–2).[3] The resistance of Mytilene, the death of Memnon in June, and the withdrawal of the Greek mercenaries by Darius gave the Macedonians a breathing space. Alexander had sent 500 talents to Hegelochus and had ordered him to hold the Hellespont (C. 3. 1. 19), i.e. with his Macedonian fleet; and 600 talents to Antipater and the officers responsible for the defence of the Greek cities (see Volume II, 639). Alexander had issued orders directly to the members of the Common Peace who had provided naval contingents in 334: they were to put their squadrons to sea 'in accordance with their treaty obligations as his allies' (Arr. 2. 2. 3; C. 3. 1. 19–20). Despite some opposition at Athens (P*Phoc* 21. 1) and perhaps elsewhere these orders were obeyed and the Greek fleet of 160 triremes was soon at sea (compare C. 4. 5.

---

[1] In his assessment of A.'s decision Bosworth 141–3 omits any consideration of the relative numbers of the fleets; he seems at the end of his disquisition to regard A. as falling into 'a colossal error'.

[2] To entrust this valuable weapon of war to 'hostages' would have been the height of stupidity. The concept is academic (hostages were taken in Greece in 1943–4 not to serve as troops, but to be shot if their compatriots fought against the occupying powers); the Athenian ships were retained because they were the pick of the Greek fleet.

[3] Probably on this occasion Memnon defeated the fleet of the Mytileneans (Frontin. 2. 5. 46).

14). One Macedonian officer made a daring strike with some ships supplied by Euboea and the Peloponnese against an enemy squadron at Siphnos (Arr. 2. 2. 4–5). But this was exceptional. The main policy was one of defence, and fortifications were built for the protection of passage through the narrows of the Euripus Channel by Chalcis (Str. 447).

In the late summer and autumn of 333 the next commander, Pharnabazus, gained many successes. He captured Mytilene, took possession of Tenedos and Samothrace, and penetrated the Hellespont to win a footing at Callipolis on the European shore (see Fig. 1). Darius was now within an ace of achieving his purpose, the control of the Hellespont. However, his admiral Aristomenes and his fleet were destroyed there by the Macedonian fleet and a flotilla of the Greek fleet (C. 4. 1. 36 'classis Macedonum ex Graecia accita'), probably in December 333.[1] This victory was to prove as decisive as the battle of Aegospotami had been in 405, although its consequences were not so immediate. For Pharnabazus received unexpected help on the Asian coast from those Persian commanders and their Greek mercenaries who came north after the battle of Issus in November 333, and his fleets spanned the central Aegean from Andros and Siphnos in the west to Chios, Cos, and Halicarnassus (see Fig. 7), so that Alexander's communications across the Aegean Sea were cut (2. 13. 4 and C. 4. 1. 34 and 37).[2] Now, if ever, was the opportunity for any dissident states of the Greek mainland to offer bases to the Persian fleets; but no, they stayed loyal to the Common Peace. Sparta alone joined Persia. Even she could not enlist the support of any Greek state. The Spartan king, Agis III, accepted ten ships and a financial subsidy, which enabled him to engage the services of 8,000 Greek mercenaries (C. 4. 1. 39; D.S. 17. 48. 1). He threw his energies into the naval war. But he was too late to affect the issue. Already in midsummer 332 the Persian fleet was depleted by the desertion of 200 Phoenician and Cyprian ships which joined Alexander at Tyre; and Macedonian military and naval forces and the Greek fleet recovered points on the Asian coast and Chios and Cos, where they were helped by popular risings (Arr. 3. 2. 3–6; C. 4. 5. 14–18).

Towards the end of 332 Rhodes joined Alexander and the centre of the conflict shifted to Crete; for the Persians might still mount another offensive at sea, if they were in control of Crete and Egypt. While both sides fought in Crete, Agis at last found some sympathizers in some

---

[1] Both the Macedonian fleet and the reconstituted Greek fleet were to protect the Hellespont (C. 3. 1. 19 and 20); but Hegelochus was forestalled by Aristomenes (Arr. 2. 2. 3).

[2] On the other hand Badian in *Hermes* 95 (1967) 176 maintains that 'the hope of defeating the Macedonian army by sea was gone' with the defeat of the Persians at Issus.

Peloponnesian states;[1] but this was too late for the war at sea. For
Alexander entered Egypt in December 332 and the Persian fleet was
hamstrung. Amphoterus, the Macedonian admiral, drove the Persians
and the Spartans out of Crete, defeated some pirates, and sailed to the
Peloponnese with reinforcements consisting of 100 Phoenician and
Cyprian ships, in order to encourage those states which were loyal to
the Common Peace (C. 4. 8. 15; Arr. 3. 6. 3). Alexander's ships—
Macedonian, Greek, Phoenician, Cypriot, and Egyptian—held undisputed sway in the summer of 331. The naval war was at an end.

A new thalassocracy of unparalleled extent had been won. Alexander
had gained the prize which had eluded Xerxes and Athens: the control
of the whole Eastern Mediterranean and the possession of the straits
leading to the Black Sea. He had won it with a minimum of Macedonian
and Greek casualties, and yet his victory at sea was as epoch-making as
his victory over Darius at Gaugamela was to be in terms of land power.
The foundation of his success was political. The appeasement of Athens
by diplomatic methods kept in dock a fleet of over 300 triremes which
could have played a major part.[2] It was enough for Alexander that she
should provide only twenty ships. The aims of the Common Peace, the
programme of freeing the Greek states from the rule of Persia, the
promise of autonomy, and the favouring of democracy held the Greek
fleet together and gained more support in the islands and on the Asiatic
coast than the programme of the Persian admirals who used Greek
mercenaries as marines and pirate vessels as auxiliaries, imposed
tyrannies or oligarchies, and proposed to re-establish the 'Peace of
Antalcidas' with its two corollaries, the enslavement of the Greek cities of
Asia and the support of Spartan hegemony in Greece. By his strategy
Alexander avoided any set battle at sea and yet prevented Persia from
winning the vital bases. But the final victories at sea were won by
fighting, and the credit for them was shared by the Macedonian fleet,
the Macedonian commanders, and the Greek fleet. One consequence—
the accession of the fleets of Phoenicia, Cyprus, and Egypt—was bound
to diminish the importance of the Greek fleet in the balance of naval
power within the thalassocracy of Macedonia.

3. *Relations with the Greek states*

Relations between an island state and Alexander were based either on
membership of the Common Peace or on a treaty of alliance (e.g. at

[1] The passage at Arr. 3. 6. 3 is mistranslated by Robson in the Loeb edition as 'things had
taken a turn towards revolt in his favour'. The dating is disputed. I support Bosworth 279 against
Badian, Borza, Wirth, and Lock, whom he cites.
[2] The navy list of Athens' fleet in 330/29 was twelve quadriremes and 392 triremes (*IG* II^2.
1627. 266 f. and 275 f.).

Arr. 2. 1. 4 κατὰ συμμαχίαν in the case of Mytilene). In consecutive chapters Arrian gives an example of each, Tenedos having its agreement 'with Alexander and the Greeks', and Mytilene in Lesbos simply 'with Alexander' (2. 2. 2 and 1. 4).[1] These agreements carried different obligations. For example, offenders from Chios as a member of the Common Peace were tried by the Court of the Common Peace (*GHI* 192, 15). On the other hand, some Lesbian offenders were tried by the court of their own state in the island (3. 2. 7; C. 4. 8. 11–13), others by Alexander (*GHI* 191, 99), and others under an agreed procedure which stemmed from Alexander's *diagramma* (191, 129–30 and *SEG* 12. 1 and 16, being lines 20 and 28 of Heisserer 123 f.). Again in Lesbos Alexander rewarded Mytilene with money and 'a large grant of territory' (C. 4. 8. 13). This land was taken probably from the king's territory on the mainland. Such a grant of land was not within the competence of the Council of the Common Peace.

During the struggle between Macedonia and Persia the faction strife which was already endemic in many states of the eastern Aegean took on a new impetus. With each change a new faction took power. Thus Chios had fought against Macedonia in 341/0; but in 335, if not earlier, it was a member of the Common Peace and, as such, a member of a common alliance with Macedonia. Then in 333 it resisted Memnon, but fell through betrayal from within and became an ally of Persia (2. 1. 1). Finally the popular party invited the help of Hegelochus, in 332, who defeated the Persian garrison and took over the island. The regulations which were then made by Alexander as *hegemon* have survived (*GHI* 192).[2] There was to be a democratic constitution, a new code of laws, and a banishing of those responsible for betraying the

---

[1] The clear difference is obfuscated by E. Badian's assumption in 'Alexander the Great and the Greeks in Asia' in *Ancient Society and Institutions* (Oxford, 1966) 50 that Arrian's distinction is 'probably mere inaccuracy', or Bosworth's idea that the omission of 'and the Greeks' is a 'stylistic variation' (*C* 181). It is then easy for them to argue that A. broke his obligations to the Common Peace by using different methods of trial for persons from Chios and persons from Mytilene, for instance, as in Badian 53. Brunt, L 124 n. 2, thinks Arrian mistaken. There is a better understanding of these passages in V. Ehrenberg, *Alexander and the Greeks* (Oxford, 1938) 20 ff., against whom Tarn's arguments were weak in 2. 201. n. 6. We do not know why some islanders joined the Common Peace and others did not, but it was probably due to preference on both sides and to opportunity when the Persian fleet was controlling most of the Aegean Sea. The verb ἐπανάγεσθαι in line 14 of *GHI* 192 is best explained like ἐπαναφέρεσθαι πρὸς Ἀλέξανδρον in line 7 as meaning 'be referred to A.', who was on the way to, or already in, Egypt.

[2] This dating by Tod is preferable to that proposed by Heisserer 79–95, namely 334. Heisserer's view that Memnon took Chios in 335 (his pp. 83 and 93) overlooks the fact that Memnon campaigned only on land (D.S. 17. 7. 3 and 8–10); and if a Macedonian garrison was placed there in 334 and Chios was captured despite it in 333, as Heisserer supposes, Arrian would surely have mentioned that garrison, since he mentioned the garrison of A. at Mytilene (2. 1. 4). On my view Memnon 'won it over' (D.S. 17. 29. 2) through treachery from within (2. 1. 1) in 333. Thus from A.'s point of view Chios was then guilty of 'revolt' (*apostasis* 3. 2. 5) from the Common Peace.

island to Persia from all Common Peace territories. Further, any persons so responsible, but still in Chios, were to be tried 'before the Council of the Greeks', and any such elsewhere were to be liable to arrest 'in accordance with the decree of the Greeks'. Any dispute arising between those in Chios and the returning exiles was to be tried by Alexander, and the drafted code of laws was to be submitted to him. Here we see Alexander as *hegemon* trying to check victimization through discriminatory verdicts and laws. Those of the pro-Persian leaders who were subsequently caught by the Macedonian fleet were imprisoned that winter at Elephantine in Egypt, probably until they could be sent safely through the Aegean to the Greek mainland for trial by the Council of the Greeks. For Alexander insisted on the establishment of law and proper legal procedures, and he put a stop to lynching and persecution (as we see at Ephesus, 1. 17. 12). In a second letter to Chios he called a halt to indictments on the charge of Medism and requested honourable treatment for a Chian citizen whom he regarded as a personal friend and as a sincere patriot (*SEG* 22. 506).[1]

There had been faction strife also in Eresus, a city-state on the island of Lesbos, with which Alexander made a treaty of alliance, as with Mytilene. Here between *c.* 350 and *c.* 340 a tyranny headed by three brothers had been in power, and it had been succeeded by a democracy which set up altars to Zeus Philippius, presumably because Philip had had a hand in promoting the change. Its life was short; for before the agreement was made between Alexander and the Greeks in late 336 there was already another set of tyrants in power ([Dem.] 17. 7). They fled in 334, only to return with Memnon in 333, whereupon they committed a number of atrocities against their fellow citizens. In 332 the Macedonians gained control of Lesbos and brought the leader of the Eresus tyrants, Agonippus, to Alexander in Egypt, by whom he was sent back to be tried by a court of the restored democracy. He and his colleague were executed.[2] In accordance with normal Greek practice, reprisals were taken against the families of the condemned tyrants, and the relatives of both sets of tyrants were duly exiled. At an unknown date Alexander asked the democracy to consider in its court whether the descendants of the first set of tyrants should be restored or continue in exile; the verdict was the latter. The relatives of the second

---

[1] Well discussed by Heisserer 96–116.

[2] The order and the dating of events are disputed. Tod (*GHI* 191) has the above order, except that he puts the installation of the second set of tyrants early in A.'s reign (despite [Dem.] 17. 7, unless he means at the very start). Griffith in Volume II. 720 f. has the same order and dating down to the installation of the second set. Heisserer 27–78 carries the first down to 334, and introduces the second set in 333 (despite [D.] 17. 7). Bosworth 179 f. has tyrants continuously until they meet with trouble in 332; this requires them to change political horses rapidly with impunity, which seems very unlikely.

set were exiled by a judgement of Alexander, and this judgement was confirmed later by Philip Arrhidaeus. In the inscriptions which give us this information we can see that Alexander insisted on the democracy following legal procedures and instituting trials with a secret ballot.

Mytilene as an ally of Alexander defied Memnon in 333. When it was compelled to submit, Pharnabazus installed a garrison, made a restored exile tyrant, banished the previous leaders, and exacted a heavy financial penalty; and perforce the state allied itself with Persia and accepted the 'Peace of Antalcidas', a fossil some fifty years old (Arr. 2. 1. 2–5). A year later Mytilene was liberated by Hegelochus and was rewarded for its loyalty, as we have seen above (p. 73). The exiles were recalled, the tyrant (if he survived) was tried in the local court and a democracy was set up. Alexander issued a *diagramma* which was expressly designed to bring the two factions of the Mytileneans into concord (Heisserer 123 ll. 28–30, with his restoration).

We may assume that Rhodes yielded to Memnon in 333; for we should have learnt from Arrian, were it otherwise. Then in 332 during the siege of Tyre ten Rhodian triremes made their way to Alexander (2. 20. 2), and after the fall of Tyre the city of Rhodes surrendered itself and its harbours into Alexander's hands (C. 4. 5. 9). Here too there must have been changes of faction, and probably a *diagramma* was issued by Alexander in favour of reconciliation; for a garrison was placed there, as at Chios, and it was removed later, probably after the end of the actions in Crete (C. 4. 8. 12). There is no sign that Rhodes became a member of the Common Peace. It simply remained an ally of Alexander, to the mutual satisfaction of both parties.

Greek cities on the Asiatic mainland formed a separate category. They were not admitted to membership of the Common Peace, and there is no evidence that the question of admission ever arose. Modern scholars have expressed surprise or disapproval, because they have associated liberation from Persian rule with membership of the Common Peace.[1] Greeks of the 330s probably had no such expectations. Athens and Sparta had 'liberated' Greek cities from Persian rule, not in order that they should become free members of the Hellenic League or the Peloponnesian League, but in order that they should enter the power system of the 'liberator'. So now the 'liberated' Greek cities entered Alexander's power system, the Kingdom of Asia, as subjects of the King, but by his grace with a preferential status, paying a 'contribution' for the war and not 'tribute' and dealing directly with the King. Such was the status of Aspendus, for instance. But when

---

[1] In this controversial matter Ehrenberg, *Alexander and the Greeks* makes a better case than E. Badian in *Ancient Society and Institutions* (Oxford, 1966) 37 f.

Aspendus went back on its obligations, it was made tributary both to Alexander as King of Asia and to Macedonia and also made subject to the orders of Alexander's deputy, the satrap; and at the moment it had to pay an indemnity, provide hostages for good conduct, and accept Alexander's ruling in a border dispute (Arr. 1. 27. 4). Athens had done no less to an 'ally' who broke her agreement in the 450s, and Alexander's methods now served as a model for the treatment of Greek cities within a kingdom.

The Greeks of the islands and of the Asiatic mainland preferred the rule of Alexander to the rule of Persia,[1] particularly because Alexander favoured democracy, while Persia relied on cliques or tyrants, and because the restored democratic leaders obtained the general support of the electorate. The real centre of disaffection was on the Greek mainland, at Sparta, which stood outside the Common Peace and had good reason to hate Macedonia. Philip had had her excommunicated by the Amphictyonic Council in 346, had thwarted her attempts to reconstitute an alliance in the Peloponnese, and had finally deprived her of some border territories and maintained the independence of Messene and Megalopolis. When Sparta refused to recognize Philip, Alexander, and the Common Peace, she was left in proud, but impotent, isolation. When her hated rival, Thebes, was in danger, Sparta did not go to her aid either in 338 or in 335; and when she decided in 333 to side with Persia against Macedonia, she was too late to affect the course of the war at sea, as we have seen, but she did obtain what she had lacked, a large enough subsidy of Persian gold to hire eventually 10,000 Greek mercenaries (Dinarch. 1. 34) and maintain her own army on a war footing.

In the last months of 331 Sparta faced a difficult choice. More than a year of war in alliance with Persia against the forces of the Greek League and Macedonia at sea had ended in utter failure. Prudence might now have advised capitulation. But some factors seemed to favour the continuation of war, not at sea, but on the Greek mainland. Most important of all, Sparta had the military means; for her forces were more than twice as large as they had been for some generations thanks to the Persian subsidy, which would however become a wasting asset if they delayed. On the other hand, the forces of Macedonia were widely dispersed and over-strained: the army of Antipater, drained by the sending of 6,500 Macedonians to the East, was now at a low ebb, and Alexander himself was far away in Mesopotamia. The news of Memnon's large-scale rising in Thrace (see p. 54 above) seemed to promise that Antipater's army would be further depleted and pinned

[1] As a change from enslavement to autonomy; see *SIG* 278. 3, Priene marking the new era with the words αὐτονόμων ἐόντων Πριηνέων.

down in the north. There were also political changes in some Peloponnesian states whereby anti-Macedonian leaders were coming into the ascendancy, and this might be a token that Greek opinion generally was moving towards a war of 'liberation' (D.S. 17. 62. 3–6). Yet Sparta must have realized that she had irreconcilable enemies in the Peloponnese—Messenia, Megalopolis, and Argos (cf. Isoc. 5. 74)— and that north-eastern Greece from Boeotia to Thessaly was likely to support the Common Peace and Macedonia. Much would depend upon the attitude of Athens and Aetolia, as at the time of Thebes' rising, and it was discouraging for Sparta that Athens had recently congratulated Alexander on his victories and he had released Athenian prisoners of war, captured at the Granicus river.

The news of Alexander's victory at Gaugamela on 1 October 331 and of his advance to Babylon may have contributed to the decision of the Spartan people; for it was clear he would not turn back to Greece. So they marched under the command of Agis and engaged the forces of the Macedonian commander Corragus, which represented the Greek League and Macedonia as keepers of the Common Peace. Sparta's full levy and her 10,000 mercenaries were completely victorious, and her success brought two states into alliance with her, Elis and Achaea apart from Pellene (see Fig. 10). These states renounced their membership of the Common Peace, laid themselves open to attack by members of the Common Peace (*GHI* 177, 20 f.), and accepted the hegemony of Sparta, as in the days of the Peloponnesian League. Their example was followed later by Arcadia apart from Megalopolis. Elsewhere Sparta's approaches were rejected, and in particular Athens did not move from her membership of the Common Peace and her alliance with Macedonia.[1]

Early in 330 Sparta did not deploy the forces of her coalition against the Macedonian garrison of Acrocorinth or show the flag in central Greece, but instead she and her allies laid siege to Megalopolis, which was of particular concern to Sparta herself. Her strategy suited Antipater admirably. Having come to terms with Memnon and received a huge sum of money from Alexander (3. 16. 10), he reinforced his relatively small Macedonian army of some 1,500 cavalry and 12,000 phalanx infantry (D.S. 17. 17. 5) with perhaps some Balkan troops and certainly large numbers of Greeks, loyal to the Common Peace, who were willing to serve (Athenians not among them). It was probably April or May of 330 when Antipater led an army, reputedly of 40,000 men, into the Peloponnese (D.S. 17. 63. 1) and won near Megalopolis a hard-fought, but decisive, victory over an

---

[1] The sequence of events is clearly given in Aeschin. 3. 165 and Dinarch. 1. 34, and there is no reason to rearrange them, as Tarn did in *CAH* 6. 445. For Athens' hostility to Sparta in the war see *IG* II². 399 with *BSA* 79 (1984) 229 ff.

army numbering 2,000 cavalry, 20,000 citizen troops, and 10,000 mercenaries.[1] In particular the Macedonian pikeman outfought the Spartan hoplite, and Agis died fighting heroically. Losses of the Spartan coalition were 5,300 killed, and of Antipater's coalition 3,500 killed according to D.S. 17. 63. 3, but 1,000 and very many wounded according to C. 6. 1. 16. It was, in the words of Alexander 'a battle of mice'.[2]

Antipater, who had acted as deputy of the *hegemon*, now asked the Council of the Greek League to decide on the fate of the insurgents. Was Sparta to be destroyed, as Thebes had been? The Council imposed an indemnity of 120 talents on Elis and Achaea, which was to be paid to Megalopolis, arrested the ringleaders of the revolt in Tegea and probably other Arcadian cities (D.S. 17. 73. 5–6; C. 6. 1. 20), and referred the decision about Sparta to the *hegemon* himself, to whom Sparta was ordered to send fifty leading Spartiates to be held as hostages and also envoys to plead her case (Aeschin. 3. 133). Alexander showed surprising clemency; for he pardoned Sparta. It was also a sound piece of statesmanship, as Philip had realized (Volume II. 618 f.). For the course of the war had shown that the existence of Sparta was a source of disunity among those Greek states which might otherwise combine against him. On her side Sparta had shown more courage than intelligence in her continuation and conduct of the war; and Elis and Achaea were fortunate in escaping with a fine, as compared with what had happened to Thebes. It is probable that all three states and the Arcadian states were admitted to the Common Peace, Sparta for the first time.[3]

[1] For the mercenaries see Dinarch. 1. 34; they are omitted by D.S. 17. 62. 7–8. The meaning of the latter passage is uncertain. If Diodorus' phrase 'most of the Peloponnesians' does not include the Lacedaemonians, then we may add Sparta's forces *pandemei*. This makes a total of almost 40,000. Berve 2. 9, much followed by others, is mistaken in putting Agis' forces at 22,000 in all; for he included the 10,000 mercenaries in the figure of 20,000 soldiers expressly recruited by 'most of the Peloponnesians' in D.S. 17. 62. 7. Thus the view of R. Lane Fox, *Alexander the Great* (London, 1973) 252, that the odds were 'two to one' in numerical strength in favour of Antipater, seems to be incorrect. For the size of Antipater's army we may compare that of Epaminondas, namely 40,000 hoplites, when he invaded the Peloponnese.

[2] P*Ages* 15. 4 'myomachia', being contrasted with the A.'s own epic fight against Darius, just as the 'batrachomyomachia' was contrasted with the Homeric epic.

[3] The chronology of the war is much disputed, because Diodorus and Curtius are at variance. The *terminus post quem* is given by the arrival of Macedonian reinforcements between Babylon and Susa in November/December 331, they having set out before trouble broke out, and the *terminus ante quem* by the imminent journey of the Spartan envoys when Aeschines made his remark in 3. 133 in August 330. Diodorus is probably right in putting the final decision of Sparta after the news of Persia's defeat at Gaugamela (17. 62. 1). For various views see E. Badian, 'Agis III', *Hermes* 95 (1967) 190 f.; E. N. Borza, 'The end of Agis' revolt', *CP* 66 (1971) 230 f.; G. L. Cawkwell, 'The crowning of Demosthenes', *CQ* 19 (1969) 171 f.; Brunt, L 1. 480 ff.; G. Wirth, 'Alexander zwischen Gaugamela und Persepolis', *Historia* 20 (1971) 617 f. For the final settlement see E. I. McQueen in *Historia* 27 (1978) 53–8.

The failures of Greek resistance to Macedonia can be epitomized in the words 'united we stand, divided we fall.' Only a few mainland states fought at Chaeronea in 338, and none of them except Achaea fought again in 331/0. Thebes was abandoned even by the few states which had intended to help her in 335. Other Greek states fought against the resisting states in 335 and in 331/0. This situation was due to the long traditions of inter-state rivalry and warfare on the mainland and to the internal politics of individual states. Thus in 330, although Athens had not moved to help either side, Lycurgus in prosecuting Leocrates claimed that 'the freedom of Greece' was buried with the fallen at Chaeronea, and Aeschines failed to win even a fifth of the votes in his attack on the policy of Demosthenes. In fact, though not in spirit, the only form of unity lay still in the Common Peace.

Although Alexander could not command the allegiance of the Greek states to the spirit of the Common Peace, he could and, as far as we can tell, did respect the letter of the Agreement (*syntheke*) which he had made in 336 as *hegemon*. This was demonstrated particularly by the poor case which the speaker of the pseudo-Demosthenic speech, *On the Articles of Agreement with Alexander*, put forward late in 331. The omissions are highly significant. There was no raising of points which modern scholars might raise: the right of Macedonia to hegemony, the position of Alexander as *hegemon*, the destruction of Thebes, the disbanding and the recall of the Greek fleet, the non-admission of 'liberated' Greek states on some islands and in Asia to the Common Peace, and Alexander's treatment of pro-Persian Greeks, e.g. from Chios. We may conclude that in all these matters Alexander had not acted *ultra vires*. The charges actually made are trivial. They were based on the more or less tacit assumption that the *hegemon* was bound to observe the rules and regulations imposed on the member states by the Charter of the Common Peace. But the assumption was false; for the *hegemon* clearly had emergency powers. Thus just as he approved a change of government from oligarchy to democracy at Ambracia (D.S. 17. 3. 3), so he or his deputy approved or facilitated changes of government at Messene and Pellene, which the speaker represented, not necessarily with truth, as becoming close oligarchies or tyrannies ([Dem.] 17. 4 and 10).[1] As events were quickly to prove, these changes of government were in the interest of the Common Peace; for they were among the factors which kept Messene and Pellene loyal during the war of Agis.

As allies of Macedonia in the joint war against Persia, the members of the Common Peace had no grounds for complaint. Alexander was

---

[1] As regards the tyrants at Eresus in [Dem.] 17. 7 see p. 74 above.

personally correct in his treatment of 'the Greeks'. Spoils were dedicated in the names of 'Alexander and the Greeks'; captured works of art were restored to their Greek owners; and large bounties were given to the allies at the end of their service in 330 (Arr. 1. 16. 7; 3. 16. 7–8 and 19.5). The war of revenge for the profanation of the Greek temples by Xerxes which 'the Greeks' had declared (D.S. 16. 89. 2) was brought to a dramatic conclusion by the burning of the Persian palace at Persepolis.

The dealings of Alexander with the Greek states did not begin or end with the members of the Common Peace. They began with the states of the Amphictyonic League. A list of the 'temple-building' delegates in 327 is remarkable for the large number of states which were represented; this surely indicates a high degree of reconciliation and cooperation. Argos had nine delegates out of forty-five. She may have taken a lead as the rival of Sparta and as the homeland of Alexander's family. Alexander's contacts with Greek states went far beyond those of the Common Peace. He was in treaty with probably all Greek states east of the Ionian and Sicilian Seas. While Alexander dealt with the Council of the Common Peace on all matters which fell within its competence, he did not use it as a channel of communication with Greek states in general. In his attempts to check the excesses of political faction and in his proposal that the Greek states should each recall and reinstate its own exiles, he preferred rightly to address the Greek states directly. For he was concerned with a problem which was not particular to the members of the Common Peace and did not fall within the sphere of competence of the Council of the Common Peace.

The announcement (*diagramma*) of Alexander's request that Greek states should recall all their exiles and restore to their exiled owners any confiscated territory, except for men under a curse and those exiled from Thebes, was made first at Susa to the army and later at Olympia to an audience at the Olympic festival which included more than 20,000 exiles. Alexander chose these occasions because he was addressing his request not to the members of the Common Peace alone, as Tarn and others have supposed, but to all states within his sphere of influence.[1] The announcement was not an 'order', as hostile critics suggested (e.g. Hyp. *Dem.* 18, *epitagmata*) but the starting-point for a

---

[1] A. Heuss, 'Antigonos Monophthalmos u. d. griech. Städte', *Hermes* 73 (1938) 135, accepts as genuine A.'s letter which was read out at Olympia (D.S. 18. 8. 4). It was addressed to τοῖς ἐκ τῶν Ἑλληνίδων πόλεων φυγάσι, i.e. to the exiles from the Greek states in general and not merely to those which participated in the Common Peace. That phrase may be genuine; but I do not think that A. would have committed himself and Antipater to the use of compulsion in advance (as the last sentence of the letter does). J. 13. 5. 2 had the exiles from all Greek states in mind: 'omnium civitatum exsules'.

dialogue, during which envoys were sent to Alexander, for instance at Babylon (D.S. 17. 113. 3).

Who would benefit from this restoration of exiles? It has sometimes been suggested that the return of the exiles would strengthen the pro-Macedonian parties in the states.[1] But a moment's reflection shows that this was not so. For those who had been exiled since the rise of Macedonia to power were not the supporters, but the enemies, of Macedonia. For example, the men in exile from Tegea had supported Sparta against Alexander. Yet, as we know from an inscription (*GHI* 202, 57–66), special steps were taken by Alexander to protect them from any victimization by loyal citizens of Tegea on their return; for his *diagramma* laid down strict principles which attest his humane concern for exiles (ibid. 2–3, 10–11, etc.). How greatly the modern world would benefit from such a measure! The reaction of the Greek world at the time may be summed up in the words of D.S. 18. 8. 6 (tr. R. M. Geer): 'people in general welcomed the restoration of exiles as a good thing', i.e. 'for a good purpose' (ὡς ἐπ' ἀγαθῷ γινομένην; cf. LSJ⁹ s.v. ἐπί B III 2).

The restoration of confiscated territory to a dispossessed population (such as the Palestinian Arabs today) was likely to be resisted by the current owners. In particular Athens had expelled the population of Samos in 365 and seized the territory for her own citizens; and the Aetolians had acted similarly at Oeniadae in Acarnania. It would be absurd to suppose that the gratitude of the dispossessed would weigh more than the enmity of Athens and the Aetolian League in terms of power politics. That Alexander was prepared to incur that enmity is a measure of his sincerity and of his determination to establish more settled conditions in the Greek world of city-states. We do not hear of any attempt by Alexander to restore the survivors of Olynthus and Galepsus within the Macedonian kingdom to their original territories.[2] But it is probable that they had already been settled in new towns founded by Philip and Alexander.

Although Athens resented Alexander's plan, she behaved correctly in the matter of Harpalus. As one of Alexander's treasurers, this Macedonian officer had relieved a famine at Athens by sending shipments of grain, and for this he had been made an Athenian citizen. During Alexander's absence in India Harpalus embezzled funds and in the summer of 324 he fled with 6,000 mercenaries, thirty ships, and 5,000 talents to Sunium in Attica. The Assembly refused, on the recommendation of Demosthenes, to grant him asylum, and he moved

[1] As alleged in D. 18. 8. 2.
[2] This point was hinted at by Demosthenes in speaking at Olympia (*PDemosth* 9. 1).

on with his forces to Taenarum in the Peloponnese. From there he returned with the money but in a single ship, hoping to buy support. Once again he was disappointed. Indeed the Athenians arrested him, as the Macedonians had requested. However, he escaped and fled to Crete, where he met his death. These events at Athens took place between the announcement at Susa and the announcement at Olympia.[1]

In this year, 324, Alexander addressed two further requests to the Greek states in general. First, he asked that they should establish cults in honour of his dead friend Hephaestion as 'hero'. Such heroization of a dead man had been granted voluntarily in the past, for instance to Brasidas and Timoleon. Alexander's request was accepted. Some cults were established in 323. Second, he asked that he himself should be granted 'divine honours'. Precedents were rare; but one was apposite for the would-be liberator of Samos, for his predecessor in that role, Lysander, had been worshipped at Samos *c.* 404. Moreover, some Greek cities in Asia in 334/3 and Thasos and Rhodes later had on their own initiative granted Alexander divine honours and established a cult with its own shrine, sacrifices, and games. But it was unique that the request was made by the would-be recipient. What were Alexander's motives? His chief motive was the desire for glory: to be recognized by the Greeks as a benefactor of exceptional degree.[2] To this may be added a political motive. A request from so powerful a person was likely to be accepted by many as a veiled order, and the general acceptance of him as a god would enhance his authority in the Greek world. This request, then, may be seen as a first, perhaps tentative step on the road towards establishing a ruler cult in the Greek world.

As Alexander had no doubt anticipated, the Greek states granted him 'divine honours', sometimes with sarcasm (e.g. Demosthenes at Athens remarking 'Let him be a son of Zeus... or Poseidon, for all I care') and sometimes no doubt with real gratitude. In 323 worship of him was inaugurated with shrines, altars, and statues (e.g. at Athens, Hyp. 1. 31, 6. 21), and games were held in his honour (by the Ionians, Str. 644).[3] Envoys came 'from Greece' to greet Alexander as a god.

---

[1] The chronology is in doubt. See D.S. 17. 108. 6–8; C. 10. 2. 2–4; P*Demosth* 25; and the discussion by E. Badian, 'Harpalus', *JHS* 81 (1961) 41 ff.

[2] His desire to see Olympias deified after death (C. 9. 6. 26; 10. 5. 30) was to give her glory, not political power. Habicht 35 and C. F. Edson in *CP* 53 (1958) 64 stress A.'s desire for glory in this connection.

[3] The second passage in Hyperides refers probably, but not necessarily, to Athens (see Habicht, *Studien* 28 f. and 246 f.). The people of Ephesus wrote of A. as 'a god' (Str. 641). A cult of A. as a god, son of Ammon, was probably established at Megalopolis in 323 before A.'s death (Paus. 8. 32. 1); see E. Fredricksmeyer, 'Alexander's deification', *AJAH* 4 (1979) 1 f. The evidence is well assembled by Berve 1. 96 ff. Lucian, *DMort* 391, said that some added A. in his life to the twelve gods, built him temples, and made sacrifice to him.

They were crowned and they crowned Alexander with golden crowns, as 'sacred envoys come to honour a god' (Arr. 7. 23. 2).[1] That was in Babylon shortly before his death. Had he lived to fulfil his plans, he would have built three great temples in Delos, Dodona, and Delphi and three more in Macedonia, all in honour of the leading gods whom Greeks and Macedonians shared. For whether he himself was recognized as a god or not, his duty to the Greek gods was his first priority, as he showed in his hearing of embassies at Babylon (D.S. 17. 113. 4). They repaid him in true Greek fashion: he died young.

4. *The effects of Alexander's career on the Greek states*

It remains to assess the cultural, social, and economic effects of Alexander's career on the Greek world. Alexander, like Philip, regarded himself as a Greek of Temenid descent. Tutored by Aristotle in contemporary Greek thought and deeply influenced by the *Iliad*, the lyric poetry of Pindar, and the plays of the Attic dramatists, he intended from the outset to make Greek culture the hallmark, not only of his own court, but of his Kingdom of Asia. Philip had shown him the way by recruiting able men from the Greek city-states (Isoc. 5. 19) and employing the finest artists, as the paintings and offerings in the royal tombs of Aegeae testify. Alexander surrounded himself with Greek writers, philosophers, scientists, and engineers, and he employed the leading painters, sculptors, and actors. No king has ever been a greater patron of the arts. He brought from Greece the most famous artists to compete in festivals of the arts at Memphis, Tyre, and Ecbatana, and at other places of which we do not know (3. 1. 4; PA 29. 1–6). The cities which he founded in Asia were designed to become centres of Greek culture in terms of education, performance, architecture, and town-planning, as we know from the excavation of Ai-Khanum.[2].

Whether he founded seventy cities or less, each with a start usually of 10,000 adult male citizens, Alexander had no difficulty in providing the necessary component of Greek-speaking people.[3] He used Macedonians unfit for active service, discharged Greek mercenaries, camp-followers, and then hundreds of thousands of Greeks from the homeland. The flow of men and families to Asia alleviated the social

[1] See Fredricksmeyer, op. cit. 3–5. The expression 'from Greece' takes its meaning from the context, namely Greece in general as A. was at Babylon (Arr. 7. 23. 2) rather than the Greek mainland in particular as Habicht *Studien* 22 argues ('die festländische Städte'). But Greece in general here did not include Asia Minor, parts of which were mentioned in Arr. 7. 23. 1.

[2] On the south bank of the Oxus (Amu) in that part of Afghanistan which borders on Russia.

[3] The only figure in the ancient tradition is 70 (P*Mor* 328 E), which is more likely to be correct than the calculations of Tarn 1. 132 and 2. 232 ff. and of others. That such a number was possible is shown by Seleucus planting fifty more.

problems arising from overpopulation and unrest in Greece. This Isocrates had foreseen, when he wrote as follows to Philip: 'By founding cities in Asia you will settle in permanent abodes the vagrants who lack the means of subsistence and commit outrage on anyone they meet' (Isoc. 5. 120). The new world which he opened to Greek enterprise absorbed not only a plethora of displaced persons, but also great numbers of skilled craftsmen and professional men who chose to emigrate from their own states. Our sources mention 3,000 actors and athletes from Greece performing in a single festival at Ecbatana (7. 14. 10; P*A* 72. 1) and the teaching of the Greek language to Asian army recruits (we know of some 50,000 from P*A* 47. 6 and Arr. 7. 23. 1 and 7. 6. 1) and, we may add, to native settlers in the new cities. The scale of emigration from Greece was such that the citizen population even of Athens, the most prosperous city of the Greek mainland, shrank by perhaps a quarter during Alexander's lifetime.[1]

This is not to say that Alexander solved the unending problem of fourth-century Greece, the unemployed mercenaries. At first the war at sea and on land gave employment on both sides to hundreds of thousands of soldiers,[2] marines, and oarsmen, but the defeat of Persia and the gradual pacification of the East reduced their field of employment. Large numbers settled in Alexander's new cities, and some may have returned to settle in their home states. But there were many tens of thousands who were not willing to abandon their career, but found themselves unemployed in Asia in 324. Alexander planned to settle these mercenaries perforce in new cities which he intended to plant throughout Persis; but the bulk of them—perhaps 50,000—made their way to the coast and crossed over to Greece, where they caught up with the survivors of another group, originally 3,000 strong, who had quarrelled among themselves and left their cities in Asia (D.S. 17. 99. 5–6; C. 9. 7. 1–11). For the situation in Asia in 323 was such that unemployed mercenaries had less chance of employment there than in Greece. If Alexander had lived to return to the eastern Mediterranean, they would have fled westwards to seek employment with his enemies.

The population which remained on the Aegean islands and in the Greek mainland gained in prosperity, as the lucrative markets of Asia became available and Alexander imposed peace on the high seas of the eastern Mediterranean. Within the mainland there was a shift of emphasis. Thessaly and other states north of the Isthmus gained most

[1] From 'approaching 40,000' *c.* 360 in H*HG* 528 to the '31,000 of 322 B.C.' in A. W. Gomme, *The Population of Athens in the fifth and fourth centuries B.C.* (Blackwell, Oxford, 1933) 8 and 19. For a different view see A. H. M. Jones, *Athenian Democracy* (Oxford, 1957) 76 and 149.

[2] Paus. 1. 25. 5 and 8. 52. 5; Pausanias' number, some 50,000 in Persian lands, is in line with other numbers; see H*HG* 667. As late as 326 A. was joined by nearly 6,000 cavalry and over 30,000 infantry from Greece, being 'allies and mercenaries' (D.S. 17. 95. 4).

from service in Asia and from the economic growth of Macedonia. The north-western states benefited from service in Italy under the Molossian king, Alexander, and some of them developed the Epirote Alliance *c.* 330.[1] The Isthmus states flourished with the increase in maritime commerce. The Peloponnese fell behind and suffered most in the war of Agis. In 324/3 the Greek states were overshadowed by the power and the personality of Alexander, and the political leaders at the time were supporters of the Common Peace; but there was certainly a strong latent opposition among those who longed for the hegemonies they had lost and favoured an aggressive unilateral foreign policy.

The economic revolution which Alexander brought about by putting the hoarded treasure of the Persian kings into circulation in the form of coinage and by imposing settled conditions over a huge area had its repercussions on the economy of the Greek homeland. Greek services, Greek goods, and Greek shipping were in high demand and were purchased with Alexander's strong currency. The abundance of that currency in the Greek world made it unnecessary and increasingly unprofitable for individual Greek city-states to produce their own silver currencies, which were more and more limited to a purely local circulation. Even city-states which had been relatively strong in earlier Greek finance, such as Larissa in Thessaly and Sicyon in the Peloponnese, cease to mint a coinage in silver late in the fourth century.[2] This did not affect their prosperity. Indeed the resources of the cities of the Aegean area, the mainland, and Crete, were such that they were able to survive four years of shortfall in grain, the main foodstuff, in 330–326 by importing the surplus of Cyrene's harvests (*GHI* 196). But rising prosperity and increasing productivity were not a panacea for the troubles of a society which coupled affluence with destitution. For prosperity increased the holdings of the wealthy, particularly in the ownership of slaves, but it did not benefit the poorer citizens, who had to compete with slave labour. Thus the gap between the capitalists and the non-capitalists merely widened, and the disparity promoted the desire of the one for authoritarian government and of the other for social and economic revolution. The prohibitions in the Charter of the Common Peace (*GHI* 177) and the basic assumptions of Aristotle in the *Politics*,[3] which was unfinished at the time of his death in 322, are ample testimony to the chronic instability of the world of Greek city-states.

---

[1] H*E* 557; H*HSE* 16.

[2] See Martin ch. 2 and especially pp. 58 f. for Larissa, and 176 f. for Sicyon; the theory that A. had a Macedonian mint at Sicyon has been overthrown, as Martin points out, citing the work of H. Troxell in *ANSMN* 17 (1971) 44 ff.

[3] He regarded a state dole as water poured into a faulty pot. Rather, he thought, the state should distribute its surplus revenue to the destitute citizens to set them up as small capitalists (Arist. *Pol.* 1320^{a}29–^{b}4). For the problems of Greek states at this time see H*HG* 521–32.

IV

ALEXANDER AND THE MACEDONIANS

1. *Manpower and maintenance*

MACEDONIA's military resources were of two kinds: the 'Macedones' proper, who constituted the king's field army and held the right to attend the Assembly, and the local reserves or 'militiamen', organized for home defence and not having that right. In 336 Alexander inherited a field army of some 28,000 Macedones. Of these he took to Asia mainly the older age-groups (J. 11. 6. 4 f. with rhetorical exaggeration), no doubt because the *sarissa* phalanx was perfected only by long training; in consequence 1,000 of them were over age in 331 (C. 5. 2. 16) and 10,000 in 324. His field army for Asia numbered 1,800 cavalrymen and 12,000 phalangites, all being Macedones, and at least 900 non-Macedones, being light cavalry from within the kingdom (D.S. 17. 17. 3–4). He left under Antipater's command a field army mainly of the younger age-groups, numbering 1,500 cavalry and 12,000 infantry, the former including perhaps 1,000 Companion Cavalrymen and the latter being probably all phalangites.[1] The troops of both field armies were armed and equipped by the king. The militiamen were the local levies of the cantons and the towns. They probably provided their own weapons and equipment, were trained locally, and did not normally serve outside the kingdom.

Alexander needed reinforcements in the very year that he crossed to Asia. The officers whom he sent to Macedonia were ordered 'to enlist as many men as possible from the land' (1. 24. 2 ἐκ τῆς χώρας), that is, volunteers from the local militia. No other source is likely; for Antipater's field army, which consisted of the already enlisted and trained men, was not to be depleted. The officers brought back 300 cavalry and 3,000 infantry (1. 29. 4). These figures tell us nothing of Alexander's losses, but something of the willingness of militiamen to opt for service overseas in the field army and so become Macedones.[2] Later, in 332, Alexander sent officers 'to collect young soldiers' (D.S. 17. 49. 1; C. 4. 6. 30), and a year later 500 cavalrymen and 6,000 infantrymen arrived soon after the battle of Gaugamela (D.S. 17. 65. 1;

---

[1] See H*A* 26 f. for these figures, and D.S. 16. 85. 5 for Philip's field army. The number of Macedonians already in Asia was very small.

[2] See Volume II 163 f., 647, and 651.

C. 5. 1. 40). They had no doubt received training in Macedonia and en route, and on their arrival they were distributed over the Companion Cavalry squadrons and the phalanx brigades (3. 16. 11). These young soldiers were presumably taken both from those destined for Antipater's field army and from those intended for the militia.[1]

When we recall that Philip's entire army in 359 numbered 10,000 Macedones, it is remarkable that within three years Alexander could muster almost four times as many men. The explanation is that the kingdom in 334 was more than twice as large as in 359, and that the birth-rate of boys born in 359 to 350 was much higher than it had been in the years before 377, because conditions and prospects had improved in Philip's early years. Moreover, in 359 Macedones had come only from Lower Macedonia and Eordaea, whereas now they came from Upper Macedonia as well and also from new towns planted elsewhere by Philip. Thus Alexander gathered the harvest of Philip's policy, so that the field armies rose in all to 38,000 Macedones in 331.

For his campaigns thereafter Alexander took no more men from Macedonia. The war of Agis showed him the danger of doing so, and he was by now able to attract huge numbers of Greeks and Thracians (e.g. almost 36,000 on one recruiting drive, D.S. 17. 95. 4 and C. 9. 3. 21). In his last year he intended to leave probably 6,700 Macedones of the phalanx as part of his multiracial army in Asia,[2] and to restructure his army for the Mediterranean campaign by repatriating 10,000 overage 'citizen' troops (D.S. 17. 109. 1) and bringing out under Antipater's command 10,000 'Macedones in their maturity' (7. 12. 1 and 4 Μακεδόνας τῶν ἀκμαζόντων). These men were evidently to come from Antipater's field army of men, who being of the younger age-groups in 334 were now older by ten years.

Antipater had presumably replaced wastage by enlistment of men reaching military age. In 331 his field army (he had been given some 13,500 Macedones in 334) forced the insurgent Memnon to make a settlement (see p. 54 above). In spring 330 it formed the spearhead of an army totalling 40,000 men which invaded the Peloponnese, the rest of that army being formed by contingents of the Greek allies and perhaps some Balkan troops. The victory of the Macedonian phalangites over the Spartan hoplites in set battle was the decisive factor, and

---

[1] Plb. 12. 19. 1 = *FGrH* (Callisthenes) F 35 mentioned 800 cavalry and 5,000 infantry coming to A. as he was about to invade Cilicia, i.e. in summer 333, 'from Macedonia'. As a place in central Macedonia was the natural mustering point, it is likely that Callisthenes was giving men of many origins and not just Macedonians. This group is not to be confused with the party of Macedonians who joined A. at Gordium in April 333 (1. 29. 4). See Walbank, *C* 2. 371, Brunt, L 1. lxxii, and R. D. Milns in *GRBS* 1966. 159 ff. I disagree with Brunt, L 2. 490, who proposes 'the arrival of a very considerable force of Macedonian recruits' between 326 and 323, for which there is no support in the sources.

[2] See H*A* 240 for this figure.

Antipater made terms without attacking the confederate forces in the town of Sparta (D.S. 17. 63. 1–4; C. 6. 1. 1–16). Alexander's division of the Macedones, the best troops of the world, between Europe and Asia had been shrewdly calculated. Had he lived beyond 323, he would have concentrated most of them in the eastern Mediterranean, and they together with the enormous fleet he was about to build in the dockyards of Cyprus, Cilicia, Syria, and Phoenicia would have overawed any resistance in Greece.

The cost of maintaining Macedonia's armed forces, including the fleet (see pp. 24 above), was borne by subventions from Persian treasure, converted into currency. Higher rates of pay and bounty, remission of tax for the dependants of casualties (1. 16. 5), provision for war orphans, education of soldiers' sons, cancellation of soldiers' debts (7. 5. 1–3 and 12. 1–2), special equipment such as silver shields, and other signs of royal favour show how vital it was for Alexander to keep his Macedones sweet. He legitimized their liaisons as marriages in Asia, and he urged repatriated Macedonians to beget sons at home, in order to maintain the flow of recruitment. His control of the army in Asia was remarkable; for he handled the sit-down at the Hyphasis and the mutiny at Opis so skilfully that he retained the respect and the love of his men to the moment of his death. The toughness[1] and the devotion of his soldiers were indispensable to his success. As Cleitus said to Alexander, 'your achievements are in great part those of the Macedones' (4. 8. 5).

2. *Tendencies towards disunity*

Splits in the unity of Alexander and his Macedonians arose from matters of policy. Philotas, Cleitus, Callisthenes, and other leading officers and officials detested Alexander's promotion of the Kingdom of Asia, his recruitment of Asians into Macedonian units, and his adoption of Asian ceremonial and manners; and they took actions which led to open rifts. Their resentment was probably a general cause of the conspiracy of the Royal Pages. The Macedonian soldiers shared that detestation and resentment, and this led to their mutiny at Opis (7. 6. 2–5 and 8.2). Alexander emerged triumphant then, but they still hated his policy. It was probably from dislike of his Asian policy rather than for any other reason that the Macedonians in Asia refused to

---

[1] This physical toughness is incompatible with a malaria-ridden society, such as is supposed by E. N. Borza in *AJAH* 4 (1979) 111 and Adams and Borza 17 ff. In this matter experience is important. It is therefore relevant that I have lived among peasants in North Greece who suffered from benign tertian malaria. They were debilitated and apathetic. The Yiannitsa plain and the Sarigol—corresponding to Bottiaea and Eordaea—were notoriously such areas as a result of endemic malaria until the late 1940s.

grant him the divine honours which he sought from them (C. 4. 7. 31; 8. 5. 5; 10. 5. 11).

The constitutional machinery of the Macedonian kingdom travelled to Asia; for it was the king and the Macedones of his army who decided matters of state. At some critical moments Alexander consulted the Assembly, persuading it to endorse his plans of conquest and bringing cases of suspected treason before it. He enunciated the principles of the trust which a king must establish between himself and his people: he must tell the truth and he must persuade, not dictate. Alexander was as good as his word. Such acts as the execution of Parmenio and the killing of Cleitus were accepted by the Macedonians as acts committed for the sake of the state. And he accepted the will of the Macedones at the Hyphasis river. There was also an important part of the state system which moved with him, the School of Royal Pages; this School came out to Asia in 331 (C. 5. 1. 42; cf. Arr. 4. 13. 1), and the Pages he trained between 331 and 323 were destined to play leading roles.

The other part of the Macedonian kingdom operated in Macedonia during his absence. Antipater carried out the duties of the king as commander of the armed forces of Macedonia in Europe, and he deputized for Alexander as *hegemon* of the joint Greek and Macedonian forces. He was responsible too for the conduct of army and navy finances (Alexander repeatedly sent him large sums of money) and he initiated diplomacy with the Council of the Greeks of the Common Peace. We may assume that he acted as the king's deputy in regard to the Macedonian Assembly; for instance, he may have had a hand in the Assembly's decision to pay the unusually large sum of 5 talents to the Delphic Amphictyony in autumn 325.[2] While he managed these affairs of state, the organs of local government were continuing to function normally, e.g. in finance, where they made their own contributions to religious shrines of southern Greece and appointed their own *theorodokoi*.[3] After the death of Alexander the Molossian in Italy in 331, Antipater exercised some control over the Chaones and the Cares (these tribes held the lands between Parauaea, a Macedonian canton, and the mouth of the Adriatic Sea), and over the Illyrians, Triballians, and Agrianians.[4]

[1] C. 4. 7. 31 'immortalitatem affectantem'; C. 8. 5. 5 'caelestes honores'; C. 10. 5. 11 'divinos honores...appellatione'. These passages refer not to *proskynesis* but to a god-like status, such as he requested the Greek states to grant him.
[2] *Mélanges G. Daux* (Paris, 1974) 22 f. and H*SPA* 462, the sum being given by 'Macedones' and not by 'Alexander'.
[3] *SIG* 269 L and *IG* iv 617. 17.
[4] *FGrH* 156 (Arrian) F 1. 7; 100 (Dexippus) F 8, 3; see H*SPA* 471 f. and H*HSE* 14 f. and 19. 'Antipater sent 3,000 Illyrian infantry', e.g. in 327 (C. 6. 6. 35).

3. *The religious obligations of the monarchy*

One function of the monarchy was to carry out certain religious observances which were protective of itself and of the state. While Alexander was abroad, these were conducted by Alexander and his half-brother Arrhidaeus in Asia (C. 10. 7. 2) and, it seems, by the queen mother, Olympias, in Macedonia. This is to be inferred from what happened with Craterus after the death of Alexander. Then, while the new king, Philip Arrhidaeus, stayed in Asia, Craterus was to proceed to Macedonia and undertake 'the care and all that makes for the protection of the kingship' (*FGrH* 100 (Dexippus) F 8. 3); and Antipater was to act in Macedonia as military commander of a wide area. The duties of Craterus were those of 'the most prestigious office in Macedonia'. We may for convenience call it the *prostasia*, the word used by Dexippus.[1]

Who was the predecessor of Craterus in this office? The answer is probably Olympias from 334 to 324. In Macedonia she will have sacrificed daily at dawn as Alexander did in Asia, and she was by virtue of her office in charge of the religious ceremonials and festivals of state. On one occasion she sent an expert in ritual to Alexander with the recommendation: 'He knows how to conduct all your ancestral ritual sacrifices, both the Argeadic[2] and the Bacchic, and all the sacrifices offered on your behalf by myself' (Athen. 14. 659 f., his name being 'Pelignas the server'). Offerings of thanksgiving for victory were sent by Alexander to Olympias (*FGrH* 151 (Fr. Sabbait.) F 1; P*A* 25. 6), and in connection with the victory at Issus and the capture of treasure at Damascus Olympias made offerings at Delphi which were officially recorded there in 331 (*SIG* 252 N 5 ff.). After Alexander's recovery from his illness at Tarsus, she made a dedication to the goddess Hygieia at Athens in 333. Like Craterus later, she was probably the keeper of the king's purse and property in Macedonia (cf. J. 13. 4. 5, cited below, p. 103 n. 2), and it may have been in this capacity that she was the official recipient of corn sent from Cyrene to relieve Macedonia twice during the years of drought, 330–326 (*SEG* 9. 2). She may have presided at court and been concerned with the training of the Royal Pages until they moved to Asia (cf. C. 7. 1. 37–8).

In some situations Olympias acted in conjunction with Alexander or with his deputy, Antipater. Thus complaints were lodged at Athens in

---

[1] See H*SPA* 474 ff., where comparison is made with a similar *prostasia* of the Molossian kingship.

[2] As emended by Kaibel. 'On your behalf' rather than 'preliminary sacrifice' makes better sense for προθύεται in the context. So also E. A. Fredricksmeyer in *CP* 61 (1966) 180.

331/0 in the names of Olympias and Alexander (Hyp. *Eux.* 31–2, Teubner) and the demand for the arrest of Harpalus in 324 was sent to Athens by Antipater and Olympias (D.S. 17. 108. 7). Olympias and Alexander were constantly in correspondence. Alexander was deeply attached to her. When Olympias and Antipater quarrelled, as they frequently did, Alexander was inclined to support her 'through his sense of piety towards the divine being' (D.S. 17. 118. 1); and when Antipater redoubled his letters of complaint against her, Alexander is said to have replied that one tear of his mother wiped away 10,000 letters (*PA* 39. 13). Finally, perhaps late in 324, Alexander made new arrangements: Antipater was to come out to Asia, and Olympias was to be replaced in Macedonia by her daughter Cleopatra and she herself was to act instead of Cleopatra as queen mother of the infant king Neoptolemus in Molossia.[1] In case she might feel slighted, he announced his intention of obtaining divine honours for her in the event of her death (C. 9. 6. 26 and 10. 5. 30).

4. *National growth and ecumenical concepts*

The economic change in Macedonia must have been breath-taking. In his last years Philip had spent almost all his resources, and Alexander crossed to Asia with only small reserves in hand. Then as victory followed victory Alexander sent more and more gold and silver bullion and coin to Amphipolis and Pella. Of all the mints in Europe and Asia that of Amphipolis was the most prolific; it has been calculated that it issued over a period of eighteen years some 13,000,000 silver tetradrachms. Amphipolis and Pella provided gold and silver coin for the West, for the Balkans and mainly for the area north of the Taurus range in Asia. Among their issues until 328 there were the coins of Philip which had become so popular. Damastium, coining silver for the West until 325, and Philippi, coining gold and silver until *c.* 328, were subsidiary mints. Whereas Philip had used the Attic standard in gold and the Thracian in silver, Alexander adopted the Attic standard only. It had prevailed in the eastern Mediterranean and it now became the ecumenical standard. Macedonia, a backwater in 359, was by the late 330s the leading banker and the leading employer in the world and the wealthiest state in Europe, exploiting her central position in the Balkan network of communications and developing her maritime commerce.

---

[1] The change is known from *PA* 68. 4 in the context of the changing world after the return of Nearchus in January 324; and it took place after July 324, when 'Antipater and Olympias' demanded the arrest of Harpalus. This date is defended in H*SPA* 473 ff. against the dating to 331 or earlier by Berve, Tarn, Franke, and others. Later propaganda attributed the change to a flight by Olympias from Antipater (Paus. 1. 11. 3; D.S. 18. 49. 4).

One sign of prosperity in the central Balkans was the continuing coinage of the Paeonian kings, Patraus *c.* 335–315 and Audoleon *c.* 315–285, which was issued in tetradrachms, drachms, and tetrobols. Its favourite emblem, a cavalryman wearing a plumed helmet, celebrated the fame of the Paeonian squadron of cavalry which served in the field army of Alexander.

The coinages of Alexander in gold and in large silver units (Pl. I *a*, *b*), commemorating his victories in Asia, were designed primarily for such large-scale operations overseas as paying and supplying his armed forces, constructing harbours, docks, and fleets, and building and equipping new cities.[1] For the history of Macedonia in Europe we turn rather to his coinage in small silver units and in bronze. For instance, coins which bear the head of a young Heracles and on the reverse an eagle (Pl. I *c*) or two eagles were issued as drachms, hemidrachms, diobols, and obols and also as bronze pieces; these evidently form a group intended for local exchange in and near Macedonia. The designs hark back to Amyntas III, the founder of this dynasty within the royal house; for while the head of Heracles was used earlier Amyntas was the first to introduce the eagle into the repertoire.[2] Of the lesser emblems the *thyrsos* and the thunderbolt were native to Macedonian religion, while the *protome* of Pegasus had reference probably to the cults of eastern Macedonia. Another group of bronze coins carried the emblems of Philip II into the reign of Alexander: Heracles and a selection of his weapons, a head of Apollo laurel-wreathed, a two-horsed chariot, a thunderbolt, and a young head wearing a diadem with no ends (probably representing Caranus, the mythical founder). The lesser emblems on this last issue—a dolphin and a torch—are associated with Amphipolis. The mint for these coins was probably there. It is interesting that these coins give no indication of Alexander's conquests in Asia and that, as on the coins of Philip, the title **ΒΑΣΙΛΕΩΣ** is not used.[3]

The greatest opportunities for money-making by individual Macedonians were in service overseas. For Alexander gave most generous pay and bounties to his soldiers and veterans, in order that those at home should be eager to join him in Asia (7. 8. 1 and 12. 1–2). The senior officers in particular accumulated fortunes in Asia. Some, like Philotas and Harpalus, lived extravagantly and ostentatiously (PA 48. 3), others kept ten or more horses (C. 7. 1. 34), and others, on

[1] See *SNG* v. 4 Pl. 70 no. 3379 for the Paeonian coinage and H*A* 156 f. for a summary account of A.'s coinages.

[2] Gaebler III. 2. 168–170; III. 2. 159 no. 3 and Volume II. 171 for Amyntas III.

[3] Similarly only one of 426 silver coins of A., which were found in a hoard just west of the Koritsa basin carried the title *basileus*—a clear proof that A. did not use the title in Europe. See the report in *Iliria* 1985. 1. 191.

becoming satraps, hired mercenary forces and lived like petty kings. But Alexander enforced discipline on officers and men alike. He punished breaches of discipline and misconduct with severity and without respect for station. He insisted on maintaining the Macedonian traditions of toughness and austerity and even on Macedonians using the Macedonian dialect of Greek among themselves (C. 6. 9. 34–6); and this insistence generally won the approval of 'the Macedones who could not endure to impair any jot of their native customs' (C. 8. 5. 7). It seems that Alexander was anxious to introduce new methods of selecting officers which would favour the rougher and tougher type of soldier—men such as Atarrhias (C. 5. 2. 2–5). We know nothing of the effects of the new affluence on Macedonia itself. We may conjecture that prosperity brought contentment and that capital wealth resulted in the large-scale acquisition of slaves in areas where they had been rare or lacking. A general rise in the standard of life and an increase in trade must have helped to consolidate the position of the new towns in Upper Macedonia and to homogenize their mixed populations.

Macedonia's spectacular success made the Macedonians more conscious than ever of their own nationality, of their distinctness as a people from the Greeks of the Common Peace and from their Balkan neighbours, and of their incomparable prowess in war. At the same time their experience of a wider world made them more aware of their Greek speech and Greek religion, and on the Greek side there was a general acceptance of the Macedonians as members of the Delphic Amphictyony and of the Hellenic race, even though little love was lost between Greeks and Macedonians. It was partly this sense of Macedonian nationalism which bred opposition to Alexander in his army in Asia and brought him less recognition in Macedonia than he thought he deserved. The people at home had had only a short experience of Alexander as king, and his prolonged absence did not endear him to them. It is true that untold wealth came to them from him, but so did casualty lists, wounded soldiers, and reports of their men being planted in new towns at the farthest confines of the world. The evidence of their disgruntlement may be seen in their refusal to grant him the divine honours which they had granted to Philip, the king *par excellence* of the Macedonian homeland and the creator of the greater Macedonian state.

The aim of Alexander to create a Kingdom of Asia and not a Macedonian empire in Asia, similar to the Macedonian empire in the Balkans, was formally approved when he was publicly proclaimed 'King of Asia', presumably by the Macedones in his army (PA 34. 1 βασιλεὺς δὲ τῆς Ἀσίας Ἀλέξανδρος ἀνηγορευμένος ἔθυε κτλ.)[1], but it must have seemed unreasonable, and even quixotic, to Macedonians at home. The reports which came in the letters of the soldiers and on the lips of returning veterans must have been very disquieting. He believed himself to be a son of Ammon (so they heard), he was sacrificing to Egyptian and Babylonian gods, he wore Asian dress, he brought Asians into crack Macedonian units, he wanted his Macedonians to do obeisance to him, and he consulted Egyptian, Persian, and Babylonian soothsayers. The men on the spot had more understanding of Alexander's mind, and they were given higher rewards and posts and seats of honour than Greeks, Persians, Medes, and so on. Those at home did not receive such personal benefits at his hands, and they must have resented such behaviour in a Macedonian king.

One thing is certain. Alexander did turn increasingly to a faith in Zeus Ammon of Libya and in Sarapis, the Egyptian god of healing; in Egyptian, Persian, Babylonian, and Syrian priests and diviners; and in a physical after-life for which—no doubt on his orders—his corpse was mummified in oriental style and not cremated in the Macedonian manner. He had broken completely with the Homeric form of burial which he had carried out for Philip at Aegeae. It was this development which tended to distance him somewhat from his Macedonian followers in the last year of his life. But to the end he retained his mesmeric hold on the affection of those who had fought under his command and at his side in so many campaigns. It was the personality of Alexander which held his diverse worlds together: Greece of the Common Peace, Macedonia as a kingdom of many races, the Balkan empire, and the new-born Kingdom of Asia. If he had lived another thirty years, he might have created bonds which would have held them together in some lasting form of unity; for he, if anyone, was a worker of miracles in war and in statesmanship. But fate ruled otherwise.

---

[1] See H*A* 148 and E. Fredricksmeyer, in *CP* 56 (1961) 167 n. 39. In his dedication at Lindus he named himself as 'having become Lord of Asia' (*FGrH* 532 F 1. 38). See my article in *Antichthon* 1987 (pp. 73 ff.) for the Kingdom of Asia. The title *basileus* was used only on coins minted in, and intended primarily for, Asia, where A. was 'King of Asia'. On the other hand the coins for Europe did not have the title; for the name alone was traditional for the kings of Macedon.

V

THE LEGACY OF ALEXANDER AND THE OUTBREAK OF CIVIL WAR AMONG THE MACEDONIANS

1. *The sources*

WE owe our knowledge of the period 323–301 mainly to Hieronymus of Cardia, who according to D.S. 18. 42. 1, wrote a *History of the Successors*. In the course of a very long life, traditionally *c.* 364–260, he held many high diplomatic, military, and administrative posts under successively Eumenes, Antigonus Monophthalmus, Demetrius, and Antigonus Gonatas; thus he was well placed to know the leading Macedonians and to understand the Macedonian background to this troubled period. He was evidently a very competent and rather factual historian. We can make allowance for a tendency to favour his masters (cf. F 15) and especially his fellow townsman Eumenes. His general viewpoint was that of a naturalized Macedonian rather than that of a citizen of an independent Greek *polis*. His form of exposition and his literary style were regarded as tedious, so that he was little read except by earnest historians, and in consequence only very few fragments of his work have survived (*FGrH* 154). What we know of his *History* is due to secondary writers whose works do survive: especially Diodorus, Justin's epitome of Trogus, Arrian's *Events after Alexander*, and some of the *Lives* by Plutarch and Nepos. For it is certain that they drew to a very great extent upon Hieronymus, and that the similarities spanning their works are due to their use of him as a common source.[1]

At what precise point did Hieronymus begin the *History of the Successors*? One would expect with the day of Alexander's death. This is suggested too by the alternative title, preserved in Suidas, *What was done in succession to Alexander* (τὰ ἐπὶ Ἀλεξάνδρῳ πραχθέντα). Moreover, the earliest fragment for this period concerns a description of Alexander's funerary car (F 2). We find further evidence of this start in Photius' epitomes of Arrian and of Dexippus, a writer who himself followed Arrian's meaning closely but used different terms. Arrian

---

[1] This has been admirably demonstrated by Hornblower 18 ff. with special reference to Diodorus. The criticism of Hieronymus' work as unreadable in bulk comes from Dion. Hal. *De comp. verb.* 4. 30 = *FGrH* 154 T 12.

chose Hieronymus as his main source for his *Events after Alexander*;[1] for Hieronymus had those very qualifications of being a participant and a practical man, which had caused Arrian to choose Ptolemy and Aristobulus as the main sources for the *Anabasis Alexandri* and Nearchus for the *Indike*.[2] Now Arrian 'started from the very death of Alexander' (ἄρχεται ἀπ᾽ αὐτῆς τῆς τοῦ βασιλέως τελευτῆς, in the Teubner edition by Roos of Arrian, II. 253) and treated of 'the *stasis* within the army [it began on that very day] and the proclamation of Arrhidaeus as king' (τήν τε στάσιν τῆς στρατιᾶς καὶ τὴν ἀνάρρησιν, F 1a). He evidently took this start from the work of Hieronymus. It is the same in two independent writers who also used Hieronymus as their main source. For Diodorus begins at 18. 2. 1 with 'Alexander having died childless, anarchy and much *stasis* ensued concerning the leadership'; and Justin at 13. 2 marks the incipient 'discordia' and proceeds to an attempt to create a new regime ('ad formandum rerum praesentium statum').

We learn most about Hieronymus from the epitomes by Photius of Arrian and Dexippus. For it was the habit of Arrian (followed closely by Dexippus) to select one main source—here Hieronymus—and to mark any deviations from that source by describing them as 'stories' (τὰ λεγόμενα), as we have seen in the *Anabasis*. On the other hand Diodorus does not give such a clue. He seems to have supplemented Hieronymus with items favourable to Ptolemy, which came from some historian at Ptolemy's court or even from Ptolemy himself;[3] and he drew upon some technical writers, such as probably Biton and the Rhodian Zeno. In his opening chapters Diodorus repeated points he had made in Book 17, such as the handing of the ring to Perdiccas (17. 117. 3 and 18. 2. 4). Justin used at times another source or sources, e.g. on the Lamian War and the battle of Gabiene. Plutarch drew sometimes on a source which was hostile to Eumenes, and he gave a pro-Athenian picture which was alien to Hieronymus.

By far the longest account of the seven days which followed the death of Alexander is in Curtius (10. 5–10). The first chapter, 10. 5, includes in the description of Alexander's last moments a conversation with his friends, the handing of his ring to Perdiccas, the order that he should be buried at (the shrine of Zeus) Ammon, and the matter of divine honours. This is fiction; for the record in the *King's Journal*, as abbreviated and paraphrased by Arrian and Plutarch independently, and the agreement in general of Ptolemy and Aristobulus, whose

---

[1] So P. A. Stadter, *Arrian of Nicomedia* (Chapel Hill, 1980) 148; and R. H. Simpson, 'Abbreviation of Hieronymus in Diodorus', *AJPh* 80 (1959) 376.

[2] Hieronymus presumably had access to the *King's Journal* of Antigonus (Polyaen. 4. 6. 2), even as Ptolemy had to that of Alexander. Thus there is every reason to accept as correct the figures for Antigonus' forces as preserved by Diodorus.

[3] As suggested by Stadter, loc. cit.

accounts were 'not far from'[1] Arrian's version of the *Journal*, show that
Alexander lost his voice and was probably delirious at that time (earlier
he had talked of the forthcoming campaign). This fiction cannot come
from Hieronymus, who knew Alexander's friends and had access to
official records as well as to their chief compiler, Eumenes. Rather it is
the work of Cleitarchus, writing before Aristobulus and Ptolemy and
preferring sensationalism to veracity. The scenes of mourning, the
imagined thoughts of Macedonians and of Persians, and the memories of
Sisygambis are the product in part of Cleitarchus' fertile imagination.
The suicide of Sisygambis makes a sensational climax (10. 5. 24).[2]
Curtius himself has added his own rhetorical touches, no doubt, and the
final assessment of Alexander in 10. 5. 26–37 may well be the work of
Curtius alone. The same ingredients, but in a rather different order and
with other additions, are to be found in Justin (12. 15–16 and 13. 1);
and Trogus as abbreviated by Justin passed a more hostile judgement on
Alexander than Curtius was later to do. It seems, then, that Trogus also
made some use of Cleitarchus.

The incidents which led eventually to the election of two kings and
of Perdiccas as their manager were described by Diodorus, Justin, and
Arrian in such a manner that we may attribute the similarities to their
use of Hieronymus as a common source. For example, both Diodorus
(18. 2. 3) and Justin (13. 3. 2) represent Meleager as an emissary sent
by the cavalry and then as a deserter to the infantry, which made him
its leader, and Arrhidaeus as a mere pawn in the game. On the other
hand, Curtius gave an entirely different account in which Meleager
from the very start opposed Perdiccas and canvassed the support of the
infantry, and Arrhidaeus played the decisive part as a man of sense and
moderation (10. 8. 2, 6, 8, and 15–22). We can only conclude that
Curtius was using a source other than Hieronymus. Some of the details
may well be historically correct.[3] At the same time Curtius invented a
great deal. For him and for his readers there was an obvious parallel
between the election of Arrhidaeus in 323 and the election of Claudius
in A.D. 41. We can see that the numerous speeches put in the mouths of
his characters were free compositions by Curtius and that the general

[1] Arr. *An.* 7. 26. 3 οὐ πόρρω δὲ τούτων. Scholar after scholar has taken these words out of
context. Their meaning in the context is plain: they refer not to the length of Ptolemy's last book
and of Aristobulus' last book, but to the contents of their narratives, being close to the narrative of
the *King's Journal*. The point is important to Arrian, because he is going on to show the falseness of
acts and words which were given in other accounts, such as A.'s death-bed conversation about his
successor. The passage is mistranslated by E. I. Robson in Loeb 2. 295. Brunt, L 2. 295 'have
recorded no more than this' with his note 'no further details' is correct in the context; but his note
that 'they stopped with A.'s death' is ambiguous. For further discussion see H*THA* 3–10.
[2] As in D.S. 17. 118. 3.
[3] Thus C. mentions A.'s diadem, armour, and robe being laid on the throne (10. 6. 4). This set
of objects has been found in the royal tombs at Vergina.

confusion and the picture of unruly troops eager for booty were closer to what happened in A.D. 41 than in 323 B.C.

We conclude, then, that the *History* of Hieronymus was used, though to varying extents, by Arrian from the outset of his work, by Diodorus from 18. 2. 1, and by Justin from 13. 2. 1 onwards.[1] The most accurate summary of Hieronymus' opening part has come to us in Photius' epitome of Arrian, *Events after Alexander*, to which Photius' summary of Dexippus (*FGrH* 100) is ancillary. On the other hand, the account of Curtius is in general untrustworthy; but it may contain details which are historical, because he read widely and had a scholarly interest in various aspects of the Macedonian kingdom.

For the rest of Diodorus Book 18 and for Books 19 to 20 the main source for Macedonian affairs was Hieronymus, especially in Asia where Hieronymus served during the time covered by these books. For affairs in Greece Diodorus drew sometimes upon a different source, who was most probably the historian he had used for Greek affairs in Books 16 and 17, Diyllus of Athens. This is apparent, for instance, in the account of the Lamian War in 18. 8–13 and in the description of Polemaeus' actions in Greece in 19. 77–8. This author was particularly interested in Athenian affairs, the follies of the demagogues and the decrees of the people, and he delighted in giving numbers and names, unlike Hieronymus. He lacks Hieronymus' bias in favour of Antigonus. He is a source whose information seems to have been obtained in Greece and to be accurate in general.[2] The best study of the chronology of 323–301 is that of Beloch (4. 2. 235 ff.), which is followed mainly here. Particular problems are treated in the footnotes.

2. *The succession*

As we approach the problem of the succession[3] in 323, it is well to make some general observations. In the first place, most kings or

---

[1] In this I differ from Hornblower 88 f., who has the narrative of Hieronymus start with the revolt in Bactria, so that for her Diodorus' regular use of Hieronymus starts at 18. 7. 1. She sees D.S. 18. 2–6 as a 'bridge passage' (her p. 94), in which Diodorus was drawing both on his old source for A. (which she assumes was Cleitarchus and so believes that Cleitarchus included the burial of A. in his work) and on the new source, Hieronymus. I do not think that Diodorus used two sources concurrently for the same theatre of operations here or elsewhere.

[2] I have already argued in H*THA* 73–4 that the author on whom Diodorus drew at 18. 9 was Diyllus. Schubert 243 f. is of the same opinion; so also is Schwahn 145. The lack of continuity between 19. 78. 4 and 20. 45 is explained best if we suppose that Diodorus followed Diyllus for the former passage and Hieronymus for the latter passage. On Diyllus in D.S. 17 see H*THA* 32 f., 81 f., and 160 f.

[3] Differing accounts of the succession will be found in F. Schachermeyr, *Alexander in Babylon u. die Reichsordnung nach seinem Tod* (Vienna, 1970); M. J. Fontana, *Le lotte per la successione di Alessandro Magno* (Palermo, 1960); and R. M. Errington, in *JHS* 90. 49 ff. with an Appendix on Curtius' use of Hieronymus in *JHS* 74. 73 ff. Here the matter is handled *ab initio*.

regents of Macedonia were polygamous. Thus between 359 and 357 Philip took four wives (Audata, Phila, Philinna, and Olympias), and between 339 and 337 at least two more wives. Similarly between 327 and 324 Alexander took three wives (Roxane, Stateira, and Parysatis). The chief purpose of polygamy was to ensure that there was a choice of male children for the succession. All the wives enjoyed the status of queen, and if a priority was given by the king it was accorded probably to the mother of the king's intended heir.

As all the children of these marriages belonged to the royal house, an order of precedence was arranged, presumably by the king, for his sons. If the son he intended to succeed was an adult, that son ranked first. If the son was still under age, his guardian ranked first, and other sons, whether adult or not, came after him.[1] The guardianship of a prince was normally entrusted to the closest agnate, who was an uncle in most cases. Thus Aëropus was guardian of Orestes, Ptolemy Alorites of Perdiccas, and Philip of Amyntas.[2] If a minor became king, his guardian frequently, but not always, acted on his behalf. The technical term for guardian was ἐπίτροπος.[3] There was no term in Greek for our word 'regent'.

Although the king could indicate who was his intended successor, the decision was vested in the Assembly of Macedones. As soon as a king died, the available Macedones met under arms in an Assembly in order to elect a new king. They were not bound by the dead king's wishes. They made their own choice, but in practice only from members of the royal house. If the Macedones subsequently changed their minds, it lay in their power to meet and depose the current king and elect another to the throne.

At the time of Alexander's illness his next-of-kin was Arrhidaeus, a half-brother perhaps older than himself (see Volume II, 225 and 679 n. 5). As the son of Philip and Philinna, he ranked first in the order of precedence, and we find him following Alexander in the carrying out of state sacrifices and state ceremonial. But after a normal boyhood he had been afflicted by a disease which left him not fully *compos mentis* (*PA* 77. 7–8 and 10. 2 οὐ φρενήρης; cf. App. *Syr.* 52). He was thus incapable of holding any administrative or military position, but he was not so badly handicapped that he was put under the charge of a guardian. The next in precedence were Perdiccas and Leonnatus, as we may infer from later events. They were members of the royal house

---

[1] See Volume II. 135 f., 170, and 182.
[2] See Volume II. 135 f. for the possible case of Alcetas being guardian of the seven-year-old boy who was the son of Perdiccas and Cleopatra.
[3] E.g. in Aeschines 2. 29 with Schol. and D.S. 14. 37. 6. The Latin equivalent is 'tutor', as in J. 7. 5. 9 and C. 10. 7. 8.

in a collateral branch or branches (C. 10. 7. 8) and they had held and still held important military commands. Next after them (and after the other royals, if there were any) came the leading Friends of Alexander.

In his last days Alexander lost the power of speech and probably of reason. Although a similar fever had preceded the death of Hephaestion, Alexander seems to have assumed that he would survive. Thus he died without indicating whom he wished to be his successor.[1] Meanwhile those nearest to him, and especially Perdiccas and Leonnatus, must have considered who was the best candidate. The first in the order of precedence, Arrhidaeus, seemed to them unsuitable; for his actions as king would be unpredictable and certainly irresponsible, and he would inherit a position which would require the highest military and administrative abilities. Next in precedence, it seems, was Perdiccas, brave, capable, and experienced, and after him came Leonnatus with similar qualifications, both being of the royal blood. In the younger generation there was a son of Alexander by Barsine, a Persian noblewoman. She was the widow first of Mentor and then of Memnon, brothers from Rhodes, who had had a fine record of service as commanders for Persia. This son, Heracles, had been born probably in 327/6, but out of wedlock;[2] for he was the child of a long-lasting liaison which Parmenio had advised Alexander to form. If there had been legitimate sons available, Heracles would not have been considered; but conditions in 323 were abnormal. Finally, Roxane was some seven months pregnant.[3] She had already born a son who had died in infancy (*Epit. Metz.* 70), and if this pregnancy should result in a boy he would be the natural heir. But for the two months until the sex of the child was known, and for many years thereafter if the child was a male, the state would be in the hands of the child's guardian or guardians. Such then were the possibilities, while the king lay dying, which were considered by the leading Friends and Bodyguards.

But there was another factor in the situation, the Macedones of the armed forces at Babylon. They were deeply devoted to the descendants of Amyntas III and in particular to Philip II and Alexander, as they showed when they insisted on parading past him as he lay dying (Arr.

---

[1] Arr. *An.* 7. 25–6 and P*A* 76–77. 1. For arguments in favour of the official record see H*THA* 4 ff.

[2] The source of P*A* 21. 7–9, Aristobulus, is dependable, and the word ἅψασθαι means not to marry, but to have intercourse with (LSJ[9] s.v., III 5). See also P*Eum* 1. 7; C. 10. 6. 11–13; J. 11. 10. 2 and 13. 2. 7; App. *Syr.* 52; Suidas s.v. *Antipatros*. The doubts of Tarn 2. 330 ff. are not justified. Heracles was born probably in 327/6 (D.S. 20. 20. 1 giving his age in 310/9) rather than in 324/3 (as in J. 15. 2. 3); for J. 13. 2. 7 called him a boy ('puer') rather than a baby in 323. When A. died, Heracles was being brought up, not at the court, but at Pergamum. This suggests that he was not regarded officially as a member of the royal family (J. loc. cit. and, much later, D.S. 20. 20. 1). Tarn's views were refuted by P. A. Brunt in *Riv. fil.* 1975. 22 ff.

[3] So J. 13. 2. 5, which is to be preferred to C. 10. 6. 9.

An. 7. 26. 1). Their mood in 323 was uncertain. The unity which they
had shown during the campaigns had been split by the mutiny at Opis,
by the sending away of 10,000 veterans, and by the drafting of Asians
into what had become a multiracial army. Discontent was aggravated
by the fact that the generous bounty which Alexander had promised to
those Macedonians who were to stay in Asia after the mutiny at Opis
(Arr. *Succ.* 1. 32) had not yet been paid. No one could have foretold
with confidence what the decision of the Macedonians would be.

It was this uncertainty which caused the leading Friends and
Bodyguards to proceed by stages on their own initiative and not to
convene immediately a full Assembly of all available Macedones. First,
they met under arms themselves and discussed alternative courses.[1]
They adopted the proposal of Perdiccas: to await the birth of Roxane's
child, and to set up Leonnatus, Perdiccas, Craterus, and Antipater as
guardians of the child *in utero* and thereafter, should it prove to be a
boy. All those present took an oath of obedience to the four guardians.
They then reported their own decision to the Macedonian cavalrymen, who were summoned, it seems, to parade under arms. The
cavalrymen adopted the decision and took an oath of obedience to the
four guardians (D.S. 18. 2. 2; J. 13. 2. 14 and 3. 1). The leading
Friends and Bodyguards intended next to convene the Macedonian
infantrymen, obtain their agreement, and exact their oath of obedience.[2] The final step would then be to convene a full Assembly of all
Macedonians at Babylon. Its decision would be an act of state.

In proceeding thus by stages the Friends and the Bodyguards may
have had in mind a precedent set by Alexander. He had put a proposal
to a picked force of Macedonians, obtained their vote of approval, and
then taken the matter to the entire army, which had concurred with
that vote (*PA* 47. 1–4). But in the present case great issues were
involved. The Friends and the Bodyguards were planning to exclude
Arrhidaeus even from consideration, and to place their chosen representatives in a position of power, which they had every chance of
retaining whether as guardians of an infant king, if Roxane should
bear a son, or as *ipso facto* rulers, if she did not. A self-selecting caucus of
leading generals, backed by the Macedonians of the Royal Army,
might well have been the best body to rule a huge and ethnically
diverse area, such as we have seen in the U.S.S.R. But this plan was
overthrown by the Macedonian infantrymen who stood firm on the
democratic rights of the Macedonian Assembly.

The Macedonian infantrymen did not wait to be convened. Being
resentful that they—a majority in any full Assembly of Macedones—

---

[1] The report of the discussions, both in J. 13. 2. 5–12 and in C. 10. 6. 5–7. 5, is fictional.
[2] D.S. 18. 2. 2 fin. ἀξιοῦντες πειθαρχεῖν αὐτοῖς.

had not even been consulted, they met under arms of their own accord, hailed Arrhidaeus under the name of Philip as king, and selected an Infantry Guard to protect him.[1] However, their assembly was not a properly constituted Assembly of the Macedones. They had simply put up an alternative plan and made their intentions clear.

The leading Macedonians, having taken the oath of obedience to the four guardians, sent some of their own number to try to persuade the Macedonian infantrymen to accept their plan and take the oath of obedience (D.S. 18. 2. 2. fin.; J. 13. 3. 2). But on their arrival two of the envoys, Meleager and Attalus, abandoned their mission and approved what the infantrymen had done; they were then appointed as the leaders of the infantry. It was probably at this point that Meleager, treating the assembly of the infantrymen as if it were a properly constituted Assembly of the Macedones, presided over a formal election of Arrhidaeus as king. In the course of it he put on his cuirass as the supporter of the new king, and the infantrymen, clashing their pikes against their shields, promised to kill any pretender to his throne (C. 10. 7. 14). Then the infantrymen, led by Meleager and the king, forced their way into the royal quarters, where the corpse of Alexander was being guarded in the traditional manner by his Friends and Bodyguards and by the Royal Pages (J. 13. 3. 4; D.S. 18. 2. 3; C. 10. 7. 16). In order to avoid bloodshed Perdiccas, as the leading Bodyguard, and his supporters withdrew. As they left they declared Meleager and the other leaders guilty of treason in violating the traditional procedure for protecting the corpse of the king.[2] Meleager may have thought that possession of the corpse would help the infantry to enforce its wishes. But the only effect was to deepen the rift between the infantry and the cavalry, which now made separate armed camps, one in Babylon and the other in the open plain.

Fighting was averted by Perdiccas. He harangued the infantrymen with the greatest eloquence and gained their consent to a compromise, which was thereafter accepted separately by the cavalry. So at last a properly constituted Assembly of all Macedones under arms was convened. It deliberated in the presence of the corpse, so that 'His

---

[1] J. 13. 3. 1, the Guard consisting presumably of selected *pezhetairoi* (rather than *asthetairoi*), as in Theopompus (*FGrH* 115) F 348. See Griffith in Volume II. 705. Beloch 4. 1. 65 and others have maintained that 'the Macedonian infantry would have nothing to do with any son of an Asiatic mother'. This is an absurd view. The infantry accepted any son of the Asiatic Roxane in advance as king, gave her a guard in the remaining months of her pregnancy (App. *Syr.* 52 οἱ μὲν Μακεδόνες...ἐφύλαξαν γὰρ δὴ καὶ τὴν κυοῦσαν), was prepared to fight for his rights, and when he was born elected him king and gave him the name 'Alexander'. Beloch and others have swallowed the typically Roman race prejudice of Justin and Curtius, who included it in fictitious speeches of their own invention (J. 13. 2. 9 and C. 10. 6. 13).

[2] This is not stated in our sources, but seems to be the ground on which Meleager and some others were executed subsequently.

Majesty' could be witness to their decisions.[1] It then proceeded to elect Arrhidaeus king on condition that, if Roxane's child should be a boy, he also should be king (Arr. *Succ.* F 1, 1), and to vote particular powers to four men. Perdiccas was to be 'manager of the kingship' (D.S. 18. 2. 4 *epimeletes tes basileias*), viz. of Arrhidaeus. He was also to be the commander of the royal forces in Asia (including Egypt) and the king's senior officer in Asia (the title 'chiliarch' being employed). Meleager was to be associated with Perdiccas as his deputy. Craterus was to hold the *prostasia* ('protection') of the kingship of Arrhidaeus; this gave him control of the royal property and purse in Macedonia. Antipater was to be general in charge of Macedonia and Greece.[2]

This final decision of state saved the monarchy, whether Roxane should bear a son or not. By electing Philip Arrhidaeus, the Assembly ensured that the same family within the royal house would continue to hold its hereditary authority (C. 10. 7. 15). Moreover, the Assembly had upheld its democratic right and had no intention of relinquishing it. The clear-cut system of administration which it had created had its own checks and balances. Perdiccas had been elected commander of the Royal Army and chiliarch; but Meleager was a counterweight as commander of the infantry and deputy-chiliarch. Craterus and Antipater not only balanced one another in Europe; they counterbalanced Perdiccas and Meleager, of whom they were independent. The sovereign authority was to lie with the king and Assembly, as it had done in the past.

Now that the settlement had been made, the army was purified in preparation for the funeral of the dead king. In the course of this traditional ceremony the cavalry rode towards the infantry, both groups being fully armed, within an area marked by the two halves of a disembowelled dog. On this occasion the cavalry was led by the king and the elephants were with him. When the advancing cavalry and elephants were bearing down on the infantry which was in phalanx formation, the king issued the command that 'the mutineers' (i.e. those condemned as such by Perdiccas) should be handed over to him.

---

[1] J. 13. 4. 4 'posito in medio Alexandri corpore ut maiestas eius testis decretorum esset'. This passage has the ring of authenticity; it foreshadows A.'s presiding genius at D.S. 18. 60. 6–61. 2.

[2] For a full discussion of the *epimeleia* and the *prostasia* see H*SMO*. The former term was used, according to Smith 145, in the Babylonian Chronicle, 'umman sarri' being Akkadian for ἐπιμελητὴς τῶν βασιλέων. The arrangements are clearly stated in J. 13. 4. 5 (which is to be preferred to C. 10. 7. 8–9); in Arr. *Succ.* 1. 3, where ἡ ξύμπασα βασίλεια means 'the entire Kingdom of Asia', for which kingdom see H*A* 150 f. and 261 f. (so Bengtson, *Strat.* 1. 89); and in Dexippus (*FGrH* 100 F 8, 3–4). During the last weeks of his life A. may have appointed Perdiccas to the office of Chiliarch, if only to its staff duties (P*Eum* 1. 5; cf. Arr. *An.* 7. 14. 10). For different interpretations of these arrangements see W. W. Tarn in *CAH* 6. 461, Beloch 4. 2. 307 f., Errington 55 f., Bosworth in *CQ* 21. 130, and Wehrli 32. For 'pecunia' meaning property see H*SMO* 157 n. 11. Huge sums and estates were involved.

Perdiccas as chiliarch identified thirty men, arrested them, and had them executed. It is possible that they were thrown under the elephants, which then trampled them to death before the eyes of the horrified phalanx. Soon afterwards Meleager was executed as leader of the mutiny.[1] Thus Perdiccas, 'a man of blood', took his revenge. He acted henceforth without a deputy, but he held the infantrymen to obedience by fear, and not by affection. He relied only on the cavalry.

It was probably at the time when the settlement was being made that Perdiccas brought before the Assembly of the Macedones the plans of Alexander.[2] These were known through written orders issued by Alexander to Craterus in 324 (D.S. 18. 4. 1), through verbal orders issued by Alexander before and during the early days of his illness (Arr. *An.* 7. 12. 4 and 25. 2 f.) and through 'memoranda' (ὑπομνήματα) in the king's archive, which was kept by Eumenes and other secretaries and formed the kernel of the *King's Journal*. The need to reconsider orders arose during the negotiation of the settlement; for Craterus had been ordered originally to replace Antipater as general in Europe and, we may assume, to start on some of Alexander's plans.

The Assembly abandoned the impending campaign in Arabia and the circumnavigation of the Arabian peninsula, and it decided not to carry out the projects of the memoranda on the grounds that they were 'too grandiose and too difficult to accomplish'. Among these projects were the building of 1,000 warships larger than triremes, of naval facilities, and of a road along the North African coast; the construction of three great temples in Macedonia, three in Greece, and one enormous one at Troy; the raising of a tomb for Philip which would rival the greatest of the pyramids; and the creation of new urban centres and the transplantation of populations from Asia to Europe and vice versa in the interest of racial concord and intermarriage.[3] There are no good grounds for accepting the view of Tarn and others that 'the memoranda' as retailed by Perdiccas were forged by him; indeed all the projects are entirely of a scale appropriate to Alexander

---

[1] Arr. *Succ.* 1. 4 mentions the presence of the king, and Perdiccas terrifying the rest of the infantry (he refers to them as *to plethos*); the act which caused the terror may well have been the throwing of the mutineers under the feet of the elephants, as described in C. 10. 9. 18. The number of mutineers was given as thirty by D.S. 18. 4. 7, and as 300 by Curtius. Since the source of Arrian and Diodorus drew on Hieronymus, as we have argued above, they are to be preferred to Curtius. Justin, based ultimately on Hieronymus, seems to have substituted a Roman method of dealing with a mutiny and secret orders on the part of Perdiccas (13. 4. 8); his account should be regarded as not historical. Briant 252 preferred Curtius' 300 to Diodorus' thirty; he did not analyse their sources.

[2] D.S. 18. 4. 2–6, our main source for this, placed the meeting of the Assembly (τὸ κοινὸν τῶν Μακεδόνων πλῆθος) before the punishment of the mutineers.

[3] See also Paus. 1. 25. 5 and 8. 52. 5, Arr. *An.* 7. 19. 5, and Plb. 10. 27. 3.

and consonant with the purposes which Alexander had in mind.[1] The Assembly was wise to abandon them; for neither Philip Arrhidaeus nor Perdiccas was capable of leading the Macedonians on such enterprises. The expansion of Macedonia halted abruptly and, it was to prove, decisively.

It was after the killing of Meleager[2] that Philip Arrhidaeus issued the orders for the administration of the Kingdom of Asia which Perdiccas and his associates had prepared (Arr. *Succ.* 1a. 5 [Perdiccas] ὡς Ἀρριδαίου κελεύοντος ἔγνω; cf. App. *Syr.* 52).[3] The supporters of Perdiccas now reaped their reward. For example, Ptolemy was made satrap of Egypt, Libya, and the so-called Arabian borderlands, whereas Cleomenes was reduced to a subordinate position. Leonnatus was offered the satrapy of Hellespontine Phrygia; in accepting it, he became subordinate to Perdiccas rather than being his equal as a member of the royal family. Lysimachus was rewarded with the command of Thrace, the Chersonese, and the neighbours of the Thracian tribes from the north coast of the Black Sea to Salmydessus (Fig. 3). Antipater and Craterus, who had not been involved in the ructions at Babylon, were left to handle Macedonia, the Agrianes, the Triballi, the Illyrians, North Epirus, and 'all the Greeks' (that is, of the Common Peace).[4] See Fig. 8. There was one independent area on the mainland: the lands of the Molossi, the Thesproti, and the Atintanes, who had formed the 'Epirote Alliance' in 330 or so.[5] Here Olympias, the guardian of the child king Neoptolemus, wielded paramount authority as the effective head of the Molossian royal house. Soon after Alexander's death she arranged for the recall of the king exiled by Philip in 342, Arybbas, in order that he could be co-king with Neoptolemus and command the forces of the Epirote Alliance. She may have been anticipating trouble.

Attention was now paid to the dead king. The corpse was embalmed by Egyptian and Chaldaean priests, presumably in accordance with the known wishes of Alexander; for this marked a radical change from

[1] Reasons for regarding the plans as genuine are given in H*A* 300–4; *contra* Tarn 2. 378 ff. and F. Hampl in Griffith 308 ff.

[2] This is the time in Arr. *Succ.* 1. 5 and C. 10. 10. 1, but not in D.S. 18. 3 f.

[3] These arrangements appear, for instance, in the dating in an inscription at Lagina in Caria as 'the first year of Philip being king' and of 'the satrap being Asander'.

[4] Most fully defined in Arr. *Succ.* 1. 7 and Dexippus F 8, 3. See H*SPA* 471 ff. for the geography. The definitions in Arrian are from the viewpoint of Macedonia, so that ὡς ἐπὶ τὰ ὄρη τὰ Κεραύνια ἀνήκοντα means westwards from Macedonia to the Ceraunian range on the coast, i.e. what we call 'North Epirus'. That his authority ran for part only of Epirus is confirmed by the words of Dexippus, ὅσα τῆς Ἠπείρου. Bengtson, *Strat.* 1. 31 'das ganze epirotische Gebiet' is thus incorrect. Préaux 1. 128 misconstrues the Arrian passage as 'Arrien…ajoute: la Grèce à Cratère'.

[5] See H*E* 537 and 559 and my commentary in H*HSE* 14 ff. on the important inscription of the *theorodokoi* in *SEG* 23. 189. The supposition of Bengtson *Strat.* 30, that Epirus (or a part of it) was included in the Greek League rests on no evidence, as far as I am aware.

the form of burial accorded to his father. The embalmed body was crowned with a diadem and placed in a gold coffin, which was lined with scent-giving herbs (C. 10. 10. 13). As the corpse was to be taken to Aegeae, a funerary car had to be constructed, and this task was entrusted to an associate of Perdiccas, called Arrhidaeus. Alexander's corpse still lay in Babylon when Roxane gave birth to his son, probably in August 323. The baby was named 'Alexander' by 'the Assembly of the Macedones' (Dexippus 1b, 5 τὸ Μακεδόνων πλῆθος; cf. Arr. *Succ.* 1a. 8), and from that day Alexander IV was co-king with his uncle Arrhidaeus.

Thus the Macedonians and the Molossians found themselves to be each the subjects of two kings, one an adult and the other a minor. In accordance with Macedonian practice it is probable that Arrhidaeus, as the closest agnate on the male side, became the elected guardian of the baby. In any case Perdiccas kept the two kings with him, and it was Perdiccas who commanded the Royal Army and held the office of chiliarch.[1] He was assisted by Seleucus as commander of the Companion Cavalry (D.S. 18. 3. 4) and by Cassander, a son of Antipater, as commander of the Royal Bodyguard (J. 13. 4. 18), i.e. the Cavalry Guard. Thus the troubles which had arisen over the succession were brought to an end, and the struggle for power among the generals was resolved. The authority of Perdiccas in Asia was unquestioned; and wherever he went he had Philip Arrhidaeus follow 'like a mute in a play' (*PA* 77. 7).

The lack of an operative king was to prove an almost fatal disadvantage in a monarchical state with the commitments of Macedonia. There was no unquestioned centre of loyalty, no single authority set above all others, no impartial awarder of patronage. It is arguable that the Assembly of the Macedones should have elected Perdiccas as king with or without the addition of a baby king. As it was, Perdiccas ruled as an opportunist leader, created out of *stasis* and dependent upon the support of a clique. What he had done, others could attempt to do. He might well fall through *stasis*.

One weakness was his lack of standing in Europe. Absent from Macedonia for eleven years, he had no understanding with Antipater, and no connection with the Greeks of the Common Peace. He tried to remedy this at once by sending letters in the name of King Philip Arrhidaeus to the Greek states in which he reaffirmed 'the (Common) Peace and the constitutions established by Philip' (D.S. 18. 56. 2; cf. *GHI* 177, 14 which refers to 'the constitutions' then). He respected the

[1] Technically he was the king's 'manager' (ἐπιμελητής, D.S. 18. 2. 4; cf. 'regum cura' J. 13. 4. 5), and he held 'the stewardship of the whole kingdom' (ἐπιτροπὴ τῆς ξυμπάσης βασιλείας, Arr. *Succ.* 1. 3), that is, of all the Kingdom of Asia.

'autonomy' of Ephesus as a Greek city in Asia by sending a political prisoner there 'to be tried in accordance with the laws' (Polyaen. 6. 49). The Macedonians who took the letters to the Greek mainland states commended Antipater to them for his excellent qualities as the representative of the Macedonian state. But the mood of many in Greece was revealed by the remark of Hyperides: 'We are aware that he is an excellent master, but we have no need of any, however good' (P*Mor* 850 A).

3. *The Lamian War and a rising of Greek soldiers in Asia*

At the time of his death Alexander had four particular plans in view: the settling in Persis of a huge number of Greek mercenaries, the redistribution of some 20,000 Macedonians between Macedonia and Asia, the building of a battle fleet perhaps of 1,000 vessels in the southeastern Mediterranean (D.S. 18. 4. 4; J. 13. 5. 7), and the restoration of innumerable exiles to the Greek states. Some of the dangers involved in these plans became apparent before his death. Tens of thousands of Greek mercenaries fled to the coast, where an Athenian mercenary commander, Leosthenes, raised a fleet and shipped them over to the Greek mainland. Entering into secret negotiations with Athens, Leosthenes kept a large force of mercenaries in readiness for action at Taenarum in the Peloponnese. The 10,000 Macedonians under the command of Craterus reached Cilicia when the Greek mercenaries had already escaped to mainland Greece. See Figs. 7 and 10.

Alexander had known in 324 that Athens was making preparations for war rather than surrender Samos to the Samian exiles,[1] and he had proclaimed his intention to come in person and punish Aetolia for having expelled the inhabitants of Oeniadae (P*A* 49. 15). As he planned to conquer Arabia during the winter and spring of 323/2,[2] he expected to deal with any threat from Athens and Aetolia in the latter half of 322. With this end in view, Craterus and his 10,000 Macedonian veterans were to hold Cilicia and protect the east-Mediterranean harbours until early summer 322. By then most of the new battle fleet would be at sea. It would escort the convoys which were to carry Craterus and his 10,000 Macedonians to Macedonia and bring out to Cilicia Antipater and his Macedonian troops. Thereafter Macedonia

---

[1] See *FGrH* 126 (Ephippus) F 5. The inference from A.'s letter, whether spurious or not, that A. let Athens keep Samos, is a false one; for the letter indicates only that A. would not have acted as Philip had done in 338. For a discussion of this point, citing earlier views, see I. Worthington, '*IG* II². 370 and the date of the Athenian Alliance with Aetolia', *ZPE* 57 (1984) 142 ff.

[2] See H*A* 300 f. and n. 138. The 10,000 Macedonians of serviceable age in Macedonia were evidently to stay in Macedonia until such time as A. wanted them in Syria, which he expected to reach in 322.

would be protected by a strong holding force, and Alexander would cross to mainland Greece at the head of a huge fleet and an exceedingly powerful army, if it should prove necessary. The chances were high that Athens, Aetolia, and any other dissident states would be intimidated and accept restoration of the exiles.

The opponents of Alexander in Athens had suffered a set-back in spring 323; for Demosthenes and other leaders had been disgraced on a charge of corruption. Even so, the democracy showed its hostility to Alexander by giving asylum to two men of Ephesus who were wanted by the Macedonians (Polyaen. 6. 49), and it entered into secret negotiations with Leosthenes. When the news of Alexander's death reached Athens in midsummer 323, there was only a small Macedonian fleet in commission, and that fleet was threatened by the fleet of Rhodes which had just expelled a Macedonian garrison. The 10,000 Macedonians under Craterus were likely to be marooned in Cilicia. The main army was far away in Babylonia, and it was split by dissension about the succession to the throne. The situation seemed very favourable for Athens, if she wished to break away from the Common Peace and reject the hegemony of Macedonia. Phocion and other leaders of the propertied class advised caution, but Hyperides and other orators persuaded the Assembly to embark on a war of liberation, probably early in September 323.[1] They proposed to free any Greek state which was still occupied by a Macedonian garrison; one of them was Ephesus. The Assembly decreed that a fleet of forty quadriremes and 200 triremes[2] should be equipped for action and that 70 per cent of the citizen army up to the age of forty were to prepare themselves for service abroad. Arms from Athenian stocks and 50 of the 350 talents left at Athens by Harpalus were sent to Leosthenes, so that he could muster a large mercenary army. Envoys were sent far and wide. Many states and tribes of the mainland joined Athens: Argos, Sicyon, Epidaurus, Phlius, Troezen, Elis, and Messenia in the Peloponnese, and Phocis, Leucas, the tribes between Phocis and Thessaly, the Athamanes, and some of the Molossians.[3] Farther afield, some Illyrian tribes and some Thracian tribes promised to support the anti-Macedonian coalition. But the response of the islanders and the maritime states was disappointing. Only Rhodes and

---

[1] The date may be inferred from *IG* II[2] 1. 367, which concerns an embassy of the Athenians to the Phocians. See Beloch 4. 1. 69 n. 1, and the probable restorations and the commentary of A. N. Oikonomides in *Ancient World* 5 (1982) 123 ff. The Athenians called it 'the Hellenic War', but Hieronymus canonized it as 'the Lamian War'; see N. G. Ashton in *JHS* 104 (1984) 152–7.

[2] Emending D.S. 18. 10. 2 to accord with the evidence of the Navy Lists, on which see Additional Note, p. 122 below. That Athens ever manned so many ships is not attested.

[3] See *HE* 561. For the alliance between Aetolia and Athens see *IG* II[2]. 370, *SEG*. 21. 299, and the article of I. Worthington, cited in n. 1, p. 107 above.

Carystus sided with Athens. The others probably had more sympathy for the Samians who had been in exile since 365, and they had every reason to be afraid of Athenian imperialism. Even so, the allied fleet was probably twice as large as any Macedonian fleet in the Aegean basin[1] (D.S. 18. 9–11. 2).

Antipater did not seize the initiative as Alexander had done in 336, when he entered Thessaly and marched south. Instead, he offered one of his daughters in marriage to Leonnatus and asked Leonnatus and Craterus to bring their armies urgently to Macedonia. Meanwhile Leosthenes and 8,000 experienced mercenaries sailed from Taenarum and landed in Aetolia, which joined the coalition and put its army of 7,000 men under his command. The only states of eastern-central Greece which stayed loyal to the Common Peace were the Boeotian League, which feared that the insurgents would restore Thebes, and the Euboean League, which had suffered from Athenian imperialism in the past. Leosthenes marched his army into Boeotia, where he joined hands with an Athenian army of 500 citizen cavalry, 5,000 citizen infantry, and 2,000 mercenaries, and inflicted a defeat on the forces of Boeotia and Euboea.[2] As he moved north to adopt a defensive position at Thermopylae (see Fig. 6), his army was increased to some 30,000 men by the contingents of neighbouring peoples. These successes were impressive, but they had been won at the expense of other Greeks and not of Macedonians.

Antipater found himself short of 'citizen soldiers' (D.S. 18. 12. 2), that is of Macedones proper, the first-line soldiers. In 334 he had been left with 13,500 Macedones, but Alexander had required reinforcements for the campaign in Asia and his demands had halted or impaired recruitment for the home army. Now Antipater gave to his own deputy 'sufficient soldiers' and permission to recruit as many men as possible, in order to hold the frontiers against the Illyrians and the Thracians. He himself set off south with only 600 cavalry (for he counted on the accession of some 2,000 Thessalian cavalry, ever faithful to Macedonia since early in Philip's reign) and a phalanx of 13,000 infantry. A Macedonian fleet of 110 triremes (D.S. 18. 12. 2), which happened to be in home waters, accompanied him and provided supplies in Thessaly. There he picked up 'a great force' of Thessalian cavalry. Marching on towards Thermopylae, he engaged the confederate army in set battle. At the very outset the Thessalian cavalry deserted to the Athenians. Antipater's Macedonian cavalry must have been destroyed. But the

---

[1] The estimate of some 350 ships which is given by Cary 382 may be near the mark for the entire Greek fleet at its strongest moment.

[2] Hyp. 4. 5. 15 ff. mentions Macedonians also; they evidently included the garrison of the Cadmea.

phalanx was undefeated. Antipater led it back, to Lamia, strengthened the fortifications, and brought supplies and artillery from his fleet into the city.[1] The decision to hold Lamia was brilliant; for it deterred Leosthenes from invading a weakly held Macedonia and joining hands perhaps with the Illyrians and the Thracians (Fig. 6).

The confederates tried to take Lamia by assault, but in vain. They adopted the usual Greek method: circumvallation with a wall and a ditch. This was nearing completion late in 323, when the Macedonians made a sortie and one of the Greek casualties was Leosthenes. Antipater offered to negotiate. The Greeks demanded unconditional surrender, which he rejected. There was optimism and rejoicing in Athens, and Demosthenes came back from exile. During the autumn the coalition of Greek states had developed its system of organization. A Council of delegates, elected by each state, conducted the policy and the finances of 'the Greeks'; gave the hegemony by land and sea to Athens; and called her generals—Leosthenes, succeeded by Antiphilus, and those in command of the fleets—'the generals of the Greeks'.[2] Each state's contingent had its own national commander. The Council denounced the Greek League which Philip and Alexander had promoted as an abuse of Greek liberty; planned to drive out any Macedonians; and allied itself with some Illyrians and Thracians. The Council took the Greek League of 480 as its model, and its spokesmen saw the Macedonians as the successors of the Persians.

The war at sea (of which we have little information) was of vital importance. Control of the Bosporus and the Hellespont was crucial both for the food supply of Athens and for the inter-continental communications of the Macedonians; and the Rhodian fleet, if reinforced, could prevent the army of Craterus in Cilicia from venturing to cross the Aegean Sea. It is probable that the fleets of Athens and her allies operated both in the Hellespont and near Rhodes during the autumn of 323. Thus the Macedonian fleet was able to nurture Antipater at Lamia and also to land mixed forces of Macedonians and mercenaries for raids on the Attic coast.[3] At some unknown date a part of the Greek fleet returned and imposed a full blockade on Lamia by sea. Meanwhile the Macedonian fleet was in home waters, covering the construction of many new warships at Pella and Amphipolis, for which much money was available (D.S. 18. 12. 2).

Antipater could not escape from Lamia, unless help were to come

---

[1] Polyaen. 4. 4. 2; D.S. 18. 12. 3–4. Lamia was then about a mile from the sea.

[2] Paus. 1. 25. 5. A *synhedros* from Carystus was honoured in 306 for his part in the war 'on behalf of the liberty of the Greeks' (*IG* ii². 1. 249; for the phrase cf. D.S. 18. 10. 2), and what appears to be a list of member states included Cephallenia in the west and a state in Thrace (ἀπὸ Θράκης), of which the name is lost (*CIA* ii no. 184). For the term 'the Greeks' see D.S. 18. 15. 7–8.

[3] *PPh* 25. 1.

from Lysimachus or Leonnatus. Of the two Lysimachus had his own problems. For on entering his province, Thrace, he had under his command merely 2,000 cavalry and 4,000 infantry. He found himself opposed by an insurgent army of 8,000 cavalry and 20,000 infantry under the leadership of Seuthes, the king of the Odrysians. With characteristic audacity Lysimachus fought a pitched battle. He was, rightly, confident in the fine quality of his men, and he inflicted severe casualties on the Thracians. But he could achieve little with such small numbers, and it was only after the end of the Greek war that he made a final settlement with Seuthes. He was left on the throne, but accepted Macedonian suzerainty (D.S. 18. 14. 2–4). Leonnatus, being under the orders of Perdiccas, had been told to help Eumenes acquire the satrapy of Cappadocia. He was about to do so when the pro-Macedonian tyrant of Cardia crossed the Hellespont and delivered the request of Antipater for immediate help. Leonnatus did not hesitate. Macedonia was in every way more important than Cappadocia, and Leonnatus may have had personal ambitions. As a member of the royal house, he might be able to take control of Macedonia, and it was for this reason that Cleopatra, the sister of Alexander, who still held the *prostasia* of the kingship at Pella, offered herself in marriage to Leonnatus. She had done this secretly by letter; for she was competing with Antipater in the marital field and perhaps in terms of the ultimate control of Macedonia.[1]

Whatever his personal motives were, Leonnatus took his army across the straits, recruited more men in Macedonia, and entered Thessaly with 1,500 cavalry and more than 20,000 infantry. By this time (probably early spring 322) the Greek army besieging Lamia had dwindled to 22,000 infantry, because the Aetolians and some other units had gone home; but it still had 3,500 cavalry, and these included the famous Thessalian cavalry, 2,000 strong. Leonnatus, it seems, had not made any preconcerted plan with Antipater. Consequently when the Greek commander, Antiphilus, heard of the approach of Leonnatus, he slipped away from the lines of circumvallation and caught the Macedonians in the open plain of Thessaly. His superior cavalry won a cavalry engagement, in which Leonnatus fell, fighting gallantly. The Macedonian phalangites withdrew in formation to higher ground and beat off all cavalry attacks, while the Greek infantry stayed at a respectful distance. Antiphilus failed to intercept the army of Antipater, when it abandoned Lamia and joined the Macedonians of Leonnatus. By following a hilly route Antipater avoided the Thessalian cavalry and withdrew into Macedonia.[2] Antiphilus did not try to

---

[1] D.S. 18. 14. 5; P*Eum* 3. 8–9, although the version of Hieronymus, a friend of Eumenes, may not be altogether true.

[2] D.S. 18. 15. 1–7; Arr. *Succ.* 1. 9; J. 13. 5. 14–16.

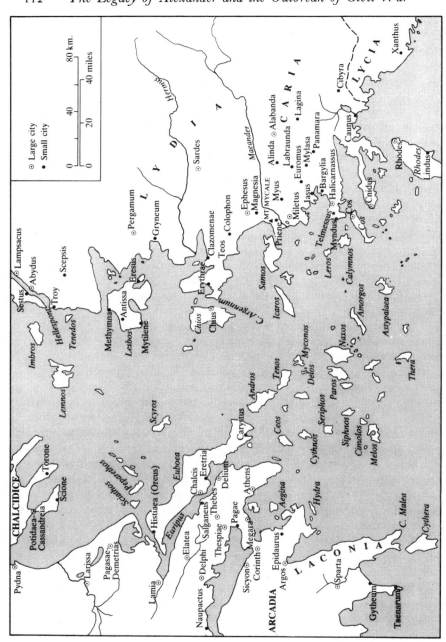

FIG. 7. THE AEGEAN BASIN

invade. He was deterred perhaps by the natural strength of the southern frontier of Macedonia, and he may later have been ordered by the Council of the Greeks to wait in Thessaly. In any case his inaction gave Antipater the respite which he needed.

While the Greek army waited, fateful events occurred at sea (see Fig. 7). At the start of the sailing season the Greek fleets lay at several scattered stations: one at the Hellespont, another in the south-eastern Aegean to prevent any reinforcements sailing from Cilicia to Macedonia, and a third, consisting only of Athenian ships, in home waters to safeguard Attica. The Macedonian admiral, Cleitus, concentrated all available ships, from whatever source, in the Thermaic Gulf and then defeated the enemy fleets piecemeal: first in late spring the Greek fleet off Abydus; then in May or June the Greek fleet in the south-east off Amorgos; and finally in the summer, with 240 ships, the Athenian fleet, which consisted of some ships surviving from the earlier battles and others stationed to protect Attica, the whole amounting to 170 ships, in two battles probably in the Maliac Gulf. Superior strategy and fighting power thus re-established Macedonian thalassocracy and broke the Athenian navy, the very backbone of Greek sea power.[1]

After the battle of Amorgos the seas were safe for Craterus to bring 6,000 of his 10,000 Macedonian veterans from Cilicia to Macedonia. He landed perhaps at Amphipolis. For on his way to join Antipater he raised 4,000 infantry and 1,500 cavalry to supplement his Macedonians and 1,000 Persian Archers and Slingers. When they met on the lower Peneus near the Macedonian frontier, Antipater took command of the joint forces, being 'more than 40,000 heavy-armed infantry, 3,000 Archers and Slingers and 5,000 cavalry' (D.S. 18. 16. 5). On the other hand, the Greek army had declined during its period of inactivity, as city-state units and individuals absented themselves, so that only 25,000 infantry and 3,500 cavalry remained. Their only hope was the superb Thessalian cavalry. Antipater forced a battle at Crannon in central Thessaly on 5 Metageitnion (*PCam* 19. 8), i.e. in late August 322. He managed to avoid the opening cavalry engagement taking place between the two infantry lines (as had happened with Leonnatus), and it was the charge of the Macedonian phalanx which decided the issue. For the Greek infantry was driven back, with the loss of 200 Athenians and 300 others, onto higher ground, and the Greek cavalry, which had been gaining the upper hand, disengaged

---

[1] *IG* ii². 298 and 493 (Abydus); *FGrH* 239 (Marmor Parium) B 9 and P*D* 11. 4 (Amorgos); D.S. 18. 15. 8–9 (Athens home fleet), where the reading Ἐχινάδας may have referred to islands—now lost to the coast—off the Malian town Echinus. The name 'Sea-urchin islands' may well have been given to more than one set of such islands, and not only to those off Oeniadae, as in Droysen 2. 65. See Additional Note for the Navy Lists, p. 122 below. The course of the naval war is very uncertain.

and joined the infantry. Outmanœuvred and outnumbered, the Greek commanders sought terms for the Greeks collectively, but Antipater insisted on dealing separately with individual states. When Antiphilus and Menon, the Thessalian cavalry commander, refused to treat on these terms, Antipater did not attack the Greek army; for he had lost 130 Macedonians and was anxious to conserve his best troops. Instead, he captured city after city by storm or negotiation and made a treaty with each one, thus disbanding in effect the Thessalian League. Meanwhile the Greek army dispersed. By the time that Antipater entered Thebes, all the insurgent states had concluded separate treaties with him except Athens and the Aetolian League. Even they did not combine their forces.

Meanwhile at Athens the party leaders changed. Hyperides and Demosthenes fled, and Demades and Phocion were sent by the people to ask for terms. Antipater demanded and obtained an unconditional surrender; for Athens, cut off by sea and by land, had no hope of withstanding a blockade, and the spirit which had enabled Athens to resist for four months in 405/4 was lacking now. What was Macedon to do with the ringleader of the insurgents, the state which had broken its oaths of membership of the Common Peace and of alliance with Macedon? The decision lay entirely with Antipater, advised no doubt by Craterus.[1] He had grown to manhood at a time when Athens, as the leading Aegean state, threatened the very existence of his country, and he had seen her act as the leading opponent in 349–347 and 341–338 and then as the chief instigator of Thebes in 336 and 335. Now at the age of seventy-five Antipater may have decided that the lenient policy of Philip and Alexander had not won, and never would win, the loyalty of the democracy, and that a new policy was needed. In theory he could have emulated Alexander, referred the matter to the Council of the Common Peace, and obtained a vote to destroy the city, as Alexander had done with Thebes. But he chose instead to reduce Athens to the status of a controlled and weakened subject state. Democracy was to be replaced by 'the ancestral property-based polity'. The new government was to pay a financial indemnity in excess of the cost of the war, the anti-Macedonian leaders were to be delivered to Antipater, and a Macedonian garrison was to be stationed at Munychia overlooking the Piraeus.[2] These conditions, *mutatis mutandis*, had been imposed by Athens on breakaway allies in the periods of her hegemony.

On a day in late September 322, when the Eleusinian Mysteries were starting (P*Cam* 19. 8), a Macedonian detachment marched through the city and occupied the Munychia. The Athenians had

---

[1] Craterus may have wanted to invade Attica and blockade the city (P*Ph* 26. 5–7).
[2] P*Ph* 27. 5.

already condemned Demosthenes, Hyperides, and others to death on the proposal of Demades. The agents of Antipater found them taking sanctuary in temples; Demosthenes committed suicide on Calauria, and the others were dragged off to Antipater who had them executed in October. In Athens 'the ancestral property-based polity' was set up (*PPh* 27. 3): the right to vote in elections and on policy was limited to citizens possessing property worth 2,000 drachmae, these being some 9,000 in number,[1] and the remainder were struck off the register of electors (D.S. 18. 18. 4; *PPh* 28. 4). In addition to paying the huge indemnity the state had to provide for the Athenian refugees from Samos; for the island was awarded by Perdiccas, acting on behalf of Philip Arrhidaeus, to the exiled Samians. Conditions in Attica became so appalling that thousands of Athenians emigrated to Thrace, where Antipater provided territory and a city, no doubt at the expense of rebels there.[2] Similar puppet governments were imposed on the other defeated city-states (D.S. 18. 69. 3), and Deinarchus was appointed 'manager of the Peloponnese'; anti-Macedonian leaders were executed and their supporters were banished beyond 'the Ceraunian mountains and Cape Taenarum' (*PPh* 29. 4). Thus the word of Antipater became law for most of the Greek mainland.[3] His obvious forerunner was the Spartan Lysander in 404.

The Aetolian League fought for its existence through the winter of 322/1. Its army of some 10,000 men took to the high mountains; but severe weather, lack of supplies, and great inferiority in numbers brought them to the verge of surrender. They were saved by a split in the Macedonian high command. Antipater and Craterus had recently been joined by Antigonus, who had said that Perdiccas intended to cross into Europe with the royal forces and depose them from their commands. Believing this to be true, Antipater and Craterus decided to forestall Perdiccas by crossing into Asia, and this they did, but only by making a hasty peace with the Aetolian League. Thus the 'Greek War', which we call the Lamian War, came to an end which was less disastrous for the Greeks than it might have been.

---

[1] A similar number qualified in 411 (see H*HG* 408 n. 1).

[2] The number of citizens below the property limit of 2,000 drachmae is uncertain. In the last stage of the naval war Athens manned 170 ships with crews totalling some 30,000 men, and we must therefore assume a population of at least 20,000 *thetes*. The figures in D.S. 18. 10. 2 and 11. 3 suggest a zeugite population of 14,000 or so. Thus the total population of citizens may have been around 34,000. The figures in D.S. 18. 18. 5, namely 9,000 above the property limit and 22,000 'displaced from their fatherland', come close to that total; but we should have to assume that Diodorus has misapplied the figure 22,000. *PPh* 28. 7, saying that 'those voted out of the constitution' were 12,000, is not acceptable as it stands. For the uncertainty see Gomme 18. We do not know how many went to Thrace.

[3] Suidas s.v. *Deinarchos*; Plb. 9. 29. 2–4; and D.S. 18. 18. 8 for honours showered on Antipater by his Greek agents.

There were lessons to be learnt on the Greek side. Some Greeks saw in the war an expression of national resistance to a foreign power, as in 480; but others saw the war as a means of Athens and Aetolia keeping imperial gains and perhaps adding to them. This ambivalence weakened the coalition itself and restricted its growth; for while many remained neutral, Sparta as a state and many individuals elsewhere sided actively with the exiled Samians.[1] Even so, the coalition fielded 40,000 heavy infantry, excellent cavalry, and at least 350 ships (manned by some 70,000 men), a sufficient force to hold Macedonia proper in check. But it was no longer a question of Macedonia alone: the coalition had to face the multiracial forces organized and trained by Alexander. Of those forces 50,000 soldiers and some 50,000 men manning a fleet superior in skill decided the issue.[2] The Macedonian phalanx was once again invincible, and the Athenian navy was driven off the seas.

The effects of the war were entirely bad. The concept of the Common Peace was rejected by the Greeks and discarded by Antipater. The Greek states now had no form of unity and no barrier against renewed strife between state and state and faction strife within each state. The semblance of liberty *vis-à-vis* Macedonia and the hope of collaboration with Macedonia were at an end. Antipater had deliberately reversed the policy of Alexander, replacing co-operation with repression, conciliation with dictation, and arbitration with intervention. He had foolishly created a system which could only be maintained by political intrigue and Macedonian manpower.[3]

Meanwhile in Asia the first challenge to the authority of Macedonia came from Greek soldiers whom Alexander had settled in the cities he had founded in the 'upper satrapies' of the Iranian highlands and the adjacent areas. Mostly ex-mercenaries who had served with Alexander for years, they organized themselves into a formidable force of 3,000 cavalry and 20,000 infantry and decided to return to Europe, by fighting if necessary (others had escaped without opposition; see p. 84 above).[4] Perdiccas took up the challenge. Acting on behalf of the

---

[1] The entire Lacedaemonian community abstained from food for one day and gave the equivalent of that food in money to the exiled Samians ([Arist.] *Econ.* 2. 2. 9). See C. Habicht in *Chiron* 5 (1975) 45 ff.

[2] It is clear from these numbers that non-Macedonians were employed in very great numbers, probably Thracians for the army, and north-Aegean Greeks, Cilicians, and Phoenicians for the navy.

[3] The judgement of Hieronymus, as reflected in D.S. 18. 18. 6, is very favourable to Antipater; for his settlement is represented as in the best interests of Athens. For Macedonian garrisons see Paus. 7. 10. 4, and for Philip's policy see Volume II. 612.

[4] Beloch 4. 1. 67, who rejects the intention of the mercenaries to go home, says that they had a 'strong Asian contingent' with them. He cites no evidence. It may stem from his equally baseless idea that the Persian aristocracy wanted to rebel.

king, he drew 800 Macedonian cavalrymen and 3,000 Macedonian infantrymen from the King's Army by lot, ordered them to kill any Greeks they mastered and to take their goods as booty. The Assembly chose Pithon to command the force.[1] It was to be supplemented with 8,000 cavalry—the arm in which the Greeks were weak—and 10,000 infantry, who were to be sent on the orders of Perdiccas by the satraps of the intervening areas. These were mainly Asians, trained on Alexander's instructions, and a large part of them came presumably from Pithon's own satrapy, Media. When the two armies met, a detachment of the Greeks withdrew from the action, and those who fought on were outfought and accepted terms. In particular their safety was guaranteed under oath. But when they had laid down their arms, the Macedonians, mindful of Perdiccas' orders and eager for booty, killed the defenceless Greeks and made off with their goods (D.S. 18. 4. 8 and 7. 1–9). The incident illustrates the bitter feeling between Greek and Macedonian, the callousness of Perdiccas, and the bad faith of the Macedonian troops. At the same time it is remarkable that it was the Macedonians who were able to use the Asian troops, and that the Greek troops were not able to enlist Asians in support of a rebellion.

4. *The outbreak of civil war in 321 B.C.*

The unifying factor for all Macedonians, wherever they were, was always love of the royal family. To maintain loyalty to the two kings of 322 was the responsibility of Antipater and Craterus in Macedonia and of Perdiccas as chiliarch in Asia. Another force for unity among Macedonians, when they faced Greeks and Asians, was the *esprit de corps* of the Macedonian troops. The city foundations of Alexander provided widespread and significant support for Macedonian rule, in that they supplied trained troops, financial strength, and commercial centres throughout Asia, and it was they above all who led the way in the adoption of Greek speech and of Graeco-Macedonian institutions. Another factor which encouraged unity was the royal currency and the *koine* of free trade which embraced south-east Europe, the Black Sea coasts, Asia as far as the Indus valley, Egypt, and Cyrene. The divisive elements among the Macedonians were the personal ambitions of the generals, the jealousy between individual units of the Macedonian army, and the inherent weakness by position of the home country, which was no longer at the centre, but rather at the edge, of the huge area under Macedonian rule.

---

[1] D.S. 18. 7. 3 ἑλομένου. The emendation to ἑλόμενος, followed in the Loeb text, is unacceptable; for τοῦ πλήθους is no way to refer to a special group of troops.

The size of the King's Army at Babylon is uncertain. It may have comprised 10,000 cavalry, which was Macedonian, Thracian, Greek, and predominantly Asian, 15,000 front-line infantry of Macedonian, Thracian, and Greek origins, 50,000 Asian infantry and the Indian elephants trained for war.[1] The satraps also had armies under their immediate control; for Alexander's separation of civil and military powers broke down after his death.

Perdiccas chose as his first undertaking a campaign against Ariarathes, the usurper of Cappadocia, who had 15,000 excellent native cavalry, 30,000 infantry, which included a force of Greek mercenaries, and large reserves of money (D.S. 18. 16. 1). In the course of it he intended to test the loyalty of his satraps in Asia Minor; he ordered Leonnatus, satrap of Lesser Phrygia, and Antigonus, satrap of Greater Phrygia, Lycia, and Pamphylia, and no doubt other satraps, to join him in ousting Ariarathes and in making Eumenes satrap of Cappadocia. On the other hand, he did not call on Craterus, who was in Cilicia with the 10,000 Macedonian veterans; for Craterus was not subordinate to Perdiccas. Early in 322 Leonnatus was setting out to join Perdiccas, when he was diverted by the appeal of Antipater for help against the insurgent Greeks and crossed into Europe. Before doing so, he revealed to Eumenes as a secret his intention to marry Cleopatra and seize Macedonia. When Leonnatus fell in action, the secret was divulged by Eumenes to Perdiccas. Antigonus, finding himself no longer between the armies of Leonnatus and Perdiccas, paid no heed to his orders. In the course of the summer Perdiccas, accompanied by King Philip and commanding the King's Army and some satraps' forces, won two set battles, killed or captured 9,000 men, and tortured to death Ariarathes and his family (P*Eum* 3; D.S. 18. 16. 2–3). By this time Craterus was on his way with his army to help Antipater in north Greece. As Perdiccas was on good terms with Antipater, he may well have been satisfied with the distribution of Macedonian forces.

After some punitive operations in Pisidia, Perdiccas moved to Cilicia. While he was on the way, a daughter of Antipater, Nicaea, came to marry him; for Perdiccas had asked Antipater to confirm their friendship by this marriage. At about the same time Antipater gave another daughter, Phila, in marriage to Craterus, on whom he heaped many presents. As two of Antipater's sons were serving with Perdiccas, it must have seemed likely in autumn 322 that this triumvirate would hold together and would preserve the unity of the Macedonian world

---

[1] See H*A* 218 and 240 for the numbers at A.'s disposal, on which this estimate is based. They include among the Macedonian infantry the 3,000 'descendants of the Hypaspists' (οἱ ἐκ τῶν ὑπασπιστῶν) for whom see *CQ* 28 (1978) 133 and 135.

in loyalty to the kings.[1] Indeed it was a sign of unity during the winter that Antipater referred the matter of Samos to the kings, and that Perdiccas decided it in a manner which Antipater evidently wished.

The first incidents which upset the situation were initiated by women of the royal house.[2] Olympias was a bitter enemy of Antipater, and during the Lamian War she had impelled the Molossian king Arybbas (her protégé: see p. 108 and H*E* 561) to take the side of the Greek insurgents. Although Arybbas went over to the Macedonians during the war, it seemed likely that Olympias would be punished for her action as soon as Antipater and Craterus were able to overcome the Aetolian League. What Olympias needed now was influence at the real seat of power, the court of Perdiccas. Her daughter Cleopatra, the sister of Alexander, had already tried to inveigle Leonnatus into opposing Antipater, and she had just been ousted by Craterus from her position in Macedonia as 'guardian of the kingship'. Olympias now proposed to bestow the hand of Cleopatra in marriage on Perdiccas. So during the winter of 322/1 Cleopatra established herself at Sardes in Lydia and entered into secret communication with Perdiccas. He had to choose between Nicaea, the daughter of Antipater, and Cleopatra, a most prestigious member of the royal house. Meanwhile another of Philip's daughters, Cynane whose mother was an Illyrian princess, had entered the field. She had a daughter Adea, renamed Eurydice, whom she had born to Amyntas, son of Perdiccas III, *c.* 336. In the winter of 322/1 Eurydice was rising fifteen years of age; but she was a precocious girl, already trained in armed combat by her mother and as brave as a lioness. Cynane intended to marry Eurydice to King Philip, and the two women set off from Pella with a small armed force. They were held up at the river Strymon on the orders of Antipater,[3] but they fought their way through, crossed the Hellespont, and were then intercepted by Alcetas, the brother of Perdiccas, who had no wish to see his control of Philip weakened by such a marriage. As Cynane persisted, Alcetas killed her in accordance with the orders of Perdiccas. But the Macedonian soldiers were outraged. They insisted on Eurydice marrying the king, and Perdiccas was compelled to agree, in order to avert a mutiny (Arr. *Succ.* 1. 22; Polyaen. 8. 60).

---

[1] The Greek term for such a coalition was κοινοπραγία. Ptolemy's marriage to another daughter of Antipater, Eurydice, may have taken place at this time; see Beloch 4. 2. 178 f.

[2] A sinister example had been set by Roxane, who with the connivance of Perdiccas killed A.'s Persian wives, Stateira and Parysatis (P*A* 77. 6). Perhaps they were also pregnant, and any male child they bore might have become a rival heir.

[3] Droysen 2. 93. n. 2 inferred that Antipater went in person to the Strymon and therefore that Cynane's departure happened before the campaign in Aetolia. But the wording of Polyaenus (8. 60) shows that while Antipater sought to prevent her he was not himself among 'those who were trying to stop' her at the crossing of the Strymon.

The disciplining of Antigonus for disobeying the king's orders was another source of division. During the winter Antigonus was summoned to stand trial on a charge of treason before the Assembly of the Macedonians of the King's Army. After a period of procrastination he and his son Demetrius eventually fled on some Athenian ships which were probably evacuating Athenian refugees from Samos.[1] On joining Antipater and Craterus, who were still campaigning against the Aetolians, he alleged that Perdiccas intended to marry Cleopatra, invade Macedonia, and get rid of Antipater and Craterus;[2] and as an indication of Perdiccas' purposes he cited the execution of Cynane. Whatever the intentions of Perdiccas really were, Antipater and Craterus believed Antigonus. They made peace with the Aetolians and prepared to forestall Perdiccas by invading Asia themselves. Another disruptive figure was Ptolemy, satrap of Egypt, who had strengthened his own position by seizing the treasure amassed by Alexander's unscrupulous financial officer, Cleomenes, and by annexing Cyrenaica to his satrapy late in 322. Ptolemy was on excellent terms with Antipater, whose daughter Eurydice he had married; and it was natural for Antipater and Craterus to seek and obtain a promise of assistance from Ptolemy in their intended campaign against Perdiccas. Meanwhile Ptolemy managed to gain possession of the corpse of Alexander, which, it was commonly believed, had magical powers and would bring success to the country in which it lay, like the corpse of Oedipus.[3] With the connivance of Arrhidaeus, the officer in charge of the arrangements, the funerary car carrying the corpse was diverted at Damascus and taken, not to Aegeae in Macedonia, but to Memphis in Egypt. This was interpreted as an act of rebellion against King Philip and Perdiccas (Arr. *Succ.* 1. 25).

In this sea of troubles Perdiccas acted, apparently without negotiat-

[1] The chronology given above is based on the following points. Occupation of the Munychia during the Eleusinian Mysteries was in late September 322; the fate of Samos was referred to Perdiccas at that time; and the campaign against the Aetolians fell in winter 322/1. This war was still undecided in late winter, say in March 321 (D.S. 18. 25. 1–2). Antigonus reached Antipater at that time. Terms were then made with the Aetolians, *c.* April 321. During the winter Perdiccas had decided the future of Samos (D.S. 18. 18. 9); and Athenian cleruchs were evacuated by Athenian ships early in the spring of 321. Antigonus escaped on one of them (D.S. 18. 23. 4). Cynane's journey was made in the winter; for her journey and her death preceded the flight of Antigonus, who reported it to Antipater (Arr. *Succ.* 1. 22–4). For different chronologies see Errington 61 ff. and in *Chiron* 5 (1975) 51 ff., and H. Hauben in *Anc. Soc.* 8 (1977) 85 ff. The departure of the Athenian cleruchs from Samos has been dated 'zu Beginn des Jahres 321' by C. Habicht in *Chiron* 5 (1975) 47. He dates the decree in honour of Antileon to this year (his p. 49).

[2] It is simplistic to accept Antigonus' picture of these motives; for Antigonus had personal aims of his own. All our sources, as they derive from Hieronymus, are hostile to Perdiccas. If Antigonus had presented himself for trial, as Ptolemy did later, it is arguable that the split between Antipater and Perdiccas would not have occurred.

[3] Aelian, *VH* 12. 64.

ing. He sent Eumenes with gifts to Cleopatra, and stated that he had decided to send Nicaea away and marry Cleopatra.[1] News of this was passed by the satrap of Lydia, Menander, to Antigonus and so to Antipater and Craterus, who interpreted it as a sign of outright hostility. For them the great danger was that, if the two kings, the two royal women, and Perdiccas were to bring the King's Army into Europe, the Macedonian people in Europe would stay loyal to the royal house and discard Antipater, Craterus, and Antigonus. Rather than face that danger they and the officers whom they called together for consultation decided to invade Asia with all speed (D.S. 18. 25. 4). Meanwhile Perdiccas consulted his Friends and his officers on the strategy to be pursued. They decided to deal first with Ptolemy and then to invade Europe and take over Macedonia (D.S. 18. 25. 6, resumed at 29. 1).[2] In May or June 321 the King's Army began its march from Pisidia to Egypt. Eumenes was sent with a separate force and with an overriding authority to hold Asia Minor. It was there that the first blood was shed in the civil war. For Eumenes, staunchly loyal to Perdiccas, led his army against that of Neoptolemus, satrap of Armenia, who had defected from Perdiccas to Antipater and Craterus. That was in June or early July.[3] Meanwhile Perdiccas was on his way from Damascus towards Egypt.[4] No doubt in the name of the kings, he had ordered Ptolemy to present himself at the frontier of his satrapy; and it was probably there that Ptolemy, being tried before the Assembly of the Macedonians of the King's Army,[5] was acquitted of 'the charges'. Moreover, the verdict was an indication that the majority did not want to fight a civil war against Ptolemy and that they would prefer a negotiated settlement. That too was probably the

---

[1] The statement of F. Chamoux in *AM* 3. 64, that Cleopatra married Leonnatus and Perdiccas, is incorrect.

[2] Not a doublet, as Briant 195 ff. proposed for his theory of not one, but two consultations being made by Perdiccas; he is followed by H. Hauben in *Anc. Soc.* 8 (1977) 96.

[3] When Eumenes' troops were about to engage the army of Craterus, they crowned themselves with ears of corn, presumably ripe, that is, around July (*PEum* 6. 11). Then the battle against Neoptolemus, being ten days earlier (*PEum* 8. 1), was in late June or early July.

[4] Arr. *Succ.* 1. 28 παραγίγνεται ἀπὸ Δαμάσκου Περδίκκας ἐπ' Αἴγυπτον seems to me to mean this and not what Briant 264 supposes, that Perdiccas had already arrived in Egypt.

[5] Arr. *Succ.* 1. 28 ἐπὶ τοῦ πλήθους (cf. 8 fin. τὸ πλῆθος), not before a Council (which Briant 154 f. supposes to have been the norm after the reign of A.). Some scholars have rejected Arrian as reported by Photius on the grounds that Ptolemy would have been in great personal danger in presenting himself for trial; but Ptolemy was fully aware of his own popularity with the Macedonians and of the phalanx's dislike of Perdiccas. Briant 265 has suggested that Ptolemy was tried not now, as Arrian has it, but after the death of Perdiccas on charges made before his death, and he cites D.S. 18. 36. 6, as if it supported his interpretation. However, Arrian is a more dependable user of Hieronymus than Diodorus is. It should be noted too that Arrian went on to say that Perdiccas attacked 'despite the unwillingness of the Assembly' (τοῦ πλήθους), and that in D.S. 18. 36. 6 Ptolemy's defence of his resistance in Egypt is entirely apposite for the day after the death of Perdiccas, when Ptolemy wanted a reconciliation.

desire of Ptolemy; for there was little point in his appearing for trial, if he intended to fight in any case. With characteristic obstinacy and rancour Perdiccas proceeded to invade Egypt. The first blood was shed in an engagement by the Nile, which was provoked by Perdiccas in July.[1] The two kings and Eurydice were in the camp of Perdiccas, but the war was not in fact between those loyal to the monarchy and any dissenters, but between Perdiccas and the generals who opposed him.

Navy Lists of 325/4 and 323/2. In an article in *BSA* 72 (1977) 1 ff. N. G. Ashton is correct in applying the figures in the lists to the end of the archon year. The stocks then were as follows: 360 triremes and 50 quadriremes in June/July 324, and 315 triremes and (on an almost certain restoration) 50 quadriremes in June/July 322. The list for 324/3 is missing; but since Athens in 324 foresaw a probable war over Samos looming in 322, she probably increased her stock with new ships before June/July 323. The drop in June/July 322 we may attribute to losses of 50 or so triremes in the actions of the Greek fleets off Abydus and off Amorgos. The number of Athenian ships at sea in June/July 322 according to the Navy List was 49 quadriremes (on the same restoration) and probably 94 triremes (Ashton 7 gives the possible restorations), totalling 143 ships. At 18. 15. 8 Diodorus says that while Antiphilus waited in Thessaly (through summer 322) the Macedonians were in the ascendancy at sea, which can only mean after their victories off Abydus and off Amorgos over the Greek fleets. Now they faced the Athenian fleet. It equipped others above those it had (i.e. above the 143 ships as we have interpreted the list) and put 170 ships to sea. Cleitus' fleet of 240 ships defeated the Athenian admiral of this fleet in two engagements, probably in the Malian Gulf, as a large number of Athenian ships were destroyed off 'the Echinades islands'. It is evident that Diodorus omitted altogether the account of the naval war in the eastern Aegean, which he could have drawn from the history of Hieronymus, and concentrated his attention on the destruction of the sea power of Athens. Ashton's theory that the battle of Amorgos happened a few days before the end of the year 323/2, but that Athenian losses in that battle were not included in the list dating to the end of that year seems implausible; for the *euthyne* of outgoing officials involved a check.

---

[1] Before the flooding of the Nile and after the first victory of Eumenes, which was reported to Perdiccas in Egypt; thus in late July. The subsequent death of Perdiccas, being in the Attic year 321/0 (*FGrH* 239 (Marmor Parium) B 11), was after June/July 321. For a different chronology see Errington 75 f., who overestimates the value of the Babylonian Chronicle in Smith 140 ff.; see also H. Hauben in *Anc. Soc.* 86, following Briant 216 ff.

VI

THE CIVIL WAR AND THE SPLITTING OF THE MACEDONIAN STATE

1. *Some general factors in the civil war*

THE members of the royal house, whether dead or alive, played a most important role. Their presence alone made a form of rule legitimate. Thus the possession of Alexander's corpse and the institution of a cult of Alexander 'with heroic honours' at Alexandria endowed Ptolemy's government of Egypt with a special aura of authority.[1] When Eumenes claimed to have seen Alexander in a dream and then set up a throne of Alexander complete with Alexander's diadem, wreath, sceptre, and armour, the Macedonian soldiers gave their allegiance to him and accepted his orders as those of Alexander himself. Seleucus made a similar claim to good effect in Babylonia in 312.[2] Most remarkable of all, the treasuries established by Alexander throughout Asia were respected and kept for his constitutionally elected heirs for a period of seven years. Only after his decisive victory did Antigonus, the most ruthless of rebels, dare to raid those treasuries for his own purposes, and even then he felt it necessary to represent himself as the duly authorized 'manager of the kings'.

In the eyes of the Macedonians the supernatural quality of the royal house was not peculiar to Philip and Alexander. It extended to all their relatives. For that very reason they insisted on electing as king the son of Philip, half-witted though he was, and naming him 'Philip'; and then on electing the baby son of Roxane as king and naming him 'Alexander'. In the past the gods had favoured the house of Amyntas, and it was the belief of the soldiers that the gods would continue to do so if only that house remained in power. It was therefore essential that the kings should be seen to be kings. Decrees and orders were issued always in their names, and it was their presence—whether dead[3] or alive—that conferred legality upon all acts of state.

The women also of the royal house were venerated by the Macedonians. When one of Philip's daughters, Cynane, was killed by Alcetas, the Macedonian soldiers mutinied. They were appeased only by the fulfilment of Cynane's wish, that Philip III should marry Cynane's

[1] D.S. 18. 28. 4–5. [2] D.S. 18. 60. 4–61. 3; Polyaen. 4. 8. 2; D.S. 19. 90. 4.
[3] D.S. 18. 60. 6.

daughter Adea, and it was probably they who renamed her Eurydice (the name of Philip's mother). This marriage of uncle and niece concentrated the legacy of the great Philip in a striking manner. Although she was only in her early teens, Eurydice claimed to represent the wishes of the king. Her complaints against 'the managers of the kings' created such an uproar among the Macedonian soldiers that the managers resigned. Antipater was elected in their place. Eurydice attacked him too, and it was only with difficulty that Antipater persuaded her to abandon her claim.[1] There was great respect also for Cleopatra, the sister of Alexander. If she had associated herself with the kings or if she had strengthened the royal house by marrying one of the ambitious generals who sought her hand, she might have played an important role. Instead, she stayed unmarried at Sardes, and in the end she met the fate of the uncommitted notability in this age of violence, assassination. Her aim was perhaps to keep herself clear of the civil war.[2] The most prestigious woman in the royal house was Olympias, widow of Philip and mother of Alexander. Moreover, during most of Alexander's absence in Asia she had held the most respected constitutional office in Macedonia, the *prostasia* of the monarchy (see p. 90 above). When she was deprived of it, she held a similar office in Molossia, and there she stayed in her fear of Antipater and then of his son, Cassander, until 317. Finally Polyperchon, as the general in power in Macedonia, invited her to return, in order to undertake 'the management' of Alexander IV and to have the dignity of a royal position.[3] In this capacity she took decisive and disastrous actions.

The Macedonian state consisted of two parts: the royal house and the Assembly of Macedones.[4] Before and during the civil war this Assembly was attended by those Macedonians who were with the king or kings at the time of a meeting being convened. Their decisions were final, for instance, in abandoning Alexander's plans, in electing the kings, and in electing one or more 'managers of the kings'. It was to this Assembly as the organ of authority that Eurydice appealed in the name of her husband, the king; she seems to have asked it to make her and not 'the managers' the representative of the kings.[5] This Assembly exercised also its traditional role in judging allegations of treason and in executing anyone found guilty.[6] The members of the Assembly had

---

[1] D.S. 18. 39. 2–4; Arr. *Succ.* F 9, 33.   [2] D.S. 20. 37. 4; Arr. *Succ.* F 11, 40.

[3] D.S. 18. 49. 4 τὴν ἐπιμέλειαν τοῦ Ἀλεξάνδρου...καὶ τὴν βασιλικὴν προστασίαν. See HMSO 159 for the probable meaning of *prostasia* here.

[4] Different terms were used by different writers: C. 10. 7. 3 'contio' and 7 'milites'; Arr. *Succ.* F 1, 8 τὸ πλῆθος; D.S. 18. 36. 6 ἐκκλησία; 36. 7 and 39. 2 οἱ Μακεδόνες. For other examples see p. 173 below.

[5] Arr. *Succ.* F 9, 31 Πείθωνα καὶ Ἀρριδαῖον μηδὲν ἄνευ αὐτῆς ἠξίου πράττειν.

[6] D.S. 18. 37. 2 and 19. 23. 4.

rights apart from its meetings: for instance, to receive the bounty promised by Alexander for service in Asia. When Antipater temporized, he narrowly escaped death at their hands.[1] The Macedonian soldiers who were serving elsewhere, and not in proximity to the kings, regarded themselves as part of the Macedonian state. If a general was sensible, he sought their favour and, if possible, their oath of loyalty. Craterus and Eumenes were particularly successful in handling them. But the soldiers were largely free agents, ready to change their allegiance, as Eumenes found at the end.

All the candidates for power, except Cassander, came from the group of commanders (*hegemones*) who had served under Philip or/and Alexander. Each candidate needed the support of a group of 'Friends', who would act as subordinate commanders or govern satrapies in his interest. It was prudent for him to consult the Friends sitting in Council (*synhedrion*) on matters of policy and as a primary court, as Alexander had done on occasion.[2] These Friends were often fickle, either deserting their leader[3] or themselves killing him, as they killed Perdiccas. The bitterness of feeling which grew up among the officers resulted in the atrocities which they committed against one another, Antigonus for instance burning alive a rival general, Antigenes.

As success or failure depended entirely on military power, each candidate did all he could to retain or gain the services of the best troops in the world: the Companion Cavalry and the Macedonian phalangites. But since they were limited in number, he needed as many native troops as he could raise, whether in the Balkans, Asia, or Egypt. Many tens of thousands had been trained in Alexander's lifetime, and soon other tens of thousands were equipped and trained, sometimes in Macedonian weaponry and tactics. The magic of Alexander's name, which is attested by the very early development of the *Alexander*

---

[1] Arr. *Succ.* F 9, 32–3; Polyaen. 4. 6. 4; Arr. *An.* 7. 8. 1 reading ἐπιδώσει μένουσιν, as proposed in H*A* 321 n. 113 and adopted by Brunt, L 2 ad loc.

There should be no doubt, *pace* Errington 67 n. 132 and E. Badian in Adams and Borza 105, that Arrian's Greek is correct: τὰ παρὰ Ἀλεξάνδρου ὑποσχεθέντα αὐτοῖς ἐπὶ τῇ συστρατείᾳ χρήματα. 'The campaigning with Alexander.' was what distinguished the veteran fighters. There are several references to it for individuals and for troops in Diodorus (e.g. 19. 82. 1 Pithon ὁ συνεστρατευμένος μὲν Ἀλεξάνδρῳ and 19. 90. 3 τοὺς Ἀλεξάνδρῳ συνεστρατευκότας). Both Arrian and Diodorus derived the expression from Hieronymus, a contemporary of the events. We know from Arr. *An.* 7. 12. 2 that A. gave a bounty of a talent each to the 10,000 veterans who had campaigned with him for their services up to their discharge. The other veterans who continued to serve had the expectation of a similar bounty; and it appears from Arr. *An.* 7. 8. 1 ἐπιδώσει μένουσιν (so all MSS.) that A. had promised to give it to them in due course. To suppose that Perdiccas is to be read or postulated in place of A. is gratuitous. Moreover, there is no ground for supposing that Perdiccas had failed to pay his troops from 323 to 321. See further in *GRBS* 25. 58. n. 21.

[2] D.S. 18. 25. 4–5, passing a *dogma*, and 19. 48. 1, allocating satrapies.

[3] E.g. D.S. 18. 29. 5. See M. M. Austin in *CQ* 36 (1986) 462, with bibliography.

Romance, was a potent factor especially among the Persians. This was demonstrated in a remarkable banquet at which Persian officers and men and other Asian troops who had fought under the command of Alexander joined in the sacrifices to Alexander and Philip.[1]

The ships of the navies were manned by native oarsmen[2]—Greeks, Phoenicians, Cypriots, Cilicians, Lycians, and Egyptians. It was only the officers and the marines who were Macedonians or Greeks in Macedonian service. Lastly, there were tens of thousands of mercenaries of many races. The most prized were the Greek mercenaries, hired in already organized bands and loyal usually to a regular paymaster. Money was of supreme importance for the building of navies and the hiring of large mercenary forces. When Antigonus seized the treasuries of the kings in Asia, he was soon able to outnumber the combined forces of his rivals in ships and men.

The factor in the civil war which has been most often underestimated is the loyalty of the Macedonian soldiers to the kings and later to the surviving king. They had elected them and they continued to regard them as kings. The Macedonian throne was never vacant until the death of Alexander IV.[3] That occurred in 309, but was not generally known until 307/6, after which the winning generals dared to call themselves 'kings' and at last to coin in their own names.

2. *From the Aetolian rising to Nicanor's victory at sea (321–318 B.C.)*

We turn now to the civil war and to its effect primarily in Europe, with which this *History* is concerned. The first Macedonian to set a Greek state against the authority of European Macedonia was Perdiccas. When he was threatened by the coalition of Antipater, Craterus, and Antigonus, he entered into secret, but ineffective, negotiations with Demades, the leading politician at Athens, and he concluded an agreement with the Aetolian League. It was at his request that an Aetolian army of 400 cavalry and 12,000 infantry in spring 321 took the field against Polyperchon, whom Antipater had left as general in Macedonia with responsibility for Greece and other areas. The Aetolians began by settling a grudge they had against the West Locrians. They ravaged their territory and captured some small towns, an inauspicious start in a so-called war of liberation. But they went on to defeat a Macedonian force and to win over the greater part of Thessaly, a notable achievement which brought their joint forces up to 1,500 cavalry and 25,000 infantry. They planned to invade Macedonia, probably by the Volustana pass (see Fig. 6), and to bring to battle

---

[1] D.S. 19. 22. 1–3 and P*Eum* 14. 3.   [2] Arr. *Succ.* F 10, 6.
[3] See pp. 161 and 193 below.

the Macedonian army which had been depleted by the drafts accompanying Antipater, Craterus, and Antigonus to Asia. But before they could do so, their false start caught up with them. The Acarnanians, avenging the Locrians, entered Aetolia and ravaged the territory, with the consequence that the Aetolian citizen soldiers returned to defend their homes. While they were absent, Polyperchon took the offensive. He invaded Thessaly and won a decisive victory. Once again the disunity of the Greeks played into Macedonian hands, and the Macedonian soldier showed himself superior in battle. We do not know what terms Polyperchon gave to the Aetolian League (D.S. 18. 38).

In this year victory attended the coalition of Macedonian rebels, for Ptolemy repelled the Royal Army at the Nile and Perdiccas was murdered by his own officers. The fruits of victory were reaped mainly by Antipater at a meeting of armies and generals at Triparadeisus in Syria. He made it clear, as Ptolemy had done, that his rebellion had been against Perdiccas and not against the kings, whom he intended to take into his benevolent charge. He overcame the challenge of Eurydice (see p. 124 above), and he was elected 'manager of the kings with full powers' by the Assembly of the Macedones, which was attended by the soldiers of the Royal Army and also by those of the army brought by Antipater from Macedonia.[1] The surviving supporters of Perdiccas—namely Eumenes, Alcetas, Attalus (son of Andromenes), and fifty or so others—were condemned to death as public enemies by the Assembly. Since the kings were there, these were constitutional acts of state. Antipater then appointed his friends and supporters to governmental posts in Egypt and Asia; this he did, no doubt, in the names of the kings as their executive 'manager'. The appointments were formally approved by the Assembly of Macedones (cf. 19. 55. 3).[2]

Antipater's immediate task was war with Eumenes, Alcetas, and Attalus, who held parts of Asia Minor with formidable armies, especially of cavalry. Antipater's own army, that which he had

---

[1] The two armies were clearly distinguished in the sources, e.g. when Antipater was almost attacked by the royal army and escaped to his own army's camp across the river (Arr. *Succ.* F 9, 33 and Polyaen. 4. 6. 4), and in Arr. loc. cit. 38 τῆς δυνάμεως δὲ τῆς πρόσθεν ὑπὸ Περδίκκᾳ τεταγμένης and 43 τῆς τε ξυνδιαβάσης αὐτῷ εἰς Ἀσίαν.

[2] *IG* ii². 401. 7–10, τοῦ καθ[εσ]τῶτο[s σατρά]που ὑπὸ βασιλ[έων] καὶ [Ἀντιπάτ]ρου καὶ τ[ῶν ἄ]λλων Μ[ακεδ]όνων gives the three authorities: the kings, Antipater, and the Assembly of Macedones other than the kings and their manager. Thus the king is not *ipso facto* a member of the Assembly. In relation to the satrap Antipater may be cited here in his capacity not as manager, but as chiliarch in succession to Perdiccas; for that is what is meant by App. *Mithr.* 8 Ἀντίπατρος ἐπὶ τῷ Περδίκκᾳ τῆς ὑπὸ Ἀλεξάνδρου γενομένης γῆς ἐπιτροπεύων, 'Antipater being governor in succession to Perdiccas of the territory which had come under the control of Alexander'; for a similar phrase was used by Arrian (*FGrH* 156 F 1. 3) for the appointment of Perdiccas as chiliarch: τὸ δὲ ἦν ἐπιτροπὴ τῆς ξυμπάσης βασιλείας, for which see p. 103 with n. 2 above.

brought from Macedonia, was dependable. The Royal Army was far from dependable, for it had behaved mutinously in its demand for the promised bounties. When Antipater made the settlement at Triparadeisus he detached the most troublesome unit, the 3,000 Silvershields, from the Royal Army and sent it to Sousiane with Antigenes, the newly appointed satrap. He now put the rest of this army under the command of his close associate, Antigonus, to whom he had just allocated a generous part of Asia Minor (Pamphylia, Lycaonia, Lycia, and Greater Phrygia); and he appointed as its second-in-command his son Cassander with the title 'chiliarch of the cavalry'. It continued to be 'the Royal Army', attendant upon the kings and their court.[1] The appointment of Cassander was a gesture of friendship towards Antigonus;[2] and in addition Antipater arranged the marriage of his daughter Phila to a son of Antigonus, Demetrius. The two armies campaigned under the overall command of the kings and Antipater; for the court moved with him, as it had done with Perdiccas.

Late in 321 Antipater lost the appetite or the will-power to continue indefinitely in Asia as supreme commander in what was proving to be a difficult war.[3] He was nearly eighty, and he had lived his long life almost entirely in Macedonia. He was a man of a past generation. Had Philip and Alexander lived a normal span, they would now, at the ages of sixty and thirty-five, have been contemporaries of Antigonus and Cassander; but Antipater had grown up in the pre-Philip era of Macedonia's weakness, and he had little or no experience of the wider world which Alexander had created. He decided to move the kings, their court, and a Royal Army to Macedonia as the *fons et caput regni*.[4]

In preparation for his departure he appointed Antigonus 'general of Asia' with the right to call upon the troops of the satraps, but only for the duration of the war. He redistributed a part of each of the two armies. He gave from his own army to Antigonus 8,000 Macedonian phalangites, 500 Companion Cavalry, and 500 (probably) allied cavalry;[5] and he left seventy elephants with him. On the other hand he took over from the army of Antigonus the Macedonian phalangites and some Companion Cavalrymen who had served for many years in Asia. As he led his army towards the Hellespont, it was these troops

---

[1] Arr. *Succ.* F 9, 38 τοὺς βασιλέας φρουρεῖν τε καὶ θεραπεύειν.

[2] It was later represented as due to Antipater's distrust of Antigonus (D.S. 18. 39. 7); but that was an example of hindsight.

[3] Arr. *Succ.* F 11, 41 οὐκ ἐθάρρει.   [4] The phrase is that of J. 13. 6. 11.

[5] Arr. *Succ.* F 11, 43 ὡς...διαπολεμήσων and D.S. 18. 40. 1 διαπολεμήσων. The numbers in the text are derived from a corrupt passage in Arrian. Of them the 8,000 there is certified by the repetition of it in D.S. 19. 29. 3; the words then to be supplied before πεντακοσίους are probably ἱππέας συμμάχους because these troops fought next to the Companion Cavalry in D.S. 19. 29. 4; and ἴσους for the Companion Cavalry refers to πεντακοσίους (cf. D.S. 19. 27. 5 ἴσοι). See further my comments in *GRBS* 25 (1984) 59 n. 26 and *CQ* 28 (1978) 134.

which mutinied again, demanding their bounties. Antipater lulled them into obedience with promises, but he took the wise precaution of crossing the Hellespont at night with the kings, Eurydice, Roxane, probably Heracles and Barsine,[1] the Royal Bodyguards and the Royal Pages. Next day the army, complete with seventy elephants, crossed to European soil. It was a notable homecoming for Alexander's veterans. That they were disgruntled when they compared the achievements of Alexander with those of the senior officers since his death is not surprising.

Antipater's decision had important implications. The centre of gravity in the world created by Alexander lay both strategically and economically in the region of Syria, and any powerful commander there could call on the manpower of the Levant for his navy and on the Asian peoples for his army. Moreover, he had within his reach the treasuries situated in Cilicia, Media, and Persia and the revenues of many rich satrapies. On the other hand, Macedonia was on the periphery of that world; and because it was frequently distracted by the Greek states, it did not have the manpower or the resources to control the world of Alexander. By moving the kings to Macedonia, Antipater created an imbalance in the structure, which it was going to be difficult, or even impossible, to redress.

The veterans of Alexander's campaigns who had been brought home, some by Craterus and now others by Antipater, were bound for some years to form the majority in any full Assembly of the Macedonians in Macedonia, and their loyalties were to the members of the royal house and to the older generation of commanders. On the other hand, the Macedonians allocated by Antipater to Antigonus had not seen a king in person since spring 334, and they were therefore less strongly attached to Alexander and to his branch of the royal house; and they had little except the name in common with those of Alexander's Macedonians who were still serving in Asia (for instance the famous Silvershields). Such lines of demarcation between the armies of Antipater and of Antigonus and of the eastern satraps help us to understand the actions these armies took in the continuing civil war.

Antipater returned to two loyal supporters, Lysimachus 'general of Thrace' and Polyperchon, his own deputy in Macedonia and the adjacent areas. The Greek states were now under control, for Antipater's partisans held power in the individual states, and his garrisons occupied many key points. His methods with Greek dissidents were drastic and direct, since he had abolished the Council of the Common Peace. For example, Demades of Athens was found to have been in

---

[1] Str. 794 mentions 'the children of Alexander'.

treasonable correspondence with Perdiccas. When he and his son came to Pella, Antipater condemned them to death on that evidence, and let his son Cassander, it was said, execute them with his own hand.[1] The only state outside his sphere of control was the Epirote Alliance, within which Olympias and Thessalonice, a daughter of Philip by Nicesipolis, were living at the Molossian court. When Antipater's health declined, he brought Cassander home to help 'manage the monarchy in Macedonia'. And in summer 319, when he lay dying, he remembered his bitter struggles with Olympias when she had held the *prostasia*, and he uttered words of advice for the future. 'Never allow a woman to preside over the monarchy' (τῆς βασιλείας προστατῆσαι).[2]

During his last illness, according to our sources, Antipater 'appointed' Polyperchon as 'the manager of the kings' and Cassander as Polyperchon's deputy. The decision, however, lay with the Assembly of the Macedonians at Pella. 'The eager desire of the Macedones'—being mainly veterans of Alexander—'turned to Polyperchon.' They elected him 'manager', it seems, and gave nothing to Cassander.[3] The choice was perhaps not wise. A brave highlander, a scion of the Tymphaean royal family, a marvellous dancer, and a good drinker, Polyperchon was still a vigorous sixty-year-old; but he had not risen above the rank of brigadier under Alexander, and he had not had the experience even of governing a satrapy. He had no standing in the eyes of Antigonus or Ptolemy or Peucestes, for instance, and he had little influence with the Macedonian soldiers in Asia.

A new round of civil war was started on the initiative of Cassander, a ruthless and ambitious man, who saw no future in staying with

---

[1] D.S. 18. 48. 1–4; Arr. *Succ.* F 9, 14–15; P*Ph* 30. 10, emended; P*D* 31, 4–6; only Diodorus had Cassander do the killing, and he may have derived it from Athenian propaganda to the detriment of Cassander.

[2] D.S. 19. 11. 9. The Greek phrase in itself can be either general in meaning, as at D.S. 18. 75. 2, or specific to the *prostasia*. See H*SMO* 159.

[3] D.S. 18. 48. 4 and P*Ph* 31. 1. The 'appointing' by Antipater has been held by Droysen 2. 1. 177 and 185 and others (e.g. Préaux 1. 130) to have been conclusive. If so, and Cassander was in fact second in authority to Polyperchon, it is difficult to see why he did not stay and exploit his position in Macedonia. Diodorus resumed his account at greater length in 18. 54 with the remarks that 'Cassander had failed to obtain the commanding position in Macedonia...and saw that the strong desire of the Macedones had turned towards Polyperchon' (ἀποτετευχὼς τῆς κατὰ τὴν Μακεδονίαν ἡγεμονίας...ὁρῶν δὲ τὴν τῶν Μακεδόνων ὁρμὴν κεκλιμένην πρὸς τὸν Πολυπέρχοντα). This desire, it seems to me, was shown not in the circumstances of Antipater's appointment in his last illness, but in the Assembly of the Macedones, which was needed to elect 'the manager of the kings' as in the case of Antipater himself. Diodorus was not interested in the constitutional procedures of the Macedonians here any more than he was at 18. 2. 4. What caused Cassander to go and serve as a subordinate officer of Antigonus was that he failed to be elected number two to Polyperchon, who turned instead to Cassander's enemy, Olympias. The generation gap between Polyperchon and Cassander, noted in D.S. 18. 48. 4, accounts largely for the enmity between the two men and the attitude of the veterans to Cassander; the latter had no wish to make Cassander their master as chiliarch. For other motives see W. L. Adams in *AM* 3. 18 ff. For the Assembly's part see H*SMO* 160.

Polyperchon. He had good friends in the commanders of the Macedonian garrisons in Greece, and especially in Nicanor, whom he installed at Munychia in Athens shortly before his father's death; and he inherited ties with the oligarchic governments in the Greek states. He had too a considerable following among those Macedonians who had been beneficiaries of Antipater's long period of command in Macedonia. He opened secret negotiations with Ptolemy, who had shown his independence of any central authority by stealing the corpse of Alexander and proclaiming that Alexander's dying wish had been to be buried at the shrine of Zeus Ammon.[1] These negotiations resulted in an alliance later, but in the meanwhile Cassander and his friends left Macedonia for the camp of Antigonus, who had increased his army to 70,000 men and acquired large amounts of money.[2] Antigonus sympathized with Cassander's plan to rebel against Polyperchon, and he promised to give an army and a fleet to Cassander. The plot of this triumvirate was reported to Polyperchon by Cleitus, a loyalist satrap who had been driven out by Antigonus, and his report was confirmed when Antigonus confiscated 600 talents at Ephesus which were on their way by sea from Cilicia to the kings in Macedonia.[3]

Polyperchon convened a council of his commanding officers and other leading persons in Macedonia and sought their advice. With their approval he disregarded Antipater's dying words and sent for Olympias, asking her to undertake 'the management of the infant son of Alexander and stay in Macedonia, having the dignity of a royal position'. She accepted the invitation; for it was for her a return to 'the favoured and honoured position she had held before, in the lifetime of Alexander'.[4] The Assembly of the Macedonians, we may assume, appointed her to the office of manager in the hope that by adding her name to those of the kings they would attract more adherents to the royal cause among the Macedonians in Asia. It mattered little that Olympias did not transfer her residence to Macedonia, the reason being that she was afraid of Cassander's supporters there.[5] Polyperchon and Olympias, each acting separately in the names of the kings, sent envoys to Eumenes and other commanders in Asia and asked them to attack Antigonus as the leading rebel. They hoped in this way to deflect Antigonus and Cassander from crossing into Europe.

Antigonus had had a similar idea. Although a part of his army was besieging Eumenes at Nora (on the frontier of Cappadocia and

---

[1] J. 12. 15. 7 and C. 10. 5. 4; cf. J. 13. 4. 6 and D.S. 18. 28. 3, which shows a knowledge of the idea. The ultimate source was probably Cleitarchus; see H*TAH* 40.

[2] D.S. 18. 50. 3.   [3] D.S. 18. 52. 6–7.

[4] D.S. 18. 49. 4, quoted in p. 124 n. 3 above; J. 14. 5. 1; D.S. 18. 65. 1 τὴν προϋπάρχουσαν ἀποδοχὴν καὶ τιμὴν Ἀλεξάνδρου ζῶντος. For τιμή meaning honour and not an office see H*SMO* 159.

[5] D.S. 18. 57. 2; cf. Nepos, *Eum.* 6. 1.

Lycaonia), he invited Eumenes to join him against Polyperchon. His envoy, Hieronymus of Cardia, brought a form of words which emphasized loyalty to the kings at the outset, but mentioned only Antigonus in the proposed oath of loyalty which Antigonus was asking Eumenes and his men to take. Eumenes composed a different version in which loyalty was 'to Olympias and the kings' as well as to Antigonus. He then submitted both versions to the Macedonians of the besieging force and invited them to choose in the absence of Antigonus. They chose Eumenes' version. Eumenes and his men took the oath.[1] The siege was lifted, and Eumenes and his troops departed. When Hieronymus brought the new version to Antigonus, he had a cold reception; for Antigonus had no intention of taking that form of the oath. Eumenes had once again played a winning trick.

Soon after leaving Nora Eumenes received letters from Macedonia. In one 'Polyperchon and Philip the king' appointed him satrap of Cappadocia and ordered him to make war on Antigonus. For his past efforts Eumenes was to receive 500 talents and to draw as much more as he needed for the war from the treasure of the kings in Cilicia. If he should require more troops than he could muster as 'commander of all Asia with full powers', Polyperchon and the kings would bring the royal army from Europe to Asia. On the other hand, if Eumenes should come to Europe, Polyperchon offered him an equal share in the management of the kings.[2] In another letter Olympias invited him to come to Macedonia and take over and educate the infant son of Alexander, who, she said, was 'the object of plots'. Accordingly she asked Eumenes to come to the rescue of 'the kings and herself, since he was the most loyal of their friends that were left' (she had known him at Philip's court and during Alexander's period in Europe). She expressed her distrust of 'this succession of so-called managers', and she asked Eumenes whether she should stay in Molossia or return to Macedonia. He urged her not to return until a decision was reached in the war.[3]

For whatever reason—loyalty, self-interest, hatred of Antigonus, or a combination of the three—Eumenes devoted himself to the royalist cause with zest. He knew that Polyperchon and the kings had sent orders to the loyalist satraps that they should support him. He therefore marched at speed into Cilicia, persuaded Antigenes and Teutamus, commanders of the Silvershields and keepers of the kings' treasury, to accept him by telling of a dream about Alexander, and then set up a tent with Alexander's throne for the joint planning of operations (see p. 123 above). By this quick move he anticipated

[1] *PEum* 12; cf. D.S. 18. 50. 4–53. 5.   [2] D.S. 18. 57. 3–4, 58. 1, and 59. 4.
[3] *PEum* 13. 1; D.S. 18. 58. 2–4; Nepos, *Eum.* 6. 1 with apocryphal advice.

Ptolemy and Antigonus, who were both trying to gain control of the treasury. His own force and the Silvershields now marched to Phoenicia and then to the East, where they met the eastern satraps and persuaded them to accept the orders sent by the kings and fight against Antigonus.[1]

Polyperchon could not have hoped for a better ally than Eumenes, for Eumenes kept Antigonus in the East until the winter of 317/6. Then at Gabiene he was betrayed by the Silvershields in exchange for their families and baggage, which Antigonus had captured (Polyaen. 4. 6. 13). On the insistence of Antigonus' Macedonians Eumenes was executed as 'a public enemy' in accordance with their earlier vote (see p. 127 above). It was ironical that Eumenes had been loyal to the kings, first with Perdiccas and then with Polyperchon as 'manager of the kings', whereas Antigonus had instigated civil war first against Perdiccas and then against Polyperchon. What earned Eumenes the hatred of the Macedonians who had come with Antipater to Asia and now served with Antigonus was the killing of Craterus and the opposition to Antipater.

Meanwhile in Europe in 319 Polyperchon and his advisers decided on a new policy towards the Greek states, in the hope of winning them over from Cassander. This policy was made public in the form of a resolution (*diagramma*), which Hieronymus included in his history. A part of it verbatim and some of Hieronymus' comments have survived in the history of Diodorus,[2] and from them we can understand the nature of an official Macedonian document. The authors of the resolution, 'we', were 'the kings and the *hegemones*' (Polyperchon, being one of the *hegemones*, had bound himself to follow the majority view of 'the Friends', among whom were the other *hegemones*). The association of the two was probably traditional (see Volume II. 136 concerning the treaty of Perdiccas II with Athens). The resolution was addressed to 'the Greeks' in the sense of the Greeks of the Common Peace.[3]

Since the kings and the commanders of Macedonia were claiming to re-establish the Common Peace which Antipater had abolished, the resolution used the original catchwords, liberty and autonomy, the latter now being assumed to mean a democratic government. It recalled the letters which had been sent after the death of Alexander to all the states (i.e. of the Common Peace), and it drew attention to the principle therein of maintaining 'the peace and the constitutions which Philip our father had established'.[4] 'We', the resolution proclaimed,

[1] D.S. 19. 15. 3.   [2] D.S. 18. 56 and *SVA* 403. III.
[3] D.S. 18. 55. 4 τὴν τῶν βασιλέων καὶ τῶν ἡγεμόνων εἰς τοὺς Ἕλληνας εὔνοιαν, and 18. 56. 1.
[4] Echoing phrases in the treaty between Philip and the Greeks in *GHI* 177, e.g. τὰ[ς πολιτείας τὰς οὔσας] παρ' ἑκάστοις.

'are establishing the peace[1] and the constitutions as in the time of Philip and Alexander'; and 'we are restoring those expelled or exiled by the generals', i.e. by Antipater and his officers.

The arrangements for the restoration of the exiles were like those of Alexander in 324 (see p. 80 above). The exceptions were those guilty of murder, sacrilege, and 'treason' (the last meaning violation of the terms of the Common Peace). If any discrepancies should arise between the regulations of Philip and those of Alexander, the ruling should be given by the kings and the *hegemones*. 'The Greeks' were all to forbid any act of aggression against Macedonia;[2] if anyone broke this ban, he was to be exiled with loss of property. Athens was to have what she had possessed in the time of Philip (e.g. Samos), with the exception of Oropus which was to remain independent. And 'the Greeks' were to pay heed to Polyperchon, who was appointed by the kings to look after these matters.[3]

The *diagramma* was carefully worded to recall the principles and the practices of the past, in the hope that it would win credence among the Greeks and confer on Polyperchon's government the respectability of an honourable precedent. But it was entirely specious. There was no move and no intention to reconstitute a Council of the Common Peace as an organ of self-government. Polyperchon's aim was to use the democratic factions against the oligarchic factions which Cassander and his associates were supporting in the Greek states. This was made abundantly clear by an immediate fiat from Polyperchon to 'Argos and the remaining states' to exile the leaders installed by Antipater, and in some cases to execute them and confiscate their property.[4] There was no question of bringing these leaders to trial before the Council of the Common Peace.

The effects of Polyperchon's policy can be seen most clearly at Athens. There Cassander's friend Nicanor was in command of the garrison at Munychia, and he was on friendly terms with Phocion, the leader of the party put in power by Antipater. Nicanor extended his hold by seizing the Piraeus. Then at the invitation of intending revolutionaries at Athens a Macedonian army commanded by Polyp-

---

[1] D.S. 18. 56. 3 κατασκευάζομεν ὑμῖν εἰρήνην, πολιτείας δὲ τὰς ἐπὶ Φιλίππου καὶ ᾽Αλεξάνδρου. One may compare A.'s phrase in his letter to Darius: τὴν εἰρήνην ἣν τοῖς Ἕλλησιν κατεσκεύασα (Arr. *An.* 2. 14. 6). Bosworth 232 suggested that the phrase in A.'s letter was a backward projection from the Hellenistic period; but it is much more likely that the actual letter of 333 B.C. was cited by Ptolemy. The phrase was then repeated with this precedent in mind in 319 B.C., in the normal sequence of historical events.

[2] D.S. 18. 56. 7. Cf. *GHI* 177, 10–11.

[3] D.S. 18. 56. 7 προστετάχαμεν δὲ καὶ περὶ τούτων καὶ τῶν λοιπῶν Πολυπέρχοντι πραγματεύ-εσθαι. Cf. D.S. 18. 8. 4, where A. made a similar reference to Antipater: γεγράφαμεν δὲ Ἀντιπάτρῳ περὶ τούτων.

[4] D.S. 18. 57. 1; cf. *PPh* 32. 1. See Wehrli 108.

erchon's son Alexander appeared in Attica, and a swarm of returning 'democratic' exiles restored the democracy by deposing existing officials and electing new ones.[1] Some of the deposed were executed, others were exiled, and others escaped.

Phocion and his friends were accused of 'treason', i.e. of betraying the Common Peace. They were taken to the camp of Polyperchon in Phocis and tried there before a Macedonian *synhedrion*, in which Philip III and his Friends presided, and a deputation from the Athenian democracy prosecuted. The erratic behaviour of the half-witted king made a nonsense of the proceedings. The matter was then passed to Athens for decision, together with a letter from the king as follows: 'I have decided that the men are traitors; but since the Athenians are a free and autonomous people I give the decision to them.' In the trial before the Athenian Assembly there was such an uproar that no systematic defence was possible, and a show of hands passed sentence of death on the prisoners and also on others who were absent.[2] Phocion drank the hemlock in May 318; it was a sad end for an elderly statesman with a long record of faithful service to Athens. The democratic party was now politically in control. But Nicanor held its harbour, into which Cassander sailed with thirty-five ships and 4,000 soldiers, provided and paid by Antigonus.

The faction strife which racked the mainland states had less effect on the war between Polyperchon and Cassander than the moves of the Macedonian forces. The fleet of Polyperchon, which was based on Pella, was sent under the command of Cleitus to the Propontis, where it was joined by most of the Greek cities and by the forces of Arrhidaeus, an enemy of Antigonus (see Figs. 1 and 7). If Cleitus could hold these waters, he would prevent any army from crossing from Asia into Europe and he would cut the supply line of Cassander's fleet which lay at the Piraeus. In response Nicanor sailed from the Piraeus, joined forces with Antigonus' fleet from Ephesus, and despite adverse weather forced an engagement in the waters south of the Bosporus in summer 318. Cleitus won a brilliant victory, sinking or crippling thirty, and capturing forty, of the 130 enemy ships.

While Cleitus' men celebrated their victory, Antigonus staged a dawn attack on their camp and their anchorage with some light-armed troops, who had been transported overnight from the Asiatic side on

---

[1] D.S. 18. 65. 6.

[2] The accounts in D.S. 18. 64–7, PPh 33–6, and Nepos, *Phoc.* 2–4 have much in common. The trial before the king is more fully described by Plutarch, who seems to have supplemented Hieronymus with a rhetorical source; but the essence is given in D.S. 18. 66. 3 and Nepos, *Phoc.* 3 'ex consilii sententia in custodiam coniectus [sc. Phocion] Athenas deductus est, ut ibi de eo legibus fieret iudicium.' The charge of the prosecution, according to Nepos, was that Phocion had betrayed the Piraeus to Nicanor, thereby committing προδοσία.

ships supplied by Byzantium, and with his best Macedonian phalangites on board his remaining ships (D.S. 18. 72. 5–9; Polyaen. 4. 6. 8). The surprise was complete. Cleitus and his flagship alone escaped, and on landing in Thrace he was captured and killed by the soldiers of Lysimachus.[1] Nicanor kept his reconstituted fleet in the north-east Aegean and from there he supplied Cassander, who was now blockading Athens and soon captured Salamis and Aegina.[2]

Antigonus turned south and gained possession of the entire seaboard as far as Phoenicia, where his ally Ptolemy had already staked out his claim. Antigonus now held the key position between the two chief champions of the kings, Polyperchon in the West and Eumenes in the East.

3. *Polyperchon, Olympias, and Cassander (318–316 B.C.)*

Before and during Cleitus' naval operations Polyperchon was campaigning on the Greek mainland with the royal army of the kings and the allied contingents of the 'liberated' Greek states. When he entered Attica from the north in early summer 318, he had 20,000 Macedonian infantry, 4,000 Greek allied infantry, 1,000 cavalry, and sixty-five elephants—the first war elephants to enter Greece. His troops were far too many for a beleaguered Attica to feed, so he left a detachment under Alexander to besiege the Piraeus, and he passed on to the Peloponnese. There the proclamation of liberty and autonomy had led to the usual round of executions and banishments with the swing to restored democracies, and only Megalopolis remained faithful to oligarchy and Cassander. Its massive walls were manned by 15,000 men, free and liberated, and their commander, Damis, had served with Alexander and had had experience of elephants in war. Polyperchon built siege-towers higher than the walls, cleared the battlements with his catapult fire, and undermined a stretch of wall by sapping. When the pit-props in the sap were burnt, a long stretch of wall including three towers collapsed. The defenders fought so well from the collapsed rubble that they held off the attacking Macedonians while palisades and a second wall were being constructed.

During the night before the expected assault Damis buried sets of caltrops, made with huge nails, in shallow trenches along a central cleared passage, which led towards the second wall. On either side of the passage he posted his catapults, slingers, archers, and javelin-men. Next day the Macedonians cleared more of the debris and then attacked, their elephants being in advance and following the cleared

---

[1] D.S. 18. 72; Polyaen. 4. 6. 8, misplacing the battle in the Hellespont.
[2] D.S. 18. 69. 1–2; Polyaen. 4. 11. 1; Paus. 1. 15. 1, 25. 6, and 35. 2.

passage-way. As the mahouts urged them on, the elephants were struck by a hail of fire and their feet were impaled by the caltrops, so that maddened by pain they turned and trampled on the supporting troops, who fled in confusion. Discouraged by this disaster, Polyperchon left a detachment to maintain a blockade of Megalopolis. He led the royal army back to Macedonia, in case Antigonus should bring his huge army into Europe.[1]

The ineffectiveness of Polyperchon and the failure of his fleet enabled Cassander to put further pressure on Athens by capturing Panactum on the land-route northwards and by intensifying his blockade. See Fig. 9. In spring 317 Athens sued for terms and accepted the following: to be friends and allies of Cassander, accept his garrisoning of the Munychia 'until he should complete the war against the kings', recognize the independence of Salamis, enjoy complete control of her own resources within Attica, and 'elect' an Athenian citizen of Cassander's nomination as 'manager of the state'—a Macedonian term.[2] Cassander nominated Demetrius of Phalerum, an able philosopher and an already experienced politician in his thirties. Demetrius chose a *via media* between Antipater's narrow oligarchy and Polyperchon's democracy by limiting the political franchise to some 21,000 owners of property worth 1,000 drachmae.[3] The rest of the population enjoyed all other citizen rights. But this 'moderate oligarchy' was little more than a façade; for Demetrius was virtually a dictator, although he and his friends were duly elected to formal magistracies. He kept Athens peaceful and prosperous for ten years under the shadow of Cassander's authority.

Soon after the setting up of Demetrius as 'manager', Nicanor and his ships, which were bedecked with the spoils of victory, sailed into the Piraeus, and he resumed his post as garrison commander on Munychia. But Cassander distrusted him. He played a confidence trick on Nicanor, had him arrested, and brought him before an Assembly of the Athenians, who condemned him to death on criminal charges. He was executed.[4] The thalassocracy which Nicanor had consolidated was used to good effect by Cassander; for he made a landing in strength on the coast of Macedonia, contacted his supporters, and removed a

---

[1] D.S. 18. 68–72.

[2] The same specious combination of nomination and 'election' was practised later by Antigonus in the wording of *SEG* 3. 122: κατασταθεὶς στρατηγὸς ὑπό τε τοῦ βασιλέως Ἀντιγόνου καὶ [ὑπὸ τοῦ δήμου] χειροτονηθείς.

[3] Antipater had drawn the line at 2,000 drachmae, which produced only 9,000 persons. The census in Athen. 272 c was 'of those inhabiting Attica' and not of those fit for military service, as Gomme 18 f. was inclined to suggest.

[4] Polyaen. 4. 11. 2, where ἐψηφίσαντο is appropriate to an Athenian Assembly. D.S. 18. 75. 1 reduced the process to one word: ἐδολοφόνησεν.

number of elephants from their pastures, presumably near Pella. There was a swing in favour of Cassander in the Greek states of the mainland, and the summer of 317 saw war there between the armies of Cassander and Polyperchon, mainly in the Peloponnese. The details are not known.[1]

Whatever developments took place in Greece, the Aegean, or Asia, Macedonia remained the vital centre. There the kings resided and the court and the constitution operated as they had done for centuries. The kings went on campaign with their general Polyperchon to Phocis, as we know from D.S. 18. 68. 2, and presumably to the Peloponnese in 318. Acts of state were published in the names of the kings. Their names were associated with those of the leading *hegemones* in treaties and proclamations.[2] The adult king, Philip III, sat with the Friends at the trial of the Athenian leaders, and in theory it was he and they who debated matters of policy. The parties in the civil war were those loyal to the kings and those in rebellion against them; and it was in these terms that Hieronymus described the war in his history.[3]

In practice the responsibility for initiating and executing policy fell upon Polyperchon as the duly elected 'manager of the kings', and he was careful to share that responsibility with the Friends. He and they decided after the death of Antipater to reinforce the royalist position by adding the prestigious name and influence of Olympias. So they invited her to take over 'the management' of Alexander IV (he had been in the charge hitherto of his uncle and guardian Philip III and the royal ladies, Eurydice and Roxane) and to resume her royal position at court. She accepted the office and proceeded to issue orders. Thus she instructed Nicanor to restore Munychia and the Piraeus to Athens, and she informed the Athenians of that instruction; and it was no empty gesture, for Nicanor was frightened into professing obedience, and the Athenians were hopeful of a real 'autonomy' because of Olympias' past favours to Athens and her newly established position.[4]

---

[1] D.S. 18. 75 and 19. 35. 7 (the elephants). Polyaen. loc. cit. may suggest a voyage by sea, and Theophr. *Char.* 8 may belong here; see Beloch 4. 2. 436 ff. for speculations. Beloch 4. 1. 439, Dušanić 40, and W. L. Adams 20 n. 13 held that Philip III conferred authority to administer the kingdom on Cassander in Macedonia; but the phrasing of J. 14. 5. 3 suggests a written order, such as Olympias had sent to Eumenes.

[2] D.S. 18. 55. 4; *Hesp.* 37 (1968) 222, recording the dedication of 'the Doric building' at Samothrace by 'the Kings Philippos and Alexandros', in the period 323–316. For the equal rights of the two kings see Ch. Habicht in *Akten d. VI. Internat. Kong. f. gr. u. lat. Epigraphik, München 1972* (Munich, 1973) 375; S. M. Burstein, in *ZPE* 24 (1977) 223 ff. and W. Meckel in *ZPE* 40 (1980) 249 f.

[3] As reflected in D.S. 18. 55. 2, 68. 3, and 74. 3, for example.

[4] D.S. 18. 65. 1–2, keeping the MS. reading δεδογμένας τιμάς. The honours had been conferred officially by the Assembly, quite apart from the sense of δεδογμένας.

She communicated directly with Eumenes and asked him, among other things, to take charge of Alexander IV in Macedonia (as she being in Molossia was unable to do); and she wrote, separately from 'the kings and their manager Polyperchon', to the commanders of the Silvershields and the governors of satrapies and instructed them to obey the orders of Eumenes.[1] It is true that her instructions were in line with the policies of Polyperchon and the Friends. But the importance of them was that she spoke with the royal voice on behalf of 'the kings and herself' and more generally of 'the house and family of Philip [meaning Philip II] and the children of Alexander [meaning Alexander IV and Heracles]' (Nepos, *Eum.* 6). Soon afterwards she decided not to return to Macedonia.

The influence of Olympias with the Macedonian soldiers at home and overseas was an important element in the royalist cause. To those at home, being mainly of the older generation, she stood for Philip in particular; and to those overseas she was the mother of Alexander and the grandmother of the king they had elected, Alexander IV. Her importance in their eyes was apparent from the form of the oath 'to Olympias and the kings' which was preferred by the soldiers of Antigonus as well as by those of Eumenes (see p. 132 above). That her instructions to Peucestes and the satraps in the east were obeyed in general both by them and by their soldiers was due in part to her prestige.

But the involvement of Olympias was attended by dangers. In 317, when Polyperchon was in Greece trying to stem the rising tide of support for Cassander, he sent Alexander IV and Roxane to Olympias in Molossia and he left Philip III and Eurydice in Macedonia. Whatever his motives—fear of Cassander's supporters or fear of Eurydice—it was a mistake to divide the royal family into two parts. Eurydice took immediate advantage of the situation. She knew that many of the Macedonian soldiers who had supported her claim to speak for Philip III in Asia were now present in Macedonia, and she made some pact with the party of Cassander in Macedonia. Whether she worked only through the Assembly of the Macedones or was also elected to hold the *epimeleia* of the monarchy, she achieved a *coup d'état*.[2] When she learnt that Olympias was planning to return to Macedonia, she invited Cassander to come from the Peloponnese and help her, and she sent orders in the name of Philip III to Polyperchon and Antigonus to hand over their armies to Cassander, 'to whom the

---

[1] *PEum* 13. 1; D. 18. 58. 2–3 and 62. 2; Nepos, *Eum.* 6 fin.

[2] D.S. 19. 11. 1 τῆς βασιλείας προεστηκυῖα probably means 'being at the head of the kingdom' (as in D.S. 18. 60. 3) i.e. speaking and acting on behalf of the king. Thus she was able 'on his behalf' to distribute gifts and make promises of future benefits.

king had transferred the administration of the kingdom.'[1] Her challenge to Olympias and Polyperchon was so direct that a clash was inevitable.

Olympias was not the woman to hesitate. She sought, but failed to win, the armed support of the Epirote Alliance for an invasion, but nevertheless she and Alexander IV set off with an army mustered by Polyperchon and with the royal forces attendant on the Molossian king, Aeacides. See Fig. 8. In a region called 'Euia' on the Molossian–Macedonian frontier, they found Eurydice and Philip III with their Macedonian army.[2] Bloodshed was averted by the desertion of Eurydice's Macedonian soldiers; for they had no taste for civil war, respected Olympias, and remembered Alexander. Philip III and his entourage were taken prisoner forthwith, and Eurydice was captured while escaping towards Amphipolis. Thus her initiative ended in disaster, and worse was to follow.

Olympias was a passionate and embittered woman, some sixty years old. Restored to Macedonia after an absence of seven years and in sole charge of the young king, she took a cruel revenge. She kept Philip III and Eurydice in prison under such appalling conditions that she began to lose favour with the Macedonians. Then, in September 317, she had some Thracian soldiers stab Philip III to death and sent to Eurydice a sword, a noose, and a dose of poison with the order to kill herself. Eurydice, a girl of nineteen years, washed the corpse of Philip, so that it was ready for burial, and then hanged herself with her girdle.

The act of regicide was not enough for Olympias. She had to take revenge on Antipater and Cassander. So she selected 100 leading Macedonians who had supported Eurydice and Cassander, and she had them executed as traitors.[3] One of them was Nicanor, a brother of Cassander. Then she destroyed the tomb of another brother, Iollas, on

[1] J. 14. 5. 3 'in quem regni administrationem rex transtulerit'. This was presumably Justin's translation of τὴν ἐπιμελείαν τῆς βασιλείας in his source, being Hieronymus. Bengtson *Strat.* 87 n. 1 held that it translated τὴν ἐπιμελείαν τῶν βασιλέων, which is not only incorrect linguistically, but obscures the significant 'rex', indicating a rejection of 'reges' by Eurydice. It may be recalled that the Macedonian infantrymen in 323 had wished to make Arrhidaeus sole king at first. Beloch 4. 1. 439, Dušanić 40, and W. L. Adams, op. cit. 20 n. 13, held that Philip III appointed Cassander during his raid on Macedonia (D.S. 18. 75. 1 and 19. 35. 7, mentioned on p. 137 above); but Justin's text suggests a written order (see n. 1 p. 138 above).

[2] Paus. 1. 11. 3; J. 14. 5. 9 'finibus'; D.S. 19. 11. 2 ἐν Εὐίοις τῆς Μακεδονίας. Justin seems to be preferable here to Diodorus, who had Olympias restored before the armies met. Both passages show that 'Euia' (neuter plural) is not to be identified with the Εὐία of Ptolemy 3. 13. 32, which is in Dassaretis and so a long way north of the Macedonian frontier with Molossia (see Volume I. 64). The persons called 'Euiestae' came from the region; and since an inscription mentioning them was found near Kozani (*AJA* 42 (1938) 249), it is probable that Euia was a region containing a strategic pass near by, e.g. the pass of Siatista. I have shown it so on Fig. 8.

[3] She probably persuaded the Assembly to pronounce them public enemies, as the Assembly had done in Asia when it passed sentence on some fifty supporters of Perdiccas and might have done on Sibyrtius (D.S. 18. 37. 2 and 19. 23. 4).

the ground that as Alexander's cupbearer he had administered poison and was responsible for Alexander's death. The civil war of atrocities and propaganda thus spread to the homeland. The responsibility lay with Eurydice and Olympias rather than with Polyperchon, who was dominated by Olympias' force of personality and prestige.

The actions of Eurydice and Olympias shattered the united front of the royalist cause, which since 323 had used the terms 'the kings' and recently 'Olympias and the kings'. It was remarkable how consistently that cause had been maintained in Asia; for the keepers of the royal treasuries in Cilicia and Media and at Susa had refused to issue money except on the order of 'the kings', the Silvershields had rejected all advances by the rebels, and the eastern satraps had raised very large forces of Macedonians, Greeks, Thracians, and Asians to defend the rule of 'the kings'.[1] Self-interest no doubt played its part, for the officers hoped to receive military commands and satrapal posts, and the soldiers high pay and large bounties. But men had also a genuine veneration for Philip II and Alexander III, a veneration which was felt also by the Persians;[2] and Olympias at first basked in the reflected glory. When Eumenes as the leading royalist wished to encourage his men, he put out a false story, in summer 317, that Olympias, having taken charge of Alexander IV, had regained the kingship and kingdom of Macedonia[3] and had killed the rebel Cassander, and that Polyperchon was bringing the pick of 'the royal forces' to Asia in order to crush the rebel Antigonus. The truth came as a rude awakening: the cold-blooded murder of Philip III and the savagery of Olympias.

Cassander exploited the new situation. Rebel though he was, he had been given the semblance of respectability by Eurydice, when she had appointed him in the name of Philip III 'administrator of the kingdom'. For whatever reason, he had left Eurydice in the lurch,[4] preferring to stay with his Greek allies besieging Tegea. Yet later in this same year, 317, he suddenly abandoned those allies (D.S. 19. 35. 1) and marched north. He had chosen the moment to suit his personal interest. The forces of Olympias and Alexander IV were widely scattered (see Fig. 5). Alexander, son of Polyperchon, waiting probably in southern Aetolia to invade the Peloponnese; the Aetolians holding the pass of Thermopylae; Polyperchon covering the pass of Volustana between Perrhaebia and Elimea; and Olympias probably at

---

[1] D.S. 18. 58. 1 and 62. 1–2; 19. 15. 5, 17. 3, and 18. 1; D.S. 18. 62. 5–6; and D.S. 19. 14. 4–8 and 24. 1.

[2] D.S. 19. 22. 1 and 3; cf. 19. 15. 4.

[3] D.S. 19. 23. 2 κεκόμισται τὴν Μακεδονίας βασιλείαν. The word βασιλεία has a double meaning, 'kingship' and 'kingdom', which are combined in the Greek concept.

[4] One can only speculate that Cassander either wanted Eurydice to fail or, anticipating her failure, had no intention of becoming involved.

Aegeae with some élite troops which were protecting the members of the royal house—Alexander IV, Roxane, Thessalonice, and the orphaned daughters of Perdiccas' sister—and in addition a Molossian princess called Deidameia, who was a daughter of Aeacides, and some relatives of Olympias' leading supporters in Macedonia (D.S. 19. 35. 5). By quickness of movement and by using sea transport, Cassander landed unopposed in Thessaly and marched towards Perrhaebia. Informed of his approach, Olympias sent troops ahead to occupy the Petra pass which leads from Pieria to Perrhaebia (see Fig. 17), moved her court forward to Pydna, and appointed Aristonoüs as her commander-in-chief for the campaign. But Cassander anticipated her. He sent one force under Callas to pin down Polyperchon and another to occupy the Petra pass—it arrived first and kept possession—and then at the head of his main force he descended towards Pydna.

Olympias and her court could have escaped by sea. She chose to stay at Pydna, in the belief that her other forces, her friends in Macedonia and her Greek allies would come to her aid. It was a false hope. Alexander invaded the Peloponnese; most of Polyperchon's army deserted when Callas offered them higher pay; and another of Cassander's generals, Atarrhias, occupied the passes between Macedonia and Epirus against the forces of the Epirote Alliance. It was Aeacides, the Molossian king, who had persuaded the Epirote Alliance to support Olympias; but on finding the passes blocked the Epirote troops mutinied. When the mutineers were sent home by Aeacides, they persuaded the authorities of the Epirote Alliance to banish Aeacides and the troops which had stayed with him. The Epirote Alliance then made an alliance with Cassander. He sent another general, Lyciscus, to be 'manager' (*epimeletes*) of its affairs.[1] Indeed it was only in central and eastern Macedonia that Olympias' officers had some success against the forces which were sent north by Cassander (D.S. 19. 50. 7).

The blockade of Pydna proceeded inexorably through the winter months (see Fig. 18). Cassander surrounded the fortified hill (now much eroded on the seaward side) with a palisade of stakes 'from sea to sea', blocked all landward approaches with his army, and patrolled the waters off shore with his fleet.[2] Starvation led to cannibalism among the defenders, and in answer to their appeal Olympias let some of the emaciated soldiers depart. Cassander had them carried round the cities of Lower Macedonia. A plan to escape on a quinquereme was betrayed. At last, in spring 316, Olympias capitulated, obtaining only

---

[1] D.S. 19. 36. 2–5; Paus. 1. 11. 3–4. See H*E* 561 ff. for the situation in Epirus.
[2] See H*Pydna* 31 for a description of the site and 32 n. 5 for a report of stakes being found in the Karagats river-bed.

one condition from Cassander, the promise of her personal safety. Her commander at Pella surrendered, but Aristonoüs held on at Amphipolis. Olympias ordered Aristonoüs to surrender, and he did so on Cassander's promise of his personal safety.

Cassander had no intention of honouring his promises. Since Aristonoüs was highly regarded as a Bodyguard of Alexander, Cassander did not bring him to trial. Instead, he arranged for the relatives of his enemies to do him to death. At his instigation an Assembly of Macedones conducted a trial, at which Olympias was neither present nor represented, and the relatives of the Macedonians she had killed were the prosecutors. The Assembly passed a sentence of death. Cassander then offered to smuggle her on a ship to Athens, but she had the good sense to refuse. Instead, she asked to make her own defence 'before an Assembly of all Macedones' (the first Assembly no doubt having been hastily convened).[1] Cassander did not risk such a confrontation. He sent a section of 200 soldiers to kill her, but not a single one dared face her. However, the relatives of her victims were at hand. They were let in and killed her, fearless and indomitable to the end. Cassander was said to have left her corpse unburied.[2] He tried to blacken her memory by spreading the allegation that she had instigated the murder of Philip II, honoured the assassin Pausanias (J. 9. 7. 1–11; *PA* 10. 6–7), and roasted Cleopatra and her baby to death (Paus. 8. 7. 7).

During the period 323–316 the huge amounts of gold and silver which had been accumulated in Asia by Alexander were kept under the control of the kings, and the officers and troops in charge of them obeyed no orders except those of the kings or the kings' representatives. There were further issues of Alexander's own coinages in gold staters and silver tetradrachms (Pl. I*a* and *d*),[3] and alongside them coins were minted with the title **ΒΑΣΙΛΕΩΣ ΦΙΛΙΠΠΟΥ** or **ΒΦΙΛΙΠΠΟΥ** in gold and silver, and sometimes just **ΦΙΛΙΠΠΟΥ** in bronze; this last form appeared also on coins minted at Lampsacus in silver and at Sidon in gold and silver.[4] Philip III's gold staters carried the head of Athena

---

[1] For a similar instance see *PA* 47. 1–4, where A. overcame the reluctance of his army by persuading a part only in the first instance to follow him in his expedition eastwards. Errington, *Gesch. Mak.* 120 does not mention Olympias' request.

[2] D.S. 19. 51. 3–5; J. 14. 6. 6–12. The statement about Olympias is not necessarily true, because Hieronymus, whom Diodorus was following, was an advocate of Antigonus' cause.

[3] Gaebler III. 2. 173 n. 1.

[4] Gaebler III. 2. 170 f.; *SNG* v Pl. 65 and 66. A large hoard of silver coins, found west of the Koritsa basin in Dassaretia and reported in *Iliria* 1985. 1. 167 ff., had 426 Alexander coins, of which only one had the title *basileus*, and 42 Philip III coins all with the title. The proportion shows that there were large issues in Europe of the Alexander silver coins after his death. All these coins, tetradrachms, and drachms alike, had the head of Heracles and on the reverse Zeus enthroned and holding an eagle.

and on the reverse a Nike with a stylis, and his silver tetradrachms and drachms the head of a young Heracles and on the reverse Zeus enthroned with an eagle on his outstretched arm. These were in the tradition of Alexander's first coinages after the battle of Issus.[1] Philip's stater and tetradrachm both carried the letters of two mint-officials: **M** and **ΛY** (the former appearing also on some Alexander tetradrachms). Two of Philip's bronze issues had **ΛY** towards the edge. There was no connection here with the general Lysimachus. The bronze coins were issued probably for local exchange within Macedonia and the Balkan area. They carry traditional features, such as the rider on a prancing horse, the head of Apollo laurel-wreathed, the club of Heracles, and his bow and quiver.[2]

An *exhedra* or resting-place for pilgrims was dedicated by 'Kings Philip [and] Alexander to the Great Gods' at the famous sanctuary in Samothrace, where Philip II and Olympias had met during their initiation into the cult of the Cabeiri. It had a fine façade of white marble with six Doric columns, carried an inscription of dedication in large letters on the architrave, and was in a conspicuous position near the entrance to the sanctuary. It has been conjectured that the large Hall of Initiation with its apsidal end and evidence of frescoes in several colours was built by the same two kings; but the dedicatory inscription has not been found.[3] It is impossible to tell which of the 'managers of the kings' was responsible for initiating this policy.

4. *Cassander, Polyperchon, and Antigonus (316–315 B.C.)*

Thus in spring 316 the cause of the rebels triumphed both in Europe and in Asia. It might seem to us natural for them to have proclaimed a republic. They did not do so, because the Macedonians and the Asians were wedded to kingship as the only acceptable political form, hallowed by centuries of tradition and reaching its acme in the achievements of Philip and Alexander. Thus when the victorious Antigonus entered Persia, he was held worthy of 'royal status' by the Persians (D.S. 19. 48. 1). The Macedonian soldiers, whose support was essential to any Macedonian commander, had no use for republicanism, even though many of them had followed Cassander,

---

[1] See H*A* 284 (a) and (b).

[2] I stress my point about the letters **ΛY**, because Gaebler III. 2. 172 nos. 5 and 6 sought to identify them with Lysimachus in the case of the Alexander IV bronze coins.

[3] See H. A. Thompson in *M–G* 179 and A. Frazer in *M–G* 195. A third building, the great Altar, has been attributed to Arrhidaeus; but the restoration of the fragmentary inscription is uncertain, and I consider it unlikely that in A.'s lifetime Arrhidaeus was able to make his own dedication, quite apart from his absence in Asia for eleven years and being of unsound mind. See n. 32 by H. A. Thompson in *M–G* 188 for references.

Antigonus, and Ptolemy in their war against the kings and Polyperchon in pursuit of power, booty, high wages, and bounties. Nor were they disappointed. Antigonus, for example, gave ample satisfaction to his supporters in the months after his victory; for he awarded satrapies to some of his leading officers and large sums to his soldiers. As he moved westwards, he seized for himself the enormous treasuries of Alexander which had hitherto been respected in Media, at Susa, and in Cilicia. But the satisfaction of their desires did not mean that in 316 the soldiers would have accepted either a republic or Antigonus as their king, if he had proposed it.

The centre of attention was Alexander IV, now seven years old. Cassander placed him and his mother Roxane at Amphipolis for safe-keeping,[1] because the civil war was far from finished. He himself married Thessalonice, the daughter of Philip II and so the aunt of Alexander IV, and it is to be presumed, though nowhere stated in the extant accounts, that Cassander was appointed 'manager' of his nephew by marriage. For Cassander's aim was to make his position legitimate. It was with this purpose that in summer 316 he gave a magnificent funeral at Aegeae to the remains of Philip III and Eurydice (they had been killed nine months before) and to those of Eurydice's mother, Cynane (she had been killed in Asia six years before). Thus Cassander constituted himself defender of the monarchy and the champion of the surviving members of the Temenid house.[2]

He advertised his own importance by giving his name to a new city which he founded, Cassandreia, on the promontory of Pallene.[3] The refugees who survived from the destruction of Olynthus by Philip in 348 and the citizens of the small towns of Pallene were drafted into the

---

[1] D.S. 19. 52. 4, adding the removal of the Royal Pages and the treatment of the king as if he were a private person, belongs to the propaganda of Antigonus (cf. 19. 61. 3), which Diodorus' source, Hieronymus, was anxious to promote and justify. In fact the Royal Pages, being recruited at the age of fourteen, were too old to be associated with Alexander IV, who was only six or seven. Diodorus also says that Cassander had already decided to kill Alexander and his mother; that happened six years later!

[2] D.S. 19. 52. 5; *FGrH* 73 (Diyllus) F 1. Diodorus implies that Cassander was acting 'in a regal manner'. But it was in every way appropriate that Cassander arranged the funeral, as he had been appointed 'administrator of the kingdom' by Philip III and Eurydice (J. 14. 5. 3–4) and was acting now in that capacity for the child king. The supposition of Tarn in *CAH* 6. 482 that Cassander thereby 'claimed to be the successor of the old national kings, Perdiccas III and Philip II...and in effect treated Alexander [?III or IV or both] as an illegitimate interloper' reveals a total misunderstanding of the importance which Alexander III and Alexander IV had in the eyes of the Macedonians in 316. Tarn's view has been frequently repeated, e.g. by Cary 20 and 25, who wrote of 'Alexander's dynasty coming to an end in 316' and of 'Alexander's vacant throne' in that year. See also W. L. Adams 24 f.

[3] Tarn, loc. cit., 'the name shows that Cassander treated Alexander IV as formally deposed', has been generally accepted; but it is to be noted that Alexander III was not king when he founded his first 'Alexander city', and that we do not know of any new city being named after a child king.

new city. He founded also Thessalonica, named after the aunt of Alexander IV, and peopled it with the inhabitants of many neighbouring towns. Both cities flourished as centres of the trade which flowed from the Balkans to the Thermaic Gulf and thence into the Aegean world.[1] See Figs. 3 and 7.

Cassander's first task was to defeat Polyperchon and his son Alexander, who were respectively in Aetolia and in the Peloponnese. Having called up all fit Macedonians, no doubt in the name of Alexander IV, Cassander fought his way through the pass of Thermopylae, which the Aetolians were defending, and he gained the approval of the Boeotian League for a new project, the refounding of Thebes. His aim was to create in central Greece a counterweight to the powerful Aetolian League. At the same time his action was interpreted as a reversal of the policy of Alexander, the destroyer of Thebes. It was therefore welcomed by Athens, where Cassander's nominee Demetrius was in control, and by states as far afield as Italy and Sicily, which sent men or money to rebuild the walls and the public buildings of Thebes.[2]

As the Isthmus was securely held by the army of Alexander, Cassander transported his soldiers in boats and his elephants on barges built for the purpose to Epidaurus (see Fig. 10). He then forced Argos to come over to his side, gained the support of Hermione, and campaigned successfully in Messenia; but he failed in his main purpose, to draw Alexander into battle. At the end of 316 he returned as he had come, leaving a garrison at Argos and placing a covering force at the northern end of the Isthmus. This, however, was not his only theatre of operations; for he had sent another army into Asia, which was successful in penetrating as far inland as Cappadocia (D.S. 19. 60. 2), a very important recruiting ground for cavalry. It is arguable that Cassander should have concentrated both his armies against Alexander at the Isthmus and forced a battle with a view to gaining complete control of the Greek mainland in this critical year. But he wanted, it seems, to establish the right of Alexander IV to rule also over Asia,[3] where he knew that his previous associate, Antigonus, was extending his personal power.

The year 315 was dominated by the sixty-seven-year-old Antigonus, who was as capable, ruthless, and ambitious as Cassander. His own constitutional position was clear enough. He had been duly appointed at Triparadeisus in 321 by Antipater as manager of the kings and by the Assembly of the Macedones as 'general of the royal army' and 'general in Asia'; but only for the duration of the war against Eumenes

---

[1] Str. 7 frs. 21, 24, 25, and 27.   [2] D.S. 19. 52. 6; 53. 1; 54. 2.

[3] Cary 22, limiting Cassander's aims and outlook to Europe, failed to note this passage.

(D.S. 18. 39. 7 and 40. 1). His victory in the winter of 317/16 terminated that appointment. Thenceforth he held no office. Yet he was *de facto* in command of a huge army. He proceeded then to act as if he were 'Lord of Asia', and he was welcomed as such by the Persians; for they being aware of his desire to emulate Alexander in being King of Asia greeted him with the honours due to a king (D.S. 19. 48. 1; cf. Polyaen. 4. 6. 13 fin.).[1] He behaved in an arbitrary manner in awarding the commands of the satrapies; for while he consulted his Friends, he did not take his proposals to the Assembly of Macedones for confirmation. Those he feared most were the officers who had earned higher distinctions than he had during the reign of Alexander: in particular three of Alexander's Bodyguards, being Pithon, Peucestes, and Seleucus. He lured Pithon into a trap and prosecuted him first before the Council of his Friends and then before the Assembly of the Macedones. Pithon was convicted and executed (D.S. 19. 46; Polyaen. 4. 6. 14).[2] He deposed Peucestes from his satrapal command and expelled him from his satrapy, Persis, without rhyme or reason (D.S. 19. 48. 5–6). And although Seleucus, as satrap of Babylonia, paid every honour to Antigonus, he was treated as a subordinate under suspicion and wisely fled to the court of another Bodyguard, Ptolemy, satrap of Egypt (D.S. 19. 55. 2–3). The most blatant example of Antigonus' autocratic behaviour was his seizure of the treasuries of the kings at Ecbatana, Susa, and Cyinda (in Cilicia); for he took what others had respected since the death of Alexander in 323.

Within the confines of Asia Antigonus relied on the power of money and the loyalty of the well-paid non-Macedonian troops under his command; for there was no organized army in Asia to oppose him. It was when he planned to enter Europe, and in the words of Seleucus to win 'all the kingdom of the Macedones' (D.S. 19. 56. 2), that he needed to present himself not as an autocratic potentate, but as a royalist, a champion of Alexander IV. The necessary sleight of hand was not beyond him. He planned first to attract to his side the two men in Europe who had an untarnished record of loyalty to the Crown, Polyperchon and Alexander; for if he could win their support, he would accuse their enemy in Macedonia, Cassander, of being a rebel. His agent, Aristodemus, set off for Laconia with 1,000 talents. With

---

[1] The last words of Polyaenus, Ἀντίγονος δὲ ἁπάσης τῆς Ἀσίας βασιλεὺς ἀνηγορεύθη echo those of *PA* 34. 1, concerning Alexander III after his victory at Gaugamela, βασιλεὺς δὲ τῆς Ἀσίας Ἀλέξανδρος ἀνηγορευμένος. Since no general called himself 'king' until much later, these words may have occurred in a longer text which Polyaenus has abbreviated and have referred to the 10,000 Persians in the army and not to the Macedonians.

[2] If both authors were abbreviating a longer account by Hieronymus, Antigonus may have made use of both stages, as Alexander III had done in dealing with Philotas (C. 6. 8. 1–15).

Sparta's permission he recruited 8,000 mercenaries within her territory (mainly at Taenarum), and offering this army and much money as a bait he persuaded Polyperchon to accept appointment by Antigonus as 'general of the Peloponnese', and Alexander to visit Antigonus in Phoenicia, where a treaty of friendship with Antigonus was concluded (D.S. 19. 61. 1).

Now that the scenario was established, Antigonus convened an Assembly of all Macedones in the vicinity, that is of his soldiers, who for the most part had been brought from Macedonia by Antipater in 321, and of the ex-soldiers who had settled in Phoenicia.[1] Their loyalties, he knew, were to the Crown in the person of Alexander IV. Moreover, these soldiers looked back to the great Assembly at Triparadeisus, where their general, Antipater, had made the definitive constitutional settlement. It was in furtherance of that settlement that they had hunted down and executed 'the public enemy', Eumenes, and they had in principle supported Antipater and then his general in Europe, Polyperchon, as successive managers of the kings and now of the surviving king. The speech of Antigonus was, no doubt, a *tour de force*, as the summary in D.S. 19. 61. 1–2 indicates. He denounced Cassander as the murderer of Olympias, the incarcerator of Roxane and the king, the violator of Thessalonice in a forced marriage, the friend of Macedonia's bitterest enemies—the Olynthians and the Thebans—and the usurper of the Macedonian throne. The Assembly roared out in anger. Antigonus made the proposal that Cassander should be declared a public enemy unless he razed the cities of Cassandreia and Thebes, restored Alexander IV and Roxane from prison to their people, and agreed to obey Antigonus 'as the properly constituted general and as the one who had taken over the management of the monarchy' (D.S. 19. 61. 3 τῷ καθεσταμένῳ στρατηγῷω καὶ τῆς βασιλείας παρειληφότι τὴν ἐπιμέλειαν Ἀντιγόνῳω). The proposal was carried: it became 'the decree of the Macedones with Antigonus', τὰ δεδογμένα τοῖς μετ' Ἀντιγόνου Μακεδόσι (D.S. 19. 62. 1).

To borrow a term from the game of chess, Antigonus had castled very neatly. But so had Cassander; for the Assembly of Macedones in Macedonia had, no doubt, elected Cassander to be both 'general' and 'manager of the king'. Antigonus was thus the first to take the formal step which split the Macedonian state into two separate Assemblies, each claiming to be a sovereign body. Three of Antigonus' enemies—

---

[1] D.S. 19. 61. 1. The Loeb edition misprints as παρεπιδημόντων, and the translation by R. M. Geer 'of the aliens who were dwelling there' is misleading in that it implies aliens of any race, although he corrects that implication in his footnote. Errington, *Gesch. Mak.* 129 called them Antigonus' 'sonstigen Anhänger'.

Ptolemy, Lysimachus, and Seleucus—were also on the side of the king; for they had been appointed as satraps by the properly constituted Assembly, first of Perdiccas at Babylon and then of Antipater at Triparadeisus, and they, like Cassander, were now fighting on behalf of Alexander IV against the rebel Antigonus. This war of words was not meaningless. By his decree Antigonus did confirm the loyalty of his own Macedonians to himself, and he hoped to obtain the obedience of the generals and the satraps of the 'upper satrapies', who had hitherto suspected Antigonus of aiming to depose the kings and seize power himself, but might now be persuaded to see in him the staunch royalist, the avenger of Olympias, and the defender of Roxane, Thessalonice, and Alexander IV (cf. J. 15. 1. 3).

On the same occasion Antigonus persuaded his Assembly to decree that all the Greeks should be free, ungarrisoned, and autonomous (D.S. 19. 61. 3). This was the antithesis of the policy which had been instituted by Antipater and inherited by Cassander; and it was a return to the declared policy of Philip II and Alexander III, which Polyperchon had resuscitated. Antigonus' aim was forward-looking: to split Macedonian policy in the Aegean and in Europe, and to win over the Greek states to his side. He publicized his policy in Greece. But so did Ptolemy; for he too declared himself in favour of freedom for the Greek states, and he had a powerful fleet as well as economic resources to implement the policy. The effect of all this on the Greek states was, foreseeably, a new outbreak of *stasis*, fomented by external interventions. The effect of splitting the Macedonian state was bound to be damaging to the status and the resources of Macedonia.

Could such divisive policies have been avoided? Antipater had managed to unite the Macedonian armies after the death of Perdiccas; and in theory Antigonus might have done so after the death of Eumenes. What prevented this happening was the naked ambition of Antigonus and his cavalier treatment of Seleucus; for when Antigonus did have second thoughts and sought a friendly settlement with Ptolemy, Lysimachus, and Cassander, they had already seen behind his mask and they had been forewarned by Seleucus (D.S. 19. 56. 1–4). Even so, they did not reject Antigonus' overtures. They sent envoys, who were brought before the Council of Antigonus' Friends in Syria. There they proposed a sharing of the treasure seized by Antigonus and a division of the satrapies, which would extend the spheres of Cassander and Lysimachus into parts of Asia Minor and of Ptolemy into Syria, re-establish Seleucus as satrap of Babylonia, and leave Antigonus in charge of the remaining satrapies in Asia which were both numerous and rich in resources. All four were to be united, no doubt, in recognition of Alexander IV as the king of Macedon.

Quadripartite settlement of this kind might have worked; indeed it was to re-emerge after four years of civil war. The proposals of the envoys received a harsh reply, not apparently from the Council of Friends, but from Antigonus himself. He preferred war, civil war, to any form of compromise (D.S. 19. 56. 4–57. 2; J. 15. 1. 1–2).

VII

THE AMBITION OF ANTIGONUS, THE END OF THE TEMENID HOUSE, AND CLAIMS TO KINGSHIP

1. *The abortive civil war and the treaty of 311 B.C.*[1]

ANTIGONUS started his war with enormous financial reserves—more than 45,000 talents—as compared with those of his opponents, and he was able to buy or requisition all he wanted in the way of men and materials. In consequence he expected to overcome quickly his most serious disadvantage, the total lack of a fleet (D.S. 19. 58. 6). He hired 8,000 loggers, 1,000 teams and their teamsters, and thousands of shipwrights, who converted the cedars and cypresses of Mt. Lebanon into warships, some of unparalleled size,[2] in the shipyards of Tripolis, Byblus, and Sidon; and other shipwrights worked in Cilicia and in Rhodes with local or imported timber. Even so he had to wait till 313 before he had a fleet large enough to dominate the Aegean. His enormous resources enabled him too to mount a large-scale siege of Tyre, which was as necessary for him as it had been for Alexander, because in each case the Phoenician fleet, led by Tyrians, was in service with his enemies. But the siege cost Antigonus fifteen months of effort. In terms of strategy he boxed cleverly against all his opponents, but failed to concentrate on knocking out the one who mattered most, Ptolemy, the leading sea power in 315 and 314. Because he engaged on so many fronts and was a man of sixty-seven, he had need of capable and experienced lieutenants. These he rarely had; for his own ruthless methods had liquidated or alienated the most experienced commanders. Instead, he relied greatly on young men of his own family—two nephews,

---

[1] The evidence for this section comes mainly from D.S. 19. 57–105. Despite Diodorus' own confusion at 19. 77. 1, the chronology is made clear in the narrative by the mentions of winter quarters for 314/13 at 19. 68. 5 and 69. 2, 313/12 at 19. 77. 7, and 312/11 at 19. 89. 2. Diodorus seems to have drawn for the Macedonian world on two sources: Hieronymus, favourable to Antigonus and giving such details as army and navy strengths (e.g. 58 and 62), and Diyllus, favourable to Ptolemy, less detailed in military and naval matters and more interested in internal Greek affairs (e.g. 63–4). Some obscurities, such as what happened to Cassander's garrison in Apollonia in 70. 7, 78. 1, and 89. 1, may be due to changes of source or to Diodorus' incompetence, or both.

[2] See W. W. Tarn, *Hellenistic Military and Naval Developments* (Cambridge, 1930) 132.

Polemaeus (so in IG II². 1. 469) and Dioscourides, and his son Demetrius, who started disastrously and paid little heed to his older advisers who had served with Alexander (Nearchus, Philip, and Pithon).

When Antigonus started, he was virtually Lord of Asia. His position was gradually eroded. In 315 Asander, satrap of Caria, joined his opponents and opened up a new front which cost Antigonus much effort and soon drew him from his chosen and best base, Phoenicia, to the highlands of Turkey in Greater Phrygia. While he was there, the inexperience of Demetrius was exploited by Ptolemy, who fought a pitched battle at Gaza, killed 500 (mainly Macedonians), and captured 8,000 (mainly mercenaries).[1] He took over Phoenicia and Syria for a short time. During it he enabled Seleucus to reach Babylonia and open up a new front, which sapped the resources and the reputation of Antigonus. On whom could Antigonus rely to hold that front? He sent Demetrius, whose tactics of raiding and plundering merely alienated the peoples of the eastern satrapies. It was the reverses in Asia which led Antigonus to make peace in 311.

His four opponents were faithful to their pact. Antigonus tried, but failed, to make a separate peace with Ptolemy in 315 (19. 64. 8) and then with Cassander in 314 (19. 75. 6). Ptolemy and Seleucus saved Cyprus from Antigonus (19. 57. 4; 62. 5; 79. 4–5) and intervened in Caria when Antigonus planned to invade Europe (19. 68. 2–4); and they tried to help Cassander in Greece in 315 (19. 62. 5 and 64. 4). Lysimachus was steadfast in guarding the gateway to Europe at the Hellespont and the Bosporus; he made that his first priority in the allied cause (19. 73 and 77. 7). Cassander had to bear the brunt of Antigonus' offensive on the Greek mainland. At first he operated in Cappadocia, Caria, and the Hellespont (19. 57. 4; 68. 2), which helped his colleagues; and later, when he was confined to Europe, his unabating resistance drew troops from Antigonus which might have been used against Ptolemy and Lysimachus. It was primarily the mutual co-operation of these four men which thwarted the ambition of Antigonus. They preserved the position of Alexander IV.

The objective of Antigonus was Macedonia. It was the heart of 'all the kingdom of the Macedones', on which he had set his sights, and it was also the most vulnerable of the territories of the coalition. We shall follow its history in greater detail for the years 315–311.

Cassander had three main theatres of operation: his western and northern neighbours, Greece north of the Isthmus, and the Peloponnese. These were in decreasing order of importance for the safety of

---

[1] 19. 80–5; *PD* 5. For losses D.S. 19. 85. 3 is preferable.

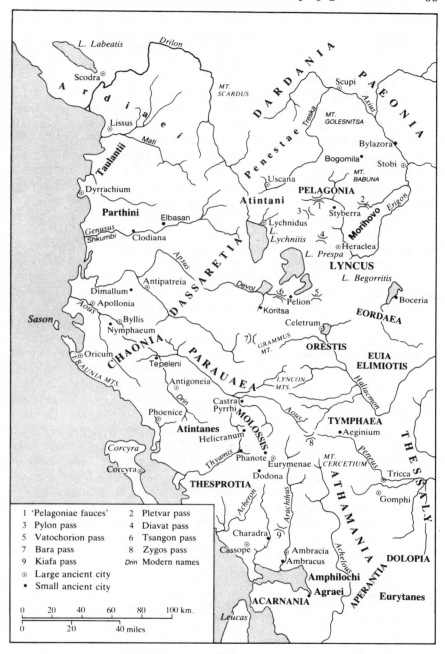

FIG. 8. WESTERN MACEDONIA AND THE ADRIATIC COAST

Macedonia itself. We shall consider each in turn. The recently formed Epirote Alliance held an integral position in the first theatre (see Fig. 8). It was immediately adjacent to Macedonia, its large army had been trained in Macedonian weaponry and tactics during the period of Philip's protectorate, and it had shown its prowess in Italy under the command of the Molossian king, Alexander. Geographically it lay between Aetolia, Cassander's most dangerous Greek enemy, and Corcyra, whose seapower provided an entry to Leucas, Apollonia, and Epidamnus; and the Illyrians, who had become familiar with Macedonian weaponry and tactics during the campaigns of Alexander the Great in the Balkans and in Asia. In 317 the Epirote Alliance, comprising southern and central Epirus, had made alliance with Cassander and had accepted his general Lyciscus as its 'manager and general' (19. 36. 5 ἐπιμελητὴν ἅμα καὶ στρατηγόν; see also p. 103 above).[1] In the first capacity Lyciscus had wide administrative powers in Epirus. In the second he commanded the Epirote levy in place of the new Molossian king, Neoptolemus II, a minor, whom the Molossians elected to succeed the banished Aeacides.[2] For two years this alliance, which made Epirus into a protectorate under Macedonian administration, gave to Cassander a continuous area of control from the Ionian Sea to the Thermaic Gulf.

While this alliance held good, Cassander tried to rectify what was evidently a dangerous situation in Illyris—a combination or an incipient combination of Corcyra, the two Greek cities on the coast, and the group of Illyrian tribes ruled by Glaucias, the Taulantii. In 314 Cassander attacked Apollonia. He captured it at the first onslaught (19. 67. 6). Advancing north and crossing the Genusus (Shkumbi),[3] he defeated the army of Glaucias, tricked the people of Epidamnus by making a feigned retreat (Polyaen. 4. 11. 4), and placed a garrison in the city. He left Glaucias on his throne under a treaty which required him not to attack any of Cassander's allies. Among these were the tribes of the Epirote Alliance, into which the Chaones had entered during the period of Lyciscus' management.[4] In this year Lyciscus was in Acarnania, no doubt because Neoptolemus II had come of age and taken military command. The fact that Cassander in person had conducted the campaign in the north-west showed its

---

[1] One of several passages which show that the *epimeletes* was not a military commander, as has been maintained often, e.g. by Hornblower 13 with other references. See H*SMO* 157 n. 15.

[2] See Klotzsch 112 n. 1 and H*E* 567 on P*Pyrrh* 2. 1; *contra* Cross 106 f. and Franke, *AE* 44. Neoptolemus, son of Alexander (ob. 330) and Cleopatra (married in 336), was born probably in 332, as he came of age at eighteen *c.* 314.

[3] 19. 67. 6 has 'Hebrus' mistakenly. The error is probably Diodorus's.

[4] *SIG* 653. 4 having 'Apeirotai round Phoenice', not 'Chaones round Phoenice', who honoured Lyciscus. See H*E* 567 and 641.

importance in his eyes. Probably during it he founded a Macedonian stronghold, Antipatreia (Berat), on the inland side of the coastal plain between Epidamnus and Apollonia.[1]

In 313 the whole arrangement collapsed. Glaucias laid siege to Apollonia. A passing Spartan adventurer, Acrotatus, did his good deed by persuading Glaucias and Apollonia to make a treaty, which involved the departure of Cassander's garrison. Meanwhile trouble arose in Epirus. The exiled Molossian ex-king, Aeacides, the enemy of Cassander, seized the throne by a *coup d'état*, raised a strong army of anti-Macedonian tribesmen, and planned to join the forces of the Aetolian League. Fortunately a Macedonian army in Acarnania, commanded by Cassander's brother, Philip, intercepted and defeated the Epirotes. He captured fifty of Aeacides' most influential supporters and sent them in chains to Cassander. Then, as Aeacides and part of his force had escaped and joined the Aetolians, he won a victory over them. Aeacides died during or after the action (19. 74. 5; Paus. 1. 11. 4). Corcyra took advantage of the confusion in Epirus to send help to Apollonia and Epidamnus, overpowered Cassander's garrison in the latter and gave the city to Glaucias (19. 78. 1). Apollonia was now free and hostile to Macedonia.

In 312 further trouble was caused when the Molossians elected Aeacides' brother, Alcetas, to be king. Since Alcetas II was a declared enemy of Cassander, the Macedonian general in charge of Acarnania, Lyciscus, invaded South Epirus at once and encamped near the capital city of the Cassopaeans, 'Cassopia' (19. 88. 1–3). Alcetas sent his older sons, Alexander and Teucer, to the cities of the Epirote Alliance to muster the full levy. He brought such troops as he had close to the camp of Lyciscus, whereupon being much outnumbered they deserted to Lyciscus. Alcetas took refuge in a strongly fortified city, Eurymenae (Kastritsa, at the southern end of the Lake of Ioannina),[2] and when Lyciscus came up in pursuit he was caught between Alcetas and the new levy and suffered defeat with heavy loss. However, another Macedonian general with an army arrived on the scene, defeated Alcetas and his sons, and captured Eurymenae, which was plundered by the Macedonians and razed to the ground. Cassander arrived at the head of an army soon afterwards. He negotiated with Alcetas, who had escaped to a stronghold, and recognized him as king on condition that the Epirote Alliance and Macedonia entered into a treaty of friendship. This was after all what Cassander wanted: amity between the two states and not a war of mutual attrition. But Alcetas was an unwise choice; for his dictatorial behaviour resulted in the assassination

---

[1] HE 567.　　　[2] HE 526 f.; for different views see Cabanes 123.

of him and two younger sons during a popular rising (19. 89. 3; Paus. 1. 11. 5).[1]

After coming to terms with Alcetas Cassander advanced through North Epirus to Apollonia. His intelligence must have been faulty; for he found outside the walls a great army of the citizens and their allies, among whom were certainly the Illyrians and probably the Corcyraeans. He attacked, but his relatively small force was defeated with serious loss and he withdrew to Macedonia, as winter was at hand. The Corcyraeans celebrated the victory by helping the people of Leucas to expel Cassander's garrison.

As Cassander withdrew towards Macedonia, he received news of another danger. See Fig. 3. A northern-Illyrian tribe, the Autariatae, was moving southwards in a mass migration and threatening the northern frontier of his kingdom.[2] Instead of opposing them with force, he made a treaty of alliance and gave them lands to cultivate within the kingdom, close to its northern frontier, no doubt on condition that they would do military service at his request. In this policy he was following the example of earlier kings and in particular Philip II.[3]

Fear of invasion by the northern barbarians was a common bond between Cassander and his brother-in-law Lysimachus. In the previous year, 313, some northern Thracians and the neighbouring Scythians joined some Greek cities on the Black Sea coast, which had expelled garrisons imposed by Lysimachus.[4] Well known for his daring, Lysimachus marched at speed across Thrace and over Mt. Haemus to Odessus. The threat of siege was enough there and at Istria. But when he moved towards the instigator of the revolt, Callatis, he met large forces of the Thracians and the Scythians who were in alliance with the Greek cities. Undeterred by numbers, he attacked at once. The Thracians deserted to him, and the Scythians were defeated and driven beyond his frontier. Meanwhile Antigonus was quick to take advantage of Lysimachus' absence in the north. He sent a fleet with an expeditionary force into the Black Sea and a separate land army into eastern Thrace, which marched probably up the Black Sea coast towards Callatis. Seuthes, king of the Odrysians, saw his chance

---

[1] We have no information about the Molossian king of the other branch, Neoptolemus II. He was overshadowed by Aeacides and Alcetas II, and then became sole king after this event, probably in 311.

[2] J. 15. 2. 1–2, where 'dum haec aguntur' pins the event to the year 312, while 'deinde' marks some passage of time, in fact some years. His statement that the migration was caused by a plague of frogs and mice may have been borrowed from a better attested example in App. *Illyr.* 4.

[3] *Macedonia* 63; J. 8. 6. 1.

[4] On the general situation there see G. Mihailov in *AM* 1. 84 and D. M. Pippidi in *AM* 2. 392 ff.

of winning independence and occupied the Haemus pass with a large force. Lysimachus heard only of the two expeditions sent by Antigonus. He left a detachment to maintain the siege of Callatis and hastened to the Haemus pass, which to his surprise was occupied. He attacked, and the result of a long action was that he lost 'not a few men', inflicted enormous casualties, and routed the enemy completely. He cornered and captured the separate land army (19. 73), and he sent envoys ahead to Byzantium. There Antigonus was knocking at the door, offering alliance. He had recalled his great fleet from Greek waters and brought a large army to the Asiatic side of the Propontis. Now was his chance to cross unopposed into Europe and march upon Macedonia. When the Byzantines heard of Lysimachus' victories and of his approach to their territory, they decided to remain neutral. Antigonus withdrew to winter quarters in Phrygia late in 313. Lysimachus alone of Alexander's generals came close to him in generalship.

The Greek mainland was the chief cockpit for the forces of Cassander and those of Antigonus (see Fig. 10). By supporting minority governments of an oligarchic character and supplying them perforce with garrisons, Cassander tied down too many troops and diminished his striking power. As champion of liberty, autonomy, and democracy, Antigonus imposed no garrisons (though his generals did for emergencies) and kept his troops on the offensive. As the forces of the two great powers passed to and fro over the small Greek city-states, the worst excesses of that *stasis* which Thucydides had described so vividly became a commonplace. For instance in 315 Cassander's general, Apollonides, burnt 500 democratic partisans alive at Argos, and Cassander himself let his oligarchic partisans have their way with their opponents at Orchomenus in Arcadia, with the result that suppliants were torn from the shrine of Artemis and slaughtered 'in breach of universal Greek standards of conduct' (19. 63). Similar atrocities occurred at Dyme in Achaea, where Antigonus' mercenaries joined in a massacre (19. 67).

The Peloponnese nearly passed into Cassander's control in 315, while Antigonus was building his fleet. Cassander even persuaded Polyperchon's son, Alexander, to change sides and become his own 'general of the Peloponnese', and he presided over the Nemean Games. But in 314 Aristodemus, the general of Antigonus, held his own, while Cassander was busy in central Greece and Epirus; and in 313, with Cassander deeply involved in the north-west area, the generals of Antigonus acquired all the Peloponnese except Sicyon, held by Alexander's widow, Cratesipolis, and Corinth, held by Polyperchon. The fighting then moved north of the Isthmus, except that one of Antigonus' generals, Telesphorus, turning adventurer, seized Elis city and plundered Olympia, and that Polemaeus went to convert Telesphorus and repaid the 500 talents of loot to the god of Olympia, Zeus (19. 87. 3).

Greece north of the Isthmus was the base Antigonus needed for launching an attack on Macedonia itself. There were at this time three military states of importance. Of these the Thessalian League seems to have remained neutral, or at least inactive. The Aetolian League was consistently opposed to Cassander, and in 314 when Alexander, the son of Polyperchon, who stood well with the Aetolians, changed sides, Aristodemus addressed the Assembly of the Aetolian League and confirmed its alliance with Antigonus. The Boeoian League supported Cassander in 316 when he refounded Thebes, but the presence of his garrison on the Cadmea was viewed with disfavour. Athens no longer counted as a military state; but it still had a fleet and its ruler, Demetrius of Phalerum, was dependent on Cassander.

In 314 Cassander moved with a large army into Acarnania, then at war with Aetolia, and persuaded the Acarnanians to concentrate their people in a number of walled cities, so that they would be better able to defend themselves (see Fig. 12). He left Lyciscus with a sufficient force to stiffen their resistance, and on his way to Epirus he brought Leucas into his alliance. In 313 a Macedonian invasion of Aetolia from Acarnania was planned, but it had to be postponed, because the Macedonian forces were diverted to Epirus. Their success there so alarmed the Aetolians that they and the Boeotians sent envoys to Antigonus in Asia and entered into a formal alliance with him, no doubt on the promise of military aid. Aware of this danger, Cassander took steps to block Antigonus' naval approaches to Boeotia through the Euripus channel. See Fig. 1. Since Athens threatened the southern entry, and Cassander's garrison at Chalcis controlled the narrows, Cassander took a fleet of thirty ships and an army to the northern entry and laid siege to Oreus (Histiaea). When his fleet was blockading the harbour and the city was about to fall to a violent assault, help arrived in the form of twenty ships from the Peloponnese and 100 ships from Asia. Fire-ships nearly destroyed the fleet of Cassander, but with the help of reinforcements sent by Athens (*IG* ii^2. 1. 682; D.S. 19. 75. 8) Cassander extricated himself from a dangerous situation.

In this year, 313, Antigonus was making a supreme effort to win the war. One army and one fleet were liberating the Greek cities on the Carian and Ionian coasts and installing democratic governments, which would help to isolate Asander, the satrap of Caria, from contact with his allies, Ptolemy and Seleucus. Another army and another fleet were on their way to pin down Lysimachus in north-eastern Thrace and prevent him from returning to hold the European side of the

Hellespont. As his fleets dominated the central Aegean basin (Fig. 7), he inspired the formation of a League of Islanders with Delos as its centre.[1] Now Antigonus sent an armada off to liberate Greece: 150 warships carrying 500 cavalry and 5,000 infantry, and twenty fully manned ships of the Rhodians, who espoused the cause of liberation. The supreme commander was Polemaeus, a nephew of Antigonus. He brought his armada through the southern entry and anchored near Aulis on the Boeotian coast, where he was joined by an army of the Boeotian League, which consisted of 1,300 cavalry and 2,200 infantry. He built a fortified camp at Salganeus on the mainland side of the narrows, facing Chalcis, and summoned the fleet operating off Oreus to join him. The combined forces, totalling some 60,000 men, were supplied mainly from granaries in Boeotia.[2] Cassander abandoned the siege of Oreus, moved his soldiers to Chalcis, and sent for help, primarily from the Euboeans, who were hostile to the Boeotians. He was in a desperate position.

At this point Antigonus made a fatal error. He recalled the entire fleet to Asia, where it was to support him personally in command of a large army for his planned invasion of Europe. As we have seen, the plan miscarried; for the envoys of Lysimachus persuaded the Byzantines to stay neutral. The departure of the entire fleet from Salganeus had meanwhile crippled the effectiveness of the army of Polemaeus and destroyed the reputation of Antigonus. Cassander had guessed the purpose of Antigonus, but he kept his sense of timing. Leaving his brother Pleistarchus in charge of Chalcis, he took his army across to Attica, captured Oropus on the way to Thebes, and formed an alliance with Thebes. Only then, when Polemaeus was cut off from Attica, did Cassander set off for Macedonia, in case Antigonus had crossed into Europe and was on the way to the eastern frontier of Macedonia. So ended the campaigning season of 313.

Throughout 312 Cassander was operating in Epirus and Illyris. Polemaeus and his Boeotian allies had a free hand. They defeated the garrisons of Cassander and gained possession of Chalcis, Oropus, Thebes, and probably Opus, and they received Thebes, Phocis, and Euboea into the alliance of Antigonus. To the west the Aetolian League was their staunch ally, and to the south they entered Attica and their presence caused Demetrius of Phalerum to open negotiations with Antigonus in Asia (D.S. 19. 78. 4). Apart from the episode of

---

[1] Known only from inscriptions. See Wehrli 113 ff. and Buraselis 67. Delos itself was freed probably in 314.

[2] Including 250 warships 'from Asia' alone. In 315 Antigonus had there 240 warships (19. 62. 8), and by 313 many more had come off the stocks. He had in addition a fleet in the Black Sea and a fleet in his home waters, i.e. off Phoenicia and Cilicia.

Telesphorus (pp. 157–8 above), Polemaeus had established a very sound foundation for an invasion of Macedonia in 311, if Antigonus should resume the offensive which he had initiated in 313. However, it was not to be so. For 312 saw also the crushing defeat of Demetrius at Gaza, the opening of a new front by Seleucus, and the ineffective raid by Demetrius on the adherents of Seleucus.[1]

[In 311] the group of Cassander, Ptolemy, and Lysimachus terminated hostilities against Antigonus and signed a treaty, wherein the following provisions were made. Until Alexander, son of Roxane, should reach maturity,[2] Cassander was to be general of Europe, Lysimachus was to be in charge of Thrace, and Ptolemy was to be in charge of Egypt and the contiguous states in Libya and Arabia, but Antigonus was to hold the leading position in all Asia, and the Greeks were to be autonomous. (D.S. 19. 105. 1).[3]

Although Antigonus chose later to represent himself as having granted a treaty at the request of the others, the fact is that the treaty set the seal upon the utter failure[4] of the war aims which he had publicly announced. He had set out in 315 to free the king and Roxane from (alleged) imprisonment, to force Cassander to his knees, and to become himself 'the properly constituted general and the one who had taken over the management of the monarchy' (D.S. 19. 61. 3). Now he left the king and Roxane in the care of Cassander, recognized Cassander as general in Europe, and confined himself to Asia (excluding Egypt). In 315 he had indeed been the leading authority in all Asia, but now he was still challenged by Asander in Caria and his word went for nothing in the easterly group of satrapies. His expenditure of men and money had been totally destructive and self-damaging. Even in relation to the Greek city-states he had achieved nothing of permanence. If he honoured the treaty, he would withdraw all his troops from Greece and desert his Greek allies. Thereafter the enactment of the articles giving the Greeks 'freedom and autonomy'[5] would be in fact at the discretion of each ruler within his own area.

---

[1] Marmor Parium (*FGrH* 239 B 16) put the defeat off Gaza in 312/11.

[2] At the age of eighteen, i.e. in summer 305. This was probably the age at which the Royal Pages graduated for full-time military service. We see from the case of Neoptolemus II that Molossian princes came of age at eighteen.

[3] This is a summary of the treaty, not a text of it. Préaux 1. 186 writes of 'zones d'influence', a vague term not used in ancient Greek. The areas were no doubt defined in the text of the treaty. Even in the summary they are quite precise, and Diodorus ends the section with a precise phrase for each general: τὴν ὑφ᾽ ἑαυτὸν τεταγμένην χώραν (19. 105. 4).

[4] Hieronymus, it seems, put a better complexion on the matter, and his influence through the text of Diodorus has misled many scholars. For instance, Rostovtzeff's judgement on the treaty of peace as 'a great diplomatic victory for Antigonus' (Rostovtzeff, *SEM* 1. 13) could hardly be farther from the truth.

[5] 'Freedom' was omitted by Diodorus, but can be supplied from other treaties. It is included in Antigonus' letter to Scepsis (see Welles 3 l. 2).

Ptolemy and Lysimachus kept the areas which they had had since 323. Cassander gained a much better position than he had had in 315. Then he had been one of the contestants for power in Greece, opposed by Polyperchon and Alexander and denounced by Antigonus as an imposter, a rapist, and a murderer. Now he was recognized as the protector of the king and Roxane and as 'the general of Europe', i.e. the officer in control of the south-west Balkans, Macedonia, and Greece, a control which had in the past been judged compatible with the 'freedom and autonomy' of the Greek states.[1] These three did not bring Seleucus into the treaty.[2] On the other hand, they did not undertake to help Antigonus enforce his leadership over all Asia, and in any event they had no means geographically of sending help to Seleucus. He was left to fight his own battles outside the treaty.

The most important (and the most neglected) clause in the treaty is 'until Alexander, son of Roxane, should reach maturity'. It conditions all four appointments[3] both in the Greek language and in common sense. The Greek runs as follows in describing the treaty between two parties—the trio and Antigonus:

ἐν δὲ ταύταις ἦν Κάσανδρον μὲν εἶναι στρατηγὸν τῆς Εὐρώπης μέχρι ἂν Ἀλέξανδρος ὁ ἐκ Ῥωξάνης εἰς ἡλικίαν ἔλθῃ, καὶ Λυσίμαχον μὲν τῆς Θρᾴκης κυριεύειν, Πτολεμαῖον δὲ τῆς Αἰγύπτου καὶ τῶν συνοριζουσῶν ταύτῃ πόλεων κατά τε τὴν Λιβύην καὶ τὴν Ἀραβίαν, Ἀντίγονον δὲ ἀφηγεῖσθαι τῆς Ἀσίας πάσης, τοὺς δὲ Ἕλληνας αὐτονόμους εἶναι.[4]

The opening μέν is answered by the δέ of the other party, Antigonus, and the article about the Greeks is added with a δέ. As the phrase μέχρι ἄν...ἔλθῃ is common to all the clauses except the last, it is placed at the end of the first clausula; so too κυριεύειν, being common to Lysimachus and Ptolemy, is placed last in the first clausula. In common sense it is obvious that in the future, (if and) when Alexander should come of age his authority would not be limited to Cassander's fief and exclude, for

---

[1] See p. 133 above and Bengtson *Strat.* 1. 46 f.

[2] The attempt of Beloch 4. 1. 133 to foist Seleucus into this treaty has no merit; see Cary 384 and Simpson 29 f.

[3] Not so Cary 28 f., who applies it expressly to Cassander's appointment only, while Tarn in *CAH* 6. 489 and Rostovtzeff, loc. cit., did so without comment. Wehrli 53 raised the issue, but gave no ruling himself.

[4] The word κυριεύειν was used both of Lysimachus and Ptolemy. It is a very common and non-technical word in Diodorus (e.g. 19. 48. 6 [Xenophilus] κυριεύων τῶν ἐν Σούσοις χρημάτων). The expression used for Antigonus ἀφηγεῖσθαι τῆς Ἀσίας πάσης is reminiscent of Arrian's explanation of Perdiccas' office as chiliarch, ἐπιτροπὴ τῆς ξυμπάσης βασιλείας, which in that context meant charge of all the Kingdom of Asia (F 1 a 3; see p. 103 above). It seems that all commentators except J. Kromayer in *DLZ* 1912. 2663 and Errington, *Gesch. Mak.* 130 f., have assumed that the clause about Alexander reaching maturity applied to Cassander alone. Were the others rejecting the kingship of Alexander publicly except for the area of Macedonia itself, and doing so six years in advance?

instance, Thrace. No, the preservation of the king's rights ran for the whole area—for Europe, Asia, and Egypt—but not for the Greeks, who were to be 'free and autonomous'. In fact Alexander did not reach maturity. Was Cassander the only one to be affected by his demise? The answer is clear in the same chapter of Diodorus: 'Cassander, Lysimachus, and Ptolemy, and Antigonus too, and their associates were freed from the fears which they expected to arise from the king' (i.e. from Alexander becoming king indeed at the age of eighteen). They no longer had any need to account for their stewardship on that dread day.

The treaty has been hailed by some scholars who look for precedents to subsequent events as a treaty recognizing the 'Successor Kingdoms' as sovereign states.[1] At the time it was not so interpreted. There was no question then of denying the right of Alexander IV to continue as elected king and on reaching his majority to assume the reins of government. The four leaders of 311 were not called 'Successors' (διάδοχοι), but generals, satraps, and perhaps chiliarch, as men had been under Alexander the Great.[2] The treaty looked forward not to a splitting up of the areas conquered by Alexander into a number of sovereign states, but to Alexander's son and heir taking control of the whole area with a team of generals and satraps who were at peace with one another. It was a dream, alas, which did not come true.

2. The end of the Temenid house and the beginnings of the Successor Kingdoms[3]

That the Temenid house ruled was apparent from the coinage of Macedonia. As we have seen, Philip III coined in gold, silver, and bronze, and after his death it seems that coins were issued for the first time in the name of Alexander IV. The chief reason for believing this is that his issues were only a hemidrachm in silver and four types in bronze, presumably for circulation in Macedonia and the Balkan area from 315 until his death was officially announced.[4] In my opinion the hemidrachm carries the head of the boy king, a delightful portrait (Pl.

---

[1] e.g. *SVA* III no. 428 and p. 44 'seine Bedeutung liegt in der gegenseitigen Anerkennung der Diadochenreiche (mit Ausnahme des Reichs des Seleukos) als de facto souveräner Staaten.' Also Will 56.

[2] When Diodorus has to use a general term, he writes δυνάσται or occasionally οἱ περὶ Κάσανδρον καὶ Πτολεμαῖον καὶ Λυσίμαχον (19. 105. 1; cf. 20. 76. 7).

[3] For this period D.S. Book 20 and *PD* supplement one another. Both are derived from the account of Hieronymus. It seems that Justin drew for 15. 3. 1–15 and 4. 10 on a biographical source, i.e. on Satyrus' *Lives* for Lysimachus and Seleucus (as perhaps for J. 9. 7, J. 12. 14 and J. 12. 16; see H*THA* 88 ff. and 111 f.). For 15. 2. 3–17 and 4. 11–22 Justin was probably indebted to Hieronymus and added some stories from another source.

[4] Gaebler III 2. 171 ff. dates the coins to 323–311, overlapping those of Philip III.

I *e*); he wears a diadem without ends, as the youthful Caranus, founder of the house, does on coins of more than one reign (Volume II. 138 and 171).[1] The reverse of the hemidrachm has a rider on a prancing horse, with a running lion under the horse, and on one type a spearhead, and on another type a three-pronged weapon;[2] the lesser emblems may refer to hunting, the sport of the Macedonian kings. Bronze coins show the head of Apollo, laurel-wreathed, and have the same reverse as the hemidrachm; or the head of a young Heracles and on the reverse his club and bow; or a thunderbolt in the centre of a Macedonian shield and on the reverse a plumed helmet. The name **ΑΛΕΞΑΝΔΡΟΥ** appears alone on most of these coins; on one bronze of his type the word **ΒΑΣΙΛΕΩΣ** appears; and **ΛΥ** occurs on four of Gaebler's six types (Pl. I *e*). As I maintained earlier, the **ΛΥ** had nothing to do with the general Lysimachus when it occurred on the coins of Philip III, and it seems to me that here too we find the same mint-official operating.[3]

During the war of 315–311 there had been heavy fighting for the Macedonian field army in Epirus and Illyris, and for Macedonian soldiers in eastern Thrace. Elsewhere the generals were careful to take turns in any one theatre, e.g. in Cyprus, where Antigonus' forces operated in 315 and Ptolemy's in 313. When rival forces were in one theatre, they tended to avoid confrontation: thus Polemaeus stayed inactive at Salganeus while Cassander was in action near by, and when Cassander withdrew to Macedonia Polemaeus went into action. The huge fleet of Antigonus did not fight in Greek waters or in the Propontis; it was used rather in a game of manœuvre and counter-manœuvre rather like a queen in chess. It was different with the Greeks. Plenty of them were killed in alternating waves of *stasis* by their fellow citizens and sometimes by the troops of the intervening generals. On the comparatively rare occasions when forces of Macedonians faced one another, they often either made a truce or changed sides or surrendered and were re-employed (D.S. 19. 59. 2; 60. 2; 63. 4; 73. 10; 75. 1; 92. 4). In the one pitched battle, at Gaza, those killed were little more than 500, while 8,000 were taken prisoners of war (19. 85. 3). In the night operation at Myus there were perhaps no casualties at all, since Demetrius 'mastered the enemy without a battle' (19. 93. 2). That was the ideal achievement for a Macedonian commander (cf. Polyaen. 4. 6. 7).

---

[1] I have not seen this suggestion elsewhere.   [2] Gaebler calls it a 'Dreizack'.

[3] Gaebler accepts the view of L. Müller, *Die Münzen des thrak. Königs Lysimachos* 39 f., that Lysimachus 'als Statthalter erst in Namen Philipps III., dann Alexanders IV. und schliesslich nach des letzeren Tode, als es keinen König mehr gab, dessen Name angebracht werden konnte' minted some coins which Gaebler names on his p. 172, note to no. 5. See p. 144 above for **ΛΥ** on coins of Philip III.

The losses which the Macedonians had suffered in the north-west area seem to have weakened the position of Cassander in Macedonia and caused him to take no action in Greece. In 310 the Autariatae were once again on the move. They broke into the kingdom of Macedonia, overran the upper Axius valley, and brought Cassander and his army into action. He restored the authority of the Paeonian king Audoleon in this area, came to terms with the Autariatae, and settled 20,000 of them, together with their wives and children, in the border territory of Parorbelia (see Figs. 1 and 3). Meanwhile, despite the treaty, Antigonus kept his nephew Polemaeus and his forces in Greece; and he tried to win over his aged contemporary Polyperchon, who was an enemy of Cassander and held the important key to the Peloponnese, Corinth. In 310 Polemaeus, feeling slighted perhaps by Antigonus' intrigue with Polyperchon, made an alliance with Cassander and sent troops to help Phoenix rebel against Antigonus and hold the cities of the Hellespont. Also in 310 Ptolemy accused Antigonus of breaking the agreement about the autonomy of the Greeks by installing garrisons in some cities, and he sent an expeditionary force to Cilicia Tracheia, where it drove out Antigonus' troops. Casting his net wider, he asked the Greek cities in the domains of Cassander and Lysimachus to join with him against Antigonus. Although the main theatre of operations for Antigonus was in the East against Seleucus, he sent armies to the Hellespont and to Cilicia. Thus civil war broke out again in 310. It was destined to last for nine years (D.S. 20. 2. 3 and 19. 1–5).

In the summer of 309 Polyperchon and his army (estimated at 20,000 infantry and 1,000 cavalry in 310; see D.S. 20. 20. 3)[1] marched from Aetolia through western Thessaly to the border of the Macedonian canton, Tymphaea, where he had his own supporters as a scion of the royal house of the Tymphaei (see Fig. 8). He was escorting Barsine and her son Heracles, whom he intended to place upon the throne of Macedonia. Cassander and his army were encamped at the frontier. Fearing that his Macedonians would desert and favour the restoration to power of the royal house in the person of Heracles, Cassander persuaded Polyperchon that it was better for Polyperchon to kill Heracles and receive every honour and high command from Cassander than to make Heracles king and find himself rapidly displaced by other favourites. The result was that the armies disbanded, Heracles and his mother Barsine were murdered, and Polyperchon, recovering his

---

[1] The figures for 310 came evidently from Hieronymus. As Polyperchon 'was collecting money' then for his enterprise, we may be sure that he drew large subsidies from Antigonus and that he recruited mercenaries in the Peloponnese. The figures may not include the Aetolian levy which joined him presumably in 309. Polyperchon was already in touch with dissidents inside Macedonia.

estates in Macedonia and commanding an army of 4,000 Macedonian infantry and 500 Thessalian cavalry in accordance with his agreement with Cassander, set off for the Peloponnese, but was diverted by the opposition of the Boeotians and some Peloponnesians into Locris, where he spent the winter of 309/8. His callous duplicity had in effect made him a mere lieutenant of his old enemy, Cassander.

The statements of Diodorus that Heracles was 'about seventeen years old' in the archon year 310/9 and 'king' in 309/8 agree with a remark in J. 13. 2. 7 that Heracles was a boy ('puer') in 323. On the other hand, his half-brother Alexander, born in August 323, became thirteen early in that archon year and was then five years off maturity.[1] Those Macedonians, and they must have been very many, who viewed the renewal of civil war with disgust, saw the best way to peace and unity in the election of Heracles as active reigning king. Cassander's fears of his own Macedonians deserting to join Heracles were well and truly founded. To kill Heracles was to deprive the Macedonians of that hope and to relieve Cassander's fears—but only for a few years. For if Alexander were to become active king in 305, one of his first acts would be to avenge the death of his half-brother. Cassander could escape from that situation only by killing Alexander beforehand. One murder necessitated another murder, as it did for Macbeth.

It has generally been maintained that Cassander killed Alexander before he instigated Polyperchon to kill Heracles.[2] This view is based on the fact that Diodorus mentioned the killing of Alexander at 19. 105. 2, a chapter which came within his narrative of the archon year 311/10. But the deduction that the killing was therefore within that year is mistaken. It was the treaty at 19. 105. 1 which Diodorus was dating. At 19. 105. 2 he was looking forward to the future effects of the treaty: the ambitions of the generals, the killing of Alexander, and then the generals developing 'royal hopes', each holding his domain 'as if it were a kingdom won by the spear' since 'no one any longer existed to succeed to the realm'.[3] Diodorus had the years 310–306 in mind. The killing of Alexander—which he did not mention again—fell within that span of years.

Two authors mentioned the killing of Heracles before the killing of Alexander, and they attributed both to Cassander as the instigator.

[1] D.S. 20. 20. 1 and 28. 1. J. 15. 2. 3 made Heracles 'over fourteen', perhaps confusing Heracles and Alexander. See Beloch 4. 2. 124.
[2] So Tarn in *CAH* 6. 493, Beloch 4. 1. 138 f., Cary 29 f., Rostovtzeff, *SEH* 1, Wehrli 57 f., Will 55, and Errington, *Gesch. Mak.* 120 and 131.
[3] This chapter marked the climax of the Macedonian narrative of his Book 19. He made similar forward-looking climaxes in Book 18 (the rise of Cassander) and Book 20 (the decisive battle of the civil war).

Pausanias (9. 7. 2) represented Cassander as 'destroying the whole house of Alexander in that he handed over Olympias to be stoned by Macedonians who were embittered against her, and he killed with drugs the sons of Alexander, both Barsine's son Heracles and Roxane's son Alexander.' Justin (15. 2. 3) gave more details.

Lest Alexander's son Heracles, who had passed fourteen years, might be called to the throne through the favour with which men regarded his father's name, Cassander ordered that he and his mother Barsine be killed secretly ('tacite'), and that their corpses be covered with soil, so that there should be no grave to betray the murder, and he killed the other son too and his mother Roxane with the same deception, as if he had not committed crimes enough against the king himself first and then against his mother Olympias and his son [viz. Heracles].[1]

These two passages outweigh a brief summary in the Prologue of Trogus XV in which the order is reversed, probably because the epitomator was more interested in Alexander than in the (unnamed) other son.[2]

Cassander, then, killed Alexander and his mother after, and not before, the pact with Polyperchon, i.e. at the earliest in the summer of 309, during which Alexander became fourteen. That age was important, because boys became Royal Pages at fourteen, and Alexander would be ready to become one in August 309. Justin's mention of 'having passed fourteen years' may have been mistakenly applied by him to Heracles; it may have gone with Alexander in Justin's source. In any case the suggestion that Alexander was killed in the summer of 309 is compatible with the analysis of the bones in Tomb 3 under the Mound at Aegeae (Vergina), which are those of a boy who died when he was between eleven and fourteen years of age. This boy was certainly the last king of that branch of the Temenid house, Alexander IV.[3]

Why did Cassander have Alexander and his mother killed at that particular time? He had had them in his power since 316. During those years he had found them a great asset, because their presence in Macedonia and the Macedonians' recognition of Alexander as king conferred legitimacy on Cassander's position as manager of the king's affairs and general in Europe. Tarn divined a change in 311. The article in the treaty which said that appointments were 'until

---

[1] Pausanias and Justin may have used a common source in mentioning Olympias and attributing both sets of killings to Cassander. The source was perhaps Satyrus (see *HTHA* 109 ff. on the alleged part of Cassander in the death of Alexander).

[2] In *Prol.* 14 the epitomator changed the historical sequence in putting the defeat of Polyperchon before Cassander's possession of Munychia. In the same way the order of importance rather than of chronological sequence was followed in placing the death of Alexander IV before that of Heracles in the entry for 310/9 in Marmor Parium (*FGrH* 239 B 18).

[3] See *HRTV* 116, where the phrase 'there is no possible alternative' was used.

Alexander should reach maturity' was, he thought, 'a direct invitation to Cassander to murder Alexander's son.'[1] If Tarn is right, why did Cassander wait two years? In fact there was no change. The situation in Macedonia after the treaty was as it had been before it: Alexander was still an asset which no other general had. And there were six years to run before Alexander would come of age. It was in 309 that the situation changed. Then, when the two armies of Macedonians were encamped close to one another, Cassander saw the desire of many Macedonians, probably an outright majority, to be rid of Cassander and to have a member of the royal house, adult and active, on the throne. Secondly, and soon after, Alexander reached the age to join the group of Royal Pages. Diodorus, drawing on Hieronymus, noted the effect of the second change at 19. 105. 2: 'Cassander saw that Alexander, the son of Roxane, was growing up (αὐξόμενον) and that certain men were spreading their views throughout Macedonia, that the proper course was to bring the boy out of guarded quarters and hand over to him his father's kingdom. It was fear for himself' which made Cassander act as he did. Tarn's remark (*CAH* 6. 493), that 'all the dynasts except Seleucus...were in fact equally guilty'[2] is incorrect. They had neither the need nor the opportunity to kill Alexander in 309.

The accounts of the killing differ. Diodorus wrote as if Alexander and his mother were kept in prison under harsh conditions from 316 onwards (19. 52. 4). That is about as probable as the remark at 19. 52. 4 that Cassander had decided in 316 to kill Alexander and his mother! Such misrepresentations were part of the propaganda which Antigonus issued and Hieronymus retailed (e.g. at 19. 61. 3). What Cassander rightly did from 316 onwards was safeguard the heir and his mother from assassination or from being kidnapped by raiding forces (Cassander himself had made a successful raid in 317). A guard was therefore mounted outside Alexander's quarters in a stronghold (the citadel of Amphipolis in 316). According to Diodorus, Cassander ordered the captain of this guard to kill the boy and his mother, hide the corpses, and inform no one of what had happened (19. 105. 2). Justin (15. 2. 5) had them killed 'with the same deception', i.e. the killing was done secretly and the corpses were covered with soil. Pausanias had them killed with drugs. The truth may be beyond discovery. But the main point is not in doubt: the fate of Alexander and his mother was concealed for some time, perhaps for years, even in Macedonia, and it was not finally confirmed outside Macedonia—say in Babylon—until 306. For the last year of Alexander's reign as sole king in the

---

[1] *CAH* 6. 489. So too Errington, *Gesch. Mak.* 131 'das Todesurteil'.　　[2] *CAH* 6. 493.

Babylonian record was his 10th year, 307/6.[1] It was then, in 306, that Antigonus and after him the others called themselves kings; for they had abstained 'as long as any sons of their own king could have survived' (J. 15. 2. 13 and 14).

Other notable killings marked the renewal of civil war. Ptolemy confirmed his control of Cyprus by eliminating a king at Paphos whom he suspected of intriguing with Antigonus. A posse of soldiers surrounded the palace and ordered the king to kill himself. When he did so, the rest of his family committed suicide by staying indoors and setting fire to the building (20. 21). When Ptolemy's generals lost their foothold in Cilicia Tracheia, Ptolemy himself led an expedition to capture Phaselis and Xanthus, where he drove out the garrisons of Antigonus and no doubt imposed his own. At Caunus he received one citadel by surrender, but had to leave the other in the hands of Antigonus' garrison. Changes of garrison were, as usual, attended by partisan reprisals among the citizens. At Cos he met Polemaeus and his band of soldiers, whom he had summoned in summer 309 from Chalcis. On the ground that Polemaeus was subverting his men, Ptolemy had him arrested and forced him to drink hemlock. His soldiers were distributed among the units of Ptolemy's army (20. 27). It was at this time that Chalcis became a member state of the Boeotian League, which was increasing in strength.[2]

In 308 Ptolemy sailed with a large fleet from Myndus (on the Asiatic

---

[1] The fragmentary 'Babylonian Chronicle concerning the Diadochi', published and translated in Smith 140 f., has been the centre of controversy. My interpretation is as follows. For the author of this Chronicle the 1st regnal year of Philip III was 324/3 (the Babylonian year beginning normally *c*. April, but varying with intercalation of lunar months); his 8th and last year was 317/16 (see Smith 127). Greek chronology, dealing with archon years beginning *c*. June, started Philip in 323/2 and ended his reign during his 7th year, 317/16 (e.g. D.S. 19. 11. 5). The Chronicler, proceeding in his sequence of named years, made the 1st regnal year of Alexander (then sole king) 316/15, and the 10th and last 307/6 (see Smith 137 and in *Revue d'Assyriologie* 22 (1925) 184; and R. A. Parker and W. H. Dubberstein, *Babylonian Chronology* (Chicago, 1942) 18). Within the Chronicle the following events were dated expressly by regnal years. Philip crossed to Europe in his 5th year = 320/19 and was in Macedonia in his 6th year = 319/18. The royal forces of (probably) Eumenes operated in his 7th year = 318/17. His reign ended in the course of his 8th year = 317/16. Antigonus and Seleucus were at war in Alexander's 6th and 7th years = 311/10 and 310/9. Uncertain events occurred in his 9th and 10th years = 308/7 and 307/6. The 1st year of Seleucus as king followed = 306/5. The last entry is to some extent supported by the 1st regnal year of Ptolemy being 305/4 in the Marmor Parium (*FGrH* 239 B 23). It is clear that the death of Alexander was officially recorded first in the course of the Babylonian year 306/5, in Babylon (see Beloch 4. 2. 167). It is important to remember that the translation of years and especially of months from the Greek system, beginning *c*. June, and from the Macedonian system, beginning *c*. October, into the Babylonian system, beginning *c*. April—each with its own random intercalation—did not make for accuracy. One has to reckon inclusively; and not exclusively as in Cary 384. For a different interpretation of the Chronicle's early years, which assumes that Philip's 1st regnal year was 323/2 and so pushes the whole series down by a year, see Errington 75 f. A convenient table of months under various systems is given by Parker and Dubberstein, op. cit. 24.

[2] Known from *IG* ii². 1. 469. Eretria and Oropus also became members; see Beloch 4. 2. 426 ff.

coast opposite Cos), passed through the Cyclades, and landed at the Isthmus of the Greek mainland. During his period of thalassocracy after 313 Antigonus had controlled the Cyclades and the Asiatic coast facing Greece through the councils of three Leagues which he created or revived: the Island League with a centre at Delos, the Ilian League of Aeolian cities with a centre at Ilium, and the Ionian League. But after the treaty of 311 Antigonus was fully stretched by his campaigns against Seleucus, and his fleet went out of commission. Moreover, Antigonus lost his footing on the Greek mainland; for Polemaeus in 310 and Polyperchon in 309 went over from him to Cassander. In 309 Polemaeus tried to change sides again and persuade Ptolemy to use his thalassocracy and invade Greece. The results were disastrous for Polemaeus, as we have seen, but the fact that Ptolemy accepted his approaches showed that he was prepared to act on his own both against Antigonus on the Asiatic coast and against Cassander in Greece.

Why did Ptolemy make this change of policy? The answer seems to be connected with members of the royal family.[1] When Heracles and Barsine were sent in 310 from Pergamum to join Polyperchon, it must have alarmed his aunt Cleopatra, the sister of Alexander, who was living not far away at Sardes. She quarrelled with Antigonus, perhaps over the involvement of Heracles in the civil war. Then in summer 309 came the killing of Heracles and Barsine, and the *entente* between Polyperchon and Cassander. Cleopatra must have feared for the safety of Alexander IV and looked for an ally. She chose Ptolemy, whose fleet held the seas, and her hope may have been to land in Macedonia. Ptolemy had his own plans. He had seen Polyperchon nearly succeed, and he knew that the killing of Heracles had alienated many of Cassander's supporters in Macedonia. He was always *persona grata* with Macedonian soldiers and was the guardian of Alexander's tomb. Now was his chance to gain 'the following of the Macedonians' (20. 37. 4). They had shown themselves aware of the rights of Alexander IV, Eurydice, Olympias, and recently Heracles. Now they would support Cleopatra. If he and Cleopatra could take over Alexander IV and Macedonia, and if his fleet ruled the eastern Mediterranean, he would be in a powerful position. But he could do so only if he had Cleopatra with him and if he gained the co-operation of a number of Greek states.

Everything went wrong. Cleopatra was stopped as she tried to leave Sardes and join Ptolemy in Greece. She was killed on Antigonus' order by a group of women, of whom some were promptly executed by

---

[1] Not mentioned by Cary 31 in his assessment of the 'political somersaults of Ptolemy', and underestimated by Tarn in *CAH* 6. 494 f., who thought that Ptolemy 'aimed at controlling Greece'.

Antigonus on a charge of conspiracy. Hoping to hide his own part in the affair, Antigonus gave Cleopatra a royal funeral (20. 37. 3–6). Meanwhile Ptolemy, who had always proclaimed himself a liberator, began well by ejecting a garrison (of Cassander's men) from Andros and liberating Corinth and Sicyon from the autocratic rule of Cratesipolis, the widow of Polyperchon's son, Alexander. The Boeotians and the Peloponnesians who had resisted Polyperchon seemed to be his natural allies. He required the Peloponnesians to contribute supplies and money, as well as men, in the cause of liberation. They agreed, but did nothing. By now he knew of the death of Cleopatra.[1] The plan was stillborn. He made peace with Cassander on the basis of the *status quo* and withdrew his fleet to Egypt at the end of the sailing season of 308 (20. 37. 1–2). Cassander had had a lucky escape with no expenditure of effort on his part.

In 307 his Greek allies expected Ptolemy to return to his garrisoned bases at Corinth and Sicyon and to carry the war of liberation northwards through central Greece.[2] But it was now the turn of Antigonus to play the part of liberator. See Fig. 7. In May/June 307 his son Demetrius sailed from Ephesus with 5,000 talents and a reconstituted fleet of 250 warships. Happening on good weather and boldly seizing the initiative, he sailed straight into the Piraeus and announced through his herald that the day of liberation had come. He was greeted with the applause of the populace, while his marines passed inside the walls of the Piraeus. Demetrius of Phalerum withdrew into the city, accepted an offer of safe conduct for himself and his associates, and went via Thebes to join Ptolemy in Egypt, whom he regarded as a stronger patron than Cassander, even after eleven years of service with the latter. Munychia was captured quickly, and its fortifications were razed in the following year.[3] Athens was indeed free. Full democracy was restored, a treaty of friendship and alliance was concluded with Demetrius, and the most extravagant honours were piled upon Demetrius and Antigonus as 'the Saviour Gods'. Antigonus responded by withdrawing his garrison from Imbros and presenting the island to Athens, and he sent 230,000 bushels of grain to compensate for the loss of the corn supply from the Black Sea ports (for Cassander's ally Lysimachus controlled the Hellespont; see P*D* 12. 5). He sent also

---

[1] This reconstruction cannot be regarded as more than probable. Diodorus reports all the events of one region for one archon year and then turns back to those of another region for the same year; he does not mark correlations in time between the events of one region and those of another. The Marmor Parium (*FGrH* 239 B 19) put Cleopatra's death in 309/8.

[2] He had already been in touch with Demetrius of Phalerum and could have won him over to his side; for in 307 the fleet of Demetrius was taken to be that of Ptolemy.

[3] Marmor Parium (*FGrH* 239 B 20–1) put the flight of Demetrius in 308/7 and the razing of Munychia in 307/6.

sufficient ship-timber to build 100 triremes; for his intention was to recreate the Athenian fleet and use it against his rivals. During his first burst of energy Demetrius had freed Megara from Cassander's garrison, prevented his soldiers from plundering the city and declared it free (P*D* 9. 5). Thereafter he seems to have wasted several months in philandering and extravagance. His initial success, more brilliant than that of Ptolemy, brought him the alliance of the states which regarded themselves as free or had been liberated by Ptolemy, and Antigonus sent him instructions to convene representatives of the allied states, re-establish the Hellenic League (as it had been in the days of Philip and Alexander), and concert future measures 'in the interest of Greece' (20. 46. 5), no doubt for war against Cassander.

Cassander was indeed at his lowest ebb. Ptolemy and Demetrius had stripped him of his allies in Greece and had expelled his garrisons. During 307 Glaucias, king of the Taulantii, who was in league with Epidamnus, Apollonia, and Corcyra, invaded Epirus with an army, put the anti-Cassander party in power in Molossia, and placed a twelve-year-old son of Aeacides, called Pyrrhus, on the throne with guardians representing that party (P*Pyrrh* 3. 3; J. 17. 3. 21). The western frontier of Macedonia was now at risk (see Fig. 8). Within Macedonia many Macedonians had been alienated by the killing of Heracles in 309, and perhaps even more now if there were rumours that Alexander and Roxane had disappeared.

Thus all the circumstances seemed to be in favour of Demetrius, the Greeks, the Molossians, and Glaucias, if they should undertake a joint invasion of Macedonia in spring 306. At this moment Antigonus showed that lack of judgement which he had shown in 313. He recalled all his forces from Greece, leaving his unfortunate allies to sink or swim on their own for what was to be almost three years. His forces were redeployed against Ptolemy's forces in Cyprus; for his first priority now was to overthrow Ptolemy. When Ptolemy's fleet came up to the relief of Salamis in Cyprus, Demetrius won a brilliant victory. Leaving ten ships to blockade the sixty ships of Ptolemy's brother, Menelaus, in Salamis harbour, Demetrius engaged Ptolemy's fleet of about 140 warships and 200 transporters carrying 10,000 infantrymen, with his own fleet of some 150 warships. He captured seventy warships and all the transporters with cargoes of men, money, and materials. Ptolemy escaped with only eight ships.[1] The forces of Menelaus—sixty ships, 1,200 cavalry, and 12,000 infantry—capitulated. Demetrius was generous in victory. He rewarded his Athenian squadron of thirty

---

[1] 20. 49–52, a full account including the *aristeia* of Demetrius; P*D* 15. 2–16. 4 from a different source; and Polyaen. 4. 7. 7. For numbers see Cary 385 f. Marmor Parium B 21 has the capture of Cyprus in 307/6.

172 The Ambition of Antigonus and the End of the Temenid House

quadriremes by giving the city 1,200 sets of armour, accorded a military funeral to all the enemy dead, and let his captives go free without paying a ransom. As master now of all the cities of Cyprus, both Greek and Phoenician, Demetrius organized a defence force of 600 cavalry and 16,000 infantry.

The next objective was Egypt. In late October 306 Antigonus, now nearing eighty, set out from Gaza with an army of eighty-three elephants, 8,000 cavalry, and 80,000 infantry, and Demetrius sailed alongside the army with 150 warships and 100 transporters of supplies and equipment, despite the pilots' forecast of bad weather at 'the setting of the Pleiades' c. 1 November (20. 73. 3). This forecast was only too correct. Much of the fleet was wrecked on the harbourless coast, Ptolemy's defences on the line of the Nile were too strong, the supply system began to fail, and Antigonus faced disaster. He obtained the approval of his officers and men and withdrew to Gaza. He planned, he said, to return. Instead, in 305 he attacked Rhodes, a neutral state, and enlisted the services of the enemies of Rhodes, the pirates.[1] So much for the cause of Greek liberation! During a year-long siege Ptolemy, Lysimachus, and Cassander supplied the gallant Rhodians with great quantities of grain and pulse, and Ptolemy sent 1,500 soldiers as well. Envoys from the Greek states of the mainland, headed by Athens, and finally envoys from the Aetolian League urged Demetrius to break off the siege. In 304 Demetrius made the following terms. Rhodes was to enjoy her own revenues, be autonomous and ungarrisoned, and ally herself with Antigonus, except in any campaign against Ptolemy. Rhodes delivered to Demetrius 100 hostages as a guarantee that she would observe the terms (20. 99. 3). The siege of Rhodes, like the invasion of Egypt, had proved pointless and ineffectual.

During these three years the generals became 'kings'. Non-Macedonians had indeed called some of them 'kings' as a form of flattery; the Persians, for instance, after the defeat of Eumenes called Antigonus king, 'the barbarians' called Seleucus king (PD 18. 2), and the Athenians called Demetrius and Antigonus kings after the liberation of Athens (PD 10. 3). But for all Macedonians, including the generals, there was only one king after 317, Alexander IV. The last year of his reign, according to the Babylonian Chronicle,[2] began c. April 307, and within that year and certainly by its end c. March 306 his death was accepted as certain. No male of the Temenid house survived.

---

[1] Rhodes had maintained friendly relations with all the generals. It was true that her ports were used especially by ships trading with and from Egypt and that she imported her cereals from Egypt; but that was no reason for Antigonus to pick a quarrel with her (20. 81–82. 3).

[2] Published and translated by Smith 126 ff. This Chronicle concerns the Diadochi.

Antigonus stepped into the vacant position after the great victory of Demetrius in Cyprus in 306. The procedure he used was similar to the traditional one in electing a Macedonian king in Macedonia. The fullest account is in PD 18. The acclamation of Antigonus and Demetrius as kings was made at the headquarters of Antigonus in or near Syria by τὸ πλῆθος, meaning, as at D.S. 18. 4. 3, the Assembly of the Macedones at that place (J. 15. 2. 10 translated the Greek as 'populus'; App. *Syr.* 9. 54 had 'the army'). Thereupon the Friends of Antigonus crowned him immediately (ἀνέδησαν, i.e. with a diadem). As Demetrius had been acclaimed king, it was natural for Antigonus to send a diadem to him (he was still in Cyprus) and address him as king. Of what territories did Antigonus and Demetrius claim to be kings? Our texts do not tell us. But if we recall the words of Seleucus, that Antigonus aimed to win 'all the kingdom of the Macedones' (D.S. 19. 56. 2), and the claim of Antigonus, 'to have taken over the management of the kingdom' (19. 61. 3), there can be little doubt that he was claiming now to succeed Alexander IV as ruler of the kingdom, i.e. of all lands ruled by that Alexander and his father, Alexander the Great.[1]

Ptolemy moved next. He was acclaimed king by οἱ ἐν Αἰγύπτῳ (sc. Μακεδόνες) (PD 18. 1);[2] they are called 'the army' in J. 15. 2. 11 and 'his personal army' ὁ οἰκεῖος αὐτοῦ στρατός, i.e. the Macedonian army, in App. *Syr.* 9. 54. Since Ptolemy was making, and about to make, common cause with Seleucus, Lysimachus, and Cassander against Antiochus, he did not claim to rule over 'all the kingdom of the Macedones'; for had he done so, he would have been in danger of losing his allies. This was true also of the other three, when their turn came. Each, it seems, was elected king over what he then held, as we can infer from passages in Diodorus, who drew probably on Hieronymus. At 19. 105. 4, writing collectively of the generals, he said that 'each of those who had authority over races or cities...held the territory subject to himself as if it were a kingdom won by the spear' (ὡσανεί τινα βασιλείαν δορίκτητον); and at 20. 53. 4, in writing of their elevation to kingship, he mentioned the territories of Lysimachus and Cassander as 'those originally granted to them' and he described Seleucus as having 'acquired in addition the upper satrapies' (προσκεκτημένος, i.e. in addition to the original grant of the satrapy of Babylonia).

When the death of Alexander IV was made public in Macedonia, his corpse was cremated and given a magnificent burial in the family's tumulus at Aegeae, not far from the burial of his grandfather, Philip II. This was presumably the first act of Cassander, when he was duly

---

[1] So too Tarn in *CAH* 6. 499.
[2] In 305/4 according to the Marmor Parium (*FGrH* 239 B 23).

acclaimed 'king of the Macedonians'. The statue base, which has been found at Dium by Professor Pantermalis, was set up probably after the coronation. It carried the following inscription:

βασιλεὺς Μακεδόν[ων]
Κάσσανδρος Ἀντιπ[άτρου]
Διὶ ᾿Ολυμπίωι

Statues of the kings were erected in the *temenos* of Zeus Olympius at Dium (Plb. 4. 62. 2), and this was done probably when they were elected to the throne.[1] It seems that Cassander issued now his own regal coinage, only in bronze (Pl. I *f*). His favourite head was that of a young Heracles, the ancestor of the Temenid house and appropriate in his youthfulness to Cassander as a man of the younger generation, and he made much use of the accoutrements of Heracles—the club and the quiver. On the reverse of some coins he had a lion, both couchant and standing while teasing a spear (as on the coins of Amyntas III). On other issues he placed the head of Athena, or the head of Apollo with the tripod on the reverse. A naked rider is portrayed with his right arm extended and raised in a position of salute, as on coins of Philip II.[2] The emphasis on Heracles and the choice of emblems from the coinages of Amyntas III and Philip II show that Cassander wished to stress his connection with the Temenid house through his queen, Thessalonice, the daughter of Philip II. The practice of using the gold and silver coinages of Alexander III continued through Cassander's reign.

Antigonus put his name and the title **ΒΑΣΙΛΕΩΣ** on the gold and silver coinages which advertised his claim to succeed Alexander III as ruler of Alexander's world. For they were very similar to the coinages issued by Alexander in Asia after his victory at Issus. Now Antigonus celebrated the victory of his fleet at Cyprus (see P*D* 17. 6 and 18. 1) with the head of Athena and on the reverse the Nike with naval emblems on his gold coinage, and he claimed to rule by placing on his silver coinage the head of a young Heracles and on the reverse Zeus the

---

[1] *Proc. 8th Epigr. Conf.* 271. Adams in *AM* 3. 25 f. prefers his interpretation of P*D* 18. 2, that Cassander was not elected King until ?301, to the statements of D.S. 20. 53. 3–4 οἱ λοιποὶ δυνάσται and J. 15. 2. 12, which are derived from Hieronymus. The use which Cassander made of the title may have been idiosyncratic, as Plutarch indicates. Ptolemy and Seleucus became kings in 305/4 (Marmor Parium B 23 and *Iraq* 1954. 205); Lysimachus and Cassander are not likely to have delayed. Préaux 1. 183, 'c'est aux armes que chacun des diadoques demanda d'établir son titre à la royauté', needs to find victories for Ptolemy, Seleucus, Lysimachus, and Cassander for this view to be convincing. For the views of Gruen, 'Coronation', see below, p. 192 n. 3 and p. 193 n. 2.

[2] Gaebler III. 2. 176 f. He attributed two coins which lack **ΒΑΣΙΛΕΩΣ** to the years before Cassander became king. But this lack is not decisive; for one coin of a type which normally had **ΒΑΣΙΛΕΩΣ** is without it (his no. 4). Cassander was obviously wise not to coin in his own name until he became king. His bronze coins circulated widely in central Thrace; see Youroukova 24.

King seated on a throne with an eagle on his outstretched hand. His son Demetrius commemorated the victory and advanced the same claim on his gold coinage with his name and **ΒΑΣΙΛΕΩΣ**, and he placed a striding Poseidon with poised trident and on the obverse a Nike on a ship's prow on his silver tetradrachms (Pl. I*g*). These coinages presumably were issued alongside those of Antigonus *c.* 306–301.[1] It was perhaps in these years rather than later that Lysimachus issued his royal coinage with his name and title and placed on his silver tetradrachms the magnificent portrait head of Alexander wearing the horns of Ammon (Pl. I*i*).[2] In this coinage he proclaimed his loyalty to the Temenid house and in particular to the memory of the Alexander to whom he had been a Bodyguard. This was a personal loyalty which the other Successor Kings did not express on their coinages.

There was a distinction between Antigonus and Demetrius who claimed the universal rule, and the other four kings who ruled each over a region, respected one another, and regarded Antigonus and Demetrius as impostors. This led inevitably to the combination of the four kings against Antigonus and Demetrius in 303–301 (foreshadowed by Diodorus at 20. 2. 3 and described as a working agreement at 20. 106 under the archon year 302/1).

Let us return now to the mainland of Greece. Since her liberation Athens had renovated her defences and built a fleet from her own resources and from Antigonus' subsidies of money and ship-timber. Because she was stronger at sea than Cassander in 306, she let thirty quadriremes sail with Demetrius to Cyprus. In summer 306 Cassander invaded Attica. Athens allied herself with Aetolia, and with Aetolian help withstood the attack (Paus. 1. 26. 3). Strengthened with further subsidies from Antigonus and provided with sets of armour by Demetrius, she brought Boeotia into alliance in 305 and forced Cassander to abandon the siege of Elatea in Phocis and retire to the north of Thermopylae (Paus. 1. 26. 3; 10. 8. 7 and 34. 3). Athens was jubilant. She needed only Demetrius and his huge forces to give Cassander's Macedonia the *coup de grâce*. By now Cassander had built a fleet, and the Greek successes merely united his Macedonians. On the Greek side the unprovoked attack on Rhodes alienated those who had hitherto sided with Athens and Antigonus. Boeotia even joined

---

[1] Gaebler III. 2. 179 f.

[2] Gaebler III. 2. 172 nos. 5 and 6, being a silver half-drachm and a bronze coin, carry a monogram, which corresponds with the first two letters of Lysimachus; but it is most unlikely that he coined in his own name and used that abbreviation. The explanation is surely that the name of a mint-official began with those two letters, as in the reign of Philip III (see *SNG* LXV 3207).

Cassander and put a garrison into Chalcis. No Greek state helped Athens when Cassander invaded Attica in 304, captured and garrisoned Phyle and Panactum (PD 23. 2), and laid siege to the city. Meanwhile his fleet defeated the Athenian fleet decisively, liberated Salamis, and set it up as a separate state (Polyaen. 4. 11. 1; Paus. 1. 35. 2). The Peloponnese was overrun by another Macedonian army under Polyperchon, who took over Corinth from Ptolemy's garrison and ravaged the territories of any states friendly to Athens (D.S. 20. 100. 6). Athens had one last hope. She appealed to Demetrius for help.

On the advice of the Aetolian League, Demetrius broke off the siege of Rhodes and sailed with 330 warships and a large army to Aulis in Boeotia (see Fig. 7). He liberated Chalcis,[1] made Boeotia accept neutrality, and brought Aetolia into alliance. As Cassander hastened northwards for Macedonia, he was defeated and 6,000 of his Macedonians deserted to Demetrius (PD 23. 1; D.S. 20. 100. 6). Demetrius turned south for a winter of dissipation in Athens, quartering himself and his prostitutes (of both sexes, it was said) in the Parthenon. In 303 Demetrius went not to Macedonia, but to the Peloponnese, which was no threat to him, but offered easy victories. By the end of the year he overcame all enemy garrisons and declared the Peloponnesians free,[2] though he put his own garrison into Acrocorinth. At Argos he married a Molossian princess, Deidameia, daughter of Aeacides, who had been betrothed to Alexander IV; this strengthened his ties with the Molossians hostile to Cassander, and gave him a connection with the last legitimate king of Macedonia. His hopes of Molossian support were dashed in 302, when a change of power in Molossia brought Neoptolemus back and caused Pyrrhus to flee to Demetrius.

In spring 302 Demetrius crowned his policy of liberation. At the Isthmian festival, to which he had summoned delegates from all liberated tribal states and city-states in Greece, he and they founded an organization named by them 'the Greeks' and by modern scholars 'the Hellenic League'. We know of this from PD 25. 3 and from an important inscription, found at Epidaurus, of which the best text is in SVA no. 446. I refer to this text by sections and lines, e.g. v. 141, in what follows. The founding states went on to form an offensive and defensive alliance between 'the Greeks' and 'the kings Antigonus and Demetrius' (PD 25. 3 and SVA v. 141).[3]

Initially a military coalition was thereby created to fight a joint war

---

[1] Marmor Parium (*FGrH* 239 B 24) put the liberation of Chalcis in 304/3.

[2] He made an alliance with each liberated state, e.g. with Sicyon (*SVA* III. 445), on which see *Studies Edson* 166.

[3] Revealed in a fragmentary inscription at Epidaurus, *IG* IV². 104. 1. 68; for text and commentary see *SVA* III. 446 with a select bibliography. See also *Hesp.* 9 (1940) 348 ff.

of liberation against Cassander. Demetrius was elected supreme commander of its joint forces (*PD* loc. cit. ἡγεμών; D.S. 20. 102. 1 and 106.
1), and he was to appoint 'the presidents of the Council of the Greeks'
during this war (*SVA* III. 91). Sizes of military and financial contributions by the member states were fixed, and scales of fines for any
shortcomings were laid down. Wartime meetings of the Council were
to be held wherever 'the presidents and the king' (i.e. Demetrius) 'or
the general appointed by the kings' (*SVA* III. 71; more precisely at III.
68 'the general left[1] in charge of joint defence by the kings') should
decide. Thus, like Philip II and Alexander III, Antigonus and
Demetrius represented themselves as the champions of 'the Greeks' in a
war of liberation from oppressors.

Demetrius and the delegates drew up regulations also for the
conduct of the organization in peacetime. The alliance between 'the
Greeks' and the kings was to be for all time in the form 'Antigonus and
Demetrius and their descendants' (*SVA* v. 140 f.) with reciprocal
guarantees not to overthrow the constitutional framework of each
party.[2] In peacetime the meetings of the Council were to be at the
centres for the Panhellenic Games, the presidents were to be selected
by lot, and a 50-per-cent attendance of councillors was required as a
quorum. Regulations were laid down for judicial and presumably
financial proceedings, in which the presidents acted, not as advisers,
but as channels of communication. The Council's decisions were
binding on the member states, and a councillor could not be prosecuted by his member state for his part in decision-making. The
undertakings of the member states towards one another have not
survived. 'Friendship' (Schmitt in *SVA* I. 8) implies no intervention or
acts of war (so probably *SVA* v. 144 f.), and the regulations governing
a Common Peace may well have been the traditional ones. This
peacetime organization was modelled on that which had obtained in
the reigns of Philip II and Alexander III. When the war against
Cassander was finished, it was anticipated that 'Antigonus and
Demetrius and their descendants' would be kings of Macedon in
Macedonia.

The concern of Demetrius for the freedom of the Greeks may have
been praiseworthy in itself, but it was strategically unwise. Instead of
attacking Cassander at his weakest moment, Demetrius gave him a
year and a half's respite. When Cassander tried to treat for terms in
303, Antigonus demanded total surrender. Thereupon Cassander
began diplomatic negotiations with the other kings, which were
inevitably protracted over many months before an agreed plan of

---

[1] e.g. at Corinth probably, when Demetrius was commanding forces in Central Greece.
[2] The guarantee survives only for the Kings, but may be assumed for 'the Greeks'.

operations was made.[1] In 302 Cassander was to undertake a holding operation in north Greece. Lysimachus' army, reinforced by a part of Cassander's army, was to invade Asia. Seleucus was to march from the upper satrapies and join Lysimachus. Ptolemy was to invade Syria. The intention was to force a decision in Asia, not in Europe.

Cassander and his Thessalian allies occupied the passes leading from central Greece into Thessaly (see Fig. 6). What with constitution-making, assessing, and calling up the contingents of 'the Greeks', it was high summer before Demetrius arrived with his forces. Unable to force the passes, he landed troops on the coast of Phthiotis and extended his bridgehead gradually. A war of manœuvering followed between Cassander's mobile army of 2,000 cavalry and 29,000 infantry and Demetrius' huge army of 1,500 cavalry, 8,000 Macedonian infantry, 25,000 infantry from the states of Greece, 15,000 Greek mercenaries, and 8,000 light-armed freebooters. A true son of Antipater, Cassander played out time, and in the autumn Demetrius received the expected summons from Antigonus: he was to bring his forces to Asia as quickly as possible. Cassander was only too happy to grant the terms which Demetrius proposed, but would be unable to enforce; they included the freedom of the Greek states both in Greece and in Asia (D.S. 20. 111. 2).[2] When Demetrius sailed to Ephesus, the army of 'the Greeks' seems to have faded away. Cassander regained control of southern Thessaly and sent a further force of 500 cavalry and 12,000 infantry to help Lysimachus.

Lysimachus and a force supplied by Cassander crossed in the early summer of 302 into Asia, where two of Antigonus' generals with their troops deserted to him.[3] When Antigonus came up from Syria, Lysimachus used brilliant evasive tactics until winter arrived. By then only a part of Cassander's further reinforcements had reached him, the rest having been intercepted by Demetrius' ships or drowned in a storm in the Black Sea. Just before winter set in, Seleucus marched into Cappadocia with 480 elephants, 100 scythed chariots, 12,000 cavalry, and 20,000 infantry. Late in the year Ptolemy invaded Syria; but he was deceived by a false report that Lysimachus and Seleucus had been defeated, and he drew his army back into Egypt.

In 301 the decisive battle was fought at Ipsus in Phrygia. Lysimachus and Seleucus, both very able generals trained by Alexander, had 400 elephants, 120 chariots, 10,500 cavalry, and 64,000 infantry; they faced seventy-five elephants, 10,000 cavalry, and 70,000 infantry. The opening cavalry engagement was won by Demetrius. He pursued too

---

[1] D.S. 20. 106; P*D* 28. 1–2; J. 15. 2. 15–17; Orosius 3. 23. 41, following Justin.
[2] Marmor Parium (*FGrH* 239 B 26) placed the truce in 302/1.
[3] Marmor Parium B 25 put the crossing into Asia in 303/2.

far, leaving part of his phalanx exposed. Seleucus moved his elephants into the gap and rode round the exposed part of the phalanx with his Royal Guard of cavalry, until the phalangites there deserted. The rest of the phalanx was routed.[1] Antigonus fell in action, awaiting his son's return. Thus the instigator of two, or even three, phases of civil war met his deserts, death and total defeat.

[1] For the campaign and the battle see P*D* 28–9; D.S. 20. 107–9; Polyaen. 4. 7. 4 and 12. 1.

VIII

SOME FEATURES OF THE TRANSITIONAL PERIOD 323–301 B.C.

WHEN Philip and Alexander were organizing their relations with the Greeks, it was appropriate to write of 'the *poleis*'; but when Demetrius and Antigonus were doing so in 302, the treaty mentioned the presidents as coming from 'tribe or *polis*', ἐξ ἔθνους ἢ πόλεως.[1] The priority of the *ethnos* in that phrase was symptomatic of the revolutionary change in the ranking of the *ethnos* vis-à-vis the *polis* in terms of real power. In the same way kingship was an eccentric institution in Greek thinking in the middle of the fourth century. It was accepted as the central political phenomenon by the end of the century.

We may take Aristotle in his *Politics* as a representative of the general Greek view in the middle decades of the fourth century. Then the *polis* ranked first in prestige. As compared with it the *ethnos* or tribal state was far inferior. Kingship was not natural for Greeks (1287^a); but it was appropriate for some of the 'barbarians', because barbarian peoples were servile (1285^a20) and they sometimes produced an outstandingly able family (1288^a7–10). He noted (not entirely to their credit) that some *ethne* and some of the kingships to which they were prone were interested primarily in military achievements: for example, Scythians, Persians, Thracians, and Celts, and Macedonians who once had a law that a man who had not killed an enemy must wear a halter instead of a belt (1324^b11–17).

Onto such general views Aristotle grafted some remarks which sprang from his own experience at the Macedonian court after 343. He drew a distinction between despotic kingship and 'hereditary constitutional kingship' (κατὰ νόμον καὶ πατρικαί, 1285^a19–28). A holder of the latter ruled over 'willing' men, was guarded by citizen guardsmen and used his Friends to enlarge and implement his administrative and executive powers (1285^a25 and 1287^b30). He observed that in relation to the common people kingship developed as a means of favouring capable persons and safeguarding their estates (1310^b8 and 1311^a1); and that the constitutional king aims at 'what is noble' (τὸ καλόν) and pursues what leads to personal 'honour' (τὰ δ' εἰς τιμήν). One may perhaps catch an echo of Aristotle lecturing his pupil Alexander; but it

---

[1] *GHI* 192, 12–13; *SVA* III 446 III 71.

is proper to recognize the truth of Aristotle's observation in the case not only of Alexander the Great, but also of Ptolemy and Demetrius. When he gave examples of kings who were capable of benefiting their *ethne*, he mentioned the kings of the Macedonians and the Molossians in that they had acquired additional territory ($\chi\acute{\omega}\rho\alpha$, 1310^b35-40).

By 301 the *ethne* were far more powerful than the *poleis*. Macedonia itself was a community of *ethne*, an enlarged *ethnos* (see Thuc. 2. 99. 2 and 6, and J. 8. 6. 2 'ex multis gentibus nationibusque unum regnum populumque constituit'). Molossia, Thesprotia, and Chaonia also were tribal communities, both individually and as a group, when they combined in the later phase of the Epirote Alliance. Aetolia, Acarnania, Thessaly, Phocis, Locris, and Boeotia (not always including Thebes) acted increasingly during this period as ethnic units, and these units were more formidable in land warfare after 322 than any *polis*, even Athens. It was not so much that the *poleis* declined in themselves. Indeed Athens showed herself capable of producing a very large navy, and she continued to lead in many ways. What the *poleis* failed to do, except for a short period in the Lamian War, was to combine with one another and to create a close-knit community which would have been able to match the military resources of Macedonia.

An important factor in this transitional period was the aura of kingship. Alexander's pursuit of what was noble, his winning of personal honour, and his military achievement won a reputation for kingship which became immediately apparent in the *Alexander Romance*, a mirror of unsophisticated Greek and barbarian opinion. His career marked the apotheosis of kingship in the eyes and hearts not only of the Macedonians, but also of the peoples in the Kingdom of Asia. When his family died out, it was unthinkable there that his successors should be anything but kings, not only because they held military command and possessed military skill, but also because they conferred benefits upon the peoples of their realm. Greek philosophers might deride kingship in the tradition of Callisthenes, but the new regard for kingship had its effect even in the Greek *poleis*. The extravagant honours which Athens heaped upon Demetrius were indicative not only of the leading *polis*'s minor status in power politics, but also of gratitude and respect for the beneficent power of a king.[1] But, as Aristotle saw, Macedonian kingship was a particular form of kingship—constitutional, hereditary, militaristic, and concerned to serve its peoples. It is misleading to call the kingships of the late fourth century 'Hellenistic'. If 'Hellenistic' means 'imitative of the Greeks' or 'using the Greek language, but not being Greek', it is both inappropriate (for

---

[1] Similarly the League of Islanders established festivals separately in honour of Antigonus and Demetrius, as the holders of power at sea. See Buraselis 78 ff.

the model of this kingship was not found in the Greek *polis*) and negative rather than positive. The fact is that what emerged in those years were Macedonian kingships and in some sense, as we shall see, Macedonian kingdoms.

For some centuries the *poleis* had derived their strength from their urban society, their capitalistic system, and their commercial activity. During that time the *ethne*, for instance in north-west Greece, had been living a primitive, semi-nomadic existence, and they had used not sophisticated methods of exchange, but simple barter, whenever their herdsmen, peasants, hunters, fishermen, or brigands rose above the level of mere subsistence (1256[a]40). But the reigns of Philip and Alexander saw in the lands north of the Greek *poleis* a meteoric development of the *ethnos*, which moved suddenly from a semi-nomadic system to one of settled agriculture, urban centres, and growing capitalism.[1] Recent excavations have revealed for the first time the massive walls and the great size of such cities as Dium, Aegeae, Edessa, and Pella, built not on a hill-top, but set on flat or rolling ground and encompassed by finely built walls some 5 or 6 kilometres in length.[2] Within Philip's lifetime these and others yet to be uncovered were cities in the modern sense with closely built houses and large populations.

Similar changes occurred in Epirus. When our evidence is best, in 360–355, the tribesmen were living in the open or in villages (κατὰ κώμας), and then in the wake of the Macedonians of Upper Macedonia they adopted a settled life and built urban centres such as Cassope, Eurymenae, and Phoenice. By the first decade of the third century Epirus had become a land of many well-fortified cities, smaller but more numerous than those of Macedonia and built generally on hills.[3] There too the cities were centres of commerce and culture, and it was from them that the levies of trained soldiers were raised, e.g. by the sons of Alcetas in 312 (D.S. 19. 88. 3 ἐπὶ τὰς πόλεις). These social and economic developments went together with the expansion of the Molossian state—on which Aristotle commented, as we have seen—and with the creation of the Molossian coalition, which enabled the Molossian king, Alexander, to campaign in Italy. There followed *c.* 330 the birth of the Epirote Alliance, consisting at first of the southern Epirote tribes and later including also the Chaonians of northern Epirus.[4] This community of *ethne*, having, like its Macedonian cousin,

---

[1] See Volume II. 658 ff. and especially Arr. *An.* 7. 9. 2–3 and J. 8. 5. 7.

[2] This statement is based on visits to these sites and to the kindness of the excavators, Professors Pantermalis, Andronicos, Petsas, and Vavritsas, and Mrs. Siganidou. The foundation courses at Dium and Edessa are strikingly similar in style, and the excavators have attributed them to the time of Philip II, rightly in my opinion.

[3] H*E*, esp. 532, 553 f., and 659 f., and H*HSE* 19 f.

[4] H*E* 525 ff. (esp. 531), 537, 559 f., and H*HSE* 16 and *SIG* 653. 4.

a communal name οἱ Ἀπειρῶται, was developed by Pyrrhus into a powerful kingdom of the Macedonian type with a much greater military potential than any city-state of Greece.

The urban centres in Macedonia and Epirus were not independent city-states (though also called πόλεις), but privileged communities within a kingdom. They resembled the Greek *poleis* in many social and economic aspects, but they were different in that they were contained within a powerful state and accepted the rule of a king. Developments of a similar kind were taking place in the kingdom of Glaucias in Illyria and in the area ruled by Lysimachus in Thrace; and more importantly in Alexander's Kingdom of Asia, where his city-foundations and others planted by generals and kings were developing into great centres of economic and military strength. Within the Greek peninsula Cassander created Cassandreia and Thessalonica by bringing together the inhabitants of small towns,[1] and he refounded Thebes with help from many parts of the Greek world. The Acarnanians were persuaded to move from their small towns into large urban centres at Agrinium, Sauria, and Stratus.[2] Demetrius moved the population of Sicyon to a new site and redeveloped the city as 'Demetrias'.[3]

The culture of the free citizens of these cities may be labelled Greek or Macedonian or Graeco-Macedonian, with equal justice. It was Greek in the sense in which Isocrates had written of a common outlook or intelligence as Greek, regardless of race.[4] It was Macedonian in that the Macedonian kings for two centuries had been adopting much of Greek thought and art, attracting to their court the best artists and thinkers (as Athens had done in her period of greatness) and contributing something of their own taste. The discoveries which have been made recently not only at Pella and Aegeae (Vergina) but also at Dion, Lefkadhia, Mikhaniona, and Derveni have shown that this culture was not limited to the court, but was widespread in Lower Macedonia.

The most striking additions to our knowledge are the frescoes which have survived on the walls of funerary monuments.[5] It was already known that a famous painter, Zeuxis, was employed by Archelaus to paint the walls of the palace at the new capital, Pella, late in the fifth century.[6] Now we have actual frescoes, a generation later, in the tomb of Amyntas III at Aegeae (ob. 370). Painted in four colours, these frescoes in their vigour and naturalism have revolutionized our ideas of fourth-century painting; for the control of composition, the perspec-

---

[1] D.S. 19. 52. 2–3; Str. 330 frr. 21 and 24; D. H. 1. 49. 4. See D.S. 20. 29. 1 for Lysimacheia and 20. 47. 5 and 108. 1 for Antigoneia in Syria. E. I. Mikroyiannakis discusses Cassander's policy in founding cities, in *AM* 2. 225 ff.; and J. A. Alexander the status of Cassandreia in *AM* 1. 127 ff.
[2] D.S. 19. 67. 3–4.   [3] D.S. 20. 102. 2–4.   [4] Isoc. *Panegyricus* 50.
[5] The best reproductions are in Andronicos, *V*.   [6] See Volume II. 149.

tive, and the colour contrasts in the Rape of Persephone by Pluto are masterly. The painting of the Royal Hunt, a generation later, on the façade of the tomb of Philip II (ob. 336) shows how this art developed with the use of seven colours. See Fig. 2. The purity of colour is worthy of Raphael, and the skill of composition and of draftsmanship on this 18-foot-long panel is paralleled only by the painting which one must imagine was the model for the Alexander Mosaic, portraying Alexander in the battle of Issus. The strength and the naturalness of attitudes of the huntsmen and their horses are such as we have seen in the Rape of Persephone, but there is an even greater skill in the use of perspective, and a new mastery in the portrayal of the hunted animals and of the trees and flowers of the forest glade. Paintings such as these were the models for those which have survived at Pompeii and Herculaneum.[1]

The development of funerary architecture has also been revealed by excavation. The cist tomb of Amyntas III, originally crowned by a small tumulus,[2] is not unusual except for its frescoes and its size, but the tomb of Philip II is the earliest known example of a new architectural form, which was certainly invented in Macedonia and came into fashion only in Macedonia and in adjacent regions. The exact specification of such a tomb was provided *c*. 350 B.C. by Plato in *Laws* 947 D, when he wanted it to be used for the leading statesmen of his ideal state.

Their tomb shall be constructed underground, in the form of an oblong vault of spongy stone, as long-lasting as possible, and fitted with couches set side by side; in this, when they have laid him who is gone to his rest, they shall make a mound in a circle round it and plant thereon a grove of trees, save only at one extremity, so that at that point the tomb may for all time admit of enlargement, in case there be need of additional mounds for the buried.[3]

The source of this specification was surely Plato's pupil, Euphraeus, the philosopher in residence at the Macedonian court, who may have attended the burial of Alexander II in 368 or that of Perdiccas III in 359.[4] The tomb of Philip II at Aegeae corresponded exactly with the

[1] For commentaries see Andronicos, *V* and articles by P. H. von Blanckenhausen and N. Yalouris in *M–G* 251 ff. and 263 ff., and Pollitt 191 f. with Fig. 204.

[2] The tumulus was traditional; see C. 7. 9. 21 and H*PT* 332. For such large built cist tombs of the Geometric period at Argos see HR*TV* 115.

[3] The translation is that of R. G. Bury in the Loeb edition. 'Spongy stone' is the *pōros* stone which was used for all three tombs, and the circular tumulus was built over, rather than 'round', the tomb. 'Need of additional mounds' is inaccurate; the meaning is 'need of mounded earth' as opposed to the tree-growing ground, so that another burial could be put into the earth of the mound.

[4] See Volume II. 188 for Euphraeus. The attendance of cavalrymen and infantrymen in full armour, leading the funeral procession in the *Laws*, was a Macedonian practice as we see from Arr. *An*. 2. 12. 1.

specification, even to the circular tumulus with the possibility of adding another burial at one extremity, but it was even grander in that it had two chambers and an ornamental façade. This type of built tomb, covered by a tumulus of soil, fulfilled its function of housing and preserving the remains of the dead and the offerings placed there for their use in an after-life. The paintings within the tomb and on the façade were in honour of, and for the delight of, the buried persons, and not for public spectacle. The architectural design is most pleasing. The vaulted roof,[1] so suitable for sustaining the massive weight of soil, gives an upward lift, which contrasts with the rectangular forms of the tomb (for there is no pediment above the façade of the tombs of Philip II and Alexander IV). The noble façade of Philip's tomb, with its attached pillars, tall doors, and beautiful fresco, invests this variation on the theme of the cist tomb under a tumulus with the dignity of a religious monument.[2] See Pl. II.

Within the next generation the Macedonian 'built tomb', as it is often called, attained its standard form with the addition of a rather shallow pediment and architectural details as in a Greek temple above the façade. Thus in the tomb excavated by K. A. Rhomaios at Aegeae the temple-like effect is heightened by the tall Ionic pillars, the narrow panel for the fresco with its floral design, and the magnificent portal. A superb marble throne, with griffins on the arms, left by the tomb-robbers, shows that it was a royal tomb; if the date *c.* 300 is correct, the occupant of this tomb which holds an important position close to the ancient city may well have been Cassander.[3] The Great Tomb at Lefkadhia, usually dated to the same period, is much more pretentious, with its double storey and second set of pillars on the façade (as on the façade of Pythippus at Thasos). Here paint is used with great skill to produce a novel effect, namely to create the illusion that a painted scene or an architectural detail is not flat, but in relief.[4] The dead man is portrayed as in life, wearing a white cuirass over a purple-red *chiton*. He stands expectant while Hermes is motioning him towards the doorway, beyond which the two judges of the underworld are awaiting his arrival. The amazing quality of the figures is due to the naturalness

---

[1] For the vault see HRTV 115 n. 11, with references to those who held that the vault came into use only after A.'s expedition to Asia.

[2] The fullest account is in Andronicos, *V*; for a commentary see S. G. Miller in *M–G* 153 ff. She is inclined to judge the building as if it were freestanding (her p. 155); but it was to be buried at once and for ever, and the function of the façade was religious, not architectural or illusionistic. The Macedonian vaulted crypt, as a tomb or/and shrine, has had an amazingly long life in Christian architecture.

[3] K. A. Rhomaios, ὁ Μακεδονικὸς τάφος τῆς Βεργίνας (Athens, 1951). See Miller, loc. cit. 155 ff. with Figs. 7, 8, and 9.

[4] Ph. M. Petsas, ὁ τάφος τῶν Λευκαδίων (Athens, 1966) and Miller, loc. cit. 153 ff. with Figs. 1–5 and *M–G* 194 Fig. 6 for Pythippus' façade.

of their postures and the clever use of colour and shading, which makes them stand out from the light background as if in relief sculpture.[1] Here too we see the antecedent of Roman painting at Pompeii and Herculaneum.

Another Macedonian art was mosaic with rounded pebbles, which provide a subtler interplay of reflected light than the flat tesserae of Roman mosaic. Pella has yielded striking examples of late-fourth-century mosaic, which show the vigour and the naturalism we noted in the frescoes of the tombs at Aegeae. A remarkable effect is achieved by the use of white pebbles for the figures of men and animals against a dark background. The Stag Hunt mosaic has an outer border of the breaking-wave design, which is the same whether you look at the black pebbles or at the white pebbles (Pl. IV). There follows a rectangular frame in white, which encloses an amazingly delicate and intricate floral design, and then another rectangular frame in white, within which the central picture is presented. The figures there of the two huntsmen with flying cloak, naked bodies, and raised weapons are superbly arranged over the faltering stag, its dark eye looking towards the viewer.[2]

Macedonia led the way also in metallurgical skills, not surprisingly, as she had such large deposits of gold, silver, copper, and iron. The discoveries at Trebenishte and at Sindos and Sedhes show that these skills had a long history in Macedonia, and the objects found in the tombs of Philip II and Alexander IV mark the zenith of the metal-working art. The gold wreaths of oak-leaves and acorns and the gold wreath of myrtle leaves with insects in the blossoms are as fine as anything anywhere; for they show in metal the delicacy of observation and of touch which we see in the frescoes and the mosaics. There were many references in literature to the gold and silver goblets, vessels, and spoons which were to be seen in use in Macedonia, and the forty-five silver vessels and spoons in these two tombs reveal to us how attractive they were in shape and in finish. The tiny heads at the base of the handles rival the five ivory heads from Philip's tomb in expressiveness and variety. They stand supreme in miniature work. Nor should we omit the ceremonial shield in gold, silver, and ivory, the gold-engraved greaves, the iron cuirass with gold fittings, the iron helmet, and the silver-gilt diadem with the snakeskin design.[3] Equal artistry is shown

---

[1] See *M–G* 256 and 266.

[2] Ph. M. Petsas, 'Mosaics from Pella', *La Mosaïque gréco-romaine* (Paris, 1965) 41 ff. and *Archaeology* 17 (1964) 74 ff.; and for commentary M. Robertson in *M–G* 241 ff. with his Figs. 1 and 2, and Pollitt 41 with Fig. 35.

[3] The best reproductions are in Andronicos, in *Macedonia*, and in *Philip of Macedon*, edd. M. B. Hatzopoulos and L. Loukopoulou. See also *M–G* 141 ff. and 123 ff. for the jewelry and vessels, on which R. A. Higgins and B. Barr-Sharrar comment.

in the coinages of Philip and Alexander which set the fashion for the Hellenistic period, and a similar grasp of architectural principles appears in the palaces and the town planning, with which we shall deal later. Enough has been said to show that Macedonia in the time of Philip and Alexander was a great innovator in painting, mosaic, funerary architecture, and metal-working, and that its influence on subsequent generations was seminal and longlasting. The Macedonian element in what we call Hellenistic civilization was an important one, whether we look to South Italy, Egypt, Antioch, or Aï Khanum.

The effects of the civil wars of 322–301 were superficial, though with some exceptions. The wars were waged between armies of professional soldiers and sailors of almost all races within the Macedonian world: professional in the sense that they were well paid and highly trained and sought regular employment. Battles on land were decided often by manœuvre and counter-manœuvre rather than by bloody conflict; desertions were common and the defeated were taken prisoner and often re-employed at once. This was true even of the Lamian War. Exceptional events were the massacre of the Greek mercenaries in 323, the death in battle of 8,000 of Eumenes' men in 320, and the killing of 5,000 soldiers by the 3,000 Silvershields in their famous charge in 317.[1] In battles at sea ships were frequently captured 'with their crews' intact, and it was usual to pick up survivors in the water.[2] It is probable that more lives were lost in storm than in battle, for instance in the abortive invasion of Egypt by Antigonus and Demetrius and in the attempt of Macedonian reinforcements to cross the Black Sea. Great expenditures on armaments, whether by Cassander, Athens, or Antigonus, had the merit of providing employment. There were regional losses caused by pillaging and ravaging—notably in Babylonia after 311 and in mainland Greece in 304—but it must be admitted that the presence of garrison troops and the movement of large armies and fleets created markets for those who had supplies to sell.[3]

The general picture was one of increasing prosperity and urbanization, in spite of the civil wars. The tradition of responsible and capable government which Alexander had inaugurated was maintained in the eastern-Asian satrapies by Peucestes, Seleucus, Tlepolemus, Stasanor, and Oxyartes, for instance, and the competent administration of Egypt and the western-Asiatic satrapies enabled Ptolemy and Antigonus to pay for their massive armaments. Egypt in particular exported vast amounts of foodstuffs, for instance to Rhodes in peace and also under

---

[1] D.S. 18. 7. 2–9; 18. 40. 8; 19. 43. 1.

[2] D.S. 18. 45. 4; Polyaen. 4. 6. 9; D.S. 20. 52. 4 and 6. For desertion by crews see Polyaen. 4. 6.

[3] M. M. Austin in *CQ* 36 (1986) 465 notes the importance of pillaging, especially in the third century.

siege.[1] This general prosperity was of greater benefit to the Greek cities in Asia, the Phoenician cities of the Levant, and Alexandria in Egypt, than to the cities of the Greek mainland. But the size of Athens' fleet in the Lamian War and again in 306, and the proverbial wealth of Rhodes as the entrepreneur of maritime trade show that they enjoyed larger revenues than ever. The comedies of Menander give us an insight into the life of a prosperous and sophisticated society of citizens, resting, as in the past, on a substructure of impoverished and slave labour. Macedonia was one of the leading beneficiaries of increasing trade within the Balkan area of which she held the central position and within the Mediterranean; for her exports of foodstuffs, timber, minerals, and weaponry were much in demand. The great palace at Aegeae was built in this period, and the superb mosaics in large rooms at Pella are 'indications of the magnificence of the capital of the Macedonian kings'.[2]

The generals followed the example of Alexander in using Balkan troops and in training Asiatics in the Greek language and Macedonian weaponry. Thus Antigonus, for instance, had 'about 5,000 men of all sorts of races who were armed in the Macedonian style' in his phalanx at Gabiene.[3] Huge armies and navies were recruited very largely from Greeks, Egyptians, islanders, Phoenicians, Balkan peoples, and all varieties of Asiatics: for instance, about 100,000 men in 360 warships and 200 transporters in and off Salamis in Cyprus, 120,000 men on land and sea invading Egypt under Antigonus and Demetrius, and 150,000 men in the conflict at Ipsus. The proportion of Macedonians was very small, as in the last years of Alexander's life. For instance, at the battle of Paraetacene in 317 out of a total of 65,000 infantrymen there were 6,000 Macedonians on Eumenes' side and 8,000 on Antigonus' side; and the proportion must have been much smaller at Ipsus. Yet these Macedonian troops were of the greatest importance, militarily and politically. We shall therefore attempt to determine the numbers and the dispositions of the various groups.

First-line Macedonian infantrymen under arms in 323/2 may be estimated as follows. A: 15,000 in Macedonia. B: 10,000 (or thereabouts) veterans in Babylonia. C: 10,000 veterans with Craterus in Cilicia. D: 3,000 'descendants of the Hypaspists', i.e. the sons of the Silvershields, also in Babylonia.[4] I shall refer to them by these letters.

[1] D.S. 20. 81. 4 and 96. 1.
[2] *Macedonia* Pls. 110, 116, and 117, and Petsas, *Pella* 28, 113, and 123 ff. For personal wealth see Athen. 128–30.
[3] D.S. 19. 27. 6.
[4] Thus Antipater took 13,000 Macedonian infantry into Greece, while leaving Sippas in Macedonia with 'sufficient troops' and orders to raise more (D.S. 18. 12. 2); and A. had planned shortly before to take 10,000 or so from Macedonia to replace the returning veterans (Arr. *An.* 7.

When Craterus and Antipater crossed from Europe to Asia in 321, leaving an unsettled situation, they took perhaps, at a guess, 3,000 men of A and Craterus brought back most of the 6,000 veterans of C who had fought at the battle of Crannon.[1] Of these the 3,000 stayed with Antigonus down to Ipsus; the 6,000 mostly joined Antigonus, who had rather more than 5,000 of them in 320 (D.S. 18. 40. 7), but in the winter of 320/19 he sent 3,000 of them to Macedonia (Polyaen. 4. 6. 6). The 4,000 veterans of C who were left behind in Cilicia served at first under Neoptolemus and Alcetas; those under Neoptolemus went via Eumenes to Antigonus late in 321, and those under Alcetas reached Antigonus in 319 (D.S. 18. 50. 1). So perhaps 3,000 of these the C veterans were with Antigonus. In all, then, Antigonus had 8,000 Macedonian infantrymen, as at Paraetacene in 318 (D.S. 19. 29. 3).[2]

The B veterans ran a different course: with Perdiccas, his two successors, and Antigonus as the Royal Army, unruly and mutinous in demanding a bounty, and then transferred to Antipater and taken back to Macedonia in winter 321/0 except for the 3,000 Silvershields (*FGrH* 156 (Arrian) F 9. 32 and 11. 44). Those 3,000 Silvershields and their descendants, the 3,000 of D, collected the treasure from Susa in 321, joined Eumenes when he came to Cilicia, and betrayed him to Antigonus in 317.[3] Thereafter the Silvershields were split up and disappeared from history, whereas their descendants served Antigonus as Hypaspists until his death. There were in addition small numbers of Macedonian infantrymen with Ptolemy and Lysimachus, and a sprinkling of ex-soldiers in the new cities of Alexander.

If our analysis is correct, the Macedonian infantrymen who had served with Alexander had almost all returned to Macedonia by 319, except two very elderly groups—the 3,000 veterans of C and the 3,000 Silvershields. The departure of the infantrymen was a matter of great political importance. They had always been nationalistic in a narrow sense. For instance, although Greek speech was the norm in Alexander's army, these Macedonians used the Macedonian patois among themselves and even flattered their brilliant Greek commander,

12. 4). For B (in the text) see H*A* 240 and 245; the figure of 13,000 in C. 10. 2. 8 does not specify Macedonians, but may be correct for them, if group D was formed by then and was included. For C see D.S. 18. 4. 1. For D see Hammond in *CQ* 28 (1978) 133 n. 21, and 135, citing other views.

[1] Droysen 2. 1. 71, 'er hatte die 10,000 Veteranen aus dem grossen makedonischen Heere...mit sich', misreads D.S. 18. 16. 4. In point of fact 4,000 veterans stayed in Asia.

[2] *FGrH* 156 (Arrian) F 11. 43, where a noun has dropped out after πεντακοσίους, because 500 is appropriate for the Companion Cavalry, and because 8,000 recurs in D.S. 19. 29. 3 (although his remark that Antipater had given *these* 8,000 men to Antigonus is not correct). See *CQ* 28. 134.

[3] *FGrH* 156 (Arrian) F 9. 35 and 38 may both refer to the Silvershields; if not, the 'roughly 3,000 mutinous Macedonians' may have included some of 'the descendants of the Hypaspists', a group which apparently moved with the Silvershields (D.S. 19. 28. 1).

Eumenes, by acclaiming him in it.[1] They were resentful if any other troops were treated with honour. They hated the introduction of Asians first in parallel units and then in mixed units, and Alexander's policy towards the Asians altogether. They were thus a dangerous element in the post-Alexander period, when Macedonian and Asian had to serve and live together. The infantrymen who did continue in Asia—apart from the two groups we have mentioned—were the 3,000 'descendants of the Hypaspists' by mixed marriages, the descendants of the 10,000 veterans by mixed marriages (Arr. *An.* 7. 12. 2) and the 'descendants of the settlers in the upper satrapies' (D.S. 19. 29. 2). They had every reason to support the Asian policy of Alexander. The other Macedonian infantrymen who stayed in Asia—the 3,000 brought from Macedonia in 321—were destined to take their wives and make their fortunes in Asia over the next twenty years. Thus the way was cleared, more by accident than by intention, for the Asian policy of Alexander to be implemented.

The military value of the Macedonian veteran infantrymen can hardly be overestimated. They crushed the rising of the 23,000 Greek settlers so drastically that others stayed in their cities; the group that went to Greece with Craterus turned the scales at Crannon; and a few hundred veterans enabled Seleucus to win Babylonia.[2] But by 319 the veterans of Alexander had fulfilled their function in Asia in a military sense. They had ensured Macedonian ascendancy in an astonishing manner. When they left Asia, the lands 'won by the spear' were firmly held and even extended, huge new armies of Asians trained by Macedonians and commanded by Macedonians were taking control, and the flow of Macedonian soldiers who were the fruit of mixed marriages was beginning to compensate for the departure of the veterans. Part at least of Alexander's plans for an Asian army was being realized.

There is less evidence for the numbers of Macedonian cavalrymen, that is of Companion Cavalrymen and the *asthippoi*[3] brought from

---

[1] *PEum* 14. 5, treating him as one of themselves. On another occasion Eumenes appealed to their *amour propre* by sending a Macedonian officer to address the Macedonian phalanx in the patois (*PSI* 12. 2 (1951) no. 1284, republished by A. B. Bosworth in *GRBS* 19 (1978) 227 ff. with commentary). I do not agree with the deduction of Bosworth and E. Badian that these Macedonians did not understand or speak Greek (Badian in *M–G* 41); for they fail to realize that φωνή is normally used of dialect (e.g. Thuc. 6. 5. 1 and 7. 57. 2) and γλῶσσα of language, as in the word δίγλωσσος (Arr. *An.* 3. 6. 6). In giving Eumenes a bodyguard of 1,000 Macedonians they treated him as if he were a king (cf. D.S. 17. 110. 1; J. 12. 12. 4 and 13. 3. 1).

[2] The force in D.S. 19. 90. 1 and 3 (cf. App. *Syr.* 9. 54 with more troops) included 'soldiers who had campaigned with A.'.

[3] For the *asthippoi* and the application of the figure 800 see Hammond in *CQ* 28 (1978) 128 ff. For the meaning of this word and of *asthetairoi* as 'townsmen-cavalry' and 'townsmen-companions' see Hammond, ibid., comparing the contraction of πεζοὶ ἑταῖροι into πεζέταιροι. Bosworth 252

Macedonia in 321. At Paraetacene in 318 there were altogether 2,500 of the former, and the *asthippoi* together with 'the descendants of the settlers in the upper satrapies' (of Asia) numbered 800. Thus, apart from the *asthippoi*, they were all men with long service in Asia or men recruited in Asia. Their estates and their future lay in Asia, where they served for the rest of the period of which we are writing. Militarily they remained the élite cavalry. Politically they provided the advisers, administrators, and subordinate commanders of the generals and after 306 the 'kings'.

Macedonia itself had received back its heroes,[1] the nationalistic veterans, who had shown their wishes in the mutiny at Opis. They themselves and the example they set maintained the military superiority of the Macedonian phalanx in Europe. Even if its cavalry deserted or were defeated, the phalanx fought on to win in the end. Politically the veterans had great influence. They brought the elderly Polyperchon to power, put too much faith in a Eurydice or an Olympias, and were personally involved in the cause of Antipater's son versus Antigonus' son. Thus in 304 6,000 Macedonians deserted Cassander for Demetrius (*PD* 23. 1). They were renowned for their instability, their changeableness—τὸ τῶν Μακεδόνων εὐμετάβολον (D.S. 19. 51. 3); and it was this defect in them and their descendants in Europe which tore Macedonia apart time after time.

During this period Macedonia was always short of 'citizen soldiers', i.e. Macedones proper, as Diodorus remarked at the beginning of the Lamian War: ἐσπάνιζε γὰρ ἡ Μακεδονία στρατιωτῶν πολιτικῶν, 18. 12. 2. She made up the deficiency by recruiting men within the kingdom (some were not originally Greek-speaking, but were of Paeonian, Thracian, or Illyrian origin),[2] and this had the effect of fusing the various *ethne* into a unity. In addition the policy of planting foreign peoples within the borders of the kingdom was continued, for instance when Cassander planted large groups of Autariatae in 312 and 310. Some of these Autariatae were recruited and served with pay, but they changed sides readily and were not dependable. Lysimachus lost 2,000

continues to derive the *asth-* from a postulated adverb ἄσιστα (better Greek would be ἀσσότατοι or with Aeschylus ἄσσιστοι). He overlooks the planting of towns in Upper Macedonia (see J. 8. 5. 7 and 6. 1, 'in finibus ipsis' and 'in extremis regni terminis'; and Volume II. 660 f.). Excavation has shown us Heraclea Lyncestis near Bitola and a town near Florina at Xenia (*AR* 1982–3. 37); HH *Via Egnatia* 1. 141 saw another town of this time near Petres.

[1] See *PA* 71. 8 for honours paid to veterans in Macedonia.

[2] In 323 and 322, in D.S. 18. 12. 2, 14. 5 and 16. 4, Sippas was told to recruit soldiers, Leonnatus recruited 'many Macedonian soldiers', Craterus enlisted 4,000 soldiers ἐν παρόδῳ, which probably included Macedonia, and Perdiccas hoped to get drafts of recruits from Macedonia (J. 13. 6. 6). As the source of these passages was Hieronymus, the information is dependable. It shows conclusively that Macedonia had not been drained of its reserves in men by Alexander.

by desertion and massacred another 5,000 in case they should desert in 302.[1] The use of non-citizen troops from within the kingdom explains the difference between Antipater's army of 13,000 Macedonians in 323 (D.S. 18. 12. 2) and Cassander's army in 302: for even after the desertion of 6,000 Macedonians and the sending of troops to Lysimachus, Cassander had 29,000 infantry and 2,000 cavalry for his campaign in Thessaly.[2]

During the civil wars, wherever there were large groups of Macedonian soldiers, they maintained the traditions of the Macedonian constitution. The Macedones, rightly called by Diodorus 'citizen soldiers' (στρατιῶται πολιτικοί), met in Assembly to elect kings and managers of kings or king, to confirm the appointments of generals and satraps, to carry measures of political importance, and to conduct trials. In Greek authors the Assembly was named τὸ κοινὸν τῶν Μακεδόνων πλῆθος (D.S. 18. 4. 3), οἱ Μακεδόνες (18. 4. 6), τὸ πλῆθος (*FGrH* 156 F 1. 7 and *PD* 18. 1), ἡ κοινὴ ἐκκλησία (D.S. 19. 61. 1), and ἡ ἐκκλησία (18. 30. 2); and in Justin's Latin 'Macedones' (14. 1. 1), 'contio' (13. 3. 8), 'exercitus' (15. 2. 11, electing Ptolemy king), and 'populus' (15. 2. 10, electing Antigonus and Demetrius kings).[3] Sometimes the Macedones of an Assembly were defined more closely. Olympias asked to be tried before 'all Macedones', viz. of Macedonia. When Antigonus had measures carried by 'the Macedones with Antigonus', the Macedones were not only his soldiers, but also Macedones resident there, viz. ex-soldiers (D.S. 19. 61. 1 and 62. 1). In the homeland itself these institutions were ancient and endemic (see Volume II. 160 f. and *CQ* 30 (1980) 461 ff.). The transplantation and

---

[1] D.S. 20. 113. 3 and Polyaen. 4. 12. 1. It is probable that the Autariatae were among the troops sent in two groups by Cassander to Lysimachus (20. 107. 1 and 112. 1–4). F. Papazoglou in *Misc. G. Novak* (ed. Mirosavljević, Zagreb, 1970), 335 gives a different interpretation.

[2] D.S. 20. 110. 4. The army included probably men from Thessaly, but not from Epirus, where the situation was unstable. Tarn's statement in *CAH* 6. 468, that Antipater and Craterus crossed to Asia in 321 'with 32,500 men chiefly Macedonians', is extraordinary; he seems to have taken and misapplied the figure in D.S. 18. 24. 1. While Antipater took a part of their forces towards Cilicia, Craterus went towards Eumenes with '2,000 cavalry and 20,000 infantrymen among whom were the majority of Macedonians famous for deeds of valour', the majority, that is, of the veterans Craterus had had in Cilicia.

[3] This is not a complete list, of course, but just examples of what figures in our texts. It is obvious that authors like Diodorus and Polyaenus, uninterested in the details of constitutional procedures, simply said '*A* appointed *B*'. In particular I disagree with the view of Gruen, 'Coronation' 256, that the generals decided to appoint themselves 'kings' and so created a 'personal, charismatic' form of monarchy. Anyone can call himself 'king', as in the game 'king of the castle'; but what makes a real king is the backing of the people who elect him. Thus 'coronation' did not signify just 'an exalted prestige' (his p. 262). Sometimes one author will give only one stage, and another author will give a different stage. Thus D.S. 19. 46.4 has Pithon condemned in a court of 'those participating in the Council' (ἐν τοῖς μετέχουσι τοῦ συνεδρίου), and Polyaen. 4. 6. 14 before 'the Assembly of the Macedones' (τὸ κοινὸν τῶν Μακεδόνων), i.e. of the Macedones with Antigonus. Unless *synhedrion* is here synonymous with *koinon*, we see two stages in the process of convicting Pithon.

the perpetuation of these institutions were important factors in retaining the Macedonian character of Alexander's world.

There was continuity likewise in the two kings, and after Philip's death in the one king. The fact that they were incapable of ruling did not impair the continuity of the royal house; and the kings were equipped with all the traditional paraphernalia and ceremonial. Thus the two kings had seven *somatophylakes*,[1] although they were incompetent or too young for combat respectively. Even if the Crown was administered by a 'manager', it was the Crown which appointed the generals and the satraps and made their tenure of power legal. It is very illuminating that Antigonus strained every nerve to represent himself not as a rebel, but as 'the properly constituted general and the one who has taken over the management of the monarchy' (D.S. 19. 61. 3). If one could claim connection with the royal house, the Temenidae, that was a great asset for an ambitious general, as it had been for Perdiccas and Leonnatus. Ptolemy sought that asset by claiming to be the child of a cousin or a mistress of Philip II.

When the death of Alexander IV was officially known, the generals tried to justify their claim to be 'kings'. Antigonus harked back to his original, but time-limited, appointment as general of Asia, and he no doubt reaffirmed his claim to universal rule (as in D.S. 19. 61. 3).[2] On the other hand, Ptolemy, Lysimachus, and Seleucus claimed, with justification, that they were 'keeping the parts which had been given originally to them' (D.S. 20. 53. 4; cf. Arr. *Succ.* F 1, 5, and 7, and F 9. 34–5). Cassander had no such claim; but we may assume that he had been formally elected 'manager of the king' in Macedonia in 316.

---

[1] Probably from the time of their election, and even for the final months of Roxane's pregnancy, according to Appian (*Syr.* 52). If so, those of Philip were replaced by new ones at Triparadeisus (*FGrH* 156 (Arrian) F 9. 38); those of Alexander IV are mentioned in *IG* ii². 561, dated *c.* 307–301 B.C. They were not normally attendant upon the king except in battle; and I doubt if they were abolished in 316 by Cassander, as S. M. Burstein has suggested in *ZPE* 24 (1977) 223 f., citing D.S. 19. 52. 4. See W. Heckel in *ZPE* 40 (1980) 249 f. commenting on *IG* ii². 561 as evidence for the two kings sharing the rule equally.

[2] The aim of Antigonus to obtain the universal rule was noted already in P*Eum* 12. 1 τῇ γνώμῃ τὴν ὅλην περιβαλλόμενος ἡγεμονίαν. Gruen, 'Coronation' 259 sees no difference between Antigonus' claims and those of the others who became kings. In D.S. 19. 61. 3–4, however, Antigonus demanded that Cassander (then in Macedonia) should obey him, that Greece should be free under his own aegis, and that the generals and satraps of 'the upper satrapies' should support him. It is true that he claimed to be acting on behalf of 'the kings from Alexander', i.e. Philip III and Alexander IV; but the intention of controlling the whole of Alexander's legacy is surely clear, and it became more realistic with the removal of Alexander's heirs. His first act after being proclaimed king was to launch a large-scale invasion of Egypt. That did not indicate that he had reduced his claims. Gruen lays much emphasis on P*D* 18. 2 τῶν ἄλλων αὐτὸν βασιλέα καὶ γραφόντων καὶ καλούντων, as if it meant that Antigonus recognized Cassander as king, but in the context Plutarch is writing of their subjects calling these generals—Ptolemy, Lysimachus, Seleucus, and Cassander—kings, so that I take τῶν ἄλλων to mean 'the other people' and not 'the other kings'.

Some of the kings made the additional claim that they had won further lands 'by the spear'. Thus Ptolemy had been authorized in 321 to acquire (and had in fact acquired) further lands to the west of Egypt (ὅ τι περ ἄν...δορὶ ἐπικτήσηται), and Seleucus 'acquired in addition the upper satrapies' (D.S. 20. 53. 4 προσκεκτημένος).[1] This concept of a kingdom as being territorially defined with additional land won by the spear was very old in Macedonia (Thuc. 2. 99; Arist. *Pol.* 1310ᵇ38 κτησάμενοι χώραν). Alexander had applied it in pre-empting his conquest of Asia at the Hellespont as δορίκτητον (D.S. 17. 17. 2, derived from Diyllus), and the fact that Ptolemy had twice defended Egypt against attack entitled him in his opinion to 'hold the land as won by the spear' (D.S. 18. 39. 5 and 20. 76. 7 δορίκτητον ἔχειν τὴν χώραν).

Every person within such a kingdom was subject to the king. It was he who granted various forms of privilege and status; and in particular he granted full citizenship to those who were to become Macedones. It was the Macedones of the moment who elected and acclaimed a new king in these new kingdoms. Antigonus recognized no kingdom but his own. The other four kings recognized one another's kingdoms. Thus four of the so-called 'Hellenistic' kingdoms came into being, each based on Macedonian precedent. One of the four was 'Macedonia', an area which had been very largely cut off from Thrace, Asia, and Egypt since the return of Antipater in the winter of 321/0.

The Macedonians respected all members of the ruling house, both the living and the dead. They were horrified by the treatment of Cynane, of Eurydice and Philip, of Olympias, of Cleopatra, and of Heracles. Alexander's spirit lived. The succession was decided in the presence of his corpse (J. 13. 4. 4). He was present at the deliberations of Eumenes and his staff, and he inspired a dream which led Eumenes to victory. The favour of Philip and Alexander was sought by the sacrifices which the armies of Eumenes and Peucestes made at Persepolis.[2] The honouring of Alexander's mummified body in Alexandria brought his blessing upon Ptolemy and Egypt.[3] When the death of Alexander IV was made public, he was buried in a monumental tomb within the tumulus which contained the tombs of the deified kings, Amyntas III and Philip II.[4] Other members of the royal house were buried 'royally': Philip Arrhidaeus, Eurydice, and Cynane; Cleopatra (D.S. 20. 37. 6); and later Olympias, whom Alexander had

---

[1] Lysimachus tried to acquire land north of the Danube in 'the desert of the Getae' (Str. C 305); this attempt is dated by F. Papazoglou, *Misc. G. Novak* loc. cit. (p. 192 n. 1), on the evidence of App. *Illyr.* 4 to before 302 B.C.

[2] D.S. 19. 22, which should be compared with its predecessor in Arr. *An.* 7. 11. 8–9.

[3] See Athen. 201 d for the continuing worship of Alexander.   [4] H*RTV* 16.

intended to deify after death.[1] When Antigonus became a king, he accorded the honour of 'royal' burial to his son Phoenix (D.S. 20. 73. 1). That burial and the association of Demetrius in the kingship marked the continuation of a Macedonian belief, that the kingship was vested in a family rather than in an individual. The other new kings took note.

Whatever they called themselves, the great men of the civil wars depended, as Alexander had done, on the co-operation of their Friends. They used marriage to bind to themselves some of their friends and allies of whatever race (Seleucus marrying a Bactrian princess, Lysimachus a Persian aristocrat); for they practised polygamy, like the Macedonian kings. They lavished large estates and honorific gifts on their friends and helpers (P*Eum* 8. 7. and D.S. 20. 28. 2–3), consulted them frequently in council, and promoted them to command satrapies or armies. Each great general had his special bodyguard and cavalry squadron (*agema*), and he maintained his own School of Pages.[2] He had his own courtiers (called collectively ἡ θεραπεία), and there was in his army a hierarchy of military and racial rank (e.g. at Persepolis and in burial, P*Eum* 9. 2). Thus the generals were copying the methods and reproducing the court of Alexander in a great many ways. What they lacked was the ability to inspire trust and loyalty in their Friends and even in their relations. For in a civil war the stakes were high, and there was no traditional tie between the dynast and his leading commanders.

In a passage which may perhaps be derived from Timagenes,[3] those who contended for the 'successionem regni' were contrasted with Alexander to their advantage (J. 13. 1. 10–15). Such a judgement is ludicrous. Alexander acquired the empire, originated the principles of its structure, and devised the methods of controlling and developing it. His successors tore the empire apart, impaired the principles of

---

[1] For the mounded tomb (*tymbos*) of Olympias see the epitaph cited by C. F. Edson in *Hesp.* 18 (1949) 87 and his discussion of it. The two mounded tombs of Olympias and Neoptolemus (an Aeacid) may be those north of Korinos, which are marked as 'T T' on Fig. 17; only one of the pair has been excavated.

[2] The guards were known as ὑπασπισταί (e.g. Polyaen. 4. 11. 2). Pages fought as cavalry units (D.S. 19. 28. 3 τῶν Εὐμένους παίδων εἴλας δύο, totalling 100 boys, and 19. 29. 5 ἐκ τῶν ἰδίων παίδων εἶλαι τρεῖς, being the Pages of Antigonus). The term ἴδιοι παῖδες was evidently a technical one; it occurs also in connection with Eumenes in Polyaen. 4. 8. 4 ἡγεμόνας μετὰ τῶν ἰδίων παίδων. At a time when the generals did not claim themselves to be kings, it was natural to use the expression ἴδιοι παῖδες, instead of the βασιλικοὶ παῖδες of Arr. *An.* 4. 16. 6 (cf. 'puerorum regia cohors' in C. 10. 7. 10). The translation 'slaves' by R. M. Geer in the Loeb edition of Diodorus is incorrect, but has been widely accepted.

[3] H*THA* 109 and 186 n. 48. It is from the same source that Justin seems to have derived his sketch of Lysimachus in 15. 3. Trogus was much more concerned with the march of events than with the sort of anecdotes which occur in 15. 3. The early part of the sketch of Seleucus may be from the same source, but the latter part, 15. 4. 10–25, comes from Trogus, as *Prol.* 15 indicates.

administration,[1] and eroded the idea of unification. They showed ability in handling huge armies and navies, preserving the economic strength of most regions, fostering the development of urban centres, and managing their personal advancement. The most divisive, destructive, and ruthless was Antigonus.[2] He was closely rivalled in these respects by Cassander, but Cassander combined his unlovable qualities with the ablest strategic sense of them all. Ptolemy was unique in his *savoir faire*. Lysimachus was probably the most able. He won control of Thrace with tiny forces (D.S. 18. 14. 2–4), extended his authority along the west coast of the Black Sea, and created a very strong kingdom. He rivalled Alexander in personal prowess and in generalship, and he promoted what Philip and Alexander had initiated, the Hellenization of Thrace.

Hellenization is a term of imprecise meaning. The 23,000 Greek settlers in Asia and the city-states of the Greek mainland were the chief opponents of the Macedonians; and the only settlers who are known to have gone out from Athens of their own will headed for the West, not for the East. Greek individuals of the mainland, the islands and the cities of the Asian shore were a different matter. What attracted them was money to be earned in all fields of enterprise in the new world. Greeks were in great demand and ample supply as mercenary soldiers and sailors (though rivalled as soldiers by Thracians in the eastern satrapies), and as entertainers and athletes and artists in the festivals and at the courts of the dynasts (e.g. D.S. 20. 108. 1). Their skills as traders and craftsmen ranked high throughout the East, and they could command high wages and acquire capital in the cities founded by Alexander and the Successors. There they were accorded a privileged status; for together with a small number of Macedonians they were needed to develop the cities as centres of Graeco-Macedonian culture and capitalism. The miracle of this period was the progress of Hellenization in this sense of the word despite the civil wars, and the two powers behind that miracle were the genius of Alexander and the brilliance of fourth-century Greek civilization.[3] There was no continuation of the racial exclusiveness of the fifth-century city-state. Rather the attitude of Alexander to marriage predominated. For in the East especially Greeks and Macedonians must often have taken Asians as legitimate wives, and it was significant of the current attitude that Seleucus and Sandracottus (Chandragupta) legalized intermarriage between Europeans and Indians by a mutual treaty (Str. 724).

---

[1] Especially Antipater and Cassander *vis-à-vis* the Greek city-states and Antigonus *vis-à-vis* the Persians, e.g. at D.S. 19. 48. 5.

[2] See Beloch 4. 1. 167 f. for a different appreciation.

[3] My view of that civilization is given in H*HG*, esp. 582–95.

PART TWO

FROM THE BATTLE OF IPSUS TO THE DEATH OF ANTIGONUS DOSON

IX

FROM IPSUS TO THE END OF CASSANDER'S DYNASTY (301–294 B.C.)

1. Cassander's last years (301–297 B.C.)[1]

EVER since the defeat of Eumenes in 317 and the capture of the immense resources which followed on this the ambitions of Antigonus had threatened the positions of the rival generals. In 316 he had rejected the advances of Ptolemy, Lysimachus, and Cassander[2] and he made it clear to Cassander in 315 that he meant to take control of Greece and Macedonia, albeit as manager of the two kings.[3] The agreement of 311 was made by Antigonus at the expense of Seleucus[4] and once his hands were free Antigonus concentrated his attack on Ptolemy and refused to consider any compromise with Cassander.[5] In the eyes of his rivals Antigonus intended in 302 to seize Macedonia and then despoil them of their kingdoms.[6] The defeat at Ipsus, the death of Antigonus, and the flight of Demetrius ended what was to prove the only attempt to unite the homeland and the conquests of Alexander under a single rule.

The spoils of victory were now up for bargaining. On hearing of the battle Cassander crossed over from Macedonia to Asia Minor for a conference with Lysimachus and Seleucus, at which the territories of Antigonus were divided;[7] where the three met is not known. In 316

---

[1] The sources for the period from Ipsus (301) to the seizure of the Macedonian throne by Antigonus Gonatas in 277/6 are scanty. Something of the sound tradition established in the lost work of Hieronymus of Cardia (which probably went down to 272) can be recovered from Plutarch's *Lives* of *Demetrius* and *Pyrrhus* and from Trogus Pompeius, whom we possess only in the summary of Justin (Books 15–17) and the contents lists of the various books which survive as *Prologi*. Diodorus used Hieronymus extensively, but unfortunately from Book 21 onward his work exists only in fragments. Those from Books 21 and 22 are relevant for this period. Plutarch's *Demetrius* and *Pyrrhus* also draw on the *Macedonica* of Duris of Samos, which covered Macedonian affairs from 370/69 to 281/0; the tone of this work was hostile towards Macedonia. A little information is recorded by Memnon of Heraclea, a writer of the first century A.D., who used the *History* of the third-century historian Nymphis for the affairs of the area surrounding the Bosphorus and the Black Sea. Otherwise one is reduced to scraps of information surviving in Diogenes Laertius' compendium on the lives of the philosophers, Frontinus' *Stratagems*, Pausanias, the Elder Pliny, and Athenaeus, along with a number of inscriptions and papyri, which are mentioned where relevant. The chronology is difficult to establish and depends on combining information of various kinds; the Athenian archon list is assured only down to 292/1 and for occasional periods later in the century. [2] D.S. 19. 57. 1–2. [3] D.S. 19. 61. 2–4.
[4] D.S. 19. 105. 1. [5] D.S. 20. 106. 1–2. [6] D.S. 20. 106. 4.
[7] App. *Syr.* 55 τὴν Ἀντιγόνου γῆν διενέμοντο; Plb. 5. 67. 8; cf. Niese 1.351 n. 3.

Cassander had been appointed manager of the king's affairs and general of Europe,[1] a position which recalled the title of 'manager plenipotentiary' of the kings which the Macedonians had granted at Triparadeisus to his father Antipater.[2] But since the death of Alexander IV his claim to be king of Macedonia was open to challenge, as Antigonus had demonstrated. Cassander's hopes and ambitions after Ipsus are therefore clear. His first aim must beyond doubt have been to have the victorious allies validate his rule in Macedonia. He may earlier have cherished the further hope of acquisitions in Asia Minor—if indeed it was he and not Asander, the satrap of Caria, who demanded Cappadocia and Lycia in the ultimatum presented to Antigonus in 315.[3] But any such ambitions were now in the past, for Cassander's only direct contribution to the victory had been to send his brother Pleistarchus with a contingent consisting of 12,000 foot and 500 horsemen, and thanks to a chapter of accidents most of these were either taken prisoner or lost in a storm.[4] He could not therefore expect great rewards since, as Seleucus later observed sourly to Ptolemy, 'it was only just that those who were victorious on the battlefield should dispose of the spoils.'[5] However, Pleistarchus himself received territory in Cilicia. Later, having lost Cilicia to Demetrius (see below, p. 205), he is found in Caria where, after the peace of 311, Eupolemus had held a *dynasteia* aligned with Cassander. It was, however, as an independent ruler that Pleistarchus occupied these areas and his only use to Cassander was as an outpost against Demetrius. The links were loose and when at a later date Pleistarchus found himself in trouble, it was first to Seleucus, and only afterwards to Cassander, that he turned. Cassander himself, we may assume, claimed the throne of Macedonia and was granted a free hand in mainland Greece,[6] where of course Demetrius still had substantial possessions.

How far Cassander could exploit the situation there was bound to depend on his own skill and political adroitness and the extent to which he judged control of Greece essential to the safety of Macedonia. It is not easy to estimate his success, given the scantiness of our sources. It has been suggested that his death four years later in 297 may indicate that his ambition and drive were already flagging.[7] That, however, is pure speculation and there is evidence which points against it.[8] On an objective assessment there was much to encourage him. The Athenians had sent troops to help the Antigonids at Ipsus, as allies or

---

[1] J. 14. 5. 3.   [2] D.S. 18. 39. 2 ἐπιμελητὴν...αὐτοκράτορα.   [3] D.S. 19. 57. 1.

[4] D.S. 20. 112. On Cassander's maritime weakness see Buraselis 36.

[5] D.S. 21. 1. 5. This was said of Ptolemy's seizure of Coele–Syria. This region had been assigned to Seleucus, who chose not to press his claim for the time being. On Pleistarchus' position see Buraselis 22–33.   [6] Cf. Will 1². 80.

[7] Fortina 117.   [8] See below, pp. 207–8, for his activities in the Adriatic region.

perhaps as mercenaries,[1] but the news of the catastrophe at once brought about a political upheaval at Athens. Demetrius had many enemies there, who detested his arrogant and despotic ways and licentious conduct,[2] and the pro-Antigonid government under Stratocles was now forced to resign and gave way to a moderate regime committed to a policy of neutrality towards the various dynasts.[3] This political change was perhaps more easily effected if, as is likely, Demetrius had already withdrawn his garrison from Athens before the Ipsus campaign.[4] It was not long before the Athenians were able to give a practical demonstration of their new policy.

From Ipsus Demetrius had fled to Ephesus, where his fleet was stationed. From there he made a detour, sailing to Cilicia to collect his mother Stratonice along with various moneys left there, before returning to Ephesus by way of Salamis in Cyprus.[5] He still held a considerable empire in Asia, which included Parium, Lampsacus, Abydus, Clazomenae, Erythrae, Ephesus, and Miletus in western Asia Minor, Tyre and Sidon in Phoenicia, Cyprus and the Cyclades, all accessible to his fleet;[6] but his immediate concern was to assure his position in Greece, for here was his main reservoir of manpower. Moreover, he had left ships and money along with his wife Deidameia at Athens. But on reaching the Cyclades he was met by an Athenian embassy, which informed him that a decree had recently been passed denying all kings entry into Athens and reported that Deidameia had been sent with due honours to Megara. Restraining his anger, Demetrius sent an embassy to Athens requesting that at least his fleet, including a 'thirteen', should be returned to him; and to this the Athenians agreed. Whether he also recovered his money is not known.[7] It seems likely that Demetrius carried out these negotiations

---

[1] See below, p. 204 n. 2.   [2] *PD* 24, 27; Fortina 112.

[3] The latest inscription with a decree sponsored by Stratocles is *IG* ii². 640, dated to the second prytany of 301/0 (August/September 301).

[4] Cf. D.S. 20. 111. 1–2. A decree for Aristomachus of Argos, dated to the first half of the 240s (Habicht, *Unters.* 124–5) refers to the withdrawal of troops ὑ[πὸ...] from the city (*IG* ii². 774 = *ISE* 1. 23, l. 28), following aid sent by an earlier Aristomachus, and it seems likely that A. Wilhelm (*Wien. Sitzb.* 202. 5 (1925) 15–34) is right in filling the lacuna ὑ[πὸ Δημητρίου] and referring the elder Aristomachus' help to the period immediately before and after the removal of Demetrius' troops in 301. Moretti (*ISE* 1. 23) thinks it unlikely that a decree passed at a time when Athens was under the control of Antigonus Gonatas would have referred to Demetrius' withdrawal; but the alternatives ὑ[πὸ Κασσάνδρου] or ὑ[πὸ Λαχάρους] are hard to reconcile with the statement in the decree that at that time συγκ[ατ]έστησεν Ἀ[θηναίων τὸν δῆμον ἀσφα]λῶς εἰς τὰ μακρὰ τείχη καὶ τὸμ Π[ειραι]ᾶ.

[5] D.S. 21. 1. 4b. According to *PD* 30. 2, he went direct from Ephesus to Greece, but the discrepancy is probably due to Plutarch's having omitted the detour to collect Stratonice and his treasury.

[6] D.S. 20. 107. 1–3, 5; 111. 3; 113. 2 (Sidon); *SIG* 322 (Miletus); *PD* 32. 7 (Sidon and Tyre). On Ephesus see below, p. 206 n. 1. On the Cyclades see Newell, *Coinages* 44.

[7] *PD* 30. 2–31. 2.

from Delos. An extract from the accounts of the *hieropoioi* records that 'when the king had sailed away, they removed the excrement from the shrine with hired labour at a cost of 23 drachmas.' The date of this somewhat discreditable visit was probably 301.[1]

The Athenians were not alone in their reaction to Ipsus. Indeed, Demetrius very soon discovered that his European empire had already crumbled. True, he retained his hold on Euboea, where there is no interruption in the annual issue of Euboean League coinage, silver and bronze;[2] otherwise little was now left of the League of Corinth set up by Antigonus and Demetrius in 302, apart from a few cities around the Isthmus together with the Argolid and parts of Achaea and Arcadia. It has been argued that the League still maintained a nominal existence and that both Pyrrhus, whom Demetrius now designated as his representative in Greece, and Antigonus Gonatas later[3] operated there with the authority and title of general of the Hellenic League.[4] This is not impossible, but if in fact the League did still survive in an attenuated form, it was now no more than a juridical disguise for a handful of Macedonian possessions. Having placed garrisons in the few loyal cities, Demetrius sailed off to the Chersonese to attack Lysimachus' possessions there.[5] It was certainly a stroke of luck for Cassander that Demetrius, with that instability and lack of determination which increasingly characterized him after his father's death, was so easily deflected from the attempt to rebuild a base in Greece.

To what extent Cassander had himself contributed to the collapse of the Antigonid position in Greece is not clear. His policy there had been a mixture of military force and diplomacy. Already in 301 before Ipsus he had tried once to seize the important city of Elatea in Phocis, which commanded the main road south into Boeotia and Attica, but had been forced to abandon the siege by the Athenian Olympiodorus, perhaps helped by Aetolian troops; the Phocians celebrated their deliverance by dedicating a bronze lion to Apollo at Delphi.[6] Once Demetrius had left for the Chersonese, Cassander made another attack on Elatea, probably in 300, and this time managed to take it.[7] It was

---

[1] Cf. *IG* XI. 2. 146 ll. 76–7 ὅτε ὁ βασιλεὺς ἐξέπλευσεν, τὸγ κόπρον ἐξενέγκασιν ἐκ τοῦ ἱεροῦ μισθωτοῖς **ΔΔⱵⱵⱵ**; on the date see Th. Homolle, *Les Archives de l'intendance sacrée à Délos* (Paris, 1887), 114 f.; Buraselis 58 n. 74.

[2] See Picard, *Chalcis* 263–7, who points out that D.L. 2. 140 and 143 give no support to the view that Demetrius lost control of Euboea after Ipsus (so Beloch 4. 2. 462).

[3] So Bengtson, *Strat.* 1. 164–7, comparing *PD* 31. 2 ἀπολιπὼν ἐπὶ τῆς Ἑλλάδος with *IG* IV. 1². 68 ll. 68–9, ὁ στρατηγὸς ὁ ὑπὸ τῶν βασιλέων ἐπὶ τῆς κοινῆς φυλακῆς καταλελειμμένος.

[4] Cf. Beloch 4. 1. 213; Lévêque 106–7.

[5] *PD* 31. 2–4; *PPyrrh* 4. 5; cf. Polyaen. 4. 12. 1; Buraselis 58.

[6] Paus. 10. 18. 6, 34. 3; Flacelière 47 n. 8; 53. Cassander had lost Elatea to Xanthippus in 304 (*SIG* 361B).

[7] The evidence for its acquisition is that Cassander's son, Philip IV, died there in 297 (Eus.1.

very likely their alarm at this threat to their confederacy that led the Aetolians to annex Locris and southern Phocis, to serve as a bulwark on their eastern flank.[1] Shortly afterwards they made a treaty of alliance and mutual assistance with the Boeotians, in which the 'Phocians with the Aetolians'—the phrase distinguishes them from the Phocians now under Cassander—come in as partners on the Aetolian side.[2] The alliance benefited the Boeotians by assuring them some help in the event of any future attack by Demetrius.[3]

These moves were a set-back for Cassander, since they hindered any further expansion to the south. As to his reaction, there are some clues. A Theban inscription (*IG* VII. 2419)[4] lists various cities and rulers who contributed to the costs of rebuilding the city after the reconstitution in 316. Lines 35–40, though fragmentary, mention two kings whose gifts fall later than those of a third king, whose name is also missing, but whose dedication of a tithe from Rhodian spoils identifies him as Demetrius (ll. 30–4). Holleaux argued that the two kings must be Cassander and Lysimachus and the date of their contributions *c.* 299. He also believed that Boeotia must at that time have been under Cassander;[5] but the Aetolo-Boeotian treaty, which was not of course known when Holleaux republished *IG* VII. 2419 in 1895, rules this out.[6] Cassander's contributions must be interpreted on the assumption that (like Lysimachus) he did not control Boeotia in 299. His gift to Thebes is susceptible of two explanations. Following the conclusion of the Aetolo-Boeotian treaty he may have sought to placate the Boeotians by a timely gift to Thebes. Alternatively he may have hoped, in a more Machiavellian fashion, in this way to strengthen and conciliate a city which he had himself refounded, but which, ever since the days of Epaminondas and even before, had been at loggerheads

241 Sch.); that he died while attacking it seems less likely, cf. Flacelière 55. Its seizure could have occurred at any time between 301 and Cassander's death in 297, but the actions of Boeotia and Aetolia suggest that it was in 300.

[1] See Flacelière 55–7; 65, who points out (56 n. 3) that although the precise boundaries between the Aetolian and Macedonian parts of Phocis cannot be determined, the whole plain of the Cephissus must have been in Cassander's hands.

[2] *IG* IX. 1². 1. 170 = *SIG* 366 = *SVA* 463 (the most recent and the best text); cf. Lévêque 136 n. 3. This treaty could just possibly belong to 292/1, which is when Schmitt dates it; but 300/299 is more likely. On the failure of the Aetolians to send help to Thebes in 293/2 see below, p. 221 n. 4. For other suggested dates see Schmitt, *SVA* 463 commentary (p. 99), and the discussion of Flacelière 57–68.

[3] Cf. Flacelière 62.   [4] See especially Holleaux, *Études* I. 1–40 (text on pp. 39–40).

[5] This is a deduction from a supposed attack made by Cassander on Athens in 301/0; but this attack is a chimera, since the occasion when Olympiodorus 'saved Piraeus and Munychia' (Paus. 1. 26. 3) has been shown by Habicht (*Unters.* 102–7) to belong either to 305 or to one of the years immediately before Ipsus (303–301) and more probably the former, since in 304 Boeotia fell under Demetrius, thus constituting an obstacle to any invasion of Attica (Habicht, loc. cit. 107 n. 65).   [6] Assuming that its date is 300 (see above, n. 2).

with the other cities of Boeotia and had only recently been admitted to membership of the Boeotian League.[1]

Lysimachus' gifts to Boeotia have their counterpart in the good relations which he enjoyed about this time with Athens. An Athenian decree honouring the poet Philippides (it was probably passed in 283/2)[2] records how this man had gone as envoy to Lysimachus and had persuaded the king to send a gift of 10,000 *medimni* of corn and a new yard-arm and mast for the Panathenaic ship to Athens. In addition to burying the Athenian dead (from Ipsus) at his own expense, he had also secured the release of the prisoners and of certain opponents of the Antigonids, who had been banished to Asia from Athens and had there fallen into the hands of Lysimachus. This mission of Philippides to Lysimachus is probably to be dated to 299/8, and his friendly response, like his gifts to Boeotia, represented a way of working against Demetrius. As for the Athenians, they interpreted neutrality to mean maintaining friendly and profitable relations with all parties, in so far as that was feasible. It must have been shortly before Philippides' mission to Lysimachus that they had dispatched an embassy to Cassander, for in the second prytany of 299/8 (September 299) an Athenian decree was passed honouring Poseidippus, a member of a well-known Athenian family, for help in this embassy.[3]

As to its purpose, there are various possibilities. It may have been sent to make peace with Cassander following the recent war in which, as we saw, Athens had participated on Demetrius' side. Or peace may already have been made earlier, in which case this embassy had some other end in view. The question of the relations between Athens and Cassander at this time has been unnecessarily complicated by the assumption that there had been active hostilities between the king and the democratic regime set up in 301. A papyrus (*FGrH* 257a = *POxy* 2082), containing fragments of a chronicle dealing with these years, mentions (ll. 8–9) an Athenian expedition (στρατεία) which took place shortly before a political upheaval at Athens. In this Charias, its leader, seized the acropolis and was subsequently tried and, along with some colleagues, executed. Hunt, who originally published the papyrus, took the expedition to be part of the fighting against Cassander in 301.[4] But if, as Habicht has shown,[5] the internal upheaval at Athens

---

[1] Cf. Roesch 417–39; he puts the re-entry of Thebes into the League at the end of 309 or early in 308 (along with Chalcis and Eretria).

[2] *SIG* 374 (archon Euthius); for its date see Habicht, *Unters.* 99 n. 24.

[3] *SIG* 362 (archon Euctemon); for another decree honouring Poseidippus see *IG* ii². 649. Treves, 'Dopo Ipso' 90, thinks Lachares was behind this embassy, but there is no evidence for his influence at this date.

[4] See Jacoby, *FGrH* ii b p. 850; De Sanctis, *Scritti* 1. 355.

[5] Habicht, *Unters.* 16–21. H. Heinen, *Gött. gel. Anz.* 233 (1981) 184, regards 300 as a

occurred in the early months of 297, the expedition mentioned on the papyrus[1] can hardly have been earlier than 298, and so must have taken place after the Athenian embassy to Cassander. So, whatever its purpose, this expedition can hardly have been directed against the king of Macedonia.[2]

Meanwhile, in the wider field outside Greece events were working to Demetrius' advantage. The alliance of convenience which had led to Ipsus and the destruction of Antigonus became strained when Ptolemy, instead of sending forces for the common effort, used the opportunity to annex Coele–Syria, which the allies had assigned to Seleucus. In 300/299 Ptolemy made a close alliance with Lysimachus, clinched by marriages involving two of his daughters: Arsinoe married Lysimachus himself and Lysandra his heir Agathocles. For Seleucus the obvious counter-measure was an alliance with Demetrius, and he sent messengers to the latter, who was busy operating against Lysimachus in the Chersonese, asking for his and Phila's daughter Stratonice in marriage.[3] Demetrius at once set sail for Syria, making a landing in Pleistarchus' kingdom of Cilicia on the way and exploiting the absence of Pleistarchus (who had unwisely gone to upbraid Seleucus for his volte-face) to carry off 1,200 talents from Cyinda.[4] At a conference at Rhosus an alliance was made. The main clauses are unrecorded, but they probably included an undertaking to assist one another; in addition it was agreed that Seleucus should marry Stratonice. Demetrius took possession of Cilicia and sent his wife Phila, who after a long period of separation had now rejoined her husband, to Macedonia to ensure that Cassander, her brother, took no action over the expulsion of Pleistarchus. In this she was apparently successful.[5] Demetrius may possibly have given Cassander an undertaking not to interfere west of the Aegean; but in any case Cassander was not perhaps sorry to see Pleistarchus humiliated.[6]

possibility. In its favour is the statement in *POxy* 1235 ll. 105–12 that Menander wrote the *Imbrioi* in the archonship of Nicocles (302/1) for the Dionysia, but that owing to the tyrant Lachares it could not be performed; but Wilamowitz's emendation of ἐπὶ Νικοκλέο[υς to ἐπὶ Νεικίου (archon 296/5) has been generally accepted and, as Habicht points out, the earlier date is hard to reconcile with the continued production of private documents characteristic of the democratic regime down to 298/7 (see below, p. 207 n. 4).

[1] It may be the same expedition for which Ameinias, later executed together with Charias, was honoured on a stele published by B. D. Meritt, *Hesperia* 11 (1942) 278 ff. no. 53; this expedition is said to be ἐν Ταρνέα[ι], which is unidentified.
[2] The chronological sequence established by Habicht also excludes the view of Fortina 116, that the expedition took place in the late summer of 301 after Ipsus and aimed at eliminating the garrisons left behind by Demetrius.
[3] PD 31. 5.
[4] PD 32. 1; Diodorus here goes back to Hieronymus; cf. Hornblower 69 n. 168.
[5] PD 32. 4. For the view that Demetrius offered Cassander assurances see F. Stählin, *RE* s.v. *Kassandros* col. 2311.
[6] For ineffective help sent to Pleistarchus by Lysimachus see Buraselis 24.

This alliance between Demetrius and Seleucus was accompanied by other diplomatic activity. A decree of Ephesus (*OGI* 10) honouring Nicagoras of Rhodes, who had been sent there on a goodwill mission by Demetrius and Seleucus, shows that the alliance was widely publicized, for Ephesus was not the only city to receive this attention.[1] Furthermore Seleucus, who had carefully avoided a breach with Ptolemy over Coele–Syria, used his influence to arrange a treaty between him and Demetrius, probably in 299/8. Demetrius' wife Deidameia, Pyrrhus' sister, had conveniently died shortly after joining her husband in Cilicia, and in confirmation of the treaty it was agreed that Demetrius should marry Ptolemy's daughter, Ptolemais—an agreement that was only to be honoured ten years later.[2] As a further guarantee of Demetrius' good faith Pyrrhus consented to go as hostage to Alexandria. The arrangement with Seleucus did not last long, however, but ended in a quarrel over Cilicia, which Seleucus demanded that Demetrius should sell to him as part of the marriage settlement with Stratonice.[3] When that was refused he asked Demetrius to give him Tyre and Sidon instead; but when Demetrius rejected both demands, relations between the two became understandably strained. These diplomatic moves did not affect Cassander directly and little is recorded of him during these years. He was active behind the scenes at Athens; and events in the Adriatic during the last months of his life suggest that he was hoping to revive his earlier ambitions in that area.[4]

At Athens the following circumstances led to a seizure of power by Lachares, who seems to have been a supporter of Cassander.[5] Charias, the general over the hoplites (ὁ ἐπὶ τῶν ὅπλων τεταγμένος)[6] had become unpopular because of food shortages, for which he was held responsible.[7] He had therefore occupied an unnamed stronghold, perhaps the Museum hill, and upon being expelled from there, had seized the acropolis with the help of accomplices (see above, pp. 204–5).

---

[1] Ephesus had a special claim on the attention of the kings, since from 302/1 it was within Demetrius' realm (above, p. 201 n. 5; cf. *OGI* 9); and subsequently, between 300 and 297, Demetrius was involved as the ally of Ephesus in a war against Priene, where Hieron as tyrant had gone over to Lysimachus (cf. *SIG* 363). On the distress caused at Ephesus by this war and a moratorium on debt see *SIG* 364, with the commentary of Asheri, *Leggi greche* 42 ff., 108 ff. But Nicagoras is said to have been sent to both Ephesus and τοὺς ἄλλους Ἕλληνας (*OGI* 10 l. 3).

[2] See below, p. 232 n. 8.

[3] This seems implied by PD 33. 1, where Demetrius says that he will not consent to pay for the privilege of having Seleucus as his son-in-law. Evidently Seleucus regarded Cilicia as a marriage dowry.

[4] For his activity in the Adriatic in 314 see above, pp. 154–5.

[5] Cf. Paus. 1. 25. 7. He may well derive this information from Hieronymus, who was hostile to both Cassander and Lachares.

[6] On his antecedents see Habicht, *Unters* 17 n. 82; Davies, *APF* 193 no. 5604.

[7] *FGrH* 257a F1.

Lachares, who was general in charge of the mercenaries (ὁ τῶν ξένων ἡγούμενος) succeeded in ejecting him from the acropolis too, had him arrested and tried, and secured the execution of the whole group.[1] These events, as we have seen,[2] are probably to be dated to the early months of 297. They left Lachares in a dominant position, though he suffered a set-back when, shortly afterwards, the Piraeus troops which he had used against Charias revolted, brought about a secession of the Piraeus and held the port under separate control until Demetrius recovered Athens and Piraeus in 295/4.[3] According to Pausanias, Cassander, 'having a terrible hatred of the Athenians', now persuaded Lachares to make himself tyrant. Despite this statement, it seems clear, however, that this final step was not taken until after Cassander's death and that until then democratic institutions and lawcourts continued to function.[4] But Lachares may well have been in touch with Cassander for some time before that. If this was suspected, it could go some way towards explaining the secession of the Piraeus and its troops.

The area where Cassander was active during the last months of his life was Corcyra. Cleonymus of Sparta had seized the island in 302,[5] but had been expelled shortly afterwards—perhaps by Agathocles, though the sources mention no name.[6] In 298 or 297 Cassander sailed round the Peloponnese to attack Corcyra. His purpose is not clear; but his actions suggest an interest in the Adriatic coast which, had events turned out differently, might have been further developed. As it is, this episode merely foreshadows the later ambitions of Philip V. On reaching Corcyra, Cassander landed troops and besieged the city by land and sea. He was on the point of success when Agathocles, arriving from Sicily, got part of his forces ashore, while the remainder, presumably operating from shipboard, succeeded in setting all the Macedonian ships on fire. A hard-fought battle ensued around the ships, the Macedonians being desperate to save the fleet and the

---

[1] Ibid. F2.   [2] See above, p. 204 n. 5.

[3] Accepting De Sanctis's reconstruction of *FGrH* 257a F 2 ll. 1–6 (*Scritti* 357):

> [τὸ Μουσ?]εῖον καταλαβ[ὼ]ν
> [φρουροὺς] οὓς κατέστη[σ]εν Χάρι-
> [ας μετὰ] τῶν Πειραϊκῶν στρα-
> [τιωτῶν] ἐξέβαλεν

On the secession of Piraeus see Polyaen. 4. 7. 5.

[4] Paus. loc. cit. described him as προεστηκὼς...τοῦ δήμου; and Habicht, *Unters.* 18–19, draws attention to the uninterrupted publication of private Athenian documents at least till 298/7.

[5] D.S. 20. 105. Cleonymus came from Metapontum in South Italy, which he had seized. Diodorus, following Duris, says that he hoped to use Corcyra as a base for interference in Greece, but rejected offers from both Demetrius and Cassander.

[6] Trog. *Prol.* 15 'cui oblata Corcyra'—but by whom is not stated. See Fortina 119; F. Stähelin, *RE* s.v. *Kassandros* col. 2311.

Siceliotes determined to give a good account of themselves against 'the troops who had conquered Europe and Asia alike'.[1] Fortunately for the Macedonians, Agathocles did not realize how near he was to destroying the enemy and so failed to launch against them the force which he had brought ashore. The Macedonians were able to save their fleet and effect their escape.[2]

Shortly afterwards in May 297,[3] Cassander died at Pella. Eusebius and Syncellus speak of a wasting illness, but Pausanias (9. 7. 2) is more specific, diagnosing the disease as dropsy and internal worms, and interprets it as divine punishment for Cassander's cruelty towards the house of Alexander.[4] Cassander had played a notable part in the destruction of Alexander's empire and its splintering among a succession of separate kings. But it is arguable that only Alexander could have kept it together; and Macedonia itself owed Cassander a very real debt. Of his utter ruthlessness there is no question. But over a period of twenty years (from 317 to 297) he had played his cards adroitly, outstripping Polyperchon in the struggle to follow Antipater and warding off attacks both from Ptolemy and from Antigonus and his son. In Macedonia he had consolidated his own position in a series of astute moves. By conniving at the execution of Olympias in retribution for her murder of Eurydice and Philip III Arrhidaeus, and by following this up in 310 with the assassination of Alexander IV and Roxane, he had rid himself of all representatives of the Argead house who might challenge his authority. Meanwhile his marriage to Thessalonice, the daughter of Philip II, provided him with a claim of sorts to represent the Argeads himself. By the time of his death he had already established a dynasty which looked back beyond himself to the Macedonians' appointment of his father Antipater as *epimeletes* of the kings.

Cassander's power in Greece was based mainly on garrisoned strong-points, including the fort of Munychia at Athens. There, however, he relied primarily on his protégé Demetrius of Phalerum to maintain the loyalty of the city until his expulsion by Demetrius Poliorcetes in 307. At home Cassander, like Philip II, strengthened Macedonia by introducing settlers from beyond the frontiers, such as the Autariatae, and under his control the number of available troops

---

[1] D.S. 21. 2. 1–3 (source uncertain); Fortina 118–19.

[2] Fortina 119 says that the entire fleet was destroyed; but Diodorus does not say so, and had it been so Cassander could not have extricated his forces.

[3] According to *FGrH* 257a it was in the latter part of the intercalary month, the second Artemisios. The year is Ol. 120, 3 (298/7); cf. Porph. *FGrH* 260 F 3 (64).

[4] Eus. 1. 231 f. Sch.; Syncellus 265A 504 Bonn; Paus. 9. 7. 2, perhaps going back to Hieronymus. On famous people who died (or are alleged to have died) of phthiriasis (being eaten by worms) see T. W. Africa, *CA* 1 (1982) 1–17.

increased substantially. This was due not only to the introduction of settlers, but also to his skill in refraining from involving his subjects in a succession of wars. This policy ensured that a new generation of Macedonians grew up to take the place of those who had gone off to Asia, never to return—though the gain must be qualified, since the presence of Macedonians overseas suggests that many continued to slip away to try their fortunes in the new kingdoms of Asia and Egypt. A few, it is true, returned home rich, but they were a minority. Cassander was also responsible for two great urban foundations (both probably in 316), which were to play an important role in the later history of the country. About twenty-six villages at the head of the Thermaic Gulf were united in a synoecism which he named Thessalonica after his wife, and the cities of Pallene, including Potidaea and the remnants of the Olynthians, were incorporated in a foundation named Cassandreia after himself. Though they are shown by inscriptions to have been Macedonian cities, they had substantial Greek populations and indeed Cassandreia contained many Greeks from the Chalcidian cities.[1]

Since Alexander's departure for Asia, Macedonia had suffered culturally from the absence of a royal court, and the existence of a regency had been no substitute. Both Antipater and Cassander, however, did something to make up for this. Antipater, like Philip II, had enjoyed close relations with Aristotle who, indeed, named him as his executor[2] when he died in 322. He was himself a man of some culture and, according to an entry in Suidas, the author of letters and of a history of Perdiccas' Illyrian Wars.[3] Cassander maintained his father's links with the Peripatetic school. He put the philosopher Demetrius of Phalerum in charge at Athens and appointed Aristotle's son-in-law (and adopted son) Nicanor as Macedonian commander in Munychia (though he later executed him for treason).[4] He was on good terms with Theophrastus, who dedicated his book *On Kingship* to him,[5] with the orator Dinarchus,[6] a pupil of Theophrastus and Demetrius of Phalerum, and with Euhemerus.[7] Like Alexander, Cassander was also passionately devoted to Homer,[8] and he was a patron of the visual arts; Pliny (*HN* 35. 110) records his association with Philoxenus of Eretria and Athenaeus (11. 784 c) that with

---

[1] Str. 7 fr. 21, 24 (Thessalonica); D.S. 19. 52. 2 (Cassandreia), Olynthians included. See F. Papazoglou, *AM* 3. 195–210 (Macedonian cities).

[2] D.L. 5. 11.

[3] Suidas s.v. *Antipatros*; cf. J. Kaerst, *Philol.* 51 (1892) 620–1, who however gives strong arguments for regarding at any rate the letters as a Hellenistic forgery.

[4] Athen. 12. 542 f; *PPh* 31. 1–2; D.S. 18. 75. 1.

[5] D.L. 5. 42, 49 = fr. 125 Wimmer; according to Athen. 4. 144 e, the authenticity of this treatise was queried.

[6] *PMor* 850 c-d.   [7] D.S. 6. 1. 4.   [8] Athen. 14. 620 b.

Lysippus of Sicyon. These links must have been reflected to some extent in court life at Pella, though details specifically relevant to Cassander's domination are lacking.[1]

2. *Philip IV, Antipater II, and Alexander V (297–294 B.C.)*

Cassander's death in 297 ushered in a period of weak and unstable government in Macedonia, in which the mounting pressures at one moment threatened even that most durable of Macedonian institutions, the monarchy itself. This was to last for twenty years until 277, when the son of Demetrius Poliorcetes made himself king. His accession introduced a new dynasty, which occupied the Macedonian throne for over a hundred years. No meaningful history of the country throughout these two decades can ignore the moves and counter-moves of the rival kings, who had their eyes on Macedonia either as a prize in itself or as a stepping-stone to greater things.

In Macedonia the weaknesses were quick to appear. Cassander's son Philip IV succeeded his father unopposed; but, like him, the young man died of a wasting disease four months later, at Elatea,[2] leaving as natural successors only his two younger brothers, Antipater and Alexander. At their mother's instigation it was agreed that they should rule jointly. No record has survived of the constitutional procedures which led to the accession of Philip IV and that of his brothers; but the Macedonian Assembly no doubt gave formal approval to the obvious dynastic heir or heirs in each case. The connection with Philip II must have dispelled any possible hesitation. Antipater cannot have been more than sixteen; and Cassander's widow Thessalonice, though we are not told that she was officially appointed his guardian,[3] seems to have exercised considerable influence over both sons.[4] The queen preferred the younger boy, Alexander, and insisted that Antipater should share the kingship with him. As the half-sister of Alexander the Great and a daughter of Philip II, she evidently commanded sufficient prestige to have her way, though it was by no means obviously in the interest of the state. A boy king was bad enough. Two boy kings ruling

---

[1] On art in Macedonia in the Hellenistic period generally see J. Touratsoglou, *Macedonia: 4000 years of Greek History and Civilization*, ed. M. B. Sakellariou (Athens, 1983), 170–91.

[2] *FGrH* 257a F 3; Porph. *FGrH* 260 F 3 (sect. 5): death at Elatea; Eus. 1. 241 Sch.; J. 15. 4. 24. What Philip was doing in Elatea is not recorded. He may have been on a campaign (cf. Beloch 4. 2. 168). According to Paus. 9. 7. 3 ἀπήγαγεν ὑπολαβοῦσα νόσος φθινώδης.

[3] She is nowhere so described; see R. M. Errington, *Chiron* 8 (1978) 126 n. 124, against Beloch 4. 2. 127–8; Lévêque 111. But a queen acting as guardian is not out of the question in Macedonia, any more than in Illyria, where Teuta became regent after Agron's death (see below, p. 333 n. 6).

[4] J. 16. 1. 1–2.

together could only compound the dangers.[1] However, this joint
monarchy lasted from Philip IV's death in autumn 297 until the spring
of 294. The division of the kingship was an indication of weakness and
a recipe for intervention. There were at the time three possible serious
claimants to the Macedonian throne—Lysimachus in Thrace, Demetrius Poliorcetes, and Pyrrhus the Molossian; it was the two latter who
offered the more immediate threat to the shaky house of Cassander.

Of the two, Demetrius had set his eyes on Athens. He resented its
defection and was waiting for the chance to recover this all-important
Greek base. There Lachares was still in power, though the secession of
the Piraeus[2] caused him some embarrassment and even obliged him
to strip the statue of Athena of its gold to pay his mercenaries.[3] The
winter of 296/5 saw an unsuccessful rising against him[4] and after this
was suppressed Lachares converted his position into an open tyranny.
The council was reorganized (and presumably filled with his supporters) and the first prytany of the new regime began in Elaphebolion
(March) 295. The suppression of democratic features can be detected
in the inscriptions, in which for the remainder of his year of office the
archon Nicias (296/5) is designated ἄρχων ὕστερος.[5] The fact that
Lachares' coup coincided with the Dionysia (10–16 Elaphebolion)[6]
explains Menander's failure to stage his *Imbrioi* on that occasion.[7] It
was probably the setting up of Lachares' tyranny that precipitated
Demetrius' intervention at Athens.

In the spring or early summer of 295 he crossed from Asia Minor,
hoping that these recent events at Athens would render the city easy to
take; but he lost most of his ships in a storm off the Attic coast and
made no headway in his subsequent attacks on Attica.[8] So while a
new fleet was being assembled in Cyprus and the Peloponnese he
marched against Messene,[9] where he sustained a wound in the jaw
from a catapult. On his return to Attica he seized Rhamnus and

---

[1] Lévêque 126, assumes that the kingdom was divided into two halves, with Alexander ruling
west of the Axius and Antipater the area east of that river. The Axius was indeed the later
dividing line between Lysimachus and Pyrrhus (see below, p. 230, n. 1), but there is no evidence
that Alexander and Antipater divided the realm geographically. It is inconceivable that the
Macedonians would have acquiesced in such a division.
[2] See above, p. 207 n. 3. [3] *FGrH* 257a F 4.
[4] Paus. 1. 29. 10. On the events down to Demetrius' capture of Athens see Habicht, *Unters.*
1–13.
[5] *IG* ii². 644 l. 16 (Munychia); B. D. Meritt, *Hesp.* 11 (1942) 281 no. 54 restored as Ν[ικίου
ἄρχοντος τοῦ ὑστέρου]; *IG* ii². 645; see Habicht, *Unters.* 2 n. 9. Similarly, Phaedrus appears in
Nicias' archonship as στρατηγὸς ὑπὸ τοῦ δήμου χειροτονηθεὶς ἐπὶ τὴν παρασκευὴν δίς (*IG* ii². 682 ll.
21–3 = *SIG* 404).
[6] Cf. W. S. Ferguson, *Hesp.* 17 (1948) 133–5; Mikalson 125, 137, 189–90.
[7] See above, p. 204 n. 5. [8] *PD* 33. 1–3.
[9] *PD* 33. 3 εἰς Πελοπόννησον παρῆλθε; this suggests a land-route rather than sailing round the
peninsula. On what pretext he attacked Messene is not known.

Eleusis, ravaged the countryside, and imposed a blockade of the city which was savagely enforced against grain ships attempting to get through. He also seized Aegina and Salamis.[1] In the course of the winter famine grew more acute and Demetrius finally managed to take Piraeus; according to Polyaenus (4. 7. 5) he had first tricked the dissident garrison into supplying him with arms. In the spring of 294 Ptolemy sent 150 ships against him, but by then Demetrius had assembled his new fleet of 300 ships and the Egyptian admiral did not dare sail closer than Aegina.[2] Pyrrhus sent no help to Ptolemy on this occasion, perhaps hoping to avoid an open breach with Demetrius, or, more likely, not yet disposing of sufficient resources for such intervention (see below, pp. 213–14).[3] Discouraged by the departure of the Egyptian ships, Lachares now gave up all hope of further resistance and fled to Boeotia. Later, in 291 or 290, when Boeotia fell to Demetrius, he managed to escape to Delphi and from there to Lysimachus.[4] For a time the Athenians continued to resist, but by April they could hold out no longer. Accordingly they opened the gates and sent envoys to Demetrius.[5] Demetrius treated Athens generously, providing the city with 100,000 medimni of much-needed grain, and reinstituted democratic magistrates.[6] On the proposal of Dromocleides a decree was passed, granting Demetrius possession of Piraeus and Munychia;[7] in addition he garrisoned the Museum.[8] The same autumn Demetrius planned to extend his base by seizing Sparta. Invading the Peloponnese, he defeated King Archidamus near Mantinea and pressed on into Laconia, where in a further battle against the Spartans he killed 200 and took 500 prisoners.[9]

While Demetrius was busy enforcing his authority in mainland

---

[1] PD 33. 4. 5; Polyaen. 4. 7. 5; Demetrius hanged one captain and his crew whom he captured while running grain into Athens.

[2] PD 33. 7.   [3] So Lévèque 123.

[4] Paus. 1. 25. 7–8; Polyaen. 3. 7. 1; Holleaux, *Études* 1. 88 n. 3; Wehrli 174; cf. Flacelière 73. Pausanias asserts that he was murdered in Coroneia for the golden shield and golden robes of Athena he was said to have brought with him; but according to the papyrus *FGrH* 257a F 4 he had taken the gold from the statue to pay his soldiers (above, p. 211 n. 3).

[5] PD 34. 1 ἀνεῴγνυσαν τὰς ἐγγὺς πύλας καὶ πρέσβεις ἔπεμπον; see Habicht, *Unters.* 4–6. Though *IG* ii². 646, a decree honouring Herodorus of Cyzicus for help given to [οἱ πρέσβεις οἱ] πεμφθέντες ὑπὲρ τῆς ε[ἰρήνης πρὸς τὸ]ν βασιλέα Δημήτριον, might imply negotiations, the opening of the nearest gates surely suggests unconditional surrender. H. Heinen (*Gött. gel. Anz.* 233 (1981) 281) argues that the gates were opened merely to let the envoys out, not to let Demetrius in; but that would hardly be worth mentioning since obviously envoys cannot go through a locked gate. Moreover, when Demetrius did march in (PD 34. 3), the people, ordered to assemble in the theatre, clearly had no idea what their fate was to be. The envoys had been sent to surrender and, presumably, to plead for mercy.

[6] PD 34. 5 κατέστησεν ἀρχὰς αἳ μάλιστα τῷ δήμῳ προσφιλεῖς ἦσαν.

[7] PD 34. 6 γνώμην...τῷ βασιλεῖ τὸν Πειραιᾶ παραδοθῆναι καὶ τὴν Μουνυχίαν. But according to Polyaen. 4. 7. 6–7 the Piraeus at least was already in Demetrius' hands.

[8] PD 34. 7.   [9] PD 35. 1–2.

Greece, Pyrrhus the Molossian had also been improving his position. As we saw, he had accompanied Demetrius to Greece in his flight from Ipsus and had for a time acted as his representative at Corinth when Demetrius sailed north to attack Lysimachus (above, p. 202). But after the agreement between Ptolemy and Demetrius in 299/8, the latter sent Pyrrhus to Egypt as a hostage to underwrite the compact.[1] Nothing is known of the terms on which Pyrrhus agreed to become a hostage, but he must have gone willingly. Very soon he transferred his allegiance from Demetrius to Ptolemy and married Antigone, a daughter of Ptolemy's influential mistress, Berenice, by her former husband.[2] A little over a year later, in 297, Ptolemy restored Pyrrhus to his native land of Epirus.[3] The personal relationship set up between Ptolemy and Pyrrhus was a warm one: they are said to have addressed each other as father and son.[4] But Ptolemy had an axe of his own to grind. He was well aware of the long-standing feud between Pyrrhus' family and Cassander's, and though Cassander was probably dead when the restoration took place,[5] it no doubt suited him to see a vigorous rival, friendly to himself, established on the western flank of Macedonia to worry Cassander's successor. Pyrrhus would be a useful counterweight should Demetrius make any move against Macedonia[6] —a distinct possibility in the unstable conditions which followed Cassander's death. The terms on which Pyrrhus had gone back to Epirus were that he and Neoptolemus, the present ruler, should share power. But very soon Pyrrhus had his rival assassinated, claiming to have discovered that Neoptolemus was plotting his own death.[7] Shortly afterwards, when Antigone died prematurely, Pyrrhus married Lanassa, the daughter of Agathocles of Syracuse, thereby obtaining Corcyra as a marriage settlement.[8] Set in the context of Cassander's disastrous enterprise, this alliance had clear anti-Macedonian implications, inasmuch as Agathocles had been instrumental in Cassander's defeat. It consolidated the power of Epirus and provided Pyrrhus with a navy. His new marriage did not, however, lead to any breach with Ptolemy; and when in 294 Pyrrhus failed to render assistance to the

[1] PPyrrh 4. 5; above, p. 206. [2] PPyrrh 4. 6–7.
[3] PPyrrh 5. 1; Paus. 1. 11. 5. [4] PPyrrh 6. 7; for parallels cf. Herman, 18 n. 28.
[5] Lévêque 110 dates Cassander's death to 298, but with this brought down to 297 (see above, p. 208 n. 3) it can still have preceded Pyrrhus' restoration.
[6] Against the view that Ptolemy restored Pyrrhus with the connivance of Demetrius see Lévêque 111 n. 4, who points out that Paus. 1. 6. 8 implies that he saw the restoration of Pyrrhus as directed against Demetrius.
[7] PPyrrh 5. 1–14; cf. Lycophron 1042. The circumstantial account in Plutarch is favourable to Pyrrhus. Its source may be Hieronymus (so Lévêque, 64 n. 4), but this is hypothetical; the account could equally well draw on Pyrrhus' own *Memoirs*. How far it is true we cannot say.
[8] PPyrrh 9. 2; D.S. 21. 4, 22. 8. 2; Lévêque 125. The account of an attack on Corcyra by Pyrrhus in Paus. 1. 11. 6 is to be rejected; cf. Lévêque 197.

Ptolemaic fleet when it approached Athens (see above, p. 212) this was not entirely due to lukewarmness on Pyrrhus' part. For by this time Pyrrhus had probably enough on his hands at home without directly challenging Demetrius in Attic waters.

In the autumn of 294 Antipater, now about nineteen and increasingly irritated at the domination of Thessalonice and his shared rule with Alexander, murdered his mother and, according to Plutarch, drove out his brother.[1] We are not told that Alexander was forced into exile, but he was certainly expelled from Pella. In retaliation he appealed, unwisely, to both Pyrrhus and Demetrius. The latter was still in the Peloponnese, where he had just defeated the Spartans (above, p. 212 n. 9), and his response to the appeal was delayed. For this delay the sources offer various explanations. In the *Pyrrhus* (6. 4) Plutarch says that Pyrrhus was held up by other business in hand (ὑπὸ ἀσχολιῶν); but in the *Demetrius* (35. 5–6) he attributes his withdrawal from Sparta to the receipt of bad news from Asia, where Lysimachus had seized the cities under his control and Ptolemy had annexed all Cyprus except for Salamis, where his children and mother were under siege. There is no reason to doubt the truth of this; and it is likely that Ptolemy had also seized Tyre and Sidon.[2] This unwelcome news may well have reached Demetrius while he was near Sparta. But it was hardly the cause of his withdrawal, since he could do nothing immediately to reverse the situation in Asia (nor does he seem to have tried); whereas the news from Macedonia called for early action. It was therefore probably the latter that led Demetrius to abandon his Peloponnesian enterprise. Plutarch seems to have introduced the report from Asia as an illustration of the quirks and changes brought about by Fortune (*Tyche*).

Pyrrhus, however, was nearer and acted with greater speed. On receiving Alexander's appeal he marched quickly from Epirus to Macedonia, probably by way of Aeginium and Beroea. Alexander soon found that he had brought in a dangerous ally. In return for his aid Pyrrhus demanded[3] that Alexander should surrender Tymphaea

---

[1] P*D* 36. 1; P*Pyrrh* 6. 3; Paus. 9. 7. 3; D.S. 21. 7.

[2] Cf. Beloch 4. 2. 327–8; I. L. Merker, *Anc. Soc.* 5 (1974) 119–26 (coin hoards from Galilee in Tyre); Habicht, *Unters.* 66; cf. Buraselis 88 n. 201. The capture of these places is more usually dated to 288 (so Will 1². 96–7; E. T. Newell, *Tyrus Rediviva* (New York, 1923), 15–23; Wehrli 184; Shear 72), but the hoard published by Merker seems decisive.

[3] P*Pyrrh* 6. 4; the MS. reading Παραλίαν and Νυμφαίαν. Tymphaea lay to the east of northern Pindus and included the headwaters of the Venetikos river; it came close to modern Grevena and extended southwards as far as the headwaters of the river Peneus. Parauaea is the area west of Pindus draining into the upper valley of the river Aous and containing the towns of Permet and Leskovik; on both areas see H*E* 680–2. Woodward in A. J. B. Wace–A. M. Woodward, *BSA* 18 (1911–12) 181, followed by Lévèque 127 n. 5 and 184, would locate Parauaea along the upper waters of the Haliacmon; but this area formed part of Orestis.

and Parauaea and, of the acquired regions subject to Macedonia, Ambracia, Acarnania, and Amphilochia. The young king had no alternative but to accede to these terms. In addition Pyrrhus seized Atintania, which lay on his side of Parauaea.[1] Of these outlying provinces, Ambracia had been Macedonian for some time, but whether it had been acquired under Alexander, Antipater (after the Lamian War), or Cassander (at the time of his expedition into north-west Greece), is uncertain. Acarnania had been Macedonian since Cassander intervened in 314 and left Lyciscus there to protect the province.[2] Amphilochia, like Acarnania, had probably fallen into Cassander's hands about the same time.[3] All these states will now have been incorporated in the Epirote Alliance; and Pyrrhus moved his capital to Ambracia.[4]

By these concessions Alexander undid much of the work both of Philip II and of his own father, Cassander,[5] but the direct responsibility was that of Antipater, who had precipitated the crisis by attacking his brother. After taking over his new possessions, Pyrrhus now advanced on Antipater and set about expelling him from the rest of Macedonia.[6] Learning nothing from the price Alexander had had to pay for Pyrrhus' help, Antipater now in his turn looked to outside support, appealing to Lysimachus, his father-in-law.[7] Since he was at this time fully occupied on his Thracian frontier fighting the Getae, Lysimachus (it is alleged) resorted to diplomacy or, more accurately, chicanery: he sent a forged letter to Pyrrhus, purporting to come from Ptolemy, urging him to bring his campaign to an end in consideration of a payment of 300 talents.[8] According to Plutarch, Pyrrhus at once recognized the letter as a forgery, since the opening words were 'King

---

[1] Cf. H*E* 568 n. 2, who points out that the area is still Epirote in Plb. 2. 5. 6.

[2] D.S. 19. 67. 3–5. It now became Epirote and was probably attached directly to Pyrrhus on terms defined in a now lost treaty between Pyrrhus and the Acarnanian League (cf. Lévêque 189 n. 5 for references). At Ausculum in 279 Pyrrhus had some Acarnanian mercenaries (D.H. 20. 1. 2); this creates a problem if Acarnania had been annexed, but the solution is hardly to emend the text of Plutarch to read *Ἀθαμανίαν* or *Ἀτιντανίαν* in place of *Ἀκαρνανίαν* (see Lévêque 190–1, who lists other possible solutions).

[3] Cf. Lévêque 194 n. 1.

[4] Str. 7. 7. 6; Florus 1. 25. 2; Zon. 9. 21; H*E* 568–9. It is also unlikely that Pyrrhus acquired Athamania in the upper valley of the Achelous at this time; see Lévêque 194–5.

[5] Cf. Lévêque 128.

[6] P*Pyrrh* 6. 5; προεμένου δὲ τοῦ νεανίσκου ταῦτα μὲν αὐτὸς εἶχε φρουραῖς καταλαβών, τὰ δὲ λοιπὰ κτώμενος ἐκείνῳ περιέκοπτε τὸν Ἀντίπατρον. The words τὰ λοιπά mean 'the rest of Macedonia' or 'the rest of what was now Antipater's kingdom'. Lévêque 128 rightly observes that Antipater held onto the areas east of the Axius. But περιέκοπτε need not imply that the process of stripping Antipater was completed. The imperfect can bear an inceptive sense: 'he set about stripping Antipater'.

[7] P*Pyrrh* 6. 6; for the relationship between Antipater and Lysimachus, whose daughter Eurydice he had married, cf. J. 16. 2. 4.

[8] P*Pyrrh* 6. 7–8.

Ptolemy to King Pyrrhus, greeting', instead of the more familiar 'the father to the son, greeting'. In fact the whole anecdote is dubious for, despite having seen through the trick, Pyrrhus appears to have followed Lysimachus' advice, just as if the letter had been genuine. In any case, it was in Pyrrhus' interest not to become involved in a campaign which would certainly have led to hostilities with Lysimachus; and he probably knew that Alexander had also appealed to Demetrius, who might therefore be expected to appear very soon in Macedonia.

Accordingly a treaty was made between the brothers.[1] In describing this, Plutarch has an odd story. As preparations were being made to sacrifice a bull, a boar, and a ram to seal the oaths, the ram fell down dead of its own accord—an incident which aroused general mirth—and when the *mantis* interpreted this as a sign that one of the three kings would die, Pyrrhus used this as an excuse for refusing to take part in the peace. This did not prevent the reconciliation taking place; but Pyrrhus was not officially a party to it.[2] His role was not essential, since officially he was supposed to be merely helping Alexander; and Justin (10. 1. 8) speaks of 'incohatam intra fratres reconciliationem'. The story of the ram's death and its sequel may be apocryphal; the irrelevant detail—the amusement of the crowd, the name of the *mantis*—may be there simply to give verisimilitude to what looks like a *vaticinium ex eventu*—for Alexander was to die very soon afterwards. But the story could also have been invented to explain why Pyrrhus was not himself a party to the agreement.

Pyrrhus had already returned to Epirus, no doubt taking with him the 300 talents which, according to Lysimachus' letter, Antipater was to pay him, when Demetrius arrived to find peace made between the brothers, the kingdom diminished and divided, and no role for himself.[3] He had welcomed Alexander's appeal, since he was naturally attracted by the prospect offered by Macedonia, with its resources of men and money, quite apart from its special claim as the homeland of Philip and Alexander and all the other kings. Shaken by the news of his losses in Asia, Demetrius must have seen this new opening as an unforeseen gift of Fortune, another turn of her incalculable wheel.[4] But having met him at Dium, Alexander at once set out to coax him into leaving. Plutarch tells the story of a plot by Alexander against Demetrius' life, reminiscent of that in his *Pyrrhus*, which culminated in

[1] PPyrrh 6. 8.   [2] PPyrrh 6. 8–9.
[3] PPyrrh 7. 1; PD 36. 3; D.S. 21. 7 (inaccurate); Paus. 1. 10. 1, 6. 6, 9. 7. 3; Eus. 1. 231 Sch.; Trog. Prol. 16; J. 16. 1. 18–19; Oros. 3. 23. 51.
[4] PD 25. 3–4. His long-term plans can only be guessed at. Lévèque and Buraselis both argue with some plausibility that he still hoped to follow in Antigonus' footsteps and saw Macedonia as a useful base from which to extend his power to the Aegean and Asia Minor.

Neoptolemus' assassination and perhaps derived from the same source. According to this, Demetrius discovered a conspiracy to kill him after supper and so excused himself from attending the drinking; he then alleged duties in the south, retired—accompanied by Alexander—to Larissa, and there had the young man murdered.[1] Plutarch's version excuses Demetrius; but the outcome was wholly to his advantage and the siting of the murder away from Macedonia suggests that he had planned it, thus outwitting Alexander. The young man had shown great *naïveté* in his dealings with both Pyrrhus and Demetrius.

Alexander's death threw his troops into a panic, but they soon recovered their composure when Demetrius requested a meeting with them. At this he had little difficulty in persuading them to proclaim him king of Macedonia.[2] Such is Plutarch's account (*Demetr.* 37), and he goes on to say that the change was welcome to 'the Macedonians at home' (τοῖς οἴκοι Μακεδόσιν), who recalled with hatred Cassander's crimes against the house of Alexander. Their warmer memories of the elder Antipater benefited Demetrius, who was married to Antipater's daughter Phila, and whose son by her was Antipater's grandson. This account probably goes back to Hieronymus, who accompanied Demetrius on this expedition into Macedonia.[3] It is entirely credible. According to Justin (16. 1. 9), however, the decisive events occurred later: 'occupato...Macedoniae regno caedem [sc. Alexandri] apud exercitum excusaturus [in] contionem vocat'; and he records a speech, which must be regarded as fictitious, though it puts forward plausible arguments. This version would imply that the real recognition came in an Army Assembly in Macedonia. But it is clear from the more trustworthy account in Plutarch that this had already happened at Larissa at the hands of the troops accompanying Alexander. The speech in Justin must be regarded as a rhetorical exercise. It can hardly be the worked-up version of one delivered at Larissa, following a telescoping of events by Justin,[4] since Plutarch (*Demetr.* 37. 2) says that Demetrius had no need to make a long speech (οὐ μακρῶν ἐδέησεν αὐτῷ λόγων), such was the temper of Alexander's troops; and it is highly unlikely that, having won over the army at Larissa and having been saluted by them, Demetrius then submitted himself to a repeat performance before an official Army Assembly in Macedonia. It appears then that on this occasion a small body of troops, including the Royal Bodyguard and the king's Friends, took a decision on behalf of the Macedonian People, who tacitly accepted

---

[1] *PD* 36. 4–37. 15.   [2] *PD* 37. 2.
[3] The next year Demetrius left him behind as the governor of Thebes; see below, p. 220. On Hieronymus as the source here see Hornblower 69.
[4] So R. M. Errington, *Chiron* 8 (1978) 127.

it—tacitly because when Plutarch, following Hieronymus, describes the change as not unwelcome to the Macedonians at home and explains why, he is not referring to any speech delivered before an assembly at Pella, but characterizing the general attitude as Hieronymus had experienced it. It is clear[1] that in the events leading up to the recognition of Demetrius as king by the troops at Larissa (acting under pressure from Demetrius' own superior forces) one decisive factor must have been the attitude of the Friends constituting Alexander's Council. Their willingness, for whatever reasons, to transfer their allegiance to Demetrius, was clearly crucial to the whole operation.

Antipater quickly realized the danger that confronted him; the troops at Larissa had spoken for the whole nation. Justin (16. 2. 4) implies that he fled from Macedonia to take refuge with Lysimachus, who naturally gave him shelter. Apart from the ties arising from his being Antipater's father-in-law, the latter's claim to the Macedonian throne could be usefully exploited by Lysimachus, who was now free to play his own hand, sheltering behind the legitimacy of Antipater, but prepared to jettison his protégé whenever the appropriate moment came—which is what in fact was to happen.[2]

Demetrius' accession to the throne of Macedonia was probably in 294.[3] That it took place with the connivance of Pyrrhus[4] is unlikely. As to why Pyrrhus remained quiescent in the face of this challenge, one can only speculate. He may have had problems with the Illyrians, but there is no evidence of this. It is on the whole most probable that at this stage he was not prepared to confront his former ally and patron, or else did not yet control military resources adequate for such an undertaking. Alternatively, as Lévêque suggests,[5] he may have suspected that Demetrius, given his restless ambition, would soon be away on some enterprise or other, from which he, Pyrrhus, could profit. Meanwhile, as king of Macedonia, Demetrius found himself obliged to impose harsh measures on the Greek cities, which clashed directly with the Antigonid claim to be liberators. In consequence, he soon attracted the hatred and obloquy with which kings of Macedonia were traditionally regarded in Greece.

---

[1] Errington, loc. cit.

[2] D.S. 21. 7 and P*Mor* 530 c both wrongly assign the responsibility for Antipater's death to Demetrius; but see J. 11. 2. 4.

[3] See Lévêque 132 n. 3, for other suggested dates. But, as Habicht, *Unters.* 21 observes, the chronology of this period must be based on firm dates derived (wherever possible) from the Athenian inscriptions in preference to the chronographers; and the dating of the overthrow of Lachares to early April 294 implies that Demetrius ascended the Macedonian throne the same autumn.

[4] So P. Treves, *Riv. fil.* 59 (1931) 372 f.   [5] Lévêque 133.

X

DEMETRIUS, PYRRHUS, AND LYSIMACHUS
(294–285 B.C.)

1. *Demetrius as king of Macedonia (294–287 B.C.)*

DEMETRIUS occupied the throne of Macedonia for over six years without ever disciplining his restless nature to the pursuit of a single consistent policy, or deciding whether to concentrate realistically on ruling Macedon effectively or to follow the will-o'-the-wisp of a universal empire. His first three years were spent in mainly futile activity in central Greece, where an independent and unfriendly Boeotia stood between Thessaly, which he controlled, and the Antigonid possessions, viz. the Megarid, Attica, and parts of the Peloponnese—and, if Picard is right, he continued to hold Euboea after Ipsus.[1] Almost immediately—before the end of 294—he resolved to attack the Boeotian League. By dispatching a herald to convey a declaration of war to the Boeotarchs assembled in Orchomenus only one day before his army seized Chaeronea[2] (having evidently overrun east Locris and that part of Phocis which lay north of the Cephissus en route), he caught the Boeotians unprepared and cut them off from all hope of getting reinforcements from their Aetolian allies.[3] They quickly capitulated and Demetrius 'made amicable arrangements with the Boeotian cities'. They were not to last long.

The next year, encouraged by the arrival at Thebes of a Spartan army under Cleonymus and by the friendly attitude of the Aetolians, who gave him free passage through the areas under their control after he had crossed the Corinthian Gulf at Rhium, and perhaps of other states discontented with Demetrius' domination, the Boeotians revolted. Their leader was Peisis of Thespiae, a former Antigonid supporter, who had fought in the Boeotian squadron which helped Antigonus relieve Opus in 313/12.[4] Demetrius' reaction was swift. He

---

[1] For Demetrius' control of Thessaly cf. PD 39. 1; on his continued possession of Euboea after Ipsus see above, p. 202 n. 2.

[2] Polyaen. 4. 7. 11. Lévêque 131 argues that Demetrius took over Boeotia on his way north to meet Alexander; but this contradicts the order of events in PD loc. cit.

[3] For the treaty between Aetolia and Boeotia see SVA 463. Its date is probably 300/299; see above, p. 203 n. 2.

[4] PD 39. 2; Flacelière 72–3; Cloché, *Thèbes* 208; Wehrli 174. Wehrli accepts Holleaux's view (*Études* 1. 38 n. 3) that Lysimachus was behind the revolt. There is no evidence for this.

at once marched on Boeotia and upon his arrival Cleonymus slipped away and the Boeotians surrendered. It was either now or earlier that Demetrius imposed garrisons and appointed Hieronymus of Cardia, the historian, as '*epimeletes* and harmost' over the whole of Boeotia. But in order to placate the growing hostility he treated his leading opponents with a show of generosity, establishing Peisis himself, for instance, as polemarch at Thespiae. But such a gesture merely emphasized the autocratic nature of the appointment and the interference with the city's independence and democratic government which it entailed.[1] It was in marked contrast to the professions and policy of Antigonus and showed to what extent Demetrius, in ascending Cassander's throne, had perforce taken over his methods of controlling Greece as well.

Shortly afterwards, probably in 292, the Boeotians revolted yet again.[2] Demetrius had laid himself open to this action by a characteristic diversion, undertaken at short notice when an unforeseen opportunity presented itself. Lysimachus, who was campaigning in Thrace near the Danube, was taken prisoner by the king of the Getae, Dromichaetes,[3] and on learning of this Demetrius could not resist the temptation to set out at once for the Hellespont in the hope of turning Lysimachus' misfortune to his own advantage. But Dromichaetes, perhaps realizing that the removal of Lysimachus would bring him face to face with Demetrius,[4] released his captive. On learning of this Demetrius reversed his march; but the Boeotians, resentful and no less hot-headed than he, had already rebelled. By the time Demetrius himself reached Boeotia, however, they had been defeated by his son, Antigonus, whom he had left in charge in Greece, and all except the Thebans had surrendered.[5] Demetrius therefore set about besieging their city.

The siege of Thebes dragged on through the winter of 292/1 and in the following spring, as soon as the passes were clear, Pyrrhus of Epirus attempted a diversionary campaign. Probably following the most direct route from Ambracia through Athamania to Gomphi (near mod. Mouzaki), he overran Thessaly, perhaps hoping thereby to drive

Lysimachus' dedication of a statue of Adeia in the Amphiareum (*SIG* 373) indicates that the king was on good terms with the Boeotians, but nothing more. For Peisis' presence at Opus see *ISE* 2. 71.

[1] P*D* 39. 3–5. For Demetrius' policy of installing garrisons see also P*D* 33. 1, 34. 7 (Athens); P*Pyrrh* 10. 7 (Corcyra); J. Briscoe in Garnsey and Whittaker 149.

[2] P*D* 39. 6 οὐ πολλῷ...ὕστερον; the phrase is too vague to sustain the argument that both revolts must have been in the same year (so Wehrli 175–6).

[3] D.S. 21. 11 f.; Str. 7. 302, 305; Paus. 1. 9. 6; Memnon, *FGrH* 434 F 5. 1; Polyaen. 7. 2. 5; Suidas s.v. *anadrome, Dromichaites*.

[4] So plausibly, Wehrli 175–6.

[5] P*D* 39. 6–7; an inscription from Acraephiae honours the ilarch Eugnotus, who fell in this battle (P. Perdrizet, *BCH* 24 (1900) 70–4).

a wedge between Demetrius and his base in Macedonia or even envisaging an advance into Macedonia itself. No details of the affair have survived, however, other than the fact that Demetrius quickly ejected Pyrrhus from Thessaly, where he now stationed 10,000 hoplites and 1,000 cavalry, no doubt along the western approaches.[1] That done, he returned to Thebes. The siege dragged on in a long and hard-fought struggle. Demetrius brought up his siege-engines, including the famous 'helepolis' used at Rhodes, but progress was slow and casualties heavy. In his irritation Demetrius spared neither himself—he was wounded in the neck from a catapult bolt—nor his men. His callous attitude towards casualties won him the reproof of his son Antigonus —if we may believe an anecdote which will go back to Hieronymus and is designed to bring credit on the young prince.[2] When towards the end of 291, or even early in 290, Thebes fell at last, Demetrius treated it with compassionate leniency. Only a handful of the leading spirits in the revolt were executed and a few more banished. But Demetrius installed Macedonian troops and a royal governor, and this meant an end of democratic institutions until 287 (see below, p. 228 n. 2).[3]

If the Aetolians took part in this war, it has left no trace in our sources.[4] Certainly their failure to assist Pyrrhus in his inroad into Thessaly suggests some degree of mutual mistrust. But there was no doubt on which side their sympathies lay, and if at any time they should decide to combine whole-heartedly with Pyrrhus against him, the results for Demetrius could be disastrous. Together, Macedonia and Thessaly could raise perhaps 30,000 or even, at a maximum, 35,000 men, compared with 12,000 to 20,000 from Epirus and some 12,000 from Aetolia. These are estimated figures and the equation must allow for several imponderables, such as the number of Macedonians (as distinct from mercenaries) that Demetrius would require for frontier defence and the number who could safely be enrolled from the

---

[1] PD 40. 1–2. PPyrrh 7. 3 καταδρομαὶ τῆς Θεσσαλίας ἐγεγόνεισαν ὑπ' ἐκείνου is attributed to this occasion by Lévêque 137 n. 3, but the pluperfect, taken together with the words καὶ πρότερον, should indicate an earlier period. These raids were perhaps made by Pyrrhus when on his way to answer Alexander's appeal, or on some other unrecorded occasion. But if they occurred before 294, it is strange that Alexander solicited Pyrrhus' help against Antipater. So perhaps Plutarch is here in error (as he is a few lines further on when he states that Demetrius defeated the Aetolians) and the raids in question are those which took place now.

[2] The siege may have lasted over a year. Thebes probably fell towards the end of 291 or even early in 290 (but certainly before Demetrius' trip to Corcyra; see below, pp. 223 n. 5 and 224 n. 1); cf. Lévêque 131. For other passages from Hieronymus designed to bring credit to Antigonus see PD 40. 1–4; PPyrrh 31. 4, 34. 7–11.

[3] The number executed was variously given as ten (D.S. 21. 14. 1), thirteen (PD 40. 6), or fourteen (D.S. 21. 14. 2). On the interference with democratic institutions see Roesch 436–8. It was probably now that Demetrius set up a Macedonian mint in Thebes; see Newell, *Coinages* 130.

[4] Tarn, *AG* 41 n. 8; Flacelière 73.

Greek cities controlled by Macedonia. But the estimate is near enough to show that a full-scale attack by the massed forces of Epirus and Aetolia was not something that Demetrius could contemplate with equanimity.[1]

Demetrius' march on the Hellespont and later events from 287 onwards indicate clearly that he never fully abandoned his ambition to recover his father's kingdom in Asia. In that context it was essential for him to be rid of the threat of a united attack by Pyrrhus and the Aetolians before turning east. But apart from that—and it would probably be wrong to see any action of Demetrius as part of a rational plan conceived in a long perspective—both foes were an obstacle to full control of central and southern Greece. It was Demetrius' way to hold several possibilities in his mind simultaneously. So while he planned to move west against the Aetolians, he was also making provision for a more active policy in the Aegean—whether peaceful or military—by his new foundation about this time of Demetrias, a synoecism of the villages of the Magnesian peninsula around a core consisting of Pagasae.[2]

A decade earlier, in 302, Demetrius had thwarted an attempt by Cassander to incorporate several communities into Phthiotic Thebes, and so to transform it into the strongest city on the Gulf of Pagasae.[3] The great rival of Thebes was Pagasae, which vied with it for the privilege and profit of handling the corn, meat, hides, and wool exported from the plains of Thessaly.[4] Demetrius' new foundation was intended to pre-empt any such claim, using a better site with a better harbour than that of Pagasae, of which it became the successor. Demetrias stood on and around the hill of Palati, some 7.5 kilometres south and west of Volo. The circuit of the walls was 7.8 kilometres in length and enclosed an area of 262.5 hectares. It took in the northern sector of Pagasae, which was incorporated as a deme in the new city. Demetrias was in due course to develop into the main port for Macedonia and Thessaly and, especially in the late third and early second centuries, it acquired a cosmopolitan population from many parts of Greece.[5] Its great days were, indeed, to come in the reign of

---

[1] The calculations are those of Tarn, *AG* 64 ff., 424 ff. While admitting that Cassander's army had defeated the combined forces of Aeacides of Epirus and Aetolia in 313, Tarn points out that Aeacides had not commanded the full forces of Epirus and that since then Epirus had expanded at the expense of Macedonia, while the Aetolians had also acquired new territories. See also Lévêque 138.

[2] Str. 9. 4. 15 C 428; *PD* 53. 7; Livy 35. 31. 9; D.L. 4. 39. Cf. Buraselis 89 with n. 206; *Pagasai und Demetrias; Demetrias I*; E. Meyer, *RE* Suppl. 9 s.v. *Demetrias* cols. 24–6; Wehrli 196–9. For Pagasae as a deme of Demetrias see *SIG* 1157.

[3] D.S. 20. 110.   [4] On this trade see Stählin 67; Westlake 5 n. 5.

[5] Cemeteries to the south of the city have revealed graves of men from Magnesia itself, Macedonia, the islands (including those as far afield as Sicily), Asia Minor, Syria, and Phoenicia. For the evidence see Stählin 74.

Philip V, for pottery discovered in recent excavations[1] has shown clearly that the large and impressive royal palace, which stood on height 33 to the north of the 'sacred *agora*',[2] dates not, as had been assumed, to the reign of Antigonus Gonatas, but to that of his grandson, Philip V. Strabo (9. 4. 15) informs us that Demetrias included both Pelion and Ossa within its territory and commanded the passes around Tempe. It must therefore have represented a synoecism of the whole Magnesian peninsula, which thus became in effect an adjunct to Macedonia rather than a part of Thessaly. Thessaly was of course subject to the control of the king of Macedonia. But it remained nominally independent and when a king of Macedonia wished to see some policy adopted in a Thessalian city, he wrote with suggestions rather than orders.[3] The control exercised from this new royal foundation with a royal garrison must inevitably have been far closer and it will have operated throughout the whole of Magnesia and all the surrounding parts of Thessaly. It was not without reason that Philip V, for whom, as we have just seen, Demetrias became a favoured residence, described it—along with Chalcis and Corinth—as one of the three 'fetters of Greece'.

In 290 Demetrius was presented with an unexpected chance to hit at both Pyrrhus and the Aetolians. Some four or five years previously Pyrrhus had contracted a marriage with Lanassa, the daughter of Agathocles of Syracuse, by which she brought him Corcyra as her dowry.[4] Weary of Pyrrhus' polygamous habits and the favours he showed to his other wives, Lanassa now invited Demetrius to accept her hand in marriage and with it Corcyra, where she had taken refuge. Apart from any personal motivation, this move was clearly linked with a change in policy on the part of her father and should be seen primarily in that context; for shortly afterwards Agathocles dispatched his son Agathocles as envoy to Demetrius, who in return sent Oxythemis, one of his leading Friends, to Syracuse to arrange an alliance (289).[5] As a naval base in Demetrius' hands, Corcyra could damage the Aetolians as much as Pyrrhus, and Demetrius lost no time in accepting Lanassa's offer and sailing at once to Corcyra—whether from Macedonia or from Athens is not stated. Leaving a garrison in the

---

[1] See in *Demetrias I*: P. Marzolff, 5–16, 17–45; I. Beyer and others, 59–74 (excavations 1970), 75–143 (excavations 1971).

[2] For evidence of its existence in 192 see Livy 35. 31. 9–10; and see below, p. 479.

[3] Cf. Philip V's letters to Larissa on creating new citizens (*SIG* 543).

[4] See above, p. 213 n. 8.

[5] P*Pyrrh* 9. 2 (Lanassa marries Pyrrhus), 10. 5 (her approach to Demetrius). On the negotiations with Agathocles see D.S. 21. 15, 16. 5 (an improbable story that Oxythemis placed Agathocles on the funeral pyre while still alive). On Oxythemis see *IG* ii². 558 = *SIG* 343; Robert, *Hellenica* 2 (1946) 29 n. 6; Athen. 6. 253 a, 14. 614 f, gives a false impression of his importance in Demetrius' court.

city, he then proceeded to Athens, where, as a gesture against the
Aetolians (who controlled the approaches to Delphi), he held the
Pythian games in Metageitnion (August–September) 290. It was
probably on that occasion that the Athenians chanted the famous
ithyphallus, which lauded Demetrius as a god, not like other gods far off
and invisible, but here in very flesh, and urged him to take action
against the Aetolians.[1] The conjunction of divine status for Demetrius
and the call for an Aetolian war was no coincidence. It was designed to
represent the forthcoming campaign as a sacred war or crusade, just as,
seventy years later, Demetrius' great-grandson, Philip V, was to
represent his war against the Aetolians as designed to liberate Delphi
from the usurping power.[2] Meanwhile Corcyra (and Leucas, which
went with it)[3] provided Demetrius with an outpost in the West,
overlooking commerce between Greece, and more particularly Sicyon
and Corinth, and the cities of Sicily and Magna Graecia. But whatever
Agathocles' plans (and he died in 289/8), it is unlikely that Demetrius
was looking seriously to the West. Judging by his subsequent policy, he
regarded Corcyra, and especially Leucas, as a useful base against
Aetolia.[4]

In 289 Demetrius invaded Aetolia from Macedonia, probably by
way of the Spercheius valley and the route over into the Achelous basin
past the site of modern Karpenisi, and having ravaged the country,
advanced north into Epirus, keeping well inland from the coast.[5]
Meanwhile Pyrrhus had marched to the rescue of the Aetolians by the
most direct route through Amphilochian Argos, Stratus, and Agrinium, with the result that the two kings missed each other.[6] But
Demetrius had left a large force behind to continue the ravaging of
Aetolia—probably a strategic error—and after a fierce battle, which
included a bloody personal duel between Pantauchus and Pyrrhus
along Homeric lines, the Macedonian force was cut to pieces and

---

[1] On the holding of the Pythia of 290 in Athens see PD 40. 7–8; Flacelière 75–7; and for the
singing of the *ithyphallus* then (rather than at the Great Eleusinia of 290; so Flacelière 65 n. 1) see
Lévêque 142 n. 7. The text of the *ithyphallus* (in Duris) is in *FGrH* 76 F 13 = Athen. 6. 253 d–f.
[2] Cf. Flacelière 76; for Philip V's propaganda cf. Plb. 4. 25. 8.
[3] Cf. Athen. 6. 253 c.
[4] For the view that Demetrius planned an active policy in the west see P. Treves, *Rend. Linc.*
1932, 171–2.
[5] PD 41. 2; PPyrrh 7. 4. On the route see Lévêque 144–5 (with sketch-map on p. 143);
according to Béquignon 24, the ancient road went rather further to the south along the Vistritza.
The account in the *Pyrrhus* has Demetrius defeat the Aetolians, but they will hardly have faced a
pitched battle. This section of the *Pyrrhus* is in other respects inaccurate (see above, p. 221 n. 1)
and the reference to ravaging the land (in the *Demetrius*) is much more plausible; cf. Flacelière
77–8 n. 2; Wehrli 179 n. 39.
[6] PD 41. 3; PPyrrh 7. 4. Lévêque 145 sends Demetrius via Agrafa, Granitsa, and Sacaretsi (cf.
A. Philippson, *Thessalien und Epirus* (Berlin, 1897) 339–58), but this seems an unnecessarily
roundabout way.

Pyrrhus took 5,000 prisoners.[1] Thus the expedition ended in disaster for Demetrius, who is next heard of lying ill at Pella.[2] The Aetolian campaign was clearly intended to strike at both enemies and not simply to keep the troops quiet, as Plutarch alleges—though Demetrius may well have taken soundings among the Macedonians and decided that a western expedition would not be unpopular.[3] His defeat, however, dealt him a blow from which in the long run he never recovered.[4] In both the *Pyrrhus* and the *Demetrius* Plutarch stresses the admiration which the Macedonians felt for Pyrrhus, whom they compared with Alexander to the detriment of Demetrius. The losses in Aetolia will also have added to Demetrius' unpopularity in Macedonia, where he had already a name for arrogance, extravagance, and contempt for both the rights of the Macedonian people and the obligations of kingship.[5]

Pyrrhus' victory brought him great prestige in Epirus; and shortly afterwards, perhaps in 288,[6] on hearing that Demetrius lay ill at Pella, he invaded Macedonia. His route is uncertain; but if the *castra Pyrrhi* at Mesogephyra close to Konitsa got its name on this occasion,[7] Pyrrhus will have taken one of two routes, either the northern route via modern Leskovik, Koritsa, and the Tsangon pass to Bilisht and Florina, or that followed by Philip V in the opposite direction in 198, on his way to occupy the pass of the Aous, viz. up the Sarandoporos and over the watershed near Kotili down to Argos Orestikon and Kastoria.[8] Rallying support along the way, Pyrrhus got as far as Edessa before

---

[1] PD 41. 3; PPyrrh 7. 6–10. The account may be a contamination of Hieronymus and Proxenus (Lévêque 146), with the latter responsible for the epic colouring. But the fact of the duel need not to be rejected; Scipio Aemilianus fought such a duel in Spain a century later and in 222 M. Claudius Marcellus won *spolia opima* in single combat at Clastidium.

[2] PD 43. 1.

[3] PD 41. 1. Campaigning to keep the troops contented is a theme found elsewhere (cf. PPyrrh 12. 8), but need not be wholly a *topos*, as Lévêque 163 suggests.

[4] Cf. Lévêque 146.

[5] PD 41. 4–5; PPyrrh 8. 1, 11. 8 (resentment at Demetrius' behaviour). His preparations for an eastern policy may also have been unpopular; cf. J. V. A. Fine, *AJP* 61 (1940) 143; Buraselis 43 n. 226.

[6] According to PPyrrh 10. 2, Pyrrhus' invasion of Macedonia took place shortly after (ὀλίγῳ ὕστερον) his victory in Aetolia; but the phrase is vague and could easily refer to an event the following spring. Since there is good reason to date the joint attack which led to Demetrius' expulsion from Macedonia in spring 287 (see below, p. 228 n. 2) it is more likely that Pyrrhus' first invasion, which reached Edessa, was in 288, than that a whole year without any recorded events intervened between the two invasions.

[7] The other date when Pyrrhus could have camped at Mesogephyra is 274; but this is much less likely (see below, p. 261).

[8] For the former of these routes see N. G. L. Hammond, *BSA* 31 (1931–2) 141 (his route 2), for the latter Hammond, *BSA* 61 (1966) 46 with Map 1 on p. 20; *HE* 275–6. As a variant Pyrrhus could have taken the northern route but descended to Kastoria and thence via the Kleisoura of Mt. Vitsi to Amindaion and Edessa. The route up the Sarandoporos is now a first-class motor road, which, however, continues east to Neapolis before turning north to Kastoria.

being confronted by a large Macedonian army raised by Demetrius' Friends and generals, since the king himself was still ill. Pyrrhus, who did not intend his attack to develop into a major assault on Macedonia, fell back and Demetrius recovered sufficiently to patch up an agreement with him, the terms of which are unrecorded.[1] In fact Demetrius, characteristically, already had his eyes elsewhere and was busy building up a large army and navy for a campaign in Asia Minor, evidently in the hope of restoring the Antigonid empire in the East. With this in mind he had already assembled 98,000 infantry and 12,000 cavalry and laid down the keels for 500 ships at the Piraeus, Corinth, Chalcis, and Pella. The absence of Demetrias from this list is striking, but perhaps the new city was not yet sufficiently developed by 288 to cope with shipbuilding on a large scale.[2]

This vast military and naval programme is reflected in the increasingly large issues of coinage by various Macedonian and Greek mints under Demetrius' control throughout these years. The various series of his European coinage have been convincingly identified and analysed by E. T. Newell, who distinguishes the issues of the two great Macedonian mints at Pella and Amphipolis from others emitted by mints at Demetrias, Thebes, Chalcis, and (perhaps) Sicyon. Newell identified six series consisting mainly of tetradrachms, but also including gold staters (and some other values such as drachmas and a certain amount of bronze). These evidently all belong to the years during which Demetrius was king of Macedonia—though Newell's assumption that each series represents the output of exactly one calendar year (a procedure perhaps more suited to the coining practices of a state or city with annually elected magistrates) seems less likely now that it is known that Demetrius' expulsion from Macedonia was in 287, not 288.

During this period two changes took place in the style and legend of Demetrius' Macedonian coins. The first occurs in the third series (dated by Newell to 292/1) where, in place of Nike on a prow (celebrating the Antigonid victory at Salamis) the obverse of the tetradrachms now carries Demetrius' own portrait, adorned with bull's horns. The second change occurs halfway through the fourth series, which must have been minted approximately in 291/0. This involved a

[1] PD 43. 2; PPyrrh 10. 1–4. In the *Pyrrhus* passage Plutarch claims that Pyrrhus' invasion was intended only as a plundering expedition (ἐπιδρομήν τινα καὶ λεηλασίαν) but when he encountered no opposition, but only men anxious to volunteer in his army, he marched on to Edessa. Hammond sends him via Metsovo, Milia, Grevena, and Kozani (*BSA* 32 (1951–2) 141 n. 3; cf. Lévêque 148 (with sketch-map on p. 149)). But see above p. 225 for the likelihood that he took the easier northern route.

[2] PD 43. 4–7; some of the ships were 'fifteens' and 'sixteens'. The number of troops (rounded off in PPyrrh 10. 3) need not be regarded as exaggerated, if they included garrison troops and mercenaries (Niese 1. 174; Tarn, *AG* 71 n. 42). On the omission of Demetrias, despite the proximity of the forests of Mt. Pelion, see Buraselis 90 n. 209.

reversal in the order of the words constituting the legend. Hitherto this had read **ΔΗΜΗΤΡΙΟΥ ΒΑΣΙΛΕΩΣ** (or, on a stater of series 1, simply **ΔΗΜΗΤΡΙΟΥ**). Now, and on all Demetrius' later coins, the wording is invariably **ΒΑΣΙΛΕΩΣ ΔΗΜΗΤΡΙΟΥ**. It would, however, be a mistake to read a political meaning into this change of style,[1] since a similar variant in the word-order is to be found on the bronze coins of Cassander and on silver tetradrachms of Gonatas.

Of the royal mints which Newell has identified, that at Chalcis in particular shows a considerable and constantly growing output of money, which no doubt served to finance the building of new ships in the dockyards of this important city. But the greatest increase in production, as demonstrated by the large number of dies and known specimens, occurs in the Macedonian mints at Pella and, more especially, Amphipolis. Diodorus mentions Pella as one of Demetrius' centres for shipbuilding, but the evidence of the coinage suggests even more activity at Amphipolis, which of course lay closest to Mt. Pangaeum and its silver supplies and to those of Stagira. Indeed, the sixth and last series from Amphipolis seems to have been the largest single issue ever put out from any of Demetrius' mints. These various coinages reveal very clearly the size of the military and naval effort Demetrius was making at this time, the threat which it must have presented to his enemies, and the burden of taxation which it will have laid on the inhabitants of his empire.[2]

News of what was afoot soon reached the other kings and spread general alarm. Recalling his father's ambitions, they were apprehensive at the menace which Demetrius in his turn represented, now that he controlled Macedonia and at least part of Greece.[3] Sometime in 288, therefore, Seleucus, Ptolemy, and Lysimachus made an alliance against him and sent a joint embassy to Pyrrhus urging him to ignore his agreement with Demetrius and to attack Macedonia. Plutarch speaks of a series of letters to Pyrrhus, which implies negotiations, but he does not record what Pyrrhus was offered. It seems likely, however,

---

[1] See Gaebler III. 2. 177 no. 9 with Pl. XXXII. 10; Merker, 48–9.

[2] On Demetrius' European coinage see Newell, *Coinages* 76–100 nos. 65–92 (Pella); 77–124 nos. 93–138 (Amphipolis); 125–30 nos. 139–41 (Thebes); 131–6 nos. 143–5 (Demetrias); 137–42 nos. 146–52 (Chalcis), nos. 153–4 (Euboean); 144–7 nos. 155–9 (?Sicyon-Demetrias; cf. D.S. 20. 102. 3: hypothetical). On the Chalcis coins see Picard, *Chalcis* 266–7. An indication of the financial pressure laid on Demetrius' subjects is to be seen in the heavy tribute imposed on Eretria, which the philosopher Menedemus persuaded Demetrius to reduce to 150 talents (D.L. 2. 140)—though both this and the original figure of 200 talents look like an exaggeration. For the subsequent lifting of this burden by Ptolemy I see *SIG* 390 l. 16: [κ]αὶ τῶν εἰσφορῶν κουφίσας (referring to the islanders). For evidence of public debts owed both to the temple at Delos and to individuals at this time see the evidence assembled by Buraselis 90–1 n. 219.

[3] As king of Macedonia he would not command a great deal of support in Greece; see, against Tarn, *AG* 89–109, Will I². 96.

that he demanded, and was granted, Macedonia, for he was clearly taken aback by Lysimachus' later claim that the kingdom should be divided and, even though he gave way to this, he succeeded in keeping the larger share.[1] The agreement was followed by joint action. In the spring of 287 Ptolemy sent a fleet into Greek waters to stir up revolt against Demetrius—especially, as events were to show, at Athens. The Cyclades were taken under Ptolemaic control and the island of Andros, which furnished a convenient base for action on the mainland, was seized and garrisoned.[2] From Thrace Lysimachus invaded Macedonia and captured Amphipolis with the help of supporters within the city,[3] while Pyrrhus, ignoring his pact with Demetrius, came in shortly afterwards from the west, probably via Metsovo, Grevena, and Kozani, and from there advanced directly on Beroea, whence he ravaged the country widely.[4]

As to what happened next, the sources disagree. According to the most likely account, Demetrius who was at the time in Greece, probably supervising his naval works there, left his son in charge, returned to Macedonia, and advanced against Lysimachus,[5] but, on then hearing that Pyrrhus had taken Beroea, suddenly found his army to be on the brink of mutiny. Judging that Macedonian troops might

---

[1] PD 44. 1; PPyrrh 11. 1 (repeated letters); J. 16. 2. 1–2. On the danger should Demetrius succeed in uniting Greece see Tarn, AG 71. On the division of Macedonia cf. PPyrrh 12. 1; Paus. 1. 10. 2. See Lévêque 152 n. 2; below, p. 230 n. 1.

[2] PD 44. 3. When, later in 287, Athens revolted from Demetrius (see below, p. 230 n. 3) the Athenian Callias was able to transport 1,000 Ptolemaic mercenaries from Andros to the mainland to help safeguard the bringing in of the harvest; cf. Shear 2–4 ll. 18–23; 68. It is just possible that Ptolemy had held Andros continuously since 308, but unlikely after the defeat at Salamis in 306: cf. Habicht, *Unters.* 66. It is clear from *IG* xii. 7. 506 = *SIG* 390 (a decree of the Nesiote League found on the small island of Nicouria, in honour of Philocles, king of Sidon, and Bacchon, the Ptolemaic nesiarch) that the League came under Ptolemaic control in the reign of Ptolemy I and this probably took place in 287 (Will 1². 96). Habicht, *Unters.* 63 n. 79, 66, would date the Ptolemaic acquisition of the Nesiote League a year later in 286/5, but his argument that Demetrius would not have contemplated sailing across the Aegean without the certainty of a peace with Ptolemy is not a strong one, since when Demetrius built his fleet he controlled the Cyclades and had he continued to do so he might well have planned to sail to Asia without making peace.

[3] Polyaen. 4. 12. 2.

[4] PPyrrh 11; PD 44; Trog. *Prol.* 16; J. 16. 2. 1–2; Oros. 3. 23. 54–5; Cic. *Off.* 2. 26; Paus. 1. 10. 2. On Pyrrhus' route see Lévêque 148–9, 154 n. 3. Lévêque supposes that Pyrrhus had come this way the previous year also, but on that occasion he probably took a more northerly route; see above, p. 225 n. 8. According to Pausanias, Demetrius defeated Lysimachus, but this is quite inconsistent with both the mutinous condition of the Macedonian army afterwards and Lysimachus' claim to share Macedonia with Pyrrhus; cf. Lévêque 153 n. 3. Pausanias' account is to be rejected. R. M. Errington, *Chiron* 8 (1978) 128, argues that the men (τινές) who urged Demetrius to go were 'influential nobles', but Plutarch does not say so (as he might well have done) and the situation seems to be one in which the rank and file asserted their wishes; the men who opposed Demetrius had to pluck up their courage (τολμήσαντες: PD 44. 8; ἐτόλμων: PPyrrh 11. 12) to address him.

[5] PD 44. 4: τὸν μὲν υἱὸν ἐπὶ τῆς Ἑλλάδος κατέλιπεν. Hammond, *BSA* 31 (1931–2) 141.

more readily fight against an Epirote than a general of Macedonian stock, he marched west to Beroea. It was too late. The Macedonians, responding to the praises of Pyrrhus sung by the citizens of Beroea and influenced by infiltrators from Pyrrhus' camp, resolved to be rid of their unpopular king. Eventually some of the soldiers plucked up courage to approach Demetrius face to face and bade him go. Once he saw that he had lost all support, Demetrius slipped quietly away to seek temporary refuge in Cassandreia, where his wife Phila, in despair, took her own life by poison. From Cassandreia he made his way to Greece to rally his remaining supporters in the cities. Meanwhile, at Beroea, Pyrrhus took over the Macedonian camp and was there acclaimed king of the Macedonians by the army.[1]

2. *The kingdom divided between Pyrrhus and Lysimachus* *(287–285 B.C.)*

Demetrius lost his hold on Macedonia for several reasons. Military disaster in Aetolia, arrogance towards a proud and independent people, and an extravagant naval programme in preparation for the invasion of Asia had combined to render him thoroughly obnoxious to the Macedonians. His final collapse was due to military pressure from two directions and, though it was Pyrrhus who forced Demetrius to go, he was not able to assert control over the whole kingdom. Lysimachus insisted firmly upon his share, and Pyrrhus, who (according to Plutarch)[2] did not yet fully trust the Macedonians, agreed reluctantly to divide the kingdom. How this was done constitutionally and what role the Macedonians played in the arrangements is not recorded; but clearly they must have regarded it as no more than a temporary measure. According to Pausanias (i. 10. 2), Pyrrhus received the

---

[1] For the date of Pyrrhus' accession to the throne of Macedonia there have been several suggestions ranging from April/May 288 to autumn 287; see Lévèque 156, 178–80 (on Porphyry's dates in Eusebius and Syncellus). According to Porphyry, Demetrius reigned as king of Macedonia for six years (Eus. *FGrH* 260 F 3 sect. 6: from 293/2 to 288/7; 294/3 is assigned to Cassander's sons) and according to Syncellus (*Chron.* 265 d-266 b, pp. 505–6; 270 b, p. 513), he was king in Thessaly for 6 years 6 months. *PD* 44. 7 assigns him 7 years. His accession was in autumnn 294, a date determined by that of the overthrow of Lachares (see above, p. 212 n. 4; similarly his expulsion by Pyrrhus must be related to the revolt of Athens, which can be independently dated to June 287 (see below, p. 230 n. 3). In favour of dating Pyrrhus' invasion in 288 is the argument that the allies would be anxious to attack Demetrius before his fleet was ready; and *PD* 45. 5–46. 1 might suggest that after leaving Macedonia Demetrius spent a considerable time visiting Greek cities before he got round to granting *politeia* to Thebes and Athens revolted. But this passage of Plutarch is not to be pressed so hard. As Habicht (*Unters.* 60 n. 63) points out, Athens cannot conceivably have delayed nine months after Demetrius' disaster in Macedonia before deciding to revolt. The likelihood is, therefore, that the joint action of Ptolemy, Lysimachus, and Pyrrhus, culminating in the events at Beroea, fell in the spring of 287. This fits Plutarch's seven years and it is not in disagreement with Porphyry, given Eusebius' assignment of 294/3 to Cassander's sons.

[2] *PPyrrh* 12. 1.

greater part. Our surviving sources do not say where the line of division lay, but there can be little doubt that it was along the river Axius.[1]

For Demetrius support in Greece proper was now essential and he set about visiting the main cities as a private citizen, hoping by an exhibition of uncharacteristic humility to revive sympathy for his cause. For, despite the loss of Macedonia, he had not relinquished his wider ambitions. Among the cities he visited was Thebes where, after consolidating his position elsewhere,[2] he restored independence. Such progress as he had made received a serious jolt, however, when, in June 287, the Athenians revolted.[3] Olympiodorus was elected general and, with a specially raised force, which included old men and children, he attacked the Macedonian mercenary garrison. In this he was assisted by a section of the garrison itself under a Macedonian officer, Strombichus,[4] whom the nationalists had evidently bribed to join them. Their success in doing this suggests that some at least of his troops felt no great allegiance to Demetrius. Having failed to crush the revolt, the Macedonian garrison commander, Spintharus, retreated to the fort on the Museum hill, which Olympichus, with Strombichus' help, now stormed and captured with the loss of only thirteen men; Pausanias (1. 29. 13) saw their tombs in the Cerameicus. At the same time Callias of Sphettus, who was serving as a mercenary captain with the Ptolemaic garrison on Andros, and obviously was operating with Ptolemy's consent, brought 1,000 of the troops stationed there over to the Attic coast and so ensured that the harvest (of 287) was brought in safely from the fields despite attempts by the Macedonian troops from the Piraeus to destroy it.[5] In this highly important action he was assisted by his brother, Phaedrus of Sphettus, who had remained at Athens and had been elected general over the hoplites (see above, p. 206 n. 6) in the year of Cimon's archonship, 288/7. Phaedrus was later the recipient of an honorary decree which, among other listed

---

[1] Cf. Beloch 4. 1. 236 n. 3. When, in 294, Lysimachus seized the whole kingdom, his decisive meeting with Pyrrhus was at Edessa (PPyrrh 12. 10), which would have been unlikely had Pyrrhus held territory east of the Axius. According to Paus. 1. 10. 2, after the division Lysimachus ἐπῆρξε Νεστίων καὶ Μακεδόνων. The Nestii must be the Thracians around the river Nestus, not Macedonians.

[2] PD 46. 1: ἐπεὶ δ' ἅπαξ ὥσπερ εἰς βασιλικὴν τὴν ἐλπίδα κατέστη καὶ συνίστατο πάλιν σῶμα καὶ σχῆμα περὶ αὐτὸν ἀρχῆς, Θηβαίοις μὲν ἀπέδωκε τὴν πολιτείαν; on the meaning of πολιτεία here see Roesch 436–7, who argues that Thebes had been deprived of its independence after the second Boeotian revolt in 292. The Thebans probably now began issuing coins as a mark of independence (Newell, Coinages 130 and Pl. XV. 7).

[3] On the Athenian revolt see PD 46. 1; Paus. 1. 2. 1–2; IG II². 666–7, a decree for the Macedonian mercenary captain Strombichus (two copies); Shear 1–4 ll. 11–26. On the date see Habicht, Unters. 48–62; it occurred in the archonship of Cimon (288/7). For Demochares' part in the revolt see PMor 850 F–851 F.

[4] Strombichus is a Macedonian name; cf. D.S. 20. 103. 5; Launey 1. 305 n. 2.

[5] Shear 2–4 ll. 15–16 τῆς χώρας ἐμ πολέμωι οὔσης ὑπὸ τῶν ἐκ τοῦ Πειραέως.

achievements, praised his zeal in getting in the corn 'in difficult times'.[1]

Demetrius' response to the liberation of Athens was quicker and more decisive than the Athenians had anticipated. Assembling forces from such cities in southern Greece as he still held (the most important was of course Corinth), he marched from the Peloponnese and laid Athens under siege.[2] At this, the Athenians sent a message to Pyrrhus begging him to come to their aid. Some fighting now took place, in which Callias was wounded, though not seriously; and the Athenians sent the Academic philosopher Crates (he was later to be head of the school) to mediate with Demetrius.[3] The upshot was that peace was made—not indeed between Demetrius and Athens, but between Demetrius and Ptolemy, with a cessation of hostilities against Athens apparently written into the agreement.[4] The evidence for this curious arrangement is to be found in the Athenian decree for Callias passed by the Council and People in the archonship of Sosistratus (270/69). The negotiations leading to the settlement took place at the Piraeus, which was still held by Demetrius, and Ptolemy was represented by Sostratus of Cnidus, one of his leading Friends.[5] On Sostratus' invitation and with the agreement of the Athenian generals and Council Callias led an embassy to him to discuss Athenian interests and how they might be safeguarded in the peace terms. The conditions laid down were not easy for the Athenians to accept, for Piraeus, Munychia, Salamis, and the Attic fortresses at Eleusis, Phyle, Panactum, and Sunium were all to be left in Demetrius' hands; but they had little choice and on Phaedrus' advice both the Council and Assembly approved the peace.[6]

---

[1] IG II². 682 (= SIG 409) ll. 35 ff. τὸν σῖτον ἐκ τῆς χώρας καὶ τοὺς ἄλλους καρποὺς αἴτιος ἐγένετο εἰσκομισθῆναι; cf. Habicht, *Unters.* 53. This inscription, which gives the decree passed in his honour *c.* 255/4, relates how περιστάντων τεῖ πόλει καιρῶν δυσκόλων Phaedrus maintained peace in the χώρα. The καιροὶ δύσκολοι will refer to the period before Demetrius arrived and invested Athens (so Habicht) rather than the earlier threat of an attack from the Ptolemaic fleet (so Shear 69). The latter interpretation would imply that Phaedrus acted in support of the Macedonian cause and a similar objection applies to H. Heinen's proposal (*Gött. gel. Anz.* 233 (1981) 192) to date Phaedrus' activity in bringing in the grain to the beginning of Cimon's year of office in 288; Heinen does not specify what the καιροὶ δύσκολοι would then be.

[2] PD 46. 1. Shear 2–4 ll. 16–18: Δημητρίου παραγιγνομένου ἐκ Πελοποννήσου μετὰ τοῦ στρατοπέδου ἐπὶ τὸ ἄστυ. On the likelihood that the army was assembled at Corinth see Shear 16; Bengtson, *Strat.* 2. 345–62.

[3] PD 46. 2; for Crates' πρεσβευτικοὶ λόγοι found among his papers after his death see D.L. 4. 32.

[4] Shear 2–4 ll. 34–40.

[5] *Pros. Ptol.* 6. 16555; Str. 17. 1. 6 C 791. It was Sostratus who dedicated the famous Pharos at Alexandria. On him see further Fraser 1. 18–20 with notes; Shear 23–5. His activity in Greece about this time is attested by inscriptions at Delos and Delphi.

[6] IG II². 682 (decree for Phaedrus) ll. 36–7 συμβουλεύσας τῶι δήμωι συντελέσαι...; Habicht, *Unters.* 56. The recovery of these possessions remained a major aim of Athenian policy: cf. IG II². 657 ll. 34–6 ὅπως ἂν διαμένει ὁ δῆμος ἐλεύθερος ὢν καὶ τὸν Πειραιᾶ κομίσηται καὶ τὰ φρούρια τὴν

This treaty between Ptolemy and Demetrius meant that Ptolemy had withdrawn from the triple alliance which had brought about Demetrius' expulsion from Macedonia. For Demetrius it held obvious advantages. He could now advance against Lysimachus free from the fear that Ptolemy might attack or interfere with his possessions in Greece. As for Ptolemy, he had probably already got as much as he could hope to get for the time being. He had held Cyprus since 294,[1] and now in 287, by annexing the Cyclades, he had also acquired the patronage over the Island League.[2] He had moreover strengthened his position relative to Greece by installing garrisons, perhaps on other islands, but certainly on Andros, which was excellently placed for surveying and (as events at Athens had shown) for intervening in Greek affairs. He would no doubt have liked to remove Athens more completely from the Macedonian sphere; but in 294 he had failed to prevent Demetrius from taking it, despite his fleet of 150 ships,[3] and he was probably unwilling to face further humiliation by pressing the issue further. In addition, he probably knew that Athens had appealed to Pyrrhus and was anxious to settle matters with Demetrius before the new king of western Macedonia arrived to complicate them.[4] For Athens the peace was a limited success. The city was free and there was no longer a garrison on the Museum hill; but there was still an Antigonid presence in Attica. This, however, was all that Ptolemy was at this moment prepared to underwrite.

Demetrius beyond doubt saw the peace as a green light from Ptolemy sanctioning an attack on Lysimachus;[5] and soon afterwards, late in 287, he set sail for the coast of Asia Minor, 'to wrest Caria and Lydia from Lysimachus'.[6] His fleet was much smaller than that originally planned, for of the 500 keels laid down[7] those at Pella had been lost along with Macedonia. His land forces amounted to 11,000 foot and an unspecified number of cavalry. On arriving at Miletus, Demetrius celebrated his marriage with Ptolemais, the daughter of Ptolemy I and his ex-wife Eurydice (a dynastic alliance agreed ten years previously),[8] as an indication to the world at large that good relations once more existed between the Ptolemaic and Antigonid

---

ταχίστην; cf. Habicht, *Unters.* 78 n. 13. For an unsuccessful attempt to recover Piraeus in 286 see below, p. 237 n. 3. Eleusis was recovered, however, by Demochares (who was restored from exile in 286/5 in the archonship of Diocles) sometime between July 286 and April 284 (cf. P*Mor* 851 F; Shear 84–5; Habicht, *Unters.* 25 n. 25), an event which Habicht, *Studien* 44 associates with the splitting of the Athenian generalship ἐπὶ τὴν χώραν into two separate commands.

[1] See above, p. 214 n. 2.   [2] See above, p. 228 n. 2.   [3] See above, p. 212 n. 2.
[4] Cf. Beloch 4. 1. 133 n.
[5] On this see Buraselis 96–103. Between his arrival and departure Demetrius cannot have spent very long at Athens (cf. Habicht, *Unters.* 54 n. 40).   [6] PD 46. 4.
[7] See above, p. 226 n. 2.   [8] PD 32. 6; see Seibert, *DV* 30 ff.; Buraselis 95.

houses.[1] Demetrius' possessions in Greece had already been placed under his son Antigonus Gonatas when he hastened back to Macedonia the previous year. They consisted of Corinth and a few other places in the Peloponnese, Piraeus and the Attic fortresses, Euboea, Boeotia, Phocis, and Demetrias.[2]

Demetrius had evidently already sailed for Asia when Pyrrhus arrived belatedly at Athens. After sacrificing on the acropolis, the latter thanked the Athenians for the confidence they had shown in him, but (if we can believe Plutarch) offered them the sound advice to admit no kings within their walls in future.[3] Shortly afterwards he too made peace with Demetrius, a move which served the interests of both, for it ensured that Pyrrhus would send no help to Lysimachus while it allowed Pyrrhus to consolidate his position in western Macedonia. In fact it suited Pyrrhus to leave Demetrius free to attack Lysimachus, since he naturally resented the latter's annexation of the eastern half of the country. The terms of the peace are not recorded, but they can be confidently deduced from the circumstances in which it was made. They must have confirmed the *status quo*, recognizing Pyrrhus as king of Macedonia and Demetrius' possession of the Piraeus and the other Attic strongholds, including Salamis; and presumably the freedom of Athens was acknowledged by both parties.[4]

Once Demetrius was safely away in Asia, however, Pyrrhus soon broke this agreement (incited, Plutarch tells us, by Lysimachus)[5] and seized Thessaly, which by this time could reasonably be considered a natural appendage to Macedonia—though either Antigonus managed to maintain his hold on Demetrias[6] or Pyrrhus did not press his attack on that stronghold. He did, however, try to take some other unspecified Macedonian garrison posts in Greece.[7] Pyrrhus was now in a

---

[1] Buraselis 102–3.

[2] See above, p. 219; Bengtson, *Strat.* 1. 166. For Demetrius' control of Euboea see Picard, *Chalcis* 263–7; above, p. 202 n. 2.

[3] P*Pyrrh* 12. 6–8: this passage seems to distinguish between the making of peace and Pyrrhus' action against Thessaly εἰς Ἀσίαν ἀπάραντος αὐτοῦ, but the Athenians will hardly have admitted Pyrrhus into the city if Demetrius was still near by, and at war with him. The statue in Pyrrhus' honour, mentioned by Paus. 1. 11. 1, may have been set up on this occasion (Lévêque 161 n. 2).

[4] Cf. Beloch 4. 1. 232–3 n. 2; Lévêque 161; Lemnos and Imbros were in Lysimachus' hands; cf. Habicht, *Unters.* 79 n. 21.

[5] P*Pyrrh* 12. 8 πεισθεὶς ὑπὸ Λυσιμάχου. Plutarch gives as a reason the need to exercise the army, a theme which also appears in P*D* 41. 1 to explain Demetrius' attack on Aetolia. Tarn, *AG* 102, points out that if the earlier agreement between Pyrrhus and Lysimachus (above, pp. 227–8) contained a clause pledging mutual assistance if either should be attacked by Demetrius, Lysimachus may have invoked it to secure Pyrrhus' co-operation in a move which was of course very much in Pyrrhus' own interest.

[6] When Demetrius died in 283, Antigonus conveyed his body by sea for burial at Demetrias (P*D* 53. 4). Since Demetrias can hardly have been lost and recovered by then, it follows that Antigonus held it against Pyrrhus now and against Lysimachus two years later.

[7] P*Pyrrh* 12. 8.

very strong position. He controlled territories stretching from the Axius to the Adriatic and southwards to the Achelous and Thermopylae;[1] but later events[2] suggest that many Macedonians resented their incorporation in what was virtually an Epirote empire and that Pyrrhus never firmly established himself in their affections. So long as Demetrius was actively campaigning against Lysimachus, he remained a factor in the situation imposing caution on all his rivals. But after some early successes—for example he captured Sardes and Miletus[3] —he was confronted by Lysimachus' son Agathocles and withdrew into the interior of Asia Minor and from there moved eastwards into Armenia and Media. After heavy losses from sickness and famine he finally became entangled with Seleucus and after mass desertions was persuaded to surrender to him. As a result he spent the last years of his life in honourable captivity. Demetrius became a prisoner in 285 and he died in the course of 283.[4]

For Lysimachus the failure of Demetrius' enterprise and the news that he was a prisoner in Seleucus' hands seemed like an invitation to attack Pyrrhus, who was still nominally his ally. The following campaign, which is described briefly in P*Pyrrh* 12, presents several difficulties. According to this, Lysimachus found Pyrrhus encamped at Edessa and managed to cut off his supplies. What is unclear is why Pyrrhus was at Edessa. Was he anxious about his communications with Epirus? Or was he perhaps expecting trouble, of which we know nothing, from the north-west? If neither of these suppositions is true, his mobilization of the army can only mean that he had some inkling of Lysimachus' intentions. But in that case it is hard to see how Lysimachus—we do not know whether he set out from Cassandreia Lysimacheia, or Amphipolis—could have got so far west as to cross the Axius without any challenge from Pyrrhus (who must surely have had some kind of intelligence service in Lysimachus' half of Macedonia). One cannot therefore rule out the possibility that Plutarch has omitted an earlier confrontation east of Pella and near the Axius, the result of which was to force Pyrrhus to withdraw to a position on the edge of the hills, despite the fact that this imperilled his supply line (since the natural source of supplies for an army at Edessa would be the coastal

---

[1] Beloch 4. 1. 238.   [2] P*Pyrrh* 12. 9–12.
[3] Buraselis 104 n. 277; Müller, *MV* 73 ff. (Miletus); P*D* 46. 6 (Sardes). He also held Caunus (ibid. 49. 5).
[4] P*D* 46–52. The events described in 46–50 extend into 285. The winter mentioned in 47. 6 will be that of 286/5 since there can hardly have been enough time after Demetrius' departure from Greece in the autumn of 287 for him to reach Miletus, marry Ptolemais, and acquire various towns in western Asia Minor before going into winter quarters for 287/6 (cf. Niese 1. 381–2). It follows that Demetrius' capture and Lysimachus' expulsion of Pyrrhus from Macedonia were in 285. Demetrius died during his third year of captivity (P*D* 52. 5).

plain to the south-east). What is scarcely credible is that Pyrrhus, anticipating an attack from Lysimachus, chose Edessa as his first position, thus voluntarily surrendering Pella, the capital, and all that Pella meant in terms of prestige and the claim to rule Macedonia.

Lysimachus at once followed up his tactical advantage with a propaganda campaign among the leading Macedonians (τοὺς πρώτους τῶν Μακεδόνων: PPyrrh 12. 10) in which he played upon their nationalistic feelings of superiority to their Epirote king. The upshot was that Pyrrhus, sensing that he had lost the game, fled to Epirus.[1] Whether Lysimachus was hailed king of Macedon now or earlier, when he seized the eastern part of the country, is not recorded. There is some evidence that Pyrrhus had already been hedging his bets in a secret alliance with Demetrius' son Antigonus, who had been left in control of the Antigonid possessions in Greece. This agreement, which was probably entered into after Pyrrhus' seizure of Thessaly, and so in the winter of 286/5 or even a little later, is referred to in a fragment of Phoenicides' *Fluteplayers (Auletrides)*,[2] in which, according to Hesychius, the poet jokes about a secret treaty, which will be that made between Pyrrhus and Antigonus. This compact—probably a defensive alliance against Lysimachus—was evidently widely enough known at the time of the play's performance for the Athenian audience to take the point. But since the year in which the *Auletrides* was performed at the City Dionysia is not recorded, the passage affords no help in dating the alliance or the expulsion of Pyrrhus from Macedonia.[3] Pyrrhus may have been tempted to take this step in view of the advanced age of his ancient patron, Ptolemy Soter, who was now eighty and unlikely to afford him much further help. Nor can it have pleased Pyrrhus that Ptolemy's intervention at Athens had forestalled his own response to the Athenian appeal. Since then Soter had moved closer to Lysimachus, whom he saw as a useful counterweight against Seleucus. For Seleucus still maintained his claim to Coele–Syria. Indeed it may well

---

[1] PPyrrh 12. 9–12; J. 16. 3. 1–2.

[2] CAF 3 p. 333 fr. 1; Hesych. s.v. Δύνασαι σιωπᾶν. Two characters remark: α. Δύνασαι σιωπᾶν; β. ὥστε τοὺς τὰς διαλύσεις συντιθεμένους κεκραγέναι, (γύναι), δοκεῖν. Cf. A. Körte, RE s.v. Phoenicides col. 380.

[3] Beloch 4. 2. 107 argues that the evidence from Phoenicides dates Pyrrhus' expulsion from Macedonia to 284. But, although Paus. 1. 10. 2 refers to Lysimachus fighting Pyrrhus and Antigonus, it does not imply that the agreement between the two latter was made after Demetrius was taken prisoner (as Beloch asserts); nor does the reference to the treaty in Phoenicides imply that it was still in force. Consequently, even if it were true that the *Auletrides* was staged in March/April 284 (which is hypothetical), the passage in question would not be proof that Pyrrhus had not yet been expelled from Macedonia. No safe conclusions about the end of Pyrrhus' reign in Macedonia can be drawn from Porphyry's list of kings contained in Eusebius, since the Macedonian list assigns him only 7 months, a palpable mistake, and the Thessalian list gives him 3 years 4 months in the table, and 4 years 4 months in the text, both far too long. For a plausible explanation of these errors see W. S. Ferguson, CP 24 (1929), 27–31; Lévèque 168, 178–80.

have been in 285 that Ptolemy Philadelphus, who was raised by his father to be co-regent in that year, sealed a new relationship with Lysimachus by marrying his daughter Arsinoe.[1] In these circumstances a *rapprochement* with Antigonus was a wise move for Pyrrhus to take. And indeed Pausanias refers to fighting between Lysimachus and Antigonus, which may imply that Antigonus sent troops to help Pyrrhus at the Axius or at Edessa.[2]

Lysimachus' seizure of the whole of Macedonia in 285 greatly strengthened his relative position among the competing rulers. The battle of Ipsus had left him with a kingdom embracing much of Asia Minor as well as Thrace. Now his western frontiers reached the borders of Epirus and he could reasonably hope to build up an Aegean empire— a prospect alarming both to Seleucus and to the Ptolemies. His kingdom comprised Thrace as far as the Danube (but excluding Byzantium), Macedonia and Thessaly (but not Demetrias), and Asia Minor, with the exception of Pontus, Bithynia, and various principalities in Paphlagonia.[3] In addition, following Demetrius' capitulation to Seleucus, he had managed to gain control over Lemnos, Samothrace, and Samos, and he also exercised some influence in Delos.[4] South of Thessaly the Phocians were warmly disposed to him. It was during one of the next few years (284–281) that the Phocian Xanthippus, son of Ampharetus, who had freed Elatea in 304 only to see it fall into Cassander's hands *c.* 300,[5] once again liberated it by expelling Antigonus' garrison. He then bound it by an alliance to Lysimachus, who had given him financial aid for the enterprise. The Phocians celebrated Xanthippus' achievement with a metrical epigram lauding his deeds on a monument (which also records the earlier exploits of Xanthippus) in the sanctuary of Pythian Apollo at Delphi.[6] A dedication at Delphi implies good relations with Aetolia, and indeed the Aetolians too enjoyed Lysimachus' patronage,[7] and rewarded him by naming two towns in Aetolia Lysimacheia and Arsinoe (after his queen) respectively.[8]

---

[1] Schol. Theoc. 17. 128; on the date of the marriage cf. Beloch 4. 2. 182.

[2] Paus. 1. 10. 2.　　[3] On Lysimachus' kingdom at this time see Will 1². 99, 101–2.

[4] Cf. Phylarchus, *FGrH* 81 F 29 (=Athen. 6. 255 a); *IG* 11². 672 (Lemnos); *IG* xii. 8. 150 (=*SIG* 372) (Samothrace); *Inschr. Priene* 37 ll. 96, 130 f. (Samos); *IG* xi. 4. 542 (=*SIG* 381) (Delos); Buraselis 154 n. 151.　　[5] See above, p. 202 n. 7.

[6] *SIG* 361; *HGE* 89; Beloch 4. 2. 369; Flacelière 81. J. Pomtow (on *SIG* 379) has plausibly suggested that the Delphic proxeny conferred in the Delphic archonship of Heracleides on Prepelaus, a Macedonian known for his services as an ambassador of both Cassander and Lysimachus (cf. D.S. 19. 64. 3, 68. 5; 20. 102. 1, 103. 1, 103. 4, 107. 4; *SIG* 353 (Ephesus 302/1) l. 4; 379; *OGI* 5 = Welles, *RC* 1), was in recognition of his having acted as Lysimachus' agent on this occasion.

[7] An honorary decree voted for Androbolus, an Aetolian from Naupactus, at Cassandreia during Lysimachus' reign (*SIG* 380) is evidence for good relations.

[8] Arsinoe was a new name for Conope; both lay west of the modern Lake Lysimacheia. Str. 10. 22. 2 C 460 calls Arsinoe a foundation of Arsinoe 'the wife and sister of Ptolemy II'; but her

At Athens, it is true, the picture was somewhat different. In the days immediately following the liberation it was Athenian policy to cultivate good relations with any ruler opposed to the Antigonids, whose control of the Attic strongholds was still deeply resented. In particular, this meant Ptolemy, Pyrrhus, and Lysimachus[1] and two embassies to Lysimachus were headed by Demochares, who, after being exiled in 303, had been recalled when democracy was restored.[2] From these embassies Demochares returned triumphantly with subsidies amounting to 130 talents. The erection of a statue to Lysimachus at Athens may have been in recognition of his gift.[3] After 285, however, when Lysimachus became master of the whole of Macedonia, relations with Athens cooled. For this there were several reasons. First, the Athenians resented the expulsion of Pyrrhus, whom they regarded as a friend, from western Macedonia.[4] Then again, at some date after 285/4, Lysimachus had driven Ariston, the son and heir of their friend, King Audoleon, out of Paeonia and had annexed the country.[5]

connections with Aetolia are more likely to date from the period when she was Lysimachus' wife than after her return to Alexandria. Cf. F. Bölte, *RE* s.v. *Lysimacheia* col. 2554. For doubts see P. M. Fraser, *BCH* 78 (1954) 60 n. 3. Tarn, *AG* 119, believes that Aetolian friendship with Lysimachus came to an end when he became master of the whole of Macedonia; against this see Flacelière 80 n. 2. Aetolia had no reason to be hostile to Lysimachus unless he showed signs of advancing south of Thessaly (which he did not).

[1] Cf. Tarn, *AG* 101–2. For embassies sent to Ptolemy at this time see Habicht, *Unters.* 77 n. 6, listing various embassies, decrees, and gifts, which testify to the continual support lent by Alexandria to Athens. Athens also cultivated good relations with Boeotia, returning the town of Oropus; cf. G. De Sanctis, *Riv. fil.* 54 (1926) 222 ff.; R. Étienne and P. Roesch, *BCH* 102 (1978) 374. See *ISE* 1. 15 (decree honouring Athenian taxiarchs who had taken part in the *Basileia* festival at Lebadeia in 281/0). Relations were renewed with Aetolia, since from 286 onwards Athens was represented at the Pythia (Habicht, *Unters.* 77).

[2] According to P*Mor* 851 E, he was restored in the year of Diocles' archonship (286/5), the year after the liberation of Athens. His return may have been delayed for reasons unknown to us (cf. Habicht, *Unters.* 51; *contra*, H. Heinen, *Gött. gel. Anz.* 233 (1981) 91). For his exile in 303 see L. C. Smith, *Historia* 11 (1968) 114–18.

[3] P*Mor* 851 E; for Athenian embassies to Lysimachus at this time cf. *IG* ii². 657 ll. 31–8; 662 ll. 12–14; 663 ll. 6–10; and for embassies from Lysimachus to Athens and other Greek states see *IG* ii². 662 ll. 7–10; 663 ll. 2–4. The statue to Lysimachus may, however, have been set up earlier; cf. Habicht, *Unters.* 77 n. 8. Demochares succeeded in recovering Eleusis for Athens (P*Mor* 851 F; cf. *IG* ii². 1682 for building undertaken there soon after), either by force or diplomacy. This was some compensation for a disastrous attempt to get back Piraeus in 286, which failed with the loss of 426 lives (Polyaen. 5. 17. 1; Paus. 1. 29. 10; Ferguson, *HA* 150–1. The funerary epigram for Chaerippus (*ISE* 1.13) *may* connect with this incident).

[4] See above, pp. 231 and 233, for his role in the liberation.

[5] Cf. Polyaen. 4. 12. 3. Paeonia had been a vassal state under Philip II and Alexander, when its rulers were nevertheless allowed to coin (Volume ii. 251 and 506 for Lyppeius; Moretti, *ISE* 2. 79 n. 3 for two tetradrachms of Diplaus). Lysimachus evidently sought to impose Macedonian control over the kingdom. Audoleon was already king in 310 (D.S. 20. 19); for his gift of corn to Athens in 285/4 (archon Diotimus) see *IG* ii². 654 = *SIG* 371. A coin of Leon, the father of the later King Dropion (cf. *ISE* 2. 79) suggests either that some parts of Paeonia remained independent of Lysimachus or, more probably, that the Macedonian conquest of the kingdom did not survive the chaotic years following Lysimachus' death. On the later relations of Paeonia and Macedonia see

Thirdly, if we may accept a plausible suggestion of Habicht,[1] the embassies exchanged between Lysimachus and Athens were probably concerned with the return of the islands of Lemnos and Imbros to Athens—but proved fruitless. It was not until 281, and at the hands of Seleucus and his son Antiochus, that the Athenians were to recover these possessions.[2] If this is so, Lysimachus' loss of Athenian goodwill is not surprising. Yet it cannot have been a very serious matter for the king himself, for after 285 Lysimachus held a dominating position astride the straits, which made him hard to challenge in either Europe or Asia. He could well afford to ignore any unpopularity created by his oppressive policy.[3] That his power was nevertheless to suffer a swift decline was largely the result of errors of policy and acts of folly in his personal life. The events to which they gave rise are a lively illustration of those quick reversals of fortune which are characteristic of the history of Macedonia in the age of the Diadochi.

below pp. 267–8. According to Paus. 1. 9. 7 = *FGrH* 154 F 9, Lysimachus also invaded Epirus. Despite the fact that Pausanias attributes the statement to Hieronymus, it is to be rejected as an error; see the discussion in Lévêque 169–71.

[1] *Unters.* 80.

[2] Cf. *IG* ii². 672 (decree for Comeas, an Athenian hipparch, envoy to Seleucus I); Phylarchus, *FGrH* 81 F 29 (= Athen. 6. 254 f); Habicht, *Gottmenschentum* 89–90. G. Saitta, *Kokalos* 1 (1955) 131–4, who accepts Pausanias' evidence, argues for dating this invasion of Epirus to 287 at the time of the peace negotiations between Demetrius and Pyrrhus; but there is no trace of an open breach between Pyrrhus and Lysimachus at this time and Pyrrhus' seizure of Thessaly in 286 was on the urging of Lysimachus (above, p. 233). Moreover, as Hornblower 247 points out, Pausanias normally observes a chronological order in his excursuses. Here, that would imply dating Lysimachus' invasion of Epirus before the joint action of Pyrrhus and Lysimachus in 287, which is hardly possible. Jacoby, on *FGrH* 154 F 9, sees a confusion in Pausanias with the later plundering of the royal tombs at Aegeae by Pyrrhus' troops (P*Pyrrh* 26. 6–7; see below, p. 262 n. 6), which is plausible. But Hornblower's suggestion, that the two events were linked through Pyrrhus' being in camp at Edessa when Lysimachus expelled him, is based on the false belief that Aegeae was at Edessa.

[3] See Str. 4. 1. 21 C 640; P*Ph* 29. 2; Buraselis 95. The evidence for Lysimachus' administration is all from Asia, however; there is none from Macedonia. In some places he tried to repair injustices committed by Antigonus; but he showed little regard for the traditions of the cities and he enforced heavy taxation. See (with bibliography) Will 1². 101–2.

XI

THE YEARS OF CHAOS (285–277/6 B.C.)

THE origins of the disaster that struck the house of Lysimachus go back to the year 300/299 when, in the manœuvring that followed Ipsus,[1] he made an alliance with Ptolemy Soter and confirmed it with a double marriage: Lysimachus himself married Arsinoe, Ptolemy's daughter by Berenice, while Lysimachus' son and heir, Agathocles, whose mother was Nicaea, the daughter of the regent Antipater, married Arsinoe's elder half-sister Lysandra, Ptolemy's daughter by Eurydice. Arsinoe bore Lysimachus three sons, and as they grew up she became jealous of Agathocles' position as heir and set about poisoning his father's mind against him in the interest of her own children and, in particular, of the eldest, Ptolemy. Her perseverance eventually bore fruit when Lysimachus, probably in 283/2,[2] was persuaded to put his eldest son to death on a trumped-up charge of treason.[3] In fear for herself and her family, Lysandra took refuge with Seleucus. She was accompanied in her flight by her children, her brother, Ptolemy Ceraunus (who had joined her at Lysimachus' court, probably after Ptolemy I divorced their mother Eurydice a little before 287),[4] and Alexander, a son of Lysimachus by an Odrysian concubine.[5]

[1] See above, p. 205. On Lysimachus' marriage see Seibert, *DV* 93–6.

[2] The murder occurred 'brevi...tempore' after an earthquake, which took place at Lysimacheia in 287/6 (J. 17. 1. 1). Justin gives the impression that Seleucus' war against Lysimachus broke out fairly soon after Agathocles' murder, and Paus. 1. 10. 3 ff. also suggests a rapid sequence of events between the murder and Lysimachus' own death at Corupedium in 281. On the whole, then, 283/2 seems a likely date (Heinen, *Unters.* 17–18) though 284/3 is also possible (Will 1². 100).

[3] See J. 17. 1. 3–6; Memnon, *FGrH* 434 F 5. 6; Paus. 1. 10. 3–4; Trog. *Prol.* 17; Str. 13. 4. 1 C 623; Longega 44 f. and 455 attempts to determine the origins of these sensational accounts, but they are all too brief for certainty; cf. Heinen, *Unters.* 6. Pausanias has a version of the Phaedra or Potiphar's wife story, in which Agathocles rejects Arsinoe's advances. Justin attributes Agathocles' death to poison, while according to Memnon poison failed and Agathocles was murdered in prison by Ptolemy Ceraunus. It is unlikely that Ceraunus was involved; see next note.

[4] Eurydice was already divorced and living in Miletus in 287 when Demetrius married her daughter Ptolemais (*PD* 46. 5; above, p. 232 n. 8). The sources disagree about when Ceraunus joined Seleucus. Memnon (*FGrH* 434 F 8. 2) dates this after Corupedium in February 281 (see below, p. 241 n. 4) but inconsistently, since he also has Seleucus offer to set him on the Egyptian throne when his father died—despite Ptolemy's having already died in 282. App. *Syr.* 62 and Nepos, *de reg.* 3. 4 send Ceraunus to Seleucus direct from Egypt whereas Paus. 1. 16. 2 makes him a refugee from Lysimachus. He probably fled along with Lysandra after Agathocles' murder. Memnon (loc. cit. F. 5. 6) involves Ceraunus in Agathocles' murder. But Ceraunus had nothing

These events provoked hostility towards Lysimachus throughout his kingdom, and when the opposition was savagely suppressed,[1] more than one of his generals defected to Seleucus. Reading the signs, Seleucus, despite the fact that he was seventy-seven and Lysimachus seventy-four,[2] felt encouraged to make a late bid for the throne of Macedonia. Seleucus was at this time ruler over a large area of western Asia. His original satrapy of Babylonia (assigned to him at Triparadeisus and recovered from Antigonus in 312 after Ptolemy had routed Demetrius at Gaza) had been augmented by the conquest of the 'upper satrapies' of Iran. True, he had been forced to relinquish any claim to Gandhara, eastern Arachosia, and Gedrosia in an agreement with Chandragupta, the founder of the Mauryan empire, but this was probably a blessing in disguise, for it freed him from military responsibilities which would in all likelihood have over-taxed his resources and it planted his interests more firmly in Mesopotamia and on the shores of the Mediterranean. If he could defeat Lysimachus, Seleucus might hope to make himself master not only of Macedonia, but also of western Thrace, where Lysimachus was king (cf. Paus. 1. 9. 5).

An additional immediate incentive was a treasonable offer from a hitherto trustworthy servant of Lysimachus, Philetaerus. Philetaerus was a Paphlagonian whom Lysimachus had left in charge of the fortress of Pergamum, which contained treasure amounting to 9,000 talents.[3] But Philetaerus had recently quarrelled with the queen Arsinoe[4] and, both for this reason and, it is alleged, because of his indignation at Agathocles' execution, he now sent a messenger to Seleucus offering to join him and hand over the treasure at Pergamum: it was an offer hard to resist. And so, in the winter of 282/1, Seleucus invaded Asia Minor.[5] No account of the fighting

to gain from this and Memnon has probably compounded his other errors by confusing Ptolemy Ceraunus, the brother of Lysandra, with Ptolemy, the eldest son of Lysimachus and Arsinoe, who will have been about seventeen in 283/2 and had everything to gain from complicity in his mother's plot. See further Heinen, *Unters.* 3–20.
      [5] Paus. 1. 10. 4.

[1] J. 17. 1. 6, 'principum caedes'.   [2] J. 17. 1. 10.   [3] Str. 13. 4. 1 C 623; Paus. 1. 8. 1.
      [4] The quarrel perhaps arose out of an attempt by Arsinoe to get possession of the town of Amastris, as she had done that of Heraclea—if indeed the Eumenes to whom Lysimachus had evidently entrusted the town (Memnon, *FGrH* 434 F 9. 4) was Philetaerus' brother. See Str. 12. 3. 10 C 544; Memnon, *FGrH* 434 F 5. 1–5; Hansen 14–15.
      [5] According to the Babylonian king-list published by A. J. Sachs and D. J. Wiseman (*Iraq* 16 (1954) 203–5), Seleucus 'was killed in the land (of the) Khani' (i.e. probably the Caeni at the base of the Thracian Chersonese) in month 6 of year 31 (Seleucid era), which, by the revised chronology of Parker and Dubberstein 36, works out at 26 Aug.-26 Sept. (Jul.) 281. The decisive battle of Corupedium fell seven months earlier in Jan./Feb. 281 (J. 17. 2. 4), so Seleucus must have launched his attack on Lysimachus' Asian possessions during the winter of 282/1 (Heinen, *Unters.* 22 and, on the season, 26–7 n. 82). Heinen compares the crossing of Taurus by Antigonus I in the winter of 314/13 (D.S. 19. 69. 2) and by Maximinus in the winter of A.D. 312/13 (Lact. *de morte persec.* 45).

survives.[1] But it is clear that Seleucus' move caught Lysimachus unawares, since he was able to reach and capture Sardes,[2] another royal fortress with a valuable treasure, before Lysimachus could intercept him. The seizure of Cotiaeum in Phrygia Epictetus by Alexander, the son of Lysimachus, who had gone over to Seleucus along with Lysandra, also belongs to this stage in the war.[3] Apparently Seleucus had split his army into two parts, which advanced, one by way of the Royal Road to Ancyra and Cotiaeum and the other through the Cilician Gates and on to Iconium. Lysimachus managed to get an army across the Hellespont and marched directly against Seleucus, who was now near Sardes.

The two sides met at Corupedium, in the neighbourhood of that city.[4] The numbers and composition of the two armies are unknown,[5] but the result was a resounding defeat for Lysimachus, who was himself struck down by a Heracleote soldier.[6] Following his victory, Seleucus at once set about consolidating his position in western Asia Minor[7] before crossing into Europe to take over Macedonia. The situation there following Lysimachus' death is obscure. On the death of a king, it lay with the Macedonians to acclaim a successor. The recent internal conflicts meant that there was no unchallenged candidate, and the defeated army was poorly placed for taking what could only be a controversial decision. Our sources know nothing of any election during the following months. There is certainly no evidence that Seleucus got himself acclaimed king of the Macedonians[8] in advance

---

[1] The sources are: Str. 13. 4. 1 C 623; J. 17. 1. 7–2. 3; Trog. *Prol.* 17; Paus. 1. 10. 4–5; App. *Syr.* 62; Memnon, *FGrH* 434 F 5. 7; Porph. *FGrH* 260 F 3. 9; Eus. 1. 234 Sch.

[2] Polyaen. 4. 9. 4. The commandant Theodotus was persuaded to hand over the city and its contents. Seleucus subsequently coined here (cf. Heinen, *Unters.* 31–2).

[3] Polyaen. 6. 1. 12. See Heinen, *Unters.* 29–30, for various interpretations of the trick played by Alexander to capture this city.

[4] App. *Syr.* 62 puts the battle in Hellespontine Phrygia; but a funerary monument for a Bithynian Menas, who was killed fighting Κούρου...ἐ]μ πεδίω[ι] and Φρυγίοιο παρὰ ῥοόν, establishes that this Corupedium is identical with the 'plain of Cyrus' mentioned along with the river Phrygius near Sardes (Str. 13. 4. 5 C 626; 4. 13 C 629). This conclusion is independent of whether the battle in which Menas fell was this one or some other conflict. For the inscription see G. Mendel, *BCH* 24 (1900) 380; B. Keil, *Rev. Phil.* 26 (1892) 257–62; Beloch 4. 2. 458–61; L. Robert, *BCH* 59 (1933) 490 n. 3; P. Roussel in Glotz–Roussel–Cohen, 4. 1. 372 n. 86; Magie 2. 727 n. 5, 783 n. 8; Launey 1. 434 n. 4; Heinen, *Unters.* 28.

[5] If the funerary inscription for Menas is from this battle (see the previous note), it indicates that Seleucus had a contingent of Bithynians on his side and that Lysimachus' army contained Thracians and Mysians (for Menas killed one of each).

[6] Cf. Memnon, *FGrH* 434 F 5. 7. Lysimachus' remains were handed over to his son Alexander and buried at Lysimacheia. According to another tradition he was buried by one Thorax of Pharsalus (App. *Syr.* 64).

[7] For the details, which do not concern us here, see Heinen, *Unters.* 37–46; and, for the virtual annexation of the Aegean by Ptolemy at this time, Buraselis 155.

[8] A cuneiform inscription from Borsippa (F. H. Weissbach, *Die Keilinschriften der Achaemeniden*, Vorasiat. Bibl. 3, (Leipzig, 1911) 132 f. col. 1, ll. 4 f.) was read by several scholars (quoted in

of his crossing into Europe; and within the kingdom there were rival claimants. First, there was Arsinoe, never negligible, and skilful at gaining her ends.[1] She had awaited the result of Corupedium at Ephesus and, on hearing the bad news, had escaped to Cassandreia,[2] which she then proceeded to hold as a private strong-point. As she no doubt foresaw, the possession of Cassandreia would be an important factor in any struggle for power in Macedonia. Her obvious move was to have her eldest son Ptolemy, who was by this time seventeen or eighteen years old[3] and officially Lysimachus' heir, proclaimed king as his father's successor. But there is no firm evidence that she did so, though Justin, describing Ceraunus' later offers, speaks of the kingdom belonging to her children.[4] Not everyone in Macedonia, however, was prepared to admit that claim. Agathocles' supporters were hardly likely to welcome the accession of Arsinoe's son, especially if—as seems to be the case—he was already suspected of complicity in Agathocles' execution. But whether the latter had left an heir—he could only have been a child—on which the loyalty of his faction could focus is not known, since our sources speak only of Lysandra's children, without indicating whether they included a son. There was also Pyrrhus, who had already ruled for two years in western Macedonia. He might well lodge a claim to the kingdom, if he saw any chance of pressing it successfully. But while Seleucus was busy taking over Lysimachus' possessions in Asia Minor, Pyrrhus had become master of Corcyra,[5] and already his eyes were on Italy.

Late in August or early in September (281) Seleucus crossed the Hellespont, with the object of taking over by force the rest of Lysimachus' possessions, including Thrace and Macedonia. Memnon

---

Heinen, *Unters.* 46 n. 163) as if it described Seleucus as 'king of the Macedonians', but it is now generally agreed (cf. Aymard, *Études*, 103 f.; A. L. Oppenheim in J. B. Pritchard, *Ancient Near Eastern Texts Relating to the Old Testament*[2] (Princeton, 1955) 317) that the correct reading is 'Seleucus the king, the Macedonian'. The question whether the victory of Corupedium in fact gave Seleucus rights over Macedonia (for the long controversy on the subject between C. F. Lehmann-Haupt and F. Reuss see the summary in Heinen, *Unters.* 46–8) would be of no importance, had it not later become the basis for the claim made by Antiochus III to Thrace and the Thracian Chersonese (Plb. 18. 51. 3 Σελεύκου...κρατήσαντος τῷ πολέμῳ πᾶσαν τὴν Λυσιμάχου βασιλείαν δορίκτητον γένεσθαι Σελεύκου); it also appears in Memnon, *FGrH* 434 F 5. 7 ἡ τούτου [sc. Λυσιμάχου] ἀρχὴ προσχωρήσασα τῆι τοῦ Σελεύκου μέρος κατέστη, and J. 17. 2. 5 'regnumque Macedoniae, quod Lysimacho eripuerat, cum vita pariter amittit [sc. Seleucus].'

[1] Memnon, *FGrH* 434 F 5. 4 ἦν γὰρ δεινὴ περιελθεῖν ἡ Ἀρσινόη.
[2] On her escape see Polyaen. 8. 57.
[3] At the time of Arsinoe's marriage to Ptolemy Ceraunus (winter 281/0) his younger brother Lysimachus was sixteen (J. 24. 3. 5).
[4] J. 24. 2. 2 'sororis filios, quorum regnum occupaverat'.
[5] Paus. 1. 12. 1; J. 25. 4. 8; Corcyra must have broken away from Demetrius in 287 after his expulsion from Macedonia. See Lévêque 125–6.

says[1] that he had a longing to see his native land (which he had not visited for fifty years). Such a motive cannot be excluded, but it is more likely to be romantic surmise; certainly Seleucus' main object was much more practical. Since he evidently expected to remain, at any rate for some time, in Europe, he left Asia in the hands of his son Antiochus.[2] The size of Seleucus' army is not recorded, but it must have been substantially the force which had gained the victory at Corupedium, perhaps reinforced by some of Lysimachus' defeated troops.[3] Seleucus' ultimate plans and the role of Macedonia in these must, however, remain obscure since no sooner had he landed near Lysimacheia than he was murdered by Ptolemy Ceraunus.[4] This brutal act was clearly the outcome of a carefully prepared plan, for Ptolemy immediately followed it up by securing the nearest thing he could obtain to a legitimizing of his position as king of Macedonia. Mounting a horse, he fled from the scene of his crime to Lysimacheia whence he shortly afterwards emerged wearing a diadem and, accompanied by an impressive bodyguard, returned to receive the acclamation of Seleucus' leaderless forces.[5] What exactly had happened in Lysimacheia is not clear; but the likelihood is that Ceraunus there had himself proclaimed king—perhaps by the leading officers of the garrison, but more likely by such assembly of the troops stationed there as could be regarded, at a pinch, as representing 'the Macedonians'. The support of Seleucus' army was vital to his cause, but as it was composed of Greeks and barbarians[6]—their status is not known—they were not entitled to validate his rule inside Macedonia.[7]

Ceraunus' murder of Seleucus is not unnaturally condemned in our

---

[1] Memnon, *FGrH* 434 F 8. 1. The word is πόθος, which is often used to describe Alexander's urges (cf. V. Ehrenberg, *Alexander and the Greeks* (Oxford, 1938) 52–61); Brunt, 1. 469–70 App. V. 3.

[2] Memnon, loc. cit.

[3] There is no record of what happened to the survivors of Lysimachus' army; cf. Ritter 109 ff.; Heinen, *Unters.* 49 n. 179.

[4] Memnon, *FGrH* 434 F 8. 3; App. *Syr.* 62; Str. 13. 4. 1 C 623; Paus. 1. 16. 2, 10. 19. 7; *PMor* 555 BC; Pliny, *HN* 6. 31; J. 17. 2. 4 f.; Trog. *Prol.* 17; Eus. 1. 235 f., 249 f. Sch.; Oros. 3. 23. 63 f.; *Orac. Sib.* 5. 836 ff. Geffcken.

[5] Memnon, *FGrH* 434 F 8. 3 ἵππου ἐπιβὰς πρὸς Λυσιμαχίαν φεύγει, ἐν ἧι διάδημα περιθέμενος μετὰ λαμπρᾶς δορυφορίας κατέβαινεν εἰς τὸ στράτευμα, δεχομένων αὐτὸν ὑπὸ τῆς ἀνάγκης καὶ βασιλέα καλούντων, οἳ πρότερον Σελεύκωι ὑπήκουον.

[6] Paus. 1. 16. 2. If Seleucus had had substantial Macedonian troops, it is unlikely that Pausanias would have included these under 'Greeks'. This would not of course exclude the presence of some Macedonians in his entourage.

[7] See Heinen, *Unters.* 61–3. R. M. Errington, *Chiron* 8 (1978) 130 agrees in the main with Heinen, but argues that there was not necessarily an acclamation by troops in Lysimacheia, since acceptance by the 'chief men and army officers' would be enough. The combination of assuming the diadem and acquiring a bodyguard (δορυφορία is an armed guard, not just an escort) suggests a formal recognition which, on Macedonian precedent, would involve such troops as were present in the city. According to Trog. *Prol.* 17, 'creatus ab exercitu rex'; this probably refers to the action of Seleucus' army, despite the inaccurate use of *creare*.

sources as a savage and impious act of ingratitude towards a king who had provided him with support and shelter. But in the months since Corupedium Ptolemy must have become increasingly aware that Seleucus had nothing more to offer him. Memnon's statement[1] that Seleucus had originally promised to secure Ceraunus the succession in Egypt must, it is true, be rejected both on the grounds of its inherent improbability and, if Ceraunus fled to Seleucus in 283/2, on chronological grounds as well, since Philadelphus had already become sole king in Egypt upon the death of Soter in 283. A more reasonable hope for Ceraunus, and one that had been fostered by the group of refugees from Lysimachus' court, was that with the overthrow of Lysimachus the throne of Macedonia would be at their disposition and—especially if Lysandra had no male offspring—that meant that it would fall to Ceraunus. But Seleucus' resolve to leave Asia under Antiochus and to invade Europe showed that he intended to become king of Macedonia himself and that he was renewing in extreme old age the plan that Antigonus and Demetrius had formerly pursued for a single kingdom embracing at any rate the European and Asiatic components of Alexander's empire. If Ptolemy was to achieve anything, it was essential to get rid of Seleucus before he could gain a firm footing in Macedonia. He chose the place and the moment well, since apart from the prestige which he possessed as a son of Ptolemy Soter, he could also command allegiance from the forces in Lysimacheia by representing himself as Lysimachus' avenger[2]—and that despite his known links with his sister Lysandra, Agathocles' widow. Her fate is unknown. She and her family may have perished in the aftermath of Ptolemy's murderous attack on Seleucus. Be that as it may, it was no disadvantage to Ceraunus that they seem to have disappeared from the story from this time onwards.[3]

The support of Seleucus' army was an important factor in Ceraunus' plans, and it is likely (though not attested) that he had taken steps in advance to ensure the goodwill of some of the officers. When the army accepted him as king—'perforce', according to Memnon[4]—he was free of all fear of immediate disaster; but he had still several obstacles to overcome. An early challenge came from Antigonus, who, on hearing of Ptolemy's coup at Lysimacheia, launched a joint military and naval expedition with the apparent intention of seizing Macedonia

---

[1] Cf. Memnon, *FGrH* 428 F 8. 2 ὑποσχέσεσι λαμπρυνόμενος, ἃς αὐτῶι Σέλευκος προύτεινεν, εἰ τελευτήσειεν ὁ γεινάμενος, ⟨εἰς⟩ τὴν Αἴγυπτον, πατρῴαν οὖσαν ἀρχήν, καταγαγεῖν.

[2] Cf. J. 17. 2. 6 'cum et in gratiam memoriae Magni Ptolomei patris et in favorem ultionis Lysimachi ambitiosus ad populares esset.'

[3] Their whereabouts at the time of Seleucus' murder is unknown. That they fell victim to rioting following this is possible, but beyond proof; cf. Heinen, *Unters.* 52 n. 192.

[4] *FGrH* 434 F 8. 3 ὑπὸ τῆς ἀνάγκης.

first.[1] Antigonus clearly controlled an effective fleet, probably including some of Demetrius' ships, which will have returned to join him
after the latter's disaster in Asia.[2] But Ptolemy proved to have the
advantage, since he was now in control of Lysimachus' fleet, and this
included allied contingents like the considerable squadron from Heraclea which, according to the biased account in Memnon, contained
'sixes', quinqueremes, and 'deckless ships' (*aphraktoi*) as well as a
famous 'eight' with a huge crew and a lion as its crest, and played an
outstanding role in the battle. With this fleet Ptolemy successfully
repulsed Antigonus' attack, forcing him to withdraw to Greece—to
Boeotia, according to Memnon. The scene of this naval battle is
unknown, but Memnon's account suggests that it took place before
Ptolemy had advanced from Lysimacheia into Macedonia; perhaps
then it was fought somewhere near the Thracian Chersonese.[3]
Antigonus, it is true, attacked with an army as well as a fleet; but this
need not have involved intimate tactical collaboration between the
two arms. Antigonus may well have aimed at drawing out Ceraunus'
fleet and challenging him on the sea before he reached Macedonia,
while the army endeavoured to be first at Pella. Certainly it was only
after he had defeated Antigonus Gonatas that Ceraunus entered
Macedonia and took over the kingdom.[4]

One of Ceraunus' first acts on seizing power was to make a friendly
approach to his half-brother Ptolemy II, but its results seem to have
been negligible.[5] Next, and probably after Gonatas' attack,[6] he took
steps to establish good relations with Pyrrhus and Antiochus.[7] Justin
suggests that there were wars with both to be ended, but no record of
any fighting has survived. Antiochus was in any case tied up with
internal problems. Not only had he to face the revolt of Heraclea
Pontica, which was allied to Byzantium and Calchedon and supported
by Mithridates of Pontus, but in addition he had to deal with a
rebellion in Seleucis itself and with Ptolemaic annexations along the
south-west coast of Asia Minor, including the island of Samos, Caria,
and perhaps various strong-points in Lycia, Pamphylia, and western

---

[1] Memnon, *FGrH* 434 F 8. 4–6; J. 24. 1. 8–2. 1. Both agree in putting Antigonus' attack
before Ceraunus' intrigue to secure Cassandreia by marrying Arsinoe and this is preferable to the
account in J. 17. 2. 6–10, which reverses the order of these two events; see Heinen, *Unters.* 64.

[2] Cf. Tarn, *AG* 119; Buraselis 152 n.   [3] Cf. Heinen, *Unters.* 65.

[4] Memnon, *FGrH* 434 F 8. 6 Πτολεμαῖος δ' ἐπὶ Μακεδονίαν διέβη καὶ βεβαίως ἔσχε τὴν ἀρχήν.

[5] J. 17. 2. 9 ff.; cf. Heinen, *Unters.* 74.

[6] J. 17. 2. 10 suggests that Ceraunus made his settlement with Pyrrhus foreseeing war with
Antigonus and Antiochus, which would put it at the very beginning of his reign in 281; but
Antigonus' attack was before Ceraunus left Thrace (see above, n. 1).

[7] J. 24. 1. 8 'Ptolomeus pulso Antigono cum regnum totum Macedoniae occupasset, pacem
cum Antiocho facit adfinitatemque cum Pyrrho rege data ei in matrimonium filia sua iungit';
Trog. *Prol.* 17 'bella cum Antiocho et Pyrro composuit.'

Cilicia.[1] In view of these many threats Antiochus had appointed an officer, Patrocles, to represent him in Asia Minor and he was clearly in no position to take the offensive against Ceraunus, however much he resented his father's murder; indeed a termination of what may have been no more than a technical state of war was plainly to his advantage.

Whether Ceraunus was involved in hostilities with Pyrrhus[2] is also doubtful. As a former ruler over part of Macedonia, Pyrrhus was a potential threat, especially in view of his wide-ranging ambitions and incalculable character. But fortunately for Ceraunus, he was already negotiating with the Tarentines, who had solicited his help against Rome and, probably in May 280, he crossed over into Italy.[3] Among his forces he is said to have included 5,000 infantry, 4,000 cavalry, and fifty elephants, provided by Ceraunus on a two-years loan.[4] These figures may need adjustment; but even so they are sufficiently large to support the impression, derived from Justin,[5] that in loaning these forces Ceraunus was subject to considerable pressure. It was of course very much in his interest to see Pyrrhus safely away in Italy, perhaps—with luck—never to return. He could not foresee the calamitous situation which was soon to arise when the Gauls invaded Macedonia and found it denuded of these substantial forces. The compact with Pyrrhus was sealed in the usual fashion of the day by a marriage settlement, Pyrrhus marrying Ceraunus' daughter (her name is unknown).[6] Justin also asserts that Pyrrhus appointed Ceraunus to act as his 'vindex regni' (i.e. in Epirus) during his absence, but this statement is probably due to confusion with Pyrrhus' own son Ptolemy, who is elsewhere described as 'custos regni'.[7]

According to Justin (17. 2. 13), Pyrrhus requested the loan of transports from Antigonus and financial help from Antiochus. It has been generally assumed that both kings acceded to his demand, but

---

[1] On this see Will 1². 137–42.

[2] Despite Trog. *Prol.* 17 (quoted above, p. 245 n. 7); see Lévêque 277.

[3] See Lévêque 277 ff.; Heinen, *Unters.* 69.

[4] J. 17. 2. 14. The figures are not easily reconciled with those of an army which, according to P*Pyrrh* 15, amounted to 20,000 infantry, 2,500 archers and slingers, 3,000 cavalry, and 20 elephants; but Pyrrhus need not have taken all the forces lent by Ceraunus with him at the outset. See Lévêque 278 n. 2; Heinen, *Unters.* 72–4; Nachtergael 127 n. 5.

[5] J. 17. 2. 14 'Ptolomeus, cui nulla dilationis ex infirmitate virium venia esset....'

[6] J. 17. 2. 15, 24. 1. 8 (quoted above, p. 245 n. 7). Rejection of Justin's statement that Ceraunus was left as 'vindex regni' (see the next note) need not invalidate his reference to this marriage (so Lévêque 278).

[7] J. 17. 2. 15 (Ceraunus); 18. 1. 3 'relicto custode regni Ptolomeo filio annos xv nato'. Tarn, *AG* 134 n. 47, accepts the truth of the statement that Ceraunus was left as 'vindex regni' and Heinen, *Unters.* 71 n. 273 sees no contradiction between the son as internal 'guardian of the realm' and Ceraunus as its foreign protector. A confusion nevertheless seems to me more likely (cf. Lévêque 278).

Justin does not say so. He merely records the request without saying whether it was granted. Ruehl has indicated a lacuna in the text of Justin at this point (17. 2. 13) and indeed the word 'sed', with which the next sentence opens, suggests that there is a contrast between Ceraunus, who was not able to plead weakness of resources as an excuse for putting Pyrrhus off (and therefore sent the above-mentioned forces) and the other two who have just been referred to. Lévèque[1] does not believe that there is a lacuna; but 'sed' makes little sense on any other assumption and the likelihood is that a now missing sentence explained that Antigonus and Antiochus excused themselves from responding to Pyrrhus' request to send troops, the former no doubt because of his recent defeat at the hands of Ceraunus, the latter because of his commitments in Asia. The threats with which Pyrrhus accompanied his demand for assistance from Antigonus in 275 at the time of the battle of Beneventum (J. 25. 3. 1–2) are best explained on the assumption that his earlier request had met with a rebuff.

In the meantime, and probably during the winter of 281/0, Ptolemy set about disarming the opposition of Arsinoe, Lysimachus' widow, and the faction supporting her and her sons (who were with her in the stronghold of Cassandreia).[2] After failing to dislodge her by force,[3] Ceraunus made a volte-face and offered to marry her (despite the fact that she was his half-sister). His purpose in doing this is represented differently in the two passages of Justin which constitute the main source for the succeeding events. According to the first (17. 2. 6–8), he intended to forestall any opposition from Arsinoe's sons, whereas the second (24. 2. 1–3. 10) represents him as plotting to kill them. These two versions may correspond to two successive stages in Ceraunus' plan; but it is more likely that both rest on pure surmise concerning Ceraunus' motives.[4] Arsinoe's justified doubts were set at rest when Ptolemy swore oaths in the temple of Zeus that he would not only make her his queen, but also take no other wife, and that he would have no children except by her. He even promised to share the

---

[1] Lévèque 278 n. 1.

[2] See on this J. 17. 2. 6–8; 24. 2. 1–3. 10 (both accounts are hostile to Ceraunus and his death at the hands of the Gauls is seen as retribution for his crimes against Arsinoe); Memnon, *FGrH* 434 F 8. 7. Cf. Heinen, *Unters.* 75.

[3] J. 24. 2. 4 'armis contendisse'.

[4] Heinen, *Unters.* 81–3 sees Arsinoe's agreement with Ceraunus as a compromise, in which the interests of her eldest son were sacrificed to her own; and he suggests that Ceraunus' decision to murder the other two boys and expel Arsinoe may represent a change in policy in response to the elder son's flight and alliance with the Illyrian king Monunius (see below). This is clearly possible but, as Heinen recognizes, it cannot be proved. Justin's source is of course Pompeius Trogus; but whether Trogus is here following Hieronymus, one can only speculate. For the period of Alexander, where we have alternative versions, Trogus seems to have drawn on several sources (H*THA* 86–115). The same is likely to be true here too.

kingdom with her sons by Lysimachus. According to Justin,[1] her eldest son Ptolemy warned her against accepting Ceraunus' promises; whether this is true or not, he soon afterwards fled from Macedonia—wisely if, as seems likely, he had been involved in the plot against Agathocles. An impressive wedding was held, presumably at Pella, where Ceraunus crowned Arsinoe queen before the Army Assembly.[2] For Ceraunus this marriage was intended to secure the possession of Cassandreia, and Arsinoe, installed as queen, invited her husband to the city, presumably in order to take over its control. In a formal procession of welcome he was met by Arsinoe's two younger sons, Lysander and Philip, aged sixteen and thirteen respectively, both garlanded for the occasion. But once he had occupied the citadel he had them both murdered—in their mother's presence, according to the highly dramatic account in Justin.[3] Arsinoe herself was allowed to escape, first to Samothrace and from there to her half-brother Ptolemy II in Egypt, where a not undistinguished future as queen awaited her.[4]

The outcome of this disagreeable story was that Ceraunus now fully controlled all Lysimachus' European possessions, including Macedonia. But Ptolemy, the son of Lysimachus and Arsinoe, was still at large and, probably in the spring of 280, appears in alliance with Monunius, an Illyrian chieftain.[5] According to Trogus (*Prol.* 24), Ceraunus now fought a war inside Macedonia against the Illyrian Monunius and Ptolemy the son of Lysimachus. The two allies evidently invaded from the north-west; but nothing is known of the outcome of the war, which is omitted by Justin, neither how long it lasted nor whether the Gallic invasion brought it to an end. Despite the order of events in the prologue of Trogus, which puts the attack first, it probably occurred

---

[1] J. 24. 2. 4 'mandat velle se cum filiis eius regni consortium iungere'; 2.9 (his oath) 'neque in contumeliam eius se aliam uxorem aliosve quam filios eius liberos habiturum.'

[2] J. 24. 3. 2 'ad contionem quoque vocato exercitu capiti sororis diadema imposuit reginamque eam appellat.' Cf. Ritter 114 ff.

[3] J. 24. 3. 4–8. The trick of a marriage to obtain a vital fortress was also employed by Antigonus Gonatas at Corinth in 245 (P*Arat* 17)—though no murder was involved on that occasion; see below, p. 305 n. 3.

[4] J. 24. 3. 9; cf. Will 1². 105, 149. Samothrace seems to have been independent at this time; cf. Fraser, *Samothrace* 5 ff.; Will 1². 160. How long Arsinoe stayed on Samothrace is unknown. That she remained there until Antigonus was master of Macedonia (276), furthering the claims of Ptolemy son of Lysimachus (so W. W. Tarn, *JHS* 46 (1926) 161), seems unlikely.

[5] Cf. N. G. L. Hammond, *BSA* 61 (1966) 246, who argues convincingly against the view of F. Papazoglou, *Historia* 14 (1965) 163, that there was at this time a single Illyrian state of which Monunius was king. The name of Monunius is not uncommon and the tridrachms struck at Dyrrachium bearing that name (cf. P. Gardner, *BMC Thessaly to Aetolia* (London, 1883) 801–3 and Pl. XIV 10–11; Head 316) may be those of another Monunius. Çeka, *Questions* 24–6, would date them to 350–335. Against taking this Monunius to be the king of the Dardanians, however (see below, p. 253 n. 1), is the fact that when the Gauls attacked Ptolemy Ceraunus, the king of the Dardanians offered him help.

after Arsinoe had been ousted from Cassandreia—and indeed from Macedonia itself.[1]

While all this was happening in Macedonia, Antigonus, whose prestige had suffered a serious blow in his naval defeat at Ceraunus' hands, was facing a revolt in Greece. There various cities expelled their Macedonian garrisons and a joint army led by Areus, the ambitious king of Sparta, crossed the Corinthian Gulf and, avoiding a direct clash with Antigonus, launched an attack on his allies, the Aetolians,[2] the pretext being the hoary complaint that they had seized the Crisaean plain, sacred to Apollo.[3] According to Justin,[4] 'nearly all the states of Greece' were involved in this action, but that is an exaggeration. Athens took no part, and though Argos and Megalopolis probably expelled their Macedonian garrisons now, they certainly did not march out under a king of Sparta.[5] The allied army made the mistake of scattering to plunder and burn and fell a prey to Aetolian guerrilla troops hiding in the hills; according to Justin's highly unlikely account, 500 Aetolian shepherds slew 9,000 of the pillagers and put the rest to flight. But, whatever the real losses, this expedition proved a complete disaster and its main importance perhaps lies in the fact that among the cities which expelled their garrisons were Dyme, Patrae, Pharae, and Tritaea in western Achaea.[6]

Areus' failure had discredited Sparta's leadership; indeed, according to Justin, Spartan calls for help to renew the war were rejected on the grounds that the true Spartan aim was domination, not the freedom of Greece.[7] It was perhaps distrust of Sparta, together with the prospect of Macedonian retaliation, that now led the four Achaean cities which had joined the revolt to combine in order to re-establish the ancient Achaean Confederation, which had fallen apart in the decades follow-

---

[1] Trog. *Prol.* 24 'bellum quod Ptolomaeus Ceraunus…cum Monunio…et Ptolomaeo…habuit utque Arsinoen sororem suam imperio Macedonicarum urbium exuit'. Unless this refers to Arsinoe's expulsion from Macedonia *in toto*, it might suggest that she had controlled other cities besides Cassandreia. But the wording cannot be pressed, since one cannot tell what exactly stood in Trogus' text.

[2] How long Antigonus had been allied to the Aetolians is unknown.

[3] J. 24. 1. 3–4.

[4] J. 24. 1. 1–2 'interim in Graecia dissidentibus inter se bello Ptolomeo Cerauno et Antiocho et Antigono regibus omnes ferme Graeciae civitates ducibus Spartanis…in bellum prorumpunt'; on the reference to war between Ceraunus and Antiochus see above, p. 245 n. 7. Despite J. 24. 1. 8, which places Antigonus' attack and Ceraunus' agreement with Antiochus after the events in Greece, it is unlikely that these occurred earlier than the spring and summer of 280.

[5] Cf. Habicht, *Unters.* 83–4; on the revolt generally see Will 1². 108. Boeotia and Megara sent contingents to Thermopylae in 279 (Paus. 10. 20. 3–4), so they may have thrown off Antigonus now; cf. Tarn, *AG* 132 n. 44.

[6] On the revival of the Achaean League at this time see pp. 299–300 below.

[7] J. 24. 1. 7 'dominationem eos, non libertatem Graeciae, quaerere'. On this campaign see Flacelière 80–5.

ing Alexander's death.[1] The decision to reconstitute the league was taken in Ol. 124. 4 (281/0) and the first *strategos* year was dated May 280–May 279. This event attracted little attention at the time, but it marked the birth of a new political organization which would play a leading role in the affairs of Greece and Macedonia throughout the next 130 years.

Areus had avoided a direct clash with Antigonus but he, discouraged from any further immediate attempt to gain Macedonia, now transferred his activities to the north-east and to Asia Minor, where he soon became involved in a war with Antiochus. It was probably now that he placed his half-brother Craterus, the son of Phila and Alexander's general Craterus, in charge of Corinth, a command which included many of the other Antigonid possessions in Greece (see below, p. 270). In Asia Seleucus' death had been followed by a widespread movement of revolt involving Nicomedes of Bithynia and a 'northern coalition' around Heraclea Pontica (see above, pp. 245–6). Nicomedes now appears also as Antigonus' ally against Antiochus. Trogus (*Prol.* 24) describes this war between Antigonus and Antiochus as fought in Asia; but Antigonus may also have seized parts of Thrace. What sparked the war off is not recorded; but it seems likely, in view of the general problems confronting Antiochus (see above, p. 245) that Antigonus exploited the trouble with Bithynia to renew his claim to territory in Asia Minor,[2] or alternatively that he tried to build up a base in Thrace, and Antiochus regarded this as threatening.[3]

The war lasted 'a long time' (χρόνον συχνόν), according to Memnon.[4] The phrase is elastic; but the fact that both kings made identical contributions of 500 mercenaries to the Greek force which assembled against the Gauls at Thermopylae in the late summer or early autumn of 279[5] is not evidence that they had already made peace by then. It

---

[1] Plb. 2. 41. 2; see Walbank, *C* 1. 232–4. The new league was founded at the same time as Pyrrhus' crossing into Italy i.e. May 280. For Achaean chronology between then and the liberation of Corinth in 243/2 see Walbank, loc. cit. Errington, *Philop.* 266–71, defends Mommsen's alternative chronology, based on the assumption that Polybius is using inclusive reckoning, but this scheme only works if the introduction of a single general in place of two (Plb. 2. 43. 1) took place twenty-five years after the accession of Aegium, Bura, and Ceryneia, whereas on the most natural interpretation of Polybius it was twenty-five years after the reconstitution of the League in 280/79. It also involves a misunderstanding of Plb. 2. 43. 3: τετάρτῳ δ' ὕστερον ἔτει τοῦ προειρημένου [sc. Μάργου] στρατηγοῦντος. This means that Sicyon was liberated in the fourth year after Margus was general (for the present participle cf. Plb. 3. 114. 6), not 'four years later, when Margus was general'.

[2] Cf. Beloch 4. 1. 561; Ferguson, *HA* 155.

[3] Cf. Buraselis 112, who compares Demetrius Poliorcetes' attack on the Chersonese shortly after Ipsus (see above, p. 202 n. 5).

[4] On the war and the peace see Memnon, *FGrH* 434 F 10; J. 24. 1. 1, 25. 1. 1; *OGI* 219 = *Inschr. Ilion* 32 = Austin, *HW* 139; cf. L. Robert, *Am. Stud. Pap.* 1 (1966) 175–211.

[5] Paus. 10. 20. 5.

could equally well be taken to show that they were still at war and that neither was prepared to put himself at a disadvantage in relation to the other. Though we cannot be certain, the likelihood is that peace was not made until 278,[1] when it was accompanied by the arrangement that Antigonus should marry Phila, the half-sister (and stepdaughter) of Antiochus, who, being the daughter of Antigonus' own sister Stratonice, was also his niece.[2] This peace between the two powers had the immediate advantage of leaving Antigonus free to exploit the chaotic conditions in Macedonia; but it had a more important result in the long run, since it ushered in a period of peace between the Macedonian and Seleucid kingdoms, which was to remain a solid and lasting feature among the many shifting political alignments of the third century. In making it, Antiochus in effect renounced all claim to the Macedonian throne, and Antigonus that to the Asian part of Lysimachus' dominions.[3] That Antigonus formally gave up all claim to eastern Thrace is unlikely;[4] but in practice he seems to have exercised no influence there.

In discussing the peace between Antiochus and Antigonus we have run ahead; for both the war and the peace that ended it must be considered against the disruption of normal life which occurred in the Balkan peninsula during the years from 280/79 onwards. The cause of this disruption was an invasion by Gallic tribes[5] who wrought havoc throughout the whole length of Macedonia and penetrated Greece as far south as Delphi. The forces behind this large folk-movement lay outside Macedonia itself and were probably multiple. Since 400 the western Gauls had been on the move and by this time they may have acquired a taste for raiding; but there were other, and probably more important, factors, such as the population increase and famine stressed in the ancient sources,[6] pressure from the Germans further to the

---

[1] See on this Bengtson, *Strat.* 2. 336 n. 1; Nachtergael 142 n. 78.

[2] *Vita Arati*, ed. Westermann, 53 and 60; Seibert, *DV* 33. The wedding was celebrated in Macedonia after Antigonus had acquired the kingdom in 277/6.

[3] Cf. Buraselis 114–19 against Will 1². 109, who thinks Antigonus renounced all ambitions in Asia generally.

[4] So Tarn, *AG* 168; Beloch 4. 2. 355 ff.; *contra* Bengtson, *Strat.* 2. 336 ff. See Buraselis 117–18.

[5] The sources are D.S. 22. 3–5, 9; J. 24. 3. 10–5. 11 (the main sources for events in Macedonia); Memnon, *FGrH* 434 F 8. 8 (death of Ceraunus); Syncellus, *FHG* 3. 696. 6; Paus. 1. 4; 10. 19. 5–23 (the invasion as a whole); a few inscriptions, of which the most important is *SIG* 398 from Cos (= Austin, *HW* 88). The fullest treatment is now that in Nachtergael 1–205. Contemporary writers who will have dealt with the affair are Hieronymus, Nymphis of Heraclea (an important source for Memnon), and Psaon of Plataea, and perhaps Demetrius of Byzantium and the younger Eratosthenes; Phylarchus and Timaeus may have touched on the Gauls, but if so only in digressions. Of the two versions in Pausanias, the second is longer but less reliable. To determine which original sources lie behind those now available is no longer feasible. The tradition is uniformly hostile to Ceraunus.

[6] Memnon, *FGrH* 434 F 8. 8 διὰ λιμόν.

north, and the pull exercised by the rich lands of the Mediterranean. Technical advances in La Tène civilization may also have rendered the Gauls more capable of migration and more formidable to those they encountered. As to how much each of these—and other—factors counted for in the final analysis, one can only speculate. Certainly the invasion was not a catastrophe for which the southern peoples had themselves no responsibility, for the many coins of Philip II found in the Danube area testify to contacts with Macedonia in the fourth century in the form of trade or perhaps of subsidies paid for help against the troublesome Illyrian Autariatae.[1] At some unspecified date Cassander is reported to have attacked one body of Gauls in what is now Bulgaria and to have driven them back into the Haemus.[2] But now, a little before 280, perhaps encouraged by the political crisis following the death of Lysimachus, they began to push further south, not as a migratory horde with all their belongings, but organized in bands out for plunder; the women and children remained behind in an unnamed location further north. The movement began with a raiding party led by Cambaules which got as far as Thrace, but then retired, since its numbers were not sufficient to face Greek armies.[3] Subsequently, in spring or early summer 280, this preliminary raid was followed by further incursions by three groups under separate leaders, each following a different route.[4]

Of these groups the first, under the command of Cerethrius, attacked the Triballi and the Thracians, the second under Brennus and Acichorius came south into Paeonia, clearly following the Axius valley, while the third group under Bolgius (or Belgius: so Pausanias) invaded Macedonia by way of Illyria. All three groups threatened Macedonia, which they saw both as a source for plunder and as an obstacle to be overcome before they could reach the rich plains of Thessaly and the wealth of central and southern Greece. It is difficult to assess the seriousness of Ceraunus' defensive measures, since the scanty sources are all hostile and give a picture of a young man urged on by pride and folly to self-destruction. In lending troops to Pyrrhus he had perhaps acted with little choice,[5] but in the events leading up to the fatal battle Justin (or his source) carefully builds up a tragic

[1] Cf. Nachtergael 8 n. 7 for bibliography on Macedonian coins found in the Balkans and the Danube valley.

[2] Seneca, *QN* 3. 11. 3 (quoting Theophrastus); Pliny, *HN* 31. 53. Niese 1. 304 n. 4 dates this around 310, Nachtergael 12 n. 13 some ten years later.

[3] Paus. 10. 19. 4.

[4] Paus. 10. 19. 6–7; Pausanias mentions the places they made for in reverse order, putting Thrace, for instance, before the Triballi and Macedonia before Illyria. See Nachtergael 129. On the chronology see below, Appendix 2.

[5] See above, p. 246 nn. 4–5.

narrative of a man spurred on by the furies that avenge the murder of kinsmen ('parricidiorum furiis agitatus') to invite the inevitable consequences of *hybris*. Whereas even kings who had not been attacked ('reges non lacessiti') had hastened to offer payment to the barbarians unasked—who were they? Balkan chieftains? or a mere rhetorical foil?—Ceraunus alone heard of their approach unmoved; and lest this should sound like laudable courage, it is made clear that he was rash enough to go out to meet them with only a few undisciplined troops. His boastful pride showed itself not only in his reception of the Gallic envoys who came offering peace in return for Danegeld—his reply was to demand their leaders as hostages—but also in his insulting rejection of 20,000 troops offered to him by the king of the Dardanians. Thus the story builds up to an inevitable climax with the prophetic moral obligingly enunciated by the Dardanian king.[1]

Severely wounded and taken alive, Ptolemy was decapitated and his head paraded before his troops to dishearten them. According to Memnon, he was thrown by his elephant and torn to bits by Gauls 'as he deserved'. Syncellus also attributes elephants to him in this battle: evidently they had not all been sent to Italy with Pyrrhus. In a single surviving fragment Diodorus (22. 3) adds one detail: 'being young and inexperienced in war' Ptolemy rejected his Friends' advice to wait for reinforcements which had not yet arrived.[2] From this dramatic account and the few details with which it can be supplemented no convincing picture of the geography of the campaign nor of Macedonian policy or tactics can be recovered.

In Ceraunus' place the Macedonians elected his brother Meleager,[3] but deposed him two months later as inadequate, appointing instead Antipater, the son of Cassander's brother Philip. He reigned for 45 days only—the length of time that the Etesian winds usually blew,

---

[1] J. 24. 4. 6–11; cf. 4.11 'inclitum illud Macedoniae regnum brevi immaturi iuvenis temeritate casurum dicit.' J. G. Droysen, *Kleine Schriften zur alten Geschichte* 1 (Leipzig, 1893) 92, sought to identify the king of the Dardanians with Monunius (see above, p. 248 n. 5), but there seems no reason why he should have made a sudden volte-face and deserted Ptolemy the son of Lysimachus.

[2] On D.S. 22. 3 see Heinen, *Unters.* 89 n. 340. Ptolemy's youth is stressed by both Justin ('immaturus iuvenis') and Diodorus (τὴν...ἡλικίαν νέος ὢν παντελῶς), but he was over thirty at the time of his death.

[3] According to PPyrrh 22. 1–3, Pyrrhus received the news of Ceraunus' death just after his own victory at Ausculum, and was faced with the choice between going to Sicily and returning to try his fortunes in Macedonia. However, Lévêque 558, seems to go beyond the evidence when he interprets this news from Greece as proof of strong support for Pyrrhus in Macedonia. Plutarch speaks merely of a message from Greece (not Macedonia) and this reads more like an indication by Pyrrhus' private Greek informants that there was now an opportunity for him in Macedonia (which needed a king) than an appeal by Macedonians to come and seize the throne with their support.

hence his nickname, Etesias.[1] Then, because he failed as leader of the army, he was deposed by a certain Sosthenes who, though elected king, declined the royal title. Sosthenes controlled Macedonia for two years, after which he died, leaving the country without a ruler—though Porphyry mentions a Ptolemy and an Arrhidaeus as holding some sort of partial authority.[2] Sosthenes seems to have been appointed *strategos*, like Antigonus Doson fifty years later.[3] Why he rejected the kingship is not known; he may have preferred the lesser post in view of his own lack of royal connections.[4] It is possible (but by no means certain) that Sosthenes is to be identified with one of Lysimachus' officers mentioned in a letter sent by him to Priene (*c*. 285).[5]

Sosthenes' office as general lasted for two years, from about June 279 to the middle of 277,[6] and during that time he was occupied fighting the Gauls,[7] various pretenders, and Antigonus Gonatas, after the latter's peace with Antiochus (above, p. 251) left him free to turn to Thrace and Macedonia. Sosthenes had been elected general in recog-

---

[1] We hear of an Athenian embassy to Antipater, led by Demochares to try to secure help in expelling Antigonus from the Piraeus; P*Mor* 851 E (*psephisma* for Demochares); cf. Heinen, *Unters.* 58.

[2] Porph. *FGrH* 260 F 3. 10; Eus. 1. 235 Sch.; J. 24. 5. 12–6. 3 (omitting Meleager and Antisthenes); D.S. 22. 4. According to Diodorus, Meleager was a brother of Ptolemy, son of Lagus, but this seems like a confusion, since it is not clear what a brother of Ptolemy I could be doing in Macedonia at this time. The names of Ptolemy and Arrhidaeus suggest royal connections, but the identity of these men is unknown. Diodorus mentions an Alexander, who may be identical with Arrhidaeus.

[3] According to J. 24. 5. 14, many nobles were anxious to claim the kingship, but Sosthenes, having defeated the Gauls (see below, p. 254 n. 1), was acclaimed king by the army; he refused the title, however, and 'non in regis, sed in ducis nomen iurare milites compulit'. That he was 'ignobilis' (cf. Porphyry in Syncellus, τῶν δημοτικῶν) is unlikely, especially as Justin also calls him 'unus de Macedoniae principibus'.

[4] For a full discussion of Sosthenes' position cf. Bengtson, *Strat.* 2. 381–6, who sees it as a kind of 'diminished kingship', harking back to a time before the monarchy was set up and lacking royal dignity and the expectation of passing the office on to a successor, rather than as a republican measure (so Beloch 4. 1. 565); Nachtergael 131 n. 22. L. Mooren, *EHW* 206 nn. 2–3 and 233–40, suggests that Sosthenes was attempting to put into practice the proposal made by Ptolemy at Babylon in 323, that the state should be run by a board of generals (C. 10. 6. 15; J. 13. 2. 12). But we hear nothing of such a board under Sosthenes. That the tetradrachms with the inscription *Sosthieni* on the reverse, found in a hoard at Bjelovar (Slavonia) and published by K. Pink, *Num. Zeitschr.* 77 (1957) 7–17 and Pl. 1, recall the name of this Sosthenes is dubious. When Eusebius (1. 236 Sch.) says of Sosthenes that διʼ ὅλων δύο ἐτῶν προστὰς τῶν πραγμάτων ἀποθνήσκει, the word προστάς means simply 'being in charge', and is not evidence that he held an official title of *prostates*.

[5] *OGI* 12 = Welles, *RC* 1. 11. The name is restored and might equally well be Sopater or some other name beginning with Σω-.

[6] See Appendix 2.

[7] Sosthenes' struggle against the Gauls is mentioned on a late third century inscription regulating a territorial quarrel between Gonnus and Heracleum (Helly no. 93 ὁ κατὰ Σωσθέ[ν]ην πόλεμος). It was probably in his honour too that the town of Sosthenis, lying between Hypata and Spercheiae, was named or renamed by the Aetolians; cf. F. Stählin, *RE* s.v. *Sosthenis* cols. 1198–9; G. Daux, *BCH* 58 (1934) 164 n. 2; Nachtergael 131 n. 22.

nition of his success in defeating Bolgius.[1] But shortly afterwards, still
in the summer of 279, he was faced with a more serious invasion under
Brennus, who commanded a much larger expedition—the sources give
exaggerated figures and the true numbers cannot be recovered[2]—in
order to exploit the opportunities for plundering more effectively than
Bolgius had done. One group of 20,000 led by Leonnorius and
Lutarius broke away in Dardania and made its way into Thrace;
eventually this group passed over into Asia.[3] The main body of Gauls,
however, came down through Macedonia, where they defeated Sosthenes, though not without suffering substantial losses.[4] After ravaging the country they went on to attack Delphi, where a combination of
bad weather and stout resistance by the Greeks brought about their
complete defeat and the collapse of the expedition. The survivors were
too demoralized to cause much damage as they retreated north,
pursued by the Greeks—first the Aetolians and later the Malians and
Thessalians.[5] The Thessalians' role in the invasion was ambiguous.
According to Justin,[6] they and the Aenianians had joined the
barbarians 'ad praedae societatem', whereas later on Thessalians—
probably different ones—took part in the pursuit. This may suggest
that Macedonian control of Thessaly had broken down and that the
cities went their own way, when faced by the Gallic invasion. Of the
surviving Gauls (Justin and Diodorus claim that there were none!)
some led by Bathanattus reached the Danube and others settled
around the junction of the Save and the Drave and later turn up as the
Scordisci.[7]

One group had been left behind by Brennus when he marched
south, in order to defend what at that time the Gauls regarded as their
homeland,[8] and they, probably late in 278 or early in 277 (since
Antigonus and Antiochus had now made peace) armed a force of
15,000 infantry and 3,000 cavalry and, after defeating the Getae and

---

[1] J. 24. 5. 12 'contracta iuventute et Gallos victoria exultantes compescuit et Macedoniam ab
hostili populatione defendit.'

[2] See J. 24. 6. 1; Paus. 10. 19. 3; Polyaen. 7. 35. 1; D.S. 22. 9. 1. According to Justin there were
150,000 foot and 15,000 cavalry. Diodorus makes it 150,000 foot and 10,000 cavalry (with camp
followers and 2,000 wagons), Pausanias 152,000 foot and 20,400 cavalry, each attended by two
grooms. These are the exaggerated figures one would expect in a description of such a frightening
episode as the Gallic attack on Delphi.

[3] See Livy 38. 16. 1–9 for the adventures of this band, who seized Lysimacheia by 'fraus' and
occupied the whole Chersonese. Eventually they tricked Antiochus' governor, Antipater, into
giving them ships, while some of them were brought over into Asia Minor by Nicomedes of
Bithynia to help in a war against Zipoetes.

[4] Cf. J. 24. 6. 1–4 (Sosthenes' defeat); D.S. 22. 9. 1 has a lacuna, but the surviving text speaks
of Brennus losing many men in Macedonia.

[5] Paus. 10. 23. 13–14.   [6] J. 24. 7. 2.

[7] Posidonius, *FGrH* 87 F 48 (Bathanattus); J. 32. 3. 8 (Scordisci).

[8] J. 25. 1. 2 'ad terminos gentis tuendos relicti'.

Triballi in Thrace, made demands on Antigonus. At this time
Antigonus seems to have been established—if temporarily—on the
European side of the straits. According to Justin he was in Macedonia,[1] but the site of the subsequent battle against the Gauls was
Lysimacheia, hence it seems probable that his present position was in
the neighbourhood of the Thracian Chersonese. Antigonus' eyes were
still on Macedonia and he had made a further attempt to invade the
country from Asia in 278. But once again he had been driven out,
probably by Sosthenes,[2] and had been forced to retire to Asia. By
277, however, he had evidently made some headway and had a footing
on the northern shore near Lysimacheia.[3] How he came to be there
we do not know; perhaps, as Tarn suggested,[4] he was called in by the
Greek cities, who had already experienced the ravages of the band led
by Leonnorius and Lutarius. Justin relates[5] how the Gauls sent
envoys to Antigonus, who aroused their greed by a great display of
wealth and then laid an ambush for them by leaving his camp
apparently deserted. When night came, the Gauls plundered the camp
and were attacking the ships when Antigonus' troops fell upon them
and inflicted such slaughter that he was able to set himself up in
Macedonia without any fears henceforth of attacks either from the
Gauls or from any other of his fierce neighbours. The story is riddled

---

[1] J. 25. 1. 1 'cum in Macedoniam reverteretur'; the use of 'reverti' probably refers to
Antigonus' unsuccessful invasion following the assassination of Seleucus (see above, pp. 244–5) or
that of 178.
[2] The evidence is in Philodemus, ed. A. Mayer, *Phil.* 71 (1912) 226 [...]νων κράτησας τῆς
Μακε[δο]νίας ἐκπίπτει πά[λιν εἰς τὴν] 'Ασίην. See Appendix 3.
[3] For the site of the battle see D.L. 2. 141.   [4] *AG* 165.
[5] The sources for the battle of Lysimacheia are D.L. 2. 141; J. 25. 1. 1–2. 7. The victory was
celebrated at Eretria in a decree moved by the philosopher Menedemus, which referred to the
king as having come into his own (μάχῃ νικήσας τοὺς βαρβάρους παραγίνεται εἰς τὴν ἰδίαν)—a
phrase commonly used of those returning from exile: Tarn, *AG* 166 n. 104—and it is mentioned in
an honorary decree for Heracleitus dating to around 250 (cf. Habicht, *Unters.* 71), which speaks of
the erection of *stelai* (so A. N. Kontoleon, *Akte des 4. Internationalen Kongresses für griechische und
lateinische Epigraphik (Wien, 1962)* (Graz–Vienna–Cologne, 1964) 196–7, reading στήλ]ας rather
than γραφ]άς) containing a narrative τῶν [τῶι βασιλεῖ π]επραγμένων πρὸς τοὺς βαρβάρους ὑπὲρ
τῆς τῶν Ἑλλήνων σωτηρίας (*SIG* 401; cf. J. and L. Robert, *Bull. épig.* 1965, 142). For a coin of
Antigonus with the words βα-σι and Λυσιμαχέων see F. M. Heichelheim, *AJP* 64 (1943) 332–3;
Nachtergael 179 n. 233. It has been argued that Antigonus was helped towards his victory at
Lysimacheia partly by a panic among the Gauls inspired by the god Pan. This hypothesis is based
on the evidence of silver tetradrachms showing a horned Pan superimposed on a Macedonian
shield on the obverse and on the reverse Athena Alcidemus and the words βασιλέως Ἀντιγόνου
together with bronze coins with Athena's head on the obverse and on the reverse Pan setting up
or crowning a trophy with the letters βα and a monogram of Antigonus (Head 232); cf. Merker
39–52; below, Appendix 4 pp. 594–5. Nachtergael (177–9 and esp. n. 231) has shown that there
is no good reason to connect these coins with the battle, for which no source records any panic or
intervention of Pan, nor is Pan depicted on the coin specifically linked with the victory by the
word Λυσιμαχέων (see above). Pan had long had an established place in the Macedonian
pantheon and on Macedonian coinage (cf. F. Brommer, *RE* Suppl. 9 s.v. *Pan* cols. 996–7; Gaebler
III. 2. 158 nos. 2 and 3 (Amyntas II) and Pl. xxix. 28–9).

with inconsistencies. It suggests that Antigonus showed the Gauls his wealth and forces in order to intimidate them, not having realized that this would further incite their greed. But then, when they approach by night, we find that the king has after all foreseen their move and, having stripped the camp in advance, has hidden his forces in a wood—presumably in order to fall on the Gauls when they enter the camp. But in fact, after some hesitation, they overrun the camp and are attacked only when they begin to plunder the ships—and that too by the rowers and such troops as had fled, along with their wives and children. The men planted in the wood are not mentioned again. This disjointed and illogical narrative suggests that Antigonus was in command of a mercenary army, whose ἀποσκευή (baggage) was near the ships, and that the Gallic attack was perhaps more of a surprise to him than Justin implies. If that is so, his victory was the fortunate outcome of an incident which very nearly went disastrously wrong.

The remnants of the defeated Gauls turned inland into Thrace, where they founded a kingdom at Tylis, which was to last until about 212.[1] But Antigonus was able to press his advantage and to take over Macedonia. Whether Sosthenes was now dead is not clear, though it is likely. But there were certainly others still in Antigonus' way. Over the next few months he defeated Antipater Etesias who, after being dethroned, apparently still maintained a following somewhere in Macedonia. Antigonus used Gallic mercenaries under their leader Ciderius to defeat him and then had trouble with his soldiers over their payment.[2] Antipater escaped to make his way to Egypt, where his name turns up on a papyrus twenty years later, still enjoying his nickname Etesias and described as a great player of dice. Philadelphus no doubt encouraged him and kept him for future use as a possible pretender against Antigonus.[3] Antigonus also had to deal with Apollodorus, who had established a tyranny at Cassandreia.[4] This city, which had belonged to Arsinoe, had later been assigned by Ptolemy Ceraunus to his mother Eurydice, but afterwards—perhaps on Ceraunus' death—it had fallen under the tyranny of Apollodorus, who had allied himself with Antiochus. After a ten-months siege Antigonus enlisted an 'arch-pirate', the Phocian Ameinias, to gain

---

[1] Cf. Plb. 4. 46. The site of the kingdom (cf. Trog. *Prol.* 25, 'quas regiones Tyleni occuparunt') is uncertain. G. Mihailov, *Athen.* 39 (1961) 33–44 locates it near Adrianople, but Danov 369 n. 8, favours Gerov's location near Cabyle some 200 km. further north.

[2] Polyaen. 4. 6. 17.   [3] *P. Cair. Zen.* 1. 50.019. 6; cf. Nachtergael 168 n. 192.

[4] D.S. 22. 51–2; Trog. *Prol.* 25; Polyaen. 2. 29. 1, 4. 6. 18 (use of Ameinias), 6. 7. 1–2 (his rise to power); P*Mor* 555 B; Paus. 4. 5. 4–5; Seneca, *de ira* 2. 5. 1; *de benef.* 7. 19. 7; Dio Chrys. 19. 52. 1–2, 61. 2; Aelian, *VH* 14. 41. The sources agree in assigning to him the traditional tyrannical vices, including sacrificing a baby and drinking its blood to seal a compact with his fellow conspirators. On Apollodorus see further A. Fuks, *Anc. Soc.* 5 (1974) 71 = *Social Conflicts in Ancient Greece* (Jerusalem–Leiden, 1984) 29 (cf. Will 1² 212).

entry into the city by a trick and so captured it. Antigonus had also, it appears, to deal with Ptolemy the son of Lysimachus, which he did, though no details survive.[1] There were certainly other problems which have escaped the record; but by the middle of 276 Antigonus was master of Macedonia, where no organized government had existed since the death of Sosthenes.[2]

The kingdom he had won for himself was a land racked and weakened by civil war and barbarian invasion. Its power and influence had declined catastrophically in comparison with the rival kingdoms and what was most needed now was a strong ruler who would ensure a period of peace in which to build up and consolidate its wealth and its manpower.

---

[1] Cf. *FGrH* 260 F 3. 11 (Armenian version of Eusebius). Ptolemy later turns up occupying a royal domain near Telmessus, obtained it seems from Philadelphus, and later still as governor of Telmessus itself under Ptolemy III (*OGI* 55); cf. H. Volkmann, *RE* s.v. *Ptolemaios* (13) col. 1596.

[2] On the chronological problems of Antigonus' reign see Appendix 2 pp. 581–3.

XII

ANTIGONUS GONATAS: THE EARLY YEARS
(276–261 B.C.)

1. *Antigonus II and Pyrrhus (276–272 B.C.)*

As a result of the battle of Lysimacheia the Antigonid dynasty had at last acquired a territorial base and Macedonia a new royal house. Hitherto Antigonus' power had been based on his solid block of possessions in central Greece—Corinth, Piraeus, and the Attic fortresses, Euboea, Boeotia, and Phocis—reinforced by his father's great foundation in Magnesia, Demetrias. In recent years, however, his military and naval operations had been mainly around the Chersonese, an area formerly part of Lysimachus' dominions. No figures are recorded for the army and fleet which were under his command, nor is it clear from where he derived his financial support—though his later association with pirates (whom he used both to recover Cassandreia and, probably, to harass Attica in the Chremonidean War) may suggest that, like Philip V later in the century, he was not excessively scrupulous as to how he filled his coffers. Now, however, the acquisition of Macedonia for the first time provided him with a regular source of wealth from the taxes and the extensive mines and forests of that kingdom.

As king of Macedonia his position was immeasurably improved. But for several years Antigonus' hold on his kingdom remained precarious. Almost at once he had to face a very real threat from Pyrrhus, who after his defeat at Beneventum at the hands of the Romans—probably in the summer of 275[1]—made threatening demands for aid from Antigonus and Antiochus to enable him to stay on in Italy. When both alike refused him help,[2] he recrossed the Adriatic in the autumn of that year,[3] resumed without opposition his control over Epirus and southern Illyria,[4] and set about organizing an attack on Antigonus. Once already Pyrrhus had been king of Macedonia: why not again? Neither in making these plans nor in putting them into operation is

---

[1] Cf. Lévêque 527.
[2] Cf. J. 25. 3. 1–2; Paus. 1. 13. 1; Polyaen. 6. 6. 1. Pyrrhus demanded both men and money from Antigonus (with threats, according to Justin); see above, p. 247. Polyaenus says that he offered Antigonus a συμμαχία.
[3] On the date cf. Lévêque 535.　　　　　　　　　　　　　[4] For Illyria see App. *Ill.* 7.

there any reason to think that Pyrrhus was receiving any help from outside. Both numismatic and epigraphic evidence show him to be on good terms with the Aetolian League,[1] but nothing indicates that the Aetolians gave him direct assistance against Antigonus. Nor is it to be supposed that Ptolemaic policy or aid played any part in Pyrrhus' plans. Tarn argued[2] that in invading Macedonia Pyrrhus was in effect acting as the agent of Ptolemy II. At this time Ptolemy was married to his sister Arsinoe II, Lysimachus' widow. It was she who, on this hypothesis, was ambitious to see her son Ptolemy established on the Macedonian throne and her husband is supposed to have concurred in this plan, with the object of securing the Cyclades against Macedonian attack. But the thesis is unsupported and wholly improbable. There is no evidence that Ptolemy II provided Pyrrhus with any subsidy, nor will either Ptolemy or Arsinoe have harboured the naïve illusion that if Pyrrhus gained the Macedonian throne he would be anyone's man but his own. It is therefore highly unlikely that Ptolemy (who was at this time fully occupied with the revolt of his half-brother Magas in Cyrene) had any part in Pyrrhus' invasion of Macedonia.[3]

For his invasion Pyrrhus commanded 8,000 infantry and 500 cavalry—but little money.[4] With these forces and a number of Gauls, who joined him, no doubt, as mercenaries,[5] he set out in the spring of 274 on what appears to have been envisaged as a raiding expedition into Macedonia.[6] But when a number of towns went over to him and 2,000 Macedonian troops changed sides (just as in 287),[7] he allowed the expedition to develop into a full-scale attack on Antigonus.[8] Pyrrhus' behaviour was entirely in character, for he was always ready to alter his aims at the slightest nod from Fortune. According to Plutarch, he fell upon Antigonus at a place called the Narrows (τὰ Στενά). In the battle which ensued Pyrrhus began by cutting to pieces

[1] A stater of the Aetolian League (Head p. 334) has an obverse identical with that of a gold stater issued by Pyrrhus and it seems likely that both were the product of the Syracusan mint (Lévêque 572, 692). In addition, certain Aetolian coins of this period carry an Epirote monogram (Flacelière, 189); and *SIG* 369 records the setting up of a statue to Pyrrhus in gratitude for his restoration of Callium, destroyed by the Gauls (Paus. 10. 22. 3–4). Cf. Lévêque 572–3, dating this inscription to 274–2.   [2] *AG* 259 ff.

[3] It is, however, equally unbelievable that the Ἀντίγονός τις φίλος τοῦ Φιλαδέλφου Πτολεμαίου who, according to Schol. Callim. *Hymn to Delos* 2. 70 ff. (Pfeiffer), furnished Ptolemy with Gallic mercenaries against Magas, is Gonatas (so Beloch 4. 2. 508; Buraselis 156, is dubious). Launey (1. 496–7) is surely right to regard this man as one of Ptolemy's Friends sent to recruit in Macedonia or Asia Minor—perhaps the Antigonus who conveyed corn and forces to the Rhodians during the siege of 304 (D.S. 20. 98. 1; cf. Launey 1. 303). So this text provides no evidence of friendly relations between Antigonus Gonatas and Ptolemy II.   [4] P*Pyrrh* 26. 3.

[5] Ibid. 26. 4.   [6] Ibid. 26. 5 ὡς ἁρπαγῇ καὶ λεηλασίᾳ χρησόμενος.

[7] See above, pp. 228–9.

[8] On the campaign and battle see P*Pyrrh* 26. 5–9; Paus. 1. 13. 2; J. 25. 3. 5; Ampel. 28. 3; D.S. 22. 11. 1.

Antigonus' rearguard, made up of Gallic mercenaries (who fought well). He then forced the troops in charge of the elephants to surrender and, 'relying on fortune rather than good judgement', attacked the phalanx. The phalangites, demoralized by the destruction of the Gauls and the loss of the elephants, readily responded to Pyrrhus' appeal to go over. Antigonus fled with a few horsemen and occupied the coastal cities, thus virtually surrendering the interior of Macedonia to his opponent. Though Plutarch does not actually say so, the opening of the fighting with an attack on the Macedonian rearguard suggests that Pyrrhus had succeeded in getting a force round Antigonus' lines to attack him from behind. Such a manœuvre may have contributed substantially to the Macedonian distress.

The site of this major battle is not clearly indicated in our sources. Lévêque has argued[1] that τὰ Στενά must be the gorge of the Aous south-east of Tepeleni, where Flamininus defeated Philip V in 198. But a site so far west cannot be reconciled with Pyrrhus' capture of towns and the surrender of Macedonian troops before the battle took place. It has been generally assumed that the *castra Pyrrhi* where Philip paused in his retreat in 198, and which must have been near Mesogephyra, a little to the north-west of Konitsa, in the vicinity of the modern frontier between Greece and Albania,[2] got its name on this occasion and so confirms a western site for the battle. But Pyrrhus can just as well have camped near the Aous crossing during his invasion of Macedonia in 288,[3] in which case the location of *castra Pyrrhi* is irrelevant to the site of the battle in 274. It seems more likely that for this one should think rather of a position further east inside Macedonia itself, such as the gorge of Kleisoura on Mt. Vitsi, east of Kastoria.[4] Both generals employed Gallic mercenaries, and Pyrrhus later dedicated the shields of those who fell fighting in Antigonus' army at the shrine of Athena Itonia in Thessaly.[5] Beloch[6] took this to indicate that the battle was fought in Thessaly, but this is not a good argument, since the shields from the slain Macedonians were dedicated in Epirus

---

[1] Lévêque 561–2; on the Aous passes see N. G. L. Hammond, *JRS* 56 (1966) 39–54; H*E* 279. Tarn, *AG* 264, locates the battle in Macedonia, yet in a footnote speaks of the Aous pass.

[2] Livy 32. 13. 12; cf. N. G. L. Hammond, *BSA* 32 (1931/2) 145; *JRS* 56 (1966) 53; H*E* 280; Walbank, *Ph* 153 n. 2; Lévêque 562 n. 3 (listing other views on the location).

[3] See above, p. 225 n. 7.

[4] On this see Hammond, Volume I. 106 and Map 8; and above, p. 225 n. 8.

[5] For the dedicatory epigram by Leonidas of Tarentum see *Anth. Pal.* 6. 30; P*Pyrrh* 26. 10; Paus. 1. 13. 2; D.S. 22. 11. 1. It reads:

τοὺς θυρεοὺς ὁ Μολοσσὸς Ἰτωνίδι δῶρον Ἀθανᾷ
Πύρρος ἀπὸ θράσεων ἐκρέμασεν Γαλατᾶν
πάντα τὸν Ἀντιγόνου καθελὼν στρατόν, οὐ μέγα θαῦμα·
αἰχματαὶ καὶ νῦν καὶ πάρος Αἰακίδαι.

[6] 4. 1. 573 n. 1.

at Dodona.[1] It seems more likely, as Tarn suggested,[2] that the dedication to Athena Itonia was intended to win the favour of the Thessalians.

Pyrrhus' unexpected victory[3] gave him control of most of Macedonia and Thessaly and left Antigonus precariously based on the coastal area. From Thessalonica, whither he fled, he could still maintain his fleet, which was vital for his communications with the Antigonid positions further south.[4] Of Pyrrhus' seizure and subsequent occupation of much of Macedonia few details have survived. Polyaenus (2. 29. 2) records the capture of Edessa by Cleonymus of Sparta, who had joined up with Pyrrhus and was soon to exercise a marked influence on his policy.[5] This passage of Polyaenus indicates that some strongpoints held out for a time and that Pyrrhus' victorious progress was not so unchallenged as other sources suggest. But in any case Pyrrhus soon showed his habitual gross lack of finesse in dealing with the Macedonian people. In particular, he kept too slack a rein on his Gallic mercenaries, allowing them to violate and plunder the royal tombs at Aegeae (modern Vergina)[6] and afterwards failing to punish them, since he required their future services. As a result the initial enthusiasm for Pyrrhus quickly abated and he was soon highly unpopular in Macedonia. His second reign there was brief, which is perhaps why it is omitted from Porphyry's Macedonian and Thessalian king-lists;[7] only a passage in Syncellus' *Chronography*[8] mentions it among the several short reigns which followed the death of Ceraunus.[9]

---

[1] Paus. 1. 13. 3: the dedication here reads:

Αἵδε ποτ᾽ Ἀσίδα γαῖαν ἐπόρθησαν πολύχρυσον,
αἵδε καὶ Ἕλλασιν δουλοσύναν ἔπορον.
νῦν δὲ Διὸς ναῶ ποτὶ κίονας ὀρφανὰ κεῖται
τὰς μεγαλαυχήτω σκῦλα Μακεδονίας.

Launey 1. 500 n. 2, suggests that Pyrrhus' dedications to Lindian Athena recorded in the Lindian Temple Chronicle (*FGrH* 532 F 1 c 40) were also of spoils from this battle.

[2] *AG* 265.

[3] The Armenian version of Eus. *FGrH* 260 F 31. 4, records a later defeat of Pyrrhus at 'Derdion' at the hands of Antigonus' son Demetrius, but this seems to be a confusion with Demetrius' expulsion of Pyrrhus' son Alexander in 262/1 (J. 26. 2. 11); see Jacoby ad loc. Derdion is unknown.

[4] J. 25. 3. 7. On Antigonus' fleet see above, p. 245, n. 2. It probably included ships that had formerly belonged to Lysimachus and Ceraunus.

[5] Cf. Lévêque 577 (identifying Aegeae with Edessa).

[6] P*Pyrrh* 26. 11–13; D.S. 11. 2, 12.   [7] Cf. Beloch 4. 2. 115.

[8] Syncell. *Chron.* p. 507, 267 a, 'Meleager, Antipater, Sosthenes, Ptolemy, Alexander, and Pyrrhus, in all three years, according to Diodorus'. On this text see below, Appendix 2 p. 581.

[9] Lévêque 564–5 follows Svoronos in attributing Pyrrhus' Macedonian bronze coins to this second spell as king of Macedonia. These (Lévêque Pl. VII. 17) comprise three closely related types, showing a monogram of the king's name in the middle of a Macedonian shield and on the reverse **ΒΑ/ΣΙ ΠΥΡ** beneath a pointed helmet, the whole being enclosed in an oak-leaf crown. These issues take up the types found on coins emitted by Antigonus Gonatas, and must therefore be later than these (cf. Gaebler III. 2. 189 no. 15; Pl. XXXIV. 11). Another issue (Lévêque 564–5;

Late in 274 or (more probably) early in 273[1] Pyrrhus returned home to Epirus, leaving Macedonia under his son Ptolemy. His hold on Macedonia was perhaps already weakening, but in any case he had been persuaded by Cleonymus to take up yet another new scheme—an invasion of the Peloponnese with the immediate object of putting the exiled Cleonymus on the Spartan throne.[2] Pyrrhus' move was very much to Antigonus' advantage and he was quick to exploit it. He recruited more Gallic mercenaries and, with Pyrrhus out of the way, attacked his son Ptolemy. His attack was unsuccessful, however, and, according to Justin's probably exaggerated account, Antigonus was forced to seek safety in hiding with a small retinue of seven companions.[3] Pyrrhus' wider aims can only be guessed at and, in considering a character so volatile and incalculable as his, rational analysis is neither easy nor perhaps especially relevant. But, in addition to serving Cleonymus' ends, which cannot have been very important to him as king either in Epirus or Macedonia, he clearly hoped to cut away that centre of support in Greece which, from Ipsus onwards, had been so important to Antigonus.[4] Many Greeks were no doubt waiting with judgement suspended to see how events would turn out. One caustic comment survives in a fragment of the diatribe *On Poverty* by the Cynic Teles, in which he records the gibes directed by Bion of Borysthenes against Pyrrhus the tomb-robber and Antigonus the cowardly runaway.[5]

Pl. VII. 16), showing a head of Zeus crowned with laurel and on the reverse an eagle on a thunderbolt carrying the monogram ΤΑΡ , is also regarded by Svoronos and Lévèque as a Macedonian issue of Pyrrhus. Gaebler (III. 2. 5 no. 36) dates it much later, under Philip V or Perseus at the earliest; and he interprets the monogram as **ΠΑΡ** *(ωραίων)*, which he takes to be a reference to Paroraea. Lévèque bases his view (a) on the fact that some specimens are overstruck coins of Poliorcetes or Gonatas, and (b) on the known use of the monogram **ΠΑΡ** to represent **ΑΠΕΙΡΩΤΑΝ** on voting tablets. But, according to B. V. Head (*BMCoins Macedonia* 15 no. 65) this issue is found as an overstrike on a coin of one of the later Macedonian kings, with a Macedonian shield (obverse) and a crested helmet (reverse). And is it really likely that Pyrrhus would stamp coins minted in Macedonia with a monogram meaning **ΑΠΕΙΡΩΤΑΝ**? On the whole, then, this issue is probably better assigned to the second century. See also Franke, *Münzen* 1. 244, 251; Head 234.

[1] On the chronology of the events between Pyrrhus' invasion of Macedonia (274) and his Peloponnesian expedition (272) see Lévèque 632–5. Beloch dated Pyrrhus' seizure of Macedonia to 274, Tarn set it in spring 273; the former conforms more closely to the sequence of events in Plutarch and is to be preferred.

[2] PPyrrh 26. 14–19; Parthen. *Erot.* 23; Paus. 1. 13. 4, 3. 6. 2–3.

[3] J. 25. 3. 8 'non iam reciperandi regni spem, sed salutis latebras ac fugae solitudines captat.' Lévèque 59 and 570, thinks that the emphasis on Antigonus' disasters points to the use of Hieronymus as the original source to which Justin here looks back; but one cannot do more than speculate. Tarn, *AG* 265 n. 19 is clearly dubious about the reality of this second defeat, which does not seem to have hampered Antigonus to any appreciable extent.

[4] Cf. Lévèque 578–9; PPyrrh 26. 19–20, says that the size of his army indicated that he aimed at seizing the whole Peloponnese. [5] *Teletis reliquiae*[2] (ed. Hense) 43.

Pyrrhus delayed his invasion of the Peloponnese until early in 272. He then began his campaign by ferrying a substantial army across the Corinthian Gulf at Pleuron near its mouth;[1] this consisted of 25,000 infantry, 2,000 cavalry, and twenty-four elephants.[2] Since he had returned to Epirus in 275 with only 8,500 men (out of an original 30,000),[3] the question arises: where had he got the fresh forces for this new army? His growing unpopularity in Macedonia makes it unlikely that he had called out the national levy in that part of his dominions and it seems more probable that any Macedonians (and Greeks) in his forces came as volunteers. The bulk of his army will have been raised within his own dominions, which indeed included not only Epirus proper, but also southern Illyria, extending as far north as Epidamnus, together with Amphilochia and Acarnania to the south. That this was the main source of his troops is indicated by the fact that later, during his attack on Sparta, a picked force under the command of Pyrrhus' son Ptolemy consisted of 2,000 Gauls and Chaonians—the former clearly mercenaries.[4] For Pyrrhus, indeed, much depended on the attitude of the Peloponnesians. They, according to Justin,[5] were impressed by his reputation as a general and by his campaigns in the West; and he sought to win them away from Antigonus by emphasizing the overworked slogan of 'eleutheria'.[6] At Megalopolis he was attended by embassies from Sparta, Athens, Achaea, and Messene.[7] The matters discussed are not recorded, but there can be little doubt that the Athenians' main concern was to be rid of the Macedonian garrison now stationed in the Piraeus, a grievance which, four years later, was to lead them into the Chremonidean War.[8] The Achaean Confederacy, which had recently been revived in opposition to Macedonia and had been augmented in 275/4 by the accession of Aegium,[9] could also be expected to welcome any opponent of Antigonus. Messene is more of a problem. According to Pausanias,[10]

---

[1] This route must be deduced from J. 25. 4. 4, where Beloch 4. 1. 575 n. reads 'cum copias Chersoneso < Aetolica in Peloponnesum > transposuit'; this solution to an otherwise incomprehensible passage has been accepted by Flacelière (189) and Lévêque (584) and is certainly attractive. For the 'Aetolian Chersonese' i.e. the area between the mouth of the Achelous and the Euenus, see Ptol. 3. 14. 2.

[2] PPyrrh 26. 19–20; cf. Launey 1. 11–12.   [3] PPyrrh 26. 3.

[4] On the extent of Pyrrhus' dominions see HE 586–8. For the composition of Ptolemy's force at Sparta see PPyrrh 28. 2; for Pyrrhus' own forces at Sparta see 30. 4 (Gauls and Molossians); 32. 1 ff. (Gauls). See Griffith, *Merc.* 64.

[5] J. 25. 4. 5.

[6] PPyrrh 26. 21 ἔφη γὰρ ἐλευθερώσων τὰς ὑπ' Ἀντιγόνῳ πόλεις ἀφῖχθαι.

[7] PPyrrh 26. 20 (Sparta); J. 25. 4. 4 (Athens, Achaea, Messene). By sending delegates to the Amphictyonic Council in the spring and autumn of 272 Sicyon also made an anti-Macedonian gesture (see below, p. 273 n. 7).

[8] Habicht, *Unters.* 110–11.   [9] Plb. 2. 41. 13.

[10] Paus. 1. 13. 6, 4. 29. 6. On the Messenians see Lévêque 589.

the Messenians sent help to Sparta; but this may mean either that their embassy to Pyrrhus was merely exploratory or else that they later changed their mind about where their interests really lay. In general Pyrrhus was welcomed. His statue, erected in the Altis at Olympia by the Elean seer Thrasybulus—he was later to be one of the murderers at Elis of the pro-Macedonian Aristotimus[1]—may suggest that Elis joined Pyrrhus,[2] and Megalopolis, which had been free of Antigonus since 280,[3] gladly opened its gates to a king who was proposing to attack Sparta. The 'liberation' of Alipheira and the expulsion of Aristolaus, the Macedonian officer in charge there, by Cleonymus[4] may belong to this year. Argos was divided in sentiment and, according to Pausanias,[5] sent help to Sparta. In general, the cleavage of interest was between factions favouring Pyrrhus or Sparta rather than between supporters of Pyrrhus and Antigonus. Ptolemy, significantly, seems to have played no part in the conflict, perhaps not wishing to take sides against either Pyrrhus or the Spartans.[6] Once Pyrrhus was dead, support for Athens and Sparta could be unambiguously aimed at Antigonus. In the meantime Ptolemy leaned towards caution. But it can be argued that in 272 he let slip the opportunity to strike with greater hopes of success the blow against his main enemy which was to end in disaster when it came four years later.

Though it is far from clear just how the change came about, by the middle of 272[7] Antigonus had recovered Macedonia and expelled Pyrrhus' garrisons. It seems likely that, in order to build up his army, Pyrrhus had rashly stripped Macedonia of all but a mere skeleton occupying force; and many of his supporters in Macedonia may well have volunteered to join the Peloponnesian expedition. Be that as it may, from his base on the coast Antigonus experienced little difficulty in overrunning the whole country and expelling Pyrrhus' son Ptolemy.[8] This done, he showed a statesmanlike understanding of the main issue, which was to destroy Pyrrhus at all cost, lest he should attempt to seize the Macedonian throne yet a third time. With this aim in mind, Antigonus was even prepared to assist his old enemy Sparta, hiring for the purpose a body of mercenaries led by Ameinias of Phocis, whom he had used earlier to recover Cassandreia from the tyrant

---

[1] P*Mor* 253 B.   [2] Paus. 6. 14. 9.   [3] See p. 249 n. 5.

[4] Cf. *SEG* 25. 447; T. Schwertfeger, *Chiron* 3 (1973) 85–93 (dating Pyrrhus' invasion of the Peloponnese to 273). That Aristolaus, the Macedonian commander, is the dedicator of a statue to Ptolemy II (Paus. 6. 17. 3) and must therefore be assumed to have left Antigonus' service for Ptolemy's, is highly hypothetical.

[5] Paus. 1. 13. 6.   [6] So Lévêque 589.

[7] On this date see Lévêque 607; previous writers set the recovery too early.

[8] Ptolemy turns up shortly afterwards outside Sparta, where he had joined his father (P*Pyrrh* 28. 2).

Apollodorus.[1] Pyrrhus had already invested Sparta when Ameinias' troops arrived; but when shortly afterwards Areus, who had been fighting in Crete on behalf of Gortyn (at the behest of Ptolemy II), returned to Sparta with 2,000 men, it became apparent that Pyrrhus' attack had failed. After a long struggle, which is described in the sources in sensational detail,[2] the Spartans succeeded in beating off Pyrrhus' attacks and he fairly soon lost his zest for the siege and called it off in order to march back to Argos.

Argos had been independent since perhaps 280,[3] but sympathies there were divided. An aristocratic faction led by Aristippus favoured Antigonus, while the democrats under Aristeas supported Pyrrhus. Plutarch represents the division as a personal feud between the two politicians and no doubt personal animosity played a part in the conflict, which reached a climax with the arrival of the news that Antigonus had come south and would soon reach Argos in person on his way to catch Pyrrhus at Sparta. It is likely that Antigonus came by sea to avoid any entanglement with the Aetolians (who had let Pyrrhus cross the Gulf without hindrance) and he will have disembarked at Corinth.[4] It was in swift response to Aristeas' appeal that Pyrrhus marched north from Sparta, harassed by Spartan troops under Areus (who succeeded in killing Pyrrhus' son Ptolemy in a skirmish).[5] Antigonus, however, who had a shorter distance to come, reached Argos first and took up a position on the neighbouring heights, probably to the north of the city. On his arrival Pyrrhus succeeded in entering the city by night, either by force (so Pausanias) or more probably having been let in by Aristeas (so Plutarch).[6] According to Plutarch, his entry followed an Argive attempt to persuade both kings to leave; Antigonus agreed and gave his son as hostage for his sincerity, but though Pyrrhus also agreed, he was not believed since he offered no surety.

Once inside, Pyrrhus was held up by a serious problem. How was he to get his elephants with their towers under the city gates? The Argives

---

[1] P*Pyrrh* 29. 11. On Ameinias and Cassandreia see above, p. 257 n. 4.

[2] P*Pyrrh* 27–30; Paus. 1. 13. 6–7; Polyaen. 8. 49; J. 25. 4. 6–10.

[3] It will have gained its independence from Antigonus at the time of his conflict with Ptolemy Ceraunus; cf. Lévêque 608 n. 4; Tarn, *AG* 132 n. 44.

[4] Cf. Lévêque 607–8.

[5] P*Pyrrh* 30. 4–11, 31. 1.

[6] The main sources for the fighting at Argos are P*Pyrrh* 31–4; Polyaen. 8. 68; Paus. 1. 13. 7–8; Val. Max. 5. 1 ext. 4. Of these the most important is Plutarch, whose account probably derives mainly from Hieronymus, with some contamination from Phylarchus and Proxenus; cf. Tarn, *AG* 449 and Lévêque 614–15 (against the view that Plutarch's source is Phylarchus; so Beloch 4. 1. 575). A number of passages in other authors are less important and record the unreliable tradition that Pyrrhus was besieging Argos (so Schol. Ovid. *Ibis* 301; *de vir. illustr.* 35. 10; Syncell. *Chron.* 271b p. 515), with Antigonus within the city (so J. 25. 5. 1) when Pyrrhus met his death. For other minor sources and discussion see Lévêque 613–31.

meanwhile occupied the Aspis and appealed to Antigonus for help. He sent in his son Halcyoneus and a relief force under his generals. Fighting continued throughout the night and the Argives got some help from a body of 1,000 Spartans and Cretans under the command of Areus. Towards dawn Pyrrhus tried to retreat amid great confusion, to which the elephants contributed substantially, and in the course of this the king was killed by a tile thrown by a woman from an adjoining roof.[1] Pyrrhus' severed head was taken by Halcyoneus to Antigonus, who drove him away 'calling him impious and barbarous' and 'burst into tears, recalling Antigonus his grandfather and Demetrius his father, who were examples in his own family of a reversal of fortune.'[2] The tears may or may not be true. The victor weeping over the vanquished enemy and recalling or foreseeing disasters of his own is a common literary theme in Hellenistic times.[3] Pyrrhus' body was cremated[4] and his son Helenus, who surrendered, was allowed to return to Epirus, where his elder brother, Pyrrhus' son Alexander II, who was also the grandson of Agathocles of Syracuse, succeeded his father and was granted generous terms by Antigonus. He was in fact left in possession of Tymphaea, Parauaea, and Atintania as a useful barrier against the Illyrians from farther north.[5]

By his resolution and wisdom in following Pyrrhus into the Peloponnese Antigonus had confirmed the lesson of Lysimacheia and was now the unchallenged ruler of Macedonia. His immediate concern was to consolidate his position within the kingdom, give the land and its people an opportunity to recover from the disasters of the last decades, and make sure that the garrisons or friends of Macedonia were firmly entrenched in Greece and capable of warding off any attack, direct or indirect, that might come from Alexandria.

2. *Macedonia and Greece (272–268 B.C.)*

The fighting and disorder of the last decade had involved territorial losses on the eastern and northern frontiers of Macedonia, and Antigonus could not hope to recover all that had gone immediately. In the confusion following Cassander's death Paeonia had achieved

[1] For variants in the details, unimportant here, see Lévêque 622–6.
[2] For this incident see PPyrrh 34. 7–11; Val. Max. 5. 1 ext. 4; J. 25. 5. 2.
[3] Cf. e.g. Antiochus III weeping over Achaeus and Scipio Aemilianus over the ruins of Carthage (Plb. 8. 20. 9, 38. 5. 2).
[4] According to Paus. 1. 13. 8 and 2. 21. 4, Pyrrhus was buried at Argos, and Tarn (*AG* 240 n. 1) accepts this. But Val. Max. 5. 1 ext 4 and J. 25. 5. 2 agree that his remains went back to Epirus, and Ovid, *Ibis* 303–4, implies that they were buried in Ambracia. See Lévêque 627–30.
[5] On the 'greater Epirus' which still remained under the control of Alexander II see Cabanes 77–80; on Macedonian policy cf. H. Dell, *CP* 62 (1967) 98.

independence under its king Audoleon,[1] and Lysimachus' reoccupation of the area[2] was short-lived. Whether Paeonia was already under Leon, Audoleon's son, at the time when Antigonus acquired the throne of Macedonia is uncertain. At some date, however, Antigonus Gonatas annexed Paeonia. This is indicated by the existence of a city named Antigoneia in the neighbourhood of Banja.[3] But when this took place is unknown.[4] Later we find Dropion, the son of Leon, ruling there. Pausanias (10. 13. 1) saw a bison's head in bronze dedicated by him at Delphi, and another inscription (*SEG* 13. 263 = *ISE* 2. 79), also at Delphi, records a dedication made by him to Apollo. Further, there is a dedication to Dropion at Olympia[5] by the κοινὸν τῶν Παιόνων, which describes him as 'founder', κτιστήν, probably of the reconstituted state. This combination of king and *koinon* recalls the relationship of Pyrrhus and the *koinon* of the Molossians, though indeed the word *koinon* is commonly found among communities in Epirus and Macedonia and may represent some local word for 'community'. So Pouilloux dates this dedication to the time of Demetrius II.[6] If that is correct, it would suggest that by then Paeonia had become once more independent of Macedonia since the reign of Gonatas, an assumption which gains some support from Philip V's seizure and garrisoning of Bylazora in 217[7] as a defensive measure against the Dardanians.

In Thrace too Antigonus made no immediate move. As we saw,[8] there is no evidence that his treaty with Antiochus I involved Antigonus in renouncing all claim to territory east of the Nestus. The

---

[1] On Paeonia see Volume I. 418–19. On Audoleon see above, p. 237 n. 5. Pyrrhus married one of his daughters (P*Pyrrh* 9. 2).

[2] See above, p. 237 n. 5.

[3] For Antigoneia-on-the-Axius see Pliny, *HN* 4. 34 and the Peutinger Table; it probably stood at the entrance to the Iron Gates. See Tarn, *AG* 321, and Volume I. 172–4.

[4] For discussion see Tarn, *AG* 320 f.; H. Gaebler, *ZfN* 37 (1927) 244 (but his attribution there of certain Paeonian coins with the monogram Δ to Dropion is to be rejected; cf. Gaebler III. 2. 5 no. 35, reading Δο(βήρων); 206 no. 1 n.); Lenk, *RE* s.v. *Paiones* col. 2406; Bengtson, *Strat.* 2. 340 n. 1.

[5] *SIG* 394. See J. Pouilloux, *BCH* 74 (1950) 22–32; J. Bousquet, ibid. 76 (1952) 136–40; Leschhorn 284–7.

[6] He argues that good relations between Dropion and Delphi (indicated by the dedications there) point to good relations between Dropion and Aetolia, hence that the Olympian dedication (assuming that it is roughly contemporary) is likely to belong to a time when Aetolia and Macedonia were at loggerheads. R. Mack, *Grenzmarken und Nachbarn Makedoniens im Norden und Westen* (Diss. Göttingen, 1951) 154 f., adds the argument that by the time of Demetrius II the Achaean and Aetolian leagues were already providing a pattern for other states to copy. It must, however, be admitted that neither argument is conclusive.

[7] Plb. 5. 97. 1–2 κατελάβετο Βυλάζωρα...ὥστε διὰ τῆς πράξεως ταύτης σχεδὸν ἀπολελύσθαι τοῦ φόβου τοῦ κατὰ Δαρδανίους. For a different view of the fortunes of Paeonia see Hammond, Volume II. 652, 666, and 669 and below pp. 385–6, who argues that, after becoming a client kingdom of Macedonia under Philip II, Paeonia remained so throughout the third century and that Philip V occupied Bylazora as a new city and did not take it from the Paeonians.

[8] See above, p. 251 n. 4.

fact that the mint of Lysimacheia continued to produce coins of Lysimachus and never went over to issuing coins of Antiochus I suggests that the area east of the Nestus remained a sort of no man's land between the two kingdoms.[1] To the west, as we have noted,[2] Tymphaea and Parauaea had been left in Epirote hands as a buffer area against the Illyrians. In all three regions Antigonus seems to have gone for a speedy settlement, which would leave him free to deal with the problems which were of most immediate concern. It was not that the interior, and the barbarians who lived there, did not interest Antigonus. Indeed, his reversion to Pella as his capital represents a return to a more traditional Macedonian policy in contrast to Cassander and Demetrius, whose preoccupation with events in Greece shows itself in their new coastal foundations at Cassandreia and Demetrias, neither in Macedonia proper. But for the moment matters in Greece claimed Antigonus' attention. First and foremost there was the question of Thessaly, and this Antigonus had already dealt with before the threat from Pyrrhus materialized. The evidence lies in the Delphic records for 277, which show the Thessalians presiding at the meetings of the Amphictyonic Council even after it had fallen under Aetolian control. Since, however, states directly under Macedonia normally refrained from sending representatives to Council meetings,[3] the absence of the Thessalians from the Council from 276 onwards is a clear indication that by then Macedonia had reasserted its control of Thessaly.[4]

Even before this Antigonus was in possession of Demetrias. This new creation of Demetrius Poliorcetes served as the northern terminal of the vital sea-route running via Chalcis and the Piraeus to Corinth. Philip V later dubbed Demetrias, Chalcis, and Corinth 'the fetters of Greece' and together they ensured Macedonian control over central Greece and the Isthmus area. They were usefully supplemented by the Piraeus, which a Macedonian force occupied (probably without a

---

[1] Cf. Newell, *WSM* 353; Will 1². 211. [2] See above, p. 267 n. 5.

[3] See on this Flacelière 193 ff.; Tarn, *AG* 276 ff.; Bengtson, *Strat.* 2. 348–9; Will 1². 216–18; Walbank, *CAH* 7. 1². 229–32.

[4] *SIG* 399, dated to 277 (cf. G. Klaffenbach, *Klio* 35 (1939) 194, against Flacelière 112 ff., who makes it 278) shows the Aetolians controlling two votes, probably those of Ozolian Locris and Heraclea-on-Oeta, and the Thessalians presiding and controlling two votes. In *SIG* 405, dated to 276 (Klaffenbach, loc. cit.; Flacelière, loc. cit., and makes it 277), the Aetolians preside and the Thessalians are no longer there (and do not reappear until the second century), clear proof that Thessaly is once more under Macedonian control. In 276 the Aetolians control a third vote, and Flacelière has plausibly suggested that this represents that of the Dolopians, who will now have entered the Aetolian Confederation. On the subordinate position of Thessaly relative to Macedonia see Plb. 4. 76. 2 (under Philip V) Θετταλοὶ γὰρ ἐδόκουν μὲν κατὰ νόμους πολιτεύειν καὶ πολὺ διαφέρειν Μακεδόνων, διέφερον δ' οὐδέν, ἀλλὰ πᾶν ὁμοίως ἔπασχον Μακεδόσι καὶ πᾶν ἐποίουν τὸ προστατόμενον τοῖς βασιλικοῖς.

break) from 294 to 229.[1] Antigonus had continued to garrison these strongholds even before his recovery of Macedonia and it was perhaps while he was preparing to attack Antiochus I in 280/79 that he entrusted the command centring on Corinth to his half-brother Craterus, the son of his mother Phila by her earlier husband, Alexander's general Craterus.[2] Craterus was older than Antigonus and his ancestry was equally distinguished; but throughout his life he remained entirely loyal to the king. His official title as commander at Corinth is not recorded, but his sphere included parts of the Peloponnese, the Piraeus, Euboea (with Chalcis), and Megara. When Antigonus acquired Megara is uncertain, but it was probably between 272 and 268, since Megara was certainly in Macedonian hands during the Chremonidean War.[3] A passage in Teles (Περὶ φυγῆς (ed. Hense) 23) refers to Lycinus, one of Antigonus' Friends (πιστευόμενος παρ' Ἀντιγόνῳ), as phrourarch in Megara.[4]

Euboea also seems to be under Macedonian influence at this time. Demetrius Poliorcetes had revived the Euboean League, probably before 301, as an 'act of liberation' and it continued to support him, even after Ipsus. Beloch argued[5] that shortly after this battle both Chalcis and Eretria fell away from Demetrius, but the evidence is slender and, as Picard has demonstrated, there is no interruption in issues of the coinage of the Euboean League such as one would expect, had any major political change occurred. Picard has made a good case for dating certain issues of the federal coinage between 304 and 290, after which all federal coinage was suspended.[6] What this means in terms of Macedonian control of Euboea is not entirely clear. That Euboea generally remained under the aegis of the Antigonids is undoubted; but despite the fact that after 277 states under Macedonian control, which were entitled to send *hieromnemones* to Delphi, did

---

[1] On this controversial question cf. Habicht, *Unters.* 95–112. According to Paus. 1. 26. 3, Olympiodorus accomplished his greatest achievement Πειραιᾶ καὶ Μουνυχίαν ἀνασωσάμενος. This, Habicht argues, refers to his preserving it from seizure in 305, not to his recovery of it later. For discussion see H. Heinen, *Gött. gel. Anz.* 223 (1981) 196–205; Musti, *Pausania* 1. 359.

[2] On Craterus see Tarn, *AG* 195; Fellmann 50–1; P. Schoch, *RE* s.v. *Krateros* cols. 1621 f.; Bengtson, *Strat.* 1. 131, 2. 347–52. Craterus is mentioned in a letter of Epicurus which must date to between 280 and 277 (cf. *P. Hercol.* 1418 col. 32a; A. Vogliano, *RFIC* 54 (1926) 320; 55 (1927) 501 ff.; De Sanctis, *Scritti*, 1. 493–500; G. Arrighetti, *Epicuro, Opere* (1960) 425–6 no. 49; Habicht, *Unters.* 99 n. 28). Craterus' loyalty to Antigonus is praised in P*Mor* 486 A.

[3] Cf. Heinen, *Unters.* 170 f.; J. 16. 2. 1 f.; Trog. *Prol.* 26 for the crushing of Gallic mercenaries at Megara by Antigonus.

[4] The relevant words are παρ' ἡμῖν ἐφρούρει φυγὰς ὢν ἐκ τῆς Ἰταλίας and it is thought for various reasons that Teles, the author of Stoic–Cynic diatribes, was from Megara (cf. A. Modrze, *RE* vA 1 (1934) s.v. *Teles* (2) col. 381).

[5] Beloch 4. 2. 462; but D.L. 2. 14, which he quotes, does not justify this conclusion; see Picard, *Chalcis* 263 ff. For the coinage, ibid. 267.

[6] For these federal coins, which he numbers 7–21, see Picard, *Chalcis* 174–5. Picard here shows that Chalcis and the Euboean League coined alternately and not simultaneously.

not normally do so, so long as the Aetolians controlled the Amphictyonic Council, Eretria sent *hieromnemones* in 276 (not 277, as Flacelière),
274, 273, 272 and 271, and Euboea in 267.[1] This suggests that the
Euboeans were at least nominally independent. On the other hand,
that independence did not amount to hostility, since the *hieromnemon* in
274[2] was Menedemus of Eretria, a warm supporter of Antigonus, who
had proposed a decree in his honour following the victory at Lysimacheia three years earlier.[3] Had there been a breach with Antigonus or
a successful revolt, Menedemus would clearly not have been chosen.[4]
In fact, the situation in Eretria changed immediately afterwards. The
city switched its allegiance, and Menedemus was now forced to flee
and sought refuge in the Amphiareum at Oropus.[5] The defection of
Eretria was beyond doubt the result of Pyrrhus' seizure of Macedonia
in 274: the *hieromnemon* sent to the Amphictyony in 273 was Aeschylus
of Eretria, Menedemus' enemy and an opponent of Antigonus.[6]

The trouble at this time extended to Chalcis. As Picard has shown,
numismatic evidence indicates that Chalcis too revolted about 273; the
revolt was soon suppressed, but the activities of the Chalcidian mint
were suspended and no Chalcidian coins were issued between that year
and the defection from Antigonus of Alexander, Craterus' son and
successor at Corinth (see below, p. 301).[7] The situation in Histiaea, at
the northern extremity of Euboea, is slightly puzzling. Histiaea was
independently represented on the Amphictyonic Council from 266 to
255,[8] and probably occupied the Euboean seat mentioned on an
inscription of 267.[9] As Tarn saw,[10] the presence of Histiaean delegates
at Delphi implies some degree of independence from Macedonia; but
this need not mean complete alignment in the Aetolian camp. After
255, however, all Euboean representation at Delphi ceases, which must
imply that Antigonus had strengthened his hold there; and if the
victory over the Ptolemaic fleet off Cos belongs in that year,[11] he
probably took advantage of his consequent increase in prestige and
power and of the disappearance of any threat from Ptolemy to tighten

[1] Flacelière App. I lists nos. 3, 5, 6, 7, 8, 9, and 12.   [2] Flacelière App. I list no. 5.
[3] D.L. 2. 142 (after Lysimacheia); see above, p. 256, n. 5.
[4] So correctly Picard, *Chalcis* 268.
[5] D.L. 2. 142; here he was in contact with Hierocles, the commander of the Piraeus.
[6] Ibid. 2. 141; cf. Flacelière 188 n. 3.
[7] Picard, *Chalcis* 174–5; 'Group 2' of the coins which Picard identifies as Chalcidian were
issued between the suspension of federal coinage in 290 and 273. For the next twenty years or so
(down to the revolt of Alexander of Corinth) there were neither federal nor Chalcidian issues.
[8] Flacelière 193.
[9] Flacelière 391, App. I list no. 12, archon Athambos; Picard, *Chalcis* 271.
[10] Tarn, *AG* 293–4; his dates require adjustment in view of the subsequent redating of several
Delphic documents. Picard, *Chalcis* 268–9, questions whether Histiaea was truly independent. It
was probably 'free', but controlled by friends of Antigonus (cf. W. W. Tarn, *CAH* 7. 216).
[11] See Appendix 4.

his grip on the important island of Euboea. Picard has pointed out[1] that Histiaea continued coining tetrobols throughout the century, which perhaps seems strange after 255, when the disappearance of the Histiaeans from among the Delphian *hieromnemones* clearly indicates the subjection of Histiaea to Macedonia. The emission of these coins both before and after that date seems to imply that throughout Histiaea remained a loyal supporter of Macedonia.

As governor of Corinth, Craterus exercised some control over, and derived some strength from, the pro-Macedonian tyrannies which appear at various dates from now on in several Peloponnesian cities. The leading state in the Peloponnese, Sparta, under its king Areus, remained implacably hostile to Macedonia; the help which Antigonus, from motives of self-interest, had given to Sparta against Pyrrhus in 277 brought only a temporary and half-hearted interruption of this hostility, which was fanned by Areus' ambition to play the part of a Hellenistic king in a manner well outside normal Spartan tradition. Against Antigonus Sparta looked for support to Ptolemy II and, once Pyrrhus' death had freed Ptolemy from any conflict of interests, there was nothing to hinder his making an alliance with Sparta. The exact date of this alliance is not known.[2]

The earliest of the tyrannies to arise after Pyrrhus' defeat was that of Aristotimus at Elis, which belongs to the period immediately after Pyrrhus' invasion of the Peloponnese.[3] According to Pausanias, he had Antigonus' backing in seizing power, but failed to establish himself firmly. Within six months he had fallen to a conspiracy of several leading citizens, including one Cylon, who killed the tyrant at the altar of Zeus Soter, where he had taken refuge, and the seer Thrasybulus, who was earlier a supporter of Pyrrhus.[4] Craterus came to Aristotimus' rescue, but he had only got as far as Olympia when he learnt that the tyrant was dead.[5] At Megalopolis Aristodamus succeeded in setting up a tyranny which was to last until around 250.[6] One of the most famous episodes of his period of rule was the defeat and death of

---

[1] *Chalcis*, 271; see also L. Robert, *Num. grecque* 179 ff.

[2] On Ptolemy's failure to support Sparta, an old friend, see above, p. 265 n. 6. It is, however, clear that he had made an alliance with Sparta before Athens and Sparta made the compact that led to the Chremonidean War in 268 (*SVA* 476 ll. 21 f. Λακεδαιμόνιοι φίλοι καὶ σύμμαχοι τοῦ βασιλέως ὄντες Πτολεμαίου). See P. Cloché, *REA* 48 (1946) 29–61; Heinen, *Unters.* 126–7.

[3] J. 26. 1. 4 dates Aristotimus' tyranny among the movements which followed Pyrrhus' death and Antigonus' victory. On Aristotimus see also Paus. 5. 5. 1; P*Mor* 249 F, 250 F, 253 B. Justin's omission of all mention of Antigonus' support does not imply that he questioned the truth of this (as Tarn, *AG* 278 seems to suggest). It is significant that the refugees from Aristotimus' tyranny found refuge in Aetolia.

[4] See above, p. 265 nn. 1–2 on Thrasybulus; his part in the murder is mentioned in P*Mor* 253 B. For the names of the other tyrannicides see Paus. 5. 5. 1.

[5] P*Mor* 251 B.

[6] Paus. 8. 27. 11 says that he was called Aristodamus the Good (χρηστός).

Acrotatus of Sparta at his hands,[1] but all that is known for certain about the date of this incident is that it occurred before 255.[2] When Aristodamus seized power and what role Antigonus (or Craterus) played in this are alike unknown.

The sequence of events which led to Aristomachus' tyranny at Argos is also obscure. It is likely that he was the son of the Aristippus who represented Macedonian (and aristocratic) interests at the time of Pyrrhus' appearance there in 272,[3] since Aristomachus' son bore that name. Beloch[4] may well be right in suggesting this relationship, for Phylarchus' comment (quoted by Plb. 2. 59. 5) that the second Aristomachus, who was the son of Aristomachus I, was 'not only a tyrant, but sprung from tyrants (ἐκ τυράννων πεφυκέναι)'—in the plural—confirms the hypothesis that it was the Macedonian supporter Aristippus who first set up the Argive tyranny after Pyrrhus' death, and that he thereby established a dynasty consisting of himself, his son Aristomachus I, and his grandsons Aristippus and Aristomachus II.[5] The antecedents and the persistence of this dynasty of tyrants do not, however, imply that all its members were inseparably bound to Antigonus. Indeed, it is not by any means certain that they held power without a break for, as we shall see,[6] in the late 250s a group of exiles living in Argos was able to plot against the tyrants of Sicyon and Megalopolis with impunity—though this is perhaps a warning against our assuming either that there was invariably solidarity between tyrants or that all alike were sponsored by Macedonia.

Another important Peloponnesian city, Sicyon, was governed by a succession of tyrants, whose links with Macedonia are also by no means firmly established. The presence of Sicyonian *hieromnemones* at the Amphictyonic Councils held in spring and autumn of 272 suggests that in that year the city was independent of Macedonia[7] and their subsequent absence from the lists may indicate that Sicyon now fell under a pro-Macedonian tyrant, perhaps the Cleon mentioned by

[1] P*Agis* 3. 7; Paus. 8. 27. 11.
[2] Cf. *SIG* 430, a Delphic dedication to Acrotatus' infant son as 'King Areus' in 255/4 (archon Emmenidas: Flacelière 397 App. I list no. 21 for the date; cf. Nachtergael 273, who favours 255/4 while admitting 259/8 as a possibility). This inscription is evidence that Acrotatus' death was no later than 255, but whether it occurred in the latter stages of the Chremonidean War or the early 250s is not certain. See Tarn, *AG* 304 n. 84, whose dates require revision, but who disposes of Bousquet's argument that the Areus of *SIG* 430 is Areus I (a view still held; see, *contra*, Nachtergael 266 ff.; Walbank, *CAH* 7. 1². 237 n. 31). On the whole, the later date for Acrotatus' death is more likely than one which would imply yet another Spartan expedition after the disaster of Areus' death in 265.
[3] See above, p. 266. 　　　　　　　　　　　　　　　　　[4] 4. 1. 579 with n. 3.
[5] On this family of tyrants see Will 1². 218; Wilhelm, *Beiträge* 110 ff.; *Sitz. Wien* 202. 5 (1925) 15 f.
[6] See below, pp. 296–8.
[7] Flacelière 388–9, App. I lists nos. 7 and 8 (archons Archiadas and Eudoxus II).

Plutarch.[1] How long this tyranny lasted is unknown, but it was followed by the joint magistracy of Timocleidas and Cleinias, the father of Aratus.[2] After Timocleidas' death Cleinias governed alone. According to Plutarch he was a guest-friend of both Antigonus and Ptolemy and evidently tried to keep Sicyon neutral in the conflict of the great powers. Apart from these cities the only place in the Peloponnese of which we have information around this time is Troezen, where Cleonymus of Sparta had expelled a Macedonian garrison installed by Craterus,[3] perhaps in 278.[4] But its allegiance at the end of the 270s is unknown.

The picture is clearly incomplete, indeed fragmentary—perhaps partly because Hieronymus' *History* ended with the death of Pyrrhus, and the tradition derived from Phylarchus is hardly a satisfactory substitute. But the available evidence is certainly not enough to support the claim that at this time Antigonus rested his power in the Peloponnese on pro-Macedonian tyrants. Twice in Polybius, once in a speech attributed to the Aetolian Chlaeneas and once as his own view, Antigonus is alleged to have planted tyrannies in Greece on a large scale.[5] As a general policy this is true only at a later date, when the revolt of Alexander and the subsequent loss of Corinth to Aratus forced Antigonus to fall back on a system which did not include the possession of the Acrocorinth.[6] For the period immediately following Pyrrhus' death his policy was more eclectic, with some tyrants, some garrisons, and here and there a tolerated neutrality, and with Craterus' troops on Acrocorinth to oversee and coordinate.

The Athenians, however, like the Spartans, remained implacably hostile to Macedonia and from 277 until 264 they regularly sent *hieromnemones* to the Amphictyonic Council.[7] But since 294 Athens had been obliged to submit to the indignity of a Macedonian garrison

---

[1] P*Arat* 2. 1.

[2] According to Paus. 2. 8. 2 Timocleidas was a tyrant along with one Euthydemus, and both were expelled by Cleinias. Euthydemus was in fact the Sicyonian *hieromnemon* to the Amphictyonic Council in autumn 272 and *should* (perhaps) be anti-Macedonian. But Plutarch, who is here following Aratus' *Memoirs*, is more likely to be right in making Timocleidas the colleague of Cleinias rather than co-tyrant with Euthydemus.

[3] Polyaen. 2. 29. 1; Frontin. 3. 6. 7.

[4] The incident falls between the installation of Craterus at Corinth (*c*. 280/79) and Cleonymus' expulsion from Sparta (*c*. 275); cf. Beloch 4. 1. 562 n. 1; Tarn, *AG* 163. The context of *SEG* 13. 341 = *ISE* 1. 62 (statue of Diomedes of Troezen, who freed the city) is uncertain.

[5] Plb. 2. 41. 10 πλείστους γὰρ δὴ μονάρχους οὗτος ἐμφυτεῦσαι δοκεῖ τοῖς Ἕλλησι; 9. 29. 6 (Chlaeneas) οἱ δὲ τυράννους ἐμφυτεύοντες, οὐδεμίαν πόλιν ἄμοιρον ἐποίησαν τοῦ τῆς δουλείας ὀνόματος. Cf. Plb. 2. 42. 3, 43. 8; 9. 29. 6. Other relevant passages are J. 26. 1; Trog. *Prol.* 26 (referring more generally to *dominatio* and attributing this to the period after Pyrrhus' death).

[6] See Fellmann 47–63.

[7] Cf. Flacelière 386–94, App. I lists nos. 3–16; on the dating of lists 1–4 (277–275 rather than 278–276) see G. Klaffenbach, *Klio* 32 (1939) 194; Nachtergael 195–6.

in the Piraeus.[1] In 272, as it appears, the Athenians made a treaty or, more probably, renewed an earlier treaty with the Aetolians;[2] this seems mainly to have been concerned with ensuring Athens redress against alleged illegal action such as we find in many *asylia* agreements. Hence it can hardly be interpreted as specifically aimed at Macedonia; nor is its precise date assured within the period 277–266/5. But the passing of a decree, proposed by his son Laches, in 271/0, in honour of Demochares, who had played a leading part in the rising against Poliorcetes in 287,[3] was a gesture of unmistakable defiance towards the Antigonid house. Furthermore, a measure passed in the winter of 270/69 in honour of Callias, which speaks warmly of Ptolemy II, indicates that in the 270s there were frequent exchanges of embassies between Athens and Egypt and in the light of what was to happen two years later these take on a clearly anti-Macedonian significance, as part of the background of the great rising of 268.[4]

Before turning to this we must, however, first consider the Aetolians and their role in Greece during the years between Antigonus' accession and the outbreak of the Chremonidean War. The Aetolians had gained much prestige from their courageous defence of Delphi at the time of the Gallic invasion (279)[5] and this they exploited to secure acquiescence in their seizure of Delphi itself and to dominate the Amphictyonic Council which administered the shrine. The growth in Aetolian power during the sixty years following the Gallic attack is reflected in broad outline in the growth in the number of votes on the Amphictyonic Council controlled by the Aetolians. This they brought about by appropriating the votes on the Council which belonged by tradition to states which were now incorporated in the Aetolian League. The details are subject to some uncertainty owing to three factors. First, the documents giving the names and cities of representatives cannot always be dated with accuracy and this will continue to be true until the table of Delphic archons is completely assured. Secondly, though an increase in the number of Aetolian representatives must imply the acquisition of, or at least the claim to, new territories, one can often only speculate on which these were, since the representatives to which they entitled the Aetolians could come from anywhere in the Confederacy. Thirdly, the Aetolians may have maintained a claim to territories (and sent *hieromnemones* to Delphi on that basis) even after losing control over them. All this was made easier by the fact that the

---

[1] Habicht, *Unters.* 95–112.

[2] *SVA* 470 = *IG* ix². 1. 176; on the date see Flacelière 190. Previously scholars had dated this treaty after 228 (so Klaffenbach) or even later, but it must belong to a time when the Athenians were sending *hieromnemones* to the Amphictyonic Council.

[3] See above, p. 230 n. 3. For the decree see P*Mor* 850 f–851 f (the year is that of Pytharatus).

[4] See Shear 3–4, ll. 40–78; Habicht, *Unters.* 48, 85.   [5] See above, p. 255 n. 5.

king of Macedonia refrained from exercising any vote to which Macedonia was entitled, so long as the Council was under Aetolian control, a practice which also applied (with a few possible exceptions) to states within the Macedonian sphere of interest.[1]

For the years between Antigonus' accession and the outbreak of the Chremonidean War in 268 the position is, however, fairly clear. As we have already seen,[2] the Aetolians controlled two votes—probably those of Ozolian Locris and Heraclea-on-Oeta—in 277, to which they added a third vote in 276; this was pretty certainly that of the Dolopians. In 272 they exercised five votes, probably through having incorporated Aeniania, which was still sending its own *hieromnemones* in autumn 273,[3] and the records from Athambus' archonship, in autumn 268, show Aetolia exercising six votes, after having annexed Doris in 271/0.[4] Thus in under ten years the Aetolians had extended their territory eastward as far as the Malian Gulf and could therefore block Macedonian movement by land into southern Greece via the historic route through the pass of Thermopylae. So far, however, there had been no open hostility,[5] for although the Aetolians had allowed Pyrrhus to cross the Corinthian Gulf into the Peloponnese in 272 in a move clearly directed against Antigonus, the latter had been careful to bring his forces into the Peloponnese by sea, so as to avoid a clash with the Aetolians.[6] In the long run Aetolian expansion in central Greece was bound to run up against Macedonian interests; but before any serious conflict had time to develop here, Antigonus had to cope with a full-scale revolt in southern Greece led by Athens and Sparta and apparently stimulated by Ptolemy II.[7] This, the so-called Chremonidean War, was to prove his most serious challenge since the death of Pyrrhus.

3. *The causes of the Chremonidean War*

The Chremonidean War, like so many other events in the early third century, is shrouded in queries and uncertainties through lack of a satisfactory literary source. The war itself has to be reconstructed from brief passages in Pausanias, Justin, and Plutarch, supplemented by a handful of inscriptions; and the same absence of firm evidence dogs any

[1] See above, p. 255 n. 5.   [2] Ibid.
[3] Cf. Flacelière 191, with App. I nos. 6–7.
[4] Cf. Flacelière App. I no. 11 (autumn 268). J. Bousquet, *BCH* 62 (1938) 359 ff. has shown that Doris became Aetolian in 271/0; but that the one for autumn 268 is the earliest surviving list of *hieromnemones* after autumn 271. See Will I². 228.
[5] It is noteworthy, however, that the Aetolians gave asylum to those expelled from Elis by Aristotimus (above p. 272 n. 3) and they may have assisted them to recover their country. Cf. Flacelière 194.
[6] See above, p. 266 n. 4.
[7] On the events leading up to this war and Ptolemy's role in it see the next section.

attempt to discover its causes.[1] The most important document for this purpose is an inscription recording the Athenian decree which approved the alliance with Sparta at the outset of the war, and giving the actual text of the treaty of alliance (σπονδαὶ καὶ συμμαχία) between the two cities. This decree was proposed by Chremonides, one of the leaders of the anti-Macedonian faction at Athens at this time, who in consequence gave his name to the war. It was passed in the year of Peithidemus' archonship, and though the date of this has been the subject of long debate, 268/7 now appears to be the most probable year.[2] The decree enumerates the allies lined up behind the two cities—Elis (now rid of its tyrant Aristotimus),[3] the Achaeans, Tegea, Mantinea, Orchomenus, Phigaleia, Caphyae, and some un-named Cretan cities allied to Sparta;[4] it denounces Antigonus for unjust and treacherous behaviour;[5] and it indicates that the move-ment has the support of Ptolemy II, with whom Sparta had already made an alliance.[6] The wording of this Athenian decree, which is really a call to arms, gives some indication of the panhellenic themes which were invoked in the propaganda of the war. It includes a rhetorical appeal to the historic days when Athenians and Spartans had united in friendship and alliance to resist those seeking to ensnare the cities; and the same panhellenic note is also struck in a somewhat later inscription from Plataea, which records a decree of the *koinon* of the Greeks honouring Glaucon, Chremonides' brother, for his atten-tion to the shrine of Zeus Eleutherius at Plataea.[7] Clearly Athens and

---

[1] The sources for the war are Paus. 1. 1. 1, 7. 3, 3. 6. 4–6; J. 26. 2; P*Agis* 3. 4. For the causes of the war D.L. 2. 24 has an anecdote about Zeno, but the main evidence lies in the decree of Chremonides (*SIG* 434–5 = *SVA* 3. 476) and a decree of the *koinon* of the Greeks honouring Glaucon, his brother (cf. R. Étienne and M. Piérart, *BCH* 49 (1975) 56 ff.).

[2] Inscriptions imply that a state of war existed in the Athenian archonships of Menecles and Nicias (cf. *IG* ii/iii². 665 = *SIG* 386; *IG* ii/iii². 666–7). Heinen, *Unters.* 100–17, has argued convincingly for dating Menecles to 267/6 and Nicias to 266/5; and, since the decree of Chremonides must precede these, there is a good case for dating Peithidemus' year to 268/7. See further Heinen, *Unters.* 201 n. 435; Habicht, *Unters.* 116 n. 11.

[3] See above, p. 272 n. 3.

[4] *SVA* 476 ll. 23–7. The Cretan cities in question are probably Gortyn, Itanus, Olus, Aptera, Rhethymna, Polyrrhenia, and Phalasarna, though this is not certain (cf. van Effenterre 203–4; Heinen, *Unters.* 132); in any case there is no indication that they played an active role in the war.

[5] *SVA* 476 ll. 31–33: κοινῆς ὁμονοίας γενομένης τοῖς Ἕλλησι πρός τε τοὺς νῦν ἠδικηκότας καὶ παρεσπονδηκότας τὰς πόλεις. Heinen, *Unters.* 120 favours W. W. Tarn's view (*JHS* 54 (1934) 33 ff.) that there is a reference to σπονδαί contracted in 279 between Antigonus and the Greek cities in view of the Gallic invasion; but παρασπονδεῖν may be used very generally and without reference to a particular treaty, as often in Polybius. See Walbank, *C* 1. 108 (on 1. 43. 2) quoting Heuss, *VG* 71 n. 'παρασπονδεῖν...ist im allgemeinen ein Ausdruck für unredliches Verhalten.'

[6] *SVA* 476 ll. 16–19, 21–2. For a dedication by Ptolemy II to Areus I at Olympia see *SIG* 433.

[7] R. Étienne and M. Piérart, *BCH* 99 (1975) 51–75. The date of this decree is uncertain but it is evidently later than the end of the Chremonidean War. Buraselis (*AE* 1982 (1984) 136–59) argues that it was passed after Glaucon's death and probably between 250 and 245 (see below, p. 303 n. 1).

Sparta sought to represent their revolt against Macedonia as an echo of the Persian and Lamian wars and as a rising of Greece against enslavement.

However, the war was more than a revolt of Greek cities, for the decree stresses Ptolemy II's role in supporting the cause of Greek freedom 'following the policy of his ancestors and of his sister'.[1] Why, after his father's active intervention in the Athenian revolt against Demetrius Poliorcetes in 287,[2] Ptolemy II (who succeeded in 285) had neglected his many opportunities to hamper and oppose Antigonus throughout the last twenty years, is not clear. And it is equally puzzling that, after encouraging Athens and Sparta to revolt against Macedonia in 268, he then apparently gave them so little help. Various explanations have been suggested.[3] One view makes Arsinoe II the driving force behind a new policy.[4] True, she was already dead when the war broke out, but, on this hypothesis, Ptolemy was loyally following her aim, which was to secure the throne of Macedon for her son by Lysimachus. This imaginative theory lost much of its attraction once it was realized that the Ptolemy who figures for a time as Philadelphus' co-regent was not the son of Lysimachus.[5] Heinen still regards it as probable;[6] but the reference to Arsinoe in the decree of Chremonides need not be more than a gesture of respect, and even if it is more, Ptolemy II is not likely to have instigated a war primarily to further the interests of his stepson, once Arsinoe was dead. If Arsinoe's ambitions played any part in the events leading to the Chremonidean War (and this is not impossible), it was certainly much more modest than many scholars have assumed.[7] Other views of the causes of the war have been advanced. Will[8] has emphasized the absence of all documentary support for, or probability in, Rostovtzeff's theory[9] that Ptolemy hoped to thwart a supposed plan of Antigonus to make the Piraeus a trading rival to Rhodes and Delos or Tarn's belief[10] that the Athenians had aligned themselves with Ptolemy in order to ensure a regular supply of Egyptian corn. However, the real problem is not so much to explain why Ptolemy put himself behind the rising, but why, having done so, he gave it such meagre backing. Habicht[11] has

---

[1] See above, p. 278 n. 6.   [2] See above, p. 230 nn. 3–4.
[3] See esp. Heinen, *Unters.* 97 ff.; Will 1². 221–2.
[4] So Tarn, *AG* 90 ff.; *CAH* 7. 705 ff.; cf. Bouché-Leclercq, *Lagides* 1. 188.
[5] Cf. M. Segre, *Clara Rhodos* 9 (1938) 181 ff.; on 'Ptolemy the Son' see Appendix 4 pp. 589–92.
[6] *Unters.* 97–100. Heinen admits that the naming of a street in Alexandria after 'Arsinoe(?) Chalcioecus' (*P. Lond.* 7. 1986 l. 17)—the epithet is that of Athena in Sparta but 'Arsinoe' is restored—is no evidence for diplomatic activity by Arsinoe in Sparta (so Longega 106).
[7] The theory of U. Koehler (*Berl. Sitzb.* 1895, II. 976 ff.) that Arsinoe intervened with her husband on behalf of a group of Alexandrian intellectuals, who included Greek exiles and maintained links with anti-Macedonian circles at Athens, goes beyond any firm evidence.
[8] 1². 220–2.   [9] 1. 215 ff.   [10] *AG* 221 ff.   [11] *Unters.* 111–12.

argued that this is most easily explained if the main initiative for the war came not from Ptolemy, but from Athens and Sparta themselves. Against this is the fact that the Ptolemaic alliance with Sparta certainly antedated the treaty recorded in *SVA* 476, and so clearly indicates Ptolemy's readiness to fish in troubled waters. His inadequate support is not therefore to be explained by the assumption that he was a reluctant patron from the outset, tagging along behind Athens and Sparta.

Ptolemy had in fact adequate reasons to act against Antigonus at this time. The growth of Macedonian power in Greece since Pyrrhus' death gave him sufficient cause to welcome a Greek revolt against Antigonus. For with a strong Macedonia there was always the possibility that Antigonus might once more revive his family ambitions in the Aegean, where a Macedonian presence was rightly regarded as a threat to Egypt;[1] and Will has argued plausibly[2] that after his victory over Pyrrhus Antigonus at once set about restoring Macedonian naval power by building new ships. This seems extremely likely, for naval communications with the Peloponnese were essential to Macedonia (see above, p. 262 n. 4). Moreover, shipbuilding presented few problems in Macedonia, which had rich supplies of timber, excellent docks at Pella and Amphipolis, and skilled craftsmen. How many, and what types of ships were built is not recorded. Nor have they made much impression on the scanty tradition of this war, though there is some evidence that Antigonus proceeded against Athens with ships;[3] and the fact that operations to bring in the corn in the first year of the war were severely hampered, may point to the presence of Macedonian vessels. Any growth in Macedonian naval power presented a threat to Alexandria, particularly now that Antigonus was on good terms with the Seleucids. This explanation of Ptolemaic policy—it cannot be more than a likely hypothesis—gains some confirmation from what happened after the war, when Antigonus used the pretext of the Second Syrian War to sail into the waters off the coast of Asia Minor and there defeated the Ptolemaic navy off Cos in 255.[4] Macedonian naval power may in fact have been both a major factor in leading Ptolemy to provoke the Chremonidean War and an explanation of why he played so ignominious a role in waging it.

---

[1] Cf. Bengtson, *Gesch.*[4] 407; Buraselis 157; Walbank in Adams and Borza 217–19.

[2] 1². 219–21.

[3] Paus. 1. 1. 1 ναυσὶν ἅμα ἐκ θαλάσσης κατείργεν, which, as Heinen points out (*Unters.* 190 n. 393), could mean 'he pressed them hard (cf. Hdt. 6. 102)'. According to Paus. 3. 6. 4, Antigonus moved on Athens πέζῳ τε καὶ ναυσίν; and Athenian problems over corn may imply the presence of Macedonian ships off Attica (cf. *SEG* 24. 154, a decree for the *strategos* Epichares, who got in the grain; on this see below, p. 283 n. 4). But the danger *may* have come from pirates in the pay of Antigonus. [4] See below, p. 291 and Appendix 4.

Thus the various parties to the war had each their own separate aims. Ptolemy sought to check the rise of Macedonian power in the Peloponnese and the beginnings of a forward naval policy in the Aegean, Athens hoped to recover the Piraeus and the other Attic strongholds held by Antigonus and so rid herself completely of the humiliating symbols of occupation, and Areus I sought to reaffirm a traditional Spartan hegemony over the Peloponnese. In 268/7 these convergent interests came together in the Athenian decree of Chremonides and the outbreak of the Chremonidean War.

4. *The Chremonidean War*

The Greek revolt led by Athens and Sparta presented Gonatas with his most alarming challenge since he had established himself on the throne of Macedonia. The war had to be won if the Macedonian position in Greece was to be maintained; and since the time of Philip II control of Greece had been regarded as a central tenet of Macedonian policy. Furthermore, a base in southern Greece was highly desirable, should the son of Demetrius Poliorcetes at any time decide on a forward policy in the Aegean. Against the new coalition Antigonus had one strong advantage, his possession of Corinth, and so of interior lines; indeed, as events were to show, it was his ability to prevent an effective juncture between his enemies' forces by way of the Isthmus that was, more than anything else, to decide the issue. To balance any assistance the Greeks might receive from Alexandria, Antigonus could hope for help from Antiochus I; but apart from some Gallic mercenaries, who may have come from him,[1] there is no indication that any such help actually reached Antigonus.

The two main sources for the war are Paus. 3. 6. 4–6 and J. 26. 2. 1–8.[2] The chronology of the events there described is bound to be speculative, but Heinen has suggested very plausibly that, taken together, these accounts point to three Spartan campaigns, occurring in the three successive summers of 267, 266, and 265, since D.S. 20. 29. 1 seems to indicate that Areus met his death in 265.[3] Following the declaration of war, the Spartan king led an expedition north in 267, but was forced to fall back through shortage of supplies.[4] Pausanias

---

[1] See below, p. 282 n. 1.

[2] See also D.S. 20. 29; P*Agis* 3. 7. For the interpretation adopted here see Heinen, *Unters.* 199–202, criticizing McCredie 110 ff., who argues that Areus made only one expedition, which reached Attica and ended in his death near Corinth on the way back.

[3] According to Diodorus, Areus (who ascended the throne in 309/8) reigned for 44 years; and since he normally includes only one of the two terminal years in calculating intervals, this should put Areus' death in 265/4. In favour of 265 rather than 264 see Heinen, *Unters.* 173–5, 201–2.

[4] Paus. 3. 6. 6 Ἀρεὺς δέ, ὡς σφισι τὰ ἐπιτήδεια ἐξανήλωτο, ἀπῆγεν ὀπίσω τὴν στρατίαν.

BOEOTIA

Thebes

Tanagra *Asopus* Oropus

Rhamnus

Panactum

Cephisus

▲ *MT. PARNES*

Phyle

Cephisus

THRIASIAN
PLAIN

MEGARID

Eleusis

Athens
Museum ▲ *MT. HYMETTUS*
Munychia Phalerum
Salamis Piraeus
Heliupolis
Salamis Sphettus

Koroni

Saronic Gulf

Vuliagmeni

— — Approximate frontiers
of Attica in 268
⊙ Urban centres
■ Fort and garrisons *c.* 268–261
▲ Mountains
Koroni Modern names
0   5   10   15 km.

0   5   10 miles

Laurium

LAURIUM

Patroklou Charax

Pr. Sunium

FIG. 9. ATTICA

does not tell us how far beyond the Isthmus he penetrated on this
occasion, but the view that he advanced into Attica, leaving an
undefeated Macedonian garrison force in his rear, seems unlikely.[1]
In 266 Areus again marched north and this time he was assisted by a

[1] Cf. Heinen, *Unters.* 201 n. 36.

revolt at Megara of Gallic mercenaries in Antigonus' employ. The background and details of this incident are obscure. Antigonus evidently marched or sailed south to Corinth soon after war broke out and with forces in Attica laid siege to Athens. The Gallic mercenaries,[1] who may have been sent by Antiochus, were perhaps engaged in taking Megara, but this is uncertain since the date when Megara fell into Antigonus' hands is not known. Polyaenus and Aelian, however,[2] mention an incident during the siege of the city, in which the Megarians used pigs to induce a panic among Antigonus' elephants. Whether that was now or earlier,[3] and at what date Antigonus installed Lycinus, a Greek from Italy, as phrourarch in Megara,[4] are alike questions we cannot answer.

Antigonus suppressed the Gallic mutiny with considerable carnage[5] and pressed on with the siege of Athens; and Areus retired to a safer position (presumably south of the Isthmus). In the next year he made yet a third attempt to break the Isthmus line, but was defeated near Corinth by Macedonian troops under Antigonus and lost his life in the fighting.[6] This reconstruction is attractive, but by no means certain. The campaigns here assigned to 267 and 266 may in fact have been one and the same. The essential point is, however, that thanks to his control of the Isthmus Antigonus was able to prevent the union of his two enemies.

An important element in the Isthmus defences has recently been revealed with the investigation by R. Stroud[7] of a tower (giving an extensive view across the Isthmus and the Saronic Gulf), an enclosure, and a rubble wall on Stanotopi, the eastern extremity of Mt. Oneium, and two rubble walls blocking routes through the gap between Stanotopi and Mt. Oneium proper. The bulk of the pottery associated with these sites dates to the period 350–275 and it seems likely that this important defence system was built either by Philip II (who will certainly have occupied the site) or early in the period of the Diadochi. As Stroud points out, this complex must have been occupied during the Chremonidean War, in order to block land movement across the Isthmus and also to forestall any acts which the Ptolemaic admiral

---

[1] That they were mercenaries employed by Antigonus (a fact not made clear by Justin) is indicated by Trog. *Prol.* 26 'ut defectores Gallos Megaris delevit'. See C. B. Welles, *Klio* 52 (1970) 487, for an epitaph on Brikkos, a citizen of Apamea-Celaenae, who fell fighting as leader of a body of Gauls against Areus. It seems likely that these mercenaries had reached Antigonus through the good services of Antiochus I; cf. Will 1². 227.

[2] Aelian, *Nat. anim.* 11. 14, 16. 36; Polyaen, 4. 6. 3. The same story is associated with one of Pyrrhus' battles in Aelian, *Nat. anim.* 1. 38.

[3] See Heinen, *Unters.* 170–2 for discussion; he favours the view that Gonatas took Megara during the Chremonidean War.

[4] See above, p. 270 nn. 3–4.　　　　[5] J. 26. 2. 1–6.　　　　[6] P*Agis* 3. 7.

[7] Cf. R. Stroud, *Hesperia*, 40 (1971) 127–45; the historical conclusions are on pp. 139–45.

Patroclus (see below) might have been tempted to take against Cenchreae. Antigonus' firm control of the Isthmus certainly goes some way towards explaining the failure of the Ptolemaic forces stationed in Attica to furnish Areus with any effective help.[1]

In fact, despite having provoked the war,[2] Ptolemy gave the allies little aid—though perhaps rather more than has frequently been supposed. Pausanias (1. 1. 1) attests the sending of the Ptolemaic admiral Patroclus to Greece and the stationing of a Ptolemaic force on the island of Gaidhouronisi (Patroklou), 4.5 kilometres west of Cape Sunium, probably in 268/7 at the beginning of the war. McCredie has shown from the evidence of pottery and Ptolemaic coins that there were Ptolemaic strong-points at this time at Koroni, Vuliagmeni, and Heliupolis, as well as at Patroklou Charax on Gaidhouronisi.[3] But that is not the only evidence of Egyptian help. An Athenian decree,[4] passed probably in 267/6, in honour of Epichares, who had held the post of general ἐπὶ τὴν χώραν τὴν παραλίαν during the archonship of Peithidemus (268/7), indicates that Rhamnus on the north-east coast of Attica was in Athenian hands (and not, as had previously been supposed,[5] in those of Antigonus). Epichares, who controlled an area of some 30-stades radius, had ensured the bringing in of the corn and fruit harvest and had protected the vines. He had taken steps to apprehend and punish certain Athenians who had collaborated with pirates,[6] and he had provided accommodation for Patroclus' soldiers who had brought help to Athens. That the pirates were in the pay of Antigonus is not stated, but seems very likely. The mention of pirates reminds us of the Glaucetas who operated under Antigonus I and was captured by the Athenian Thymochares of Sphettus in 315/14,[7] Timocles who fought against Rhodes in the interest of Demetrius I and was captured by the Rhodians in 304,[8] and Ameinias, the Phocian

---

[1] J. 26. 2. 16 mentions Ptolemaic troops as well as Spartan in his account of the destruction of the Gauls. See below, p. 284 n. 4.

[2] See above, p. 279; on the meagreness of his support cf. Paus. 1. 7. 3 ἀπ' αὐτοῦ οὐδὲν μέγα ἐγένετο ἐς σωτηρίαν Ἀθηναίοις.

[3] The evidence for other sites is not decisive for the Chremonidean War. For discussion see Heinen, *Unters.* 159–67, with a useful map on p. 164. The presence of Ptolemaic coins certainly suggests that of Ptolemaic troops, since Ptolemaic coins are rarely found abroad in purely commercial contexts (cf. Will 1². 179 n. 1). The dating of the pottery found at Koroni to the time of the Chremonidean War (E. Vanderpool, J. R. McCredie, A. Steinberg, 'A Ptolemaic camp on the east coast of Attica', *Hesperia* 31 (1962) 26–61) was queried by G. R. Edwards (*Hesperia* 32 (1963) 109–11) and V. R. Grace (ibid. 319–34); but the excavators have defended their view successfully (*Hesperia* 33 (1964) 69–75).

[4] *SEG* 24. 154; originally published by B. Chr. Petrakos in *AD* 22. 1 (1967) 38 ff.; cf. J. and L. Robert, *Bull. épig.* 1968, 247. A full text and commentary in Heinen, *Unters.* 152–9.

[5] So Pouilloux, *Rhamnonte* 118.

[6] ll. 21–3 ἐκόλασε δὲ καὶ τοὺ[ς κ]αθηγουμένους εἰς τ[ὴ]ν χώραν τοῖς πειραταῖς, λαβὼν καὶ ἐξετάσας αὐτούς, ὄν[τα]ς ἐκ τῆς πόλεως, [ἀξίω]ς ὧν ἔπραττον.

[7] *SIG* 409 ll. 10–14.

[8] D.S. 20. 97. 5.

284   *Antigonus Gonatas: The Early Years*

'archpirate', who had earlier helped Antigonus himself to take Cassandreia.[1] Later Philip V was to use the Aetolian Dicaearchus to plunder the Aegean islands and assist the Cretans against Rhodes.[2] The decree for Epichares supports the archaeological evidence, which shows Ptolemaic troops, though probably in small numbers, operating at various points in Attica. But Pausanias records Patroclus' reluctance to attack the Macedonians by land in support of Areus' invasion in 267.[3] This suggests that in 266 Ptolemaic forces may once again have advanced towards the Isthmus, but that when Antigonus crushed the Gallic mutineers, they (like the Spartans) retired 'in tutiora'.[4]

The main Ptolemaic help for the allies seems to have come from operations directed from the islands, in particular from Arsinoe (Coresia) on Ceos, which was probably Patroclus' main base.[5] There is also evidence for his presence at Thera and at Itanus and Olus in Crete.[6] If any corn was sent, this action has left no trace in the evidence. Indeed, taken as a whole Ptolemaic aid was unimpressive. Why this was so remains a mystery. Perhaps Ptolemy lacked a firm commitment to the war he had played a large part in provoking, or he may have been diverted by unrecorded Macedonian naval activity in areas more vital to his interests, such as Asia Minor. But, for whatever reasons, he failed to give adequate backing to Areus in his attempt to break through the lines at Corinth and he brought little help to the beleaguered Athenians.[7]

In contrast to Ptolemy, Antigonus fought with vigour: for him, of course, more was at stake. His personal intervention against Areus in 267 and 266 was decisive in preventing a juncture between the Spartan and Athenian armies and in 265 caused Areus' death at Corinth.[8] At the same time he directed attacks by land and sea against Attica. As we have seen (above, p. 283), his use of pirates acting in conjunction with supporters in the city had embarrassed the general Epichares in the first year of the war. There is, however, evidence that the pressure was

---

[1] See above, pp. 257–8. Pirates were often enrolled as mercenaries; cf. D.S. 20. 110 (8,000 in Demetrius' army invading Thessaly in 302; they were perhaps freebooters).

[2] Plb. 18. 54. 8–12; D.S. 28. 1.

[3] Paus. 3. 6. 5 οὐκ εἰκὸς εἶναι σφᾶς Αἰγυπτίους τε ὄντας καὶ ναύτας Μακεδόσιν ἐπιέναι πεζῇ.

[4] J. 26. 2. 7.

[5] On the site of Arsinoe see Robert, *Hellenica* 11–12. 146 ff.; Heinen, *Unters.* 150 n. 240. For Patroclus' stay on Ceos cf. *IG* xii. 5. 1061 ll. 2–4.

[6] For Thera cf. *IG* xii. 3. 320 = *OGI* 44; Heinen, *Unters.* 148–9; for Itanus and Olus cf. *IC* iii. 4. 3 ll. 4 ff.; ibid. i. 22. 4A ll. 35–42; Heinen, *Unters.* 143–8; see also Will 1². 226. For a possible explanation of the remoteness from Greece of these Ptolemaic naval forces see below, p. 290.

[7] See also above, pp. 278–9, for discussion of Ptolemy's commitment to the war.

[8] Trog. *Prol.* 26 'regemque Lacedaemoniorum Area Corinthi interfecit [sc. Antigonus]'; P*Agis* 3. 4.

maintained, in the shape of two honorific Athenian inscriptions[1] recording decrees passed in 266/5 and referring to events of 267/6. Of these the first is a decree of the Assembly for the Athenian ephebes of the year of Menecles' archonship (267/6), who had satisfactorily carried out their duties, including the guarding of the Museum hill in time of war, and the second (which exists in two fragmentary copies) honours a certain Strombichus, who had originally served in the Macedonian garrison on the acropolis, but had joined the Athenians in 288/7 (see above, p. 230 n. 4) and now in 266/5 did further service to the Athenian cause, in recognition of which he was awarded Athenian citizenship. Another decree of 266/5,[2] referring to the sacrifice carried out by the archon, includes on this occasion the unusual phrase 'for the health and safety of the crops on the land' (ἐφ' ὑγιείαι καὶ σωτηρίαι...τῶν καρπῶν τῶν ἐν τῆι χώραι), evidently introduced because of the presence of hostile Macedonian forces in Attica. These inscriptions in fact tell us very little beyond what is self-evident about the effects of the war on Attica. The surprising thing is that, even after Areus' death in 265, and with it an end to all hope of help from the Peloponnese, the Athenians managed to hold out for another three years.[3]

One factor may have been a diversion in the north. It was probably in 262/1 that Macedonia was invaded by Alexander II, the king of the Molossians and *hegemon* of the Epirote League.[4] Justin tells us that he sought to avenge the death of his father Pyrrhus, and no doubt he hoped to exploit Antigonus' difficulties in Greece. That he was incited by Ptolemy Philadelphus, as Bevan believed,[5] is neither attested in the sources nor inherently likely. Realizing that this invasion must take precedence over the affairs in central Greece, Antigonus marched north to confront Alexander, and the attack quickly ended in failure. Alexander was driven out of Macedonia[6] and, following on that, from Epirus itself, so that he was compelled to seek refuge in Acarnania.[7] His expulsion from Epirus created a dangerous situation

---

[1] *IG* II/III². 665 (= *SIG* 385), honouring the Athenian ephebes; *IG* II/III². 666–7 (= *SIG* 386–7) for Strombichus. Both decrees were passed in the year of Nicias (266/5) and refer to that of Menecles (267/6). On the dating of Peithidemus, Menecles, and Nicias (Otryneus) see Heinen, *Unters.* 113.

[2] *IG* II/III². 668 (= *SIG* 388). [3] Paus. 3. 6. 6 ἐπὶ μακροτάτου.

[4] J. 26. 2. 9–3. 1. Justin's statement that Antigonus was deserted by his troops and defeated by Alexander and in consequence lost Macedonia is clearly a false echo of Antigonus' defeat at the hands of Pyrrhus' son Ptolemy in 274 or 273 (see above, p. 263 n. 3).

[5] Bevan, *Ptol. Dyn.* 67.

[6] If the army which expelled him was commanded by the future Demetrius II 'puer admodum' (as J. 26. 2. 11 asserts), his command may have been only nominal; but in any case this passage is highly unreliable (see above, n. 4). It should however be noted that Perseus held such a command at the age of thirteen (Livy 31. 28); cf. Tarn, *AG* 304 n. 83.

[7] J. 26. 3. 1.

on the northern frontiers of Aetolia and it may have been this context of shared apprehension that brought Aetolia and Acarnania briefly together to make the treaty of alliance which Will has plausibly dated to this period.[1]

Antigonus took Alexander's invasion very seriously. He was hardly likely to forget how successful Alexander's father Pyrrhus had been in winning support in Macedonia. To cover his withdrawal to the north he seems to have made a peace with Athens[2] in the autumn of 262. But once Alexander had been expelled, Antigonus returned to Attica, where the war again broke out as if the peace had been no more than a truce. If Polyaenus is to be believed, the Athenians had used their reserve corn as seed and now found themselves in a desperate situation. Very soon they were suffering from famine and were compelled to capitulate in the spring of 261.[3]

This disaster brought a temporary end to Athenian independence and a period of occupation which was to last for some years. Besides the forces already present in the Piraeus and Munychia, Athens was now obliged to admit a Macedonian garrison onto the Museum hill, where it exercised control over the city itself and the territory of Attica.[4] There were also Macedonian units at various other points—Eleusis, Rhamnus, and Sunium and the frontier posts at Panactum and Phyle.[5] Antigonus also made changes in the internal administration of Athens. The post of hoplite general was abrogated, since there was no longer to be an independent Athenian army, though the two regional commanders, the στρατηγοὶ ἐπ' Ἐλευσῖνος and ἐπὶ τὴν παραλ-ίαν, were retained.[6] These posts were filled, however, by men appointed by the king, whose choice was then ratified by the people. The only known example of this procedure is that furnished by a

---

[1] *IG* ix. 1². 1. 3A = *SVA* 480 (found at Olympia in 1879). For this dating see Will 1². 227–8, with a full discussion. For other suggested dates see Schmitt, *SVA* 480. The alliance did not outlive for very long the circumstances in which it was made.

[2] Polyaen. 4. 6. 20, who interprets the peace as a trick to cause the Athenians to sow most of their corn, so that when the Macedonians returned and denied them access to their fields they could be starved out. That this is an *ex eventu* interpretation is convincingly argued by Heinen, *Unters.* 177–80. The peace is described by Polyaenus without a chronological context, but it best suits 262 and the circumstances created by Alexander's invasion of Macedonia.

[3] The evidence is in Paus. 3. 6. 6; Polyaen. 4. 6. 20; Philodemus, Περὶ τῶν Στωικῶν col. iii = Apollodorus, *FGrH* 244 F 44; it is conveniently assembled in *SVA* 477; see also Heinen, *Unters.* 180–1. Philodemus dates the peace to the archonship of Antipater. That this fell in 262/1 is confirmed by the strong arguments of R. Étienne and M. Piérart (*BCH* 99 (1975) 59–62) in favour of placing the Delphic archon Pleiston, not in 266/5 (so Daux and Nachtergael), but in 262/1; for Pleiston's year of office will then be the last in the sequence in which Athens is represented at the Delphic Amphictyony (*ISE* 75). It follows that by 260/59 (Peithagoras) or 261/0 (Delphic archon unknown) Athens was under Macedonian control; and the Athenian archon Antipater will have held office in 262/1. See Habicht, *Unters.* 74 n. 40; *Studien* 13 n. 1.

[4] Paus. 3. 3. 6; Philodemus, loc. cit. (n. 3).

[5] See Habicht, *Studien* 55–9 on these posts.   [6] Ibid. 43–7.

decree honouring the general Apollodorus passed by the *isoteleis* of Rhamnus.[1] In this Apollodorus is described as 'appointed general by King Antigonus and voted [by the people] to the coastal command' (κ]ατασταθεὶς στρατηγὸς ὑπό τε τοῦ βασιλέως Ἀντιγόνου καὶ [ὑπὸ τοῦ δήμου] χειροτονηθεὶς ἐπὶ τὴν χώραν τὴν παραλίαν). But it is likely that the same procedure was regularly used in filling all the *strategiai*. There is some evidence that Antigonus also appointed a governor of Athens to whom the generals were subordinated. According to Hegesander,[2] Demetrius, the grandson of Demetrius of Phalerum, was designated *thesmothetes* by Antigonus and Habicht has argued that, since there is no evidence that Antigonus nominated archons, this title was applied to the governor of Athens in preference to the now offensive word *epistates*. Finally, Antigonus appears to have substituted a single post of ὁ ἐπὶ τῇ διοικήσει for the former board bearing that title.[3]

These measures ensured that henceforth the city was under the effective control of friends of Macedonia. But from the formal aspect the changes were not very radical and this suggests that Antigonus was anxious to go a considerable way in softening the blow. Whether these constitutional modifications were embodied in the peace treaty or imposed at the time of the capitulation—or both—is unknown.[4] For the Athenians the outcome was deeply humiliating, however much Antigonus might seek to disguise the fact. Chremonides and Glaucus both fled to Egypt. The activity of the Assembly was much curtailed; indeed it was restricted to passing resolutions which met with Macedonian approval.[5] The minting of coinage was suspended and was perhaps not resumed until 229—though whether this was a cause or a result of the progressive economic decline which afflicted Athens from this time onwards, is not clear.[6] The military defeat of Athens also coincided with the end of a cultural era. Zeno of Citium died about the end of the Chremonidean War, and the comic poet Philemon around the same time; and Philochorus' execution for treasonable communications with Alexandria brought an end to the writing of Athenian local

---

[1] Cf. Pouilloux, *Rhamnonte* 118 no. 7 = *SEG* 3. 122 = *ISE* 1. 22. The *isoteleis* are a group of non-citizens of a higher status than metics, since they have been accorded a position equal to that of citizens in relation to taxes. Habicht, *Studien* 49–59, has shown clearly that a fragmentary Eleusinian decree honouring a general Demetrius (*IG* II². 1285 = *SEG* 3. 123), which has sometimes been adduced as evidence that hipparchs were also appointed by the same method as *strategoi*, contains no reference to Antigonus and is irrelevant in this connection.

[2] In Athen. 4. 167 f. See Habicht, *Studien* 18–19. Ferguson, *HA* 183, and Tarn, *AG* 307 assume that Demetrius was appointed as one of the lesser archons.

[3] Habicht, *Studien* 15.

[4] Paus. 3. 6. 6 suggests the former, Polyaen. 4. 6. 20 the latter; but neither is a source which merits to be pressed closely.

[5] Cf. Rhodes 78 ff.; Habicht, *Studien* 20–4.

[6] T. Hackens, *BCH* 93 (1969) 706 and n. 23; Habicht, *Studien* 34–42. There is no direct evidence for any ban on coining.

history.[1] A few years later, in 256/5 or 255/4, Athenian freedom was nominally restored,[2] with the withdrawal of the garrison from Athens and the removal of the Macedonian governor. This represented a real change in the situation of Athens, which could once more resume its status as a sovereign state—though the continued occupation of the Piraeus and Munychia ensured that the city remained politically shackled.

That Antigonus was unable to curb Sparta in the same way was the happy result of her geographical position; but the loss of Areus was compounded by the death of his son Acrotatus while attacking Megalopolis at some date before 255,[3] and Sparta was not to constitute a danger for Macedonia for the next few decades. Antigonus' hold on Corinth, which his half-brother Craterus governed as his loyal deputy, placed him in a strong position relative to the Peloponnese, where Argos in particular was friendly. But further north the situation was less satisfactory for Macedonia. There is no independent evidence for fighting in central Greece. On the other hand, a decree of the Amphictyonic Council[4] refers to the widespread distress experienced in those parts in what is probably the year 261/0. The Council of that year had prevailed on both Antigonus and Ptolemy, as well as other states, to grant safe conduct to those who would be visiting the Pythian games of (presumably) 260/59. Evidently the war was now over, but the inscription indicates to what extent normal traffic and in particular the holding of Amphictyonic meetings had been disrupted, probably by considerable fighting, throughout its duration: τῆς συ[νόδου τῶν Ἀμφικτυόνων ἐν] Θερμοπύλαις διὰ τὸν πόλε[μον διακωλυθείσης ἐπὶ χρό]νον πολύν. The Council of 261/0 are praised by their successors of 260/59 for having organized the first meeting since this interruption. The tone of the decree is strictly neutral. But in the Delphic archonship of Pleiston (262/1),[5] at a time when the fate of Athens was either imminent or already decided, the Council had given some indication of where Aetolian sympathies lay, by choosing the moment of Antigonus' triumph to register its acceptance of Philadelphus' request to recognize the Alexandrian *Ptolemaieia* proclaiming the divinity of Ptolemy Soter

---

[1] Cf. Heinen, *Unters.* 204–5.

[2] See below, p. 293 n. 4. On what was involved see J. Briscoe in Garnsey and Whittaker 149; J. Pouilloux, *BCH* 70 (1946) 489–96, who regards the concessions as of little substantial importance (*contra*, Habicht, *Studien* 20).   [3] See above, p. 273 nn. 1–2.

[4] *Delphes* 3. 1. 479 = *SEG* 2. 261 = *ISE* 2. 76 (with bibliography). The most probable date for the decree is 260/59, and the Council honoured in it will be that of 261/0, a year for which the name of the Delphic archon is unknown (see above, p. 286 n. 3). See Heinen, *Unters.* 139 ff.; Moretti ad loc. (*ISE* 2. 76).

[5] See above, p. 286 n. 3. The acceptance is recorded in *ISE* 2. 75. On the delay see Étienne and Piérart, art. cit. (above, p. 286 n. 3) 62–7; Habicht, *Gottmenschentum* 258–9 (with the correction of the date of Pleiston's archonship in *Unters.* 75 n. 46).

—almost twenty years after the setting up of the festival. Heinen suggests[1] that this action was a *quid pro quo* for Ptolemy's grant of *asphaleia* in the following year; but the two matters are probably independent of each other. On the other hand, in accepting the *Ptolemaieia* the Aetolians were clearly indicating that they were not over-impressed by Antigonus' subjugation of Athens.

The Aetolian League and the Delphic Amphictyony had both been at pains to observe neutrality in the war, but it was an unfriendly neutrality as far as Macedonia was concerned.[2] Moreover, the Aetolian League had used the years of disturbance to make further acquisitions which could only embarrass Macedonia. The evidence for this is once again to be found in the details of the *hieromnemones* attending meetings of the Amphictyonic Council. In the Delphic archonship of Damaeus (265/4) the Locrians (probably the Epicnemidian Locrians around Scarpheia and Thronium) were still exercising one vote, but for the next year (that of Damosthenes) this disappears and instead, under Damosthenes and Pleiston (262/1), the Phocian vote goes up from two to three, an increase which evidently reflects the annexation of Epicnemidian Locris by Phocis.[3] The archonship of Peithagoras, which is most likely to have been in 260/59, marks the beginning of a new distribution of voting power. Phocis had apparently lost one vote to Aetolia, which now had seven votes, and that suggests that by this time Epicnemidian Locris had been absorbed into the Aetolian League, which thus acquired a seaboard on the straits of Euboea. This expansion continued in the following years, for shortly afterwards the Aetolian votes rose from seven to nine. The two additional votes will reflect the annexation of part of Phocis (probably the southern area around Mt. Parnassus) and perhaps the western part of Phthiotic Achaea. In both these states the existence of cities facilitated such a partial transfer.[4] These acquisitions brought the Aetolians ever nearer to the Gulf of Pagasae and increased the threat to Macedonian communications with southern Greece. In consequence, the possession of Corinth became if anything even more central to Antigonus' strategy for controlling Greece and, with it, the firm control of Piraeus and the coastline of Attica, to secure his line of communication. So long as this fortress was in the loyal hands of Craterus all was well. But, as events were later to show, so great a concentration of power in a single man would very quickly constitute a danger, should Craterus' eventual successor ever waver in his loyalty to the king.

---

[1] *Unters.* 140. Heinen, who was writing before the publication of the article by Étienne and Piérart (above, p. 286 n. 3), accepts an early dating for both *ISE* 2. 75 and *ISE* 2. 76.

[2] See also Flacelière 196–7; Will 1² 230–1 (with bibliography).

[3] Cf. G. Klaffenbach, *Klio* 20 (1926) 68–81.

[4] Cf. Flacelière 198–201, who suggests that the Aetolians annexed the part of Phocis around Parnassus and, in Phthiotic Achaea, Melitaea, and the western part of the region; Nachtergael 281.

XIII

ANTIGONUS GONATAS: THE NAVAL
SITUATION (261–251 B.C.)

OR the decade following the conclusion of the Chremonidean
War almost no information has survived which might throw light
on Macedonian policy and any reconstruction of either aims or
events is open to correction as new evidence appears. Such evidence as
we have at present suggests that during the next few years Antigonus
followed up his victory in Greece with a policy of naval expansion
which took the Macedonian fleet into Ptolemaic waters. What kind of
ships he built is not known, but since he had Egypt in mind the
majority must have been quinqueremes and quadriremes. Later both
Philip V and Perseus built and used *lembi*, but against the Ptolemaic
fleet larger vessels are certainly more likely. The oarsmen presumably
came from the maritime cities of Macedonia, but marines will have
been enrolled from Macedonian soldiers. That this was a new initiative
undertaken after 261, is, however, by no means certain. Indeed, Will
has plausibly dated the revival of a Macedonian naval policy to the
year after Antigonus' defeat of Pyrrhus and has argued that it was
largely in response to this policy that Ptolemy incited Athens and
Sparta to revolt.[1] Moreover, the relatively weak support given to the
Greeks by Patroclus is more readily understandable if the efforts of the
Ptolemaic fleet during the war were hampered by the need to deal with
Macedonian naval activity in other waters—for example off the coast
of Asia Minor.[2] But on our present evidence this can be no more than
speculation.

For the period after the war a background against which Macedonian naval expansion may possibly have taken place is furnished by the
Second Syrian War between Ptolemy II and Antiochus II, which
broke out in 260 and lasted until 253. This war seems to have been the
result of Ptolemy II's determination to exploit Seleucid weakness at the
beginning of a new reign (Antiochus II having succeeded his father in
261).[3] One of the few events which we can assign to it is the revolt at
Miletus of 'Ptolemy the Son'—probably Ptolemy II's co-ruler—

---

[1] Will 1². 219–21; see above, pp. 278–9.
[2] See above, pp. 279, 283–4; and cf. Walbank in Adams and Borza 218–20.
[3] On the war see Will 1². 234–9, with discussion and bibliography.

assisted by a certain Timarchus, who followed up his revolt by making himself tyrant in the city, where he continued to rule until expelled by Antiochus' confidant, Hippomachus.[1] The war was brought to an end in *c.* 253, after Antiochus had made gains in Ionia, Cilicia, and Pamphylia,[2] and peace was sealed with a marriage alliance between Antiochus II himself and Berenice, the daughter of Ptolemy II. By divorcing Laodice in order to contract a new marriage, Antiochus was laying up much future trouble for himself. But what concerns us here is the question whether Antigonus intervened in any way in this war. Help from Antigonus would no doubt have been welcome and might have seemed a suitable *quid pro quo*, if indeed it was Antiochus I who sent the Gallic mercenaries who mutinied at Megara to help in the Chremonidean War.[3] Unfortunately there is no direct and uncontrovertible evidence to settle this matter one way or the other.[4] There is, however, the relevant problem of the naval battle of Cos.

This battle was fought near Leucolla off the island of Cos between Antigonus II and Ptolemy's admiral Patroclus. Some hints concerning its historical context are to be found in an anecdote retailed by Phylarchus,[5] according to which Patroclus, on some unspecified occasion, sent Antigonus a present of large fish and green figs 'as an indication of what would happen to him, just as the Scythians did to Darius, when he was invading their country. For the Scythians, Herodotus tells us [4. 131], sent a bird, an arrow, and a frog.' Antigonus, we are told, at once solved the riddle: 'either we must be masters of the sea (*thalassokratein*) or else we must eat figs', that is, go short![6] If the story is true, the message was a challenge and the anecdote has point only if Antigonus took up the challenge and won. The location of the battle, close to Philadelphus' birthplace, the island of Cos, sacred to him as Delos was sacred to Apollo (according to Theocritus 17. 66–70), implies a Macedonian campaign in the southeastern waters of the Aegean, near Caria and the Sporades. The date of the battle of Cos has been the subject of long controversy. In Appendix 4[7] I give the reasons which seem to me to favour dating it to 255 and making it an incident in the Second Syrian War, with Antigonus

---

[1] On these events see Appendix 4 p. 590. The revolt at Miletus was in 259 and the overthrow of Timarchus sometime before the death of Antiochus II in 246.

[2] Cf. H. Heinen, *CAH* 7² 1. 419. [3] See above, p. 282.

[4] On this see, most recently, Will 1². 238–9, who vigorously defends a sceptical position.

[5] Athen. 8. 334 a = *FGrH* 81 F 1; cf. Heinen, *Unters.* 191–2.

[6] See my discussion of the story, art. cit. (above, p. 290 n. 2) 213–15. In 201/0 Philip V's army was in fact obliged to eat figs, when trapped in the Bay of Bargylia: Plb. 16. 24. 9 = Athen. 3. 78 e–f.

[7] In the article mentioned above (p. 290 n. 2), 2, I put Cos in the spring of 261 at the end of the Chremonidean War. This still seems to me to be possible, but Buraselis 146–51, has given various reasons which make 255 a more attractive date.

intervening as an ally of Antiochus. But, as I there insist, an alternative date is 261, after Athens had fallen but before the Chremonidean War was officially over; for by that time (it was the archon year of Tharsynon at Delos)[1] the Delian records find it possible to speak of health, peace, and wealth existing (in the Aegean?). On balance, however, the arguments for 255 seem the stronger.

Antigonus celebrated his victory with a dedication on Delos. According to Athenaeus (probably quoting Moschion),[2] Antigonus dedicated his flagship there and it has been plausibly suggested that it was placed in the Neorion or 'Hall of the Bulls', which is now known to have been adapted at a later date to take a larger ship than the one planned for in the original construction in the late fourth century. Why Moschion (or Athenaeus) refers to the ship as ἱερὰν τριήρη is obscure. It is perhaps called 'sacred' because it was dedicated, but a Hellenistic flagship at this date cannot have been anything smaller than a quinquereme. It has been argued that in celebration of his victory Antigonus instituted the 'vase-festivals' of the *Antigoneia* and the *Stratoniceia* on Delos in 253.[3] But it is hard to see why there should have been a two-year interval between a victory in 255 and their institution in 253, or why festivals set up to celebrate that victory should have been named after Antigonus himself and his sister Stratonice.[4] Antigonus did, however, also celebrate his victory at Cos by the erection on Delos of a portico bounding the north of the *hieron*. On its eastern side stood the so-called 'Monument of the Ancestors', which contained statuary representing at least ten of his forebears. Both these monuments were dedicated appropriately to Apollo.[5]

There is no evidence that Gonatas continued to operate against Ptolemy after his victory off Cos. Indeed, a Delian inscription[6] of 255 testifies that there was peace in that year (the archonship of Antigonus II). Whether this implies a formal peace or merely peaceful conditions in the Aegean is not clear. The use of a similar expression in 261 certainly coincided with the formal end of the Chremonidean War, but it does not follow that Antigonus made a separate peace with Ptolemy in 255.[7] If, in fact, his participation in the war was merely on the basis

---

[1] *IG.* XI. 2. 114 ll. 1 ff. ['Eπ' ἄρ]χοντος Θαρσύνοντος τοῦ X[οι]ρύλου ὑγίεια εἰρήνη πλοῦτος ἐγένετο.   [2] Athen. 5. 209 e; see for discussion Appendix 4 pp. 595–6.

[3] See Appendix 4 pp. 598–9 for the argument of Buraselis and criticism of it.

[4] The victory of Andros was probably celebrated by the institution of the vase-festivals of the *Paneia* and *Soteria* in 245. These titles have quite a different sound about them (see Appendix 4 pp. 592–3), being named exceptionally after the god or gods to whom the offering was made.

[5] For a description see F. Courby, *Délos* 5. *Le portique d'Antigone ou du nord-est* (1912) 38–40; see further Durrbach, *Choix* nos. 35 and 36; Bruneau 552 f.   [6] *IG* XI. 2. 116.

[7] The presence of Argive *theoroi* in Alexandria in September 254 (*P. Lond.* 7 no. 1973 ll. 5 ff.) is not proof of a formal peace between Antigonus and Ptolemy, despite the likelihood that Argos was at this time in Antigonus' sphere of interest.

of bringing help to Antiochus as the victim of aggression, a separate peace would not be necessary.[1] A passage in Diogenes Laertius (4. 6. 39) informs us that while he was in Athens after his victory Antigonus received many appeals.[2] The context of Diogenes' story implies that these appeals were on behalf of Athens; and it is in fact this that makes the passage the strongest piece of evidence in favour of dating Cos in 255, since such a crop of petitions centring on Athens must surely have been appeals for the removal of the Macedonian garrison. That it would have seemed worth while making such an appeal in 261, immediately after the city had capitulated, is highly improbable. But in 255, following the battle of Cos, there were excellent reasons for pointing out that Antigonus' decisive naval victory had removed all danger from Egypt, thus rendering the Macedonian garrison in Athens superfluous. It appears that the appeal was successful for, according to Eusebius, it was either in 256/5 or 255/4[3] that Antigonus 'gave freedom to Athens'; and this statement is confirmed by Pausanias, who reports (3. 6. 6) that τοῖς μὲν ἀνὰ χρόνον αὐτὸς ἤγαγεν ἑκουσίως τὴν φρουρὰν Ἀντίγονος.[4] For Athens this was a substantial concession, though the continued Macedonian occupation of the Piraeus with Munychia, and the presence of Macedonian garrisons at other strongpoints[5] placed an effective curb on what the Athenians were free to do—which was, briefly, anything that the king of Macedonia approved of. The removal of Macedonian troops from Athens is certainly not to be regarded as a relaxation of Antigonus' interest in southern and central Greece. As has already been noted,[6] from 255 onwards no *hieromnemones* from Histiaea appear at the Amphictyonic Council, whence it seems likely that Antigonus followed up his victory off Cos by intensifying his control of Euboea.

Antigonus' successes on land in the Chremonidean War and at sea in his victory over the Ptolemaic fleet at Cos resulted in a general strengthening of the Macedonian position in the Aegean. But that is not to say that the Egyptian thalassocracy had been permanently

---

[1] For discussion see Will I². 238, with arguments against Otto, *Beiträge* 44 ff.; *Philol.* 86 (1931) 416 f., who argued for a separate peace between Antigonus and Ptolemy. Will rightly observes that one cannot use a presumed peace in 255 to support a presumed war before that date.

[2] See Appendix 4 pp. 596–8.   [3] See Appendix 4 p. 596 n. 8 (for references).

[4] Cf. Habicht, *Studien* 16 n. 16, who links the evidence of Eusebius and Pausanias on this point. For bibliography concerning the restoration see above, p. 288 with n. 2.

[5] On the occupation of Rhamnus, Eleusis, Panactum, Phyle, Salamis, and Sunium see Habicht, *Studien* 56–9. Piraeus, Salamis and Sunium remained in Macedonian hands until 229 (*PArat* 34. 5–6, Paus. 2. 8. 6) and Rhamnus is likely to have gone with them. But the other forts—Eleusis, Phyle, and Panactum—were probably restored to Athens sometime between 240 and 235, a likely date being after Demetrius II's acquisition of Boeotia (see below, p. 326).

[6] See above, p. 271.

broken or substantially impaired. The institution of the *Antigoneia* and the *Stratoniceia* vase-festivals in 253[1] certainly suggests that Alexandrian control of Delos was no longer effective in that year. It is true that Delos was an international shrine and Egyptian control would not necessarily exclude a private dedication by another ruler. It is, however, rather unlikely that two years after his great victory over Ptolemy Antigonus would have chosen Delos for his dedication, if Ptolemy was still master of the island. A weakening of the Ptolemaic position in the Aegean is further attested by the fact that no nesiarch of the Island League is known after 260.[2] But this evidence is far from proving a complete collapse of Ptolemaic power. Several inscriptions which mention a King Antigonus, from Syros, Ios, Minoa on Amorgos, Cimolos, and Cos (together with a similar inscription from Poiessa on Ceos, which does not mention the king's name),[3] have been taken as evidence for an Antigonid domination of the islands. But so long as it remains uncertain whether the Antigonus in question is Gonatas or Doson, these documents provide no independent evidence for the domination of the Aegean by Antigonus II. Indeed, the only clear reference to Macedonian possessions there under Gonatas is to Andros, which was in Macedonian hands when Aratus sailed for Egypt in 251.[4] It has also been held that a passage in Athenaeus (9. 400 d, quoting Hegesander of Delphi) indicates that Antigonus possessed Astypalaea, in the south-east Aegean.[5] But the inscription *IG* XII. 3. 204 suggests that the place was Ptolemaic. Hegesander merely mentions a plague of hares occurring there during Antigonus' reign; he does not say that Antigonus owned the island and, since he is known to have deliberately avoided writing about the Ptolemies,[6] no weight can be attached to this passage. Nor is it safe to build very much on an anecdote related by Sex. Empiricus.[7] In this Sostratus, when sent as envoy by Ptolemy to Antigonus and faced with unpalatable proposals, quoted to the latter Iris' words to Poseidon (Homer, *Iliad* 15. 201 ff.) in which she suggested that the earth-shaker might change the reply she was to convey back to Zeus. By this deft quotation Sostratus caused

---

[1] Cf. Bruneau 518 ff., 557 ff.; Buraselis 143.

[2] Cf. I. L. Merker, *Historia* 19 (1970) 159 ff.; Will 1². 233. This would of course support a date of 261 for the battle of Cos as well as (or even in preference to) 255.

[3] *IG* XI. 4. 1052 and supplement (Syros); XII. 5. 570 (Ceos), 1008 (Ios); XII. 7. 221–3 (Amorgos); T. W. Jacobsen and P. M. Smith, *Hesperia* 37 (1968) 184–99 (Cimolos); *GDI* 3611 (Cos); cf. Will 1². 232, 238–9.

[4] Cf. P*Arat* 12. 2 (accepting Palmerius' reading Ἀ⟨ν⟩δρίας for the MS. Ἀδρίας; Bergk emended to Ὑδρίας or Ὑδρείας).

[5] Cf. Fraser–Bean 157 n. 1.

[6] Cf. F. Jacoby, *RE* s.v. *Hegesandros* (4) col. 2600; he wrote on the kings of Macedonia and Syria: 'die Ptolemäer fehlen ganz gewiss nicht zufällig.'

[7] *adv. math.* 1. 276.

Antigonus to think again. Buraselis[1] interprets the story to mean that Sostratus, in the course of negotiations for peace between the two kings, warned Gonatas not to regard his victory at Cos as giving him more than a local thalassocracy in the Aegean; but this is surely to read too much into the anecdote, and Heinen is rightly sceptical.

Buraselis has argued[2] that the difficulty in gaining a clear picture of Macedonian domination in the Aegean following Cos is due partly to Ptolemy's having succeeded, around the year 250, in staging a counter-offensive which largely cancelled out Antigonus' gains. There are three pieces of evidence which may point to such a comeback. The first is the founding of the *Ptolemaieia* festival on Delos by Ptolemy II in 249.[3] But this need only indicate that at that date Delos was not under the direct control of Antigonus, just as Antigonus' dedication of 253 indicated that the island was not under the direct control of Ptolemy; and, as we shall see below,[4] Gonatas' loss of Chalcis and Corinth as a result of the revolt of Alexander, the son of Craterus, will certainly have involved a catastrophic decline in Antigonus' naval effectiveness in the Aegean. Secondly, there is a reference *en passant* in Ps.-Aristeas (and following him in Josephus) to a naval victory of Ptolemy II over Antigonus,[5] an incident nowhere else mentioned. And finally a letter from Ptolemy's *dioiketes* Apollonius, dated January 250,[6] conveys orders for the marshalling and dispatch of a naval force, and this the editors have suggested is to be brought into relation with the vase-festival of the *Ptolemaieia* of 249. In a period when clues are thin on the ground these statements cannot be ignored. They come together satisfactorily, if around 250 Ptolemy sought out and defeated Antigonus' fleet, thereby to some extent reversing the result of Cos. But one would like to know where such a battle took place, why Antigonus' fleet was available and what the background was in terms of Antigonid and Ptolemaic policies. Until more evidence is available a query must attach itself to this hypothetical Ptolemaic recovery. Whatever the truth of this, however, it seems clear that during the fifties Ptolemy had not been completely ousted from his maritime supremacy in the Aegean. But the next developments in the struggle between the two rivals were to take place once again on the Greek mainland.

---

[1] Buraselis 165–7; on this story see also Tarn, *AG* 386 f.; Heinen, *Unters.* 196 f.; Fraser 2. 53 f.
[2] 170–1.   [3] Cf. *IG* XI. 2. 298 l. 76.   [4] See below, p. 301.
[5] See Appendix 4 p. 591 n. 4. Without necessarily accepting Tarn's view (*AG* 131 n. 43) that this is a confusion with the battle between Antigonus and Ptolemy Ceraunus, one must admit the validity of his observation that the story in Aristeas and Josephus appears to refer to a date early in Ptolemy's reign.
[6] Cf. P. M. Fraser and C. H. Roberts, *Chron. d'Égypte* 24 (1949) 289–94.

XIV

ANTIGONUS GONATAS: THE LAST YEARS
(251–239 B.C.)[1]

1. *The revolt of Alexander (251–245 B.C.)*

So long as Craterus, Antigonus' loyal half-brother, held Corinth, Macedonian power in central Greece was solidly based. But at the end of the fifties Craterus died. His death coincided with the startling rise to authority of a young Greek from Sicyon and together these two events shattered the basis of Antigonid power around the Isthmus. There had been little warning of this catastrophe, for the situation in this area and in the Peloponnese seemed wholly favourable to Macedonia. Megalopolis was in the strong hands of the tyrant Aristodamus, who still ruled there with the connivance and support of Antigonus.[2] Argos, it is true, apparently stood outside the Macedonian sphere of interest, for (as we shall see), in the years up to, and including, the spring of 252, it harboured a group of refugees hostile to tyrants and especially tyrants sponsored by Macedonia. Further, it is perhaps significant that in September 254 Egyptian records[3] show Argive *theoroi* present in Egypt; but as their purpose is not known— they may have been there to invite participation in the Nemea of 253—it is perhaps inadvisable to use their visit as an indication of the political sympathies of the city at this time, other than to note that the *theoria* would suit an unaligned Argos better than one closely linked to Antigonus.

It was in Sicyon, however, that the significant developments occurred. There Cleinias had successfully entertained friendly relations with Antigonus and Ptolemy alike, both during his joint magistracy with Timocleidas and after the latter's death as sole magistrate.[4] But in 264

---

[1] The main sources for the last decade or so of Antigonus' reign are Plutarch's *Lives* of Aratus and Agis of Sparta, based largely on the *Memoirs* of Aratus and the *History* of Phylarchus respectively (see Walbank, *A* 3 ff.); see also Paus. 2. 8. 1–4; Cic. *Off.* 2. 80–2. Phylarchus was a contemporary of Aratus and composed twenty-eight books of *Histories*, covering the period from 272 to the death of Cleomenes III in 220/19. He wrote in a sensational manner, appealing to the emotions of his readers, and was also a partisan of Sparta, which helps to explain the violent criticism of his work in Plb. 2. 56–63. For the chronology see Plb. 2. 43. 1–6, with Walbank, *C* 1. 234 ff.

[2] On Aristodamus see above, pp. 272–3.

[3] *P. Lond.* 7 no. 1973; cf. H. I. Bell, *Symb. Osl.* 5 (1927) 32–7; Urban 22 n. 88; Buraselis 165.

[4] See above, pp. 273–4.

FIG. 10. THE PELOPONNESE

he was assassinated by Abantidas,[1] who then ruled as tyrant for twelve years until, in 252, he was in turn murdered, by a man named Deinias (possibly the historian of Argos)[2] and by Aristotle 'the logician'. When Abantidas' father Paseas seized power, he in turn was assassinated by a certain Nicocles, who now himself became tyrant. There is no reason to think that Macedonia was directly involved in any of these events. But, as we know from Plutarch,[3] the royal Macedonian stud was at this time situated on Sicyonian territory and this is a clear indication that Nicocles was at least no enemy of Antigonus. That assumption is confirmed by the fact that, when a little later Aratus attacked Sicyon and set Nicocles' palace ablaze, the people of Corinth all but started out to bring help.[4]

Nicocles' tyranny was of brief duration. For Aratus, Cleinias' son, who upon his father's murder in 264 had found refuge in Argos and had been brought up there by family friends, was now twenty years old and the recognized leader of a group of Sicyonian exiles and other refugees from tyranny. Relying on Cleinias' family connections, Aratus made approaches to Antigonus and to Ptolemy Philadelphus.[5] But when no aid was forthcoming from either, he decided to act on his own initiative, relying solely on the help of his immediate friends, who included Ecdelus of Megalopolis, a pupil of Arcesilaus of the Athenian Academy and later to become famous as a fanatical foe of tyrants everywhere.[6]

In May 251,[7] in a well-organized coup, Aratus seized and liberated Sicyon and expelled its tyrant. Shortly afterwards he restored many political exiles, including eighty refugees from Nicocles and some 500 who had been in exile, in some cases for as long as fifty years.[8] This

---

[1] P*Arat* 2. 2; Paus. 2. 8. 2. Cleinias' son Aratus was seven years old. Since Aratus was born in 271 (Plb. 2. 43. 3: he was twenty in 251), Cleinias' murder was in 264.
[2] *FGrH* 306 T 1 = P*Arat* 3. 4.   [3] P*Arat* 6. 2; cf. Urban 21–2 n. 87.   [4] P*Arat* 9. 1.
[5] According to P*Arat* 4. 2, Nicocles suspected that Aratus was making approaches to Antigonus and Ptolemy. Urban 16–18, doubts the truth of these approaches at this stage; and certainly one might have expected a favourable reaction from Ptolemy to any project for overthrowing a tyranny friendly to Macedonia. But Nicocles only ruled for four months. Consequently, if Antigonus *was* asked for help, but ἠμέλει καὶ παρῆγε τὸν χρόνον (P*Arat* 4. 3), Aratus' first approaches must have taken place under Paseas (or even Abantidas).
[6] P*Arat* 5. 1. On Ecdelus and Demophanes (and the variant forms of their names) see K. Ziegler, *Rh. Mus.* 83 (1934) 228–33; Walbank, *C* 2. 223–4. These two men were later to enhance their reputation as liberators by their activities in Cyrene; cf. Will 1[2]. 245.
[7] Cf. P*Arat* 5–9 for a detailed account of the coup (based on Aratus' *Memoirs*); Plb. 2. 43. 3. P*Arat* 53. 5 gives the month of Aratus' coup as Daisios, which is the equivalent of May in the Macedonian calendar (it is equated with the Attic Thargelion: P*Cam* 19. 7; *PA* 16. 2). If, however, Daisios was a Sicyonian month (so Errington, *Philop.* 268 n. 2), the equation with Thargelion will not necessarily be valid. Errington himself puts the coup in February/March 249, i.e. at the end of the Achaean year 250/49, for it occurred in the eighth year before the liberation of Corinth (Plb. 2. 43. 4) in 243/2; and by inclusive reckoning Errington makes that the eighth year after 250/49. I am not at all persuaded that this chronology is preferable to that set out in *C* 1. 234.
[8] P*Arat* 9. 4.

group will have included hard-line anti-Macedonian politicians, expelled after Ipsus[1] and never restored by any of the subsequent tyrants or indeed by Cleinias, the cautious guest-friend of both Antigonus and Ptolemy. According to Plutarch,[2] Aratus now found Sicyon regarded with hostility by Antigonus, and it is a reasonable assumption that the cause of this hostility was not merely the expulsion of the tyrant, but also the fact that among the restored exiles Sicyon now harboured many bitter enemies of Macedonia. In the same passage Plutarch also states that Sicyon was the object of plots from outside. Obviously a city which had experienced so stormy a history since Ipsus and now had to cope with a variety of exiles—together, no doubt, with their dispossessors—within its walls, was particularly vulnerable to outside intrigue. It was to help solve this desperate problem and free Sicyon from its isolation that Aratus took a bold and far-reaching step, which was to reveal him as an imaginative statesman of a high order—and a formidable enemy of Macedonia. This was to bring Sicyon into the Achaean League as a full member. In doing so he made the decisive move towards transforming a small and rather insignificant ethnic association into a federal body potentially capable of wide extension throughout southern, and perhaps also central, Greece.[3]

The Achaean League, which embraced the Achaean cities along the southern shore of the Gulf of Corinth, had been active during the fifth century, but from about the middle of the fourth century little is heard of it, and during the period from Alexander's death until 281/0 it had apparently ceased to function.[4] In the last year of Ol. 224 (281/0), however, Dyme, Patrae, Tritaea, and Pharae had come together to reconstitute the Confederation, and the first 'Achaean year' of the new dispensation was reckoned May 280 to May 279.[5] In 275/4 these cities were joined by Aegium, which controlled the federal shrine of Zeus Homarius; and shortly afterwards Bura was brought in by the rest of the Achaeans, who killed its tyrant, whereupon Iseas the tyrant of Ceryneia resigned and joined his city to the League.[6] In 251 the Achaean League had become an effective state embracing ten cities, the other three being Leontium, Aegeira, and Pellene.[7] Since 255/4 its

---

[1] Cf. Porter 53 note on 9. 4; he quotes Schorn for this suggestion (cf. Freeman 280 n. 1).

[2] P*Arat* 9. 5: Aratus saw Sicyon φθονουμένην ὑπ' Ἀντιγόνου...διὰ τὴν ἐλευθερίαν; see Urban 24.

[3] Plb. 2. 43. 3; P*Arat* 9. 6; on the significance of this see Walbank, *A* 37–8.

[4] Cf. Plb. 2. 40. 5 διαλυθέντος τοῦ τῶν Ἀχαιῶν ἔθνους ὑπὸ τῶν ἐκ Μακεδονίας βασιλέων.

[5] Plb. 2. 41. 12; cf. 4. 60. 10. The union of these cities was a sequel to Gonatas' naval defeat at the hands of Ptolemy Ceraunus in 280 and links with Areus' defeat in Aetolia; see above, pp. 244–5, 249; cf. Urban 5–13.   [6] Plb. 2. 41. 13–15.

[7] Plb. 2. 41. 7–8 with Walbank, *C* 1. 230–2. An inscription (*SEG* 1. 74) shows Olenus as an eleventh member at some date after 272, but this city had disappeared by the time Polybius was writing.

chief officer was a single general (*strategos*), who entered office in May. Re-election was permitted, but not in consecutive years. By bringing Sicyon into this hitherto purely ethnic confederation Aratus strengthened it immeasurably as an instrument of anti-Macedonian agitation and military action in the northern Peloponnese.

This independent alignment of Sicyon and its new position within the Achaean League was a set-back for Antigonus. But worse was soon to come. In the first place, it was about this time—either just before or just after Aratus' liberation of Sicyon—that Ecdelus joined a fellow Megalopolitan, Demophanes, in assassinating Aristodamus, the tyrant of Megalopolis. This deprived Antigonus of one of his strongest supporters in the Peloponnese and it was probably in response to this set-back that he lent his help to Aristomachus (who was probably the son of Aristippus and a friend of Macedonia) in re-establishing the tyranny in Argos. In that way Argos might be expected to serve as a bulwark on the south side of Corinth and so present a firm obstacle to further Achaean expansion.[1] But more important than the defection of Sicyon and Megalopolis was the death of Antigonus' half-brother Craterus. In his place as governor of Corinth the king appointed Craterus' son, Alexander, thus confirming the impression that this important fortress was to stay under the control of a half-independent dynasty.

The union of Sicyon with the Achaean League did nothing in itself to resolve the serious financial problems arising out of the restoration of the exiles and the claims and counter-claims to property which that involved. A gift of 25 talents 'from the king' might have gone a little way (but not far) towards a solution, but Aratus preferred to use it for ransoming prisoners of war. The identity of the king who proferred this gift has been much discussed.[2] Holleaux, pointing out that the last king to be mentioned previously by Plutarch was Antigonus, argued that it was he who was indicated here; and this view has been widely followed. But it leaves unexplained why Antigonus, who was last referred to as hostile to Aratus, should suddenly send him a gift and why, having received it, Aratus should almost immediately afterwards see 'that his only hope lay in the generosity of Ptolemy.'[3] The possibility remains that Antigonus now made an unsuccessful attempt to buy Aratus' support. But it seems more likely that the king who sent the 25 talents was Ptolemy Philadelphus.

---

[1] On the problems which surround the beginnings of this dynasty of tyrants at Argos see above, p. 273.

[2] P*Arat* 11. 2; cf. Holleaux, *Études* 3. 43–6 = *Hermes* 41 (1906) 475–8; discussion in Will 1². 321.

[3] P*Arat* 12. 1; cf. Porter xli; and for a balanced discussion Urban 25–9, who finally leaves the identity of the king an open question, given the possibility that Antigonus may have been trying unsuccessfully to buy Aratus' support.

The Macedonian position in Greece suffered yet a further disastrous blow when, probably in 249, Craterus' son Alexander, the new governor of Corinth, revolted from Antigonus and declared himself independent.[1] An inscription from Eretria[2] in honour of Arrhidaeus, one of Alexander's supporters, gives the latter the title of king and also furnishes evidence that in defecting Alexander took much of Euboea with him, since the governor of Corinth also controlled Chalcis. Eretria hailed Alexander as a benefactor, who had liberated the city from Antigonus; and the Euboean League was now reconstituted. The evidence for this comes from the coinage. Picard, in his study of the coins of Chalcis and the Euboean League, has identified five annual issues,[3] which evidently covered the period of Alexander's control.

The revolt was no doubt the fruit of a long-maturing ambition in the son of Craterus.[4] But its timing must also be considered against the background of what was happening simultaneously around the Isthmus of Corinth. For the new governor almost immediately found himself attacked by Aratus, perhaps in return for Ptolemaic help. In the winter of 250/49, faced with financial problems which threatened to tear the newly established Sicyonian democracy apart, Aratus had made a hazardous journey to Alexandria to solicit Ptolemaic subsidies.[5] He had embarked from Methone, a harbour in Messenia, but when he had rounded Malea he was driven north by heavy weather and forced to land on Andros, where he narrowly escaped capture by Antigonus' garrison. From Andros he eventually continued his journey on a timely Roman ship to Caria, and thence to Egypt. The commander of the Macedonian garrison on Andros seized Aratus' ship as enemy property,[6] a fact which indicates that Antigonus regarded himself as at war with the Achaeans. In Alexandria Aratus extracted a welcome subsidy of 150 talents for Sicyon, 40 of which he took back

---

[1] Many scholars set Alexander's revolt in 252; cf. Will 1². 316. But the order of events in Trogus, *Prol.* 26, on which this view rests, is not chronologically based. For the arguments in favour of dating Alexander's revolt to 249 see Urban 14 ff.

[2] *IG* XII. 9. 212 Ἀλέξανδρον τὸν βασιλέα εὐεργέτην γεγενημένον τοῦ δήμου τοῦ Ἐρετριέων; (but see Errington, *Gesch. Mak.* 253 n. 36, reporting an (unpublished) new reading of this inscription by R. Billows, which renders βασιλέα doubtful); see also Suidas s.v. *Euphorion*: Ἀλεξάνδρου τοῦ βασιλεύσαντος Εὐβοίας, υἱοῦ δὲ Κρατεροῦ.

[3] *Chalcis* 273–4 nos. 22–6. Picard dates Alexander's revolt to 253/2, but the issues can equally well cover the years 249–245. He argues that certain independent issues from this period indicate that Carystus and almost certainly the northern part of Euboea were not included in the revival of the League. Presumably they remained aligned with Antigonus.

[4] Alexander may have been further encouraged to revolt if Antigonus did in fact suffer a naval defeat at the hands of Ptolemy in 250; but this remains hypothetical. See above, p. 295.

[5] P*Arat* 12. 1–13. 6; 'Andros' depends on an emendation of the reading τῆς Ἀδρίας in 12. 2. The alternative 'Hydria' is impossible. See Porter xlii–xliii; Urban 27 n. 115; Buraselis 173 n. 208.

[6] P*Arat* 12. 4 τὰ μέντοι κομιζόμενα καὶ τὴν ναῦν καὶ τοὺς θεράποντας ἀπέφηνε πολέμια καὶ κατέσχε.

with him, while the rest was to be sent on in four instalments. This method of delivery was hardly adopted because Ptolemy was short of ready cash or because of the dangers of the journey. It was clearly intended to ensure that Aratus gave him a *quid pro quo* in political terms.

Plutarch informs us[1] that Aratus attacked Corinth while Alexander was in control there, but ceased these attacks once the Achaeans had made an alliance (συμμαχία) with him. Clearly those attacks were directed against Alexander in his role as Antigonus' governor and it is likely that they played a part in persuading him to revolt.[2] Once he had revolted, he had an obvious interest in coming to terms with Achaea, since he was now the object of attacks from Antigonus himself. In his attempt to recover Corinth Antigonus arranged for Aristoma-chus of Argos to attack Alexander from the south while Macedonian forces, including an Athenian contingent, marched against him from the Piraeus. The main evidence for these attacks comes from inscriptions. A decree passed by Athenian cleruchs on Salamis[3] in honour of Antigonus' general in the Piraeus (and other fortified places), Heracleitus of Athmonon, the son of Asclepiades, shows that among the dangers against which he had to guard were attacks on the territory of Salamis[4] by pirates, encouraged by Alexander to sail out from Corinthian territory raiding and kidnapping. Heracleitus was the successor of the earlier phrourarchs stationed in the Piraeus, but since he was now in charge of Antigonus' remaining possessions in Greece, his post had apparently been upgraded to that of *strategos*.[5]

How long the desultory fighting around Corinth continued is uncertain, but it ended in an agreement decidedly in Alexander's favour. An Athenian honorary inscription praises Aristomachus of Argos[6] for refusing to make a separate peace with Alexander, when he might well have done so, and instead insisting that the Athenians

---

[1] P*Arat* 18. 2 ὁ δ' Ἄρατος ἔτι μὲν καὶ Ἀλεξάνδρου ζῶντος ἐπεχείρησε τῇ πράξει (MS. πατρίδι), γενομένης δὲ συμμαχίας τοῖς Ἀχαιοῖς πρὸς τὸν Ἀλέξανδρον ἐπαύσατο (the πρᾶξις is the seizure of Corinth).

[2] Those who date Alexander's revolt to 253/2 assume the attacks are against Alexander as independent ruler. Against this see Urban 37–8 with n. 158.

[3] *IG* II[2]. 1225 = *SIG* 454 στρατηγὸς ἐπὶ τοῦ Πειραιέως καὶ τῶν ἄλλων τῶν ταττομένων μετὰ τοῦ Πειραιέως. Heracleitus is also honoured in an Athenian decree (*IG* II[2]. 677: for improved readings by Kondoleon see Habicht, *Unters.* 71 n. 18).

[4] *SIG* 454 l. 17 πειρατικῶν ἐκπλεόντων ἐκ τοῦ Ἐπιλιμνίου. P. Monceaux, *BCH* 6 (1882) 534, plausibly suggested that the unknown *Epilimnios* (perhaps better 'the *Epilimnion*') is a sanctuary of Poseidon situated near Schoenus (cf. Hesych. s.v. *Epilimnios*); see Brulé 3 n. 4, who argues that the pirates were Cretans.

[5] Cf. Bengtson, *Strat.* 2. 349–50; Habicht, *Studien* 51–2.

[6] *ISE* 1. 23 = *IG* II[2]. 774 with improved readings by A. Wilhelm, *Sitz. Wien* 202. 5 (1925) 15–34. To the bibliography in Moretti, *ISE* ad loc. add Habicht, *Unters.* 124–5, who dates it to the first half of the 240s.

should be included. It also reveals the fact that peace had been bought only at the cost of an indemnity of 50 talents, which Aristomachus had generously provided. To what extent this peace between Athens and Argos on the one hand and Alexander on the other involved Antigonus or had his approval, must be a matter for speculation, for Antigonus is not mentioned in the Athenian decree for Aristomachus. The two cities are hardly likely to have broken away from Macedonia to the extent of making a separate peace without consulting Antigonus.[1] It does not of course follow that Antigonus also agreed to grant peace to his rebellious governor or to that governor's allies, the Achaean League. On the other hand, with the withdrawal of Athens and Argos from the conflict actual hostilities must have died down, and though for Antigonus to have made a humiliating treaty with Alexander would have meant according *de iure* recognition to his occupation of Corinth and Chalcis, Aratus' later reference (see below, p. 309 n. 3) to his seizure of Corinth as an ἀδικία suggests that a formal peace was made between Antigonus and the Achaean League. Be that as it may, despite the qualified loyalty of Argos and Athens, based on self-interest in the one case and the absence of choice in the other, the Macedonian position around the Isthmus and in the Aegean had suffered a disastrous blow, which left Antigonus substantially weakened.

2. *The recovery of Corinth and the naval battle of Andros (245 B.C.)*

Antigonus, meanwhile, could derive no satisfaction from the growing prestige of the Aetolians. For it was about this time, in the year of Polyeuctus' archonship at Athens (either 247/6 or, more probably, 246/5),[2] that they made a public gesture to draw attention throughout Greece to their position of eminence and influence at Delphi and to remind the Hellenic community of their past services to the Greek world. For in that year they reorganized the annual Delphic *Soteria*, set up to commemorate the delivery of the shrine from the Gallic marauders in 279, as a panhellenic festival, to be celebrated every fourth year. By accepting the invitation to this festival the Greek cities would in effect be acknowledging the Aetolian claim to control Delphi and the Amphictyonic Council. That was a claim which, by its boycott of the Council, Macedonia had consistently refused to recognize. But

---

[1] Cf. Habicht, *Studien* 25. K. Buraselis, *AE* 1982 (1984) 158 argues that Athens became neutral and that the decree of the Hellenic *koinon* at Plataea, in honour of Glaucon, was passed posthumously in the period of Alexander's rule at Corinth and was partly designed to win Athens over to a policy of outright revolt from Antigonus.

[2] The date of Polyeuctus' archonship is a focal point for the chronology of the Athenian archons in the mid-third century. See, most recently, C. Pélékidis, *BCH* 85 (1961) 53–68; Μέλετες 39, 58 n. 81 (246/5); Nachtergael 211 ff. (246/5).

there was a certain ambiguity in Antigonus' position relative to Aetolia at this time, due to the strained relations existing between Aetolia and the expanding Achaean League.

The rift between Achaea and Aetolia suddenly widened in 245, when Aratus, now twenty-six years old and elected general of the League for the first time, celebrated the attainment of this office with an attack on the Aetolians, who had attempted a coup at Sicyon shortly before its liberation from Nicocles in 251.[1] Crossing the Corinthian Gulf, he ravaged the countryside of Locris and Calydon.[2] He also persuaded the Boeotians, who had taken no part in the proceedings of the Amphictyonic Council since 256 in their resentment at the Aetolian annexation of southern Phocis,[3] to go to war with the Aetolians. But when the Aetolians invaded Boeotia and the Boeotian general Abaeocritus called on Aratus for help, he was unable to get his troops across the Isthmus in time to save the Boeotian army from a disastrous defeat at Chaeronea, in which Abaeocritus himself and 1,000 of his men perished.[4] In consequence of this Boeotia passed into the Aetolian sphere of influence (probably making a treaty of *isopoliteia*) and was, it seems, obliged to surrender Opuntian Locris, which she had annexed in 272; but she did not lose her entitlement to send representatives to the Amphictyonic Council.[5] The result of Chaeronea was to strengthen Aetolia and to inflict humiliation on the Achaean League. It has been argued[6] that these events are to be seen in the context of the struggle to recover Corinth by Antigonus, who planned to use the Aetolians against the Achaeans. On this hypothesis Aratus' raid across the Gulf into Locris and Calydon was an unsuccessful attempt to divert the Aetolians from attacking Achaea's allies in Boeotia. But, according to Polybius, it was the Achaeans who took the initiative in egging on the Boeotians to go to war with the Aetolians. Nor is it clear how the Aetolian conquest of Boeotia was to help Antigonus in his main aim, the recovery of Corinth. It is indeed true that the battle of Chaeronea cost the Achaeans an ally, but the outcome can hardly have afforded substantial satisfaction to Antigonus.

Fortunately Antigonus could afford to neglect Aetolian success in Boeotia, for already events were moving towards a Macedonian triumph as impressive as it was unforeseen. Late in 246 or early in 245

---

[1] P*Arat* 4. 1.   [2] P*Arat* 16. 1.

[3] Cf. Flacelière 200 and 207; and see above, p. 289, for the rise in the number of Aetolian votes.

[4] Plb. 20. 4. 4–5; P*Arat* 16. 1.

[5] Cf. G. Klaffenbach, *Klio* 32 (1939) 199 n. 2; Flacelière 208 nn. 2 and 3; Beloch 4. 2. 432. For Boeotian *isopoliteia* with Aetolia see Porter 58 on P*Arat* 16. 1.

[6] Urban 46–7.

Alexander, the Macedonian usurper in Corinth, died. Plutarch[1] alleges that Antigonus procured his death by poison, but such accusations were commonplace when medical knowledge contained large gaps, and the story may be dismissed. Alexander's widow Nicaea, who now felt herself isolated, received a proposal from Antigonus that she should marry his son Demetrius. Nicaea jumped at this offer and Antigonus hastened to Corinth. A fragmentary inscription, bearing a decree of Eleusinians and Athenians stationed at Eleusis, refers to his visit.[2] He came from Eretria in Euboea through Attica, pausing at Eleusis *en route*, and on arriving in Corinth made arrangements for the proposed marriage between his son and Nicaea. On the day of the ceremony, as the wedding procession proceeded to the theatre, Antigonus detached himself and ascended the Acrocorinth, where he beat on the gates and was quickly admitted by the astonished guards.[3] By this bold stroke he recovered the citadel lost when Alexander revolted; and along with Corinth he took possession of the rest of Alexander's splinter-kingdom. Persaeus, the pupil of Zeno and himself a noted Stoic philosopher, was placed in charge of the Acrocorinth.[4] In Euboea, as we have seen, Alexander of Corinth had withdrawn Macedonian garrisons from the cities and had reconstituted the Euboean League, at any rate in the southern part of the island, with an independent coinage.[5] Antigonus reversed these measures, suspending the functioning of the League and abolishing the coinage. Macedonian garrisons were reinstated. The 'marriage' was apparently forgotten and Nicaea is not heard of again in relation to Demetrius. Indeed, Demetrius' current wife Stratonice, the sister of Antiochus II of Syria, seems to have maintained her position at the Macedonian court for several further years.[6]

The recovery of Corinth and Chalcis and the end of the breakaway kingdom of Alexander thus unexpectedly reversed Antigonus' position at the Isthmus. It would have crowned his success in southern Greece generally if he could have bought off the hostility of the Achaeans and it seems highly probable that it was now, after the recovery of Corinth, that he made a determined effort to win over Aratus with gifts of sacrificial meat—the implications of such a gift being no doubt far greater than its content. When this had no effect, however, he attempted to discredit him with Ptolemy by publicly asserting that Aratus had changed camps and was now an adherent of Macedonia—

[1] P*Arat* 17. 2. Plutarch doubts the story since he add ὡς λέγεται.
[2] Cf. *IG* II². 1280; Habicht, *Studien* 59–61; cf. Dinsmoor 188; Launey 2. 1040 n. 2.
[3] P*Arat* 17. 2–7; Polyaen. 4. 6. 1. [4] P*Arat* 18. 1.
[5] See above, p. 301.
[6] Stratonice eventually fled from Pella to the Syrian court, but the date and circumstances of her flight are uncertain; see below, pp. 322–3 for discussion.

tactics which proved equally unsuccessful in shifting the young man's allegiance.[1]

Though he failed to win over Aratus and the Achaeans, Antigonus soon found other ways to build on his victorious coup at Corinth. What ships were present at Corinth when he got it back is not recorded,[2] but his possession of the Isthmus and southern Euboea now made all the difference to his position in southern Greece and encouraged him to undertake more active intervention against Ptolemy III Euergetes, who had succeeded his father Ptolemy II in 246, the very same year that the death of Antiochus II had placed Seleucus II on the Seleucid throne. Whatever the truth about the alleged naval defeat of 250,[3] Antigonus must in the meantime have been busy at Demetrias building up his fleet to make up for the ships which he will have lost as a result of Alexander's defection. In 246 the accession of the new kings on the thrones of Egypt and Syria was quickly followed by the outbreak of a new war between the two powers, the so-called Laodicean War. At that time Antigonus was still handicapped by his loss of the areas under the control of Corinth. But once Corinth had been recovered (probably early in 245) he felt far less restricted and in possession of sufficient naval resources to enter the war and strike a blow against Egypt in alliance with Seleucus II.

This blow took the form of a major naval victory off Andros. The date of this battle and the circumstances which led up to it have been the subject of long debate. In Appendix 4 I set out the evidence and attempt to show that it supports the view that this Macedonian victory was won in 245. We may in fact possess the names of two Ptolemaic admirals involved in the battle. According to Trogus,[4] Antigonus conquered 'Opron' in a naval battle. 'Opron' is probably Sophron, the governor of Ephesus under Antiochus II. After the latter's death Sophron fell foul of his widow Laodice, and after narrowly escaping execution at her hands,[5] fled to take up service with Ptolemy III Euergetes. A certain Ptolemy 'Andromachou' (later to be murdered at Ephesus) seems also to have fought at Andros. He was probably a bastard son of Ptolemy II, who had been brought up as the son of a leading landowner, Andromachus 'Myriarouros'.[6] On the Macedonian side all the evidence points to Antigonus having commanded the fleet in person (like Demetrius I and, later on, Philip V).

---

[1] P*Arat* 15. 1–5. On the date of this approach see Walbank, *A* 43; Habicht, *Studien* 61 n. 114. It was in 245, despite the reference to Aratus' first generalship (245/4) in P*Arat* 16, for, as Habicht points out, P*Arat* 15 concludes Plutarch's account of Aratus' political beginnings.

[2] There were twenty-five there when Aratus seized Corinth two years later; cf. P*Arat* 24. 1.

[3] See above, p. 295.   [4] Trog. *Prol.* 27.

[5] Athen. 13. 593 b–d; Appendix 4 pp. 590–1.

[6] *P. Haun.* 6; Athen. 13. 593 a; Appendix 4 pp. 588–9.

The sequence of events which brought the Ptolemaic and Antigonid fleets together in the neighbourhood of Andros is not recorded. Two circumstances may offer a clue.[1] Buraselis has argued, very plausibly,[2] that in the extract dealing with Ptolemy 'Andromachou' (*P. Haun.* 6. 1. 7) one should read αἱρεῖ κ' αἰνον; this reference to the seizure of Aenus would suggest an expedition against the Thracian coast led by Ptolemy 'Andromachou', at the outset of the Laodicean War, but before the battle of Andros; and this hypothesis gains support from a famous inscription from Adulis,[3] which mentions the Hellespont and Thrace as conquests of Ptolemy Euergetes. Secondly, Andros is known to have been in Antigonus' hands at the time of Aratus' voyage to Egypt in 251/0.[4] Whether its garrison had defected to Alexander in 249 is unknown. But if so it must have returned to Antigonus along with Corinth and Chalcis. The Ptolemaic fleet which Antigonus encountered off the island may therefore have been sent to try to seize this important island, relatively near to the Greek coast, following the annexation of areas in the region of Thrace. In the absence of further evidence this must, however, remain speculation.[5]

Antigonus' victory at Andros was a brilliant sequel to the recovery of Corinth, and Antigonus celebrated it by inaugurating two vase-festivals at Delos in the same year (245), designed in their unusual names, the *Soteria* and the *Paneia*, to indicate their political significance.[6] For, unlike all the other Delian vase-festivals, these two were named after the gods to whom they were dedicated, the *Theoi Soteres*—probably Zeus Soter and Athena Soteira—and Pan who, though he possessed a cult on Delos, was especially prominent at Pella.[7]

3. *Aratus' seizure of Corinth and the aftermath (245–243 B.C.)*

The recovery of Corinth and the naval victory of Andros represented an impressive strengthening of the Macedonian position in the Aegean

---

[1] See Buraselis 172–3.

[2] Buraselis 127, whose suggestion has the approval of C. H. Roberts. Buraselis points out that it is known from the *asylia* inscriptions from Cos (R. Herzog and G. Klaffenbach, *Abh. Berl. Ak.* 1952 no. 1, 19) that Aenus was Ptolemaic in 242.   [3] *OGI* 54 ll. 14 ff.

[4] See above, p. 301.   [5] So, rightly, Buraselis 173–4.

[6] On these festivals see Appendix 4 pp. 592–4.

[7] On the cult of Pan in Macedonia, especially under the Antigonids, see Launey 2. 934–7; Bruneau 560 n. 6; Gaebler III. 2. 185 ff.; Ph. Borgeaud, *Recherches sur le dieu Pan* (Geneva, 1979) 169 n. 135; E. L. Brown, 'Antigonus surnamed Gonatas' in G. W. Bowersock (ed.), *Arktouros. Hellenic studies presented to B. M. W. Knox* (Berlin–New York, 1979) 303 ff. See, however, the sober reservations of W. K. Pritchett, *The Greek State at War* 3 (Berkeley–Los Angeles–London, 1979) 32–4, especially against the unfounded suggestion that there was an epiphany of Pan at the battle of Lysimacheia.

and of Antigonus' hold on the areas around the Isthmus and the northern Peloponnese. But the Aetolians, meanwhile, were showing their strength south of the Corinthian Gulf. An inscription dating from about this time, found on the site of Phigaleia,[1] records a treaty of *isopoliteia* between that city and Messenia, which had been sponsored by the Aetolians, acting as allies of Phigaleia. Whether close relations between Aetolia and Messenia predated this treaty or resulted from it, it undoubtedly signifies an increase of Aetolian intervention in the Peloponnese. About the same time Megalopolis fell into the hands of a tyrant, Lydiades.[2] Lydiades may have gained power with Macedonian connivance; but there is no direct evidence for this nor indeed that he was in any straightforward sense a Macedonian protégé—though his tyranny suited the interests of Antigonus. At some time during his tyranny (and perhaps now, at the outset) Lydiades ceded Alipheira to Elis, for reasons which Polybius does not specify.[3] This concession may have been in recompense for help given at the time Lydiades became tyrant or, as Urban suggests, for some other reason, such as the ransoming of prisoners.[4] In addition, Elis may now have gained possession of Triphylia, a region which counted itself Arcadian,[5] for Triphylia was subsequently returned to the Achaean League, of which Megalopolis was by then a member.[6]

How far these moves damaged Macedonia is not clear. Antigonus cannot have regarded an extension of Aetolian influence in the western Peloponnese unmoved. On the other hand, tyrannies in Megalopolis and Argos[7] were some check on this expansion and even more on that of the Achaeans, who now found themselves hemmed in on all sides, especially to the east, where Antigonus was again firmly ensconced on the Acrocorinth in the place of their recent ally, Alexander. At once, therefore, Aratus set about planning to take this key fortress from the Macedonian king. He was brilliantly successful in carrying out this enterprise early in his second term of office as general of the League, in the summer of 243.[8] Having first ensured collaboration from within by buying the help of two Syrian mercenaries serving in the Macedo-

---

[1] *SIG* 472 = *SVA* 495; cf. Plb. 4. 6. 11.

[2] The account of a battle of Mantinea fought about 250 between Sparta under Agis on the one hand and a combined army of Mantineans, Megalopolitans (under Lydiades and Leocydes), and Achaeans and Sicyonians (under Aratus) (Paus. 8. 10. 5) on the other contains so many improbabilities that it must be dismissed as unhistorical; see, most recently, Urban 38–45.

[3] Plb. 4. 77. 9–10 (with Walbank, *C* ad loc.). Paus. 5. 6. 1 mentions an Aetolian officer Polysperchon, who used Samicum as a bulwark against the Arcadians; and he may have been behind the Elean acquisition of Cynaetha and Psophis at this time. See Walbank, *JHS* 56 (1936) 67–8; below, p. 312 n. 1.

[4] See Urban 87 n. 412.   [5] X. *Hell.* 7. 1.26 Ἀρκάδες ἔφασαν εἶναι.

[6] Plb. 18. 47. 10; Livy 32. 4. 4–5.   [7] See above, p. 300, for Argos.

[8] For the detailed account of the operation, derived from Aratus' *Memoirs*, see P*Arat* 18. 2–24. 1.

nian garrison, Aratus chose a midsummer night with a full moon to lead a force of 400 picked men to the Phliasian gate in the west of the city and, having made an entry at this point, climbed up the slope of the Acrocorinth and attacked and seized the citadel. At daybreak the main Achaean army reached Corinth, and Aratus, now master of the city, addressed the people in the theatre. Concerning the fate of the Macedonian governor two accounts survive. According to the Stoic tradition he committed suicide; but there was also a malicious and less likely version, according to which he escaped to lead a life of leisure.[1].

At one blow Aratus had nullified all Antigonus' careful diplomacy and had all but put Macedonia back where she was six years earlier after the revolt of Alexander. Along with Corinth Aratus captured twenty-five Macedonian ships, 500 horses, and 400 Syrian mercenaries. The port of Lechaeum was secured, an Achaean garrison—400 hoplites together with fifty dogs and their guards—was placed on the Acrocorinth and shortly afterwards Cenchreae, the other harbour, was in Achaean hands.[2] Aratus' coup has been generally regarded as a breach of international law. Polybius, following Aratus' own *Memoirs*, refers to it as an injustice (ἀδικία) towards Antigonus.[3] True, he does so in a context in which Aratus is giving Antigonus Doson's view of the affair, so as to emphasize the king's hostility towards him at the time he was negotiating to secure Macedonian help against Cleomenes (see below, pp. 348–9).[4] But the word ἀδικία clearly suggests that Aratus' action, perpetrated in a period of *de facto* or even *de iure* peace between the League and Macedonia (see above, p. 303) was a breach of accepted convention. In the same way he was later to show little scruple about observing the normal rules where Achaean interests were involved.[5] On this occasion the gains were spectacular, for the fall of Corinth had opened up the Isthmus to the Achaeans and it was rapidly followed by the entry of Megara, Troezen, and Epidaurus into the League.[6] These acquisitions established the federal authority firmly on the Saronic Gulf, and placed a wedge of hostile territory between Antigonus' nearest outposts in Attica and his allies, the tyrants of Argos

[1] Paus. 2. 8. 4, 7. 8. 3; *Index Stoic. Herc.* col. xv. The other version is in P*Arat* 23. 5–6; Athen. 4. 162 d; Polyaen. 6. 5. Cf. K. Deichgräber, *RE* s.v. *Persaios* col. 927. Tarn, *AG* 398 n. 9, accepts the Achaean version; *contra* U. von Wilamowitz-Moellendorff, *Antigonos von Karystos* (Berlin, 1881) 108 n. 10.

[2] P*Arat* 24. 1, 29. 1–3 (Cenchreae).

[3] Plb. 2. 50. 9 τὴν ἐξ αὐτοῦ προγεγενημένην ἀδικίαν περὶ τὸν Ἀκροκόρινθον εἰς τὴν Μακεδόνων οἰκίαν.

[4] Cf. Urban 121 n. 102.

[5] Cf. P*Arat* 25. 5 for his fine by the Mantineans acting as arbitrators concerning his attack on Aristippus of Argos.

[6] P*Arat* 24. 3; cf. *SVA* 489 (=*SEG* 11. 401) for an agreement governing the accession of Epidaurus to the League.

and Megalopolis. Beloch[1] has estimated that the League now controlled territory amounting to 5,500 square kilometres and this sudden accession of strength to Achaea represented a challenge both to Antigonus—who felt his position in Attica and Euboea to be seriously threatened—and to the Aetolians, whose hopes of Peloponnesian expansion were now much less rosy.

4. *The Aetolian alliance (243–241/0 B.C.)*

The Achaean challenge to Macedonian domination in central and southern Greece soon became translated into fact, for in the spring of 242, while still general, Aratus initiated raids on Attica and Salamis along the easy route now open to him across the Isthmus and through Megara.[2] A recently redated document from Athens has been taken as evidence that the Athenians were anticipating some such raid in 243 before the Achaean capture of Corinth. This is an inscription[3] from the year of Diomedon's archonship, now assigned with all but complete certainty to 244/3,[4] which deals with an Athenian fund (*epidosis*) derived from a levy imposed on landowners mainly from the *mesogaia*, which had been set up, apparently in conditions of emergency, in March/April 243. The purpose of this fund was to provide money to pay for enough military protection to ensure that the fruit harvest of 243 could be brought in in safety. It has been argued[5] that the threat to the harvest came from Aratus, who might have been expected to take some action in response to Antigonus' recovery of Corinth as soon as he entered office in May 243; and that the Athenian mistake lay simply in expecting an invasion of Attica rather than what Aratus did carry out—the seizure of Corinth. This explanation of the Athenian *epidosis* of 243 cannot, however, be correct, for until Aratus had taken Corinth and acquired Megara he had no feasible approach route to Salamis and Attica. Whatever threatened Attica in the early months of 243—it may for example have been piratical incursions encouraged by the Aetolians, such as we hear of at other times[6]—it cannot have been an Achaean invasion.

The Athenians were as unresponsive to the pressure from Achaea as

---

[1] Beloch 4. 1. 621 n. 3.

[2] P*Arat* 24.3. On the date see, most recently, Habicht, *Studien* 29 n. 87.

[3] *IG* ii². 791; republished by B. D. Meritt, *Hesperia* 11 (1942) 287–92 no. 56. See Pélékidis, *Μέλετες* 42–56; Habicht, *Studien* 26–33.

[4] Habicht, *Unters.* 133 ff.; *Studien* 68, 77; Will. 1². 258; G. Daux, *BCH* 164 (1980) 115–16.

[5] See Habicht, *Studien* 30.

[6] E.g. Bucris' raid, referred to in *SIG* 535 ll. 5 ff. (229/8: Heliodorus' archonship; see below, p. 328 nn. 2–3). But could raids on this scale explain what sounds like provision to meet a serious emergency? Pélékidis, *Μέλετες* 53–6, argues that Aratus' raid on Athens was in 243.

Aratus himself had been to Antigonus' propagandist campaign to win him over to Macedonia. In fact the Achaeans, who were indirectly pensioners of Ptolemy since Aratus made Sicyon a member of the League, now pinned their colours firmly to the mast by appointing Ptolemy Euergetes *hegemon* of the Confederation 'by land and sea'. Urban[1] dates this appointment to before Aratus' capture of Corinth in 243, but Plutarch puts it later. It seems likely that it was an honorary appointment in the sense that Ptolemy did not expect, and was not expected, to direct Achaean operations. But it sealed the friendship between Ptolemy and the League and is no doubt a pointer to Ptolemaic financial support for such military operations as Aratus was now initiating against Antigonus' posts in Attica.

Antigonus' response to Aratus' seizure of Corinth was indirect.[2] According to Polybius,[3] he entered into a compact with his old enemy, the Aetolians, to partition Achaea. Who took the initiative in this agreement is not clear. Polybius says that it was the Aetolians, but he may be indulging his well-known dislike of the rival federation.[4] In any case, it suited both parties very well. As part of the compact Antigonus evidently connived at a similar agreement between Aetolia and Epirus (under Alexander II) to partition Acarnania between them—a plan which was in part carried out.[5] This agreement implies that good relations existed, or were established, between Antigonus and the Epirote League (which at this time controlled much of southern Illyria: see above, p. 264) and, as a corollary, that Antigonus had in this way rendered the whole of his western frontier secure. About the same time Aratus made an alliance with Sparta.[6] Whether this occurred before the accession to the Eurypontid throne of Agis IV, perhaps in 243, is uncertain; and so, necessarily, are Aratus' reasons for

[1] Cf. Urban 52–3. He argues that Ptolemy's *hegemonia* was more than an honorary position and that the Achaean attacks on Athens and Salamis were undertaken at his instigation. There is no evidence that this was so.

[2] Wherever possible, Antigonus seems to have opted for indirect methods, which did not involve the mobilizing of Macedonians and the loss of Macedonian lives. Hence his use of tyrants, mercenaries, or (as here) allies.

[3] 2. 43. 10, 45. 1; 9. 34. 6, 38. 9; P*Arat* 43. 9; cf. Walbank, *JHS* 56 (1936) 69–70.

[4] Tarn, *AG* 400 and Beloch 4. 1. 628 f. follow him in making this an Aetolian plan.

[5] Plb. 2. 45. 1; 9. 34. 7, 38. 9 (confused); J. 26. 3. 1; 28. 1. 1. The Aetolians took eastern Acarnania with Stratus, Oeniadae, Metropolis, and Phoetiae, Epirus, western Acarnania, and Leucas. See Walbank, *C* 1.239–40.

[6] This alliance is implied by P*Arat* 13–15, where Aratus invites help from Sparta against an Aetolian invasion and then dismisses τοὺς συμμάχους (P*Arat* 15. 5). Urban 52 n. 234, queries the making of a new alliance on the grounds that there had been no hostility between Achaea and Sparta. He regards Ptolemaic help to Achaea as far more important than Spartan. But Aratus' call for Spartan help implies a specific, and probably recent, agreement between the two states. Whether *SVA* 455 can be brought into this context is, as Urban rightly says, rather dubious. The date of the alliance is uncertain. It may indeed have been made before Agis' accession to the throne.

making it. One obvious common interest lay in defensive measures against Lydiades, the new tyrant of Megalopolis; and if the alliance was concluded after Antigonus' compact with the Aetolians, that too can have been a reason for it.

However this may be, there was no opportunity to put the terms of the alliance into operation until 241. In the spring of that year the Aetolians, either instigated by Antigonus or else perhaps alarmed at an unsuccessful attempt by Aratus to take the town of Cynaetha (mod. Kalavryta), which lay on the northern verge of Arcadia and was at this time under the control of their allies in Elis,[1] invaded the Peloponnese by way of Boeotia and the Megarid. Aratus, whose intelligence was good, had foreseen the invasion and sent an appeal to Sparta. Agis therefore marched north with an impressive Spartan army, which inspired some alarm in Aratus and the richer inhabitants of the cities of Achaea,[2] for Agis was already known to harbour plans for a radical change in land tenure in his native city and it was feared that this might be intended for export. At a joint war council it was decided, however, to adopt Aratus' proposal and avoid a pitched battle, since the harvest was already in,[3] and Agis and his forces were dismissed together with a substantial part of the Achaean army. Agis was at the time involved in an internal struggle with his political adversaries on account of his reforms, and his absence from Sparta proved disastrous to him. Shortly after his return he was forced to take sanctuary and, having been persuaded to come out, was put to death. His early end and the collapse of the attempt to restore Spartan military might by reconstituting the Spartan citizen body do not concern us here except as a foretaste of the later movement headed by Cleomenes III, which was to lead indirectly to a remarkable revival of Macedonian influence in Greece.

As for Aratus, his dismissal of Achaean and Spartan troops proved premature, for shortly afterwards the Aetolians, on their way back from Arcadia, attacked Pellene in eastern Achaea. As they plundered the town, Aratus fell upon them, however, and inflicted a defeat and heavy losses.[4] This Aetolian invasion was not an isolated incident, for we hear of other Aetolian plundering attacks in the Peloponnese about this time, on Lusi and as far as Taenarum by Timaeus, probably along with Charixenus, on the Argive Heraeum by Pharycus, and on the temple of Poseidon at Mantinea.[5] These raids, referred to out of

---

[1] Cf. Walbank, *JHS* 56 (1936) 64–71; Plb. 9. 17. 1–10.   [2] P*Agis* 14.

[3] P*Arat* 31. 1–2. Urban 55 argues that the plan was changed because the Aetolians appeared to be making for Arcadia through the Argolid and so to present no danger to Achaea.

[4] P*Arat* 31. 1–32. 6.

[5] Plb. 9. 34. 9; for Timaeus and Charixenus Plb. 4. 34. 9; P*Cleom* 18. 3.

context at a much later date, cannot be firmly assigned to any particular year. For several of them 240 seems a plausible date (though Beloch puts the raid of Timaeus and Charixenus in 244, and the same could be true of Pharycus' raid on the Argive Heraeum).[1] Some of them, moreover, may have been carried out from an Aetolian base in Messenia, in which case they need not have any connection with the invasion of 241. They form part of the continuing hostilities between the Achaeans on the one side and Macedonia and Aetolia on the other. These hostilities were brought to an end in 240, perhaps as part of a comprehensive peace settlement.[2] This did not prevent Aratus continuing to put pressure on Argos as an outpost of Macedonia.[3] For a peacetime attack on Aristippus, who had succeeded Aristomachus as tyrant there, the Achaeans were arraigned before a Mantinean court—perhaps the Mantineans were acting as arbitrators—and condemned to pay the somewhat nominal fine of 40 *minae*.[4] This was probably in 240, and in the same year Aratus made several unsuccessful raids on Athens and the Piraeus.[5] Already, before the peace with Aetolia, he had gained possession of Cynaetha.

5. *The end of Antigonus' reign (241–239 B.C.)*

Apart from contracting the Aetolian alliance, Antigonus remained strangely inactive during the years following his loss of Corinth. He was an old man and perhaps no longer capable of reacting energetically to disaster or provocation. It was probably in the winter of 240/39 that he died, aged eighty.[6] Despite the setbacks experienced in Greece during his last years, he had, throughout his long reign, deserved well of Macedonia. He had given the country peace and a chance to recover from the weakness and devastation of the years between Cassander's death in 298 (or 297) and his own accession. Where fighting was necessary, he deliberately spared his national troops by leaving them to farm the land and rarely calling out the levy. Instead he used mercenaries—Greeks, Illyrians, and Gauls from the Balkans—

---

[1] Beloch 4. 1. 620; that Argos was under a pro-Macedonian tyrant need not necessarily have deterred the Aetolians from attacking the Heraeum.
[2] P*Arat* 33. 1–2.   [3] P*Arat* 25. 1–6.
[4] P*Arat* 25. 5. For Antigonus' support for Aristippus see P*Arat* 26. 1.
[5] P*Arat* 33. 2–6.
[6] Demetrius II, Gonatas' successor, reigned for ten years and died in spring 229, when the Romans crossed into Illyria (Plb. 2. 44. 2); consequently Antigonus' death fell in the Olympiad year 240/39. Since he reckoned his first regnal year, exceptionally, as 283/2, following Demetrius I's death in 284/3 (see Appendix 2 pp. 581–2) and reigned for forty-four years (according to the Greek version of Eus. 1. 238. 10 Sch.), his last full year was 241/0 and he died in the course of 240/39, as Porphyry states (Ol. 135. 1): *FGrH* 260 F 3. 12. His death probably took place in spring 239 (cf. Ehrhardt 140).

for his fighting and garrisoning. Unfortunately no firm figures exist for Macedonian manpower under the Antigonids until we reach the reign of Antigonus III and the battle of Sellasia (222). It has been argued that the minting of an adequate and reliable silver coinage by Antigonus II indicates the prosperity of his reign.[1] But this is hardly true. The main purpose of his coining is more likely to have been to meet military demands than to further commercial ends and its volume has been greatly exaggerated. Not only under Antigonus, but also under his successors, Demetrius II and Antigonus III, there was really very little Macedonian silver currency. It is clear that there was no attempt to impose a monopoly of Macedonian coinage such as was practised from 305 onwards in Egypt and in the second century in Pergamum.[2] Judging from finds, Macedonian coins were outnumbered by foreign even in Macedonia, Thessaly, and Euboea, while outside those areas they are hardly to be found at all.[3] In fact Macedonia did not in this period attain anything like the level of wealth to be found in Egypt and some other Hellenistic states. In 168 the land tax brought in only a little over 200 talents a year.[4] In stable conditions the rich agricultural lands of the coastal plain, the still extensive forests, a source of timber and pitch, essential for shipbuilding, the silver mines of Pangaeum, and a little gold all contributed usefully to the wealth of the kingdom; but the results cannot be quantified.

Abroad Antigonus had pursued a consistently cautious foreign policy directed towards the security of Macedonia. After the Gallic invasion of 280/79 he was hardly likely to neglect his northern frontiers, and his defences there were evidently effective, for no record has survived of such trouble as his successors were to face on this front. But he limited himself to a defensive policy there and the evidence of coin finds suggests that he exercised no influence in Thrace and the Danube area, where after the time of Lysimachus and Demetrius Poliorcetes the connections seem to be mainly with the Seleucids and to some extent the Attalids.[5] It therefore looks as if Antigonus did not use Thrace as a recruiting area for mercenaries, unless indeed mercenaries recruited there were paid in something other than Macedonian coin.[6]

---

[1] Cf. Rostovtzeff, *SEH* I. 253. On the coinage of Antigonus II see Merker 39–52, with the criticisms of Ehrhardt 75–8. See further Appendix 4 pp. 594–5.

[2] Cf. O. Mørkholm, *Historia* 31 (1982) 297–301.   [3] Cf. Ehrhardt, 75–109.

[4] P*Aem* 28. 4.

[5] Cf. *IGCH* nos. 448–50, 853–4, 859–61, 866–7 (the latter contains two Attalid coins and the only Ptolemaic coin recorded in a Balkan hoard), 870–2, 874, 887–8. The only hoard containing a Macedonian coin is no. 889; Ehrhardt 79–80. See especially G. Mihailov, *Athenaeum* 39 (1961) 33–44.

[6] The volume of Macedonian silver which can be deduced from the number of surviving specimens—even assuming that all the 'Antigonus' coins are issued by Gonatas—can hardly have been sufficiently large to finance the hiring of mercenaries and paying of officials by the

In the south the problems were different. Towards the expanding Aetolian League Antigonus had been patient and unprovocative, refraining from retaliatory measures when the Aetolians continued to incorporate one after another of the states lying between Thessaly and Attica in their confederation. Where a more headstrong king like Pyrrhus might have challenged this expansion and launched himself into a wearisome conflict, Antigonus apparently took no steps to make good his loss of the mainland route south, but was content to rely on his ships to ferry his forces over to Euboea, whence an alternative route was available, linking Macedonia and Demetrias with his garrisons at Chalcis, the Piraeus, and Corinth.

These garrisons constituted the central element in Antigonus' system of control over Greece as far as, and somewhat beyond, the Isthmus of Corinth. They were supplemented by his sponsorship of tyrants, more especially in his later years, in Argos, Megalopolis, and other smaller cities such as Phlius and Hermione. The purpose of this system was basically defensive. It was intended to debar any rival—and this in effect meant Ptolemy, his only serious opponent after the compact with Antiochus in 278—from effective access to Greece.[1] This pattern of defence was challenged in the Chremonidean War, but unsuccessfully, since Philadelphus proved a broken reed and brought wholly inadequate help to Sparta and Athens. Antigonus bided his time and in 255 responded vigorously with his naval victory at Cos. This was inconclusive in its long-term results, but for a time at least it diminished the effectiveness of the Ptolemaic supremacy in the Aegean and reasserted the naval traditions and ambitions of the Antigonid house. Ten years later Antigonus taught Ptolemy III a similar lesson by intervening in the Laodicean War to defeat his admirals off Andros, perhaps thereby warding off a new Ptolemaic threat to him in Macedonia by sea and on the Thracian frontier.

Until 249 the Macedonian system in Greece served its purpose well. But the revolt of Alexander was a blow from which it never fully recovered. Antigonus' reaction was to rely increasingly on pro-Macedonian tyrants. But many of these found themselves under growing pressure from the Achaeans, whose seizure of the Acrocorinth shortly after Antigonus had got it back completed the destruction of Macedonian power from the Isthmus southwards. Subsequently either senile inertia or unrecorded trouble on the northern frontier prevented

government and the paying of taxes by the inhabitants of Macedonia. Foreign trade to and from Macedonia must to a large extent have used other currencies, and the same may have been true for the paying of mercenaries. See Ehrhardt 80, 162.

[1] The Ptolemaic outpost at Methana in the Argolid must have been an irritant, but there is no evidence that Alexandria used it for provocative ends.

Antigonus taking any direct steps—other than by his alliance with Aetolia—to recover lost positions.

Antigonus, it is recorded, was a pupil of Zeno and a Stoic by conviction.[1] His generous spirit is the subject of several anecdotes, in particular one which recounts how, when he found his son ill-treating some of his subjects, he reproved him, saying that 'our kingship is a kind of glorious servitude (*endoxos douleia*).'[2] But it would be a mistake to make too much of this in assessing Antigonus' work as a king and a statesman, for there is no evidence that Stoic theories of kingship exercised the least influence on his policy. Though he was joined at court by Persaeus, it was primarily as a politician and officer that the Stoic served him, as would any other of his Friends. As a man, Antigonus Gonatas is attractive[3] and leaves a favourable impression. He was humane and modest, he rejected flattery, and his relations with his family, and especially with his sons, were excellent—something that cannot be said of all Hellenistic, or indeed all Antigonid, rulers. But his death left many problems for his son Demetrius, who may indeed already have been shouldering part of the burden in Antigonus' last years.

---

[1] Aelian, *VH* 12. 25; cf. Tarn, *AG* 34 ff., 230 ff. Tarn rightly observes that at the time Antigonus invited Zeno to Pella, he 'must have already forgotten more about the art of governing than Zeno had ever learnt.'

[2] Aelian, *VH* 2. 20.

[3] The meaning of 'Gonatas' is as obscure as it was when Tarn published his biography of the king in 1912 (see *AG* 15 n. 1). It may just possibly mean 'knock-kneed' and be a soldiers' nickname. A connection with Gonni in Thessaly (so Porphyry in Eus. 1. 237 Sch.; *FGrH* 260 F 3. 12) cannot be correct.

XV

DEMETRIUS II (239–229 B.C.)[1]

1. *The situation in 239 B.C.*

DEMETRIUS II was born *c.* 275[2] and he was in his middle thirties when he succeeded his father in the winter of 240/39.[3] Whether Antigonus had already made him co-ruler is uncertain, though likely. An act of manumission from Beroea,[4] dated to Peritios (January/February) of the 27th year of the reign of Demetrius, has generally been referred to Demetrius II and taken to indicate that he had been co-ruler with Gonatas since, at the latest, 257/6. It is indeed true that there is no trace of any co-regency in two inscriptions from the late years of Antigonus Gonatas and that one from the 3rd year of Demetrius' own reign, recording an alliance with Gortyn, ignores any co-regency in its dating. It has therefore been argued[5] that the Demetrius of the Beroea manumission is Demetrius I. But Demetrius I did not become king until 306 and, since he died in 283,[6] he cannot have reached his 27th regnal year. Moreover, the letter forms of the Beroea manumission document (*SEG* 12. 314) point to a date in the second half of the third century at the earliest. One would therefore have to assume, first that those setting up the manumission inscription, *ex hypothesi c.* January 280, being uncertain who was king in that part of Macedonia, decided to date it posthumously by the regnal year of

---

[1] The sources for Demetrius' reign are poor. There is no consecutive account. J. 28. 1–3 is concerned mainly with events in Epirus. Plutarch's *Life of Aratus* contains a few details, derived mainly from Aratus' *Memoirs*; and Polybius has very little (cf. 2. 44. 1–2). Much depends on a few inscriptions, which are mentioned below as they become relevant. The chronology rests largely on that of the Athenian archons, none of whom is datable with absolute certainty.

[2] Cf. Ehrhardt 198; Tarn, *AG* 302–4. His mother Phila married Antigonus Gonatas *c.* 276 (see above, p. 251, n. 2); and he is alleged to have commanded the army which defeated Alexander of Epirus late in the Chremonidean War (J. 26. 2. 11)—though this passage is full of inaccuracies (see above p. 285 nn. 4 and 6) and at the most his command is likely to have been nominal.

[3] See above, p. 313 n. 6.

[4] *SEG* 12. 314 = *ISE* 2. 109; to the bibliography listed in Moretti's edition add Ehrhardt 145; R. M. Errington, *Anc. Mac.* 2. 115–22; P. Cabanes, *Iliria* 11. 2 (1981) 81.

[5] See Errington, loc. cit. (n. 4). The inscriptions are *SIG* 459 = *SEG* 12. 311 (Demetrius' letter to Harpalus, *epistates* at Beroea, dated to Gonatas' 36th year (248/7)); Herzog–Klaffenbach no. 6 l. 19 (a Coan inscription recording a decree of Amphipolis recognizing the *asylia* of the Asclepieum, dated to Gonatas' 41st year (243/2)); and *SVA* 498 = *IC* 4. 167 (alliance dated to Demetrius' 3rd year (238/7, since his 1st year was equated with Ol. 135. 1 (240/39)).

[6] See above, p. 234 n. 4.

Demetrius, who had died three years earlier, and secondly that for some unexplained reason the inscription was re-engraved between fifty and a hundred years later. The combination of these two hypotheses seems highly unlikely. In particular, the Beroean authorities would hardly adopt this curious posthumous dating in January 280, when Ptolemy Ceraunus was unquestionably king, with Pyrrhus out of the way (since 285), Lysimachus and Seleucus both dead, and the Gauls not yet on the scene. The manumission decree from Beroea is therefore to be taken as evidence for a co-regency of Demetrius II with his father, which was not however incorporated into the official titulature of either Gonatas' or Demetrius' reign, though it was taken account of in this private document. The founder of the Antigonid dynasty, Antigonus Monophthalmus, had similarly made his son Demetrius co-regent from the time he took the royal title.

In fact Demetrius had probably been taking an ever more important share in Macedonian government during Gonatas' last years and there will have been no suggestion of any opposition to his succession. As king he inherited several serious problems. The growing power of the Aetolians threatened Thessaly and their control of Thermopylae continued to deny Macedonia the mainland route to the south. In the Peloponnese and around the Isthmus of Corinth Aratus and the Achaeans had shattered Gonatas' well-tried system of garrisons and well-disposed tyrants, which represented the first line of defence against any other Hellenistic power with designs on Macedonia.[1] Fortunately there was at present nothing to be feared from Ptolemy III, whose fleet had suffered a serious defeat off Andros in 245;[2] and neither Antigonus nor Demetrius took any action, as far as we know, to interfere with the continued Ptolemaic occupation of Methana on the coast of the Argolid.

In assessing Demetrius' prospects on his accession, one must consider how Macedonia stood in relation to her neighbours at this date. The situation in Paeonia (in the upper Axius valley) is not clear. The name of Antigoneia, a town to be located at Banja a little north of the pass of Demir-Kapu, probably indicates that it was founded by Gonatas. But he will have lost control of the area by the end of his reign, if the rule of Dropion, whom the *koinon* of the Paeonians honoured at Olympia as their founder (*SIG* 394; see above, p. 268 n. 5), is to be dated to the reign of Demetrius II and he was in fact independent, and not a client king of Macedonia.[3] To the east both Chalcidice and the coast, at least as far as Philippi, were Macedonian. A decree of Philippi from 243/2,

[1] See above, pp. 308–9.   [2] See above, pp. 306–7.
[3] On Antigoneia and on Dropion see Volume 1. 172, and above, p. 268 nn. 3–4. For Hammond's view that Paeonia remained a Macedonian client kingdom throughout this period see above, p. 268 n. 7.

which registers the intention of that city to send an escort of mercenaries to accompany Coan *theoroi* on the next stage of their journey to Neapolis on the coast opposite Thasos, has been taken as evidence that Neapolis was not at that time under Macedonian control.[1] But such an escort would hardly have been welcomed by an independent city and could well have prejudiced the reception of the Coan *theoroi*. Probably then the assignment of these troops points to the opposite conclusion, that Neapolis lay within the realm of Macedonia, but indicates that the region between Neapolis and Philippi was exposed to danger—perhaps from brigands. All these cities in Macedonia enjoyed considerable independence in local affairs and in finance.

On the other hand, despite the fact that it was at Lysimacheia that Gonatas had won his great and crowning victory, there is no evidence that he continued to exercise influence in coastal Thrace after making his agreement with Antiochus in 278.[2] Abdera certainly issued an independent coinage;[3] and in 243 both Aenus and Maronea were Ptolemaic possessions.[4] In the interior of Thrace and along the Danube there is a noteworthy absence of Macedonian coins from hoards. As we have already seen,[5] with one exception no Thracian hoard from the period covering the reigns from Demetrius I to Perseus contains Antigonid coins. It is true that we do not know in what coinage the Antigonids paid their mercenaries. If Macedonian coins were used, it is odd that so few exist from the reigns after Poliorcetes; but in fact Macedonian coins are outnumbered by non-Macedonian even in Macedonia, Thessaly, and Euboea.[6] If, then, Macedonian coins were not used in paying troops, the most likely alternative currency might be expected to be that of Athens. Yet Athenian coins too are largely absent from Balkan hoards of this period.[7] It seems a fair conclusion that the Antigonids had little influence in the Thracian and Danube areas and that they recruited few mercenaries from those parts—though indeed not many Thracian mercenaries are recorded in the sources for the mid-third century from anywhere other than Egypt.[8] This may partly reflect lacunae in our sources, but the absence of any mention of Thracians in Antigonus Doson's army at Sellasia is significant.[9]

---

[1] See Herzog–Klaffenbach no. 6 ll. 53–4; cf. J. and L. Robert, *Bull. épig.* 1953 no. 152.

[2] See above, p. 251 n. 4.

[3] Cf. H. von Fritze, *Nomisma* 3 (1909) 27–9; Ehrhardt 161 n. 8.

[4] Cf. Herzog–Klaffenbach nos. 8 (Aenus) and 9 (Maronea: fragmentary). On Aenus see above, p. 307, with the evidence of *P. Haun.* 6.

[5] See above, p. 314 n. 5 for the evidence.   [6] Ehrhardt 75.

[7] Ehrhardt 79 n. 29.

[8] Cf. Launey 1. 373, 378; the first known Thracian mercenaries in an Antigonid army in the period after 250 are to be found serving under Philip V in 219 (Plb. 4. 66. 6).

[9] Plb. 2. 65. 2–5; unless indeed the μισθοφόροι of 65. 2 included Thracians.

To the south Macedonia controlled Thessaly and its outlying areas, except for Dolopia and perhaps part of Phthiotic Achaea. Magnesia was Macedonian and together with it (probably) Peparethos.[1] Euboea was also under Macedonian control. There is some evidence[2] that at the time of Alexander's revolt, Carystus and the northern part of the island remained loyal to Antigonus. On Alexander's death and the recovery of Corinth from his widow, as we have seen, the king dissolved the reconstituted Euboean League and suspended its coinage.[3] The island was now once more firmly within the Macedonian sphere. It was, of course, vital as a staging-post for Macedonian ships *en route* for Attica or southern Greece, so long as Aetolia controlled Thermopylae. Chalcis continued to be garrisoned; and it is significant that at the time when various cities throughout the Greek world were replying to the request from Magnesia-on-the-Maeander to recognize the festival of Artemis Leucophryene (*c.* 206), the decree from Chalcis shows direct dependence on Philip V, through whose chancellery the request had been forwarded, and resembles the replies of several kings in not specifically mentioning or granting *asylia*.[4] A decree from Rhamnus praises Dicaearchus, the Macedonian commander in Eretria, for help during the Demetrian War and several decrees from Eretria honour Macedonian officers.[5] The *Antigoneia* remains an important festival at Histiaea, where the normal organs of government continue to function.[6] Around 230 Carystus issued didrachms with a royal head; and an inscription which mentions a man from Carystus sent by an Antigonus to ask for a judge from Cimolos has been dated by Kontoleon to the reign of Doson—though this, it is true, is not proof of subjection to Macedonia.[7] Whether Euboea is to be counted as nominally independent is not wholly clear. The Euboeans are not listed among the allies constituting the Symmachy set up by Antigonus Doson in 224/3,[8] but they are referred to as allies later.[9] In any case,

---

[1] Philip V held Peparethos in 209 (Plb. 10. 42. 1). When Macedonia acquired it is not known.
[2] See above, p. 301 n. 3.   [3] Above, p. 305.
[4] *Inschr. Magn.* 47 = *SIG* 561; cf. Picard, *Chalcis* 275.
[5] Cf. *IG* XII. 9. 199–200, 205–6, 212, 272. Picard, *Chalcis* 275 mentions several other Eretrian decrees honouring Macedonian officers, but several of these date to the fourth century and few can be dated at all accurately. Of those quoted here no. 212 belongs to the period when Alexander of Corinth controlled the Isthmus and Euboea.
[6] *SIG* 493 l. 23. But this festival could honour either Gonatas or Doson; cf. Habicht, *Gottmenschentum* 80 ('probably Doson').
[7] Cf. Picard, *Chalcis* 275. For the man sent to Cimolos see T. W. Jacobsen and P. M. Smith, *Hesperia* 37 (1968) 184–99; N. M. Kontoleon, *Kimoliaka* 2 (1972) 5–8.
[8] Plb. 4. 9. 4.
[9] Plb. 11. 5. 4. That they were included in the Isthmus proclamation liberating the Greeks in 197 (Plb. 18. 46. 5) suggests that by that date they were subject to Philip; but this may have happened during the First Macedonian War (cf. Plb. 10. 42. 7 with Walbank, *C* 2. 258). See also below, p. 351 n. 6.

Euboea was clearly under close Macedonian surveillance, even if its cities (other than Chalcis) were not garrisoned.[1]

In central Greece the Macedonian position was seriously compromised, however, by the steady growth and expansion of the Aetolian League, which now controlled Ozolian Locris, Heraclea-on-Oeta, Dolopia, the Aenianians, Doris, Epicnemidian Locris, southern Phocis, western Phthiotic Achaea, and the part of Malis which included Thermopylae;[2] and since the Aetolian victory over the Boeotians in 245, the latter had been closely aligned with the Aetolian League, probably on the basis of an *isopoliteia* agreement.[3] Boeotian independence was therefore under serious threat, while that of northern Phocis and the part of Malis towards Lamia was precarious. Attica was of course still a bulwark of Macedonia, with garrisons in Munychia and the Piraeus and at several strong-points in the hills and on the coast. Athens itself, though no longer occupied, was still firmly in the Macedonian sphere.[4] Further south in the Peloponnese, beyond the lost fortress of Corinth, the new king could still look to broadly pro-Macedonian tyrants in Megalopolis, Argos, Hermione, and Phlius.[5] Orchomenus too was under a tyrant, Nearchus, in 235,[6] but how he stood towards Macedonia is not recorded. Sparta continued to enjoy close relations with Achaea,[7] which, in addition to its own territory and the Dorian town of Sicyon on the southern shore of the Corinthian Gulf, now controlled a solid block of territory around the Saronic Gulf, comprising Megara, Corinth, Epidaurus, and Troezen, and was eager to expand southwards within the Peloponnese as well as eastwards into Attica as soon as an opportunity presented itself.

2. *The Epirote Alliance (239 B.C.)*

During the years after he lost Corinth to Aratus Antigonus had used the Aetolians to attack Achaea. But in 241/0, as we saw,[8] these hostilities ended, perhaps in a general peace, but certainly in a peace between the two confederations. This settlement was later converted

---

[1] For an earlier occasion (before 255) when Eretria in particular and Euboea generally seem to have received privileged treatment from Macedonia see above, pp. 270–1.

[2] See above, pp. 275–6 and 289, for Aetolian expansion as indicated by the rise in Aetolian votes on the Amphictyonic Council.

[3] See above, p. 304.   [4] See above, p. 286 and, for the liberation of Athens, p. 288.

[5] See above, pp. 300 (Argos), 308 (Megalopolis and the relation of Lydiades to Macedonia). For Phlius and Hermione see Plb. 2. 44. 6; P*Arat* 34. 7, 35. 5 (Cleonymus and Xenon hand over their tyrannies and join the Achaean League).

[6] *SVA* 499 l. 141. Mantinea, Tegea, and Caphyae later followed the same fortunes as Orchomenus; but there is no evidence that they were under tyrants nor any reason to connect them with Macedonia.

[7] Cf. Urban 64 n. 302.   [8] See above, p. 313 n. 2.

into an alliance between Aratus and Pantaleon, as representatives of
the two sides. But, although Plutarch (*Arat.* 33. 1–2) reports the peace
and the alliance as closely linked, the latter came somewhat later and
after Demetrius had succeeded to the throne of Macedonia.[1] It was
this alliance that provoked the outbreak of the so-called Demetrian
War between the new king and the two old enemies, now acting in
concert.

The events which immediately precipitated the conflict occurred in
Epirus, where close links with Macedonia had been established
through a marriage between Demetrius and the princess Phthia, the
daughter of Alexander of Epirus and his wife and half-sister Olympias,
both being the children of Pyrrhus. According to Justin (28. 1. 2–4),
Alexander died leaving Olympias with two sons, Pyrrhus and Ptolemy,
and a daughter, Phthia. When the Aetolians then proceeded to attack
the western part of Acarnania, which belonged at that time to Epirus,
Olympias 'ad regem Macedoniae Demetrium decurrit' with a proposal
that Demetrius should marry Phthia and, it is implied, help the
Epirotes to resist the Aetolians. At this point Justin describes a
supposed Acarnanian appeal to Rome and an apocryphal Roman
embassy to Aetolia, which received an insulting reception.[2] It is
generally agreed that this story has no historical reality. But the
marriage of Phthia to Demetrius is a fact and the birth of Philip V in
238/7[3] is consonant with the marriage having taken place in 239.

The question of the Macedonian–Epirote alliance is complicated by
Justin's statement that Demetrius' former wife, Stratonice, 'ad fratrem
Antiochum discedit eumque in mariti bellum impellit.' Since
Antiochus died in 246, this, if true, would date Stratonice's flight (and
Demetrius' marriage to Phthia) to 247, which is not easily reconciled
with Philip's birth in 238/7 and the fact that Demetrius did not become
king until 239. Moreover, Agatharchides (*FGrH* 86 F 20a), who also
records Stratonice's flight to Syria, agrees with Justin in dating it to the
reign of Seleucus, whom the queen allegedly tried to entice into
marriage. When this plan failed, she exploited Seleucus' absence on
campaign from Babylon to stir up trouble and, on his return, fled to
Seleuceia where she was taken and executed—a version of events
which ignores the fact that from 246 onwards Seleuceia was in
Ptolemaic hands.

As Holleaux pointed out over sixty years ago,[4] it is impossible to
extract a firm chronology either for Demetrius' marriage to Phthia or

---

[1] Plb. 2. 44. 1.   [2] Cf. Holleaux, *Rome* 5–22, exposing the falsity of this story.
[3] Cf. Walbank, *Ph* 295. It is not certain, of course, that Philip was Phthia's first child. If he
had an elder sister or sisters, the marriage could have been earlier.
[4] Holleaux, *Rome* 7–9 n. 3.

for Stratonice's flight to Syria from these contradictory accounts; and there is no independent evidence for the date of the death of Alexander of Epirus, which evidently preceded Olympias' appeal to Demetrius. It is also impossible to reconcile Justin's story that Stratonice incited Antiochus to war against Demetrius or Agatharchides' story of intrigue at Seleucus' court with what is otherwise known of Antiochus' last years and the early years of Seleucus, which were fully occupied with the Laodicean War against Ptolemy III.[1] We may therefore leave the date of Stratonice's flight and its motivation as insoluble problems on the present evidence and turn our attention to the marriage with Phthia and the Epirote appeal to the new Macedonian king, Demetrius.

It is not self-evident why Demetrius accepted Olympias' proposal, which was clearly bound to lead to a breach with Aetolia. Dell[2] suggested that Demetrius saw advantages in a close alignment with Epirus with a view to creating a strong bulwark against the Illyrians. But there is little evidence of any threat to Macedonia from the coastal Illyrians at this time. Indeed, within a few years Demetrius was himself to call on the king of the Ardiaei to help the Acarnanians.[3] It is perhaps more likely then that Demetrius' eyes were on the southern rather than on the northern frontiers of Epirus and that, since the Aetolians had made peace with Achaea, he was not unwilling to face a breach with their confederacy. Possibly he had become discontented with the compliant policy pursued by Gonatas during his last years towards the growing power which was gradually hemming in Macedonia to the south and was already denying her access to Thermopylae. Perhaps, too, he saw an alliance with Epirus as a way to save that kingdom from eventual annexation by Aetolia.

The marriage with Phthia apparently followed at once and the political implications of the alliance quickly became evident. That Demetrius sent help to Epirus to protect western Acarnania is not specifically recorded. But the Demetrius 'Aetolicus' who, according to Strabo (10. 2. 4 C 451), laid waste the district of Calydon, and so led the inhabitants of Pleuron to migrate to a new site higher up on the slopes of Mt. Aracynthus, may well be Demetrius II. Beloch argued[4]

---

[1] For an attempt to extract a consistent story of Stratonice's flight and activities at Antioch and Seleuceia see Ehrhardt 199–203. In placing the flight in 247 (before Antiochus' death), he is committed to the assumption either that the proposed marriage to Nicaea and Gonatas' recovery of Corinth fell before 246 or that Stratonice's flight had nothing to do with that marriage (still less the marriage to Phthia).

[2] *CP* 62 (1967) 98.   [3] See below, p. 333.

[4] Beloch 4. 2. 136. Accepting the identification with Poliorcetes in *CAH* 7. 1². 449, I stated that there is independent evidence that he had ravaged the area round Pleuron. That is incorrect. The only evidence for that campaign is the passage of Strabo under discussion.

that Demetrius Poliorcetes was meant, and indeed that Αἰτωλικός was a corruption of Πολιορκητικός; it was not, he rightly observed, a Greek custom to assign titles from conquered peoples. Ehrhardt has, however, plausibly suggested[1] that 'Aetolicus', like many other Antigonid nicknames, may originally have carried a taunting meaning, and could have been applied to Demetrius II as the king 'who kept on fighting the Aetolians (unsuccessfully)'. In that case Demetrius probably did bring some help to Epirus.[2] Indeed the failure of the Aetolians to continue with the annexation of western Acarnania is hard to explain on any other assumption.[3] In making his alliance with Olympias Demetrius must have been prepared to take some such action.

3. *The war against the Leagues; Attica and Argos (239–235 B.C.)*

The conversion of the peace between Achaea and Aetolia into an alliance was an event which has to be considered in relation to Demetrius' Epirote policy.[4] No source tells us whether the alliance preceded or followed the Macedonian alliance with Epirus—whether in fact it encouraged Demetrius to accept Olympias' proposal or was the Leagues' reaction to it. Nor do we know whether it was Aratus or Pantaleon who took the initiative in the negotiations. If these followed Demetrius' alliance with Epirus and his invasion of Aetolia, an Aetolian initiative is perhaps more likely—though this is not implied in Plb. 2. 44. 1, where the picture of Achaea lending loyal help to Aetolia merely reflects the historian's partisan view. The alliance in fact served the Achaean interest equally well, for it enabled Aratus to continue his attacks in Attica and the Peloponnese with a clear conscience (if the phrase has any meaning in reference to Aratus). Athens, Argos, Megalopolis, and any other outposts of Macedonian power or influence would become legitimate targets for Achaean attack while, it was hoped, Demetrius was kept active in the north.[5] Both leagues, indeed, had much to gain from weakening Macedonian power in their own corners of Greece. Since moreover it would have been open to Demetrius, without breach of recognized custom, to bring help to

---

[1] Ehrhardt 205–7; *Hermes* 106 (1978) 251–3. He cautiously leaves the question open.

[2] But was the attack on Pleuron part of this aid? Ehrhardt 218 suggests that it was made by sea along the Corinthian Gulf and so after Demetrius' seizure of Boeotia (*c.* 236). But the events of Philip V's reign demonstrate that it was possible to march over the mountains and carry out devastating attacks in Aetolian-held territory. One may doubt the presence of suitable ships in any Boeotian ports on the Gulf and such a voyage would have been in enemy waters all the way to Pleuron.

[3] Unless with Ehrhardt 189–90 one rejects the Aetolian attack on western Acarnania, recorded in J. 28. 1. 1, as being an invention to provide a background for the apocryphal Roman embassy to Aetolia.

[4] See above, p. 322.   [5] Cf. Urban 64.

Epirus under the convention of an *epimachia* without becoming involved in a full-scale war with Aetolia, one must assume that the launching of such a war suited both sides at this juncture. But these considerations are of no help in determining which alliance came first.

According to Athenian records, the Demetrian War broke out in the year of Lysias' archonship,[1] 239/8 on the most likely calculations. The evidence for the fighting is scanty and disjointed and does not permit the reconstruction of a connected account of the strategy or indeed of the objectives on either side. At the most one can identify, and within limits assign dates to, some of the events.[2] For the Achaeans the war seems simply to have provided a wider context within which Aratus could continue his attacks on Athens and Argos. Demetrius sent what help he could to his allies in the south, no doubt mainly in the form of mercenaries. An inscription discovered on the site of Gortyn in southern Crete[3] contains the text of an alliance made between that city and Demetrius II in the third year of his reign and, though it breaks off before the effective clauses are reached, enough survives to show that, like similar treaties made a decade later by Antigonus Doson with Eleutherna and Hierapytna (*SVA* 501–2), it was concerned with the sending of troops, νεανίσ[κοι.[4] It is true that the only evidence for the use of Cretans at all in Macedonian service under the Antigonids before the reign of Philip V is as members of the garrison at Demetrias.[5] That Demetrius did send mercenaries to help his allies is, however, clear from the scanty record. We hear, for example, of a 'royal force', commanded by Agias (perhaps a mercenary captain)[6] and the younger Aristomachus, thwarting Aratus' attempt to capture Argos in 235; and there were of course some mercenaries in Attica.[7] For the most part, however, the garrisons at Eleusis, Panactum, and Phyle and those at Sunium and Rhamnus consisted of Athenian

---

[1] *SIG* 485 l. 37 ἐπὶ Λυσίου ἄρχοντος, ἐν ὧι ἐνιαυτῶι ὁ πόλεμος ἐνέστη. On Lysias' date see Habicht, *Unters.* 143 (apparently superseding the suggestion on p. 135 n. 99 of a return to Beloch's date of 237/6); cf. also B. D. Meritt, *Historia* 26 (1977) 176.

[2] There is no evidence to support the view that the Leagues were either incited or supported by Ptolemy III. It is now clear that the reference to Ptolemaic assistance to Aetolia in *P. Haun.* 6 fr. 12 l. 18, is to be dated to the reign of Doson; and it is at least likely that the statues of the Ptolemaic royal house erected in Aetolia also belong to his reign. See below, p. 340 nn. 1–2.

[3] *IC* 4 no. 167 = *SEG* 13. 465 = *SVA* 498. Gortyn had been aligned against Macedonia in the Chremonidean War. See above, p. 277 n. 4.

[4] As K. Buraselis, *AE* 1981 (1983) 114–25 points out, these troops were technically allies rather than mercenaries; but no doubt financial arrangements were defined in the treaty and in practice such Cretan 'allied troops' will not have been very different from mercenaries.

[5] See Launey 2. 1152–69.

[6] *PArat* 29. 6. The name is known in Elis and Arcadia. J. Kirchner (*RE* s.v. *Agias* (3) col. 808) calls this man an Argive, but, as the commander of a Macedonian mercenary (?) force, he could have come from any Greek city.

[7] Cf. *IG* ii². 3460, referring to the Eleusinian military district.

citizens;[1] and even the generals and phrourarchs were largely Athenians. This demonstrates that, since the catastrophe of the Chremonidean War, a satisfactory *modus vivendi* had been reached between Macedonia and the government in Athens; and Habicht[2] does not exclude the possibility of a joint use of mercenaries by Macedonia and Athens in the occupied fortresses. It was no doubt partly in order to strengthen this relationship that Demetrius decided to reduce the dimensions of his problem of defending his southern possessions against the Achaeans by handing over the occupation of the Eleusinian command (see above, p. 293 n. 5) with its subsidiary forts at Phyle and Panactum to the Athenians themselves, as soon as he felt secure against attack from over the Boeotian frontier.

4. *Demetrius' invasion of Boeotia (c. 236 B.C.)*

It was probably with this object in mind as well as the wish to control a state which was linked closely with the Aetolian League (though not actually a member of it)[3], that Demetrius invaded Boeotia with his army, whereupon the Boeotians (according to Polybius) at once abandoned their links with Aetolia and 'completely submitted to Macedonia.'[4] The date of Demetrius' invasion has been much discussed, but a firm *terminus ante quem* seems now to have been established. Habicht[5] has drawn attention to an inscription containing two decrees in honour of the *strategos* Aristophanes, one that of the garrison at Eleusis, the other that of the Eleusinian *demos* (*IG* II².1299 = *SIG* 485). The inscription is later than the archonship of Cimon (237/6)[6] and probably dates to that of Ecphantus (236/5); and whereas the garrison decree emphasizes loyalty to Demetrius and Macedonia throughout, the slightly later decree of the Eleusinian *demos* makes no reference at all to the royal house. In addition, it mentions (ll. 41–2) mercenaries in the service of the citizens of Athens. These two facts suggest that by 235, when Aristophanes was *strategos* at Eleusis, that command, including the three fortresses of Eleusis, Panactum, and Phyle, had been restored to the city of Athens, though with the same Athenian general in command. In consequence Aristophanes was now

---

[1] *IG* II². 1219, 1280, 1285, 1288, 1299, 3460; Habicht, *Studien* 57.

[2] *Studien* 57, against Maier, *Mauerbauinschriften* 1. 107. The mercenaries in Athenian employ mentioned in *IG* II². 1299 ll. 21–2 belong to a period after the restoration of the Eleusinian command to Athens (see below).

[3] Above, p. 321 n. 3.

[4] Plb. 20. 5. 3 ὑπέταξαν σφᾶς αὐτοὺς ὁλοσχερῶς Μακεδόσι. See Walbank, *C* 3. 69.

[5] *Studien* 57.

[6] Cf. Habicht, *Unters.* 144 for the dates of the archons who are mentioned at ll. 60 and 64 of the inscription. 'Ecphantus' is restored, but seems certain, since he was the archon in the year after Cimon.

responsible for wall repairs at all three fortresses (ll. 65–6), a duty hitherto falling within the competence of the Macedonian-appointed phrourarchs.

This transfer of power to the Athenians implies that Demetrius had conquered Boeotia by c. 236.[1] Beloch (4. 1. 631) assumed that he came from Chalcis, but it is perhaps more likely that he shipped his army over to northern Euboea and thence direct to a port in Boeotia or Locris.[2] He is hardly likely to have come wholly by land.[3] Some support for the view that Demetrius took this route into Boeotia is provided by new evidence on the fortunes of Opus. It has been shown that while Opus was Aetolian as late as 237, by the year of the Boeotian archon Charopinus, which was probably c. 230, it belonged to the Boeotian League; and since it was independent by 228/6, when an Opuntian, Calliclidus, who carried the oracle of Trophonius concerning the reorganization of the *Ptoia* festival to Acraephiae is described as Λοκρὸς ἐσς Ὀποέντος (i.e. he is not a Boeotian) (*IG* VII. 4136. l. 1), the assignment of Opus to Boeotia must have taken place between 237 and 228/6.[4] The likelihood is that Demetrius gave it to Boeotia when it capitulated to him in c. 236 and it is tempting to associate the event with a crossing from Euboea to Opus. In consequence of this change in their fortunes the Boeotians now ceased to send representatives to the Amphictyonic Council.

Flacelière[5] assigns two Amphictyonic decrees, which list Boeotian *hieromnemones* in c. 236/5 and c. 235, but neither is firmly dated and both could be earlier, since the archon Praochus, whom he assigned to 238/7, should probably stand in 241/0[6]. Unfortunately the two lists, which record the victors at the *Soteria* of 237/6 and 233/2, have lost their preamble and are extremely fragmentary, their date depending wholly on their position on the stone.[7] Hence there is no indication of whether the Boeotians sent representatives to the Amphictyonic Council on those occasions or not: presumably not. There were certainly none in 229/8, which is likely to be the year of the archon Herys.[8]

[1] Macedonian control of Boeotia is reflected in a proxeny decree passed in the priesthood of Spintharus at Oropus (at this time Boeotian) for Autocles, the son of Aenesidemus of Chalcis (B. I. Leonardos, *AE* 1892, 49 no. 79), a man known as a *proxenos* at Delos (*IG* XI. 4. 679–80), where he is described as a φίλος of Demetrius II. Cf. Étienne and Knoepfler, *Hyettos* 298.
[2] On this frequently used route see J. O. A. Larsen, *Phoenix* 19 (1965) 122.
[3] So Feyel 101.
[4] On the annexation of Opus to Boeotia see Étienne and Knoepfler, *Hyettos* 288 ff. (date of Charopinus), 331 ff.
[5] Flacelière 402–3 nos. 30–1 (*SIG* 461 and 506).
[6] Nachtergael 280.
[7] Nachtergael 282–3 and 476–7 nos. 60 and 61.
[8] Cf. Flacelière 404 no. 32 (a) and (b); Nachtergael 476–7 no. 60 (victor list only); ibid. 280 for the date.

Against this it has been argued[1] on the basis of an inscription of 236/5 (Athenian archon Ecphantus) that at that time Boeotia was still in the Aetolian camp. In it the people of Rhamnus honours Dicaearchus, the commander of Eretria and formerly (under Gonatas) of Rhamnus and Panactum, and it records assistance recently given by him to the people of Rhamnus in conveying their flocks over to Macedonian-controlled Euboea for safety. On the assumption that the danger to these flocks came from Boeotia, Demetrius' invasion of that country has been dated after 235. But it is perhaps more likely that the threat to Rhamnus came from pirates, such as operated on other occasions in the mid-third century. For example, an Athenian decree passed in the early months of 228 (in the archonship of Heliodorus) honours a Cretan, Eumaridas of Cydonia, who had helped the Athenians a little earlier, when an Aetolian Bucris had raided the coast and had carried off captives to Crete.[2] Bucris of Naupactus was a man of consequence in Aetolia,[3] and had received *proxenia* at Delos. His raid on the Athenian coast may have been an element in the Aetolian strategy of the Demetrian War, but it may equally well have been simply a normal act of Aetolian piracy. If the citizens of Rhamnus were afraid of piratical attacks of this kind, then the decree for Dicaearchus is not relevant to the date of Demetrius' invasion of Boeotia.

Two reasons have been suggested (see above, p. 326) for that invasion: to deny Boeotia to the Aetolians and to free Attica from the threat that would arise were the Aetolians to annex that state completely. That these were not idle fears can be seen from the fact that already, before Demetrius invaded Boeotia, the Aetolians had annexed northern and western Phocis and Malis (and in particular Lamia). The evidence for this lies in an inscription (*SIG* 506) containing an Amphictyonic decree honouring Timocrates of Chios. The name of the Delphic archon is illegible, but the *hieromnemones*

---

[1] Cf. Pouilloux, *Rhamnonte* 129 ff. The inscription is no. 15 = *ISE* 1. 25. I followed this view in *CAH* 7. 1². 450.

[2] *IG* II². 44 = *SIG* 535; on Bucris' raid see Brulé 17 ff. For other examples of piratical raids on Attica see *IG* II. 746, probably to be dated to the Demetrian War (cf. Flacelière 250 n. 3); *SEG* 24. 154 (268/7, in the Chremonidean War; cf. Heinen, *Unters.* 158–9); *SIG* 454, cf. Holleaux, *Études*, 1. 375 (Salaminian decree honouring Heracleitus, Gonatas' general in the Piraeus, for help against pirates during the war against Alexander of Corinth). On security in the Attic countryside see J. H. Young, *Hesperia* 25 (1956) 122–46. The *epidosis* of 244/3 (*IG* II². 791; see above, p. 310 n. 3) may link with defensive action against the Aetolians. The decree for Eurycleides after the liberation of 229 (*IG* II². 834 = *SIG* 497 ll. 7–9) refers to the land being fallow and unsown. See also the decree for Aeschrion, the commander of the Rhamnus garrison (E. Mastrokostas *PAE* 1958 (1965) 35–6 (cf. J. and L. Robert, *Bull. épig.* 1966 no. 182) = Y. Garlan, *BCH* 102 (1978) 103–8). Habicht, *Studien* 59, connects the disruption at Rhamnus with Aratus' raids; but will they have extended as far as these coastal regions?

[3] See *SIG* 494 (Peithagoras archon at Delphi, probably 260/59: Nachtergael 272); *SIG* 500 (proxeny).

include eleven Aetolians and two Boeotians. The presence of the latter shows that this decree was passed before Demetrius annexed Boeotia, while the eleven Aetolians indicate a rise of two in the number of Aetolian votes since the archonship of Praochus (241/0).[1] According to Flacelière,[2] these will be the votes for northern Phocis and Malis. Flacelière dates this inscription to 235, but with the earlier date for the invasion of Boeotia the Aetolian annexation of these two areas must also be earlier.[3]

5. *The Achaean advance: Phylacia (235–233 B.C.)*

For many years Feyel had almost unanimous support for his view that after occupying Boeotia Demetrius went on to seize Megara.[4] But the King Demetrius mentioned in several Megarian proxeny decrees, upon which he rested this argument, is certainly Demetrius I, who controlled Megara for several years, and there is no other evidence for any break in the Achaean control there between 243 (see above, p. 309) and 224, when Megara was transferred to Boeotia (see below, p. 350). Consequently there was no hostile power in the Isthmus to prevent Aratus continuing his raids on Attica, which he had begun shortly before Gonatas died.[5] These incursions cannot be closely dated, but they may have extended throughout the greater part of Demetrius' reign. Plutarch,[6] after describing an attack carried out by one of Aratus' supporters, Erginus, a Syrian, mentions a series of raids on the Piraeus; and though he does not mention Demetrius' accession until his next chapter, his account appears to cover raids on Attica going on well into the new reign. They were pressed home with vigour and at some personal risk, since on one occasion Aratus twisted his leg 'as he fled through the Thriasian plain' and was immobilized in a litter for some time afterwards. These attacks may well have been yet another factor in Demetrius' decision to hand over the responsibility for the defence of the interior of Attica to the Athenians themselves.

Aratus also directed attacks on Argos, which was indirectly an outpost of Macedonian influence; and here, as in Attica, there was

[1] See above, p. 327 n. 6. *SIG* 461, an Amphictyonic decree honouring the philosopher Lycon, which Flacelière also dates in the early 230s (402 no. 30, archon illegible), records only nine Aetolian representatives and must precede the expansion.

[2] Flacelière 247. G. Klaffenbach's belief (*Klio* 32 (1939) 200) that one of the votes was for Phthiotic Achaea depends on his view that the Aetolians had annexed all Phocis during the Chremonidean War; against this see Nachtergael 281.

[3] If this is true, the Amphictyonic victor-list for 233/2 and perhaps even 237/6 will have contained eleven Aetolian votes. Unfortunately, this cannot be checked, since, as we have seen (above, p. 327 n. 7), both are fragmentary and do not include any *hieromnemones*.

[4] Feyel 85 ff.; his argument is decisively refuted by Urban 66 ff.

[5] See above, p. 310; P*Arat* 24. 3.

[6] P*Arat* 33.

little enthusiasm for liberation so long as this meant absorption into the Achaean League. In 235 Aratus penetrated the city by night, but failed to gain any support from the population and after holding out for a day and sustaining a spear-wound in the thigh was forced to withdraw through lack of water.[1] Later in the same year[2] he attempted an open attack by day, but was twice driven off by the tyrant Aristippus. In retaliation he seized Cleonae and, having tricked Aristippus into attacking the town, routed his troops. Aristippus was killed in the course of the flight, but a Macedonian force succeeded in installing Aristippus' brother Aristomachus in the tyranny and so kept this centre of Macedonian power intact (*PArat* 27–9).

Shortly afterwards, however, Demetrius sustained a set-back in the disappearance of the tyranny at Megalopolis. As indicated earlier,[3] there is no direct evidence that Lydiades based his power on Macedonian help; but he represented a substantial obstacle to Achaean expansion and this it was very much in Demetrius' interest to encourage. For some time the steady expansion of the Achaean League had threatened Megalopolis more and more. In 236, in the Achaean generalship of Dioetas, the Achaeans had annexed Heraea[4] and this implies that Cleitor and Telphusa were already theirs (though Elis still possessed Triphylia and Alipheira). The death of Aristippus must have caused Lydiades fresh alarm. It was a triumph for Aratus when, in 235, Lydiades sent for him to negotiate his own abdication and the incorporation of Megalopolis in the Achaean League.[5] The collapse of Lydiades' tyranny was a setback to Demetrius in so far as it removed a curb on his enemies in Achaea. But it was not in fact a very serious matter, for since the loss of Corinth the Peloponnese was more of a liability than an asset to the Macedonians. Its control was still in the forefront of Macedonian policy, partly because it provided a bulwark for the defence of Macedonia and partly no doubt because of its place in Antigonid traditions. But such control could not be exercised once an Achaean garrison held the Acrocorinth. And in the mid-thirties, with Demetrius fully occupied in central Greece, there seemed no chance of the recovery of that stronghold. In the long run, however, the accession of Megalopolis to the Achaean League was to do more harm to the Achaeans than to the Macedonians. For along with Megalopolis the League now inherited a tradition of hostility towards

[1] *PArat* 27. 2.
[2] On the chronology of these attacks (*PArat* 26–30) see Walbank, *A* 186–7.
[3] See above, p. 308.   [4] Polyaen. 2. 36; on the date see Beloch 4. 2. 224.
[5] *PArat* 30. 3–4. On the date see Walbank, *A* 169 n. 6. He was general for the third time when Demetrius died in 229, hence general in 234/3, 232/1, 230/29; consequently he must have surrendered his tyranny the previous year, 235, in time to be elected general for 234/3.

Sparta, which was to be one factor—another was the accession in the same year, 235, of a young and ambitious king, Cleomenes III, to the Agiad throne at Sparta—which would soon set Sparta and Achaea on a collision course; and this in turn was to provide Macedonia with an unforeseen opportunity to regain its foothold in the Peloponnese.

Following the accession of Megalopolis Achaea kept up the impetus of her expansion by acquiring Tegea, Mantinea, Orchomenus, and Caphyae—though for reasons that remain obscure these cities soon afterwards left Achaea and joined the Aetolian League, probably through a link of *isopoliteia*.[1] Perhaps the most likely explanation of these shifts is that the cities in question joined Achaea, not through enthusiasm for her confederacy, but out of fear, following the abdication of Lydiades; and that their sympathies were basically with Sparta (to which they switched allegiance in 229), with the result that the anti-Spartan policy now adopted by the League in response to Lydiades' pressure alienated them. They therefore joined Aetolia, an ally of Achaea, because they thought this would be more acceptable to the Achaeans and less dangerous to themselves than an undisguised defection to Sparta would have been. Finally, it was perhaps with Aetolian connivance that they went over to Sparta in 229.[2] But other explanations are possible.

On what the Macedonians were doing at this time we have virtually no information. Plutarch[3] records a battle in which Demetrius' general Bithys defeated Aratus περὶ Φυλακίαν, but the only chronological indication is that it fell in a generalship of Aratus sometime between Demetrius' accession and his death[4] and that the Macedonian commander in the Piraeus was Diogenes, who was still in command there in 229.[5] It was probably this same Bithys who received Athenian citizenship by a decree passed in the thirties,[6] but he is otherwise unknown. The site of 'Phylakia' is disputed, but it could be the Phylace

---

[1] Plb. 2. 46. 2 (seizure of Tegea, Mantinea, and Orchomenus by Cleomenes from Aetolia in 229); 57. 1 (Mantinea deserts Achaea for Aetolia); *SIG* 490 = *IG* v. 2. 344 = *SVA* 499 (treaty of accession to the Achaean League by Orchomenus). On the changes in allegiance of these four towns see Walbank, *C* 1.242–3 (on Plb. 2. 46. 2). Orchomenus was under a tyrant, Nearchus, who followed Lydiades' lead in abdicating.

[2] Cf. De Sanctis, *Scritti* 1.392; Walbank, *CAH* 7. 1². 411.   [3] P*Arat* 34. 2.

[4] The invasion of Attica which followed Bithys' victory (P*Arat* 34. 4) is described by Plutarch separately from the attacks mentioned in *Arat* 33. 2–5 and seems to be later.

[5] On Diogenes see below, p. 341 and n. 1. If he was one of the contributors to a state fund (*epidosis*) in the archonship of Diomedon (see above, p. 310 n. 3), he was already in this post in 244/3. But the evidence for that lies in an inscription (*IG* 11². 791 with new fragments in B. D. Meritt, *Hesperia* 11 (1942) 287–92 no. 56: I. 48 ...6...ης Μακε(δων)) in which Diogenes' name is restored. 'Diogenes' is the right length to fill the lacuna, but there is no certainty either that this contained the name of the commandant or that he was Diogenes.

[6] *IG* 11². 808; cf. M. J. Osborne, *Anc. Soc.* 5 (1974) 97–104; Habicht, *Studien* 25. The Delian dedication *IG* XI. 4. 1242 may be by the same Bithys.

situated about 10 miles south of Tegea (Paus. 8. 54. 2).[1] If so, Bithys must have shipped troops to Argos to march over the hills in a direct attack on Achaean territory; but his precise aims and strategy are beyond recovery.[2] The battle has generally been assigned to the year 233/2. Two years earlier is a possibility; but by 231 Demetrius was fully occupied in the north (see below). Aratus followed up his defeat with a routine attack on Attica, in which he got as far as the Academy before retiring πεισθείς—an ambiguous word, which may suggest that he was bribed to go away. Plutarch relates this invasion to a story of Athenian rejoicing over a false report of Aratus' death and an ultimatum from Diogenes to the Achaeans to hand back Corinth. Both stories are probably apocryphal.

6. *Revolution in Epirus: Demetrius and the Illyrians (233–229 B.C.)*

The final stages of the war, like the first, are associated with Epirus, where the rather swift downfall of the monarchy brought an end to such advantages as the alliance had been intended to gain for Macedonia. Once more the evidence is mainly in Justin, supplemented with an extract from Polyaenus. According to the former, at an unspecified date Olympias handed over the kingdom of Epirus to her son Pyrrhus and he, having died soon afterwards, was succeeded by his brother Ptolemy. Ptolemy himself soon perished in the course of a campaign against enemies who are not named (perhaps they were Aetolians) and Olympias did not survive her sons for very long.[3] The only remaining members of the Aeacid royal house were now Nereis and Deidameia, the daughters of Pyrrhus I.[4] Nereis was married to Gelon, the son of Hieron of Syracuse, by whom she became the mother of Hieronymus.[5] But Deidameia seems to have held some position in Epirus after Ptolemy's death and, when popular leaders seized power, to have opposed them from a base in Ambracia. She was, however, soon overwhelmed in the rising which swept the country and she perished while seeking refuge at the altar of Artemis Hegemon, either

---

[1] Beloch 4. 2. 529 rightly rules out the possibility that it is Phylace in Phthiotis.

[2] Habicht, *Studien* 59 seems to imply that Bithys' victory was in Attica, but no place called Phylakia is known there.

[3] J. 28. 3. 1–3; according to Polyaen. 8. 52, Ptolemy was assassinated at Ambracia.

[4] So Plb. 7. 4. 5; J. 28. 3. 4 gives the name as Laodamia, but see Polyaen. 8. 52 for the correct form. Polybius makes Nereis the daughter of Pyrrhus I; and cf. Livy 24. 6. 8: Hieronymus was descended from 'Pyrrhi regis, materni avi', who must be the great Pyrrhus; Paus. 6. 12. 3. This is preferable to Paus. 4. 35. 3 (she was the grandchild of Ptolemy, the grandson of Pyrrhus I). See Corradi, *Atti Acc. Torino* 47 (1911–12) 192–215; *HE* 594 (Nereis and Deidamia daughters of the younger Pyrrhus, grandson of Pyrrhus I); Seibert, *DV* 110–11; Ehrhardt 176–82.

[5] On the date of Nereis' marriage see Ehrhardt 176–82. Hieronymus was born *c.* 231/0, but there may have been earlier children who died, or girls who have dropped out of the record.

at the hands of the crowd (Justin) or slain by Milon, allegedly a matricide (Polyaenus).[1] A republic was now set up in Epirus, but was unable to impose the federal power over all the areas hitherto held by the Aeacids. It was probably now that Ambracia and Amphilochia broke away from Epirus to become members of the Aetolian League.[2]

The demise of the Epirote monarchy encouraged the Aetolians to renew their attacks on western Acarnania, which now probably also managed to assert its independence from the weakened republic of Epirus. The chronology of the Epirote revolution is uncertain, but it was probably in 231 that the Aetolians laid siege to Medeon in western Acarnania.[3] The Acarnanians, it appears, appealed to Demetrius for help, but he was unable to send any for reasons that Polybius does not record. (What these may have been will be considered later.) Unable to respond,[4] Demetrius took the dangerous step of subsidizing Agron, the king of the Ardiaei, an Illyrian people living around Scodra and as far north as the Bay of Kotor, to assist the Acarnanians. Agron accordingly sent a fleet of 100 *lembi* with 5,000 men on board to help the latter. These Illyrians were successful in defeating the Aetolian army when it looked as if the capture of Medeon was certain. The date was autumn 231, since the event coincided with the end of the Aetolian year, when the new general for 231/0 was due to take office.[5] Shortly afterwards Agron died and his widow Teuta, who took over the throne,[6] sent out a force equal in strength to that of the previous year. This force, after raiding the coast of Elis and Messenia, put in near Phoenice. Having been somewhat naïvely received into the city as friends (because enemies of Aetolia), the Illyrians conspired with 800 Gallic mercenaries in Epirote service to seize Phoenice. On news of this the Epirote League called out the federal army πανδημεί. But meanwhile the Illyrians had got a message through to the north and a second Illyrian force, commanded by Scerdilaidas, which was probably already stationed in southern Albania, advanced southwards along the Drin valley. The Epirotes divided their army, sending one section to protect Antigoneia (mod. Jerme). But those left behind were caught unawares by the troops occupying Phoenice and sustained a disastrous defeat.[7]

---

[1] On the overthrow of the Epirote royal house see H*E* 591–2.

[2] This cannot be proved. All that is known for certain is that Ambracia and Amphilochia were Aetolian at the time of the Social War early in Philip V's reign; cf. *IG* ix². 1. 31 l. 83 (223/2), where Charicles, an Ambracian, acts as guarantor for a Tarentine who receives *proxenia* from Aetolia (H*E* 602).

[3] Plb. 2. 2. 5; for the date see De Sanctis 3. 1. 293 n. 73. Medeon (cf. Thuc. 3. 106. 2) lay a little south of Katouna; cf. Leake, *NG* 3. 503, cf. 575–6.

[4] See below, p. 335.

[5] Plb. 2. 2. 7–4. 5; on the date see Walbank, *C* 1. 134 on 2. 2. 8.

[6] Plb. 2. 4. 7.   [7] Plb. 2. 5. 1–8; cf. H*E* 596.

Having suffered these losses at the hands of the troops originally
called in by Demetrius to help Acarnania, the Epirotes now turned to
the enemies of Macedonia and sent representatives to the Aetolian and
Achaean Leagues. Their call for help was favourably considered and a
joint force sent to Helicranum. An encounter with the united forces of
the Illyrians in Phoenice, which now included those of Scerdilaidas,
was imminent when Teuta suddenly recalled both divisions to deal
with a threatened defection to the Dardanians in the north of her
kingdom. Before departing, the Illyrians brought pressure to bear on
the Epirotes to switch sides yet again, in order to secure the return of
Phoenice and the liberation of its free population, and to this the
Epirotes agreed. Both they and the Acarnanians made an alliance with
Teuta, by which they abandoned their links with the Aetolians and the
Achaeans.[1]

The following spring (229) Teuta sent an even larger force to attack
the Greek cities along the coast; Epidamnus narrowly escaped capture
and Corcyra was put under siege. The representatives of these cities,
together with those of Apollonia, now jointly appealed to the Achaean
and Aetolian Leagues, who agreed to man jointly the meagre fleet of
ten vessels, which was all the Achaeans possessed; why the Aetolians
provided none is not explained. The Illyrians, reinforced by seven
Acarnanian vessels, had no difficulty in defeating the federal ships in
an engagement off the island of Paxos, probably around May or June
229.[2] Whether the threatened cities making the appeal themselves
contributed any ships is not recorded. Corcyra was now forced to come
to terms with the enemy and accept an Illyrian garrison under the
command of Demetrius of Pharos; and Epidamnus was in turn put
under siege.[3] Already, however, the Illyrians had fallen foul of Rome
and it was shortly after this that a Roman expeditionary force under
two consular commanders arrived in Greek waters. The First Illyrian
War, which lasted till spring 228, ended in a complete Roman victory
and a treaty which forbade the Illyrians to sail south of
Lissus.[4] The Roman general L. Postumius followed up his victory by
sending envoys to announce the outcome of the war to the Achaean
and Aetolian Leagues; and shortly afterwards the Senate sent further
envoys to Corinth and Athens.[5] According to Zonaras,[6] the
Romans were allowed to compete in the Isthmian Games of 228, when

---

[1] Plb. 2. 6. 1–11. H*E* 596 locates Helicranum at Chrisorrhaki about 30 km. north-west of
Ioannina.

[2] On the date of the battle of Paxos cf. Ehrhardt 231–2, who shows that the agreement
between the Epirotes and the Achaeans and Aetolians cannot have taken place before May 229.

[3] Plb. 2. 9. 1–10. 9.

[4] Plb. 2. 11. 1–12. 6; on the Roman dispositions in Illyria after the victory see H*IRM* 7–9.

[5] Plb. 2. 12. 4–6. 8.   [6] Zon. 8. 19.

Plautus won the stadium race, and at Athens the Roman envoys were admitted to the Eleusinian mysteries. These moves have been variously interpreted. But on a minimal interpretation of their significance, they revealed a certain coldness towards Macedonia—which, however, as we shall see, was at this time facing more serious problems than Roman displeasure.

7. *The end of Demetrius' reign (229 B.C.)*

The battle of Paxos (229) was the last joint operation of the Achaean and Aetolian Leagues and, though it occurred after Demetrius' death, it may perhaps be regarded as the end of the Demetrian War. In the last stages of this war the Epirotes had moved from their original position as protégés of Macedonia and had become allies of the Achaean and Aetolian Leagues, a situation which was very soon reversed in order to recover Phoenice. These switches were the result of Demetrius' ill-advised policy of inviting in the Illyrians. That he took what he must have known to be a grave risk suggests that at the time he took it he found himself in a desperate situation. Things had gone reasonably well in central Greece with the acquisition of Boeotia and Opus, and Attica was still firmly held, even after the handing over of the interior forts based on the Eleusis command to the Athenians. In the Peloponnese, it is true, Demetrius had lost some ground to the Achaeans, but, as we have seen,[1] nothing that happened south of Corinth at this time was vital to Macedonian interests. In the circumstances, what prevented his giving help himself to the Epirotes and led him to take the grave risk of buying Illyrian help instead must have been a Dardanian invasion from the north. Such an attack, led by a certain Longarus (Livy 31. 28. 1–2) is recorded by Trogus[2] as taking place shortly before Demetrius' death, and it resulted in a Macedonian defeat. It was, moreover, about the same time that the Dardanians were also active further south, where Teuta had similarly been obliged to call off her forces from Phoenice because of defections to the Dardanians in her northern districts.[3] Evidently the Dardanian tribes were in movement at this time, for reasons which we cannot now determine. But, as far as Macedonia was concerned, this was a problem which would have to await Demetrius' successor.

By the time the Romans arrived in Epirote waters, Demetrius was already dead. He died in the spring of 229, about the time they

---

[1] See above, p. 330.
[2] Trog. *Prol.* 28 'ut rex Macedoniae Demetrius sit a Dardanis fusus: quo mortuo etc.'
[3] See above, p. 334.

were preparing to cross the Adriatic.[1] His last years are shrouded in silence and we do not know whether he played any part in the events in Epirus, once he had invited in the Illyrians. The war against the Leagues must in retrospect have seemed a disaster. The initiative in the south had remained mainly with the Achaeans. Attica had resisted Aratus but, as events were soon to show, the making over of the forts to their own authority had whetted the Athenians' appetite for complete independence. Boeotia was now under Macedonian control, but could hardly be relied on;[2] and even with Opus annexed to Boeotia, communications with southern Greece remained difficult so long as the Aetolians sat astride Thermopylae. The invitation to Agron seems to have been a sudden decision to cope with a crisis. But it had far-reaching and unfortunate results, in as much as it established a link between Macedonia and Illyria at the very time that the Illyrian kingdom was about to become embroiled with Rome. The seeds of trouble were sown and were to come to fruition fourteen years later. Meanwhile the death of the king, leaving as his heir a child of nine years,[3] his son by the Epirote princess Phthia, compounded the many problems which at this moment confronted Macedonia.

---

[1] On the date of Demetrius' death see Plb. 2. 44. 2. περὶ τὴν πρώτην διάβασιν εἰς τὴν Ἰλλυρίδα Ῥωμαίων. There is no evidence that Demetrius was killed in action. J. 28. 3. 14 speaks of the Dardanians *and the Thessalians* exulting over his death; the passage cannot therefore be pressed into proving that the Dardanians could claim credit for his death.

[2] For the anti-Macedonian opposition in Boeotia see Plb. 20. 5. 5.

[3] He was seventeen in autumn/winter 221 (Plb. 4. 5. 3; the same figure is repeated for early summer 220: Plb. 4. 24. 1). See, for further discussion, Walbank, *Ph* 295–6.

XVI

ANTIGONUS DOSON (229–221 B.C.)[1]

1. *The first two years (229–228 B.C.)*

THE death of Demetrius II early in 229 was a serious blow to Macedonia. The legitimate heir, Philip, was a child,[2] who clearly could not cope with the responsibility of kingship; and a strong leader was essential in view of Demetrius' defeat by the Dardanians. The Macedonians therefore looked round for a suitable member of the royal house to step into the breach and their choice fell on Antigonus, the son of Gonatas' half-brother, Demetrius the Fair, and so, like his cousin Demetrius II, a grandson of Poliorcetes.[3] Antigonus was later known as Doson,[4] though what this signified is uncertain. According to Porphyry, he was also called Physcus, which should mean 'corpulent'.[5] Plutarch, the only source to mention the manner of his appointment, attributes the decision to 'the leading Macedonians'[6]; we have no reference to any assembly approving their choice but this need not mean that none met. Antigonus was appointed guardian (*epitropos*) to Philip and also *strategos*,[7] army commander,

---

[1] The sources for the reign of Doson are rather fuller than those for Demetrius II; but they concern mainly his relations with the Peloponnese (and to some extent Caria), with little on Macedonian relations with the peoples on the northern frontier and with the Aegean. The main source is Polybius, who devotes much of Book 2 to the events leading to the Achaean crisis and the return of Macedonia to the Peloponnese. His account, which draws largely on Aratus' *Memoirs* (but also on a Megalopolitan oral tradition) can be supplemented from Plutarch's *Lives* of *Aratus* (also largely using the *Memoirs*), *Cleomenes* (based mainly on Phylarchus), *Philopoemen* (for an incident in the battle of Sellasia), and *Aemilius Paulus*. There is also some information in Justin (28. 3. 9–4. 16) and Trog. *Prol.* 28. Frontinus and Pausanias are occasionally useful. *P. Haun.* adds something to our knowledge of the Aetolian invasion of Thessaly; and the inscriptions from Labraunda throw new light on the Carian expedition.   [2] See above, p. 336 n. 3.

[3] Cf. Eus. 1. 243 Sch.; Porph. *FGrH* 260 F 31 (6).

[4] According to Livy 40. 54. 5 (following Polybius) 'tutorem eum Graeci, ut cognomine a ceteris regibus distinguerent, appellarunt'; and Athen. 6. 251 d quotes Phylarchus Ἀντιγόνου τοῦ κληθέντος Ἐπιτρόπου. Pausanias (2. 8. 4, 6. 16. 3, 7. 7. 4, 8. 8. 11) frequently refers to Antigonus as Philip's guardian. It does not follow that ἐπίτροπος (*tutor*) translates a Macedonian word 'doson' meaning 'guardian' (though this is possible; cf. Beloch 4. 2. 139). That 'Doson' meant 'one who promised, but did not keep his promise' (*PAem* 8. 3) sounds like a poor guess, for Antigonus did hand over the kingdom to Philip on his death.

[5] Eus. 1. 238 Sch.; Porph. *FGrH* 260 F 3 (14); on the meaning of this word, which recalls Ptolemy VIII's nickname 'Physcon', see O. Hoffmann, *Die Makedonen* (Göttingen, 1906) 213.

[6] Cf. *PAem* 8. 3 δείσαντες δὲ τὴν ἀναρχίαν οἱ πρῶτοι Μακεδόνων Ἀντίγονον ἐπάγονται τοῦ τεθνηκότος ἀνεψιὸν ὄντα. See R. M. Errington, *Chiron* 8 (1978), 92–3.

[7] Cf. Plb. 20. 5. 7 Ἀντίγονος μετὰ τὸν Δημητρίου θάνατον ἐπιτροπεύσας Φιλίππου; cf. 2. 45. 2 προσεστῶτι Μακεδόνων ἐπιτροπεύοντι δὲ Φιλίππου παιδὸς ὄντος; *PAem* 8. 3 ἐπίτροπον καὶ στρατηγόν.

which recalls the office held by Sosthenes in 279–7; and he married Demetrius' widow Phthia, Philip's mother, to strengthen his position.[1] According to Porphyry,[2] followed by Eusebius, he reared no children by her so as not to jeopardise Philip's eventual succession. Antigonus remained Philip's guardian until he died.

Demetrius' death was a signal for the enemies of Macedonia to invade. In the north the Dardanians under Longarus, who had defeated Demetrius shortly before his death, were still an active threat.[3] Though our sources do not decisively indicate in what sequence Antigonus tackled the problems confronting him, it seems likely that the Dardanians must have been his first priority, especially if they had penetrated the northern frontiers. But an almost equally disastrous situation arose in Thessaly, where an insurrection was accompanied by an Aetolian invasion and the temporary annexation of many areas to the Aetolian League.[4] This is partly to be deduced from the later Aetolian possession of Phthiotic Achaea, but it is also revealed by the increase in the number of votes claimed by Aetolia on the Amphictyonic Council. In the year of the Delphic archon Herys (probably 229/8) the Aetolians still claimed only eleven votes, which included those of northern Phocis and Malis, annexed during the Demetrian War.[5] But in 225/4, the next year for which figures are available, the number has risen to fourteen.[6] The most likely explanation of these additional votes—they very soon rose to fifteen[7]—is that they are those of Thessaliotis and Hestiaeotis together with Phthiotis.[8] On the other hand, the Aetolians clearly did not continue to hold most

On Sosthenes' position see above p. 254 n. 4. Though Philip is normally called the son of Demetrius, in *Labraunda* no. 7 ll. 12–13 (cf. no. 5 l. 48) he refers to Antigonus as his father.

[1] According to Plb. 5. 89. 7, Euseb. 1. 237, 238 Sch., and Porph. *FGrH* 260 F 3, 13–14 (cf. *Etym. Magn.* 10 s.v. Δώσων), the name of Philip's mother (and Doson's wife) was Chryseis, but inscriptions call her Phthia (*Inscr. Délos* 407 l. 20; *IG* ii². 1299=*SIG* 485 (restoration appears certain)). Tarn has argued convincingly that Chryseis was a nickname for Phthia which won popular currency and eventually ousted the princess's real name in some of the written sources (*Ferguson Studies* 483–501).   [2] Cf. Porph. *FGrH* 260 F 3 (14); Eus. 1. 238 Sch.
[3] See above, p. 335 n. 2.
[4] Cf. J. 28. 3. 14, where Antigonus later 'commemorat...ut defectionem sociorum uindicauerit, ut Dardanos Thessalosque exultantes morte Demetrii compescuerit.' The 'defectio sociorum' looks like something other than the Thessalian revolt, which is mentioned separately. But there is no reference elsewhere to any other allied revolt put down by Antigonus. The order of the words 'Dardanos Thessalosque' is perhaps a slight indication that the Dardanians were dealt with first.
[5] *GDI* 2521 = *SIG* 499. See above, p. 328. On the dating of the changes in the number of votes I accept Nachtergael's scheme.
[6] See *SEG* 18. 237 (= Flacelière 404 no. 33; Nachtergael 478 no. 63), a fragmentary catalogue of victors in the musical conext at the *Soteria* (225/4); *GDI* 2525 (=Flacelière 405 no. 34, archon Nicarchus); *GDI* 2544 (=Flacelière 405 no. 35, archon Callias).
[7] Cf. *GDI* 2568 (=Flacelière 406 no. 36; Nachtergael 480–1 no. 65, 'agonothetes Xennias'), probably 217/16.
[8] See Flacelière 253; Nachtergael 284; Will 1². 361–3. The seizure of Thessaly evidently occurred too late to be reflected in the votes for 229/8.

of Thessaly throughout the 220s and one has therefore to explain the Aetolian retention of these votes. Two possibilities have been envisaged.[1] The first is that the Aetolians based their claim on the presence in Aetolia of Thessalian exiles. Exiles were not needed as representatives, however, since the Aetolians normally 'pooled' the votes of states attached to them and did not restrict the representation of a state to citizens belonging to it. Alternatively, Doson left the Aetolians holding a few cities, thus giving them a tenuous claim to votes which would not be challenged in a Council boycotted by the Macedonians. But why should he do that? A third and perhaps more likely explanation is that the Aetolians simply retained the votes as a claim on the territories in question (knowing that it would go unchallenged).[2]

Of the Aetolian defeat little is known. Frontinus, however,[3] records a stratagem by which 'Antigonus rex Macedonum' allowed Aetolian forces which he had penned up and was besieging in an unnamed town to escape and then wiped them out as they fled, thus avoiding the losses likely in a direct assault. This must be Doson, since Gonatas never fought against the Aetolians; and the incident fits easily into the campaign to expel them from Thessaly. Once master of Thessaly, Antigonus pursued them further south. An inscription from Xanthus in Lycia[4] mentions an attack by Antigonus Doson on Cytinium in Doris, while its men of military age were absent protecting Delphi, in the course of which he razed the walls and burnt the town.[5] He was

---

[1] Cf. Will 1². 363.

[2] See for discussion J. V. A. Fine, *TAPA* 63 (1932) 130–47; *AJP* 61 (1940) 129–65; M. T. Piraino, *Antigono Dosone re di Macedonia* (Palermo, 1953) 365–6.

[3] Frontin. *Strat.* 2. 6. 5.

[4] For information about this long and important inscription I am grateful to Professors P. Roesch, F. Chamoux and, especially, J. Bousquet, who is to publish it in *REG*, and who kindly made the text available to me and gave me permission to quote from it. It refers to an appeal to Xanthus from Cytinium in Doris, requesting help in the rebuilding of its walls, destroyed partly in an earthquake and then subsequently by Antigonus Doson. There had been some doubt about the date of the inscription but M. Bousquet has now firmly established this as 2 Audnaios of year 17 (l. 3 has LII, L being the abbreviation for ἔτους) of Philopator, i.e. 15 December 206. Why so long a time elapsed between the damage sustained by Cytinium and the appeal to Xanthus is not clear, but it probably links with the succession of wars—the Cleomenean, Social, and First Macedonian—which followed the attack. The appeal comes shortly after the separate peace made between Philip V and Aetolia in 206. Doson's attack can hardly be later than 228, for clearly he made peace with Aetolia before his Carian expedition. The retrospective reference to him as *basileus* (not *strategos*) need not invalidate this dating. See further F. Chamoux, *La Civilisation hellénistique* (Paris, 1981) 260; Robert, *Amyzon* 162 ff., 189.

[5] ll. 93–9 read: συμβαίνει γὰρ ἁμῶν, καθ᾽ ὃν καιρὸν
ὁ βασιλεὺς Ἀντίγονος ἐνέβαλε ἐν τὰν Φωκίδα, τῶν τε
τειχέων μέρη τινὰ καταπεπτώκειν ὑπὸ τῶν σεισμῶν πα-
96 σᾶν τᾶμ πολίων καὶ τοὺς νεωτέρους εἰσβοαθοήκε(ι)ν ἐν τὸ ἱερὸν
τοῦ Ἀπόλλωνος τοῦ ἐν Δελφοῖς· παραγενόμενος δὲ ὁ βασιλεὺς ἐν τὰν Δωρίδα τά τε τείχη ἁμῶν κατέσκαψε πασᾶν
τᾶμ πολίων καὶ τὰς οἰκίας κατέκαυσε.
96 lapis εἰσβοαθοηκεν, emend. Bousquet.

able to seize Cytinium so easily because shortly before earth tremors had already destroyed part of the walls of all the cities in Doris. We are not told why the troops of Cytinium were absent defending Delphi. But it can hardly have been against Antigonus, for had he been expected to attack Delphi, the Aetolians (and Dorians) would not have left a city ungarrisoned which stood directly on the road from Lamia and Heraclea southwards, especially one with gaps in its walls from a recent earthquake. One must assume that the Aetolians had confidence in their force in Thessaly and that it was felt safe to send Dorian troops south to protect Delphi—perhaps against pirates. The use of the word εἰσβοαθοήκε(ι)ν is inconsistent with routine garrison duties. Antigonus' onslaught was evidently unexpected and that would be so if it followed closely on the victory described by Frontinus, in which the Aetolian army suffered heavy losses. Antigonus probably marched directly south through Malis and his action is to be regarded as an act of retaliation for the Aetolian invasion of Thessaly.

The defeat of the Aetolians will have disappointed Ptolemy III, for he had supported their attack on Thessaly, possibly with funds. According to *P. Haun.* 6[1] he was an ally (συνεμάχησεν) of the Aetolians in the war against Antigonus Doson and this has been taken to indicate that other examples of Ptolemaic patronage revealed by Aetolian decrees and monuments honouring Ptolemy III and his family should be dated to the time of Antigonus Doson rather than to that of Demetrius II.[2] But it is of course possible that warm relations between Aetolia and Alexandria existed at the time of both Macedonian kings.

The war with Aetolia probably ended in 228. Polybius' distorted account[3] of a compact made in that year between Antigonus and the Aetolians (and Cleomenes of Sparta) may have this peace settlement as its kernel of truth. But meanwhile the Aetolians, the Thessalians, and the Dardanians did not make up the sum of Antigonus' troubles. Further south, in southern and central Greece, allies wavered and subject states saw an opportunity to throw off the Macedonian yoke. The Athenians at long last ejected the Macedonian garrison from the Piraeus with the co-operation of its mercenary commander Diogenes, who merely stipulated that 120 talents should be raised to pay off his

---

[1] Chr. Habicht, *ZPE* 39 (1980) 1–5, drawing on a new examination of the text of *P. Haun.* 6 by A. Bülow-Jacobsen (*ZPE* 36 (1979) 91–100), points out the significance of *P. Haun.* 6. l. 18 συνεμάχησεν Αἰτ⟨ω⟩λοῖς εἰς τὸν πρὸς Ἀντίγο[νον πόλεμον]. It had formerly been supposed that this passage referred to help given to Aetolia in the war against Demetrius (cf. W. Huss, *Chron. d'Égypte* 50 (1975) 312 ff.; *Unters.* 105 n. 7).

[2] *IG* ix. 1². 56, a group of statues for Ptolemy III and his family at Thermum (= *ISE* 2. 86); *IG* ix. 1². 202 = *Delph.* 3(4). 233 (with an additional fragment reported by Flacelière 268 n. 3); *IG* ix. 1². 203; Flacelière 268–9.

[3] Plb. 2. 45. 2; see Walbank, *C* 1. 241 ad loc.

troops. Aratus was active in this, contributing 20 talents to the subscription list in the vain hope of coaxing Athens to join the Achaean League. The main honours, however, went to the Athenian brothers Eurycleides and Micion, who sponsored the operation and subsequently directed their liberated city, pursuing a conservative policy of neutrality linked with the cultivation of Ptolemaic favour.[1] The process of liberation, set in motion in the early months of 229, was complete by the summer of that year and the Athenians celebrated the recovery of Piraeus and the other fortresses by instituting a new archon list beginning with 229/8, the year of Heliodorus.[2]

The Boeotian League, which Demetrius had taken over in 237/6,[3] now also broke its links with Macedonia. The new policy is reflected in loans made by Thespiae and Thebes to Athens for her liberation.[4] In addition Boeotia and the Phocian League (which had also thrown off Macedonian control) became allies[5] and both leagues made a further alliance with the Achaeans, depositing hostages in Achaea as a pledge of loyalty.[6] The move towards Achaea probably involved some coldness towards the Aetolians.[7] It is noteworthy that, despite the break with Macedonia, the Boeotians sent no representatives to Delphi in 229/8, the year of Herys' archonship.[8] Antigonus was unable to counter these moves immediately, though very shortly (perhaps after his march south into Doris and Phocis) he gained control of Opuntian Locris, which had probably been Boeotian since 237/6 (see above, p. 327 n. 4).[9]

In the Peloponnese too the crisis in Macedonia had repercussions. At Argos Aristomachus agreed to follow Lydiades' example and resigned his tyranny, subject to the Achaeans' providing 550 talents to pay off his mercenaries. Early in the Achaean year 229/8 Aratus as general had Argos admitted into the League and shortly afterwards Xenon, the tyrant of Hermione, and Cleonymus, the tyrant of Phlius, laid

---

[1] P*Arat* 34. 5–6; Paus. 2. 8. 6. Diogenes was granted Athenian citizenship and later his family is connected by marriage with the aristocratic family of the Eteobutadai (*IG* ii². 3474). A gymnasium for the ephebes, the *Diogeneion*, was built and named after him and an ephebic festival, the *Diogeneia*, was set up in his honour and continued to be celebrated until the third century A.D. (*IG* ii². 1011 l. 41; 1028 l. 24; 1029 l. 55; 1040; 1078; 3765; *SEG* 1. 52; Pélékidis 264–6). There is, however, no direct evidence that he received a cult; cf. Habicht, *Studien* 84. On Eurycleides and Micion see *IG* ii². 834 ll. 10–11 (decree for Eurycleides) and for Ptolemaic support see Maass 112; Habicht, *Studien* 79 ff.

[2] *IG* ii². 1706. See Habicht, *Studien* 79 n. 4.   [3] See above, p. 326, n. 4.

[4] *IG* vii. 1737–8, 2405–6; Feyel, *Contr.* 19 ff.

[5] *IG* ix. 1. 98 = *ISE* 2. 83. Roesch 359–64 makes a strong case for dating this about 228.

[6] *SIG* 519, an Achaean inscription from Aegium, records honours later voted to these hostages.

[7] Cf. Feyel, *Contr.* 122–3.

[8] Cf. Flacelière 404 App. I no. 32; Nachtergael 280 (table), 283, and 477–8 (*Actes* no. 62).

[9] Cf. Étienne and Knoepfler, *Hyettos* 331–41.

down their powers and joined Achaea, as did the island of Aegina, which had been held by Macedonia along with the Piraeus.[1] This access of new members to the Achaean League was in appearance a serious setback to the Macedonian position in Greece, but their allegiance was much less firmly rooted than Polybius implies. Within a few years the failure of the expanded League to withstand an attack from Sparta was to provide an unforeseen opportunity for a Macedonian *revanche*.

The expansion of Achaea coincided with, and may have caused, a break with Aetolia. As we saw (above, p. 334), the battle of Paxos, the last joint operation of the two leagues, took place in May or June 229. About the same time Cleomenes III of Sparta annexed the Arcadian cities of Tegea, Mantinea, Orchomenus, and Caphyae, perhaps at their request.[2] Formerly Achaean, these four cities had recently been linked to Aetolia, and their annexation by Sparta was bitterly resented in Achaea, though there was little the Aetolians could have done to retain them, even had they wished. The Spartan seizure of these cities was followed by hostilities between Cleomenes and the Achaeans. Still in 229 Cleomenes occupied the Athenaeum fortress on the border of Arcadia, and Aratus made an unsuccessful night attack on Tegea and Orchomenus. Soon afterwards, late in 229 or early in 228, the Achaeans declared war on Sparta,[3] thus initiating what was to become known as the Cleomenean War.[4] Still in Aratus' generalship (229/8) the Achaeans seized Caphyae from Cleomenes and during the ensuing summer Cleomenes invaded the central Peloponnese to take Methydrium. But Aratus persuaded Aristomachus, who had been elected general for 228/7, to decline battle at Pallantium near Tegea, despite Achaean superiority in numbers.[5]

This desultory fighting can have been of little interest to Antigonus. He had no doubt noted the sending of Roman envoys to the Achaean and Aetolian Leagues and to Athens and Corinth to announce the victory over the Illyrians and the Roman participation in the Isthmian games in April 228. The omission of Macedonia from this activity was a clear indication of Roman displeasure.[6] But Antigonus did not allow any of this to interfere with an ambitious scheme which he must have been planning in the winter of 228.

---

[1] Plb. 2. 44. 6, 60. 4; P*Arat* 34. 7, 35. 5. On Aegina, included among ἄλλα τὰ ταττόμενα μετὰ τοῦ Πειραιέως see *IG* ɪɪ². 1225 ll. 9–10.

[2] Plb. 2. 46. 2. Caphyae is not mentioned but probably went with the other three cities. On the relation of these cities to Achaea and Aetolia, see above, p. 331 nn. 1 and 2. See Ehrhardt 238–9.

[3] Plb. 2. 46. 1–7.   [4] Plb. 1. 13. 5, 2. 56. 2.   [5] P*Arat* 35. 7; P*Cleom* 4. 9.

[6] Plb. 2. 12. 8; Zon. 8. 19. See above, pp. 334–5.

2. *The Carian Expedition (227 B.C.)*

Having settled the northern frontiers and the Thessalian revolt to his satisfaction and having dealt several blows to the Aetolians—though the peace of 228 left them in control of the pass of Thermopylae— Antigonus had decided on a naval programme designed to reaffirm Macedonian interests in the Aegean and Asia Minor dormant since the reign of Antigonus Gonatas, thus recalling the maritime achievements of his own grandfather, Demetrius Poliorcetes, the victor of Salamis. His plan was for an expedition against Caria in south-west Asia Minor.[1] Its immediate purpose is obscure. There is no indication that it was directed against Ptolemy III,[2] nor indeed against Seleucus II.[3] Antigonus may have been disturbed by the recent victories of Attalus of Pergamum over Antiochus Hierax, who was in rebellion against Seleucus.[4] But speculation is hazardous, especially since (as we shall see) fresh opportunities at home were almost immediately to cause Antigonus to abandon his Asian plans, whatever they were.

We catch a glimpse of Antigonus on his outward voyage. While passing through the Euripus with his fleet he ran aground in a low ebb tide on the frontier of Boeotia near Larymna in Opuntian Locris. Apparently the Boeotians were expecting some hostile action, and federal cavalry under the command of Neon were near by. Neon took the decision to let Antigonus refloat his fleet (it met with criticism at Thebes) and subsequently he and his family figure as firm supporters of the Antigonid house in Boeotia. Antigonus continued on his way to Caria, where he could count on the support—probably negotiated in advance—of Olympichus of Alinda, formerly a representative of Seleucus II in Caria, but at this time an independent dynast.[5] The size of Antigonus' fleet is not known. The fact that he chose to sail through the Euripus is no indication that he had only a small squadron,[6] since he had some business to transact at Larymna, which may well have governed his choice of route.[7]

---

[1] The sources for the Carian expedition are still tenuous: Trog. *Prol.* 28; Plb. 20. 5. 7–11; *Inschr. Priene* 37 ll. 136 ff.

[2] Cf. Crampa, *Labraunda* 1. 125; H. Bengtson, *SBAW* 1971. 3, 27. [3] Ehrhardt 243–4.

[4] See *OGI* 274, 278, and 279 for victories of Attalus I over Hierax; on the date see Will 1². 297, following Eus. 1. 251 f. Sch. = Porph. *FGrH* 260 F 32, 8.

[5] Evidently Neon now became a *xenos* (guest-friend) of Antigonus; cf. Herman, 15.

[6] On Olympichus see Crampa, *Labraunda* 1 nos. 1–12 and 2 no. 45; see especially no. 9, an honorific decree of Mylasa for Olympichus who is there designated *strategos* of Seleucus II, and no. 7, a letter of Philip V to Olympichus dated Audnaios of Philip's 3rd year (December 219). Olympichus figures as an independent ruler among the benefactors to Rhodes following an earthquake, probably *c.* 227; see Plb. 5. 90. 1. [7] So Ehrhardt 244.

[8] Plb. 20. 7. 5 πλέων ἐπί τινας πράξεις πρὸς τὰ ἔσχατα (B.–W. τὰς ἐσχατίας) τῆς Βοιωτίας πρὸς Λάρυμναν (MSS. Λαβρύναν). The wording (especially πράξεις) suggests that Antigonus was planning some kind of hostile action against Larymna and the frontier area (τὰ ἔσχατα) between

On reaching Caria Antigonus was received at Mylasa, a city hostile to Olympichus, who was at this time in control of Iasus. It is likely that the king also took over Pedasa and Euromus,[1] but his movements cannot be reconstructed. He did however write to the Chrysaoric League granting it the possession of the shrine of Zeus at Labraunda. Philip later insisted on the return of this shrine to Mylasa, explaining in a letter which he wrote in December 219 to Olympichus, that Antigonus his father had been deceived by the priest Hecatomnus with false allegations that his family were entitled to control the temple.[2] Antigonus also intervened in a land dispute between Priene and Samos, according to a Prienean inscription which mentions an Antigonus and the 'successor to the throne, Phi[lip'.[3] Trogus states that Antigonus 'Cariam subegit'.[4] He evidently kept some possessions there to hand on to Philip, for Olympichus is later found acting as his *strategos* in Caria, a capacity in which he was the recipient of Philip's instructions concerning the treatment of Iasus and Mylasa.[5] The Carian expedition had few lasting results and gives the impression of being an irrelevant episode in Antigonus' career. This may be because evidence about it is so scanty, but an equally important reason is that soon after his return to Macedonia Antigonus was presented with new possibilities for an active policy in the Peloponnese. That he went to Caria at all indicates, however, that Illyria and Epirus—notwithstanding the Roman expedition into those waters— were not among his immediate preoccupations.

At the time Antigonus was sailing through the Euripus on his way to Caria his position was still that of 'guardian to Philip'.[6] But soon afterwards, either in the course of his Carian expedition or, more probably, shortly after his return to Macedonia, he was elected king in his own right.[7] This is clear from the fact that when, a little later, he

---

Opuntian Locris and Boeotia. Neon's cavalry may have been operating there to counter any such move or alternatively they may have been on a routine frontier patrol. Having refloated, Antigonus continued to Asia, so perhaps the *quid pro quo* for Neon's forbearance was the abandonment of whatever action Antigonus had in mind at Larymna.

[1] Cf. Robert, *Amyzon* 150; for his reception at Mylasa see Crampa, *Labraunda* 1 no. 5 (especially pp. 33 ff.).

[2] Crampa, *Labraunda* 1 nos. 5–7.

[3] *Inschr. Priene* 37 ll. 136 ff. 'Antigonus' *could* be Antigonus I; cf. Bagnall, *Administration* 172. But the text also mentions τὸν γενόμενον διάδοχον τῆς βασιλείας φι[(cf. P*Arat* 46. 2 for the same phrase used of Philip V). That the reference is to the usurper Antiochus Hierax (U. von Wilamowitz-Moellendorff, *Sitz. Berlin* 1906. 54–5) seems highly improbable.

[4] Trog. *Prol.* 28.

[5] Cf. Crampa, *Labraunda* 1 no. 5; Holleaux, *Études* 4. 146–62 (with the note of L. Robert 162 n. 1, dating these inscriptions to the beginning of Philip's reign).

[6] Plb. 20. 5. 7 ἐπιτροπεύσας Φιλίππου.

[7] Eusebius assigns a reign of 12 years to Antigonus, and Dow and Edson (*Harv. Stud.* 48 (1937) 172 ff.) argue that this misunderstanding arose from adding 3 years as *strategos* to 9 years' reign as a whole. But without knowing how these 3 years were calculated, this hypothesis cannot be used to determine the date of Antigonus' election as king.

was confronted with a mutiny at Pella, he offered to hand back the purple and diadem—a bluff which succeeded and left his constitutional position stronger than before.[1] Justin records a speech delivered by Antigonus on this occasion which mentions several events that serve to date the mutiny. Among his benefactions to the Macedonians he includes his defeat of the Dardanians and Thessalians and his suppression of defecting allies—a reference perhaps to his recovery of Opuntian Locris, though more probably to that of Thessaly—actions by means of which 'dignitatem Macedonum auxerit'. The author of this speech (which is unlikely to be based on any true record) does not appear to be aware of the Carian expedition, but the occasion of its delivery must be after Antigonus' return from Caria, since when he set out he was not yet king (see above). It was in the winter of 227/6 after these events that Antigonus received an embassy from Megalopolis which was to change all his plans. It is to the events leading up to that embassy that we must now turn.

3. The Megalopolitan embassy and the breakdown of Achaea (227–224 B.C.)

The year 227 marked a turning-point in the conflict between Cleomenes III of Sparta and the Achaean League. In May Aratus succeeded Aristomachus as Achaean general and almost at once sustained a defeat at the hands of Cleomenes at Mt. Lycaeum in Arcadia.[2] In order to strengthen his hand against the ephors, who were opposed to his policy of expansion, Cleomenes now recalled Archidamus, the exiled Eurypontid king, from Messene—a scheme which went wrong when Archidamus was murdered and Cleomenes rightly or wrongly received the blame.[3] In a second campaign he defeated Aratus again at Ladoceia near Megalopolis in a battle in which Lydiades perished, largely as a result of his own impetuousness.[4] Finally, in a third campaign he seized Heraea, introduced food into Orchomenus, which was under Achaean siege, and himself laid siege to Mantinea, which the Achaeans had taken earlier in the year.[5] At this point Cleomenes returned with a force of mercenaries to Sparta, and there assassinated four of the ephors and several of his political

---

[1] Cf. J. 28. 3. 10, implying that Antigonus had already had himself made king, 'regem se constitui laborat'.

[2] Plb. 2. 51. 3; P*Arat* 36. 1.

[3] See Walbank, *C* 1. 568–9; P. Oliva, *Sparta and her Social Problems* (Amsterdam–Prague, 1971) 234–44.

[4] Plb. 2. 51. 3; P*Arat* 36. 4–37. 5; P*Cleom* 6. 3–7.

[5] P*Arat* 36. 2–3; P*Cleom* 5. 1; Paus. 8. 28. 7; Plb. 2. 57. 2 (Achaeans take Mantinea); P*Cleom* 7. 5–6 (third campaign).

opponents and, after expelling the rest, seized autocratic power. Extensive social reforms were carried out, including the pooling and dividing up of the large estates, the cancellation of debts, and the making up of the citizen body to, perhaps, 5,000 from among the metics and *perioikoi*. The Macedonian phalanx and the fighting methods which that entailed were now introduced at Sparta and Cleomenes set about creating a military machine capable of conquering the Peloponnese, with the help of his social programme which encouraged quite unjustified hopes of revolution among the poor and disaffected in the Achaean cities.[1]

These events seemed an encouragement to those in Argos and Megalopolis (but not only there) who favoured an aggressive policy towards Sparta. But Aratus was quick to appreciate the danger from Cleomenes' new army, coupled with the appeal which his programme might have inside Achaea. He was also afraid that Cleomenes might strike an agreement with Antigonus. The Aetolians too, by letting Cleomenes take over the Arcadian cities without protest, had thrown doubts on the sincerity of their alliance with the Achaean League. Aratus could not exclude the possibility that they might revert to the kind of understanding which had served them well under Gonatas.[2] In the light of these circumstances Aratus decided, in the winter of 227/6, that it would be prudent to look for some guarantee of help should the situation deteriorate still further, and his eyes turned to Pella. Apart from its effect on Achaean morale, an open approach to Antigonus would have given Cleomenes too clear an indication of Achaean weakness.[3] Aratus therefore decided to work through Megalopolis, a city closely associated with Macedonia and one most endangered by the new access of strength and aggressive spirit at Sparta. Two Megalopolitans, guest-friends (*xenoi*) of Aratus, obtained permission from the League to go as envoys to Antigonus in order to sound out the possibility of obtaining eventual help from Macedonia.[4]

This embassy, which was to play so important a role in shaping subsequent Macedonian policy in Greece, raises many problems. Polybius and Phylarchus are agreed that Aratus was behind it, Polybius indeed treating it as evidence of Aratus' craftiness.[5] But when Aratus himself finally made a direct appeal to Macedonia in 225, he chose to represent that as a desperate measure forced on him by

---

[1] Plb. 2. 47. 3; P*Cleom* 8–11; P*Arat* 38. 4.

[2] But the triple alliance of Antigonus, Cleomenes, and Aetolia mentioned in Plb. 2. 45. 2 derives from a Megalopolitan source (it was neither in Aratus' *Memoirs* nor in Phylarchus) and is to be rejected. It is inconsistent with Cleomenes' fear of having Aetolia as an enemy (P*Cleom* 10. 11) and with Aratus' appeal for help to Aetolia in 225 (P*Arat* 41. 3). See further Urban 131 ff.

[3] Plb. 2. 47. 7 ff.   [4] Plb. 2. 47. 4–50. 2.

[5] Plb. 2. 47. 4; P*Arat* 38. 12 (evidence of Phylarchus).

circumstances and omitted all mention of the Megalopolitan embassy from his *Memoirs*.[1] Polybius, who knew of the embassy from oral traditions current in his native city,[2] leaves it unclear whether the envoys went to Pella as Achaean or as Megalopolitan representatives. He reports that in their address to Antigonus they stressed the dangers of an Aetolian attack on their city in conjunction with Sparta, presenting this as a threat to Macedonia. This danger from Aetolia seems however to be largely imaginary and is not supported by any overt act of hostility towards Achaea. It may have been a useful argument to put to Antigonus, given that the object of the mission was to ensure that Macedonian help would be there when it was needed and that in the meantime Antigonus should not entertain any possible proposals from Cleomenes. Antigonus must of course have seen the embassy as a confession of Achaean weakness: he had everything to gain and nothing to lose by giving the requested promise. The envoys returned to Achaea with a letter promising Macedonian help if it was needed; and privately they brought Aratus a report on the king's attitude. On the strength of this Aratus persuaded the Achaean Assembly to carry on the war alone for the time being. He was determined to put off making the unwelcome appeal until the last possible moment, in order to forestall any accusation of treachery.[3]

The Achaeans held out alone for two more years with varied, but gradually deteriorating, fortunes. Early in 226 Aratus defeated the Spartan Megistonous at Orchomenus,[4] but Cleomenes advertised his contempt of the Achaeans by holding theatrical performances in Megalopolitan territory.[5] Soon afterwards he seized Mantinea,[6] a city torn with internal conflict, and defeated the Achaeans at the Hecatombaeum near Dyme.[7] During the ensuing winter (226/5) a truce was arranged and Cleomenes was invited to a conference to discuss 'hegemony'—the meaning of which was probably left undefined. Illness kept the king away and Aratus worked to prevent a settlement. In 225, instead of taking office as general, his normal practice in alternate years, he got a supporter Timoxenus elected instead.[8] The Achaean position was now rendered worse by the news that Ptolemy III had transferred his subsidy from Achaea to Sparta.[9] On the other hand this alignment with Ptolemy had hitherto stood in

---

[1] P*Arat* 38. 11; cf. Plb. 2. 47. 10–11 (many matters omitted from his *Memoirs*).
[2] Hardly, as E. S. Gruen argues (*Historia* 21 (1972) 609–25), from Phylarchus; see Urban 126 ff.; Pédech, *Méthode* 160.
[3] Plb. 2. 50. 3–51. 1.   [4] P*Arat* 38. 1.   [5] P*Cleom* 12.
[6] Plb. 2. 58. 4; P*Arat* 39. 1; P*Cleom* 14. 1.
[7] Plb. 2. 51. 3; P*Arat* 39. 1; P*Cleom* 14. 4–5; Paus. 7. 7. 3.   [8] P*Cleom* 15. 1.
[9] Plb. 2. 51. 2. Polybius does not date this clearly, but it was probably in the winter of 226/5.

the way of a direct approach to Antigonus[1] and when renewed negotiations with Cleomenes fell through and he, after narrowly failing to capture Sicyon, seized Pellene, Pheneus, and Penteleum in rapid succession and took over Caphyae, it was decided to vote special powers to Aratus and to send a further embassy to Pella, including Aratus' son of the same name, to find out the price of Macedonian help.[2]

Aratus had spent some time investigating cases of disaffection at Sicyon and was engaged in a similar operation at Corinth when news reached him that Cleomenes had seized Argos during the Nemean truce.[3] For a time the Achaeans held on to the citadel, but very soon that too fell to Cleomenes.[4] A tide of pro-Spartan feeling now swept over Corinth, for the Corinthians were well aware of the likely price of Antigonus' help. Aratus got away with difficulty and Cleomenes, marching via Hermione, Troezen, and Epidaurus, all of which he seized in passing, now took possession of Corinth. With Phlius and Cleonae also in his hands, the Achaean situation was desperate.[5] An appeal was made to Athens and even to Aetolia, but to no avail.[6] Aratus escaped from Corinth to Sicyon and was virtually besieged there for three months until, in the spring of 224, he got away to Aegium. There, at the spring meeting of the Achaean assembly (April 224)[7] the envoys sent to Pella reported on the terms which Antigonus laid down as the price of his intervention. There was no longer any alternative and the younger Aratus was sent back to Pella to convey the Achaean acceptance.[8]

Various conditions were laid down by Antigonus as the price of Macedonian help and were incorporated in a formal treaty between the two states.[9] In addition some of the clauses were embodied in special laws passed in the Achaean Assembly. Antigonus was recognized as *hegemon*—the post demanded by Cleomenes and previously held by Ptolemy—'by land and sea'[10] and the Achaeans agreed not to write or send envoys to any other king without his permission;[11] they

---

[1] Plb. 2. 47. 2.
[2] P*Arat* 39. 1–5; P*Cleom* 17. 6; Plb. 2. 51. 5–7. The embassy was sent to Pella in summer 225, but there had probably been earlier negotiations between Aratus and Antigonus since Hecatombaeum.
[3] Plb. 2. 52. 2; P*Arat* 39. 5; P*Cleom* 17. 7–8.
[4] P*Arat* 44.3.   [5] Plb. 2. 52. 1–3.   [6] P*Arat* 41. 3.
[7] Will 1². 386 dates it later in 225; but see *CAH* 7. 1². 467–8 n. 54.
[8] On these see Schmitt, *SVA* 506.
[9] Cf. Plb. 4. 82. 5 ἔγγραπτος συμμαχία.
[10] P*Arat* 38. 9 κατὰ γῆν καὶ κατὰ θάλατταν αὐτοκράτωρ ἡγεμὼν ἀναγορευθείς. For Ptolemy's position cf. ibid. 24. 4. Ptolemy's post was less onerous to the Achaeans because he was so far away.
[11] Ibid. 45. 2.

also passed a law forbidding any measure contrary to the alliance with the king of Macedonia to be proposed by magistrates or approved by the Council.[1] A meeting of the Assembly must be summoned at the king's request.[2] The alliance was to be renewed annually by the taking of oaths.[3] Meanwhile, and more immediately, the Achaeans were to provide pay and food for Antigonus' army[4] and were to send hostages to Pella[5] (the younger Aratus being one) as a guarantee. How long they were to remain there is not recorded. These terms were a serious encroachment on Achaean autonomy and involved the surrender of much that Aratus had gained through a lifetime's struggle against Macedonia.

4. *Antigonus in the Peloponnese: the Symmachy (224 B.C.)*

Upon learning of the Achaean decision, Cleomenes retired from before Sicyon to take up a defensive position at the Isthmus, with his lines running over Mt. Oneium and incorporating the defences of Corinth and the walls of Lechaeum and with a palisade and trench to secure the gap between Oneium and the Acrocorinth.[6] The size of his forces is not recorded, but they were evidently well below the 20,000 he mustered the next year at Sellasia.

Meanwhile Antigonus set off south, shipping his troops over to Euboea to avoid Thermopylae, which the Aetolians refused to open to his army. The pass would be hard to force and this was no moment to challenge Aetolian neutrality.[7] From Euboea Antigonus crossed to Boeotia, where the house of Neon was now in the ascendant, and from there he continued south, skirting Cithaeron to avoid Attica, and came down to Pagae, where Aratus met him and oaths were exchanged.[8] Polybius asserts that Antigonus feared a Spartan invasion of Thessaly and therefore got in touch quickly with Aratus before setting off. But this can hardly be true and must come from the version in Aratus' *Memoirs*. It connects with the argument presented to Antigonus that if

---

[1] Livy 32. 22. 3, based on Polybius (198 B.C.), 'lege cautum testabantur ne quid, quod adversus Philippi societatem esset, aut referre magistratibus aut decernere concilio ius esset.' The clause will go back to the original agreement with Antigonus.

[2] Plb. 4. 85. 3, 5. 1. 6; perhaps Livy 27. 30. 6 ff., despite 30. 9 'sociorum concilium', which suggests something more than an Achaean council. Later similar rights were granted to the Romans in certain circumstances (Plb. 22. 12. 6 ἐὰν μὴ ... παρὰ ⟨τῆς⟩ συγκλήτου τις ἐνέγκῃ γράμματα; Walbank, *C* 3. 412).

[3] Livy 32. 5. 4 (here again the commitment to Philip must originally have been to Antigonus). For Philip's renewal of the alliance in summer 220 see Plb. 4. 26. 8.

[4] *PArat* 45. 2.   [5] *PArat* 42. 3; *PCleom* 19. 9.   [6] Plb. 2. 52. 5.

[7] Plb. 2. 52. 8; cf. Ehrhardt 262.

[8] Plb. 2. 52. 7; *PArat* 43. 1, 44. 1. On the locality and communications see L. Robert, *Rev. Phil.* 13 (1939) 116–19.

he did not help Achaea he might have to face a united army of Spartans, Aetolians—and Boeotians and Achaeans, now won over to Cleomenes!—in Thessaly.[1] From Pagae Antigonus continued south over Mt. Gerania to confront Cleomenes at the Isthmus.[2] His army consisted of 20,000 Macedonian infantry and 1,300 cavalry.[3]

The Spartan lines across the Isthmus cut off Achaea from Megara and it was probably now or at the meeting at Pagae with Aratus (who had been voted plenipotentiary powers) that arrangements were made for Megara to pass from Achaea to the Boeotian League.[4] Clearly this was one more thing over which the Achaeans had little choice. It will have assisted the Macedonian cause in Boeotia and may well have been a *quid pro quo* for Boeotian co-operation. For some time the two armies faced each other and, after an attempt at an outflanking movement via Lechaeum had failed and Macedonian supplies were beginning to run low, Antigonus had already settled for the desperate plan of marching out to the Heraeum (mod. Perachora) and shipping his army over to Sicyon,[5] when a stroke of good fortune intervened to change the whole situation dramatically. At the instigation of a certain Aristoteles, a friend of Aratus, Argos suddenly revolted from Cleomenes.[6] Aratus at once sailed with 1,500 men to Epidaurus,[7] but without waiting for him to arrive Aristoteles, with the help of Achaean troops sent from Sicyon under Timoxenus, had already risen and attacked the citadel.[8] A Spartan relief force under Megistonous was defeated and its commander killed and Cleomenes, fearing for Sparta itself, now that a hostile army was in his rear, abandoned Corinth and the Isthmus lines and marched south to try to recover Argos. He managed to penetrate the city, but met with stiff resistance inside from both the Argives and the Achaean troops.[9] It was the appearance of Antigonus' forces, however, that drove him to abandon his attempt to save Argos and to retreat over the hills to Sparta.

Before leaving the Isthmus Antigonus occupied and garrisoned the Acrocorinth.[10] He now took over Argos[11] and advanced as far as the Laconian frontier, where he annexed the fortresses in the Aegytis and Belbinatis and handed them over to Megalopolis. He then returned to Aegium for the autumn meeting of the Achaean League and after that

---

[1] Plb. 2. 52. 7, cf. 49. 6 διακινδυνεύειν ἐν Θετταλίᾳ.
[2] P*Cleom* 20. 1 τὴν Γεράνειαν ὑπερβάλλοντος.   [3] P*Arat* 43. 1.
[4] Plb. 20. 6. 7.   [5] P*Cleom* 20. 4.   [6] P*Arat* 44. 2; P*Cleom* 20. 5–6.
[7] P*Arat* 44. 3; P*Cleom* 20. 7.
[8] Plb. 2. 53. 2. Timoxenus probably held a *de facto* command in view of the absence of Aratus (the general for 224/3) with Antigonus beyond the enemy lines. On the problem and the chronology see Walbank, *CAH* 7. 1^2. 467–8 n. 55; *C* 1. 254.
[9] Plb. 2. 53. 5–6. For details of the fighting at Argos see also P*Cleom* 21. 8.
[10] Plb. 2. 54. 1; P*Cleom* 21. 4; P*Arat* 44. 5.   [11] Plb. 2. 54. 1.

sent his troops for a short spell in winter quarters at Sicyon and Corinth.[1] It was probably now that Aristomachus, who had perhaps had a hand in the defection of Argos to Cleomenes, was executed by drowning at Cenchreae. Polybius attributes the decision to Antigonus and the Achaeans and defends it, but denies that he was first tortured.[2] Aratus who, according to Plutarch,[3] had been elected general at Argos after its liberation, an unusual appointment for a non-Argive, must probably bear the main responsibility for this act. Later[4], Aratus alleged that Macedonian troops under Leontius carried out a massacre at Argos, after the departure of Antigonus on his Arcadian campaign.

It was probably in the autumn of 224,[5] while he was at Aegium, that Antigonus undertook the organization of a new inter-state alliance intended to serve as a basis for Macedonian control in Greece. This alliance traditionally and conveniently known as the Symmachy, Συμμαχία—which implies a coalition for military ends—was an up-to-date version of the Hellenic League set up by Antigonus I and Demetrius I in 302. It looked back to a notable achievement of the Antigonid house, just as the Carian expedition looked back to the naval glory of Demetrius Poliorcetes. There was thus a traditional element in its constitution—but also certain novelties. In the first place it was envisaged as a league, not of Greek cities, but of Greek leagues. Thus, if we leave Macedonia on one side, the original members were all leagues—the Achaeans, Epirotes, Phocians, Boeotians, Acarnanians, and Thessalians.[6] The Macedonians constituted an official element in the Macedonian state and were referred to as a *koinon*[7]; consequently they also qualified to take their place in the Symmachy

---

[1] Plb. 2. 54. 2–5.   [2] Plb. 2. 54; P*Arat* 44. 6.   [3] P*Arat* 44. 5.
[4] Plb. 5. 16. 6.
[5] Plb. 2. 54. 4, reporting Antigonus' appointment as commander-in-chief by 'all the allies', implies the existence of a body with a wider scope than the Achaean League and that body will be the Symmachy. The context of this passage points to autumn 224 for its organization. Errington, *Gesch. Mak.* 254 n. 17, prefers 223/2, relating the formation of the Symmachy to the needs of the 222 campaign; but a wider perspective and with it the earlier date seem more likely.
[6] Plb. 4. 9. 4 (220 B.C.); cf. 15. 1. Most of the information on the Symmachy comes from the period of the Social War when Philip was the *hegemon*. The Euboeans were not included, probably because there was no Euboean confederacy at this time; see Picard, *Chalcis* 274 (and above, p. 305). Like Opuntian Locris (see above, p. 341 n. 9), Euboea was now under the control of Macedonia (Plb. 11. 5. 4 from a speech by a Rhodian, mentioning both, is merely rhetoric). The Thessalians, who were also directly under Antigonus, were however members of the Symmachy; cf. *IG* xi. 4. 1102 = *SIG* 575 (dedication on Delos after Sellasia).
[7] See below, p. 352 n. 4, for a treaty made between Antigonus and the Macedonians and Eleutherna, and p. 361 n. 6 for the dedication of 'Antigonus and [the Macedonians]' on Delos after Sellasia. The *koinon* of the Macedonians (τὸ κοινὸν Μ[ακε]δόν[ων]) honours Philip V on Delos (*SIG* 575); and the Macedonians make a dedication on his behalf to the Great Gods on Samothrace (J. R. McCredie, *Hesperia* 48 (1979) 16). On the Macedonian *koinon* see F. Papazoglou, *AM* 3 (1983) 195–210 and below, pp. 483–4.

and no doubt sent representatives to its Council meetings—though this does not of course mean that they would do anything other than echo the wishes and intentions of the king in either discussion or the taking of decisions. The Thessalians too were subject to the king of Macedonia and had no independent policy; both peoples will have exercised a convenient vote at meetings of the Council and have voted the same way. This was the first occasion on which the Macedonians and Epirotes had been included in such a comity of states. Antigonus himself was elected commander-in-chief of the Symmachy.[1] Later Scerdilaidas, the Illyrian chieftain, was received into the alliance, but whether as an individual or as a prince of the Ardiaei is not clear; in either case, however, there can have been no insistence on the presence of a *koinon*, for the Ardiaei, as far as we know, were never a league.[2] In 220 the Polyrrhenians, Lappaeans, and their allies in Crete also joined, though whether as separate units or as a *koinon* is not known.[3] At some time after 227 Antigonus had made treaties with two other Cretan cities, Eleutherna and Hierapytna,[4] but they do not appear to have become members of the Symmachy.

Of the organization of the Symmachy a certain amount is known. Antigonus was elected president (*hegemon*),[5] but since the existence of the alliance was envisaged as continuing well into the future (as was the case with the League of 302[6]) it seems likely that provision was made for the presidency to devolve eventually on Antigonus' successor, Philip (as indeed happened[7]). The *hegemon* commanded the allied forces and was empowered to requisition troops from the separate member states.[8] There was a Council made up of representatives of the various member states, which was to be summoned when necessary by the *hegemon*[9]. This body deliberated and took decisions on the making of peace and war,[10] but the members retained considerable freedom relative to its decisions since these, at any rate if they involved hostilities, had to be ratified by each state individually before that state was committed.[11] The Symmachy possessed no separate treasury of its

---

[1] Plb. 2. 54. 4 κατασταθεὶς ἡγεμὼν ἁπάντων τῶν συμμάχων; see above, p. 351 n. 5.

[2] Plb. 4. 29. 7 συνέθετο μεθέξειν τῆς κοινῆς συμμαχίας. See Hammond, *BSA* 61 (1966) 243; F. Papazoglou, *Historia* 14 (1965) 172, for Scerdilaidas as joint ruler of the Ardiaei along with Pleuratus.   [3] Plb. 4. 55. 2.

[4] *IC* II xii (Eleutherna) no. 20 = *SVA* 501; III iii (Hierapytna) no. 1 = *SVA* 502. On these see K. Buraselis, *AE* 1981 (1983) 114–25; F. Papazoglou, *AM* 3 (1983) 208–10 (attributing them to Antigonus Gonatas).

[5] See above, n. 1. κατασταθείς (in the passage of Polybius there quoted) is the term used in connection with Philip II and Alexander in reference to the League of Corinth.

[6] For continuity in the League of Antigonus and Demetrius cf. *IG* IV². 1. 68 = *ISE* 1. 44 = *SVA* 446 I l. 15 ... ἢ τὴν βασιλείαν τὴν Ἀντιγόνου κα]ὶ Δημητρίου καὶ τῶν ἐ[κγόνω]ν καταλύωσι.

[7] On this see below, p. 369.   [8] Plb. 5. 17. 9, 20. 1.   [9] Plb. 4. 22. 2, 5. 102. 8.

[10] Plb. 5. 102. 8–9, 103. 1, 103. 7, 105. 1–2 (peace of Naupactus).

[11] Plb. 4. 26. 2, cf. 4. 30. 2 f. (Acarnanians), 6 f. (Epirotes).

own, for it was an alliance, not a super-state. And the individual members retained the right to make war independently, and indeed exercised it.[1] The resolution founding the Symmachy may have guaranteed the freedom and autonomy of the member states. Such a clause is not recorded in connection with 224, but it is perhaps implied in the decision of the members in 220 to restore those rights to the states that were to be 'liberated' from the Aetolian League.[2]

The Symmachy brought clear advantages to its members and the proposal to set it up seems to have met with general approval. The Spartans were an immediate threat to the Achaeans, but Cleomenes' career must have created alarm in central Greece as well. Phocis, Epirus, and Acarnania were moreover afraid of the extended power of the Aetolian League and welcomed the guarantees implicit in an alliance under Macedonian hegemony. The system which the member states approved did not, however, give Antigonus enough authority to dominate southern and central Greece, as he no doubt intended. For this, like Antigonus Gonatas before him, Doson needed to garrison a number of strong-points. The most important of these was the Acrocorinth, but he soon added Orchomenus and Heraea.[3] These garrisons, all of them situated in Achaean territory, remained a source of irritation in Achaea for almost as long as the Macedonian alliance lasted, but at the same time they provided the League with welcome security so long as it remained militarily weak. In effect the Symmachy conferred hegemony in Greece on Macedonia, but it also had another aspect. The inclusion in it of Acarnania, Epirus, and Phocis brought together under the presidency of the king of Macedonia a group of states all potentially hostile to Aetolia; and just as Philip II's Common Peace in Greece soon found a new *raison d'être* in the war against Persia, so too the Symmachy of Antigonus Doson, conceived out of the need to save Achaea from Cleomenes of Sparta, was through no mere stroke of chance to find its new role in a war against the Aetolian League.

That the inclusion of the western states also carried implications for the Macedonian attitude towards Rome is unlikely. An important member of Antigonus' entourage at the battle of Sellasia in 222 was Demetrius of Pharos, and to understand his position it is necessary to

---

[1] Plb. 4. 9. 5–6, where the Achaeans vote to help the Messenians without referring the issues to the Symmachy in the first instance.

[2] Plb. 4. 25. 7 lists these rights ὅτι πάντας τούτους [the states to be liberated] ἀποκαταστήσουσιν εἰς τὰ πάτρια πολιτεύματα, χώραν ἔχοντας καὶ πόλεις τὰς αὑτῶν, ἀφρουρήτους ἀφορολογήτους ἐλευθέρους ὄντας, πολιτείαις καὶ νόμοις χρωμένους τοῖς πατρίοις (probably taken from the official decree).

[3] For Orchomenus see Plb. 4. 6. 5–6; P*Arat* 45. 1. It was taken by Antigonus in 223 (Plb. 2. 54. 11), and the likelihood is that he seized and garrisoned Heraea after its submission to him in the same campaign (Plb. 2. 54. 12). For discussion see Walbank, *Ph* 17 n. 2 and *C* 1. 257, against A. Aymard's argument that Heraea was captured and garrisoned by Philip.

go back to 229/8 and the Roman–Illyrian War. In the course of that war Demetrius had deserted Teuta, the ruler of the Ardiaei, for Rome and after the settlement he retained an independent *dynasteia*[1] based on Pharos and perhaps including most of the Illyrians overrun by the Romans. To the south of Demetrius' kingdom lay the Roman protectorate set up in the aftermath of the war and consisting of the coastal plain from Epidamnus to Apollonia, together with the territories of the Atintani and Parthini, which embraced the Shkumbi valley and the area to the north of it. Soon after making peace with Rome, Teuta disappears from the records, and Demetrius, as guardian of the young heir Pinnes and husband of his mother Triteuta, has become the effective ruler of the Ardiaei.[2] According to Appian, Demetrius chose the time (225–222) when the Romans were busy fighting the Gauls in north Italy to break the treaty obligations entered into by Teuta by sailing south of Lissus on a piratical cruise.[3] In 222 he turned up in Antigonus' camp at Sellasia, probably as an ally rather than as an enlisted mercenary leader.[4] This alignment will certainly not have gone unnoticed by the Romans, who had already expressed their coldness towards Macedonia by omitting Pella from their diplomatic contacts after the First Illyrian War.[5] But that is not to say that in welcoming Demetrius Antigonus was planning some sort of western policy or seeking to pick a quarrel with Rome. There is no evidence to suggest that he was seriously interested in Rome, despite the existence of the Roman protectorate on the Adriatic coast of Illyria and up the Shkumbi valley. The Carian expedition of 227 is hard to explain if Antigonus' eyes were really on the west. It suggests that had not the Achaean collapse and the approach from Aratus offered him unforeseen opportunities in Greece, his ambitions might have developed in quite another direction. The Second Illyrian War of 219 was to put a fresh complexion on the relations between Macedonia and Illyria, but one must distinguish the plans and policy of Philip V from those of his guardian and predecessor.

5. *The defeat of Cleomenes (223/2 B.C.)*

Antigonus was in no great hurry to deal with the king of Sparta. In the long term there was much to be said for consolidating his position and his presence in the Peloponnese by prolonging the time during which Cleomenes could still threaten Achaea. There were moreover other

[1] Plb. 2. 11. 17. See H*IRM* 7.   [2] Zon. 8. 19; Dio fr. 53; Appian, *Ill.* 7.
[3] Appian, *Ill.* 8.   [4] Against H. Dell, *CP* 62 (1967) 101 see H*IRM* 10 n. 37.
[5] For the envoys sent by the consul L. Postumius to the Achaean and Aetolian Leagues and by the Senate to Corinth and Athens see above, p. 334.

ways of hitting at Cleomenes. Antigonus probably knew that towards the end of 224 he had appealed to Ptolemy III for money to hire those mercenaries whose aid was essential, if he was to face the coalition which he saw being organized against him. Ptolemy demanded that he send his mother and children as hostages and reluctantly he let them go. But meanwhile Antigonus had himself sent representatives to Alexandria, clearly in the hope of getting the subsidy to Sparta suspended.[1] In this he was not immediately successful. Having jettisoned Achaea, Ptolemy was evidently prepared to risk his money at Sparta for a little longer. But after the campaign of 223 he must have reached the conclusion that Cleomenes was no longer worth subsidizing, and ten days before the decisive battle of Sellasia in 222 Cleomenes was to receive the devastating news that his Egyptian funds were at an end. It was this that finally forced him into battle.[2]

Cleomenes opened the campaigning season of 223 in May with an unsuccessful attack on Megalopolis.[3] Soon after this sortie, and somewhat later in the spring, Antigonus marched out from winter quarters, reached Tegea in three days, and after being joined by the Achaeans, undermined the walls and captured the town. According to Polybius, he secured it before continuing south, but there is no other evidence that a Macedonian garrison was put in.[4] Next, after some skirmishing with Cleomenes along the Laconian frontier, presumably in the neighbourhood of Sellasia, Antigonus marched back to occupy Orchomenus and Mantinea and then, in a sweep into western Arcadia, he took Heraea and Telphusa.[5] Since it was now early November, he sent his Macedonians back to Macedonia till the following spring;[6] they had already spent two campaigning seasons and one winter away from home. Then, having dismissed all his other troops—whether these included any besides the Achaeans is not recorded—Antigonus passed the early part of the winter at Aegium with only the mercenaries.[7]

---

[1] P*Cleom* 22. 9.

[2] Plb. 2. 63. 1–2, quoting from Phylarchus. On the importance of money to Cleomenes at this point see also P*Cleom* 27. 1–4.

[3] Plb. 2. 55. 5, which puts the attack three months before that of late autumn 223 (Plb. 2. 55. 6). But according to Plb. 9. 18. 1–4 it fell περὶ τὴν τῆς Πλειάδος ἐπιτολήν and the heliacal rising of η Tauri in the Pleiades is 22 May. The two attacks must fall at the beginning and end of the campaigning season and 'three months' is evidently an error.

[4] Plb. 2. 54. 5–7.   [5] Plb. 2. 54. 7–13.

[6] Plb. 2. 54. 13–14 συνάπτοντος τοῦ χειμῶνος. The phrase indicates a date in the first part of November (Pédech, *Méthode* 463). P*Cleom* 25. 5 says the Macedonian troops were εἰς τὰ χειμάσια διεσπαρμένους κατὰ πόλιν. This sounds like the cities of Achaea as in 224/3, but in view of Polybius' definite statement one must assume that Plutarch has misunderstood his source, probably Phylarchus, who was referring to the cities of Macedonia. Similarly, in 197, faced with a Dardanian invasion, Philip V carried out a hasty levy of Macedonians 'per urbes' (Livy 33. 19. 3, following Polybius).

[7] Plb. 2. 55. 1.

The fact that so few incidents appear to have taken place during this year (223) indicates that Antigonus was counting on wearing Cleomenes down, especially if he lost his Egyptian subsidy, and also perhaps that he was deliberately prolonging his stay in southern Greece. Financially, this would be at the expense of the Achaeans, since they had to pay for Antigonus' army.[1] But, what was even worse for them, until Cleomenes had been finally defeated, he was still capable of inflicting considerable wounds, of which Achaea would be the recipient.

This Cleomenes very soon did. In a desperate attempt to swell his army Cleomenes freed any helots able to purchase their freedom for 5 *minae*; by liberating 6,000 in this way he acquired 500 talents, some of which he used to arm 2,000 men in the Macedonian fashion as phalangites.[2] Soon afterwards he launched a sudden attack on Megalopolis, which was poorly defended and underpopulated since the defeats at Mt. Lycaeum and Ladoceia. Seizing the city by treachery, he expelled the population, who took refuge in Messene. When they refused to join him, he razed Megalopolis to the ground and carried off all the plunder to Sparta.[3] Phylarchus valued it at 6,000 talents but Polybius' 300 talents are more likely to be accurate, in view of Cleomenes' continued financial difficulties.[4] Early the following spring (222) Cleomenes made a further demonstration. By now Antigonus had moved from Aegium to Argos, and Cleomenes led a provocative march, plundering right up to the walls of that city, and then returned past Phlius and Orchomenus to Sparta. This attempt to discredit Antigonus in Achaea had no effect except perhaps to persuade him that a set battle could no longer be postponed.[5]

Antigonus' army returned from Macedonia in early summer 222[6]

---

[1] See above, p. 349 n. 4. Since this agreement was made the Symmachy had been set up. The war against Cleomenes remained primarily a war on behalf of the Achaean League and it is likely that the financial arrangements made with Antigonus still operated. On the other hand, if the other members of the Symmachy were fighting side by side with the Achaeans, it was as members of an alliance which might well in future be called upon to fight for them. One cannot therefore exclude the possibility that each allied state was responsible for paying its own troops (which could explain why some states were not represented at Sellasia: see below, p. 357 n. 1). As for the mercenaries, we have no information, but it seems likely that their cost was shared between the states taking part in the expedition.

[2] P*Cleom* 23. 1 ff. (cf. Macr. 1. 11. 34 for an exaggerated version). The source is Phylarchus and not above suspicion. If, in fact, there were 6,000 helots with 5 minae each, money economy had penetrated Spartan life to a greater extent than might be supposed.

[3] Plb. 2. 55. 1–7.   [4] Plb. 2. 62–3.

[5] Plb. 2. 64; P*Cleom* 25–6. Ch. 26 of the *Cleomenes* is probably a doublet of ch. 25, and from Phylarchus.

[6] The sources for the Sellasia campaign are Plb. 2. 65–9; P*Cleom* 28; P*Phil* 6. The *Philopoemen* passage is probably based on Polybius' lost biography of Philopoemen. That in the *Cleomenes* mentions Phylarchus and probably derives from him. Polybius' account is detailed on the Macedonian side, especially for the centre and right wing of the battle front, and probably goes

and in June or July he advanced into Laconia with a force of 27,600 foot and 1,200 horse.[1] Of these 10,000 were phalangites and 3,000 Peltasts—as Polybius calls what were in fact a crack corps of Macedonians used either in the phalanx or for special tasks in conjunction with light-armed and mercenaries, in short the equivalent of Alexander's Hypaspists under another name. Of the remaining 14,600, 3,000 were picked men from Achaea, who were accompanied by 1,000 Megalopolitans, whom Antigonus had armed in the Macedonian fashion, since they had lost everything when Cleomenes sacked their city; 3,000 were mercenaries, distinct from 1,000 Gauls and 1,000 Agrianians, who also most likely served for pay;[2] 2,000 were Boeotians—the largest contingent after the Macedonians and Achaeans—and the Epirotes and Acarnanians furnished 1,000 each. Finally, Demetrius of Pharos brought 1,600 Illyrians, probably as an ally or *xenos* of Antigonus. The cavalry, 1,200 in all, consisted of three bodies of 300—Macedonian, Achaean, and mercenary—together with 200 Boeotians and fifty each from the Epirotes and Acarnanians. The noteworthy feature of this army—to which the Macedonians, like the rest, contributed only a part of the forces at their disposal—is the small proportion of cavalry if one compares it with the army with which Alexander crossed the Hellespont. It was an army with relatively few national troops and relied largely on mercenaries and allied contingents. Nor did all the members of the Symmachy contribute men. No troops were present from Thessaly, Phocis, Euboea, or Megara.

Having garrisoned and fortified the other passes into Laconia,[3]

---

back to a Megalopolitan informant, perhaps even Philopoemen himself. Aratus' *Memoirs* seem not to be a source. They probably contained little or nothing on the battle. After long debate, it now seems certain that the year of the battle was 222. *PCleom* 26. 1 suggests that the corn was ripe in the Argolid before the battle (i.e. it was after May); and Plb. 2. 65. 1 has Antigonus start his campaign θέρους ἐνισταμένου (perhaps May–June; cf. Pédech, *Méthode* 461). So probably the battle was fought in late June or July. See Kromayer, *AS* 1. 266–77; Walbank, *C* 1. 273–4.

[1] For Antigonus' forces see Plb. 2. 65. 2–5 with Kromayer, *AS* 1. 228 and Walbank, *C* 1. 272–5. No troops are recorded from Thessaly, Phocis, Euboea, or Megara. On Philip's Peltasts see Walbank, *Ph* 291–3. They were not light-armed, for Plb. 5. 23. 4 includes them under τὴν τῶν βαρέων ὅπλων ἔφοδον but if they are the troops mentioned in the second fragment of a military code found at Amphipolis (*ISE* 2. 114 B. 1) they wore a κότθυβος—perhaps a linen cuirass—to protect the body; cf. M. M. Markle, *AJA* 81 (1977) 327, who argues for the absence of a *thorax* from a peltast's equipment. But the κότθυβος may in fact be the protective garment of a rank-and-file phalangite, whereas the front-rank men and/or officers wore a metal *thorax*. See P. Connolly, *Greece and Rome at War* (London, 1981) 79–80.

[2] Launey 1. 517 suggests that the Gauls came under the command of a chieftain, by virtue of a treaty of alliance; even so they will have been paid, probably by Achaea (see above, p. 356 n. 1).

[3] The passes carrying the roads from Megalopolis and Asea, which joined a little to the west of the Athenaeum on Mt. Khelmos, could be covered by a force holding one of the gorges in the upper Eurotas valley, while the pass carrying the coastal road from Argos over Mt. Parnon could be conveniently held at a point near the modern monastery of Hag. Saranda south-east of Sellasia. See Kromayer, *AS* 1. 212–14 with Map 1; W. Loring, *JHS* 15 (1895) 25 ff.

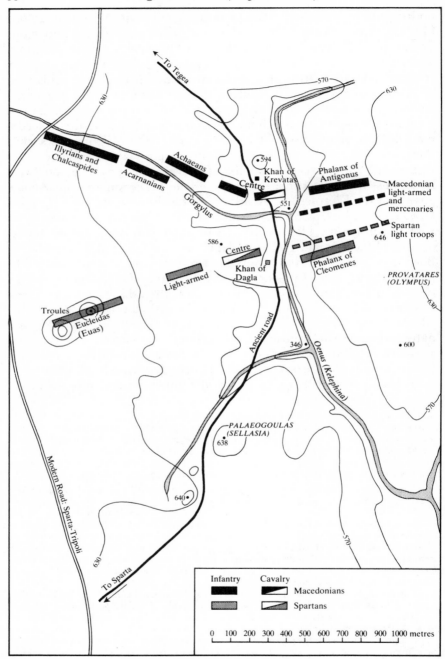

FIG. II. THE BATTLE OF SELLASIA

Cleomenes took up a defensive position near Sellasia with an army of nearly 20,000 men, astride the valley of the Oenus, along which passed the main road from Tegea to Sparta (see Fig. 11). He had chosen a point where two hills, Euas to the west and Olympus to the east, controlled the valley containing the road and river and, having fortified both hills with a trench and palisade, he stationed his *perioikoi* and allies (perhaps mainly supporters from Peloponnesian towns taken by Antigonus) on Euas under his brother Eucleidas, while he himself held Olympus with his Spartan phalanx and his mercenaries. The cavalry, supported by mercenaries, were stationed on the level ground in the valley alongside the river. Polybius, who had probably seen the site, describes Cleomenes' position as at once a battle line ready for action and a fortified camp hard to approach.[1] It was indeed a strong line, but not too strong to deter Antigonus from attack, since Cleomenes' political and financial situation compelled him to seek a battle.[2] His numbers are not recorded in detail, but his forces on Olympus probably came to around 11,000, made up of about 5,000 light-armed and mercenaries[3] and a phalanx of about 6,000.[4] If we estimate the cavalry and mercenaries stationed in the valley at about 1,000 each (this can only be a guess), we are left with about 7,000 *perioikoi* and allies as the number of troops under Eucleidas on Euas, since the total army came to a little under 20,000.[5]

Though the Oenus is clearly the modern Kelephina, the exact site of the battle has been the subject of long controversy.[6] Kromayer identified Olympus with Kotselovouni, a spur of Mt. Provatares, and Euas with Mt. Palaeogoulas. But the weakness of this location lies in its assumption that the road south to Sparta must have continued down the river to make a detour round the south side of Palaeogoulas, instead of continuing along the more natural route up the Kourmeki valley on the north-west side of that hill. A more likely location is therefore that of Pritchett, who identifies Euas with the hill of Troules (or Tourla) with its two summits, which lies north-west of Palaeogoulas beyond the Kourmeki, and Olympus (like Kromayer) with Mt. Provatares. The 'river' Gorgylus, which played an important part in Antigonus' tactics, will be the stream which flows into the Kelephina

---

[1] Plb. 2. 65. 11 οὐδὲν γὰρ ἀπέλειπε τῶν πρὸς ἐπίθεσιν ἅμα καὶ φυλακήν, ἀλλ᾽ ἦν ὁμοῦ παράταξις ἐνεργὸς καὶ παρεμβολὴ δυσπρόσοδος.

[2] On this aspect see Kromayer, *AS* 1. 214–15.   [3] Plb. 2. 69. 3.

[4] *PCleom* 28. 8.

[5] Plb. 2. 65. 7; *PCleom* 27. 11. Kromayer, *AS* 1. 227 puts the number on Euas at only 5,000, but in that case his total is too small: 6,000 + 5,000 (on Olympus) + 2,000 (in the valley) + 5,000 (on Euas) comes to only 18,000.

[6] See for bibliography Kromayer, *AS* 1. 215 ff. (map on p. 216, giving earlier suggested locations); W. W. Tarn, *CAH* 7 (1928) 885 sect. 12b; Walbank, *C* 1. 273; Pritchett, *Studies* 1. 59–70 (with Pl. 58–64).

about 250 metres south-east of the ruined Khan of Krevatas (see Fig. 11), having drained a valley to the north of Troules, which extends as far as the modern Sparta–Tripoli road. Like most of the streams here, it is dry in the summer.

Having camped for several days to the north of the Gorgylus and probed the enemy line, Antigonus drew up his forces for battle. On the right facing Euas he placed his 3,000 *chalkaspides*[1] and Demetrius' 1,600 Illyrians in alternate units (having learnt a lesson from Pyrrhus, who adapted his army to meet the more flexible Italian order by alternating maniples of phalangites and Italians[2]). Alongside these[3] were the Acarnanians and Epirotes,[4] and behind them the 2,000 Achaeans. In the valley beside the road were the 1,200 cavalry supported by 1,000 Achaean infantry and the 1,000 Megalopolitan infantry. Finally, on Olympus itself Antigonus commanded a force consisting of about 15,000 in all and made up of 3,000 mercenaries, 1,000 Agrianians, 1,000 Gauls, and the rest of the Macedonians, forming a phalanx of 10,000. The mercenaries were in front and behind them the phalangites were drawn up thirty-two deep, double the normal depth.[5] Not all this was visible to the Spartans, since the Illyrians and Peltasts (and perhaps the Acarnanians) had been sent round to the north-west of Euas in the night and had hidden themselves in the upper valley of the dried-up Gorgylus.[6] A white flag displayed from Antigonus' position on the northern slopes of Olympus was to be the signal for them to assault the hill.[7]

The battle began when this concealed force, along with the Epirotes, attacked Euas; they amounted to 6,600 men in all (i.e. 3,000 *chalkaspides*, 1,600 Illyrians, 1,000 Acarnanians, and 1,000 Epirotes).[8] Their advance up the hill left a gap in the Macedonian line, since the Achaeans had not moved forward,[9] and Cleomenes' mercenaries in

[1] Plb. 2. 66. 2. These bronze-shielded troops are probably identical with those described as Peltasts in 65. 2.   [2] Plb. 18. 28. 10.   [3] Plb. 2. 66. 6 ἐπὶ δὲ τούτοις.

[4] The MS. has Κρῆτας; this is accepted by Kromayer, and indeed Cretan troops may have come as mercenaries, perhaps through the treaties made with Eleutherna and Hierapytna (above, p. 352 n. 4). But Cretans are not mentioned in the run-down of Antigonus' forces (Plb. 2. 65. 2–5) and since the Epirotes do not occupy any other position in the order of battle, the emendation should perhaps be accepted. (On the Boeotians see the next note.)

[5] Plb. 2. 66. 7–9; the Boeotians (like the Epirotes) are not mentioned in the order of battle. Perhaps they were left in charge of the camp.

[6] Plb. 2. 66. 10. PCleom 28. 3 says that the Acarnanians also took part in this action.

[7] The source followed by PPhil 6 speaks only of a scarlet cloak on a spear, which was to be the signal for the Achaeans, and, by omitting to mention the signal to the Illyrians, suggests that they moved forward on the initiative of their own officers. This is clearly intended to defend the Achaeans who, by remaining where they were, had opened up the gap in the line.

[8] Plb. 2. 67. 1.

[9] PPhil 6. 4 τῶν Ἀχαιῶν, ὥσπερ προσετέτακτο, τὴν ἐφεδρείαν ἐν τάξει διαφυλαττόντων. In Plb. 2. 67. 2 the phrase θεωροῦντες τὰς σπείρας τῶν Ἀχαιῶν ἐρήμους ἐκ τῶν κατόπιν οὔσας should probably be translated (with Kromayer) 'seeing that the *speirai* were not covered in the rear by

the centre rushed into this gap and began attacking the Illyrians (and presumably the rest of the Macedonian right) in the rear; according to Plutarch, this was on the orders of Eucleidas.[1] This highly dangerous situation for the Macedonians was remedied, however, by the Achaean Philopoemen, who was stationed with the 300 Achaean cavalry in the centre.[2] Without waiting for orders he led the Achaean horse against the Spartan light-armed and also, probably, the Spartan cavalry.[3] The Spartan cavalry were in this way drawn off from attacking the Macedonian right, which continued up the slopes of Euas to overwhelm Eucleidas, who, instead of advancing down the hill to meet them, had awaited them on the summit. The whole of the Spartan left was routed and the remnants fled to the south-west, across the line of the modern road, and in the direction of the Eurotas.[4]

When Cleomenes observed the disaster on Euas, he took the only step open to him. Issuing from his defences and quickly bringing to an end the preliminary skirmishing, which had been going on between the light-armed and mercenaries on the two sides,[5] he charged with his phalanx. Despite Antigonus' advantage in numbers the clash was protracted and the lines surged this way and that without breaking. But when eventually Antigonus ordered his men to close ranks and deliver a concerted charge, the weight of the double phalanx of thirty-two men had its effect. The Spartans were routed, and all but 200 of their phalanx perished.[6] Cleomenes fled with a few cavalry to Sparta and then to Gytheum, whence he took ship to Alexandria, after first advising those in the city to surrender.[7]

---

the Achaeans', since it is clearly the Illyrians and not the Achaeans who are exposed to attack. Pritchett, *Studies* 1. 69. assumes (despite Plutarch) that the Achaeans had moved forward to the higher ground.

[1] Plb. 2. 67. 2; PPhil 6. 5.

[2] Plb. 2. 69. 1 τῶν 'Ἀχαϊκῶν ἱππέων ἁπάντων, μάλιστα δὲ Φιλοποίμενος.

[3] Cf. Plb. 2. 67. 6 τὴν τῶν ἱππέων συμπλοκήν, which seems to imply cavalry on both sides. According to PPhil 6. 6, Philopoemen attacked the light-armed.

[4] See Pritchett, *Studies* 1. 67–8.

[5] Plb. 2. 69. 6. For the preliminary skirmishing see 69. 3–5. According to the account in PCleom 28. 5–6, based on Phylarchus, Cleomenes charged independently of events on Euas and drove the Macedonian phalanx back 5 furlongs before the sight of Eucleidas' destruction brought him up short. This is absurd, for (a) the repulse of a phalanx twice the size and weight of the Spartan is most improbable, (b) no phalanx could be driven back 5 furlongs and then recover its formation sufficiently to turn defeat into victory. (The yielding of ground mentioned by Plb. 2. 69. 8 is obviously something quite different, a matter of yards, not furlongs).

[6] Plb. 2. 69. 7–10. Antigonus celebrated his victory with a dedication on Delos (*SIG* 518), which reads: 'King Antigonus, son of King Demetrius, and [...] and the allies from (the spoils of) the battle of Sellasia to Apollo'. The missing words can only be 'the Macedonians', as in the treaty of 215 between Philip V and Hannibal (Plb. 7. 9. 1).

[7] Plb. 2. 69. 10–11; PCleom 28. 7–29. 4.

Antigonus now entered Sparta,[1] where he 'restored the laws and constitution'—which meant that the ephorate was restored, but the kingship was left vacant. The fate of Cleomenes' social and economic measures is less certain, but probably returning exiles recovered their land, the heavy casualty list at Sellasia having facilitated this. Antigonus appointed the Boeotian Brachylles, the son of Neon, as military governor (*epistates*)[2] and deprived Sparta of Denthaliatis on the western side of Taygetus, transferring it to Messenia. It seems likely that Sparta eventually joined the Symmachy, but probably not immediately.[3] Having put these measures in motion, Antigonus, after a stay of only two days, set off north with the army of the Symmachy.

6. *The end of Antigonus' reign (222/1 B.C.)*

The reason for Antigonus' hasty departure from Sparta was that he had had news of an Illyrian invasion of Macedonia; the report spoke of a large-scale force and the ravaging of the countryside.[4] On his way back he paused at Tegea, however, to restore the old form of government, perhaps handing the city over to the Achaean League,[5] and then at Argos, where the Nemean Games, postponed from 223 because of the war, were now held.[6] Leaving Taurion in charge of the Macedonian forces in the south of Greece,[7] and perhaps empowered to deal with affairs affecting the Symmachy—or at any rate so far as they concerned the Peloponnese—Antigonus now hastened back to Macedonia, where he inflicted a decisive defeat on the Illyrians. But following the strain and excitement of the battle, coming so soon after his campaign in the Peloponnese, he began vomiting blood and fell into a decline; the symptoms point strongly towards tuberculosis.[8] He died soon afterwards, probably in 221; the month is uncertain but it was before October.[9] In the meantime he sent his ward Philip, the

---

[1] According to Paus. 2. 9. 2, Antigonus first enslaved the inhabitants of the neighbouring town of Sellasia, which had probably served as the immediate base for Cleomenes in his battle position.　　　　　　　　　　　　　　　　　　　　　　　　　　　[2] Plb. 20. 5. 12.

[3] See, however, below, p. 372.　　　　　　　　　　[4] Plb. 2. 70. 1; P*Cleom* 30. 1 πολὺν πόλεμον.

[5] When next heard of in 207 (Plb. 11. 11. 2), it is again Spartan.

[6] Plb. 2. 70. 4; for another case of postponement (in 195) see Livy 34. 4. 1 'ludicrum Nemeorum die stata propter belli mala praetermissum'.

[7] On his role there see Bengtson, *Strat.* 2. 358.

[8] P*Cleom* 30. 2–4. That he burst a blood-vessel shouting on the battle-field (so Phylarchus) is unlikely. Tarn, *Bactria* 215, comments on the prevalence of consumption among Macedonian kings, including Cassander, Philip V and Antiochus IV.

[9] Macedonian regnal years ran from 1 Dios, i.e. October, and a king's first year was reckoned as the period between his predecessor's death and the next 1 Dios. Chr. Habicht, *AM* 1. 273–9 has confirmed by his analysis of *SIG* 543 that Philip's second regnal year began on 1 Dios 221. H. Bengtson, *SBAW* 1971 no. 3, 57 puts Doson's death and Philip's accession in 222, to match his dating of Demetrius II's death to 230; but this was in 229 (see above, p. 336 n. 1).

recognized successor to the throne, on a visit to the Peloponnese.[1] According to Plutarch, Philip was instructed to attach himself especially to Aratus, but this assertion probably reflects the bias of Aratus' own *Memoirs*. If Antigonus took Philip with him to Caria in 227,[2] as seems likely, he almost certainly took him with the Macedonian army on the expedition to Greece from 224 to 222. The military experience would be invaluable and to leave him behind in Macedonia would have been politically inadvisable. So Philip had probably already met Aratus and the purpose of the special visit now may have been for him to gain a better understanding of the situation in Achaea and the affairs of the Symmachy. Antigonus' concern for Philip's political training is perhaps also to be seen in Cicero's statement in the *de officiis* that there existed letters from Antigonus to his son Philip, bidding him win over the goodwill of the multitude by well-disposed speeches and cajole the soldiers by flattering appeals. But it seems more probable that, like the letters of Philip to Alexander and Antipater to Cassander, these are Hellenistic forgeries.[3]

In his eight-years rule (229–221), part of it as *strategos* until he succeeded in being elected to the kingship, Antigonus had some remarkable achievements to his credit. By his suppression of the Thessalian revolt and his expulsion of the Aetolians and Illyrians from most of the territories they had seized—Phthiotic Achaea remained an exception—he had restored morale among the Macedonians and consolidated the realm. Later, the successful aggressive policy of Cleomenes and Aratus' refusal to allow the Achaean League to become part of a Spartan empire had enabled Macedonia to recover a position of dominance in central Greece and the Peloponnese. Besides establishing garrisons of the traditional sort at Corinth, Heraea, and Orchomenus, and appointing a Macedonian governor in Sparta, he had created a new and flexible organization, the Symmachy, with some novel features designed to capture Greek loyalty and to encourage acquiescence in the new Macedonian hegemony. Not everything indeed had turned out favourably for Macedonia. Athens and Attica were irretrievably lost. The Carian expedition had brought little gain and must be regarded as part of a plan which remains incohate, because Antigonus deliberately jettisoned it, when he saw the chance to make gains in an area more vital to long-term Macedonian interests. One result of this decision was that Macedonian naval strength was

---

[1] P*Arat* 46. 2–3 (from Aratus' *Memoirs*).

[2] That the young prince was in Asia Minor in 227 is probably implied by *Inschr. Priene* 37 ll. 136 ff.; see above, p. 344 n. 3.

[3] Cic. *de off.* 2. 48. For strong arguments in favour of the letters being spurious see J. Kaerst, *Philol.* 51 (1892) 405.

allowed to decline. The Aetolians too, though decisively defeated, were still dangerous and their hold on Delphi and Thermopylae was undiminished. It was no doubt partly with Aetolia in mind that Antigonus organized the Symmachy—though when, early in Philip's reign, the enmity of the two blocs erupted into war, it was from the Aetolians that the initiative was to come. Meanwhile, Antigonus' supporters in Greece, whether from conviction or for expediency, loaded him with honours. The first of these were accorded to him immediately after his capture of Sparta at the Nemea of 222,[1] but subsequently they were echoed in many Greek cities, including Sparta itself, where, no doubt at the instigation of those he had restored, he was hailed as benefactor (*euergetes*) and (after his death) as saviour (*soter*).[2]

In Achaea Aratus instituted a festival called the *Antigoneia* at Sicyon in his honour[3] and a similar festival is recorded from Histiaea in Euboea (an area under Macedonian control).[4] Mantinea was refounded as Antigoneia with Aratus as *oikistes*;[5] an inscription shows that, as at Sparta, Antigonus was celebrated as 'saviour and benefactor'.[6] Examples could be multiplied—for instance the altar set up to him at Epidaurus[7] and the honours voted at Geronthrae in Laconia.[8] At Olympia the Eleans set up a group of statuary[9] in which a personification of Hellas crowned 'Antigonus the guardian of Philip' and with the other hand Philip himself—perhaps an indication of the extent to which Philip, upon his accession, was to inherit all this goodwill.

---

[1] Plb. 2. 70. 5.   [2] Plb. 5. 9. 10, 9. 36. 5.

[3] Plb. 28. 19. 3, 30. 29. 3; P*Arat* 45. 3; P*Cleom* 16. 7. It is surprising to find this festival still being celebrated in 170/69 and in 166/5. In general see Porph. *FGrH* 260 F 31(5) 'he was judged worthy of honours equalling those of the gods by the Achaean people'.

[4] *SIG* 493 l. 22; cf. P. Roussel and J. Hatzfeld, *BCH* 4 (1910) 370. It is likely to be in honour of Antigonus III.

[5] Plb. 2. 56. 6 with Walbank, *C* ad loc.; cf. *IG* v. 2. 299 (better text in *SEG* 11. 1089) for honours voted there. The name Antigoneia is common on coins and inscriptions and remained the official name of the city until A.D. 125, when Hadrian renamed it Mantinea. But the old name continued to be used in common parlance and by writers (cf. Plb. 4. 21. 9, 11. 11) and is to be found in the Delphic list of *theorodokoi* of 175 (A. Plassart, *BCH* 45 (1921) 13 col. II l. 113).

[6] *IG* v. 2. 299.   [7] *ISE* 1. 46.   [8] *IG* v. 1. 1122.

[9] Paus. 6. 16. 3. This probably dates to after Antigonus' death, since both are crowned and there was no co-regency.

PART THREE

THE REIGNS OF PHILIP V AND PERSEUS

XVII

PHILIP BECOMES MASTER OF HIS COURT AND LEADER OF THE SYMMACHY

(221–218 B.C.)

1. *Sources of information*

FOR Philip's reign (chapters XVII–XX) the primary material consists of inscriptions, especially those recording his letters and instructions in military, religious, and other matters; coins, summarized by M. Price, *Coins of the Macedonians* (British Museum, London, 1974) 28–30; and monuments revealed by excavation. The chief literary source is the history of Polybius, full and detailed, based on original documents (texts of treaties, probably parts of Philip's *Journal*, memoirs, etc.) and eyewitness accounts, collected in Greece and Italy, where he lived as a hostage from 167 to 150. Born at Megalopolis a few years before 200, he became an officer and statesman of the Achaean League. In Italy he was a friend of Scipio Aemilianus and travelled with him and other Roman statesmen, and in 150 he returned to Greece. Books 1–6, which carried the narrative down to 216, may have been written before 150, and the other books after 150. Polybius condoned patriotic bias (16. 14. 6). In consequence he disparaged his country's enemies, Aetolia, Sparta, and (after 215) Macedonia; and since he admired Rome, he disparaged Rome's enemies, primarily Macedonia, of which he had no personal knowledge. His estimate of Philip is therefore very far from objective. Indeed, to quote E. S. Gruen in *Studies Edson* 180, 'his history is overwhelmingly hostile to the Macedonian king.' Polybius' history was the basis of Plutarch's *Lives* of Aratus and Flamininus and of much of Livy's history. Livy made alterations freely to the greater credit of Rome and discredit of Macedonia. He used also accounts by Roman annalists, which were biased and sometimes fictional, but gave routine Roman information correctly. Epitomes of Trogus by Justin and of Cassius Dio by Zonaras, and fragments of Trogus, Dio, and Appian mix Polybian and non-Polybian material, the latter being usually of inferior worth.

All students of the period benefit immensely from Walbank's *Historical Commentary on Polybius* in three volumes.

2. *The year of Philip's minority*

The claim of young Philip to the throne was safeguarded by the Assembly. On his father's death he was elected king at the age of eight, and his nearest male agnate in the royal house—Antigonus Doson of the cadet branch—was appointed guardian (*epitropos*)[1] and general (*strategos*),[2] i.e. commander-in-chief of the royal forces. Similar arrangements had been made for Amyntas and his uncle Philip in 359. A year or two later Doson was elected king. He continued to be Philip's guardian and he marked Philip out as his intended successor by giving him precedence in the order of the courtiers.[3] Thus an inscription at Demetrias,[4] following Macedonian protocol, was addressed to 'King Antigonus and Philip', βασιλεῖ Ἀντιγόνω[ι] καὶ Φιλίππωι. In an inscription at Priene *c*. 227 reference was made to 'King Antigonus' and 'heir to the kingdom Philip';[5] and in the dedication of statuary at Olympia *c*. 223 'Hellas was crowning Antigonus who became guardian of Philip, son of Demetrius, with one hand, and Philip with the other hand' (Paus. 6. 16. 3). There was no rival claimant in the royal house. For Doson had no adult children. He married Philip's widowed mother, Phthia; and any children they had ranked after Philip.[6]

In the course of 224 Philip, and perhaps sixteen of his contemporaries, entered the School of Royal Pages to be educated at court, to hunt with the king and to fight alongside him in war.[7] In winter 222/1 Philip stayed with Aratus 'to become acquainted through him with the states [of the Achaean League] and to be known to them' (P*Arat* 46). By then Doson was gravely ill. He drew up a will to secure the succession for Philip, who was sixteen. As there was no male agnate in the royal house, Doson named several men to become guardians of Philip (Plb. 4. 87. 6–8).In addition[8] he named four men to hold particular posts: Leontius to command the Peltasts (an élite unit, like the Hypaspists of Alexander); Megaleas to be head of the secretariat;

---

[1] Plb. 2. 45. 2; P*Arat* 8. 3; J. 28. 3. 10; Syncellus p. 508 Dindorf. Antigonus is sometimes distinguished in our sources not as 'Doson' but as 'the one who became guardian of Philip' (e.g. in Livy 40. 54. 4–5).

[2] P*Aem* 8. 3 ἐπίτροπον καὶ στρατηγόν.

[3] The years of guardianship before Doson was elected king were probably given in *FGrH* 260 (Porphyry) F 3. 14; see Jacoby ad loc. For such precedence see Volume II. 134 ff.

[4] *BCH* 1950. 42; see A. Aymard, *Aegyptus* 1952. 90–3.

[5] *Inschr. Priene* 37. ll. 136 ff.

[6] The statement in *FGrH* 260 (Porphyry) F 3. 14 that Doson did not raise his children by Phthia is most improbable; for the royal house had a dearth of children.

[7] See Volume II. 401 and the fresco of the Royal Hunt at Vergina.

[8] Apelles was a guardian; the other named persons had different appointments. *Contra* Walbank, *C* 1. 536.

Taurion to be 'in charge of Macedonian affairs in the Peloponnese';[1] and Alexander to be chancellor of the court, where he would command the Royal Bodyguard and the Royal Pages. The principle of making separate and independent appointments had been applied in 323, but there were now differences in detail. Then there had been one guardian, Philip Arrhidaeus, for the young king; now there were to be several. Then Perdiccas had been 'manager' (*epimeletes*) of the kings and also commander of the royal forces (*strategos*). Now no suggestion was made by Doson for these important posts. It seems that no 'manager' was ever appointed, and that command of the royal forces was given for each campaign by the Assembly. The lack of a central directing hand was to prove a grave disadvantage in the year or more which was to cover Philip's minority.

In 221, perhaps in July, Doson died. He left to the Macedonian Assembly 'an account of his administration' (Plb. 4. 87. 7), compiled no doubt from his own *King's Journal*. Philip was elected king. Since he was still a minor, the appointments which Doson had suggested were made.[2] One of the guardians is named, Apelles (Plb. 4. 76. 1). The hope which Polybius ascribed to Doson (4. 87. 7), that these appointments would avoid rivalry and dissension among the leading Macedonians, was to prove sadly misplaced. For even among the five named officers two rival groups emerged. There was no accepted individual, or group of individuals to formulate policy and to make proposals in the Assembly.

Macedon's enemies were quick to seize their chance. 'The Dardanians and the other neighbouring peoples, holding Philip's age in contempt, made continuous attacks', and it seems that they were not finally beaten off until Philip commanded as king in late 220 (J. 29. 1. 10–11 and Trog. *Prol.* 29). Although overlooked by Polybius, these attacks help to explain the failure of the Macedonian army to act in southern Greece until late 220. There a further weakness appeared. The hegemony of the Hellenic League was indeed vested in the Macedonian state, which then chose a Macedonian—normally the king—to act as *hegemon*.[3] During Philip's minority the chosen man was probably Taurion. He seems to have lacked initiative and to have followed the lead of Achaean generals (e.g. Plb. 4. 6. 4 and 10. 2).

---

[1] ἐπὶ τῶν κατὰ Πελοπόννησον, where there were three Macedonian garrisons; see also 4. 6. 4 and 4. 87. 1 ἐπὶ τῶν ἐν Πελοποννήσῳ βασιλικῶν πραγμάτων. Bengtson, 538, followed by Walbank, *CAH*² 7. 1. 472, held that Taurion occupied the same position towards the Greek Symmachy as Antipater had occupied in 334–323 towards the Greek League. The difference is that Taurion was subject to the government at Pella, and that in this regard Antipater was the government at Pella in the absence of Alexander in the East.

[2] Presumably by the Assembly, as in 323. See *HSMO* 160.

[3] Bengtson, *Strat.* 2. 538, thought that Taurion was *hegemon*; but if so, his inactivity is hard to explain. The Hellenic League and the Symmachy, as defined by Walbank (see p. 352 f. above), are one and the same thing.

This weakness was exploited immediately by the Aetolians, who 'felt contempt when the realm passed to a boy, Philip' (Plb. 4. 3. 3). Flourishing traditionally through acts of brigandage and war, they were opposed to the consolidation of the peace and to the extension of the Symmachy. Since the other Greek states north of the Isthmus and the north-easterly half of the Peloponnese were members of the Symmachy (apart from Athens, which was neutral), the Aetolian leaders looked for an opening in the south-westerly half of the Peloponnese, to which they had access by sea (see Fig. 10). Elis and Messenia were remarkably prosperous despite internal struggles between the haves and the have-nots and despite the hazards of piracy and brigandage, which led people to build watch-towers and fortify their farms; and it was this prosperity which led them both, and especially Messenia, to think of joining the Symmachy. The Aetolians sent a young officer, Dorimachus, 'full of Aetolian bravura and rapacity', to a small ally, Phigaleia, which was situated between Elis and Messenia. Dorimachus had 'a public mission' there; but privately he raised gangs of brigands and had them raid the farmsteads of Messenia, massacring any who resisted and carrying off cattle and humans of any kind or sex. As Messenia was on terms of 'friendship and alliance' with Aetolia, the Messenian authorities complained. Dorimachus, blustering and protesting, was sent back to Aetolia, where his friends in office, without consulting the Aetolian Assembly, commended him and committed unsolicited attacks elsewhere. According to Polybius, they made war on Messenia, Epirus, Achaea, Acarnania, and Macedonia (4. 5. 10).[1] Their fleet and that of their ally Cephallenia ravaged the coast of Epirus and delivered an attack overland on Thyrreum in northern Acarnania (see Fig. 12). Aetolian seamen seized and sold the cargo and the crew of a Macedonian 'royal merchantman' off Cythera. A group of Aetolian raiders made their way into a fortified post called Clarium in the territory of Megalopolis, where they pillaged and looted and set up a market to sell the spoil (Plb. 4. 5 and 4. 6. 1–3).

The first reaction came late in 221, when as allies of Megalopolis the general of the Achaean League, Timoxenus, and Taurion with his Macedonian garrison troops liberated Clarium. But no approach was made to the Council of the Symmachy. The Aetolian leaders exploited their indecision by mounting a full-scale Aetolian invasion of western Achaea, which they looted on their way towards Messenia. Once there, as the Messenians stayed behind their walls, the Aetolians amassed enormous quantities of loot. In mid-May the Assembly of the Achaean

---

[1] It is difficult to see how war was declared if the Assembly did not meet.

League met, voted to help Messenia, and ordered Timoxenus to conscript the Achaean levy. He procrastinated, but his successor in office, Aratus, had the levy meet at Megalopolis and arranged for his ally, Sparta, to send an army to the frontier, in case it was needed. Even then Aratus did not turn to the Council of the Symmachy. But Messenia was impressed and asked for alliance with the Achaean League. Aratus appeared to be a shrewd politician, but he proved a hopeless commander. He disbanded most of his forces; the residue of picked men was overwhelmingly defeated at Caphyae; and the Aetolians went home as they pleased, picking up more loot in Sicyonia on their way to the Isthmus of Corinth. Within a twelve-month period the Aetolians had destabilized the situation in the Peloponnese and made themselves a handsome profit by a display of lawless brigandage and ruthless opportunism.[1]

3. *Philip proves himself as a commander in war*

Coming of age at eighteen, about July in 220, Philip took control.[2] His guardians now became merely his advisers. His first command of the royal forces was against the Dardanians, with success (J. 29. 1. 10 and Trog. *Prol.* 29). It was some weeks yet before he came south. Meanwhile the Greek states were manœuvring for position. The Assembly of the Achaean League forgave Aratus, who was probably thought to be influential with Philip, and sent envoys to some other members of the Symmachy (Plb. 4. 15. 1 naming Epirus, Boeotia, Phocis, Acarnania, and Philip, but not Thessaly and Boeotia). The Achaeans wanted them each to support the acceptance of Messenia as a member of the Symmachy and a declaration of war by the Symmachy on Aetolia. To show that she was in earnest Achaea undertook to raise 10,000 infantry and 1,000 cavalry from her own forces and those of her allies, Messene and Sparta. The Assembly of the Aetolian League resolved to be at peace with all states, including the Achaean League, but only if the Achaean League cancelled its alliance with Messenia. Sparta played a double game; despite its obligations to

---

[1] Aratus may have hoped to make personal capital by winning Messenia for the Achaean League and not involving the Symmachy; but he still needed the help of Taurion (4. 10. 2 and 6).

[2] For this being the age of majority for a king see the cases of Perdiccas III in Volume II. 185 and Heracles above, p. 165. It seems likely that the Royal Pages served from the age of fourteen to their eighteenth birthday. Once aged eighteen a prince or king became qualified for military command (e.g. Alexander III at Chaeronea). A prince or a king in his minority could be given responsibility earlier (e.g. *PA* 9. 1). The decision of the Symmachy at Corinth was thus inspired by Philip himself and not, as Errington 22 holds, by 'the Macedonian Regency Council', which—if it ever existed—ceased about July 220. Even less was there a 'Council of Guardians' in 218 (but see *CAH*[2] 7. 1. 479).

'the Macedonians and Philip'[1] and its recent provision of troops to help Achaea, an opposition group made a secret pact of friendship and alliance with Aetolia. The Epirotes and Philip replied to the Achaean envoys that they were willing to support Messenia's entry into the Symmachy, but that they preferred to stay at peace with Aetolia. The fact was that no state wanted individually to provoke the savage hordes of Aetolia into raiding its own territory.

Another disturbing factor was the appearance of two fleets of Illyrian privateers, ninety in all, under the command respectively of Scerdilaidas, a prince of the Ardiaean royal house (see p. 352 above), and of Demetrius of Pharos, whose troops had distinguished themselves on the Macedonian side at Sellasia in 222. In sailing south of Lissus in Illyris, they had broken their treaty with Rome; but that did not seem to concern the Greek states. Joining forces with their Greek counterpart, the Aetolians, the Illyrians made raids on the coasts of Messenia and Achaea. Demetrius then took his squadron to raid and blackmail the Cyclades. Meanwhile the Illyrians of Scerdilaidas and the Aetolian levy led by Dorimachus struck deep into Arcadia and massacred the population of Cynaetha, a city already torn by internal strife. Aratus and the Achaean levy made no move, and the raiding forces returned unmolested to Aetolia, where Scerdilaidas was cheated of his share of the loot (4. 29. 5–6). An attempt to intercept the Aetolian fleet on its way home was made by Taurion, who bought the services of Demetrius of Pharos and his squadron when they fled from the Cyclades to the Isthmus of Corinth. They arrived two days late, raided the coast of Aetolia, and then returned to Corinth.

Such was the situation when Philip arrived at the head of the Macedonian army at Corinth (see Fig. 10). He was now the *hegemon*, appointed by the Macedonian state. He instructed the members of the Symmachy to send their delegates to Corinth (4. 22. 2), and he then advanced towards Sparta, a state outside the Symmachy, but allied with Macedonia (4. 23. 6) and in the past supportive of Achaea (4. 9. 6). An outbreak of revolutionary violence by a pro-Aetolian faction ended in the murder of some pro-Macedonian leaders at Sparta just before the arrival of Philip in the Peloponnese. Now, at Tegea, he and his Council of Friends heard a special delegation of ten Spartans defend their actions and protest their loyalty to Macedon in fulfilment of the alliance. When the Spartans withdrew, three courses may have

---

[1] 4. 16. 5; cf. 4. 24. 8. These were under an alliance between Sparta and 'the king and the Macedonians' (cf. 4. 34. 10), as contrasted with Sparta's relations with the Symmachy (4. 24. 4–6 κατ' ἰδίαν τῶν συμμάχων εἰς αὐτοὺς ἀδικήματα and τὴν κοινὴν συμμαχίαν). *Contra* A. Heuss, *Stadt u. Herrscher des Hellenismus in ihren staats- und völkerrechtlichen Beziehungen* (Leipzig, 1937) 30, and Walbank, *C* 1. 457 and 470.

been advocated: to destroy Sparta, install a pro-Macedonian regime, or let bygones be bygones. Philip decided on the last, coupled with a renewal of the alliance on both sides between Sparta and Macedon. It was a decision of principle, made less with an eye on Sparta than on the impending meeting of the Council of the Symmachy; for he wanted a willing, and not a terrorized, co-operation from the Greek states.[1]

When the Council met at Corinth with Philip presiding, it heard complaints of Aetolian aggression, brigandage, and sacrilege. The councillors resolved unanimously to declare war on Aetolia in the name of the Symmachy (hence the term 'The Social War'); they undertook to liberate any land or city which had been forced into the Aetolian League and transfer the control of Delphi from Aetolia to the Delphic Amphictyony. The resolution was morally justified. But the timing was inept; for it was ineffective, unless and until each member state as a sovereign state adopted it and raised troops to implement it. Given the Greek states' capacity for procrastination, nothing was likely to happen until the spring of 219. Aetolia now held the diplomatic initiative. When Philip tried to negotiate with her, she avoided him (4. 26. 1–6).

At the same meeting the Council admitted to the Symmachy a group of states in Crete, headed by Lyttus, their envoys having been interviewed personally by Philip as *hegemon* (P*Arat* 48. 5). It had been worsted by a rival group, led by Cnossus, then an ally of Aetolia, and it was with the help of 1,000 Aetolian soldiers that Cnossus had depopulated Lyttus by deporting all its women and children. The Symmachy sent 200 Achaeans, 100 Phocians, and 400 Illyrians, whose services—no doubt for Cretan pay—enabled the Lyttus group to stay in the field; but its action had little relevance to the situation on the mainland.

The first reaction to the resolution of the Council came from the Achaean League, where the Council and the Assembly were holding their regular early-autumn meeting. The resolution was adopted unanimously, and it was agreed to treat Aetolia as 'a prize of war', that is, its land to be plundered and its people enslaved. Philip addressed the Achaean Council in an atmosphere of mutual goodwill, and then he took his army back to Macedonia for the winter. The next reaction was that of the Aetolian League: at their annual meeting the Aetolians elected as their general Scopas, the abetter of Dorimachus, and they

---

[1] Polybius reports views expressed in the King's Council and attributes the decision to Aratus. Polybius cannot have had access to such information, and at the time, when Aratus was busy raising troops as general of the Achaean League, it is unlikely that he was a member of the King's Council. Philip had to make up his own mind and give to the allies 'an example of his own policy' (4. 24. 9 δεῖγμα τῆς ἑαυτοῦ προαιρέσεως τοῖς συμμάχοις).

sent envoys out to the mainland states. The Acarnanian League adopted the resolution and declared war on their powerful neighbour, Aetolia. The Epirote League was more circumspect: it offered peace to the Aetolian envoys, but undertook to join Philip, as soon as he acted against Aetolia (4. 30. 6–7). The replies of Phocis, Boeotia, Locris, and Thessaly are not recorded in our sources. In the Peloponnese the Symmachy's approaches were rebuffed. Messenia refused to go to war so long as the Aetolians held Phigaleia. The Spartans began by making no reply to the Symmachy and by letting an Aetolian envoy called Machatas address their Assembly. The revolutionary pro-Aetolian party then murdered the ephors-in-office in the temple of Athena of the Bronze House, appointed other ephors, elected two kings, made alliance with Aetolia, invaded the Argolid, and declared war on the Achaean League.[1] The same Aetolian envoy persuaded the Eleans to prepare to attack the Achaeans, their neighbours. Indeed the Achaean League seemed to be totally ineffective throughout the winter months. Farther afield, the envoys of the Symmachy asked Ptolemy IV not to help Aetolia in the forthcoming war.

During the winter of 220/19 Philip trained his forces and improved his defences against the Dardanians in the north. He was also concerned with the situation to the west of Macedonia (see Fig. 8). There Demetrius of Pharos was openly at war with Rome; for he overran the northern part of the Roman protectorate in Illyris (3. 16. 3), killed some pro-Roman leaders, and garrisoned Dimallum.[2] Philip's friendship with Demetrius added to Rome's fears, and in the winter Philip engaged the services of Scerdilaidas' fleet of thirty *lembi*, to operate against Aetolia. Thus Philip encouraged Scerdilaidas once again to break his treaty with Rome by sailing south of Lissus. News of all this certainly reached Rome. She prepared to send both consuls with large forces to Illyris in 219. Philip may not have foreseen this possibility when he himself embarked on his campaign against Aetolia in Greece.

Most of Aetolia is a tangle of high, forested mountain ranges. Its highland population excelled in guerrilla warfare, defending the homeland in depth and raiding far afield by land and by sea. They had fine arable land only in the west, and they had added to it by appropriating the western side of the Achelous valley from Acarnania; and they held this area with fortified and garrisoned towns and with cavalry, but they lacked heavy infantry. Philip's aim was to invade these lowlands from the west and to prepare bases for a western fleet. He marched through Thessaly, Epirus, and Acarnania, adding local

---

[1] 4. 34–6 with Walbank, *C* ad loc.
[2] Identified by tile stamps: see *SA* 1965. 1. 65 ff., *Bul. Ark.* 1974. 71 f. and H*IRM* 14 with map on p. 13.

levies to his Macedonian army of 800 cavalry, 5,000 Peltasts, and 10,000 phalanxmen, and he ravaged the wide plains of the Achelous valley and the lower Euenus valley as far as Calydon (see Fig. 12). *En route* he spent a month laying siege to Ambracus, the strongly fortified harbour of Aetolian-held Ambracia;[1] his capture of it gave him control of the Ambracian Gulf and secured his communications with Acarnania. Farther south his Macedonians captured stronghold after stronghold with spectacular courage, and his Peltasts forced the passage of the Achelous river despite the Aetolian cavalry on the far bank. He captured Oeniadae, the chief port off the mouth of the Corinthian Gulf and fortified its citadel, dockyards, and harbour to serve as a naval base.[2]

Meanwhile the Aetolians had sent out three raiding parties. The largest, commanded by Scopas, marched via Thessaly and probably the Petra pass[3] into Pieria, where he destroyed the ripening crops and collected booty. Then, turning south, he looted Dium and destroyed sacred as well as secular buildings; but the population escaped into the hills. This happened in early summer 219, when Philip began the siege of Ambracus (4. 63. 1). Another raiding party, led by Dorimachus, sailed by night to Aegeira, broke into the city, but with daylight lost cohesion as they began looting. The men of Aegeira rallied and defeated them. The third party, consisting mainly of Eleans, but led by Aetolians, overran western Achaea, which, on receiving no help from Aratus, the Achaean general, broke away and diverted its usual federal contributions to the hiring of mercenaries. This raid coincided with Philip's arrival in central Acarnania. The western Achaeans sent envoys asking him to cross the Gulf and invade Elis, but he pressed on with his main objective, the control of western Aetolia and the establishment of his base at Oeniadae. Polybius implied that his next move would have been into Elis and Achaea (4. 66. 1–2), where he would have established bases against Aetolia, but he was now diverted by news from Macedonia.

That news, according to Polybius, was that the Dardanians were preparing for an invasion of Macedonia. Later, when Philip's army reached Pella, the Dardanians abandoned the plan. Another piece of news, which Polybius did not mention, must have been the presence of large Roman naval and military forces in Illyris, where Dimallum was captured in a week and full control of the Roman dependencies was

---

[1] See H*E* 137 f.

[2] 4. 64. 5–7, the Peltasts using the close order (*synaspismos*). For Oeniadae see 4. 65. 8–11 and Walbank, *C* ad loc.; the existing rock-cut docks may be from Philip's time.

[3] He avoided Larissa and the fortified Tempe pass; thus he achieved a surprise raid first on the rich Pierian plain and then on Dium; otherwise Walbank, *C* 1. 516.

being reimposed.[1] To leave Macedonia open to attack possibly from the west as well as from the north may have seemed hazardous to Philip. As he crossed back from Acarnania to Epirus, he was met by Demetrius with the latest news, Rome's capture of Pharos, from which he had escaped with only one *lembus*. Philip received Demetrius as a friend and ally and marched rapidly to Pella. It was now high summer. The Romans stayed within the area of their dependencies and soon returned to Italy; for the actions of Hannibal in Spain were now the chief concern of Rome. Philip sent his soldiers home to garner the late harvest, and he made his headquarters at Larissa, in case the Aetolians attempted another raid on Macedonia. The loss of the autumn months for furthering the campaign to encircle Aetolia was serious; and in addition the action of Rome in Illyris had prevented the fleet of Scerdilaidas from coming to occupy Oeniadae.

In the autumn Dorimachus, elected general of the Aetolians, took his revenge on the Epirotes by invading the Molossian heartland, wreaking destruction far and wide, sacking Passaron and Dodona, and destroying the temple of Zeus there.[2] In early winter Euripidas, an Aetolian commander of 2,300 men—Eleans, mercenaries, and 'brigands'—marched through the Arcadian plateau and was about to enter and ravage the rich territory of Sicyon, when he learnt to his amazement that a Macedonian army lay at Phlius, near by (see Fig. 10). He turned back, but his army was trapped and destroyed, while he and some cavalrymen fled to Psophis, a natural citadel strongly fortified. The Macedonian success was due to the speed and secrecy of Philip's movements. He had descended from Larissa via Euboea,[3] Locris, Boeotia, and Megaris to Corinth with 400 'Court' Cavalry, 2,000 Peltasts and 3,000 'Bronze-shielded' phalangites, and with 300 Cretan allies. Entering Corinth around 22 December 219 he kept the population indoors while he sent orders to the Achaean levies to muster at Caphyae in Arcadia. He was on his way there when he fell in with Euripidas' force by sheer coincidence. At Caphyae Aratus' son of the same name, the Achaean general for this year, awaited him with more than 4,000 men. Moving fast despite snow blizzards and storming enemy-held fortresses on the borders of Arcadia and Elis, the army descended into the rich lands of Elis, collected vast amounts of loot, and overtook a swarm of refugees in a natural hide-out (like the Devil's Beef Tub near Moffat), where alone 5,000 prisoners and innumerable cattle were taken (4. 75. 2–7). Philip then withdrew to Olympia, where he sacrificed to Zeus in thanksgiving and rested his

---

[1] *HIRM* 11 ff.
[2] 4. 67; D.S. 26. 4. 7; *HE* 576 and 604; S. I. Dakaris, *Dodona* (Ioannina, 1972) 23.
[3] The Aetolians still held Thermopylae.

army, and marched to the Macedonian base at Heraea on the Arcadian side of the border. There he sold off his prisoners and booty.

The army was now ready for another lightning raid into fresh territory, Triphylia, where 600 Aetolians, 500 mercenaries paid by Elis, 1,000 citizen soldiers of Elis, and some mercenary cavalrymen, called 'Tarentines', had taken up positions at three separate fortresses. Within six days Philip stormed fortresses, won over cities, and granted terms of withdrawal to the surviving enemy forces. This spectacular success inspired the citizens of Phigaleia to drive out their Aetolian garrison and join Philip, who sent a garrison under Taurion to protect them (4. 80. 3). By the end of January 218 he advanced to Megalopolis. The Spartans, who had recently ravaged southern Arcadia and had sent a small force into Triphylia, expected an invasion, but Philip turned northwards to Argos. His Macedonians were in need of a rest. They were sent home on leave. Philip and his court stayed at Argos, the original home of the Macedonian royal house.

This winter campaign established beyond any doubt the reputation of Philip as a dashing commander and capable general, very much in the mould of the young Alexander of 335, and it confirmed the great superiority of the Macedonian citizen troops over any Greek citizen troops in courage, tenacity, physical toughness, and fighting power (4. 69. 4–7 and 71. 10). Philip led his picked men in deeds of daring, as Alexander had done; for instance at Psophis with scaling ladders and at Alipheira at the head of a rock-climbing assault party (4. 78. 6–11). The effect of the winter campaign was greatly to strengthen the position of the Achaean League; for all the frontier fortresses were handed over to League troops. Triphylia was retained under Macedonian control; for a Macedonian garrison was placed in Lepreum, and Philip appointed an Acarnanian officer as 'manager of Triphylia' (4. 80. 15 ἐπιμελητὴς τῆς Τριφυλίας). The Macedonian presence here and at Phigaleia was a protection to Messenia, which now joined Philip and the Symmachy. Sparta was defiant, but isolated and encircled. On the other hand, the sale of booty had not covered the costs of the winter campaign, and its chief object had not been achieved, the winning over of Elis. For the Eleans knew that the Macedonians would come and go, but that the Aetolians were constant neighbours with open access by sea to their coasts. To join Philip and the Symmachy would expose them to raid after raid from Aetolia.

4. *Consideration of Philip's policy*

The two campaigns of early summer 219 and of winter 219/18 revealed the limitations of both sides. The Aetolian League and its allies had mounted some minor raids by some 2,500 fast-moving troops and one great raid, perhaps by 10,000 (*pandemei* 4. 62. 1), on Pieria and Dium at harvest-time, in order to live off the land. Such guerrilla tactics caused terror and inflicted economic damage. But their cavalry and infantry were trained as marauders and not to fight in tight formations on level ground (4. 8. 10 and 11. 8). Thus they could not engage in a decisive battle. Philip had used larger numbers, perhaps 22,000 men in central Greece in proximity to Aetolia and some 10,000 men in the Peloponnese, and in addition to causing terror and economic damage he had made military gains. These, however, were expensive to hold; for his garrisons at Lepreum, Phigaleia, Heraea, Orchomenus, and Acrocorinth as well as the forces guarding Thessaly and his communications at Chalcis, were straining his manpower when he used Macedonians, and his finances when, as is probable, he relied mainly on mercenaries. He had entrusted many strongholds to the Achaeans, who tended to employ mercenaries for garrison duty. Their citizen troops, being trained for fighting in formation on flat ground (4. 11. 8), were weak in guerrilla warfare and proved men of straw in comparison with the tough and adaptable Macedonians (4. 7. 6–7, 11. 7–13, and 60. 2).[1] These remarks apply not only to Achaeans proper, but to the Corinthians, Argives, Epidaurians, and Arcadians, who also were members of the Achaean League.

The two campaigns of Philip should not be judged in isolation; for they were conceived as the foundation of a further policy—a naval offensive and an irruption into Aetolia. For the next step he needed financial help from the Achaean League as well as some shipping. In the interest of good relations he attended the late February meeting of 218, at which the Achaean Assembly elected as general a man who was to prove incompetent, Eperatus; but he was not to enter office until May. Philip went on to ravage the north-eastern part of Elis and approached the Elean authorities with an eye to negotiations; but they refused. He needed sea power to put further pressure on Elis. Addressing as *hegemon* a meeting of the Achaean League which he summoned for the purpose, he persuaded the League to provide 50 talents towards the cost of the last campaign, 17 talents a month for future campaigns (with a prepayment covering three months), 10,000 *medimni* of grain, and a number of warships (5. 1. 10–12 and 2. 4). To the last he could add some Macedonian warships, stationed at Lechaeum in the Corinthian Gulf. There he trained not Achaeans, but his Macedonians, now returned from home leave, and mercenaries for naval service. His plan, like that of Themistocles in 481, was to make

---

[1] Only Macedonians and Cretans figured in the daring assault on Psophis.

his best infantrymen into oarsmen and sailors.[1] They responded to the challenge (5. 2. 4 and 11), and a fleet of small warships and transport vessels with 6,000 Macedonians and 1,200 mercenaries left Lechaeum under oar for the west.

Philip's aim was to split his enemies by attacking Cephallenia first (see Fig. 12). He was met there by squadrons from Messenia, Epirus, and Acarnania and by fifteen Illyrian *lembi*, sent by Scerdilaidas, who was himself detained by troublesome chieftains in Illyris. The fleet was not challenged, and he landed his men to reap the harvest (in May/June) and lay siege to Pale. The wall was breached, but the assault failed. At once he sailed to Leucas, cleared the east channel, entered the Ambracian Gulf, and landed at Limnaea in Acarnania as dawn was breaking. His shipping was protected by the Epirote squadron stationed at Ambracus. The Acarnanian levy joined him by prearrangement, but he could not wait for the full Epirote levy. Speed and secrecy were essential. He knew that half of the Aetolian levy was stationed in western Aetolia (the other half had left eastern Aetolia to invade Thessaly) and that there were reserve forces in the towns. He ordered his men, perhaps 10,000 in all, to travel light, ready for action (5. 5. 14 εὔζωνοι).

Leaving Limnaea early that afternoon and apart from a break for supper marching continuously until next evening they arrived at Thermum, having covered approximately 80 kilometres in twenty-eight hours. 'The Macedonians made the march with energy' (5. 8. 3). The timing was perfect. The army crossed the Achelous at dawn to take by surprise the workers and their stock in the fields, and it occupied Thermum, the religious and political centre of the Aetolian League, with a night's rest ahead. The looting and the destruction of Thermum and the surrounding villages were carried out as acts of retaliation, marked by the writing up of the following line (a parody of Euripides, *Suppl.* 860):

ὁρᾷς τὸ δῖον οὗ βέλος διέπτατο;
'Do you see where the *dion* shaft flew to the mark?'

Here *dion* recalled Dium, and its meaning 'of Zeus' recalled Dodona, the two places so ruthlessly sacked by the Aetolians. The sack of Thermum was represented as 'the vengeance of Zeus' as much as the sack of Troy in Aeschylus' *Agamemnon* or the sack of Persepolis by Alexander and the Greeks.[2]

---

[1] For the conversion see Hammond on the decree of Themistocles in *JHS* 102 (1982) 75 ff. Philip's task was easier in that he had not triremes, but smaller warships such as penteconters and triaconters.

[2] For a similar line at Passaron see H*E* 184 and 605, to which add *Ep. Chron.* 22 (1980) 31 f. and Cabanes 246 f. Philip was condemned by Polybius (5. 9–12) for copying the Aetolians; but

The return round the south-eastern side of Lake Trichonis (Agrinion) was hazardous. The track was difficult, the ground was wooded, and the pass was overlooked by hills. During the advance Philip, unlike Flaminius at Lake Trasimene, had protected his extended column with a flanking column in the hills and a strong rearguard, and he had garrisoned the terminals at Metapa and Pamphion.[1] Now the booty and the phalangites went first, the Acarnanians and the mercenaries came next, and an ambush was laid by picked Peltasts and the Illyrians. When 3,000 Aetolians attacked the rearguard, they were caught in the ambush and fled with losses. The army destroyed every town *en route*. The next hazard was the crossing of the Achelous, since 4,000 enemy troops lay in Stratus. Philip marched to Stratus, crossed the river there with his full force facing the enemy, and later beat off an attack by making his rearguard turn about and by sending the Illyrians into action. On reaching Limnaea at the conclusion of this copybook campaign,[2] Philip sacrificed to the gods and feasted his officers. The other half of the Aetolian levy hastened back from Thessaly, but it was too late to intercept him.

The fleet sailed at once to Corinth (see Fig. 10). On the second day out of Corinth his army met the full levy of the Achaean League at Tegea by prearrangement, and the combined forces made a surprise invasion of Laconia, reaching Amyclae when the Spartans thought Philip was still in Aetolia (5. 18. 8–10). The whole of southern Laconia was pillaged and laid waste, and when the Spartans tried to intercept his army as it came north up the Eurotas valley his Peltasts and the Illyrians were skilfully deployed to defeat them (5. 22–3). He sacrificed to the gods at Sellasia, sold his booty at Tegea, and reached Corinth. He had been as bold as Athens had been timid in the fifth century in the use of sea power and of seaborne forces against enemies on the Greek mainland.

At Corinth Philip found envoys from Rhodes and Chios, who wished to negotiate a peace between Philip and the Aetolians. He encouraged them to do so; for he had done everything possible to daunt the Aetolians and their allies. A truce for thirty days was agreed, and a date was fixed for a peace conference at Rhium to be attended by delegates from both sides. At that point troubles at the Macedonian court encouraged the Aetolians to procrastinate (5. 29. 1–3). We must therefore consider the position there.

the Macedonians and the Epirotes would not have accepted less than the *lex talionis* required. Mamroth, 1935. 225 attributed some copper coins of Philip to this occasion, probably correctly.

[1] See Woodhouse 209 ff., identifying Metapa with Morosklavon (Sitaralona) and Pamphion with Petrokhori.

[2] E.g. in supply. He brought supplies from Pale to Limnaea, obtained fodder and grain east of the Achelous, captured large stocks around Thermum, and had enough to see him on the way from Limnaea.

Between July 220, when Philip attained his majority, and autumn 218 Philip was commanding the royal forces in person, instigating actions, taking decisions, and issuing orders. In Macedonia this was normal. Of course, like a king of any age, he had advisers and consulted a Council of Friends (e.g. 4. 23. 5 and 5. 22. 8); but he had the final say (e.g. 4. 24. 4–7). In the Greek states a command at the age of eighteen was an absurdity, since a citizen became eligible for office only at the age of thirty. Thus Polybius and the Greek source used by Justin (Trogus) reflected the common Greek view that Philip would be an incompetent boy[1] (4. 24. 1–3; 5. 12. 5, 16. 2, 18. 6, and 26. 4; J. 29. 1. 10 'contemptu aetatis'). But at times even Polybius had to admit Philip's ability in command (4. 77. 1 and 82. 1; 5. 18. 7 and 29. 2).

Any young king, inheriting the Friends of his predecessor, was likely to disagree with some of them. Polybius, portraying Philip as a malleable youth, was interested in what he saw as a struggle between rival advisers, especially Aratus (4. 24. 3 and 5. 28. 9)[2] and Apelles (4. 76. 1), but the real issue was one of power between the king and a group of Friends—Apelles, Megaleas, Leontius, Crinon, and Ptolemaeus. Polybius' account of this issue, being based on Greek informants friendly to Aratus and hostile to Macedonia, contains hypothetical interpretations which are of doubtful value. It is best therefore to begin with the main facts.

The first serious fracas occurred on the army's return to Limnaea in summer 218. After the king's banquet for his officers Aratus was pelted with abuse and then with stones by Megaleas and Crinon (and perhaps by Leontius, but he slipped away), and as sympathizers joined in, a riot occurred. Philip as commander-in-chief on campaign awarded the blame and fined Megaleas and Crinon 20 talents each for disorderly conduct. Once out of reach of possible pursuers, at Leucas, he held a Council of Friends which supported his action. Neither man could pay at the time; so Crinon was imprisoned, and Leontius stood bail for Megaleas (5. 14. 11–16. 10). Polybius provided antecedents, e.g. at 4. 76, some of which are far from convincing.[3]

The next fracas occurred at Corinth. On returning from the campaign in Laconia the King's Own Guardsmen (the *agema*), believing that they were losing their privileges, especially in the allocations of

---

[1] Similarly for Alexander III see H*THA* 29.

[2] 'The events are seen by Polybius through the eyes of Aratus and the Achaeans', wrote Errington in *Historia* 16. 22.

[3] Thus Leontius, commander of the Peltasts, is represented as turning tail and holding back his men in action at Pale (5. 4. 10–12) and trying to induce defeat (5. 7. 1–4), whereas in fact he and his men fought splendidly in Aetolia. The alleged excuse of the Etesian winds makes no sense for oared ships (5. 5. 5–8). That Apelles rigged the Achaean elections seems unbelievable (4. 82. 8 and 84. 1); *contra* Walbank, *Ph* 47–8.

booty, broke into the king's quarters and pillaged the tents of some senior officers. Such gross indiscipline did no credit to their commanding officers, Leontius and (probably) Ptolemaeus.[1] Philip convened all the Macedonians. His speech caused an uproar; but he ended in control and he granted an amnesty to the Guard.

The situation of Apelles was not factually related to these riots. He had been given by Philip an important appointment at Chalcis with authority over Macedonian officials in central and northern Greece (5. 26. 4–5).[2] Apparently he overstepped that authority and he failed to forward supplies to Philip (5. 2. 10). This was enough in itself for him to be recalled to Corinth, where he was given a cool reception by Philip (5. 26. 10–15). However, Philip took Apelles to Phocis on some secret negotiations, with which Apelles had probably been involved. When the king came back to the Peloponnese, he found that Megaleas had absconded, which meant that Leontius, as his bail, was liable to arrest and imprisonment like Crinon. Philip put Taurion in command of the Peltasts and sent them to Triphylia. Leontius, relieved of his command, was then imprisoned. When the Peltasts heard, they sent a deputation, offering to pay the 20 talents by subscription, and they asked that, if the arrest was on some other charge, they should be present at the trial (i.e. by an Assembly of the Army). The only effect of this, according to Polybius 5. 27. 8, was to hasten the execution of Leontius. Meanwhile Megaleas, having reached Thebes, wrote treasonable letters to the Aetolian leaders, which were intercepted in Phocis and sent to Philip.[3] An officer was sent to Thebes to bring Megaleas back to answer for his fine of 20 talents. Megaleas committed suicide. The letters seemed to Philip to implicate Apelles. So Apelles, with his favourite boy and his son, was sent ahead to Corinth under arrest. There all three 'ended their own lives.'[4] The fate of Crinon is not known. Ptolemaeus was tried later at Demetrias 'before the Macedonians', i.e. on a charge of treason (5. 29. 6). He was found guilty, and he was executed.

Polybius' informants bundled all these incidents together and

---

[1] Plb. 5. 25 had Leontius, Megaleas, and Ptolemaeus inspire the riot. This has the air of a supposition. Megaleas held no military command; the other two were liable to be cashiered for failing to control the troops under their command. If, on the other hand, Leontius and Ptolemaeus had a hand in the rioting, as Polybius implies at 5. 25. 7, the reason for their later demise is obvious.

[2] Plb. 5. 2. 8 saw this appointment as a step down for Apelles, wrongly since his authority extended into Macedonia (5. 26. 5), perhaps particularly for shipbuilding timber and oars.

[3] The exact timing at 5. 28. 4 supports the belief that these were genuine letters. Megaleas was already on the run and probably wanted asylum in Aetolia. For a different view see Walbank, *C* 1. 550.

[4] In my opinion the expression in the context meant suicide; but see Walbank, *C* 1. 552 and *CAH*² 7. 1. 480.

attributed them to a conspiracy by Apelles, Leontius, and Megaleas formed already in spring 218 (5. 2. 8); but there is little to support such a supposition.[1] Some scholars have conjectured that these and other officers disapproved of the king's naval policy or/and Peloponnesian campaigns and acted for reasons of state; but these can only be conjectures.[2] Rather, the acts of the officers and the Guardsmen are explicable in terms only of personal animosities, thwarted ambitions, grievances, and resentments, leading to mutinous behaviour. Those who pass judgement today on Philip should remember that in time of war a commander-in-chief has to enforce discipline on officers and men, and that collusion with the enemy is punishable by death. When Philip asked for judgement, he obtained the approval of the Council of Friends and the condemnation of Ptolemaeus. Suicide was generally regarded as tantamount to a confession of guilt. The most dangerous of the senior officers was Leontius. Philip acted carefully and quickly, and the execution of Leontius did not provoke a mutiny.[3] In short, Philip established his authority over the court and the army.[4]

How sound had Philip's policy been in 220/19? At the outset he faced the choice of abandoning the Greek states to their own devices or of seeking to control them. The former course would have opened the door to possible intervention by outside powers. Ptolemy Philopator, who became king in 221, might emulate his father who had once been *hegemon* of the Achaean League and had subsidized Sparta as recently as 222. Attalus I and Achaeus were active on the other side of the Aegean and both made alliance with Byzantium in 220. Antiochus III, who became king in 223, captured Seleucia-in-Pieria on the Mediterranean coast in 219. And much closer to Macedonia, Rome had sent an embassy to Aetolia in 228, claimed control of Adriatic waters from Corcyra to Lissus, and held subject territory in Illyris, not far distant from the frontier of the Macedonian kingdom. With hindsight we know that Ptolemy and Antiochus waged war over Coele–Syria in 219–217, Attalus and Achaeus quarrelled with one another in 218,

---

[1] Errington in *Historia* 16. 29 writes 'the charge [of conspiracy] is vague and uncertain' and 34 'Apelles' conspiracy remains, even at this final stage, a web of wholly unsubstantiated allegation and innuendo.'

[2] So Errington, loc. cit. 27 and Walbank, *Ph* 51 f.

[3] Analogies from the lifetime of Alexander III are relevant: the summary execution of ringleaders at Opis, the collusion of Alexander Lyncestes being judged first by the Council of Friends, the case *v*. Philotas being submitted first to the Council of Friends, the suicide of Dimnus, the death of Attalus resisting arrest, and many cases of trial before the Macedonians (see H*A* 244, 87, 181, 182, 39, 38, 181 f., and 197). In the case of Parmenio Alexander III moved quickly, but still evoked a mutinous reaction (183).

[4] Errington 35 attributes 'the fictitious conspiracy of Apelles' to Philip as a pretext for a 'purge'. But Philip dealt with each case as it arose, and the only occasion for a public trial, that of Ptolemaeus, was hardly appropriate for an announcement of a supposed conspiracy involving not Ptolemaeus, but Apelles, Megaleas, and Leontius. *Contra* Walbank, *Ph* 52 and *CAH*[2] 7. 1. 479.

Rome's actions in Illyris in 219 stopped short of a clash with Macedonia, and the actions of Hannibal in 219 and 218 diverted Rome's energies elsewhere. In 220 Philip could not have foreseen these developments. He could not have afforded to abandon the Greek states.

The alternative was to seek control of the Greek states by succeeding Doson as *hegemon* of the Achaean League and trying to force Aetolia, Elis, Messenia, and Sparta into neutrality or into the Common Peace. He followed that policy with remarkable energy and speed, and in autumn 218 he was close to success, with Aetolia eager to make peace (5. 29. 1–2). The cost in Macedonian manpower had not been heavy; for the Peltasts were regular troops, the mercenaries and the Illyrians came from elsewhere, and the Phalangites—a part of the national levy—were sent home for the harvest of 219 (4. 66. 7) and the winter of 218 (5. 29. 5). Moreover, he had developed a naval force in western waters which was effective by Greek standards, and he had won naval bases at Ambracus, Leucas and Oeniadae, which might deter Rome from seeking to expand her naval control. Under all the circumstances Philip's policy seems to have been a sound one.

The member states of the Symmachy were safeguarded only by the manning of strategic bases, especially in frontier positions. These bases were not in open country, like airfields today, but in fortified towns which were taken over for the duration of the war by the manning forces: for instance, Ambracus by Epirotes, Oeniadae by Acarnanians, Psophis by Achaeans, and Heraea by Macedonians. The town was then subject to the manning authority (e.g. Plb. 4. 6. 5; Paus. 7. 17. 5 ὑπήκοον). Macedonia, being geographically distant, had special need of these bases, if she was to lead in war; and no doubt with the approval of the Symmachy Council she had a network of bases. There is no evidence that the townsfolk of a base resented the presence of Macedonian forces; rather the reverse, as we shall see later at Dyme and Corinth (Livy 32. 22. 9 and 23. 5).

XVIII

THE CONSOLIDATION OF MACEDONIA'S POWER (217–212 B.C.)

1. *The winning of peace on the Greek mainland*

WHEN the Aetolians heard of the rioting by the King's Own Guardsmen, the flight of Megaleas, and the deaths of Apelles and Leontius, they imagined that Philip was facing serious trouble (Plb. 5. 28. 4 and 29. 3), and they knew too that his plans in Phocis had failed. They therefore postponed the date of the peace conference, and it soon became clear that they did not intend to make peace. By then the conventional campaigning season was at an end. Philip sent his Macedonian army home and established his court at Demetrias, safeguarding Thessaly. In the course of the winter some Aetolians and the Eleans, who stiffened their citizen forces with mercenaries, overran western Achaea, where the incompetent Eperatus and his inadequate troops failed to resist (Plb. 5. 30).

In 217 Philip turned first to northern Macedonia (see Fig. 3). There the Paeonians, the northernmost people of the Macedonian kingdom, had been weakened by the Dardanians, whose powerful raids were becoming a threat to Lower Macedonia. One method of checking such raids was the establishment of garrisoned strong-points, at best to stop the raiders and at least to intercept them as they returned laden with booty. Two such strong-points existed already in the Axius valley, one at Manastir at the north end of the long Demir Kapu defile and the other at Antigoneia, farther upstream near Banja. Philip now 'seized for himself the largest city of Paeonia, Bylazora, which was extremely well placed in regard to the entries from the Dardanian territory into Macedonia.' The entries were not from the Dardania of Kosovo, which lay 75 kilometres away, north of the Kačanik pass, but from the Dardania of the headwaters of the Axius river, the lower Velcka, and the wooded slopes of Mt. Golesnitsa. The routes from there came principally through Bogomila.[1] Philip evidently made Bylazora a Macedonian city and placed there a Macedonian garrison under his

---

[1] See Volume I. 79 ff. with n. 1 on p. 81 and Maps 9 and 14. Polybius does not say that Bylazora was in Dardanian hands, as Cary 166 supposed. For the geographical situation see Hammond in *Studies Mihailov* (forthcoming). Paeonia was part of the Macedonian kingdom (see Volume II 656). Walbank holds a different view (see p. 237 n. 5 above).

direct orders; no doubt he improved the fortifications (Plb. 5. 97. 2
ἀσφαλισάμενος). Like Titov Veles, Bylazora was presumably built on
both banks and had a regular crossing over the river. The next strong-
point to the north was Scupi (Skopje), a strongly fortified Paeonian
city, on the left bank of the Axius.

Philip probably used the Peltasts for the establishment of Bylazora as
a Macedonian city. He then called up the phalangites by their
territorial divisions, mustered them at Edessa, and marched to Larissa
—some 200 kilometres away—within six days. Proceeding throughout
the night on a march of some 70 kilometres he delivered a surprise
attack on Melitaea, which failed only because his scaling ladders were
short of the battlements of the unusually high walls.[1] Next he invested
the chief Aetolian base for raiding eastern Thessaly, Phthiotic Thebes,
fortified with a circuit wall nearly 3 kilometres long (see Fig. 6). He
established his army round the city in three fortified camps, linked
them with a trench and double palisade and built wooden towers at
intervals of 100 feet; thus Thebes was surrounded rapidly. While the
wall and its defenders were battered by 150 catapults and twenty-five
stone-throwers, built the previous winter at Larissa, sappers worked for
twelve days and through the last three nights and collapsed a 70-metre
length of the wall. The garrison and the citizens thereupon surrendered. He sold the population as slaves on the market, settled
Macedonians on the site, and named it Philippopolis or Philippi.[2] This
attack on the Aetolian position in eastern Greece was balanced by an
advance of Macedonian forces into east Phocis (presumably from the
Macedonian base at Chalcis) and by a minor victory over the
Aetolians at Phanoteus in southern Phocis.[3]

Meanwhile the full Aetolian levy overran and plundered Acarnania
and Epirus.[4] In this western theatre (see Fig. 12) fifteen Illyrian *lembi*
were welcomed at Leucas as friends of Macedonia. They then treacher-
ously seized four warships, stationed there by Taurion, and sent the
hulls and the crews as prizes to Scerdilaidas. Even so, ships of the
Achaeans and the Macedonians raided the lands of Calydon and
Naupactus (Plb. 5. 95. 1–3 and 11). This raid was part of an Achaean
revival, inspired by Aratus, newly elected general in May 217. He

---

[1] Philip's aim at Melitaea was to cut the Aetolians' line of communication with Phthiotic
Thebes. Polybius described the assault twice: 5. 97. 5–6, being in the historical narrative, is more
likely to be correct, and 9. 18. 5–9, being in an excursus, contains errors by Polybius. These show
how inaccurate Polybius could be. See Walbank, *C* 1. 626.

[2] Plb. 5. 99–100. Philip evidently treated the population as traitors for having joined Aetolia.
For the names see Plb. 5. 100. 8, D.S. 26. 9, and St. Byz. s.v. *Philippoi*. It is interesting to compare
Philip's method of investment and siegecraft with those of Athens at Potidaea or Syracuse.

[3] Plb. 5. 96. 4–8. A Macedonian officer 'appointed in charge of Phocis' was analogous to
Taurion 'in charge of Peloponnesian affairs'.

[4] The Aetolians could not capture the towns, for the fortifications of which see H*E* 713 ff.

persuaded the League to muster 11,000 infantry and 800 cavalry, predominantly mercenaries, and to place three warships in the Corinthian Gulf and three in the Saronic Gulf (Plb. 5. 91. 6–8). The land forces also won successes. While Taurion's Macedonians protected Arcadia and Argolis, they saved Messenia from projected raids and defeated an Aetolian–Elean raiding party in western Achaea. The net was being drawn tighter round Aetolia, and Elis and Sparta were discouraged.

At this point, in June 217, envoys from Chios, Rhodes, Byzantium, and Ptolemy came to Philip with an offer to negotiate a peaceful settlement with Aetolia. The motives of the first three are unknown. But Ptolemy was on good terms with Aetolia (see p. 340 above). He relied largely on Aetolian generals to command his troops in the war with Antiochus[1] and no doubt wanted to hire Aetolians as mercenaries. Philip welcomed the proposal and sent the envoys on to Aetolia; but in view of past experience he did not desist from operations. Embarking his troops at Phthiotic Thebes on a considerable battle fleet (12 decked ships, 8 undecked ships, and 30 lighter ships called *hemioliai*, probably built since he initiated his naval policy in 219), he sailed via Chalcis to the Isthmus of Corinth. There the lighter ships were dragged across to the Corinthian Gulf, and the decked ships, being too heavy, were sent round the Peloponnese to meet the rest in the Gulf off Patrae and Aegium (see Fig. 12). His intention, we may surmise, was to land his Macedonian field army and the bulk of Aratus' troops on territory held by Aetolia, and probably to link up with the Macedonian forces in southern Phocis and isolate Delphi. It was fear of some such action that caused the Aetolian authorities to be very eager for a settlement.

Polybius chose this moment to describe a new development. As Philip was watching the Nemean Games (in July), a courier from Macedonia came to him with the news that Hannibal had won a great victory over the Romans (at Lake Trasimene). Philip, according to Polybius, shared this news with one man only, Demetrius of Pharos, who advised him forthwith to make peace and win the support of all Greece, and to invade Illyris and then Italy as the first step on the road to the conquest of the world. 'Such arguments' filled the mind of the young king with ambition (5. 101. 6–102. 2). The advice is most probably fictional.[2] It was neither recorded at the time nor divulged to others, and it shares—thanks to Polybius and not to chance—a number of points with the later speech of Agelaus, such as winning the support of all Greece, looking to the West, and preparing for world conquest (5. 104. 6–7). Demetrius of Pharos was cast in the role of the

[1] Men such as Theodotus, Panaetolus, and Nicolaus (5. 68. 2 and 5).
[2] So too the advice of Demetrius in J. 29. 2. 1–6.

bad adviser, corrupting the young king and initiating a change in his psychology. The analogy with Herodotus' account of Mardonius misleading young Xerxes is obvious.[1] This is not to deny that Philip did consult Demetrius as the expert on the situation of Rome on the Adriatic front. But the overall decision by Philip must have rested on many other considerations than the opinions of Demetrius.

That the news of Hannibal's victory reached Philip in July is acceptable. Did it affect Philip's immediate intentions? Polybius represented his intentions in Greece as follows. At 5. 24. 11 Philip was hypocritical (συνυποκριθείς) in saying he was ready to make peace. At 5. 29. 4, after Philip had asked the member states of the Symmachy to send representatives to the peace conference, he rejoiced at the postponement of negotiations by the Aetolians, because he had always intended the negotiations to fail. At 5. 100. 10–11 Philip said he was not averse to a settlement, but paid no heed to it. Polybius' interpretation rests neither on evidence nor on probability. Why did Philip involve all the member states in a peace conference if he wanted to prevent peace? The military facts of the situation were that the armies of Philip and Aratus could win a set battle of pikemen and hoplites in a plain, a form of battle which the Aetolians had no reason to offer them, but had little hope of reducing the Aetolian highlanders in a guerrilla war.[2] What Philip wanted was what he said[3]—a favourable settlement of an expensive war—and in this he and the Achaean leaders were at one (5. 102. 3 τῶν περὶ τὸν Ἄρατον). The Aetolians were extremely anxious to avoid an invasion and therefore were eager for peace (5. 103. 2, 3, and 8).

During the preliminaries Philip threatened Elis and acquired its offshore island, Zacynthus. Peace was concluded at Naupactus in August 217 on the *status quo* by the delegates of the member states[4] in the presence of the Aetolian levy assembled without arms and of the army under Philip's command, encamped on Aetolian soil. Although the Symmachy had not achieved all its war aims (as in Plb. 4. 24. 5–8), there was no doubt that it was the winner. It had disciplined the bullying brigand among the Greek states, the Aetolian League. Peace reigned throughout Greece (for it is to be assumed that Elis and Sparta also came to terms), and the credit went to those member states which

---

[1] Hdt. 7. 5; 7. 6. 1; 7. 8. 3; 7. 9.

[2] Certainly not in the mountain ranges of South Pindus and East Aetolia, which I walked over in 1944. The difficulty of guerrilla warfare around Delphi was clear from the history of the Third Sacred War; it would have been much greater for Philip and Aratus, who depended primarily on communication by sea.

[3] Polybius wanted to represent Philip as a warmonger, to be diverted only by hopes of world conquest in the West.

[4] Plb. 5. 102. 8, 103. 1; cf. Ch. Habicht in *AM* 1. 277 f.

had fought, namely Macedonia, Epirus, Acarnania, Phocis, and the states of the Achaean League, i.e. Achaea, Corinthia, Epidaurus, Argolis, and Arcadia.[1] As *hegemon* of the Symmachy, Philip won special praise for his energetic, able leadership and for 'the beneficence of his policy' (7. 11. 8). His authority and the power of Macedonia within the Symmachy were much increased. Most of the places wrested from Aetolia during 'the Social War', as Polybius rightly called it, (Ambracus, Phoetiae and other fortresses, Oeniadae, Zacynthus, Psophis, Alipheira and other fortresses, Triphylia, Phthiotic Thebes and some places in Phocis) were held by Macedonian garrisons; but there, as at Acrocorinth, the garrisons were acting for the Symmachy as a whole.[2] Macedonia, as the hegemonic state, had borne the chief burden during the war and she continued to do so in maintaining the peace.

We must now consider the view that the news of Hannibal's victory and an Aetolian's interpretation of its significance 'prompted the allies and especially Philip to make the settlement' (Plb. 5. 105. 1). The ground for this view was prepared by Polybius at 5. 101. 6–102. 1, a passage which we have already argued was most probably fictional. The view was much elaborated by Trogus, who provided speeches for Demetrius of Pharos and for Philip, as we see from the summary of Justin at 29. 2. 1–3. 6; those speeches were clearly fictional. Is the second passage in Polybius to be judged non-fictional and to be adduced as solid evidence?

Let us begin with a précis of the passage. Agelaus, a colleague of Dorimachus and Scopas at 5. 3. 1, made the opening speech at the conference. His main points, reported by Polybius in paraphrase in indirect speech,[3] were as follows. Peace and unity in the face of a barbarian invader were best for the Greeks, especially at that time when great powers were at war in the west and the winner would invade Greece. All Greeks, and especially Philip, should take care not to weaken the Greeks and make them easy victims for invaders. Rather, Philip should concern himself with all parts of Greece, win the gratitude of the Greeks, and be protected by them against aggressors from outside. If Philip wanted action, he should pay attention to the campaigns in Italy and come in as a third party to claim world-wide

---

[1] There is no mention of action by other member states—Thessaly, Boeotia, and Euboea. Athens and probably Megara were neutral.

[2] It is important to remember that Macedonia was a member state of the Symmachy and that the Symmachy as a whole conducted the war—not, as Polybius sometimes implies e.g. at 5. 105. 3 and 107. 5, just the Achaeans or the Achaeans and Philip.

[3] Polybius was not claiming to 'reproduce a speech', and he concluded with the expression 'such things' (5. 105. 1 τοιαῦτα, as at 5. 102. 1 τοιούτοις). *Contra* Tarn in *CAH* 7. 768 'Agelaus' famous speech' and Walbank, *C* 1. 629 and 3. 774. For direct speeches in Polybius see 9. 28–39.

rule. But if he waited for the cloud in the West to settle on Greece, the Greeks might lose the chance of compounding their internal differences themselves.

Agelaus was of an age to recall the First Punic War, 'a conflict of giants'[1] by Greek standards, largely waged in Greek Sicily. It had not led to any invasion of the Greek mainland by Carthaginians or Romans. In the past Pyrrhus had won not just one, but two resounding victories over the Romans; yet he had lost the war, and Hannibal might do no better. The future was uncertain. Of course, Agelaus may have been a man of exceptional foresight; but his audience, having a knowledge of the past, would have found his views alarmist rather than practical. Polybius was of a generation which saw the invasion of Greece and Macedonia and the disastrous effects of dissension, when, ironically, Agelaus' own state was the first to join Rome. For Polybius to have composed with hindsight a piece of advice for the Greeks and Philip in 217 was perfectly acceptable by the standards of Greek historiography.[2] Herodotus had set an excellent example in the speeches of Artabanus and Demaratus. In the opinion of the present writer the points were those of Polybius and not those made in the year 217.[3] The decision of the Greeks and of Philip was determined, then, primarily by the internal situation in Greece.[4] This is not to deny that the development of events in the West was of much concern to Philip, whose kingdom was close to the Roman dependencies in Illyris.

The peace which Philip and the Symmachy negotiated for the city-states of the Greek mainland was to last from autumn 217 to autumn 211. For six years inter-state wars ceased and internal party strife seems to have died down, except in Messenia, where Philip was to intervene

---

[1] Cary 150.

[2] As in the speech of Hermocrates at Gela in Thuc. 4. 59–64, on which see Hammond in *The Speeches of Thucydides* ed. P. A. Stadter (Chapel Hill, 1973) 56 ff. For Polybius' concept of speeches the most illuminating passage is 12. 25 b 1, where he wants the historian not only to discover (and convey) what was actually said, but also to provide 'the reason' why what was said failed or succeeded, 'the reason' being what made the writing of history fruitful. In this chapter Polybius was developing the ideas of Thucydides at 1. 22. 1 (see Hammond, op. cit. 49 ff.). In the present instance Polybius could have discovered little more of Agelaus' speech than its general line, namely that the Greeks should all make peace. It was Polybius himself who added the reason in support of that line, the reason in his opinion which made that line succeed at the conference.

[3] The clichés (e.g. the linked arms and the cloud in the west) and the echoes of Thuc. 4. 59–64 came naturally to any literary man (see Walbank, *C* 1. 629). Agelaus and Lyciscus (at 9. 37. 10 'the cloud in the west' again) may have been literary men; Polybius certainly was, and he used the cloud image yet again in his narrative at 38. 16. 3.

[4] This is to shift the balance away from the views e.g. of Tarn, loc. cit. 'Peace now was vital, for he [Philip] wanted his hands free for events in Italy', and Walbank in *CAH*[2] 7. 1. 481 at the Nemean Games 'Philip received a report which led him to a sudden and complete change of policy.' On this controversial matter see O. Mørkholm in *Classica et Mediaevalia* 28 (1970) 240 ff. and *Chiron* 4 (1974) 127 ff. for the interpretation given in the text, and J. Deininger in *Chiron* 3 (1973) 103 ff. and Walbank, *Polybius* (Berkeley, 1972) 69 n. 11 for the other view.

twice. The opportunity to repair material damage[1] and restore religious practices was enjoyed generally and particularly by the Peloponnesians (Plb. 5. 106. 2), and the peace was safeguarded by the prestige of the Symmachy. At this time too the warring city-states of Crete made peace among themselves, created their own Symmachy, and elected Philip as its president (Plb. 7. 11. 9 *prostates*, and Trog. *Prol.* 29 'insulae societatem'). Nothing could testify more strikingly to the success of the mainland Symmachy and the reputation of its *hegemon*, Philip.

2. *The alliance with Hannibal and the winning of a base on the Adriatic coast*

The western area to which Philip turned his attention consisted of three regions (see Fig. 8). The western cantons of his kingdom from north to south were Pelagonia, Lyncus, Western Eordaea, and Orestis. The lakeland extended from Lychnis in the north to the plain of the Caloecini in the south, and it was neighboured to the south-west by Dassaretis, a mountainous and wooded district. The third area was that of the Roman dependencies, which included all the rich coastal plain and its harbours from south of Lissus as far as Apollonia (inclusive) and extended far inland in the north to the mountainous habitat of the Atintani. Some Macedonian kings had ruled over the second area as part of their Balkan empire, and there were still some Macedonian strongholds such as Antipatreia (Berat) in Dassaretis; but in general Philip's claim to suzerainty was little more than nominal. The Romans held as their naval base Corcyra, which threatened the harbours of Philip's ally, the Epirote League.

While Philip was engaged in Greece, Scerdilaidas broke into Macedonia, plundered a town in Pelagonia, and ravaged the western cantons. His forces overran Dassaretis and occupied Antipatreia and two other strongholds. These forays brought Scerdilaidas close to the Roman dependencies, with which he had interfered in the past; now, although Rome regarded him as her enemy, he gave her no further provocation. At the time Rome was dealing with Pinnes, the young king of the Ardiaei. Her envoys demanded arrears of tribute or, if he could not pay, the surrender of hostages (Livy 22. 33. 5; cf. Dio fr. 53), and we may conjecture that they asked for the extradition of Scerdilaidas, the young king's step-uncle. In summer 217 Rome made her first

[1] For an interesting example in Thessaly, where Philip advised Larissa to enfranchise its metics in order to cultivate lands made derelict 'through the wars', see *SIG* iii. 5 and 12 543 f.; Austin, *HW* no. 60; Ch. Habicht in *AM* i. 275 f., and E. S. Gruen in *Studies Edson* 170, citing similar actions, less securely dated, at Pharsalus and Phalanna.

diplomatic approach to Philip: her envoys demanded that he hand
over Demetrius of Pharos (Livy 22. 33. 3). Philip refused. For the
demand was such as might have been made to a Roman dependency.

On his return from Greece in autumn 217 Philip campaigned in the
west against his enemy, Scerdilaidas. He recovered the places which
the Illyrian had occupied, and he established his own control of what I
have called the second area—from Lychnis in the north to the
Caloecini in the south (Plb. 5. 108. 3–8).[1] His dependencies in the
north were now immediately adjacent to Rome's dependencies. Philip,
like Scerdilaidas earlier in the year, offered no provocation to Rome;
but proximity was hazardous. When Philip took his army home for the
winter, he may have known that Hannibal was wintering on the
Adriatic coast of Italy (in fact in northern Apulia); but their spheres of
action were poles apart.[2]

During the winter Philip used Macedonian timber and Illyrian
shipwrights to build a fleet of 100 *lembi*, small but fast ships under oar,
as compared with the heavyweight warships of the Roman and
Carthaginian navies.[3] He had trained Macedonians to row in 218
and he trained some more now. Like the Illyrians, they were to row
and fight, some fifty men to a ship (e.g. 2. 3. 1). Such a fleet could not
stand up to standard warships in a set battle. It excelled in making
surprise raids (Plb. 5. 109. 1–2), and it could defeat a smaller fleet of
lembi, such as Scerdilaidas had at his disposal (perhaps sixty *lembi*).[4]
In early summer 216 Philip and his fleet rounded the Peloponnese and
moored somewhere near Leucas until he heard, presumably from an
agent in Corcyra, that the Roman fleet was absent on service in west
Sicily. The way seemed to be clear. His fleet passed Corcyra during the
night, lay up next day off the Acroceraunian coast, and was in position
for a surprise attack the following night on Apollonia. His flagship lay
close to the mouth of the Aous river, which was navigable up to
Apollonia, and his rearmost ship was at the island of Sason, when 'as
night fell' (ὑπὸ νύκτα), a report was made to Philip that 'Roman
quinqueremes were sailing from Rhegium for Apollonia and Scerdilaidas' (Plb. 5. 110. 3).

The report was in fact true. For on hearing of shipbuilding in
Macedonia and guessing what target Philip had in mind, Scerdilaidas
had joined Rome and persuaded her to send help to him. Philip had no
means of knowing how many Roman quinqueremes were on the way;

[1] For this region see Volume I. 94 f.

[2] Polybius' suggestion at 5. 108. 4 that Philip was already intending to cross over to Italy is
unconvincing; see H*IRM* 9.

[3] Macedonia had more experience of small ships such as triaconters and penteconters than of
large warships. The king owned immense quantities of timber for building ships.

[4] See 4. 16. 9 and 5. 4. 3.

but it was clear that he might be caught between the fleet of Scerdilaidas and the Roman squadron, which would normally call at Corcyra *en route* to Apollonia. He had no harbour available in the vicinity, he carried only limited supplies of food and water, and above all he had lost the element of surprise on which he had counted for success.[1] With some such thoughts he put about and in less than two days he covered 180 miles to reach Cephallenia (Plb. 5. 110. 5). It had been an expensive and abortive expedition, and more importantly it had shown the wish of Philip to attack a leading Roman dependency, Apollonia.

Polybius poured scorn on this naval expedition. He portrayed it as the antecedent to a landing in Italy (with 5,000 men!)[2] and to the conquest of the world (Plb. 5. 101. 8–10, 102. 1, and 108. 4–5). He attributed Philip's decision to sheer panic. He supposed that if Philip had persisted he would have become master of the situation in Illyris and have captured the Roman quinqueremes in all probability (Plb. 5. 110. 9–10). The actual number of quinqueremes was ten, with perhaps 4,000 men on board; and these, together with the fleet of Scerdilaidas, which Polybius did not mention, were enough to outclass the 100 *lembi* of Philip in a battle at sea. The judgement by Polybius is typical of his attitude towards the king of Macedon.[3]

Philip was probably back in Macedonia when the news came that Hannibal had won a resounding victory at Cannae in August 216 and that almost all of South Italy had risen against Rome. During the winter Philip opened negotiations with Hannibal 'on behalf of himself, the Macedonians, and the allies' (Plb. 7. 9. 1), and he concluded in summer 215 a treaty between his group and Hannibal's group, the latter including the Carthaginians in Italy, the subjects of Carthage, and the allies of Carthage in Italy.

The treaty had two aspects, permanent and immediate. The parties were to be close friends, aid one another if attacked both then and thereafter, admit further allies to the treaty, and alter the treaty only on mutual agreement. It is important to note that, whereas in 216 Philip and the Macedonians alone had planned to attack Apollonia, they and 'the other Greeks in the Alliance' were binding themselves to Carthage for all time.[4] The decision to do so must have been taken by the Council of the Symmachy and then by the member states, which

---

[1] Had he captured Apollonia, he could have obtained reinforcements from Dassaretis and Epirus.

[2] So too J. 29. 4. 1.

[3] See further H*IRM* 15 ff., where the views of Holleaux, Badian, and Walbank were discussed. Add now Errington, *Dawn* 111 and *Gesch. Mak.* 173, and Gruen 375.

[4] For the Greeks see 7. 9. 5 and 7; for Carthage the future commitment was for the state as a whole, not just for the Carthaginian presence in Italy.

were free to adopt or reject a policy.[1] The immediate aspect concerned the current war against Rome.

'You [the Greeks] will be with us [the Carthaginians] ... until the gods grant victory to us and you, and you will help us as need may arise and we may agree.'

'If Rome seeks terms, we shall include you in any pact with the following conditions: Rome to undertake never to make war on you, not to be mistress of Corcyra, Apollonia, Epidamnus, Pharos, Dimallum, the Parthini, and Atintania, and to return to Demetrius of Pharos all his friends detained in the Roman state.'

We have only the Carthaginian document (Plb. 7. 9. 1–17).[2] It is to be supposed that the Greek document had corresponding conditions in favour of Carthage in the event of Rome seeking terms with 'the Greeks.'[3]

The interests of the contracting parties may be summarized. Hannibal's immediate interest was to secure naval bases close to Italy for the staging of reinforcements from Africa via Sicily. Corcyra and the ports of Illyris would be ideal. Reinforcements from Macedonia and Greece were of less immediate concern; and in any case they would not cross the Adriatic Sea unless Corcyra and the other ports were in their hands.[4] Carthage's permanent interest, in view of Rome's actions since the First Punic War, was to obtain the help of Macedonia and Greece in holding Rome down for ever. Macedonia's immediate interest was to expel Rome from Illyris, annex the coastal plain and its ports, reinstate Demetrius at Pharos, and settle a score with Scerdilaidas. Her permanent interest was to engage Carthage's help in holding Rome down. For many Greek city-states of the Symmachy Rome's control of Corcyra and the Greek ports on the coast of Illyris was more of a threat than for Macedonia; access to these ports was as vital to their commercial interests as it had been in the fifth century.[5] Hannibal's claim to be liberating the Greek states in Italy and Sicily from Roman rule may have excited some panhellenic sentiment; but it is probable that calculation counted for more, to be on the winning side, which looked likely to be Carthage in the year following Hannibal's victory at Cannae. With our hindsight we may argue that the Greek states in the Symmachy would have been wiser not to enter

---

[1] The wording at 7. 9. 5 implies that all the member states adopted the policy.

[2] It was captured with an envoy and probably seen later by Polybius.

[3] The treaty was, I think, between equals; for a different view see Holleaux in *CAH* 8. 119 and Walbank, *C* 2. 55 f. The annalistic tradition in App. *Mac.* 1 and Zon. 9. 4 is to be rejected.

[4] The terms given in Livy 23. 33. 10–12, including the crossing of Philip to Italy, are palpably false; they came from an annalistic source, as does the account in App. *Mac.* 1. See H*IRM* 56 n. 16. *Contra* M. Holleaux in *CAH* 8. 118 and J. Briscoe in Garnsey and Whittaker 153.

[5] Thuc. 1. 36. 2 and 44. 3; cf. *StGH* 457.

the conflict with Rome; for Carthage had no help to offer to them, and Rome might yet win and take revenge on the Greeks.

Rome was made aware of the impending agreement when she captured Xenophanes and his dispatches (Livy 23. 38. 4; cf. 23. 33 and 39. 4). Then or later she declared war on Philip, the Macedonians and the Greek city-states of the Symmachy, probably pointing out that she had committed no act of war against any of them.[1] She felt a burning resentment that they entered the war at the nadir of her fortunes, and this resentment was focused on the leader, Macedonia. She increased her squadron of warships at Tarentum and began 'to consider methods of confining Philip to his kingdom' (23. 38. 11).

The first action in implementation of the treaty was probably an attack by Philip on Corcyra late in 215, and if so, it probably succeeded, since there is no indication that a Roman fleet was stationed there in 214.[2] In that year in the summer, while Hannibal threatened Tarentum, thereby engaging the attention of the Roman fleet, Philip's fleet slipped through the Strait of Otranto (i.e. to the north of Corcyra), sailed up the Aous, and delivered a surprise attack on Apollonia. See Fig. 8. The fleet consisted of 120 *lembi biremes* (Livy 24. 40. 2), presumably having two men to an oar and so some 12,000 men aboard, and he must have built these craft since his first attempt on Apollonia in 216.[3] Philip himself led an army through Epirus[4] to join in the attack on Apollonia, a large and strongly fortified city with a circuit wall of some 4 kilometres. As the first assaults failed, Philip switched his army at night to Oricum, a small, but fortified, city. He captured it at once. Its important asset was its large inner harbour, protected by the city's fortifications and therefore safer for his fleet than the river by Apollonia.[5] Leaving a small garrison at Oricum, he continued the attack on Apollonia. Supplies came from Dassaretis and Epirus.

Meanwhile, in response to messages, a Roman fleet of warships and

---

[1] The start of the war against Philip is mentioned in App. *Mac.* 2.

[2] App. *Mac.* 1 fin. and Zon. 9. 4 mention Philip's advance to Corcyra after the capture of his envoy by Rome, i.e. in 215, and this timing makes sense of Livy's remark that the capture of the envoy delayed any action by Philip 'until the summer of that year ended' (23. 39. 4 'prius se aestas circumegit'; 'aestas' being 'summer' as at 33. 41. 13). As Livy did not go on to say what that action was, it may have been successful. What Livy's source, Polybius, emphasized was the working of 'Fortune' in the capture of the envoy and its effects. For a different view see Walbank, *Ph* 299, citing supporters of both interpretations.

[3] In 216 he had 100 *lembi*, evidently of the normal kind with one man to an oar. If he did build a new fleet, his delay until late summer 214 is explicable; and there may be some truth in Livy's remark that Philip 'seemed about to produce 200 ships' (23. 33. 10).

[4] This is the probable meaning of P*Arat* 51. 1 διαβαίνοντος εἰς Ἤπειρον αὐτοῦ, i.e. crossing from Macedonia into Epirus. This is the campaign mentioned in Philip's second letter to Larissa (*SIG* 543).

[5] For Apollonia and Oricum see *HE* 609 and 127.

transports sailed from Calabria.[1] It captured Oricum and its harbour. Reports came in that Apollonia would fall to the violent attack of the Macedonians, unless a Roman reinforcement was sent in at once. At night 2,000 men entered Apollonia unobserved. Joining the defenders, they made an unexpected sortie at night and caught the enemy off guard. Philip's losses were 3,000 men killed or captured; and his siege equipment was carried into the city. Meanwhile the Roman commander, M. Valerius Laevinus, blocked the mouth of the Aous with his large warships and trapped the Macedonian fleet which lay upriver. Philip was hopelessly outmanœuvred. He burnt part of his fleet, transported the rest, and abandoned the attempt to capture Apollonia.

These operations were reported by Livy, who used a Roman annalist as his source. The details of the report are certainly exaggerated, but the result is beyond doubt. Philip suffered a decisive defeat at sea and on land and he failed utterly to obtain a base for his fleet on the coast of Illyris. Rome now kept a fleet at Oricum (Plb. 8. 1. 6; Livy 24. 40. 17). The Straits of Otranto were effectively barred against any Carthaginian or Macedonian fleet for the future, and the Senate, in aggressive mood, allocated 'Greece and Macedonia' to Laevinus as his province (Livy 43. 44. 5).

The number of men involved in Philip's campaign and the route through Epirus suggest that some Greek forces from the Symmachy accompanied him. But the fleet of the Achaean League, which had co-operated with him in 218 (Plb. 5. 2. 4), was not present; for although Aratus, the general of the League, had been asked to participate (P*Arat* 51 συστρατεύειν), he refused to do so. Polybius, followed by Plutarch, laid great emphasis on differences between Philip and Aratus, which arose from a mysterious incident at Messene in early summer 214, that was before Philip set off on his campaign against Apollonia.

Internal troubles of a serious nature at Messene prompted Philip as *hegemon* of the Symmachy and Aratus as general of the Achaean League to bring forces to Messene. Philip arrived one day before Aratus. For what happened within that one day we have only Plutarch's account, which runs as follows. Philip urged each side in the internal struggle independently (and presumably secretly) to act against the other. The magistrates (i.e. the party in power) tried to arrest 'the demagogues' and were thereupon massacred, together with some 200 supporters, by the common people (P*Arat* 49. 3–5). Polybius had the younger Aratus attribute the massacre to Philip (7. 12. 9). This may be a case of confusing *post hoc* with *propter hoc*. The very arrival of Philip's troops, evidently expected to support the party in power, may

---

[1] Perhaps fifty warships and a part at least of a Roman legion of 4,000 men (Livy 24. 11. 3).

have been enough to spark off this internal combustion. It is indeed most unlikely that Philip wanted to promote further trouble in Messene; for in the past it was party strife which had enabled Aetolia to intervene.

On his arrival Aratus was displeased. His son Aratus, said by Plutarch to have been formerly the lover of young Philip, gave Philip the rough side of his tongue; but Philip restrained himself. Polybius and Plutarch then report a conversation between Philip and his two advisers, the bad Demetrius of Pharos and the good Aratus, as to whether Philip should garrison the towering citadel of Messene or not. Demetrius is said to have coined the happy phrase 'take the bull by both horns', i.e. seize that citadel as well as Acrocorinth, whereas Aratus advised Philip to rely on 'good faith' (πίστις). Philip took the advice of Aratus. It involved recognition of the new regime, the extreme democracy at Messene (Plb. 7. 10. 1).[1] Among those whom it exiled was one Alcaeus. He attributed his exile to Philip. He might more justly have attributed it to Aratus.

Polybius, followed by Plutarch, saw 'the massacre' as the first of Philip's grossest crimes against the deities (7. 13. 6 τῶν μεγίστων ἀσεβημάτων), and as the turning-point in the inner psychology of the young king. To Polybius the change was from a good king to a bloodthirsty tyrant (7. 13. 7); to Plutarch the innate depravity of Philip, hitherto concealed, emerged now in its naked crudity (P*Arat* 49 ἡ ἔμφυτος κακία ... ἀπεγύμνου καὶ διέφαινεν αὐτοῦ τὸ ἦθος). They wrote as if he, and not the Messenian common people, did the killing! It is wise to leave Philip's responsibility in doubt and to reserve judgement about this interpretation of his psychology.[2]

The extreme democracy at Messene soon showed its enmity towards the Symmachy. Aratus' advice seemed to have been wrong. Philip sent Demetrius of Pharos with a Macedonian force to capture the acropolis, but Demetrius failed and lost his life (Plb. 3. 19. 11). Had he succeeded, Philip would presumably have installed a moderate or oligarchic government. Later, probably in spring 213, Philip appeared before the city. When the democrats held out, he ravaged their territory, but did not bring about a change of heart. Polybius roundly condemned Philip,[3] even attributing to him the absurd idea that the Messenians would not bear him a grudge (Plb. 8. 8. 1 and 12. 1; P*Arat*

---

[1] If Philip had garrisoned the citadel, it would have been to keep the original party in power. Walbank, *C* 2. 57 suggests that 7. 10. 1 refers 'probably' to the later situation.

[2] For discussion of the affair at Messene see Walbank, *Ph* 72–5, and *C* 2. 57 and 59 f. and Gruen in *Studies Edson* 171 ff.

[3] Ravaging was, and had been for centuries, a characteristic of Greek warfare, and Philip regarded Messene as a treacherous ally. M. Holleaux in *CAH* 7. 122 accepts Polybius' condemnation.

51. 2), though he admits that other authors approved of Philip's actions in regard to Messene.

Aratus, although once again general of the Achaean League, seems not to have accompanied Philip in 213. Plutarch says that the two men were estranged for private reasons. Philip was said to have been having an affair over a long period of time with Polycratea, the wife of Aratus junior. The first to find out was Aratus senior, but he did not tell his son. Both Arati died soon afterwards, perhaps of consumption and debauchery respectively, but the gossip was that Philip poisoned them both (Plb. 8. 12. 2–6; P*Arat* 52 and 54; perhaps *Anth. Pal.* 9. 519 (Alcaeus); Paus. 2. 9. 4). When they were no more, Philip married the widow of Aratus junior, Polycratea (Livy 32. 21. 23; cf. 27. 31. 8 'spe regiarum nuptiarum'). The circumstances certainly asked for allegations of poison and a secret affair by a young king, whatever the truth may have been. We have no means of knowing.[1]

Peace reigned among the Greek states from 213 to 211, and in these years Rome was fully engaged in the siege of Syracuse, the war in Spain, and the struggle with Hannibal, who captured all of Tarentum except the citadel in 213. Philip seized the opportunity to attack the Roman dependencies in Illyris, this time from Dassaretis, where he established his authority (see Fig. 8). He captured three border strongholds, including Dimallum, and then turning north won the Parthini and the Atintani to his side. These advances enabled him to isolate Apollonia and Epidamnus, but his eyes were now set on an Illyrian city to the north of the Roman zone, Lissus, which had a harbour near the mouth of the Drilon (Drin). The city was strongly fortified with a circuit wall of some 2 kilometres, and the inhabitants had been reinforced by a large number of Illyrians from inland. In addition, there was a separate fortified site, Acrolissus, enclosing the summit of Mt. Shelbuemit, 410 m. high and steep-sided, distant about a kilometre from the circuit wall of Lissus and overlooking it. Because Arcolissus seemed impregnable, it had a relatively small garrison. There was a flat saddle of level ground between the acropolis of Lissus and the lowest slope of Acrolissus.[2]

Philip made his camp south of Lissus. He gave his men a day of rest and made an appropriate address to them (Plb. 8. 13. 5). On the following night he laid an ambush, posting picked light-armed troops

---

[1] The sequence in Livy 32. 21. 23 puts the killing of both Arati before the abduction of Polycratea. She came from Argos.

[2] The excavations of F. Prendi and K. Zheku, reported in *Iliria* 2 (1972) 239 ff., show that Lissus and Acrolissus were fortified c. 300; their Figs. 1 and 5 show the relationship between the two sites, and Fig. 4 shows the acropolis of Lissus viewed from Acrolissus. The Drilon flowed then past Lissus (see May 54 f.), not, as now, some kilometres to the north, and the sea was close to Lissus (8. 13. 6 κατὰ θάλατταν).

in some wooded ravines on the north side of Acrolissus. In the morning he marched the rest of his army round the west side of Lissus and then along its north side until he reached the saddle of level ground. The Illyrians, being much more numerous and on higher ground, made a sortie from the acropolis of Lissus. Philip sent his light-armed troops uphill to engage them. These troops fought well but they were driven back in flight to the phalangites on the level ground. The pursuing Illyrians went into the attack. Meanwhile the garrison troops ran down from Acrolissus to join in the victory, as they thought. But at that moment the Macedonians emerged from the ravines. They cut the garrison troops off from Acrolissus and chased the scattered Illyrians into Lissus. Acrolissus was occupied at once, and the assaults on Lissus were so violent that the Illyrians surrendered on the following day.[1]

This brilliant feat of arms so daunted the neighbouring Illyrians that they opened the gates of their cities. Philip's rule over territory occupied by the Ardiaei now covered the Scodra basin and reached probably to its northernmost point, the Ostrog pass.[2] His gains were at the expense of Scerdilaidas, the ally of Rome. He began now to build a fleet with Illyrian shipwrights and timber floated down the Drilon, and the payments which he made enabled the 'Lissitae' to issue their first coinage.[3] The emblems were typically Macedonian: the goat and the thunderbolt. If Lissus was captured in spring 212, the new fleet would be ready in spring 211, when he could attack Rome's last dependencies in Illyris and/or sail across to join Hannibal at Tarentum. But time was not on his side. In spring 211 the morale of the Carthaginian fleet was so low that it declined an engagement off Sicily, and Syracuse was betrayed to the Romans.

---

[1] The precise topographical detail and the king's planning suggest that the ultimate source was the *King's Journal.*

[2] At Livy 27. 30. 13 the Aetolians asked that the Ardiaei be restored to Scerdilaidas and Pleuratus. See Hammond, *Migrations and Invasions in Greece and Adjacent Areas* (New Jersey, 1976) 19.

[3] See H*IRM* 18 n. 64, and now S. Islami in *Iliria* 2 (1972) 379 ff., dating the first issue to 250–200 and rejecting N. Çeka's exact date of 229. Islami does not comment on the emblems. In *Anth. Pal.* 6. 115 Philip was described as ὁ κεραύνιος.

XIX

THE INTERVENTION AND THE WITHDRAWAL
OF ROME (211–205 B.C.)

1. *Rome and the Aetolian League in alliance*

IN 212, probably in late summer, an envoy sailing from Syracuse
to Lissus was captured by a Roman warship, and it was realized
that Philip might intervene in Italy or Sicily. According to Livy
25. 23. 9 (cf. Plb. 5. 105. 8) 'Rome was already eager for friendship with the Aetolians' that summer. But Aetolia was unresponsive;
for while Syracuse and Capua were in revolt and Carthage was
likely to succeed in Sicily and Italy, there was no expectation that
Rome would send troops to help Aetolia. In summer 211 the position
was radically different. After diplomatic exchanges Laevinus sailed
into the Gulf of Corinth, harangued a pre-arranged Assembly of
the Aetolian League, and obtained a treaty 'of friendship and
alliance'.

The terms show that Rome was the suitor. The alliance was
defensive and offensive against Philip and his Greek allies, i.e. against
the Greek Symmachy (no mention of Carthage in our source),[1] and
neither Rome nor Aetolia was to make a separate peace with them.
Aetolia was to command by land and Rome by sea, provided that
Rome sent at least twenty-five quinqueremes. The theatre of operations was to extend northwards to Rome's southernmost dependency,
Corcyra; no limit was set to south or east in our sources. Rome was to
help Aetolia acquire Acarnania, and to give to Aetolia the land and
the buildings of any city taken by force, whether by Rome alone or in
conjunction with Aetolia. The spoil in these cases—movables including humans—was to go to Rome or in a joint operation be shared. It
is probable, but not demonstrable, that if an enemy city came over to
Rome willingly, it was to become a dependent of Rome or be granted
'friendship and autonomy' (in which case it could enter the Aetolian
League). If Aetolia captured a city by force, she took everything; and
if a city came over to her, it could be brought into the Aetolian
League. The same terms were offered to Elis, Sparta, Attalus of

---

[1] Part of the treaty is preserved in Greek = *SEG* 13. 382, on which see A. H. McDonald in *JRS*
46. 153 ff. Summaries in Livy 26. 24. 8–13; J. 29. 4. 5; Plb. 9. 39. 3 and 11. 5. 4. See Walbank, *C* 2.
11–13 and 162 f. with references to modern literature. The date is disputed; see Rich 155 ff.

Pergamum, Pleuratus, and Scerdilaidas, if they should wish to join in the war against Philip and his allies.[1]

It was a treaty of expediency between unscrupulous partners. No principles of liberty or morality were proclaimed. Rome aimed to retain her footing in Illyris, defeat or pin down Philip with the help of a coalition, and obtain loot, and even dependent states, in Greece. Aetolia wanted loot, domination, and victory over Philip; she enlisted Roman aid as readily as Sparta had enlisted Persian aid against Macedonia in 333. It was a diplomatic triumph for Rome, countering the alliance between Hannibal and Philip, and it was to prove far more formidable, because Rome provided what Carthage failed to provide, a fleet which was a decisive factor in the balance of power in Greece. For the Roman quinqueremes outclassed their opponents' warships, landed an assault force of 4,000 soldiers on occasions, and were later reinforced by the fleet of Attalus. Laevinus demonstrated his naval superiority at once (in autumn 211) by overruning Zacynthus and capturing Oeniadae, Philip's naval base since 219.[2] Henceforth he controlled the entry to the Corinthian Gulf (see Fig. 12).

Philip was in winter quarters at Pella when he heard of Rome's alliance with Aetolia. He did not resort to diplomacy; for he and his people were as committed as Rome was to imperialism, that is to maintaining, and if possible extending, control over other states. He went into action at once, probably when Laevinus was at Zacynthus and Oeniadae, to discourage his numerous enemies. With the ships from Lissus and an army from Macedonia he delivered attacks on Oricum and Apollonia, but without success. His fleet sailed on to Corcyra, perhaps raiding it when it was undefended, but did not dare to steal past the Roman fleet off Zacynthus and Oeniadae and head for Macedonia. It returned to Lissus and became a wasting asset.[3] He ravaged the territory of Scerdilaidas in the upper valley of the Black Drin, captured a Dardanian town, Sintia (probably near Gostivar), reinforced his garrison at the Tempe pass with 4,000 men, captured the capital of the Maedi in the middle Strymon valley, and ravaged

[1] Plb. 11. 5. 4 named them as Boeotia, Euboea, Phocis, Locris, Thessaly, Epirus, and 'most of the Peloponnesians'. He omitted Acarnania.

[2] Livy 26. 24. 15–16; 27. 32. 2 (4,000, of whom some may have been oarsmen; cf. Rich 179 n. 248).

[3] In Livy 26. 24. 15–25. 3 the timing is vague (indeed 'hibernanti' is wrong; see Walbank, *Ph* 303), because Livy wrote separately of Laevinus in the south and Philip in the north. The overlap in operations is at 26. 24. 16, where Philip was thought to be too deeply involved 'in war with his neighbours' to think of Italy and the Carthaginians and Laevinus therefore came back to Corcyra. In Livy's account 'the war with his neighbours' can only be that with the Dardanians (Oricum and Apollonia were bases for crossing to Italy) at 26. 25. 3. Zonaras alone mentions Philip's advance to Corcyra (9. 6 fin.), which most scholars have rejected, but Hammond supported in *JRS* 58. 19 n. 67.

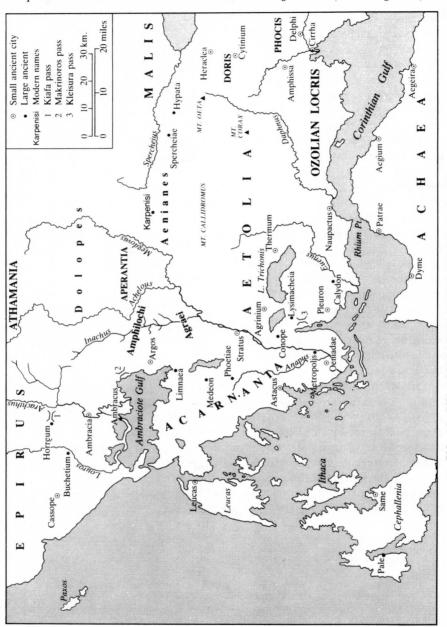

FIG. 12. THE APPROACHES OF THE GULF OF CORINTH

their territory.[1] These operations showed his commitments and his limitations. Whereas Philip II had subjugated his neighbours by superiority in set battle, Philip V lacked that margin of strength and relied on ravaging tactics and defensive measures at his frontiers. Philip returned from the Strymon valley when he heard that Aetolia was about to invade Acarnania, his staunchest ally. But the threat passed; for the Acarnanians sent their non-combatants to their ally, Epirus, and took an oath—from boys of fifteen to men of sixty—to fight to the death against their inveterate enemies.[2] Aetolia abstained.

During 210 and spring 209 Rome and Aetolia succeeded in bringing Elis, Messenia, and Sparta into their alliance, and the Aetolian Assembly elected Attalus of Pergamum to be their general for 209. They used their sea power to capture Anticyra in Phocis[3] and Aegina in the Saronic Gulf. The Roman troops sacked both cities so brutally that, to quote Polybius on Rome's general practice, one saw 'not only corpses of people, but dogs cut in two and limbs hacked off animals' (10. 15. 5; cf. 9. 42. 5). Such was the fate of a defeated enemy of Rome.[4] Aetolian, Roman, and in spring 209 Pergamene, troops held the approaches to Thermopylae (see Fig. 6), but Philip fought his way as far as Lamia and in spring 209 was about to follow up two victories there, when a delegation from neutral states—Athens, Chios, Rhodes, Egypt, and Athamania—asked him to seek a peaceful solution. Forgoing his present advantage and in good faith Philip negotiated a thirty-days truce and a peace conference thereafter at Aegium in Achaea. When he attended the conference, the aim of Rome and Aetolia became clear. A Roman fleet advanced to Naupactus, Attalus and his fleet reached Aegina, and the Aetolians made impossible demands: the surrender of Atintania, the Scodra basin, and Pylus in Messenia. Philip had been duped. The naval encirclement was complete. A Carthaginian fleet which came close to Corcyra turned back, as his own fleet of *lembi* had done in 211.[5]

Through the summer of 209 the Peloponnese was the scene of indecisive operations, during which Philip acquired much loot and the

---

[1] Livy 26. 25. 1–8. The dedication of ten pikes, ten pikemen's shields ('peltas'), and ten helmets by Philip to Athena of Lindus was made probably after this campaign (*FGrH* 532 F 1 C 42); for it celebrated a victory over 'Dardanoi and Maidoi'. He was described as 'destroyer of the Dardaneis' in *Anth. Pal.* 6. 115.

[2] Livy 26. 25. 9–17. For Epirus see H*E* 610 and Rich 174 n. 175; *contra* Cabanes 254 ff.

[3] Livy or his manuscript seems to err in giving Anticyra 'of Locris' (26. 26. 2).

[4] Greeks and Macedonians treated only a treacherous ally in this way, and that rarely, or a state guilty of impiety, e.g. in a 'Sacred War'.

[5] Livy 27. 15. 7 and 30. 16. The date is uncertain, and communication between a fleet in the Sicilian Sea and Philip near Lamia or on the way to Aegium was very slow, if not impossible. Livy's suggestion of a concerted attack by Carthage, Bithynia, and Philip on the Roman fleet is a fantasy.

Achaean League defeated the Aetolians and Eleans. In the autumn the Roman fleet joined that of Attalus at Aegina, and Philip marched north. He went in haste, covering in ten days the distance from Elis to Demetrias in Thessaly. For the Dardanians, led by Aëropus, probably a pretender to the Macedonian throne,[1] had obtained Lychnidus through the treachery of the garrison commander, reduced eastern Dassaretis, and invaded the upper Haliacmon valley (see Fig. 3). They returned with immense booty, including 20,000 prisoners, before Philip could engage them. This was the most serious blow of the war.[2]

Prospects in spring 208 were grim, with Macedonia shaken, all his Greek allies requesting help, Illyrians and Thracians said to be about to invade, the Aetolians dug in at Thermopylae, and the twenty-five quinqueremes of Rome and thirty-five of Pergamum ready to advance towards the Thermaic Gulf. A promise by Prusias of Bithynia to send ships had come to nothing. Philip fought back, like a beast at bay, as Polybius put it. First, he raided Dardania. Then, basing his army in Thessaly (see Fig. 6), he established forward troops and a signalling system by beacon in Peparethos, Euboea, and Phocis (Plb. 10. 42. 7–8). This system enabled him to parry an enemy landing at Opus; for by marching 60 miles in a day and forcing the passage of Thermopylae, he defeated the Pergamene forces at Opus[3] and nearly captured Attalus. The incident was more important than it appeared; for Attalus withdrew his fleet to Asia, where Prusias had invaded Pergamene territory, and the Romans withdrew theirs to Aegina.[4]

Philip conducted a campaign in Locris and Phocis for two purposes: to cut the communications of Aetolia with the Roman fleet and to secure his own route to the Peloponnese. His success there encouraged him to outmanœuvre the Roman fleet. His small fleet of seven quinqueremes and twenty *lembi* slipped past the Roman base to the Isthmus and was hauled across to the Corinthian Gulf. He was now in control of the western waters and he hoped to join a Carthaginian fleet, which he knew was on the way to Aegium. In fact, before he could make contact, the Carthaginian fleet, having reached the islands off Oeniadae, turned back and disappeared.

This, the first appearance of a Carthaginian fleet in Greek waters, was an exciting event for the Symmachy. At the meeting of its

---

[1] For sons of Aëropus as traitors at the time of Philip II's death see p. 5 above and H*SPA* 547 ff. This Aëropus too was probably a member of the royal house, and the report of Philip V's death, when his sons were minors, meant a disputed succession, a *stasis* as Zonaras called it (Livy. 27. 33. 1–3; Zon. 9. 9).

[2] Livy 27. 32. 9–33. 3; J. 29. 4. 6, his number not being exaggerated perhaps, since raiding for slaves was common practice among Illyrians etc.

[3] Other Pergamene troops are attested at Lilaea in Phocis (*CAH* 8. 594 n.; *ISE* 81).

[4] Livy 28. 7. 3–11; Dio 17. 57–8; Zon. 9. 11.

delegates Philip expressed his disappointment at its failure to join him at once, but he and the delegates expected the fleet or another fleet to appear. Relations between Philip and the delegates were excellent. He marked the exclusion of the Aetolians from the Peloponnese by withdrawing his troops from Heraea and Triphylia for service north of the Corinthian Gulf. Authority passed to the Achaean League for these places, Alipheira being transferred from Triphylia to Megalopolis.[1] Philip and his allies crossed the Gulf of Anticyra, and from there delivered a raid on Erythrae in Aetolia, returning with livestock and other loot to Aegium. It was time now for him to return to Macedonia. He hauled part of his fleet across the Isthmus, eluded the Roman fleet at Aegina, and sailed up the Euripus to Demetrias. His success at sea had been very encouraging, and with the prospect of Carthaginian naval reinforcements he had the keels of 100 warships laid at Cassandreia. Before the year was out, he campaigned against the Maedi.[2]

2. *Aetolia forced to make peace*

The sequence of events in 207 and 206 is uncertain, because there is little evidence. The following reconstruction is probable only. Early in 207 Philip used his fleet in the west to capture Zacynthus, a convenient base for a Carthaginian fleet, perhaps in April. He then gave it to Amynander in exchange for the right of passage for a Macedonian army through his kingdom, Athamania (Livy 36. 31. 11) (see Fig. 12). What was the value of this right, as compared with the possession of a rich and strategically important island? The best route from Thessaly to Epirus was farther north, by the Zygos. Athamania itself offered no access to North Aetolia; for the Achelous in Athamania cuts through transverse ranges in impassable gorges. The route through Athamania had only one value: it led an army from Thessaly into the territory of Ambracia at the only point where that city was not defended by the (then) navigable river, and if the bargain with Amynander was a secret one, that army could make a surprise attack on Ambracia and cut the garrison's communications with Aetolia.[3]

---

[1] The consensus of scholars is that Philip did not withdraw his troops from, or, in the phrase of Livy 28. 8. 5–6, 'give back' these places. The authority behind Livy is Polybius, and so unquestionable on a matter of fact. The interpretation is that Livy erred, and that he should have said that Philip promised to give them back; and then that Philip did not do so *for ten years*. What a canard in terms of diplomacy! Why promise at all, if there is no intention to fulfil it? One reason for the interpretation is the mention of these places again by Livy at 32. 5. 4–6 (see p. 423 below). For the best statement of the issues involved see Aymard, *Premiers Rapports* 25 f. n. 5; 59 f., n. 53. Polybius and Livy, who loved finding fault with Philip, never accused him of a ten-year-long perjury.   [2] Livy 28. 7. 12–8. 14.

[3] *HE* 248 (Achelous), 284 (route through Athamania), 682 (Athamania), 141 (Ambracia), and for maps pp. 4, 136, and 249, and *Atlas* Map 12.

Ambracia was the linchpin of Aetolia's defences towards the north-west. In 219, when the Epirotes persuaded Philip to capture Ambracus, held by 500 Aetolians (Plb. 4. 61. 6), they wanted him to besiege Ambracia; but he did not do so, since it was strongly fortified and garrisoned by at least 1,000 Aetolians (as we may infer from the garrison at Ambracus). Now it seems that he succeeded in capturing the city in 207; for it was in his hands in 206 (App. *Mac.* 3. 1). He could then plunder the rich valley of the Sindekiniotikos (Inachus) river and turning east use the easy pass to Tatarna, which 'completely commands the route which crosses North Aetolia from east to west'. From Tatarna his army went on to ravage 'the upper part of Aetolia' (Livy 36. 31. 11 'in superiorem partem Aetoliae', translating τὴν ἄνω Αἰτωλίαν),[1] the area drained by the Agrafiotikos and the Megdovas rivers. The loot must have been mainly livestock (cf. Livy 20. 8. 9–10), which could now be brought back via Ambracia into Epirus. This is the most probable reconstruction of what happened. In any case the raid was a blow to Aetolian morale (Livy, loc. cit. 'fractis animis') and it caused Aetolia to ask Rome for help in the summer of 207. In response, the Roman fleet left Aegina, rounded the Peloponnese, and reached its base, Corcyra, perhaps in July. Its recall may have been due in part to the situation in Italy, where Hasdrubal had been trying to join Hannibal, then in Apulia. But in late June he failed, being killed at the battle of the Metaurus, and Hannibal withdrew to Bruttium. When the Aetolian Assembly met in early autumn 207, proposals for peace were put forward by some neutral states (App. *Mac.* 3, this being the first of the two attempts; Plb. 11. 4. 1–6. 10, mentioning Hannibal being in Bruttium at 6. 1). Philip and Aetolia might well have agreed to a peace on the *status quo*; but Rome held Aetolia to the terms of the treaty and insisted on continuing the war (App. *Mac.* 3. 1). Aetolia agreed, presumably on a Roman promise of substantial help; for Rome had huge forces under arms in this year.

The chief concern of Rome was to close the only route between Carthage and Hannibal, that via Zacynthus and Ambracia, and Aetolia's chief concern was to stop Philip's raids by capturing Ambracia. As Appian put it (*Mac.* 3. 1), 'the Senate blocked the [proposed]

---

[1] H*E* 244 ff.; Woodhouse 35. The expression is not used of Aetolia elsewhere; but its applications to Epirus (Plb. 4. 67. 1 τοὺς ἄνω τόπους τῆς ᾽Ηπείρου, including the plateau of Dodona over 2,000 feet high) and to Macedonia (with plateaux 2,000 to 3,000 feet high) indicate that Upper Aetolia was high land. The contrast was with the lowlands e.g. of coastal Macedonia (Thuc. 2. 99. 1) and here with the low-lying central basin and the coastal plain to the south, which Woodhouse saw as forming a union (his p. 8; cf. A.Philippson, *Die griech. Landschaften* (Frankfurt, 1958) 2. 2. 360). Thermum was in the central basin. This raid was therefore different from that on Thermum (Plb. 11. 7. 2). The point has not been considered by those who believe that there was only one invasion (they are listed in Walbank, *C* 2. 278).

treaty and was sending to the Aetolians [in fulfilment of] the alliance a force of 10,000 infantry and 1,000 cavalry, and together with them the Aetolians captured Ambracia.' Having had no loot at Ambracia, which reverted intact to Aetolia, the Roman army landed at Dyme and sacked it completely (Livy 32. 22. 10 'ab exercitu Romano'), before sailing to Italy at the end of autumn.[1]

Philip soon retook Ambracia (App. *Mac*. 3. 1). In early summer 206, at harvest time, he went south from Ambracia into the central basin and ravaged as far as Thermum.[2] This second raid brought Aetolia to despair, and pleas to Rome were unavailing (Plb. 11. 7; Livy 32. 21. 17 'nequiquam opem Romanorum implorantis'). At the Aetolian Assembly of autumn 206 the neutral states mediated again. The situation in the Peloponnese was favourable for peace, because an able Achaean general, Philopoemen, had defeated the Spartans decisively at Mantinea in June 207, and Aetolia's other allies, Elis and Messenia, were isolated. So Aetolia and her Greek allies had no choice but to make peace, and when the Roman commander, Sulpicius, who attended the conference, tried to justify Rome, he was shouted down (App. *Mac*. 3. 1). Philip and the Symmachy obtained 'the terms which Philip wanted' (Livy 29. 12. 1). Speculation about these terms is inconclusive.[3] 'Peace and friendship' were established between the two groups. Only Rome took no part. She remained at war with Philip and the Symmachy and their ally, Hannibal.

[1] The operations against Ambracia do not figure in Livy's continuous narrative for these years, and this has led some to believe that there were none (e.g. Holleaux, *Rome* 245 n. 2 and Walbank, *Ph* 99 n. 9). They rely also on Livy's statement at 29. 12. 1 that 'affairs in Greece had been neglected in this two-year period'. However, Livy himself refers back to incidents of that period which his source must have described, but which Livy has omitted in his own narrative: the capture of Zacynthus, the bargain with Amynander, the raid into Upper Aetolia, and the Roman sack of Dyme. Thus there certainly was in one of these two years at least an 'exercitus Romanus' (Livy 32. 22. 10), sea borne and not land-based, under the command of a consul (32. 21. 17) in Greece. Livy omitted its activities, presumably because he had a very crowded narrative in 28. 10–29. 12, and they did not redound to Rome's credit. The gap is filled by the annalistic account in App. *Mac*. 3. It tells us about the 'exercitus Romanus' and enables us to see the purpose of Philip's deal with Amynander. We should view this account with suspicion if it recorded a great triumph by Rome; but in fact it shows the Roman possession of Ambracia to have been transitory.

An inscription found at Arta (Ambracia) may show Philip to have been there at this time. In it 'Philippos' and six 'fellow magistrates' made a dedication. As he heads the list and as he alone has no patronymic or attribution, he is most probably *the* Philip, the king, honoured in the same way as Attalus had been honoured by the Aetolians. Cabanes 548 with Pl. 4, having added *prytanis* ('magistrate') where no letter survives after 'Philippos', rejects my view (see *HE* 611 with Fig. 32); but he fails to explain the lack of a patronymic and the reason for singling out one of a board of magistrates for this distinction.

[2] Livy 36. 31. 11 'fractis animis', referring to the raid of 207; Livy 32. 21. 17 'mediterranea', translating τὰ μεσόγαια, as at Plb. 4. 61. 3, and referring to the raid as far as Thermum (Plb. 11. 7. 2) in 206, after which the Aetolians requested Roman aid in vain ('nequiquam'). Ignorance of the topography of Athamania, Ambracia, and Aetolia has led some to fuse the two raids into one. See the summary of views in Walbank, *C* 2. 278 and add Rich 139, who opts for one raid.

[3] See the judicious notes of Walbank, *Ph* 100 f. for the extensive literature on the subject.

3. *Rome and her allies make peace with the Greek Symmachy*

As far as the Greek states were concerned, the Symmachy and its *hegemon*, Philip, had repeated the triumph of 217 over Aetolia and its allies; moreover, they had excluded the Romans from Greece with the exception of Corcyra. The peace in Greece was not one of reconciliation or true 'friendship'. Yet it might have been long-lasting if the Greeks had been living in isolation; but as it was the Symmachy was still at war with Rome and Attalus. No attempt to negotiate a peace with them seems to have been made. Rome no doubt accused her treaty partner, Aetolia, of breaking the treaty by making a separate peace, and Aetolia could have accused Rome of a similar breach in not helping to capture Acarnania and in failing to send twenty-five quinqueremes in 206. Both states had acted dishonestly. Macedonia had a better image, at least in Greek eyes. She had undertaken the lion's share, outfought all opponents, and helped her allies. Her standards in warfare were more civilized than those of Rome (see Plb. 11. 5. 6–7). For example, at Dyme the population was enslaved and sold or deported by the Roman forces; and in the past, at Aegina, the Roman commander had refused at first to let such slaves be ransomed and relented only in deference to Greek custom (Plb. 9. 42. 5; cf. 11. 5. 8 and 22. 8. 9). Now Philip bought the freedom of the Dymaeans, wherever they were serving as slaves, and restored them to their ruined city (Livy 32. 22. 10). It was a lesson in human rights which was lost on the Romans, but appreciated by the Greeks.

In spring 205 Rome took the initiative. She sent a new commander, P. Sempronius Tuditanus, with thirty-five warships and 11,000 soldiers to Epidamnus.[1] He negotiated with the Parthini and laid siege to Dimallum; for he wanted to open up the land-route between Epidamnus and Apollonia in a season of the year when the coastal plain was flooded (see Fig. 8). Philip was too quick for him. Withdrawing to Apollonia and refusing an offer of battle, Sempronius waited for a reply from Aetolia. For he had sent fifteen warships and part of his army to persuade Aetolia to re-enter the war. The answer was no; for the Aetolians, deserted by Rome the year before, had no desire to win Illyris for Rome.[2] A stalemate ensued. Sempronius had no hope of

---

[1] There are no grounds for equating the force sent to Epidamnus in Illyris (Livy 29. 12. 3) with the force sent to help the Aetolians in Greece (App. *Mac.* 3. 1), as Rich 174 n. 172 does, mentioning 'the coincidence in numbers' which was achieved only by emending Livy's text to match Appian's text—a textual legerdemain indeed.

[2] Livy 29.12. 3, 'vixdum pace facta', seeks to narrow the time interval between the peace in Greece in autumn 206 and the dispatch of the Roman force in spring 205; for he implies that in terms of campaigning seasons Rome acted quickly enough. Livy's suggestion, that if Aetolia had not made peace, the Roman force would have been sent to help Aetolia, is unjustified.

reinforcements from Rome, and Philip had no hope of defeating the Roman fleet with his *lembi* which lay at Lissus. The strongly fortified Greek cities of the coast were tied to Rome by economic interest as well as by past experience. To the south Epirus, as a member of the Symmachy, had suffered severely through the loss of her usual outlets for trade, Oricum in the north and Ambracia in the south, and through Rome's control of Corcyra and its Channel. She opened negotiations first with Sempronius and then with Philip, and with their agreement called a conference at her northern centre, Phoenice.

The discussion was carried out by Philip and Sempronius in the presence of Amynander, the magistrates of the Epirote League, and those of the Acarnanian state. It was agreed that Rome should hold the Parthini, Dimallum, and two other towns, which protected the land-route between Epidamnus and Apollonia, and Philip was to hold Atintania, which gave him free access to Lissus and the Scodra basin. The peace was not between Rome and Macedonia alone; for Attalus and Pleuratus on the Roman side, and the Greek states of the Symmachy and Prusias, king of Bithynia, on the Macedonian side were participants. Thus in 205 all hostilities ended over a wide area.[1]

Philip had broken his treaty with Carthage by making a separate peace; but he can hardly be blamed, in that the Carthaginian fleet had failed twice to come to his aid. Rome had her hands free for the projected invasion of Africa; her foothold in Illyris was secure, and she felt no need to help Pleuratus. Philip had made little headway against the Roman dependencies, but he had driven a wedge between them and Pleuratus and he held Lissus on the Adriatic coast. Rome and Macedonia were immediate neighbours under the peace, and that did not make for a real détente.[2]

Philip's control of Lissus and the Scodra basin was reflected in a hoard of coins found at Selcë, north-east of Lake Scodra. It contained sixteen coins of Epidamnus, two of Apollonia, twelve or thirteen of the 'Skodrinoi', six of 'King Genthios', and one of the 'Lissitai'. The striking fact is that the coins of the Skodrinoi, all of copper, carry Macedonian emblems: the Macedonian shield with a star of curving

---

[1] Livy 29. 12. 11–16. Livy included on the Roman side Sparta, Elis and Messenia (they were however already at peace with Macedonia and the Symmachy), Troy and Athens. See Walbank, *Ph* 103 n. 6 and in *Studies Edson* 340, and Rich 150 for views on the correctness or not of Livy. I agree with the view of Habicht, *Studien* 138 f. that Troy and Athens were wrongly included, an annalist having added them. See also App. *Mac.* 3. 2 and Zon. 9. 11. Our sources do not mention Lissus and Scodra in the account of the treaty; and the deduction which I make is that Philip continued to hold them, whereas May 52 argued Philip had withdrawn from there before 207, despite the lack of evidence to that effect.

[2] The chronology of events in this chapter is uncertain. That given here is based on my interpretation of the texts. Rich 148 f. gives an earlier date for the Peace of Phoenice on grounds which I find unconvincing.

rays in the centre of the shield, and on the reverse the Macedonian helmet with its characteristic side-flap.[1] The Lissus coin had other Macedonian emblems, a goat and, on the reverse, a thunderbolt; we commented on this coin above (p. 399). Sir Arthur Evans, who obtained the hoard, held that these coins were minted only when Macedonia was in control of the region.[2] This interpretation was denied by May (48 ff.) on the grounds that Gaebler had dated all the copper coins of Philip to the years after 186 B.C., by which time Macedonian control had ceased. However, I argue below (p. 463 ff.) that Gaebler was mistaken and that Philip coined in copper from early in his reign. I consider, therefore, that Evans was right in his attribution of these particular coins to the period of Philip's control of Lissus and the Scodra basin. Otherwise it is very difficult to account for the use of Macedonian emblems only.[3]

---

[1] As in Gaebler III 2. 193 no. 23; for the star with curving rays (called volute rays) see Gaebler III 1. Pl. 1 nos. 8 and 9.

[2] In *Num. Chron.* 20 (1880) 269 ff.

[3] In the reign of Philip V cities and regions put their names on coins; and the same thing happened here, Skodrinoi and Lissitai probably being regional names rather than city names. The bronze coins of Gentius used only Illyrian emblems, once his own coinage was established; see p. 531 below.

XX

PHILIP'S EXPANSIONIST POLICY AND THE ENCIRCLEMENT OF MACEDONIA
(205–198 B.C.)

1. *Philip's naval offensive*

WE have only scraps of information for the years after the peace of Phoenice. Philip campaigned against the Dardanians, who lost more than 10,000 men in a major defeat (Bardylis in 358 had lost 7,000 men), and he executed five leading Macedonians (D.S. 28. 2). The two events may be interconnected, if the Dardanian invasion of 209 was in support of a pretender, who had sympathizers in Macedonia (p. 404 above). Four fragments (Plb. 13. 10) mention places in Thrace; but the inference that Philip campaigned at those places is no more than probable. There are several mentions of Heracleides, an adventurer from Tarentum, who became one of Philip's Companions and was cast by Polybius in the role of the bad adviser, like Demetrius of Pharos. He was said to have engineered the killing of the five Macedonians, and to have advocated the senseless and impetuous behaviour by Philip which was to ruin his kingdom (D.S. 28. 2; Plb. 13. 4 and 18. 54. 8–10). Alleged instances of such behaviour were the following. Philip sent envoys to the Cretans (he was president of their league), urging them to war against Rhodes (Plb. 13. 4. 2; cf. D.S. 27. 3). Then he sent Heracleides as a secret agent to Rhodes, where he burnt thirteen ship-sheds with their contents and escaped by sea (Plb. 13. 5. 1–6; Polyaen. 5. 17. 2). Philip employed another agent, an Aetolian called Dicaearchus, to practise piracy, blackmail the islanders, and subsidize the Cretans in the war against Rhodes (D.S. 28. 1). At the time Philip's connection with these two agents was not known. It was said later that Philip had secretly given Dicaearchus twenty ships. It is impossible to decide what truth there was in these allegations, which were retold by Polybius.[1]

In 204 or spring 203 the hand of a daughter of Philip was sought in marriage to the six-year-old king of Egypt, Ptolemy Epiphanes. The request was made by Sosibius and Agathocles, who had taken charge of the young king. They hoped to enlist Philip's aid against Antiochus

---

[1] There have been numerous conjectures, summarized by Walbank, *C* 2. 416 ff.

the Great. For Antiochus, having brilliantly reconstituted the Seleucid empire in the East, was likely to challenge Egypt's right to possessions in Coele–Syria (in the Orontes valley) and in the Aegean area. Philip procrastinated, wisely, because Sosibius died and Agathocles was killed, probably in 202. In the winter of 203/2 Philip was offered by Antiochus, and accepted, a secret alliance against Egypt, the terms of which were not known to later writers.[1] No doubt Antiochus was to have Coele–Syria and Phoenicia, and Philip Samos (the Egyptian naval base in the Aegean) and Caria (where Doson had operated). The wickedness of their plan to divide the possessions of the infant king of Egypt was denounced vigorously by Polybius (15. 20. 1), and it was indefensible in idealistic terms. In fact Philip chose Antiochus as the stronger and more dependable ally, avoided any operations in a theatre as remote as Egypt and Coele–Syria, and expected not to be hindered by Antiochus in his own plans.

The combined action of the Roman and Pergamene fleets on the Aegean coast of Greece in the recent war must have alerted Philip to a new danger. If the Roman fleet should return and together with its allies rule the waters of the Aegean Sea, it would be able to support a Roman army in Boeotia or Thessaly and to cut the corn-route from the Black Sea to Macedonia. If such a situation should develop, Macedonia would be at great risk; for she lacked the manpower to put into operation both a fleet and an army. It had to be one or the other; and whichever it was, the deployment of men would diminish the labour force for agriculture and make importation of corn essential. It may have seemed desirable to Philip to anticipate such a danger by gaining control of the corn-route and by destroying Rome's potential naval allies at a time when Rome was otherwise engaged and he himself could put all his forces into the naval effort. At the same time he was surely actuated by the desire for revenge and by the hope of acquiring territories.[2]

In spring 202 Antiochus invaded Coele–Syria successfully and in 201 he laid siege to Gaza. Philip meanwhile was pursuing his naval policy. His fleet had been built partly in 208 and partly since the peace, and he aimed to gain control of the north Aegean, where he had the alliance of his relative by marriage, Prusias, king of Bithynia (see Figs. 1 and 7). Several cities in the strategic area of the Hellespont and the Bosporus were members of the Aetolian League and had Aetolian

[1] Different terms were suggested by Plb. 3. 2. 8 and App. *Mac.* 4. 1. According to Livy 31. 14. 5 and J. 30. 2. 8 (cf. Trog. *Prol.* 30) they were to divide Egypt and its wealth. Action in accordance with the treaty is in Plb. 16. 1. 9, and intended action in Plb. 16. 10. 1. See Walbank, *C* 2. 471 ff.

[2] J. Briscoe in Garnsey and Whittaker 155 regarded Philip's policy as one of 'sheer and unashamed aggressive imperialism'. Philip no doubt had a similar opinion of the policies of Rome, Pergamum and Aetolia.

generals as governors. Philip, no doubt with threats of force, persuaded Lysimacheia in the Chersonese and Calchedon at the entrance to the Bosporus to dismiss their Aetolian general and accept a Macedonian garrison under treaties of 'friendship and alliance'; and he gave the same terms to Perinthus, which he persuaded to break off from Byzantium. He and Prusias then approached Cius, an inland city of Bithynia, which had an Aetolian general, but was torn by internal strife. When negotiations failed and the kings laid siege to Cius, envoys from Rhodes and other neutral states tried to arrange a peaceful settlement. While Philip stalled, the city fell. It was razed and its population enslaved. Myrlea, its neighbour towards the coast, suffered the same fate. The sites were taken over by Prusias, and the cities which he built were named Prusa and Apamea (after his wife).[1]

Philip tried later to justify himself by arguing that the war against Cius had been not his, but Prusias' war (Plb. 18. 4. 7). The agreement between the two may have been, as between the Romans and the Aetolians, that one took the spoil and the other the city, so that the fate of Cius, being in Prusias' kingdom, lay with him. At the time both were held responsible by Greek opinion, which was outraged by these acts of enslavement (*andrapodismos*). An even more shocking instance followed, in which Philip alone made the decision. On its way home the fleet put in at Thasos, an independent state in a strategic position off the Macedonian coast, and the Macedonian general gained admission to the city on promising to respect its liberty. Once in the city Philip captured and enslaved the population, and he left a garrison to hold the site. His actions in this year were bound to undermine his position as *hegemon* of the Symmachy and to reduce his reputation to the level of his former adversaries, Aetolia and Rome.[2]

In the latter part of 202 Aetolian envoys asked Rome to make an alliance with Aetolia against Macedonia. They were rebuffed, according to Livy 31. 29. 4, with the peremptory answer: 'Why, Aetolians, do you come to us, without whose agreement you made your peace with Philip?' News of this encouraged Philip to press on with his naval plans; for if he could rule the Aegean, he would isolate Attalus, keep Rome out of eastern waters, and compete with Egypt or Antiochus, as need might arise. He had already a considerable fleet in Macedonia; he added ships and oarsmen from dependent states (App. *Mac.* 4. 1) and from his allies (Plb. 16. 7. 6), including states recently won over and Prusias. Setting sail early in spring 201, he reduced the Cyclades to obedience and forced the Samians to admit him to their harbour,

[1] Plb. 15. 23. 9; 18. 3. 11 and 4. 5–6; *SVA* 549; Plb. 18. 2. 4 and 44. 4; and for Cius Plb. 15. 21–22. 1; 18. 3. 12 and 4. 7; Str. 563 (Prusias) συγκατασκάψαντι καὶ ταύτην καὶ Μύρλειαν.
[2] Plb. 15. 24. 1–6; Livy 33. 30. 3.

which was the base of an Egyptian squadron.[1] Since he was still on good terms with Egypt, he fitted out some of the Egyptian ships and had them join his fleet. He now had fifty-three large, decked warships, a smaller number of medium-sized, undecked vessels, and 150 *lembi* and 'sawfish', these being very fast, but small (16. 2. 9). More than 30,000 men were involved.[2]

At Samos he will have learnt that a Rhodian fleet had sailed north to join its allies, Byzantium and Attalus (see Fig. 7). Taking the same route, he won the support of the coastal cities and then passed Cape Argennum at the south end of the Chios Channel and laid siege to Chios town. If he could capture it, he would be well placed to confine the enemy to northern waters and cut the Rhodians off from Rhodes. But the enemy were too quick. Seizing the north end of the Channel, they threatened his supplies. He decided to row away suddenly southwards and reach a friendly coast before the enemy could catch up (16. 2. 4). Again the enemy were too quick. Attalus' fleet came up with Philip's eastern wing just short of Cape Argennum and forced it to turn about and engage (16. 2. 8). Meanwhile the Rhodian fleet, rowing from a more distant station, but with greater speed, overtook the rearmost ships of Philip's slower western wing and forced that part of the fleet to put about and engage (16. 2. 7 and 4. 4).[3] Thus two battles developed, one on either side of the Channel (16. 5. 8–9). The Rhodians excelled in oarsmanship and manœuvre. They and their allies had in all sixty-five large warships, nine medium-sized vessels, and three triremes.

The large warships proved superior in action. For they could cripple medium-sized and small ships by driving into them amidships or on the side (e.g. 16. 3. 4); and if ships became locked together, their marines had the advantage of greater height and a solid deck as compared with less large ships. Of the marines the Macedonians were the most effective (16. 3. 9 and 4. 13). Whenever the Rhodians had sea room, they rammed and disengaged with great skill (16. 4. 5 and 14–15), but when the fighting became closer they suffered from attacks by the *lembi* and 'sawfish', which were interspersed among the larger ships (16. 4. 10). In very close combat the Rhodians rammed an opponent bow to

---

[1] For the sequence of events, which is disputed, see Walbank, *C* 2. 497 ff. Plb. 16. 2. 9 indicates the Philip fitted out some ships at Samos before he went to Chios, and App. *Mac.* 4. 1 mentions Samos before Chios, though he has Philip capture both.

[2] The estimate is based on Plb. 1. 26. 7, where a quinquereme had 120 marines and 300 oarsmen; it is suggested above that a *lembus* had fifty men who both rowed and fought; and a trireme had about twenty marines and 180 crew. The largest ship mentioned in the battle was Philip's flagshap, a *dekeres*, with presumably twice as many oarsmen as a quinquereme.

[3] The main lines are clear, but Polybius used the terms 'left' and 'right' in a confusing manner; see Walbank, *C* 2. 504.

bow (ἔμπρωρρα), having perhaps a protector (like a cow-catcher on a locomotive) which lifted the enemy bow so that any damage the enemy ram did was above the water-line, whereas the Rhodian ram holed its opponent under the water-line (16. 4. 11–12).[1]

A separate engagement developed between the two kings. Philip, having kept a few ships in reserve at the islets off Cape Argennum, caught Attalus and two quadriremes out of formation and forced him to run his ships ashore on the mainland coast, whence he and his crews escaped to Erythrae (16. 6. 1–8). After this the fleet of Attalus withdrew northwards to its mainland base. The Macedonian western wing disengaged and joined the eastern wing. The Rhodian fleet retreated to Chios harbour. Philip claimed the victory, because his fleet stayed on the scene of the action; but it was a hollow victory in that his losses were greater, both of men drowned or lost on hostile coasts and of ships sunk and abandoned. The battle was in itself indecisive.[2]

Soon afterwards it seems that the Rhodians sailed home, leaving the Chios Channel open for Philip to attack the realm of Attalus and ravage the countryside within a radius of some 50 miles round Pergamum. His army defeated the army of Attalus, failed to capture the superbly fortified city, and obtained only moderate booty; for the population had had time to remove their valuables and stock to fortified refuges. Philip acted as he had done in Aetolia, sacking temples and shrines and destroying statues of gods (16. 1). Attalus appealed to the Aetolian League to help by invading Macedonia (Livy 31. 46. 4); but the League's peace with Philip held firm. His secret pact with Antiochus was also of benefit; for Zeuxis, a Macedonian general of Antiochus at Sardes, sent him some supplies, as he marched south to attack Rhodes. He engaged the Rhodian fleet, which was not supported by any allies, off the island of Lade and captured two quinqueremes with their crews, whereupon the rest hoisted sail and fled; only their speed saved the Rhodians from disaster (16. 14. 5 and 15). He then captured the Rhodian territory on the mainland, including Prinassus, where he fooled the defenders by piling up soil at his end of his sappers' tunnels and pretending the saps had undermined the walls (16. 11; Polyaen. 4. 18. 1).

Philip's strategy so far had been admirable. True, Polybius censured

---

[1] I take the word to mean 'bow on', whereas ἀντιπρώρους here means that the ships faced one another in a more general sense (as at 16. 4. 7). The Rhodian device and the text of Polybius are both uncertain.

[2] Polybius used Rhodian sources of information, which greatly exaggerated Philip's losses and Rhodian successes; see Walbank, *C* 2. 509 f. and, for views on who won, 2. 503 f. See a dedication by Attalus after the battle 'against Philip and the Macedones' in *OGIS* 283. Mamroth, 1935. 233 saw a reference to Philip's victory in the prow of a warship on a copper coin of the king. The Egyptians suffered casualties (16. 7. 6.).

him for not sailing to Egypt after the battle off Lade (16. 10. 1); but to have done so with the Rhodian fleet threatening what would have been immensely long lines of communication would have been insane. Philip's next step should have been to muster his naval allies, including some Cretan cities,[1] and then to attack or blockade Rhodes into making terms. Instead he turned inland to the north and gained possession of four more Greek cities. Meanwhile Attalus and Rhodes joined forces. Their fleets blockaded Philip's army and navy in the Bay of Bargylia throughout the winter,[2] when Philip's supply problems were solved only with the help of Zeuxis. In spring 200 he escaped at night by a trick and sailed direct to Macedonia. Part of his army stayed to control his possessions in Asia. But they were of little value without that superiority of sea power, which had been his main purpose in the long year of campaigning.[3]

Philip's actions had been inspired by a restless desire for power. He aimed to encircle the Aegean basin from the Bosporus to Crete and from the Peloponnese to Caria. He was inspired no doubt by the achievements of his predecessors on the Macedonian throne; but he had an immediate purpose, to establish a thalassocracy in the Aegean and to build an empire capable of withstanding two equally ambitious states, Rome in the West and Antiochus in the East. His successes of 203–201 proved to be phantoms. Miletus and Hiera Come might pay him honours,[4] but the Greek cities were moved less by any gratitude than by fear of suffering at his hands as Cius, Myrlea, and Thasos had suffered. His naval successes disappeared in the débâcle at the Bay of Bargylia. His ambitions had overrun his resources, and he failed totally to put Rhodes out of action.

2. *The involvement of Rome*

Meanwhile Rome imposed terms of peace on Carthage in 201. Attalus and Rhodes were quick to invoke the victor's aid; their envoys in autumn 201 reported the pact between Philip and Antiochus, which had become known, and complained of Philip's attacks on the Greek cities of Asia (as well as elsewhere). Rome offered no aid, but she appointed three Romans (C. Claudius Nero, M. Aemilius Lepidus, and P. Sempronius Tuditanus) to act as a commission of inquiry, and

---

[1] Gortyn led the pro-Macedonian group, but we know little of the Cretan War; see Errington, *Philop.* 39 ff.

[2] His fleet was evidently much less strong than it had been in the summer; he may then have had some Cretans among his allies. His own fleet, having been at sea so long, may have deteriorated.

[3] Polyaen. 4. 18. 2; Livy 33. 18. 6 and 9; *BCH* 28 (1904) 346 ff.

[4] Plb. 16. 15. 6; *BCH* 11 (1887) 104.

she allotted 'Macedonia' as a province to the incoming consul, P. Sulpicius Galba, for the year 200. The Senate certainly was preparing for war, and with its support early in 200 Sulpicius proposed to the Comitia Centuriata that war be declared against 'King Philip and the Macedonians'. The Comitia refused to pile war on war.[1] The proposal thus lapsed for the time being, but the three commissioners frequently mentioned the proposal in the diplomatic negotiations which they now opened with Egypt, Epirus, Amynander of Athamania, the Achaean League, and Athens. Their purpose was to confirm or establish friendly relations, collect charges against Philip, and assess each state's attitude in the event of war being declared against Macedonia. At the moment they enjoyed diplomatic immunity under the pact of Phoenice, whereby Rome was at peace with Philip, the Greek Symmachy, and Prusias of Bithynia.

There were plenty of charges against Philip at Athens. Acarnania had demanded an indemnity from Athens for the summary execution of two young Acarnanians, who had entered Demeter's temple at Eleusis during the Mysteries when they were not initiates. Athens had refused; and Acarnania had asked Macedonia for help. When the request came, Philip had just reached Macedonia in his flight from the Bay of Bargylia, in spring 200, and Attalus and the Rhodians had brought their fleets to Aegina. He sent troops to join the Acarnanian army in ravaging Attica, and some Macedonian ships seized four Athenian warships with their crews in the waters off the Piraeus. At this point the fleets of Attalus and Rhodes intervened. They recovered the four Athenian ships and protected the coast of Attica. Attalus was given a hero's welcome at Athens, Rhodes was honoured with a reciprocal exchange of citizenships (*isopoliteia*), and the three Roman commissioners—who had just reached Athens—basked in the glory of their allies. Anti-Macedonian feeling had been running high for some months. The tribal names 'Antigonis' and 'Demetrias' had been abolished in favour of a new one, 'Attalis'. Now all statues of Macedonian kings were smashed and all honorary mentions of them in inscriptions were deleted. Attalus and the Rhodians quickly persuaded the Athenian Assembly to join them (and, no doubt they implied, to join Rome later). Athens declared war on Macedonia in April or May. The Rhodian fleet then proceeded to most of the Cyclades and won their alliance.[2]

Philip, being at war with Attalus and Rhodes, struck at once at his

[1] Livy 31. 2. 1, 6. 1 and 3; App. *Mac.* 4. 2 The last and J. 30. 3 add some incorrect details from an annalistic source.

[2] Livy 31. 14. 7–10 and 15. 5; Plb. 16. 25–26, for Athens' hostility towards Philip see *Hesp* 5. (1936) 419 ff. and McDonald and Walbank 200 ff. For the sequence of events at Athens see Habicht, *Studien* 144–50. The Macedonian garrisons in Paros, Cythnos, and Andros held firm (Livy 31. 15. 8).

new enemy. Enraged by the insults to his ancestors, he sent a Macedonian army, commanded by 'Jumbo' Nicanor, to ravage Attica ruthlessly as far as the walls of the city. The three commissioners, who had made diplomatic play with the proposal which had in fact been rejected by the Comitia, now served the substance of that proposal as an ultimatum on Philip: Rome would continue at peace only if Philip undertook to attack 'no Greek state' and to compensate Attalus for 'the wrongs done to him' at a sum to be determined by arbitration.[1] They did not wait for an answer. They sailed off to Rhodes, probably because they knew that the ultimatum had not been ratified at Rome.

Philip did not reply to the ultimatum (he presumably knew of the Comitia's rejection). He continued to prosecute the war with his enemies. See Fig. 10. Attica was ravaged by Macedonian troops based on Corinth and Euboea, temples and statues in the countryside were destroyed, her shipping was attacked by Macedonian warships operating from Chalcis, and her supplies of corn from the Black Sea coast were cut off by Philip who captured city after city on the Thracian coast, gained complete control of the Chersonese, and laid siege to Abydus on the Asiatic coast. Attalus, Rhodes, and Cyzicus sent only trifling aid to Athens and to Abydus. Athens had entered into alliance also with Aetolia, the anti-Macedonian group of cities in Crete, and Egypt; but they provided nothing. In late summer 200 she sent envoys, led by Cephisodorus, to Rome to beg for aid, for her situation was desperate.[2]

When the envoys arrived, they found that the Comitia had accepted the Senate's proposal to declare war on Macedonia. They waited hopefully, and they may have been joined by envoys from Egypt, who supported Athens' request (Livy 31. 9. 1–5). Meanwhile preparations for war were mounted, and the next stage of Roman procedure was entrusted to the most junior of the three commissioners at Rhodes, M. Aemilius Lepidus. He had to present to Philip in person a demand for reparation ('rerum repetitio'), and in the event of refusal a notice of war ('indictio belli').[3] He arrived outside Abydus, just as the last survivors were surrendering. For Philip had isolated Abydus by surrounding it with a stockade and blocking the harbour entrance, had undermined and collapsed a stretch of the circuit wall, and had overcome a desperate resistance at an inner wall.[4]

---

[1] Plb. 16. 27. 2–3. For this interpretation see McDonald and Walbank 197.

[2] Livy 31. 16; Plb. 16. 30. 7; 31. 3; Paus. 1. 36. 5–6 (for the date of the record of Cephisodorus see McDonald and Walbank 198 f.); *Hesp.* 5 (1936) 419 ff.

[3] Livy 31. 8. 1–4. For the procedure see Livy 7. 6. 7 and McDonald and Walbank 192 ff.; for a different view see J. W. Rich, *Declaring War in the Roman Republic in the Period of Transmarine Expansion* (Brussels, 1976) 82 ff.

[4] Plb. 16. 29–34, with a moving account of suicide pacts among the defenders who included Pergamene and Rhodian soldiers.

Lepidus was brought before Philip and presented Rome's demand. Philip was to compensate Attalus and Rhodes for injuries done to them, respect the possessions of Egypt (Philip had captured some of them in Thrace), and 'not make war on any Greek state' (τῶν Ἑλλήνων μηδενὶ πολεμεῖν). If Philip should accept this demand, there would be peace; otherwise, war. When Philip objected (justifiably) that Rhodes was the aggressor, Lepidus made the smart rejoinder: 'What of Athens, Cius, and Abydus? Were they the aggressors?' The aim of Lepidus was to cut discussion short. Rome's demand was not open to qualification. Philip, realizing it was a question not of international law, but of either submitting to, or resisting, Rome, replied, according to Polybius, 'I ask Rome not to break the treaty [of peace at Phoenice] nor to go to war with us. Failing that, if Rome goes to war, we shall defend ourselves gallantly, calling the gods to our assistance.'[1]

The determination of the Senate (not of the Comitia, which showed reluctance) to cripple Macedonia, whether by restricting its foreign policy or by war, is not in doubt. International law was irrelevant; for Rome had no legal justification, since Philip had kept the treaty of peace and Rome's only ally in the East, Attalus, had been the aggressor.[2] The Senate presented a fiat in terms which represented Rome as the champion of Attalus, Rhodes, Egypt, and all Greek states; a fiat so timed that a Roman army crossed the Adriatic before Philip returned from Abydus to Macedonia (Livy 31. 18. 9). It was a crude and cunning ultimatum.

The motives actuating the senators varied from man to man. They probably included the desire to extend Rome's power eastwards, to punish Philip for having allied himself with Hannibal, to prevent the expansion of Macedonia, and themselves to dominate Greece. Fear of an invasion of Italy by Philip and Antiochus, once the pact between them was known, was probably not a motive with many; for neither of them had a huge fleet, and Antiochus' forces were still engaged in the war with Egypt.[3] Concern for all Greek states was paraded for propaganda purposes; it meant nothing to the destroyers of Tarentum, Syracuse, Oeniadae, and Aegina.[4]

[1] Plb. 16. 34. 1-7. Polybius does not say that Lepidus declared war; it is thus unlikely that he did. Rather, Rome deferred its declaration (which was already decided in principle) until its army was about to go into action in Illyris, in order to catch Philip on the wrong foot, as Livy 31. 8. 3 'in finibus regni quod proximum praesidium esset' may indicate.
[2] See Habicht, *Studien* 158; see also Harris 212 ff. and M. H. Crawford, *The Roman Republic* (Sussex, 1978), 65 ff.
[3] For this motive see especially Holleaux, *Rome* 306 ff. and *CAH* 8. 158 ff., G. T. Griffith in *Cambridge Historical Journal* 5. 1 (1935) 7-9, and McDonald and Walbank 206, where it is said to lead to 'preventive action' or 'preventive war'. Errington, *Gesch. Mak.* 183 is closer to my view.
[4] Later writers tried to justify Rome by changing the order of events and by inventing details

The arguments which the consul as the representative of the ruling élite presented to the Comitia were of a different order, at least as reported by Livy 31. 7. 'The choice is not of war or peace, since Philip is mounting war by land and sea, but whether you send the army overseas or let the enemy into Italy. The last war, if nothing else, has taught you how great the difference is.' The campaigns of Pyrrhus and Hannibal in Italy were rehearsed, and the lesson was clear. 'Let Macedonia rather than Italy be the scene of war; let the enemy's cities and fields be laid waste with fire and sword.' Ordinary people knew little or nothing about the Macedonians except that they had conquered the East and that their power now was far greater than that of Pyrrhus had been. Such arguments carried them into war, but the serving soldiers were war-weary and the Senate was therefore chary of making war farther afield than was necessary.

Philip preferred peace with Rome. He had sufficient commitments already, and his chief concern was to impose his will on Athens, Attalus, and Rhodes. The Roman procedure gave him no chance of prolonging the peace on his own terms. He had either to accept dictation or to fight. His decision to fight expressed the spirit of the Macedonian royal house and the Macedonian people. In diplomacy he had been outmanœuvred; for Rome was stealing the flag of 'autonomy', which had hitherto been flown by Philip and the Symmachy on the Greek mainland, and she was collecting an array of ready-made allies.

3. *The Romans attack from the west*
(Figure 8)

First in the field, two Roman legions established a bridgehead on Macedonian territory by destroying the walls and massacring the population of Antipatreia (Berat), garrisoning Codrion (probably Rrmait), and capturing Cnidus (unidentified). These successes brought Pleuratus the Illyrian, Bato, king of the Dardanians, and Amynander, king of Athamania, to the camp of the consul, Sulpicius. He planned to co-operate with Pleuratus and Bato in a spring invasion of Macedonia, and he urged Amynander to bring Aetolia into the war.[1] The Roman fleet also acted with speed. Thirty ships held Corcyra and blockaded Epirus. Twenty ships sailed at once to occupy

---

of the pact between Philip and Antiochus; see McDonald and Walbank 182 f. and 203 f., and Habicht, *Studien* 153 ff.

[1] Livy 31. 27 and 28. 1–2. See H*IRM* 42 f. for a full study of the campaign. For Antipatreia (Berat) see *SA* 1 (1964) 184 and *Iliria* 13 (1983) 119 ff.; and for Rrmait near Miräke see *BUST* 1963. 4. 3 ff. and *Iliria* 2 (1972) 25 ff., where the name is Irmaj (see *JRS* 56 (1966) 43 n. 14).

the Piraeus as a naval base, and with some Rhodian and Athenian ships made a dawn raid on Chalcis, destroying its arsenal and granaries. Philip responded by raiding Attica with 300 cavalry and 5,000 infantry and destroying sacred as well as secular buildings; his attacks on the walls failed, but the Athenians did not dare to make a sortie. Philip led his army on to Argos, where the Achaean Assembly was discussing, not the coming of Roman forces to Greece, but their local war with Nabis, king of Sparta. While Philip had been in the Aegean, he had not helped the Achaeans and relations had cooled. Now Philip offered to invade Laconia, if the Achaeans would help him to garrison Corinth, Chalcis, and Oreus. The Assembly refused. It was clear that the Achaean League was thinking of joining Rome. On his way north Philip ravaged Attica thoroughly and then went into winter quarters.[1] His fleet had made no attempt to challenge the fleets of Attalus, Rhodes, Rome, and Athens, which held the Saronic Gulf and the central Aegean.

During this autumn Rome was active also on the diplomatic front. An alliance was made with Rhodes and Athens. The three commissioners proceeded from Rhodes to Syria, where Antiochus had defeated the resurgent forces of Egypt at Panium, late in 200. They learnt that Antiochus had no intention of supporting Philip in the war, and they invited Antiochus to send envoys to Rome. Going on to Egypt, they were royally received and exchanged assurances of friendship. Thus, despite the war between Antiochus and Ptolemy, Rome kept on good terms with both, and later the envoys of Antiochus were given an honorific reception at Rome.[2] The anti-Macedonian cities in Crete may have declared for Athens and Rome. But the Aetolian League stayed neutral despite pressure from Amynander and Athens; for they distrusted Rome and feared Philip.

Rome's diplomacy succeeded for several reasons. She had created a new image of herself as the champion of autonomy for the Greek states; and this posture was made more plausible by her dissociation from Aetolia, which could now be blamed for the past destruction of Aegina and Anticyra, and her association with Rhodes and Athens, advocates of peaceful trade.[3] On the other hand Philip's claim to uphold autonomy as *hegemon* of the Symmachy rang hollow after his treatment of Thasos. Then Rome's military and naval power seemed to make a victory over Macedonia almost a certainty; for in 212/11 she had had

[1] Livy 31. 22. 4–26. 13.
[2] Livy 31. 2. 3–4 and J. 30. 3. 3 (both false, drawn from an annalistic source); Livy 33. 20. 8; Plb. 16. 27. 5; see Walbank, *Ph* 316 f. and *JRS* 27. 204 f.
[3] Rome had respected the autonomy of Epidamnus, Apollonia, and Oricum, and their trade had prospered from close contact with Italy.

200,000 soldiers and 125 large warships, whereas Macedonia's own army numbered some 20,000 soldiers, and her fleet had already failed against those of Attalus and Rhodes alone. The temptation to join what seemed to be the winning side was very strong. Last, but not least, if Rome should win, her forces might well go back to Italy and leave the Greek states free; for during her alliance with Aetolia she had made no territorial acquisitions. But Macedonia would always overshadow the Greek states of the mainland and might threaten their liberties.

For the defence of Macedonia in 199 Philip posted his fleet at Demetrias and his army in the north-west, one group under Perseus at the Pelagonian pass and the main force near Heraclea in Lyncus (see Fig. 8). He hoped to hold a wedge of country separating the Illyrians of Pleuratus and the Dardanians of Bato from the Roman army. The main problem for Sulpicius was supply. He advanced from his base camp into the lakeland, where he could commandeer supplies and forage. First contact was made between reconnoitring cavalry forces south of Lake Lychnitis. Philip then brought all his forces to check Sulpicius. He had 20,000 infantry and 2,000 cavalry to face some 30,000, of whom perhaps 25,000 were infantry of the line, supported by a small force of cavalry, some elephants brought from Carthage, and Illyrian auxiliaries.[1] Being stronger in infantry, Sulpicius offered battle on open ground. Philip did not engage; for, having no reserves, he dared not risk the possibility of heavy casualties. As his army was more mobile and stronger in cavalry, he hoped to block Sulpicius' advance by holding fortified positions, attack his foraging parties, and make him retire for lack of supplies. He nearly succeeded at Ottolobus, a region south of Lake Lychnitis; but he lost a cavalry engagement through getting onto marshy ground and was lucky himself to escape. He disappeared at night, in the manner of Hannibal. Sulpicius went north through the lakeland and into Pelagonia, where his army gathered the harvest. He headed next for the Monastir gap, but his column of march was suddenly attacked by Philip, who emerged from side routes. Sulpicius retreated. Philip fortified a position at the narrows by the Erigon, and Sulpicius dared not pass it; but he was saved by the arrival of the Illyrians and the Dardanians. Their light troops rendered Philip's position untenable. He slipped away again and fortified the next narrows, the Lyncus pass, a defile between two parallel ridges. Sulpicius sent a turning force to capture the eastern ridge, while a legionary group was making a frontal attack with locked shields in close order (a *testudo* or 'tortoise' formation).[2]

---

[1] Livy 31. 34. 7 with the better MS. reading 'MM'; 31. 8. 6; 14. 2–3; 19. 2 and 4 (supplies).
[2] Livy 31. 33. 3–39. 15. For geographical detail see Volume I. 60–5, 70 f., 99 f., and 116, and HH *Via Egnatia* I. Lyncus pass = Kirli Dirven.

As the season was now advanced and Philip covered the approach to central Macedonia, Sulpicius ravaged Eordaea, Elimea, and Orestis, where Celetrum (Kastoria) surrendered to him, and crossed the mountains into Dassaretis, where he captured and garrisoned Pelion. He intended to use Pelion as an advanced base in 198 for a drive into central Macedonia.[1] He had failed to bring Philip to battle; but he had damaged the western cantons, encouraged a pro-Roman party in Orestis, and lowered the military reputation of Macedonia. This last achievement had brought Aetolia into the war. The armies of Aetolia and Amynander broke their way into Thessaly and Perrhaebia, ravaging and looting ruthlessly, and then turned back with the intention of capturing Gomphi in south-west Thessaly (see Fig. 6). Philip sent most of his cavalry and light-armed north, where they inflicted losses on the retreating Dardanians, and marched south with lightning speed to rout the unsuspecting Aetolians with heavy losses. The survivors escaped with Amynander through Athamania.[2] Philip tried to capture Thaumaci in southern Thessaly, but it was reinforced and held by the Aetolians. The enemy fleet made raids as far as Acanthus in Chalcidice. They sacked and enslaved the populations of Anticyra in Phocis and Oreus in north Euboea. Then the separate flotillas went to their home bases.[3] Macedonia's defences, though shaken, were still intact.

Philip's achievement had been due to the professionalism of the Macedonian army. He increased its strength by withdrawing garrisons from Lysimacheia in the Chersonese and from Orchomenus, Heraea, Alipheira, and the district of Triphylia—all of which Achaea was to take over. His hope that the Achaean League might declare for Macedonia was not fulfilled. Throughout the winter he trained his Macedonians and his mercenaries continuously, and he was cheered by the news that the Roman army had mutinied after its gruelling campaign.[4] His plan for 198 was to wear down the enemy with similar tactics and obtain a reasonable settlement.

Philip's army was the first to move. An advance party crossed the Pindus range into Parauaea, a canton of Epirus, and occupied the Antigoneia pass, thus barring any Roman entry into Epirus through the Drin valley (see Fig. 13). His purpose was twofold: to strengthen his party in Epirus and to draw the Roman army away from its intended course, the invasion of central Macedonia via Pelion, in

---

[1] Livy 31. 40. 1–6.   [2] 31. 40. 7–43. 3.
[3] 31. 45. 1–47. 3; Paus. 7. 7. 9 (Oreus also called Histiaea).
[4] Plb. 18. 4. 5–6; Livy 32. 5. 4–9. The Romans had suffered severely from lack of supplies, since they depended largely on foraging (Livy 31. 33. 5; 36. 5–7; 38. 1; 39. 3–4; P*Flam* 4. 1; Dio 18. 58; Zon. 9. 15. 4).

conjunction probably with attacks by the Illyrians and Dardanians in the north and by the Aetolians and Amynander in the south. When Philip arrived with the main body, he concentrated all his forces within the near-by Aous pass, from which he could enfilade the entry into Epirus and keep his communications open with Macedonia (see Fig. 8). Moreover, if the Romans did march to Pelion, he could move quickly to Antipatreia and cut their lines of supply. If they came south, they would be far from the Dardanians and they would be prevented by him from making contact with the Aetolians.[1]

Philip's position was reported by Charops, a pro-Roman Epirote, to the successor of Sulpicius, P. Villius, who thereupon moved from Corcyra to the mainland and brought his army to the junction of the Aous and the Drin, where he pitched camp, 8 kilometres away from Philip's position, now fortified with field works ('ditches, rampart, and towers') in the narrow defile between towering cliffs (see Fig. 13). Forty days passed during which the Romans took no action. In the course of them Villius was replaced by Titus Flamininus, who brought reinforcements of 800 cavalry and 8,000 infantry, but still hesitated to attack and the Epirote magistrates arranged a meeting between Philip and Flamininus to discuss terms of peace. Philip offered to liberate cities captured by himself, but not those held by his ancestors, and to accept arbitration over questions of compensation. Flamininus demanded the surrender of all places outside Macedonia proper and rejected arbitration. Philip broke off negotiations with the question: 'What harsher terms could you impose if you had defeated me?'[2]

Flamininus then delivered frontal assault after frontal assault, without success and with considerable loss, as his flanks for 3 kilometres were raked by missiles from the catapults, 'stone-throwers', and skirmishers on the high rocks, and his leading troops failed to break through the serried pikes of the phalangites on the level ground, where the defile was narrowest. No progress seemed possible, until a detour leading to a position above the Macedonian lines was suggested by some local shepherds. Their bona fides was guaranteed by Charops. A force of 300 cavalry and 4,000 infantry was sent with them to travel mainly by night and at dawn on the third day to indicate their arrival by smoke signal. Just before dawn on the arranged day Flamininus sent three columns into the attack. The flanking columns soon ground to a halt, and the centre column could not penetrate the line of the

---

[1] For routes and topography see H*IRM* 39 ff., referring to earlier accounts and writing from personal knowledge of the area, and Hammond, 'Antigonea in Epirus', *JRS* 61 (1971) 112 ff. The pass led to the largest city in the area. The inscribed voting discs with the city's name are decisive, despite N. Çeka in *Monumentet* 5–6 (1973) 7 ff., who dates the city far too late; see H*E* 209 ff., 668 f., and 720.

[2] Livy 32. 6. 1–4; 8. 2; 9. 6–10. 7; D.S. 28. 11; P*Flam* 3.

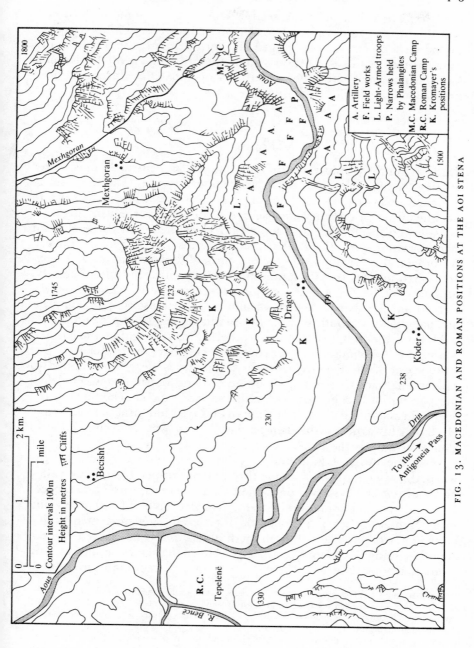

FIG. 13. MACEDONIAN AND ROMAN POSITIONS AT THE AOI STENA

phalanx. Then the smoke was seen. The Romans charged with shouts, and the turning force on the heights shouted in reply. Philip retreated to the eastern end of the gorge. Our pro-Roman sources probably exaggerated his losses at 2,000 men; they did not give the Roman losses, which were certainly greater, as they had suffered from artillery fire in the long defile.[1]

4. *Operations in Thessaly and the conference at Nicaea* (Figure 6)

Philip withdrew rapidly to the high country of central Pindus. After waiting some days to observe the movements of Flamininus, he marched to Tricca in west Thessaly. Flamininus pardoned the Epirote League for its past enmity and secured its neutrality; the Romans were not allowed to plunder, and some Epirote soldiers joined the Roman forces as volunteers. The fleet and supply ships moved from Corcyra to Ambracia, in order to send convoys through Athamania to Thessaly, and when all was ready Flamininus brought his army into Thessaly, probably by the Zygos pass, and joined forces with Amynander by Mt. Cercetium (Mt. Koziakas). It was now early August 198; for Flamininus had spent a month in Epirus, organizing the system of supply.

Philip had no hope of holding southern Thessaly against the Roman army, the Aetolians, and Amynander. He therefore evacuated five cities south of the Peneus river; the populations were transplanted to Macedonia and the buildings were burnt. The alternative was to leave the populations to be enslaved and the cities to be occupied by the enemy in accordance with the Roman and Aetolian practice hitherto.[2] He based his army in the Tempe pass, which was as impregnable to frontal assault as the Aous pass.

With the news of Flamininus' victory the Aetolians went on the warpath, ravaging and looting through the upper Spercheus valley and south-west Thessaly. Some small towns were captured and sacked. From others the population fled, not always to safety; for those fleeing from Xyniae, 'a great number of disordered, unarmed men and a crowd of women and children with them, were massacred by the Aetolian soldiers' (Livy 32. 13. 14). The Athamanes, reinforced by Roman troops, laid siege to Gomphi, the Macedonian stronghold.

---

[1] 32. 10. 9–12. 7; P*Flam* 4–5. 1; Zon. 9. 16; App. *Mac.* 5–6. For the differences in our sources see H*IRM* 52 n. 38. That Livy used an annalist at some points is clear from 32. 6. 5–8, which mentions a (fictitious) campaign for Villius. The Romans captured Philip's camp, but no Macedonian soldiers, as far as the report goes.

[2] Livy 32. 12. 8–13. 9; Plb. 18. 4. 2. These cities had been closely associated with Macedonia since Philip II's reign, and a Macedonian general directed defence in Thessaly (see *Studies Edson* 194 ff.). For the supply system see Livy 32. 15. 5–7 and H*E* 283 f.

When it capitulated, other fortresses followed suit; meanwhile the countryside was ravaged. At sea the combined fleets of Rome, Attalus, and Rhodes, totalling about 100 large warships and also supply ships, captured a number of Aegean islands and attacked Macedonian bases in Euboea. Eretria suffered the same fate as Oreus, the sack yielding 'statues and works of ancient art' beyond expectation and the population being enslaved. Carystus surrendered and was spared. The derelict sites of Oreus and Eretria were taken over by the Macedonians, who had their headquarters at Chalcis.[1] The fleet turned south to capture Cenchreae and threaten Corinth.

Philip hoped to stave off the Roman army until the end of the season, when he might obtain terms. To this end he put garrisons of picked Macedonian troops in at least three strongly fortified towns: Aeginium, overlooking the Thessalian side of the Zygos-pass route, which the Romans found too strong to attack; Phaloria, by Mt. Cercetium, where 2,000 Macedonians fought stubbornly but were overwhelmed; and Atrax, by the Peneus west of Larissa, where the Romans broke down part of the wall, but were hurled back by the serried ranks of long pikes. Phaloria was sacked and burnt. Philip's plan succeeded, in that Flamininus marched south into Phocis where some cities surrendered, others resisted, but were captured, and Elatea offered stiff resistance. Flamininus now, in October, took steps to bring the Achaean League into the war. His army was just across the Gulf, and the combined fleets were at Cenchreae, when he arranged for his brother Lucius, commander of the Roman fleet, Attalus, Rhodes, and Athens, but not Aetolia, to send envoys to a conference held at Sicyon.[2]

The newly elected general of the Achaean League, Aristaenus, favoured Rome; but the delegates of the member states were divided in their sympathies. Philip too managed to send envoys; for the Achaean League was a neutral state in the major war, though it was at war with Nabis. The issue hung in the balance for three days. The proximity of overwhelming Roman forces was probably the deciding factor. The League made alliance with Rome against Macedonia and sent troops and siege-engines for the attack on Corinth, a member of the League, but opposed to Rome. The representatives of three states left the conference in disgust: Dyme, Megalopolis, and Argos. To break the oaths of alliance by attacking their ally seemed to them unprincipled. The Macedonian garrison of Corinth, supported by the citizens and reinforced by 1,500 soldiers sent from Chalcis, beat off all attacks, to the disappointment of the Achaean League, to which Flamininus had promised the city as a reward.[3]

---

[1] 32. 16–17. 2; Paus. 7. 8. 1; Zon. 9. 16. 2; Plb. 18. 45. 5.
[2] 32. 15. 1; 15. 4 and 8; 17. 4–18. 9; 19. 1–5.
[3] 32. 19. 6–23. 13.

In Phocis Elatea was taken by storm and looted. The garrison and the population escaped into the citadel, and rather than storm that too, Flamininus accepted its surrender on condition that the Macedonians and the people should go free. At Opus, where the citadel was held by a Macedonian garrison, some of the townspeople wanted to bring in the Aetolians, others the Romans; and it was the latter who took the town. At this point a herald arrived from Philip, proposing a conference and Flamininus accepted. A standstill would give the Roman army a much-needed rest and prevent Philip from regaining cities in Thessaly and elsewhere. It was a sign of what might happen that Argos, on which the Achaean League had imposed a garrison of 500 young citizen soldiers, had brought in a Macedonian force and ejected the Achaeans. Moreover, Flamininus had personal ambitions: if peace was to be made, let it be now so that he could be the peacemaker, or if it was to be war, let him be continued in his command, since the time for elections at Rome was approaching.[1]

The conference began in November and lasted three days at Nicaea near Thermopylae. A detailed account survives in Plb. 18. 1–10; it is the source of shorter statements elsewhere.[2] On the first day Flamininus and the delegates of his allies, namely Pergamum, Rhodes, Aetolia, Athamania, Athens, and Achaea, put forward their demands, which were naturally maximal. On the second day Flamininus and Philip had a separate discussion at which Flamininus learnt what Philip was prepared to concede (18. 8. 8–10) and (as can be inferred from later developments) advised Philip how to proceed. The concessions were regarded as inadequate by Flamininus' allies; the meeting was adjourned. On the third day Philip made the proposal (no doubt inspired by Flamininus) that, if the present negotiators could not agree, the matters under discussion should be referred to the Senate. All Flamininus' allies rejected the proposal; they would rather continue the war (18. 9. 6). However, Flamininus insisted that nothing could be settled without the Senate's approval, and he persuaded his allies to take their demands to Rome. A truce for two months was then concluded, Philip agreeing to the condition laid down by Flamininus, that he would withdraw his garrisons from Phocis and Locris. The nominated envoys of all participants set off for Rome (18. 10. 7–11). It was a tacit, and to many an unwelcome, admission that the future of the Greek states and of Macedonia lay in the hands of the Roman Senate and People.[3]

---

[1] 32. 24. 25; 32. 1–8; P*Flam* 5. 6. and 7. 1.

[2] 32. 32. 6–36. 10; P*Flam* 5–7. 1; App. *Mac.* 8; J. 30. 3. 8; Zon. 9. 16. 4.

[3] See Walbank, *C* 2. 548–62, citing the extensive bibliography, to which add Errington, *Dawn* 149 f.

XXI

THE DEFEAT OF THE MACEDONIAN ARMY
AND THE ROMAN SETTLEMENT (197–196 B.C.)

1. *The hearing at Rome and preparations in the field*

THE vision of the Senate extended beyond the Greek peninsula and Macedonia to the Aegean Sea and the Asian shore, where Rhodes and Attalus had proved such staunch allies. Rome's interests there had been affected by the activities of Antiochus' generals in 198. Before Flamininus engaged Philip at the Aoi Stena, Attalus sent envoys to report that while his army had been helping Rome against Philip his kingdom had been invaded by the forces of Antiochus, and to ask Rome either to send her troops to protect his kingdom or to allow him to withdraw his own forces. The Senate replied that Attalus and Antiochus should make peace as they were 'allies and friends of the Roman People', and it undertook to send envoys to remind Antiochus that the Roman People was using the forces of Attalus against their common enemy, Philip. When the envoys reached Antiochus, he withdrew his army from the kingdom of Attalus 'in respect for their authority' ('legatorum Romanorum auctoritate'). Attalus showed his gratitude by giving a golden crown to Rome and thanking the Senate late in 198, before the Senate granted a hearing to the delegates from Greece and Macedonia.[1] It must have seemed feasible to the delegates from Greece that Rome's authority might make Philip withdraw his forces from their territories.

Meanwhile the Senate and the People went ahead with their own business. In December the allocation of provinces to the new consuls was held up by two tribunes, who persuaded the Senate to keep both consuls in Italy and to prolong for a further year the commands of Titus Flamininus and Lucius Flamininus against Macedonia. Reinforcements were voted for them: 300 cavalry, 6,000 Roman infantry, and 3,000 'naval allies' (mainly from the Greek cities in South Italy). Supplies were also sent to Greece: a vast quantity of grain from Africa, and foodstuffs and clothing from Sicily and Sardinia. Masinissa contributed ten elephants and 200 cavalry. Two previous commanders in Greece—Sulpicius and Villius—were appointed to the staff of

---

[1] Livy 32. 8. 9–16 and 32. 27. 1.

Flamininus.[1] These arrangements made sense only if the Senate intended to go to war with Macedonia.

Philip's envoys for the hearing by the Senate had little freedom of manœuvre. The king had already refused the Senate's demand as conveyed by Flamininus, that he withdraw 'from all of Greece' and restore the possessions of Ptolemy to Ptolemy (Plb. 18. 1. 13–14). Then, by what was probably a breach of confidence, Flamininus had revealed that Philip was willing to make certain concessions in return for peace: namely to give to Aetolia Pharsalus and Larissa, but not Phthiotic Thebes; to Rhodes the Peraea, but not Iasus and Bargylia; to Achaea Corinth and Argos towns, but not their citadels; to Attalus the captured ships and crews; and to Rome places in Illyris lost to Philip since 205.[2] Thus, when the hearing did start and the envoys of the Greek states were invited to speak first, they knew what bids to make.

'They all condemned Philip roundly,' says Polybius. In essence they appealed to the Senators as 'liberators of Greece' to break 'the fetters', as Philip himself had once called them, by making him remove his troops from Corinth, Chalcis, and Demetrias; and if he refused, they asked the Senate to renew the war. It was then the turn of the Macedonian envoys to present their prepared statement. They were not allowed to do so. Instead they were asked by the Senate whether they would surrender Corinth, Chalcis, and Demetrias. They said that they had had no instruction about these places from Philip and could not answer for him. The Senate did not deign to consult Philip. It voted forthwith to continue the war and entrusted the conduct of it to Flamininus.[3]

On the Roman side the truce had been a trick to enable Flamininus' friends to engineer the prolongation of his command, and his divulging of what Philip had been willing to concede was calculated to make the Greek delegates raise their demands to an unacceptable level. The hearing was a sham, in that the Senate had decided beforehand to continue the war for its own reasons; and no attempt to conceal the fact was made in that Philip was not given an opportunity to reply at all. The Senate got possession of Phocis and Locris at no cost. Polybius accorded the highest praise to Flamininus for his astute and successful calculations.[4] On the other side, Philip may have been misled; but he was glad to have gained the two months for regrouping his forces and even the return of his garrisons from Phocis and Locris may have been to his advantage.

Philip paid now for his past policy. He had succoured his allies and defended his dependants by supplying garrisons to counter the ma-

[1] Livy 32. 27. 2 and 28. 1–12.   [2] Plb. 18. 8. 8–10; Livy 32. 35. 9–11.
[3] Plb. 18. 11–12. 1; Livy 32. 37.   [4] Plb. 18. 12. 2–5.

rauding tactics of Aetolia, Rome, and Dardania by land and of
Attalus, Rhodes, and Rome by sea. Now he needed the men from
those garrisons for a decisive battle; for *in toto* they must have
exceeded 20,000 men.[1] However, he either could not or would not
bring the garrisons back from Caria and Thrace; he had to hold his
northern frontier against the threat of Illyrians and Dardanians; and
he kept his garrisons in Illyris to face other Roman forces. During this
winter he withdrew one garrison from the Peloponnese, but the
withdrawal had unforeseen consequences. This was at Argos. Philip
struck a bargain with Nabis, king of Sparta, who took the city and
promised to return it, if Philip should win the war against Rome.
Nabis then played him false by coming to terms with Rome, Attalus,
and Achaea, sending 600 Cretan mercenaries to serve with Flamininus and concluding a truce with the Achaean League; the credit for
this deal was due to Attalus, who was rewarded by the Achaeans with
a cult in his honour at Sicyon.[2] Elsewhere Philip left his garrisons in
position—at Corinth, a garrison of 1,500 Macedonians and a further
defence force of 4,500 men; at Chalcis, his base of operations for
Euboea; at Demetrias and Phthiotic Thebes, on which he may have
hoped to base his field operations; and at other strong-points in
Thessaly.

The absence of so many men on garrison duty left Philip desperately
short of troops for the defence of Macedonia. Livy, drawing on
Polybius, gives the following description.

'On learning from his envoys that there was no hope of peace Philip
conducted a conscription through all the cities of his kingdom. The great lack
of mature soldiers was due to casualties sustained over many generations in
continual wars; in his own reign too a great number had fallen in naval battles
against Rhodes and in land battles against Rome. So he was enlisting boys
over sixteen years of age as soldiers and recalling to the colours such veterans
as had some strength left.'

The description rings true. But Philip was able to enlist further men at
the end of this year.[3]

As Philip intended to operate in Thessaly, the situation there was

[1] A considerable city, such as Phaloria, had 2,000 'Macedonians', i.e. Macedonian troops
being mainly mercenaries (Livy 32. 15. 1 in 198 B.C.), and Atrax probably had more (Livy 32.
17. 7). A major base, such as Chalcis, had perhaps 5,000 men, since Philocles could draw on them
for forces of 2,000 to attack Eleusis and 1,500 to reinforce Corinth (Livy 31. 26. 1–4 and 32. 23.
11); and Demetrias, a major base with a wall circuit of 7 km., may have had a garrison as large as
that of Chalcis. Philip's garrison forces *c.* 200 B.C. were estimated at 20,000–30,000 by Niese 3.
600 n. 2 and Kromayer 104. For Corinth see Livy 33. 14. 3–5.
[2] Livy 32. 38–40; Plb. 18. 16.
[3] Livy 33. 3. 1–5 and 19. 3. The administrative centre for conscription was the town, in both
instances.

relevant to his plan (see Fig. 6). The Thessalian city-states had either an indigenous population, which was sometimes less than loyal, as at Pharsalus and Pherae, or a population or section of population implanted from elsewhere, loyal to Macedonia, as at Gomphi (Philippi), Phthiotic Thebes (also Philippi), Atrax (peopled from Perrhaebia), and Gonnus, and Demetrias (a Macedonian foundation). Philip made recommendations to the former group, as in his letter of 215 to Larissa, advising the enfranchisement of resident aliens.[1] He exercised a direct control probably over the latter group; it is probable, for instance, that the five cities in the Enipeus valley from which he removed the populations to Macedonia in 198 were of this group. In any case the removal showed that he did not intend to defend that valley, and the barren area thereby created would not help an enemy army operating in that valley. Thus we may infer his intention to adopt a line of defence marked by Mt. Titarus and the Karadagh range (to which the Cynoscephalae belong), ending in the north at Atrax and in the south-east at Phthiotic Thebes. The line was pierced by two main roads at Palaepharsalus and Pherae.

Flamininus did not disperse the Roman forces, which wintered at Elatea in Phocis. In the spring the Achaeans were ordered to tackle the Macedonian forces at Corinth, and the Rhodians to contain Philip's garrisons in Caria. Lucius Flamininus took a small force to Acarnania, which had remained loyal to Macedonia. The main Roman fleet and the reinforcements brought by Attalus were to support the Roman army in its advance. Flamininus probably had a good understanding of his enemy's plans, and he intended to force a decisive battle, but only under conditions unfavourable to the Macedonian phalanx.

2. *The campaign and the battle of Cynoscephalae* (Figure 6)

We owe our knowledge of the ensuing campaign entirely to Polybius. A large part of his account has survived, and the full account was the basis of Livy's narrative and of Plutarch's summary. Polybius himself, it may be inferred, drew on eyewitnesses, primarily Aetolians who magnified their part and also Romans and Macedonians; in addition, his own admiration of Rome and dislike of Macedonia coloured his narrative somewhat. Livy reduced the part of the Aetolians and made some errors in translating and abbreviating Polybius' account (e.g. at 33. 8. 13 and 9. 6 'right' instead of 'left'). The resulting picture is

---

[1] See Volume II. 539 f. and St. Byz. s.v. *Philippoi*; *SIG* 543 (Larissa).

detailed, but blurred, because Polybius had a lack of strategic insight and an inability to define the topography of the actions.[1]

Philip's evacuation of the towns in the Enipeus valley which he could not defend, and his holding of Atrax as a stop-point, had been well calculated. For he had kept unscathed much of Phthiotis, all Pelasgiotis, and rich areas north of the Peneus river. He had strong garrisons and well-stocked bases at Demetrias and Phthiotic Thebes, and he had advanced garrisons at Larissa Cremaste and at Echinus. Given these defences, he expected to deflect the Roman army into south-western Thessaly, remote from the sea, and in that area he had a strong garrison at Pharsalus, of which the citadel was almost impregnable. Towards the end of March he chose Dium as the base camp for training his army and collecting supplies. It was well placed for holding the narrow entries into Macedonia on either side of Mt. Olympus, the Petra pass inland, and the Tempe pass and the Heracleum narrows near the coast. But that was not the immediate reason for the choice. He intended to hold the protected areas of Thessaly, which would provide much needed cavalry and supplies. So, soon after hearing that the Roman army had left its base at Elatea in Phocis, he made Larissa his advanced base and moved his army and supply waggons along the main road towards Pherae *en route* for Demetrias and Thebes. His advance was halted by the appearance of Roman scouts near Pherae, and he never reached his intended position.[2]

What considerations would have governed his choice of position? His recruiting of the young and the old showed that he expected to be

---

[1] Kromayer, *AS* 2. 57–105 and in *Schlachtenatlas*, Röm. Abt. 2 Blatt 9, gives the fullest account, accepted in general by Walbank, *Ph* 169 f. and *C* 576 f. But his placing of the Thetideum so far from Pharsalus is inconsistent with Str. C 431 and 441; his 'level ground' in the battle is too small in area, and his march for Philip on the second day is too short. He put the Aetolian infantry at 600 (Livy 33. 3. 9), rather than at the 6,000 (*PFlam* 7. 3), which accords better with 1,200 Athamanian infantry. Pritchett, *Studies* 2. 135 follows Kromayer's 600 Aetolian infantry, but he rejects Kromayer's site for the Thetideum. He describes the areas east and south of Scotussa very well; but his description of the battle is cursory and his location of it on p. 144 does not provide any 'level ground' (Plb. 18. 22. 6, discussed on p. 439 below). J. D. Morgan, 'Palaepharsalus —the Battle and the Town', *AJA* 87 (1983) 23–54, discussing the battle of 48 B.C., has shed new light on the topography by establishing the site of Palaepharsalus by Driskoli (now Krene), the course of the main road from Pharsalus via Palaepharsalus and Crannon to Larissa, and that road's crossing of the Enipeus by Vasili (downstream from the long bridge of the main road near Pasa Magoula). No two scholars seem to have agreed on the question which ridges look like dog's heads, Cynoscephalae. The account in the text is different from those of Kromayer and Pritchett and rests in part on the article by J. D. Morgan. An important point may be mentioned here. In Plb. 18. 20. 6 at the end of the second day Philip reached a place in Scotussaean territory, Flamininus one in Pharsalian territory. Pritchett 2. 138 and others inferred that Philip entered Scotussaean territory now for the first time. On my interpretation Philip had collected supplies at Scotussa as intended at 18. 20. 2, and it is the scene of the impending battle which Polybius sought to define at 18. 20. 6 as being on or near the border of the two territories (so Walbank, *Ph* 169 no. 2).

[2] Livy 33. 3.1–6; 3. 11–4. 5 and 6. 3.

outnumbered, especially in light-armed troops. He therefore needed a position with strong flanks, the more so since his hopes of victory lay in his phalanx, which was helpless if its flanks were turned in the course of an action, and with level, or at least even, ground in the centre, so that the phalanx could charge without losing its formation. Finally, he wanted a main road for his supply route, and he was in need of the additional troops which he could obtain if his chosen position was in the vicinity of Demetrias and Thebes.

Flamininus, having had experience of the phalanx, hoped to engage the Macedonians on broken ground, where the flexible legions and his superiority in light-armed troops would be effective. That meant confronting Philip, before Philip reached his chosen position. But he chose first to deal with the Boeotian League, still in alliance with Macedonia, and at the beginning of spring he asked the aged Attalus to come from Cenchreae to Elatea—we may allow a fortnight—and then he marched with one legion from Elatea south to Thebes, where the Boeotian Assembly was in session. He passed troops into the city by a trick (Livy 33. 1. 2–7), and his speech, supported by those of Attalus (his last contribution as he died soon afterwards at Pergamum) and Aristaenetus, persuaded the Assembly to switch its alliance from Macedonia to Rome. Collecting the other legion at Elatea, he marched via Thermopylae to Heraclea, where the Aetolian Assembly, specially summoned for the purpose, voted forces of 400 cavalry and 6,000 infantry (light-armed) to serve under his command; and three or four days later he collected these troops—already conscripted in advance —at Xyniae in south Thessaly. He then marched 'rapidly' (33. 3. 9 'confestim'), collecting 800 Cretans and 1,200 Athamanians *en route*, to the walls of Phthiotic Thebes, where he hoped for collusion within, and probably tried the trick he had used at Boeotian Thebes. This time he failed. He learnt that Philip was somewhere in Thessaly. So he marched on past Demetrias and had his men make a fortified camp—the first apparently on his marches, which indicates that he meant to stay where he was, namely 6 miles short of Pherae (Velestinon). It had been a 'moderate' day's march (33. 6. 2),[1] and the ground by Pherae was unsuitable for a phalanx.

The rapidity of Flamininus' movements and then the slow pace on the last day (Plb. 18. 19. 1 βάδην) show that Flamininus was moving now into his desired position. This was a remarkable achievement, when we realize that he had marched about twice as far as Philip and beaten him to the post by a short head.[2] Such arrangements as the

[1] Livy 33. 1–2, 3. 6–10, and 5. 1–6. 2; Plb. 18. 18–19. 1; Zon. 9. 16.
[2] From Dium to Pherae is some 110 km., whereas from Thebes to Pherae is just over 200 km. by the route which Flamininus took.

summoning of the Aetolian Assembly, the conscription of groups of Greek troops, their accession on the march, and the delivery of supplies, had all been made in advance and executed without a hitch. He now enjoyed several advantages. He had prevented Philip from basing himself on Demetrias or Thebes, from adding their garrison troops to his army, and from drawing on their granaries and arsenals. He was only 3 or 4 miles away from a possible terminal for sea-borne supplies, and he was on a main road for overland supplies from south Thessaly. He was at the junction of two main roads, one running east towards Pharsalus and the other north towards Larissa, and he had chosen at his leisure the most suitable site south of Pherae from which to await or deliver attack, if Philip should appear.

It happened that Philip had camped on the very same day 4 miles north of Pherae on the Larissa road. Neither commander knew of the presence of the other until their scouts made contact around dawn in the vicinity of Pherae; and further probing on the following day led to a fierce skirmish, in which the Aetolians distinguished themselves. Philip's wish was obviously to reach Demetrias. But he could not fight his way through; for the ground below Pherae was intensively cultivated and had dry-stone walls and copses, which made it most unsuitable for a phalanx in battle order. Polybius wrote that both commanders were dissatisfied with the terrain and moved off simultaneously. See Fig. 14. Philip, he says, was eager to obtain supplies from the (large) city Scotussa.[1] That he should be short of supplies so soon suggests that he had expected to reach Demetrias and had not organized an immediate service from Larissa. What would happen beyond Scotussa? Presumably he was switching his supply service from the Larissa–Pherae road to that leading from Larissa towards Pharsalus. He therefore intended to hold a position on or by that road on ground more suitable to his phalanx. If Philip moved off first, we can see that Flamininus was able to guess Philip's intention from the direction which Philip took. Flamininus, then, followed the main road towards Pharsalus. He was, at present, well off for supplies. According to Polybius his aim was to forestall Philip by 'destroying the crops in Scotussaean territory', not to obtain them for himself. Such an aim is unacceptable; for Flamininus never entered Scotussaean territory.

For two days the armies marched westwards on roughly parallel lines, being out of touch with one another because the high southern ridge of the range of Mt. Karadagh lay between them. On the second day Philip's army marched less far, as it was rounding up supplies; but Flamininus was too far away to interfere and presumably completed a

[1] Plb. 18. 19–20. 4; Livy 33. 5. 4–6. 8. The local crops were grown west of Scotussa (Kromayer 67 f. and Stählin in *RE* s.v. *Skotoussa* 614 'das fruchtbare Kornland').

normal march. The following night saw exceptional thunder and lightning and heavy rain, and towards dawn the cloud layer settled so low on the hills that one could not see people in front of oneself. (Plb. 18. 20. 7). Despite the darkness Philip started off with the entire army, 'being eager to arrive at his intended destination', which was, on my interpretation, a place on, or covering, the Larissa–Pharsalus road. But the weather was against him. He had to encamp. He sent forward only an advance force. It was ordered to occupy the high ridge which separated him from his destination. Meanwhile Flamininus stayed in his camp near the Thetideum, or 'shrine of Thetis'; and being on lower ground he was less affected by the mist. He sent out 1,300 men towards the same high ridge, in order to see when the mist cleared where Philip was (18. 21. 1). In the mist they came unexpectedly on Philip's advance force.

Flamininus, it seems, had guessed correctly the region and the direction from which Philip would come. Moreover, he was now in Pharsalian territory (Plb. 18. 20. 6), and so able to open up a new supply route from the south. But accident played an important part in this first clash, in that his 1,300 men met not the full Macedonian army—as they would have done on a clear day—but only a comparable force, and Philip had lost the lead which he would have had on a clear day towards reaching his objective, namely, a strong position with suitable ground for his phalanx. It was this clash which led to the battle of Cynoscephalae.

We must pause to consider the size and nature of the armies. Philip had 18,000 phalangites, all Macedonians, of whom 2,000 were the élite Peltasts; then 5,500 light-armed troops, being 2,000 Thracians, 2,000 Illyrians (called Tralles), and 1,500 mercenaries of various nationalities; and 2,000 cavalry, both Macedonian and Thessalian.[1] The strength of the army lay in the phalanx of pikemen; and the supporting troops were enough to defend its flanks in a defensive position of Philip's choosing. According to Livy 33. 4. 6, the Roman forces were approximately equal except that the Aetolian cavalry gave them a slight superiority; but Livy achieved this by putting the Aetolian infantry at 600 (33. 3. 9) instead of the 6,000 which is given by P*Flam* 7. 3. On the other hand, Plutarch rated the Roman army at 'over 26,000', including the Aetolians. It may be that their common source, Polybius, accepted the official Roman version for the total. The truth is probably that the two Roman legions were at full strength at 22,000 men and that the 8,000 or more light infantry (which included 2,000

---

[1] Livy 33. 4. 4. The Thracians appear as mercenaries in Plb. 18. 22. 2, and we may assume the Tralles (cf. 31. 35. 1) were mercenaries too; those of various nationalities included Boeotians (Plb. 18. 43. 1).

Athamanians and 800 Cretans) and some 2,500 cavalry brought the total to some 32,000 men.[1] An unstated number of war elephants was an important addition; for most of the Macedonian infantry had had no experience of them and the mounts of the Macedonian cavalry could not be made to face them.

Where was the high ridge on which the first clash occurred? Kromayer and Pritchett proposed the locations for the ridge which are shown on Figure 14; but neither seemed to me to fit the purposes which I attributed to the two commanders, and to accord with the normal marching speed of Macedonian and Roman armies. On the first day, starting later than Philip had done, Flamininus marched some 16 kilometres to Eretria (Plb. 18. 20. 5), far removed from Scotussaean territory; and on the second day with a normal march of some 20 kilometres he reached a position in Pharsalian territory, which on my theory gave him control of the crossing of the river Enipeus so that supplies could come to him from the south. In the plain north of the crossing he needed an excellent water supply for his men and horses. That he found such a supply is indicated by his encamping περὶ τὸ Θετίδειον (Plb. 18. 21. 1), 'round the sanctuary of Thetis', a goddess of water.[2] The obvious place was betrayed by the village name, Zoodokhos Pege, 'Lifegiving Waters'.

Let us turn now to Philip. On the first day, leaving probably at dawn, Philip marched some 17 kilometres to camp by the river Onchestus (Plb. 18. 20. 5) beside the city of Scotussa, from which he was intending to draw supplies (Plb. 18. 20. 2 σπεύδων ἐκ ταύτης τῆς πόλεως ἐφοδιάσασθαι). On the second day, while pasturing his animals and letting men forage, he made on my theory some 12 kilometres to reach 'Melambium in Scotussaean territory' (Plb. 18. 20. 6). He too needed water in abundance. The best sources are at Khalkiades, where there are three springs. So I proposed to put Philip's camp by Khalkiadhes (see Fig. 15). His intention on the third day was to

---

[1] The number of Roman and Italian soldiers is surprisingly low, as in spring 198 Flamininus had brought 8,800 men to swell the army of Villius (Livy 32. 9. 6). In Livy 33. 3. 10 'quingenti Gortynii Cretensium duce Cydante et trecenti Apolloniatae, haud dispari armatu' the similar equipment (presumably as archers) and the partitive genitive 'Cretensium' indicate that the Apolloniatae were Cretans and not (as Aymard, *Premiers Rapports* 431 and 147 n. 52 holds) citizens of Apollonia Illyrica, which had hoplites and needed them for local defence. Philip too had Cretans (33. 14. 4). Cavalry numbers are uncertain, whether one reads 'qui tum' with A. H. McDonald or 'equitum' with others at 33. 4. 6. The 1,000 Numidian cavalry sent for the Macedonian campaign in 199 (31. 19. 4) may still have been present.

[2] Kromayer had Philip reach Ayia Triadha on the first day and spend all the second day foraging ('damit ging der Tag hin'), and Pritchett had Philip go some 8 kilometres to Mikron Perivolakion on the first day and not even reach Scotussa on the second day. See Pritchett, *Studies* 2. 111–14 and 118 for the walls of Eretria and Scotussa, both of which are identified with certainty. Pritchett proposed to give the name Onchestus to the stream by Mikron Perivolakion and to place the 'Thetideum in Pharsalian territory', at Ayios Athanasios.

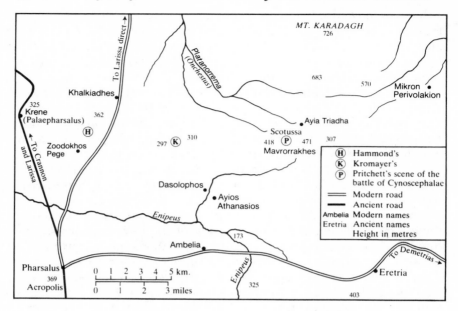

FIG. 14. THE MARCHES TO CYNOSCEPHALAE

occupy a suitable position on the Pharsalus–Larissa road, where he could deploy his phalanx to advantage; and it was by that road that supplies would be coming to him from Larissa.

The next question was where the ancient road ran. The solution was provided by J. D. Morgan in a very important article, in which he showed that the Roman road, no doubt following the course of the Macedonian road, ran through Palaepharsalus and Crannon to Larissa, and that Palaepharsalus should best be placed at Krene.[1] Thus, but for the mist, Philip would have reached his objective (Plb. 18. 20. 8 τὸ προκείμενον) and placed his army astride the Palaepharsalus–Crannon road, before Flamininus had got under way.

In October 1985 it was possible to visit the scene and to fit the details of the battle to the terrain (see Fig. 15).[2] Beginning at the recently developed upper hamlet of Khalkiadhes (Ano Khalkiadhes on Fig. 15), we walked to point 362 (now carrying a water-tank) and crossed the watershed ridge to 'K', standing for Kremaste, the name of farm-buildings on the flat upper part of the long ridge which runs

---

[1] Cited in n. 1 p. 433 above.

[2] My wife and I were accompanied by Dr. M. B. Hatzopoulos and his son Philip. I am most indebted to Dr. Hatzopoulos for his acute observation and his grasp of the tactics as we went over the ground. My wife and I returned to the scene in June 1986, partly in connection with the battle between Pelopidas and Alexander in 364 B.C.

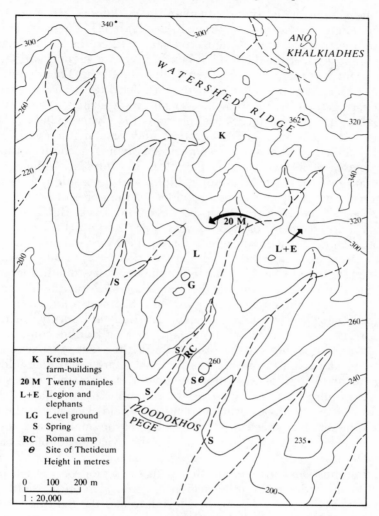

FIG. 15. CYNOSCEPHALAE

south towards the western part of Zoodokhos Pege. Walking down this
ridge we came to 'the level ground' (Plb. 18. 22. 6 τοὺς ἐπιπέδους
τόπους), marked 'LG' on Fig. 15. As we came down we noted the
parallel ridge to the east, because it was used, as we shall see, by the
elephants and one legion. The view, shown as Plate III is from 'the level
ground', looking back up the ridge to 'K' (the trees belonging mainly
to the farm-buildings) and having to the right the parallel ridge.

On coming to the next dip of the ridge I was amazed to see in the slanting rays of the early morning sun the outlines of a Roman camp and an angle of a second one beside it. See Plate III. These are marked RC on Fig. 15. The gate of the Roman camp faced the spring, marked S on Fig. 15. The ruined church is beside a second (higher) spring, and I have put a Θ there to mark the possible site of the Thetideum. The ridge, which we came down, and the parallel ridge are two of several similar ridges, springing from the very long watershed ridge, and it is probable that these ridges were known as the Cynoscephalae, 'Dog's Heads', 'rugged with broken ground and reaching a considerable height' (Plb. 18. 22. 9).[1] We resume now Polybius' account at the first clash between the two advance forces on the watershed ridge.

Because the mist was lightening, Philip sent a considerable detachment from his camp to forage for fodder for the horses. Meanwhile on the ridge his advance troops drove the enemy back. But Flamininus sent a reinforcement of 500 cavalry and 2,000 light-armed, part Aetolian and part Roman, which forced the Macedonians back onto high ground above the ridge (i.e. towards point 362). Philip answered requests for help by sending the Thessalian cavalry, one hipparchy of Macedonian cavalry,[2] and all the mercenaries except the Thracians, and they drove the enemy back downhill, but not so far as 'the level ground';[3] for the Aetolian cavalry, resisting stubbornly, held the lower slopes. Whereas Philip in his camp at Khalkiadhes could not see what was happening on the other side of the ridge, the action was visible to Flamininus from his camp. He therefore began to deploy his entire army in front of his camp. Meanwhile exaggerated reports were reaching Philip ('the enemy are on the run; now is your chance!'), and perhaps in the mistaken belief that his men held the edge of the level ground he set off at speed with the first half of the phalanx as it formed up outside his camp, and he ordered 'Jumbo' Nicanor to follow closely with the other half.[4]

Flamininus went into action first with the legion on the left of his force; for he ordered the other legion to stand firm on his right, with the elephants in front. As this first legion joined the fighting troops it drove the Macedonian light-armed and cavalry back towards the ridge. There Philip had just arrived with the first half of the phalanx,

[1] A much more detailed account of the campaign of Cynoscephalae in 364 and in 197 and more details of the Roman camp and its surroundings will be published in *JHS* 108 (1988), to which the reader is referred.

[2] I infer one hipparchy (500 horsemen in the army of Alexander the Great) from Plb. 18. 22. 2. This cavalry force certainly outnumbered that sent by Flamininus.

[3] 'The level ground' of Plb. 18. 22. 6 has to be between the Roman camp and the high ridge, and troops fighting just above it have to be visible to Flamininus at the Roman camp. See Fig. 15.

[4] Polybius is unclear. At 18. 24. 1–2 τὸ πλέον μέρος may mean the greater part of those available, since some were out foraging; and, if Philip had half the phalanx, there is exaggeration in τῶν πλείστων μερῶν at 18. 24. 7.

including the Peltasts, and had deployed his men from column of march into line to his left. His line, facing south, ran through K on Fig. 15. The retreating light-armed and cavalry took position as his right flank-guard.[1] He then doubled the depth of his formation by bringing the left-hand phalangites to the right, ordered the light-armed to cover the flank, and charged downhill, sixteen men deep, into the legion of Flamininus, which had taken the advanced troops into its own ranks. The impact of the serried pikes was irresistible. The first legion was being driven back with losses, whereupon Flamininus transferred himself to the other legion and led it, not into the battle, but up the right-hand ridge towards the watershed ridge. ('L + E' on Fig. 15). There the rest of the Macedonian phalangites, the 2,000 Thracian light-armed, and the rest of the cavalry were arriving in disorder without the benefit of a co-ordinating commander.[2] Some were making contact with the first half of the phalanx; others were beginning to descend from the high ground; yet others were on it; and others were just coming up to it. Most of them were in marching order and not yet deployed, when the elephants and then the legion in battle order struck them and quickly routed them.[3]

Thus two separate battles had developed. The link between them was made by the brilliant initiative of an unnamed officer of the second legion. He wheeled 'twenty maniples' (some 2,000 men) round out of the pursuit into an attack on the rear of the victorious Macedonian phalanx ('20 M' on Fig. 15). In hand-to-hand fighting the long pike and the packed formation of the Macedonians were terrible disadvantages; for with enemies ahead and behind them it was impossible for the pikemen to reverse their direction quickly. Moreover, the legionary had a large shield, a heavy javelin ('pilum'), and a long sword, whereas the pikemen had a small shield and a short sword or dagger. As the hitherto victorious Macedonians threw away their pikes[4] and fell in large numbers or were trying to surrender, Philip broke away with a few horsemen and infantrymen, collected Macedonians and Thracians from his broken left, and made his escape towards Larissa and Tempe. About 8,000 Macedonians lay dead, and not less than 5,000 men were taken prisoner. The Romans and their allies lost 700 men only.[5] The defeat of Macedonia was decisive.

---

[1] Other phalangites were coming up to extend the phalanx on his left.

[2] Plb. 18. 25. 6. Had Philip had a Parmenio instead of a Nicanor, he might have won the day.

[3] 18. 25. 7 The elephants caused terror and the ground was unsuitable for those groups which adopted a phalanx formation.

[4] 18. 26. 5 and 12 τὰ ὅπλα, perhaps including shields (small, but affording some protection) but primarily weapons, i.e. the long pikes useless in a mêlée and burdensome in flight.

[5] 18. 27. 6, casualties being far heavier when men were out of formation and with exposed backs in flight.

The battle of Cynoscephalae revealed the strength and the weakness of the phalanx of pikemen (see Fig. 5). With a downhill slope and on what was at first even ground, the phalanx in massed formation, with protected flanks, proved far superior to the much looser legionary formation; and the long pikes even prevented the legionaries from engaging. The weakness of the phalanx, when disrupted by uneven, rugged ground and attacked on an open flank or from behind, needs no elaboration.[1] The open order of the legion with gaps between the maniples, each of 120 men of the leading and supporting lines, enabled the legion to keep formation on uneven ground and to manœuvre flexibly; and in hand-to-hand fighting the long sword and the long shield were used with gladiatorial skill. Philip was outgeneralled. He should never have allowed Flamininus time to cut him off from Demetrias and Phthiotic Thebes and dictate the scene of the first confrontation. He failed to amass supplies at appropriate places; and in consequence he incurred a delay at Scotussa, which prevented him from reaching his destination on or near the Pharsalus–Larissa road, and his dispatch of a foraging party was a factor in slowing down the departure of troops from his camp. He should have avoided committing his phalanx to unfavourable ground and doing so in driblets. Flamininus was quicker than his opponent, seized a position of strategic and tactical value, organized his supply system admirably, chose a campsite with a view in the direction of the enemy, and showed excellent judgement in accepting defeat on his left and therefore attacking on his right. Even so, that day might have been very different if there had been no mist to delay and confuse the Macedonians, and if in the battle there had not been a senior legionary officer of initiative and insight.

Philip retreated rapidly to a defensive position at Tempe, detaching a trusted officer to burn his papers at Larissa (Plb. 18. 33. 2–3 τὰ βασιλικὰ γράμματα, including the *King's Journal* as τὰ ὑπομνήματα, which Livy 33. 11. 1 aptly translated 'commentarii regii'). There he considered his future course. He was influenced by adverse news from other fronts. The Acarnanians, after a very gallant resistance, had lost Leucas (when they heard of Philip's defeat, they entrusted their future to the discretion of Rome). The large forces of Androsthenes at Corinth had made havoc of the neighbouring areas, but they were defeated in battle by the Achaean general and confined to Corinth. In Caria the Macedonian phalanx was defeated by a flank attack, and surviving forces were limited to holding a small area.[2] Should Philip fight on or

---

[1] See the interesting discussion of the phalanx and the Roman formation in Plb. 18. 28–32, with Walbank, *C* 2. 585 ff.

[2] Livy 33. 14–18.

seek terms? The loss of half his army and the news of these set-backs left him no real choice. He must try to obtain tolerable terms.

3. *The Roman settlement*

Meanwhile the victors had fallen out. The Aetolians had sacked the king's camp while the Romans were still in battle, and now they claimed the victory was due to themselves. Flamininus was piqued by this and by a caustic poem of Alcaeus, which mentioned Aetolia first and Rome second; and also Aetolia's separate peace of 206 still rankled. At Larissa Philip's envoy came asking for a truce to bury the dead and for a meeting to discuss terms. Flamininus granted both and told the king 'to be of good cheer'. He did not consult the Aetolians, and they in their annoyance put out a rumour that he had been bribed by Philip. Before the meeting was held, he did consult his allies. Amyander wanted terms ensuring peace and the liberty of the Greek states. The Aetolians wanted Philip 'expelled' (Plb. 18. 36. 7; Livy 33. 12. 4 adding 'executed'); that meant war to the death. Flamininus then spoke of Rome's policy of peace, clemency, and sparing the vanquished —good Augustan ideas which Livy may have amplified (33. 12. 5–9)—and of the danger that, if Macedonia was destroyed, the northern barbarians would overrun Greece. When the Aetolian commander interrupted, Flamininus snubbed him. The decision was clearly to be made by Flamininus and the Senate.[1]

Events in the East were also of concern to Flamininus. There Antiochus with a large army and fleet had been advancing towards the Aegean basin, ostensibly to wrest Greek cities from the control of Ptolemy. Rhodes, as an ally of Rome, ordered Antiochus not to enter the Aegean Sea; for she suspected that he meant to join Philip against Rome. The news of the Roman victory at Cynoscephalae reached Rhodes during further negotiations. Thereupon Rhodes withdrew her order and strengthened her own grip on some of Ptolemy's Greek cities.[2] Before the meeting with Philip Flamininus became aware that Antiochus was entering the Aegean area and might join Philip. If so, the war would be prolonged; and the decision might lie with a commander other than Flamininus.

Thus Philip and Flamininus were both eager for a reasonable settlement when they and the delegates of Rome's allies met at Tempe.

---

[1] Livy 33. 10. 6; 11. 3–8; and 12. Flamininus may have given to his own soldiers ('militi' at 33. 11. 2) part of the proceeds from the sale of the loot and of the prisoners as slaves. Plb. 18. 34; 36–7; P*Flam* 8 fin. and 9. 1–2, citing Alcaeus' poem (*Anth. Pal.* 7. 247).

[2] Livy 33. 19. 8–20. 12; Plb. 18. 39. 3–4. The truce after the battle was for fifteen days, and there was then some delay before the meeting. For Rhodes see H. H. Schmitt, *Rom und Rhodos* (Munich, 1957) 76. n. 3.

Philip opened by expressing his willingness to concede all that had been demanded at Nicaea in Locris and to refer other matters to the Senate. The Aetolian delegate at once stepped up Aetolia's demands. He was mocked by Philip and rebuked by Flamininus, who censured Aetolia for having made a separate peace in 206. To cut short any further wrangling Flamininus granted Philip a four-months truce and permission to send envoys to the Senate, provided that he paid an indemnity of 200 talents and sent his son Demetrius and some leading Macedonians to Rome as hostages. Philip accepted on condition that the money and the hostages would be returned, if peace was not made. Rome's allies, who had had no effective voice in the negotiations, were permitted to send envoys to the Senate.[1]

During the four-months truce (which in fact ran its full course) Philip suffered two serious set-backs. The Dardanians broke through his frontiers, probably in August, and devastated inland parts of central Macedonia. Since Philip kept his field army at Tempe in case the truce collapsed, it took him some time to raise another army by conscription. Setting off with a force of 500 cavalry and 6,000 infantry, he caught the Dardanians while they were scattered, raiding 'around Stobi', and drove them out, inflicting heavy losses. Over the years the cantons of Upper Macedonia had suffered severely. One of them, Orestis, on the border with Epirus and Illyris, chose this moment in 197 to defect to Rome. We may suspect that their leaders had been in touch with the pro-Roman leaders in the Epirote League and with Roman forces in Illyris. As the Dardanians had been, and presumably still were, allies of Rome, their invasion was a breach of the truce; and if Rome accepted the Orestae, she would be breaking the truce which no doubt was based on maintaining the *status quo*. Philip, we assume, protested to Flamininus. He left the question of Orestis undecided and forwarded Philip's protest to the Senate.[2]

During the same four months Antiochus, now in league with Rhodes, was making a triumphant advance through Asia Minor and approached the Hellespont. Should Philip seek the alliance of Antiochus and Rhodes against Rome? He must have pondered the matter and decided that Antiochus' army was not capable of defeating the Roman army in Thessaly. He may have put more trust in Flamininus, with whom he had developed a good understanding, than in Antiochus, whom he regarded as a rival. Rome was alarmed by the

---

[1] Plb. 18. 38–9; Livy 33. 13; P*Flam* 9. 4–5; Dio 18. 60; App. *Mac.* 9. 2.

[2] Livy 33. 19. 1–5 (Dardanians). The Orestae defected during the truce (Livy 39. 28. 2 'inter indutias') in time of war 'in bello', i.e. before peace was concluded (Plb. 18. 47. 6); and Philip expected that he would be entitled to discipline them (Livy 39. 23. 6). Walbank, *C* 2. 616 put the defection in winter 198/7 and cited the views of others. Orestis had defected to Molossia in the 360s (see Volume II. 185).

advance of Antiochus, on which she received reports from Eumenes of Pergamum; indeed her intervention was requested by Lampsacus and Smyrna at Eumenes' instigation.[1] Thus both Philip and Rome had reasons for observing the truce.

Flamininus and his Greek allies were not inactive during the truce. They promoted the rise of pro-Roman politicians. The Roman *coup d'état* at Thebes had been followed by fierce party strife throughout Boeotia; and now, when the pro-Macedonian leader, Brachylles, seemed to be winning, Flamininus and the Aetolian general arranged for him to be murdered by three Italians and three Aetolians. This dastardly act caused a popular rising and the massacre of 500 of the hated Roman soldiers. Flamininus demanded an indemnity of 500 talents and was about to let the army loose on Boeotia, when the Achaeans intervened. Through their mediation the indemnity was reduced to 30 talents, and those held guilty of the massacre were handed over.[2]

At Rome the Senate proceeded with routine business, as in 198. Consular elections were held, and then the delegates from Greece and Macedonia were heard. The Senate's proposal to make peace with Macedonia was opposed by one of the new consuls, but it was carried by the Populus Romanus, probably in December 197.[3] The Senate then ascertained that the Macedonian delegates accepted the peace, the terms being stated apparently only in broad terms, and at once sent ten commissioners to settle the details of the terms in consultation with Flamininus.[4]

The commissioners arrived early in 196 with a brief in the form of a decree by the Senate (of which Plb. 18. 44 gives a summary). When it was made known, the Aetolians protested, somewhat tactlessly, that Rome was succeeding Macedonia as tyrant of Greece because she was making fast with Roman garrisons 'the fetters of Greece'—Demetrias, Chalcis, and Corinth. Philip will have protested on other grounds. For the decree not only imposed on him a further indemnity of 1,000 talents (half to be paid at once) and the surrender of his fleet except for an old flagship and five light craft, but also ordered him not to act against the Orestae.[5] The final decisions were announced in mid-

[1] Plb. 30. 31. 6; Livy 33. 38. 1–4; *SIG* 591.

[2] Plb. 18. 43 with 40. 1–4 (see Walbank, *C* 2. 601–2 and 609); Livy 33. 27. 4–29. 12 ('execrabile odium Romanorum').

[3] D. Baronowski in *Phoenix* 37 (1983) 218 ff. puts the end of the consular year in December 197 and the approval of the peace by the Comitia into 196; he reverses the chronological order of two passages in Livy, namely 33. 25. 4–7 and 33. 24. 3–7.

[4] Plb. 18. 42; Livy 33. 24. 1–7. The account in Livy 33. 25. 4–7 and 11, being from an annalistic source, is less worthy of credence.

[5] Our sources do not mention the position in Illyris. This silence suggests that Philip had already withdrawn from Lissus and the Scodra basin. May 52 reckoned that he had withdrawn before 207.

summer 196 at the Isthmian festival, when 'the fetters' were tacitly freed and Philip's protest was disregarded. The herald made proclamation as follows. 'The Roman Senate and the proconsul Titus Quinctius, having outfought King Philip and the Macedonians, liberate the peoples of Corinth, Phocis, Locris, Euboea, Achaea Phthiotis, Magnesia, Thessaly, and Perrhaebia, with freedom from garrison and tribute and with the use of their ancestral laws.' In principle all Greece was free.[1]

Flamininus was overwhelmed with congratulations, and he was soon honoured as a god in new cults at Larissa, Chalcis, Corinth, Argos, Gytheum in Laconia, in Achaea, and no doubt at many other places.[2] These honours resulted from the rise of the pro-Roman parties to power and the expulsion of the pro-Macedonian leaders.

Rome's ambitions were not limited to the Greek mainland. The senatorial decree which the ten commissioners brought from Rome laid it down that 'the Greeks in Asia and in Europe would be free and use their own laws', the Macedonian garrisons were to be withdrawn from Thasos, Lemnos, and seven named cities on the coasts of Thrace and Asia Minor, and Flamininus was to negotiate with Prusias of Bithynia for the liberation of Cius. At the Isthmian festival an embassy from Antiochus was given the first hearing by the ten commissioners, who then issued the following orders to Antiochus. He was to keep his hands off the free cities in Asia, evacuate his men from any city previously held by Ptolemy or Philip, and not to cross into Europe with any armed force. 'The Greeks are not at war any more, and they are not anyone's subjects.' The commissioners said that one of their number would visit Antiochus. That was done in October 196, by which time Antiochus had shown his disregard of the commissioners' orders by operating successfully in eastern Thrace. At the meeting when the commissioners repeated themselves, Antiochus said that Rome had no *locus standi* in Asia, eastern Thrace was inherited from Seleucus Nicator, and Ptolemy was about to marry one of his daughters.[3] These were excellent debating points, fully justified in terms of Hellenistic international law. But the cold facts were that Rome had ordered Philip to keep his hands off the Greek cities in 200 and had answered his debating points by war.

The detailed settlement of Greek affairs kept Flamininus and his army engaged for almost two years. As regards Macedonia and its

---

[1] Plb. 18. 44–6; Livy 33. 30–3. Oreus and Eretria may have been retained by Rome at first, though not among the 'fetters' of Greece. P*Flam* 10–11; App. *Mac.* 9. 2; Val. Max. 4. 8. 5.

[2] For cults see Walbank, *C* 613 f. and add *IG* xii. 9. 931.

[3] Plb. 18. 44. 2; 47. 1–4; 48. 1–2; 50. 5–52. 5 (the claim being based on conquest, at 18. 51. 4 δορίκτητον); D.S. 28. 12.

immediate neighbours (see Fig. 8), he gave Lychnis and Parthus to Pleuratus, so that Philip's frontier was on the east side of Lake Lychnitis (Ochrid). Orestis was declared independent; so too Perrhaebia[1] and Magnesia. As Philip's garrisons departed, fortifications were razed, e.g. at Demetrias (see Fig. 6). Amynander kept the forts he had won from Philip. Despite claims by Aetolia, Leucas went to the Acarnanian League, and in Thessaly a league was set up which included Achaea Phthiotis. Euboea became an independent league of cities, including Chalcis. Phocis, Dolopia, and East Locris chose to enter the Aetolian League. Corinth, Triphylia, and Heraea were awarded to the Achaean League.

When these awards had been made under the peace, Philip was advised by the Roman commissioners to send envoys to Rome on the subject of alliance (Plb. 18. 48. 4 ὑπὲρ συμμαχίας). It was evidently important for the Senate that Philip as the defeated party should sue for terms for the future, and he for his part could not afford to reject the advice. As the following part of Polybius is lost, we are not told what happened. But later events show that Philip was granted a treaty in which the cardinal point was friendship with Rome, but under which unilateral obligations were imposed upon him.[2]

In 195 the last opponent of Rome, Nabis, king of Sparta, who had refused to evacuate Argos, was attacked by the Roman fleet and army. The Romans were supported by 1,500 Macedonians (probably in accordance with the obligations of the new treaty), 10,000 Achaeans, 1,000 Achaean cavalry, 400 Thessalian cavalry, and a great many Spartan exiles; and warships were supplied by Eumenes of Pergamum and by Rhodes. Laconia was devastated and Nabis was forced to capitulate. Flamininus left him on his throne. His policy in general was to get rid of 'the disorderly scum'—Livy's phrase for the pro-Macedonian leaders—and to strengthen the grip of the pro-Roman leaders.

In 194 the Roman forces, led by Flamininus, sailed home to Italy. They were laden with loot of every kind, which had been taken almost entirely from Greek city-states. At Rome huge quantities of gold and silver, bronze and marble statuary, and armaments were carried in the triumphal procession. Before the chariot of Flamininus walked a son of Philip, Demetrius, and the son of Nabis, Armenes.[3]

---

[1] Property confiscated during the war was returned to the people of Chyretiae in Perrhaebia; see *SIG* 593 = Sherk no. 33.

[2] Plb. 18. 47. 5–13. See Appendix 5, where it is suggested that one obligation was to fight on the side of Rome in certain circumstances.

[3] Livy 34. 25. 3; 26. 9–11; 35. 1–2; 52. 4–9; P*Flam* 14. The 'disorderly scum' is at Livy 34. 51. 4 'ex omni colluvione et confusione'.

XXII

COLLABORATION AND SUSPICION BETWEEN MACEDONIA AND ROME (195–179 B.C.)

1. *Collaboration with Rome against Sparta, Antiochus, and Aetolia*

THE Macedonians had no love for Nabis of Sparta who had combined treachery and enmity at Argos, or for the Aetolians and Amynander who had contributed to their defeat at Cynoscephalae, or for the Achaeans who had repaid continuous aid with a treasonable change of allegiance. Thus they were willing enough to honour their treaty with Rome by sending troops to fight against Nabis, and Rome repaid their services with promises to release Demetrius and other hostages and to remit further instalments of the indemnity.

Rome's dealings with Antiochus followed a predictable course. His proposals first to let Rhodes arbitrate between them and then in winter 196/5 to enter into alliance were disregarded, and he campaigned again in Thrace as far as Maronea. He strengthened his diplomatic front by marrying Cleopatra to Ptolemy and Antiochis to Ariarathes, king of Cappadocia, but Eumenes of Pergamum preferred Rome to his offer of another daughter. In autumn 195 he gave asylum to Hannibal, who had fled from Carthage in fear of being victimized by Rome. As this action, normal in Hellenistic states, might be judged provocative elsewhere, Antiochus sent envoys to Rome in winter 194/3. They were sent on by the Senate to Flamininus, who turned a deaf ear to their diplomatic niceties and delivered a blunt ultimatum (no doubt, as instructed by the Senate): Antiochus must either depart from Europe and have *carte blanche* in Asia, or stay in Europe and have Rome defend the cause of Greek liberty in Asia.[1] To this ultimatum only the king could reply. So the envoys arranged for a Roman embassy to go to Asia.

Meanwhile in Greece the Aetolians were active in trying to raise a coalition against Rome. Philip refused their request. Nabis accepted and opened hostilities by attacking towns which had been transferred by Flamininus from Sparta to the Achaean League. The Roman embassy reached the court of Antiochus ahead of an Aetolian envoy.

---

[1] Livy 34. 57. 4–59. 3; D.S. 28. 15; App. *Syr.* 6; Plb. 3. 11. 1–2.

No progress was made, as neither side would yield. Then the Aetolian envoy arrived with the report that Nabis and Philip had joined Aetolia (the lie about Philip being entirely typical of Aetolian diplomacy), but he could not bring Antiochus to a decision.

In 192 a Roman fleet returned to Greek waters. With its help the Achaeans and their allies[1] checked the successful campaign of Nabis and soon blockaded him in Sparta town. Flamininus and other commissioners toured the Greek states, confirming or introducing their own supporters, for instance in Demetrias, and Flamininus attended the spring meeting of the Aetolian Assembly. There he heard the Aetolians decide to summon Antiochus 'to liberate Greece and arbitrate between them and Rome', and he was offered a further meeting 'on the banks of the Tiber' (Livy 35. 33. 8). The Aetolians seized Demetrias, but failed to take by surprise Chalcis and Sparta, where an Aetolian commander assassinated Nabis, but was overcome by a general rising. The Roman fleet, helped by Eumenes of Pergamum, held Chalcis and Corinth. At this point Antiochus took his decision. He sacrificed to Athena at Troy (as Xerxes had done in 480 and Alexander the Great in 334), and he embarked on his fleet six elephants, 500 cavalry, and 10,000 infantry from an army which was already operating near the Hellespont.[2] He and his armada joined the Aetolians at Demetrias in the Gulf of Pagasae and he was appointed commander-in-chief of the joint forces, to which Amynander of Athamania was soon recruited (see Fig. 6).

At that time, early autumn 192, Philip faced a critical decision. In the likely event of a war between Antiochus and Rome Philip held a key position. The treaty of friendship which Rome had imposed upon him in 196 was something which he need not feel bound to honour. If he should abandon Rome and join Antiochus, the reinforcements which Antiochus said would come by sea next spring, when sailing conditions were favourable, could come by land in a month or so, and the combination of Philip, Antiochus, Aetolia, and Athamania could bring or force Acarnania and Epirus into the coalition and compel Rome to fight for her foothold in Illyris. On the other hand, if Philip should honour his treaty and stay with Rome, he could continue to block Antiochus' overland communications, secure Rome's route of entry into northern Greece, and probably keep Epirus and Acarnania on the Roman side. Moreover, his own military forces were of critical

---

[1] We do not know who the allies were. Some leading men of Acarnania and Epirus attended the meeting at Tegea, probably as mediators (Livy 35. 27. 11; see *HE* 622).

[2] Livy 35. 43. 3–6; 36. 19. 11. The fleet of 100 warships was accompanied by 200 merchantmen, which ferried supplies from Asia (cf. 36. 20. 7–8). Antiochus refortified Demetrias as his base.

importance in the immediate future, whichever side he chose to join. For the nonce he stayed inactive. But with the forces of Antiochus so close to his frontiers both in Thrace and in Thessaly, neutrality meant that he did not intend to join Antiochus and Antiochus' allies.

Antiochus had chosen his time well in the sense that Rome was unlikely to send a large army overseas until early in 191. He thus had five or six months in which to bring the Greek states to his side, augment his army with more troops from Asia, and adopt his positions for meeting a Roman offensive. Diplomacy failed at the start; for it only elicited a declaration of war by the Achaean League, at the instigation of Flamininus. In December 192 a force of 500 Roman soldiers was defeated in battle on its way to Chalcis. This success prompted the accession to Antiochus of Boeotia, Chalcis, and Euboea; but they did not provide troops. As far as possible the Greek states were playing for safety. Epirus was typical. Its leaders asked Antiochus not to involve the country in war with Rome, but he might use their cities and harbours, provided he gave protection from Rome by land and sea. Antiochus made an evasive reply.[1] When Elis asked for help against the Achaeans, he sent 1,000 men. Two months had passed in ineffective policy when Hannibal gave Antiochus some timely advice in a speech, composed by Polybius and of doubtful historicity.[2] Philip, he argued, should either be enticed into the coalition or else diverted by attacks on his Thracian frontier, and Antiochus should move his fleet to Corcyra and his forces to the territory of Byllis (see Fig. 8). From these positions Antiochus, he maintained, could protect Epirus (which would then support him), oppose a Roman landing in Illyris, and go on to invade Italy. What Hannibal was not permitted to mention was the large Roman fleet at Corinth and the difficulty of supplying from Demetrias an army on the western side of the Pindus range, especially if Philip stayed with Rome and threatened the passes over the mountain range. Antiochus chose instead, together with his allies, to force the cities of Thessaly to his side and make Thessaly his base of operations.

During the autumn of 192 Rome laid the keels of fifty quinqueremes and sent Baebius in command of 3,000 men to Apollonia Illyrica around November, in case a war should eventuate. Meanwhile envoys arrived at Rome from Philip with the offer of troops, money, and grain in the event of war. That particular offer was not accepted (war had not yet been declared), but Philip was told that he would earn the gratitude of Rome if he did not fail Acilius, the consul to whom Greece was allocated for 191. Other envoys came to Rome, apparently at the

---

[1] Plb. 20. 3; Livy 36. 5. 1–8; H*E* 623.
[2] Livy 36. 7. 2–21, seen from App. *Syr.* 14 to have come from Polybius. Hannibal, a brilliant strategist by any standard, is less likely to have put forward such ideas than Polybius.

same time, from Ptolemy, Masinissa, and Carthage with similar offers. It is probable that Rome had asked the four states to say in accordance with the terms of their treaties what help they could give in the event of war. The attack on Roman troops at Delium caused Rome to declare war at the turn of the year. By then Philip had decided to side with Rome and had made contact with Baebius. His decision had been caused in part by the folly of Antiochus, who sent a pretender to the Macedonian throne to collect and bury the bones of the Macedonian dead at Cynoscephalae, thereby taunting Philip for his failure to have done so.[1]

Philip and Baebius now planned joint operations (see Fig. 6). Philip now and later was apparently not under Roman supreme command; and it was agreed that Philip should keep any places which he might capture.[2] Appius Claudius and 2,000 Roman soldiers were escorted through Macedonia to Gonnus, overlooking Larissa, which was being besieged by Antiochus. By lighting a great many camp fires Claudius gave the impression of a huge army and Antiochus withdrew hastily to Demetrias. Larissa was secured by a Roman garrison, and the Macedonian and Roman forces went into winter quarters. Antiochus unwisely wasted two months in festivities at Chalcis, his chosen base, and the discipline of his inactive army became relaxed.

In March 191 Antiochus was persuaded by the Aetolians to invade Acarnania, but on hearing that the main Roman army had landed in Illyris he hastened back to Chalcis. During his absence Philip and Baebius had been capturing cities in Perrhaebia and north Thessaly and on the Thessalian side of the Pindus passes. All was ready for the advance of the consular army through Epirus.[3] It reached Larissa with fifteen elephants, 2,000 cavalry, 20,000 infantry, and some Illyrian skirmishers. As it moved south from there, city after city surrendered and the garrisons put in by Antiochus were allowed to serve with Philip or go back unarmed to Antiochus. Altogether 5,000 soldiers joined Philip, and by liberating any Athamanian prisoners and sending them ahead he won over Athamania, from which Amynander fled to the Aetolian stronghold, Ambracia. The two-pronged advance kept the Aetolians on the defensive, and they sent only 4,000 soldiers in answer to the orders of Antiochus, who was holding a defensive position at Thermopylae. The failure of those 4,000 to hold the passes inland led to the total defeat of Antiochus' army, outnumbered by at

---

[1] See for Baebius Livy 35. 20. 12 (3,000 infantry), 35. 24. 7 ('omnibus copiis') and App. *Syr.* 16 (2,000 men sent ahead). For offers of help Livy 36. 4 and see Appendix 5 for the interpretation given here. For Antiochus Livy 36. 8. 3–5 and App. *Syr.* 16.

[2] E.g. Livy 39. 23. 10.

[3] Livy 37. 6. 1; supplies being brought by sea and through Epirus, which evidently joined Rome.

least two to one, which fled via Chalcis to Ephesus.[1] Philip was ill at the time of the battle, probably 24 April, but he sent his congratulations to the consul, Acilius Glabrio. His own policy seemed to have been justified. He had chosen the winning side and expected to share the fruits of victory.

The Romans were anxious to make a settlement in Greece as quickly as possible, because they were planning a major offensive by land and sea against Antiochus in the coming year, 190. Thus no reprisals were exacted from Euboea, Phocis, and Boeotia, when they surrendered, and in the Peloponnese Flamininus rewarded the loyal Achaean League by adding Messenia to its membership. At the same time it lost Zacynthus, which Rome took over as a naval base for the offensive by sea. The consul Acilius and Philip collaborated in operations against the Aetolians and the Athamanians. In a competitive spirit Acilius laid siege to Heraclea and Philip to Lamia, a few miles apart. Acilius succeeded first. He then granted a truce to the Aetolians and thereby deprived Philip of Lamia, which he was on the point of capturing and keeping as his possession. A division of interest was already appearing.[2] But the truce broke down. Acilius sent Philip northwards, where he captured Demetrias and other coast towns, completed the conquest of Perrhaebia, and invaded Dolopia and Aperantia.[3] Meanwhile Acilius marched south to Naupactus, where the main Aetolian forces were concentrated, and conducted a two-months siege without success. This operation enabled Philip to advance unopposed. However, Flamininus persuaded Acilius to raise the siege and grant a truce, so that the Aetolians could send envoys to Rome. Thereby he prevented Philip from making further gains of territory; for these gains were inconsistent with Flamininus' avowed policy, 'the liberation of the Greek city-states'. As all parties withdrew to winter quarters, Demetrius and probably other Macedonian hostages were returned to Philip, and a promise was made to remit the last instalments of the indemnity, if he remained loyal to Rome.[4] For Macedonia was to be an important base for the attack on Antiochus.

---

[1] Antiochus received no help from other Greek states (Livy 36. 15. 3–5); his 'liberation' had meant garrisons and the odds were heavily in favour of Rome.

[2] Plb. 20. 11 marked the division by retailing a private conversation between Philip and a captured Aetolian envoy, Nicander, in which Philip suggested that Macedonia and Aetolia should not now take advantage of one another's difficulties, the implication being that Rome was their common enemy. It is most unlikely that Philip would have been so incautious or that either of them reported the conversation, let alone faithfully, if it happened. But see Walbank, *Ph* 206.

[3] It has been suggested (see Walbank, *Ph* 207) that Philip should have invaded lower Aetolia; but the only good route through Aperantia went via the Inachus valley and was therefore exposed to attack from the Aetolian stronghold at Ambracia (see above, p. 406). Even the powerful Roman forces in 189 felt it essential to capture Ambracia before threatening to invade Aetolia.

[4] Plb. 21. 3; Livy 36. 35. 13.

The army which landed in Illyris in spring 190 was commanded by L. Cornelius Scipio and accompanied by Scipio Africanus. As they passed through Greece, they persuaded the Aetolians to accept a truce for six months and marched through Macedonia, where Philip had made elaborate preparations for their reception. He was not asked to contribute a contingent, but he allowed any Macedonian volunteers to join the Roman force. A close friendship was formed between Philip and Scipio Africanus, who announced at last that the final instalments of the indemnity were remitted. Thereafter the Senate and the Scipios rejected every offer of Antiochus to negotiate by making maximum demands, and their army won a decisive victory at Magnesia late in the year. The terms of peace for Antiochus were an indemnity of 15,000 talents (a world record at the time) and the surrender of his elephants, most of his fleet, and all lands in Thrace, and Asia west of the Taurus range. Such terms had a familiar ring for Philip, and they must have alarmed him; for he was now surrounded on all sides except to the north by peoples who were tied to the *status quo* under 'settlements' which Rome regarded as irrevocable.

Once the Roman army had passed through Macedonia to the Hellespont, the Senate had no need to humour Philip. The truce with Aetolia ended in November 190, when the Senate's demand for an indemnity of 1,000 talents and alliance or else unconditional surrender were rejected. Amynander and the Aetolians then mounted a winter offensive in mountainous terrain, drove Philip's garrisons out of Athamania, Aperantia, and Dolopia, and defeated him, when he counterattacked with 6,000 Macedonians. The Roman troops in Greece did not come to his aid. He realized that his treaty with Rome was worthless, where his own interests were concerned, and he learnt that the Senate in Rome and the Scipios in Asia were listening to accusations against himself made by Amynander.[1] However, like Rome's other allies friends, or co-belligerents—the Epirote League, the Achaean League, and Pleuratus, king of the Ardiaei—Philip responded to the request for help in the attack on Ambracia, which lasted through the summer of 189 (see Fig. 12). His elder son, Perseus, now in his early twenties, commanded a Macedonian army, which invaded Dolopia and Amphilochia and diverted an Aetolian relief force; thereafter he withdrew, ravaging as he went, but not acquiring territory. Before Ambracia fell and Aetolia could be invaded, the Aetolians obtained peace on terms which were negotiated by Athens, Rhodes, and Amynander without consultation of Philip and others who had helped Rome. The *pax Romana* was to be dictated by the Senate and the Populus Romanus.

---

[1] Plb. 21. 25. 1–7.

The provisional terms of the peace were made known at Ambracia, and envoys went to Rome from the Aetolians, the Rhodians, and the Athenians and from the Roman consul. An invitation was not extended to Philip. He therefore urged his friends in Rome, such as Scipio Africanus, to oppose the approval of the terms. These made no mention of lands and cities taken by him from the Aetolians, whereas all lands and cities taken by Rome or entering into friendship with Rome since 192 were to be exempt from interference by Aetolia. An indemnity of 500 talents was to go to Rome alone. 'The allies' were compensated only in that prisoners of war and hostages were to be returned to them by Aetolia; and here prisoners and hostages taken during the period of Rome's alliance with Aetolia against Macedonia were made an exception. The friends of Philip in Rome had no success. The terms were approved by the Senate and the Populus Romanus.[1]

When the terms of the settlement were put into effect, it seems that Amynander was given Athamania, and the Aetolians received Aperantia and most of Dolopia, despite Philip's attempt to use the influence of his friends at Rome. Even his claim to the cities which he had captured in the war in Thessaly, Magnesia and Perrhaebia, was not confirmed by Rome. And in Thrace the Roman commander chose to draw the line of the frontier between Macedonia and Thrace along an inland road, thereby excluding Maronea from Macedonia. Philip had good reason to feel affronted; the more so because Rome had rewarded the services of Eumenes of Pergamum with a grant of some Greek cities and large tracts of land.

The Roman settlements in the Balkans and in Asia Minor were not prompted by any principles of international law or considerations of services rendered by allies and friends. They were solely in the interest of Rome. Because her citizen army was to return to Italy, she annexed no territory except Cephallenia and Zacynthus, important as naval stations; for her presence in the Aegean area was to be primarily naval. She intended to control the Balkans and Asia Minor by the system known as 'divide et impera', namely by establishing a balance of relatively weak powers and using her authority to maintain it.

Aetolia occupied an important position in the system. Although Oeniadae was awarded to Acarnania and Ambracia was made a free city, Aetolia received Heraclea from Rome and her League included West Locris, East Locris, Doris, Amphilochia, Aperantia, and most of Dolopia. She was unique in being expressly tied in her foreign policy to

[1] Plb. 21. 31–2; Livy 38. 10. 3 adding Amphilochia. 'Allies' at Plb. 32. 3 and 5, and at Livy 38. 11. 2 and 4.

the will of Rome.[1] The Thessalian League, now reconstituted, was given all the cities captured by Rome except Heraclea, and it could be relied upon to be hostile both to Aetolia and to Macedonia. The independence of Orestis was maintained by Rome, and Macedonia was not allowed to expand eastwards. There Eumenes of Pergamum, an enemy of Philip, was given the Chersonese and other Thracian territory; and he and Rhodes were awarded parts of Asia Minor. It had already been made clear by the Senate that official relations with Rome, whether of 'friendship' or 'alliance', allowed of no deviation. The Epirote League had tried to ensure itself with both Rome and Antiochus in 192/1, and on the defeat of Antiochus the Roman consul said that he did not know whether to treat the Epirotes as active enemies or as defeated enemies. The threat was one of massacre and enslavement. He granted them an armistice of ninety days, during which a deputation was interrogated by the Senate at Rome. In the end the League was pardoned.[2]

Philip took every step possible to convince Rome of his pacific attitude. For instance, his coins in copper no longer carried emblems of war. Instead, they were marked with such signs of peace as an eagle standing not on a thunderbolt as in the past, but on a plough, two goats reclining, and the stern of a merchantship, and they harked back to the mythical past in showing Perseus with his weapon (the *harpe*) or expressed worship (e.g. of Artemis Tauropolus).[3]

2. *Rome's hostility and Macedonia's recovery*

The political changes which had happened during the war or as a result of the settlement were accompanied by party strife in each city-state, and the ambiguous situation of the cities held by Philip in and around Thessaly added fuel to the fire. The tension between the Thessalian League and Philip was visible in a struggle for control of the Amphictyonic League, now that Delphi was liberated. For Rome declared Delphi 'free and immune from tax' in a decree of 189. The Thessalians predominated on the Council, which sent a special envoy to Rome who accused Philip of plotting.[4] Critics of Philip knew that they would get a sympathetic hearing; for it was obvious that he had been slighted under the Roman settlement, and the Roman army on

---

[1] Plb. 21. 32. 2 and 4, specifically 'to preserve the rule and power of Rome', a vague phrase which Rome could interpret at her own pleasure.

[2] Livy 35. 36. 8–11. The League gained greatly from trade with the Roman bridgehead in Illyris. This has been demonstrated by a hoard of 441 silver coins in a hoard laid down *c.* 200 B.C. near Apollonia; for there were almost more coins of the Epirote League than of Epidamnus and Apollonia put together. See *SA* 1972. 1. 49 ff.

[3] See Mamroth, 1935. 234 f.   [4] Sherk no. 1 (Delphi); *SIG* 613 ll. 33–5.

its way back from Asia attributed an attack by Thracians to treachery on Philip's part (Livy 38. 40. 8 'non sine Philippi...fraude'). Under these conditions Philip should have been circumspect. But he courted trouble, when he moved the road, and so the frontier, to include Maronea in his kingdom, and then intervened at the request of one side in a party strife and gained control of Aenus, which was situated further to the east.

The reckoning came when envoys from Thessaly, Perrhaebia, Athamania, and Pergamum arrived at Rome, evidently by prearrangement, to lay charges against Philip. He sent his own envoys. The Senate heard all the envoys, but then deputed the decision to three commissioners, who called a meeting at Tempe in spring 185. The procedure was that of a trial with the king in the dock. The prosecuting envoys spoke first. Philip himself replied, attacking his critics, emphasizing his services to Rome, and insisting on the pact made with him by the Roman commanders in 191. That pact was at the heart of the matter. Had Philip been promised any city captured by him from the Aetolians and the Athamanians, or only such cities as had 'originally' been Aetolian? The hearing was in fact a farce, because that question could only have been answered conclusively by the Roman commanders, and one of them was sitting there in judgement as a commissioner, M. Baebius Tamphilus. He made no statement. There was no summing up. The verdict was the withdrawal of Macedonian garrisons from all cities under dispute and the limiting of the Macedonian kingdom to its 'ancient' frontiers (these, not being defined, would lead to further dispute). Charges not involving these issues were deferred for a future occasion.[1]

The commissioners then moved to Thessalonica to hear accusations by the envoys of Eumenes and by some exiles from Maronea, which Philip had to answer in person. The commissioners decided to refer the matter to the Senate, because the solution depended on what the ten Roman commissioners had said; but in the interim Philip was to remove his garrisons from Maronea and Aenus (see Figs. 1 and 3). At the end of 185 the Senate went through the whole process with envoys from the contestants and decided that the two cities should be free. To show their distrust of Philip they purposed to send out yet another commission to see that Philip carried out the various orders of that year.[2] What happened next is uncertain. Philip evidently withdrew his garrison from Maronea, because some Thracians broke into the town at night and killed many of the citizens. Polybius attributed the

---

[1] Livy 39. 23. 6–26. 14, giving a full account from Polybius; see two fragments of Polybius 22. 6. 1–6 and 6. 7.

[2] Plb. 22. 6. 1–6; Livy 39. 24. 6–14 (see Walbank, *C* 3. 184).

Thracian incursion to a plot by Philip, who supposed (according to Polybius) that no one would dare to accuse him. When the commission, headed by Appius Claudius, arrived, Philip was asked to send two Macedonian officers to Rome for interrogation without being told what the accusation was. With the agreement of the commissioners he sent one officer, Cassander. However, Cassander died *en route* somewhere in Epirus. Philip, says Polybius, poisoned him.[1] This story is on a par with the alleged plot of Philip inspiring the Thracians to attack the Roman army in eastern Thrace. The alternative is more probable, namely that the Thracians saw their chance in both cases and took it. What mattered was that the commissioners showed their distrust of Philip once more, refused to state the charge against him, and did not allow him to defend himself.

It hardly needed a session with his friends, Apelles and Philocles, as Polybius reported, for Philip to reach the obvious conclusion that the estrangement between Macedonia and Rome was public knowledge, and that he should prepare for the possibility of war. At the same time he tried to defend himself against the charges deferred from spring 185. To this end he sent his son Demetrius, Apelles, and Philocles to speak for him in Rome.[2] They faced envoys from Thessalian towns, the Thessalian League, Perrhaebia, Athamania, Epirus, Illyria, and Pergamum, who took three days to present their charges against Philip. Even the Senate shrank from divining the truth in this farrago of king-baiting; so after persuading Demetrius to read out some notes which Philip had given him the Senate abandoned that part of the inquiry, but made it clear that Philip owed his escape solely to the excellent impression which Demetrius had made both during his six years as a hostage and now at the hearing. The Senate's hope that Demetrius would succeed Philip was not concealed.

The Senate then heard the envoys of Eumenes accuse Philip of having sent help to Prusias, his ally of long standing, in a current war and of keeping his garrisons in Maronea and Aenus. Philocles answered the charges. The Senate said that it was sending a commissioner, Q. Marcius Philippus, and it would not tolerate its orders being disobeyed.[3] In spring 183, when the commissioner arrived, Philip withdrew his garrisons and obeyed some other instructions; and in winter 183/2, in accordance with the report of the commissioner, the Senate told Macedonia's envoys that Philip must not even appear to act in any way against the wishes of the Senate. In winter 182/1 Philip

---

[1] Plb. 22. 13–14; Livy 39. 34.   [2] Plb. 22. 14. 7–11; Livy 39. 35. 1–3.
[3] Plb. 23. 1–3 and 4. 16; Livy 39. 46. 6–11 and 48. 5; J. 32. 2. 3–5; App. *Mac.* 9. 6. Marcius was on terms of guest-friendship with Philip (Livy 42. 38. 8–9); this is confirmed by coins (see E. A. Sydenham, *The Coinage of the Roman Republic* (London, 1952) 56 n. 477).

kept diplomatic contact by sending Apelles and Philocles to Rome, where they learnt more about the support which Flamininus and others were giving to Demetrius.[1] No shadow of doubt was left. The Senate was determined to clip the wings of Macedonia as short as possible, and Flamininus and others were hoping to see Philip replaced by Demetrius, whom they expected to behave as a client king.

During the years of collaboration and disillusion with Rome Philip had been restoring the resources and capabilities of his kingdom. Eighteen years of peace till his death in 179—broken only by minor operations in 191 and 189—gave the country a much-needed respite and made a remarkable economic recovery possible. The most serious loss was in the number of Macedones who formed the phalanx (including the Peltasts); for with at least 10,000 killed or captured at Cynoscephalae and a further 1,000 actual and potential phalangites disappearing with the defection of Orestis, the kernel of Macedonian military power was more than cut in half. Philip now 'compelled the Macedonians to beget children and to raise them all', no doubt by methods familiar in modern times; but twenty or thirty years were needed for this policy to result in a larger reservoir of adult man-power.[2] In the meantime he could add to the normal intake, based on the previous birth-rate, of recruits for the phalanx by drawing on Greek-speaking immigrants or/and on non-Greek-speaking people within the kingdom; but this might weaken the prestige and co-hesion of the phalangite troops. We do not know what he did in this regard.

Macedonia had also suffered an overall decline in population, not only through the continuous wars abroad, but also through ravages caused by the marauding Romans, Illyrians, and Dardanians, who swept thousands of people into slavery as spoil. Philip filled some of the gaps at once by withdrawing his garrison troops from abroad—perhaps 20,000 or so (see p. 431 above); they were mainly mercenaries, but they were likely to accept settlement on the land. And he resettled in Macedonia the populations which he withdrew from cities in Thessaly, especially those of the Enipeus valley. The constant party warfare of the Greek city-states gave off waves of refugees who might be tempted to settle in Macedonia on lands which the king could make available. Moreover, 'he transplanted to Macedonia a great multitude of Thracians'; for they were skilled in agriculture, mining, and road-

---

[1] Plb. 23. 8. 1–2 and 9. 5–7; Livy 39. 53. 10–11; 40. 2–3 and 20. 5–6.

[2] Livy 39. 24. 3. The phalangites were drawn from the Greek-speaking peoples living mainly in Lower and Upper Macedonia west of the Axius river. It is these peoples who were to make up the losses. Between 1944 and 1972 Albania trebled its population by setting targets for the production of children, village by village, and by imposing the capital sentence on any form of contraception; other societies have preferred to offer rewards for large families.

making.[1] Although we know few details, the net result by the time of Philip's death was a very well-populated kingdom.

With so many new settlers available, Philip reorganized the structure of his kingdom for military and economic purposes. The peace with Rome removed the threat of invasion from the coastal areas, and he was now able to strengthen the western and northern frontiers which had been pierced by the Romans, Illyrians, and Dardanians. Polybius has preserved a memory of this reorganization, though he saw it merely as an example of the impious and criminal acts of the king at a time when he was planning to go to war against Rome.

'He transferred the enfranchised men (τοὺς πολιτικοὺς ἄνδρας) with their women and children from the most distinguished coastal cities and transplanted them to the area now called Emathia, but in earlier times Paeonia. He filled the (said) cities with Thracians and barbarians; for he supposed that they would show a more abiding loyalty in the circumstances. (23. 10. 4–5)

Here οἱ πολιτικοί were the Macedones proper, the military class from which the phalanx was recruited. They and their families were transferred to the inland Emathia, the fertile region between Bylazora (Titov Veles) and Antigoneia (north of the Demir Kapu).[2] They and their descendants were to form a military reserve for deployment against threats from the north-west from Polog, from the north down the Axius valley, and from western Thrace via Pautalia (Kjustendil). In 183 Philip founded a new city, no doubt for a settlement of Macedones proper, 'in Deuriopus near the river Erigon' and named it Perseïs in honour of his intended successor, Perseus (see Fig. 3). It was in the plain called Deuriopus, perhaps just north of the Monastir gap, which Sulpicius had traversed in the invasion of 199, and it was to be a strong-point facing the passes from the west (used by the later Via Egnatia) and the north-west (the 'Pelagoniae fauces' by Bučin). Philip may well have founded similar cities elsewhere, which have not been mentioned in our sources.[3]

The economic strength of Macedonia rested on the following

[1] For Thessaly see Livy 32. 13. 6 'homines qui sequi possent sedibus excibat' and 39. 25. 8. For political refugees from early times see the case of Mycenae (Volume II. 103) and for non-Greek peoples settled in Macedonia see Volume II. 660 f.; for road-making see Arr. *An.* 1. 26. 1.
[2] See Volume I. Map 1. For Emathia see Volume II. 145 and 657, and for Macedones in this region Volume I. 173 f., citing inscriptions. For a different interpretation see Walbank, *C* 3. 231. The move has to be from the coastal towns, not to the coastal Emathia, but to the inland Emathia.
[3] Livy 39. 53. 14–16, where 'haud procul Stobis' goes not with 'Perseïs', but with the confluence of the Erigon and the Axius. See Volume I. 69 with n. 3. and Map 9. A different location was given by Heuzey (see Volume I. 174 n. 3) and Walbank, *C* 3. 226, citing other writers. Philip II had founded a number of such cities to strengthen his frontiers' defences (see Volume II. 653–7).

resources. The great plain of Lower Macedonia and the wide cantons of Upper Macedonia, the middle and upper Axius catchment areas, and eastern Macedonia produced an abundance of cereals, and the full gathering of the great harvest was possible, when the phalanx-men were available as they were in peacetime. The Alpine pastures throughout Macedonia and the coastal pastures, irrigated by perennial rivers, supported huge herds of cattle, horses, sheep, and goats, partly transhumant and partly kept locally, which no longer suffered from the raids of marauding Romans, Illyrians, Dardanians, and Thracians. These basic staples of diet were augmented by fish from the numerous lakes, trout rivers, and silt-fed lagoons and shallows of the Thermaic and Strymonian Gulfs, and by fruit, nuts, grapes, and olives, the last especially in Chalcidice. Philip now developed these resources by settling Thracians, Gauls, and Illyrians as agricultural labourers in the rich coastal plains. The rural economy was supported by a fine road system and by the numerous market towns, from which the farmers went out to their work. Towns and cities had their own local administration and pride, and it was through them that the king channelled his communications and conducted recruitment and conscription.[1]

Macedonia exported a surplus of cereals and animal products, many kinds of timber (including wood for shipbuilding), several precious metals and finished goods, such as weapons especially for northern markets. By royal charter Philip directed the trade in timber, floated down the large rivers or felled on the coastal ranges. In these years of peace Philip 'increased the revenues of his kingdom not only by agricultural production and harbour dues. He also redeveloped old mines which had gone out of use, and he opened new mines in many places' (Livy 39. 24. 2). As the king owned all mineral resources, he was able to improve methods of extraction and subsidize prospecting with excellent effect, as Philip II had done. Thrace too had rich mines, and it is probable that many of the Thracian settlers worked in mining, as we do not hear of slave gangs in Macedonia. Gold, silver, copper, iron, lead, nickel, and molybdenum were obtained, and Macedonian workmanship in metals was of the highest order.[2]

The Macedonian king was able to deal in gold and silver in the form of bullion rather than in coinage, when he had to pay out large sums of money. This was convenient when payments were to be made in

---

[1] Plb. 4.66.7 (army home for the harvest); 23. 10. 4 (agricultural labour, not urban proletariat); Livy 42. 51. 5 'Thracibus incolis'; 45. 30. 5 'incolas quoque permultos Gallos et Illyrios, impigros cultores'; 37.7.13 (roads, bridges, culverts); 33. 3. 2 and 19. 3 ('per oppida' and 'per urbes').

[2] See Volume I. 12 ff. and Map I for the positions of mines.

bullion to Scerdilaidas at 20 talents for a year's co-belligerency (Plb. 4. 29. 7), to Cotys at 200 talents for a year's service by his cavalry (Livy 42. 67. 5), and to Gentius at 300 talents for his collaboration against Rome (Plb. 29. 4. 7). After his defeat at Cynoscephalae Philip had to pay to Rome 200 talents at the time of the truce and then an indemnity of 1,000 talents, of which 500 talents had to be paid at once (Plb. 18. 44. 7); and the indemnity to be paid by Antiochus was to be 'in fine silver' (Livy 38. 38. 13 'probi argenti'). 'Macedonian gold' was the preference of Gallic mercenaries in 277 (Polyaen. 4. 6. 17), and the Bastarnae wanted Perseus to pay 20,000 of them a huge sum of gold (P*Aem* 12. 6); in such cases bullion may have been used. Bulk quantities of refined gold and silver, measured by weight, were carried among the spoils in the triumph of Flamininus over Macedonia (P*Flam* 14. 2 χρυσίου συγκεχωνευμένου λίτρας), and as much bullion silver as coined silver was carried in the triumph of Aemilius Paullus.[1] There were very large numbers of gold 'Philippeioi' in circulation during the reigns of Philip and Perseus, as we see from their prominence in the triumphs of Flamininus and Paullus (P*Flam* 14. 2 Φιλιππείους χρυσοῦς and P*Aem* 33. 4 οἱ τὸ χρυσοῦν νόμισμα φέροντες). They had been coined by Philip II and the kings who came after him, and it seems likely that Philip V minted an issue of them; for a gold Philippic with a crude representation of Heracles, which might perhaps have been to the taste of the Bastarnae, has been attributed to Philip V.[2]

The dating of Philip's gold and silver coinage presents problems. Gaebler listed two types only of silver tetradrachm. He dated to *c.* 212 his first type, which has the diademed head of the king, bearded, and on the reverse the striding Athena, her thunderbolt poised for action, evidently Athena Alcidemus; and he thought that this Athena commemorated the success of Philip in capturing Lissus at that time. However, he failed to note that one of the two monograms on the reverse is **EP** (see Pl. I*m*), which occurs on all the bronze coins of Perseus except one in Gaebler's publication, thus making this mint-master active into the 160s. As it is highly improbable that a mint-master served for so long, we should date this type of tetradrachm much closer to the reign of Perseus.[3] Gaebler dated to immediately after 187 the second type of tetradrachm precisely because it carries the monogram of Zoilus, who was active as mint-master early in the reign of Perseus (see p. 462 below). This type bears the head of the hero

---

[1] See Meloni, *Perseo* 433 ff. for the various figures; and Youroukova 32 for coins and silver ingots together in a hoard of the mid-second century B.C. at Belitsa near Razlog.

[2] *Rev. Num.* 9 (1967) 242 ff.

[3] Gaebler III. 2. 190 no. 2 and Pl. 34. 16; for Perseus' coins see p. 503 below. For the association of the thunderbolt with Philip see *Anth. Pal.* 6. 115.

Perseus in his standard griffin-ended and winged helmet set in the centre of a Macedonian shield, and on the reverse the club of Heracles inside an oak-wreath (Pl. I*n*).[1] It is thus evident that both types of tetradrachm should be dated to the last decade or so of Philip's reign. Walbank and M. Price followed Gaebler in regarding the first type of tetradrachm as Philip's first coinage, early in his reign and in Walbank's case 'commemorative', i.e. of some victory.[2] Price dated the second type to after 196, because he saw in the griffin-end to the helmet a tribute by Philip to Rome which had a griffin on her *denarius* at this time.[3] But this is not a convincing reason; for the griffin is appropriate to Perseus and as such is found on the bronze coins of King Perseus who was not paying any tributes to Rome, and in general the griffin was part of the artistic stock-in-trade and not peculiar to Rome.

If we consider the dating of these tetradrachms *de novo*, we should note that Demetrius II coined only in bronze and that Antigonus Doson coined probably not at all (see pp. 594–5 below). The reason was that the mines, which were of course in the ownership of the king, did not yield a sufficient quantity of silver. There are no grounds for supposing that the situation changed for the better in Philip's earlier years; indeed he had to pay a heavy indemnity after 197, evidently in bullion silver (Livy 33. 30. 7–8 and 38. 38. 13 'argenti probi'). The great change came with the opening of new mines at some time after 186 in Livy's chronology. It was then that Philip produced his two types of silver tetradrachms with the mint-masters Zoilus and **EP** coming into activity in those years and continuing to act in the reign of Perseus[4]. The first type in Gaebler's list took its reverse from Antigonus Gonatas' tetradrachms, the last royal coinage in silver, and it showed the war goddess of Macedonia ready to defend her country. The adoption of the hero Perseus for the second type of tetradrachm and also for the didrachm, the drachm, and several types of the bronze

---

[1] Gaebler III. 2. 190 no. 3. He was following Mamroth, 1930, who also failed to note the occurrence of the monogram EP on the coins of both kings. Mamroth assumed that there was only one mint-master at a time, operating for several years, although two were cited together in P*Aem* 23. 6 as τοὺς ἐπὶ τοῦ νομίσματος at Pella in 167, and that minor mint-officials operated one at a time for a year only and represented themselves in the choice of a lesser emblem, e.g. a thunderbolt or a *harpe*, for their year of office. Although it is highly unlikely that a minor official rather than the mint-master or (more probably) the king himself chose the emblem ('das Beizeichen'), Mamroth went on to arrange a seven-year run for the silver coins with the head of Perseus from 186 to 179.

[2] Walbank, *Ph* 224, citing Mamroth, 1930. 290 ff. and noting that Seltman, *GC* 224 had dated this type to *c.* 201. Price 28 and 45 dated it to 'the late third century B.C.'.

[3] Price 29 'his new coinage reflects his Roman connections only in a minor detail', and 45 with the date '188–178 B.C.'; this was not something suggested by Mamroth and Gaebler.

[4] For Zoilus see Gaebler III. 2. 195 note to no. 1. For EP see III. 2. 190 no. 2 Pl. 34. 16 to the right of Athena, and 196 nos. 6–11. The monogram ⴹ stands presumably for EP on a coin mentioned in *ANSMN* 12 (1966) 61.

coins of Philip is likely to have reference to Perseus as the heir apparent; for Perseus was twenty-seven or so in 186, and the new city of 183 was named Perseïs.[1] The likelihood is increased by the fact that the hero Perseus had not been portrayed before on a royal coinage.

When did Philip obtain the precious ore to coin in gold? Most probably through opening new mines, as his predecessor Philip II had done. This suggestion is strengthened by the fact that the gold stater[2] has the head of the hero Perseus, and on the reverse the club of Heracles, both of which are on the second type of silver tetradrachm. We conclude, then, that Philip first coined in gold and silver in the years after 186, and that this coinage is an indication of the economic recovery in the years of peace and a sign indeed of prosperity.

Something similar seems to have happened in Thrace. During the prosperous period of the late fourth century and early third century a Thracian dynast called Skostokos was coining silver tetradrachms and drachms, as well as bronze pieces, with his own name. His tetradrachms have been found on the right bank of the Hebrus. During the period when the Gauls dominated the interior of Thrace, 278–216, their king Cavarus coined a very little in silver and mainly in bronze; and a dynast Adaeus issued many coins but only in bronze until *c*. 230. His territory was in south-eastern Thrace. The country recovered only slowly from the disastrous effects of the Gallic domination. Cotys, the ally of Perseus, minted coins only in bronze and not many of them.[3]

Gaebler lists twenty-six types of bronze coins of Philip, which is in striking contrast to the one type of gold and two types of silver coins. The reason surely is that Philip issued royal coinage in bronze throughout his long reign of forty-one years, and coined in other metals only in his last seven or eight years.[4] Eight of Gaebler's types carry a

---

[1] There has been much discussion of the question whether the head of the hero was made to look like Philip as king or Perseus as king or as prince. It is inconclusive and unprofitable, as the final words of Mamroth, 1930. 286 show: 'der Kopf ist das Bildnis König Philipps V., verjüngt und idealisiert als Heros Perseus oder, wie man auch sagen kann, der Heros Perseus mit den idealisierten Gesichtszügen des Königs, was praktisch auf dasselbe hinausläuft.' Nor is further speculation on Philip's motives for introducing the hero Perseus into the repertoire any more helpful; see Mamroth, 1930. 288. Some coins of this kind were wrongly ascribed to Andriscus by Gaebler; they are shown by N. Olcay, *Le Trésor de Mektepini en Phrygie* (Paris, 1965) 29 to have been minted by Philip V; his date for the deposit of the hoard *c*. 190 is a flexible one.

[2] Gaebler III. 2. 189 no. 1 and Pl. 34. 14, a beautiful specimen.

[3] See Youroukova 28 f. (Skostokos), 82 (Cavarus), 31 f. (Adaeus), and 33 f. (Cotys).

[4] Gaebler III. 2. 191–4; some issues can be related to one another, but Gaebler did not attempt any chronological arrangement or dating. He wrote in his note to no. 7 as if the monogram of Zoilus occurred on nos. 12 and 24 ff., but this is not borne out by his own descriptions and plates. For the deposits of copper in Macedonia see Volume I. Map 1. Mamroth, 1935. 219 ff. had twenty-two or twenty-four types (omitting Poseidon, for instance) and he emphasized the extraordinary number of types, as compared with the bronze issues of earlier kings. He attributed

monogram. There is one example of Zoilus' monogram and none of EP; one may infer that the other monograms were those of earlier mint-masters. Almost a quarter of the twenty-six types portray the hero Perseus, which we should date *c.* 186–179, and this would suggest that Philip coined more prolifically in bronze after 186 than earlier in his reign. An interesting feature of the royal bronze coinages is that so many deities are portrayed: Zeus, Poseidon, Athena, Artemis, Helios, Pan, Heracles, and the hero Perseus. It reminds us that Philip and the Macedonians for whom this coinage was intended were deeply religious and worshipped above all the gods and heroes of the Greek pantheon.

Philip was the first Macedonian king certainly to put a portrait of himself on the royal coinage, as distinct from the figure of the king e.g. on horseback. It occurred only on one type of tetradrachm (see Pl. I*m*); for I do not share the opinion of Gaebler that the other type of tetradrachm shows Philip's head posing as the head of the hero Perseus.[1] The gold and silver coins carry the full title of the king, **ΒΑΣΙΛΕΩΣ ΦΙΛΙΠΠΟΥ**. All his bronze coins carry abbreviations such as **ΒΑ ΦΙ** or the full title. This was necessary to distinguish them from the other bronze coinages to which we now turn.

During the reign of Philip three classes of bronze coins were issued by the Macedones, by regional groups, and by cities respectively. These were all greeted by Gaebler as 'autonomous' coinages, which became possible only with the collapse of the Macedonian empire and the weakening of the Macedonian monarchy, and he contrasted this state of affairs with the monopoly of Philip II in coinage when royal rule was at its height. 'Wie die autonome Münzprägung makedonischer Städte mit dem Erstarken der Königsherrschaft ihr Ende fand, so steht umgekehrt das Erscheinen autonomer makedonischer Landesmünzen mit dem Niedergang des Reiches in ursächlichem Zusammenhang.' He therefore dated all these bronze coinages after 185. Price raised the date to 196, i.e. to after the battle of Cynoscephalae.[2] Gaebler's theory is based on the assumption that the right of coining was a mark of political independence in classical and Hellenistic Greece. This assumption has been laid to rest recently by T. R. Martin, who has shown conclusively that city-states in Thessaly

some of the types to historical occasions and he placed those with what he regarded as peaceful symbols after 186; but in most cases he does not carry conviction.

[1] Gaebler III. 2. no. 3. Pl. 34. 18 (the hero Perseus) should be compared both with 34. 16 (the portrait of Philip) and other heads of the hero at 34. 29–30 and 35. 4, 12, 19, 20. It is possible that Alexander IV and Demetrius II were portrayed on coins (see p. 162 and p. 226 above).

[2] Gaebler III. 1. 1; Price 29 and 45 f., giving 196–168 for coins of the Macedones but 196–171 for coins of the Macedones Amphaxii. He suggested that the last of these was issued for the accession of Perseus (? hence the date 171): but this is puzzling, since Perseus acceded in 179.

continued to issue coins while they were subject to the overall authority of Macedonian kings.[1] And in Macedonia the people of Philippi and of Damastium, and the king of the Paeonians, Lycceus, issued coins although they were all subject to the Macedonian king, Philip II.[2] Gaebler, like most scholars, thought that the Macedonian monarchy was of an absolutist type and that the king directed all the affairs of all citizens. We have shown in the preceding volumes of this work that it was not so. Every free person in Macedonia had the citizenship either of a city or of a region, and he was loyal to that city or region; moreover, each city and each region had its own officials, Council, and Assembly and directed its own finances.[3] This continued to be so to the end of the Macedonian monarchy, as we shall see when the cities offered financial and other help to Perseus. Thus whether a city or region coined or not was not in itself a mark of independence or subjection, but rather a matter of whether it had the precious metal and the desire to coin. Of course cities and regions were under the overall authority of the king and were unlikely to act without his approval. In the same way coining by the Macedones was thought to indicate a rift between the king and his people and a political breakaway. But we have shown here and elsewhere that the Macedonian state consisted of two parts, the king and the Macedones, and that each had its own financial system and its own diplomatic relations.[4] For the Macedones to coin was a matter of their own convenience and not a form of political protest. Finally, the king owned all the precious metal of the mines of Macedonia. It was he who provided the precious metal for the silver and the bronze coinages of the Macedones, the cities, and the regions, and he did so because he wanted them to coin.

The reason for issuing these new coinages was economic and social rather than political. From 221 to *c.* 186, if we judge by surviving specimens, the only coinage minted by the king in Macedonia was in bronze, and in small denominations suitable primarily for local exchange and trade. At the same time the regions and the cities were mature and established, and it made good sense for them, if they so wished, to provide their own bronze coinage for the internal markets of the kingdom, and to encourage the people to move towards a fuller monetary economy. The Macedones as part of the state had their own

[1] E.g. on his p. 58 'Thessalian local coins continue to occur as significant and generally consistent percentages of the total contents of Thessalian hoards throughout the second half of the fourth century B.C.' And of Greece generally from Philip II to Perseus on p. 220: 'even the most obvious demonstration of a king's power over another state, the imposition of a garrison, demonstrably had nothing to do with the fate of the coinage of the garrisoned state.'
[2] See Volume II. 668–9.
[3] See Volume I. 86 f., 114, and 120, and II. 648 f. and 671.
[4] Especially in H*SPA* 461–5.

obligations and it was equally convenient for them to use their own coinage. They gained also financially; because there was a profit to be made when the coinage was in precious metal, once the initial expenses were covered.[1] After *c.* 186 some of these bodies coined also in silver. Finally, Gaebler's date for the commencement of these bronze coinages, *c.* 185, can be abandoned. They began probably soon after Philip came to the throne.

The coins of the Macedones with the letters **MAKEΔONΩN** show a number of deities in the traditional manner: Poseidon, Strymon the river-god, Apollo, Artemis, and Heracles, together with some of their symbols, e.g. the trident, the cithara, and the club and bow. Others have a Maenad, the stern of a ship, a horse, a shield and a helmet, such as appeared on earlier royal coinages. The Macedones coined in silver tetrobols and diobols and in bronze, and the number of types given by Gaebler was about the same for each metal.[2] The Assembly of the Macedones, which administered this coinage, did not have the heavy expenditures which called for gold coins or silver tetradrachms.

The regional coinage of Amphaxitis used the same emblems but added Zeus, Athena, Dionysus, goat, thunderbolt, and tripod. There was only one type of silver tetradrachm; it was in the last part of Philip's reign, since it carried the monogram of the mint-master Zoilus.[3] All other issues were in bronze. The issuing authority appears on one type (the tetradrachm) in full as Μακεδονων Ἀμφαξιων, on five types as Μακεδονων (or a monogram for it) with a monogram for the Amphaxii, and on two types with Ἀμφαξιων alone (Pl. I*o*). The authority is thus not all people living in Amphaxitis, but the 'Macedones' in that area, i.e. those possessing the full franchise. The regional coinage of Bottiaea drew on the same repertory and added Pan, two recumbent goats, and a pasturing cow. It had silver pentobols and two-and-a-half obol pieces, and as many bronze types as the Amphaxii. The silver coins and two bronze types have the name Βοττεατων by itself or a monogram for it, and four bronze types have Μακεδονων and a monogram for the Botteatae (Pl. I*p*).[4] Here too, though less conspicuously, it was the Macedones among the Botteatae who were the issuing authority.

Whereas earlier Paeonian coinages had been issued in the name of a king, Gaebler attributed to the time of Philip and Perseus a Paeonian

[1] See Martin 238 ff., citing *OGIS* 339, which shows Sestus instituting a bronze coinage as a source of profit, as well as a matter of civic pride.

[2] Gaebler III. 1. 26 ff. and 2. 1–3.

[3] III. 2. 3. no. 18 and Pl. 7. 21. He does not mention the monogram, which is above the delta of **MAKEΔONΩN**.

[4] III. 2. 4 f.

coinage of one type in bronze, carrying the head of Zeus, laurel-wreathed, and on the reverse a wingless thunderbolt with Παιονων above it and a monogram below, which he took to stand for Δοβηρων. It seems that these 'Paiones Doberes' of the Strumitsa region did not have a king and were well placed for local trade.[1] Another regional coinage carried a monogram, which Gaebler interpreted as standing for Παρωραιων, and it had three types in bronze, all having the same head of Zeus as the Paeonian coinage had on the obverse and an eagle or a wingless thunderbolt on the reverse.[2] As the two regions were close to one another, their sharing of emblems was natural. The issuing authority in each case was not restricted to the 'Macedones' in the region, but it consisted probably of the adult male citizens of the region.

A bronze coin with the head of a young Dionysus and on the reverse a standing goat has the inscription Θεσσαλονικης and some letters which date its issue to Philip's thirty-fourth year as king, i.e. to 187.[3] This coin of Thessalonica and various stylistic details enabled Gaebler to place some of the coins of Thessalonica, Amphipolis, and Pella within the reigns of Philip and Perseus; for example, the head of a Hermes on a coin of Thessalonica was seen by Gaebler to be a portrait of Perseus in his youth.[4] All the coins are in bronze. They draw on the usual repertory; Amphipolis is notable for the head of Strymon, the river-god, a dolphin, and a centaur, Thessalonica for a Pegasus, and Pella for Demeter, a Nike, and Athena Alcidemus who was worshipped at the city (Livy 42. 51. 2). The worship of Pan was represented by two goats butting on coins of Amphipolis and Thessalonica, and the worship of Demeter was accompanied with ears of corn and cattle on the coins of Pella.[5] Apollonia in Mygdonia and Aphytis, in Chalcidice, a religious centre for the worship of Zeus Ammon and other deities, had coined early in the fourth century; they now resumed coining in bronze for a short time and honoured respectively the local hero Olynthus and Apollo Carneios, the god of the ram.[6]

The naming of the issuing authorities of these coinages was usually simple, because the coins were intended mainly for local exchange within the kingdom. Thus it was enough to inscribe Ἀμφιπολιτων, Ἀπολλωνος (the god of Apollonia), Ἀφυται(ων), Θεσσαλονικης, and Πελλης. But it was necessary to define the 'Doberes' as 'Paeonians' in order to distinguish them from the Thracian Doberes who were also

---

[1] III. 2. 5 no. 35. See Volume I. 200 ff. with 200 n. 1 for the Doberes, and Volume II. 57 and 128 Map 4.

[2] III. 2. 5; see Volume I. 199 n. 2.

[3] III. 2. 117 no. 1.

[4] III. 2. 118 no. 5.

[5] III. 2. 33 ff. for Amphipolis; 93 ff. for Pella.

[6] III. 2. 46 f. For Aphytis see Volume II. 192; for this Apollonia as the place from which Alexander III had a squadron of Companion Cavalry see Volume II. 194 n. 2.

within the Macedonian kingdom,[1] whereas the 'Paroraei' needed no further definition. By the same standard 'Amphaxioi' and 'Botteatae' were self-explanatory. It is therefore surprising that 'Makedones' was not merely added, but given more prominence than the regional names on these coins. The best explanation of the addition is that it was the 'Makedones' alone among the inhabitants of Amphaxitis and Bottiaea who were the issuing authority.

3. *Philip's foreign policy 188–179 B.C.*

In his foreign policy Philip was debarred from Illyris, Greece, part of the southern Thracian coast, and the Chersonese by the Roman settlement, but not from the northern Balkans and most of Thrace (see Figs. 1 and 3). In 184 he deployed his reconstituted army in aid of Byzantium against marauding Thracians, won a battle, and captured Amadocus the king (Plb. 22. 14. 12 and Livy 39. 35. 4). His purpose was to subjugate the leading Thracian power, which had eliminated the Gallic kingdom of Cavarus *c.* 212 and expanded towards Byzantium (Plb. 4. 46 and 8. 22 with Walbank, *C* ad loc.). As the name indicates (see Volume II. 195), Amadocus was king of the Odrysae, who controlled the lower Hebrus valley, inland of Aenus. Philip then sent envoys to the Bastarnae, a Gallic or Germanic tribe, which had settled near the Getae on the north bank of the lower Danube, and urged them to migrate westwards, presumably as his allies against other Thracian tribes and the Dardanians, but not to invade Italy, as Livy, loc. cit. suggested.[2] Then or later he obtained the alliance of another Gallic tribe, the Scordisci, who held the region of Belgrade, where the Save joins the Danube (J. 32. 3. 5 and 8).

In spring 183 Rome forced him to withdraw his garrisons from Maronea, Aenus, and other towns, which had provided his base of operations in 184. But in summer 183 his army marched probably on the route which Alexander III had followed (above, p. 34) into the central plain, where he captured and garrisoned Philippoupolis (Plovdiv) and made a pact with the Odrysian king (Plb. 23. 8. 6–7 πίστεις). Then, ravaging the western part of the plain, he reduced the Bessi in the upper reaches of the Hebrus river, and the Dentheletae, who were probably around Sofia. The latter bordered the Agrianes, faithful allies of Macedonia, who lived in the headwaters of the

---

[1] See Volume I. 200 f. with 200 n. 1; when Thucydides mentioned Doberus at 2. 98. 2, he qualified it as the Paeonian one for the same reason (ἐς Δόβηρον τὴν Παιονικήν).

[2] The suggestion was taken from Plb. 22. 14. 12 χάριν τῆς προκειμένης, as Papazoglou *CBT* 163 n. 108 observed, and it was derived from Roman propaganda; for the Macedonians must have known enough of the north-west Balkans to realize that such an invasion was impracticable. See Walbank, *C* 3. 200.

Strymon. This great sweep brought the main tribes of central Thrace under his control, and it was probably now that one of Philip's daughters was given in marriage to Teres.[1] We may compare Alexander III offering the hand of his half-sister Cynane to the king of the Agrianes (Arr. *An.* 1. 5. 4).

Close relations were maintained with the Bastarnae through a diplomatic mission, headed by Antigonus, and a marriage was arranged between a princess of the royal house and a prince of the Macedonian house, evidently Perseus, in the course of 182. During the summer of 181 Philip conducted a campaign which, as reported by Livy, was remarkable for the ascent of the highest peak of Mt. Haemus. The view from the top was believed to include the Adriatic and Black Seas, the Danube, and the Alps, and Livy supposed that Philip and his war council would plan the invasion of Italy from that vantage-point! Even Napoleon did not scale Mont Blanc to plan the conquest of Europe! The peak in question was probably Musala (2,925 m.) of the Rila range, the centre of Bulgarian resistance in the last war, and probably at that time the centre of resistance to Macedonian control. This was the sacred mountain of the Thracians. At the two altars which he dedicated there Philip made sacrifice to Zeus and the Sun, perhaps using the Thracian titles of these divinities; for it was an act of political and religious propaganda. He campaigned next in the territory of the Dentheletae, who were nominally his allies, and again he was probably dealing with elements of resistance. He then descended the Strymon valley and laid siege from two sides to a city called Petra, which capitulated and provided hostages. His elder son, Perseus, commanded one of the attacking forces. His younger son had been left in Macedonia as the deputy of the king 'to guard the realm' (Livy 40. 21. 6 'ad...custodiam regni'), in accordance with Macedonian custom.[2]

In 179 Philip made arrangements for a joint campaign with the Bastarnae. They were to cross the Danube with their families, march

[1] D.S. 32. 15. 5; Plb. 23. 8.4–7; Livy 39. 53. 12–14, drawing on Polybius, but changing the order of Bessi and Dentheletae. The Agrianes were still active allies; perhaps later the Dentheletae moved into the Strymon valley. But see Papazoglou, *CBT* 101 and n. 33.

[2] Livy 40. 5. 10 and 21–2. For the route from Stobi see Volume I. 198. Livy's Mt. Haemus cannot be the range north of the central plain; for it took Alexander III ten days to reach it from Amphipolis, and so Philip could not have done so from Stobi (farther away) in seven days. So too Heiland 27. The range east of the middle Strymon valley, where Maedica lies, was included in Mt. Haemus (see Volume II. 64), and the highest peak of the Rila range, Musala, is to be preferred to Mt. Vitosha, some 2,000 feet lower and at the head of the valley (but favoured by Walbank, *C* 3. 613). Mt. Rila is 'exceptionally steep and exuberantly forested' (*HA* 46, having visited Rila monastery), which fits Livy's description. This Petra, like Petra in Macedonia, was associated evidently with the Kresna defile of the middle Strymon (see Casson 20 and Fig. 12). Livy's source was probably Polybius, who mentioned the view of the two seas (Str. 313) and used the sardonic tone so evident in Livy.

east of the Haemus range and then through the central plain of Thrace, Philip having obtained free passage by his gifts to the local kings (these will have included the kings of the Odrysae, Bessi, and Dentheletae). Philip was to provide supplies, which must have been dumped in advance. Perseus went with the vanguard ahead of the Macedonian army. Philip brought the main army from Thessalonica to Amphipolis. There he was taken ill and died. Messengers from the Bastarnae were heading for Amphipolis, when news reached them of the king's death. Philip's intention had been that the combined forces would attack the Dardanians, and that the Bastarnae would settle their families probably in Polog, the region of Dardania closest to Macedonia. The chance of the king's death at this very moment upset the whole scheme. For with inadequate liaison the Bastarnae fell out with the Thracians and clashes occurred; then the Thracians fled to a high mountain, the Bastarnae pursued and were caught in a colossal storm with thunder and hail. Some leaders were killed by lightning. Believing that the gods were showing disfavour and 'the heavens were falling on them', the Bastarnae quarrelled among themselves; part returned to the Danube, others—some 30,000 men—reached the rendezvous which had been agreed with Philip (Pautalia would be a suitable place). We shall describe the sequel in the next chapter; but we may note now that Perseus had Antigonus executed, probably because Antigonus had been in charge of liaison and had failed in his duty.[1]

In gaining this control of the central plain of Thrace Philip rivalled Philip II and Alexander III, and in mounting a migration of the Bastarnae with the support of Thracian forces and those of the Scordisci he showed the extent of his influence and the thoroughness of his organizing ability. Had he lived, the Macedonian army would have joined in an attack on the Dardanians; and there is little doubt that the combined forces would have gained possession of Polog and weakened the Dardanians who lived north of the watershed range. The Bastarnae would then have settled in Polog and been friendly neighbours. Thus Philip's web of alliances would have covered a great area, extending to the Scordisci in the Save valley. Our sources[2] state that Philip intended to organize an invasion of Italy by the Bastarnae, the Scordisci, and perhaps the Thracians, with the support of Macedonia, whether clandestine or overt. For any Bastarnae in Dardania it meant a journey of some 700 kilometres via the Save valley and over the Julian Alps

[1] Livy 40. 57. 2–58. 8; Trog. *Prol.* 32. For the idea of the heavens falling see Arr. *An.* 1. 4. 8. The timing of events is not clear (40. 57. 2–3; 58. 1); but for the long delay ('plurimum temporis') at Thessalonica, Philip would have brought his army, it seems, to the borders of Dardania and met the Bastarnae there. See Hammond in *Studies Mihailov* for the Dardanians of Polog.

[2] Plb. 22. 14. 12; Livy 39. 35. 4; J. 32. 3. 5; Trog. *Prol.* 32. Papazoglou, *CBT* 161 ff. argues in favour of the plan to invade Italy.

into the plain of Trieste. To maintain an invasion from such a distance was almost impossible, and meanwhile Macedonia would have been exposed to attack by Rome and her allies from the west and from the south. The alleged plan seems rather to be a part of the Roman propaganda which preceded the outbreak of the Third Macedonian War.

Strained relations between Macedonia and Rome may have under-lain a conspiracy of late 183 which ended with the condemnation and execution of three leading Macedonians—Samus, who had grown up with Philip as a Royal Page, Pyrrichus, and Admetus—and their associates. In 182 Philip arrested and imprisoned the sons and daughters of these persons, and also of all others executed 'in accordance with a royal order'. On this occasion Polybius reported that 'as they say' (a qualification by Polybius) Philip cited a line of Homer: 'Foolish is he who kills the father and leaves the sons behind.' He might equally well have cited the customary law of Macedonia, that the relatives of those executed for treason were put to death (C. 8. 6. 28 'mos Macedonum'). According to Livy, a man and his wife from Aenea (a city famous for the festival of Aeneas, the founder of Rome) tried to escape the arrest of herself and some children, and they all committed suicide rather than be captured by the king's men. The story may be true; the setting in Aenea was chosen for its propaganda value in Rome.[1]

Philip's fears of further dissensions were certainly focused on his younger son, Demetrius, born *c.* 207, who had spent six impressionable years in Rome as a hostage (*c.* 197–191) and was openly courted still by leading senators, such as Flamininus. Demetrius probably advocated collaboration and appeasement, if not total submission to Rome; and Flamininus and others left no doubt that they hoped to see Demetrius succeed to the throne. Perseus, who was five years older and the expected heir, supported his father's policy of rearmament and readiness, if necessary, to resist Rome by armed force. In spring 182 the quarrel between the princes became public knowledge, when they and their associates clashed after a ceremonial purification of the Macedonian army, and Philip conducted an inquiry into what had happened.[2] From then on our sources, deriving from Polybius, provide an imaginative, sensational, and entirely untrustworthy account. Long speeches, clearly spurious, were provided for the father and the two

---

[1] Livy 40. 3. 7 and 4, adding to Plb. 23. 10. 8–11 the killing off of his prisoners one by one; P*Mor* 53 E. The three names occur on inscriptions: see *AM* 1. 270 n. 7; 2. 34 ff.; and *SEG* 13. 393. For Aeneas and Aenea see *HE* 385 f.

[2] Plb. 23. 3. 5–8; 7. 1–4; Livy 39. 53. 1–11 for Roman favours to Demetrius. Livy 40. 6–7 for the quarrel.

sons at the inquiry.[1] The fact that Philip left Demetrius as his deputy in Macedonia in spring 181 is twisted by Livy into a calculated slight on Demetrius. This too was the opportunity in Livy's account for Perseus to plant an agent on Demetrius, namely Didas, the king's governor in Paeonia; and then a forged letter, allegedly from Flamininus, inculpated Demetrius. In spring 180 Philip sent Didas and Demetrius to Paeonia, where, allegedly on Philip's orders, Demetrius was done to death (Livy 40. 24. 4; cf. Plb. 23. 10. 12). It is impossible to ascertain the truth; but Philip would have kept Demetrius at his court under surveillance, if he had distrusted him. Nor is the sequel, that Philip learnt of Demetrius' innocence and Perseus' guilt and intended to make one Antigonus his heir, any more credible.[2] For when Philip died in summer 179 he had full confidence in his surviving son, Perseus, whom he had sent ahead on an important mission to the Bastarnae.

4. *Philip's achievements and the organization of the kingdom*

Anyone seeking a fair appraisal of Philip would not have turned to the Romans and the Achaeans. Both were rabid republicans who regarded monarchy as tyranny; and in addition they sought to justify their relations with Macedonia. Yet they are the ultimate sources of the surviving accounts, and their prejudices are almost fused in Polybius, who combined an admiration for Rome with Achaean patriotism. The picture which Polybius drew of Philip fitted the Roman and Greek model of the tyrant as a young man of fine instincts quickly corrupted by power (4. 77. 1–4 and 7. 11. 1–11; cf. P*Arat* 49), dominated by his advisers (4. 24. 1–3; 5. 12. 5–7 and 101. 7–102. 1; 13. 4. 8), and finally a pitiable old man, pursued to the grave by the Furies of remorse for innumerable gross impieties and murderous acts (23. 10. 1–3 and 12–14). We should be on our guard against accepting such a picture as true.

Our clearest view of Philip is of him as a commander; for no one provided him with a Parmenio. His ideas and qualities were his own. He was from the start brilliant in speed of decision and movement, in

---

[1] For sensationalism see e.g., Plb. 23. 10. 1–3. Plb. 23. 11; Livy 40. 8–16. 3. On the speeches as rhetorical exercises see E. S. Gruen in *GRBS* 15 (1974) 240 f., and Edson 196 'it is impossible to regard these speeches as authentic.'

[2] For the death of Demetrius see also D.S. 29. 25; J. 32. 2. 3–10; P*Arat* 54. 7; P*Aem* 8. 9. For the sequel see Livy 40. 54–6, and for its worthlessness as evidence see Edson 199 f. Edson's view of Rome's involvement with Demetrius (his 201 f.) is closer to mine than to that of Gruen, op. cit. We differ in that Edson 201 made the Senate aim at putting Demetrius on the throne, whereas I think its aim was to split and weaken the royal house, in which it did succeed. The quarrel and the sequel have been discussed with varying degrees of acceptance and rejection; see e.g. Walbank in *JHS* 58 (1938) 55 ff., E. S. Gruen in *GRBS* 15. 221 ff. and H. J. Dell in *AM* 3. 67 ff. Heiland 10 f. blamed Rome and believed that Demetrius was poisoned on Philip's orders.

the training and application of naval and military forces, and in his daring innovations in strategy and tactics. In a long career he was outgeneralled only by Flamininus. 'Chance, which no one can command', as Thucydides remarked (4. 62. 4 and 64. 1), served him ill. The news of quinqeremes approaching came at the very moment when he was about to surprise Apollonia; the clouds were low on the one day that it mattered, at Cynoscephalae; and his death happened at the very climax of his Balkan policy. His powers of organization were remarkable, and he showed extraordinary resilience. His control of supply was masterly, except in the crucial campaign ending at Cynoscephalae. He rivalled Philip II, whom he took as his model.[1]

In assessing Philip's ability in foreign policy we must discard the prejudices of Polybius. His picture of one adviser after another changing the direction of Philip's policy is incompatible with the confident decisiveness of Philip in war. It seems that Polybius confused *post hoc* and *propter hoc*; for when Philip changed his theatre of operations, e.g. from the Peloponnese to Illyris, he inevitably turned from Aratus to Demetrius for advice. Polybius was apt to judge Philip's policies with hindsight; and looking back from the fall of Macedonia one might say that policy after policy did end in failure. But hindsight is not a fair basis of judgement. We need to evaluate each decision at the time he made it. Thus his decisions in 220 and 211 to lead the Symmachy against Aetolia were sensible and in fact justified, in that they gave peace to Macedonia and the Greek states from 217 to 211 and from 206 to 201. Rome's methods left Philip with a simple choice. The maxim that 'the strong do what they can and the weak suffer what they must'[2] had been demonstrated by Rome in 238 in the seizing of Sardinia and Corsica and the planting of a further indemnity on Carthage. In 217 Rome made her first approach to Macedonia. It was a demand to hand over the person of Demetrius of Pharos. To yield was to invite a further demand and ultimately to submit. Macedonia's tradition was one of proud independence. In refusing, Philip incurred the hostility of Rome, and in 215 he judged it prudent to enter into alliance with Carthage against the common enemy. He was not alone in believing that Rome was crippled by defeat after defeat in Italy, and he hoped to eject Rome from Illyris. As it turned out, he overestimated the value of that alliance and underestimated the resilience of Rome.

The alternative to war with Rome was coexistence and even cooperation. Philip chose the former in 205 and the latter in 196 to 179, and in each case he proved that it was a viable policy. War was Rome's

---

[1] He studied the career of Philip II, excerpting the passages concerning him from the work of Theopompus (Phot. *Bibl.* 176 p. 121a, 35 = *FGrH* 115 T 31).

[2] Thuc. 5. 89 fin.

choice in 200; and Philip should not be censured for fighting for the liberty of his country. His eastern policy is open to criticism; for there he held the initiative. He has been blamed for not bringing Antiochus into the war against Rome in 200 to 197; but at that time Antiochus showed more hostility towards Philip than towards Rome. In 192/1 Philip's low opinion of Antiochus' army was justified; to have joined Antiochus then would have been to court disaster. It was rather the pursuit of his own ambitions in Asia Minor which was misconceived; for he lacked the resources to win there, and his confidence in the treaty of peace with Rome was misplaced. Thus he weakened himself before the decisive struggle with Rome, and in addition he lost his moral superiority in the conduct of war by his treatment of Cius, Thasos, and Athens.

The final phase of his policy—the extension of his authority in the Balkans—is related more closely to his position in Macedonia. There too Polybius and Livy misunderstood or misrepresented some of his actions. The polygamy of a Macedonian king was portrayed as sexual incontinence, and any non-Macedonian wife as a concubine or prostitute; thus Philip's marriage to the Argive widow of the younger Aratus was mired with allegations of seduction (P*Arat* 51. 3).[1] The integration of Thessaly with Macedonia which Philip II had initiated was regarded as imperial exploitation. Thus the training of Thessalian boys as Royal Pages at the court of Philip V was an exercise in slavery (Livy 39. 25. 8 'in servilibus abuti ministeriis').[2] Polybius and Livy made much of Philip's cruelty in destroying cities and deporting populations from the Enipeus valley (Plb. 18. 3. 8–9 and 4. 2; Livy 32. 13. 8–9 and 39. 25. 8),[3] and in transplanting Macedonians from the coastal plain to the frontier areas of Upper Macedonia (Plb. 23. 10. 4–7; Livy 40. 3. 3–6). He was in fact following the traditional policies which had strengthened Macedonia in the past and were restoring her after the defeat at Cynoscephalae.

The military and economic nuclei of the kingdom were the Macedonian cities, *poleis*. They are attested as existing in the sixth century in some cases in Lower Macedonia and generally from the fourth century onwards in Upper Macedonia.[4] Originally independent Greek cities,

---

[1] See Volume II. 154, and in the case of Philip V's son Perseus Livy 40. 9. 2 'me subditum et paelice genitum appellant.'

[2] As in C. 8. 6. 2 'munia haud multum servilibus ministeriis abhorrentia'; see Volume II. 154 and for an early instance of a Thessalian as a Royal Page p. 168. Livy described them as 'principes iuventutis'.

[3] They were probably his 'subjects', like the Dymaeans in Achaea (Paus. 7. 17. 5), who had been dissatisfied with the Achaean League and owed their liberation to Philip (Plb. 4. 60. 4–10 and Livy 27. 31. 9), and he was saving them from the Aetolian raiders.

[4] See Volume I. 188 f. and II. 649 for literary evidence and II. 85 for coins; II. 659 ff. for fourth-century cities. F. Papazoglou has dated the development of cities too late in *AM* 3. 209.

such as Pydna and Amphipolis, were incorporated and changed into the standard Macedonian type. By the time of Philip the cities in the coastal plains were very large, strongly walled, and beautifully laid out, as we can see at Dium, Edessa, and Pella. The sites had been chosen for their position on overland routes and not primarily for purposes of defence; thus although Edessa possessed a strong acropolis on top of the cliffs, the city itself was built on a level plateau, which was closer to the plain and its roads.[1] In this respect the Macedonian city differed from the average city of peninsular Greece and also from the acropolis-type cities of Hellenistic Epirus, which were built with an eye to defence. Each city had a large, productive, and defined territory, and frontier disputes between them were settled by the decision of the king.[2] These large cities had been the model for Alexander's cities and those of his successors in Asia and Egypt, cities which lived on through the Roman Empire and the Byzantine period. The small Greek cities of the classical type on the coasts of Macedonia and Chalcidice were often transformed into the Macedonian kind, for instance Pydna;[3] or they were absorbed into new Macedonian foundations such as Thessalonica and Cassandreia. The older cities in Upper Macedonia, such as Cellis and Boceria in Eordaea,[4] were on defensible sites and rather small, like most Hellenistic cities of Epirus, whereas the recent foundations, such as Heraclea Lyncestis,[5] were often in the plain, being sited on a line of communication. One reason for their smallness was that much of the population within a city's territory lived in villages, such as 'Dourea' and 'Aleb(?e)a' (neuter plurals) in Elimea, each with its head man κωμαρχῶν.[6] The villagers were attached to the city for administrative purposes.[7]

In what follows I am adhering to the principle enunciated in Volume I. 85 and 121, that the evidence concerning the institutions of cities and tribes which comes from inscriptions of the Roman period is valid for earlier times and not due to the *pax Romana*. Each *polis* had its own citizenship, territory, and revenues, appointed its own officials,

---

[1] See HH *Via Egnatia* II.

[2] *Proc. 8th Epigr. Conf.* 259 ff. and L. Missitzis, 'A Royal decree of Alexander the Great on the lands of Philippi', *Ancient World* 12 (1985) 3 ff.

[3] See H*Pydna* 32 f.; and for Trailus see *AM* 3. 134.

[4] Described in HH *Via Egnatia* I. 141–3. For cities in Epirus see H*E* 657 ff. and 670 f.

[5] See F. Papazoglou, *Heraclée* I (Bitola, 1961) and Volume I. 41.

[6] *Proc. 8th Epig. Conf.* 305 (Ph. Petsas saw in the name of the second *kome* a survival of the Lebaea of Herodotus 8. 137. 1); for *komai* see Volume I. 89 f. (Alcomena in Deuriopus), 103 (in Lyncus; cf. *PAE* 1931. 55 f.), 107 n. 2 (in Atintania), 135 (Leibethra and Pimpleia in Pieria). For *komarchon* see *Spomenik* 71 (1931) no. 265 in an inscription seen at Ochrid.

[7] See *Bull. épig.* in *REG* 97 (1984) 453 ἔδοξε Γαζ[ωρίοις] κα[ὶ] συ[γκ]ουρούσαις κώμαις. The villages appear in Livy as 'vici', which were ordered, for instance, by the king to supply food to troops travelling on a nearby road (Livy 44. 26. 5). The cities from which the populations were moved in part to form Demetrias became *komai* of the city; see *Pagasai und Demetrias* 94 f.

and made its own decisions by majority vote.[1] Each city was an entity. When men moved from one city to another city within Macedonia, they became a resident group with only limited rights in the second city.[2] The freedom of action of a *polis* was, of course, restricted by the overall authority of the Macedonian king and the Assembly of the Macedones, who together formed the Macedonian state, and this was particularly so in matters of religion, foreign policy, and military preparedness.[3] That authority was represented in the person of a state official, called (probably in all cities) an ἐπιστάτης, and his administrative assistants, called χειρισταί. These officials conveyed the wishes of the state to the leading magistrates of the city (the 'principes' of Livy 40. 56. 8), for instance in regard to cult matters at Cos, recruitment of men in an emergency, and provision of money or supplies. These magistrates were called πολιτάρχαι.[4] The economic importance of the cities in Lower Macedonia was primarily in agriculture, arboriculture, and cattle; the people went out from them to work as 'impigri cultores' (Livy 45. 30. 5).[5] Philip strengthened this part of the economy by settling Thracian and other foreign workers in these cities. The coastal cities had the further value of engaging in maritime trade, which was encouraged by Philip, e.g. for Demetrias (Livy 39. 25. 9). As that trade developed in the latter part of his reign, the three largest ports—Pella, Thessalonica, and Amphipolis—issued coinage in their own names.[6]

---

[1] For Pellaia, the territory of Pella, see Volume I. 143; revenues *SIG* 459 (Beroea); voting at Amphipolis (Herzog–Klaffenbach no. 6 l. 34), at Morrylus and Bragylae (Volume I. 179), and at Lete (Volume I. 184).

[2] They were called *katoikoi* and the verb was used of Aenians resident at Amphipolis (Koukouli-Chrysanthaki in *AM* 2.153 κατοικούντων and 159), and as a group a *demos*, e.g. at Amphipolis a *demos* of Samothracians. Similarly at Aenus there was a δῆμος Μαρωνιτῶν and at Maronea a δῆμος ὁ ἐν Αἴνῳ (*JHS* 16 (1896) 318 no. 12). At Greia μέτοικοι was used instead of *katoikoi* (*Eph. Arch.* 1934/5. 118).

[3] See F. Papazoglou in *AM* 3. 203 f., e.g. at Amphipolis the people of Cos expressed goodwill πρὸς τὸμ βασιλέα ᾽Αντίγονον καὶ πρὸς Μακεδόνας in Herzog–Klaffenbach no. 6, ll. 24–5 and 30, and in a literary source Paus. I. 11. 3 Ἀριδαίῳ καὶ Μακεδόσιν.

[4] Plb. 5. 26. 5; Diodorus, the official in Livy 44. 44. 4 'qui praeerat urbi', was presumably the *epistates*, for which in inscriptions see *BCH* 85 (1961) 426 and Philip's letter to Archippus, the *epistates* of Greia, in *Arch. Eph.* 1934/5. 117 ff. The *kheiristes* was associated with οἱ δικασταί at Thessalonica and Amphipolis (see *AM* 2. 318 f. and *AJA* 42 (1938) 249); and he is mentioned in an inscription in Austin, *HW* no. 74 A 3 and *IG* XII. Suppl. 644. That the *principes*, who figure also in Livy 45. 29. 1, were the city's elected πολιτάρχαι is demonstrated by an inscription found at Amphipolis of the reign of Perseus (see *Studies Edson* 229 ff.), as suggested in *CP* 55 (1960) 90 ff. The *archontes* of Amphipolis in *SEG* 12 no. 373 in the reign of Antigonus Gonatas may have been politarchs. For a politarch at Olympe in South Illyris *c*. 200 B.C. see *Iliria* 1984. 2. 117. Recruitment was 'per omnia oppida regni' in Livy 33. 3. 2, and the cities sent embassies to Perseus in Livy 42. 53. 3.

[5] As they did in the 1930s. City and country were a unity, and the huge plain supported a great number of cities, which Xenophon described as 'numerous, both small (near to Chalcidice) and large (further away from Chalcidice), with Pella as the largest' (*HG* 5. 2. 13, referring to 383 B.C.).

[6] See p. 467 above. Aphytis and Apollonia Mygdonica also coined. The former had a pilgrim trade and a harbour; the latter was very wealthy and provided a squadron of Companion

The regional system ran throughout Macedonia. In Lower Macedonia each region gave its name to phalangites recruited from within it; thus Philip called up 'the men from Bottiaea' (Livy's 'Vettiorum bellicosam gentem' at 45. 30. 5) and 'the men from Amphaxitis' (Plb. 5. 97. 3), and Alexander III had a squadron of Companion Cavalry 'from Bottiaea'. As we have mentioned, the first regional coinages appeared in Philip's reign, and two of them were issued by the Bottiaei and the Amphaxii. It is thus clear that each region in Macedonia had its own finances and a corporate organization. Philip probably encouraged the competitive spirit of the regions. We may compare the county system and the cities in England, and the greater wealth of the 'home counties'.[1]

The importance of the Macedonian city in the history of town planning has been revealed by large-scale excavations, which have become possible only since 1950. At Aegeae the palace was the centrepiece, situated between the steeply rising acropolis with its gateway at the highest point and the public buildings and the houses on the lower gentle slopes to the north.[2] The flat terrace on which the palace was built during the last years of the fourth century on the orders of Cassander was artificially levelled and commanded a superb view over the great Emathian plain. The sides of the building, 104.50 m. × 88.50 m., face the points of the compass. It was remarkable for its huge open-air central court with a stylobate and peristyle of sixty Doric columns, which gave light, air, and along its periphery shade for the inhabitants and visitors (see Fig. 16). The court was no doubt used for ceremonies. There was only one main entrance, on the east side, and visitors passed through four pillared entrances before they reached the central court. The throne room, circular with niches in its walls and the base of a throne *in situ*, was entered only from the court. The royal reception rooms—E, F, and G—had one pillared entry.

The other rooms surrounding the court were *andrones* (men's rooms fitted with couches on slightly raised platforms), and they varied in size, the largest having a span of 16.74 m. for the roof-bearing timbers. One of their uses was certainly the state banquet (*symposium*) of the king and his companions.[3] The eastern section had an upper storey, of which the outer façade was decorated with Ionic columns. This storey

Cavalry for Alexander III (Arr. *An.* 1. 12. 7). I disagree here with the view in Volume II. 368 f. that the squadron came from Apollonia Chalcidica.

[1] Pella, for instance, was in Bottiaea; yet Pella and Bottiaea each had their own administration and their own coins.

[2] See Andronicos, *V*, esp. 38–51 and the bibliography at 238 f. He has most courteously taken me round the site several times.

[3] See R. A. Tomlinson, 'Ancient Macedonian Symposia' in *AM* 1. 308 ff.

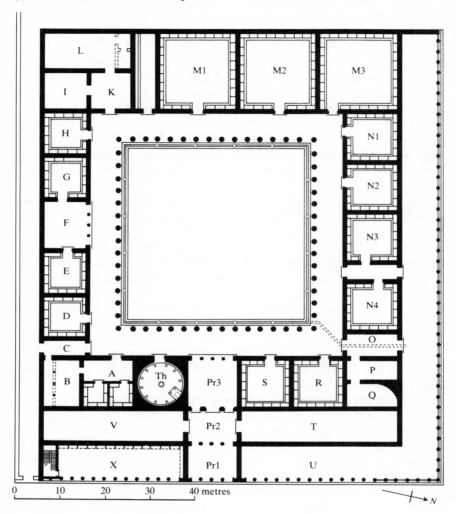

FIG. 16. THE PALACE AT AEGEAE

provided living rooms for the royal family and for those Royal Pages
who were detailed to wait upon the king. The Guardsmen were
probably billeted in V and T, and they were stationed at the main
entrance and by the staircase leading from X to the royal rooms. The
entries were few for reasons of security. Viewed from the outside, the
palace was remarkable for the colonnades of Doric columns on the east
and north sides, which provided walkways with splendid views. The
southern terrace protected the building from water and soil washed

down from the acropolis hill. The west wall of the palace served as the wall of another large building of the same general plan.

This palace served as the model for the palace which was built at Demetrias by Philip V in the years after 218. The palace walls there formed a square some 65 m. × 65 m., aligned to the points of the compass, and the central open-air court had a peristyle of thirty-six columns and was surrounded by *andrones*, similar in form to those at Aegeae.[1] As Demetrias was a harbour town, and so vulnerable to attack, the palace was protected by fortification walls with a tower at each corner, so that it resembled a medieval castle. Terraces on the south and west sides commanded fine views; for the site, on Hill 33, overlooked the harbour to the north and the surrounding land. A citadel on Hill 49, close to the palace, was no doubt occupied by the Royal Guardsmen (it was separate from the acropolis), and a 'sacred agora' with a temple of 'Athena of Iolcus' near its centre was immediately adjacent to the palace on the south side. Thus the complex of buildings was not unlike the complex at Aegeae; for there the temple of Eucleia in the mid-fourth century lay just below the palace area.

At Pella the palace area is still under excavation. What follows is very tentative, being based on a visit in 1981, when Mrs. M. Siganidou conducted me round her excavations.[2] The palace is built on a flat part of the acropolis, which occupies a gently sloping top of undulating ground, and it commands a magnificent view of the great plain and in antiquity of the landlocked harbour with its fortified keep on the 'Bean Island' (Phacus), more than 2 kilometres away. The foundation walls of the palace are exceptionally massive; they are 3.20 m. wide, faced on both sides with huge ashlar blocks (e.g. 1.5 m. × 1 m.), which were cut to fit precisely without mortar. Here too a central rectangular court was emerging, and towards one end there was a semicircular stone foundation, which may have belonged to a throne-room. Another palace, or at least a building of similar design, with equally massive foundations lay back to back with the first palace; it too had at the far end a similar semicircular foundation. The two palaces did not share a party wall, as they did at Aegeae, and there was only a tiny gap of some 6 inches between the two adjacent massive walls. At other spots similar walls were found to rest on natural rock or on layers up to 2.5 m. thick of roughly shaped large blocks or on packed soil above the

---

[1] *Demetrias I* with excellent plans. The state-house or *katagogion* at Cassope in Epirus is built on the same design and is about half the size (see H*E* 664 f. and Fig. 29 (*a*)). Large Turkish 'khans' are similar in design.

[2] I am most grateful to her for help on this and subsequent visits. See *Ergon* 1982 (1983) 20 for a preliminary statement.

rock. It is thus evident that the palaces had more than one storey. The stone for the palaces was not cut from the local rock; some of it was a bluey-grey stone from Mt. Paiko and the rest was honey-coloured from the region of Koufali (ancient Ichnae). The site had been completely cleared, even of sherds of pottery, presumably in 167, and the date of the foundation of the palace is uncertain.

That palaces on this scale existed earlier than the palace at Aegeae is demonstrated by the discovery of the palace at Ai Khanum in Afghanistan. For while it resembles the Persian palace at Persepolis in some respects, it has a large rectangular open court with a peristyle of columns and a stately entry to the court.[1] There is no doubt that Alexander and his generals and successors built their palaces overseas after the model of those in their homeland.

The layout of a Macedonian city has been revealed most clearly at Demetrias, a new city founded by Demetrius Poliorcetes between 294 and 288. A massive fortification wall, strengthened with many rectangular towers and some advanced outworks (*proteichismata*), enclosed not a single defensible hill, but a large area of hollows, level spaces, and hills; its length exceeded 8 kilometres, this being determined by choice rather than by the nature of the ground.[2] A strongly fortified acropolis stands on Hill 193. Public buildings such as the theatre were inside the walled city. The residential area was on the grid plan. The streets, all being almost 8 m. wide, ran east to west and north to south, the latter enabling the onshore winds from the sea to blow through the city (as at Alexandria in Egypt). On rising ground the streets were stepped. Each rectangular housing block measured 50.5 m. × 100.5 m. The dwellings within the blocks seem to have varied in design; this may be due to the fact that the population of the new city was not uniformly indigenous, but mixed. Drainage was channelled into stone conduits. Similar housing blocks at Pella early in the third century averaged 47 m. × 111.5 m.[3] This type of layout dated back to at least the time of Philip II, since it was employed at the new city of Priene, in which Alexander took a personal interest. The fortification walls of Pella and of Amphipolis were between 6 and 7 kilometres in length at the height of their prosperity. The average city in Lower Macedonia was smaller than these, but still large by ancient standards. They were built closer

---

[1] See the plan in *Scientific American* 247 (1982) 148 ff.

[2] *Demetrias I* Plan 1 for the excavated area. I walked over the site in 1983 and saw the massive foundations of the fortifications. *Pagasai und Demetrias* 86 estimated the number of towers at 142, and showed plans of a *proteichisma* wall, an outer tower, and an inner tower behind on pp. 32 and 36.

[3] Ph. Petsas in *Archaeology* 17 (1964) 74 ff. The grid plan was used much earlier, as at Olynthus in Chalcidice in the first half of the fourth century. For the fine houses with a central court and mosaic floors see *Macedonia* 175-7 with figures.

to the plain than such modern cities as Verria, Edessa, and Naoussa, which grew during the troubled times of the Turkish Empire and clung to the hills for safety. Between 359 and 169 Lower Macedonia was very rarely invaded, though damaged sometimes through civil war.

The Macedonians were innovators in the construction of harbours. Philip II was credited with the development of Pella as a great capital city, and one of its important assets was a riverine harbour, so constructed that it was connected with the Axius on the one hand and the sea on the other by navigable channels or canals. The harbour itself was in a lake between the two canals. As the Mediterranean Sea is almost tideless, the tidal water in the lake was almost constant; the flow from the Axius was controlled by some form of lock, because the river flooded at some times of the year. It was this type of harbour which inspired Alexander to build the great riverine harbours by the mouths of the Nile, the Euphrates, and the Indus. Demetrius Poliorcetes built two harbours for his city Demetrias. One was an open harbour on the south side, adjacent to the massive fortification wall of the city (like the medieval harbours of Rhodes or Famagusta in Cyprus). The other was a very large fortified harbour, created by the two arms of a built mole, 2.17 m. wide, which ran out into the shallow waters of the bay from points 750 m. apart on the shore line. The entrance was no doubt controlled by some form of boom and commanded by defensive works. It is remarkable that, although the Romans and the Rhodians had complete supremacy at sea during the Second and Third Macedonian Wars, they found Demetrias and its fortified harbour impregnable.[1]

Macedonia was a land of innumerable cults—Greek, Macedonian, and foreign.[2] Aegeae, Demetrias, and Dium—and no doubt other cities—each had a separate area for shrines and dedications. One centre of worship of Dionysus, a specifically Thracian-Macedonian deity, was the theatre. The earliest example yet known in Macedonia is at Aegeae, just below the palace terrace. It had only one row of seats in stone, alongside the *orchestra*, and the other seats were evidently of wood and were supported by low scaffolding set on the gently rising slope. Wooden seating had been customary in Greece until the latter part of the fourth century. One imagines that Euripides produced his

---

[1] See *Pagasai und Demetrias* 94.

[2] The list is endless in that it is increased by excavation. See W. Baege, *De Macedonum Sacris* (Halle, 1913), C. F. Edson on Macedonian cults in *OCD*[2], and S. Düll, *Die Götterkulte Makedoniens in römischer Zeit* (Munich, 1977). The last book deals mainly with the evidence after 167 B.C.; but most of the cults had their origins in earlier centuries. Nearly all the cult names in the book are Greek, and the exceptions are usually near the frontiers. We may mention Apollo Oteudanos in northern Pelagonia (probably Paeonian or Brygian), Dionysus Pyrmerylas near Sandanski, north of the Rupel Pass (probably Thracian), Dionysus Asdoules (probably Thracian), and Daimones Antanoi at Stobi (Antanoi being a constituent tribe of the Illyrian Atintanoi).

Archelaus and his *Bacchae* in this theatre late in the fifth century. The excavations at Dium have revealed two theatres, a stadium, temples of Asclepius, Demeter, and Isis, and inscriptions recording worship of Zeus Olympius, Poseidon, Aphrodite, Hecate, and Artemis Eileithyia. The gilded statues of the ruling kings which were dedicated in the sacred area at Dium remind us that the royal family led the way in promoting the worship of the Macedonian deities.[1] A fascinating shrine lies in a sunken area, fed by copious springs, just outside the massive walls of Dium. The worshipper descended on a ramp and his worship was associated with fertility and childbirth, over which Aphrodite, Artemis Eileithyia, and Isis Lochias presided at different times. A similar worship was practised just outside the acropolis wall of Pella in a sunken circular pit, lined with fine ashlar masonry, perhaps 15 m. in diameter and some 2 m. below ground level. Within it a ramp led down to a central altar, which was surrounded by hundreds of terracotta figurines of humans and of all kinds of domesticated animals. Pockets sunk elsewhere in the surface were filled with fragments of vases, which had probably been broken deliberately during the ritual ceremonies. This circular pit resembles the pit in the sanctuary of the Cabeiroi in Samothrace. The worship may remind us that these cities were inhabited not by a sophisticated population, but by simple agricultural workers who went out daily to work in the fields and to raise livestock.

In the reign of Philip V the cities were at the peak of their development, beautifully designed and magnificently appointed with public and private buildings. The remains of wall-paintings (mainly in tombs), mosaic floors of rounded pebbles which are much more colourful and luminous than those with tesserae, and of variously coloured plasters which were used to decorate walls and floors and architectural features are indicative of a very high level of achievement in the decorative arts. The discoveries at Vergina are very far from unique. They are rivalled by recent discoveries at Lefkadhia, Pella, Stavroupolis, Derveni, Amphipolis, and Trailus.

In Upper Macedonia the cities played an equally important role in the economy. Many of them had been what we call 'new towns', created by the Macedonian government to stimulate agriculture and trade and to strengthen defence; and in most cases the population was a social mix of people from Lower and Upper Macedonia and also of some non-Greek-speaking Balkan people. Philip founded Bylazora and

---

[1] D. Pantermalis in *Proc. 8th Epigr. Conf.* 271 ff. One base bore the inscription βασιλεὺς Μακεδόν[ων] Κάσσανδρος Ἀντιπ[άτρου] Διὶ 'Ολυμπίωι. For this full royal title compare *IG* VII. 3055 Ἀ[μ]ύντας Π[ερ]δί[κ]κα [Μα]κεδόνων βασιλεύ[s] and my commentary on it in Volume II. 651.

Perseïs as Macedonian cities, and he transplanted Macedonians from Lower to Upper Macedonia to strengthen existing cities or start new ones. The regional system in Upper Macedonia had been militarily important in the reign of Alexander III, when a phalanx regiment took its men from one region or sometimes two regions; but later the recruiting was by cities throughout Macedonia, and the only distinction by region in the sources was between the men of Upper Macedonia and those of Lower Macedonia (Plb. 5. 97. 3 τοὺς ἄνω Μακεδόνας).[1] The regional system in Upper Macedonia was stronger in terms of local administration than in Lower Macedonia, because the tribal traditions of each region there were still living. As in Epirus, to which Upper Macedonia was closely related in customs and dialect, each (originally tribal) group administered itself as a κοινόν, 'a community'. Such *koina* are attested in inscriptions from the early fourth century in Epirus and in inscriptions after the fall of the monarchy in Upper Macedonia; they are likely to have originated much earlier than in the fourth century in both Epirus and Upper Macedonia.[2]

The nature of 'the *koinon* of the Orestae' may be inferred from some inscriptions of the Roman Empire. When τὸ κοινὸν 'Ορεστῶν decided to make a dedication to a Roman emperor, probably Claudius, the Orestae included among its constituent tribes one on the eastern side of the upper Haliacmon and another, the Battynaei, on the western side. Each constituent tribe, as in fourth-century-B.C. Epirus, conducted its own affairs. The *ekklesia* of the Battynaei was convened by the *politarches*, who was named.[3] When we realize that the community of the Orestae had its own cantonal government and internal organization, we can understand how it was able to break away from the Macedonian state. Nor were the *koina* limited to the tribes of Upper Macedonia; for the Paeonians had their own *koinon* in the upper Axius valley in the reign of Demetrius II (239–229).[4]

[1] The same distinction had existed in the time of Alexander III; for he had 'the cavalrymen from Upper Macedonia' (Arr. *An.* 1. 2. 5), and half of his phalangites came from there and were called *asthetairoi* on my interpretation (see H*A* 27 and *CQ* 28. 128 f.).

[2] For Epirus see H*E* 525–40; for Upper Macedonia see Volume I. 88 ff., 111, 121 f., and 130 and D. Kanatsoulis in *AM* 2. Ἐλημιω[τ]ῶν τὸ κοινόν. In Epirus a large *koinon* (e.g. of 'Molossoi' or of 'Thesprotoi') consisted of several small *koina*, each being that of a constituent tribe; this was so in Pelagonia (see Volume I. 79). There were officials called πελιγόνες in Macedonia (probably Lower Macedonia in view of the dialect form) and πελιγᾶνες in Seleucid Syria, retaining the West Greek dialect form of Upper Macedonia (Str. 329 fr. 2; Hsch. s.v.); and perhaps 'adeiganes' in Plb. 5. 54. 10 (see Volume II. 649 n. 1).

[3] See Volume I. 111 ff. for references, and *Studies Edson* 229 for politarchs in the reign of Perseus.

[4] *SIG* 394; *BCH* 74 (1950) 22 ff. The Paeonians were organized in tribes (Pliny, *HN* 4. 35 'Paeoniae gentes'). Dittenberger inferred from *SIG* 394 in which Dropion was described as 'king of Paeonians and founder' (*ktisten*) that the 'Paeonian *koinon*' was established by him; but it may

The king communicated with the *koina* or regional governments through his officials. Thus in 181 Philip gave orders to 'one of his royal officers who was in charge of Paeonia' (Livy 40. 21. 9); as this officer provided a military guard, he was probably a στρατηγός. The same system obtained no doubt in the regions of east Macedonia where the Doberes and the Paroraei issued their own coinages. The king's officials may have had a hand in this (see Volume II. 668). East Macedonia was rich in cities, some founded by Paeonians in the sixth century and others founded by Macedonian kings. Each city had its own administration and officials, and it was linked to the central government by the king's ἐπιστάται.[1] The official language was Greek, while native languages were in daily use.

Central government was conducted, as we have seen, by the Macedones, being the élite citizens, to whom the citizenship had been granted by a Macedonian king for military or administrative service,[2] and by the king and his officers and officials. Some of these Macedones, holding their citizenship until death, became the local administrators in the cities and the king's officials in the cities and the regions. Meeting in Assembly as a central government, the Macedones decided some matters of policy, conducted some elections and trials, and administered their own finances. They paid honour to Philip at Samothrace as Μακεδόνες and at Delos as τὸ κοινὸν Μ[ακε]δόν[ων]. Thus the community of Macedones called itself a *koinon*, as contemporary communities did in Upper Macedonia and Epirus. The term *koinon* appeared in our sources in the reign of Alexander III (Arr. *An.* 7. 9. 5 in a speech τῷ κοινῷ τῶν Μακεδόνων) and just after his death (D.S. 18. 4. 3 τὸ κοινὸν Μακεδόνων πλῆθος).[3] It had probably originated much earlier. It was the meeting of this central government—'commune concilium gentis'—which was banned in 167 (Livy 45. 18. 6).

As executive head of the central government Philip proved himself to be a brilliant organizer and administrator both before and after the crippling defeat at Cynoscephalae. The results of his domestic and Balkan policies in the latter period were a reconstituted army of 43,000 men in 171, abundant armaments, large financial reserves, accumulated supplies, and offers of money and cereals from the cities, whose embassies expressed their loyalty to the Crown (Livy 42. 51. 11; 52. 11–13; 53. 2–4). Moreover, the Balkan policy had not only increased

---

refer rather to the founding of some city and be complimentary. In the same way Eumenes was described as 'king and founder of the *polis*' (in fact of Panion, not of Pergamum).

[1] For cities see Volume II. 96 f.; an *epistates* at Amphipolis in *SIG* 832, and in Eordaea in *AJA* 42 (1938) 250, with an office *epistasion*.

[2] For the Macedones see Volume II. 647 ff.; H*SPA* 461 ff.; F. Papazoglou in *AM* 3. 198.

[3] H*SPA* 461 ff.; *Hesp.* 48 (1978) 16; *SIG* 575.

Macedonia's manpower and resources; it had also given the Macedonian troops training and experience, which restored the morale of the phalanx brigades (Livy 42. 52. 2 and 14). His only demonstrable failure was the loss of the Orestae, now protected by the Roman settlement. Orestis apart, he rivalled Philip II in welding the diverse peoples and languages into a united kingdom.

The king depended on the loyalty of his troops and of his Friends, from whom he chose his commanding officers, leading officials, and chief advisers. Philip used clemency in dealing with a mutiny early in his reign (Plb. 5. 25. 6–7), and he issued his King's Regulations for punishing indiscipline (Austin, *HW* no. 74); in general he commanded a complete loyalty. Disloyal Friends in high places were the greatest hazard of the Macedonian kings, especially if they were members of the royal house or/and commanders of Macedonian troops. Philip dealt firmly and successfully with four cases. The first occurred in 218 (pp. 381 f. above), and in this case Philip used summary methods, consultation of the Friends in Council (Plb. 5. 16. 5) and trial in a court of Macedones (Plb. 5. 29. 6). Then in 209 his *strategos* at Lychnidus on the Illyrian frontier betrayed the city to Aëropus, probably a pretender from the royal house, and to the invading Dardanians (Livy 27. 32. 9); Philip took immediate action. In 205 or 204 five leading Friends were executed, presumably after a trial in a court of the Macedones (D.S. 28. 2); the charge was not stated in the fragment of Diodorus. The last case, in 183, resulted in the execution of three Friends and some associates (Plb. 23. 10. 9); as one of these, Samus, was a member of the royal house, being a nephew of Antigonus Doson, they probably had conspired to seize the throne. Later, he imprisoned their sons and daughters. We may deplore his methods, but the suppression of conspiracies was essential to the stability of the throne and the penalties were within Macedonian law.

The personality of Philip was painted in the blackest colours by Polybius and Livy. It was second nature with them to attribute the deaths of the two Arati, Cassander and Demetrius, to poisoning on Philip's instructions; but the accusations are unsupported. They described him as the committer of the grossest impieties against the gods. It is true that at Thermum he destroyed votive offerings in punishing the Aetolians for their sacrilege at Dodona and Dium, and in Attica his sacking of sanctuaries was unjustifiable. But there is no doubt that his life in general was one of religious faith and practice. He sacrificed to Zeus at Olympia and at Ithome, supported the cult of Asclepius at Cos, made dedications to the Cabeiroi in Samothrace and Lemnos, to Athena at Lindus, to Zeus at Panamara in Caria, and especially to Apollo in Delos, and he certainly made daily sacrifices in

Macedonia or on campaign, as Alexander III had done, dedicated spoils of the chase to Heracles, and granted land to be used for religious rites. He gave thanks to 'the gods' for the victories granted to Antigonus Doson at Sellasia and to himself at Thermum, and he built altars and made offerings to Zeus and the Sun on the summit of Mt. Haemus, and he safeguarded the revenues of the cult of Sarapis at Thessalonica. His faith embraced many deities; and his saying that 'he feared no one except the gods' is supported by the evidence.[1] His religiosity was paralleled by that of his subjects. Inscription after inscription adds to the huge number of known cults, and the religious faith of Macedonia's peoples, not shaken as in the Peloponnese by the miseries of war and revolution (Plb. 5. 106. 2–3), was the mainstay of their morale.

The strength of Philip's character and his ability to impose his will on the Macedonians and many other peoples, including the fierce Thracian tribes, were certainly rooted in his religious faith. He placed the head of Athena Alcidemus, the Macedonian goddess of war, on his first coinage, and the emblems of Heracles and Zeus were associated with the head of Perseus, whom Philip chose as his heroic model, on his later coinage. In moments of stress, like Alexander III, he called on the gods in the heat of battle (Livy 35. 18. 6). His finest monument is a dedication to Apollo, the beautifully proportioned portico beside the Sacred Way which leads from the harbour to the sanctuary at Delos. Philip may not have attained the qualities which Polybius set for an ideal Hellenistic king, 'a gentleness in rule and a magnanimous spirit' (4. 27. 10). But he had the practical virtues and qualities which the Macedonians admired: daring courage in the hunt, in battle, and in strategy, extraordinary thoroughness in administration,[2] a sense of humour and verbal wit (*PFlam* 9. 3), a love of banqueting and carousing (Livy 37. 7. 12), an affable manner, and a readiness to move freely among his people and to listen to frank speaking (Plb. 5. 27. 6). He carried his country safely through a changing world, and he bequeathed to his successor a reconstituted and powerful kingdom.

That the Macedonians paid special honour to Philip is clear from a dedication at Delos with the inscription: τὸ κοινὸν Μ[ακε]δόν[ων] βασιλέα Φίλ[ιππον βασιλέως] Δημητρίου ἀ[ρετῆς ἕνεκεν] καὶ εὐνοία[ς... 'The community of Macedones (honours) king Philip, son of king

---

[1] See Herzog–Klaffenbach, *JHS* 59 (1939) 203 (Lemnos); *FGrH* 532 F 1, C 42 (Lindus); *BCH* 28 (1904) 346 f., 354 f., (Panamara); Walbank, *Ph* 268 f. for Delos; *Anth. Pal.* 6. 114–16 (Heracles); *Arch. Eph.* 1934/5. 117 f. (grant); *AJA* 42 (1938) 251 (Thessalonica); Plb. 18. 1. 7 (saying).

[2] Attested by many letters and instructions issued by the king, e.g. for the maintenance of supply depots of grain, wine, and timber at Chalcis (*AJA* 42. 252).

Demetrius, for his excellent and loyal conduct.'[1] It is indeed probable that they paid him the highest tribute, worship as a god, associated with Sarapis and Isis; if so, he was rated in the same class as Philip II.[2] But a different comparison was drawn between the two Philips in the hostile tradition which cited an oracle by the Sibyl as follows: 'O Macedones proud of your Argead kings, a Philip on the throne is a blessing and a disaster for you. Indeed the elder will set rulers over states and peoples; but the younger will destroy all your honour, overthrown by men of the West and men of the East.' Those who mocked him for the defeat at Cynoscephalae gave him the sobriquet 'Pseudophilippus', the false Philip.[3]

[1] *SIG* 575.

[2] An inscription found at Amphipolis and published in *BCH* 18 (1894) 417 Ἀλκαῖος Ἡρακλείδου Σαραπίδι Ἴσιδι βασιλεῖ Φιλίππωι shows that *a* Philip was worshipped at Amphipolis. We know that Philip II was worshipped there from Aristides, *Symmach.* A (*Or.* 38) 1 p. 715 D, but the association of a *synnaos theos* with the Egyptian deities is anachronistic for Philip II, but very appropriate for Philip V, who was a patron, as we have mentioned, of the cult of Sarapis at Thessalonica. It was evidently a public cult, and Alcaeus, son of Heracleidas (the latter being a distinguished Macedonian name), was no doubt a Macedonian. By this time Amphipolis was an entirely Macedonian city (see A. Giovannini in *AM* 2. 466 and F. Papazoglou in *AM* 3. 203) and not a Greek city, as was supposed in *BCH* 18. 417 f.

[3] Paus. 7. 8. 8–9. The oracle was a *vaticinium post eventum*, foisted onto the Sibyl of Cumae in Italy. It probably inspired the sobriquet in Tac. *Ann.* 12.62, where the "rex Macedonum" is Philip V and the sequence of actions is emphasised by "orsi" and "missas posthac copias" (*contra* H. Furneaux ad loc.).

XXIII

COLD FRIENDSHIP BETWEEN MACEDONIA AND ROME (195–179 B.C.)

1. *The main sources of information*

MOST of our information about the reign of Perseus (179–168) is derived from Polybius, directly and indirectly. He had excellent opportunities to inform himself of what were to him contemporary events. The son of a leading statesman, he was chosen at a young age by the Achaean League to serve as one of three envoys to Ptolemy V in 181/0; he held the high office of hipparch of that league in 170/69 (Plb. 28. 6. 9); and he was with the Roman commander during part of the campaign against Perseus in 169 (28. 13. 1–6). As a detainee in Italy from 167 to 150 he will have met many Greeks and Macedonians who had played a leading part in their states, and he will have consulted copies of treaties on the Capitol. He returned to Greece in 150. After that date, when he was writing his account of the reign of Perseus, he was still able to interview some surviving participants.

He had lived for years under the shadow of Roman power, and he had every reason to avoid giving offence to Romans in his writing. As he portrayed it, to quote Walbank, 'the rise of Rome to world-empire reflected a transcendental plan, the work of Tyche', i.e. Fortune,[1] and all who opposed Rome fell into disaster through their own errors and stupidities. For example, when Roman intrigues split the Boeotian League in 172/1, Polybius did not comment on the Roman action, but censured the Boeotians for acting 'paradoxically, rashly, illogically, at random, and in a childish fit of excitement' (27. 2. 10). Again, he found the cause of the Third Macedonian War not in any action by Rome, but in the (alleged) plans of Philip for war (22. 18. 1–11). He wrote for Greeks, especially Peloponnesians, and for Romans; and not for the defeated Macedonians, whom he had no reason to defend. In regard to politicians he was at pains to justify some, including himself, and to condemn others; but he showed extreme caution in commenting on Roman leaders. Thus his version of events was from the viewpoint of Rome and not from that of Macedonia.

---

[1] *JRS* 55 (1965) 3 = *Selected Papers* (Cambridge, 1985) 160.

Polybius regarded the Third Macedonian War as the climacteric point in the rise of Rome to world empire. He described the course of the war with a wealth of detail, and in his introduction to it he challenged comparison with his great predecessors, Herodotus and Thucydides. The actions of Philip were 'the beginning of evils' (22. 18. 1 and 23. 10. 1 ἀρχὴ κακῶν), like the actions of Athens at the start of the Persian wars (Hdt. 5. 97. 3). Perseus was advised to read the treaty with Rome twice daily (Livy 44. 16. 5), a reminiscence surely of Darius being reminded daily to remember the Athenians. The analysis of its causes which Polybius advanced at 22. 18–19 was divided into πρόφασις, αἰτία, and ἀρχή in the manner (but not in the sense) of Thucydides 1. 23. 6. He certainly reserved some of his finest writing for these books, and he excelled himself in sensational descriptions and in rhetorical speeches. It is sad that so much of his text is lost.

The books of Livy for this period are derived to a great extent from the work of Polybius, then intact. Livy also gives non-Polybian material. For example, Livy introduced the most improbable story that Perseus sent envoys to Carthage, and that Carthage sent envoys to Macedonia; at Carthage they received an audience during the night! In another passage the terms of the peace granted by Rome to Philip were represented as like those granted to Carthage in 202, so that Philip, and Perseus in his turn, were expressly forbidden to lead an armed force beyond the borders of Macedonia and were banned from engaging in war against the allies of the Roman People (42. 25. 4). Then it was said that Perseus denied the validity of the agreement with Rome (42. 25. 10), which he had renewed, and that Perseus ordered the envoys of Rome to depart from Macedonia within three days (this to balance Rome's action in ordering Macedonian envoys to depart from Italy within a specified number of days, at 42. 36. 7). These non-Polybian passages, and others which depend on them, are to be rejected as inventions by Roman annalists, designed to put the blame for the war on Perseus.

Certain features in Livy's account come from Polybius. As we have seen, the correct designation of the Macedonian state was βασιλεύς X καὶ Μακεδόνες, and this is found at 42. 30. 1 and 63. 12, and 43. 19. 14, evidently from the Greek of Polybius. The attention to problems of supply and to the transportation of foodstuffs during the campaigns of the Third Macedonian War is far more prominent than in the Second Macedonian War, and the reason is perhaps that Polybius had some experience himself in organizing supplies (28. 12. 5) and took a special interest in this aspect of the contemporary campaigns, for which he could obtain information from participants.

2. *The legacy of Philip and the opening years of Perseus' reign (179–174 B.C.)*

Before Perseus ascended the throne, he was a fated man in the narrative of Polybius and in that of Livy, which was derived mainly from Polybius. Although Perseus was the eldest son and in accordance with Macedonian custom likely to succeed his father (Livy 40. 9. 8), he was represented as the bastard child of a concubine, unloved by his father and at odds with his half-brother (Livy 40. 9. 2–3 and 8). Curses were laid on Philip and his sons by the relatives of Philip's victims and they were fulfilled by the Furies setting father against son and brother against brother (Plb. 23. 10 and Livy 40. 5. 1). The fratricide was initiated by Perseus in his lust for regal power and engineered with the help of others, since Perseus was too 'woman-minded' to do the killing himself (Livy 40. 5. 3). Thereafter, Philip hated Perseus and would have had another member of the royal house, Antigonus, succeed to the throne. But Philip repented too late. Death intervened. Thanks to the doctor who concealed the king's death and sent post-haste to Perseus, the successful criminal seized the kingdom before the Macedonians realized what was happening (Livy 40. 54–57. 1). The criminality of Perseus was not confined to family horrors. He had encouraged his father's hatred of Rome and he had shared in his father's plans to make war on Rome (Livy 40. 5. 5 and 9). Given the predilections of Polybius and Livy, this was a crime in itself, a wrongheaded attempt to frustrate the course of destiny which was carrying Rome to world power. It is important to bear this Polybian background in mind, as we turn to the narrative of Perseus' reign.

The facts are that Perseus was the son of Philip and one of Philip's wives, Polycrateia, a woman of distinguished family from Argos in the Peloponnese. The transplanting of Macedonians was standard practice and is unlikely to have evoked such curses. The brothers certainly quarrelled; but there is no reliable evidence, and little likelihood, that Demetrius died from other than natural causes.[1] Philip had marked Perseus out as the intended successor by giving him major commands and calling his new city Perseïs (p. 459 above). If the story about the doctor is accepted, the doctor delayed so that Perseus could come back from Thrace and trick the Macedonians.

That Philip was planning to make war on Rome is most improbable. To the end he avoided any act of provocation and obeyed every order. He observed the terms of Rome's settlements, which governed relations only between Macedonia and Rome's protégés—the Greeks of the

---

[1] Livy 40. 24. 3–8 tells of poisoning and of smothering in order to exaggerate the heartlessness of Philip's agents; see also D.S. 29. 25 and Livy 40. 54. 1–2 and 7.

mainland, Pleuratus, Eumenes, some Greek cities in Thrace, and Rhodes. In Philip's last years central Thrace was outside the sphere of the Roman settlements and outside the orbit of Rome's interests. Our sources do not mention any complaint lodged then at Rome by any Thracians, not surprisingly, as they had no diplomatic or other contacts with Rome. It was twenty years since Rome and the Dardanians had been in league against Macedonia. If Philip had lived to support the raid of the Bastarnae on the Dardanians, he might have been taken to task by Rome; for when it suited them, the Romans had a long memory.

Philip's death was unexpected. The successor of his choice, Perseus, was in Thrace, far from the capital. It was an ideal opportunity for a rival on the spot to seek election. Such a rival, according to Livy 40. 56. 10, was Antigonus, son of Echecrates; for he was a member of the royal house, a nephew of Philip's predecessor, Antigonus Doson, and an outstanding administrator.[1] That there was a party opposed to Philip and Perseus is probable after the humiliation of Cynoscephalae and the uncertain policy towards Rome. But no chance was given to any rival. The doctor attending Philip concealed the news of the death from other people, but told Perseus so that he could return post-haste from Thrace, followed evidently by his army. Once elected, Perseus 'ordered Antigonus to be executed' according to Livy 40. 58. 8. It is more likely that Antigonus was tried on a charge of treason and executed by the Macedonian Assembly. It is perhaps indicative of a disputed succession that Perseus is said to have asked the Senate to recognize him as king (Livy, loc. cit. and 45. 9. 3; Zon. 9. 22. 2). His right to the throne was undisputed thereafter.

Philip died at a critical moment in the joint campaign by the Bastarnae and the Macedonians which he had planned against the Dardanians (see p. 470 above and Fig. 3). It seems that Perseus withdrew the Macedonian forces and took them back to Macedonia. Meanwhile the Bastarnae, having crossed the Danube in huge numbers, found that Philip's arrangements for providing supplies and for smoothing relations with the Thracians had not been implemented. Clashes with the Thracians ensued, a mighty storm terrified the Bastarnae, and a large part of them went home; the remainder, 30,000 in number, advanced under the command of Clondicus, but they found no Macedonians at the rendezvous (Livy 40. 58. 1–8). Even so the Bastarnae, it seems, defeated the Dardanians. While the fortunes of the Bastarnae were fluctuating and Perseus was absent in central

---

[1] Ch. Habicht in *Chiron* 13 (1983) 23 has established that *SEG* 13 no. 393 does not refer to this Antigonus, but to an Antiochus, son of Echecratides. Walbank, *C* 3. 274 was written before Habicht's article appeared.

Macedonia, the king of the Sapaei, called Abrupolis, crossed the frontier of Macedonia and ravaged as far as Amphipolis; he returned home with spoil from the mines of Pangaeum and from the rich countryside. The time, says Polybius, was 'after the death of Philip' (22. 18. 2).[1] Perseus retaliated at once, defeated his forces, and expelled him from his kingdom (Plb. 22. 18. 2–3; cf. Livy 42. 41. 11).

The huge numbers of the Bastarnae, like the estimated 150,000 warriors of Sitalces in 429 (Thuc. 2. 101. 2), spread alarm through the peoples of northern Greece. The fact that Perseus had not co-operated with them may have earned him some credit with the Thessalians, for instance. We hear of the campaign against Abrupolis from two inscriptions. One, found at Amphipolis, records a dedication by Perseus to Artemis Tauropolus 'from the campaigns into Thrace' (ἀπὸ τῶν εἰς Θράικην στρατειῶν) and then a dedication by 'the *demos* of the Amphipolitans'. The plural στρατειῶν means that there had been more than one campaign.[2] This meaning is borne out by the other inscription, *SIG* 643 found at Delphi, which lists Rome's grievances against Perseus in 172 (see below, p. 500). For the μέν and δέ show that the 'Thracians' formed a separate grievance from 'Abrupolis' in lines 15 ff. κ]αὶ Θράικας μὲν ὄντας ἡμετ[έρους...Ἀβρού]πολιν δέ...[ἐξέ]βαλεν ἐκ τῆς βασιλείας. That Rome did have a treaty of alliance with Abrupolis, the king of the Sapaei at the time of the campaign is mentioned in Paus. 7. 10. 6, Livy 42. 13. 5 and 40. 5 'socium atque amicum populi Romani', and App. *Mac.* 11. 2. Since Rome did not make an issue of the matter at the time (App. *Mac.* 11. 6), but raised it only later (Plb. 22. 18. 2; D.S. 29. 33; and Paus. 7. 10. 7 διὰ τὸ ἐς Σαπαίους ἀδίκημα) we may infer that it was a defensive alliance and that Abrupolis was regarded as the aggressor at the time.[3]

The next step of Perseus, still in 179, was to send envoys to Rome and to ask for a renewal, or rather reaffirmation, of the treaty of 'friendship' which was governing the relations between Macedonia and Rome at the time of his father's death. The request was granted, probably in 178. Livy added that Perseus asked that he be recognized as king by the Senate (40. 58. 8). We have suggested that he wanted this recognition, because the succession had been disputed. The agreement was a formal one with oaths taken by the envoys of both

---

[1] This phrase helps to date the expedition to 179; for App. *Mac.* 11. 6 put the retaliation by Perseus before the renewal of the treaty with Rome.

[2] We may compare Thuc. 2. 11. 1 πολλὰς στρατείας. The plural was correctly explained by Ch. Koukouli-Chrysanthaki, when she published the inscription in *Studies Edson* 229 ff., and incorrectly by J. and L. Robert in *REG* 97 (1984) 452, whose special pleading that incidents in one campaign may make several campaigns should not be accepted.

[3] See Appendix 5. Abrupolis may have invaded in support of a pretender to the Macedonian throne.

parties, and it ensured friendly relations, as long as the behaviour of both parties was friendly.[1] As we argue in Appendix 5, Perseus inherited a unilateral clause, probably to the effect that he should side with Rome in a war declared by Rome and not allow passage through his kingdom to an enemy of Rome.

Perseus had married a princess of the royal house of the Bastarnae in 182 (Livy 40. 5. 10). In 178 he married Laodice, the daughter of Seleucus IV (Plb. 25. 4. 8; Livy 42. 12. 3). It was a grand occasion. The bride was escorted to Macedonia by the fleet of the Rhodians, with whom Perseus was cultivating friendly relations; for he had recently given Rhodes a quantity of fine ship-timber, and now he rewarded the oarsmen of the bridal vessel with a golden headband apiece (Plb. 25. 4. 10). He probably made another marriage at this time, following the polygamous tradition of the Macedonian royal house.[2]

From early in his reign Perseus tried to cultivate better relations with the Greek states. As this policy appealed to Polybius, he depicted Perseus, like Philip in his young days, as an ideal Hellenistic monarch (25. 3. 4–8), who later deteriorated and sank to abject depths. Thus Polybius may have exaggerated Perseus' early stance as a philhellene (25. 3. 1 Ἑλληνοκοπεῖν; App. *Mac.* 11. 1. 4 and 7 φιλέλλην). But the policy is not to be doubted. Perseus presented himself as the benefactor of the less well-to-do and the impoverished, whereas Rome consistently supported the well-to-do. Within Macedonia he cancelled all debts due to the crown, and he liberated all prisoners who had been imprisoned for offences against the crown; and he called back to Macedonia those who had been exiled on such charges or by the civil courts. To this end he posted lists of the beneficiaries in the sanctuaries of Apollo at Delos and Delphi and at a shrine of Itonian Athena (it was probably the one at Coroneia in Boeotia). All who returned to Macedonia were to be assured of their safety and were to resume possession of the property which each had held previously (Plb. 25. 3. 1–3).[3] That Perseus could advertise his policy at Delphi was due to a change in the composition of the Amphictyonic Council, which had hitherto been pro-Roman, and which in 182 had hinted at Philip as one of 'the kings who plot against

---

[1] The renewal is described as a renewal of τὴν φιλίαν by Plb. 25. 3. 1, and by authors who probably derived information from Polybius: D.S. 29. 30, App. *Mac.* 11. 5, and Zon. 9. 22. 2. On the other hand, Livy is inconsistent. Paus. 7. 10. 6 emphasizes the element of peace in the sworn agreement: ἄγοντι εἰρήνην κατὰ συνθήκας ... ὑπερβῆναι τοὺς ὅρκους.

[2] App. *Mac.* 11. 2 was referring to current connections by marriage in his words ἐπιγαμίας βασιλικάς. The rumour that Perseus murdered one of his wives (Livy 42. 5. 4) may be discounted as part of a smear campaign.

[3] Coroneia was loyal later to Perseus and may have been specially favoured by him. Walbank, *C* 3. 276 prefers the shrine near Halus in Thessaly. Livy makes no mention of these acts by Perseus.

the Greeks' (*SIG* 630. 8). Now, in 178, two Macedonian *hieromnemones* sat on the Council 'from King Perseus'; thus Macedonia had become a member of the Amphictyony (*SIG* 636. 5–6).[1] The change indicated a radical swing of sympathy towards Macedonia in a majority of the states north of Attica.

The Aetolian League led the way in following Perseus' policy. Society in Aetolia was crippled by an immense accumulation of debt, and in consequence a revolutionary form of party strife was raging (Livy 42. 5. 7 'in seditionibus propter ingentem vim aeris alieni'; 41. 25. 1 'mutuis caedibus'). Help was obtained from Perseus in order to bring the party strife under control, and then all debts were cancelled. Similar conditions obtained in other places. Diodorus, probably drawing on a lost passage of Polybius, states that the Aetolian League cancelled debts throughout its member states. Also in Perrhaebia and in Thessaly debts were cancelled in the hope of avoiding further civil strife (Livy 42. 5. 7; D.S. 29. 33); and when Perseus marched his army through Thessaly, his presence helped 'the worse cause' and was designed 'to overthrow the better class', as Livy expressed it in his sympathy for Rome (42. 13. 8–9). The city-states of Boeotia were probably in an even worse condition than those of Aetolia and Thessaly. For the appalling situation, which Polybius had described as existing *c.* 192 (20. 6. 1–6), may even have been worsened by a severe shortage in the production of cereals there in the years after 180.[2] In addition, there was contention within Boeotia between the separatists and the federalists, who wished respectively to abolish and to strengthen the Boeotian League. Perseus supported the democratic elements and the federalists. His ascendancy was marked by the conclusion of a treaty with the Boeotian League (Livy 42. 12. 5 'Boeotorum gentem'), of which copies were set up at Thebes, 'at the most revered and famous temple' (of Boeotia) which was probably at Delium,[3] and at Delphi.

Perseus backed his policy with grants of financial aid, with the making of treaties with states where his partisans were in control, and with the offer of treaties to uncommitted states (Livy 41. 22. 7 and 42. 5. 1). He was widely hailed as philhellene, giver of benefactions, and a generous philanthropist.[4] His reputation spread rapidly to Asia Minor, where the Greek states became favourably disposed towards

---

[1] See *SIG* II p. 199 *nota finalis*. The swing was led by the Aetolian League, which now dominated the Amphictyonic League Council. For the change see Walbank in *AM* 2. 89 ff. countering the view of A. Giovannini in *AM* 1. 147 ff.

[2] See D. Hennig in *Chiron* 7 (1977) 119 ff. and P. Roesch in *Rev. Phil.* 1965. 256.

[3] The text of Livy 42. 12. 6 is often emended to read 'Delium'.

[4] Livy 41. 24. 11 'beneficio'; App. *Mac.* 11. 1 τῶν Ἑλλήνων φιλία καὶ γειτνίασις and 11. 7 φιλέλλην.

Macedonia (42. 12. 1 and 14. 9). He was still resisted by Athens and by the Achaean League which had banned the entry of Macedonians into their respective territories. Perseus tried to win the favour of the Achaean League by offering to return any escaped slaves who had taken refuge in Macedonia; but the only effect was to split the Achaean Council and exacerbate disputes between the rival leaders (41. 23–4 and 42. 12. 6). He also approached a number of states overseas, in particular Antiochus IV and Ptolemy VI (42. 26. 8).

Within the Greek mainland Perseus waged war only against his subjects, the Dolopians, who had tortured and killed his governor in Dolopia (41. 22. 4; 42. 13. 8; App. *Mac.* 11. 6). He was accused later of having sent military aid to Aetolia and Boeotia, states with which he had an alliance (App. *Mac.* 11. 1 and 7), and of having marched with an army to Delphi, probably in 174 (Livy 41. 22. 5–6).[1] These actions were not in breach of the agreement which he had renewed with Rome, and when Roman envoys went to Macedonia early in Perseus' reign they were received with gestures of goodwill (41. 24. 6). Perseus was succeeding well in re-establishing Macedonian influence in the Greek world. But the success was to prove more apparent than real, because it was to be resented by Rome.

In these years Perseus campaigned at least once against some Thracians, whom Rome claimed in 172 had been 'hers' (presumably under a treaty, whether of friendship or alliance).[2] The diplomatic ties of Rome with the Thracian region at this time are uncertain. When she compelled Philip to remove his garrisons from 'the Greek cities in Thrace' in 183 (Plb. 23. 8. 1; see p. 468 above), she is likely to have made treaties assuring the liberty of the leading cities, especially Aenus and Maronea; indeed, it was at this time that she made a treaty of alliance and friendship with Abrupolis, king of the Sapaei.[3] Although Rome accepted Perseus' right to retaliate against Abrupolis in 179, she presumably did not relinquish her treaty with the Sapaei.

In 177 the Dardanians sent a report to Rome that Perseus and the Bastarnae were in league with one another, and this report was confirmed by envoys from Thessaly. They both asked Rome for help. This led to the dispatch of a Roman commission, led by Aulus Postumius, which made contact with the Bastarnae, who lived as far away as the lower Danube valley (Plb. 25. 6. 6; App. *Mac.* 11. 1). On their return in 176 the commissioners said that there was war in Dardania (Plb. 25. 6. 2–6; Livy 41. 19. 4). Meanwhile Perseus sent envoys to Rome to declare that he had not prompted the actions of the

---

[1] *SIG* 643 τῷ]μ Πυθίων dates his visit to the Olympic year 174/3.
[2] *SIG* 643. 15. See p. 500 n. 3 below for the date.
[3] See Appendix 5 for these treaties.

Bastarnae in any way.[1] The Senate neither cleared Perseus of any accusation nor made any accusation. It simply 'ordered him to take care time and time again to be seen to be being punctilious in respecting the treaty he had with Rome' (Livy 41. 19. 6). We may infer that Perseus had kept clear of Rome's 'friends and/or allies' and that Rome had no specific complaint against him. But the warning was emphatic.

In early winter 175/4 the Dardanians acted on their own against those Bastarnae who had established themselves in Dardania and now enjoyed the support of some of the neighbouring Thracians and also of the Scordisci (see Fig. 3). Waiting for the Thracians and the Scordisci to go home for the winter, the Dardanians advanced in two columns. One was defeated. The other captured the camp which contained the women and children of the Bastarnae. At that point the account in Livy breaks off (at 41. 19. 11), but we may assume that the Bastarnae left Dardania in exchange for receiving their families.[2] Early in 174 the Bastarnae recruited an innumerable host of cavalry and infantry.[3] As it was crossing the Danube, 'intent on a raid, the ice broke under their weight and few survived.' In the short account in Orosius 4. 20. 34–5 the intended raid was 'auctore Perseo', 'at the instigation of Perseus'. This was probably a matter of suspicion and not of certainty. It may have come from the annalistic source which supposed that Perseus intended to direct the Bastarnae towards an invasion of northern Italy.[4]

The extent of Perseus' territory in Thrace is inferred mainly from the Roman settlement of 167 (see Appendix 6). His 'Macedonia' was said then to have reached Cypsela (see Fig. 3). From that place it was 22 kilometres down the navigable Hebrus to the Aegean Sea. Since he kept his hands off the coastal Greek cities, namely Abdera, Maronea,

---

[1] The association of the Roman commissioners returning and the envoys of Perseus appearing is common to Livy 41. 19. 5 and App. *Mac.* 11. 1, which can therefore be attributed to a common source, probably Polybius. Livy dated the two events within the consular year corresponding to 175, but the chronology is disputed; see Walbank, *C* 3. 282, citing rival views. Because part of the Bastarnian host returned to Apollonia and Mesembria (Livy 40. 58. 8), it is probable that these places were on the route of invasion, which then ran from the Danube estuary down the coast and went inland through the central plain to Sofia and on to Dardania.

[2] The withdrawal is apparent from Livy 41. 23. 12. That the hearing at Rome preceded this campaign follows from the pluperfect tense in Livy 41. 19. 4 and 5, compared with the imperfect and vivid present tenses in 41. 19. 7. The campaign was earlier than the next invasion by the Bastarnae. See the next note.

[3] The year is given by Orosius as 'Lepido et Mucio consulibus'. The circumstances are so different from those of the (assumed) withdrawal of the Bastarnae from Dardania in Livy that the two movements should not be telescoped into one, as has sometimes been suggested. See F. Papazoglou, *CBT* 166 ff. with n. 122 for the views of herself and others; and add Walbank, *C* 3. 288 f.

[4] E.g. in Livy 40. 57. 6–9 and 42. 11. 4 in Philip's last months.

and Aenus, he must have held extensive areas inland of the coastal strip in order to establish himself at Cypsela, and we learn from Livy 45. 29. 6 that he held 'villages, fortresses, and towns' to the east of the river Nestus. Since his communications were threatened by the Sapaei, living inland of Maronea and Lake Ismarus (Str. 7 fr. 43), he must have held the strategic area round Razlog. To the north of Cypsela his alliance with Cotys, king of the Odrysae, gave him a secure position on the main trade-route which, passing up the Hebrus valley, divides and leads overland to the central plain and to the Black Sea coast of Mesembria and Apollonia.[1] To the east he was in alliance with Byzantium, and he sent help to that city, perhaps *c.* 173.[2] The statement in App. *Mac.* 11. 1, that he had acquired Thrace, 'a great base of operations' (μέγα ὁρμητήριον), was indeed an exaggeration, but it contained an element of truth.

3. *The Senate's reaction to the successes of Perseus (174–172 B.C.)*

The Senate was alarmed more by events in Greece than in Dardania and inland Thrace. It saw itself in danger of being replaced by Perseus as the arbiter of liberty and the supporter of social justice, not least because the Greeks of the mainland now particularly resented what they saw as subjection to Rome (Livy 42. 5. 6). Therefore it sent a number of commissions to Greece, sometimes on its own initiative, sometimes at the invitation of pro-Roman leaders (e.g. 41. 22. 3 and 25. 2). A commission sent to Aetolia in 174 reported that 'the madness of the people there could not be controlled' (41. 27. 4). Another commission visited Macedonia in 174 (41. 22. 3). When the reports of the various commissions had been studied, the Senate began in 173 the long process of going to war by propitiating the Roman gods in response to various portents and by seeking to win their favour. The projected enemy was not made public, but it was generally known that it was Macedonia, as Livy indicated (42. 2. 3 'cum bellum Macedonicum in expectatione esset'). Nor was war inevitable as yet. Later in 173 envoys came to Rome from the pro-Roman parties in Aetolia and Thessaly (42. 4. 5), and Appius Claudius was sent out as a Roman commissioner. In Greece he reprimanded the leaders in Thessaly and Perrhaebia, and he imposed a compromise settlement under which an illegal form of interest on debts was disallowed and creditors were assured of repayment within a period of ten years (42. 5. 8–10).

---

[1] For Cotys see Livy 42. 29. 12 and 51. 10; Plb. 27. 12; for the route see S. Casson in *Macedonia* 255.

[2] App. *Mac.* 11. 1 and 7; Livy 42. 13. 8, 40. 6, and 42. 4. For the date see Ch. Koukouli-Chrysanthaki in *Studies Edson* 234 n. 17.

Another commissioner went to Delphi. There he persuaded the leaders of the two factions within Aetolia to agree to a reconciliation and to provide hostages as a guarantee of good faith. Marcellus placed the hostages in Corinth, which was under the control of the Achaean League. He then crossed to Aegium, where he had ordered the Assembly of the Achaean League to be convened. He complimented the Assembly on its continued banning of a Macedonian king from its territory (42. 6. 1–2).

The Senate's animosity towards Perseus was increased at this time by Eumenes of Pergamum, who presented at Rome a memorandum in which he described Perseus as making preparations for war (42. 6. 3–5). So the Senate sent five commissioners to investigate the situation in Macedonia. Still in 173 Rome and Antiochus IV, who had earlier lived as a hostage at Rome, made an exchange of embassies, and Rome renewed the friendship on the same terms which she had accorded to Antiochus III (Livy 42. 6. 6–12 wrongly called it 'societas atque amicitia').[1] The commissioners who were to visit Macedonia were instructed to go from there to Alexandria; their task there was to renew the agreement of friendship with Ptolemy VI (42. 6. 4 'amicitia').

At the beginning of the consular year, December 173,[2] the allocation of the province 'Macedonia' came under consideration as the next step on the road towards war, but a decision was postponed for purely domestic reasons (42. 10. 11–12). In 172 around April Eumenes presented himself at Rome. He was received with special honours and addressed the Senate. The speech reported by Livy includes points which Eumenes might have made.[3] He aimed to emphasize the power and the ambition of Perseus, and he urged the Senate to attack Perseus before Perseus could cross to Italy (42. 11–13). A few days later a Macedonian embassy, led by Harpalus, arrived at Rome. In addressing the Senate Harpalus gave offence by his manner, and the Senate rejected the claim which he put forward on behalf of Perseus, that nothing which Perseus had said or done was

---

[1] See Appendix 5.

[2] Walbank, *C* 3. 301, following Derow, dates the start of the next consular year to 27 November 172. Warrior prefers 15 March 171. The sequence of events after the speech of Eumenes down to the consul Licinius crossing to Greece on his interpretation (we agree on the sequence) falls three or four months later, so that the ships have to be manned and moved during midwinter (at Livy 42. 27. 3 and 7), the exchanges of envoys with Gentius across the Adriatic Sea have to be made during midwinter, and the vanguard of Roman troops has to cross to Illyris '*c.* 13 February'. Such traffic in the worst of the winter seems most improbable, since the Adriatic is a dangerous sea until late March or early April and was certainly thought to be so in antiquity.

[3] It seems unlikely that the actual speech was recorded verbatim at the time of delivery, and its content was not divulged for four or five years (Livy 42. 14. 1). Livy's speech, if derived from Polybius, rests rather on what Polybius heard from senators during his own stay in Rome and on what he thought that Eumenes might have said.

hostile in intent (42. 14. 2–3). Meanwhile a spate of embassies descended on Rome from various Greek states, and among them one from Rhodes, which had fallen out with Eumenes of Pergamum and felt vulnerable because of its friendly relations with Perseus.

On his way back from Rome Eumenes went to consult Apollo at Delphi. As he was walking up from the Pleisthenic gorge, he reached a narrow place where he and his retinue had to go in single file. There he was struck on the head and the shoulder by a couple of large rocks and was knocked unconscious. The assailants, said to have been a Cretan commander of auxiliaries named Evander and three unnamed Macedonians, ran away uphill. They killed one of their own number, allegedly because he was too slow. The other three escaped. According to Livy the four assailants had stayed with a lady called Praxo at Delphi and they had brought to her a letter from Perseus. This lady was collected and brought to Rome by the leader of the five Roman commissioners who were on a visit to Macedonia. No doubt it was she who inculpated Perseus with what was probably a forged letter; for Perseus would not have been so foolish as to commit a plan to writing, if there was a plan.[1] The leader of the commissioners brought to Rome another informer, one Remmius of Brundisium, who had a story that Perseus was planning through him to poison a number of leading Roman senators (42. 17. 3–9; App. *Mac.* 11. 7). These allegations, together with the commissioners' report on affairs in Macedonia, confirmed the resolution of the Senate to prepare for war. The Senate issued orders around July 172 that troops were to be enlisted forthwith and transported to Apollonia Illyrica, and that from there they would garrison the coastal cities in advance of the arrival of a consular army. And Roman envoys set off to offer congratulations to Eumenes, who was himself making preparations for war (42. 18. 4–5). Another king, Ariarathes IV of Cappadocia, followed Eumenes' lead and placed his son under the care of Rome (42. 19. 2–5).

Meanwhile envoys were on their way to Rome from three Thracian tribes. The names in Livy's text are corrupt. One was probably the Asti, whose lands came close to Cypsela. The envoys were asking for 'alliance and friendship'. The Senate granted them alliance 'gladly, because Thrace was in the rear of Macedonia' (42. 19. 6–7 'societatem').[2] Next, two commissioners were sent to tour Asia and the islands, especially Crete and Rhodes, in order to renew friendships and to find out whether Perseus' diplomacy had altered the attitude of

---

[1] Some have assumed that there was a plan, or have written as if it was proved; thus Adams wrote in Adams and Borza 252 'the attack was traced to Evander', although Evander was never put on trial. Heiland 33 is wisely sceptical and finds any share in the attack by Perseus most improbable.   [2] See Appendix 5.

Rome's allies (42. 19. 7–8 'sociorum'). When they returned, they assured the Senate that their friends and/or allies were loyal with the exception of Rhodes, which was wavering (42. 26. 8).[1] As the prospect of war was approaching, renewed attempts were made to placate the gods and win the favour of Jupiter Optimus Maximus (42. 20).

Envoys from Thessaly and Aetolia, who were granted an audience, evidently made charges against Perseus in the Senate (42. 25. 14; cf. 42. 4. 5). Envoys from Issa complained that Gentius, the king of a large Illyrian territory north of Lissus, had ravaged Issa and was in collaboration with Perseus with a view to making war on Rome. Some subjects of Gentius who were in Rome were not allowed to answer these complaints, but the Senate sent its own envoys to Gentius and complained of Gentius' behaviour towards Rome's allies in Illyria (42. 26. 2–6 'socii'). Those allies had included one Arthetaurus, an Illyrian dynast, a 'friend and ally'; but he had just been assassinated (42. 13. 6; cf. App. *Mac.* 11. 2). They were principally peoples within and near the Roman protectorate, who later provided troops as allies of Rome (43. 9. 7 'sociis').[2] Envoys arrived from Rhodes. They hoped to dispel Rome's doubts, but a hearing was deferred until the next consular year, beginning about December 172 (42. 26. 9). The Senate arranged for the manning and the concentration of a fleet at Brundisium and for the mustering of an army there, which was to be shipped to Illyris and hold the 'provincia Macedonia', i.e. the area of operations for war against Macedonia (42. 27).

By the summer of 172 the Senate had collected all manner of complaints and charges against Perseus. It was now ready to launch its own diplomatic offensive by sending Roman envoys to the Greek states of the mainland, the islands, and Asia. They were to carry with them a statement of the offences committed by Perseus, and a form of this statement was to be publicized at Delphi for all to see. A fragmentary inscription (*SIG* 643), which has been found at Delphi, gives a summary of the chief points in the statement.[3] We shall consider it now as an example of Rome's propaganda and of her worsening relations with Macedonia. Extensive restorations may be uncertain, but there is no doubt about the following points (I use square brackets to indicate a restoration):

---

[1] For Rhodes' relations with Rome see Appendix 5.

[2] For Rome's change of policy here see Appendix 5.

[3] Sherk no. 40 gives texts as restored by H. Pomtow and by G. Colin. The year in which it was inscribed is in doubt. J. Bousquet in *BCH* 105 (1981) 416 put it in 171 and Sherk in 171/0, while G. Daux, *Delphes au IIe et au Ier siècle* (Paris, 1936) 322 ruled out G. Colin's date after 168. I prefer 172, because it was Rome that took the diplomatic initiative, and Perseus drew up his memorandum, I think, as a reply to the Roman statement as published at Delphi and as stated by Marcius Philippus (Plb. 27. 4. 1–3).

1. Perseus is to be banned from sacred ceremonies at Delphi.
2. He has brought barbarians from beyond the [Danube] to enslave [Greeks].
3. He has broken the [sworn agreement].[1]
4. The Thracians attached to us[2]...and Abrupolis has been expelled from his kingdom by Perseus.
5. Envoys who were travelling to Rome on the matter of alliance (περὶ συμμαχίας) [have been abused by Perseus].
6. He committed an act of desperation in [trying to poison senators].
7. [The Dolopians] were deprived of freedom.
8. In Aetolia he planned (civil) war and massacres.
9. He was continually...corrupting the leading men and he was causing revolutions.
10. This has led to disasters in Pe[rrhaebia etc.] and in the barbarians becoming more a cause of fear.
11. Perseus is eager for war and intends to enslave [Greece].
12. [?His invoking of Gentius].
13. Perseus impiously attacked Eumenes the king [at Delphi].

As the last part of the inscription has not survived, there may have been a few further points.[3]

The first point sought to justify Rome in taking control of Delphi and of the Amphictyonic Council. This she now did. The other points were designed to portray Perseus as the would-be enslaver of the Greek cities, and Rome as the liberator and guarantor of liberty and as the guardian of social order. There was no attempt to prove the charges by citing any evidence. The Senate was not interested in proof or discussion. The points were paraded at Delphi in order to bias the Greek world against Macedonia.

The points listed at Delphi found their way into some of our literary sources through the intermediary annalistic writers. They appeared sporadically in Livy 42. 11–13 (in a speech by Eumenes), 42. 15–16 (Eumenes attacked at Delphi), 42. 17. 1 (the poison plot), 42. 25 (a false account of the agreement with Perseus which was blown up into an alliance at 42. 25. 12), 42. 26. 2 (Gentius in league with Perseus), 42. 36. 4 (Perrhaebia etc.), 42. 40 (in the speech of Marcius Philippus, misrepresenting the agreement with Perseus and including most of the points made at Delphi), and 42. 41–2 (a fictitious reply by Perseus, foretelling Rome's later hostility to Eumenes). They appeared also in App. *Mac.* 11. 1–2 and 4 (charges made by Eumenes and by Rome), and 11. 6–8 (a fictitious reply by the envoys of Perseus), and in D.S. 29. 30 and 33 (Aetolia, Thessaly, and Abrupolis).

---

[1] Reference to the oaths of the agreement is made by Paus. 7. 10. 6.
[2] The word ἡμετ[έρους] was probably followed by φίλους συμμάχους τε as in treaties nos. 11 and 12 in Appendix 5.   [3] See the admirable commentary in *SIG* 643.

The Roman procedure at the time is clear. The Senate decided to force Perseus into making concessions or, if he refused, to destroy him in war. Once the decision was taken, it was necessary to persuade the Roman People to go to war, because the Senate depended on the willingness of a conscript army. To this end the blessing of the gods on a just war and a prophecy of success had to be publicly obtained by ritual processes. It was also desirable to fill the ordinary citizen with fears for his property, and for this the inspired rumour that the Macedonians, the dreaded Gauls (as they believed the Bastarnae and the Scordisci to be), and hordes of Thracians were about to invade Italy was particularly effective. Propaganda in Rome's favour was to be published at Delphi and elsewhere, and the name of Perseus was to be blackened (this being an early example for us of political warfare); and envoys were to travel far and wide and build a web of alliances. Throughout the long process of preparing for the war Perseus was given no chance of making a defence at Rome or even of using the normal diplomatic channels which were open to any 'friend of the Roman People'.[1] As Livy put it, 'the minds [of the Senators] were such that they could not be taught or swayed' (42. 48. 3). They were moving deliberately towards the stark ultimatum: 'Make the reparations we demand, or we go to war.'

The motives of the Senate can only be conjectured. At this time it maintained a consistent policy towards any past enemy of either confining him or, if opportunity offered, of weakening and then destroying him. This policy was applied to Carthage (Livy 42. 23–4), to Antiochus when he attacked Egypt (44. 19. 6–14) and in turn to Philip and Perseus. Individually the senators, as members of the ruling class, were not averse to a war which might yield them fame, financial profit, and even a triumph, and the leading families of Rome owed their eminence to leadership in wars, especially when the result had been a resounding victory.

Perseus certainly wanted peace, as he showed repeatedly both before and during the course of the war, but he wanted a peace with honour and power for Macedonia. He respected his treaty obligations with Rome, because he saw himself able within them to strengthen his financial and military resources, weaken the Dardanians, expand his power in central Thrace, and restore his country's prestige with the Greek cities. He may at first have thought that Rome would not act so long as he observed his treaty obligations. But it became apparent in and after 174 that this was not so; for she was obviously unwilling to be ousted from her position as the liberator, and in effect controller, of the

---

[1] E.g. in Livy 42. 14. 2, 36. 1 and 5, and 37. 6.

Greek states. It may be that Perseus miscalculated Rome's reaction. But once that reaction was clear, he had to decide whether to hold his ground, even if it endangered the existence of Macedonia, or to change to a policy of apathy and subservience, which was at this time being imposed on Carthage.[1]

At some time during these years Perseus made a change in his coinage. The strongest monetary system in the eastern Mediterranean and the Aegean Sea was that of Rhodes and Eumenes, to which the strong Phoenician-Egyptian group was closely related. The Macedonian coinage, which had been on the Attic-Euboean standard since the time of Philip and Alexander, found itself now at some disadvantage for purposes of exchange not only in eastern areas, but also in mainland Greece (and not least in Thessaly), where Rhodian coins were becoming very popular and ousting other currencies.[2] At first Perseus issued silver tetradrachms, didrachms, and drachms on the traditional standard, the mint-master being Zoilus, who had served Philip's closing years, but then he reduced the weight of the tetradrachms by one-twelfth and that of other units by one-eleventh under a mint-master whose monogram was **AY**.[3] This change brought his coinage closer to the Rhodians' lighter standard and made exchange easier. At the same time it was a devaluation, and if he continued to pay his mercenaries, for instance, in so many tetradrachms a year, he was saving a substantial amount of silver. This form of parsimony may have earned him a reputation for stinginess. It is probable that Perseus recalled the coins of the heavier standard, melted them, and reissued the units at the reduced weight; for very few of the older tetradrachms were found in a hoard near Ioannina in Epirus, which was probably hidden in 167.[4] Perseus is likely to have made the change at a time when he could foresee the probability of war and the need for heavy expenditure. It is apparent that he issued at this time imitations of Rhodian silver coins, because a large number of such coins with the two initial letters of the mint-master Zoilus were found in a hoard in Thessaly.[5] Payments in this coinage, which was so popular in northern Greece, may have been more acceptable than in Macedonian coinage.

[1] See Livy 42. 23. [2] See Robert, *Num. grecque* 179 f. and esp. 190 and 213.
[3] Gaebler II 195 f.; Mamroth, 1928. 13 ff.
[4] See Franke, in the important article where he reaches conclusions by studying the hoards laid down at Oreus (Histiaea) perhaps in late autumn 171, at Metsovo in 171 or 170, and near Ioannina very probably in 167. The change to a lighter weight by Perseus is described by Franke as 'die logische und zwangsläufige Folge eines weitsichtigen Finanz- und Handelspolitik'. The first Ptolemy had recalled silver in circulation in Egypt in order to melt it and issue a different coinage; see Martin 225. For the Oreus hoard see Mamroth, 1928. 6 n. 2.
[5] See T. Hackens, 'La circulation monétaire dans la Béotie hellénistique', *BCH* 93 (1969) 721. This hoard, found at Metsovo in Epirus, had 1,500 Rhodian coins and some tetradrachms of Perseus and earlier Macedonian kings.

There is every indication that Perseus coined massive quantities of silver coins during his reign for the purposes both of trade and of hiring mercenaries and obtaining war material. The beautiful craftsmanship of the early coins, which is apparent in the head of the young king (Pl. I*q*), declined in the later issues, where it has been suggested that the final touches were made by hand on the minted coin and not on the negative mould. A close affinity in style and in the use of the oak-wreath has been seen between Macedonia and the Epirote League. The explanation is more likely to be found in religious and economic factors than in any political alignment of the two states;[1] for Zeus, the god of the oak-wreath, was the ancestor of the Macedonian kings as well as the god of Dodona, and the silver for Epirote coinage is likely to have come from Macedonia, since Epirus had no silver mines. The coins with the portrait head of the king carried the full title 'of King Perseus' and had on the reverse an open-winged eagle, standing on a thunderbolt, the emblem of Zeus, all set within an oak-wreath. Lesser emblems were the plough and the eight-rayed star, or those of war the club of Heracles and the *harpe*, being the weapon of the hero Perseus,[2] with whom the king liked to identify himself. The royal coinage in bronze was marked usually with the letters **BA**, short for **ΒΑΣΙΛΕΩΣ**, and sometimes with the addition of **ΠΕ**, short for **ΠΕΡΣΕΩΣ**, this being necessary in order to distinguish it from the bronze coinages of the Macedones and of the regions and cities, which we have mentioned above (pp. 464–8). These bronze coinages testify to a lively trade within the kingdom itself and with immediately adjacent areas. The royal coinage had the head, not of the king, but of the hero Perseus or of a young Heracles. An early specimen, overstruck on a coin of Philip, had the open-winged eagle standing on a plough with an ear of corn in the field, indicative of peaceful pursuits; others had the thunderbolt and the *harpe*, and one a Nike, which probably commemorated the victory over the Roman cavalry at Callicinus. Another issue had the Macedonian shield with a star of six curving rays, and on the reverse the *harpe* with a different kind of star. Perseus himself appeared on the reverse of coins bearing the head of young Heracles; he was on horseback with his right arm raised, as on coins of Philip II. These coins were designed to persuade the Macedonians that the gods were on their side.

---

[1] Franke 43 related the similarity to 'dem an der Seite Makedoniens geführten Krieg gegen Rom'; but the Epirote League took the side not of Macedonia, but of Rome against Perseus, and remained loyal to Rome when the Molossian state split off and joined Macedonia.

[2] See LSJ[9] s.v., citing Pherecydes, and Mamroth, 1928. 2 n. 1.

XXIV

THE THIRD MACEDONIAN WAR: THE INDECISIVE PHASE (172-169 B.C.)

1. *The preliminary moves*

THE preliminaries to hostilities are described in our sources mainly from the standpoint of the Romans and the Greeks and relatively little from that of the Macedonians. On the one hand Polybius wrote primarily for Romans and Greeks, and his views were transmitted by some later writers. On the other hand the annalistic writers were eager to justify Rome and paid less attention to the Greeks and the Macedonians. The chief surviving source of information is Livy. In Book 42 he created confusion by putting in sequence two accounts of the same event which were really alternatives. The event was the last hearing of envoys sent by Perseus to Rome. The annalistic account in 42. 36. 1-7 ended with the Senate's order for the envoys to leave Italy within eleven days and its ban on any further envoys coming to Italy; and the account drawn from Polybius (see 27. 6. 3) ended with the Senate's order for the envoys to leave Rome the same day and Italy within thirty days (42. 48. 1-3). The latter is clearly the historical version, and the former is to be discarded, together with the similar account in Dio 20. 22 = Zon. 9. 22. We turn next to App. *Mac.* 11. 5-9. The first envoys in 11. 5 reported the surprise of Perseus at Rome sending out her envoys (to speak) against him; and this corresponds with the envoys in Livy 42. 36. 2 reporting the surprise of Perseus that Rome was sending troops over to 'Macedonia'. The second set of envoys in 11. 5 (ὁ δ' αὖθις ἔπεμπεν ἑτέρους) was finally ordered to leave Rome the same day and Italy within thirty days (11. 9); this corresponds with Plb. 27. 6. 3, D.S. 30. 1, and the second passage in Livy. It is generally thought that Appian drew on the 'composition of an early imperial annalist';[1] if so, this annalist had put the two accounts in sequence, one from an earlier annalist and the other from Polybius, and had omitted the inconsistent details.

What of the speech delivered by the second set of envoys in Appian? It belongs in the passage derived ultimately from Polybius, and we can be sure that Polybius supplied a speech at that culminating moment in

---

[1] So A. H. McDonald in *OCD²* 87.

the relations between Macedonia and Rome. The material for the speech could have been drawn by Polybius from the memorandum which Perseus circulated to the Greek states (as we shall explain shortly) and which Polybius certainly saw at the time. But we cannot rule out some modification of Polybius' text by the intermediate imperial annalist.

When did the Senate decide to go to war? It was alarmed by Eumenes' speech and convinced by Gaius Valerius' report (Livy 42. 14. 1 and 18. 1). From that time, in summer 172, Livy wrote of 'war' (42. 18. 2 'belli administratio'; 19. 3 'bello etsi non indicto, tamen iam decreto'). However, the decision by the Roman People to make a conditional declaration of war was still to come; it was not taken until just after the inauguration of the new consuls, which happened about December 172 (42. 30. 8–31. 1). Between summer and December 172 the Senate was preparing for war.

In summer 172 Rome had no fleets and no troops east of the Adriatic Sea, and her friends and allies on the coast of Illyris would be overwhelmed if Perseus were to attack them with an army of 40,000 men. Except for Corcyra she had no dependable naval base, and the allies she had had in the Second Macedonian War were lukewarm, alienated, or even won over, by Perseus. The first step was to fit out and man a greatly superior fleet of quinqueremes in Roman waters (Livy 42. 27), and to start on the enrolment of a very large army for the 'provincia Macedonia', as the Senate called it (Livy 42. 31–35. 6). Probably in September,[1] the Senate passed a vanguard of 300 cavalry and 5,000 infantry and a strong fleet into Illyris, where the commander occupied the coastal cities and placed garrisons in advanced forts of the Illyrians and the Dassaretii (42. 18. 3 and 36. 8–9). A large army, still mustering at Brundisium, was ready, if needed, to reinforce the vanguard; for the Illyrian coastal area was the necessary bridgehead for an offensive now, as it had been in 200. At the same time Roman envoys set off on the way to Masinissa and Carthage to arrange for cavalry, elephants, and supplies and to Crete for archers; and other envoys were proceeding on diplomatic missions to Illyria, the Greek

---

[1] The dating is uncertain. Livy 42. 27. 5 reported an order for the Second Legion to reach Brundisium by the Ides of February, i.e. by late October; but this legion was not part of the vanguard (42. 32. 6). When Perseus sent his letter to the Roman envoys at Corcyra, news of the vanguard's arrival had reached him in Macedonia; for in the letter he referred to troops 'crossing to Greece' (probably to Oricum) and 'occupying cities' (i.e. coastal Greek cities, as foreseen at 42. 18. 3). The time needed for the envoys in Greece to complete their missions by January/February 171 (Plb. 27. 2. 12 ἐν τοῖς Ἕλλησι κατὰ χειμῶνα) suggests that the crossing of Sicinius' force took place not later than September. So also Heiland 20 and 42 f. 'Frühherbst'. The crossing thus happened before the arrival of the Second Legion, which was thereafter kept in Italy (42. 32. 6). For this controversial matter see Walbank in *JRS* 31 (1941) 82 ff. and *C* 3. 291 and 294. For the independence of Oricum and its relations with Corcyra and Rome see *HE* 609.

mainland, the Greek islands, Asia, and Egypt with the clear message that the Senate was contemplating war with Perseus and with any state supporting him. This was no idle threat; for everyone knew the fate, for instance, of Anticyra, Aegina, and Oreus.

The five envoys who were to go to Illyria and the Greek mainland were accompanied by 1,000 soldiers. These were to be their armed escorts. This unusual association was a form of psychological warfare, implying an imminent state of war and the readiness of Rome to back diplomacy with armed force.[1] On reaching Corcyra this group of envoys received a letter from Perseus in which he asked why troops were crossing from Italy to Greece (probably at Oricum) and 'occupying cities' (i.e. probably Oricum, Apollonia, and Epidamnus). The envoys gave not a written, but a verbal, reply that the action had been taken 'for the protection of the cities themselves' (42. 37. 5–6). The envoys and their troops then split up and set off for different destinations.

In Illyria an evasive reply was given by Gentius, ruler of a large kingdom to the north of the Roman zone, and he was marked down for destruction in the Senate's mind, unless he changed his tactic. The Epirote League, immediately to the south of the Roman zone, said it would honour its defensive alliance with Rome and a special clause therein, apparently not to make any new alliance without Rome's consent. What was more important, it sent 400 soldiers to garrison Orestis.[2] The Acarnanian League, which had had a defensive alliance with Rome in 191, was warned to deserve well of Rome now and in the future. The envoys did not press Aetolia, but waited there while a pro-Roman leader was elected general of the League. Other envoys visited Cephallenia and toured the Peloponnese, where they gave some offence. Two envoys, Marcius Philippus and Aulus Atilius, hastened to Larissa, where the Council of the Thessalian League met and promised full support.[3]

At this point envoys from Perseus came to Larissa. Having received the verbal reply from Corcyra, Perseus now asked for a personal interview with Marcius Philippus, whose father had been a guest-friend of Perseus' father. A meeting was arranged at Homolium, just south of the Macedonian frontier, probably late in November. We do not know what was said at the meeting; for the contents of the speech retailed by Livy was derived from the list of charges inscribed at Delphi

---

[1] These troops were not for garrison duties, as suggested in *JRS* 31. 83. They were far too few and we are told that allied troops were used in Orestis and at Chalcis.

[2] That this alliance had special terms is to be inferred from Polybius' phrase at 27. 15. 12 τὰ κατὰ τὴν συμμαχίαν ... δίκαια. See *HE* 621, Walbank, *C* 3. 315, and Appendix 5. For Orestis independent since 197, see p. 444 above.

[3] Livy 42. 37. 7–38. 7.

and is not authentic. At the end of the conference Marcius Philippus proposed to Perseus that he should send envoys to Rome and obtain a peaceful settlement on easy terms.[1] That was exactly what Perseus wanted. So he agreed to send envoys, who might take a month in winter to reach Rome. In fact he was being duped by Marcius Philippus, in whose good faith as a guest-friend Perseus may have put too much trust. For the Senate was already set unconditionally upon war and their envoy was playing for time within which to mount larger forces and continue the diplomatic offensive. Livy tried to palliate this act of deception by calling the following weeks a period of 'armistice' ('indutiae'), as if the two countries had already gone to war!

The Roman envoys hastened on to Chalcis in Euboea and to Boeotia, both areas being indispensable if Rome was to mount an offensive by land and sea from Thessaly. As we shall see, they succeeded in disrupting the Boeotian League, winning most of the Boeotian cities for Rome and securing the allegiance of Chalcis, where a Roman officer was now stationed. Hurrying on to Argos, where a meeting of the Achaean League Assembly had been arranged in advance, they obtained 1,000 troops from the League and sent them to serve as a garrison under the Roman officer at Chalcis. Meanwhile the envoys in the islands were promoting the cause of Rome. Their coming prompted Rhodes to equip a fleet of forty ships, ready for action, and the Greek city-states in Asia Minor inclined now towards Rome. There Eumenes of Pergamum and Ariarathes of Cappadocia were enthusiastic supporters, and Prusias of Bithynia was pursuing a neutral policy. Ptolemy, or rather his guardians, promised to provide any help Rome might want for the war (Livy 42. 29. 7). When the envoys returned in batches during the opening months of 171, the Senate was pleased with the results, although some of the older members of the House expressed disapproval of the duplicity employed by Marcius Philippus.[2]

During the absence of the envoys a further step towards war had been taken at Rome. Shortly after the beginning of the consular year the *haruspices* forecast 'victory, triumph, and extension of empire' (Livy 42. 30. 8). Perhaps early in January 171 the Roman People, meeting in the Comitia Centuriata, voted in favour of a conditional declaration of war against Macedonia. The condition was as follows. 'Unless Perseus gives satisfaction on these grounds of complaint, that he has attacked allies of the Roman People, both ravaging their land and occupying their cities, in violation of the treaty concluded with Philip and renewed with Perseus; and that in assembling armaments, army, and

---

[1] Livy 42. 39–42. That Philippus suggested some terms—no doubt tempting ones—is indicated in Livy 42. 46. 1.

[2] Livy 42. 47. 4–7; D.S. 30. 7. 1.

fleet he has laid plans for mounting a war against the Roman People'.[1] The grounds of complaint were framed to convince the Roman public that Perseus could avoid war by making recompense, and that if war should come it would be a just war. Whether the complaints were justified or not was immaterial to the Senate; for it had no intention of letting Perseus defend himself in public. It was already unconditional war for the Senate. The condition, however, had a further value: it might encourage Perseus to negotiate further and so enable Rome to occupy advantageous positions on the Greek mainland.

The envoys from Greece had already reported, probably in early February, and officers had been sent from Rome to collect troops from the vanguard in Illyris and place garrisons in Larissa and Thebes, when the envoys from Perseus were given a hearing by the Senate, about the beginning of March 171.[2] Their arguments were addressed to deaf ears. The Senate ordered them and any other Macedonians in Italy to leave the country within thirty days (Plb. 27. 6. 3; Livy 42. 48. 1–31; App. *Mac.* 11. 9). The fleet now moved to its advanced base in Cephallenia, and the newly appointed consul for the 'provincia Macedonia', Publius Licinius, set off from the capital in military uniform, an indication that he was going to war. In late March or early April he took the main army across to join the vanguard which was encamped at the Nymphaeum near Apollonia.[3] The Roman pieces were all in place for the opening gambit.

Let us turn now to the Greek states. The city-states of the mainland and the islands were far too deeply split by internal faction and by inter-state animosities to adopt any common policy towards either of the great powers. There was widespread sympathy for Macedonia, but the decisive factor was fear of Rome, as soon as her troop movements began.[4] Boeotia was an extreme example of political disintegration at this time, federalists sparring with separatists, democrats with oligarchs, and one city with another city. The Roman envoys stirred the pot with great skill. Because federalists, democrats, and some cities had risen to power within Boeotia and made alliance with Macedonia in (probably) 174/3, the envoys courted the exiles and the rival factions

---

[1] This is an excellent example of imputing to an enemy what you are doing yourself; similarly Dio 20. 22 suggested that it was Perseus who wanted a delay in order to prepare for war.

[2] Since Livy 42.36. 1 is unhistorical (see p. 505 above), the phrase 'the Kalends of June' in 42. 35. 3 does not help with the dating. We rely rather on Plb. 27. 6, which dates the hearing of Perseus' envoys to after the return of the last Roman envoys, those from Asia, perhaps in March, when sailing conditions began to improve.

[3] Livy 42. 47–9. For the Nymphaeum see H*E* 232 f. and 626. We have rejected Livy 42. 25. 1–13 as unhistorical; see p. 501 above.

[4] Cf. Plb. 24. 9. 6 διὰ τὸν φόβον. The effects of fear were as shrewdly and cynically calculated by Rome as by Hitler in the run-up to a major war. For Polybius' comments on the pro-Perseus politicians see 30. 6–8.

and cities. The Roman presence, actual and expected, caused a change of heart at Chalcis and at Thebes. There the majority now wanted alliance with Rome, and the pro-Macedonian leaders, being thrown into prison, committed suicide. Marcius Philippus and his colleagues insisted that each city-state in Boeotia must send its envoys to Rome and make submission separately. The death-knell of Boeotian federalism was sounding when the envoys left for the Peloponnese. The blame for this was assigned by Polybius to the Boeotians themselves. The Roman part in it incurred no judgement from him.[1]

Political conditions in the Peloponnese were little better than in Boeotia; for since 180 the Achaean League had been split by the rival factions which Polybius, a rising young politician himself, described very vividly (24. 8–10). The first Roman envoys in autumn 172 played upon the internal animosities and supported the separatist principle by asking individual city-states, and not the League as a whole, to support Rome against Perseus (Livy 42. 37. 7–9). They were shouted down in some assemblies, but their message went home to ambitious oligarchs. In early 171, when Marcius Philippus and his colleagues came to Argos from Boeotia, they avoided political issues and obtained what they wanted, Achaean troops to garrison Chalcis. They then returned to Rome.

Perseus must have made the critical decision in 172 not to deliver an offensive in response to Rome's open preparations at sea and in Illyris, but to work for the continuation of the peace and friendship which were assured under the current treaty with Rome. One reason for the decision may have been the failure of his envoys to win Eumenes of Pergamum, Antiochus, and Ptolemy to his side (Livy 42. 26. 8). Past enmities proved irreconcilable. He could not count on any Hellenistic monarch joining in the defence of Macedonian liberty, if the situation should deteriorate into war. His hopes of a peaceful settlement were raised by Marcius Philippus in late 172, and he was careful to respect the conditions of the standstill. Rome was less scrupulous; but then she had no intention of keeping faith in regard to the standstill or the current treaty.[2]

After the conference at Homolium Perseus drew up a memorandum on the Macedonian case and the Roman case as presented at the conference, and he concluded—correctly by ideal standards of inter-

[1] Plb. 27. 1–2; Livy 42. 37. 4, 38. 3 and 5, and 43. 4–44. 8. Suicide was probably due to fear of torture; cf. Plb. 24. 9. 13 αἰκισαμένους πᾶσαν αἰκίαν ἀποκτεῖναι.
[2] Plb. 27. 5. 7–8; 'standstill' is a better translation of Polybius' term αἱ ἀνοχαί than 'armistice' in the context. It was of fixed duration (Livy 42. 47. 10), and its conditions included a ban on movements of troops by Macedonia and by Rome. This was broken in spirit, if not in letter, when Achaean troops were sent to garrison Chalcis, and flagrantly when 2,000 Roman troops were sent to garrison Larissa before the standstill ran out (Livy 42. 47. 10–11).

national equity and legal justice—that he had much the stronger case. He circulated this memorandum to all Greek states, partly as a means of offsetting Rome's propaganda at Delphi and partly to elicit the policies of individual states. Our patchy sources tell us of replies only from Boeotia and Rhodes. Three city-states in Boeotia—Coroneia, Thisbe, and Haliartus—were in opposition to the pro-Roman separatists at Thebes, and after an exchange of envoys they asked Perseus to send them military help. He said that he could not break the terms of the standstill, and he advised them to withstand any attack by Thebes, but not to go to war with Rome (Plb. 27. 5. 7–8). This was tantamount to admitting that, if it came to war with Rome, Macedonia could not operate in central Greece. Perseus' honesty was laudable in itself, but there was a certain *naïveté* in the faith he put in his memorandum; for the policy of the small Greek states was not likely to be affected by questions of right and wrong, when two great powers were entering the arena. This was apparent in Rhodes' reply to the memorandum and to Perseus' special request that Rhodes should remain neutral and try to effect a reconciliation, if Rome should break the treaty and go to war against Macedonia (Plb. 27. 4. 5 παρὰ τὰς συνθήκας, translated by Livy 42. 46. 3 'contra foedus'): 'Perseus must not ask Rhodes to do anything which might make her position appear contrary to the wishes of Rome.'[1]

If we allow a month for news to travel in midwinter from Rome to Pella, perhaps via Gentius, Perseus learnt in February that the Roman People had voted in favour of a conditional declaration of war, and in late April that his envoys had been given a perfunctory hearing in March in a manner which could only mean war. Rome had cheated and fooled him all along the line, and Rome had won the diplomatic game almost everywhere. Justice was on his side, in that he had observed the terms of the current treaty with Rome and the terms of the standstill, whereas Rome had broken both. This was an important consideration within Macedonia, where the choice lay between humiliating concessions and stubborn resistance. Livy reported the views of Perseus' Friends, convened in Council at the palace in Pella, and the view of Perseus when he addressed his troops at Citium. The great majority of the Friends considered that appeasement by concession was useless, and that Rome's aim was to remove the Macedonian kingdom from her imperial path; the only course was war, in which victory by Macedonia would free the world from Roman imperialism (42. 50. 4–9). On this advice, in the name of honour and justice, Perseus decided on war (42. 51. 1). He sacrificed 100 animals to the Macedo-

---

[1] The request to Byzantium, then in alliance with both parties, was probably the same; but a lacuna in Livy 42. 46. 1 deprives us of information.

nian goddess of war, Athena Alcidemus, on behalf of the state and claimed the help of the gods. His address at Citium stressed the injustices committed by Rome, the duplicity of Marcius Philippus and the treacherous movement of troops during the standstill (42. 52. 6–8). When he said that the choice was one of liberty or enslavement, the army roared out a demand for action (42. 53. 1). The die was cast.[1]

2. *The resilience of Macedonia*

For a campaign in the Balkan peninsula Rome needed to control the Lower Adriatic Sea and the Ionian Sea (see Fig. 8). Her main bridgehead was the Illyrian coast opposite Brundisium; her vanguard was already in place there before the standstill, and her main army was assembling to follow, before the news reached Perseus that diplomatic relations were severed (Livy 42. 38. 3–4 and 49. 10). Rome's battle-fleet of fifty quinqueremes, with crews of which two-thirds were freedmen from Italy and one-third Italian allies, was unrivalled. However, the supply vessels which would be crossing these seas might be raided by the small fast *lembi* of Gentius, perhaps 300 in number, which were based on the coast to the north of the bridgehead. As a check on Gentius Rome had alliances probably with Issa and Pharos, Greek city-states on the like-named islands off the Dalmatian coast.[2] We hear later of a Roman officer in charge of a defence force at Issa (43. 9. 5). In this year when the main battle-fleet was in Adriatic waters Gentius played safe. He sent fifty-four *lembi*, while Issa sent twelve *lembi*, to meet the leading Roman flotilla at Epidamnus;[3] but Rome remained distrustful. The main fleet headed for Corcyra and Cephallenia, and it was followed by convoys of merchant ships which were transporting supplies of cereals and other foodstuffs from Brundisium to Apollonia Illyrica and from Naples to Cephallenia (42. 48. 10). These supplies had come from as far away as Numidia, Sardinia, and Sicily.

If Rome intended to deliver an offensive mainly from Thessaly rather than from Illyris, she needed naval bases on the east coast of

---

[1] A narrative of this period is given by W. L. Adams in Adams and Borza 237–56 with little criticism of the sources; e.g. he accepts Livy 42. 25. 1 as historical in his n. 106. Walbank in *Anc. Mac.* 2. 80–94 criticizes cogently the views of E. J. Bickerman in *REG* 66 (1953) 479 ff. and of A. Giovannini in *BCH* 93 (1969) 853 ff., and he advances his own views, with which I am in general agreement.

[2] The booty from Illyria in 167 included 220 *lembi* (45. 48. 10). For the alliance with Pharos see Appendix 5. Issa is likely to have had a similar alliance.

[3] Livy 42. 48. 8 implied that Gentius' ships came on a raid and that the Roman commander blandly assumed they were on his side and carried them off with the main fleet. But if their aim had been to raid Roman shipping they would not have been waiting inside an enemy harbour! For various views see Meloni, *Perseo* 212 f.

Greece. She obtained these by acts of duplicity during the standstill; for with the help of the Achaean League she secured Argos and Chalcis, and she put a Roman garrison into Thebes, which enabled her to control some ports on the Boeotian coast (see Fig. 7). By prearrangement Eumenes of Pergamum brought his fleet with 1,000 cavalry and 6,000 infantry to Chalcis, and there he joined the bulk of the Roman battle-fleet which, having rounded the Peloponnese, carried at least 10,000 marines (42. 56. 1–5). Naval reinforcements from Carthage, Rhodes, Samos, Calchedon, and Heraclea Pontica were sent away, because Roman thalassocracy in the Aegean Sea was now assured (cf. Plb. 27. 7. 14–16). Naval personnel laid siege to Haliartus in Boeotia, and a flotilla captured Alope and attacked Larissa Cremaste, ports on the Thessalian coast, facing north Euboea (see Fig. 6). From now the main supply lines by sea were not across the Adriatic to the north-west coast of Greece and to Illyris, but round the southern Peloponnese or from the eastern Aegean and the Black Sea ports to Chalcis in the Euripus Channel. This efficient supply system was an essential part of the campaign.

When the consul landed in Illyris in 171, he had an army of at least 2,000 cavalry and 35,000 infantry.[1] While a substantial force was no doubt left to hold the bridgehead, the main army made a rapid march through Epirus, took a difficult pass through Athamania, and arrived at Gomphi on the edge of the Thessalian plain (see Fig. 6) with much exhaustion of men and horses (42. 55. 1–5).[2] Speed was important, because the whereabouts of Perseus' army, superior in numbers and in training, was not known. But the consul was helped by the standstill; for Perseus did not move from central Macedonia until he learnt that his envoys had been ejected from Italy. Sufficient supplies were carried over the Pindus range to feed the Roman army at Gomphi, but thereafter the main supply lines were to run from Chalcis and Boeotia, and the route through the Pindus range from Ambracia to Gomphi was to play a subsidiary role. At Gomphi the consul sacrificed to the gods of Rome in gratitude for his safe arrival in Thessaly. It was a notable achievement, in that his predecessors in the earlier Macedonian wars had had to fight difficult battles before they crossed the spine of Pindus.

[1] 42. 31. 2–5. An attempt was made to recruit experienced soldiers for two legions by the prospect of loot, and the 'tribuni militum' were selected by choice and not by lot. As Livy mentioned the cavalry of the vanguard as a separate item at 42. 31. 3, it seems that the 5,000 infantry was also separate. Heiland 50 dated the crossing to the end of April 171.
[2] The route through Epirus from the Nymphaeum ran first up the Aous valley, then up the Drin valley past Antigoneia and then to Eurymenae (Kastritsa) in the plain of Ioannina. From there the consul chose neither the Zygos route via Metsovo nor the much longer route via Ambracia and Argithea to Gomphi, but a less-used route via Melissouryio into the Achelous valley at Theodhoriana and on via Mesokhora to Gomphi (near Mouzaki). I have travelled over all three; see *HE* 280 ff. for the routes and 284 for this campaign.

Rome had now reaped the full advantage from her own duplicity and from Perseus' hope of peace (emphasized by Livy at 42. 43. 3, 44. 1, and 47. 1–3 'decepto per indutias et spem pacis rege').

On the other hand, the trust which Perseus had put in Marcius Philippus and the Senate had cost him dear in terms of strategy. He had lost the chance of eliminating the Roman bridgehead, or by a threat to it of drawing the Roman army into the wild country of Dassaretis, or of holding the Aoi Stena position with flankguards, and so of keeping the Roman army out of contact with its allies in most of Greece and in the Aegean area. But there was another side to the matter.[1] Perseus had demonstrated to the Greek world, and especially to his own people, that he had made every possible effort to maintain peace, and that Rome's treachery and aggression left no alternative but war for his people, if they wished to preserve their national independence. A united Macedonia was needed in a war of survival, and Perseus clearly obtained that unity. Livy recorded it at three levels: in a Council of Friends at Pella (42. 50), in a speech to the army (42. 52. 5–53. 1), and in spontaneous deputations from the cities and regions of Macedonia (42. 53. 3–4). While some details of the descriptions, taken no doubt from Polybius, are not authentic,[2] the unanimity of the response is clear.

It was probably late in April 171[3] when the envoys came to Pella with the news that Rome chose war and was, no doubt, about to reinforce the vanguard which Perseus knew was in Illyris. During the months when he had hoped for peace he had not kept his army under arms, but sent the men to their fields. Now he convened in his palace a Council of Friends, and on the advice of the great majority he decided to meet war with war. It must have taken three weeks at least to assemble his entire army at Citium, in the plain below Edessa;[4] for the Odrysians, led by Cotys, 400 kilometres away, had to be informed and make the march. It may have been at Citium that the Assembly of the Macedones in the army voted for war; but what Livy describes is the parade of the army at Citium and the march from there day by day.

---

[1] Meloni, who often writes from hindsight, did not consider this aspect. He condemned Perseus' efforts to obtain a peaceful settlement, and therefore his honouring of the standstill, as 'absurd'; see Meloni, *Perseo* 185 and 202.

[2] At 42. 50. 10 the mention of Perseus' brother aiming at the throne was very inappropriate; at 42. 52 the size of the Roman army cannot have been known; and the war being contrived by 'fortuna' is typical of Polybius, but inapposite for Perseus.

[3] We have to work back from Livy 42. 64. 2–3, when the ripe grain in the fields was appropriate to mid-June in the Thessalian plain. Allowing a fortnight for operations after Perseus reached Sycurium and a fortnight for the march from Citium and operations before Sycurium, we put the review of the army in mid-May, the bringing of news by the envoys in late April, and the reply of the Senate to the envoys in late March.

[4] For its position see Volume I. 166 with Map 14. Heiland 53 put it at Naoussa.

The description comes ultimately from the *King's Journal* in my opinion. It is therefore dependable, if Polybius and Livy have transmitted it correctly.

The forces of the Macedonians and their allies totalled 43,000 men. There were 3,000 Macedonian cavalry and 1,000 Odrysian cavalry. There were 21,000 Macedonians of the phalanx formation and two groups of élite Macedonians, one of 2,000 and the other of 3,000, and 13,000 other infantry with their own national forms of equipment. The latter consisted of 3,000 Paeonians, Agrianians, and Thracians (the last being settlers in the kingdom); 3,000 Thracians who were 'free' in the sense that they had never paid tribute to Macedonia (see Volume II. 672 ff.); 3,000 Cretans; 2,000 Gauls; 1,000 Odrysians; 500 Aetolians and Boeotians; and 500 Greeks of various origins.[1] During the twenty-six years since the battle of Cynoscephalae the losses in Macedonia manpower had been more than made good, and the new generation of soldiers had gained some experience in action in Thrace. The non-Macedonian infantrymen, being light-armed in contrast to the phalangites, were seasoned troops, whether drawn from martial races or from groups of mercenary soldiers. It was a highly professional army as compared with the Roman forces, which contained a large proportion of raw recruits. The 'free' Thracians, the Cretans, the Odrysians, and the two Greek contingents had their own commanders. All other units were commanded by experienced Macedonian officers.[2] Perseus, the commander-in-chief, now aged forty or so, was also experienced in command.

The Macedonian army was admirably equipped from the royal arsenals, and its needs in finance and supply were covered for some years ahead. The cities throughout the kingdom had home-defence forces and reserves of money and grain, which they offered to contribute to the national cause. For the moment all that the king needed from the cities was more wheeled transport for the carriage of siege equipment, artillery, and supplies.[3] The strategic thinking of Perseus was governed by the fact that this was a once-for-all army, irreplaceable if it suffered a severe defeat. He wished, as far as it was

---

[1] Livy 42. 51 gave round numbers (as we therefore do), but he qualified five of them with the word 'ferme', 'almost', which means that he had exact numbers in at least those cases, and another with the words 'non plus quam'. He mentioned that 'almost half' of the 43,000 were 'phalangitae'. This confirms the figure of 21,000 phalangitae which is reached by subtraction; so also Meloni, *Perseo* 217. Some of the text is corrupt. About now he sent off an envoy to Antiochus, whose reply is not known (Plb. 27. 7. 15).

[2] Livy gave the citizenship of only some of the Macedonian commanders, and one of them wrongly (Didas Paeon; cf. 40. 21. 9 and 42. 58. 8). In the original list the citizenships of all Macedonian commanders was no doubt recorded.

[3] Livy 42. 51. 6; 52. 11–12; 53. 3–4. For the importance of wheeled transport see Hammond in *GRBS* 24 (1983) 27 ff.

possible, to commit it to a set battle only if he was confident of an all-out victory. In comparison Rome was a many-headed Hydra, able to replace army after army; and she had what Macedonia lacked, an unchallenged navy, which could undertake its own sphere of operations. When his army was assembled at Citium, Perseus knew that the Roman army had left its base in Illyris and was moving southwards with a lead of several days in hand,[1] and it was obvious enough that its destination was Thessaly. The immediate concern of Perseus was to seize the southern approaches to the two main passes from Thessaly into Macedonia, the Volustana pass and the Tempe pass; for the Perrhaebian and Thessalian cities, which owed their independence to the Roman settlement after the battle of Cynoscephalae, were certain to take the Roman side, if opportunity offered. As it was better to attack the Perrhaebians first as the weaker opponents and thereafter to approach the Tempe pass from the Thessalian side, thereby cutting off any garrisons in Tempe from their base, he headed for the Volustana pass.

Following the Macedonian road—the later Via Egnatia—from Citium to Boceria on the east side of Lake Begorritis (then much smaller than today), he encamped there with abundant supplies of water available. Next day he made a long march of some 40 miles (over 60 kilometres) to the Haliacmon river, where his leading troops probably went ahead to occupy the pass (see Fig. 6).[2] Next morning he surprised the three Perrhaebian cities on the south side of the pass, which surrendered although the Thessalian League had exacted hostages from them. From one of the cities, Pythium, he controlled the southern end of the Petra pass. Advancing down the Europus valley he forced the pro-Roman city of Chyretiae to surrender on the second day of his attack.[3] Mylae, strategically placed at the narrow entry to the valley, was taken by storm on the fourth day of a desperate resistance. The city was sacked and destroyed; those who survived the street fighting were sold as slaves. Swinging eastwards he encamped by Phalanna, a Thessalian town which evidently submitted; and on learning that a Roman officer and a Thessalian force under the command of the general of the Thessalian League were in possession of

---

[1] Livy 42. 53. 2. The distance from the Nymphaeum to Citium being 220 km. as the crow flies, we may allow four or five days for a messenger to proceed from one to the other through mountainous country.

[2] The area is described in Volume I. 57 and 110 and by HH *Via Egnatia* II. 128 ff. The ethnic Βοκέρριος occurs in an inscription (*Proc. 8th Epigr. Conf.* 296 and *AAA* 4 (1971) 115 f. As HH reported, water was piped to Boceria in the Hellenistic period; the water of the lake was also drinkable. See *Atlas* Map 12. For such long marches see *HA* 91 and n. 33, and C. Neumann in *Historia* 20 (1971) 196 ff.

[3] See p. 447 n. 1 above for Rome's dealings with Chyretiae.

Gyrton, he marched past it and took by surprise[1] Elatia and Gonnus in the southern vestibule of the Tempe pass. He improved the defences of Gonnus by digging a triple ditch and throwing up a rampart, placed a strong garrison in it, and made his own camp at Sicyrium on the foothills of Mt. Ossa, where there were abundant springs of water. His rapid marches had enabled him to anticipate the enemy and gain control first of the Volustana pass and then of the Tempe pass, through which supplies could now be brought forward from Dium and Heracleum by waggon and upriver by boat. His men gathered the green crops as fodder for the horses from the rich fields below Sycurium.[2]

When Licinius learnt of the Macedonian presence in Thessaly he advanced towards Larissa and made a fortified camp on the south bank of the Peneus, 3 miles short of the city. There he was joined by Pergamene forces from Chalcis, numbering 1,000 cavalry and 4,000 infantry; the entire cavalry of the Aetolian League, 500 strong; 400 Thessalian cavalry; 300 cavalry and 100 infantry from Apollonia Illyrica; and 1,500 light-armed infantry from the Achaean League.[3] Adding these cavalry forces to his Roman cavalry, 2,000 strong, he was more or less equal in numbers to the 4,000 cavalry under Perseus' command. The supply lines ran from Larissa through the Pherae gap (by Velestinon) to the ports of the Pagasaean Gulf, southwards via Crannon and Pharsalus to central Greece, and westwards to the rich area irrigated by the Peneus and the Zygos pass to Epirus.

Confident in the speed and efficiency of his cavalry and light-armed infantry, Perseus cut the Romans' communications with the Gulf of Pagasae by devastating the territory of Pherae and capturing much livestock, and thus made contact with his garrison and fleet at Demetrias. After some probing skirmishes Perseus appeared close to the Roman camp at sunrise with his entire army, the cavalry and light-armed in front and the infantry phalanx behind. The Roman legions took position inside their camp, while the cavalry and light-armed went out to engage the enemy beside a hill called Callicinus. Perseus, commanding the élite Macedonian cavalry and supported by a royal infantry battalion, routed the élite Roman cavalry and the Greek cavalry, except for 400 Thessalians, who kept formation and enabled

---

[1] Here, as in northern Perrhaebia, his cavalry will have surprised many people out in the fields.

[2] This brilliant and almost last-minute campaign has not always been appreciated. For instance, he chose to go first to Boceria to mislead the enemy about his objective. He then avoided the alternative route via Verria and Zoodokhos Pege (see Volume I. 158 f.), because it was visible to outposts at the Volustana pass. See Leake, *NG* 3. 288 f., Meloni, *Perseo* 224, and Walbank, *C* 3. 302.

[3] 42. 55. 8–10. The cavalry was particularly welcome, and Apollonia must have been asked to send cavalry for preference.

most of the defeated cavalry to escape. In this part of the engagement the Romans lost 200 cavalry and 2,000 infantry killed, and 600 were taken prisoner. The phalanx came up close behind the cavalry and was ready to attack the camp; but Perseus was not prepared to incur the heavy loss in phalangites which a determined attack on the fortified camp would have incurred. His army collected the spoil on the battlefield, the Thracian skirmishers decapitated some corpses and carried the heads on their spears, and the whole company returned in triumph to their camp.[1]

The consul arrested the commanders of the five Aetolian squadrons of cavalry, which were said to have fled first, and sent them without any trial to Rome. That night the Romans crossed to the north bank of the Peneus, putting the river between themselves and Perseus' army and fortifying a new camp. In so doing they sacrificed their control of the capital of the Thessalian League, Larissa, which was on the south bank, and they left their allies in the central plain exposed to raids by the Macedonian cavalry. Morale was low, particularly among the allies, and the Roman legions had been afraid to leave their camp during the battle. It was fortunate that at that very moment reinforcements arrived from Numidia: twenty-two war-elephants, which the Macedonian cavalry horses were not trained to face, 1,000 infantry and 1,000 cavalry, the last more than compensating for Roman losses in the battle.

Perseus moved his camp closer to Larissa. He then sued for peace, offering to make payments to Rome for the cost of the war, return to the territorial *status quo ante*, and renew the pre-war agreement with Rome. He made the offer with the support of his Council of Friends and Commanders, their hope being that Rome would henceforth respect Macedonia's strength and keep her distance (Plb. 27. 8. 1–3). The consul and his senior officers rejected the offer. If Perseus wanted peace, they replied, he must place himself and his country in the hands of the Senate, which would decide their future. Perseus made other offers subsequently, but without success. Polybius found the consul's attitude 'fine', and Livy sang the praises of Roman 'constantia'. In fact the negotiations showed that Rome had decided on war *à outrance* and that Perseus had wanted peace from the start.[2]

---

[1] Meloni, *Perseo* 229 opts for the form 'Callinicus'. The detailed account in 42. 57–59, mentioning units and naming commanders, was drawn from Polybius and ultimately in my opinion from the *King's Journal*. A lacuna in Livy's text deprives us of the account of the light-armed Thracians' tactics in attacking enemy cavalry. Livy's statement that a Cretan officer dissuaded Perseus from assaulting the Roman camp is most improbable. Neither army was ever prepared to make an attack on the other's fortified camp. For the scale of the engagement at Callicinus see A. H. McDonald in *Studies Edson* 247.

[2] Plb. 27. 8; Livy 42. 62; App. *Mac.* 9. 12; Zon. 9. 22. 5; P*Aem* 9. 2; J. 33. 1. 4; Eutrop. 4. 6. 3;

Further operations were governed by problems of supply. Both armies depended upon reaping the ripe crops and confiscating grain, and their movements were restricted by lack of water in the plain, Perseus overcoming this difficulty once with water-carts (42. 57. 10; 64. 2–3; App. *Mac.* 9. 13). The Roman army needed more supplies than it could obtain from western Thessaly and Epirus; it therefore moved camp first to Crannon and then to Phalanna in pursuit of standing crops (42. 64. 7 and 65. 1). Perseus made some attacks with a flying column on Roman foraging parties and on one occasion he captured 1,000 waggons with their teams and 600 men. This success precipitated an engagement with the Roman army which issued from camp and inflicted losses of twenty-four cavalrymen and 300 infantry.[1] The campaigning season ended indecisively with neither side willing to attack the other's fortified camp and the Roman legions unwilling to engage the Macedonian phalanx on its chosen ground, the level plain.

As Perseus withdrew for the winter, he left a garrison at Gonnus, which proved impregnable, and a reserve force at Phila. Perrhaebia, however, was recovered by the Romans, and Larissa was abandoned by its Macedonian garrison. The sympathy of the masses in the Greek states were more than ever on the side of Macedonia, not just because their sporting spirit favoured the small man, as Polybius averred, but because they disliked Rome's support of oligarchs and hated her methods.[2] Her pose as a liberator was belied by the total destruction of Haliartus, which fell after a desperate resistance by the inhabitants and by a group from Coroneia; the sale of the persons and property of all opponents at Thebes; the sacking of Malloea in Perrhaebia; and the razing of Pteleum in Phthiotis. In Illyris, too, a city which surrendered was sacked by the Roman army (43. 1. 3). During the winter greater brutality was used after the capture of Coroneia, when all survivors were sold. Even her fondest allies resented the demands for grain which Rome had made during the campaign, for instance from Athens (43. 6. 3). The concern of the Roman army was not liberation, but loot, as the recruiting officers had foreseen (42. 32. 6).

Rome's treatment of the Aetolian cavalry commanders alarmed some elder statesmen of the Epirote League. Hitherto they had honoured the League's alliance with Rome; but now they evidently came to see that this course might lead not to independence, but to loss

Oros. 4. 20. 37. Polybius and Livy called the proposed payments φόροι and 'vectigal', i.e. 'tribute'; but Justin was probably nearer the truth in calling them 'inpensa belli', i.e. 'war costs'. See Meloni, *Perseo* 236 ff.

[1] Livy 42. 64. 7–66. 10 tries to belittle the defeat. Roman losses were due in part to a new missile fired by slingers (Plb. 27. 11).

[2] Plb. 27. 9–10; Livy 42. 30. 1 and 53. 1–2. Polybius avoided analysis of Rome's unpopularity.

of it. They had personal reasons also, in that a younger politician who had been educated at Rome and had influence there was maligning them. The statesmen, named Cephalus, Antinous, and Theodotus, were all Molossians, whereas the younger man was a Thesprotian, called Charops, the grandson of the Charops who had helped Rome in the Second Macedonian War.[1] These Molossians planned to lead the Epirote League into the Macedonian camp, if an opportunity should arise.

In spring 170 Theodotus and Philostratus, another pro-Macedonian leader, hatched a clever plan. See Fig. 8. They invited Perseus to enter Epirus and kidnap the new consul, Aulus Hostilius Mancinus, on his way from Corcyra to Thessaly. The plot miscarried, because Perseus was unexpectedly delayed at the Aous bridge by Molossian guards, who were not in the know, and meanwhile the consul's host had some presage of danger and sent the consul back to the coast, whence he travelled by sea to Boeotia. The object of the plot, successful or not, was to commit the Epirote League to war with Rome and alliance with Perseus. It succeeded only to the extent that the Epirote League split apart on the issue and that the Molossian state and one or two others allied themselves with Perseus. The other states, led by the Thesprotians and the Chaonians, stayed loyal to Rome. The disintegration of the Epirote League resembled that of the Boeotian League, and it too was destined to have disastrous consequences. At the time Perseus gained much-needed allies, Orestis was threatened from both sides, and Hostilius lost the best route for supplies from Epirus to Thessaly via the Zygos pass.[2]

Early in the campaigning season Perseus made a surprise attack from Demetrias on the Roman naval base at Oreus in north Euboea. He captured four quinqueremes, towed off twenty merchantmen with their cargoes, and sank the rest which were laden with grain for the army in Thessaly. The Roman fleet, now commanded by Hortensius, toured the Thracian coast in search of supplies and loot. Putting in at Abdera, a 'friend' of Rome, as it had been declared free by her in 197 (see Plb. 18. 2. 4), Hortensius demanded exorbitant amounts of cash and grain; and when the authorities sent envoys to Rome to protest, the sailors and marines took the place by storm, beheaded the leading men, and sold the rest as slaves. After that the next Greek cities which had in the past been declared free by Rome—Maronea and Aenus—closed their harbours and gates against the fleet. Even Chalcis, the chief naval base of the Roman People, was not safe; for when the fleet

---

[1] Plb. 27. 15, followed by D.S. 30. 5, concerned himself only with their personal reasons. For Charops being Thesprotian see S. I. Dakaris in *Ergon* 1968 (1969) 51 ff. and Ch. Habicht, *Archaeologia Classica* 25–6 (1973–4) 313 ff.

[2] Plb. 27. 16 and D.S. 30. 5a. For further details see H*E* 628.

returned, temples were looted, citizens were kidnapped and sold, and private houses were requisitioned for billeting.[1] Complaints led ultimately to some redress by order of the Senate, where it was possible.

Since much of Livy's text for 170 has not survived, we know only that Hostilius attempted to invade Macedonia twice, the first time by the Volustana pass and then 'through Thessaly' (rather than through Perrhaebia), i.e. near the coast (see Fig. 6). He was outmanœuvred and had to withdraw on each occasion, and when Perseus offered an opportunity for a set battle Hortensius declined it. In a successful counter-offensive Perseus captured many cities in Perrhaebia and Thessaly, and with that front secure he entered Dardania and inflicted a crushing defeat on the Dardanians. It was possibly on this campaign that the treacherous massacre of some troops who had surrendered under a promise of safe conduct occurred, according to D.S. 30. 4.[2] In Thrace a local chieftain and the general of Eumenes, based on the Thracian Chersonese, had forced Cotys to depart from Macedonia, rewarded for his services with 200 talents, and defend his own kingdom. Perseus, therefore, entered into negotiations with the Bastarnae of the lower Danube valley. The Roman bridgehead in Illyris received from Hortensius a reinforcement of 4,000 men under Appius Claudius, who recruited another 8,000 from Rome's allies there. Claudius campaigned inland and established a base in eastern Dassaretis, perhaps at Lychnidus. Eight warships and 2,000 soldiers were sent from Italy to the Roman officer at Issa.[3] These moves alarmed Gentius.

Rome's allies on the Greek mainland had provided only small forces, mainly of cavalry, which was recruited only from the pro-Roman propertied class. An interesting inscription, recording a senatorial decree of October 170, reveals Rome's attempt to tighten her control. At Thisbe, a Boeotian city which had yielded without a struggle (see p. 511 above), the restored pro-Roman party was to fortify and occupy the acropolis and hold all offices for the next ten years, while the rest of the population—such as had not been sold as slaves—needed a permit to travel to Phocis or Aetolia. The decree defined the pro-Romans as 'those who abided by our friendship'. Farther afield Rome used threats. The cities of Crete, for instance, were instructed to recall any Cretans serving with Perseus, if the cities wished to be regarded as 'friends' of Rome rather than of Perseus. Supplies were sent from

[1] Livy 43. 4. 8–10 and 7. 5–11; D.S. 30. 6.

[2] P*Aem*. 9; Livy 44. 2. 6 and 36. 10. See Volume I. 120 for routes. He returned with much booty (P*Aem* 9. 5); 10,000 Dardanians killed is clearly an estimate, probably inflated; see Meloni 273.

[3] Livy 42. 67. 4–5 (Cotys); P*Aem* 9. 5 (Bastarnae); Livy 43. 9. 4–7 (Illyris and Issa). The name of the base is corrupt; but see 43. 10. 8 'ad Lychnidum reduxit'.

Miletus in Asia Minor and from Carthage and Masinissa; and Masinissa's offer of twelve war-elephants and 1,200 cavalry was gratefully accepted.[1]

In autumn 170 Appius Claudius walked into a trap (see Fig. 8). Misled by messengers into believing that Uscana, a Penestian city of 10,000 inhabitants guarded by a Cretan garrison, would be betrayed at dawn, he marched his force of 12,000 men by night from the Penestian frontier (near Vrbjani) and arrived in confusion at dawn only to be routed by a well-prepared attack (see Fig. 8). Some 3,000 escaped to Lychnidus. Claudius had been tempted not only by hopes of loot (Livy 43. 10. 2–3), but also by the strategic importance of the city; for if he captured it, he would cut the best line of communication between Perseus and Gentius and be much closer to the Dardanians.[2]

The incompetence of Roman commanders was matched by absenteeism among the Roman troops, who were adept at staying away on leave or obtaining early discharge (43. 14. 7 and 9–10). Regulations were tightened, and the Senate arranged to recruit 6,000 Romans and 6,000 Latin allies for the legions and 250 Roman cavalry and 300 Latin cavalry for the Macedonian theatre. The navy was also to be reinforced for 169.[3]

At Rome the Senate was approached by envoys from Antiochus and Ptolemy, the former accusing the latter of preparing to invade his possession, Coele–Syria. The Senate gave its favour to Ptolemy by renewing friendly relations; but it deferred a reply to Antiochus. Ptolemy was the more useful because he was able to send large quantities of grain to the Roman army in Greece; but his offer to mediate there for Rome and obtain peace was perhaps resented, and certainly not accepted. The dwindling reputation of Rome in Greece was a cause of anxiety to the Senate. It therefore passed decrees to protect the Greek states from exploitation and in particular from arbitrary requisitioning by Roman officers.[4]

Hortensius sent envoys to some Greek states to publicize these decrees and also to indicate his future support for pro-Roman leaders and his strong dislike for any other leaders. Thebes was advised to continue its loyal support of Rome. The leading politicians of the Achaean League, including Polybius himself, were bewildered and alarmed, but the envoys thanked the League for its military services. In

---

[1] *SEG* 19. 374 = Sherk no. 2; Livy 43. 7. 1–4, 6. 4, and 11–14.

[2] Livy 43. 10. For the location of Uscana at Kitševo see Volume I. 43 ff. with n. 1 on p. 45 giving rival views, to which may be added Meloni, *Perseo* 275 n. 3 and Walbank, *C* 3. 339.

[3] Livy 43. 12. 3–4 and 9.

[4] Such requisitioning was probably the cause of Ambracia seeking and obtaining financial aid from the Thessalian League at this time; see Ch. Habicht in *Demetrias* I. 175–80, commenting on the relevant inscription.

addressing the Assembly of the Aetolian League the envoys talked of taking the children of anti-Roman leaders as hostages for their good conduct; but they did not insist. Their presence encouraged pro-Roman leaders to accuse their opponents. The general result was 'mutual suspicion and utter disorder' (Plb. 28. 4. 13). When the Assembly of the Acarnanian League met, the envoys played the same game. This time the pro-Roman leaders asked for Roman garrisons to be placed in their cities. A rival leader, Diogenes, protested. The envoys did not proceed with the suggestion of garrisons, but they knew now which leaders might oppose them.

The tactics of Hortensius' envoys must have offset any goodwill which the senatorial decrees were designed to excite. For the envoys hoped to quell opposition by intimidation. Leading politicians in the Greek states were now beset both by fear of immediate victimization and deportation, as had happened with the Aetolian cavalry commanders, and with fear of what a Roman victory would mean in the punishment of even moderate politicians, let alone in the loss of Greek liberty. When the envoys left the Peloponnese, the moderate politicians held a discussion in which both these fears were expressed by Lycortas, who wanted, like Polybius himself, to pursue a moderate course.[1]

3. *Perseus assumes the offensive, but Philippus enters Macedonia*

Winter now set in and the Roman army dispersed into winter quarters in Boeotia. Perseus, however, had other plans (see Fig. 8). It appears that in the late autumn the people of Uscana, who were Illyrians of the Penestae tribe, rose against their Cretan garrison and called in a garrison of 4,000 Romans and 500 Illyrians. The defection of Uscana was particularly serious for Perseus. For Uscana not only blocked direct access towards Gentius; it opened two routes of invasion, one for the Romans and the Illyrians from the west via Dibra and Popovec, and the other for the Dardanians from the north via Tetovo. In the depth of the hard Macedonian winter, when snow blocked the passes from Thessaly into Macedonia, Perseus led an élite force of 500 cavalry and 12,000 infantry to Styberra (Bučinsko Kalë) in Deuriopus. Taking grain for several days and ordering the siege-train to follow, he crossed the high range with peaks of 1,450 m. and reached Uscana on the third day, having covered some 60 kilometres. When negotiations failed, the walls were assailed by day and by night, and siege-towers and penthouses with rams were brought to bear. As such a siege in midwinter was entirely unexpected, the city had no reserve of supplies.

[1] Plb. 28. 6–7.

The commanders of the Roman garrison negotiated a surrender for the Romans on condition of fair treatment for themselves, but they abandoned the Illyrian soldiers and the inhabitants, who were forced to surrender unconditionally and were sold as slaves. In a rapid campaign Perseus captured twelve fortresses and took 1,500 Roman prisoners among their garrisons. Oaeneum, the strongest town in the Artatus (Velcka) valley, held out until a ramp was built to a height greater than that of the wall and the Royal Guard led the assault. All adult males were killed, and the rest of the population was taken prisoner. No doubt they had defected, like the people of Uscana.[1]

As a demonstration of Macedonian power this winter campaign was remarkable; for it was conducted in wild country dominated by ranges 2,000 m. high. Perseus treated the people of Uscana as traitors (as Alexander III had treated the Thebans in 335), and he recouped his expenses by selling them as slaves at Styberra. The Romans he treated well; indeed their commander encouraged Roman soldiers in other garrisons to surrender (Livy 43. 19. 7). They might be valuable as a bargaining counter, if Perseus could make Rome negotiate for peace. His other concern was Gentius, to whom he sent envoys, hoping for alliance;[2] but Gentius wanted money which Perseus was not prepared to pay. He left strong garrisons in Uscana and some of the fortresses, which withstood a Roman counter-attack in the spring; and the Romans took hostages from the Parthini and from Illyrian towns near the Macedonian area, in case they should defect to Macedonia.

In Epirus Perseus reinforced his allies, the Molossians, and posted a garrison at Phanote (Raveni) in the Kalamas valley, which blocked

---

[1] Livy 43. 18–19. For the geography see Volume I. 44 f. with n. 1 and Map 9. In 1968, when I visited Kitševo, it was a thriving place with many handicrafts, and had fine stands of timber, a large breed of horses and cattle, and a fertile plateau; its resources were appropriate to a large ancient city. From Popovec it is 46 km. through high limestone country to Dibra. The visible remains at Tsepicovo are mainly Roman and the inscription in *Spomenik* 71 (1931) no. 501 showed that it was Roman Styberra. Macedonian Styberra was with little doubt at Bučinsko Kalë, where there are remains of a classical and Hellenistic city. See Volume I. 67 ff. The 'Sulcanum oppidum' of Orosius 4. 20. 38 is not otherwise known.

[2] Plb. 28. 8 and Livy 43. 20. 1. Passing north of Mt. Scardus (Šar Planina), impassable in winter, and via Prizren (which I have visited only in summer) into the White Drin valley, they followed the main river and then turned off to Scodra, where they learnt that Gentius was at Lissus. It is evident that the Romans and their Illyrian allies held the upper valley of the Black Drin and the catchment area of the Mati river; for they invaded later from the west to take Uscana, and the land immediately south and south-east of Lissus was held by Roman forces (Livy 44. 30. 7). A route through the Mati catchment area is however advocated by Kromayer, *AS* 2. 260 n. 4 and Walbank in *Iliria* 4 (1976) 269 n. 38 and *C* 3. 338. For 'Illyris deserta' see Hammond in *BSA* 61. 250 with Fig. 2; Walbank, loc. cit. placed it in the valley of the White Drin, which is not on the route through the Mati catchment area. Meloni, *Perseo* 275 ff. has an entirely different location for the campaign.

the entry from the west into the plain of Ioannina.[1] Appius Claudius added Chaonians and Thesprotians to his Roman army and with 6,000 men attacked Phanote but was beaten off. In March 169, after purifying the Macedonian army in the festival called Xandica, in Elimiotis, Perseus set off with 300 cavalry and 10,000 infantry with the intention of capturing Stratus, then in Aetolian hands (see Fig. 1). Speed and surprise were essential for success. He crossed north Pindus with much suffering of men and pack animals; for the snow was very deep on the watershed range by Mt. Citius (Avgo, 2,177 m. high). On the fourth day he camped in the plain of Ioannina, where the Molossians provided supplies and some troops. On the fifth day he made 'a huge march' via Horreum (Ammotopos)[2] and the Kiafa pass to the river Arachthus at a point 12 kilometres north of Ambracia, where a strong Roman garrison lay (see Fig. 12). He intended to march to the east of Ambracia and then south next day, but he was unlucky. The river was too high; he had to wait while his engineers built a bridge of local timber. When it was completed, in one day's march he reached (probably) the Agraean frontier,[3] where he met an Aetolian magistrate, called Archidamus, who had arranged to betray Stratus to him. Another forced march brought him within reach of Stratus, only to find that the Roman commander of Ambracia, aware of his presence through the delay at the river, had thrown a garrison of 1,000 men into the city 'that very evening' (Livy 43. 22. 2 'ipsa ea nocte') and had coincided with the arrival of 100 cavalry and 600 infantry under the command of Dinarchus, the Aetolian cavalry commander. In the absence of Archidamus it seems that his rivals had seized power in Stratus and sent to Ambracia for help, which came by sea to Limnaea and overland to Stratus. Dinarchus, it was said, had intended to join Archidamus and Perseus, but changed his mind when he found the Romans in the city. Had the chances of weather and time been different, Perseus would have taken Stratus without a blow and might have brought Aetolia and Acarnania onto his side. As it was, lacking a source of supply, he veered off into Aperantia, which accepted him, and leaving Archidamus and 800 men to garrison its chief city, he returned to Macedonia by the same route.[4]

---

[1] For Phanote being at Raveni see *HE* 676. For other identifications see Meloni, *Perseo* 256 n. 4, Cabanes 296, and Dakaris, *Thesprotia* 141. The last put it at Dholiani (for which see *HE* 86 ff.), but Dholiani was not on the direct route from Gitana to Molossia, which Hostilius would have taken on his way from Corcyra to Thessaly (see *HE* 82 Map 4).

[2] North Pindus was reckoned impassable by Christmas 1943, when I was at Pendalophos in western Macedonia. See *HE* 281 ff. and 154 ff. for 'the huge march' along the line of the old Turkish road via Pende Pigadhia, some twelve hours in good weather. For the identification of Horreum see *BCH* 109 (1985) 1. 499 ff.

[3] The text of Livy 43. 22. 1 is corrupt; see *HE* 282 for this suggestion. Each march here was of some 40 km.

[4] 43. 21. 5–23. 1. The Molossians and some other tribes proposed the march on Stratus (43.

At the same time there was fighting in Epirus (see Figs. 6 and 8). When the Romans under Claudius and his allies withdrew from their attempt on Phanote, the Macedonians and the Molossians pursued them and, probably with the help of the Atintanes, killed 1,200 of them before Claudius reached the plain called Meleon, south-east of Buthrotum. The Macedonian commander, Cleuas, then moved into Chaonia; there he drew the garrison of Antigoneia into an ambush where 500 Molossian troops smote them, inflicting 1,000 casualties and taking 100 prisoners. Claudius withdrew ineffectually into Illyris.[1]

We may pause to consider these winter campaigns. The planning and the execution of them were extremely able; for the problems of supply and the dangers of frostbite were formidable (as in the Greek campaign of 1940–1 in Albania). The speed and the endurance of the troops was maintained only by inspiring leadership and by their training and morale. In these respects the army of Perseus in that winter rivalled the army of Alexander the Great in 330/29. But the policy of Perseus is more debatable. It is true that he strengthened his north-western frontier at a critical place, and that he brought his first allies into action. Yet there was little material advantage, apart from the sale of prisoners and booty, to offset the expenditure of money, animals, and men. The Molossians and the small tribes which joined them were so involved in fighting the other Epirotes that they added nothing to the strength of the Macedonian army. On the other hand, Perseus had to tie down valuable Macedonian troops in Penestia, central Epirus, and distant Aperantia, and it was an admission of miscalculation that he had to bring 200 cavalry and 1,000 infantry back from Penestia to garrison Cassandreia against possible attack from the sea (43. 23. 7). While his men and his transport animals had been severely strained, his main objective—the Roman army in Greece—had been left in peace. The Roman commander was thus able to re-establish discipline and train legions for the impending offensive.

In Book 44 Livy presents us with a different portrayal of Perseus. The king changes from a capable leader to an idiot. Within the first ten chapters of Book 44 Perseus is rushing up and down the Pierian coast like a mad thing, mindless and incompetent (2. 12 'inops consilii'); he misses chance after chance (4. 9–10 and 6. 6), panics disastrously (6. 1–2 and 10. 1–4), is entirely witless (6. 14 and 17; 7. 1), and blames his officers instead of himself (7. 8). The heroic figure is now the gallant consul, Q. Marcius Philippus, an overweight sixty-year-old, but a man

21. 5) and wanted Perseus to attack Stratus (43. 22. 9). If the purification ceremony was the traditional one, it gives a date in early March, when the snow is usually heavy on the Epirote side of North Pindus. See *HE* 281 ff. for the geography and for readings in Livy's text.

[1] 43. 23. See *HE* 686 for 'campus Meleon'.

of magnificent spirit (4. 10). What is the explanation of this sudden change? It is not due to a change of source; for Livy was clearly drawing on the account of Polybius in the main. It is due rather to Polybius himself. In Book 43 Polybius described the campaigns from the Macedonian viewpoint and drew on Macedonian sources, ultimately in my opinion from the *King's Journal*. In Books 44 and 45 the viewpoint is Roman and in the opening part of Book 44 that of Polybius, who was present on the campaign and saw things from the Roman side. For instance, he knows how many miles were covered each day on the march across Lower Olympus. He is now embarking on the triumph of Rome, a congenial topic to his Roman readers, and praise of Rome led readily to denigration of Perseus and Macedonia. A further reason lies in Polybius' personal belief that the triumph of Rome was destined by Tyche and that anyone opposing it was a fool; and in addition he believed that a sudden change of personality (*metabole*) was psychologically probable in itself. In the summer of 169 Perseus suffered a radical change of personality, almost to a pathological degree, in the view of Polybius and so of Livy.

In fact it seems that Perseus anticipated an attack through Perrhaebia. He therefore made Dium his base; and he stationed small garrisons in four forts of the Tempe pass (44. 6. 9), 12,000 men mainly, but not all, light-armed on the Lapathus saddle, an advance guard in the Petra pass, and 10,000 light-armed in the Volustana pass.[1] His cavalry patrolled the coastal plain to deal with sea-borne raids. If the Romans attempted to carry the Petra pass, they would be enfiladed by the groups of 10,000 men and 12,000 men. His supply system ran from Elimiotis and Pieria, both grain-growing areas.

The consul for 169, Quintus Marcius Philippus, was notorious for impetuous foolhardiness in Liguria (Livy 39. 20. 5–10) and confident through his previous experience of Philip and Perseus. Coming out with 5,000 men to fill gaps in the two legions and accompanied by some able officers, he landed at Ambracia and marched to the Roman base at Palaepharsalus. He kept his predecessor, Hortensius, on his staff; and he had Gaius Marcius Figulus, his cousin, as naval commander at Chalcis. Having arranged that Figulus should make landings on the coast of Pieria and having loaded his soldiers with grain for a month, he marched into Perrhaebia and camped between Azorus and Doliche (see Fig. 6). He decided, apparently without reconnaissance, to take the route over the Lapathus saddle. Marching 7 miles a day for three days over broken, steep, and rugged ground, his advanced forces climbed onto the ridge and had their first view of

---

[1] Livy mentioned the two large forces only. We hear later of troops in the Tempe pass, and we may be sure that the Petra pass was also garrisoned.

Heracleum, Phila, and the seashore below. There they encamped and had a day's rest. The narrow saddle which formed the main pass between Olympus and Lower Olympus, apparently a mile to the north of the Roman camp, was held by the 12,000 men under the command of Hippias. They beat off all Roman attacks throughout the next two days.

Philippus was now in a quandary. Unable to break through the enemy position and unable to stay where he was, because his supply train could not cope with the rugged ground, he had either to retrace his steps with considerable loss of prestige or to find some other route towards the coast, where Figulus and the fleet would be able to land supplies. He chose the latter course, no doubt on the advice of local guides. Livy, mirroring Polybius, was enthusiastic in his praise: 'he pursued his bold undertaking superbly to the end' (44. 4. 11 'egregie ad ultimum in audaciter commisso perseveravit'). Philippus had only himself to blame for being in this difficult situation. The boldness of his descent is less striking, if we realize that his army outnumbered the force under Hippias by at least three to one. The toil of the descent and the loss of pack animals and equipment were exceptional, and at the steepest places collapsible wooden platforms were built, one below the other, so that the elephants could be brought down safely. For when the elephants were herded onto a platform, it was made to collapse gently and they slid down onto the next platform. Their trumpeting panicked the pack-horses and caused losses of animals and materials. We are not told how the overweight commander made his descent, but the troops were rarely on their feet ('minimum pedibus itineris confectum'). After four days the army reached the plain between Heracleum and Leibethra and built a fortified camp for the infantry and a separate camp in the plain for the cavalry. The fleet was no doubt at hand with supplies; for Figulus had been expecting the army to reach the coast, whether at that point or farther to the north.[1]

Perseus was now outmanœuvred.[2] His forces were widely dispersed. He withdrew northwards from Dium to meet the troops from the Volustana pass, the Petra pass, and the Lapathus saddle near Katerini.

---

[1] For the geography see Volume I. 137 ff. with Map 12. The site of Leibethra or one of its villages has been described by N. Ch. Kotzias in *AE* 1948–9 (1951) *Chronica* 25–40. See Volume I. 136. See Pritchett, *Studies* 2. 164 ff.

[2] Perseus panicking in his bath-tub (Livy 44. 6. 1–2) and his 'stultitia et segnitia' are not to be taken seriously. Livy greatly exaggerated the difficulties of Philippus probably to the greater praise of Aemilius Paullus; for example, there was no difficulty in advancing 'into Macedonia past Dium' at 44. 6. 5 and 14, as Philippus showed (this is not a reference to the Petra pass route as Pritchett *Studies* 2. 170 n. 131 maintains). Polybius was very critical of Perseus (28. 10) and blamed him for not now bribing Gentius to make an alliance. Livy's account of Perseus' follies at 44. 6. 2 and 10. 1–4 may derive from Polybius (see D.S. 30. 10–11, probably from Polybius); it is not to be accepted.

The garrisons which held Tempe pass retreated over Lower Olympus. When all the troops were together, they drew their supplies from Pydna. Meanwhile Philippus marched into Dium, from which Perseus had removed the population and the gilded statues of the kings (44. 6. 3),[1] and Roman foraging parties ranged as far north as the river Ascordus (perhaps in the hills above Aegeae). One city, Agassae or Acesae by name,[2] was captured and hostages were taken. Philippus declared it free and autonomous in order to appear as a liberator; but he had no intention of staying, since supplies were running out. He withdrew via Dium to Phila, to which grain was brought by sea and overland from Thessaly. Perseus had wisely foreseen the dilemma and withdrawal of Philippus. He now reoccupied Dium and adopted a very strong defensive position on the north bank of the river Elpeüs. He had left a strong garrison in Heracleum (Platamona), perched on a cliff above the sea. The Roman army and fleet attacked it vigorously, but it did not fall until the campaigning season was nearing an end.[3]

The Roman fleet conducted its own offensive (see Fig. 1). It landed ravaging parties on the coasts of the Thermaic Gulf and threatening Thessalonica, Aenea, and Antigoneia, but its personnel suffered casualties from roving bands of Macedonian cavalry and infantry who were waiting for them. Arriving off Cassandreia, on the site of Potidaea, which had withstood a famous siege by the Persians, the Roman commander, Gaius Marcius, met Eumenes with twenty warships of Pergamum and five from Prusias of Bithynia, who now abandoned his policy of neutrality. They tried to take the city by assault and then by blockade. But the defence force, consisting of citizens, 800 Agrianians, and 2,000 Penestae, made a sortie, caught a Roman group between the walls and an outer moat, which Perseus had added recently, and killed 600 of them. The blockade was broken by a picked force of Gauls on ten *lembi*, which slipped past the blockading ships at night and got into the city. The Romans and their allies then delivered an abortive attack on Torone and made for Demetrias, near which they came to port at Iolcus. It so happened that a Roman task force of 5,000 men had been sent to attack Meliboea, a city on the coast of Magnesia, through which Perseus kept contact with Demetrias. Perseus sent 2,000 men under Euphranor, who not only raised the siege by a surprise attack, but led his men into Demetrias by night. The Romans gave up the idea of laying siege to Demetrias,

---

[1] Perhaps there was one of himself among them. Professor D. Pantermalis has found a base there inscribed β]ασιλέως Φιλίππ[ου βα]σι[λ]εὺ[ς Π]ε[ρσεύς. The statue on this base was probably of marble. See *Proc. 8th Epigr. Conf.* 272.

[2] See Volume I. 139 n. 1, and for Ascordus I. 129.

[3] Plb. 28. 11 and Livy 44. 9. 3–9, describing a special kind of *testudo* which the Romans formed. For the site see Volume I. 135.

Eumenes went home, and the Roman fleet wintered at Sciathos and at Oreus.[1] Philippus arranged for an improved supply system to reach Phila by water and through the Tempe pass, and moved his camp to Heracleum. He received a large amount of barley and wheat from Rome's allies in Epirus, for which they were duly paid.

The honours of the year 169 lay with Perseus. He and his allies had inflicted defeats and losses on the Romans and their allies in Penestia, Illyris, Epirus, and Lapathus and had driven them away from the coasts of Macedonia and from Meliboea and Demetrias. The Macedonian forces had suffered very few casualties; their morale was high and they had recently shown their initiative and enterprise at Cassandreia and Demetrias. The winter campaigns had been much more spectacular than the failure of Philippus to force the pass in Lapathus and his sideways slither into the Pierian plain. In fact Philippus had prised open one way into Macedonia and thereby given his successor a better chance, but he himself had retreated without engaging the enemy army to the very edge of Macedonia. The stronger position of Perseus encouraged Prusias of Bithynia, his brother-in-law, and Rhodes to send envoys to Rome and advocate the making of peace. Prusias said he had acted at the instigation of Perseus. Rhodes said she had sent envoys to Perseus also on the same errand, because the prolonged war was disrupting the flow of international commerce. The Senate was not persuaded; indeed it regarded Rhodes with annoyance and suspicion.[2] Eumenes, too, was suspected of secret negotiations with Perseus in the hope of a general peace. Rhodes had sent envoys also to Philippus at Heracleum, who returned them a soft answer and advised them to intervene and make peace in the war between Antiochus and Ptolemy, which had started about the beginning of March 169 and was still undecided in the autumn.[3] Philippus may have been interested primarily in obtaining grain from Egypt.

The most significant sign that Perseus appeared to be in a more favourable position was the readiness of Gentius in autumn 169 to enter into alliance with Perseus on the promise of a payment of 300 talents. Oaths and hostages were exchanged, the ceremony at Dium being attended by a parade of the Macedonian cavalry. Gentius and Perseus sent a joint embassy of Illyrians and Macedonians to invite Rhodes to join them in the war against Rome.[4] At this time, if not earlier, Gentius was issuing bronze coins. In the Selcë hoard (see p. 409 above) there were two coins of Gentius with Macedonian emblems;[5]

---

[1] Livy 44. 10. 5–13. 11. Prusias was neutral at 42. 29. 3.
[2] 44. 14, and for Eumenes 44. 13. 9.
[3] I follow the chronology of Walbank, *C* 3. 324.   [4] Plb. 29. 3–4; Livy 44. 23.
[5] A. J. Evans in *Num. Chron.* 20 (1880) 269 ff.

perhaps the name **ΒΑΣΙΛΕΩΣ ΓΕΝΘΙΟΥ** was overstruck on coins of the Macedonian period at Lissus and Scodra. The other coins of Gentius have what is probably his head with a cap not unlike the *petasos* and a torque around his neck, and on the reverse in one case a thunderbolt and in the others a galley (i.e. a *lembus*).[1] There are copper deposits in the Mati valley.[2]

---

[1] See *SA* 1972. 1. 69 ff. for another coin of Gentius found in a burial; and for his coining see S. Islami in *SA* 1966. 1 and *Iliria* 2 (1972) 379 ff.

[2] For the copper see Hammond, *Migrations and Invasions in Greece and Adjacent Areas* (New Jersey, 1976) 75 Map 16.

XXV

THE DEFEAT OF THE MACEDONIAN STATE
(168 B.C.)

1. *The portrayal of Perseus*

FOR the final part of Perseus' reign we have relatively few fragments of Polybius' Book 29. But they are enough to show that Polybius' account was very largely used by Diodorus, Livy, Plutarch, Appian, and Dio. The unfavourable portrait of Perseus in his last year as king was certainly painted by Polybius, who found one source of Perseus' deterioration in an increasing miserliness and meanness (29. 8. 2 φιλαργυρώτατος and 8 μικρολογία), which manifested themselves in dealings not only with Eumenes, but also with the Bastarnae and Gentius (29. 9. 13). This theme recurred in D.S. 30. 19 (φιλαργυρία), Livy (44. 24. 8 and 26. 1–2 'avaritia'; 27. 8 'eadem avaritia'), P*Aem.* 12. (φιλαργυρία and μικρολογία), App. (*Mac.* 18. 1 μικρολόγος and φροντίζων χρημάτων), and Dio 20. 66 (φειδωλία). Another weakness in Perseus, according to Polybius, was folly and ignorance (29. 9. 1–2 μωροποιεῖσθαι and ἄγνοια), qualities which reappear in the accounts of Diodorus (30. 11. 1 by implication), Plutarch (*Aem.* 12. παραφρονήσας), and Appian (*Mac.* 18. 3 ὑπ' ἀφροσύνης). In Polybius' account these qualities in Perseus had surfaced earlier, when Perseus approached Gentius, and at that time his miserliness and ignorance were attributed not to lack of thought, but to heaven-sent delusion (28. 9. 4 δαιμονοβλάβειαν). This part of Polybius' analysis is preserved for Perseus' last year by Appian in *Mac.* 16, a passage which may be translated as follows:

From the summer of 169 there was at once a change (ἐκ μεταβολῆς). He became cruel and unscrupulous towards all persons. There was not a shred of decency or sense in him any longer. He who had been most persuasive in counsel, capable in planning and most daring in battle, except when lack of experience made him err, at that moment sank totally and inexplicably into cowardice and illogicality, becoming hasty, abruptly changeable, and utterly stupid, as Chance (τύχη) was beginning to desert him.[1]

This analysis of Perseus is the less convincing, because it had been

---

[1] Appian at 18. 1 attributed his meanness to divine intervention: μικρολόγος ὑπὸ θεοβλαβείας ἐς πάντα γενόμενος. He clearly took this from Plb. 28. 9. 4. See Walbank, *C* 1. 24 f. for this concept.

given in much the same words for Philip V at 4. 77. 4, 5. 10. 11, 7. 11. 1, 10. 26. 7–10, and 18. 33. 6, the only difference being that thanks to Chance (18. 33. 7 ἐκ τῆς τύχης; cf. 25. 3. 9) Philip after his defeat reverted from illogicality to logicality. Perseus stayed down, a despicable figure in the eyes of Polybius and his Roman acquaintances.

The ideas that it is a god who takes a man's wits away—usually, as here, when the god is about to destroy him—and that Chance presides over a psychological reversal of such magnitude are not really acceptable to us. We shall judge Perseus rather by his actions and consider Polybius' criticisms in each case. Another work which darkened the image of Perseus in this year was a Memoir written by Scipio Nasica; for it was consulted by Livy and Plutarch. We shall discuss it later.

To resume our narrative, we may recall that Perseus was said by Polybius to have wanted and to have attempted to obtain peace with Rome 'every year' (29. 7. 4 καθ' ἕκαστον ἔτος; cf. Livy 44. 25. 3). In this respect certainly his psychology did not change. The secret negotiations with Eumenes in winter 169/8 were undertaken in the hope that Eumenes would act as an intermediary and would engineer a peace between Rome and Macedonia (Dio 20. 66. 1). But nothing came of it. Another possible intermediary was Rhodes, with which Perseus had been in touch. It was Philippus who suggested that Rhodes should play this role in this winter, and the matter was debated in the Assembly at Rhodes. The majority voted in favour of Philippus' suggestion, and envoys were sent to Rome, Philippus, and Perseus. The vote was interpreted by Polybius as a victory for the pro-Macedonian party in Rhodes. The Assembly went on to send to the Cretan cities a request for an alliance between Rhodes and 'all the Cretans' (Plb. 29. 10; App. *Mac.* 17). On both counts the Senate was annoyed; it did not want peace, and it had reprimanded the Cretans for letting some of their citizens serve in Perseus' army.

2. *Perseus seeks allies*

As it became clear that Perseus would not obtain a peaceful settlement, he looked round for more allies. During the winter he prepared a statement for the benefit of Antiochus and Eumenes (Plb. 29. 4. 8; Livy 44. 24). He argued as follows. To monarchy the Roman Republic was by nature hostile ('natura inimica'), and its aim was to destroy all monarchies by invoking one king against another, namely Attalus v. Philip, Philip v. Antiochus, and now Eumenes and Prusias v. Perseus. The policy of the kings so far had been suicidal, and if Rome should destroy Macedonia she would go on to her next victims—Eumenes and Antiochus. What Eumenes and Antiochus ought to do was persuade

Rome to make peace with Perseus, and, failing that, regard Rome as their enemy too. This argument does not seem to be that of a deluded fool! The statement was sent openly to Antiochus.

His reply, though not known to us, was certainly in the negative, not only because Antiochus had a deep animosity towards Philip V and Perseus, but also because Antiochus hoped that, while Rome continued to be at war with Perseus, he would conquer and annex Egypt. The statement was delivered in secret to Eumenes. His reply was in the negative; he hated Perseus and he was blind to his own peril. Polybius attributed the failure of the secret negotiations to Eumenes' greed in asking for huge sums (Polybius speculates on 500 talents or 1,500 talents) and to Perseus' stinginess in refusing them. However, this attribution was part of Polybius' psychoanalytical theory about Perseus, and Polybius himself admitted that the theory was subjective and not substantiated (29. 5; enlarged by Livy at 44. 24. 7–26. 2). It is better to discard it.[1]

The alliance with Gentius had cost Perseus the promise of 300 talents. These were placed in a container, sealed, and deposited at Pella (Plb. 29. 4. 7 and Livy 44. 27. 8–9). At the start 10 talents were given to Gentius; then hostages were exchanged; some months later the container was sent to the frontier (in Penestia). By then Gentius had committed himself to war irrevocably by emprisoning two envoys from Rome and Perseus did not give him the money (Livy 44. 27. 8–12; App. *Mac.* 18. 1). Another alliance which involved a monetary transaction was formed with the Bastarnae, whose leader, Clondicus, brought 10,000 cavalry and 10,000 reserve cavalrymen on foot into the territory of the Maedi in the upper Strymon valley and encamped at Desudaba, an unidentified place (see Fig. 3). This had no doubt been prearranged by Perseus. He took half his army away from his defensive position at the Elpeüs river in southern Pieria and marched up the Axius valley to Almana, another unidentified place, which was probably between Stobi and Bylazora. He ordered the villages and cities near the road from Desudaba to Bylazora to provide grain, wine, and meat for the Bastarnae. For he had ordered the Bastarnae to come on to meet him at Bylazora (see Fig. 3). Perseus' plan was presumably to campaign against the Dardanians of Polog or/and against the Romans in northern Illyris, in conjunction with Gentius.[2]

---

[1] See the cautious scepticism of Walbank, *C* 3. 366 with references to other views on this controversial topic.

[2] The Bastarnae will have come via Sofia to reach the upper Strymon valley. If their destination was to be the Elpeüs front, they would have followed the easy route via the Strumitsa and Valandovo (see Volume I. with Map 17), and Perseus would not have taken half his army away from the Elpeüs position. The time was probably late February or early March, when the Roman army was still in winter quarters. His plan was probably to drive the Dardanians out of

The difficulties began before the two armies met. Perseus had brought gifts for the leading officers, and these included what Livy called 'a little gold' and Appian stated was 10,000 staters. Clondicus demanded immediate payment in advance for all his men. Perseus consulted his Council of Friends and commanders, to whom he explained that a force of 5,000 cavalry was as much as he needed. A message to that effect was sent to Clondicus, who set off for home with his 20,000 men and ravaged parts of Thrace on the way (Livy 44. 26–27. 7; D.S. 30. 19; App. *Mac.* 18. 1–3; P*Aem* 12. 4–6 and 13. 1).[1]

Polybius censured Perseus for stinginess in his dealings with Eumenes, Gentius, and Clondicus. But we must not forget the very heavy expenditures which Perseus must have made in the first three years of the war, the damage to the economy with so many men on continuous active service, and the cost of providing food for men and animals on campaign, garrisons in towns and probably some of the cities. And he probably had a long war in prospect. He had to save where he could. Money spent on Eumenes would have been money wasted; for he intended to stay with Rome. Gentius would have been no more committed to war against Rome, if he had received the 300 talents. When Clondicus insisted on pay in advance for 20,000 men, Perseus was surely wise to reject the request, quite apart from the colossal expense; for he intended to fight a defensive war in southern Pieria, and if Clondicus should become an enemy and attack him from the north Perseus would be between two fires.[2]

When the envoys of Gentius came to Dium, a formal parade of the Macedonian cavalry was held, and the exchange of oaths and hostages was conducted in their presence. Livy suggested that Perseus arranged this to encourage the cavalry (44. 23. 8, hinting that the Macedonians were in poor heart). On the other hand, the parade may have impressed the Illyrians, and the cavalry may have represented the Macedones in the ratification of the treaty ('foederi sanciendo', if correctly restored). When Clondicus presented his demand, Perseus consulted the Council of Friends and commanders, because he needed their advice and hoped to come to an agreed decision. Livy suggested

Polog and to join forces with Gentius. See Hammond in *Studies Mihailov* 200 f. For different interpretations of Perseus' purpose see Meloni, *Perseo* 329–35 and Walbank, *C* 3. 369 f.

[1] All deriving from an account by Polybius, who will have had it from one of Perseus' officers; for the detail betrays a Macedonian source. The proposed rate of pay is uncertain; see Griffith, *Merc.* 306 n. 2.

[2] Livy 44. 27. 4–6 suggested that Perseus could have sent the mounted Bastarnae to ravage the plain and storm the cities of Thessaly behind the back of the Romans; App. *Mac.* 18. 3 echoes the idea, which came therefore from Polybius as an example of Perseus' folly. It is, however, a naïve suggestion. The only possible entry to Thessaly was through Perrhaebia and the cavalry had no base in Thessaly and no access to supplies. Tempe was held by the Romans.

that the majority wanted to hire the Bastarnae, but were afraid to say so, and that Macedonian morale was lowered by the departure of the Bastarnae (44. 26. 12, 27. 1, and 27. 7), thus implying that Perseus was despotic and Macedonian morale was shaky. The evidence is rather that Perseus enjoyed the complete support of the army and of the people. Indeed we hear of only one Macedonian renegade, Onesimus, who was installed by the Senate in a mansion with some land at the seaside resort Tarentum (44. 16. 4–7).

Before the normal sailing season began Perseus sent out from Cassandreia forty *lembi* and five smaller craft, which headed for Tenedos (see Fig. 7). Their task was to protect merchantmen, which were carrying grain from Black Sea ports to Macedonia. At Tenedos they met Rhodian ships which they treated as friends, and they frightened off some warships of Eumenes which were blockading fifty Macedonian merchantmen. The merchantmen were escorted by ten *lembi* to Macedonian ports. Within nine days the *lembi* rejoined the fleet at Sigeum.[1] Sailing south, the Macedonians intercepted and destroyed or captured an unescorted group of thirty-five transports, carrying over 1,000 Gallic mercenaries and their mounts, which were on the way from Pergamum to join the Romans in Thessaly. They then moved into the sacred waters of Delos, where they enjoyed sanctuary alongside five Pergamene quinqueremes and three Roman quinqueremes. At night the fast *lembi* slipped out under oar and next day plundered and sank any ship bound for Macedonia, before the massive quinqueremes could come to the rescue (44. 27–9).

These successes were reported at Rhodes when the envoys from Perseus and Gentius arrived, perhaps in April.[2] They were heard first by the Council and then in an Assembly, where the debate became violent; for the pro-Macedonian leaders spoke openly in favour of Perseus and the opposition leaders protested. The decision of the Assembly was to make a friendly reply to the two kings and to reaffirm the desire of Rhodes to negotiate peace between the kings and Rome (Plb. 29. 11).

To the Senate it was obvious that the war had taken a turn for the worse. In 169 in Epirus the Molossians had become enemies and the Romans and their allies had suffered considerable losses; and the Roman force which Appius Claudius had withdrawn from Epirus was now in danger of defeat in Illyris (Livy 44. 20. 5), quite apart from any action the ambiguous Gentius might take. The Greek states, which had given very little help in 170, had played no part in the invasion of

---

[1] If the *lembi* escorted them to Cassandreia, their entire journey averaged over 30 miles a day.

[2] This month would be consistent with the Rhodians having heard of the Bastarnae reaching Macedonia, but not of their departure (44. 29. 6).

Macedonia in 169. Indeed the most faithful of them, the Achaean League, had so timed the offer of its levy that it was of no use; and it refused the request of Appius Claudius for help on the technical ground that the request had not been initialled by the consul. Polybius, who led the envoys to the consul and spoke in the Assembly which considered the request, has left a rather embarrassed account of the proceedings.[1] Even Eumenes was under some suspicion, and the gratuitous offer of Rhodes to negotiate a peace was clearly inspired by the belief that the Roman forces by land and by sea were not in the ascendant.[2] Moreover, Antiochus was taking advantage of Rome's struggle against Perseus to invade Egypt; and at the beginning of the new consular year, when envoys were heard from Ptolemy Euergetes II and Cleopatra, Antiochus appeared to be within an ace of success.

3. *Roman offensives against Gentius and in the Aegean*

The Senate decided to put more forces into the field. It was fortunate in the newly elected consul, to whom Macedonia fell by lot, Lucius Aemilius Paullus, an experienced commander in his early sixties. He had been consul in 182, and he had many friends among the senators. At his request a commission of three senators was sent to investigate the situation in 'Macedonia', i.e. in Illyris and Greece on land and sea. Its return was delayed by adverse winds which twice drove their ship back to Epidamnus. Its report[3] caused the Senate to send out substantial reinforcements and to authorize a simultaneous offensive on three fronts: in Illyris, at sea in the Aegean, and in Pieria.

In Illyris Gentius moved first (see Fig. 8). Having mustered 15,000 men and a fleet at Lissus, the southernmost city of his kingdom, he advanced into Roman territory and laid siege to Bassania, a Roman ally, which refused to yield, although it was only 5 miles from Lissus. His half-brother, Caravantius, attacked the Cavii, where one city yielded, and he ravaged the fields of another city, called Caravandis. A flotilla of eighty *lembi* set off a little later to ravage the lands of the coastal cities, Epidamnus and Apollonia. Meanwhile Appius Claudius had heard of the alliance between Gentius and Perseus, and of Gentius' arrest of the Roman envoys. He therefore moved his army (its strength is not known) out of his winter quarters at the Nymphaeum, added to it troops from Byllis, Apollonia, and Epidamnus, as he marched north,

---

[1] 28. 12–13. Polybius did not make the offer until Philippus camped near Heracleum. The League was careful to honour Philippus; see *SIG* 649.

[2] This was clearly expressed in Zon. 9. 22.

[3] Livy 44. 18. 1–5, 19. 1–3, and 20. 2–7. Aemilius was determined to wait until he was given the best possible forces for the job.

and encamped by the river Genusus (Shkumbi), where he had a rendezvous with the new Roman commander, Lucius Anicius Gallus, a praetor. Anicius had crossed over from Italy to Apollonia with two legions (totalling 600 cavalry and 10,400 infantry) and 800 cavalry and 10,000 infantry of the Italian allies; and his fleet (its size is not known) had been strengthened with a draft of 5,000 sailors. To this imposing force he added 200 cavalry and 2,000 infantry of the Parthini, the tribe of the middle Genusus valley.[1] The combined forces outnumbered those of Gentius by two to one.

As a folio of Livy's text is missing, we know little of the campaign. It seems that Anicius' fleet engaged the *lembi* of Gentius and captured a number of them. Next, Anicius engaged Gentius on land, defeated him in battle, and advanced into the kingdom, where he won the cities over by humane and clement methods. Gentius concentrated his forces in his capital, Scodra, strong in its natural position and well fortified. When Anicius approached it with his army in battle formation, the Illyrians made a sortie, were defeated, and fled into the city in such a panic that Gentius asked for and was granted a three-days truce. He hoped that Caravantius would come at any moment with a large relieving force; but it did not happen. On the third day of the truce Gentius came to the camp and surrendered himself to the praetor, who gave him a dinner with full honours and then put him under arrest. The Illyrians in Scodra surrendered, the Roman envoys were liberated, and the members of the royal family were rounded up and were sent together with Gentius and some leading Illyrians to Rome. This part of the campaign had lasted only thirty days.[2] There were certainly further operations in the northern part of Gentius' kingdom. For Anicius placed garrisons in some towns, citadels, and fortresses. Issa, Rhizon, and Olcinium, and the tribal states of the Daorsi, the Pirustae, and the northern Taulantii (not those inland of Epidamnus) came over to Rome of their own accord, but other places—such as Pharos—and tribes were reduced by force and their property was looted.[3]

[1] Livy 44. 30. The Bullini, or Bylliones, lived inland of Apollonia (see H*E* 225 ff.). For Anicius' force see Livy 44. 21. 9–10.

[2] App. *Ill.* 9, reducing the thirty days to twenty days; Livy 44. 31–32. 5; Zon. 9. 24; Eutrop. 4. 6. 4. The Cavii were probably in the Mati basin, not north of Scodra, as Meloni 355, since they would then be in the heart of Gentius' kingdom. Warships certainly escorted the transports which conveyed the army from Italy, *pace* Meloni, *Perseo* 356; for transports were very vulnerable to *lembi*, as in Livy 44. 28. 10–13.

[3] Livy 45. 26. 12–14. For Pharos see Appendix 5 p. 607. Meloni, *Perseo* 358 with n. 4 ends the whole campaign within Appian's twenty days. Until the surrender of Gentius the Roman fleet must have been supplying the 30,000 men of the army, and it operated later against the northern areas; there Caravantius held out for some time during which the Daorsi abandoned him (45. 26. 13–14 'relicto Caravantio' being contrasted with 'incolumi Gentio'). For the looting see the case of Pharos and note 45. 43. 7–8. Meloni's view, accepting what in my opinion was Roman propaganda, is that generally held; e.g. in *CAH* 8. 272.

Of the naval offensive in the Aegean we know hardly anything. The praetor Cnaeus Octavius left Italy at the same time as Anicius and Aemilius and took command of the Roman fleet at Oreus in northern Euboea. Its strength, when combined with the ships of Eumenes, was such that the Macedonian *lembi* ceased their raiding at sea and took refuge in such bases as Cassandreia, Pella, and Demetrias. With the Roman fleet dominant, supplies were carried by sea to the army in Thessaly and Pieria, and merchant ships bound for Macedonian ports were intercepted. Livy remarked that Perseus was as much afraid of the Roman fleet and the danger to his coastal areas as of the Roman army (44. 32. 6). There was an element of truth in this. For the fleet could land a large force behind his own lines, and sea-borne raiding parties could do much damage to towns and crops. Livy mentions that Thessalonica was held by 'a small garrison of 2,000 élite Macedonian troops' (loc. cit. 'caetrati'), and an officer, presumably with troops, was sent there to camp at the dockyards. Aenea received 1,000 cavalry, whose task was to protect the countryside from enemy raiding forces. The garrison at Amphipolis included 2,000 Thracians. If this was done at some other places, notably at Pella, Cassandreia, and Demetrias, perhaps 10,000 valuable troops were tied down and unable to join the main army. Although we are not informed, it is probable that some squadrons of the Roman fleet sailed north to make raids or to give the impression that they were about to do so.[1]

4. *The Roman offensive in Pieria*
(See Figure 17)

Aemilius set out from Italy at the same time as Anicius and Octavius to take command in the field. We have surprisingly little information about the Roman army in Thessaly and at Heracleum, but there is general agreement among scholars that it was only slightly smaller than the Macedonian army, which totalled 4,000 cavalry and not much less than 40,000 infantry. Of that total about 23,000 were men of the phalanx and its special Guards. Since the Macedonian battle order had become well known to Roman commanders and so to the Senate in the course of the war, we may be sure that at least 23,000 legionary infantry were provided for this campaign. Indeed a confused passage in Livy 44. 21. 3–9 suggests that Aemilius had 26,000 legionary infantry.[2]

---

[1] For such raids in 169 see Livy 44. 10–12, and for the garrisons 44. 32. 6 and 44. 4.

[2] Livy 44. 21. 2–3 and 5–8 (I take 'neque in ea provincia plus quam duas legiones esse' to be a statement, not an order). Of the planned eight legions two were to be 'for Macedonia' ('duas legiones in Macedoniam'), and the enlistment for these was to be 7,000 infantry and 200 cavalry of Roman citizenship and 7,000 infantry and 400 cavalry of 'the Latin name', and also a special corps of 600 Gallic cavalry. This force was to be sent out to Macedonia ('in Macedoniam'). Two

The remaining infantry, perhaps 13,000, came from Italy, Pergamum, Numidia, Liguria, and Crete. The Roman cavalry arm consisted of 1,200 Roman and Italian cavalry, 600 Gallic cavalry, and an unknown number of Numidian and Pergamene cavalry, the total being comparable to that of the Macedonian cavalry.[1] Perhaps half of the army had fought under Philippus, and the other half had been enlisted and sent out in 168. Aemilius' first task was to tighten up discipline, arrange various duties, and harangue the men. He had chosen personally half of the tribunes of the enlisted men, and he now took all the tribunes and the leading centurions on a reconnaissance of the Macedonian position, which occupied the far side of the river Elpeüs.[2] He saw that a frontal assault would be costly in casualties and probably unsuccessful, and he would not be able to use the arm which had been so valuable at Cynoscephalae, the squad of war elephants which had been provided by Masinissa (45. 13. 13).

We may pause to consider the magnitude of Rome's war effort. In a passage which contrasted the financial outlay of Rome with the stinginess of Perseus (*PAem* 12. 7) the figure 100,000 was given for 'the soldiers apart from the other provision' (such as the supply systems by land and by sea). Since stinginess was a Polybian theme, the figure presumably came from Polybius; in that case it was a reasonable round number for a contemporary historian to give. As we have seen, Anicius deployed 30,000 combatants and Aemilius about 43,000; and Aemilius had garrison troops in addition (44. 21. 8), perhaps 7,000. The marines on the two fleets, in the Adriatic and the Aegean, may well have numbered 20,000; for in 171 Haliartus was blockaded by 10,000 'armati' of the 'exercitus navalis' (42. 56. 5). The provision of these large forces made it possible to launch three offensives simultaneously for the first time in the wars against Macedonia, and the scale of the main offensive may be gauged from the fact that the legionary troops at Cynoscephalae had numbered 16,000 as compared with the 26,000 facing Perseus at the river Elpeüs.

The army of Perseus at the river was reckoned at 4,000 cavalry and

legions were to be sent to Illyris, and two were to serve under the other consul, Licinius. The remaining two legions were evidently the two legions already in Pieria, facing the Macedonians; they were brought up to full strength at this time, i.e. to 6,000 infantry each and 300 cavalry each. When we come to the battle of Pydna, we shall see that only two legions are mentioned in the text of Livy; but it suffers from a large lacuna. One legion, Legio II, had been destined for Macedonia in 172 (42. 27. 5). The legions of Philippus in 169 were arranged at not more than 6,000 infantry and 300 cavalry 'in each Roman legion' (43. 12. 4).

[1] These troops appear sporadically in 42. 62. 2, 43. 6. 13 and 7. 1, 44. 4. 11 and 16. 3 and *PAem* 15. 7 and 18. 4, in the battle of Pydna. That the Roman army was somewhat smaller was stated at 44. 38. 5 (in a speech composed by Livy) and *PAem* 16. 6 (a remark attributed to Friends of Perseus). See Meloni, *Perseo* 375 n. 1.

[2] 44. 21. 1–2 and 33–4. 9; *PAem* 13. 5.

'not much less than 40,000 infantry' (*PAem* 13. 4), these figures being consistent with the parade at Citium of 4,000 cavalry and 39,000 infantry in 171 (Livy 42. 51. 11). He had other forces under arms: at least 10,000 men in garrisons and on coastal defence, local reserves such as the Bisaltae (44. 45. 8), and a small number of naval personnel. There is no doubt that the military resources of Macedonia were extended to the full, and that the cost of paying very large mercenary forces was very high.

Of the army at the Elpeüs the cavalry of Macedonia itself was organized in élite squadrons, called 'Sacred Squadrons', and in standard squadrons, and they were supported by Odrysian cavalry under the command of Cotys. If the proportion was as at Citium, the Macedonians numbered about 3,000 (there had been 3,300 in 334 B.C.), and the Odrysians 1,000. The Macedonian cavalry had an almost unbeaten record over some three centuries, and it had shown itself superior to Roman cavalry in 171 at Callicinus (Livy 42. 58–9). Then Perseus had fought at the head of the Cavalry Guard, the *agema*, and had been flanked by the Sacred Squadrons. On either side of the last there had been the Royal Cavalry, analogous to the earlier Companion Cavalry. All these were 'heavy' cavalry in the sense that the horsemen wore armour, moved in a tight formation, and fought with spear or lance at close quarters. The wings at Callicinus had been held by the Thracian cavalry of Cotys and by the 'Macedonian Cavalry'; and as they were intermingled with light-armed infantrymen, these cavalrymen wore lighter armour, fought in open order, and threw javelins or shot arrows before engaging with the sword.[1] They were highly specialized, professional units. But they had one defect. Their horses had not been trained to bear the sight, trumpeting and smell of elephants; for Perseus did not possess any. He had arranged for dummies to be constructed and for trumpeting to be simulated;[2] but when the real thing appeared, as we shall see, the horses panicked.

The most prestigious Macedonian infantrymen were called after their special type of shield *peltastai* in Greek and *caetrati* in Latin. (We use the name Peltasts in this volume.) They numbered 5,000 at Citium; and from them 2,000 were 'chosen for their strength and youthful vigour' to be the Infantry Guard, the *agema* (Livy 42. 51. 4). In Pieria Perseus had only 3,000 of them, since 2,000 were serving at Pella as Household Troops. At the battle of Pydna, as we shall see, they served

---

[1] Asclepiodotus, *Tactics* 7. 1 describes the functions of the light cavalry (*akrobolistai*), and 7. 3 the formation used by the Macedonian heavy cavalry; being of the first century B.C., he is nearest in date to this period.

[2] Plb. 29. 17. 2; Zon. 9. 22; Polyaen. 4. 21; Ampel. 16. 4.

in two Infantry Guards, evidently of 1,500 each.[1] These Peltasts had inherited the role of Alexander's Hypaspists in a set battle. They fought then with the pike, *sarissa* (see P*Aem* 19. 1), either to protect the right flank of a phalanx formation attacking in oblique order, as at Issus and Gaugamela,[2] or to protect both flanks of the formation if a frontal attack or defence was intended.

The solid core of the Macedonian infantry was the phalanx. At Citium the *phalangitai* numbered some 21,000, being 'almost half' the 43,000 on parade (42. 51. 3). They were divided into brigades, called τάξεις or φάλαγγες. Each brigade in Alexander's army had had 1,500 phalangites; we do not know that this was so in Perseus' army, but a larger number is unlikely, since a brigade commander would find it difficult to control a larger unit in battle. A *phalangites* wore light body-armour, had a slightly concave bronze shield 2 feet in diameter suspended from his neck, wielded with both hands a 15-to-18-foot pike and carried a dagger (see Fig. 5). When the phalanx line was in close order (*pyknosis*), there were five pike-points in front of the first-rank man, and the men behind the fifth rank carried their pikes upright 'so as not to interfere in the turnings', e.g. to one's flank.[3] Long training, close co-operation, and physical strength were essential, and level ground was needed, especially if the phalanx was advancing in close order. It so happened that the phalanx had not fought a set battle since the battle of Cynoscephalae in 197.

The light-armed infantry at Citium, numbering 12,000, had been drawn almost entirely from the Balkan peoples, both within and outside the kingdom, and from Crete. In 168 we hear of Thracians, Paeonians, Cretans, and mercenaries, and we may assume that there were Agrianians, since they figured at Citium. These were the professional soldiers of warlike peoples, expert in their own type of warfare; Thracians, for instance, were trained to fight within the looser formation of the light-armed cavalry, other Thracians had long, heavy swords, Agrianians were javelin-men, and Cretans were archers. They fought in loose formation and were not upset by uneven ground.[4] Perseus had trained a brigade of 'elephant-fighters' (*elephantomachai*), who wore helmets with sharp spikes and carried shields with sharp spikes (Zon. 9. 22); for the elephants at Cynoscephalae had caused much panic and damage. The total number of his light-armed infantry in Pieria was about 15,000.

The scene of the approaching conflict was dominated by Mt. Olympus, 2,911 m., sacred to Olympian Zeus (see Fig. 17). On the

---

[1] P*Aem* 18. 7 mentions one *agema* of men chosen for their 'courage and age', and at 19. 1 'the Macedonians in the *agemata*', who reappear at 21. 6 as 'the 3,000 chosen men' (*logades*), all being infantrymen.   [2] See H*A* 101 Fig. 11 and 141 Fig. 14.
[3] See Asclepiodotus 5. 1–2 and 12. 9 fin.   [4] Ibid. 1. 2.

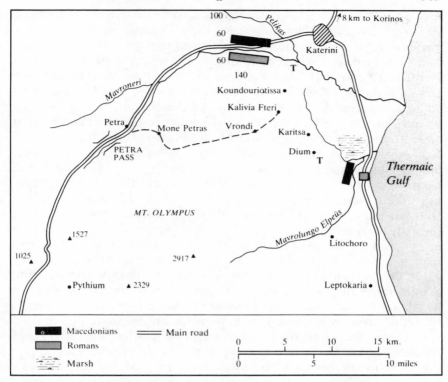

FIG. 17. THE PETRA PASS AND THE ELPEÜS POSITION

west the mountain is 'naturally linked' to Mt. Titarus, 2,194 m. (Str. 7. fr. 14 συμφυὲς τῷ 'Ολύμπῳ) by a high watershed ridge, which forms the frontier between the high plateau of Perrhaebia and the headwaters of the Macedonian river Helicon (Mavroneri). If we start from Perrhaebia, the main route, of which the Petra pass is a part, crosses this watershed ridge at a fairly level and open place (this being αἱ ὑπερβολαί in P*Aem* 16. 2), and then descends along the west side of the Mavroneri valley, which is deeply cut between the mountain sides and is forested with fir. The ancient road, first built along this route by Xerxes' army in 480, must have run, like the modern road, along the valley's steep west side with some precipitous drops to the river far below. It then descended closer to the river and went through the Petra pass, so called from a conspicuous rock, this being the best place for a blocking force to hold.[1] There was a town Petra, just as there are

---

[1] See Volume I. 123 f. I crossed from Olympus to Titarium on the watershed ridge in spring 1943 and travelled by bus from Katerini by the Petra-pass route to Elassona in summer 1978.

today a village and a monastery of that name. The route is some 28 kilometres from near Doliche (Kastri, now Dolikhi) to the exit of the Petra pass, below which the valley is joined by tributaries and is open and cultivated. A lesser route, but one closer to the Roman base at Heracleum, proceeds from Pythium (Selos) along the flank of Mt. Olympus through Kokkinopilos and then descends into the Mavroneri valley and enters the Petra pass.[1] In 168 Perseus anticipated that any turning force would be likely to use this lesser route; and he knew that on either route the strongest position for his men was at the Petra pass. Accordingly he posted troops under three commanders to hold as their bases Pythium and Petra (Livy 44. 32. 9 and 35. 11). The number of troops was almost certainly 5,000, stationed probably at three points, since there were three commanders.[2] It will be remembered that in 169, when Perseus had expected the main Roman army to attack through Perrhaebia, he had placed 10,000 men at the Volustana pass and 12,000 on the Lapathus saddle. Now his main army had to man the Elpeüs river bank which faced the main Roman army.

On the east side Mt. Olympus falls steeply to a narrow coastal plain. Winter rains and melting snows are carried down by raging torrents which are dry in summer, and one of these, the Elpeüs (Mavrolongos by Litokhoron), was chosen by Perseus for his defensive position. Its bed in the plain was always deep cut and studded with rocks and boulders; so Livy described it at 44. 8. 6. The descent from the top of the bank to the bed was some 300 paces in 168, and 'the distance between' the banks was then a little more than a Roman mile (about 95 yards short of an English mile).[3] During the winter Perseus had fortified the left bank and the ground behind it with palisades, stone walls, and built defences, and he had mounted his artillery—torsion catapults, mechanically strung bows, and stone-throwing machines —on suitable points and on towers built with timber from Mt. Olympus.[4] It was an even stronger defensive position than that occupied by Philip at the Aoi Stena. Supplies came by waggon on the

---

[1] I have not been over the lesser route, which is described by Leake, *NG* 3. 337 and Heuzey, *Olympe* 145 f. with map facing p. 9. Pritchett, *Studies* 2 Pls. 146 and 147 show a view in the Petra pass proper and the open country below the exit of the pass.

[2] The text of Livy 44. 32. 9 gives 'u' = 5 but 'milia' has to be supplied; in the Tempe pass Perseus had had garrisons at four separate places (44. 6. 9).

[3] Pritchett (*Studies* Pls. 121 and 124) shows the river-bed and his Pl. 123 shows the drop from the bank to the bed on the south side. I take 'medium spatium torrentis' at 44. 35. 17 to be the space between that bank and a similar one on the north side. The masses of detritus deposited by the river (as noted by Livy 44. 8. 6) has altered the lie of the land and pushed the coast farther into the sea, as by Dium (see Volume I. 125).

[4] Livy 44.32. 10–11 and 35. 8–9 and 21; P*Aem* 13. 5; Zon. 9. 22. For the artillery see the excellent book of E. W. Marsden, *Greek and Roman Artillery* 1 (Oxford, 1969) 166, noting the comparison with the Aoi Stena position.

main road from Pydna via Dium, only 5 Roman miles away, and were carried on the backs of women from the near-by towns.[1] Pasture was available in the swamps of the river Baphyras by Dium for the cavalry horses. Perseus knew that his position could be turned, either if the enemy marched through the Petra pass, or if the fleet landed a large force on the coast farther north (as was proposed in Livy 44. 35. 8); for then his line of supply would be cut. He had placed his troops to hold the route of the Petra pass, but he did not dare to weaken his army at the Elpeüs river further by sending considerable forces north to hold likely landing places.

Aemilius arrived in north Thessaly in early June, probably on the 7th, from which day we shall date the operations.[2] After disciplining some of the troops there he marched them through the Tempe pass on 11 June and reached the forward camp, which had been moved from Phila to the south bank of the Elpeüs (Zon. 9. 23; Livy 44. 34. 10). There he learnt of the defeat of Gentius, and this news reached the army of Perseus across the river-bed; and he met and postponed a conversation for a fortnight with the Rhodian envoys who were offering to negotiate a peace. He saw at once that the enemy's position had to be turned. After consulting his senior officers and two Perrhaebian merchants in his camp, who could act as guides, he made the following plan (see Fig. 17). Publius Scipio Nasica and Aemilius' son, Quintus Fabius Maximus, were to lead a force, probably of 5,000 men,[3] towards Pythium in such a way that they would attack the enemy there between 3 a.m. and 6 a.m. on the third day, 14 June (Livy 44. 35. 11–12 and 15). They were ordered to march their men first to Heracleum, where they were to give the impression of embarking on the fleet, which would be awaiting them with cooked rations for 5,000 men for two days. The purpose was to deceive Perseus into thinking that a large force was about to be landed on the coast north of his position. No doubt the fleet did sail north on one of the following two days. Moving only at night by a route away from habitations, probably up to the Lapathus saddle, they hid in the woods on 13 June.[4]

---

[1] See Volume 1. 126 f. Livy 44. 32. 11 gives this rare mention of women; one hopes they were commemorated like the women of North Pindus in 1940–1 by a statue.

[2] The precise dating hinges on the eclipse of 21 June, recorded by Livy 44. 37. 6 and P*Aem* 17. 7. See the discussion and references in Walbank, *C* 3. 386. The timetable here is as stated in H*Pydna* 41.

[3] In Livy 44. 35. 14 the text has 'quinque' only and 'milibus' should be added with Hertz. P*Aem* 15. 6–7 gave 8,320, evidently from Scipio Nasica (as we shall argue). Livy's 5,000 will be from Polybius, who had a number different from that of Scipio (Plb. 29. 14).

[4] Moving at night (P*Aem* 15. 8 διὰ νυκτός) and keeping away from habitation were essential in similar operations in 1943 (see H*Venture* 82 ff.). While Pritchett, *Studies* 2 159 takes them in the right direction, it would have been unwise to take them, as he does, through three places

Meanwhile, at dawn on the 12th, the Roman light-armed troops attacked the enemy light-armed and fought in the river-bed until noon, when Aemilius recalled his men.[1] Next day they attacked again and suffered quite severe losses, not so much from their immediate opponents as from the artillery fire. These attacks were sufficient to pin the enemy down and perhaps to lead Perseus to suppose that the attacks were planned to coincide with a landing from the sea to the north. On the next day, the 14th, Aemilius moved an assault force down to the seaward side of his own camp, as if about to attack where the bank shelved down to the sea. At this point in Livy's text there is a very large lacuna.

Before we return to the force led by Scipio and Fabius, we must note that Scipio wrote 'a little memoir' and sent it 'to one of the kings' (P*Aem* 15. = Plb. 29. 14). Plutarch drew on this memoir, and we see from Plutarch's account that Scipio made the events more dramatic and more to his personal credit. He exaggerated the size of his command (Polybius will have known Scipio and his memoir, but gave a less high number of men); he was the first officer to volunteer, killed a Thracian in personal combat with a lance (thus Nasica was mounted), and forced the enemy to flee with their commander still in his nightshirt. The whole episode was made more dramatic by the story of a Cretan deserter reaching Perseus and then of Perseus sending 12,000 men to the head of the pass, where Scipio smote them. In fact the timing would not fit; for with a day's lead from Heracleum for Scipio's men the 12,000 could not have reached the head of the pass in time, even if they climbed over the top of Olympus! So we may discard Scipio's account as not dependable.[2]

Between 3 a.m. and 6 a.m. on 14 June the 5,000 men of Scipio and Fabius surprised the advance post of the Macedonians who were holding the head of the pass but were asleep (Plb. 29. 15. 3). They then knocked out the other two groups of Macedonian troops,[3] cleared the Petra pass, and moved onto the foothills east of Katerini. Meanwhile a messenger will have reached Perseus. With a considerable force behind him near Katerini and with the probability that other troops would be

inhabited today and particularly through Karia (see his Pl. 151), which I knew in 1943. For the fleet see also P*Aem* 15. 7.

[1] Livy 44. 35. 16–19, using Polybius' account; cf. Plb. 29. 14. 4.
[2] See Walbank, *C* 3. 383, citing earlier writings, and H*Pydna* 43. Polybius presumably knew Nasica's memoir, but how far he was influenced by it is not known; see Walbank, *C* 1. 31.
[3] Each group was 'very small' in relation to the 5,000 men; that is the sense of Zon. 9. 23 ἐλαχίστην ... φρουράν in a short account derived from Polybius. As Petra was the narrowest point and was mentioned at P*Aem* 15. 2, I see no justification for the view of Kromayer in *AS* 2. 306 that Scipio swerved to the right and went to Kalivia Fteri instead of proceeding to Petra. See H*Pydna* 36 and Heiland 67 'kein Rechtsabmarsch'.

landed by the fleet to reinforce it Perseus realized that he might find himself trapped in his position at the Elpeüs river. During the night of the 14th 'he broke camp at speed and marched back' (*PAem* 16. 4). 'He was afraid that the enemy would attack him from behind or even seize Pydna first (for the Roman fleet was sailing along at the same time); so hastening towards Pydna he encamped in front of the city' (Zon. 9. 23). The route he took was the main road in the coastal plain, and he covered 24 kilometres to his chosen position which was 2 kilometres short of the city walls. He had time to dismantle his artillery and other material in the night, and to move it ahead on his train of wagons.

5. *The battle of Pydna*
(See Figure 18)

The chosen position was described by all our sources as 'in front of Pydna' (*PAem* 16. 5; Str. 7 fr. 22; Zon. 9. 23). It was 'in the plain before the city' (Str. loc. cit. ἐν...τῷ πρὸ τῆς Πύδνης πεδίῳ), i.e. on the enemy's side of it, and there Perseus 'began to deploy his forces for battle...as he intended to meet the Romans immediately upon their approach' (*PAem* 16. 7). The position consisted of 'a plain for the phalanx' and 'continuous ridges for the light-armed' (*PAem.* 16. 8). Since the site of Pydna in 168 is no longer in doubt, some 2 kilometres south of Makriyialos, the plain is that which extends from the latitude of the Salt Pans southwards towards Korinos, Katerini, and Dium. At its northern end it was then some 2 kilometres wide (being now diminished by the Salt Pans), and it was confined on one side by the sea and on the other side by a ridge-end 42 m. high (see Fig. 19). Looking southwards from this position one sees ahead 'the plain for the phalanx' and ahead to one's right 'continuous ridges' ending in points 42, 51, 43, and 50 m., and issuing from the valleys between the ridges two streams, which were then called the Leucus (now Ayios Yeoryios) and Aeson (now Ayios Dimitrios).[1] To the north of this position lay Perseus' fortified camp, then the Alkovitsa and Karagats rivers which provided water and pasturage near their mouths, and then Pydna, strongly walled and having seaward defences to hold the Roman fleet at bay. It was a good position for defence by the phalanx in the plain and the light-armed mainly on the ridges, or for attack if the Roman army moved close enough to the phalanx.

[1] H*Pydna* 31 ff. visited and described the site of Pydna, as Pritchett (*Studies* 2. 153 ff.) had done; since H's visit more burials have been opened in the cemeteries alongside the roads by the city. For Perseus' position see fuller details in H*Pydna* 33–6 and 38. All other scholars had placed Perseus further south, Kromayer, Heiland, Meloni, and Pritchett opting for the bank of the Mavroneri south-east of Katerini.

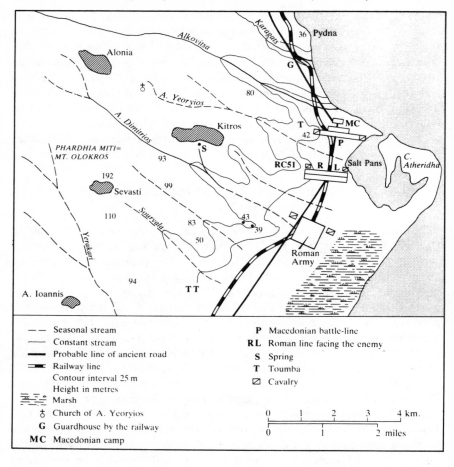

FIG. 18. POSITIONS IN FRONT OF PYDNA

The next stage of the campaign and its sequel down to the surrender of Perseus were described by three writers who were contemporary with the events: Scipio Nasica, whom we have mentioned already, a Hellenistic historian called Posidonius (*FGrH* 169), and Polybius, who knew Aemilius Paullus, members of his family, and other Roman officers, and on the other side many eminent Macedonians who were detained like himself in Italy. Scipio Nasica certainly wrote primarily about his own part in the counsels of Aemilius Paullus and in the battle itself, in which he was a mounted officer on the Roman right (*PAem* 18. 4); but there is no sign of him having written of Perseus' plans and problems or of what happened on the left half of the Roman line. Since Posidonius wrote a work of several books about Perseus and since Polybius was much interested in the behaviour of Perseus in the battle (29. 17. 3–4 and 18), we can assume that they described the battle from the side of Macedonia as well as from that of Rome, and moreover that they described the fighting on both halves of the Roman line.

The writings of these three contemporaries have been lost, and we depend chiefly on two later writers, Livy and Plutarch, whose accounts have survived. We can see clearly that their accounts drew in part on the memoir of Scipio Nasica (whether at first hand or through an intermediary) for the following passages: Livy 44. 36. 8–14 and P*Aem* 17. 1–4 (Nasica wishing to engage and Aemilius not doing so); Livy 44. 37. 10–40. 1 (the same clash of desires, but Nasica's wish shared by the staff officers and most of the army); P*Aem* 18. 4–8 (Nasica from his position on the Roman right sees the left half of the enemy line advancing); ibid. 21. 7 (Nasica's number for Roman casualties); and 26. 7 (Perseus wanted to give himself up to Nasica, in whom he had confidence). Thus we owe mainly to Nasica our knowledge of the arrival of the Roman army, its withdrawal into a camp, the reluctance of Aemilius to engage, and then the description of the fighting on one half only of the battlefield.

Since Livy was generally drawing on the account of Polybius, it is most probable that it was Polybius who incorporated some of Nasica's stories into his own account and added his own comments, such as Nasica being 'clarus adulescens' and 'egregius adulescens' (being of the Scipionic family), and also a dry criticism at Livy 45. 36. 14. On the other hand, Plutarch read widely and may well have taken Nasica's account of seeing the advancing Thracians and phalangites directly from Nasica's memoir. The emphasis on Perseus being stupid and cowardly, which is common to Livy and Plutarch, was certainly due to Polybius, for it appears in some fragments of Polybius; and the idea that the battle was precipitated by 'fortuna' at Livy 44. 40. 3 is surely derived from Polybius. On the other hand, Plutarch had the good sense to consult Posidonius as well; for Posidonius had different views from those of Polybius. Livy probably did not go beyond Polybius.[1]

While Perseus withdrew during the night from the bank of the Elpeüs, Aemilius moved from his camp on the 15th and joined the forces of Nasica, probably at a prearranged rendezvous in the foothills west of Katerini (P*Aem* 17. 1). From there they descended[2] into the

---

[1] See Walbank, *C* 3. 378 ff. for a discussion of the sources with references to earlier writings.

[2] Aemilius κατέβαινε συντεταγμένος ἐπὶ τοὺς πολεμίους. He probably thought that Perseus had positioned himself inside the walls of Pydna.

plain and followed the main coastal road towards Pydna, without making any reconnaissance, and in the heat of midday on the 16th the army in column of march came unexpectedly into sight of the Macedonian position,[1] a little more than 1 kilometre away (see Fig. 17). Perseus' scouts had seen from the hills the dust-cloud of the marching army, and he had drawn up his army in extended order for battle, with cavalry and light-armed on either flank and the phalanx in 'double formation', probably thirty-two-men deep with a front some 600 m. long (Frontin. 2. 3. 20 'phalangem duplicem').[2]

Aemilius had made a most elementary error. Granted that Perseus was slow to move, Aemilius retrieved his error by a rapid manœuvre which earned a place in Frontinus, *Strategematica*. He deployed his legionaries at top speed into three formations in line, one behind the other. The first formation in line was made up of wedge-shaped units, the point of each wedge facing the enemy, and the gaps between the wedges were filled with light-armed skirmishers who made continual sorties ahead of the line in the hope of delaying or deterring any attack.[3] The wedge-shaped units were designed to break up the uniform line of a charging phalanx. We do not know the order and disposition of the two other formations in line. Then at once Aemilius ordered his special officers to lay out a camp and place the baggage there, this being done initially by the legionaries who were escorting the baggage.[4] Once the camp was planned (on the ridge ending in point 51), Aemilius drew off the legionaries of the third formation in line, then of the second, and finally of the first, beginning with the maniple of the right wing, which withdrew behind the other maniples, i.e. to Aemilius' left, in order to man the camp. When this manœuvre was completed, the skirmishers and some cavalry were still down in the plain when the Macedonian phalanx was coming up to engage.[5] Aemilius then ordered his cavalry 'to gallop from his left wing past the front of the phalanx, the cavalrymen protecting themselves with their shields so that the points of the enemy's pikes would be broken off by the very shock of encountering the shields' (Frontin. *Strat.* 2. 3. 20). This tactic was probably designed only to halt or delay the advance of the phalanx; for the phalangites would

---

[1] Livy 44. 36. 1–2 after a long lacuna in the text describes the army arriving in the heat; this point is made again in the speech at 44. 38. 8–9 and in the narrative at 44. 40. 2. For Aemilius' surprise see P*Aem* 17. 2. Livy tried to conceal his discomfiture.

[2] The phalanx unit at this time was sixteen files deep, according to Asclepiodotus 2. 9 fin.; thus the double phalanx was thirty-two files deep. So too Kromayer, *AS* 2. 323 and n. 1.

[3] In the concise words of Frontinus, 'triplicem aciem cuneis instruxit inter quos velites subinde emisit'. Livy 44. 36. 4 stresses the speed of the deployment; see also 44. 39. 1 and 40. 2.

[4] Livy 44. 36. 6; he put the escorting troops at one-quarter of the whole at 44. 38. 6.

[5] Livy 44. 37. 1–3; P*Aem.* 17. 5–6.

have used their pikes to trip or strike the horses rather than aim at the cavalrymen's shields.[1]

Of the Macedonian line we are told that the men were fresh and already in battle order (Livy 44. 38. 11) and that the king would have been prepared to fight without reluctance (44. 37. 4). It was indeed a golden opportunity, if his phalanx had covered that 1 kilometre at a speed comparable to that of the Athenians at Marathon in 490. But he missed it, perhaps because he had for too long acted on the defensive when faced by a full Roman army. When he realized that Aemilius was withdrawing his troops onto the ridge, the phalanx did advance in fighting formation; but it arrived too late, and it was even delayed by the tactics of the Roman cavalrymen.[2]

Aemilius was doubly fortunate in the location of his camp. For the ridge-end was steep and much of the ground beside it was unsuitable for the Macedonian phalanx; and there happened by chance to be a good water supply,[3] a very rare thing in that region in June. The camp was certainly strong enough to withstand attack; and from it he had a fine view of the plain below and the camp of the enemy (*PAem* 7. 13). But he had neglected to organize a supply system. His men were short of firewood and fodder, and many of them went off scavenging in the fields (Livy 44. 40. 2–3). Perseus was fully aware of Aemilius' difficulties. He moved his camp from its original position to a new one between the Roman camp and the coast, thus preventing the Romans being supplied by their fleet. He was content to stay there until Aemilius might be forced by lack of supplies to withdraw, as Philippus had done in 169, or might choose to attack Perseus' fortified camp or his army, if it was deployed in the plain. Aemilius, it seems, had no intention of attacking the Macedonian camp.[4]

On the night of 21 June there was an eclipse of the moon.[5] According to a fragment of Polybius (29. 16), the eclipse was held generally to portend the eclipse of the king, and this encouraged the Romans and discouraged the Macedonians; and a similar account appears in Zon. 9. 23 and J. 33. 1. 7, which were thus probably based

[1] Kromayer and Meloni, *Perseo* 393 applied the passage in Frontinus not to this first contact but to the final battle, and therefore found it utterly wrong.

[2] Frontin. *Strat.* 2. 3. 20 'cum sic quoque, suspecta calliditate recedentium, ordinata sequeretur phalanx.'

[3] Livy 44. 39. 'provisam aquationem'; for the spring see H*Pydna* 35. Frontinus gave Aemilius credit for choosing this broken ground; but Aemilius had no choice in the matter.

[4] The accounts do not mention this move, which is inferred from later developments. Nasica had been critical of Aemilius for not engaging Perseus at the outset, and he was critical now of Aemilius' inaction (Livy 44. 36. 9–14 and 37. 12–40. 1).

[5] For the date see Walbank, *C* 3. 378 and 386. The interval between the 16th and the 21st is noted in Zon. 9. 23 οὐκ ὀλίγας ἡμέρας. Livy and Plutarch omitted the interval and made the situation more dramatic. See H*Pydna* 43 f.

on Polybius. According to Zonaras, Aemilius knew of the impending eclipse and warned his army beforehand. Livy tells a story which is probably apocryphal, since it occurs in a variety of authors in varying forms, namely that C. Sulpicius Gallus understood the cause of an eclipse and told the troops. Livy then adds that the Macedonians set up a clamour and a wailing in their camp; for to them the eclipse portended 'the downfall of a king and the destruction of a nation' (44. 37. 9). Plutarch has quite a different account: the Roman troops banged bronze vessels and waved blazing torches at the sky, 'as was their custom', to charm the moon back, the Macedonians did nothing of the sort, but were alarmed by this portent of the eclipse of their king, and Aemilius—aware of the natural cause, but a devout man— sacrificed eleven calves to the moon goddess, when she reappeared (PAem 17. 7–10). This account is probably historical, and its source may well have been the memoir of Nasica.[1]

During the late afternoon of June 22nd a minor clash led to an outright battle. Polybius, the source behind Zon. 9. 23, saw the clash as an accident of Chance (συμβάν τι κατὰ τύχην), and Livy adopted his view at 44. 40. 3 in the words 'fortuna, quae plus consiliis humanis pollet, contraxit certamen.' But Plutarch, still following Nasica in my opinion, tried to represent Aemilius as planning the clash for an hour when the sun would not be shining in the eyes of the legionaries (PAem 17. 12 and 18. 1). Other signs of Nasica's influence may be seen in Livy 44. 37. 10–40. 1, as we noted above (p. 549), and in PAem 17. 4, which both refer to Aemilius making sacrifices—the twenty-first effort pro- ducing the first favourable omen—instead of engaging in battle (as Nasica would have preferred). The cause of the clash was disputed in antiquity and is relatively unimportant.[2] The location was 'by a stream of no great size nearer the Macedonian camp' and 'on the right wing' (Livy 44. 40. 4 and 41. 3), i.e. of the Roman position and so by the Ayios Dimitrios. The participants were all light-armed troops posted on either bank, at first only a few and then 700 Ligurians on the Roman side and 800 Thracians on the Macedonian side.[3]

When the clash was developing, the regular infantry of the line were inside their respective camps, but in such a disposition that they could be deployed quickly into their standard formation for battle. When

---

[1] See Walbank, C 3. 386 f. and Meloni, Perseo 376 ff.; the latter attributes Plutarch's account 'probably' to Polybius.

[2] PAem 18.1–2. See Meloni, Perseo 383 ff. and HPydna 39 and 44. A horse without harness on the commemorative frieze at Delphi may refer to Plutarch's 'unbridled horse' which was said to have been the cause of the clash; see A. J. Reinach in BCH 34 (1910) 436 ff. and 449 f. and Appendix 7.

[3] Livy 44. 40. 9 describes the 800 Thracians as a 'praesidium', i.e. an outpost guarding an approach towards the camp. A lacuna follows in his text, and PAem 18. 1–2 takes up the tale.

troops began to leave the camps in order to help their comrades, Aemilius from his viewpoint saw 'the commotion of the camps' and, like a helmsman aware of a coming storm, envisaged a major battle. While he harangued his legionaries, still in camp, Scipio Nasica rode out at the head of a cavalry unit towards the scene of the clash.

[He saw] all the enemy just about to engage: first tall Thracians of terrifying aspect in their dark tunics with white greaves and gleaming oblong shields, brandishing massive curving swords above their right shoulders; next to them mercenaries with all sorts of equipment, and Paeonians mixed among them; third in succession a Guard of picked men, the élite of the Macedonians themselves in valour and in age, dazzling in gilded armour and newly dyed purple cloaks; and after them, as they were adopting their formation, the brigades of the Bronze-shield-men appearing like constellations from the camp, filling the plain with the gleam of iron and the glitter of bronze and making the hill country resound with their raucous battle-cries. (P*Aem* 18. 4–8).

The centre of the Macedonian line, held by the brigades of the White-shield-men (Livy 44. 41. 2), was beyond what Scipio Nasica could see; and beyond the centre there stretched the part of the line which corresponded to what he had seen. The whole line, including cavalry squadrons on either wing (44. 42. 2–3), was some $3\frac{1}{2}$ kilometres long, and the phalanx proper with a depth of sixteen men occupied about $1\frac{1}{2}$ kilometres in the centre.[1] Perseus, the commander-in-chief, headed some squadrons of Sacred Cavalry on the right wing.

The Macedonians were quicker to deploy than the Romans. That fact and the level ground enabled the formidable phalanx to charge into the ill-prepared Roman line. The position of the phalanx is shown on Fig. 19. The power of the phalanx in close formation, bristling with pike-points at the ready, was irresistible (Livy 44. 41. 6 'cuius [phalangis] confertae et intentis horrentis hastis intolerabiles vires'). Even the sight of it advancing swiftly filled Aemilius with utter terror—a terror which he recalled in later years (Plb. 29. 17 and P*Aem* 19. 2). As the front rank engaged, the pike-points pierced the shields of the Romans, whose swords were much outreached, and the following ranks at the word of command brought their pikes down together and thrusting with both hands and their full weight drove the points through shield, cuirass, and opponent alike (P*Aem* 19. 1–2 and 20. 1–4). The first Romans to fall were legionaries of the centre, only 400 metres from their camp; but the greatest damage was done to some Italian allies, the Peligni and the Marrucini on the right of the Roman line, who despite a gallant resistance by their first rank were forced

---

[1] See H*Pydna* 39 for these calculations.

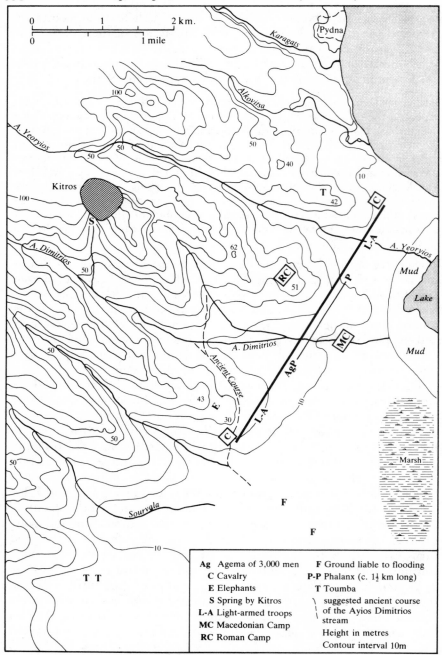

FIG. 19. THE BATTLE OF PYDNA

Ag	Agema of 3,000 men	**F** Ground liable to flooding
C	Cavalry	**P-P** Phalanx (c. 1½ km long)
E	Elephants	**T** Toumba
S	Spring by Kitros	\ suggested ancient course
L-A	Light-armed troops	\ of the Ayios Dimitrios
MC	Macedonian Camp	stream
RC	Roman Camp	Height in metres
		Contour interval 10m

back in disorder towards Mt. Olocrus (Phardhia Miti).[1] The two Guards, one at either end of the phalanx, charged with particular élan (P*Aem* 19. 1 τοὺς ἐν τοῖς ἀγήμασι Μακεδόνας). But the very impetuosity and success of the charge disrupted the long line, as parts of it charged on up the flat valley bottoms of the Ayios Yeoryios and the Ayios Dimitrios, and other parts of it were held up by the ridge-ends or delayed by ridge slopes.

Aemilius, stationed with Legio I, saw and seized his chance. Passing the order through the chain of command to the legionary soldiers,[2] he instructed them to operate not in line, but separately in groups of about 100 men (maniples), and charge into the gaps which had opened up in the enemy line, the largest of these being opposite Legio I between the Guard and the Bronze-shield-men (Livy 44. 41. 1–2). Once inside the gaps, the legionaries cut the phalangites to pieces; for it was the long sword against the dagger, the full-length shield against the 2-feet-wide shoulder-shield, and the pike was nothing but an encumbrance in fighting hand to hand (P*Aem* 20. 7–10).

As the phalanx line was crumpling under the effects of the broken ground and the attacks of the maniples, especially those of Legio II in the centre (Livy 44. 41. 6), Aemilius sent a squad of elephants and some squadrons of allied cavalry against the cavalry and the light-armed of the Macedonian left wing. The untrained horses stampeded, the 'elephant-fighters' proved ineffective, and the light-armed troops were routed, so that the left-hand units of the phalanx line were turned and encircled (Plb. 29. 17. 2; Livy 44. 41. 4–5). There the 3,000 Guardsmen, now isolated, fought to the last man, while the cavalry fled between them and the coast and joined the cavalry on the right wing (44. 42. 3). There the other Guardsmen resisted also to the last (P*Aem* 21. 6). Otherwise the fortunes of that wing are not related in our sources; but we may assume that elephants led the Roman counter-attack there and caused Perseus to withdraw all the cavalry from the battle. By then the phalanx was in a hopeless plight; for the men were being 'cut down from the front, the flanks, and the rear'. Those who escaped from the phalanx fled to the coast and swam out to sea; but the sailors who came in small boats from the warships offshore killed them without mercy. Those who turned back to the shore were trampled to death by the elephants, which had been brought by the mahouts to the water's edge (44. 42. 4–6). By nightfall the Macedonian dead numbered 'about 20,000' and 'more than 25,000'. Next morning the Leucus (Ayios Yeoryios) was still running red with blood. Within a few days 5,000 stragglers were rounded up, and 6,000 who had escaped to

---

[1] Livy 44. 40. 5 and P*Aem* 20. 1–6. For the identification see H*Pydna* 35 and 39.
[2] Aemilius had trained the army on the transmission of orders: Livy 44. 33. 7.

Pydna were taken captive. Those who got away were the 4,000 cavalry, 'almost unscathed' (44. 42. 1), and a few thousand light-armed troops. The Macedonian infantry of the line literally ceased to exist.[1]

Aemilius received undue flattery. He planned and executed the turning operation well, but then he made a gross error in marching without reconnaissance to within a kilometre of his enemy's prepared position on 16 June. When we see the effect of the charging phalanx on the day of battle, we cannot deny that if Perseus had ordered his phalanx to charge at once upon the disordered deploying legionaries he would have won as signal a victory as Aemilius won on 22 June. True, Aemilius retrieved his error by a brilliantly conducted withdrawal; but it was a matter of chance for him that the ground near by was unsuitable for the phalanx and had a fine water supply. On the day of the battle he was slower than Perseus in deploying his army. His great merit was that he saw at once how to exploit the disorder of the Macedonian phalanx and acted at speed. As at Cynoscephalae, the penetration of the phalanx by the maniples was decisive, turning what seemed to be defeat into victory. Contemporary writers covered up his defects by emphasizing his wisdom in not attacking with tired troops on 16 June, attributing his delays to the need to sacrifice, interpreting his twenty-first sacrifice as portending 'victory to those who act on the defensive' and thereby justifying his slowness in deploying on 22 June, and attributing the clash which led to the battle not to chance, but to design on his part.[2]

Perseus was given no credit. Yet the positions which he chose at the Elpeüs river, in front of Pydna and between the Roman camp and the coast cannot be faulted. The first proved impregnable. The others gave him two chances of victory. His fault was to miss the first chance through miscalculation or indecision. On the last day he lost control. Positioned far from the centre of action, he could not call the phalanx to a halt and keep it on the level ground, where it was invincible. That was a fatal error. Most of our sources portray Perseus 'in panic and despair' retreating from the Elpeüs river; riding off to Pydna when the battle was joined and making sacrifice there to Heracles, 'who would not accept the cowardly offerings of cowards'; and as the first to lead the flight from the battlefield. Posidonius alone defended Perseus against the charge of cowardice. He said that Perseus had been kicked

---

[1] The Romans spoiled, but did not bury, the dead (they had not buried the dead at Cynoscephalae). The number of dead was thus an estimate, dependable enough under the circumstances of the battle, and the 11,000 prisoners is a firm figure, since they were sold off as slaves, being part of the army's loot.

[2] See especially Livy 44. 36 and 38–9 and P*Aem* 17. 11; 18. 1.

by a horse on the previous day, rode in pain up to the phalanx during the battle, and was struck in the side by a heavy javelin. One is inclined to believe Posidonius.[1]

The final judgement is whether Perseus was justified in leading his small country into war in view of Roman aggression. Some, writing with hindsight, have condemned him outright.[2] Yet we may recall the decision of Britain in June 1940 and of Greece in October 1940. Both appeared irrational, but in the end both proved correct. Perseus and his people fought for liberty as they understood it. They might have won, but did not. The chief cause of defeat was the antiquated nature of the phalanx; for it did not adapt itself to the tactics of the Roman legions which had proved successful at Cynoscephalae.

[1] See especially P*Aem* 16. 4; Plb. 29. 17. 3–4 and 18; Livy 44. 42. 4 'princeps fugae rex ipse erat'; P*Aem* 19. 7–10. The allegation in Plb. 29. 18 and P*Aem*. 19. 3–5, that Perseus fled at the start of the battle on the pretext that he was going to sacrifice to Heracles at Pydna, is surely false. Perseus will have sacrificed at dawn, as Alexander did daily. Polybius or his informant changed the time in order to contrast Perseus as an absentee with Aemilius praying in the battle itself (19. 6).

[2] Notably Meloni, *Perseo* 213 f. 'La confederazione italica aveva sufficienti forze e volontà per imporsi su un regno ellenistico, fosse pur esso il più potente; anche il fatto che quest' ultimo fosse stato lasciato solo nella grande contesa, contribuiva a rendere l'esito non dubbio.'

XXVI

THE DISMEMBERMENT OF MACEDONIA AND THE ROMAN PEACE

1. *The final hostilities and the settlement of Illyricum*

THE story of Perseus' flight was elaborated with much detail in the accounts of Livy and Plutarch.[1] While the main pursuit by the Roman cavalry (see Figs. 1 and 3) followed the coastal road for 22 kilometres to the edge of the Emathian plain, Perseus and the cavalry forces took the military road which went through the forested foothills directly towards Pella.[2] Escaping infantrymen cursed the cavalrymen for cowardice in not engaging the enemy, and during the night Perseus and his entourage diverged from the main road and the Macedonian cavalrymen dispersed, riding for their homes. At Pella Perseus collected a large sum of money and other valuables, and during the next night with an escort of 500 Cretans, the Royal Pages, and only a few of his Friends he and his family crossed the Axius river and headed for Amphipolis. He tried to recruit troops among the Bisaltae, but in vain, and he soon took sanctuary in the holy island of the Cabeiroi, Samothrace. Meanwhile the Macedonian fleet of *lembi* left the Cyclades on hearing of the defeat of the army, and proceeded, not to Samothrace, but to Cassandreia. The Roman fleet, commanded by Cnaeus Octavius, blockaded Samothrace. A Cretan captain tricked Perseus by taking not him, but his money on board and sailing off to Crete. Then Octavius promised a free pardon and the retention of their property to the remaining Friends and the Royal Pages, who accepted the offer and brought the younger children of Perseus with them. Perseus and his eldest son, Philip, then gave themselves up. Perseus was taken to Amphipolis, where Aemilius treated him as a king on the day of his arrival and thereafter as a favoured prisoner. The Macedonian monarchy was at an end.

---

[1] Livy 44. 23; 44. 44. 4–8; 44. 45. 1 and 8–15; 45. 4. 2–7; 45. 5–8. P*Aem* 22; 23; 26–27. Zon. 9. 23; Dio 20. 3–4; and J. 33. 2. 5. For the common source of Livy and Plutarch being Polybius, see Walbank, *C* 3. 392. This holds also for Dio and Zonaras. Justin may derive from another source, as he alone gave 10,000 talents as the sum taken by Perseus to Samothrace; Livy 44. 45. 15 mentioned 2,000 with the reservation 'it is said'.

[2] See Volume 1. 138 for the 'via militaris', the Macedonian Royal Road, of Livy 44. 43. 1. In 1981 Dr. M. B. Hatzopoulos showed me the find-spot of a Roman milestone, which probably marked the line of this road; it was above the village of Livadhi. The direct road then went from there across the plain to Pella rather than round by Beroea, as I suggested in Volume 1. 138.

The victory at Pydna did not end hostilities. Aemilius made no reply to envoys and letters sent by Perseus suing for peace, until he had Perseus cornered. Then he sent three envoys to deliver the Roman ultimatum: Perseus was to commit himself and all his possessions to the mercy of the Roman People. Such an unconditional surrender was not acceptable to Perseus, predictably.[1] For Aemilius intended to impose on Macedonia a total and undeniable defeat. There is no doubt that Aemilius had ordered the soldiers and sailors not to take prisoners, or spare the wounded, or accept surrender during the fighting, whereas Perseus had taken Roman prisoners and treated them well (e.g. Livy 43. 18. 10–11 and 19. 7); otherwise the massacre of the phalangites on the shore and in the sea is inexplicable.[2] After the battle Aemilius authorized the cavalry to ravage and plunder the countryside, and this licence was extended as far as the region called Sintice, in the Strumitsa valley (44. 45. 4 and 46. 2). The infantrymen were told to spoil the thousands of dead, and they were sent in to plunder Pydna, no doubt with their usual ferocity (see pp. 453–4 above), when the surrender of the city had already been negotiated. Meliboea on the coast of Magnesia was captured by the navy and suffered the same fate. Aeginium, after a successful sortie by its garrison, was captured and was looted later (45. 27. 1–3). It controlled the route over the Zygos pass to Molossia.[3]

From Pydna the whole army moved to Pella and camped a mile from the city, probably at the so-called 'Baths of Alexander'. The treasury in the citadel was looted, but yielded only the 300 talents promised to Gentius. Other looting certainly took place, though not mentioned in the sources: for 'the exhibition of the collected loot of Macedonia—statues, paintings, and vessels of gold, silver, bronze, and ivory, made in that palace[4]—fascinated the eyes of the spectators' in 167 (45. 33. 5–6); and that exhibition did not include what the soldiers and sailors had acquired for themselves. When Aemilius reached Amphipolis, the garrison of 2,000 Thracians had been tricked into departing, and the citizen body came out to welcome the consul in the hope that the city would be spared. As the cities surrendered, they were placed under the control of Roman officers, and by the end of the

[1] Livy 44. 45. 2, 46. 1; 45. 4. 2–7; Zon. 9. 23.
[2] The emphasis was on killing in Zon. 9. 23 καταδιώξαντες τοὺς Μακεδόνας μέχρι τῆς θαλάσσης πολλοὺς μὲν αὐτοὶ ἐφόνευσαν, πολλοὺς δὲ τῷ ναυτικῷ προσπλεύσαντι ἀποκτεῖναι παρέδοσαν, and in Livy's statement that if the fighting had begun earlier in the day 'the Macedonian forces would have been entirely wiped out' (44. 42. 9 'deletae omnes copiae forent'). The source in each case was probably Polybius. A similar emphasis on killing marked the campaigns against the Illyrians: Livy 41. 4. 5–7 (in Istria c. 178) 'nemo captus' and 45. 3. 1 'caesum'.
[3] For the identification of Aeginium see HE 260 and 681.
[4] For the Baths of Alexander see Petsas, *Pella* 43. 'That palace' was the palace at Pella, and the implication is that it was looted; see also P*Aem* 28. 2–4 and 10.

campaigning season 'all Macedonian cities came under the direction of the Roman People' (45. 1. 9). The army was billeted in Amphipolis and nearby cities for the winter of 168/7, and it was available to enforce what we should call the military government of the victors.[1]

Once the kingdoms of Gentius and Perseus were 'in the power of the Roman People',[2] the Senate proceeded with its preconceived policy of weakening any kingdom, league, or city-state which was, or might become, relatively powerful. It did not matter whether these states had helped Rome, stayed neutral, or shown hostility. Thus Masinissa and his sons had contributed most to Rome's success by gifts of elephants, cavalry, infantry, and cereals,[3] and as a close second came Eumenes and his brothers, Attalus and Athenaeus, who had provided ships, cavalry, infantry, and supplies. But Rome did not reward them any more than she had rewarded Philip V in 188 (see pp. 453–4 above). Masinissa's request to visit Rome was refused, and his son's attempt to put pressure on Carthage by exacting certain hostages was thwarted by the Senate. Eumenes was treated almost with hostility, and the Senate favoured Attalus rather than him, as it had favoured Demetrius rather than Perseus, in the hope of splitting the rulers of Pergamum; and even the request of Attalus to be rewarded with the gift of Aenus and Maronea was granted only to be withdrawn.[4] When Prusias asked for some territory, the Senate did not accede; indeed it preferred to encourage the Galatians as trouble-makers for both Eumenes and Prusias.[5] And we have already described the intervention of Rome in the war between Antiochus and the Ptolemies, whereby Antiochus, aware of the defeat of Perseus, had to choose between the mailed fist or the hand of friendship and weakly agreed to withdraw from Egypt and Cyprus.[6]

Even more indicative of Rome's policy was her treatment of Rhodes, which had advocated peace between Perseus and Rome and was therefore distrusted by Rome. Her envoys played upon the animosities of the rival leaders, and the fear of Rome (for war was mooted by a Roman praetor) led the Assembly to decree that 'anyone convicted of any word or act in favour of Perseus and against Rome was to be condemned to death.' Some leaders had fled already, others committed suicide, and all who were apprehended were executed as dissidents by a verdict of the Assembly. Envoys came from Rhodes and grovelled

---

[1] It was probably closer to martial law with summary arrest and execution at the hands of the Roman officers than to British Military Government with courts martial and German barristers defending the accused in 1945–6. For the troops' misbehaviour at Amphipolis see Livy 45. 28. 9–10.

[2] Livy 45. 3. 1; 16. 7 and 44. 5.

[3] 45. 13. 13 and 14. 8.

[4] Plb. 30. 1–3 and Livy 45. 19–20. 3.

[5] See Walbank, *C* 3. 441.

[6] Plb. 29. 27; Livy 45. 10. 2 and 12. 3–8.

before the Senate, as the Carthaginians had done (see p. 503 above). But it was of no avail. Rome detached from Rhodes some parts of Caria and Lycia, and soon afterwards she transferred the control of the temple at Delos from Rhodes to Athens and made Delos a free port, which caused a disastrous decline in the revenues drawn by Rhodes from her own harbours and therefore in her ability to maintain a powerful navy.[1]

On the mainland of Greece where the Roman presence was immediate, the pro-Roman politicians led the attack on those who were accused of having favoured Macedonia or of having been lukewarm toward Rome.[2] Executions and banishments were common. The most notorious case was one in which Roman troops joined in the pogrom against the so-called dissidents. When the Council of the Aetolian League met, the Council House was surrounded by Roman troops and they helped the pro-Roman party to kill 550 leading Aetolians, banish others and confiscate all their property. When this was reported to Aemilius, he condoned the actions, but reprimanded the Roman commander for letting his troops share in the massacre.[3] Leading politicians of the Achaean League—the rival in power to the Aetolian League—were fortunate in that more than 1,000 of them were merely deported, held without trial for some seventeen years in Italy, and then sent back home—the 300, that is, who were still alive.[4] Polybius was one of them. We must not blame him for being wary in his comments on Rome's policy.

The states we have mentioned had not fought against Rome, and in the war she had not suffered heavy losses at all. Indeed at Pydna she was said to have lost only 100 men killed or even less. But there was one Greek state which had attacked Roman troops, namely the Molossian state together with probably the Atintanes, the Cassopaei, and perhaps another small tribe (see Figs. 8 and 12). After the capture of Gentius in 168 Anicius marched into Molossis, where the first city he encountered surrendered with pleas for mercy. Anicius left a garrison there. Later he encamped outside Passaron. When the people rebelled against the pro-Macedonian leaders, the latter rushed out, attacked the Romans, and were killed. The people then capitulated. Three other cities, which had intended to resist—Tecmon, Phylace, and Horreum—fell in a similar way. The army of Anicius was billeted for the winter of 168/7 in the cities of the area, acting as an army of occupation. Anicius himself went back to Illyris to meet the Roman

---

[1] Plb. 30. 4–5 and 30. 31. 9–12; Livy 45. 3. 3–8; 10. 10–14; and 20. 4–10.

[2] Livy 45. 31. 3–8 gives a general picture. Plb. 30. 6–9 provides examples of anti-Roman statesmen.

[3] 45. 28. 6–7 and 31. 1–2; Plb. 30. 11.   [4] Paus. 7. 10. 7–12.

commissioners there; but he returned to Passaron for the last part of the winter.[1]

Late in 168 the Senate prolonged for another year the commands of Anicius and Aemilius, in order that they should supervise the final settlement in each theatre in accordance with the Senate's general guide-lines and in consultation with specially appointed commissioners. Livy reported the first part of the guide-lines which applied to both areas: the Illyrians and the Macedonians were to be free, so that the world could see that Roman arms brought liberty, and in regard to the remaining kings it was to be noted that they ruled less harshly under the observant eye of the Roman People, and that if any king should attack Rome the result would be victory for Rome and freedom for his subjects.[2] This was clearly published only after the settlement was made. It was intended for the ears of the Roman People, which had as fanatical a hatred of kingship as Communists have of capitalism today.

The detailed guide-lines for Illyricum were not reported by Livy. In the winter of 168/7 the leaders of the Illyrian communities were summoned to Scodra for a conference. In accordance with the advice of the five commissioners Anicius announced that the Senate and the Roman People ordered the Illyrians to be free, and that all garrisons would be withdrawn from the towns, citadels, and forts (they had been mentioned at Scodra, Olcinium, and Rhizon). Immunity from tax would be granted to the people of Issa, the Taulantii, the Pirustae among the Dassaretii, the peoples of Rhizon and Olcinium, and the Daorsi, because they had joined Rome before the defeat of Gentius and Caravantius. The people of Scodra, the Dassarenses, the Sepelitani, and the rest of the Illyrians were to pay as tax (i.e. to Rome) half of what had been paid to Gentius. Then the kingdom was to be divided into three separate states, probably each having its own government and each sealed off from the others in respect of marriage rights and ownership of property; we may infer this from Livy's remarks that the same instructions were given for Illyricum as for Macedonia, where marriage and ownership were controlled in this way.[3]

---

[1] Livy 45. 26. 3–11 and Plb. 30. 7. 2–3. For Phanote being Raveni and Passaron Radotovi see H*E* 676 and 576 f., and for Horreum being Ammotopos see P. Cabanes and J. Andreou in *BCH* 109 (1985) 1. 520 f. Livy 45. 26. 15.

[2] Livy 45. 16. 2; 17. 1–4; 18. 1–2.

[3] 45. 18. 7; 26. 1–2 and 11–15; D.S. 31. 8. 5. One state was 'all the Labeatae', which meant the inhabitants of the Scodra basin (including Scodra and Lissus) and the lower Drilon (Drin), i.e. the catchment area of Lake Labeatis, as Lake Scodra was called. Another was the coastal belt from Olcinium to the Gulf of Rhizon (Kotor) and their neighbours inland of Kotor. The third—Livy's text being corrupt—was farther north; for it included the Daorsi of the Narenta valley and the native people of Issa island. The outlet for the trade of the Labeatae was Lissus, adjacent to the Roman sphere. Coins with the same emblems and weights of the 'Labiatae' and 'Lissitai' may belong to the first state, and those of the 'Daorsi' to the third state. H. Çeka in *Iliria*

The aim of the Senate in this settlement was to divide and dominate by indirect control, partly through pro-Roman leaders and partly through channelling each state's trade separately to Rome and Italy. The settlement was to be a strait-jacket; it could not be altered unless Rome agreed to the alteration. While the Senate claimed that the Illyrians were now free, the truth was that the Illyrians were free to obey Rome and Rome alone. Each of the new states began with much of its territory impoverished from looting and destruction by the Roman army and fleet, as we know from the case of Pharos. For when Gentius, his wife and children, his brother, and a number of leading Illyrians walked in front of the chariot of Anicius at his triumph in Rome, the vast amount of loot was remarkable even by Roman standards.[1]

2. *The settlement of Macedonia and the sack of Molossia*

The settlements for Macedonia and Molossia were deferred until later in 167.[2] Aemilius used the delay to provide further loot for the troops who were sent to sack Aeginium (mentioned on p. 559 above), Agassae, which had been 'freed' by Philippus in 169, but had then accepted Perseus, and Aenea, a famous and wealthy city, because it had resisted for longer than its neighbours. In late summer he made the grand tour, visiting the cities and shrines of mainland Greece. At Delphi he arranged for a statue or statues of himself to be erected, commemorating the victory at Pydna with the inscription 'L. Aimilius L. f. imperator de rege Perse Macedonibusque cepet' (*SIG* 652a).[3] He returned to meet ten Roman commissioners and he ordered each city to send ten leading men to Amphipolis. While they were assembling, Aemilius and the commissioners agreed to dismantle the fortifications

---

1984. 1. 15 ff. would correlate the three states with the three coinages, but that leaves the northern group stranded. J. J. Wilkes, *Dalmatia* (London, 1969) 26 f. groups the three states all in the south: he was writing before Çeka mentioned the coins. See Wilkes's map of 'The Balkan and Danubian Provinces' in *Atlas* Map 24. W. Pajakowski, *Ilirowie* (Poznan, 1981) Map 2, seems to be erroneous.

[1] For Pharos see Appendix 5 no. (16). Livy 45. 43. 1–8. On the other hand, Wilkes, loc. cit. and E. Badian, *Foreign Clientelae* (Oxford, 1958) 97 'Rome was prepared to be generous to harmless ex-enemies', find Rome to have been lenient and even generous; so too D.S. 31. 8. 5. It all depends on one's standard of comparison.

[2] The chronology is disputed. The prolongation of the commands of Anicius and Aemilius shows that both settlements were made in 167. After the Illyrian settlement Anicius went to join his army which was still in winter quarters, i.e. early in 167. Aemilius began his tour in late summer 167 (Livy 45. 27. 5); the settlement of Macedonia was in autumn 167. Meloni, *Perseo* 408 n. 3, 417 n. 3, and 468 put the tour of Aemilius in autumn 168 and the settlement in spring 167.

[3] Antissa in Lesbos was also destroyed (Livy 45. 31. 14). For the tour Plb. 30. 10; Livy 45. 27. 5–28. 6; P*Aem* 28. 1–5. For the statue or statues F. Courby *Fouilles de Delphes* 2. 3 (Paris, 1927) 302 ff., Meloni, *Perseo* 417 f., and Walbank, *C* 3. 432 with further references.

of Demetrias, which now became part of independent Magnesia, and to deprive Aetolia of Amphilochia, which afforded a good route of invasion into the Aetolian lowlands (D.S. 31. 8. 6).

The general guide-lines mentioned by Livy at 45. 18. 1–7 had been filled out with details by Aemilius and the commissioners. When the Macedonian delegates were assembled and the coffers of royal money and all of the king's papers (such as the 'commentaria regia' or *King's Journal*), had been deposited before them, Aemilius and the commissioners entered, the herald commanded silence, and Aemilius announced the terms in Latin. They were repeated in Greek by the praetor, Cnaeus Octavius.[1] The Macedonians were to be free, keeping their lands and cities, using their own laws, and electing their own magistrates. Roman garrisons were to be withdrawn. The Macedonians were to pay to Rome half of the tax they had paid to their king.[2] The land was to be divided into four regions (see Fig. 1). Each region was to be a self-governing republic. Any central assembly was banned (Livy 45. 18. 6 'commune concilium'). Intermarriage and trade in goods affecting land and buildings between the republics were banned, and salt was not to be imported. The hitherto royal estates were not to be leased, and timber suitable for shipbuilding was not to be cut by Macedonians or by anyone else. The mines of gold and silver were not to be worked, but those of iron and copper could be worked, the tax on the output being payable to Rome at half the rate payable to the king. Where the frontiers of the republics faced non-Greek tribes, armed guards might man the frontier posts.[3]

The four regions were defined as follows (though emendations in some of the texts are less than certain). The first region was the territory between the Strymon and the Nestus, extending northwards to the mountainous frontier with the Thracian tribes, but it also had Bisaltia and Heraclea Sintica west of the Strymon and certain 'towns, villages, and forts towards Abdera, Maronea, and Aenus' (these three being free Greek cities outside Macedonia).[4] The centre of government was to be Amphipolis. Livy commented on the vigour of the Bisaltae, the excellence of the soil for a variety of crops, the mines, and the strategic position of Amphipolis in blocking invasion from the east.

The second region was the land between the Axius and the Strymon, except that Bisaltia and Heraclea Sintica belonged to the first region.

---

[1] Livy 45. 29. 1–3; D.S. 31. 8. 6. For the king's papers see Plb. 30. 13. 10–11, Livy 45. 29. 1 and 31. 11 'litteras deprensas in commentariis regiis'.

[2] P*Aem* 28. 6 put the half at 100 talents a year, which seems unduly low.

[3] The sources are Livy 45. 17. 7–18; 29. 4–31. 1; 32. 1–7; D.S. 31. 8. 6–9; Str. 7 fr. 47; P*Aem* 28. 1–6. The ultimate source of them all was Polybius.

[4] See Map 9 of Volume II. 655, and Appendix 6 for the places towards Abdera etc. For Bisaltia and Heraclea Sintica see Volume I. 196 f.

It extended northwards to include all of Paeonia which lay east of the Axius until that river turns south.[1] The centre was to be Thessalonica on the Thermaic Gulf. Livy commented on the flourishing nature of Thessalonica and Cassandreia, the rich and fruitful soil of Pallene, the harbours of the promontories of Chalcidice with their access to the sea-lanes leading to Thessaly and Euboea and to the Hellespont.

The third region lay between the Axius and the lowest reaches of the Peneus. Its territory was bounded on the north-west flank by Mt. Bermium,[2] and it included Stobi in the north. Livy commented on its famous cities—Pella, Edessa, and Beroea—the warlike character of the 'Vettii' (probably the Macedonians of Bottiaea), and the intensive cultivation of the land by very large numbers of Gallic and Illyrian settlers.

The fourth region consisted of an inner band of cantons—Eordaea, Lyncus, and Pelagonia, and an outer band which extended to the frontiers of Illyris and Epirus. If some emendations of Livy's corrupt text are accepted, the cantons of the outer band were Elimiotis, Strymepalis, and Atintania; for they bordered Tymphaea (of Epirus), Dassaretis (sometimes reckoned to Epirus), and the Illyrian Parthini, Atintani, and Penestae.[3] Livy commented on the cold climate, rugged land, hard to cultivate, and inhabitants of a similar character to the terrain. Their spirit was made fiercer by their non-Greek neighbours, who shared their customs in peace and kept them alert in war. The centre of government was to be the state of Pelagonia.[4]

Other areas which had once been Macedonian were not mentioned. These were Orestis, independent for thirty years, and Dassaretis, which had served Rome well and was now made a free state, like Orestis.[5] They were well placed to inform Rome of any transgressions by the fourth republic. An inscription, recently published, records a treaty of 'friendship and alliance by land and by sea for all time' between Rome and Maronea, which would gladly report on the behaviour of the first republic.[6]

Some days later Aemilius reconvened the conference. He dictated a code of laws which was to be observed by all the republics, and he demanded the election forthwith and thereafter annually of 'council-

---

[1] See Volume I. 84.   [2] See Volume I. 73 f. for the mountain being Bermium.
[3] Livy 45. 30. 6 'quartam regionem Eordaei et Lyncestae et Pelagones incolunt; iuncta his *autincaniaestrymepalisetelimonites*'; D.S. 31. 8. 8 συνάπτει τῇ 'Ηπείρῳ καὶ τοῖς κατὰ τὴν Ἰλλυρίδα τόποις. See HE 633 for the emendations and the geography; Strymepalis is not otherwise known. See Volume II. Map 9 and Volume I. 122 n. 1 for criticism of other views.
[4] Str. 7 fr. 47 named the cities for three parts and for the fourth 'Pelagones' τὸ δὲ Πελαγόσι. See Volume I. 74 f. for the argument that it was not a town, but the state of Pelagonia. F. Papazoglou in ŽA 4 (1954) favoured a town in the Morihovo.
[5] See Volume I. 46 n. 4 and 121 f.   [6] See Appendix 5 no. (15).

lors' (*synhedroi*) for each republic. We are not told who the electors were and who were eligible for election; but the terms used by Livy and Diodorus suggest that the first elections were held within the centre of government only, i.e. within the citizenship of Amphipolis, Thessalonica, Pella, and the Pelagonian state.[1] Diodorus mentioned four officers concerned with the collection of taxes, evidently due to Rome (31. 8. 9). Aemilius then read out to the conference the names of the Macedonians who were to be deported to Italy, together with those of their sons who were over fifteen years of age. Livy defined these Macedonians as the king's Friends, Wearers of the Purple, commanders of armies, garrisons, ships, diplomatic representatives, and all who had held office under the king; we may add the Royal Pages above the first year. In other words the entire class of officers, administrators, and diplomats were to be removed and detained in Italy *sine die*.[2] The penalty for evasion was death. To show that this was no idle threat Aemilius arranged between the conferences for two distinguished Greek statesmen to be beheaded with an axe at Amphipolis—an Aetolian who had served against Rome and a Theban who had advocated alliance between Thebes and Perseus.

The aim of the Senate in partitioning Macedonia was to prevent any resurgence of power. With that end in view each republic was isolated from its fellows. The lines of division were cleverly drawn; for the great rivers—the Nestus, Strymon, and Axius—were effective barriers, difficult to cross; and the passes leading from one republic to another were few, and some of them were to come under control for the movement of Roman armies along what came to be known as the Via Egnatia.[3] The ban on the mining of gold and silver and on the logging of timber for shipbuilding, the discouragement of trade between the

---

[1] Livy 45. 29. 9 'capita regionum ubi concilia fierent' and D.S. 31. 8. 8 ἡγοῦντο δὲ πόλεις τέσσαρες. Diodorus is probably closer to the common source, Polybius, in using the word appropriate to hegemony being vested in one unit within an an association.

[2] There is no mention of exceptions, such as had been promised at Livy 45. 6. 7–9. We may compare the partition of Poland in September 1939, following 'one of the greatest battles of extermination of all time' according to the Germans (cited by Winston Churchill, *The Second World War* I (London, 1948) 398). Then the Polish officer class was executed or deported to Siberia from the Russian section. The opinion of Badian, *Foreign Clientelae*, 96 'the most liberal treatment was reserved for the humbled enemy, Macedonia', is beyond my comprehension.

[3] I enumerate the passes, with V.E. indicating the course of the Via Egnatia: between region 1 and region 2 the pass of Rendina V.E. (Volume I. 186) and Stena Dov Tepe (Volume I. 194), for which see Volume I. Map 17 on p. 180; between region 2 and region 3 the line of the Axius was reinforced by Mt. Barnous, Mt. Babuna, and Mt. Golesnitsa (see Volume I. Map 9 on pp. 62–3), through which there is only one good pass—the Pletvar pass—leading into region 4; between region 3 and region 4 the pass of Zoodokos Pege (Volume I. 158 f.) and the pass above Edessa V.E. (HH *Via Egnatia* I, 139 ff.); between region 4 and Orestis the pass of Klisoura (Volume I. 106), and between region 4 and north-western neighbours the Gryke e Ujkut or Wolf's pass west of Little Prespa Lake (*HACI* 71 ff.), the Pylon pass V.E. (Volume I. Map 6 on p. 40), and the Bučin pass from Pelagonia to Penestia (Volume I. 60).

republics, and the levying of taxes for Rome were designed to prevent an economic resurgence. The massacre on the battlefield of Pydna and the deportation of the officer class diminished the chances of any nationalist insurrection. The extent to which Macedonia had been devastated and despoiled should not be underestimated. For quite apart from what the soldiers and sailors had acquired, an unparalleled amount of spoil was provided for the triumph of Aemilius Paullus at Rome on 27–9 November 167. Its value was put at 210,000,000 sesterces by Velleius Paterculus 1. 9. 6, and it enabled the Senate to abolish direct taxation (*tributum*) throughout Italy thenceforth. This sum included more than 6,000 talents of gold and silver in the royal treasuries (Plb. 18. 35. 4); and the rest was probably obtained by the issuing of orders, as in Molossia, that all gold and silver in private possession had to be handed over to Roman officials. Moreover, all reserve stocks of grain and oil were distributed to individuals and cities in Greece at the discretion of the Roman commander.[1] Macedonia embarked on the next phase of its history crippled, impoverished, and dismembered.[2]

The Dardanians, as allies of Rome, had asked to 'recover' Paeonia, which they claimed was theirs, but, on the principle of not strengthening any state, Aemilius refused. However, he allowed them to import salt; the administrators of the third republic were to bring the salt from the coast to Stobi, and the Dardanians were to collect it at a price fixed by Aemilius.[3] In the interval between the two days of conference the names of some Greek politicians who had negotiated with, or supported, Perseus were discovered in the king's papers, and these men and others accused by the pro-Roman leaders were summoned by Aemilius and told to follow him to Rome for trial. Most of them were from Boeotia, Aetolia, Acarnania, and Epirus.[4]

From Amphipolis the army set off for Epirus. A flying column commanded by Quintus Maximus and Scipio Nasica was ordered to ravage the territory of those Illyrians who had sided with Perseus (probably some of the Penestae), and then to join the main army at Oricum, the port of embarcation for Italy (see Fig. 8). Aemilius brought the army to Passaron, the capital of the Molossian state. From

---

[1] Livy 45. 40.1–3; D.S. 31. 8. 10–12 (mentioning 500 wagonloads of statues); and P*Aem* 32–4. For corn and oil Livy 45.33. 3–4 and P*Aem* 28. 2–3.

[2] Livy and Diodorus, following Polybius, added a pro-Roman veneer. Livy represented Roman policy as beneficial to the Macedonians, who were liberated from slavery under a king and able to live happily in their republics (45. 30. 1–2; cf. D.S. 31. 8. 2 and 4), and better off with the law code of Aemilius and without the hectoring officer class. Diodorus justified the ban on mining as a relief for oppressed miners and a set-back for ambitious capitalists (31. 8. 7). These statements show only that a need was felt to justify Rome's treatment of Macedonia.

[3] Livy 45. 29. 12–13.   [4] Plb. 30. 13; Livy 45. 31. 3–9 and 11.

there he sent orders to the ten leading men of each city of the Molossians and of any other tribes which had joined Perseus: they were to collect all gold and silver and place it in the city treasury, and then they were to come to confer with Aemilius at Passaron. They were not alarmed by these orders; for Rome's settlements of the Illyrians and the Macedonians were well known, the cities had surrendered without resisting, and the pro-Macedonian leaders had either met their death or been summoned to go to Italy for trial.[1]

In fact Aemilius carried secret orders from the Senate that 'the cities were to be the booty of his army'. When the leading men were being brought to Passaron, Aemilius sent centurions to their cities to announce that the Epirotes were to be free, like the Macedonians, and that the centurions were about to remove the Roman garrisons. Next, Aemilius sent detachments of troops to all the cities, so arranging the times of their departure that they arrived on the same day. At dawn on the following day the centurions collected the gold and silver, and at the fourth hour after dawn the army was let loose on the unsuspecting population. When the looting was completed, there were 150,000 'capita humana' for the slave market, sufficient public wealth to give each cavalryman 400 denarii and each infantryman 200 denarii, and individual plunder estimated at 13 *denarii* a man. The army razed the fortification walls of the cities, some seventy in number, and marched to Oricum, driving the human and other cattle before them.[2] Central Epirus was totally depopulated. The last act of the Roman peace of 167 had been fulfilled.[3]

The ruthlessness of the Senate and the rapacity of the Roman forces were plain for everyone to see. The Senate had clearly succeeded in achieving its immediate objective: to crush any rival military power, to punish defection, opposition or even neutrality, and to exercise control

[1] Livy 45. 33. 8–34. 2.
[2] Livy 45. 34. 1–8; Plb. 30. 15 = Str. 322; P*Aem* 29; App. *Illyr.* 9; Trog. *Prol.* 33; Eutrop. 4. 8; Pliny, *HN* 4. 39. For the correctness of the figures see H*E* 635 n. 1. The most northerly razed site which I noted in my survey of Epirus is at Labovë east of Argyrokastro (ibid. 209 and 687), and the most southerly at Ammotopos (155); for the number of cities (many quite small) see 687. Polybius, the source of the main accounts, had every opportunity to be accurate. S. I. Dakaris has deduced from his excavations that the Nekyomanteion in southernmost Thesprotia and Cassope in Cassopaea were sacked at this time by the Romans. If so, the authorities of the shrine and of the Cassopaeans were among those who supported the Molossians in their alliance with Macedonia. That this was true of the Cassopaeans is made virtually certain by an issue of bronze coins with the letters **ΜΟΛΟΣΣΩΝ ΚΑΣΣΩΠΑΙΩΝ** (see Dakaris, *Cassopaea* 66 and Cabanes 304). Franke, *Münzen* 1. 82 attributed the coins to the years after 167; but that is incompatible with the sack of Molossia.
[3] The aftermath in Italy included the walking of Perseus in chains, his children, and some leading Friends before the chariot of Aemilius in the triumphal procession, and thereafter the lingering death of Perseus in a Roman gaol, of which various unpleasant accounts have survived: Livy 45. 40. 6 and 41. 10; P*Aem* 34. 1–4 and 37; D.S. 31. 9.

without committing troops to permanent occupation. But terroristic methods have long-term effects. They create the peace of desolation or impoverishment or they excite a desperate, if unsuccessful, resistance or they induce apathy in those whom they control. These effects were soon to manifest themselves in Macedonia and mainland Greece. For some two centuries the Roman Republic exacted a heavy price from the world in terms of human lives and hopes and culture. Macedonia had stood for something very different. In the reigns of Philip and Alexander she had shown how peoples of lesser military power could be brought into collaboration, make their own cultural contribution, and create a civilized world. Despite the rivalries of generals and kings, the Graeco-Macedonian world maintained its standards of civilization and prosperity. The tragedy of the Roman Republic was that it did not learn from the history of Macedonia. With the foundation of the Principate the rulers of Rome sought the collaboration of the peoples within the empire, and then what gave life and vigour to the eastern half of the Roman world was the Graeco-Macedonian civilization which we call Hellenistic and the vigorous Hellenistic city, which stemmed from the most creative period of Macedonian history.

The Formal Relations Between Macedonia and the Greeks at the End of Philip's Reign and the Start of Alexander's Reign

THE questions at issue are whether Philip (and later Alexander) was a party to the Common Peace of 338/7; whether he was simply the initiator of it or was '*hegemon* of the Common Peace' in the sense of 'sponsor and in charge of it' as in Volume II. 630; whether the Greeks of the Common Peace were allied to one another or not; and whether Philip (and later Alexander) was *hegemon* of the forces of the Greeks of the Common Peace for a specific war—that against Persia—or for a war against any enemy. Various answers have been given to these questions. Those of G. T. Griffith, together with an excellent review of the literature on the subject, are given in Volume II. 623–46. But since I find myself at variance with him on some points, I support here the views which I expressed in *A History of Greece to 322 B.C.* (Oxford, 1959) 571 ff. and 596 ff., by taking each piece of evidence and giving my interpretation of it.

As we are dealing with formal relations between two parties, it should be noted that the members of the Common Peace (οἱ τῆς εἰρήνης κοινωνοῦντες of *GHI* 177, 10; cf. 192, 13) are usually named collectively 'The Greeks' (οἱ Ἕλληνες of *GHI* 192, 11, 14 and 15), and that the Macedonian state is named either 'Macedonians' (Μακεδόνες) or 'Philip' or 'Alexander' with or without a patronymic. For the second point I gave my reasons in *CQ* 30 (1980) 461–5. It may be sufficient here to mention the treaty between Μακεδόνες and Ἀθηναῖοι (*IG* I³. 89 Μακεδ[όνο]ν Περδίκκας) c. 415; between 'Amyntas son of Arrhidaeus' and Χαλκιδεῖς with mention of Μακεδόνες in the text (*GHI* 111, 1 and 17) c. 393; and the oath taken by the Greeks not to overthrow τ]ὴν βασιλείαν [τ]ὴν Φ[ιλίππου καὶ τῶν ἐκγόν]ων, where the whole future of the monarchy in this dynasty in Macedonia is intended (*GHI* 177, 11). The practice of Greek orators and historians varied. Because the king bulked larger in their eyes, they usually referred to him and not to the people. But it should be obvious that neither term was exclusive in this context; for 'Philip son of Amyntas' and 'Macedones' were frequently alternative ways of referring to the Macedonian state.

When Arrian was writing of Alexander's treatment of some Greek envoys and mercenaries near Zadracarta in 330, he drew a clear distinction between 'the peace' and 'the alliance made with (the) Macedonians' in the phrase πρὸ τῆς εἰρήνης τε καὶ τῆς ξυμμαχίας τῆς πρὸς Μακεδόνας γενομένης 'both before the peace, and before the alliance made with (the) Macedonians' (3. 24. 5). Here 'the peace' is the Common Peace of 338/7 which brought into being 'the community of the Greeks of which Sinope had no part' (3. 24. 4 τοῦ κοινοῦ τῶν Ἑλλήνων). 'The alliance made with (the) Macedonians' is an alliance of the Greeks with the Macedonians and not an alliance of the Greek states with one another. Arrian is not pushing any view of his own. He is reporting what he found in his sources, Ptolemy and Aristobulus. They knew the facts and had no reason to misrepresent them.

We have direct contemporary evidence in the fragments of an inscription of Philip's time, which was found at Athens (*GHI* 177). What survives is an oath (itself incomplete at the end) to be taken by the Greeks, an oath which came no doubt after a statement of the terms of the agreement between the Greeks and Philip, and a list of Greek states and their votes (this list too being incomplete). The text at lines 14–15, ὅτε τ[οὺς ὅρκους τοὺς περὶ τῆ]ς εἰρήνης ὤμνυον, gives the swearing by the Greeks of 'the oaths concerning the peace' in a past tense, that is as an event in the past, prior to the current swearing of the 'oath' (ὅρκος. ὀμνύω).[1] The current oath, defined at the time of the text, includes an undertaking by the Greeks to observe 'the articles of agreement with Philip' (οὐ λύσω τὰς σ]υνθήκας τὰ[ς πρὸς Φίλιππον). 'These articles of agreement' (αἵδε αἱ συνθῆκαι in lines 5 and 16) were evidently recorded in the earlier, but lost, part of the inscription. One of the articles was an undertaking not to overthrow 'the monarchy of Philip and his descendants'. This shows that the agreement was not restricted in time, but was in perpetuity. It is certain that Philip, as the other contracting party, made a similar oath,[2] and we may conjecture that his oath included an undertaking not to overthrow the constitution of the organization known as the Common Peace.

We can infer, then, from the inscription that at an earlier date an organization for the Common Peace had been drawn up and ratified by oaths, and that now 'a treaty of agreement'[3] between the Greeks of the Common Peace and Philip was being recorded and the oath to be taken by the Greeks was being stated.

After a lacuna the text gives the votes allotted to each member state or to each group of member states for voting in the Council, but this list is unfortunately incomplete. There is no mention of contingents to be supplied or of Persia in what has survived.[4] However, some action is envisaged in the

---

[1] The difference in time is marked also in [D] 17. 10, which uses the aorist tense and gives the same definition of 'the oaths those concerning the peace', cited from the same treaty of agreement: ὅτε τοὺς ὅρκους τοὺς περὶ τῆς εἰρήνης ὤμνυσαν. The past tense shows that the oaths concerning the peace had been sworn at an earlier meeting; and the present tense ὀμνύω refers to the oath at the moment, i.e. concerning the articles of agreement. This is denied by T. T. B. Ryder, *Koine Eirene* (Oxford, 1965) 152 n. 3, 'the tense ... does not mean ... that the oaths have been taken already'; but if he wants this 'oath' to be contemporary with 'the oaths', then the Greek phrase should be either simply τὰς οὔσας παρ' ἑκάστοις (cf. *GHI* 123, 70 τῶν τε οὐσῶν πόλεων) or with the addition ὅτε τόνδε τὸν ὅρκον ὀμνύω. The singular and the plural and the definition shows that the oath (singular) and the oaths (plural) refer to different occasions; for the former concerns the article of agreement, αἱ συνθῆκαι, and the latter concerns the peace (τοὺς περὶ τῆς εἰρήνης).

[2] As the two parties do for instance in the perpetual alliance between Athens and Thessaly in 361/0 (*GHI* 147).

[3] This term, αἱ συνθῆκαι (see *GHI* 177, 5 τὰς σ]υνθήκας and restored in 177, 16 and 19), familiar also in the title of [D.] 17, is used in *GHI* 111, συνθῆκαι πρὸς Ἀμύνταν, where the συνθῆκαι include an alliance for fifty years. Thus the term here does not exclude an alliance between Philip and the Greeks; rather, it is likely by analogy to include it.

[4] This came perhaps at a third meeting. There may have been some correlation between the number of votes and the military resources of any one state; but that is not the same thing as fixing the size of a state's contingent for a war.

event of anyone violating the Common Peace; for then, so the oath runs, 'I shall go to war as the Common Council may decide and as the *hegemon* may order.' It seems probable that 'the *hegemon*' had already been appointed to deal with such an eventuality, namely Philip, since we hear of no other. If so, the implications are important. Hegemony was a long-used and well-known concept. It meant the command of allied forces in the field. The choice of Philip as *hegemon* implied the use of the allied forces of Macedonia and the Greeks, and made him their commander.

'The peace' and 'the alliance' are clearly marked in some of our secondary sources. The fullest and most interesting account is in Justin's epitome of Trogus. At 9. 5. 2 he has Philip establish the terms of 'the peace' ('pacis legem universae Graeciae ... statuit') and set up the Council ('consilium'). He then notes the separate stance of Sparta and her reasons for it. 'And then' ('deinde'), he continues, the forces of the individual states were listed 'either to help the king fend off an attack or to conduct a war, the king being commander' ('sive adiuvandus ea manu rex oppugnante aliquo seu duce illo bellum inferendum'). This is certainly language appropriate to an offensive and defensive alliance contracted between two parties, one of which is to have the hegemony—in this case between the Greeks and the Macedonians with Philip exercising the hegemony as 'dux', Justin's term for ἡγεμών. To continue with Justin, 'for there was no doubt that the Persian empire was the target of these preparations.' This sentence shows that the decision to go to war with Persia was not taken at the meeting which listed the forces of the individual states. Next in Justin the total of the forces so listed is given as 200,000 infantry and 15,000 cavalry. The important remark is then made that there was in addition to this total the army of Macedonia; for this shows that Macedonia itself was not a member of the Greek organization of the Common Peace.

Diodorus, who abbreviated the account of Diyllus drastically,[1] was interested not in the Common Peace, but in the winning of hegemony by Philip. However, Diodorus had the Common Council (τὸ κοινὸν συνέδριον) set up and functioning before Philip addressed it on the subject of war against Persia (16. 89. 3). Philip's aim was to be made πάσης τῆς Ἑλλάδος ἡγεμών; he achieved it when he was elected στρατηγὸς αὐτοκράτωρ τῆς Ἑλλάδος (89. 1 and 3; cf. 91. 1 and 6). Once elected, Philip arranged the sizes of contingents 'in accordance with the alliance' (89. 3 τὸ πλῆθος τῶν εἰς συμμαχίαν στρατιωτῶν). Thus 'the alliance' had been made before the arranging of the contingents, that is the alliance between Macedonia and the Greeks of the Common Council.

PPh 16. 4 has an interval of time between two stages. First, Demades proposed that his state (Athens) should take part in the Common Peace and in the Council of the Greeks (τῆς κοινῆς εἰρήνης καὶ τοῦ συνεδρίου τοῖς Ἕλλησιν). Second, it was only later that Athens learnt that she was required to provide triremes and cavalry to Philip, i.e. as her contribution to the allied forces over which Philip was *hegemon*, as I understand it. One action taken by the Greeks in Philip's time is mentioned by Livy, calling the Greeks 'Achaei' (as at 27. 30. 6 and 12 'concilium Achaeorum'): Belbinatis was transferred

---

[1] For Diodorus' use of Diyllus see *HSD* 84, 89 f., and 150.

from Sparta to Megalopolis 'ex decreto vetere Achaeorum quod factum erat Philippo Amyntae filio regnante' (38. 34. 8). Thus the Common Council passed a decree, which Sparta obeyed, no doubt in fear of combined action by the allied forces if she should refuse and go to war.¹

To summarize, these passages show that two things happened in the lifetime of Philip. First, the creation of a Common Peace (PPh 16. 4 τῆς κοινῆς εἰρήνης, whereas others refer simply to ἡ εἰρήνη) and the formation of a Common Council (D.S. 16. 89. 3 τὸ κοινὸν συνέδριον) for 'the Greeks' (PPh 16. 4 τοῖς Ἕλλησιν). We find these phrases in contemporary documents (GHI 177, 21–2, restored; 192, 11, 14, and 15 τῶν Ἑλλήνων). Thus οἱ Ἕλληνες is the name of the organization which had its members, Council, decrees, votes, magistrates, finances, courts, armed forces, and *hegemon*, and which was to exist in perpetuity (so binding itself to Philip and his descendants in GHI 177, 11). What do we call this organization? Not a city-state, a πόλις, but a community, a κοινόν; in fact, as Arrian correctly named it, τὸ κοινὸν τῶν Ἑλλήνων (3. 24. 4). Second, the alliance between 'the Greeks' and 'the Macedonians' (Arr. 3. 24. 5 τῆς ξυμμαχίας τῆς πρὸς Μακεδόνας γενομένης). This led at once to the appointment by the Council of Philip as *hegemon* of the allied forces (*hegemon* occurring first in GHI 177, 22).

There is no suggestion in the texts that Macedonia was a member state of the Common Peace of the Greeks; nor indeed should we expect it, since Macedonia was not regarded as one of the community of Greek city-states. Nor is there any indication that the Greek states of the Common Peace entered into alliance with one another. Rather, they committed themselves 'to fight against anyone violating the Common Peace' (GHI 177, 21), i.e. to combine in an *ad hoc* coalition, which we call 'collective security'. But when the alliance between the Greeks and Macedonia was formed, and when a war was declared by both parties, a *hegemon* of their joint forces was needed. Philip was chosen to be *hegemon* by land and by sea (Plb. 9. 33. 7). We think of his hegemony in relation to Persia. But the Greeks at the time were thinking of war against any violator of the Common Peace, and they swore in the event of such a violation to act 'in accordance with the decision of the Common Council and the orders of the *hegemon*' (GHI 177, 23). The conditions governing the actions of the *hegemon* were evidently laid down in 'the articles of agreement with Philip' (GHI 177, 5 τὰς σ]υνθήκας τὰ[ς πρὸς Φίλιππον...).²

Let us turn now to the time of Alexander. For this we have an original document in the letter of Alexander to Darius in Arr. 2. 14. 4–9, which is in my opinion a paraphrase of a letter preserved in the *King's Journal*. In it Alexander made the accusation that Persian envoys had attempted in his own reign 'to overthrow the peace which I organized³ for the Greeks' (2. 14. 6 τὴν εἰρήνην ἣν τοῖς Ἕλλησι κατεσκεύασα). As we have seen, such an attempted

¹ The transference was dated by the reign of Philip, probably because Philip was involved in the judgement as *hegemon*.
² This restoration seems to be required by the oath not to overthrow the monarchy of Philip. But the further restoration Μακεδόνα in the text of GHI looks improbable; for Philip was usually called 'Philip' or 'Philip (son) of Amyntas'.
³ A tactful word, used again by Polyperchon in 319 B.C. (D.S. 18. 56. 3).

violation obliged the Greeks and the Macedonians as allies to act together against the would-be violator. In the eyes of Alexander Persia started the enmity (2. 14. 6). Alexander used the traditional name for the members of the Common Peace, οἱ Ἕλληνες. In the same letter Alexander referred to the Persian invasions in the time of Darius and Xerxes. 'Your ancestors', he wrote, 'by invading Macedonia and the rest of Greece (τὴν ἄλλην Ἑλλάδα) wronged us.' Here he lumps Macedonians and Greeks as 'us', meaning 'us Greeks' as opposed to the Persians. So he continues 'I being appointed *hegemon* of the Greeks and desiring to avenge ourselves on the Persians crossed to Asia'. Here again 'the Greeks' comprises Macedonians and the other Greeks of the preceding sentence. Thus, as I understand the letter, Alexander, like his father, stressed two facts, that he had organized the Common Peace for the Greeks and that he held the hegemony over the joint forces of the Macedonians and the Greeks. Another passage in Arrian may preserve the exact words which were put upon the spoils he dedicated to Athena at Athens: 'Alexander (son) of Philip and the Greeks except the Lacedaemonians, from the barbarians occupying Asia'. As in previous alliances of a similar kind, the hegemonic power comes first and the aggregate of allies follows: 'the Athenians and their allies' and 'the Lacedaemonians and their alliance' (*GHI* 27).[1] Here 'Alexander (son) of Philip' is, as we have seen, one way of referring to the Macedonian state.

The secondary sources were interested less in the Common Peace than in Alexander's skill in winning the position of *hegemon*. The assassination of Philip rendered that position vacant. States which had exercised hegemony over some of the Greeks in the past were unwilling now to yield it, according to D.S. 17. 3. 1 and 4, Athens to 'the Macedones' and Thebes 'to Alexander'. So Alexander canvassed support for his hegemony first from the Thessalians, then from the Amphictyonic Council, then with a show of force from Thebes and Athens, and finally from the Council of the Greeks (D.S. 17. 4. 1, 2, and 9). The Council appointed him στρατηγὸν αὐτοκράτορα, this being Diodorus' periphrasis for ἡγεμόνα (cf. 16. 89. 3). Justin likewise has Alexander elected 'dux' (11. 2. 5), his word for *hegemon* (as at 9. 5. 4). Arrian has abbreviated his sources drastically at 1. 1. 1–3: he goes straight to the crucial election in the sentence 'assembling all the Greeks who were within the Peloponnese, he requested from them the hegemony of the expedition against the Persians, which they had already granted to Philip, and he gained his request from each state individually, excepting the Lacedaemonians.' In fact the Council must

---

[1] Thus Ἀθηναῖοι καὶ οἱ σύμμαχοι in *GHI* 123, 26 and 60 and [τοι Λακεδαιμόνιοι συμ] μαχία τ' ἀν[εθεν] in *GHI* 27. Where hegemony is not an issue, the Greeks could be mentioned first and the Macedonians could follow as 'allies', as seems to be the case in *SIG* 665. 19–20, where judgements in a joint court are described as αἱ ἐν τοῖς Ἕλλησιν καὶ συμμάχοις κρίσεις. For in this case 'the allies' can only be the Macedonians. The judgements themselves were given in a border dispute between Sparta and Megalopolis; and those judgements (or one of them) were probably incorporated in the decree of the Council of the Greeks in the time of Philip which is mentioned in Livy 38. 34. 8 (see above). They are mentioned too in Plb. 9. 33. 12. But this is a matter of controversy into which we cannot enter here; see G. T. Griffith in Volume II. 617 f. and especially 627 with notes 4 and 5. For a similar joint court see *GHI* 123, 57. For A. being a judge in the court of the Greeks see Polyaen. 4. 3. 24.

have been attended also by the representatives of some if not all states north of the Isthmus. Presumably Arrian mentioned only those 'within the Peloponnese', because his sources had described already the support granted or ceded by the states north of the Isthmus. Again, it was not a personal matter. Alexander was at the head of the Macedonian army (D.S. 17. 4. 4), and he was requesting a Macedonian hegemony within an already constituted alliance of Macedonia and the Greeks of the Common Peace.[1]

This alliance was not overlooked by our secondary sources. Diodorus has the Council of the Greeks vote 'to join in the expedition (συστρατεύειν) against the Persians in requital for the wrongdoing to the Greeks' (17. 4. 9). Arrian, drawing on Ptolemy and Aristobulus, calls the Greek troops (other than the mercenaries) who joined the expedition 'allied' (e.g. 1. 14. 3, 24. 3, 29. 3; 2. 7. 3, 8. 9, 9. 1; 3. 11. 10, 12. 4, 19. 5). This is not peculiar to him; for Curtius reports the order issued in 333 B.C. by Alexander 'that the allies in accordance with the treaty should send warships to guard the Hellespont', that is, in accordance with the treaty of alliance between Macedonia and the Greeks (3. 1. 20 'ex foedere naves sociis imperatae quae Hellesponti praesiderent').

'The peace' in Greece was also important for Alexander. What had happened in stages with Philip—first the Common Peace, then the alliance, then the appointment of Philip as *hegemon* to lead the allied forces against any violator of the peace (*GHI* 177, 21) and any external enemy, now specified as Persia—were all *faits accomplis* for Alexander. The fact that he took over the whole package did not blind him to its constituent parts. Alexander himself claimed to have 'organized the peace for the Greeks', 'been appointed *hegemon* of the Greeks', and undertaken a war 'of retaliation for Persian wrongdoing to us' (Arr. 2. 14. 4). When Philip was assassinated, Alexander chose to regard himself as *hegemon* of the Greeks, entitled to deal with any violator of the Common Peace, whether of the principles laid down in its charter (transmitted in part in *GHI* 177) or of resolutions made by the Council since the declaration of war against Persia. In this sense Diodorus listed intended or actual violations: Aetolia voting to restore persons exiled from Acarnania, Ambracia changing its constitution and expelling its garrison, Thebes voting to expel its garrison, and others eager (vaguely) for 'autonomy' (17. 3. 3–5, 'autonomy' being in contrast to the conditions of the Common Peace). Alexander with his usual skill chose to overlook these intended or actual violations. He pressed on to his objective, election as *hegemon*.

In 335 B.C. it was a different matter. The Common Peace, the alliance of Macedonia and the Greeks, the appointment of Alexander as *hegemon*, and the joint war against Persia were established facts in the political situation, when the Theban assembly voted to renounce its obligations and the Theban troops

---

[1] It was of course a request which could be refused. For that reason Arrian repeated the word 'requested' (1. 1. 2), and Diodorus emphasized A.'s tactful words when he 'persuaded' the Greeks to elect him *hegemon* (17. 4. 9). There was a velvet glove on his iron hand. He has used similar tact in Thessaly; and one of his arguments there may have survived in D.S. 17. 4. 1, that the hegemony was inherited from his father (τὴν πατροπαράδοτον ἡγεμονίαν), but if so it was an untruth.

attacked the Macedonian garrison in the citadel. On arriving outside Thebes, Alexander invited any Thebans to come to him and 'share in the common peace of the Greeks' (D.S. 17. 9. 5 μετέχειν τῆς κοινῆς τοῖς Ἕλλησιν εἰρήνης). They did not do so, thus confirming their violation of the conditions of the Common Peace and bringing upon themselves the clause of collective security (*GHI* 177, 20 πολεμήσω τῷ[ι τὴν κοινὴν εἰρήνην παρ]αβαίνοντι). In attacking the garrison on the citadel, the Thebans violated the terms of the treaty of alliance between Macedonia and the Greeks to which they were a party. So those of the Greeks who did send troops to help the *hegemon* were described correctly as 'allies' in their conduct of the war by J. 11. 3. 8 'Phocenses et Plataeenses et Thespienses et Orchomenii, Alexandri socii, victoriaeque participes', and by Arr. 1. 9. 9 τοῖς μετασχοῦσι τοῦ ἔργου ξυμμάχοις. When the city had fallen, Alexander handed over the decision to the Greek side of the alliance, that is from the Macedonian point of view 'to the allies'; and it was 'the allies' who decided what was to be done to Thebes and in Boeotia (Arr. 1. 9. 9–10 as cited and again οἱ ξύμμαχοι ἔγνωσαν). They met of course in their own chamber, the Common Council of the Greeks.

In 330 b.c. there was another violation of the Common Peace. Action was taken by Antipater and by those Greeks who were loyal to the alliance (D.S. 17. 63. 1 τῶν συμμαχούντων Ἑλλήνων), and the terms were referred to the Council of the Greeks for decision (D.S. 17. 73. 5 ἐπὶ τὸ κοινὸν τῶν Ἑλλήνων συνέδριον). The legal forms were correctly observed in each case. And when in 330 b.c. the Common Council voted to entrust the decision to the *hegemon*, it too was acting within its legal rights.

We know nothing in detail about 'the articles of agreement with Philip' (*GHI* 177, 5 τὰς σ]υνθήκας τὰ[ς πρὸς Φίλιππον). When Alexander persuaded the Greeks to elect him as their *hegemon* by land and sea, there is no doubt that 'articles of agreement with Alexander' were made. One article was evidently the right to depute his authority as *hegemon*. On leaving for Greece he 'entrusted the Greeks to Antipater' (Arr. 1. 11. 3 τοὺς Ἕλληνας Ἀντιπάτρῳ ἐπιτρέψας). Thus he gave to Antipater the command of allied forces, both Greek and Macedonian, if they were required to maintain the constitution of the Common Peace and to deal with any violator of the Common Peace. Similarly in Asia he chose deputies to command the Thessalian cavalry and the 'allied cavalry' at the Granicus river and later (Arr. 1. 14. 3 οἱ ξύμμαχοι ἱππεῖς). That the hegemony of Macedonia was unrestricted and ubiquitous is clear from [D.] 17. 22. For the speaker's claim is that 'the Macedonians' (20) by their misconduct in the waters off the Hellespont had lost the right to keep 'their hegemony by sea' τὴν κατὰ θάλατταν ἡγεμονίαν. One is reminded inevitably (as the speaker intended, no doubt) of Spartan misconduct in 478 b.c. and their loss of 'the hegemony by sea' to Athens. In each case the hegemony was a reality.

There is no doubt that Alexander had other deputies of his hegemonic authority than Antipater operating on the Greek mainland. In complaining of acts by 'Alexander' and by 'the Macedonians' the speaker of [D.] 17 quotes the conduct of τοὺς συνεδρεύοντας καὶ τοὺς ἐπὶ τῇ κοινῇ φυλακῇ τεταγμένους (17. 15). The Councillors, we know, were Greeks, elected in all probability by their own states;[1] it follows that 'those appointed in charge of common defence' were the Macedonians, or at least officers chosen by Macedonia, i.e. by Alexander. It was written in the articles of agreement, says the speaker, that they should concern themselves with preventing any breaches of the regulations of the Common Peace in the member states; but they (οἱ δέ) have done the contrary, even conniving at such breaches, and should therefore be executed. It is clear that these officers were extensions of the hegemonic authority, like the commissioners of the Athenian hegemony in the allied cities in the fifth century (οἱ ἐπίσκοποι).

These officers appear with the same title in an inscription, found at Athens, which publicized the rates of pay and the supplies of rations for troops serving under the command of Alexander, presumably on the mainland of Greece, since the record was set up at Athens and no doubt at other member states of the Common Peace. The inscription states that 'those appointed in charge of the common defence' shall set this up (i.e. publicize the rates etc.) at Pydna; and we may infer that this was for the benefit of Macedonians on service. These particular officers were presumably deputed to do this, because they were representatives of the Macedonian king ('The Greeks' alone could not have ordered things to be done in Macedonia) and because their duties included details of military service in 'the common defence'.

They are recognizable also in Curtius as 'those who guard the Greek cities' (3. 1. 20 'eos qui Graecas urbes tuebantur', where 'urbes' translates πόλεις, the term used for the Greek member states in [D.] 17). Then, in 333 B.C., Alexander sent 600 talents to Antipater and to them in connection with the defence of the Greek peninsula and islands against the Persian fleet. Their duties here, as in [D.] 17. 15, are primarily with the Greek member states ('Graecas urbes').[2]

Finally, we should note that Alexander dealt with the Greek city-states not only through the articles of agreement between the Greeks of the Common Peace and himself,[3] but also through individual treaties. The speaker at [D.] 17. 26 complains that the Macedonians sailed a trireme into the Piraeus 'in contravention of the common agreements between us and them' (παρὰ τὰς κοινὰς ἡμῖν πρὸς αὐτοὺς ὁμολογίας). These agreements are resumed in the words καθάπερ οὐδὲ τῶν προειρημένων in contrast to 'the common resolutions', τῶν κοινῶν δογμάτων, that is, the resolutions of the Greeks of the Common Peace.

---

[1] As was surely required by the agreement in the charter that the 'the Greeks' should be free and autonomous ([D.] 17. 8). The office of εἰρηνοφύλαξ to which Demosthenes wished to be elected by the Athenians in Philip's last year according to Aeschines 3. 159 may well have been the office of σύνεδρος. For εἰρηνοφύλαξ like Ἑλλησποντοφύλαξ was probably an Attic word coined by Aeschines for his ironical purpose (see Griffith in Volume II. 644). So too T. T. B. Ryder in *CQ* 26 (1976) 85 ff. If this is correct, the Athenians themselves elected their representatives to sit on the Common Council.

[2] That Macedonian officers should be concerned with the financial matters for the troops provided by 'the Greeks of the Common Peace' is less surprising if we recall that Athenian officers—the Hellenotamiae—handled the moneys of the Allies from the outset (Thuc. 1. 96. 2).

[3] Especially in *GHI* 192, where traitors to the cause against Persia could be banished 'from all states sharing in the peace' κατὰ τὸ δόγμα τῶν Ἑλλήνων, and Alexander as *hegemon* made his own arrangements, in 332.

To return to the questions at the beginning of this Appendix, we conclude that Philip was not a party to or member of the Common Peace, not '*hegemon* of the Common Peace'.[1] He merely initiated its conception and organized its development; Alexander likewise claimed to have organized it. The Greeks of the Common Peace were not allied to one another, but they were committed to that form of joint action which we call 'collective security'. The Greeks and the Macedonians entered into an offensive and defensive alliance in perpetuity, including a promise to maintain each other's constitution. The Greeks conceded the hegemony to Macedonia. It was exercised by Philip as *hegemon*, and then by Alexander as *hegemon*. The joint forces under the command of the *hegemon* were employed both to enforce obedience to the regulations of the Common Peace at home and to undertake a joint war against Persia. Alexander's deputies, chosen by himself, included Antipater, officers appointed in charge of 'the Common Defence', and probably others unknown to us.

---

[1] Such a phrase in Greek—ἡγεμὼν τῆς κοινῆς εἰρήνης—is without parellel and would be inappropriate to the meaning of ἡγεμών, which involves the leading of troops.

APPENDIX 2

The Chronology of the Years 281–276 B.C.

FOR the years between Lysimachus' death and the recognition of Antigonus Gonatas as king of Macedonia some dates are firm, but many are only approximate. The Babylonian king-list (A. J. Sachs and D. J. Wiseman, *Iraq* 16 (1954) 202–11) now firmly dates the assassination of Seleucus I by Ceraunus to month 6 of year 31 (S.E.) i.e. 26 August–25 September 281; and Corupedium, which occurred seven months earlier (J. 17. 2. 4), was therefore in January/February 281 (see above, p. 240 n. 5). The list of kings preserved in Eusebius—it is derived from Porphyry for the Macedonian kings and probably from Porphyry for the Thessalian kings (identical names, but not identical figures in all cases for this period)—assigns a reign of 1 year 5 months to Ptolemy Ceraunus, which brings his death to January/February 279.

Ceraunus was followed by Meleager, who reigned for 2 months (the Greek table of Macedonian kings gives him 1 year 2 months, clearly an error; D.S. 22 says 'only a few days') and he by Antipater Etesias, who reigned for 45 days (cf. D.S. ibid.; the Armenian list of Macedonian kings says 40 days, again an error). In *C* 1. 49–51, I argued that Antipater's nickname should have meant that he reigned at the time of the Etesian winds and so in July/August rather than May/June; but Nachtergael 135 rightly points out that Porphyry (in both the Greek and the Armenian versions of Eusebius) says that he reigned χρόνῳ τοσῷδε οἱ ἐτησίαι πνέουσι, 'da ebenso lange zeit die jährigen [sic!] winde wehen', which is consonant with Antipater's having ruled *as long a time* as the Etesian winds blow, without necessarily ruling *at the same time*. This chronology also receives some confirmation from Memnon, *FGrH* 434 F 8. 8, whose figure of 2 years for Ceraunus (πολλὰ καὶ παράνομα ἐν δυσὶ διαπραξάμενος ἔτεσι) will be the result of calculating his reign from the death of Lysimachus, the previous king. Plb. 2. 41. 2 includes Ceraunus' death within Ol. 124, which would require it to have taken place before summer 280. This cannot be made to fit the evidence for the Gallic invasion and must therefore be discarded as a loose attempt to include as many approximately synchronous events as possible within the one Olympiad. On the other hand, if the battle of Ausculum was fought in the summer of 279 (it could be a little earlier; cf. Lévêque 399), the statement in P*Pyrrh* 22. 2 that Pyrrhus got the news of Ceraunus' death just afterwards can be reconciled with a date of January/February 279 for that event without much difficulty, given the general confusion and probable delay in communications with the Balkan peninsula at the time.

The evidence concerning the Gallic attack is as follows. Plb. 1. 6. 5 dates the Gallic ἔφοδος to the year after the Tarentine appeal to Pyrrhus, which was in the consul year 281; if that is equated with the Olympiad year 281/0, the ἔφοδος can fall in 280/79, which fits a date of autumn 280 for Bolgius' irruption into Macedonia. Bolgius is unlikely to have set off in winter, but if Ceraunus perished in January/February 279, he clearly did not delay his start until the spring of that year. Pausanias (10. 19. 6–7) tells us that the Gauls invaded via Ilyria and they may well have spent some time on the way. Thus the evidence of Plb. 1. 6. 5 is consistent with the chronology proposed. Polybius (2. 20. 6) dates Pyrrhus' crossing to Italy two years before the débâcle at Delphi. That was in Ol. 125. 2 = 279/8 (Paus. 10. 23. 14) and there was snow at Delphi. Pyrrhus' crossing was in Ol. 124. 4 (Plb. 2. 41. 11) and either in May (if one accepts the implications of PPyrrh 15. 1 that the storm he ran into was παρὰ ὥραν) or earlier, perhaps in March (if one prefers the statement in Dio, fr. 40. 6 οὐδὲ τὸ ἔαρ ἔμεινε). In either case one is in the early months of 280 and so in Ol. 124. 4 = 281/0. This evidence fits a Gallic débâcle at any time during the winter of Ol. 125. 2 = 279/8. Since Brennus did not set out until the return of Bolgius in the early months of 279, and yet will hardly have waited until winter, it seems reasonable to date his start to late summer or autumn 279 and his death in the early winter of that year. The return north in wintry conditions contributed to the catastrophe of the rest.

The dates of the war between Antiochus and Antigonus have been discussed above (pp. 250–1). There is no firm and decisive evidence on when the war began or when the treaty of peace was made; but it seems likely that Antigonus will have freed himself from this entanglement before intensifying his efforts to recover Macedonia. And for this one must turn back to the king-lists. According to D.S. 22. 4 (from Syncellus), the reigns of Meleager, Antipater Etesias, Sosthenes, Ptolemy, Alexander, and Pyrrhus of Epirus amounted in all to three years; clearly Syncellus has misunderstood or misrepresented his source. What Diodorus must have said was that from the accession of Meleager to the end of the chaotic period i.e. down to the time when Antigonus gained full control of Macedonia (but *not* including the later invasion of Pyrrhus) came to three years. Meleager's accession has been dated to February 279. Three years brings us to February 276—or, in Olympiad years, it covers the period from Ol. 125. 1 (280/79) to Ol. 125. 4 (277/6). These figures can be checked from the king-lists in Porphyry, according to which Meleager reigned 2 months, Antipater 45 days, Sosthenes 2 years (or in the Thessalian list 1 year), with anarchy lasting 1 year 2 months (in the Greek table of the Macedonian kings; the Thessalian list gives 2 years 2 months, perhaps because Sosthenes lost control of Thessaly earlier). On either reckoning (of the years assigned to Sosthenes and to 'anarchy') the total amounts to about 3 years 6 months. Starting from February 279 this brings us down to September 276. Within this period Sosthenes will have been in control from about June 279 to June 277, which would fit Antigonus' unsuccessful attack in the summer of 278 and his victory at Lysimacheia in the late summer or autumn of 277. The siege of Cassandreia alone lasted for 10 months (above, p. 257), so that it will have been 276 before Antigonus was in control of the whole of Macedonia.

It is clear that Antigonus did not count his regnal years from 277/6 or 276/5. His successor, Demetrius II, died at the time when the Romans crossed into Illyria (Plb. 2. 44. 2). That, as Holleaux has demonstrated (*Études*

4. 9–25), was in spring 229, since it was shortly after the battle of the Paxos islands (which has to be in 229, since by 228 the Achaeans have broken off relations with the Aetolians). The date of Demetrius' death is also confirmed by the fact that Aratus of Sicyon, who was general of the Achaeans from May 229 to May 228, initiated negotiations for the surrender of Athens before the previous generalship expired: hence Demetrius must have died before May 229, and so in the Olympiad year 230/29. Ten years' reign (confirmed by the king-lists in Porphyry) brings us back to Olympiad year 240/39, the year of Antigonus' death; this probably fell in spring 239 (Ehrhardt 140). From 276/5 to 240/39 is 37 years inclusive; but a decree from Amphipolis replying to the invitation to attend the *Asclepieia* of Cos (Herzog–Klaffenbach no. 6 l. 19) is dated to Gorpiaios (i.e. July/August) of Antigonus' 41st year. It follows, therefore, that Antigonus began counting his regnal years from an earlier date than 276/5.

According to Eus. 1. 238. 10 Sch. (confirmed by Ps.-Lucian, *Macrob.* 11, quoting a historian Medeius) Antigonus reigned for 44 years and according to the Armenian version (Eus. 1. 237 Sch.; *FGrH* 260 F 3. 12) 43 years. The tables in each case assign him fewer years, viz. 33 (Armenian) and 34 (Greek), but this is evidently because both the Greek and Armenian texts (Eus. 1. 237–8. 11; *FGrH* 260 F 3. 12) say that he ruled for 10 years in Greece before becoming king of Macedonia. The Thessalian list has 34 years 2 months (text) and 33 years 2 months (table), presumably for the same reason. Of these variants 44 years seems the most likely and this suggests that Antigonus began to number his regnal years from his father's death in 283 (above, p. 234, n. 4). Normally a Macedonian king counted the period from the death of his predecessor to the last day of the next Hyperberetaios as his first year, subsequent regnal years beginning on 1 Dios (Walbank, *Ph* 297; Habicht, *AM* 1. 273 f.). But Antigonus was not yet king of Macedonia and in any case we do not know how long it took the news of his father's death to reach him in Europe.

That Antigonus did in fact reckon 283/2 (Mac.) and not 284/3 (Mac.) as his first regnal year is confirmed by a passage in Philodemus (*P. Herc.* 155 fr. 8. 5 and 339 col. 5), which seeks to show that at no time before 277 was Antigonus in a position to claim control of all Macedonia. As one of the dates relevant for such a claim he mentions the Athenian archonship of Euthius, 283/2 (Habicht, *Unters.* 99 n. 24), presumably because that is Antigonus' first regnal year. (On this see further Appendix 3 p. 585). This involves dating the Coan embassy, which was received at Amphipolis and elsewhere in Antigonus' 41st year, to 243/2, Gorpiaios of year 41 being July/August 242; and the Macedonian year 240/39 will be Antigonus' 44th regnal year.

The statement in the king-lists that Antigonus ruled for 10 years in Greece before becoming king of Macedonia takes one back from 277/6, not to Demetrius' death in 283, but to his departure for the East in 287/6, the date from which Antigonus had *de facto* control over the Antigonid possessions in Europe. In fact, Antigonus ruled as king of Macedonia, not for 44 years (the number of his regnal years, calculated from 283/2) but for 37 years (calculated from his gaining full control of Macedonia in 276); and this figure is the one to be found in Porphyry's table listing the reigns of the Macedonian kings in Olympiad years, for here Antigonus is said to have reigned from Ol. 126. 1 (=276/5) to Ol. 135. 1 (=240/39), a total of 37 years. For fuller discussion see M. Chambers, *AJP* 75 (1954) 385–94, 'The first regnal year of Antigonus Gonatas', on whose findings the last paragraph is based. The king-lists can be conveniently consulted in Beloch 4. 2. 115–18.

APPENDIX 3

Philodemus on the Stoics

AN important text for Gonatas' career around 281–77 is Philodemus, Περὶ τῶν Στωικῶν (P. Herc. 155 fr. 8. 5 and 339 col. 5), published by A. Mayer, Philol. 71 (1912) 225–32. The relevant fragment is part of Apollodorus' (?) demonstration that the exaggerated figures for the length of Zeno's life given by Demetrius of Scepsis (101) and Apollonius of Tyre (98) are derived from forged letters purporting to be part of a correspondence between Zeno and Antigonus Gonatas (cf. D.L. 7. 6 f.), in which Zeno claims to be eighty (or, according to another reading, ninety) in Antigonus' first year as king of Macedonia. It gives a brief and often illegible account of events in the relevant years, which would have made it impossible for Gonatas to have written in the terms recorded in his 'letter' in the Athenian archonship of either Euthius (now fixed as 283/2) or Anaxicrates (279/8). Hence the letters must be forged and the conclusions resting on them must be rejected. The printed text, which is based on two supporting papyri, unfortunately contains restorations which depend on Mayer's assumptions about the context and these have introduced both confusion and the risk of circular argument. Mayer prints the relevant passage as follows (loc. cit. 226):

ὅσα [γεγ]ραφω[σ
ἀπ[οτ]ρέψαντος [αὐτὸν] τοῦ μ[ία]ν λαμβάνειν
[τ]ὴν βασιλείαν καὶ μετὰ τὴν Λυσιμάχου τελευ[τὴν
παρέ]χ[οντ'] αἱ σπονδ[α]ὶ ⟨τῷ⟩ Γονατᾷ καὶ [Λακό]νων
5 κρατήσας τῆς Μακε[δο]νίας ἐκπίπτει πά[λιν εἰς τὴν]
Ἀσίην, εἶθ' ὕστερον ἔ[τεσιν γ̄] [νικήσας Κελ]-
τοὺς τοῦ βα[σ]ιλ[ε]ύειν Μακε[δόνων ἤρξατο]
ὥστ' εἶτ' ἐπ' Εὐθίου γρά[ψας, ἑαυτῷ μὲν εἶ]πε
πείθ[εσθαι] Μακεδό[νων συλλήβδην] πάντας,
λ[έγω]ν ἑαυτὸν [ἄρχειν τῶν Μα]κε[δόν]ων, οὔ[πω]
δ'] εἶχε τ[ότ' ὄντως βα]σιλ[είαν], εἶτ' ἐπ'
Ἀναξικ[ράτους ἔγραψεν...

However, Mayer also prints the reading of both papyri in capitals, scrupulously putting dots under doubtful letters and bracketing all restorations. Thus the word [Λακό]νων in l. 4 is shown as wholly bracketed in one text and has only the letters νων in the other. The restoration depends on Mayer's belief (op. cit. 231) that the reference is to the defeat of Areus and the Spartans in the conflict referred to in J. 24. 1. 6. It is, however, highly implausible, since Justin is describing a victory of Antigonus' allies, the Aetolians, not of the king himself. It has nevertheless misled A. C. Johnson and W. W. Tarn into discussing [Λακό]νων as if some form of that word stood in the text. Johnson, in fact, emended it (CP 9 (1914) 267 n. 2) to [Μακ⟨εδ⟩ό]νων—though he later preferred [Ἀθη]νῶν (*CP* 19 (1924) 68)—and Tarn used it to propound a wholly unconvincing thesis (*JHS* 54 (1934) 34 n. 42) that it referred to a people, the Lacones (with an omicron), in eastern Macedonia. 'It has naturally nothing to do with Sparta', he explains—despite the fact that it is because of Sparta that it has been inserted into the text by Mayer, the omicron being Mayer's solecism. Earlier, in *AG* 477 addenda, Tarn himself had tacitly emended to [Λακώ]νων. Many of Mayer's restorations in the later lines are based on the forged letters in Diogenes Laertius and are quite plausible, though in the middle of l. 9 Μακεδόνας is preferable to Μακεδόνων (so already A. Grilli, *RFIC* 91 (1963) 288). In l. 6 ἔ[τεσιν γ̄] is a bold restoration since only the ε figures visibly, superimposed above the line: other restorations would be equally plausible, e.g. (if the reference is to Lysimachus) ἐ[ν Θρακῆι]. In l. 4, as Nachtergael, 143 n. 78 (cf. A. Grilli, *RFIC* 91 (1963) 288), points out, παρέχονται σπονδαί is the obvious transcription, rather than Mayer's παρέχοντ' αἱ σπονδαί, which involves an unlikely elision of παρέχονται. This point has been missed. Indeed, through some aberration, both W. W. Tarn (*JHS* 54 (1934) 34 n. 44) and Lévêque (574) assume the word elided to be παρέχοντο [sic]. The imperfect would of course be παρείχοντο, but a present tense is required here (cf. ἐκπίπτει). In l. 7 A. Grilli (*RFIC* 91 (1963) 288) also reads ἄρχεται instead of ἤρξατο, clearly an improvement. In l. 2 A. C. Johnson (*CP* 19 (1924) 67 n. 2), not unreasonably uneasy at μίαν, made the attractive suggestion that one should read τοῦ μ[ὴ ἀ]ν[α]λαμβάνειν. Only the reading in pap. 155 is involved here since in pap. 339 the whole of the relevant phrase is illegible.

What we are dealing with in this passage is a very brief refutation of the thesis that at any time before 277 Antigonus was in such a position of power in Macedonia as would allow Zeno to speak of him as in control of all the Macedonians. In particular, it is asserted, that was impossible in the archonship of Euthius (283/2), which is thus confirmed as the 1st regnal year (i.e. from 1 Dios 283) of Gonatas, following the death of Poliorcetes in the year 284/3 (see M. Chambers, *AJP* 75 (1954) 385–94); it is in fact the year from which he chose to date his reign (see Appendix 2). Zeno's claim was equally impossible for the year of Anaxicrates, 279/8, the first year in which the Macedonian throne was unoccupied, since Ceraunus had perished in January/February 279 and Meleager and Antipater had together ruled another three and a half months. Apollodorus' demonstration is very succinct and, whether deliberately or not, does not mention Ptolemy Ceraunus by name. It concludes that in Euthius' archonship Antigonus did not possess Macedonia nor (probably, since the text here is substantially restored) did he yet have any kingdom at all. What excluded the archonship of Anaxicrates we can only surmise, since the text breaks off at this point. The demonstration is supported by four facts (there may have been more in the full text). The last of these, εἶθ' ὕστερον...ἤρξατο (or ἄρχεται), it is generally and correctly agreed, must refer to Antigonus' victory at Lysimacheia in 277. But clearly one may not use ἔ[τεσιν γ̄] as evidence that what preceded happened three years earlier. Before that three other facts are listed: (1) ll. 2–3: someone prevented someone else from taking possession of the kingdom; in the context the person prevented must be Antigonus and the kingdom Macedonia. And this was apparently before Lysimachus' death at Corupedium in January/February 281. (2) ll. 3–4: after Lysimachus' death Antigonus was granted a truce (which must logically have been such that it debarred him from proceeding against Macedonia). (3) ll. 5–7: having conquered X, someone, presumably Antigonus, was driven out of Macedonia and back to Asia; it was after that that he beat the Gauls and began to rule the Macedonians.

The first problem is to identify the treaty granted to Antigonus. The phraseology suggests that the truce was somehow imposed on him; indeed Tarn (*JHS* 54 (1934) 34) asserted that παρέχοντ' αἱ σπονδαί [*sic*] implied that he had been defeated and drew the untenable conclusion that Athens had recovered the Piraeus. The phrasing would however be equally appropriate if for some overriding reason (not necessarily defeat) Antigonus had had to accept a truce which would debar him from attacking Macedonia. The most obvious occasion for such a truce is the Gallic invasion of 280/79. That is in fact how the σπονδαί are interpreted by Heinen (*Unters.* 67) and Nachtergael (143). Following Ceraunus' accession, Antigonus had attacked him unsuccessfully (October 281) and it was probably this set-back which precipitated the widespread rising in Greece, while Areus of Sparta attacked his allies in Aetolia (see above, pp. 244–5, 249). The σπονδαί mentioned by Philodemus were probably entered into around 280/79 in view of the Gallic threat, in which case Ceraunus may also have been included (cf. B. D. Meritt, *Hesperia* 4 (1935) 577), since, as Heinen (*Unters.* 67) points out, he had a very marked interest in a settlement (cf. J. 24. 1. 8). This agreement would debar Antigonus from any further attempt on Macedonia so long as it remained in force and that is the point Apollodorus wished to make. The σπονδαί cannot be the peace made between Antigonus and Antiochus, since far from preventing Antigonus acting against Macedonia, that treaty laid the way open for him to do so.

If, however, the σπονδαί are a general Greek agreement made in or around the winter of 280/79, in view of the threat from the Gauls—Philodemus mentions only the effect on Antigonus, since that is his concern in this argument—the next event to be mentioned, Antigonus' victory over someone or other and his expulsion from Macedonia to Asia, cannot be the attack which he made on Ceraunus shortly after the latter's accession (so Nachtergael 168 n. 191), since that attack took place *c.* October 281, well before the σπονδαί. It must be another attack occurring perhaps in 278 after the Gauls had retreated and at a time when the monarchy was in suspension. Evidently Antigonus made gains but was driven back, probably by Sosthenes, and retired to Asia. By this time he had already made peace with Antiochus (who was not included in the earlier σπονδαί); that would explain why Antigonus' presence in Asia was tolerated. The battle of Lysimacheia in the spring of 277 at last gave him victory and the Macedonian throne. If this sequence of events is correct, it will no longer be possible to restore ε[...] as ἔ[τεσιν γ̄].

APPENDIX 4

The Battles of Cos and Andros

SOMETIME during the third century a king 'Antigonus' won naval victories over Ptolemaic fleets off Cos and Andros.[1] These victories are plainly significant for the history of Macedonian–Egyptian naval relations and for our understanding of Macedonian policy in the Aegean. Unfortunately there is no agreement about the date and historical context of either battle or even about which 'Antigonus' was concerned. There is a vast literature on the subject: see below, pp. 599–600, for a selection of the more recent publications. For several of the problems involved firm solutions cannot be reached on the evidence now available. This appendix is intended simply to indicate the reasoning behind the dates accepted in the text.

1.

I shall consider Andros first.

(a) For this battle three passages of Plutarch are relevant.

Mor. 183 c (among sayings of Ἀντίγονος ὁ δεύτερος) μέλλων δὲ ναυμαχεῖν πρὸς τοὺς Πτολεμαίου στρατηγούς, εἰπόντος τοῦ κυβερνήτου πολὺ πλείονας εἶναι τὰς τῶν πολεμίων ναῦς 'ἐμὲ δέ,' ἔφη, 'αὐτὸν παρόντα πρὸς πόσας ἀντιτάττεις;'

Mor. 545 B καὶ Ἀντίγονος ὁ δεύτερος τἆλλα μὲν ἦν ἄτυφος καὶ μέτριος, ἐν δὲ τῇ περὶ Κῶ ναυμαχίᾳ τῶν φίλων τινὸς εἰπόντος, 'οὐχ ὁρᾷς ὅσῳ πλείους εἰσὶν αἱ πολέμιαι νῆες;' 'ἐμὲ δέ γε αὐτόν,' εἶπεν, 'πρὸς πόσας ἀντιτάττετε;'

Pel. 2 Ἀντίγονος ὁ γέρων ὅτε ναυμαχεῖν περὶ Ἄνδρον ἔμελλεν, εἰπόντος τινὸς ὡς πολὺ πλείους αἱ τῶν πολεμίων νῆες εἶεν, 'ἐμὲ δ' αὐτόν', ἔφη, 'πρὸς πόσας ἀντιστήσεις;'

The anecdote related seems to be about Gonatas. Plutarch tells it once in connection with the battle of Cos, once with the battle of Andros, and once without naming the battle.[2] This confusion lends some support to the view that the same king fought both battles (for in that case they would be more likely to be confused in people's minds) and the natural implication is that both battles were victories for Gonatas.

(b) One of the two battles is referred to in Trog. *Prol.* 27 'Ut Ptolomaeus Adaeum (MSS. *eum* or *adeum*) denuo captum interfecerat et Antigonus proelio navali Oprona vicerit.' ('Antigonus' is a preferable reading to 'Antigonum', found in older editions: cf. A. Momigliano, *CQ* 44 (1950) 108 n. 1.) This passage records one of a number of events which took place in Asia between

---

[1] The revival by Fellmann 92–9 of Reiske's view that there was only *one* battle (Fellmann argues that 'Cos' is a corruption of 'Ceos') has not won support; it is unlikely, if not entirely impossible.

[2] E. Bikerman, *REA* 40 (1938) 377 assumes that it is Andros that is mentioned in error; but it can just as well have been Cos.

the beginning of the Third Syrian War (246) and the death of Ziaelas of Bithynia at the hands of the Galatians (*c.* 230) and is followed by a further section dealing with events of Asia related to the defeat and death of Antiochus Hierax (226). Consequently Beloch (4. 2. 516 ff.) argued that the Antigonus mentioned here must be Doson. But Tarn (*JHS* 29 (1909) 265 ff.) had already shown (a) that the *Prologi* cannot be used to determine the relative chronology of events occurring in different areas, and (b) that it was the habit of the compiler to append a short 'historical introduction' when mentioning any important figure for the first time. In the case of Doson this 'introduction' occurs in *Prol.* 28 (which also contains the first mention of Demetrius II). In view of this the Antigonus who defeated Opron has to be Gonatas, not Doson.[1] On the possible identity of Opron see below, p. 591. The Adaeus (the name is an emendation) who was executed about the same time by Ptolemy (III Euergetes) may be a Thracian dynast from near Cypsela, known from a New Comedy fragment (Athen. 11. 468 f.; cf. Buraselis 122–3). But this is uncertain and does not help us to date Opron's naval defeat, whether at Andros or at Cos.

(c) There is also important, though obscure, evidence in *P. Haun.* 6,[2] which contains what appears to be a series of short biographies of members of the Ptolemaic royal house. Among these is 'Ptolemy Andromachos' or 'Ptolemy Andromachou', so-called (ἐπικλησιν), who captured certain only partially decipherable places, *perhaps* fought a naval battle at Andros (ll. 7–8, ναυμαχησας απελ[|ανδρον), and finally fell a victim to certain people who murdered him at Ephesus (ll. 11–13, καταστασιασθεις υπο των[εν εφεσωι κατεσφαγη δα[|επιβουλην συστησαμενην.) A comparison with Athen. 13. 593 a shows beyond doubt that the Ptolemy of this papyrus is 'Ptolemy the son of Philadelphus the king, ὁ τὴν ἐν ᾿Εφέσῳ διέπων φρουράν', who was there plotted against by Thracians (probably mercenaries) and took refuge in the temple of Artemis, where he was murdered. The word διέπω frequently has the meaning 'control as someone's deputy' (see LSJ[9] s.v., quoting *P. Tebt.* 522 and *P. Lond.* 3. 908. 19, both, like *P. Haun.* 6, second century A.D.) and this man would appear to be a Ptolemaic commander in Ephesus, who fell a victim to a seditious mutiny. There is no suggestion in either *P. Haun.* 6 or Athen. 13. 593 a that he was in any way disloyal to Egypt.[3] If *P. Haun.* 6 contains a reference to Andros and we can date the death of this Ptolemy, we have a *terminus ante quem* for the battle. Fraser,[4] to be sure, has suggested other possible restorations such as ἀπ[έβαλε ναῦν...αῦτ] ανδρον vac.; but Bülow-Jacobsen's revision of the papyrus rules out ἀπ[έβαλε and the combination of ναυμαχήσας and ανδρον supports the view that the reference is to that battle.

If the Ptolemy of *P. Haun.* 6 is identical with the Ptolemy of Athen. 13. 593 a, why in the latter is he 'the son of Philadelphus' and in the former

[1] Cf. A. Momigliano, *CQ* 44 (1950) 108; Buraselis 123–4.
[2] *P. Haun.* 6 pp. 37–45; for a revised text see Bülow-Jacobsen.
[3] A. L. Oikonomides, *ZPE* 50 (1984) 148–50 restores *P. Bour.* 6 to give a reference to the death of Ptolemy the Son at Ephesus. This is uncertain and in any case adds nothing of relevance to the problem considered here.
[4] *CQ* 44 (1950) 117; Bülow-Jacobsen 92 shows that the papyrus has απελ[.

'Ptolemy called Andromachus or Andromachou' (either is grammatically possible)? That this nickname means 'fighter at Andros' (assuming the name to be Ptolemy 'Andromachus')[1] is highly unlikely, for such a nickname given to the loser in a battle would be unparalleled in relation to Egypt. Moreover, if the battle in which 'Opron' was defeated was Andros, any such taunting nickname would have been more properly applied to him; and it cannot have been at Cos, for reasons to be considered shortly (pp. 595–9). Buraselis has suggested a more plausible explanation of the nickname;[2] assuming the name to be Ptolemy 'Andromachou', it means 'Ptolemy who was called "the son of Andromachus"'—while in fact being the son of someone else, viz. Philadelphus. On this hypothesis (which would explain his inclusion in a list of members of the royal family), the Ptolemy of *P. Haun.* 6 was a bastard son of Philadelphus, whose mother was married off to an Andromachus, who brought him up as his son, though he was widely recognized to be the son of the king. The Andromachus chosen for this role may well have been the Andromachus 'Myriarouros' mentioned on three Egyptian papyri from the period between 253 and 249.[3] Buraselis has observed that in 251/0 a Ptolemy Andromachou was priest of Alexander and the *Theoi Adelphoi* and that in the same year Bilistiche, known as a concubine of Philadelphus, was *kanephoros* in the same cult:[4] was she, he asks, Ptolemy Andromachou's mother? We do not know; but whatever view one takes of this plausible connection with Bilistiche, the hypothesis that Ptolemy was a known bastard of Philadelphus, brought up as the son of Andromachus, provides a satisfactory and convincing explanation of the different names given to him in Athen. 13. 593 a and *P. Haun.* 6 and of his inclusion in the royal list contained in the papyrus.

(d) The evidence concerning Ptolemy 'Andromachou', who perhaps fought at Andros, has been complicated by the assumption that he is identical with the mysterious 'Ptolemy the Son', who revolted against his father Philadelphus.[5] The evidence for this revolt is in Trog. *Prol.* 26 'ut in Asia filius Ptolomaei regis socio Timarcho desciverit a patre'; and some broad limits can be established for its date:

i. The general scope of Trog. *Prol.* 26 covers events in Europe between the beginning of the Chremonidean War (*c.* 268) and Aratus' capture of Corinth (243). It mentions the revolt of 'Ptolemy the Son' and Timarchus (the only event relevant to the Ptolemaic kingdom) between the death of Antiochus II (246) and the death of Demetrius the Fair at Cyrene (250). But since it concerns Egypt, this revolt could fall at any point within the general scope of Book 26.

ii. For several years between 267 and 259 a 'Ptolemy the Son' figures in Egyptian documents[6] as co-ruler with Philadelphus. The last known dated

---

[1] As suggested by P. Maas (*Year's Work in Classical Studies* 1939–45, 2); cf. A. Momigliano, *CQ* 44 (1950) 112. Against it see Buraselis 128 ff.

[2] Buraselis 131.

[3] *P. Cair. Zen.* 3. 59318 ll. 8 f.; 59325 ll. 12 f.; E. Van 't Dack, *Chron. d'Égypte* 36 (1961) 184 ff. (full discussion of this Andromachus). See Buraselis 131.

[4] *P. Cair. Zen.* 2. 59289 ll. 3. 14; *P. dem. Zen.* 6B; *Pros. Ptol.* 3. 5066; 6. 14717; Buraselis 133 n. 95.

[5] So still, e.g. by A. L. Oikonomides, art. cit. (p. 588 n. 3 above).

[6] On Ptolemy the Son see Welles, *RC* pp. 75–6; H. Volkmann, *RE* s.v. *Ptolemaios* (20) ('der Sohn') cols. 1666–7. His regency is attested between 267 and 259. See below, p. 592 n. 1.

papyrus bearing his name is *P. Cair. Zen.* 59003 (April/May 259) and it has been plausibly suggested that the omission of his name from all papyri after 259 and its deletion from the Revenue Laws papyrus of that year (*P. Rev.* col. 1) result from his revolt in 259. Timarchus, who, according to Trog. *Prol.* 26, assisted him, is known from Polyaen. 5. 25 and Frontin. 3. 2. 11.[1] He was an Aetolian adventurer who, after joining in the revolt of Ptolemy the Son, established himself as tyrant in Miletus. His overthrow may well be referred to in *OGI* 226, where Hippomachus, a confidant of Antiochus II, is praised for restoring freedom and democracy to that city. According to App. *Syr.* 65 it was in recognition of his expulsion of Timarchus from Miletus that Antiochus was there accorded the title of *Theos*, which later became his cult name. From this it follows that Timarchus' expulsion from Miletus fell within Antiochus II's reign (261–246). A date of 259 for the revolt of Ptolemy the Son and Timarchus would thus fit the evidence and would support the identification of Ptolemy the Son with Philadelphus' co-ruler.

(e) The subsequent fate of Ptolemy the Son is unknown, since all references to him are from the years before 259. An example is the letter of Ptolemy II to Miletus, *RC* no. 14, in connection with which Welles has a detailed discussion of Ptolemy the Son. This letter is accompanied by a Milesian decree which mentions danger threatening Miletus 'by land and sea'. The date of this letter is probably to be put in 262/1[2] with Welles and Orth.[3] It mentions 'my son and Callicrates' (otherwise familiar as a Ptolemaic admiral) as present at Miletus. The identity of Ptolemy the Son is still debated, but to call him 'Ptolemy of Ephesus'[4] is to make the unproved and unlikely assumption that he is identical with Ptolemy Andromachou, who perished in the mutiny at Ephesus and, as a corollary, that the events of Athen. 13. 593 a, occurred immediately after Ptolemy the Son's revolt in 259.[5]

(f) There is a further piece of evidence about a son of Philadelphus in a letter of Olympichus, a dynast active in Caria *c.* 240–210, to the city of Mylasa (Crampa, *Labraunda* 1. no. 3),[6] which mentions earlier decisions to deal with a local problem, which envoys from Mylasa have referred to Olympichus. These include various pronouncements (χρηματισμοί) and a communication from Sophron and from Ptolemy the brother of King Ptolemy III to Mylasa and finally a decision taken by Olympichus himself, in response to a letter from King Seleucus (II: 246–225), to free the city. The letter contains no indication of when the pronouncements by Sophron and Ptolemy were conveyed to Mylasa. But Sophron may be a man known as an enemy of Laodice. According to Athen. 13. 593 b–d (following Phylarchus), a certain

---

[1] Cf. H. Hommel, *Chiron* 6 (1976) 321 n. 7.

[2] This date is preferable to 276/5, proposed by Tarn and Rostagni; cf. Welles, RC, p. 73. For the full inscription with the Milesian decree see A. Rehm, *Milet.* 1. 3 (1914) no. 139 pp. 300–7.

[3] Orth 25, 30–1.   [4] Cf. Will 1². 226 and 236; H. Heinen, *CAH* 7². 1. 415.

[5] A. Momigliano, *CQ* 44 (1950) 113–15, dates the rebellion of Ptolemy the Son to *c.* 259, but despite his identification of Ptolemy Andromachou with Ptolemy the Son, he leans towards *c.* 258 as a likely date for Andros. But if Ptolemy Andromachou fought in the battle, the combined evidence of *P. Haun.* 6 and Athen. 13. 593 a would exclude a date for Andros after his death.

[6] Crampa, *Labraunda* 1 pp. 13–21.

Sophron was in charge of Ephesus (ὁ ἐπὶ τῆς 'Εφέσου) under Antiochus II, fell foul of Laodice (presumably following Antiochus' death in 246), and fled to Ephesus, narrowly escaping death at her hands. It has been suggested that this man found safety by defecting to Ptolemy III, an obvious move for anyone threatened by Laodice.[1] If that were so, he could be the Sophron mentioned in Olympichus' letter. It would still remain problematical whether it was in the Seleucid or Ptolemaic interest that Sophron and Ptolemy had written to Mylasa; but the fact that Ptolemy is described as 'the brother of King Ptolemy' strongly suggests that his action fell during the reign of Euergetes (and so after 246) and it is far less likely that he would be so designated if he was identical with the mysterious Ptolemy the Son, now a Seleucid official.[2] It therefore seems to follow that Sophron and Ptolemy 'the brother of the king' are Ptolemaic officials in Caria. Sophron is likely to have been subordinate to the king's brother, but their mutual relationship is uncertain.

If this reconstruction is accepted (and it contains much that is hypothetical), the Sophron who *ex hypothesi* went over from the Seleucids to Ptolemy III in 246 may well be the 'Opron' who, according to Trogus, *Prol.* 27, was defeated in a naval battle by an Antigonus who was probably Gonatas (see above, pp. 587–8); but that identification is uncertain[3] and not essential to the argument. If that battle was at Andros—it can hardly have been the one off Cos (see below, pp. 595–9) and no third naval victory of Gonatas over the Ptolemaic fleet is known[4]—what of Ptolemy Andromachou who, according to the most probable interpretation of *P. Haun.* 6, was also a Ptolemaic admiral in that battle? This duplication of admirals would be a serious difficulty, if there was only one Ptolemaic commander at Andros. But we do not know how the precise structure of command in the Ptolemaic navy operated in a battle at this time.[5] A single commander could not control the development of a battle throughout its whole area,[6] for there was no quick

---

[1] Buraselis 135–6; Chr. Habicht, *Gnomon* 44 (1972) 169 rejects the identification of the Sophron of Athenaeus with the Sophron of *Labraunda* no. 3; against this see Huss, *Unters.* 204 n. 197.　　　　　　　　　　　　　　　　　　　[2] Cf. J. Seibert, *Gött. gel. Anz.* 226 (1974) 206 f.

[3] Note too that the name Opron is not unknown in Egypt; cf. *P. Teb.* 3. 2. 890 ll. 14, 172 ('Όπρωνι and 'Όπρωνος; 2nd cent. B.C. cf. A. L. Oikonomides, *ZPE* 50 (1984) 151)—a fact which weighs against the assumption that 'Opron' in Trogus must be a corruption.

[4] In this context I am ignoring the mysterious battle mentioned in Aristeas 180 (Wendland) and Josephus, *AJ* 12. 93, for that was allegedly a victory for Ptolemy in any case; see above, p. 295 n. 2 for Buraselis' suggestion that it occurred around 250.

[5] A good deal has been written about the post of navarch in the Ptolemaic navy; see especially I. L. Merker, *Historia* 19 (1970) 141–60, 'The Ptolemaic officers and the League of Islanders'; H. Hauben, *Callicrates of Samos. A Contribution to the Study of the Ptolemaic Admiralty* (Studia Hellenistica 18, Louvain, 1970); *Het Vlootbevelhebberschap in de vroege diadochentijd (323–301 voor Christus)* (Brussels, 1975). Hauben has shown that there was no overall admiral till *c.* 280, but that even after then the notion of 'naval commander' covered a great variety of different commands with various degrees of subordination. More than one officer could well be associated with a victory, just as, for example, the names that spring to mind in connection with the defeat of the Spanish Armada are those of Francis Drake and John Hawkins, though the overall command was in the hands of Lord Howard of Effingham.

[6] Cf. Hauben, *Het Vlootbevelhebberschap* (see the previous note) 120 (on the battle of Salamis): 'Een uitgrebreide formatie als die van Ptolemaios kon en het gevecht onmogelijk door één man

way of giving detailed commands to meet changing circumstances at a
distance. It is, moreover, significant that Plutarch (*Mor.* 183 c) refers to
Gonatas being about to fight a naval battle against τοὺς Πτολεμαίου
στρατηγούς (see above, p. 587 and below p. 595). That may have been at Cos,
but if there was more than one senior officer at Cos, the same is likely to have
been true at Andros. Sophron (or Opron) could have been Ptolemy III's high
admiral at Andros and Ptolemy Andromachou his co-commander—perhaps
even nominally his superior. His role at Andros is mentioned in *P. Haun.* 6,
however, because the biographer is concerned with Ptolemy's career, not with
who was in supreme charge of the fleet on that occasion.

(g) It is important to distinguish clearly between 'Ptolemy the Son', who
revolted in *c.* 259 and then disappears from the record,[1] and Ptolemy 'son of
King Ptolemy', 'so-called son of Andromachus', 'the brother of Ptolemy
(III)', who was active as a loyal Ptolemaic commander after 246, conducting
campaigns[2] and fighting at Andros (along with Opron, or Sophron) and
eventually meeting his death at Ephesus at the hands of mutineers. There is no
good reason to make these two men identical (other than their common
paternity) for 'the son of Andromachus' served as a loyal commander with a
successful career (down to his death) in the Ptolemaic service.[3] On the dating
suggested above, the battle of Andros was an event in the Laodicean War. We
have no other evidence that Gonatas took part in that war. But our knowledge
of this period is so slender that that is not a strong objection to a hypothesis
which accounts economically for the rest of the evidence.

(h) *The vase-festivals.* A group of festivals is known from Delos, instituted by
kings or private individuals, in relation to which a sum of money was
deposited and the interest on it used to pay for the annual dedication of a vase
to either the Delian Triad (Apollo, Artemis, and Leto) or some other god or
gods. These festivals were usually named after the person making the
dedication or the person in whose honour it was made, but in two instances,
the *Paneia* and the *Soteria*, instituted by Antigonus Gonatas in 245, they were
named after the god or gods to whom the offering was made. There has been a
long argument about whether the institution of a vase-festival by a Ptolemy or
an Antigonid carried political implications for the control of Delos.[4] It is

worden overzien.' At Salamis Ptolemy commanded the left; the names of those commanding the
other squadrons have not been preserved.

[1] Cf. Huss, *Unters.* 203 n. 195; Chr. Habicht, *Ath. Mitt.* 72 (1957) 220 n. 74; Ph. Derchain,
ZPE 61 (1985) 35–6; and, for an inscription of Xanthus dated Peritios of year 26 of Philadelphus
(*c.* December 260–January 259), Robert, *Amyzon* 124–7.

[2] See *P. Haun.* 6. l. 7. These campaigns do not directly concern us here, but with Bülow-
Jacobsen's reading ιρει κ′ αινον κ′ πολλα there is a very good chance that Buraselis 128 is right in
seeing a reference to Aenus (probably the Thracian city rather than one in Asia, as A. Bülow-
Jacobsen, *ZPE* 36 (1979) 91–100, esp. 94). According to Buraselis this suggestion has the
approval of Colin Roberts.

[3] For the distinction between the two see Buraselis 136 n. 106; M. Segre, 'Una genealogia dei
Tolemei e le "imagines maiorum" dei Romani', *Rend. Pont. Acc.* 19 (1942–3) 277–80; P. M.
Fraser, *CQ* 44 (1950) 118.

[4] On this question see Will 1². 323 (who thinks the *Soteria* was a reply to the Aetolian
reorganization of the Delphic *Soteria*, which commemorated the Gallic defeat); Tarn, *AG* 378 ff.;
E. Bikerman, *REA* 40 (1938) 376; Buraselis 141–4; Bruneau 5. Fellmann 82 makes a probably

demonstrably not true that only a power controlling Delos could set up such a festival there. But at any rate in the first half of the third century it seems likely that neither an Antigonid nor a Ptolemy would have set up a vase-festival on Delos at a time when the island was under the direct control of the rival house. There is a parallel of sorts for this in the Antigonid boycotting of the Aetolian-controlled Delphic Amphictyonic Council. As we have seen, in 245 Antigonus Gonatas established two vase-festivals, the *Paneia* and the *Soteria* (of which the first vases were dedicated a year later in 244).[1] As is the case for all the other vase-festivals, the occasion which prompted their setting up is not recorded; and this has led to a long controversy. Bikerman[2] argues that the names of the festivals do not in themselves suggest the commemoration of a victory in battle. This is not wholly true, for these two festivals are unique within the group in being named after gods, and so in directing attention to them rather than to the founder. Gods are thanked for benefits conferred or hoped for. Pan had a cult on Delos,[3] but his choice as the recipient of a festival by Antigonus must rest on his importance in Macedonia, where his cult was particularly favoured at Pella and by Gonatas himself,[4] who represented him on Macedonian coins. The *Theoi Soteres*, to whom the *Soteria* was dedicated, may be Zeus Soter and Athena Soteira who are linked in some of the oldest Delian records[5] and were especially popular in the Hellenistic period; but Tarn (*AG* 380) thought they were 'Apollo of Delos and the gods associated with him'. This emphasis on Gonatas' patron deity and gods who bring salvation is surely best explained as commemorating some important event.

What that was has been much debated. Momigliano[6] thinks that it may have been Gonatas' recovery of Corinth from the widow of Alexander (an event perhaps more advantageous than glorious). But if the battle of Andros was in 246 or (more probably) in 245, that would furnish a reason for such a celebration.[7] One result of that victory must have been to loosen (if not to destroy) the Ptolemaic hold on the Cyclades;[8] and though one did not have to *control* Delos in order to make the ordinary type of dedication there, it is hard to imagine that Gonatas would have chosen (or been allowed) to celebrate a naval victory over Ptolemy with festivals bearing such names as

valid distinction between the *Soteria* and the *Paneia* and the normal run of vase-festivals; see below, p. 599 n. 1.

[1] *IG* xi. 2. 298 l. 88. For full documentation of Antigonid vase-festivals at Delos see Bruneau 557–64.   [2] *REA* 40 (1938) 376.   [3] Bruneau 561.
[4] Cf. Bruneau 560; E. Bikerman, *REA* 40 (1938) 376 n. 5; and especially Launey 2. 934–6 and Merker 46 (Pan-head tetradrachms struck at Pella). But against the theory that there was an epiphany of Pan at Lysimacheia see Pritchett, *The Greek State at War* 3: *Religion* (Berkeley–Los Angeles–London, 1979) 32–4.
[5] Cf. Bruneau 235. But in the only inscription mentioning the gods to whom the festival is dedicated there is a lacuna and θεοῖς Σωτῆροι is Tarn's (plausible) restoration (*AG* 381 n. 33) comparing *OGI* 214 l. 15.
[6] *CQ* 44 (1950) 115.
[7] Cf. Buraselis 144–5. The *Soteria* took place in the month of Hecatombaion (July/August), which would fit a victory in the spring before the dedication. Whether the *Paneia* was also in Hecatombaion is unknown.
[8] The Adulis inscription (*OGI* 54 l. 7) still laid claim to the Cycladic islands on the accession of Euergetes in 246.

Soteria and *Paneia*, if the island was still firmly under Ptolemy's control (see above).

(i) *Coinage*. Before leaving Andros, note must be taken of the argument of I. L. Merker[1] that the Macedonian tetradrachms bearing a head of Poseidon on the obverse and on the reverse Apollo holding a bow and seated on a ship's prow inscribed **ΒΑΣΙΛΕΩΣ ΑΝΤΙΓΟΝΟΥ** (see Pl. I*k*) were issued by Antigonus Doson and commemorate a victory at Andros in 227 in a naval battle linked with his Carian expedition; this view (which in a new form renews that originally propounded by Niebuhr) has won the approval of G. Roux and M. Price.[2] There are in fact four issues of gold and silver coinages, all on the Attic standard, bearing the name of Antigonus. The emblems on these coins seem to have been chosen as likely to appeal to the Macedonians. The first of these,[3] which includes a gold stater bearing (obv.) the head of Athena and (rev.) **ΑΝΤΙΓΟΝΟΥ ΒΑΣΙΛΕΩΣ** (vertically downwards) and Nike with a naked torso, and a tetradrachm with (obv.) the head of a youthful Heracles and (rev.) **ΑΝΤΙΓΟΝΟΥ ΒΑΣΙΛΕΩΣ** (vertically) and Zeus with naked torso on a throne facing left (with sceptre and eagle), was attributed by Gaebler and others to Antigonus I, but by Newell[4] more convincingly to early in Gonatas' reign. A second issue[5] consists of silver and depicts (obv.) the head of Pan on a Macedonian shield and (rev.) Athena Alcidemus, the Macedonian goddess of war, holding a shield and hurling a thunderbolt and the words **ΒΑΣΙΛΕΩΣ ΑΝΤΙΓΟΝΟΥ** (vertically downwards) (see Pl. I*j*). Some specimens show Athena facing left, others show her facing right. The reverse also bears a helmet, sometimes a basket (*kalathos*) and sometimes a X; but the helmet, which is commonest, only appears along with the left-facing figure. A third issue, also consisting of tetradrachms,[6] has (obv.) Poseidon with flowing locks and (rev.) **ΒΑΣΙΛΕΩΣ ΑΝΤΙΓΟΝΟΥ** (horizontal) on a ship's prow, on which sits Apollo facing left and holding a bow. The fourth issue[7] (see Pl. I*l*) consists of drachmas and depicts (obv.) a bearded Zeus (or Poseidon) and (rev.) Athena Alcidemus, as on the Pan-head tetradrachms. It is the third of these issues (see Pl. I*k*) which Merker assigns to Doson.

His argument is based on the evidence from several hoards containing Pan-head and Poseidon-head tetradrachms. Ehrhardt[8] has subjected it to detailed criticism and points out that five of the ten hoards on which it rests are from outside Greece; the Antigonid coins contained in them are all strays. The Greek hoards too do not allow firm conclusions about the relative priority of Pan-head and Poseidon-head coins—though they do suggest that the latter

---

[1] Merker 39–52. For the silver tetradrachms see Price, Pl. XIII no. 72.

[2] G. Roux, 'Le Neoria et le vaisseau délien (Paus. 1. 29. 1)', *BCH* 105 (1981) 70–1; Price 28, who sees in the figure of Apollo on the reverse of these tetradrachms a reference to Doson's (hypothetical) alliance with Antiochus Hierax. For P. R. Franke, Νομισματικὰ Χρονικά (1972) 30, these tetradrachms celebrate a victory of Doson off Caria. Beloch 4. 2. 506–18 also made Andros a victory for Doson.

[3] Gaebler III. 2. 179 nos. 1–3 and Pl. XXXII. 21 and 22.

[4] Newell, *Coinages* 14 n. 1; cf. Merker 39.

[5] Gaebler III. 2. 185–6 no. 1; cf. Merker 45. I ignore slight variations, listed by Merker.

[6] Gaebler III. 2. 187 no. 4; Merker 39–40.   [7] Gaebler III. 2. 187 no. 5; Merker 40.

[8] 75–110.

are later (though not necessarily as late as Doson). As Ehrhardt observes,[1] to assign the Poseidon-heads to Doson would render it necessary to bring down the date of the earliest Acarnanian federal coins,[2] which show an Apollo apparently derived from the Apollo on the reverse of the Poseidon-head coins, from the 250s to the 220s. Though certainty is impossible on present evidence, the Poseidon-head coins should probably continue to be assigned to Gonatas.[3]

In any case it seems clear that the 'Antigonus' coinages cannot at present contribute anything to the problem of dating the battle of Andros (or the battle of Cos). Even if the Poseidon-head coins could be firmly assigned to Doson (which they cannot), their 'naval' character, as indicated by Apollo on the ship's prow, need not necessarily mean that Doson won a naval victory. They could just as well be a reference to the Carian expedition or a reminiscence of the great victory off Salamis in Cyprus won by Doson's grandfather, Demetrius Poliorcetes. If they were minted by Gonatas, they may (but need not) refer to one of the two victories off Cos or Andros.[4] Importance has been attached to the figure of Apollo, a god especially associated with the Seleucids. For Merker Apollo indicates Doson's association with Antiochus Hierax. But Apollo could equally well hint at Gonatas' alliance with Seleucus II. Apollo too has nothing to contribute to the argument.

Summing up the discussion so far, there is a strong case for thinking that the battle of Andros was a victory of Antigonus Gonatas over the Ptolemaic admiral Sophron (supported by Ptolemy 'the so-called son of Andromachus', a bastard son of Philadelphus) in the course of the Laodicean War, with Antigonus coming in as an ally of Seleucus II. And if, as seems likely, Antigonus will hardly have ventured out into the Aegean with a war-fleet before his recovery of Corinth, 245 seems more likely than 246. We may now turn to the battle of Cos.

2.

There are four passages capable of throwing a somewhat murky light on the battle of Cos. The first is P*Mor* 545 B (quoted above, p. 587), where Gonatas' remark about his inferiority of numbers is referred to that battle. Whether or no the story really belongs to Cos—as we saw, P*Mor* 183 C does not name the battle and P*Pel* 2 connects it with Andros—the conclusion nevertheless holds good that Gonatas fought a naval battle at Cos and almost certainly won it. This is confirmed by Athen. 5. 209 e. Here, after describing the great ship sent by Hieron to Ptolemy, Masurius continues (probably still quoting Moschion): παρέλιπον δ' ἕκων ἐγὼ τὴν Ἀντιγόνου ἱερὰν τριήρη, ᾗ ἐνίκησε τοὺς Πτολεμαίου στρατηγοὺς περὶ Λεύκολλαν τῆς Κῴας, ἐπειδὴ καὶ τῷ Ἀπόλλωνι αὐτὴν ἀν-

---

[1] 78 n. 19.

[2] Head 333 fig. 188; cf. W. Schwabacher in *Robinson Studies* 2. 219–20.

[3] Buraselis 163 reverts to the view of Gaebler (III. 2. 187 no. 4) and E. Bikerman (*REA* 40 (1935) 370) that Gonatas issued the Poseidon-heads, but he does not consider Merker's arguments or Ehrhardt's reply.

[4] Gaebler III. 2. 187, thinks that they celebrate Cos.

ἔθηκεν.[1] Tarn has shown[2] that the dedication must have been at Delos, for Apollo is not the principal god at any other shrine where the dedication could possibly have been made. The 'sacred trireme' here referred to is probably identical with τὸ ἐν Δήλῳ πλοῖον mentioned by Pausanias (1. 29. 1) and the Ἀντιγόνου ναυαρχὶς Ἴσθμια of PQC 676 D. Couchoud and Svoronos[3] suggest that this ship was dedicated in the *Neorion* or Hall of the Bulls, and since the archaeological evidence pointed to a late-fourth-century date for that building, Vallois[4] propounded the hypothesis that it was originally put up by Poliorcetes to hold a ship celebrating his victory at Salamis, but that it was left unfinished and was subsequently completed and dedicated by Gonatas after Cos. This argument, which looked at first sight highly implausible, has since received some unexpected confirmation from G. Roux's demonstration[5] that the building was indeed modified at a later stage to take a larger ship. True, there is some difficulty in identifying Pausanias' large ship καθῆκον ἐς ἐννέα ἐρέτας ἀπὸ τῶν καταστρωμάτων and the dimensions of the *Neorion* with the ship which Athenaeus calls a 'sacred trireme'.[6] In any case, the identification would not help us with the date of the battle.

On this D.L. 4. 39 takes us rather further. This passage, from Antigonus of Carystus, concerns the character of Arcesilaus, who refused to make any personal request to Antigonus. It states that μετά τε τὴν Ἀντιγόνου ναυμαχίαν πολλῶν προσιόντων καὶ ἐπιστόλια παρακλητικὰ γραφόντων αὐτὸς ἐσιώπησεν. 'The' sea-battle of Antigonus is likely to be the battle of Cos, his first naval victory,[7] and since the scene of the appeals and the contrasted silence of Arcesilaus is Athens, the occasion must fall after Antigonus' capture of the city in 261 and before he 'restored its freedom' in 256/5 or 255/4.[8] If the battle of Cos was an event in the Chremonidean War (the only war around this time for which hostilities between Antigonus and the Ptolemies are independently recorded), it must have taken place in the spring of 261,[9] following the

---

[1] Meineke's emendation of ἐπειδή to ὅπου δή is unnecessary and misleading. The meaning is 'and in fact' (cf. Soph. *Elec.* 352; E. Bikerman, *REA* 40 (1938) 370 n. 3; Buraselis 148; and Bruneau 554).

[2] W. W. Tarn, *JHS* 30 (1910) 202–21.

[3] P. L. Couchoud and J. Svoronos, *BCH* 45 (1920) 270–80.

[4] R. Vallois, *L'Architecture hellénique et hellénistique de Délos* 1 (Paris, 1944), 42.

[5] Art. cit. (above, p. 594 n. 2).

[6] Beloch 4. 2. 506 n. 1 regards ἱερὰν τριήρη as corrupt since, as he fairly points out, Gonatas' flagship cannot have been a trireme. Perhaps the phrase ἱερὰν τριήρη has slipped in through a reminiscence of the famous Athenian 'sacred triremes', earlier the Paralos and Salaminia (or Delia), later the Ammonia, the Demetrias, and the Antigonis (cf. F. Miltner, *RE* s.v. *Paralos* (8) cols. 1209–11).

[7] Cf. A. Momigliano, *CQ* 44 (1950) 114, who also observes that Patroclus' challenge to Gonatas (see below, p. 597) makes little sense if Gonatas had already won one naval battle.

[8] Eus. 2. 120 Sch.; it is not clear whether this occurred in the year of Abraham 1760 = Ol. 131. 1 (256/5) Greek version, or 1761 = Ol. 131. 2 (255/4), Armenian version; cf. Beloch 4. 1. 598 n. 5; Bengtson, *Strat.* 2. 373 (255/4). On the date see also W. Kolbe, *Gött. gel. Anz.* 1916. 470 n. 1; A. Wilhelm, *Abh. Berl. Ak.* 1939 no. 22 p. 27. Cf. Paus. 3. 6. 6.

[9] Will 1². 225. Antigonus' flagship, which sprouted parsley and was therefore called the *Isthmia* (P*Mor* 676 D), *may* be the ship dedicated after Cos, but (ignoring the miracle) its name need not imply that the battle was fought in an 'even' year in the Julian calendar to match the Isthmian games (so Will 1². 225, following W. W. Tarn, *CAH* 7 (1928) 262). As Tarn himself

capitulation of Athens and before the period of 'peace' in the Aegean attested as existing during the Delian archonship of Tharsynon (261);[1] and the view assigning Cos to the Chremonidean War has been thought to gain some support from an anecdote in Athen. 8. 334 a (from Phylarchus: *FGrH* 81 F 1) in which the Ptolemaic admiral Patroclus presents a riddling challenge to Antigonus, almost certainly with the implication that Antigonus, who solved the riddle, must also have accepted Patroclus' challenge and defeated him.[2] In that case the resultant battle was Cos; and that assumption fits the fact that Patroclus was already known as an admiral active during the Chremonidean War.

The connection of this anecdote with that war is plausible but not compelling; for clearly Patroclus may have continued to hold his command after the Chremonidean War was over, hence all that can be deduced from the inclusion of his name is that the battle, if not an event of the Chremonidean War, should not fall too long after it. There is, of course, no reason why Patroclus should not have held the command of the Ptolemaic fleet at Cos, just because Athen. 5. 209 e and P*Mor* 183 ε (a passage which does not actually name Cos) speak of τοὺς Πτολεμαίου στρατηγούς in the plural. As we have already seen, we are ill informed as to how the Ptolemaic naval command actually functioned in the course of a battle. There is, however, an alternative date for the battle which is in many ways more plausible. In the first place, 'peace' is also attested in the Aegean in 255, the year of the Delian archon Antigonus II (*IG* XI. 2. 116); and Buraselis[3] is only the latest scholar to date the battle of Cos to around that year. Such a date is far easier to reconcile with the story in Diogenes Laertius, for the account there of Arcesilaus' subsequent appeal to Antigonus on behalf of his native *polis*, Pitane, suggests that the other appeals were made on behalf of Athens and were, most probably, attempts to secure Antigonus' withdrawal of the Macedonian garrisons from the Museum (and Piraeus). If that is so, these appeals are more likely to have been made some time after Antigonus captured Athens than immediately after its fall; the wording of the passage indeed suggests that the new factor was Gonatas' naval victory and that it was this that prompted the ἐπιστόλια παρακλητικά. Moreover, the passage implies that there had been some lapse of time during which Gonatas had made several visits to Athens and Arcesilaus had declined to visit him, despite his warm relations with Hierocles, the Macedonian governor of Piraeus and Munychia. The appeals were made, presumably, on the

suggested earlier (*AG* 345), the ship may have been built at Corinth and so called as a compliment to that city.

[1] For the Delian archons see Beloch 4. 2. 97–101. The 'peace' of Tharsynon's archonship is of course sufficiently explained by the conclusion of the Chremonidean War, whether this included the battle of Cos or not.

[2] Buraselis 159 associates the anecdote (see above, p. 291) with the Chremonidean War and takes the figs as a symbol of Attica. In consequence he does not regard Patroclus as the Ptolemaic commander at Cos. But the anecdote surely implies that Gonatas accepted the challenge. Hence the incident is to be placed just before Cos, whenever that is dated.

[3] Buraselis 150; cf. Beloch 4. 2. 509 ff.; W. Peremans, 'La date de la bataille navale de Cos', *Ant. class.* 8 (1939), 401 ff., both of whom, however, prefer 256 to 255.

grounds that the sea victory freed Antigonus from any danger, so that in consequence he could afford to be generous and remove his garrisons. And so he did—though only from Athens, not from Piraeus—in 256/5 or 255/4 (see above, p. 596 n. 8).

This date for the battle of Cos (255) is open to the objection that there is no independent indication that Antigonus was involved on the Seleucid side in the Second Syrian War. That is indeed true, but the difficulty is not a serious one, given the scarcity of evidence for that war. It has also been assumed that in order to explain how 'peace' comes to be mentioned in the Delian records of 255 either Antigonus must have made a separate peace with Ptolemy after his victory or the Second Syrian War was itself over by then.[1] The reference to peace in Delian records of 255 is, however, something that has to be explained whether Cos was in that year or not. One possibility is, indeed, that the war was over by this date; but that is rather unlikely, for Clarysse[2] has recently observed that several cleruchic grants made in Egypt in 253 are best explained by a peace which falls in that year. But it does not by any means follow that Antigonus Gonatas made a separate peace in 255.[3] The reference to 'peace' at Delos may have a purely local significance. Such a peace in the Aegean would certainly have been the result of the victory off Cos, regardless of any diplomatic sequel. Moreover, if Cos was in 255, the cessation of Histiaean representation on the Amphictyonic Council after that year may be a reflection of Antigonus' increased pressure and prestige.[4]

Whether the vase-festivals of the *Antigoneia* and the *Stratoniceia* instituted by Antigonus in 253 (*IG* XI. 2. 287) are also to be associated with Antigonus' victory at Cos is another matter. Buraselis has argued[5] that they did celebrate that victory; but it is not clear why there should have been nearly two years' delay, as is the case if a victory in 255 was not celebrated until February/March 253. Nor do the names of the two festivals immediately suggest a victory celebration, as do those of the *Soteria* and the *Paneia*. The *Stratoniceia* was set up in honour of Gonatas' sister Stratonice, who was successively the wife of Seleucus I and Antiochus I and who may have died about this time (though that is hypothetical).[6] It may well be that neither of these two festivals was linked to any specific political or military event. Their names are those of the persons celebrated and resemble in form those of the

---

[1] For a separate peace see W. Otto, *Abh. Bay. Akad.* 34. 1 (1928) 45 ff.; it has been linked with the anecdote in Sext. Emp. *adv. math.* 1. 276 (cf. Tarn, *AG* 386 f.; Heinen 196 f.; Fraser 2. 53 f. on this anecdote). See also E. Bikerman, *REA* 40 (1938) 381.

[2] In D. J. Crawford *et al.*, *Studies in Ptolemaic Memphis* (Louvain, 1980) 85–9.

[3] The anecdote in Sext. Emp. *adv. math.* 1. 276, in which a Ptolemaic envoy, Sostratus, addresses Gonatas as Poseidon (with Ptolemy as Zeus!), has been linked with the supposed peace negotiations after Cos between Antigonus and Ptolemy (see above, p. 295 n. 1). But the persons involved cannot be surely identified and nothing can be built on this (Heinen, *Unters.* 196–7)

[4] See above, p. 271 nn. 8–10; p. 293, n. 6.   [5] 150–1.

[6] That it commemorated the daughter of Antiochus I, whose marriage to Antigonus' son, Demetrius II, may have taken place about this time (Beloch 4. 2. 157; so too P. M. Fraser and C. H. Roberts, *Chron. d'Égypte* 24 (1949) 292 n. 4; Ehrhardt 199 n. 10), is less likely for she was not βασίλισσα (as the Delian records style her).

other seventeen vase-festivals. The *Soteria* and *Paneia*, with their unusual titles, are probably exceptional in celebrating events leading to a major political change in the Aegean.[1]

The evidence therefore favours the view that the battle of Cos was a naval victory over the Ptolemaic fleet won early in 255 as part of Antigonus' intervention in the obscure Second Syrian War; it was followed by *de facto* peace in the neighbourhood of Delos and it led Antigonus to make some concessions to Athens. But an alternative date at the end of the Chremonidean War in 261 cannot be excluded.[2]

Summary of conclusions

1. *Cos*: a victory of Antigonus Gonatas over the Ptolemaic fleet commanded by Patroclus (with other commanders under him). It shows Gonatas intervening in the Second Syrian War, but only briefly, and may be tentatively dated to early in 255.

2. *Andros*: probably fought in the early part of 245 between Antigonus Gonatas and the Ptolemaic admiral Sophron (supported by Ptolemy the so-called son of Andromachus, a bastard son of Ptolemy II). It shows Antigonus taking part in the Third Syrian (Laodicean) War as an ally of Seleucus II.

Both battles were victories for Antigonus.

Bibliography

For early bibliography see Beloch 4. 2. 506–18; W. W. Tarn, *CAH* 7 (1928) 882; and the full discussion in Fellmann 66–99. New life was injected into the discussion by the publication of the Copenhagen papyri by T. Larsen (P. *Haun.*) and the Olympichus inscriptions by Crampa, *Labraunda* above, pp. 590 f.; but the gains have been smaller than was hoped. The more important recent contributions are:

E. Bikerman, 'Sur les batailles de Cos et d'Andros', *REA* 40 (1938) 368–83 (Cos: 263–1; Andros: Gonatas, but date unknown).

W. Peremans, 'La date de la bataille navale de Cos', *Ant. Class.* 8 (1939) 401 ff. (Cos: 256).

M. Segre, 'Una genealogia dei Tolemei e le "imagines maiorum" dei Romani', *Rend. Pont. Acc.* 19 (1942–3) 269–80.

A. Momigliano and P. Fraser, 'A new date for the battle of Andros. A discussion', *CQ* 44 (1950) 107–16 (A. M.), 116–18 (P.F.) (A. M.: Cos: 262; Andros: *c.* 258).

I. L. Merker, 'Studies in the sea-power in the eastern Mediterranean in the century following the death of Alexander' (Princeton dissertation, unpublished, 1958: microfilm from Ann Arbor).
'The silver coinage of Antigonus Gonatas and Antigonus Doson', *ANSMN* 9 (1960) 39–52 (Andros: Doson).

H. Heinen, 193–7 (Cos: 261).

F. P. Rizzo, *Studi ellenistico-romani* (Palermo, 1974) (Andros: 228).

---

[1] See Fellmann 82: 'Die Ἀντιγόνεια and Στρατονίκεια ...sind fromme Stiftungen, sie waren nicht das Ergebnis von Siegen und Bündnissen.' He contrasts the Σωτήρια and Πάνεια as 'Siegesfeste', which by their title are singled out from all the other vase-festivals.

[2] See Heinen, *Unters.* 196, whose own preferences is for 261.

E. Will, 1^2. 224–6, 237–9, 368–70 (Cos: 262; Andros: undecided).

K. Buraselis, 119–51 (Cos: 255/4; Andros, 246/5).

Chr. Marck, *Die Proxenie* (Frankfurt/Main, 1984), 227–80, 'Probleme der delischen Gechichte' (as Buraselis).

A. L. Oikonomides, 'The death of Ptolemy "the Son" at Ephesus and *P. Bouriant* 6', *ZPE* 50 (1984) 148–50.

'Opron and the battle of Andros', *ZPE* 50 (1984) 151–2.

APPENDIX 5

The Formal Relations of Macedonia and Some Other Greek States with Rome

ON this subject I differ from recent interpretations. They are fully set out by
E. S. Gruen in his two volumes and lead him to the following conclusions: 'All
but one of the epigraphical treaties are definitely later than 167.' Where a
treaty with Heraclea Pontica existed, it was 'a mere exchange of pleasantries
for Rome'. 'The title φίλος or φίλος καὶ σύμμαχος frequently signified no more
than a courteous appellation.' 'Designation [by Rome] of a foreign state as
φίλος καὶ σύμμαχος does not prove the existence of a treaty.'[1] It is not possible
here to review the arguments on which he has based his conclusions. It must
suffice for me to present the evidence and put forward the grounds for my
interpretation.

Macedonia and the Greek states developed a sophisticated system and
terminology for inter-state agreements, usually called συνθῆκαι. Thus the
'settlement' (αἱ διαλύσεις), i.e. of a war, 'peace' (εἰρήνη), 'friendship' (φιλία),
and 'alliance' (συμμαχία) could be either separate or combined within an
'agreement'.[2] For example, in 220 'a settlement was made ... that there
(shall) be peace and friendship for all time between Prusias and Byzantium'
(ἐγένοντο διαλύσεις ... εἶναι Προυσίᾳ καὶ Βυζαντίοις εἰρήνην καὶ φιλίαν εἰς τὸν
ἅπαντα χρόνον, Plb. 4. 52. 4–6). In this treaty we have an example of φιλία
without συμμαχία. The combination of φιλία and συμμαχία in an 'agreement'
was very common (e.g. in 323 between Athens and Aetolia); indeed it is
tempting to say that 'friendship' in such an agreement was only complimentary. But the fact is that the connotation which each had was different. For
φιλία by itself meant a particular relationship between states.[3] For example,
c. 393 Amyntas III of Macedonia and the Chalcidian League undertook not
to enter into φιλία with certain states, except by mutual agreement (GHI 111,
20). Pyrrhus in 280 offered Rome τὴν φιλίαν καὶ τὰς διαλύσεις (PPyrrh 18. 2),
and Antiochus III in 189/8 made an agreement of φιλία 'for all time' with
Rome (Plb. 21. 42. 1). Justin, probably drawing on the Hellenistic historian
Satyrus,[4] emphasized the point in his hendiadys, when he described the

---

[1] E. S. Gruen, *The Hellenistic World and the Coming of Rome* (Berkeley, 1984). The citations are
from pp. 16, 47, 48, 55. He discusses the evidence in detail in his Appendix A.

[2] Livy 34. 57. 7–11 mentioned the same four elements: the settlement terms, peace, friendship
('in pacem atque amicitiam'), and alliance ('foedus societatis'). That the elements often overlap
was apparent to me in the Agreement of Plaka in February 1944, which made the settlement,
terminated hostilities and provided a form of alliance for ELAS and EDES. See C. M.
Woodhouse, *Apple of Discord* (London, n.d.) 303 f.

[3] As Gruen observed on p. 71, 'in the Hellenistic world φιλία was a recognised category of
international relationship.'

[4] See H*THA* 111.

agreement between Alexander the Molossian and the Romans and others as 'foedus amicitiamque' (12. 2. 12).

The Hellenistic system and its terminology were well known to the Senate through its dealings with Greek cities in Italy and Sicily and with Alexander and Pyrrhus. When Rome made diplomatic contacts with states east of the Adriatic, it had no option but to adopt the Hellenistic system; for one city-state, strong though it was, could not impose its own system on innumerable eastern states. We can see from a number of inscriptions that Rome accepted Hellenistic terminology; for where we have the Greek version of an agreement between a Greek state and Rome, we know that the version was agreed to by Rome. It is to be assumed that the Latin version corresponded to the Greek version. This is basic to any international agreement. In nos. 11 and 12, cited below, the Senate wrote of φίλος σύμμαχός τε ἡμέτερος in a normal Hellenistic manner.[1]

Of the literary sources we are guided by Polybius, a contemporary, versed in politics and accurate in details, and by Diodorus and Appian, when they are thought to draw on Polybius. Livy, however, is unreliable; he was prepared to distort, was sometimes inaccurate and also drew on some inferior sources.[2] Polybius does not use a separate vocabulary of terms when he turns from treaties between two Greek states to a treaty between Rome and a Greek state. He knew that Greek politicians and the Senate used the same diplomatic terminology, not only from his own personal experience, but from the fact that he saw copies of treaties both on the Capitol at Rome during his long detention there and in various Greek states.

The following list of agreements, though far from complete, contains most of those which occur in our text and some others which are relevant. They are arranged in chronological order.

(1) In 229/8 the relations between some Illyrian tribes (familiar with Hellenistic terminology), the Greek cities on the Illyrian coast, and Corcyra with Rome were those of φιλία (Plb. 2. 11. 6 and 11; App. *Illyr.* 2. 7), some directly, others after 'deditio'. The agreement of φιλία with Pinnes contained rules for his future behaviour (App. loc. cit. and Plb. 2. 12. 3, summarizing the συνθῆκαι).[3] That these were formal written agreements seems unavoidable; for merely spoken expressions of 'friendship' and of rules for the future between persons of different languages would have been transient and worthless. I conclude that the alliance between Gentius and Perseus in Plb. 29. 3. 6 was written down and sworn to by each party.

(2) Part of the treaty between Rome and Aetolia in 211 has been preserved in an inscription (*SEG* 13. 382; see p. 400 above). The coincidence of the terms in the inscription with those reported by Polybius (11. 5. 5) and Livy (26. 24. 11) shows that the surviving account of Livy was based on a lost passage in Polybius, who had knowledge of the original treaty.[4] Incontrovertibly Rome

---

[1] The copy at Rome no doubt read 'amicus atque socius'.

[2] He used an annalistic source at 42. 25 and he was so inaccurate that he reported Rome's *amicitia* with Perseus of section 1 as 'amicitia et societas' in section 12.   [3] See H*E* 598 f.

[4] See A. H. McDonald in *JRS* 46 (1956) 153 ff. I do not see why Gruen 16 puts this treaty 'in a separate category'; it belongs with the other treaties of the period.

and Aetolia entered into a treaty of alliance in Hellenistic terms (Plb. 11. 5. 5 τὰς συνθήκας and 18. 38. 7 κατὰ τὴν ἐξ ἀρχῆς συμμαχίαν) and into a treaty of friendship and alliance in Roman terms (Livy 26. 24. 8 'in amicitiam societatemque populi Romani' and 26. 26. 3 'ex pacto'). No doubt the treaty contained both elements.[1] Copies were set up on the Capitol and at Olympia to publicize this pact. Polybius may well have seen both.

The process by which the treaty was initiated and finalized was Roman rather than Hellenistic. The Roman commander of armed forces against Philip presented himself at the head of a fleet, and he and the Aetolian commanders agreed on the terms of a treaty of friendship and alliance (J. 29. 4. 4–5; Livy 26. 24. 8). One of the terms was that the Aetolians should wage war by land on Philip 'at once' (Livy 26. 24. 10 'extemplo'). The treaty was confirmed, forthwith by the Aetolian Assembly, but only after a long delay by the Senate and People (Livy 26. 24. 14–15). There is no doubt in my opinion that the Roman commander had been instructed by the Senate to seek these particular terms.

(3) Attalus I of Pergamum claimed in 189 to have been one of the first of all in Asia and Greece to partake of φιλία καὶ συμμαχία with Rome, and his actions showed him in the capacity of 'ally' (Plb. 21. 20. 3–5; Paus. 7. 8. 9).[2] The reference was probably to the year 210 or thereabouts.

(4) Byzantium *c.* 200–197 had a 'foedus' at the time of the Roman war against Philip (Tac. *Ann.* 12. 62), and sent forces to help Rome against Antiochus and against Perseus, presumably as an 'ally'.[3]

(5) In 197 negotiations in the field were prolonged and then a hearing at Rome was granted to envoys from Philip and from 'Flamininus and the allies' concerning the agreement of Rome with Philip (Plb. 18. 42. 1 ὑπὲρ τῶν πρὸς Φίλιππον συνθηκῶν; Livy 33. 24. 5, omitting the envoys of the allies). The Messenians (Plb. 18. 42. 7 and Livy 34. 32. 16) were among 'the allies', and so probably were the Eleans.[4] When Philip's envoys had said he would accept the decisions of the Senate, ten commissioners were sent out to settle 'the terms of peace' (Livy 33. 24. 7 'leges pacis'). They brought with them a decree of the Senate as their brief περὶ τῆς πρὸς Φίλιππον εἰρήνης (Plb. 18. 44. 1) and split up into groups. One group discussed with Philip the matters on which it had instructions. 'In particular they kept advising Philip to send to Rome about alliance (ὑπὲρ συμμαχίας), in order that he should not be thought to be biding his time and longing for the appearance of Antiochus' (18. 48. 4).[5]

Polybius creates the impression on his reader that the commissioners wanted Philip to clear himself of any suspicion that he was playing for time to

---

[1] As the alliance of Aetolia and Athens in 323 did with its opening words φιλία καὶ συμμαχία. A. H. McDonald, op. cit. 155 proposed to restore εἰς τὰν φιλίαν in the missing part of the inscription.

[2] Attalus was offered *amicitia* in 211 according to Livy 26. 24. 9. See Walbank, *C* 3. 112 for various interpretations, which include a merely verbal understanding.

[3] Gruen discusses this period in *CSCA* 6. 128 f. See now E. Grzybek, *Mus. Helv.* 37 (1980) 56 ff., who argues convincingly for 200–197. He failed to explain 'Pseudophilippus' in the passage of Tacitus; but see Paus. 7. 8. 8–9 and p. 487 with n. 3 above.

[4] See Walbank, *C* 2. 607. Sparta also claimed 'friendship and alliance' with Rome (Livy 34. 31. 5 'vetustissimum foedus' and 34. 32. 1 'amicitia et societas cum Pelope').

[5] See Walbank, *C* 2. 620 'probably implying a regular *foedus*' and mentioning another view.

join Antiochus. But it was not as simple as that. The commissioners had the interest of Rome in mind, and 'advice' was a polite word for pressure, which Philip was in no position to resist. 'On the king accepting the suggestions, they left him at once.' They had achieved their purpose, and—although the fragment of Polybius breaks off at this point—Philip must have sent an embassy to Rome to ask for an alliance.

Why did Rome use this procedure? The fundamental facts were that the Senate intended to go to war against Antiochus; that it wanted Philip to be on the side of Rome in that war, whenever it might break out; and that it was not prepared as the victor to ask Philip to grant an alliance to Rome. So the matter was delegated to the commissioners. Just as they were given discretion (Plb. 18. 45. 10 ἐπιτροπὴν αὐτοῖς δεδόσθαι) to deal with Corinth, Acrocorinth, Demetrias, and Chalcis, so they were authorized to give this 'advice' to Philip when they thought fit. Once Philip sued for alliance,[1] the Senate could impose its own terms and write them into the final form of the treaty with Philip, αἱ πρὸς Φίλιππον συνθῆκαι.

Because the relevant part of Polybius is lost, we do not know the terms of Rome's treaty with Philip. They were probably such as were granted to Aetolia in 189, under which Aetolia had to side with Rome in a war declared by Rome and Aetolia had not to permit passage through its territory to any enemy of Rome. Philip's actions in 195, 192, and 191 were certainly compatible with such an obligation under the treaty.

Was there any article protecting Philip from attack? If the restorations in *SIG* 591. 65 ff. are accepted, Lampsacus asked the Romans to include Lampsacus in the treaty which Rome had contracted with Philip (see Walbank, *C* 2. 614). What Lampsacus needed urgently was protection against the army of Antiochus. It follows, then, that 'the treaty with the king' gave Philip some form of protection in the event of Antiochus going to war with Philip. Such an undertaking by Rome was compatible with the formal relationship of φιλία between Rome and Macedonia.[2]

(6) The treaty of the Epirote League with Rome *c.* 196 included terms of alliance (Plb. 27. 15. 12 τὰ κατὰ τὴν συμμαχίαν δίκαια); it was a defensive alliance and probably had the same requirement as the next treaty.[3]

(7) A treaty of the Acarnanian League with Rome, which was invoked in 191, had probably been made *c.* 196. According to Livy 36. 12. 2, 8, and 10 it seems that it was a defensive alliance and had the requirement that Acarnania should not make alliance with any other state without Rome's approval. ('nullam se novam societatem nisi ex auctoritate imperatorum Romanorum accepturos').

(8) The treaty of Aetolia with Rome in 189 has been preserved as αἱ

---

[1] Philip was to sue as the defeated party. It was important to the Senate that he should do so; for everyone knew that Macedonia had not been invaded after the battle of Cynoscephalae.

[2] Cited by Walbank, *C* 3. 275. That the chief element in the treaty was 'friendship' is clear from the fact that when Philip operated together with the Roman commanders against Antiochus the command had not been prearranged (e.g. Livy 39. 23. 10), as it would have been in a full-scale treaty of alliance.

[3] For both see *HE* 621 and Walbank, *C* 3. 315. The evidence of Polybius outweighs Livy 36. 35. 8–9, on which Gruen 33 relies.

συνθῆκαι by Polybius (21. 32. 1–15) and as a 'foedus ictum' by Livy 38. 11, following Polybius. Most of the clauses concerned τὰ τῆς εἰρήνης (Plb. section 15), but some governed future relations, namely that Aetolia should have the same enemies as Rome, should fight against those enemies in the event of a war by Rome, and should not allow free passage or provide any services to hostile forces moving 'against the Romans or the allies and friends of the Romans'. The treaty contains no undertaking by Rome.[1]

The process was as in (2) above. The commander in the field named the terms which were sent to the Aetolian Assembly and accepted by it, and Aetolian envoys went to Rome to make their representations (we may compare the process with Philip at Plb. 18. 38. 2 and 39. 5). The final version of the treaty was concluded with oaths at Rome (Plb. 21. 32. 15). The commander in the field had no doubt been told by the Senate what terms to propose during the foreseeable negotiations (Livy 38. 8–10) and one of these was the reduction of the indemnity from 1,000 to 500 talents.[2]

(9) A treaty of Heraclea Pontica with Rome, usually dated *c.* 188, is cited as συνθῆκαι by Memnon (*FGrH* 434 F 18. 10). Under it the two parties were to be not only φίλοι, but σύμμαχοι ἀλλήλων καθ' ὧν καὶ ὑπὲρ ὧν δεήθειεν ἑκάτεροι. It was an offensive and defensive alliance on equal terms for the contracting parties. They were to record τὰς ὁμολογίας ἴσους καὶ ὁμοίας on bronze plaques and to set them up, one in the temple of Zeus on the Capitol and the other in the temple of Zeus at Heraclea. Among the 'socii' who sent ships to help Rome against Perseus in 171 was Heraclea ex Ponto (Livy 42. 56. 6).[3]

(10) A treaty of Cibyra in southernmost Phrygia with Rome is known from a fragmentary inscription (*OGIS* 762), which W. Dittenberger dated by 'palaeographical and orthographical considerations' *c.* 188. The historical situation was that the city's leaders (described by their rivals as 'the tyrant and his friends') persuaded the consul in the field to accept them into 'friendship' (πρὸς τὴν φιλίαν, Plb. 21. 34. 3), and this led to the making of a treaty.[4] 'The *demos* of the Cibyratae' had 'to help the *demos* of the Romaei', if anyone should first make war on the *demos* of the Romaei or if anyone should transgress the treaty (τὰς συνθήκας); and the agreement of both parties was required for any addition to or subtraction from the treaty. Thus it was a

---

[1] Plb. 21. 32. 2 and 15 and Livy 38. 11 represent themselves as giving the terms in full. Restorations in the text of Polybius are accepted here as in Walbank, *C* 3. 131–6.

[2] It would not have been left to the discretion of the Roman commander to alter such a large sum of money.

[3] This is the treaty which Gruen 48 regarded as 'a mere exchange of pleasantries for Rome'. As no. 4 shows, Rome had a serious policy of supporting Greek city-states in this part of Thrace.

[4] The lettering is the best indication for the dating. The argument of Gruen 732, that the *demos* of the Cibyratae is incompatible with the tyrant and his friends ruling, overlooks the fact that Rome was using normal diplomatic language and not commenting on the other party's set-up. She in fact supported right-wing set-ups and not democracy. An inscription from Alabanda, in the same region, was dated in *BCH* 10 (1886) 304 ff. and *REG* 11 (1898) 258 ff. to *c.* 188 in accordance with the character of the letters (*REG* 10. 305); in it an envoy was rewarded with a bronze statue for his success (κατώρθωσεν) when he had gone to renew τὴν ὑπάρχουσαν οἰκ[ειό]τητα καὶ φιλίαν ... καὶ ποιήσασθαι συμμαχίαν. Alabanda built a temple in honour of 'the City of Rome' before 170 (Livy 43. 6. 5–6). Gruen 733 ff. would lower the date of the inscription to 170 or to after 80.

defensive alliance on equal terms, but with some other (unknown) clause. The treaty was to be recorded on bronze plaques, one to be set up at Rome on the Capitol and the other at Cibyra. Later, *c.* 167, Cibyra obeyed instructions from Rome in handing over a refugee (Plb. 30. 9. 19).

(11) An inscription (*Inschr. v. Magnesia am Meander* (Berlin, 1900) I no. 93) records a decree of the Senate, which was dated by O. Kern on the grounds of the lettering to 'eine Reihe von Jahren nach 190'. The Senate names the *demos* of Magnesia as being already then καλοῦ καὶ ἀγαθοῦ καὶ φίλου συμ[μάχου τε ἡμετέ]ρου, 'fine and good and our friend and ally'. Thus the original alliance was still earlier.

(12) The same inscription names the *demos* of Priene as καλοῦ καὶ ἀγαθοῦ καὶ φίλ]ου σ[υ]μμάχου τε ἡμετέρου. The inscription is important in giving us the Senate's own terminology.[1]

(13) Envoys from Chalcis at Rome in 170 related their services to Rome both long before ('vetera') and during the war with Perseus and protested against looting by Roman troops of their property as 'the possessions of allies of the Roman people' (Livy 43.7. 10 'fortunas sociorum populi Romani'; cf. 43. 8. 6 'socii atque amici'). The alliance was probably made soon after 191, since Chalcis set up a worship of Titus Flamininus about then (*PFlam* 16. 5–7) and Rome needed to secure Chalcis as a naval base.

(14) Abdera suffered even more than Chalcis at the hands of the Roman troops in 170. The envoys of Abdera complained later at Rome that their attempts at the time to appeal to the consul and to the Senate had been frustrated, and that their city had been stormed and looted. The complaint was justified because Abdera was not under Macedonian occupation at the time; for if it had been, the behaviour of the Roman troops would have been in accordance with Rome's normal standards of warfare. Abdera, then, like the other Greek cities in Thrace, had probably been declared 'free' by Rome, when Philip withdrew his garrisons from Thrace in 183 (Plb. 23. 8. 1; cf. 23. 3. 3 πάσας τὰς πόλεις); for Rome's policy towards these Greek cities was to guarantee their freedom (e.g. in the cases of Aenus and Maronea see Livy 37. 60. 7). It was probably from Abdera as a free city that Rome had been able to make alliance with Abrupolis and the Sapaei.[2] Now in 170 Rome 'restored' the freedom of Abdera and made such reparation as was possible.[3]

(15) 'Friendship and alliance by land and by sea for all time' between Maronea and Rome was recorded at Maronea in an inscription which has just been published in full.[4] Neither party is to allow passage or to supply corn,

---

[1] See also *Inschr. Priene* 216 IV. Sherk no. 7 follows Holleaux, *Études* 446 in dating the inscription to *c.* 175–160.

[2] Paus. 7. 10. 6–7; their king was Abrupolis, 'socius atque amicus' and 'socius populi Romani' in Livy 42. 13. 5 and 41. 10. Perseus acted against the Sapaei in 179/8, at which time Abrupolis was in alliance with Rome (see p. 492 above). It was because of this alliance that Rome insisted in later negotiations that Abrupolis was to be reinstated (D.S. 29. 33).

[3] Livy 43. 4. 12–13 and 8. 7. Aenus and Maronea presumably had the same status as Abdera in 170, for these coastal cities of Thrace were often grouped together (see e.g. Plb. 18. 48. 2; 22. 13. 1; 23. 1. 4, 3. 1 and 3, 8. 1–2). Aenus and Maronea had had the good sense to close their gates to the Roman fleet in 170 (43. 7. 9–10).

[4] D. Triantaphyllos in Θρακικὴ ᾿Επετηρίς 4 (1983).

arms, ships, or money to anyone attacking the other party or the other party's subjects. If anyone should first make war on 'the *demos* of the Romaei or their subjects', 'the *demos* of the Maronitai' is to help them; and vice versa. The agreement of both parties is required for any addition to or subtraction from the treaty. The alliance is to be recorded on bronze plaques, one to be set up at Rome on the Capitol and the other at Maronea in the Dionysion. The Greek wording betrays the fact that the original draft was made in Latin, because such phrases as πολεμίους καὶ ἀντιπολεμίους and δόλῳ πονηρῷ were unusual in Greek and came from the Latin expressions 'hostes et inimicos' and 'dolo malo'. The inscription mentions some men of Aenus who 'had been judged free ὑπὸ Λευκίο[υ]' and now ranked as citizens of Maronea.[1] The name 'Lucius' affords a clue for the dating of the inscription. It probably stood alone in the text (we may compare App. *Mac.* 7 συνέθεντο τῷ Λευκίῳ). In this context the Lucius was Lucius Aemilius Paullus, who did declare Aenus and Maronea 'free' in accordance with the Senate's decision in winter 168/7 (Plb. 30. 3. 7). Thus the Aenians at Maronea benefited from that declaration. In the case of Maronea it seems that this treaty of 'friendship and alliance' between 'the *demos* of the Maronitai' and 'the *demos* of the Romaei' was concluded under the final settlement of 167.

(16) An inscription from Pharos on the Adriatic island of Hvar was published by L. Robert, who attempted to fit it into a historical context just after 229 and then stultified his attempt by concluding from the style of the lettering 'que l'inscription ne peut être placée avant le cours du II siècle.'[2] Robert was a superb judge of the date of the lettering. So let us look within the second century at the Roman war of 168 against Gentius, who sent eighty *lembi* then to raid the territory of Epidamnus and Apollonia (Livy 44. 30. 14) and left 220 *lembi* after his defeat (45. 43. 10). His fleet was based well to the north, in the islands and gulfs; he had certainly acquired Issa, which came over to Rome during the war, and presumably Pharos. The account of the naval campaign is lost in a large lacuna at Livy 44. 30. 14; but the Roman navy was evidently more successful than the army in winning loot, because equal rewards were given to the sailors and to the more prestigious soldiers (45. 43. 7). Since Pharos was not mentioned with Issa as having defected to Rome (at 45. 26. 13), we may deduce that it was captured by Roman forces and (typically) looted. In the inscription Pharos has been almost annihilated and begs Paros for help, and the context is that 'the Senate and People of Rome, being friends and kindly to the city of the Pharians, gave the city back to us [i.e. the Pharians] and ... [probably 'renewed'] the alliance.'[3] After the sack, then, Rome made Pharos independent in view of past φιλία and did something about 'the alliance', i.e. which Pharos had had before 168.[4]

[1] Ibid. 437 f. with some explanations of their status.
[2] In *Hellenica* 11–12 (1960) 505 ff.; cf. J. Bousquet in *BCH* 85 (1961) 589 ff. and *SEG* 23 (1967) 489. P. S. Derow in *JRS* 74 (1984) 234 has expressed his support of the third-century date.
[3] Robert's restorations have been accepted as correct. As he said on p. 510 'la mention du Sénat et du peuple romain n'est pas douteuse.'
[4] As Robert remarked, the definite article means that there had been an alliance earlier, whether we restore ἀνενεώσαντο or not. He reaffirmed his view in *Bull. Epigr.* 1963 no. 129 p. 143.

We conclude that Rome and Pharos had had a pact of φιλία καὶ συμμαχία before 168.

These inscriptions and literary references show a very understandable readiness in the states east of Italy and in Rome herself to enter into treaty relations with one another. It is obvious too that the inscriptions which have survived by chance are only a small fraction of the sum of such inscriptions at the time.[1]

The evidence I have cited enables us to see to some extent the outlines of Roman policy. In what follows I use the term 'unequal' to indicate that Rome imposed a unilateral obligation on the other contracting party. (A) *c.* 229 Rome committed herself to treaties of φιλία (see (1) above), which were probably equal with the Greek states and unequal with the Illyrian tribes (see (1)). In this area her policy may have been unchanged for a couple of decades; for in 211 the offer to Pleuratus and Scerdilaidas was of 'amicitia' only. But by 191 there were 'socii' in Illyris who provided troops to fight at Rome's side (Livy 26. 24. 9; 36. 1. 8). (B) between *c.* 211 and perhaps 200 she entered into φιλία καὶ συμμαχία of an equal character with Aetolia, Attalus, and probably Byzantium (see (2)–(4)). (C) in dealing with Macedonia and north-west Greece in 197/6 Rome engaged herself in φιλία of an unequal character (see (5)–(7)); and she made a treaty of a similarly unequal character with Aetolia in 189 (see (8)). (D) from 188 to probably 178 Rome entered into φιλία καὶ συμμαχία of an equal character with a considerable number of Greek states (see (9)–(13)); and in 167 with Maronea (no. 15). The date and nature of no. 16 are uncertain.

Other evidence enables us to understand better what the various treaties implied for Rome and for her partner in each case. Entering into φιλία affected one's foreign policy with regard to that partner only. Thus the Rhodians' relationship of φιλία with Rome (Plb. 28. 2. 2 and 16. 7) left her uncommitted in other directions, as Polybius remarked at 30. 5. 6–9: 'they did not wish to couple themselves and prejudice themselves by entering into sworn treaties but rather by staying uncommitted (ἀκέραιοι) to profit from the hopes which each state had (of gaining their support).' So too in 170 Lampsacus, like Rhodes, wanted an 'amicitia' with Rome (Livy 43. 6. 9). But φιλία had two disadvantages: it did not commit the parties to defend one another, and it was open to one party to judge the other party's behaviour 'unfriendly and go to war'. Accordingly Rhodes later sued for συμμαχία (30. 5. 4, 21. 1, and 23. 2–4); and Rome chose to take Lampsacus 'in sociorum formulam' (Livy 43. 6. 9–10, with the reading of V).

The equal treaties of φιλία καὶ συμμαχία in B and D committed the contracting parties to a joint foreign policy, and if need should arise to joint action against an enemy whether potential or actual. It suited Rome so to commit Aetolia, Attalus and Byzantium against Philip *c.* 211–200, and then many Greek states against Philip and Perseus from 188 onwards. In the latter phase Rome entered into φιλία καὶ συμμαχία with many other tribes and states according to our literary sources. One need only mention Issa (Livy 42. 26. 6

---

[1] Gruen in his Appendix A did not take into account all those I have mentioned here.

'socii'), Bassania (44. 30. 8 'socii'), Arthetaurus (42. 13. 6 'socius atque amicus'), Abrupolis (42. 13. 5 'socius atque amicus'; 42. 41. 10 'socius populi Romani'),[1] both Arthetaurus and Abrupolis as φίλοι καὶ σύμμαχοι (App. *Mac.* 11. 2), three Thracian tribes (42. 19. 6 'societatem amicitiamque petentibus'), and the Achaean League (Plb. 23. 4. 12, renewing τὴν συμμαχίαν). Rome made these treaties with a view to confining Perseus, as she had confined Philip (Plb. 22. 17. 2), and to acquiring bases for attack upon him (e.g. in Thrace, Livy 42. 19. 7).

The unequal treaties of φιλία in C imposed a unilateral limitation on the other party which was in the interest of Rome. We see another example in the treaty of φιλία 'for all time' between Antiochus III and Rome in 189/8 (Plb. 21. 43–44. 1) with specific limitations on Antiochus' actions for the future; and those limitations were inherited by Antiochus IV, when the treaty was renewed in 173 (Livy 42. 6. 10; wrongly calling it 'societas atque amicitia' at 42. 6. 8). When Rome had a treaty of this type, it was easier for her to withdraw her 'friendship'. Thus the mere threat to do so, when the Roman envoy refused to shake hands with Antiochus (Plb. 29. 27. 1–3), caused Antiochus IV to withdraw his army from Egypt in 168.

Whatever the nature of the agreement, it was completed by an exchange of envoys and often of expensive gifts. It was a costly undertaking for a small Greek state or distant tribe. Nevertheless, great numbers of envoys converged on Rome. Their reasons are not far to seek. The ruthlessness of Rome in 210/9 and 206 'for purposes of terrorization' (καταπλήξεως χάριν, Plb. 10. 15. 5), the massacres committed by the Aetolians as Rome's allies in 198 (Livy 32. 13. 12–15), the blackmail and looting by Roman forces in Asia Minor in 189, and the wanton savagery of Roman troops for instance at Chalcis, Coronea, and Abdera in 170 (Livy 43. 4. 5–11 and 7. 5–10) made it desirable at almost any price to obtain an agreement with Rome, which would or might avert such horrors. The minimum was 'friendship'. Already by 192, after the defeat of Philip, there was a class of states on the Greek mainland which had achieved that (Plb. 21. 30. 4 and 32. 13 ὅσαι ... εἰς φιλίαν ἦλθον ʹΡωμαίοις). After the defeat of Antiochus 'almost all states in Asia sent envoys to Rome' in 189 (Plb. 21. 18. 2). In 184/3 'a mass of envoys from (mainland) Greece, unparalleled in number' waited upon the Senate at Rome (Plb. 23. 1. 1); and again 'most of the Greek cities' in 172.[2] They came in such numbers precisely because agreements of 'friendship' and of 'alliance' were being concluded and confirmed. When Rome made up her mind to go to war, she sent envoys to check that earlier agreements were being maintained and to make new ones.

---

[1] The alliance was with the king and the Sapaei (Paus. 7. 10. 6–7). Another treaty of φιλία καὶ συμμαχία was made by Rome with king Ariarathes v and his Cappadocian people (Plb. 31. 3. 1; D.S. 31. 19. 8; Str. 540; cf. Plb. 32. 10. 4).

[2] What Polybius had to say of these envoys and of the agreements made is very well supported by the inscriptions, e.g. in a treaty 'for all time' (no. 15 and Plb. 21. 43. 1), recorded on the Capitol etc. (nos. 10 and 15; Livy 26. 24. 14 re no. 2; *FGrH* 434 F 18, 10), alteration only by mutual agreement (nos. 10 and 15; Plb. 21. 43. 27); sailing prohibitions (Plb. 2. 12. 3 with App. *Illyr.* 2 and Plb. 21. 43. 14); refusal of passage and of services (nos. 8 and 15; Plb. 21. 32. 3 and 43. 2); and the term φίλος καὶ σύμμαχος (nos. 11 and 12 and implied in no. 16; Plb. 21. 20. 3; App. *Mac.* 11. 2). After all, his contemporaries had access to the originals.

For example, she sent envoys as far afield as the Bastarnae on the lower Danube in 177 (Plb. 25. 6; App. *Mac.* 11. 1), evidently through the northern Aegean and the Black Sea, and dispatched teams of envoys to Asia and the islands, to Ptolemy, and to the mainland Greek states in 173 and 172 (Livy 42. 6. 4; 19. 7–8, and 37–38. 7).[1]

[1] This appendix owes much to discussion with Dr. M. B. Hatzopoulos, Louisa D. Loukopoulou, C. V. Crowther, and as always Professor F. W. Walbank.

APPENDIX 6

Some Holdings of Perseus in Thrace
(See Figure 3)

IN the settlement of 167 an area east of the Nestus river was allocated to the first division of Macedonia. This area is described in two passages, both of which are derived from a common source, the lost account of Polybius. They are as follows:

Livy 45. 29. 6: trans Nessum ad orientem versum qua Perseus tenuisset, vicos, castella, oppida, praeter Aenum et Maroneam et Abdera.

D.S. 31. 8. 8: τὰ πρὸς ἀνατολὴν τοῦ Νέστου ἐρύμην καὶ τὰ πρὸς Ἄβδηραν καὶ Μαρώνειαν καὶ Αἶνον.

The first passage is translated in the Loeb edition, for instance, as follows. 'Across the Nessus to the eastward the villages, forts and towns which Perseus had held except Aenus, Maronea and Abdera.' The difficulty arising from this translation is that Perseus is not said elsewhere to have occupied these three important cities. If he had done so before the outbreak of the Third Macedonian War, the seizure of the cities would have been an immediate ground for complaint. Yet no such complaint was made. After the outbreak of war he had no opportunity to campaign in Thrace. The difficulty disappears if we give to 'praeter' the meaning in Lewis and Short s.v. II as '*past, by, before, in front of, along*. A Lit. of place (rare but class.)', citing 'praeter oram Etrusci maris Neapolim transmisit' in Livy 40. 41. 3. With this meaning 'what Perseus had held' were 'the villages, forts, and towns[1] by Aenus, Maronea, and Abdera'. A similar meaning is to be attached to 'praeter' in Livy 37. 56. 4, describing the settlement of Asia, in which Rome granted to Eumenes 'Telmesson...et castra Telmessium praeter agrum qui Ptolemaei Telmessii fuisset' and to the Rhodians 'Lycia...extra eundem Telmessum et castra Telmessium et agrum qui Ptolemaei Telmessii fuisset'. Here the word for 'except' is 'extra' (as in 37. 56. 2), and the meaning of 'praeter' has to be either 'the castra beyond (or by) the estate etc.', or 'as well as', which Walbank, *C* 3. 173 supported for 37. 56. 4. At 44. 6. 5 'praeter' means 'beyond' or 'past', and is like 'ad' at 44. 6. 14.

The Diodorus passage in the Loeb edition has been amended to fit the meaning of 'praeter' in the Loeb edition of Livy, so that it becomes ἐρύματα πλήν in place of ἐρύμην καί. But there is no palaeographical justification for substituting eleven letters for nine letters and for rejecting the intelligible καί. Dindorf read ἐρύματα καί. I suggest ἐρυμνὰ καί, keeping the same number of letters and comparing X. *An.* 5. 7. 31 τὰ ἐρυμνά. The translation then is 'the

---

[1] Livy's 'vicos, castella, oppida' is reminiscent of Polybius' phrase in the context of the Thracian coastal cities ἐρυμάτων καὶ τόπων καὶ πόλεων (22. 11. 4).

strong positions to the east of the Nestus and the strong positions towards Abdera, Maronea, and Aenus cities'.[1] The three cities had been declared 'free' earlier (Livy 43. 4. 12 Abdera before 170; Plb. 30. 3. 7 the other two in winter 168/7).

Taking the two passages together we can infer that Polybius wrote, more or less, of the places towards the east of the Nestus which Perseus had held, namely the strong positions, the villages, and the towns towards Abdera, Maronea, and Aenus cities. Why were these places added to the first division of Macedonia under the Roman settlement? The answer is that they controlled the approaches to the Via Egnatia, as the Macedonian road came to be called. It ran inland of the coastal Greek cities, and it had to be protected against the marauding Thracian tribes, who had inflicted heavy losses in men and loot on the Roman army in 188 (Plb. 21. 47; Livy 38. 40. 3–41. 15). D.S. 31. 8. 9, following Polybius, made the point that they (the Roman commissioners) stationed troops 'in the farthest regions of Macedonia because the neighbouring tribes were threatening' (ἐν δὲ τοῖς ἐσχάτοις τῆς Μακεδονίας τόποις διὰ τὰς τῶν παρακειμένων ἐθνῶν ἐπιβουλὰς κατέστησαν στρατιώτας). That these troops were Macedonians and not Romans may be inferred from Livy's use of 'permisit [Aemilius]' in the sentence, derived from Polybius, 'permisit ut praesidia armata in finibus extremis haberent' (45. 29. 14). The strong positions overlooking the road were as important to these troops, as they had been to those of Perseus.

---

[1] The same meaning attaches to πρός in πρὸς ἀνατολήν and πρὸς Ἄβδηραν, but one needs a different word in English.

APPENDIX 7

The Monument Dedicated at Delphi by Aemilius Paullus
(See Figure 20)

WHILE visiting Delphi in the summer of 167, Aemilius saw more than one
column-base which Perseus had intended to use for his personal dedications.
With wry humour Aemilius set up his own monuments on the bases,
commemorating his own victory at Pydna. Fragmentary reliefs from one
column-base were found and published by Th. Homolle, 'Le trophée de Paul-
Émile à Delphes,' *Mélanges Boissier* (1928) 298 ff. They were examined more
thoroughly by Reinach in *BCH* 34 (1910) 436 ff. and by M. Van Essen in
BCH 52 (1928) 239 f. I begin with their interpretations which are not entirely
convincing, and I add some points of my own about the shields and the dress
of the combatants. A number in brackets in my text refers to a numbered
figure as shown in Fig. 20.

The relief on the north face seems to portray the clash which led to the
battle. For the centre of the relief is occupied by a horse without harness or
rider (5), which corresponds with the mention of 'the unbridled horse' in
P*Aem*. 18. 1 ἀχάλινον ἵππον ἐξελάσαντας. On either side of the horse, fighting is
portrayed not between infantrymen and infantrymen, but between scattered
cavalrymen and infantrymen. The viewer sees on the left two cavalrymen (1,
2) attacking an infantryman (3), who carries a large circular shield, decorated
with characteristic Macedonian emblems in relief, and a collapsed horse, its
rider wearing a flying cloak, a tunic over a cuirass, which has lappets, and a
kilt (4). The infantryman is not a phalangite because the phalangites' shields
were 'light targes' (P*Aem* 20. 10 ἐλαφρα πελτάρια) slung from the shoulder (19.
2 τάς τε πέλτας ἐξ ὤμου περισπασάντων); and there is no room for him to have
been armed with a pike. In any case we should not expect to find any
phalangites at this stage in the engagement. The cavalryman (4) beside the
infantryman wears the same kind of lappets as Alexander the Great wears in
the Alexander Mosaic, portraying the battle of Issus. On the viewer's right,
two infantrymen (6, 7) wearing short tunics are clearly Italians, since one has
the full-length oval shield of the Ligurians in P*Aem* 18. 2 and 20. 3–4 and Livy
44. 33. 9. The infantryman (8) beaten to one knee has a large circular shield
like the shield of the infantryman (3) to the viewer's left of the runaway horse.
Thus the Italian (or Roman) cavalrymen and Ligurian infantrymen are
getting the better of their opponents. Those opponents are a Macedonian
infantryman (as his helmet suggests) to the left of the runaway horse (3, 5), a
Macedonian cavalryman (4) on the collapsed horse (as his flying cloak and
lappets suggest), a Thracian infantryman (8) on one knee (as his lack of a
helmet and short trews suggest), and two Thracian cavalrymen (9, 10) with a
distinctive cross-rib on the front of the large circular shield which one is

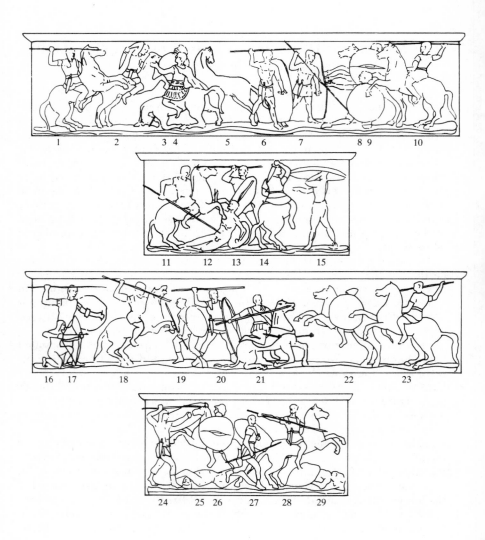

FIG. 20. THE FRIEZE OF AEMILIUS PAULLUS AT DELPHI

carrying. I differ herein from Reinach who held that the infantrymen with the large circular shield were the 'Bronze-shield-men', οἱ χαλκάσπιδες.

The east face shows an Italian infantryman (24) thrusting his long oval shield at the horse of a Thracian (or Macedonian) cavalryman (26) who has a large circular shield with the distinctive cross-rib, and on the viewer's right another Italian infantryman (27) and an Italian (or Roman) cavalryman (28) and a dead infantryman (29) lying prostrate with the same type of shield as the infantryman (3) to the left of the runaway horse was holding. I differ from Reinach who thought that the man lying prostrate was a 'Bronze-shield-man', a phalangite.

On the south face two fragmentary figures (16–17, 18) appear to be attacking one infantryman (19). We shall consider this unsatisfactory area later. In the centre there is a standing infantryman (20) with his left arm holding a long oval Ligurian shield and with his right hand raised as if he is about to strike a cavalryman (21) on a collapsed horse from behind. The relief is too worn to reveal what he is holding in his raised right hand. The opinion of Reinach, that the central infantryman is about to throw the ensign into the ranks of the enemy (as Salvius did in the main battle of P*Aem* 20. 1) is most improbable; for that happened not when cavalry and infantry were skirmishing but when the massed phalanx of infantrymen alone was charging into the Ligurian and other Italian infantrymen (P*Aem* 20. 1–2). On the right there are two cavalrymen (22, 23), one with a large circular shield and the other without a shield who is in pursuit and about to strike with a spear in his raised arm.

The west face is very worn. It appears that three infantrymen were in action against two cavalrymen.

An entirely new study with excellent photographic plates of the monument was published by H. Kähler, *Der Fries vom Reiterdenkmal des Aemilius Paullus in Delphi* (Berlin, 1965). His interpretation differs in several points from those of Homolle and Reinach, and it is not in all respects convincing. Before I turn to his study, I make some remarks about what we have considered already, in order to clear the ground. I shall give references to the plates in Kähler's publication in the form 'K Pl. 1' etc.

As I understand it, the Roman cavalryman (e.g. 1 and 23) wears a broad-belted short tunic with short sleeves and also a short undergarment which is visible below the tunic; both tunic and undergarment are straight at the lower end, sometimes with a nick in the material. See K Pls. 2, 3, 4 at the left edge, 17, and 20. He may wear a close-fitting helmet (K Pls. 3, 4 at the left, and 17). The Roman cavalrymen do not carry any shield. The opposing cavalrymen (e.g. 9 and 26) carry a shield when they are still in motion (K Pls. 7, 16, 18, 19, and 21); there is a strong cross-rib on the front of two shields (K Pls. 7 and 18) and probably not one on a third (K Pl. 16). The cavalryman on the collapsed horse (4) on K Pl. 4 either had a sunk head or his head has been knocked off subsequently. His belt is different from that of the Roman cavalrymen, and his flying cloak and pleated kilt are known Macedonian features (K Pl. 4). The other cavalryman on the collapsed horse (21) in Pl. 15 has the tied ends of his flying cloak below his neck and wears a very short tunic, loose below the belt, while he sits on a horsecloth; the cloak in particular shows he is on the Macedonian side. The cavalryman (14) on the badly damaged relief of the West face seems to be Roman, because he has short sleeves, a broad belt, a short tunic, and an undergarment (to the spectator's right on K Pl. 11; compare Pl. 17). The infantryman to his right (15) is defending himself with a shield raised above his head; he corresponds with the Roman infantryman (24) who had a similar way of defending himself on K Pl. 18. The man (13) standing to the spectator's left of the cavalryman is shown by his shield with its marked cross-rib to be on the Macedonian side; and the man (12) over whom he is standing is being protected. All the casualties in fact, are on the Macedonian side; and the two naked corpses (25 and 29) probably represent Gauls with longish hair and a big frame, since we know that Perseus had 2,000 Gauls when he mustered his army at Citium, and that Gauls sometimes fought in the nude (e.g. Plb. 2. 28. 8; 3. 114. 4; Livy 38. 21. 9 and 26. 7).

The Roman infantryman (e.g. 6) on the reliefs has the long shield of the Ligurian in Pls. 6, 14, 15, 18, and 19. He wears a short plain tunic, belted (Pls. 6, 14, 18, and 19), and in two cases we see the end of a short undergarment (Pls. 14 and 19). Of the opposing infantrymen one (3) has a well-defined helmet (Pl. 4) and a decorated circular shield; another (8) has a similar shield, but no helmet, and he wears trews (Pl. 7). One (12) appears to be naked, and one (13) with a shield seems to be wearing a very short tunic (both on Pl. 10). Of the two naked corpses one (29) is under a decorated circular shield.

I turn now to the publication of H. Kähler. As regards the north face, being his and my figures 1–10 (see his p. 34), we are in agreement. On the south face, being his and my figures 16–23, we agree that the central figure 20 is not about to throw an ensign, as Homolle and Reinach supposed, but is holding a weapon in his raised right hand. But Kähler makes the cavalryman 21 on the collapsed horse a Roman, whereas I make him a Macedonian and suppose that the central figure is about to strike him from behind. Then Kähler makes both cavalrymen to the right, 22 and 23, Roman, whereas I make 22 a Thracian or Macedonian cavalryman and 23 a Roman cavalryman about to strike 22 from behind. To the left of the central figure (20) he makes the man (19) who seems to be about to fell a Roman, whereas I think he is on the Macedonian side, a Gaul, if he is naked, as he appears to be. Nothing is left of the cavalryman 18; but he is for Kähler a Macedonian and for me a Roman. The two figures on the extreme left, 16 and 17, as compared with K Pl. 12, are so much restored in Kähler's drawing and so difficult to match with his Pl. 12 that I pass them over without comment, except to say that the pleated tunic end and the circular shield are appropriate to a Macedonian and not to a Roman as Kähler has it. We agree on the east face, figures 24–9. But on the west face, where he makes the collapsed man (12) and the man (13) standing over him Romans, I hold they are on the Macedonian side, as the cross-rib on the shield seems to indicate. The cavalryman on the left (11) is for him a Macedonian and for me a Roman; but only a bit of his horse is visible.

Thus my conclusions vary from those of my three predecessors. I believe that the reliefs on all four faces portrayed actions during the initial clash, which was started by the runaway horse. While the literary accounts mention light-armed infantry on both sides, it is obvious that there were outposts of light-armed cavalry as well. Thus it is appropriate that we should see cavalrymen portrayed as well. The details of armament and dress suggest that the portrayal is meant to be not traditional but realistic. The Romans, being on my interpretation 1, 2, 6, 7, 11, 14, 18, 20, 23, 24, 27 and 28 are winning or about to win; and their opponents, being 3, 4, 8, 9, 10, 12, 13, 15, 17, 19, 21, 22, 25, 26, and 29, are dead, collapsing, or about to be struck. In this phase of the action, then, the Romans are winning; that was no doubt what the commissioner of the relief wanted, namely Aemilius Paullus. The following phases of action were no doubt shown in the reliefs on the other columns, which were mentioned by Plb. 30. 10. 2 (a contemporary and dependable witness) as being crowned with 'statues' and not just one statue of the successful general. The details of dress and armament vary on the Macedonian side. It is not possible to be sure which are Macedonians (?a Macedonian officer, mounted, on K Pl. 4), Thracians, Agrianians, and so on, but the Gauls do seem to be recognizable.

LIST OF DATES

304	Demetrius saves Athens.
303	Demetrius in the Peloponnese.
302	Cassander holds up Demetrius in Thessaly. Lysimachus campaigns in Asia.
301	Battle of Ipsus in the summer.
300	Demetrius attacks Lysimachus in the Chersonese. Cassander takes Elatea.
300/299	Alliance between Ptolemy and Lysimachus. Alliance between Demetrius and Seleucus.
299/8	Treaty between Ptolemy and Demetrius.
298	Agathocles prevents Cassander seizing Corcyra.
297	Lachares' coup at Athens. Death of Cassander in May and of Philip IV four months later. Antipater and Alexander elected joint kings.
295	Lachares seizes tyranny at Athens in spring. Demetrius in the Peloponnese.
295/4	Demetrius recovers Piraeus.
294	Lachares flees from Athens in spring. Demetrius seizes Athens and attacks Sparta. Antipater expels Alexander from Pella in the autumn. Demetrius murders Alexander and is acclaimed king by the army at Larissa. Antipater flees to Lysimachus. Demetrius takes over the Boeotian League.
293	Demetrius suppresses Boeotian revolt.
c. 293/2	Demetrius founds Demetrias.
292	Lysimachus prisoner of the Getae. Further Boeotian rebellion.
291	Pyrrhus invades Thessaly in spring; expelled by Demetrius. Demetrius suppresses Boeotian revolt and garrisons Thebes.
290	Demetrius marries Lanassa and acquires Corcyra.
289	Demetrius invades Aetolia and is defeated by Pyrrhus.
288	Pyrrhus invades Macedonia but is checked at Edessa. Seleucus, Ptolemy, and Lysimachus allied against Demetrius.

287	Demetrius expelled from Macedonia; Macedonians acclaim Pyrrhus king.
	Athens revolts from Demetrius in June.
	Peace between Ptolemy and Demetrius.
	Demetrius attacks Lysimachus.
	Pyrrhus seizes Thessaly.
286/5	Pyrrhus makes secret agreement with Antigonus.
285	Demetrius prisoner of Seleucus.
	Lysimachus acquires all Macedonia.
283	Ptolemy II succeeds Ptolemy I in Egypt.
283/2	Lysimachus executes his son Agathocles.
282/1	Seleucus advances into Asia Minor in winter.
281	Lysimachus killed at the battle of Corupedium in January/February.
	Seleucus assassinated in August/September.
	Ceraunus defeats Antigonus at sea.
	Ceraunus makes peace with Antiochus and Pyrrhus.
281/0	Achaean Confederation reconstituted.
	Ceraunus marries Arsinoe and murders her sons in the winter.
	Greek revolt against Antigonus.
280	Pyrrhus crosses to Italy in May.
	Antigonus at war with Antiochus.
	Bolgius invades the Balkan peninsula in autumn.
279	Death of Ptolemy Ceraunus in January/February.
	Macedonians elect Meleager king; he reigns for two months.
	Antipater reigns in Macedonia for 45 days from April.
	Sosthenes general in Macedonia in June.
	Antigonus attacks Macedonia.
	Brennus' invasion in autumn.
279/8	Destruction of the Gauls in winter.
278	Peace between Antigonus and Antiochus.
	Sosthenes drives Antigonus from the Thracian Chersonese.
277	Battle of Lysimacheia.
276	Antigonus firmly established as king in Macedonia.
	Thessaly brought under Antigonus.
275	Pyrrhus returns from Italy to Epirus.

274   Pyrrhus invades Macedonia; victory at 'the Narrows'.
Gallic mercenaries plunder tombs at Aegeae.

273   Pyrrhus in Epirus; his son Ptolemy defeats and expels
Antigonus from Macedonia.

272   Pyrrhus invades the Peloponnese; Antigonus recovers Macedonia.
Death of Pyrrhus at Argos.

271/0   Athenian decree for Demochares.

270/69   Athenian decree for Callias.

268/7   Alliance between Athens and Sparta (decree of Chremonides).
Outbreak of war against Macedonia.

267   Areus' first advance to the Isthmus.
Antigonus beseiges Athens.

266   Areus' second advance north.
Antigonus suppresses revolt of Gallic mercenaries in Megara.

265   Areus' third advance north: his death near Corinth.

264   Cleinias assassinated at Sicyon.

262   Alexander II, king of the Molossians, invades Macedonia.

261   Athens capitulates.
Antiochus II succeeds Antiochus I.

260   Outbreak of the Second Syrian War.

257   Demetrius becomes co-regent with Antigonus.

255   Antigonus' naval victory over Ptolemy II off Cos.

255/4   Athens granted its freedom.

253   End of the Second Syrian War.
Antigonus institutes *Antigoneia* and *Stratoniceia* vase-festivals
at Delos.

251   Aratus liberates Sicyon in May.

c. 250   Possible naval victory of Ptolemy over Antigonus.
Death of Craterus.

250/49   Aratus visits Alexandria in the winter.
Achaean attacks on Corinth.

249   Alexander of Corinth declares himself independent.

249–7 Alexander allied to Achaea.
       Athens and Argos make peace with Alexander.

246   Accession of Ptolemy III in Egypt and Seleucus II in Syria.

246/5 Aetolians reorganize *Soteria*.
       Death of Alexander of Corinth.

245   The Aetolians defeat the Boeotians at Chaeronea.
       Antigonus recovers Corinth.
       Antigonus' naval victory over Ptolemy III off Andros.
       Antigonus institutes the *Soteria* and *Paneia* vase-festivals at
       Delos.

244   Lydiades becomes tyrant at Megalopolis.

243   Aratus takes Corinth in summer.

242   Aratus begins raids on Salamis and Attica.
       About now Antigonus' alliance with the Aetolians and
       Aratus' alliance with Sparta.

241   Aetolian invasion of the Peloponnese; Aratus' victory at
       Pellene.
       Agis of Sparta put to death.

241/0 Achaeans make peace with Macedonia and Aetolia.

240/39 Demetrius II succeeds Antigonus II in the winter.

239   Aetolians attack Epirote Acarnania.
       Alliance between Macedonia and Epirus; Demetrius mar-
       ries Phthia.
       Alliance between Achaea and Aetolia.

239/8 Outbreak of Demetrian War: Macedonia against Achaea
       and Aetolia.

238/7 Birth of Philip V.

237/6 Demetrius' alliance with Gortyn.

236   Demetrius conquers Boeotia.
       Achaeans annex Heraea.

235   Aratus twice attacks Argos; Aristippus killed at Cleonae.
       Aristomachus tyrant at Argos.
       Lydiades resigns his tyranny.
       Cleomenes III becomes king at Sparta.

234/3 Bithys' victory at Phylacia.
(or   Aratus invades Attica.
235/4) Collapse of Epirote monarchy; republic set up in Epirus.

231–29   Demetrius fighting against Dardanians under Longarus.

231   Aetolians besiege Medeon; Demetrius hires Agron to assist
         the Acarnanians.
         Agron defeats the Aetolians in autumn. Death of Agron.

230   Illyrians seize Phoenice; Epirote appeal to Achaea and
         Aetolia.
         Epirote peace with Illyrians.

229   Dardanian victory over Demetrius.
         Death of Demetrius in spring.
         Macedonians appoint Antigonus Doson Philip's guardian
         and general.
         May/June, battle of Paxos.
         Cleomenes annexes Arcadian towns.
         Romans arrive in Illyria; First Roman-Illyrian War begins.
         Athens fully liberated in summer; Boeotia and Phocis also
         throw off Macedonia.
         Antigonus deals with the Dardanians.
         Cleomenes occupies the Athenaeum. Aratus attacks Tegea
         and Orchomenus.

228   Antigonus defeats the Aetolians in Thessaly and invades
         Doris; he sacks Cytinium and acquires Opuntian Locris.
         Peace between Macedonia and Aetolia.
         Aratus seizes Caphyae; Cleomenes takes Methydrium.

227   Antigonus' Carian Expedition.
         The Macedonians elect Antigonus king.
         Antigonus suppresses a mutiny at Pella.
         Spartan victories at Mt. Lycaeum and Ladoceia.
         Cleomenes' coup at Sparta.

227/6   Megalopolitan embassy to Antigonus.

226   Cleomenes seizes Mantinea; victory at Hecatombaeum.

226/5   Negotiations between Achaea and Sparta.

225   Cleomenes takes more Achaean cities.
         Achaean embassy to Antigonus.
         Cleomenes takes Argos, Hermione, Troezen, Epidaurus,
         and Corinth.

224   Achaeans accept Antigonus' terms in April.
         Antigonus faces Cleomenes at the Isthmus of Corinth.
         Argos revolts from Cleomenes.
         Antigonus campaigns in the Peloponnese.
         Symmachy set up at Aegium in the autumn.

223 Cleomenes attacks Megalopolis in May.
Antigonus takes Orchomenus, Mantinea, Heraea, and Telphusa; he winters at Aegium.
Cleomenes takes and sacks Megalopolis.

222 Battle of Sellasia in June/July.
Antigonus defeats the Illyrians.

222/1 Philip sent to the Peloponnese.

221 Death of Antigonus Doson before October.
Philip elected king and guardians appointed.

220 Aratus defeated at Caphyae.
Philip comes of age and campaigns in Dardania and Laconia.
Social War declared by the Symmachy against Aetolia.

219 Philip captures Oeniadae.
Aetolians raid Dium, Passaron, and Dodona.

218 Winter campaign of Philip in the Peloponnese.
Naval offensive by Philip and invasion of Aetolia.

217 Bylazora seized by Philip.
In July Philip learns of Hannibal's victory at L. Trasimene.
In August peace concluded between the Symmachy and Aetolia.

216 Philip fails to surprise Apollonia in Illyris.
In winter Philip opens negotiations with Hannibal.

215 In summer Macedonia and her allies make alliance with Carthage, her subjects, and her allies in Italy.
Philip and Aratus at Messene.

214 Philip defeated by Rome at Oricum and Apollonia.
Philip and Aratus again at Messene.

213 Birth of Perseus.

212 Philip occupies Lissus and the Scodra basin.
Rome again rebuffed by Aetolia.

211 Alliance of Rome and Aetolia in late summer.
Laevinus captures Oeniadae.

210 Romans sack Anticyra and Aegeira.
They and their allies hold Thermopylae.

209 In summer peace conference at Aegium fails.
In autumn Dardanians invade Macedonia.

208   Carthaginian fleet reaches islands off Oeniadae.
Philip and his allies secure the Peloponnese.

207   Through a bargain with Amynander Philip captures Ambracia.
Philip overruns northern Aetolia.
Peace feelers fail.

206   Rome and Aetolia capture Ambracia.
Philip recaptures Ambracia and invades central Aetolia.
Aetolia makes a separate peace with the Symmachy.

205   Fighting in Illyris.
Peace made at Phoenice between Rome and the Symmachy.

204   Philip defeats the Dardanians.
Philip intrigues against Rhodes.

203   Philip builds a fleet.
In winter secret alliance of Philip and Antiochus.

202   Philip and Prusias campaign in the Propontis.
Philip destroys Thasos.

201   Philip's naval war against Attalus and Rhodes.
Philip blockaded in the Bay of Bargylia.

200   Roman commissioners visit Greece.
Philip at war with Athens.
In August Lepidus demands reparations from Philip at Abydus.
Romans advance in Illyris.

199   Romans ravage western Macedonia.
Philip drives Aetolians out of Thessaly.

198   Philip in position at the Aoi Stena.
In October the Achaean League joins Rome.
Two-month truce in the winter.

197   In June battle of Cynoscephalae.
In December peace is agreed but terms to be settled.

196   In June/July peace terms announced.
In October Antiochus rebuffs the Roman commissioners.

195   Flamininus defeats Nabis.
Hannibal joins Antiochus.

194   Roman forces leave Greece.

193   Negotiations between Rome and Antiochus.

192   In the spring Aetolians invite Antiochus to help against Rome.
In late October Antiochus lands in Greece.

191   In April Antiochus withdraws to Ephesus.
Philip, fighting on Rome's side, gains territory.

190   Rome makes a truce with Aetolia to last until November.

190/89 Winter, Antiochus is defeated at Magnesia.

189   Roman siege of Ambracia.
Peace made between Rome and Aetolia.

188   Roman settlement of Asia.

187   Philip occupies Aenus and Maronea.

186   Revival of Macedonia's economy.

185   Roman commissioners visit Macedonia.

184   Romans favour Demetrius.

183   Philip withdraws from Aenus and Maronea.
Perseïs founded.

182   Perseus and Demetrius quarrel.

181   In spring and summer Philip campaigns in Thrace.

180   Death of Demetrius.

179   In summer Philip dies and Perseus succeeds.

178   Macedonians become members of the Delphian Amphictyony.

177   Dardanians complain against Perseus at Rome.

176   Rome warns Perseus to respect the treaty.

175/4 Winter, Dardanians operate against the Bastarnae.

174   Perseus consolidates his position in Thrace.
Roman commissioners visit Greece and Macedonia.

173   Eumenes denounces Perseus in a memorandum.

172   Eumenes denounces Perseus in a speech to the Senate.
Rome publicizes her case against Perseus in Greece.
About September the Roman vanguard crosses to Greece.
Late November Perseus meets Philippus.

172/1 Winter, a standstill in relations between Perseus and Rome.

171   Probably in January the Roman people approves a motion
        for war.
        Probably in April Perseus decides on war.
        Operations in Thessaly.

170   Molossia joins Macedonia.
        Romans fail to enter Macedonia.
        In autumn Appius Claudius is routed at Uscana.

170/69 Winter, Perseus campaigns in Penestia.

169   Spring campaign of Perseus fails at Stratus.
        In summer Philippus enters Pieria.
        In autumn Gentius joins Perseus.

168   April/May, Roman offensive against Gentius.
        On 22 June the battle of Pydna.
        Anicius in Epirus.

168/7   Roman armies winter in Epirus and at Amphipolis.

167   Winter/spring, settlement of the Illyrian area.
        Summer tour of Greece by Aemilius.
        Late summer, settlement of Macedonia.
        Autumn, sack of Molossia.

GENERAL INDEX

In some entries the main reference is italicized.

632 *General Index*

29; revolt of, 56–67; 76, 78–80, 114, 146, 148, 158 f., 170, 181, 183, 203, 204 n. 1, 219–21, 226, 227 n. 2, 230, 341, 343, 380, 392, 434, 445, 494, 509 f., 511, 519, 576 f.
Thebes, Thebans (Phthiotic), Figs. 1, 6; 68, 178, 222, 386 f., 389, 430 f., 432–5, 442
Themistocles, 378
Theodhoriana, 513 n. 2
Theodotus, commandant in Sardes, 241 n. 2
Theodotus, Molossian, 520
Theophrastus, 52, 209
theorodokoi, 89, 105 n. 5
Thera, Fig. 7; 284
Thermaic Gulf, Figs. 1, 6; 113, 146, 154, 209, 404, 460, 565
Thermopylae, Figs. 1, 6; 15, 57, 109, 141, 146, 175, 234, 249 n. 5, 250, 276, 318, 320 f., 323, 336, 349, 364, 376 n. 3, 403 f., 428, 434, 451
Thermum, Figs. 1, 12; 340 n. 2, 379, 407 n. 1, 485 f.
Thespiae, Fig. 10; 59 f., 64, 68, 220, 341, 577
Thesprotia, Figs. 1, 6, 8; 105, 181, 520, 525, 568 n. 2
Thessalian Cavalry, 11, 15, 68; in Lamian War, 109–14; 165, 440, 447, 517, 577
Thessalian League, 15–17, 63, 114, 158, 351; revived, 455; 507 f., 516, 518, 522 n. 4
Thessaliotis, Fig. 6; 338
Thessalonica, Figs. 1, 3; 146, 209, 262, 467, 470, 475 f., 486, 487 n. 2, 529, 539, 565 f.
Thessalonice, daughter of Philip II, 130, 142, 145, 148 f., 174, 208, 210, 214
Thessaly, Figs. 1, 6; 15, 77, 85, 109, 122, 126 f., 142, 178, 219–23, 233, 235 f., 238 n. 2, 252, 255, 261 f., 269, 284 n. 1, 314 f., 318, 320, 336 n. 1, 338–40, 345, 349–52, 357, 363, 371, 374, 378–80, 385, 401 n. 1, 404 f., 412, 424, 426, 431, 444, 446, 450, 454–7, 465 n. 1, 474, 492, 494–7, 500 f., 512, 516–21, 535 n. 2, 536, 539, 565, 575, 576 n. 1, 581
Thetideum, 433 n. 1, 436, 440
Thisbae, Fig. 10; 511, 521
Thrace, Thracians, Figs. 2, 3; 215, 220, 228, 236, 240, 241 n. 5, 242, 250–2, 254–6, 268, 307, 314 f., 319, 431, 440 f., 446, 448, 450, 453–9, 463, 468 f., 476, 490 f., 495, 497, 502, 515, 520, 535, 539, 542, 549 f., 564, 588, 605 n. 3, 606, 609; Perseus in, 611 f.; on monument of Aemilius Paullus, 613 f.
Thrasybulus, of Elis, 265, 272
Thriasian Plain, Fig. 9; 329
throne-room, 477
Thucydides, 489
thunderbolt, 92, 163, 410, 461, 466, 504
Thymochares, of Sphettus, 283

Thyrreum, 370
thyrsos, 92
Tiber, R., 449
Timaeus, Aetolian commander, 312 f.
Timagenes, 195 n. 3
Timarchus, tyrant at Miletus, 291, 589 f.
timber, forests, 259, 279, 314, 382 n. 2, 392, 460, 493, 524 n. 1, 544, 564, 566
Timocleia, 65
Timocleidas, Sicyonian, 274, 296
Timocles, pirate, 283
Timocrates, of Chios, 328
Timoxenus, Achaean general, 347, 350, 370 f.
Tirana, 40, 47
Titarium, 543 n. 1
Titarus, Mt., Fig. 1; 432, 543
Titov Veles, 386, 459
Tlepolemus, 187
torch, 92
Torone, Fig. 7; 529
town-planning, 83, 187, 477
Trailus, 475 n. 3
Trajan, Mt., Fig. 4; 46
Tralles, Tralleis, 51, 436
transfers of population, 104, 458 f., 474, 483
Trasimene, L., Battle of, 380, 387
Trebenishte, 186
triaconter, 24 f., 26 n. 1, 379 n. 1
Triballi, Fig. 3; 32, 34, 36, 38, 48, 51, 53, 59, 89, 105, 252, 256
tribute, 38, 50, 53, 62, 519 n.
Tricca, Figs. 1, 6, 8; 426
Trichonis, L., Figs. 1, 12; 380, 382
Trieste, 471
Triparadeisus, 128 f., 146, 148, 193 n. 1, 200, 240
Triphylia (Peloponnesus), Fig. 10; 308, 330, 377, 382, 389, 405, 423
Tripolis (Syria), 151
trireme, 24 f., 26 n. 1, 66, 69, 72, 109, 122, 573, 578
Tritaea, Fig. 10; 249, 299
Triteuta, 354
Troad, 24
Troezen, Fig. 10; 108, 274, 309, 321, 348
Trogus Pompeius, as source, 23, 27, 29–31, 95, 97, 389, 409 n. 1
Troules, Mt., Fig. 11; 359 f.
Troy, Fig. 7; 104, 379, 449
Tsangon Pass, Fig. 8; 43 f., 44 n. 1, 49, 225
Tsepicovo, 524 n. 1
Turks, 48, 152
Tyche, 488, 527, 532 f., 549, 552
Tylis, kingdom of, 257
Tymphaea, Figs. 1, 6, 8; 57, 130, 164, 214, 267, 269, 565
Tyre, 31, 75, 83, 151, 201, 206, 214

PLATES

PLATE I. COINS OF THE KINGS AND THE REGIONS

a. Alexander III, double stater, Oxford, *SNG* LIII 2756 (p. 92)
b. Alexander III, tetradrachm, Oxford, *SNG* L 2645 (p. 92)
c. Alexander III, bronze, Cambridge, like G XXXI 23 (p. 92)
d. Philip III, tetradrachm, Oxford, *SNG* LXV 3207 (p. 143)
e. Alexander IV, drachm, Berlin, like G. XXXII 4 (p. 163)
f. Cassander, bronze, Cambridge, like G. XXXII 7 (p. 174)
g. Demetrius I, tetradrachm, Oxford, *SNG* LXVII 3244 (p. 175)
h. Demetrius I, tetradrachm, Oxford, *SNG* LXVII 3248 (p. 175)
i. Lysimachus, tetradrachm, Cambridge, like Price no. 70 (p. 175)
j. Antigonus II, tetradrachm, Oxford, *SNG* LXVII 3258 (p. 594)
k. Antigonus II, tetradrachm, Oxford, *SNG* LXVII 3264 (p. 594)
l. Antigonus II, drachm, Oxford, *SNG* LXVII 3262 (p. 594)
m. Philip V, tetradrachm, Cambridge, like G. XXXIV 16 (pp. 461 and 464)
n. Philip V, tetradrachm, Oxford, *SNG* LXVII 3267 (p. 462)
o. Makenones Amphaxioi, tetradrachm, Oxford, *SNG* LXVIII 3288 (p. 466)
p. Botteatai, tetrobol, Oxford, *SNG* LXVIII 3289 (p. 466)
q. Perseus, tetradrachm, Oxford, *SNG* LXVIII 3276 (p. 504)

a

b

c

d

e

f

g

h

i

j

k

l

m

n

o

p

q

PLATE II. The façade of Tomb 2 at Vergina (see also Fig. 2).

PLATE III. *a* The battlefield at Cynoscephalae, looking from 'the level ground' to the ridge at 'K' and to the parallel ridge on the right (p. 439).

PLATE III. *b* The Roman camp (p. 440).

PLATE IV. The Stag Hunt mosaic, from Pella (p. 186).

DATE DUE

GAYLORD

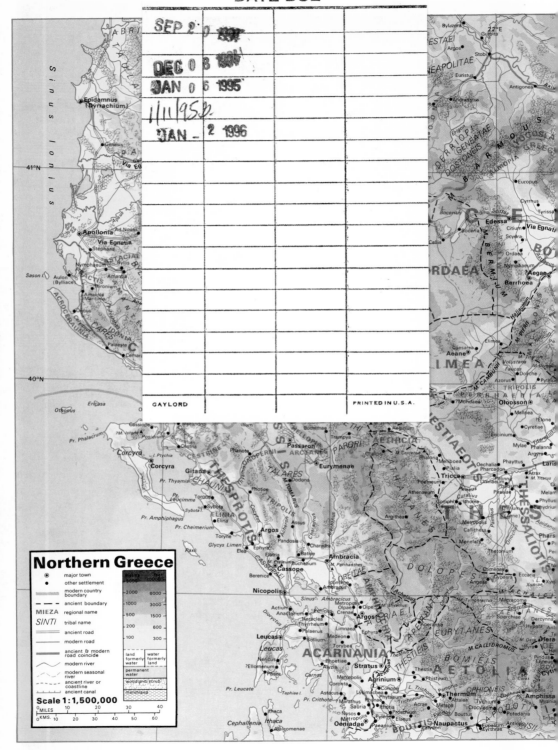

Northern Greece

⊙ major town
• other settlement
▦ modern country boundary
--- ancient boundary
MIEZA regional name
SINTI tribal name
— ancient road
— modern road
— ancient & modern road coincide
〜 modern river
〜 modern seasonal river
∙∙∙ ancient river or coastline
∎∎∎ ancient canal

metres	feet
3000	10000
2000	6000
1000	3000
500	1500
200	600
100	300

land formerly water
water formerly land
permanent water
woodland/scrub
marshland

Scale 1 : 1,500,000

MILES 0 10 20 30 40
KMS. 0 10 20 30 40 50 60